FOR REFERENCE
DO NOT REMOVE
FROM THIS ROOM

West's

FLORIDA
PROBATE CODE

with

RELATED LAWS

AND

COURT RULES

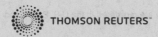 THOMSON REUTERS™

Mat #41603299

© 2015 Thomson Reuters

ISBN 978–0–314–67231–5

This publication was created to provide you with accurate and authoritative information concerning the subject matter covered; however, this publication was not necessarily prepared by persons licensed to practice law in a particular jurisdiction. The publisher not engaged in rendering legal or other professional advice and this publication is not a substitute for the advice of an attorney. If you require legal or other expert advice, you should seek the services of a competent attorney or other professional.

West's and Westlaw are registered in the U.S. Patent and Trademark Office.

PREFACE

This soft cover volume brings together in a concise and convenient format statutes and rules of court pertaining to Florida probate, estate taxation, guardianship, and related laws. Designed for convenient use in the office or courtroom.

WHAT'S NEW

The product contains the text of the Florida Statutes pertaining to probate and guardianship law and procedure as amended through Ch. 232 (End) of the 2015 First Regular Session and Special "A" Session of the Twenty-Fourth Legislature, and the Florida Supreme Court rules pertaining to probate and guardianship procedure as amended by court orders received through August 15, 2015.

This pamphlet includes new enactments or important amendments relating to guardianship.

A combined index is provided at the end of the volume to assure quick access to the law.

CONTACT US

For additional information or research assistance call the West reference attorneys at 1-800-REF-ATTY (1-800-733-2889). Contact our U.S. legal editorial department directly with your questions and suggestions by e-mail at editors.us-legal@thomsonreuters.com.

THE PUBLISHER

November, 2015

THOMSON REUTERS PROVIEW™

This title is one of many now available on your tablet as an eBook.

Take your research mobile. Powered by the Thomson Reuters ProView™ app, our eBooks deliver the same trusted content as your print resources, but in a compact, on-the-go format.

ProView eBooks are designed for the way you work. You can add your own notes and highlights to the text, and all of your annotations will transfer electronically to every new edition of your eBook.

You can also instantly verify primary authority with built-in links to WestlawNext® and KeyCite®, so you can be confident that you're accessing the most current and accurate information.

To find out more about ProView eBooks and available discounts, call 1-800-344-5009.

TABLE OF CONTENTS

FLORIDA STATUTES

TABLE OF CONTENTS

FLORIDA RULES OF COURT

COMBINED INDEX

(Page I–1)

FLORIDA STATUTES

TITLE VII

EVIDENCE

CHAPTER 90

EVIDENCE CODE

UNIFORM RULES OF EVIDENCE

Table of Jurisdictions Wherein Rules Have Been Adopted

For text of Uniform Act, and variation notes and annotation materials for adopting jurisdictions, see Uniform Laws Annotated, Master Edition, Volumes 13A–13H.

Jurisdiction	Laws	Effective Date	Statutory Citation
Arizona		9–1–1977	17A A.R.S. Rules of Evid., Rules 101 to 1103.
Arkansas	1987, No. 876		A.C.A. Rules of Evid., Rules 101 to 1102.
California			West's Ann.Cal.Evid.Code, §§ 1 to 1605.
Colorado		1–1–1980	West's C.R.S.A., Title 13 App., Evid. 101 to 1102.
Delaware		7–1–1980	D.R.E. 101 to 1103.
Florida..............	1976, c. 76–237	7–1–1977	West's F.S.A. §§ 90.101 to 90.958.
Hawaii	1980, c. 164	1–1–1981	HRS §§ 626–1 (Hawaii Rules of Evidence, Rules 100 to 1102) to 626–3.
Iowa................		7–1–1983	Iowa R.Evid., Rules 5.101 to 5.1103.
Kansas			K.S.A. §§ 60–401 to 60–472
Kentucky	1990, c. 88 Sup.Ct. Order	7–1–1992	KRE 101 to 1104.
Maine...............		2–2–1976	Rules of Evidence, Rules 101 to 1102.
Michigan		3–1–1978	Rules of Evidence, Rules 101 to 1102.
Minnesota		7–1–1977	50 M.S.A.Evid. Rules 101 to 1101.
Mississippi..........	Sup.Ct. Order 9–24–1985	1–1–1986	M.R.E. 101 to 1103.
Montana	1976, En.Sup. Ct. Ord. 12729	7–1–1977	Rules of Evidence, Rules 100 to 1008.
Nebraska	1975, L.B. 279	8–24–1975	R.R.S.1943, §§ 27–101 to 27–1301.
Nevada..............	1971, c. 775		N.R.S. § 47.020 to 52.295.
New Jersey	Sup.Ct. Order 9–15–1992	7–1–1993	N.J.R.E. 101 to 1103.
New Mexico	1973, S.C.Order	7–1–1973	NMRA, Rules of Evidence, Rules 11–101 to 11–1102.
North Carolina	1983, c. 701	7–1–1984	G.S. § 8C–1, Rules 101 to 1102.
North Dakota		2–15–1977	NDR Evid.Rules 101 to 1103.
Ohio		7–1–1980	Rules of Evidence, Rules 101 to 1103.
Oklahoma[1]..........	1978, c. 285	10–1–1978	12 Okl.St.Ann. §§ 2101 to 3103.
Oregon	1981, c. 892	1–1–1982	ORS 40.010 to 40.585, 41.415.
South Dakota			SDCL 19–9–1 to 19–18–9.
Tennessee...........		1–1–1990	Rules of Evidence, Rules 101 to 1008.
Texas		3–1–1998	Rules of Evidence, Rules 101 to 1009.
Utah...............		9–1–1983	Rules of Evidence, Rules 101 to 1103.
Vermont............		4–1–1983	Rules of Evidence, Rules 101 to 1103.
Virgin Islands			5 V.I.C. §§ 771 to 956.
Washington		4–2–1979	Rules of Evidence, Rules 101 to 1103.
Wisconsin	Sup.Ct. Order, 59 W.(2d), page R9	1–1–1974	W.S.A. 901.01 to 911.02.
Wyoming............		1–1–1978	Rules of Evidence, Rules 101 to 1104.

[1] The Oklahoma rules, as amended by L.2002, c. 468, retains the basic format and many of the provisions of the Uniform Rules of Evidence (1974), but now also contains many of the major provisions of the Uniform Rules of Evidence (1999). Accordingly, the citation of the Oklahoma rules is set forth in the tables for both the 1974 and 1999 Rules of Evidence. The Notes of Decisions for Oklahoma Rules of Evidence since 2002 are included with the 1999 revised act.

90.101. Short title

This chapter shall be known and may be cited as the "Florida Evidence Code."
Laws 1976, c. 76–237, § 1.

90.102. Construction

This chapter shall replace and supersede existing statutory or common law in conflict with its provisions.

Laws 1976, c. 76–237, § 1.

Cross References

Common law in force,
 Generally, see § 2.01.
 Crimes and offenses, see § 775.01.
Construction of statutes, generally, see § 1.01 et seq.
Prohibited laws, see Const. Art. 1, § 10.
Repealed statutes, not revived by implication, see § 2.04.

90.103. Scope; applicability

(1) Unless otherwise provided by statute, this code applies to the same proceedings that the general law of evidence applied to before the effective date of this code.

(2) This act shall apply to criminal proceedings related to crimes committed after the effective date of this code and to civil actions and all other proceedings pending on or brought after October 1, 1981.

(3) Nothing in this act shall operate to repeal or modify the parol evidence rule.

Laws 1976, c. 76–237, §§ 1, 5, 7; Laws 1978, c. 78–361, § 1. Amended by Laws 1981, c. 81–93, § 1, eff. Oct. 1, 1981.

Cross References

Applicability in probate and guardianship proceedings, see Probate Rule 5.170.
Criminal prosecutions, see Const. Art. 1, §§ 15, 16.
Due process, see Const. Art. 1, § 9.
Juvenile delinquency proceedings, see Const. Art. 1, § 15.
Motions to suppress evidence in criminal proceedings, see Criminal Procedure Rule 3.190.
Stipulations, recording parol agreements, see Civil Procedure Rule 1.030.
Uniform Commercial Code, parol evidence,
 Accommodation, negotiable instruments, see § 673.4191.
 Contract for sale, see § 672.202.
 Sale or return, see § 672.326.
Witnesses in criminal proceedings, see § 914.001 et seq.

90.104. Rulings on evidence

(1) A court may predicate error, set aside or reverse a judgment, or grant a new trial on the basis of admitted or excluded evidence when a substantial right of the party is adversely affected and:

(a) When the ruling is one admitting evidence, a timely objection or motion to strike appears on the record, stating the specific ground of objection if the specific ground was not apparent from the context; or

(b) When the ruling is one excluding evidence, the substance of the evidence was made known to the court by offer of proof or was apparent from the context within which the questions were asked.

If the court has made a definitive ruling on the record admitting or excluding evidence, either at or before trial, a party need not renew an objection or offer of proof to preserve a claim of error for appeal.

(2) In cases tried by a jury, a court shall conduct proceedings, to the maximum extent practicable, in such a manner as to prevent inadmissible evidence from being suggested to the jury by any means.

(3) Nothing in this section shall preclude a court from taking notice of fundamental errors affecting substantial rights, even though such errors were not brought to the attention of the trial judge.

Laws 1976, c. 76–237, § 1; Laws 1977, c. 77–174, § 1. Amended by Laws 2003, c. 2003–259, § 1, eff. July 1, 2003.

Cross References

Due process, see Const. Art. 1, § 9.
Evidence, see Civil Procedure Rule 1.450.
Exceptions unnecessary, objections, see Civil Procedure Rule 1.470.
Harmless error,
    Generally, see § 59.041.
    Criminal cases, see § 924.33.
Juveniles, delinquency proceedings, trial without jury or other requirements, see Const. Art. 1, § 15.
Motions to suppress evidence in criminal proceedings, see Criminal Procedure Rule 3.190.
New trial or arrest of judgment, see Criminal Procedure Rule 3.580.
New trial or rehearing, see Civil Procedure Rule 1.530.
Pleadings, amendment to conform to evidence, see Civil Procedure Rule 1.190.
Presence of defendant, foundation for introduction to jury, see Criminal Procedure Rule 3.180.
Proof of official records, see § 90.955.
Rights of accused, fair trial, see Const. Art. 1, § 15.
Self-incrimination,
    Beverage Law violations, see § 568.08.
    Federal court orders, see § 914.05.
    Insurance Code, see § 624.322.
    Privilege, see Const. Art. 1, § 9.
    Public service commission hearings, see § 366.09.
    Witnesses in criminal proceedings, see § 914.04.

90.105. Preliminary questions

(1) Except as provided in subsection (2), the court shall determine preliminary questions concerning the qualification of a person to be a witness, the existence of a privilege, or the admissibility of evidence.

(2) When the relevancy of evidence depends upon the existence of a preliminary fact, the court shall admit the proffered evidence when there is prima facie evidence sufficient to support a finding of the preliminary fact. If prima facie evidence is not introduced to support a finding of the preliminary fact, the court may admit the proffered evidence subject to the subsequent introduction of prima facie evidence of the preliminary fact.

(3) Hearings on the admissibility of confessions shall be conducted out of the hearing of the jury. Hearings on other preliminary matters shall be similarly conducted when the interests of justice require or when an accused is a witness, if he or she so requests.

Laws 1976, c. 76–237, § 1. Amended by Laws 1995, c. 95–147, § 471, eff. July 10, 1995.

Cross References

Alibi, notice of, see Criminal Procedure Rule 3.200.
Competency of witnesses,
    Generally, see § 90.601 et seq.
    Criminal proceedings, see § 914.07.

For Annotative Materials, see West's Florida Statutes Annotated

Confessions,
    Availability to accused, see § 925.05.
    Motions to suppress, see Criminal Procedure Rule 3.190.
    Suppression, appeal by state, see § 924.071.
Cross-examination of adverse witnesses, see Civil Procedure Rule 1.450.
Disqualification of witnesses, see § 90.603.
Evidence, see Civil Procedure Rule 1.450.
Foreign states, procedure when offenses are committed outside state, see § 918.03.
Functions of court and jury, see § 90.958.
Guilty pleas, offer, withdrawal, etc., see § 90.410.
Impeachment of witnesses, see § 90.608 et seq.
Interpreters and translators, appointment, see § 90.606.
Judicial notice, taking of, see § 90.201 et seq.
Mental condition of defendant, hearing, see Criminal Procedure Rule 3.210.
Mode and order of interrogation and presentation, see § 90.612.
Motions to suppress evidence, see Criminal Procedure Rule 3.190.
Offenses committed in other counties, determination, see § 918.04.
Opinions and conclusions, admitting or excluding, see § 90.701 et seq.
Preliminary criminal proceedings, see Criminal Procedure Rule 3.120 et seq.
Privileges, assertion and recognition, see § 90.501 et seq.
Relevancy of evidence, see § 90.401 et seq.
Security of communications, see § 934.01 et seq.
Self-incrimination,
    Beverage Law violations, see § 568.08.
    Federal court orders, see § 914.05.
    Insurance Code, see § 624.322.
    Privilege, see Const. Art. 1, § 9.
    Public service commission hearings, see § 366.09.
    Witnesses in criminal proceedings, see § 914.04.
Speedy trial, right to,
    Generally, see Criminal Procedure Rule 3.191.
    Constitutional guarantee, see Const. Art. 1, § 16.
View by jury, determination, see § 918.05.

90.106. Summing up and comment by judge

A judge may not sum up the evidence or comment to the jury upon the weight of the evidence, the credibility of the witnesses, or the guilt of the accused.

Laws 1976, c. 76–237, § 1.

Cross References

Functions of court and jury, see § 90.958.
Instructions to jury in criminal cases, see § 918.10; Criminal Procedure Rule 3.390.
Judicial comment on verdict, see Criminal Procedure Rule 3.451.

90.107. Limited admissibility

When evidence that is admissible as to one party or for one purpose, but inadmissible as to another party or for another purpose, is admitted, the court, upon request, shall restrict such evidence to its proper scope and so inform the jury at the time it is admitted.

Laws 1976, c. 76–237, § 1.

Cross References

Evidence, see Civil Procedure Rule 1.450.
Exclusion of relevant evidence on grounds of prejudice, confusion, etc., see § 90.403.

90.108. Introduction of related writings or recorded statements

(1) When a writing or recorded statement or part thereof is introduced by a party, an adverse party may require him or her at that time to introduce any other part or any other writing or recorded statement that in fairness ought to be considered contemporaneously. An adverse party is not bound by evidence introduced under this section.

(2) The report of a court reporter, when certified to by the court reporter as being a correct transcript of the testimony and proceedings in the case, is prima facie a correct statement of such testimony and proceedings.

Laws 1976, c. 76–237, § 1; Laws 1978, c. 78–361, § 2. Amended by Laws 1995, c. 95–147, § 472, eff. July 10, 1995; Laws 1995, c. 95–286, § 5, eff. July 1, 1995.

Cross References

Admissibility of duplicates, see § 90.953.
Admissibility of other evidence of contents, see § 90.954
Discovery, depositions and interrogatories, admission of remainder of, see Civil Procedure Rules 1.330, 1.340.

90.201. Matters which must be judicially noticed

A court shall take judicial notice of:

(1) Decisional, constitutional, and public statutory law and resolutions of the Florida Legislature and the Congress of the United States.

(2) Florida rules of court that have statewide application, its own rules, and the rules of United States courts adopted by the United States Supreme Court.

(3) Rules of court of the United States Supreme Court and of the United States Courts of Appeal.

Laws 1976, c. 76–237, § 1; Laws 1978, c. 78–361, § 21.

Cross References

Certified copies of statutes, see § 15.03.
Common law,
    Crimes, application of common law of England, see § 775.01.
    Law in force, see § 2.01.
County court records prior to 1875, judicial notice, see § 28.16.
Fundamental errors affecting substantial rights, judicial notice, see § 90.104.
Photographic enrolling, see § 11.07.
Rulemaking proceedings, judicial notice by agency, Administrative Procedure Act, see § 120.54.
Secretary of State to have custody of original statutes, see § 15.01.
Territorial court records, judicial notice, see § 28.15.

90.202. Matters which may be judicially noticed

A court may take judicial notice of the following matters, to the extent that they are not embraced within s. 90.201:

(1) Special, local, and private acts and resolutions of the Congress of the United States and of the Florida Legislature.

(2) Decisional, constitutional, and public statutory law of every other state, territory, and jurisdiction of the United States.

(3) Contents of the Federal Register.

(4) Laws of foreign nations and of an organization of nations.

(5) Official actions of the legislative, executive, and judicial departments of the United States and of any state, territory, or jurisdiction of the United States.

(6) Records of any court of this state or of any court of record of the United States or of any state, territory, or jurisdiction of the United States.

(7) Rules of court of any court of this state or of any court of record of the United States or of any other state, territory, or jurisdiction of the United States.

(8) Provisions of all municipal and county charters and charter amendments of this state, provided they are available in printed copies or as certified copies.

(9) Rules promulgated by governmental agencies of this state which are published in the Florida Administrative Code or in bound written copies.

(10) Duly enacted ordinances and resolutions of municipalities and counties located in Florida, provided such ordinances and resolutions are available in printed copies or as certified copies.

(11) Facts that are not subject to dispute because they are generally known within the territorial jurisdiction of the court.

(12) Facts that are not subject to dispute because they are capable of accurate and ready determination by resort to sources whose accuracy cannot be questioned.

(13) Official seals of governmental agencies and departments of the United States and of any state, territory, or jurisdiction of the United States.

Laws 1976, c. 76–237, § 1; Laws 1977, c. 77–174, § 1; Laws 1978, c. 78–361, § 3.

Cross References

Certified copies of statutes, see § 15.03.
County court records prior to 1875, judicial notice, see § 28.16.
Documentary evidence, certificates issued under authority of Congress, see § 92.20.
Due process, right to notice and hearing, see Const. Art. 1, § 9.
Foreign countries, proof of execution of instrument for record, see § 695.03.
Fundamental errors affecting substantial rights, judicial notice, see § 90.104.
Pleading official documents or acts, see Civil Procedure Rule 1.120.
Public records, see § 90.955.
Rulemaking proceedings, judicial notice by agency, Administrative Procedure Act, see § 120.54.
Seals, judicial notice provided for,
    Department of Labor and Employment Security, see § 440.44.
    Internal improvement trust fund trustees, see § 92.17.
    Parole and probation commission, see § 947.05.
    Soil conservation districts, see § 582.20.
Secretary of State to have custody of original statutes, see § 15.01.
Territorial court records, judicial notice, see § 28.15.
Validation of lands, etc., recording in foreign judgment book, see § 75.10.

90.203. Compulsory judicial notice upon request

A court shall take judicial notice of any matter in s. 90.202 when a party requests it and:

(1) Gives each adverse party timely written notice of the request, proof of which is filed with the court, to enable the adverse party to prepare to meet the request.

(2) Furnishes the court with sufficient information to enable it to take judicial notice of the matter.

Laws 1976, c. 76–237, § 1.

Cross References

County court records prior to 1875, judicial notice, see § 28.16.
Fundamental errors affecting substantial rights, judicial notice, see § 90.104.
Rulemaking proceedings, judicial notice by agency, Administrative Procedure Act, see § 120.54.
Territorial court records, judicial notice, see § 28.15.

90.204. Determination of propriety of judicial notice and nature of matter noticed

(1) When a court determines upon its own motion that judicial notice of a matter should be taken or when a party requests such notice and shows good cause for not complying with s. 90.203(1), the court shall afford each party reasonable opportunity to present information relevant to the propriety of taking judicial notice and to the nature of the matter noticed.

(2) In determining the propriety of taking judicial notice of a matter or the nature thereof, a court may use any source of pertinent and reliable information, whether or not furnished by a party, without regard to any exclusionary rule except a valid claim of privilege and except for the exclusions provided in s. 90.403.

(3) If a court resorts to any documentary source of information not received in open court, the court shall make the information and its source a part of the record in the action and shall afford each party reasonable opportunity to challenge such information, and to offer additional information, before judicial notice of the matter is taken.

(4) In family cases, the court may take judicial notice of any matter described in s. 90.202(6) when imminent danger to persons or property has been alleged and it is impractical to give prior notice to the parties of the intent to take judicial notice. Opportunity to present evidence relevant to the propriety of taking judicial notice under subsection (1) may be deferred until after judicial action has been taken. If judicial notice is taken under this subsection, the court shall, within 2 business days, file a notice in the pending case of the matters judicially noticed. For purposes of this subsection, the term "family cases" has the same meaning as provided in the Rules of Judicial Administration.

Laws 1976, c. 76–237, § 1. Amended by Laws 2014, c. 2014–35, § 2, eff. May 12, 2014.

Cross References

County court records prior to 1875, judicial notice, see § 28.16.
Fundamental errors affecting substantial rights, judicial notice, see § 90.104.
Rulemaking proceedings, judicial notice by agency, Administrative Procedure Act, see § 120.54.
Territorial court records, judicial notice, see § 28.15.

90.205. Denial of a request for judicial notice

Upon request of counsel, when a court denies a request to take judicial notice of any matter, the court shall inform the parties at the earliest practicable time and shall indicate for the record that it has denied the request.

Laws 1976, c. 76–237, § 1.

Cross References

Fundamental errors affecting substantial rights, judicial notice, see § 90.104.
Rulemaking proceedings, judicial notice by agency, Administrative Procedure Act, see § 120.54.

90.206. Instructing jury on judicial notice

The court may instruct the jury during the trial to accept as a fact a matter judicially noticed.

Laws 1976, c. 76–237, § 1; Laws 1978, c. 78–361, § 4.

Cross References

Fundamental errors affecting substantial rights, judicial notice, see § 90.104.
Instructions to jury in civil actions, objections, see Civil Procedure Rule 1.470.
Instructions to jury in criminal actions,
    Generally, see Criminal Procedure Rule 3.390.
    Additional or corrective instructions, time, see Criminal Procedure Rule 3.540.
    Attempt, conviction, see Criminal Procedure Rule 3.510.
    Degree of offense, see Criminal Procedure Rule 3.490.
    Lesser included offense, see Criminal Procedure Rule 3.510.
    New trial, grounds, refusal or erroneous instructions, see Criminal Procedure Rule 3.600.
    Recall for additional instructions, see Criminal Procedure Rule 3.420.
    Return for supplemental instructions, see Criminal Procedure Rule 3.410.
    Review, see § 924.33.
    Standard jury instructions, see Criminal Procedure Rule 3.985.
    Taking into jury room, see Criminal Procedure Rule 3.400.
Rulemaking proceedings, judicial notice by agency, Administrative Procedure Act, see § 120.54.

90.207. Judicial notice by trial court in subsequent proceedings

The failure or refusal of a court to take judicial notice of a matter does not preclude a court from taking judicial notice of the matter in subsequent proceedings, in accordance with the procedure specified in ss. 90.201–90.206.

Laws 1976, c. 76–237, § 1.

Cross References

Judicial notice,
    Administrative law and procedure, see § 120.54.
    County court records prior to 1875, see § 28.16.
    Fundamental errors affecting substantial rights, see § 90.104.
    Real estate commission, rules and bylaws, see § 475.05.
    Territorial court records, see § 28.15.
Matters which may be judicially noticed, see § 90.202.

90.301. Presumption defined; inferences

(1) For the purposes of this chapter, a presumption is an assumption of fact which the law makes from the existence of another fact or group of facts found or otherwise established.

(2) Except for presumptions that are conclusive under the law from which they arise, a presumption is rebuttable.

(3) Nothing in this chapter shall prevent the drawing of an inference that is appropriate.

(4) Sections 90.301–90.304 are applicable only in civil actions or proceedings.

Laws 1978, c. 78–361, added subsec. (4); Laws 1976, c. 76–237, § 1; Laws 1978, c. 78–361, § 5.

Cross References

Bail, right to, exception, see Const. Art. 1, § 14.
Civil courts of records, jurisdiction, see Const. Art. 5, § 5.
Codicils, revocation, reinstatement of prior will, see § 732.508.
Commercial code, presumption defined, see § 671.201.
Driving under influence, see § 316.1934.
Error not affecting substantial rights of accused, see § 924.33.
Estate tax prima facie liability, see § 198.32.
Evidence as to death or status, see § 731.103; Probate Rule 5.170.
Foreign will, authority to convey, see § 734.104.

Joint wills, see § 732.701.
Judicial sales, value of property sold, see § 45.031.
Legitimacy of child, artificial insemination, see § 742.11.
Names, variances, recorded instruments, see § 689.19.
Negotiable instruments,
    Consideration, see § 673.3031.
    Date of instrument, see § 673.1131.
    Holder in due course, see § 673.3081.
Offense occurring within state, see § 910.005.
Order of liability of endorsers, see § 673.4151.
Original instrument unavailable and record destroyed, acknowledgment, see § 92.27.
Personal property taxation, value, see § 199.232.
Possession, legal owner of property, see § 95.13.
Prima facie evidence,
    Bills of lading, insurance policies, etc., see § 671.202.
    Fingerprints, judgments, felony convictions, see § 921.241.
Process, doing business within state, see § 48.181.
Recording instrument from time of filing, see § 695.11.
Tax assessments, standard measure of valuation, see § 195.032.
Value of tangible property as that shown on return, see § 199.232.
Vesting of joint bank account in survivor, see § 655.79.

90.302. Classification of rebuttable presumptions

Every rebuttable presumption is either:

(1) A presumption affecting the burden of producing evidence and requiring the trier of fact to assume the existence of the presumed fact, unless credible evidence sufficient to sustain a finding of the nonexistence of the presumed fact is introduced, in which event, the existence or nonexistence of the presumed fact shall be determined from the evidence without regard to the presumption; or

(2) A presumption affecting the burden of proof that imposes upon the party against whom it operates the burden of proof concerning the nonexistence of the presumed fact.

Laws 1976, c. 76–237, § 1.

Cross References

Presumption, defined, see § 90.301.
Will contests, presumption of undue influence, see § 733.107.

90.303. Presumption affecting the burden of producing evidence defined

In a civil action or proceeding, unless otherwise provided by statute, a presumption established primarily to facilitate the determination of the particular action in which the presumption is applied, rather than to implement public policy, is a presumption affecting the burden of producing evidence.

Laws 1976, c. 76–237, § 1.

Cross References

Presumptions, generally, see § 90.301.

90.304. Presumption affecting the burden of proof defined

In civil actions, all rebuttable presumptions which are not defined in s. 90.303 are presumptions affecting the burden of proof.

Laws 1976, c. 76–237, § 1.

Cross References

Alibi, see Criminal Procedure Rule 3.200.
Cross-Claims and counterclaim, see Civil Procedure Rule 1.170.
Defenses, affirmative, pleading, see Civil Procedure Rule 1.110.
Legitimization by marriage, see § 732.108.

90.401. Definition of relevant evidence

Relevant evidence is evidence tending to prove or disprove a material fact.

Laws 1976, c. 76–237, § 1.

Cross References

Compromise and offers to compromise, see § 90.408.
Cross-examination, see § 90.612.
Impeachment evidence, see § 90.608 et seq.
Limited admissibility, see § 90.107.
Offers to plead guilty, nolo contendere, or withdrawn pleas of guilty, see § 90.410.
Opinion testimony, see § 90.701 et seq.
Payment of damages or medical expenses, see § 90.409.
Preliminary questions, see § 90.105.
Privileged matter, see § 90.501 et seq.
Religious beliefs or opinions, see § 90.611.
Rulings on evidence, see § 90.104.
Subsequent remedial measures, see § 90.407.

90.402. Admissibility of relevant evidence

All relevant evidence is admissible, except as provided by law.

Laws 1976, c. 76–237, § 1.

Cross References

Compromise and offers to compromise, see § 90.408.
Cross-examination, see § 90.612.
Impeachment evidence, see § 90.608 et seq.
Limited admissibility, see § 90.107.
Offers to plead guilty, nolo contendere, or withdrawn pleas of guilty, see § 90.410.
Opinion testimony, see § 90.701 et seq.
Payment of damages or medical expenses, see § 90.409.
Preliminary questions, see § 90.105.
Privileged matter, see § 90.501 et seq.
Religious beliefs or opinions, see § 90.611.
Rulings on evidence, see § 90.104.
Subsequent remedial measures, see § 90.407.

90.4025. Admissibility of paternity determination in certain criminal prosecutions

If a person less than 18 years of age gives birth to a child and the paternity of that child is established under chapter 742, such evidence of paternity is admissible in a criminal prosecution under ss. 794.011, 794.05, 800.04, and 827.04(3).

Added by Laws 1996, c. 96–215, § 8, eff. Oct. 1, 1996; Laws 1996, c. 96–409, § 2, eff. Oct. 1, 1996; Laws 1999, c. 99–2, § 27, eff. June 29, 1999.

90.4026. Statements expressing sympathy; admissibility; definitions

(1) As used in this section:

(a) "Accident" means an occurrence resulting in injury or death to one or more persons which is not the result of willful action by a party.

(b) "Benevolent gestures" means actions that convey a sense of compassion or commiseration emanating from human impulses.

(c) "Family" means the spouse, parent, grandparent, stepmother, stepfather, child, grandchild, brother, sister, half-brother, half-sister, adopted child of parent, or spouse's parent of an injured party.

(2) The portion of statements, writings, or benevolent gestures expressing sympathy or a general sense of benevolence relating to the pain, suffering, or death of a person involved in an accident and made to that person or to the family of that person shall be inadmissible as evidence in a civil action. A statement of fault, however, which is part of, or in addition to, any of the above shall be admissible pursuant to this section.

Added by Laws 2001, c. 2001–132, § 1, eff. June 1, 2001.

90.403. Exclusion on grounds of prejudice or confusion

Relevant evidence is inadmissible if its probative value is substantially outweighed by the danger of unfair prejudice, confusion of issues, misleading the jury, or needless presentation of cumulative evidence. This section shall not be construed to mean that evidence of the existence of available third-party benefits is inadmissible.

Laws 1976, c. 76–237, § 1; Laws 1978, c. 78–361, § 6.

Cross References

Mode and order of interrogation and presentation, see § 90.612.
Rulings on evidence, see § 90.104.

90.404. Character evidence; when admissible

(1) Character evidence generally.—Evidence of a person's character or a trait of character is inadmissible to prove action in conformity with it on a particular occasion, except:

(a) *Character of accused.*—Evidence of a pertinent trait of character offered by an accused, or by the prosecution to rebut the trait.

(b) *Character of victim.*—

1. Except as provided in s. 794.022, evidence of a pertinent trait of character of the victim of the crime offered by an accused, or by the prosecution to rebut the trait; or

2. Evidence of a character trait of peacefulness of the victim offered by the prosecution in a homicide case to rebut evidence that the victim was the aggressor.

(c) *Character of witness.*—Evidence of the character of a witness, as provided in ss. 90.608–90.610.

(2) Other crimes, wrongs, or acts.—

(a) Similar fact evidence of other crimes, wrongs, or acts is admissible when relevant to prove a material fact in issue, including, but not limited to, proof of motive, opportunity, intent, preparation, plan, knowledge, identity, or absence of mistake or accident, but it is inadmissible when the evidence is relevant solely to prove bad character or propensity.

(b) 1. In a criminal case in which the defendant is charged with a crime involving child molestation, evidence of the defendant's commission of other crimes, wrongs, or acts of child molestation is admissible and may be considered for its bearing on any matter to which it is relevant.

2. For the purposes of this paragraph, the term "child molestation" means conduct proscribed by s. 787.025(2)(c), s. 787.06(3)(g), former s. 787.06(3)(h), s. 794.011, excluding s. 794.011(10), s. 794.05, former s. 796.03, former s. 796.035, s. 800.04, s. 827.071, s. 847.0135(5), s. 847.0145, or s. 985.701(1) when committed against a person 16 years of age or younger.

(c) 1. In a criminal case in which the defendant is charged with a sexual offense, evidence of the defendant's commission of other crimes, wrongs, or acts involving a sexual offense is admissible and may be considered for its bearing on any matter to which it is relevant.

2. For the purposes of this paragraph, the term "sexual offense" means conduct proscribed by s. 787.025(2)(c), s. 787.06(3)(b), (d), (f), or (g), former s. 787.06(3)(h), s. 794.011, excluding s. 794.011(10), s. 794.05, former s. 796.03, former s. 796.035, s. 825.1025(2)(b), s. 827.071, s. 847.0135(5), s. 847.0145, or s. 985.701(1).

(d) 1. When the state in a criminal action intends to offer evidence of other criminal offenses under paragraph (a), paragraph (b), or paragraph (c), no fewer than 10 days before trial, the state shall furnish to the defendant or to the defendant's counsel a written statement of the acts or offenses it intends to offer, describing them with the particularity required of an indictment or information. No notice is required for evidence of offenses used for impeachment or on rebuttal.

2. When the evidence is admitted, the court shall, if requested, charge the jury on the limited purpose for which the evidence is received and is to be considered. After the close of the evidence, the jury shall be instructed on the limited purpose for which the evidence was received and that the defendant cannot be convicted for a charge not included in the indictment or information.

(3) Nothing in this section affects the admissibility of evidence under s. 90.610.

Laws 1976, c. 76–237, § 1. Amended by Laws 1990, c. 90–40, § 2, eff. June 1, 1990; Laws 1993, c. 93–156, § 26, eff. Oct. 1, 1993; Laws 1995, c. 95–147, § 473, eff. July 10, 1995; Laws 2001, c. 2001–221, § 1, eff. July 1, 2001; Laws 2008, c. 2008–172, § 9, eff. Oct. 1, 2008; Laws 2011, c. 2011–220, § 2, eff. July 1, 2011; Laws 2012, c. 2012–97, § 14, eff. July 1, 2012; Laws 2014, c. 2014–160, § 15, eff. Oct. 1, 2014.

Cross References

Abatement of nuisances, evidence of character and reputation, see § 60.05.
Character of witness as impeachment, see § 90.609.
Conviction of crime involving dishonesty or false statement, see § 90.610.
Impeachment, see § 90.608 et seq.
Limited admissibility, see § 90.107.
Religious beliefs or opinions, see § 90.611.
Threats made to expose one to public disgrace,
   Generally, see § 836.05.
   Public servants, see § 838.021.

90.405. Methods of proving character

(1) **Reputation.**—When evidence of the character of a person or of a trait of that person's character is admissible, proof may be made by testimony about that person's reputation.

(2) **Specific instances of conduct.**—When character or a trait of character of a person is an essential element of a charge, claim, or defense, proof may be made of specific instances of that person's conduct.

Laws 1976, c. 76–237, § 1; Laws 1978, c. 78–361, § 7. Amended by Laws 1995, c. 95–147, § 474, eff. July 10, 1995.

Cross References

Conviction of crime involving dishonesty or false statement, impeachment, see § 90.610.
Credibility of witnesses, evidence of truth and veracity, see § 90.609.
Cross-examination, see § 90.612.
Impeachment, see § 90.608 et seq.
Religious beliefs or opinions, evidence of credibility, see § 90.611.

90.406. Routine practice

Evidence of the routine practice of an organization, whether corroborated or not and regardless of the presence of eyewitnesses, is admissible to prove that the conduct of the organization on a particular occasion was in conformity with the routine practice.

Laws 1976, c. 76–237, § 1.

Cross References

Opinion testimony by lay witnesses, see § 90.701.
Uniform Commercial Code,
    Contract for sale, see §§ 672.202, 672.208.
    Course of dealing and usage of trade, see § 671.205.
    Implied warranty, sales, usage of trade, see § 672.314.

90.407. Subsequent remedial measures

Evidence of measures taken after an injury or harm caused by an event, which measures if taken before the event would have made injury or harm less likely to occur, is not admissible to prove negligence, the existence of a product defect, or culpable conduct in connection with the event. This rule does not require the exclusion of evidence of subsequent remedial measures when offered for another purpose, such as proving ownership, control, or the feasibility of precautionary measures, if controverted, or impeachment.

Laws 1976, c. 76–237, § 1; Laws 1977, c. 77–174, § 1. Amended by Laws 1999, c. 99–225, § 13, eff. Oct. 1, 1999.

90.408. Compromise and offers to compromise

Evidence of an offer to compromise a claim which was disputed as to validity or amount, as well as any relevant conduct or statements made in negotiations concerning a compromise, is inadmissible to prove liability or absence of liability for the claim or its value.

Laws 1976, c. 76–237, § 1.

Cross References

Claims against estates, see § 733.708.
Claims settlements, guardian and ward, see § 744.387.
Contribution among tortfeasors, see § 768.31.
Malpractice, immunity from liability, see § 766.101.
Probate, personal representative, powers and duties, see § 733.612.
Release or covenant not to sue, tort claims, see § 768.041.
Tort actions against state or state agencies, see § 768.28.
Unfair or deceptive acts and practices relating to vehicles, demand letters, see F.S.A. § 501.98.
Wrongful death actions, court approval, see § 768.25.

90.409. Payment of medical and similar expenses

Evidence of furnishing, or offering or promising to pay, medical or hospital expenses or other damages occasioned by an injury or accident is inadmissible to prove liability for the injury or accident.

Laws 1976, c. 76–237, § 1.

Cross References

Malpractice, immunity from liability, see § 766.101.

90.410. Offer to plead guilty; nolo contendere; withdrawn pleas of guilty

Evidence of a plea of guilty, later withdrawn; a plea of nolo contendere; or an offer to plead guilty or nolo contendere to the crime charged or any other crime is inadmissible in any civil or criminal proceeding. Evidence of statements made in connection with any of the pleas or offers is inadmissible, except when such statements are offered in a prosecution under chapter 837.

Laws 1976, c. 76–237, § 1; Laws 1978, c. 78–361, § 8.

Cross References

Degrees of crime,
    Generally, see Criminal Procedure Rule 3.170.
    Felonies and misdemeanors, see § 775.081.
Guilty plea,
    Acceptance of plea, see Criminal Procedure Rule 3.172.
    Arraignment, see Criminal Procedure Rule 3.160.
    Determination of punishment, see Criminal Procedure Rule 3.700 et seq.
    Entry, see Criminal Procedure Rules 3.160, 3.170.
    Lesser offenses or degrees, see Criminal Procedure Rule 3.170.
    Presence of defendant, see Criminal Procedure Rule 3.180.
    Right of appeal, see § 924.06.
    Trial of accused at place of arrest, see § 910.035.
    Withdrawal of plea, see Criminal Procedure Rule 3.170.
Indemnification of corporate officers, directors, employees, or agents, see § 607.0850.
Nolo contendere,
    Acceptance of plea, see Criminal Procedure Rule 3.172.
    Presentence investigation reports, see § 921.231.
    Right of appeal, see § 924.06.
    Trial of accused at place of arrest, see § 910.035.
Not guilty plea, transfer of proceeding to original place of trial, see § 910.035.
Perjury, see § 837.011 et seq.
Plea discussions and agreements, see Criminal Procedure Rule 3.171.
Pleas, see Criminal Procedure Rule 3.170.
Presence of defendant, see Criminal Procedure Rule 3.180.

90.501. Privileges recognized only as provided

Except as otherwise provided by this chapter, any other statute, or the Constitution of the United States or of the State of Florida, no person in a legal proceeding has a privilege to:

(1) Refuse to be a witness.

(2) Refuse to disclose any matter.

(3) Refuse to produce any object or writing.

(4) Prevent another from being a witness, from disclosing any matter, or from producing any object or writing.

Laws 1976, c. 76–237, § 1; Laws 1978, c. 78–361, § 9.

Cross References

Accident reports, see § 316.066.
Adoption hearings and records, confidentiality, see § 63.162.
Attendance, criminal cases,
Generally, see § 914.03.
Reading of deposition, see Criminal Procedure Rule 3.190.
Compulsory process, favor of accused, see Const. Art. 1, § 16.
Contempt, failure to make discovery, see Civil Procedure Rule 1.380.
Continuing duty to disclose, see Criminal Procedure Rule 3.220.
Criminal contempt, departure without leave of court, see § 914.03.
Depositions,
Generally, see Criminal Procedure Rule 3.190.
Failure to attend and proceed, see Civil Procedure Rule 1.310.
Extradition, see § 942.01 et seq.
Hostile, leading questions, see Civil Procedure Rule 1.450.
Indirect criminal contempt, compulsory process for attendance, see Criminal Procedure Rule 3.840.
Legislature, compelling attendance, see Const. Art. 3, § 5.
Medical review committee hearings, immunity from testifying at civil actions, see § 766.101.
Parole revocation hearings, compelling attendance, see § 947.23.
Production of books and papers, generally, see Civil Procedure Rules 1.280, 1.350, 1.410.
Self-incrimination, immunity, see §§ 914.04, 914.05.
Subpoenas, see Civil Procedure Rule 1.410.
Supplementary proceedings, refusal to answer, see § 56.29.
Tampering with witnesses, see § 914.22.
Usury prosecution, immunity of witness, see § 687.071.
Venue change, attendance, see Criminal Procedure Rule 3.240.

90.5015. Journalist's privilege

(1) Definitions.— For purposes of this section, the term:

(a) "Professional journalist" means a person regularly engaged in collecting, photographing, recording, writing, editing, reporting, or publishing news, for gain or livelihood, who obtained the information sought while working as a salaried employee of, or independent contractor for, a newspaper, news journal, news agency, press association, wire service, radio or television station, network, or news magazine. Book authors and others who are not professional journalists, as defined in this paragraph, are not included in the provisions of this section.

(b) "News" means information of public concern relating to local, statewide, national, or worldwide issues or events.

(2) Privilege.— A professional journalist has a qualified privilege not to be a witness concerning, and not to disclose the information, including the identity of any source, that the professional journalist has obtained while actively gathering news. This privilege applies only to information or eyewitness observations obtained within the normal scope of employment and does not apply to physical evidence, eyewitness observations, or visual or audio recording of crimes. A party seeking to overcome this privilege must make a clear and specific showing that:

(a) The information is relevant and material to unresolved issues that have been raised in the proceeding for which the information is sought;

(b) The information cannot be obtained from alternative sources; and

(c) A compelling interest exists for requiring disclosure of the information.

(3) Disclosure.— A court shall order disclosure pursuant to subsection (2) only of that portion of the information for which the showing under subsection (2) has been made and shall support such order with clear and specific findings made after a hearing.

(4) Waiver.— A professional journalist does not waive the privilege by publishing or broadcasting information.

(5) Construction.— This section must not be construed to limit any privilege or right provided to a professional journalist under law.

(6) Authentication.— Photographs, diagrams, video recordings, audio recordings, computer records, or other business records maintained, disclosed, provided, or produced by a professional journalist, or by the employer or principal of a professional journalist, may be authenticated for admission in evidence upon a showing, by affidavit of the professional journalist, or other individual with personal knowledge, that the photograph, diagram, video recording, audio recording, computer record, or other business record is a true and accurate copy of the original, and that the copy truly and accurately reflects the observations and facts contained therein.

(7) Accuracy of evidence.— If the affidavit of authenticity and accuracy, or other relevant factual circumstance, causes the court to have clear and convincing doubts as to the authenticity or accuracy of the proffered evidence, the court may decline to admit such evidence.

(8) Severability.—If any provision of this section or its application to any particular person or circumstance is held invalid, that provision or its application is severable and does not affect the validity of other provisions or applications of this section.
Added by Laws 1998, c. 98–48, § 1, eff. May 12, 1998.

Cross References

Waiver of privilege by voluntary disclosure, see § 90.507.

90.502. Lawyer-client privilege

(1) For purposes of this section:

(a) A "lawyer" is a person authorized, or reasonably believed by the client to be authorized, to practice law in any state or nation.

(b) A "client" is any person, public officer, corporation, association, or other organization or entity, either public or private, who consults a lawyer with the purpose of obtaining legal services or who is rendered legal services by a lawyer.

(c) A communication between lawyer and client is "confidential" if it is not intended to be disclosed to third persons other than:

1. Those to whom disclosure is in furtherance of the rendition of legal services to the client.

2. Those reasonably necessary for the transmission of the communication.

(2) A client has a privilege to refuse to disclose, and to prevent any other person from disclosing, the contents of confidential communications when such other person learned of the communications because they were made in the rendition of legal services to the client.

(3) The privilege may be claimed by:

(a) The client.

(b) A guardian or conservator of the client.

(c) The personal representative of a deceased client.

(d) A successor, assignee, trustee in dissolution, or any similar representative of an organization, corporation, or association or other entity, either public or private, whether or not in existence.

(e) The lawyer, but only on behalf of the client. The lawyer's authority to claim the privilege is presumed in the absence of contrary evidence.

(4) There is no lawyer-client privilege under this section when:

(a) The services of the lawyer were sought or obtained to enable or aid anyone to commit or plan to commit what the client knew was a crime or fraud.

(b) A communication is relevant to an issue between parties who claim through the same deceased client.

(c) A communication is relevant to an issue of breach of duty by the lawyer to the client or by the client to the lawyer, arising from the lawyer-client relationship.

(d) A communication is relevant to an issue concerning the intention or competence of a client executing an attested document to which the lawyer is an attesting witness, or concerning the execution or attestation of the document.

(e) A communication is relevant to a matter of common interest between two or more clients, or their successors in interest, if the communication was made by any of them to a lawyer retained or consulted in common when offered in a civil action between the clients or their successors in interest.

(5) Communications made by a person who seeks or receives services from the Department of Revenue under the child support enforcement program to the attorney representing the department shall be confidential and privileged as provided for in this section. Such communications shall not be disclosed to anyone other than the agency except as provided for in this section. Such disclosures shall be protected as if there were an attorney-client relationship between the attorney for the agency and the person who seeks services from the department.

(6) A discussion or activity that is not a meeting for purposes of s. 286.011 shall not be construed to waive the attorney-client privilege established in this section. This shall not be construed to constitute an exemption to either s. 119.07 or s. 286.011.

Laws 1976, c. 76–237, § 1. Amended by Laws 1992, c. 92–138, § 16, eff. July 1, 1992; Laws 1994, c. 94–124, § 12, eff. July 1, 1994; Laws 1995, c. 95–147, § 1378, eff. July 10, 1995; Laws 2000, c. 2000–316, § 1, eff. July 1, 2000.

Cross References

Abuse of developmentally disabled persons, attorney-client privilege, see § 415.107.
Accountant-client privilege, see § 90.5055.
Champerty and maintenance, see § 877.01.
Homeowners' associations, inspection of records, see § 720.303.
Protective order, discovery, see Civil Procedure Rule 1.280.
Real estate cooperative association records, see F.S.A. § 719.104.
Voluntary disclosure, waiver of privilege, see § 90.507.

90.5021. Fiduciary lawyer-client privilege

(1) For the purpose of this section, a client acts as a fiduciary when serving as a personal representative or a trustee as defined in ss. 731.201 and 736.0103, an administrator ad litem as described in s. 733.308, a curator as described in s. 733.501, a guardian or guardian ad litem as defined in s. 744.102, a conservator as defined in s. 710.102, or an attorney in fact as described in chapter 709.

(2) A communication between a lawyer and a client acting as a fiduciary is privileged and protected from disclosure under s. 90.502 to the same extent as if the client were not acting as a

fiduciary. In applying s. 90.502 to a communication under this section, only the person or entity acting as a fiduciary is considered a client of the lawyer.

(3) This section does not affect the crime or fraud exception to the lawyer-client privilege provided in s. 90.502(4)(a).

Added by Laws 2011, c. 2011–183, § 1, eff. June 21, 2011.

90.503. Psychotherapist-patient privilege

(1) For purposes of this section:

(a) A "psychotherapist" is:

1. A person authorized to practice medicine in any state or nation, or reasonably believed by the patient so to be, who is engaged in the diagnosis or treatment of a mental or emotional condition, including alcoholism and other drug addiction;

2. A person licensed or certified as a psychologist under the laws of any state or nation, who is engaged primarily in the diagnosis or treatment of a mental or emotional condition, including alcoholism and other drug addiction;

3. A person licensed or certified as a clinical social worker, marriage and family therapist, or mental health counselor under the laws of this state, who is engaged primarily in the diagnosis or treatment of a mental or emotional condition, including alcoholism and other drug addiction;

4. Treatment personnel of facilities licensed by the state pursuant to chapter 394, chapter 395, or chapter 397, of facilities designated by the Department of Children and Families pursuant to chapter 394 as treatment facilities, or of facilities defined as community mental health centers pursuant to s. 394.907(1), who are engaged primarily in the diagnosis or treatment of a mental or emotional condition, including alcoholism and other drug addiction; or

5. An advanced registered nurse practitioner certified under s. 464.012, whose primary scope of practice is the diagnosis or treatment of mental or emotional conditions, including chemical abuse, and limited only to actions performed in accordance with part I of chapter 464.

(b) A "patient" is a person who consults, or is interviewed by, a psychotherapist for purposes of diagnosis or treatment of a mental or emotional condition, including alcoholism and other drug addiction.

(c) A communication between psychotherapist and patient is "confidential" if it is not intended to be disclosed to third persons other than:

1. Those persons present to further the interest of the patient in the consultation, examination, or interview.

2. Those persons necessary for the transmission of the communication.

3. Those persons who are participating in the diagnosis and treatment under the direction of the psychotherapist.

(2) A patient has a privilege to refuse to disclose, and to prevent any other person from disclosing, confidential communications or records made for the purpose of diagnosis or treatment of the patient's mental or emotional condition, including alcoholism and other drug addiction, between the patient and the psychotherapist, or persons who are participating in the diagnosis or treatment under the direction of the psychotherapist. This privilege includes any diagnosis made, and advice given, by the psychotherapist in the course of that relationship.

(3) The privilege may be claimed by:

(a) The patient or the patient's attorney on the patient's behalf.

(b) A guardian or conservator of the patient.

(c) The personal representative of a deceased patient.

(d) The psychotherapist, but only on behalf of the patient. The authority of a psychotherapist to claim the privilege is presumed in the absence of evidence to the contrary.

(4) There is no privilege under this section:

(a) For communications relevant to an issue in proceedings to compel hospitalization of a patient for mental illness, if the psychotherapist in the course of diagnosis or treatment has reasonable cause to believe the patient is in need of hospitalization.

(b) For communications made in the course of a court-ordered examination of the mental or emotional condition of the patient.

(c) For communications relevant to an issue of the mental or emotional condition of the patient in any proceeding in which the patient relies upon the condition as an element of his or her claim or defense or, after the patient's death, in any proceeding in which any party relies upon the condition as an element of the party's claim or defense.

Laws 1976, c. 76–237, § 1. Amended by Laws 1990, c. 90–347, § 40, eff. Oct. 1, 1990; Laws 1992, c. 92–57, § 1, eff. April 3, 1992; Laws 1993, c. 93–39, § 19, eff. Oct. 1, 1993; Laws 1995, c. 95–147, § 475, eff. July 10, 1995; Laws 1999, c. 99–2, § 28, eff. June 29, 1999; Laws 1999, c. 99–8, § 5, eff. June 29, 1999; Laws 2006, c. 2006–204, § 1, eff. July 1, 2006; Laws 2014, c. 2014–19, § 30, eff. July 1, 2014.

Cross References

Medical information, release for research purposes, see § 405.01 et seq.

Mental and medical examination in civil actions, see Civil Procedure Rule 1.360.

Mental condition of defendant, hearing to determine, see Criminal Procedure Rule 3.210.

Mental institution clinical records, see § 394.459.

Microfilming of records of state institutions, see § 402.19.

Patient threats, disclosure by psychiatrist to warn victim or law enforcement agency, see § 456.059.

Protective order, discovery, see Civil Procedure Rule 1.280.

Report of mental or physical examination to be furnished patient, see § 456.057.

90.5035. Sexual assault counselor-victim privilege

(1) For purposes of this section:

(a) A "rape crisis center" is any public or private agency that offers assistance to victims of sexual assault or sexual battery and their families.

(b) A "sexual assault counselor" is any employee of a rape crisis center whose primary purpose is the rendering of advice, counseling, or assistance to victims of sexual assault or sexual battery.

(c) A "trained volunteer" is a person who volunteers at a rape crisis center, has completed 30 hours of training in assisting victims of sexual violence and related topics provided by the rape crisis center, is supervised by members of the staff of the rape crisis center, and is included on a list of volunteers that is maintained by the rape crisis center.

(d) A "victim" is a person who consults a sexual assault counselor or a trained volunteer for the purpose of securing advice, counseling, or assistance concerning a mental, physical, or emotional condition caused by a sexual assault or sexual battery, an alleged sexual assault or sexual battery, or an attempted sexual assault or sexual battery.

(e) A communication between a sexual assault counselor or trained volunteer and a victim is "confidential" if it is not intended to be disclosed to third persons other than:

1. Those persons present to further the interest of the victim in the consultation, examination, or interview.

2. Those persons necessary for the transmission of the communication.

3. Those persons to whom disclosure is reasonably necessary to accomplish the purposes for which the sexual assault counselor or the trained volunteer is consulted.

(2) A victim has a privilege to refuse to disclose, and to prevent any other person from disclosing, a confidential communication made by the victim to a sexual assault counselor or trained volunteer or any record made in the course of advising, counseling, or assisting the victim. Such confidential communication or record may be disclosed only with the prior written consent of the victim. This privilege includes any advice given by the sexual assault counselor or trained volunteer in the course of that relationship.

(3) The privilege may be claimed by:

(a) The victim or the victim's attorney on his or her behalf.

(b) A guardian or conservator of the victim.

(c) The personal representative of a deceased victim.

(d) The sexual assault counselor or trained volunteer, but only on behalf of the victim. The authority of a sexual assault counselor or trained volunteer to claim the privilege is presumed in the absence of evidence to the contrary.

Added by Laws 1983, c. 83–284, § 1, eff. June 24, 1983. Amended by Laws 1995, c. 95–147, § 476, eff. July 10, 1995; Laws 2002, c. 2002–246, § 1, eff. July 1, 2002.

90.5036. Domestic violence advocate-victim privilege

(1) For purposes of this section:

(a) A "domestic violence center" is any public or private agency that offers assistance to victims of domestic violence, as defined in s. 741.28, and their families.

(b) A "domestic violence advocate" means any employee or volunteer who has 30 hours of training in assisting victims of domestic violence and is an employee of or volunteer for a program for victims of domestic violence whose primary purpose is the rendering of advice, counseling, or assistance to victims of domestic violence.

(c) A "victim" is a person who consults a domestic violence advocate for the purpose of securing advice, counseling, or assistance concerning a mental, physical, or emotional condition caused by an act of domestic violence, an alleged act of domestic violence, or an attempted act of domestic violence.

(d) A communication between a domestic violence advocate and a victim is "confidential" if it relates to the incident of domestic violence for which the victim is seeking assistance and if it is not intended to be disclosed to third persons other than:

1. Those persons present to further the interest of the victim in the consultation, assessment, or interview.

2. Those persons to whom disclosure is reasonably necessary to accomplish the purpose for which the domestic violence advocate is consulted.

(2) A victim has a privilege to refuse to disclose, and to prevent any other person from disclosing, a confidential communication made by the victim to a domestic violence advocate or

any record made in the course of advising, counseling, or assisting the victim. The privilege applies to confidential communications made between the victim and the domestic violence advocate and to records of those communications only if the advocate is registered under s. 39.905 at the time the communication is made. This privilege includes any advice given by the domestic violence advocate in the course of that relationship.

(3) The privilege may be claimed by:

(a) The victim or the victim's attorney on behalf of the victim.

(b) A guardian or conservator of the victim.

(c) The personal representative of a deceased victim.

(d) The domestic violence advocate, but only on behalf of the victim. The authority of a domestic violence advocate to claim the privilege is presumed in the absence of evidence to the contrary.

Added by Laws 1995, c. 95–187, § 7, eff. July 1, 1995. Amended by Laws 1998, c. 98–403, § 127, eff. Oct. 1, 1998.

Cross References

Domestic violence centers, see § 39.905.

90.504. Husband-wife privilege

(1) A spouse has a privilege during and after the marital relationship to refuse to disclose, and to prevent another from disclosing, communications which were intended to be made in confidence between the spouses while they were husband and wife.

(2) The privilege may be claimed by either spouse or by the guardian or conservator of a spouse. The authority of a spouse, or guardian or conservator of a spouse, to claim the privilege is presumed in the absence of contrary evidence.

(3) There is no privilege under this section:

(a) In a proceeding brought by or on behalf of one spouse against the other spouse.

(b) In a criminal proceeding in which one spouse is charged with a crime committed at any time against the person or property of the other spouse, or the person or property of a child of either.

(c) In a criminal proceeding in which the communication is offered in evidence by a defendant-spouse who is one of the spouses between whom the communication was made.

Laws 1976, c. 76–237, § 1; Laws 1978, c. 78–361, § 10.

Cross References

Bigamy, see § 826.01 et seq.
Competency of evidence and witnesses in criminal cases, see § 914.07.
Conveyances between spouses, see § 689.11.
Evidence as to death or status, see Probate Rule 5.170.
Handicapped persons, cruelty, report, see § 415.107.
Nonsupport as offense, see § 856.04.
Personal injuries, joinder of spouse, see § 46.031.
Protective order, discovery, see Civil Procedure Rule 1.280.

90.505. Privilege with respect to communications to clergy

(1) For the purposes of this section:

(a) A "member of the clergy" is a priest, rabbi, practitioner of Christian Science, or minister of any religious organization or denomination usually referred to as a church, or an individual reasonably believed so to be by the person consulting him or her.

(b) A communication between a member of the clergy and a person is "confidential" if made privately for the purpose of seeking spiritual counsel and advice from the member of the clergy in the usual course of his or her practice or discipline and not intended for further disclosure except to other persons present in furtherance of the communication.

(2) A person has a privilege to refuse to disclose, and to prevent another from disclosing, a confidential communication by the person to a member of the clergy in his or her capacity as spiritual adviser.

(3) The privilege may be claimed by:

(a) The person.

(b) The guardian or conservator of a person.

(c) The personal representative of a deceased person.

(d) The member of the clergy, on behalf of the person. The member of the clergy's authority to do so is presumed in the absence of evidence to the contrary.

Laws 1976, c. 76–237, § 1; Laws 1977, c. 77–174, § 1; Laws 1978, c. 78–361, § 11. Amended by Laws 1995, c. 95–147, § 477, eff. July 10, 1995.

Cross References

Religious freedom, guarantee, see Const. Art. 1, § 3.

90.5055. Accountant-client privilege

(1) For purposes of this section:

(a) An "accountant" is a certified public accountant or a public accountant.

(b) A "client" is any person, public officer, corporation, association, or other organization or entity, either public or private, who consults an accountant with the purpose of obtaining accounting services.

(c) A communication between an accountant and the accountant's client is "confidential" if it is not intended to be disclosed to third persons other than:

1. Those to whom disclosure is in furtherance of the rendition of accounting services to the client.

2. Those reasonably necessary for the transmission of the communication.

(2) A client has a privilege to refuse to disclose, and to prevent any other person from disclosing, the contents of confidential communications with an accountant when such other person learned of the communications because they were made in the rendition of accounting services to the client. This privilege includes other confidential information obtained by the accountant from the client for the purpose of rendering accounting advice.

(3) The privilege may be claimed by:

(a) The client.

(b) A guardian or conservator of the client.

(c) The personal representative of a deceased client.

(d) A successor, assignee, trustee in dissolution, or any similar representative of an organization, corporation, or association or other entity, either public or private, whether or not in existence.

(e) The accountant, but only on behalf of the client. The accountant's authority to claim the privilege is presumed in the absence of contrary evidence.

(4) There is no accountant-client privilege under this section when:

(a) The services of the accountant were sought or obtained to enable or aid anyone to commit or plan to commit what the client knew or should have known was a crime or fraud.

(b) A communication is relevant to an issue of breach of duty by the accountant to the accountant's client or by the client to his or her accountant.

(c) A communication is relevant to a matter of common interest between two or more clients, if the communication was made by any of them to an accountant retained or consulted in common when offered in a civil action between the clients.

Laws 1978, c. 78–361, § 12. Amended by Laws 1995, c. 95–147, § 478, eff. July 10, 1995.

Cross References

Lawyer-client privilege, see § 90.502.
Privileges, generally, see § 90.501.
Protective order, discovery, see Civil Procedure Rule 1.280.
Public accountancy generally, see § 473.302 et seq.
Similar provision in accountancy law, see § 473.316.
Voluntary disclosure, waiver of privilege, see § 90.507.

90.506. Privilege with respect to trade secrets

A person has a privilege to refuse to disclose, and to prevent other persons from disclosing, a trade secret owned by that person if the allowance of the privilege will not conceal fraud or otherwise work injustice. When the court directs disclosure, it shall take the protective measures that the interests of the holder of the privilege, the interests of the parties, and the furtherance of justice require. The privilege may be claimed by the person or the person's agent or employee.

Laws 1976, c. 76–237, § 1. Amended by Laws 1995, c. 95–147, § 479, eff. July 10, 1995.

Cross References

Protective order, discovery, see Civil Procedure Rule 1.280.
Restraint of trade, invalid contracts, see § 542.33.
Theft, embezzlement and unlawful copying of trade secrets, see § 812.081.
Trade-marks and trade-names, generally, see § 495.011 et seq.

90.507. Waiver of privilege by voluntary disclosure

A person who has a privilege against the disclosure of a confidential matter or communication waives the privilege if the person, or the person's predecessor while holder of the privilege, voluntarily discloses or makes the communication when he or she does not have a reasonable expectation of privacy, or consents to disclosure of, any significant part of the matter or communication. This section is not applicable when the disclosure is itself a privileged communication.

Laws 1976, c. 76–237, § 1; Laws 1978, c. 78–361, § 13. Amended by Laws 1995, c. 95–147, § 480, eff. July 10, 1995.

Cross References

Accountant-client privilege, waiver, see § 90.5055.
Failure to object to competency in depositions not to constitute waiver, see Civil Procedure Rule 1.330.
Preliminary questions pertaining to privilege, see § 90.105.

90.508. Privileged matter disclosed under compulsion or without opportunity to claim privilege

Evidence of a statement or other disclosure of privileged matter is inadmissible against the holder of the privilege if the statement or disclosure was compelled erroneously by the court or made without opportunity to claim the privilege.

Laws 1976, c. 76–237, § 1.

Cross References

Exclusion of evidence in civil proceedings, see Civil Procedure Rule 1.450.
Preliminary determination as to privilege, see § 90.105.
Suppression of evidence, motion, see Criminal Procedure Rule 3.190.

90.509. Application of privileged communication

Nothing in this act shall abrogate a privilege for any communication which was made prior to July 1, 1979, if such communication was privileged at the time it was made.

Laws 1976, c. 76–237, § 1. Amended by Laws 1981, c. 81–259, § 41, eff. Aug. 4, 1981.

90.510. Privileged communication necessary to adverse party

In any civil case or proceeding in which a party claims a privilege as to a communication necessary to an adverse party, the court, upon motion, may dismiss the claim for relief or the affirmative defense to which the privileged testimony would relate. In making its determination, the court may engage in an in camera inquiry into the privilege.

Laws 1976, c. 76–237, § 1.

Cross References

Depositions, scope of examination, see Civil Procedure Rule 1.280.
Motion to suppress, see Criminal Procedure Rule 3.190.
Orders for protection of parties and deponents, see Civil Procedure Rule 1.310.
Refusal to make discovery, see Civil Procedure Rule 1.280.

90.601. General rule of competency

Every person is competent to be a witness, except as otherwise provided by statute.

Laws 1976, c. 76–237, § 1.

Cross References

Criminal cases, competency of witnesses, see § 914.07.

90.603. Disqualification of witness

A person is disqualified to testify as a witness when the court determines that the person is:

(1) Incapable of expressing himself or herself concerning the matter in such a manner as to be understood, either directly or through interpretation by one who can understand him or her.

(2) Incapable of understanding the duty of a witness to tell the truth.

Laws 1976, c. 76–237, § 1. Amended by Laws 1995, c. 95–147, § 482, eff. July 10, 1995.

Cross References

Religious beliefs or opinions, see § 90.611.

90.604. Lack of personal knowledge

Except as otherwise provided in s. 90.702, a witness may not testify to a matter unless evidence is introduced which is sufficient to support a finding that the witness has personal knowledge of the matter. Evidence to prove personal knowledge may be given by the witness's own testimony.

Laws 1976, c. 76–237, § 1. Amended by Laws 1995, c. 95–147, § 483, eff. July 10, 1995.

Cross References

Expert testimony, see § 90.702.

90.605. Oath or affirmation of witness

(1) Before testifying, each witness shall declare that he or she will testify truthfully, by taking an oath or affirmation in substantially the following form: "Do you swear or affirm that the evidence you are about to give will be the truth, the whole truth, and nothing but the truth?" The witness's answer shall be noted in the record.

(2) In the court's discretion, a child may testify without taking the oath if the court determines the child understands the duty to tell the truth or the duty not to lie.

Laws 1976, c. 76–237, § 1. Amended by Laws 1985, c. 85–53, § 3, eff. July 1, 1985; Laws 1995, c. 95–147, § 484, eff. July 10, 1995.

Cross References

Affirmation as equivalent to oath, see § 1.01.
Attorneys at law, administration of oaths, see § 454.17.
Chief Financial Officer may administer oaths, issue subpoenas, see § 17.05.
Clerks of certain courts, power to administer, see § 34.13.
Grand jurors, see § 905.10.
Guardian's oath, see § 744.347.
Notary public, power to administer, see § 117.03.
Oath of trial jurors in criminal proceedings, see Criminal Procedure Rule 3.360.
Perjury,
    Contradictory statement, see § 837.021.
    Nonofficial proceedings, see § 837.012.
    Official proceedings, see § 837.02.
Public employees, oath, see § 876.05 et seq.
State attorney, administration of oath by, see § 27.04.

90.606. Interpreters and translators

(1)(a) When a judge determines that a witness cannot hear or understand the English language, or cannot express himself or herself in English sufficiently to be understood, an interpreter who is duly qualified to interpret for the witness shall be sworn to do so.

(b) This section is not limited to persons who speak a language other than English, but applies also to the language and descriptions of any person, such as a child or a person who is mentally or developmentally disabled, who cannot be reasonably understood, or who cannot understand questioning, without the aid of an interpreter.

(2) A person who serves in the role of interpreter or translator in any action or proceeding is subject to all the provisions of this chapter relating to witnesses.

(3) An interpreter shall take an oath that he or she will make a true interpretation of the questions asked and the answers given and that the interpreter will make a true translation into English of any writing which he or she is required by his or her duties to decipher or translate.

Laws 1976, c. 76–237, § 1. Amended by Laws 1985, c. 85–53, § 2, eff. July 1, 1985; Laws 1995, c. 95–147, § 485, eff. July 10, 1995.

Cross References

Failure to perform duties as interpreter, penalty, see § 839.24.

90.6063. Interpreter services for deaf persons

(1) The Legislature finds that it is an important concern that the rights of deaf citizens be protected. It is the intent of the Legislature to ensure that appropriate and effective interpreter services be made available to Florida's deaf citizens.

(2) In all judicial proceedings and in sessions of a grand jury wherein a deaf person is a complainant, defendant, witness, or otherwise a party, or wherein a deaf person is a juror or grand juror, the court or presiding officer shall appoint a qualified interpreter to interpret the proceedings or deliberations to the deaf person and to interpret the deaf person's testimony, statements, or deliberations to the court, jury, or grand jury. A qualified interpreter shall be appointed, or other auxiliary aid provided as appropriate, for the duration of the trial or other proceeding in which a deaf juror or grand juror is seated.

(3)(a) "Deaf person" means any person whose hearing is so seriously impaired as to prohibit the person from understanding oral communications when spoken in a normal, conversational tone.

(b) For the purposes of this section, the term "qualified interpreter" means an interpreter certified by the National Registry of Interpreters for the Deaf or the Florida Registry of Interpreters for the Deaf or an interpreter whose qualifications are otherwise determined by the appointing authority.

(4) Every deaf person whose appearance before a proceeding entitles him or her to an interpreter shall notify the appointing authority of his or her disability not less than 5 days prior to any appearance and shall request at such time the services of an interpreter. Whenever a deaf person receives notification of the time of an appearance before a proceeding less than 5 days prior to the proceeding, the deaf person shall provide his or her notification and request as soon thereafter as practicable. In any case, nothing in this subsection shall operate to relieve an appointing authority's duty to provide an interpreter for a deaf person so entitled, and failure to strictly comply with the notice requirement will not be deemed a waiver of the right to an interpreter. An appointing authority may require a person requesting the appointment of an interpreter to furnish reasonable proof of the person's disability when the appointing authority has reason to believe that the person is not so disabled.

(5) The appointing authority may channel requests for qualified interpreters through:

(a) The Florida Registry of Interpreters for the Deaf;

(b) The Division of Vocational Rehabilitation of the Department of Education; or

(c) Any other resource wherein the appointing authority knows that qualified interpreters can be found.

(6) No qualified interpreter shall be appointed unless the appointing authority and the deaf person make a preliminary determination that the interpreter is able to communicate readily

with the deaf person and is able to repeat and translate statements to and from the deaf person accurately.

(7) Before a qualified interpreter may participate in any proceedings subsequent to an appointment under the provisions of this act, such interpreter shall make an oath or affirmation that he or she will make a true interpretation in an understandable manner to the deaf person for whom the interpreter is appointed and that he or she will repeat the statements of the deaf person in the English language to the best of his or her skill and judgment. Whenever a deaf person communicates through an interpreter to any person under such circumstances that the communication would be privileged, and the recipient of the communication could not be compelled to testify as to the communication, this privilege shall apply to the interpreter.

(8) An interpreter appointed by the court in a criminal matter or in a civil matter shall be entitled to a reasonable fee for such service, in addition to actual expenses for travel, to be paid out of general county funds.

Laws 1980, c. 80–155, §§ 1 to 5, 7 to 9, eff. Oct. 1, 1980. Amended by Laws 1981, c. 81–259, § 42, eff. Aug. 4, 1981; Laws 1990, c. 90–123, § 1, eff. June 21, 1990; Laws 1993, c. 93–125, § 2, eff. Oct. 1, 1993; Laws 1995, c. 95–147, § 486, eff. July 10, 1995; Laws 1999, c. 99–8, § 6, eff. June 29, 1999; Laws 2002, c. 2002–22, § 18, eff. April 11, 2002.

90.607. Competency of certain persons as witnesses

(1)(a) Except as provided in paragraph (b), the judge presiding at the trial of an action is not competent to testify as a witness in that trial. An objection is not necessary to preserve the point.

(b) By agreement of the parties, the trial judge may give evidence on a purely formal matter to facilitate the trial of the action.

(2)(a) A member of the jury is not competent to testify as a witness in a trial when he or she is sitting as a juror. If the juror is called to testify, the opposing party shall be given an opportunity to object out of the presence of the jury.

(b) Upon an inquiry into the validity of a verdict or indictment, a juror is not competent to testify as to any matter which essentially inheres in the verdict or indictment.

Laws 1976, c. 76–237, § 1. Amended by Laws 1995, c. 95–147, § 487, eff. July 10, 1995.

Cross References

Calling witnesses by court, see § 90.615.
Disqualification of judge who is material witness for party, see § 38.02.
Disqualification of juror for interest in subject matter of cause, see § 40.013.
Interest of judge, disqualification, see § 38.10.
Judge as party, effect of attempted judicial acts, see § 38.01.
Polling jury in criminal action, see Criminal Procedure Rule 3.450.
Qualification of jurors, see § 40.01.
Request of jury to review evidence or for additional instructions in criminal proceedings, see Criminal Procedure Rule 3.410.
Waiver of grounds of disqualification of judge by parties, see § 38.03.

90.608. Who may impeach

Any party, including the party calling the witness, may attack the credibility of a witness by:

(1) Introducing statements of the witness which are inconsistent with the witness's present testimony.

(2) Showing that the witness is biased.

(3) Attacking the character of the witness in accordance with the provisions of s. 90.609 or s. 90.610.

(4) Showing a defect of capacity, ability, or opportunity in the witness to observe, remember, or recount the matters about which the witness testified.

(5) Proof by other witnesses that material facts are not as testified to by the witness being impeached.

Laws 1976, c. 76–237, § 1; Laws 1978, c. 78–361, § 14. Amended by Laws 1990, c. 90–174, § 1, eff. Oct. 1, 1990; Laws 1995, c. 95–147, § 488, eff. July 10, 1995.

Cross References

Adverse witness, interrogation, see Civil Procedure Rule 1.450.
Depositions, use for impeachment of deponent, see Civil Procedure Rule 1.280; Criminal Procedure Rule 3.220.
Injury to person or property, written statements, see § 92.33.
Records destroyed by fire, impeachment of sworn copies, see § 92.26.

90.609. Character of witness as impeachment

A party may attack or support the credibility of a witness, including an accused, by evidence in the form of reputation, except that:

(1) The evidence may refer only to character relating to truthfulness.

(2) Evidence of a truthful character is admissible only after the character of the witness for truthfulness has been attacked by reputation evidence.

Laws 1976, c. 76–237, § 1; Laws 1978, c. 78–361, § 15.

Cross References

Admissibility of character evidence, see § 90.404.
Exclusion of evidence for prejudice, confusion, or waste of time, see § 90.403.
Perjury,
    Contradictory statement, see § 837.02.
    Nonofficial proceeding, see § 837.012.
    Official proceeding, see § 837.02.
Proof of character, methods, see § 90.405.

90.610. Conviction of certain crimes as impeachment

(1) A party may attack the credibility of any witness, including an accused, by evidence that the witness has been convicted of a crime if the crime was punishable by death or imprisonment in excess of 1 year under the law under which the witness was convicted, or if the crime involved dishonesty or a false statement regardless of the punishment, with the following exceptions:

(a) Evidence of any such conviction is inadmissible in a civil trial if it is so remote in time as to have no bearing on the present character of the witness.

(b) Evidence of juvenile adjudications are inadmissible under this subsection.

(2) The pendency of an appeal or the granting of a pardon relating to such crime does not render evidence of the conviction from which the appeal was taken or for which the pardon was granted inadmissible. Evidence of the pendency of the appeal is admissible.

(3) Nothing in this section affects the admissibility of evidence under s. 90.404 or s. 90.608.

Laws 1976, c. 76–237, § 1; Laws 1978, c. 78–361, § 16. Amended by Laws 1995, c. 95–147, § 489, eff. July 10, 1995.

Character evidence, when admissible, see § 90.404.
Juvenile criminal records, privileged information, see § 985.04.
Methods of proving character, see § 90.405.
Pardons, see Const. Art. 4, § 8; F.S.A. § 940.01.

90.611. Religious beliefs or opinions

Evidence of the beliefs or opinions of a witness on matters of religion is inadmissible to show that the witness's credibility is impaired or enhanced thereby.

Laws 1976, c. 76–237, § 1. Amended by Laws 1995, c. 95–147, § 490, eff. July 10, 1995.

90.612. Mode and order of interrogation and presentation

(1) The judge shall exercise reasonable control over the mode and order of the interrogation of witnesses and the presentation of evidence, so as to:

(a) Facilitate, through effective interrogation and presentation, the discovery of the truth.

(b) Avoid needless consumption of time.

(c) Protect witnesses from harassment or undue embarrassment.

(2) Cross–examination of a witness is limited to the subject matter of the direct examination and matters affecting the credibility of the witness. The court may, in its discretion, permit inquiry into additional matters.

(3) Leading questions should not be used on the direct examination of a witness except as may be necessary to develop the witness's testimony. Ordinarily, leading questions should be permitted on cross-examination. When a party calls a hostile witness, an adverse party, or a witness identified with an adverse party, interrogation may be by leading questions.

The judge shall take special care to protect a witness under age 14 from questions that are in a form that cannot reasonably be understood by a person of the age and understanding of the witness, and shall take special care to restrict the unnecessary repetition of questions.

Laws 1976, c. 76–237, § 1. Amended by Laws 1995, c. 95–179, § 1, eff. May 10, 1995; Laws 2000, c. 2000–316, § 2, eff. July 1, 2000.

Adverse witness, examination, see Civil Procedure Rule 1.450.
Compelled testimony tending to incriminate, immunity, see § 914.05.
Exclusion of evidence for prejudice, confusion, or waste of time, see § 90.403.

90.613. Refreshing the memory of a witness

When a witness uses a writing or other item to refresh memory while testifying, an adverse party is entitled to have such writing or other item produced at the hearing, to inspect it, to cross-examine the witness thereon, and to introduce it, or, in the case of a writing, to introduce those portions which relate to the testimony of the witness, in evidence. If it is claimed that the writing contains matters not related to the subject matter of the testimony, the judge shall examine the writing in camera, excise any portions not so related, and order delivery of the remainder to the party entitled thereto. Any portion withheld over objection shall be preserved and made available to the appellate court in the event of an appeal. If a writing or other item is not produced or delivered pursuant to order under this section, the testimony of the witness concerning those matters shall be stricken.

Laws 1976, c. 76–237, § 1. Amended by Laws 1995, c. 95–147, § 491, eff. July 10, 1995.

Cross References

Recorded recollections, hearsay exceptions, see § 90.803.

90.614. Prior statements of witnesses

(1) When a witness is examined concerning the witness's prior written statement or concerning an oral statement that has been reduced to writing, the court, on motion of the adverse party, shall order the statement to be shown to the witness or its contents disclosed to him or her.

(2) Extrinsic evidence of a prior inconsistent statement by a witness is inadmissible unless the witness is first afforded an opportunity to explain or deny the prior statement and the opposing party is afforded an opportunity to interrogate the witness on it, or the interests of justice otherwise require. If a witness denies making or does not distinctly admit making the prior inconsistent statement, extrinsic evidence of such statement is admissible. This subsection is not applicable to admissions of a party-opponent as defined in s. 90.803(18).

Laws 1976, c. 76–237, § 1; Laws 1978, c. 78–361, § 17. Amended by Laws 1995, c. 95–147, § 492, eff. July 10, 1995.

Cross References

Admissions, hearsay exceptions, see § 90.803.
Hearsay statements attacking or supporting credibility of declarant, see § 90.806.

90.615. Calling witnesses by the court

(1) The court may call witnesses whom all parties may cross-examine.

(2) When required by the interests of justice, the court may interrogate witnesses, whether called by the court or by a party.

Laws 1976, c. 76–237, § 1.

Cross References

Adverse witness, examination, see Civil Procedure Rule 1.450.
Confrontation by witnesses, see Const. Art. 1, § 16.
Judge as witness, see § 90.607.

90.616. Exclusion of witnesses

(1) At the request of a party the court shall order, or upon its own motion the court may order, witnesses excluded from a proceeding so that they cannot hear the testimony of other witnesses except as provided in subsection (2).

(2) A witness may not be excluded if the witness is:

(a) A party who is a natural person.

(b) In a civil case, an officer or employee of a party that is not a natural person. The party's attorney shall designate the officer or employee who shall be the party's representative.

(c) A person whose presence is shown by the party's attorney to be essential to the presentation of the party's cause.

(d) In a criminal case, the victim of the crime, the victim's next of kin, the parent or guardian of a minor child victim, or a lawful representative of such person, unless, upon motion, the court determines such person's presence to be prejudicial.

Added by Laws 1990, c. 90–174, § 2, eff. Oct. 1, 1990. Amended by Laws 1992, c. 92–107, § 1, eff. July 1, 1992; Laws 1995, c. 95–147, § 493, eff. July 10, 1995.

90.701. Opinion testimony of lay witnesses

If a witness is not testifying as an expert, the witness's testimony about what he or she perceived may be in the form of inference and opinion when:

(1) The witness cannot readily, and with equal accuracy and adequacy, communicate what he or she has perceived to the trier of fact without testifying in terms of inferences or opinions and the witness's use of inferences or opinions will not mislead the trier of fact to the prejudice of the objecting party; and

(2) The opinions and inferences do not require a special knowledge, skill, experience, or training.

Laws 1976, c. 76–237, § 1. Amended by Laws 1995, c. 95–147, § 494, eff. July 10, 1995.

90.702. Testimony by experts

If scientific, technical, or other specialized knowledge will assist the trier of fact in understanding the evidence or in determining a fact in issue, a witness qualified as an expert by knowledge, skill, experience, training, or education may testify about it in the form of an opinion or otherwise, if:

(1) The testimony is based upon sufficient facts or data;

(2) The testimony is the product of reliable principles and methods; and

(3) The witness has applied the principles and methods reliably to the facts of the case.

Laws 1976, c. 76–237, § 1. Amended by Laws 2013, c. 2013–107, § 1, eff. July 1, 2013.

Cross References

Admissibility of relevant evidence, see § 90.402.
Competency of witnesses, see § 90.601 et seq.
Definition of relevant evidence, see § 90.401.
Definitions, expert witness fees, see § 92.231.
Depositions, expert witness, see Civil Procedure Rule 1.390.
Exclusion of relevant evidence, grounds, see § 90.403.
Inspection, copying, experts' reports or statements, see Criminal Procedure Rule 3.220.
Limitation on number of experts, pretrial conferences, see Civil Procedure Rule 1.200.
Mental condition, accused, appointment of experts to examine, see Criminal Procedure Rule 3.210.
Personal knowledge, foundation for testimony of witnesses, see § 90.604.
Retardation residential programs, testimony at hearings, see § 393.11.
Uniform Foreign Depositions Law, see § 92.251.

90.703. Opinion on ultimate issue

Testimony in the form of an opinion or inference otherwise admissible is not objectionable because it includes an ultimate issue to be decided by the trier of fact.

Laws 1976, c. 76–237, § 1.

Cross References

Admissibility of relevant evidence, see § 90.402.
Competency of witnesses, see § 90.601 et seq.
Definition of relevant evidence, see § 90.401.
Definitions, expert witness fees, see § 92.231.
Depositions, expert witness, see Civil Procedure Rule 1.390.
Exclusion of relevant evidence, grounds, see § 90.403.
Inspection, copying, experts' reports or statements, see Criminal Procedure Rule 3.220.

Limitation on number of experts, pretrial conferences, see Civil Procedure Rule 1.200.

Mental condition, accused, appointment of experts to examine, see Criminal Procedure Rule 3.210.

Personal knowledge, foundation for testimony of witnesses, see § 90.604.

Retardation residential programs, testimony at hearings, see § 393.11.

Uniform Foreign Depositions Law, see § 92.251.

90.704. Basis of opinion testimony by experts

The facts or data upon which an expert bases an opinion or inference may be those perceived by, or made known to, the expert at or before the trial. If the facts or data are of a type reasonably relied upon by experts in the subject to support the opinion expressed, the facts or data need not be admissible in evidence. Facts or data that are otherwise inadmissible may not be disclosed to the jury by the proponent of the opinion or inference unless the court determines that their probative value in assisting the jury to evaluate the expert's opinion substantially outweighs their prejudicial effect.

Laws 1976, c. 76–237, § 1. Amended by Laws 1995, c. 95–147, § 495, eff. July 10, 1995; Laws 2013, c. 2013–107, § 2, eff. July 1, 2013.

Cross References

Admissibility of relevant evidence, see § 90.402.

Competency of witnesses, see § 90.601 et seq.

Definition of relevant evidence, see § 90.401.

Definitions, expert witness fees, see § 92.231.

Depositions, expert witness, see Civil Procedure Rule 1.390.

Exclusion of relevant evidence, grounds, see § 90.403.

Inspection, copying, experts' reports or statements, see Criminal Procedure Rule 3.220.

Limitation on number of experts, pretrial conferences, see Civil Procedure Rule 1.200.

Mental condition, accused, appointment of experts to examine, see Criminal Procedure Rules 3.210.

Personal knowledge, foundation for testimony of witnesses, see § 90.604.

Retardation residential programs, testimony at hearings, see § 393.11.

Uniform Foreign Depositions Law, see § 92.251.

90.705. Disclosure of facts or data underlying expert opinion

(1) Unless otherwise required by the court, an expert may testify in terms of opinion or inferences and give reasons without prior disclosure of the underlying facts or data. On cross-examination the expert shall be required to specify the facts or data.

(2) Prior to the witness giving the opinion, a party against whom the opinion or inference is offered may conduct a voir dire examination of the witness directed to the underlying facts or data for the witness's opinion. If the party establishes prima facie evidence that the expert does not have a sufficient basis for the opinion, the opinions and inferences of the expert are inadmissible unless the party offering the testimony establishes the underlying facts or data.

Laws 1976, c. 76–237, § 1. Amended by Laws 1995, c. 95–147, § 496, eff. July 10, 1995.

Cross References

Admissibility of relevant evidence, see § 90.402.

Competency of witnesses, see § 90.601 et seq.

Definition of relevant evidence, see § 90.401.

Definitions, expert witness fees, see § 92.231.

Depositions, expert witness, see Civil Procedure Rule 1.390.

Exclusion of relevant evidence, grounds, see § 90.403.

Inspection, copying, experts' reports or statements, see Criminal Procedure Rule 3.220.

Limitation on number of experts, pretrial conferences, see Civil Procedure Rule 1.200.
Mental condition, accused, appointment of experts to examine, see Criminal Procedure Rules 3.210.
Personal knowledge, foundation for testimony of witnesses, see § 90.604.
Retardation residential programs, testimony at hearings, see § 393.11.
Uniform Foreign Depositions Law, see § 92.251.

90.706.   Authoritativeness of literature for use in cross-examination

Statements of facts or opinions on a subject of science, art, or specialized knowledge contained in a published treatise, periodical, book, dissertation, pamphlet, or other writing may be used in cross-examination of an expert witness if the expert witness recognizes the author or the treatise, periodical, book, dissertation, pamphlet, or other writing to be authoritative, or, notwithstanding nonrecognition by the expert witness, if the trial court finds the author or the treatise, periodical, book, dissertation, pamphlet, or other writing to be authoritative and relevant to the subject matter.

Laws 1978, c. 78–361, § 18.

90.801.   Hearsay; definitions; exceptions

(1) The following definitions apply under this chapter:

(a) A "statement" is:

1. An oral or written assertion; or

2. Nonverbal conduct of a person if it is intended by the person as an assertion.

(b) A "declarant" is a person who makes a statement.

(c) "Hearsay" is a statement, other than one made by the declarant while testifying at the trial or hearing, offered in evidence to prove the truth of the matter asserted.

(2) A statement is not hearsay if the declarant testifies at the trial or hearing and is subject to cross-examination concerning the statement and the statement is:

(a) Inconsistent with the declarant's testimony and was given under oath subject to the penalty of perjury at a trial, hearing, or other proceeding or in a deposition;

(b) Consistent with the declarant's testimony and is offered to rebut an express or implied charge against the declarant of improper influence, motive, or recent fabrication; or

(c) One of identification of a person made after perceiving the person.

Laws 1976, c. 76–237, § 1; Laws 1978, c. 78–361, § 19. Amended by Laws 1981, c. 81–93, § 2, eff. Oct. 1, 1981; Laws 1995, c. 95–147, § 497, eff. July 10, 1995.

Cross References

Confrontation with witnesses, see Const. Art. 1, § 16.
Personal knowledge of witnesses, necessity, see § 90.604.
Preliminary questions of admissibility, etc., see § 90.105.
Prior statements of witnesses, extrinsic evidence, see § 90.614.
Rulings on evidence, see § 90.104.
Statements, admission of remainder of, see § 90.108.

90.802.   Hearsay rule

Except as provided by statute, hearsay evidence is inadmissible.

Laws 1976, c. 76–237, § 1.

90.803. Hearsay exceptions; availability of declarant immaterial

The provision of s. 90.802 to the contrary notwithstanding, the following are not inadmissible as evidence, even though the declarant is available as a witness:

(1) Spontaneous statement.—A spontaneous statement describing or explaining an event or condition made while the declarant was perceiving the event or condition, or immediately thereafter, except when such statement is made under circumstances that indicate its lack of trustworthiness.

(2) Excited utterance.—A statement or excited utterance relating to a startling event or condition made while the declarant was under the stress of excitement caused by the event or condition.

(3) Then-existing mental, emotional, or physical condition.—

(a) A statement of the declarant's then-existing state of mind, emotion, or physical sensation, including a statement of intent, plan, motive, design, mental feeling, pain, or bodily health, when such evidence is offered to:

1. Prove the declarant's state of mind, emotion, or physical sensation at that time or at any other time when such state is an issue in the action.

2. Prove or explain acts of subsequent conduct of the declarant.

(b) However, this subsection does not make admissible:

1. An after-the-fact statement of memory or belief to prove the fact remembered or believed, unless such statement relates to the execution, revocation, identification, or terms of the declarant's will.

2. A statement made under circumstances that indicate its lack of trustworthiness.

(4) Statements for purposes of medical diagnosis or treatment.—Statements made for purposes of medical diagnosis or treatment by a person seeking the diagnosis or treatment, or made by an individual who has knowledge of the facts and is legally responsible for the person who is unable to communicate the facts, which statements describe medical history, past or present symptoms, pain, or sensations, or the inceptions or general character of the cause or external source thereof, insofar as reasonably pertinent to diagnosis or treatment.

(5) Recorded recollection.—A memorandum or record concerning a matter about which a witness once had knowledge, but now has insufficient recollection to enable the witness to testify fully and accurately, shown to have been made by the witness when the matter was fresh in the witness's memory and to reflect that knowledge correctly. A party may read into evidence a memorandum or record when it is admitted, but no such memorandum or record is admissible as an exhibit unless offered by an adverse party.

(6) Records of regularly conducted business activity.—

(a) A memorandum, report, record, or data compilation, in any form, of acts, events, conditions, opinion, or diagnosis, made at or near the time by, or from information transmitted by, a person with knowledge, if kept in the course of a regularly conducted business activity and if it was the regular practice of that business activity to make such memorandum, report, record, or data compilation, all as shown by the testimony of the custodian or other qualified witness, or as shown by a certification or declaration that complies with paragraph (c) and s. 90.902(11), unless the sources of information or other circumstances show lack of trustworthiness. The term "business" as used in this paragraph includes a business, institution, association, profession, occupation, and calling of every kind, whether or not conducted for profit.

(b) Evidence in the form of an opinion or diagnosis is inadmissible under paragraph (a) unless such opinion or diagnosis would be admissible under ss. 90.701–90.705 if the person whose opinion is recorded were to testify to the opinion directly.

(c) A party intending to offer evidence under paragraph (a) by means of a certification or declaration shall serve reasonable written notice of that intention upon every other party and shall make the evidence available for inspection sufficiently in advance of its offer in evidence to provide to any other party a fair opportunity to challenge the admissibility of the evidence. If the evidence is maintained in a foreign country, the party intending to offer the evidence must provide written notice of that intention at the arraignment or as soon after the arraignment as is practicable or, in a civil case, 60 days before the trial. A motion opposing the admissibility of such evidence must be made by the opposing party and determined by the court before trial. A party's failure to file such a motion before trial constitutes a waiver of objection to the evidence, but the court for good cause shown may grant relief from the waiver.

(7) Absence of entry in records of regularly conducted activity.—Evidence that a matter is not included in the memoranda, reports, records, or data compilations, in any form, of a regularly conducted activity to prove the nonoccurrence or nonexistence of the matter, if the matter was of a kind of which a memorandum, report, record, or data compilation was regularly made and preserved, unless the sources of information or other circumstances show lack of trustworthiness.

(8) Public records and reports.—Records, reports, statements reduced to writing, or data compilations, in any form, of public offices or agencies, setting forth the activities of the office or agency, or matters observed pursuant to duty imposed by law as to matters which there was a duty to report, excluding in criminal cases matters observed by a police officer or other law enforcement personnel, unless the sources of information or other circumstances show their lack of trustworthiness. The criminal case exclusion shall not apply to an affidavit otherwise admissible under s. 316.1934 or s. 327.354.

(9) Records of vital statistics.—Records or data compilations, in any form, of births, fetal deaths, deaths, or marriages, if a report was made to a public office pursuant to requirements of law. However, nothing in this section shall be construed to make admissible any other marriage of any party to any cause of action except for the purpose of impeachment as set forth in s. 90.610.

(10) Absence of public record or entry.—Evidence, in the form of a certification in accord with s. 90.902, or in the form of testimony, that diligent search failed to disclose a record, report, statement, or data compilation or entry, when offered to prove the absence of the record, report, statement, or data compilation or the nonoccurrence or nonexistence of a matter of which a record, report, statement, or data compilation would regularly have been made and preserved by a public office and agency.

(11) Records of religious organizations.—Statements of births, marriages, divorces, deaths, parentage, ancestry, relationship by blood or marriage, or other similar facts of personal or family history contained in a regularly kept record of a religious organization.

(12) Marriage, baptismal, and similar certificates.—Statements of facts contained in a certificate that the maker performed a marriage or other ceremony or administered a sacrament, when such statement was certified by a member of the clergy, public official, or other person authorized by the rules or practices of a religious organization or by law to perform the act certified, and when such certificate purports to have been issued at the time of the act or within a reasonable time thereafter.

(13) Family records.—Statements of fact concerning personal or family history in family Bibles, charts, engravings in rings, inscriptions on family portraits, engravings on urns, crypts, or tombstones, or the like.

(14) Records of documents affecting an interest in property.—The record of a document purporting to establish or affect an interest in property, as proof of the contents of the original recorded or filed document and its execution and delivery by each person by whom it purports to have been executed, if the record is a record of a public office and an applicable statute authorized the recording or filing of the document in the office.

(15) Statements in documents affecting an interest in property.—A statement contained in a document purporting to establish or affect an interest in property, if the matter stated was relevant to the purpose of the document, unless dealings with the property since the document was made have been inconsistent with the truth of the statement or the purport of the document.

(16) Statements in ancient documents.—Statements in a document in existence 20 years or more, the authenticity of which is established.

(17) Market reports, commercial publications.—Market quotations, tabulations, lists, directories, or other published compilations, generally used and relied upon by the public or by persons in particular occupations if, in the opinion of the court, the sources of information and method of preparation were such as to justify their admission.

(18) Admissions.—A statement that is offered against a party and is:

(a) The party's own statement in either an individual or a representative capacity;

(b) A statement of which the party has manifested an adoption or belief in its truth;

(c) A statement by a person specifically authorized by the party to make a statement concerning the subject;

(d) A statement by the party's agent or servant concerning a matter within the scope of the agency or employment thereof, made during the existence of the relationship; or

(e) A statement by a person who was a coconspirator of the party during the course, and in furtherance, of the conspiracy. Upon request of counsel, the court shall instruct the jury that the conspiracy itself and each member's participation in it must be established by independent evidence, either before the introduction of any evidence or before evidence is admitted under this paragraph.

(19) Reputation concerning personal or family history.—Evidence of reputation:

(a) Among members of a person's family by blood, adoption, or marriage;

(b) Among a person's associates; or

(c) In the community,

concerning a person's birth, adoption, marriage, divorce, death, relationship by blood, adoption, or marriage, ancestry, or other similar fact of personal or family history.

(20) Reputation concerning boundaries or general history.—Evidence of reputation:

(a) In a community, arising before the controversy about the boundaries of, or customs affecting lands in, the community.

(b) About events of general history which are important to the community, state, or nation where located.

(21) Reputation as to character.—Evidence of reputation of a person's character among associates or in the community.

(22) Former testimony.—Former testimony given by the declarant which testimony was given as a witness at another hearing of the same or a different proceeding, or in a deposition taken in compliance with law in the course of the same or another proceeding, if the party against whom the testimony is now offered, or, in a civil action or proceeding, a predecessor in interest, or a person with a similar interest, had an opportunity and similar motive to develop the testimony by direct, cross, or redirect examination; provided, however, the court finds that the testimony is not inadmissible pursuant to s. 90.402 or s. 90.403.

(23) Hearsay exception; statement of child victim.—

(a) Unless the source of information or the method or circumstances by which the statement is reported indicates a lack of trustworthiness, an out-of-court statement made by a child victim with a physical, mental, emotional, or developmental age of 16 or less describing any act of child abuse or neglect, any act of sexual abuse against a child, the offense of child abuse, the offense of aggravated child abuse, or any offense involving an unlawful sexual act, contact, intrusion, or penetration performed in the presence of, with, by, or on the declarant child, not otherwise admissible, is admissible in evidence in any civil or criminal proceeding if:

1. The court finds in a hearing conducted outside the presence of the jury that the time, content, and circumstances of the statement provide sufficient safeguards of reliability. In making its determination, the court may consider the mental and physical age and maturity of the child, the nature and duration of the abuse or offense, the relationship of the child to the offender, the reliability of the assertion, the reliability of the child victim, and any other factor deemed appropriate; and

2. The child either:

a. Testifies; or

b. Is unavailable as a witness, provided that there is other corroborative evidence of the abuse or offense. Unavailability shall include a finding by the court that the child's participation in the trial or proceeding would result in a substantial likelihood of severe emotional or mental harm, in addition to findings pursuant to s. 90.804(1).

(b) In a criminal action, the defendant shall be notified no later than 10 days before trial that a statement which qualifies as a hearsay exception pursuant to this subsection will be offered as evidence at trial. The notice shall include a written statement of the content of the child's statement, the time at which the statement was made, the circumstances surrounding the statement which indicate its reliability, and such other particulars as necessary to provide full disclosure of the statement.

(c) The court shall make specific findings of fact, on the record, as to the basis for its ruling under this subsection.

(24) Hearsay exception; statement of elderly person or disabled adult.—

(a) Unless the source of information or the method or circumstances by which the statement is reported indicates a lack of trustworthiness, an out-of-court statement made by an elderly person or disabled adult, as defined in s. 825.101, describing any act of abuse or neglect, any act of exploitation, the offense of battery or aggravated battery or assault or aggravated assault or sexual battery, or any other violent act on the declarant elderly person or disabled adult, not otherwise admissible, is admissible in evidence in any civil or criminal proceeding if:

1. The court finds in a hearing conducted outside the presence of the jury that the time, content, and circumstances of the statement provide sufficient safeguards of reliability. In making its determination, the court may consider the mental and physical age and maturity of the elderly person or disabled adult, the nature and duration of the abuse or offense, the relationship of the victim to the offender, the reliability of the assertion, the reliability of the elderly person or disabled adult, and any other factor deemed appropriate; and

2. The elderly person or disabled adult is unavailable as a witness, provided that there is corroborative evidence of the abuse or offense. Unavailability shall include a finding by the court that the elderly person's or disabled adult's participation in the trial or proceeding would result in a substantial likelihood of severe emotional, mental, or physical harm, in addition to findings pursuant to s. 90.804(1).

(b) In a criminal action, the defendant shall be notified no later than 10 days before the trial that a statement which qualifies as a hearsay exception pursuant to this subsection will be offered as evidence at trial. The notice shall include a written statement of the content of the elderly person's or disabled adult's statement, the time at which the statement was made, the circumstances surrounding the statement which indicate its reliability, and such other particulars as necessary to provide full disclosure of the statement.

(c) The court shall make specific findings of fact, on the record, as to the basis for its ruling under this subsection.

Laws 1976, c. 76–237, § 1; Laws 1977, c. 77–174, § 1; Laws 1978, c. 78–361, § 20. Amended by Laws 1985, c. 85–53, § 4, eff. July 1, 1985; Laws 1987, c. 87–224, § 11; Laws 1990, c. 90–139, § 2, eff. Oct. 1, 1990; Laws 1990, c. 90–174, § 3, eff. Oct. 1, 1990; Laws 1991, c. 91–255, § 12, eff. July 1, 1991; Laws 1995, c. 95–147, § 498, eff. July 10, 1995; Laws 1995, c. 95–158, § 1, eff. July 1, 1995; Laws 1996, c. 96–330, § 2, eff. July 1, 1996; Laws 1998, c. 98–2, § 1; Laws 2003, c. 2003–259, § 2, eff. July 1, 2003; Laws 2013, c. 2013–98, § 1, eff. Jan. 1, 2014; Laws 2014, c. 2014–200, § 1, eff. Oct. 1, 2014.

Validity

For validity of subsec. (24) of this section, see Conner v. State, 748 So.2d 950 (1999).

Cross References

Abstracts of title, see § 703.01 et seq.
Accident reports, admissibility, see § 92.33.
Acknowledgments, see § 92.50 et seq.
Adjutant General's office, records, see § 250.10.
Administrative Procedure Act, see § 120.50 et seq.
Alteration of copies of records as forgery, see § 831.04.
Arbitration proceedings, depositions, see § 682.08.
Authentication or identification of evidence, see § 90.901 et seq.
Birth certificates, see § 382.013 et seq.
Buildings, sanitary condition, certificates, see § 92.21.
Certified copies, validated conveyances, admissibility, see § 694.09.
Certified copies of records of certified copies, see § 92.13.

Character evidence,
    Generally, see § 90.404.
    Methods of proving character, see § 90.405.
    Witness' character, impeachment, see § 90.609.
Chattel mortgages, records and recordation, see § 698.01 et seq.
Congress, certificates issued, see § 92.20.
Contracts for sales of realty, records, see § 696.01 et seq.
Conveyances, records and recordation, see § 695.01 et seq.
Corporate records, inspection by shareholders, see § 607.1602 et seq.
Corporation records, production and examination of, see § 607.1601.
Death certificates, see § 382.019.
Deeds and powers of attorney, record for 20 years or more, see § 92.08.
Department of Highway Safety and Motor Vehicles, records, see § 321.23.
Depositions, summary procedure, civil actions, see § 51.011.
Depositions in civil actions, see Civil Procedure Rule 1.280 et seq.
Depositions in criminal actions, see § 902.17; Criminal Procedure Rules 3.190, 3.220.
Dissolution of marriage, evidence, see § 382.025.
Documentary evidence, filing and marking, see Civil Procedure Rule 1.450.
Florida Historical Resources Act, see § 267.011 et seq.
Governmental agency reports, building, housing or health code violations, see § 92.40.
Insurance department records, see § 624.312.
Judgments and decrees, certified copies, see §§ 92.05, 92.07.
Juveniles, court records, inadmissibility, see § 985.04.
Liquor violations, exemption from prosecution, see § 568.08.
Marriage licenses, see § 382.021 et seq.
Medical, psychiatric, and psychological examination and treatment of child, admissibility of medical report at hearing,
    see § 39.407.
Missing persons, official findings and reports, see § 92.30 et seq.
Motion to suppress illegally obtained admissions, see Criminal Procedure Rule 3.190.
Offers to plead guilty or nolo contendere, withdrawn guilty pleas, see § 90.410.
Personal knowledge of witnesses, necessity, see § 90.604.
Photographic or electronic copies as evidence, see § 92.29.
Portions of records as evidence, see § 92.19.
Preliminary questions of admissibility, etc., see § 90.105.
Prior statements of witnesses, extrinsic evidence, see § 90.614.
Public business, records open to inspection, see § 286.011.
Public records, see §§ 90.955, 119.01 et seq.
Records destroyed by fire, abstracts in evidence, etc., see § 92.25 et seq.
Records of certified copies as evidence, see § 92.13.
Rulings on evidence, see § 90.104.
Secretary of State, records, admissibility of photographic copies, see §§ 15.03, 15.16.
Self-authentication of public records, etc., see § 90.902.
Self-incrimination by production, see § 443.171.
State lands, certificates respecting conveyances, etc., see §§ 92.16, 92.17.
State officials, certificates, see § 92.18.
Tax deeds, evidence of title, see § 92.24.
United States deeds and patents, copies, see § 92.14.
Vital statistics, see § 382.003 et seq.

90.804. Hearsay exceptions; declarant unavailable

(1) **Definition of unavailability.**—"Unavailability as a witness" means that the declarant:

(a) Is exempted by a ruling of a court on the ground of privilege from testifying concerning the subject matter of the declarant's statement;

(b) Persists in refusing to testify concerning the subject matter of the declarant's statement despite an order of the court to do so;

(c) Has suffered a lack of memory of the subject matter of his or her statement so as to destroy the declarant's effectiveness as a witness during the trial;

(d) Is unable to be present or to testify at the hearing because of death or because of then-existing physical or mental illness or infirmity; or

(e) Is absent from the hearing, and the proponent of a statement has been unable to procure the declarant's attendance or testimony by process or other reasonable means.

However, a declarant is not unavailable as a witness if such exemption, refusal, claim of lack of memory, inability to be present, or absence is due to the procurement or wrongdoing of the party who is the proponent of his or her statement in preventing the witness from attending or testifying.

(2) Hearsay exceptions.—The following are not excluded under s. 90.802, provided that the declarant is unavailable as a witness:

(a) *Former testimony.*—Testimony given as a witness at another hearing of the same or a different proceeding, or in a deposition taken in compliance with law in the course of the same or another proceeding, if the party against whom the testimony is now offered, or, in a civil action or proceeding, a predecessor in interest, had an opportunity and similar motive to develop the testimony by direct, cross, or redirect examination.

(b) *Statement under belief of impending death.*—In a civil or criminal trial, a statement made by a declarant while reasonably believing that his or her death was imminent, concerning the physical cause or instrumentalities of what the declarant believed to be impending death or the circumstances surrounding impending death.

(c) *Statement against interest.*—A statement which, at the time of its making, was so far contrary to the declarant's pecuniary or proprietary interest or tended to subject the declarant to liability or to render invalid a claim by the declarant against another, so that a person in the declarant's position would not have made the statement unless he or she believed it to be true. A statement tending to expose the declarant to criminal liability and offered to exculpate the accused is inadmissible, unless corroborating circumstances show the trustworthiness of the statement.

(d) *Statement of personal or family history.*—A statement concerning the declarant's own birth, adoption, marriage, divorce, parentage, ancestry, or other similar fact of personal or family history, including relationship by blood, adoption, or marriage, even though the declarant had no means of acquiring personal knowledge of the matter stated.

(e) *Statement by deceased or ill declarant similar to one previously admitted.*—In an action or proceeding brought against the personal representative, heir at law, assignee, legatee, devisee, or survivor of a deceased person, or against a trustee of a trust created by a deceased person, or against the assignee, committee, or guardian of a mentally incompetent person, when a declarant is unavailable as provided in paragraph (1)(d), a written or oral statement made regarding the same subject matter as another statement made by the declarant that has previously been offered by an adverse party and admitted in evidence.

(f) *Statement offered against a party that wrongfully caused the declarant's unavailability.*—A statement offered against a party that wrongfully caused, or acquiesced in wrongfully causing, the declarant's unavailability as a witness, and did so intending that result.

Laws 1976, c. 76-237, § 1. Amended by Laws 1990, c. 90-139, § 3, eff. Oct. 1, 1990; Laws 1990, c. 90–174, § 4, eff. Oct. 1, 1990; Laws 1995, c. 95–147, § 499, eff. July 10, 1995; Laws 2005, c. 2005–46, § 2, eff. July 1, 2005; Laws 2012, c. 2012–152, § 1, eff. April 27, 2012.

Cross References

Accused's right of confrontation, see Const. Art. 1, § 16.
Arbitration proceedings, depositions, see § 682.08.
Authentication or identification of evidence, see § 90.901 et seq.
Depositions, summary procedure, civil actions, see § 51.011.
Depositions in civil actions, see Civil Procedure Rule 1.280 et seq.
Depositions in criminal actions, see § 902.17; Criminal Procedure Rules 3.190, 3.220.
Documentary evidence, filing and marking, see Civil Procedure Rule 1.450.
Missing persons, official findings and reports, see § 92.30 et seq.
Motion to suppress illegally obtained admissions, see Criminal Procedure Rule 3.190.
Offers to plead guilty, etc., withdrawn guilty pleas, see § 90.410.
Personal knowledge of witnesses, necessity, see § 90.604.
Preliminary questions of admissibility, etc., see § 90.105.
Prior statements of witnesses, extrinsic evidence, see § 90.614.
Self-incrimination,
    Beverage Law violations, see § 568.08.
    Federal court orders, see § 914.05.
    Insurance Code, see § 624.322.
    Privilege, see Const. Art. 1, § 9.
    Public service commission hearings, see § 366.09.
    Witnesses in criminal proceedings, see § 914.04.

90.805. Hearsay within hearsay

Hearsay within hearsay is not excluded under s. 90.802, provided each part of the combined statements conforms with an exception to the hearsay rule as provided in s. 90.803 or s. 90.804. Laws 1976, c. 76–237, § 1.

Cross References

Accused's right of confrontation, see Const. Art. 1, § 16.
Authentication or identification of evidence, see § 90.901 et seq.
Documentary evidence, filing and marking, see Civil Procedure Rule 1.450.
Impeachment by evidence of conviction and crime, see § 90.610.
Personal knowledge of witnesses, necessity, see § 90.604.
Preliminary questions of admissibility, etc., see § 90.105.
Prior statements of witnesses, extrinsic evidence, see § 90.614.

90.806. Attacking and supporting credibility of declarant

(1) When a hearsay statement has been admitted in evidence, credibility of the declarant may be attacked and, if attacked, may be supported by any evidence that would be admissible for those purposes if the declarant had testified as a witness. Evidence of a statement or conduct by the declarant at any time inconsistent with the declarant's hearsay statement is admissible, regardless of whether or not the declarant has been afforded an opportunity to deny or explain it.

(2) If the party against whom a hearsay statement has been admitted calls the declarant as a witness, the party is entitled to examine the declarant on the statement as if under cross-examination.

Amendment Notes:; Laws 1976, c. 76–237, § 1. Amended by Laws 1995, c. 95–147, § 500, eff. July 10, 1995.

Cross References

Accused's right of confrontation, see Const. Art. 1, § 16.

Authentication or identification of evidence, see § 90.901 et seq.
Character of witness, opinion and reputation evidence, see § 90.609.
Documentary evidence, filing and marking, see Civil Procedure Rule 1.450.
Impeachment by evidence of conviction and crime, see § 90.610.
Personal knowledge of witnesses, necessity, see § 90.604.
Preliminary questions of admissibility, etc., see § 90.105.
Prior statements of witnesses, extrinsic evidence, see § 90.614.

90.901. Requirement of authentication or identification

Authentication or identification of evidence is required as a condition precedent to its admissibility. The requirements of this section are satisfied by evidence sufficient to support a finding that the matter in question is what its proponent claims.
Laws 1976, c. 76–237, § 1.

Cross References

Admission of facts and genuineness of documents, see Civil Procedure Rule 1.370.
Conveyances, proof of instruments, see § 695.10.
Death or status, authenticated copy of death certificate in probate proceedings, see § 731.103.
Depositions, authentication, see Civil Procedure Rule 1.310.
Judicial notice, see § 90.201 et seq.
Pretrial admission of facts and documents, see Civil Procedure Rule 1.200.
Proof of public records, see § 90.955.
Records destroyed by fire,
    Abstracts, use as evidence, see § 92.25 et seq.
    Conveyances, see § 695.15.
    Land title suits, see § 92.28.
    Sworn copies as evidence, see § 92.26.
    Wills, see § 733.207.
Relevancy conditional on fact, see § 90.104.

90.902. Self-authentication

Extrinsic evidence of authenticity as a condition precedent to admissibility is not required for:

(1) A document bearing:

(a) A seal purporting to be that of the United States or any state, district, commonwealth, territory, or insular possession thereof; the Panama Canal Zone; the Trust Territory of the Pacific Islands; or a court, political subdivision, department, officer, or agency of any of them; and

(b) A signature by the custodian of the document attesting to the authenticity of the seal.

(2) A document not bearing a seal but purporting to bear a signature of an officer or employee of any entity listed in subsection (1), affixed in the officer's or employee's official capacity.

(3) An official foreign document, record, or entry that is:

(a) Executed or attested to by a person in the person's official capacity authorized by the laws of a foreign country to make the execution or attestation; and

(b) Accompanied by a final certification, as provided herein, of the genuineness of the signature and official position of:

1.   The executing person; or

2. Any foreign official whose certificate of genuineness of signature and official position relates to the execution or attestation or is in a chain of certificates of genuineness of signature and official position relating to the execution or attestation.

The final certification may be made by a secretary of an embassy or legation, consul general, consul, vice consul, or consular agent of the United States or a diplomatic or consular official of the foreign country assigned or accredited to the United States. When the parties receive reasonable opportunity to investigate the authenticity and accuracy of official foreign documents, the court may order that they be treated as presumptively authentic without final certification or permit them in evidence by an attested summary with or without final certification.

(4) A copy of an official public record, report, or entry, or of a document authorized by law to be recorded or filed and actually recorded or filed in a public office, including data compilations in any form, certified as correct by the custodian or other person authorized to make the certification by certificate complying with subsection (1), subsection (2), or subsection (3) or complying with any act of the Legislature or rule adopted by the Supreme Court.

(5) Books, pamphlets, or other publications purporting to be issued by a governmental authority.

(6) Printed materials purporting to be newspapers or periodicals.

(7) Inscriptions, signs, tags, or labels purporting to have been affixed in the course of business and indicating ownership, control, or origin.

(8) Commercial papers and signatures thereon and documents relating to them, to the extent provided in the Uniform Commercial Code.

(9) Any signature, document, or other matter declared by the Legislature to be presumptively or prima facie genuine or authentic.

(10) Any document properly certified under the law of the jurisdiction where the certification is made.

(11) An original or a duplicate of evidence that would be admissible under s. 90.803(6), which is maintained in a foreign country or domestic location and is accompanied by a certification or declaration from the custodian of the records or another qualified person certifying or declaring that the record:

(a) Was made at or near the time of the occurrence of the matters set forth by, or from information transmitted by, a person having knowledge of those matters;

(b) Was kept in the course of the regularly conducted activity; and

(c) Was made as a regular practice in the course of the regularly conducted activity,

provided that falsely making such a certification or declaration would subject the maker to criminal penalty under the laws of the foreign or domestic location in which the certification or declaration was signed.

Laws 1976, c. 76–237, § 1; Laws 1977, c. 77–174, § 1. Amended by Laws 1995, c. 95–147, § 501, eff. July 10, 1995; Laws 2003, c. 2003–259, § 3, eff. July 1, 2003.

Cross References

Court records,
    Circuit court final orders, etc., see §§ 92.05, 92.07.
    Dissolution of marriage, see § 28.101.
    Prior county courts, see § 28.16.
    State judgments and decrees, see § 92.07.
    Superior courts, see § 28.15.
    U.S. district court judgments, see § 92.06.
Deeds and conveyances, admissibility and proof,
    Certified copies of records of certified copies as evidence, see § 92.13.
    Destruction of recorded conveyances, rerecording, see §§ 92.25 et seq., 695.15.
    Portions of records as evidence, see § 92.19.
    Recorded deeds of 20 years or more, see § 92.08.
    Reversal of deeds, effect, see § 92.09.
    U.S. deeds and patents, copies as evidence, see § 92.14.
Deeds and powers of attorney of record for twenty years or more, see § 92.08.
Judgments, decrees, etc., prior to circuit courts, see § 28.14.
Judicial notice generally, see § 90.201 et seq.
Official findings and reports, presumption of authority to issue or execute, see § 92.32.
Proof of public records, see § 90.955.
Public records, proof, see § 90.955.
Records, portions as evidence, see § 92.19.
Re-establishment of lost papers and documents, see § 71.011 et seq.
Seals, judicial notice, see § 90.202.
Tax deeds as evidence of title, see § 92.24.
Third party documents, prima facie evidence of authenticity, see § 671.202.
United States deeds and patents, see § 92.14.

90.903. Testimony of subscribing witness unnecessary

The testimony of a subscribing witness is not necessary to authenticate a writing unless the statute requiring attestation requires it.

Laws 1976, c. 76–237, § 1.

Cross References

Agreements concerning succession, attestation, see § 732.701.
Alteration of attested document, criminal sanctions, see § 831.01.
Anatomical gifts, attestation, see § 765.514.
Construction lien satisfactions, see § 713.21.
Forgery of attested document, criminal sanctions, see § 831.01.
Lawyer-client privilege, execution of attested documents, see § 90.502.
Power of appointment, attestation of release, see § 709.02.
Proof of wills, see § 733.201.
Ward's choice of guardian, attestation, see § 744.312.
Wills, attestation requirements, see § 732.502.

90.91. Photographs of property wrongfully taken; use in prosecution, procedure; return of property to owner

In any prosecution for a crime involving the wrongful taking of property, a photograph of the property alleged to have been wrongfully taken may be deemed competent evidence of such property and may be admissible in the prosecution to the same extent as if such property were introduced as evidence. Such photograph shall bear a written description of the property alleged to have been wrongfully taken, the name of the owner of the property, the location where the alleged wrongful taking occurred, the name of the investigating law enforcement officer, the date the photograph was taken, and the name of the photographer. Such writing shall be made under oath by the investigating law enforcement officer, and the photograph shall be identified by the signature of the photographer. Upon the filing of such photograph and writing with the law enforcement authority or court holding such property as evidence, the property may be returned to the owner from whom the property was taken.

Laws 1984, c. 84–363, § 4, eff. Oct. 1, 1984.

90.951. Definitions

For purposes of this chapter:

(1) "Writings" and "recordings" include letters, words, or numbers, or their equivalent, set down by handwriting, typewriting, printing, photostating, photography, magnetic impulse, mechanical or electronic recording, or other form of data compilation, upon paper, wood, stone, recording tape, or other materials.

(2) "Photographs" include still photographs, X-ray films, videotapes, and motion pictures.

(3) An "original" of a writing or recording means the writing or recording itself, or any counterpart intended to have the same effect by a person executing or issuing it. An "original" of a photograph includes the negative or any print made from it. If data are stored in a computer or similar device, any printout or other output readable by sight and shown to reflect the data accurately is an "original."

(4) "Duplicate" includes:

(a) A counterpart produced by the same impression as the original, from the same matrix; by means of photography, including enlargements and miniatures; by mechanical or electronic rerecording; by chemical reproduction; or by other equivalent technique that accurately reproduces the original; or

(b) An executed carbon copy not intended by the parties to be an original.

Laws 1976, c. 76–237, § 1.

Cross References

Admission of facts and genuineness of documents, see Civil Procedure Rule 1.370.
Certified copies of deeds, mortgages, etc., see § 695.19.
Circuit court clerks, vouchers and cancelled warrants, see § 28.30.
Comparison of disputed writings, see § 92.38.
Death certificates, see § 382.025.
Photographic or electronic copies as evidence, see § 92.29.
Recorded instruments destroyed by fire, see § 695.15.
State treasurer, records, see § 17.64.
Transportation department records, see § 334.196.
Vital statistics, see § 382.004.

90.952. Requirement of originals

Except as otherwise provided by statute, an original writing, recording, or photograph is required in order to prove the contents of the writing, recording, or photograph.

Laws 1976, c. 76–237, § 1; Laws 1977, c. 77–174, § 1.

Cross References

Abstracts of title, evidence, see § 703.08.
Birth certificates, see §§ 382.015, 382.025.
Certified copies of deeds, mortgages, etc., see § 695.19.

Circuit court clerks, vouchers and cancelled warrants, see § 28.30.
Death certificates, see § 382.025.
Department of Highway Safety and Motor Vehicles, records, see § 321.23.
Financial institutions, records, see § 655.91.
Photographic copies as evidence, see § 92.29.
Recorded instruments destroyed by fire, see § 695.15.
State treasurer, records, see § 17.64.
Transportation department records, see § 334.196.
Vital statistics, see § 382.004.

90.953. Admissibility of duplicates

A duplicate is admissible to the same extent as an original, unless:

(1) The document or writing is a negotiable instrument as defined in s. 673.1041, a security as defined in s. 678.1021, or any other writing that evidences a right to the payment of money, is not itself a security agreement or lease, and is of a type that is transferred by delivery in the ordinary course of business with any necessary endorsement or assignment.

(2) A genuine question is raised about the authenticity of the original or any other document or writing.

(3) It is unfair, under the circumstance, to admit the duplicate in lieu of the original.

Laws 1976, c. 76–237, § 1. Amended by Laws 1992, c. 92–82, § 57, eff. Jan. 1, 1993; Laws 1999, c. 99–2, § 29, eff. June 29, 1999.

Cross References

Certified copies,
    Abstract of title, evidence, see § 703.08.
    Birth certificates, see §§ 382.015, 382.025.
    Consumer finance, see § 516.22.
    Death certificates, see § 382.025.
    Recorded instruments destroyed by fire, see § 695.15.
    Recording certified copies of deeds, mortgages, etc., see § 695.19.
Corporations, evidentiary effect of copy of filed document, see § 607.0127.
Microfilm copies of records,
    Bills and joint resolutions, see § 11.07.
    Circuit court clerk, vouchers and cancelled warrants, see § 28.30.
    Financial institutions, see § 655.91.
    Highway patrol records, see § 321.23.
    Instruments filed for recordation, see §§ 696.05, 696.06.
    State treasurer, see § 17.64.
    Teachers retirement system ledger sheets, see § 238.03.
    Transportation department records, see § 334.196.
    Vital statistics, see § 382.004.
Photographic or electronic copies as evidence, see § 92.29.
Records destroyed by fire,
    Abstracts, use as evidence, see § 92.25 et seq.
    Conveyances, see § 695.15.
    Land title suits, see § 92.28.
    Sworn copies as evidence, see § 92.26.
    Wills, see § 733.207.

90.954. Admissibility of other evidence of contents

The original of a writing, recording, or photograph is not required, except as provided in s. 90.953, and other evidence of its contents is admissible when:

(1) All originals are lost or destroyed, unless the proponent lost or destroyed them in bad faith.

(2) An original cannot be obtained in this state by any judicial process or procedure.

(3) An original was under the control of the party against whom offered at a time when that party was put on notice by the pleadings or by written notice from the adverse party that the contents of such original would be subject to proof at the hearing, and such original is not produced at the hearing.

(4) The writing, recording, or photograph is not related to a controlling issue.

Laws 1976, c. 76–237, § 1; Laws 1977, c. 77–174, § 1. Amended by Laws 1995, c. 95–147, § 502, eff. July 10, 1995.

Cross References

Admission of facts and genuineness of documents, see Civil Procedure Rule 1.370.
Examination of parties or property, see Civil Procedure Rule 1.360.
Official findings and reports, presumption of authority to issue or execute, see § 92.32.
Pretrial hearing, see Civil Procedure Rule 1.200.
Re-establishment of lost papers and documents, see § 71.011 et seq.
Records destroyed by fire,
    Abstracts, use as evidence, see § 92.25 et seq.
    Conveyances, see § 695.15.
    Land title suits, see § 92.28.
    Sworn copies as evidence, see § 92.26.
    Wills, see § 733.207.
Refusal to make discovery, see Civil Procedure Rule 1.380.

90.955. Public records

(1) The contents of an official record or of a document authorized to be recorded or filed, and actually recorded or filed, with a governmental agency, either federal, state, county, or municipal, in a place where official records or documents are ordinarily filed, including data compilations in any form, may be proved by a copy authenticated as provided in s. 90.902, if otherwise admissible.

(2) If a party cannot obtain, by the exercise of reasonable diligence, a copy that complies with subsection (1), other evidence of the contents is admissible.

Laws 1976, c. 76–237, § 1.

Cross References

Certificate of state officer, prima facie evidence of fact, see § 92.18.
Certificates issued under authority of Congress, see § 92.20.
Certified copies,
    Abstract of title, evidence, see § 703.08.
    Birth certificates, see §§ 382.015, 382.025.
    Consumer finance, see § 516.22.
    Death certificates, see § 382.025.
    Recorded instruments destroyed by fire, see § 695.15.
    Recording certified copies of deeds, mortgages, etc., see § 695.19.
Certified copies of records of certified copies as evidence, see § 92.13.
Corporations, evidentiary effect of copy of filed document, see § 607.0127.
Court records, admissibility and proof,
    Circuit courts, judgments and decrees prior thereto, see § 28.14.
    County court records prior to 1875, see § 28.16.

Court records—Cont'd
    Final judgments and decrees of courts of record, see §§ 92.05, 92.07.
    Portions of records as evidence, see § 92.19.
    Powers of attorney of record for 20 years or more, see §§ 92.08, 92.09.
    State judgments and decrees generally, see § 92.07.
    Superior court records, see § 28.15.
    U.S. District Court judgments and decrees, see § 92.06.
Deeds and conveyances, admissibility and proof,
    Certified copies of records of certified copies as evidence, see § 92.13.
    Destruction of recorded conveyances, rerecording, see §§ 92.25 et seq., 695.15.
    Portions of records as evidence, see § 92.19.
    Recorded deeds of 20 years or more, see § 92.08.
    Reversal of deeds, effect, see § 92.09.
    U.S. deeds and patents, copies as evidence, see § 92.14.
Hearsay exceptions, records admissible, see § 90.803.
Maps and plats, photographs presented for recording, see §§ 171.091, 177.091.
Microfilm copies of records,
    Bills and joint resolutions, see § 11.07.
    Circuit court clerk, vouchers and cancelled warrants, see § 28.30.
    Financial institutions, see § 655.91.
    Highway patrol records, see § 321.23.
    Instruments filed for recordation, see §§ 696.05, 696.06.
    State treasurer, see § 17.64.
    Teachers retirement system ledger sheets, see § 238.03.
    Transportation department records, see § 334.196.
    Vital statistics, see § 382.004.
Pleading official documents or acts, see Civil Procedure Rule 1.120.
Public records, examination, see § 119.01 et seq.
Records destroyed by fire,
    Abstracts, use as evidence, see § 92.25 et seq.
    Conveyances, see § 695.15.
    Land title suits, see § 92.28.
    Sworn copies as evidence, see § 92.26.
    Wills, see § 733.207.
Requirement of originals, see § 90.952 et seq.
Self authentication of public records, see § 90.902.
Tax deeds, evidence of title, see § 92.24.

90.956. Summaries

When it is not convenient to examine in court the contents of voluminous writings, recordings, or photographs, a party may present them in the form of a chart, summary, or calculation by calling a qualified witness. The party intending to use such a summary must give timely written notice of his or her intention to use the summary, proof of which shall be filed with the court, and shall make the summary and the originals or duplicates of the data from which the summary is compiled available for examination or copying, or both, by other parties at a reasonable time and place. A judge may order that they be produced in court.

Laws 1976, c. 76–237, § 1. Amended by Laws 1995, c. 95–147, § 503, eff. July 10, 1995.

90.957. Testimony or written admissions of a party

A party may prove the contents of writings, recordings, or photographs by the testimony or deposition of the party against whom they are offered or by that party's written admission, without accounting for the nonproduction of the original.

Laws 1976, c. 76–237, § 1. Amended by Laws 1995, c. 95–147, § 504, eff. July 10, 1995.

Cross References

Admission of facts and genuineness of documents, see Civil Procedure Rule 1.370.
Refusal to make discovery, see Civil Procedure Rule 1.380.

90.958. Functions of court and jury

(1) Except as provided in subsection (2), when the admissibility under this chapter of other evidence of the contents of writings, recordings, or photographs depends upon the existence of a preliminary fact, the question as to whether the preliminary fact exists is for the court to determine.

(2) The trier of fact shall determine whether:

(a) The asserted writing ever existed.

(b) Another writing, recording, or photograph produced at the trial is the original.

(c) Other evidence of the contents correctly reflects the contents.

Laws 1976, c. 76–237, § 1.

TITLE XIV

TAXATION AND FINANCE

Cross References

Osceola County Expressway Authority, tax exemption, see F.S.A. § 348.9960.

CHAPTER 198

ESTATE TAXES

Cross References

Estates of decedents, see § 731.005 et seq.
Payment of federal and state estate and death taxes, apportionment, see § 733.817.
Taxation, confidentiality and information sharing, see § 213.053.

198.01. Definitions

When used in this chapter the term, phrase or word:

(1) "Department" means the Department of Revenue.

(2) "Personal representative" means the executor, administrator, or curator of the decedent, or, if there is no executor, administrator, or curator appointed, qualified, and acting, then any person who is in the actual or constructive possession of any property included in the gross estate of the decedent or any other person who is required to file a return or pay the taxes due under any provision of this chapter.

(3) "Person" means persons, corporations, associations, joint stock companies, and business trusts.

(4) "Transfer" shall be taken to include the passing of property or any interest therein, in possession or enjoyment, present or future, by inheritance, descent, devise, succession, bequest, grant, deed, bargain, sale, gift, or appointment in the manner herein described.

(5) "Decedent" shall include the testator, intestate, grantor, bargainor, vendor, or donor.

(6) "Resident" means a natural person domiciled in the state.

(7) "Nonresident" means a natural person domiciled without the state.

(8) "Gross estate" means the gross estate as determined under the provisions of the applicable federal revenue act.

(9) "Net estate" means the net estate as determined under the provisions of the applicable federal revenue act.

(10) "Tangible personal property" means corporeal personal property, including money.

(11) "Intangible personal property" means incorporeal personal property including deposits in banks, negotiable instruments, mortgages, debts, receivables, shares of stock, bonds, notes, credits, evidences of an interest in property, evidences of debt and choses in action generally.

(12) "United States" when used in a geographical sense includes only the 50 states and the District of Columbia.

(13) "Generation-skipping transfer" means every transfer subject to the federal generation-skipping transfer tax in which transfer the original transferor is a resident of this state at the date of original transfer or the property transferred is real or personal property in this state.

(14) "Original transferor" means any grantor, donor, trustor, or testator who by grant, gift, trust, or will makes a transfer of real or personal property that results in a federal generation-skipping transfer tax.

(15) "Federal generation-skipping transfer tax" means the tax imposed by chapter 13 of the Internal Revenue Code of 1986, as amended.[1]

Laws 1933, c. 16015, § 2; Comp.Gen.Laws Supp.1936, § 1342(81); Laws 1969, c. 69–106, §§ 21, 35; Laws 1971, c. 71–377, § 44; Laws 1980, c. 80–153, § 1. Amended by Laws 1989, c. 89–356, § 3, eff. July 6, 1989.

[1] 26 U.S.C.A. § 2601 et seq.

198.015. Domicile of decedent

(1) For the purposes of this chapter, every person shall be presumed to have died a resident and not a nonresident of the state:

(a) If such person has dwelt or lodged in the state during and for the greater part of any period of 12 consecutive months in the 24 months next preceding death, notwithstanding the fact that from time to time during such 24 months such person may have sojourned outside of this state, and without regard to whether or not such person may have voted, may have been entitled to vote, or may have been assessed for taxes in this state; or

(b) If such person has been a resident of Florida, sojourning outside of this state.

(2) The burden of proof in an estate tax proceeding shall be upon any person claiming exemption by reason of alleged nonresidency. Domicile shall be determined exclusively in the proceedings provided in this chapter, and orders relating to domicile previously entered in the probate proceedings shall not be conclusive for the purposes of this chapter.

Laws 1977, c. 77–411, § 1. Amended by Laws 1995, c. 95–147, § 1031, eff. July 10, 1995.

198.02. Tax upon estates of resident decedents

A tax is imposed upon the transfer of the estate of every person who, at the time of death, was a resident of this state, the amount of which shall be a sum equal to the amount by which the credit allowable under the applicable federal revenue act for estate, inheritance, legacy, and succession taxes actually paid to the several states exceeds the aggregate amount of all constitutionally valid estate, inheritance, legacy, and succession taxes actually paid to the several states of the United States (other than this state) in respect of any property owned by such decedent or subject to such taxes as a part of or in connection with his or her estate. All values shall be as finally determined for federal estate tax purposes.

Laws 1933, c. 16015, § 3; Comp.Gen.Laws Supp.1936, § 1342(83); Laws 1971, c. 71–202, § 1; Laws 1982, c. 82–38, § 3. Amended by Laws 1995, c. 95–147, § 1032, eff. July 10, 1995.

Cross References

Exemptions from inheritance and estate taxes, see § 198.44.
Limitations upon inheritance and estate taxes, see Const. Art. 7, § 5.

198.021. Tax upon generation-skipping transfers of residents

A tax is hereby imposed upon every generation-skipping transfer in which the original transferor is a resident of this state at the date of original transfer, in an amount equal to the amount allowable as a credit for state legacy taxes under s. 2604 of the Internal Revenue Code of 1986, as amended,[1] to the extent such credit exceeds the aggregate amount of all constitutionally valid taxes on the same transfer actually paid to the several states of the United States other than this state.

Laws 1980, c. 80–153, § 2. Amended by Laws 1989, c. 89–356, § 4, eff. July 6, 1989.

[1] 26 U.S.C.A. § 2604.

198.03. Tax upon estates of nonresident decedents

A tax is imposed upon the transfer of real property situate in this state, upon tangible personal property having an actual situs in this state, upon intangible personal property having a business situs in this state and upon stocks, bonds, debentures, notes, and other securities or obligations of corporations organized under the laws of this state, of every person who at the time of death was not a resident of this state but was a resident of the United States, the amount of which shall be a sum equal to such proportion of the amount of the credit allowable under the applicable federal revenue act for estate, inheritance, legacy, and succession taxes actually paid to the several states, as the value of the property taxable in this state bears to the value of the entire gross estate wherever situate.

Laws 1933, c. 16015, § 4; Comp.Gen.Laws Supp.1936, § 1342(84); Laws 1953, c. 28031, § 1.

198.031. Tax upon generation-skipping transfers of nonresidents

A tax is hereby imposed upon every generation-skipping transfer in which the original transferor is not a resident of this state at the date of the original transfer but in which the property transferred includes real or personal property in this state, in an amount equal to the amount allowable as a credit for state legacy taxes under s. 2604 of the Internal Revenue Code of 1986, as amended,[1] reduced by an amount which bears the same ratio to the total state tax credit allowable for federal generation-skipping transfer tax purposes as the value of the transferred property taxable by all other states bears to the value of the gross generation-skipping transfer for federal generation-skipping transfer tax purposes.

Laws 1980, c. 80–153, § 3. Amended by Laws 1989, c. 89–356, § 5, eff. July 6, 1989.

[1] 26 U.S.C.A. § 2604.

198.04. Tax upon estates of alien decedents

A tax is imposed upon the transfer of real property situate and tangible personal property having an actual situs in this state and upon intangible personal property physically present within this state of every person who at the time of death was not a resident of the United States, the amount of which shall be a sum equal to such proportion of the credit allowable under the applicable federal revenue act for estate, inheritance, legacy, and succession taxes actually paid to the several states, as the value of the property taxable in this state bears to the value of the estate taxable by the United States wherever situate. For the purpose of this section, stock in a corporation organized under the laws of this state shall be deemed physically present within this state. The amount receivable as insurance upon the life of a decedent who at the time of death was not a resident of the United States, and any moneys deposited with any person carrying on the banking business by or for such decedent who was not engaged in business in the United States at the time of death, shall not, for the purpose of this section, be deemed to be physically present in this state.

Laws 1933, c. 16015, § 5; Comp.Gen.Laws Supp.1936, § 1342(85). Amended by Laws 1995, c. 95–147, § 1033, eff. July 10, 1995.

198.05. Administration of law by Department of Revenue

The Department of Revenue shall, except as otherwise provided, have jurisdiction and be charged with the administration and enforcement of the provisions of this chapter.

Laws 1933, c. 16015, § 6; Comp.Gen.Laws Supp.1936, § 1342(86); Laws 1969, c. 69–106, §§ 21, 35.

198.06. Examination of books, papers, records, or memoranda by the department

(1) The department, for the purpose of ascertaining the correctness of any return, or for the purpose of making a return where none has been made, may examine any books, papers, records, or memoranda, bearing upon the matter required to be included in the return; may require the attendance of persons rendering return or of any officer or employee of such persons, or of any person having knowledge in the premises, at any convenient place in the county in which such person resides, and may take his or her testimony with reference to the matter required by law to be included in such return, and may administer oaths to such persons.

(2) If any person summoned to appear under this chapter to testify, or to produce books, papers, or other data, shall refuse to do so, the circuit court for the county in which such person resides shall have jurisdiction by appropriate process to compel such attendance, testimony, or production of books, papers, or other data.

Laws 1933, c. 16015, § 6; Comp.Gen.Laws Supp.1936, § 1342(86); Laws 1969, c. 69–106, §§ 21, 35. Amended by Laws 1995, c. 95–147, § 1034, eff. July 10, 1995.

Cross References

Failure to produce records, penalty, see § 198.36.
Taxpayer rights, see § 213.015.

198.07. Appointment of agents by department; bonds of agents; may administer oaths; credentials

(1) The department may appoint and remove such examiners, appraisers, attorneys and employees as it may deem necessary, such persons to have such duties and powers as the department may from time to time prescribe. The salaries of all examiners, appraisers, attorneys and employees employed by the department shall be such as it may prescribe, and such examiners, appraisers, attorneys and employees shall be reimbursed for travel expenses as provided in s. 112.061.

(2) The department may require such of the examiners, appraisers, attorneys and employees as it may designate to give bond payable to the state for the faithful performance of their duties in such form and with such sureties as it may determine, and all premiums on such bonds shall be paid by the state.

(3) All officers empowered by law to administer oaths and the examiners, appraisers and attorneys appointed by the department may administer an oath to all persons giving any testimony before them or to take the acknowledgment of any person in respect to any return or report required under this chapter.

(4) All examiners, appraisers and attorneys appointed by the department shall have for identification purpose proper credentials issued by the department and exhibit the same upon demand.

Laws 1933, c. 16015, § 6; Comp.Gen.Laws Supp.1936, § 1342(86); Laws 1963, c. 63–400, § 19; Laws 1969, c. 69–106, §§ 21, 35.

Cross References

Bonds of officials, see § 113.07.

198.08. Rules

The department has authority to adopt rules pursuant to ss. 120.536(1) and 120.54 to enforce the provisions of this chapter and may adopt, as rules, such rules and regulations as are promulgated with respect to the estate tax or generation-skipping transfer tax provisions of the Revenue Act of the United States insofar as they are applicable hereto. The department may from time to time prescribe such forms as it shall deem proper for the administration of this chapter.

Laws 1933, c. 16015, § 6; Comp.Gen.Laws Supp.1936, § 1342(86); Laws 1969, c. 69–106, §§ 21, 35; Laws 1980, c. 80–153, § 4. Amended by Laws 1998, c. 98–200, § 14, eff. July 1, 1998.

198.11. Appointment of special appraisers

The department may employ special appraisers for the purpose of determining the value of any property which is, or is believed by the department to be, subject to the tax imposed by this chapter, and such special appraisers shall be paid such compensation as said department shall deem proper.

Laws 1933, c. 16015, § 6; Comp.Gen.Laws Supp.1936, § 1342(86); Laws 1969, c. 69–106, §§ 21, 35.

198.13. Tax return to be made in certain cases; certificate of nonliability

(1) The personal representative of every estate required by the laws of the United States to file a federal estate tax return shall file with the department, on or before the last day prescribed by law for filing the initial federal estate tax return for such estate, a return consisting of an executed copy of the federal estate tax return and shall file with such return all supplemental data, if any, as may be necessary to determine and establish the correct tax under this chapter. Such return shall be made in the case of every decedent who at the time of death was not a resident of the United States and whose gross estate includes any real property situate in the state, tangible personal property having an actual situs in the state, and intangible personal property physically present within the state.

(2) Whenever it is made to appear to the department that an estate that has filed a return owes no taxes under this chapter, the department shall issue to the personal representative a certificate in writing to that effect, which certificate shall have the same force and effect as a receipt showing payment. The certificate shall be subject to record and admissible in evidence in like manner as a receipt showing payment of taxes. A fee of $5 shall be paid to the department for each certificate so issued.

(3) Every person required to file a return reporting a generation-skipping transfer under applicable federal statutes and regulations shall file with the Department of Revenue, on or before the last day prescribed for filing the federal return, a return consisting of a duplicate copy of the federal return.

(4) Notwithstanding any other provisions of this section and applicable to the estate of a decedent who dies after December 31, 2004, if, upon the death of the decedent, a state death tax credit or a generation-skipping transfer credit is not allowable pursuant to the Internal Revenue Code of 1986, as amended:

(a) The personal representative of the estate is not required to file a return under subsection (1) in connection with the estate.

(b) The person who would otherwise be required to file a return reporting a generation-skipping transfer under subsection (3) is not required to file such a return in connection with the estate.

Laws 1933, c. 16015, § 7; Comp.Gen.Laws Supp.1936, § 1342(87); Laws 1953, c. 28031, § 2; Laws 1955, c. 29718, § 2; Laws 1969, c. 69–106, §§ 21, 35; Laws 1971, c. 71–202, § 2; Laws 1980, c. 80–153, § 7; Laws 1984, c. 84–325, § 1; Laws 1985, c. 85–342, § 38. Amended by Laws 1995, c. 95–147, § 1035, eff. July 10, 1995; Laws 1999, c. 99–208, § 4, eff. May 26, 1999; Laws 2007, c. 2007–106, § 7, eff. July 1, 2007; Laws 2008, c. 2008–4, § 35, eff. July 1, 2008; Laws 2011, c. 2011–86, § 1, eff. May 31, 2011; Laws 2013, c. 2013–172, § 1, eff. Oct. 1, 2013.

Retroactivity

The introductory paragraph of Laws 2011, c. 2011–86, § 1, provides:

"Retroactive to January 1, 2011, subsection (4) of section 198.13, Florida Statutes, is amended to read:"

The introductory paragraph of Laws 2013, c. 2013–172 § 1, provides:

"Retroactive to January 1, 2013, subsection (4) of section 198.13, Florida Statutes, is amended to read:"

Cross References

Penalty for false return, or false statement, see §§ 198.38, 198.39.

198.14. Failure to make return; extension of time for filing

To obtain an extension for filing a Florida return, the personal representative shall file with the department a copy of the federal extension request within 30 days after filing such request with the federal taxing authorities. If the federal taxing authorities grant an extension of time for filing a return, the department shall allow a like extension of time for filing if the personal representative files a copy of such federal extension with the department within 30 days after receiving an approved federal extension. An extension of time for filing a return shall not operate to extend the time for payment of the tax. If any person fails to file a return at the time prescribed by law or files, willfully or otherwise, a false or fraudulent return, the department shall make the return from its own knowledge and from such information as it can obtain through testimony or otherwise. Any such return so made by the department shall be prima facie good and sufficient for all legal purposes.

Laws 1933, c. 16015, § 7; Comp.Gen.Laws Supp.1936, § 1342(87); Laws 1955, c. 29718, § 3; Laws 1969, c. 69–106, §§ 21, 35; Laws 1987, c. 87–102, § 2.

Cross References

Failure to make return, penalty, see § 198.37.
False return, penalty, see § 198.38.
Failure to pay tax, criminal penalty, see § 198.40.

198.15. When tax due; extension; interest; penalty

(1) The tax imposed by this chapter is due and payable on or before the last day prescribed by law for paying the federal estate tax pursuant to the initial estate tax return and shall be paid by the personal representative to the department. The department shall extend the time for payment of the tax or any part of the tax if the time for paying the federal estate tax is extended, provided the personal representative files with the department a copy of the approved federal extension notice within 30 days after receiving such notice. No extension shall be for more than 1 year, and the aggregate of extensions with respect to any estate shall not exceed 10 years from the due date. In such case, the amount in respect of which the extension is granted shall be paid on or before the date of the expiration of the period of the extension, unless a further extension is granted. If the time for the payment is thus extended, there shall be collected, as part of such amount, interest thereon at the rate of 1 percent per month of the amount due from the due date of the tax to the date the same is paid.

(2) For any tax that is due on or after July 1, 1991, and that is not paid by the due date or by the due date of any extension granted by the department, in addition to any other penalties, a

specific penalty shall be added to the tax in the amount of 10 percent of any unpaid tax if the failure is for not more than 30 days, or 20 percent of the aggregate of any unpaid tax if the failure is for more than 30 days.

Laws 1933, c. 16015, § 8; Comp.Gen.Laws Supp.1936, § 1342(88); Laws 1953, c. 28031, § 3; Laws 1969, c. 69–106, §§ 21, 35; Laws 1971, c. 71–202, § 3; Laws 1976, c. 76–261, § 1; Laws 1977, c. 77–411, § 2; Laws 1980, c. 80–24, § 1; Laws 1980, c. 80–153, § 8; Laws 1984, c. 84–325, § 2; Laws 1985, c. 85–342, § 39; Laws 1987, c. 87–102, § 3. Amended by Laws 1991, c. 91–112, § 8, eff. July 1, 1991; Laws 1992, c. 92–320, § 3, eff. Jan. 1, 1993.

198.155. Payment of tax on generation-skipping transfers

(1) The person liable for payment of the federal generation-skipping transfer tax shall be liable for the tax imposed by ss. 198.021 and 198.031.

(2) The tax imposed by ss. 198.021 and 198.031 is due upon a taxable distribution or taxable termination as determined under applicable provisions of the federal generation-skipping transfer tax.

(3) The tax becomes delinquent the day after the last day allowed for filing a return for the generation-skipping transfer.

(4) The tax shall be paid to the Department of Revenue.

(5) If the tax, or any portion thereof, is not paid before it becomes delinquent, it shall bear interest at the rate of 1 percent per month for each month or fraction thereof that it is delinquent.

Laws 1980, c. 80–153, § 21.

198.16. Notice of determination of deficiency in federal tax to be filed with department

(1) It shall be the duty of the personal representative to file with the department within 60 days after a final determination of any deficiency in federal estate tax has been made, written notice thereof.

(2) If, after a duplicate federal return of a generation-skipping transfer has been filed with the Department of Revenue, the federal authorities increase or decrease the amount of the federal generation-skipping transfer tax, an amended return shall be filed with the department showing all changes made in the original return and the amount of increase or decrease in the federal generation-skipping transfer tax.

(3) If, based upon any deficiency and the ground therefor, it shall appear that the amount of tax previously paid is less than the amount of tax owing, the difference, together with interest at the rate of 1 percent per month from the due date of the tax, shall be paid upon notice and demand by the department. In the event the personal representative or person required to return and pay such tax shall fail to give the notice required by this section, any additional tax which shall be owing may be assessed, or a proceeding in court for the collection of such tax may be begun without assessment at any time prior to the filing of such notice or within 30 days after the delinquent filing of such notice, notwithstanding the provisions of s. 198.28.

Laws 1933, c. 16015, § 9; Comp.Gen.Laws Supp.1936, § 1342(89); Laws 1953, c. 28031, § 4; Laws 1955, c. 29718, § 4; Laws 1969, c. 69–106, §§ 21, 35; Laws 1977, c. 77–411, § 3; Laws 1980, c. 80–153, § 9.

198.17. Deficiency; hearing by department

If upon examination of any return a tax or a deficiency in tax is disclosed, the department shall proceed to determine all questions involving such tax or deficiency. Such tax or deficiency

in tax shall be assessed and paid together with the penalty and interest, if any, applicable thereto, within 60 days after such demand as may be included in the department's order.
Laws 1933, c. 16015, § 10; Comp.Gen.Laws Supp.1936, § 1342(90); Laws 1955, c. 29718, § 5; Laws 1963, c. 63–559, § 19; Laws 1969, c. 69–106, §§ 21, 35; Laws 1978, c. 78–95, § 54.

Cross References

Court proceedings relating to taxation, see § 194.171.

198.18. Failure to pay tax; penalties; delinquent or deficient taxes, interest

(1) If any part of a deficiency in tax due under the provisions of this chapter is due to negligence or intentional disregard of the provisions of this chapter or the rules and regulations issued pursuant hereto, with knowledge thereof but without intent to defraud, there shall be added as a penalty 10 percent per month of the total amount of the deficiency in tax to a maximum of 50 percent of the tax due; and, if any part of such deficiency is willfully made with intent to defraud, there shall be added as a penalty 100 percent of the total amount of such deficiency, which penalty shall become due and payable upon notice and demand by the department. The personal representative shall be liable to the state personally and on his or her official bond, if any, for any loss to the state accruing under the provisions of this section through the personal representative's negligence or willful neglect. No interest shall be collected upon the amount of any penalty. The department may settle or compromise such penalties pursuant to s. 213.21.

(2) Any deficiency in tax or any tax payment not received by the department on or before the due date as provided in s. 198.15, in addition to any other penalties, shall bear interest at the rate of 1 percent per month of the amount due from the due date until paid. The department may settle or compromise such interest pursuant to s. 213.21.
Laws 1933, c. 16015, § 11; Comp.Gen.Laws Supp.1936, § 1342(91); Laws 1955, c. 29718, § 6; Laws 1969, c. 69–106, §§ 21, 35; Laws 1976, c. 76–261, § 2; Laws 1977, c. 77–174, § 1; Laws 1980, c. 80–153, § 10; Laws 1981, c. 81–178, § 2; Laws 1987, c. 87–6, § 50; Laws 1987, c. 87–101, § 30. Amended by Laws 1992, c. 92–320, § 4, eff. Jan. 1, 1993; Laws 1995, c. 95–147, § 1036, eff. July 10, 1995.

Cross References

Failure to pay tax, criminal penalty, see § 198.40.

198.19. Receipts for taxes

The department shall issue to the personal representative, upon payment of the tax imposed by this chapter, receipts in triplicate, any of which shall be sufficient evidence of such payment and shall entitle the personal representative to be credited and allowed the amount thereof by any court having jurisdiction to audit or settle his or her accounts. If the personal representative files a complete return and makes written application to the department for determination of the amount of the tax and discharge from personal liability therefor, the department as soon as possible, and in any event within 1 year after receipt of such application, shall notify the personal representative of the amount of the tax; and upon payment thereof the personal representative shall be discharged from personal liability for any additional tax thereafter found to be due and shall be entitled to receive from the department a receipt in writing showing such discharge; however, such discharge shall not operate to release the gross estate of the lien of any additional tax that may thereafter be found to be due, while the title to the gross estate remains in the personal representative or in the heirs, devisees, or distributees thereof; but after such discharge is given, no part of the gross estate shall be subject to such lien or to any claim or demand for any such tax after the title thereto has passed to a bona fide purchaser for value.

Laws 1933, c. 16015, § 12; Comp.Gen.Laws Supp.1936, § 1342(92); Laws 1969, c. 69–106, §§ 21, 35; Laws 1980, c. 80–153, § 11. Amended by Laws 1995, c. 95–147, § 1037, eff. July 10, 1995.

198.20. Failure to pay tax when due, department's warrant, etc.

If any tax imposed by this chapter or any portion of such tax be unpaid within 90 days after the same becomes due, and the time for payment be not extended, the department shall issue a warrant directed to the sheriff of any county of the state in which the estate or any part thereof may be situated, commanding the sheriff to levy upon and sell the real and personal property of such estate found within his or her county, for the payment of the amount thereof, with such interest and penalties, if any, as may have accrued thereon or been assessed against the same, together with the cost of executing the warrant, and to return such warrant, to the department and pay to it the money collected by virtue thereof, by a time to be therein specified, not less than 60 days from the date of the warrant. The sheriff thereupon shall proceed upon the same in all respects, with like effect, and in the same manner prescribed by law in respect to executions issued against property upon judgments of a court of record, and shall be entitled to the same fees for services in executing the warrant as are now allowed by law for like services to be collected in the same manner as now provided by law. Alias and pluries warrants may issue from time to time as said department may deem proper until the entire amount of the tax, deficiency, interest, penalties, and costs have been recovered.

Laws 1933, c. 16015, § 13; Comp.Gen.Laws Supp.1936, § 1342(93); Laws 1969, c. 69–106, §§ 21, 35. Amended by Laws 1995, c. 95–147, § 1038, eff. July 10, 1995.

Cross References

Executions, issuance, etc., see § 56.011 et seq.
Taxpayer rights, see § 213.015.

198.21. Tax due payable from entire estate; third persons

If the tax or any part thereof is paid or collected out of that part of the estate passing to or in possession of any person other than the personal representative in his or her capacity as such, such person shall be entitled to a reimbursement out of any part of the estate still undistributed or by a just and equitable contribution by the person whose interest in the estate of the decedent would have been reduced if the tax had been paid before the distribution of the estate or whose interest in the estate is subject to an equal or prior liability for the payment of tax, debts, or other charges against the estate, it being the purpose and intent of this section that, so far as is practical and unless otherwise directed by the will of the decedent, the tax shall be paid out of the estate before its distribution; but the department shall not be charged with enforcing contribution from any person.

Laws 1933, c. 16015, § 14; Comp.Gen.Laws Supp.1936, § 1342(94); Laws 1969, c. 69–106, §§ 21, 35; Laws 1980, c. 80–153, § 12. Amended by Laws 1995, c. 95–147, § 1039, eff. July 10, 1995.

Cross References

Apportionment of estate taxes, see § 733.817.

198.22. Lien for unpaid taxes

Unless the tax is sooner paid in full, it shall be a lien for 12 years upon the gross estate of the decedent, except that such part of the gross estate as is used for the payment of charges against the estate and expenses of its administration, allowed by any court having jurisdiction thereof, shall be divested of such lien, and except that such part of the gross estate of a resident decedent as is transferred to a bona fide purchaser, mortgagee, or pledgee, for an adequate and full consideration in money or money's worth shall be divested of such lien and such lien shall then attach to the consideration received for such property from such purchaser, mortgagee, or pledgee. If the department is satisfied that no tax liability exists or that the tax liability of an estate has been fully discharged or provided for, it may issue a waiver releasing any or all property of such estate from the lien herein imposed.

Laws 1933, c. 16015, § 15; Comp.Gen.Laws Supp.1936, § 1342(95); Laws 1957, c. 57–108, § 1; Laws 1959, c. 59–1, § 13; Laws 1969, c. 69–106, §§ 21, 35; Laws 1977, c. 77–411, § 4.

Cross References

Taxpayer rights, see § 213.015.

198.23. Personal liability of personal representative

If any personal representative shall make distribution either in whole or in part of any of the property of an estate to the heirs, next of kin, distributees, legatees, or devisees without having paid or secured the tax due the state under this chapter, or having obtained the release of such property from the lien of such tax either by the department or pursuant to s. 198.32(2), he or she shall become personally liable for the tax so due the state, or so much thereof as may remain due and unpaid, to the full extent of the full value of any property belonging to such person or estate which may come into the personal representative's hands, custody, or control.

Laws 1933, c. 16015, § 16; Comp.Gen.Laws Supp.1936, § 1342(96); Laws 1980, c. 80–153, § 13. Amended by Laws 1995, c. 95–147, § 1040, eff. July 10, 1995; Laws 1999, c. 99–208, § 5, eff. Jan. 1, 2000.

Cross References

Apportionment of estate taxes, see § 733.817.

198.24. Sale of real estate by personal representative to pay tax

Every personal representative shall have the same right and power to take possession of or sell, convey, and dispose of real estate, as assets of the estate, for the payment of the tax imposed by this chapter as he or she may have for the payment of the debts of the decedent.

Laws 1933, c. 16015, § 17; Comp.Gen.Laws Supp.1936, § 1342(97); Laws 1980, c. 80–153, § 14. Amended by Laws 1995, c. 95–147, § 1041, eff. July 10, 1995.

198.25. Actions to enforce payment of tax

Actions may be brought within the time or times herein specified by the department to recover the amount of any taxes, penalties and interest due under this chapter. Every such action shall be brought in the county where the estate is being or has been administered, or if no administration be had in this state, then in any county where any of the property of the estate shall be situate.

Laws 1933, c. 16015, § 18; Comp.Gen.Laws Supp.1936, § 1342(98); Laws 1969, c. 69–106, §§ 21, 35.

198.26. No discharge of personal representative until tax is paid

No final account of a personal representative shall be allowed by any court unless and until such account shows, and the judge of said court finds, that the tax imposed by the provisions of this chapter upon the personal representative, which has become payable, has been paid. The certificate of the department of nonliability for the tax or its receipt for the amount of tax therein certified shall be conclusive in such proceedings as to the liability or the payment of the tax to the extent of said certificate. In the case of a nontaxable estate, the court may consider the affidavit prepared pursuant to s. 198.32(2) as evidence of the nonliability for tax.

Laws 1933, c. 16015, § 19; Comp.Gen.Laws Supp.1936, § 1342(99); Laws 1955, c. 29718, § 7; Laws 1969, c. 69–106, §§ 21, 35; Laws 1980, c. 80–153, § 15. Amended by Laws 1999, c. 99–208, § 6, eff. Jan. 1, 2000.

198.28. Time for assessment of tax

The amount of estate tax due under this chapter shall be determined and assessed within 4 years from the date the return was filed, or within a period expiring 90 days after the last day on which the assessment of a deficiency in federal estate tax may lawfully be made under applicable provisions of the Internal Revenue Laws of the United States, whichever date last occurs, and no suit or other proceedings for the collection of any tax due under this chapter shall be begun after such date; provided, however, that in the case of a false or fraudulent return or of a failure to file a return, the tax may be assessed, or a proceeding in court for the collection of such tax may be begun without assessment, at any time.

Laws 1933, c. 16015, § 21; Comp.Gen.Laws Supp.1936, § 1342(101); Laws 1953, c. 28031, § 5; Laws 1955, c. 29718, § 8.

198.29. Refunds of excess tax paid

(1) Whenever it appears, upon the examination of any return made under this chapter or upon proof submitted to the department by the personal representative, that an amount of estate tax has been paid in excess of the tax legally due under this chapter, the amount of such overpayment, together with any overpayment of interest thereon shall be refunded to the personal representative and paid by the Chief Financial Officer; such refund shall be made by the department as a matter of course regardless of whether or not the personal representative has filed a written claim therefor, except that upon request of the department, the personal representative shall file with the department a conformed copy of any written claim for refund of federal estate tax which has theretofore been filed with the United States.

(2) Notwithstanding the foregoing provisions, no refund of estate tax shall be made nor shall any personal representative be entitled to bring any action for refund of estate tax after the expiration of 4 years from the date of payment of the tax to be refunded, unless there shall have been filed with the department written notice of any administrative or judicial determination of the federal estate tax liability of the estate, whichever shall last occur, and such notice shall have been so filed not later than 60 days after the determination shall have become final.

(3) For the purpose of this section, an administrative determination shall be deemed to have become final on the date of receipt by the personal representative or other interested party of the final payment to be made refunding federal estate tax or upon the last date on which the personal representative or any other interested party shall receive notice from the United States that an overpayment of federal estate tax has been credited by the United States against any liability other than federal estate tax of said estate. A final judicial determination shall be deemed to have occurred on the date on which any judgment entered by a court of competent jurisdiction and determining that there has been an overpayment of federal estate tax becomes final.

(4) Nothing herein contained shall be construed to prevent a personal representative from bringing or maintaining an action in any court of competent jurisdiction, within any period

otherwise prescribed by law, to determine any question bearing upon the taxable situs of property, the domicile of a decedent, or otherwise affecting the jurisdiction of the state to impose an inheritance or estate tax with respect to a particular item or items of property.

(5) Notwithstanding any other provision of this section, estate tax may not be refunded pursuant to any allegation that the decedent was a resident of another state unless this state is a party to any compromise agreement between the decedent's estate and the other state or unless this state is allowed to intervene as a party in any action in the other state in which the residency of the decedent is at issue.

Laws 1933, c. 16015, § 22; Comp.Gen.Laws Supp.1936, § 1342(102); Laws 1955, c. 29718, § 8–A; Laws 1969, c. 69–106, §§ 21, 35; Laws 1980, c. 80–153, § 17. Amended by Laws 1989, c. 89–356, § 2, eff. July 6, 1989; Laws 2003, c. 2003–261, § 176, eff. June 26, 2003.

198.30. Circuit judge to report names of decedents, etc.

Each circuit judge of this state shall, on or before the 10th day of every month, notify the department of the names of all decedents; the names and addresses of the respective personal representatives, administrators, or curators appointed; the amount of the bonds, if any, required by the court; and the probable value of the estates, in all estates of decedents whose wills have been probated or propounded for probate before the circuit judge or upon which letters testamentary or upon whose estates letters of administration or curatorship have been sought or granted, during the preceding month; and such report shall contain any other information which the circuit judge may have concerning the estates of such decedents. In addition, a copy of this report shall be provided to the Agency for Health Care Administration. A circuit judge shall also furnish forthwith such further information, from the records and files of the circuit court in regard to such estates, as the department may from time to time require.

Laws 1933, c. 16015, § 23; Comp.Gen.Laws Supp.1936, § 1342(103); Laws 1955, c. 29718, § 9; Laws 1969, c. 69–106, §§ 21, 35; Laws 1973, c. 73–334, § 20; Laws 1980, c. 80–153, § 18. Amended by Laws 1995, c. 95–147, § 1042, eff. July 10, 1995; Laws 1998, c. 98–191, § 14, eff. July 1, 1998.

198.31. Duties and powers of corporate personal representatives of nonresident decedents

If the personal representative of the estate of a nonresident is a corporation duly authorized, qualified, and acting as personal representative in the jurisdiction of the domicile of the decedent, it shall be under the duties and obligations as to the giving of notices and filing of returns required by this chapter, and may bring and defend actions and suits as may be authorized or permitted by this chapter, to the same extent as an individual personal representative, notwithstanding that such corporation may be prohibited from exercising, in this state, any powers as personal representative; but nothing herein contained shall be taken or construed as authorizing a corporation not authorized to do business in this state to qualify or act as a personal representative, an administrator, or in any other fiduciary capacity, if otherwise prohibited by the laws of this state, except to the extent herein expressly provided.

Laws 1933, c. 16015, § 24; Comp.Gen.Laws Supp.1936, § 1342(104); Laws 1980, c. 80–153, § 19.

198.32. Prima facie liability for tax

(1) The estate of each decedent whose property is subject to the laws of the state shall be deemed prima facie liable for estate taxes under this chapter and shall be subject to a lien therefor in such amount as may be later determined to be due and payable on the estate as provided in this chapter. This presumption of liability shall begin on the date of the death of the decedent and shall continue until the full settlement of all taxes which may be found to be due

under this chapter, the settlement to be shown by receipts for all taxes due to be issued by the department as provided for in this chapter.

(2) Whenever an estate is not subject to tax under this chapter and is not required to file a return, the personal representative may execute an affidavit attesting that the estate is not taxable. The form of the affidavit shall be prescribed by the department, and shall include, but not be limited to, statements regarding the decedent's domicile and whether a federal estate tax return will be filed, and acknowledgment of the personal representative's personal liability under s. 198.23. This affidavit shall be subject to record and admissible in evidence to show nonliability for tax. This subsection applies to all estates, regardless of the date of death of the decedent.

Laws 1933, c. 16015, § 25; Comp.Gen.Laws Supp.1936, § 1342(105); Laws 1969, c. 69–106, §§ 21, 35; Laws 1971, c. 71–202, § 4; Laws 1980, c. 80–153, § 20. Amended by Laws 1999, c. 99–208, § 7, eff. Jan. 1, 2000; Laws 2005, c. 2005–280, § 2, eff. July 1, 2005.

198.33. Discharge of estate, notice of lien, limitation on lien, etc.

(1) Where no receipt for the payment of taxes, or no affidavit or certificate of nonliability for taxes has been issued or recorded as provided for in this chapter, the property constituting the estate of the decedent in this state shall be deemed fully acquitted and discharged of all liability for estate and inheritance taxes under this chapter after a lapse of 10 years from the date of the filing with the department of an estate tax return, unless the department shall make out and file and have recorded in the public records of the county wherein any part of the estate of the decedent may be situated in this state, a notice of lien against the property of the estate, specifying the amount or approximate amount of taxes claimed to be due to the state under this chapter, which notice of lien shall continue said lien in force for an additional period of 5 years or until payment is made. Such notice of lien shall be filed and recorded in the book of deeds in the office of the clerk of the circuit court; provided, where no receipt for the payment of taxes, or no affidavit or certificate of nonliability for taxes, has been issued or recorded as provided for in this chapter, the property constituting the estate of the decedent in this state, if said decedent was a resident of this state at the time of death, shall be deemed fully acquitted and discharged of all liability for tax under this chapter after a lapse of 10 years from the date of the death of the decedent, unless the department shall make out and file and have recorded notice of lien as herein provided, which notice shall continue said lien in force against such property of the estate as is situate in the county wherein said notice of lien was recorded for an additional period of 5 years or until payment is made.

(2) Notwithstanding anything to the contrary in this section or this chapter, no lien for estate and inheritance taxes under this chapter shall continue for more than 20 years from the date of death of the decedent, whether the decedent be a resident or nonresident of this state.

Laws 1933, c. 16015, § 26; Comp.Gen.Laws Supp.1936, § 1342(106); Laws 1953, c. 28031, § 6; Laws 1955, c. 29718 § 10; Laws 1957, c. 57–108, § 2; Laws 1969, c. 69–106, §§ 21, 35. Amended by Laws 1995, c. 95–147, § 1043, eff. July 10, 1995; Laws 1999, c. 99–208, § 8, eff. Jan. 1, 2000.

Cross References

Service charges of clerk of circuit court, see § 28.24.

198.34. Disposition of proceeds from taxes

All taxes and fees levied and collected under this chapter shall be paid into the Treasury of the state to the credit of the General Revenue Fund.

Laws 1933, c. 16015, § 28; Comp.Gen.Laws Supp.1936, § 1342(108); Laws 1951, c. 26869, § 10.

198.35. Interpretation and construction

When not otherwise provided for in this chapter, the rules of interpretation and construction applicable to the estate and inheritance tax laws of the United States shall apply to and be followed in the interpretation of this chapter.

Laws 1933, c. 16015, § 32; Comp.Gen.Laws Supp.1936, § 1342(111); Laws 1977, c. 77–411, § 5; Laws 1979, c. 79–34, § 1; Laws 1980, c. 80–16, § 1; Laws 1982, c. 82–38, § 1.

198.36. Failure to produce records; penalty

Whoever fails to comply with any duty imposed upon him or her by this law, or having in his or her possession or control any record, file, or paper, containing or supposed to contain any information concerning the estate of the decedent, or, having in his or her possession or control any property comprised in the gross estate of the decedent, fails to exhibit the same upon request to the department or any examiner, appraiser, or attorney appointed pursuant to this chapter, who desires to examine the same in the performance of his or her duties under this chapter, shall be liable to a penalty of not exceeding $500 to be recovered, with costs of suit, in a civil action in the name of the state.

Laws 1933, c. 16015, § 27; Comp.Gen.Laws Supp.1936, § 1342(107); Laws 1969, c. 69–106, §§ 21, 35. Amended by Laws 1995, c. 95–147, § 1044, eff. July 10, 1995.

198.37. Failure to make return; penalty

Any person required under this chapter to pay any tax, or required by law or regulations made under authority thereof to make a return, keep any records, or supply any information for the purposes of the computation, assessment, or collection of any tax imposed by this chapter, who willfully fails to pay such tax, make such return, keep such records, or supply such information, at the time or times required by law or regulations, is, in addition to other penalties provided by law, guilty of a misdemeanor of the first degree, punishable as provided in s. 775.082 or s. 775.083.

Laws 1933, c. 16015, § 27; Comp.Gen.Laws Supp.1936, § 7473(3–a); Laws 1971, c. 71–136, § 97; Laws 1987, c. 87–6, § 62; Laws 1987, c. 87–101, § 36. Amended by Laws 1991, c. 91–224, § 11.

198.38. False return; penalty

Any person who willfully aids or assists in, or procures, counsels, or advises, the preparation or presentation under, or in connection with any matter arising under, this chapter of a false or fraudulent return, affidavit, claim, or document shall (whether or not such falsity or fraud is with the knowledge or consent of the person authorized or required to present such return, affidavit, claim or document) be guilty of a felony of the third degree, punishable as provided in s. 775.082, s. 775.083, or s. 775.084.

Laws 1933, c. 16015, § 27; Comp.Gen.Laws Supp.1936, § 7473(3–a); Laws 1971, c. 71–136, § 98.

198.39. False statement in return; penalty

Whoever knowingly makes any false statement in any notice, affidavit, or return required to be filed or made under this chapter is guilty of a misdemeanor of the first degree, punishable as provided in s. 775.082 or s. 775.083.

Laws 1933, c. 16015, § 27; Comp.Gen.Laws Supp.1936, § 7473(3–a); Laws 1971, c. 71–136, § 99; Laws 1987, c. 87–6, § 63; Laws 1987, c. 87–101, § 37. Amended by Laws 1991, c. 91–224, § 12; Laws 1999, c. 99–208, § 9, eff. Jan. 1, 2000.

198.40. Failure to pay tax, evasion of tax, etc.; penalty

Any person required under this chapter to collect, account for, and pay over any tax imposed by this chapter who willfully fails to collect or truthfully account for and pay over such tax, and any person who willfully attempts in any manner to evade or defeat any tax imposed by this chapter or the payment thereof, shall, in addition to other penalties provided by law, be guilty of a felony of the third degree, punishable as provided in s. 775.082, s. 775.083, or s. 775.084.

Laws 1933, c. 16015, § 27; Comp.Gen.Laws Supp.1936, § 7473(3–a); Laws 1971, c. 71–136, § 100.

198.41. Effectiveness of this chapter, etc.

This chapter shall remain in force and effect so long as the Government of the United States retains in full force and effect as a part of the Revenue Laws of the United States a Federal Estate Tax, and this chapter shall cease to be operative as and when the Government of the United States ceases to impose any Estate Tax of the United States.

Laws 1933, c. 16015, § 29; Comp.Gen.Laws Supp.1936, § 1342(109).

198.42. Short title

This chapter may be cited as the "Estate Tax Law of Florida."

Laws 1933, c. 16015, § 1; Comp.Gen.Laws Supp.1936, § 1342(80).

198.44. Certain exemptions from inheritance and estate taxes

The tax imposed under the inheritance and estate tax laws of this state in respect to personal property (except tangible property having an actual situs in this state) shall not be payable:

(1) If the transferor at the time of death was a resident of a state or territory of the United States, or the District of Columbia, which at the time of death did not impose a death tax of any character in respect to property of residents of this state (except tangible personal property having an actual situs in such state, territory, or district); or

(2) If the laws of the state, territory, or district of the residence of the transferor at the time of death contained a reciprocal exemption provision under which nonresidents were exempted from said death taxes of every character in respect to personal property (except tangible personal property having an actual situs therein), and provided that the state, territory, or district of the residence of such nonresident decedent allowed a similar exemption to residents of the state, territory, or district of residence of such decedent.

Laws 1931, Ex.Sess., c. 15747, § 1; Comp.Gen.Laws Supp.1936, § 1342(70). Amended by Laws 1995, c. 95–147, § 1045, eff. July 10, 1995.

TITLE XV

HOMESTEAD AND EXEMPTIONS

CHAPTER 222

METHOD OF SETTING APART HOMESTEAD AND EXEMPTIONS

222.01. Designation of homestead by owner before levy

(1) Whenever any natural person residing in this state desires to avail himself or herself of the benefit of the provisions of the constitution and laws exempting property as a homestead from forced sale under any process of law, he or she may make a statement, in writing, containing a description of the real property, mobile home, or modular home claimed to be exempt and declaring that the real property, mobile home, or modular home is the homestead of the party in whose behalf such claim is being made. Such statement shall be signed by the person making it and shall be recorded in the circuit court.

(2) When a certified copy of a judgment has been filed in the public records of a county pursuant to chapter 55, a person who is entitled to the benefit of the provisions of the State

Constitution exempting real property as homestead and who has a contract to sell or a commitment from a lender for a mortgage on the homestead may file a notice of homestead in the public records of the county in which the homestead property is located in substantially the following form:

NOTICE OF HOMESTEAD

To: (Name and address of judgment creditor as shown on recorded judgment and name and address of any other person shown in the recorded judgment to receive a copy of the Notice of Homestead).

You are notified that the undersigned claims as homestead exempt from levy and execution under Section 4, Article X of the State Constitution, the following described property:

(Legal description)

The undersigned certifies, under oath, that he or she has applied for and received the homestead tax exemption as to the above-described property, that ___ is the tax identification parcel number of this property, and that the undersigned has resided on this property continuously and uninterruptedly from   (date)   to the date of this Notice of Homestead. Further, the undersigned will either convey or mortgage the above-described property pursuant to the following:

(Describe the contract of sale or loan commitment by date, names of parties, date of anticipated closing, and amount. The name, address, and telephone number of the person conducting the anticipated closing must be set forth.)

The undersigned also certifies, under oath, that the judgment lien filed by you on   (date) and recorded in Official Records Book ___, Page ___, of the Public Records of _____ County, Florida, does not constitute a valid lien on the described property.

YOU ARE FURTHER NOTIFIED, PURSUANT TO SECTION 222.01 ET SEQ., FLORIDA STATUTES, THAT WITHIN 45 DAYS AFTER THE MAILING OF THIS NOTICE YOU MUST FILE AN ACTION IN THE CIRCUIT COURT OF _____ COUNTY, FLORIDA, FOR A DECLARATORY JUDGMENT TO DETERMINE THE CONSTITUTIONAL HOME-STEAD STATUS OF THE SUBJECT PROPERTY OR TO FORECLOSE YOUR JUDGMENT LIEN ON THE PROPERTY AND RECORD A LIS PENDENS IN THE PUBLIC RECORDS OF THE COUNTY WHERE THE HOMESTEAD IS LOCATED. YOUR FAILURE TO SO ACT WILL RESULT IN ANY BUYER OR LENDER, OR HIS OR HER SUCCESSORS AND ASSIGNS, UNDER THE ABOVE–DESCRIBED CONTRACT OF SALE OR LOAN COMMIT-MENT TO TAKE FREE AND CLEAR OF ANY JUDGMENT LIEN YOU MAY HAVE ON THE PROPERTY.

This ___ day of _____, 2___.

_____
(Signature of Owner)

_____
(Printed Name of Owner)

_____
(Owner's Address)

Sworn to and subscribed before me by _____ who is personally known to me or produced _____ as identification, this ___ day of _____, 2___.

Notary Public

(3) The clerk shall mail a copy of the notice of homestead to the judgment lienor, by certified mail, return receipt requested, at the address shown in the most recent recorded judgment or accompanying affidavit, and to any other person designated in the most recent recorded judgment or accompanying affidavit to receive the notice of homestead, and shall certify to such service on the face of such notice and record the notice. Notwithstanding the use of certified mail, return receipt requested, service shall be deemed complete upon mailing.

(4) A lien pursuant to chapter 55 of any lienor upon whom such notice is served, who fails to institute an action for a declaratory judgment to determine the constitutional homestead status of the property described in the notice of homestead or to file an action to foreclose the judgment lien, together with the filing of a lis pendens in the public records of the county in which the homestead is located, within 45 days after service of such notice shall be deemed as not attaching to the property by virtue of its status as homestead property as to the interest of any buyer or lender, or his or her successors or assigns, who takes under the contract of sale or loan commitment described above within 180 days after the filing in the public records of the notice of homestead. This subsection shall not act to prohibit a lien from attaching to the real property described in the notice of homestead at such time as the property loses its homestead status.

(5) As provided in s. 4, Art. X of the State Constitution, this subsection shall not apply to:

(a) Liens and judgments for the payment of taxes and assessments on real property.

(b) Liens and judgments for obligations contracted for the purchase of real property.

(c) Liens and judgments for labor, services, or materials furnished to repair or improve real property.

(d) Liens and judgments for other obligations contracted for house, field, or other labor performed on real property.

Laws 1869, c. 1715, § 1; Rev.St.1892, § 1998; Gen.St.1906, § 2520; Rev.Gen.St.1920, § 3875; Comp. Gen.Laws 1927, § 5782; Laws 1973, c. 73–334, § 20; Laws 1977, c. 77–299, § 2; Laws 1983, c. 83–40, § 1. Amended by Laws 1995, c. 95–147, § 1195, eff. July 10, 1995; Laws 2000, c. 2000–258, § 25, eff. July 1, 2000; Laws 2005, c. 2005–241, § 17, eff. June 17, 2005.

Cross References

Conveyances between husband and wife, see § 689.11.
Descent of homesteads, see § 732.401.
Devise of homestead, see § 732.4015.
Homestead exemptions, duty of property appraiser, see § 196.141.
Homesteads,
    Disabled veterans, tax exemption, see § 196.091.
    Exemption from taxation, see § 196.031.
    Exemptions, see Const. Art. 7, § 6; Const. Art. 10, § 4.
    False information to obtain exemption, penalty, see § 196.131.
    Permanently and totally disabled veterans, tax exemption, see § 196.081.
    Public assistance payments, enforcement, see § 414.28.
Public lands, laws authorizing sale not to impair homestead laws, see § 270.10.

222.02. Designation of homestead after levy

Whenever a levy is made upon the lands, tenements, mobile home, or modular home of such person whose homestead has not been set apart and selected, such person, or the person's agent or attorney, may in writing notify the officer making such levy, by notice under oath made before any officer of this state duly authorized to administer oaths, at any time before the day appointed for the sale thereof, of what such person regards as his or her homestead, with a description thereof; and the remainder only shall be subject to sale under such levy.

Laws 1869, c. 1715, § 2; Rev.St.1892, § 1999; Gen.St.1906, § 2521; Rev.Gen.St.1920, § 3876; Comp. Gen.Laws 1927, § 5783; Laws 1977, c. 77–299, § 3; Laws 1983, c. 83–40, § 2. Amended by Laws 1995, c. 95–147, § 1196, eff. July 10, 1995.

Cross References

False information to obtain homestead exemption, see § 196.131.
Killer, entitlement to insurance proceeds resulting from death of victim, see § 732.802.

222.03. Survey at instance of dissatisfied creditor

If the creditor in any execution or process sought to be levied is dissatisfied with the quantity of land selected and set apart, and shall himself or herself, or by his or her agent or attorney, notify the officer levying, the officer shall at the creditor's request cause the same to be surveyed, and when the homestead is not within the corporate limits of any town or city, the person claiming said exemption shall have the right to set apart that portion of land belonging to him or her which includes the residence, or not, at the person's option, and if the first tract or parcel does not contain 160 acres, the said officer shall set apart the remainder from any other tract or tracts claimed by the debtor, but in every case taking all the land lying contiguous until the whole quantity of 160 acres is made up. The person claiming the exemption shall not be forced to take as his or her homestead any tract or portion of a tract, if any defect exists in the title, except at the person's option. The expense of such survey shall be chargeable on the execution as costs; but if it shall appear that the person claiming such exemption does not own more than 160 acres in the state, the expenses of said survey shall be paid by the person directing the same to be made.

Laws 1869, c. 1715, § 3; Laws 1873, c. 1944, § 1; Rev.St.1892, § 2000; Gen.St.1906, § 2522; Rev.Gen. St.1920, § 3877; Comp.Gen.Laws 1927, § 5784. Amended by Laws 1995, c. 95–147, § 1197, eff. July 10, 1995.

222.04. Sale after survey

After such survey has been made, the officer making the levy may sell the property levied upon not included in such property set off in such manner.

Laws 1869, c. 1715, § 4; Rev.St.1892, § 2001; Gen.St.1906, § 2523; Rev.Gen.St.1920, § 3878; Comp. Gen.Laws 1927, § 5785.

222.05. Setting apart leasehold

Any person owning and occupying any dwelling house, including a mobile home used as a residence, or modular home, on land not his or her own which he or she may lawfully possess, by lease or otherwise, and claiming such house, mobile home, or modular home as his or her homestead, shall be entitled to the exemption of such house, mobile home, or modular home from levy and sale as aforesaid.

Laws 1869, c. 1715, § 5; Rev.St.1892, § 2002; Gen.St.1906, § 2524; Rev.Gen.St.1920, § 3879; Comp. Gen.Laws 1927, § 5786; Laws 1977, c. 77–299, § 1. Amended by Laws 1995, c. 95–147, § 1198, eff. July 10, 1995.

222.061. **Method of exempting personal property; inventory**

(1) When a levy is made by writ of execution, writ of attachment, or writ of garnishment upon personal property which is allowed by law or by the State Constitution to be exempt from levy and sale, the debtor may claim such personal property to be exempt from sale by making, within 15 days after the date of the levy, an inventory of his or her personal property. The inventory shall show the fair market valuation of the property listed and shall have an affidavit attached certifying that the inventory contains a correct list of all personal property owned by the debtor in this state and that the value shown is the fair market value of the property. The debtor shall designate the property listed in the schedule which he or she claims to be exempt from levy and sale.

(2) The original inventory and affidavit shall be filed with the court which issued the writ. The debtor, by mail or hand delivery, shall promptly serve one copy on the judgment creditor and furnish one copy to the sheriff who executed the writ. If the creditor desires to object to the inventory, he or she shall file an objection with the court which issued the writ within 5 days after service of the inventory, or he or she shall be deemed to admit the inventory as true. If the creditor does not file an objection, the clerk of the court shall immediately send the case file to the court issuing the writ, and the court shall promptly issue an order exempting the items claimed. Such order shall be sent by the court to the sheriff directing him or her to promptly redeliver to the debtor any exempt property under the levy and to sell any nonexempt property under the levy according to law.

(3) If the creditor files an objection, he or she shall promptly serve, by mail or hand delivery, one copy on the debtor and furnish one copy to the sheriff who executed the writ. Upon the filing of an objection, the clerk shall immediately send the case file to the court issuing the writ, and the court shall automatically schedule a prompt evidentiary hearing to determine the validity of the objection and shall enter its order therein describing the exempt and nonexempt property. Upon its issuance, the order shall be sent by the court to the sheriff directing him or her to promptly redeliver to the debtor any exempt property under the levy and to sell the nonexempt property under the levy according to law.

(4) The court shall appoint a disinterested appraiser to assist in its evidentiary hearing unless the debtor and creditor mutually waive the appointment of such appraiser. The appraiser shall take and file an oath that he or she will faithfully appraise the property at its fair market value and that he or she will file a signed and sworn appraisal with the court as required by law. Notice of the time and place of the inspection of the property for the purpose of its appraisal shall be given by the appraiser to the debtor, creditor, and sheriff, at least 24 hours before the inspection is made. The appraiser shall be entitled to a reasonable fee as determined by the court for his or her services. The appraiser's fee shall be taxed as costs, but no costs shall be assessed against the debtor for the proceedings under this section if the debtor prevails on his or her claim of exemption. The court may require the creditor to deposit a cash bond, a surety bond, or other security, conditioned on the creditor's obligation to pay reasonable appraisal expenses, not to exceed $100.

(5) During the pendency of proceedings under this section, the sheriff shall safeguard the property seized under the writ, and the creditor shall deposit sufficient moneys with the sheriff to pay the cost of such safeguarding until the property is sold or redelivered to the debtor. When the sheriff receives a copy of a court order identifying which property has been declared exempt and which property has been declared not exempt and ordering the sale of the property not exempt from levy, he or she shall sell the property.

(6) The party who successfully maintains his or her claim at the time of the evidentiary hearing may be entitled to reasonable attorney's fees and shall be entitled to costs. The costs shall include, but not be limited to, appraisal fees, storage fees, and such other costs incurred as a result of the levy.

(7) No inventory or schedule to exempt personal property from sale shall be accepted prior to a levy on the property.

Laws 1985, c. 85–272, § 5; Laws 1987, c. 87–224, § 61. Amended by Laws 1995, c. 95–147, § 1199, eff. July 10, 1995.

222.07. Defendant's rights of selection

Upon the completion of the inventory the person entitled to the exemption, or the person's agent or attorney, may select from such an inventory an amount of property not exceeding, according to such appraisal, the amount of value exempted; but if the person so entitled, or the person's agent or attorney, does not appear and make such selection, the officer shall make the selection for him or her, and the property not so selected as exempt may be sold.

Laws 1869, c. 1715, § 8; Rev.St.1892, § 2004; Gen.St.1906, § 2526; Rev.Gen.St.1920, § 3881; Comp. Gen.Laws 1927, § 5788. Amended by Laws 1995, c. 95–147, § 1200, eff. July 10, 1995.

222.08. Jurisdiction to set apart homestead and exemption

The circuit courts have equity jurisdiction to order and decree the setting apart of homesteads and of exemptions of personal property from forced sales.

Laws 1881, c. 3246, § 2; Rev.St.1892, § 2005; Gen.St.1906, § 2527; Rev.Gen.St.1920, § 3882; Comp. Gen.Laws 1927, § 5789.

Cross References

Jurisdiction of circuit courts, see Const. Art. 5, § 5; F.S.A. § 26.012.

222.09. Injunction to prevent sale

The circuit courts have equity jurisdiction to enjoin the sale of all property, real and personal, that is exempt from forced sale.

Laws 1881, c. 3246, § 1; Rev.St.1892, § 2006; Gen.St.1906, § 2528; Rev.Gen.St.1920, § 3883; Comp. Gen.Laws 1927, § 5790.

Cross References

Injunctions, see § 60.01 et seq.; Civil Procedure Rule 1.610.

222.10. Jurisdiction to subject property claimed to be exempt

The circuit courts have equity jurisdiction upon bill filed by a creditor or other person interested in enforcing any unsatisfied judgment or decree, to determine whether any property, real or personal, claimed to be exempt, is so exempt, and in case it be not exempt, the court shall, by its decree subject it, or so much thereof as may be necessary, to the satisfaction of said judgment or decree and may enjoin the sheriff or other officer from setting apart as exempt property, real or personal, which is not exempt, and may annul all exemptions made and set apart by the sheriff or other officer.

Laws 1881, c. 3246, § 3; Rev.St.1892, § 2007; Gen.St.1906, § 2529; Rev.Gen.St.1920, § 3884; Comp. Gen.Laws 1927, § 5791.

Cross References

Conveyances between husband and wife, see § 689.11.
Fraudulent transfers, see § 726.101 et seq.
Jurisdiction of circuit courts, see Const. Art. 5, § 5; F.S.A. § 26.012.

222.11. Exemption of wages from garnishment

(1) As used in this section, the term:

(a) "Earnings" includes compensation paid or payable, in money of a sum certain, for personal services or labor whether denominated as wages, salary, commission, or bonus.

(b) "Disposable earnings" means that part of the earnings of any head of family remaining after the deduction from those earnings of any amounts required by law to be withheld.

(c) "Head of family" includes any natural person who is providing more than one-half of the support for a child or other dependent.

(2)(a) All of the disposable earnings of a head of family whose disposable earnings are less than or equal to $750 a week are exempt from attachment or garnishment.

(b) Disposable earnings of a head of a family, which are greater than $750 a week, may not be attached or garnished unless such person has agreed otherwise in writing. The agreement to waive the protection provided by this paragraph must:

1. Be written in the same language as the contract or agreement to which the waiver relates;

2. Be contained in a separate document attached to the contract or agreement; and

3. Be in substantially the following form in at least 14–point type:

IF YOU PROVIDE MORE THAN ONE–HALF OF THE SUPPORT FOR A CHILD OR OTHER DEPENDENT, ALL OR PART OF YOUR INCOME IS EXEMPT FROM GARNISHMENT UNDER FLORIDA LAW. YOU CAN WAIVE THIS PROTECTION ONLY BY SIGNING THIS DOCUMENT. BY SIGNING BELOW, YOU AGREE TO WAIVE THE PROTECTION FROM GARNISHMENT.

_____(Consumer's Signature)_____(Date Signed)_____

I have fully explained this document to the consumer.

_____(Creditor's Signature)_____(Date Signed)_____

The amount attached or garnished may not exceed the amount allowed under the Consumer Credit Protection Act, 15 U.S.C. s. 1673.

(c) Disposable earnings of a person other than a head of family may not be attached or garnished in excess of the amount allowed under the Consumer Credit Protection Act, 15 U.S.C. s. 1673.

(3) Earnings that are exempt under subsection (2) and are credited or deposited in any financial institution are exempt from attachment or garnishment for 6 months after the earnings are received by the financial institution if the funds can be traced and properly identified as earnings. Commingling of earnings with other funds does not by itself defeat the ability of a head of family to trace earnings.

Laws 1875, c. 2065, § 1; Rev.St.1892, § 2008; Gen.St.1906, § 2530; Rev.Gen.St.1920, § 3885; Com.Gen. Laws 1927, § 5792; Laws 1981, c. 81–301, § 1; Laws 1985, c. 85–272, § 6. Amended by Laws 1993, c. 93–256, § 2, eff. Oct. 1, 1993; Laws 2010, c. 2010–97, § 1, eff. Oct. 1, 2010.

Cross References

Alimony and support money, garnishment, see § 61.12.
Attachment, see § 76.01 et seq.
Damages for injuries to employees, see § 769.05.
Fraternal benefit societies, benefits not attachable, see § 632.619.
Garnishment, see § 77.01 et seq.
Unemployment compensation benefits, see § 443.051.

222.13. Life insurance policies; disposition of proceeds

(1) Whenever any person residing in the state shall die leaving insurance on his or her life, the said insurance shall inure exclusively to the benefit of the person for whose use and benefit such insurance is designated in the policy, and the proceeds thereof shall be exempt from the claims of creditors of the insured unless the insurance policy or a valid assignment thereof provides otherwise. Notwithstanding the foregoing, whenever the insurance, by designation or otherwise, is payable to the insured or to the insured's estate or to his or her executors, administrators, or assigns, the insurance proceeds shall become a part of the insured's estate for all purposes and shall be administered by the personal representative of the estate of the insured in accordance with the probate laws of the state in like manner as other assets of the insured's estate.

(2) Payments as herein directed shall, in every such case, discharge the insurer from any further liability under the policy, and the insurer shall in no event be responsible for, or be required to see to, the application of such payments.

Laws 1872, c. 1864, § 1; Rev.St.1892, § 2347; Laws 1897, c. 4555, § 1; Laws 1903, c. 5165, § 1; Gen.St.1906, § 3154; Rev.Gen.St.1920, § 4977; Comp.Gen.Laws 1927, § 7065; Laws 1955, c. 29861, § 1; Laws 1959, c. 59–333, § 1; Laws 1963, c. 63–230, § 1; Laws 1970, c. 70–376, § 1; Laws 1971, c. 71–355, § 51. Amended by Laws 1995, c. 95–147, § 1202, eff. July 10, 1995.

Cross References

Decedent's estate exempt from creditors, dispensing without administration, see § 735.301; Probate Rule 5.420.
Fraternal benefit societies, benefits exempt from attachment, see § 632.619.

222.14. Exemption of cash surrender value of life insurance policies and annuity contracts from legal process

The cash surrender values of life insurance policies issued upon the lives of citizens or residents of the state and the proceeds of annuity contracts issued to citizens or residents of the state, upon whatever form, shall not in any case be liable to attachment, garnishment or legal process in favor of any creditor of the person whose life is so insured or of any creditor of the person who is the beneficiary of such annuity contract, unless the insurance policy or annuity contract was effected for the benefit of such creditor.

Laws 1925, c. 10154, § 1; Comp.Gen.Laws 1927, § 7066; Laws 1978, c. 78–76, § 1.

Cross References

Attachment, see § 76.01 et seq.
Determination of cash surrender value, see § 627.476.
Disability income benefits, exemption, see § 222.18.
Garnishment, see § 77.01 et seq.

222.15. Wages or reemployment assistance or unemployment compensation payments due deceased employee may be paid spouse or certain relatives

(1) It is lawful for any employer, in case of the death of an employee, to pay to the wife or husband, and in case there is no wife or husband, then to the child or children, provided the child or children are over the age of 18 years, and in case there is no child or children, then to the father or mother, any wages or travel expenses that may be due such employee at the time of his or her death.

(2) It is also lawful for the Department of Economic Opportunity, in case of death of any unemployed individual, to pay to those persons referred to in subsection (1) any reemployment assistance or unemployment compensation payments that may be due to the individual at the time of his or her death.

Laws 1917, c. 7366, § 1; Rev.Gen.St.1920, § 4979; Comp.Gen.Laws 1927, § 7068; Laws 1941, c. 20407, § 1; Laws 1963, c. 63–165, § 1; Laws 1969, c. 69–106, §§ 17, 35; Laws 1973, c. 73–283, § 1; Laws 1979, c. 79–7, § 10; Laws 1983, c. 83–174, § 5. Amended by Laws 1995, c. 95–147, § 1203, eff. July 10, 1995; Laws 2003, c. 2003–36, § 7, eff. Oct. 1, 2003; Laws 2011, c. 2011–142, § 96, eff. July 1, 2011; Laws 2012, c. 2012–30, § 52, eff. July 1, 2012.

222.16. Wages or reemployment assistance or unemployment compensation payments so paid not subject to administration

Any wages, travel expenses, or reemployment assistance or unemployment compensation payments so paid under the authority of s. 222.15 shall not be considered as assets of the estate and subject to administration; provided, however, that the travel expenses so exempted from administration shall not exceed the sum of $300.

Laws 1917, c. 7366, § 2; Rev.Gen.St.1920, § 4980; Comp.Gen.Laws 1927, § 7069; Laws 1941, c. 20407, § 2; Laws 1963, c. 63–165, § 2. Amended by Laws 2012, c. 2012–30, § 53, eff. July 1, 2012.

Cross References

Decedent's estate exempt from creditors, dispensing without administration, see § 735.301; Probate Rule 5.420. Payroll deductions, see § 215.28.

222.17. Manifesting and evidencing domicile in Florida

(1) Any person who shall have established a domicile in this state may manifest and evidence the same by filing in the office of the clerk of the circuit court for the county in which the said person shall reside, a sworn statement showing that he or she resides in and maintains a place of abode in that county which he or she recognizes and intends to maintain as his or her permanent home.

(2) Any person who shall have established a domicile in the State of Florida, but who shall maintain another place or places of abode in some other state or states, may manifest and evidence his or her domicile in this state by filing in the office of the clerk of the circuit court for the county in which he or she resides, a sworn statement that his or her place of abode in Florida constitutes his or her predominant and principal home, and that he or she intends to continue it permanently as such.

(3) Such sworn statement shall contain, in addition to the foregoing, a declaration that the person making the same is, at the time of making such statement, a bona fide resident of the state, and shall set forth therein his or her place of residence within the state, the city, county and state wherein he or she formerly resided, and the place or places, if any, where he or she maintains another or other place or places of abode.

(4) Any person who shall have been or who shall be domiciled in a state other than the State of Florida, and who has or who may have a place of abode within the State of Florida, or who has or may do or perform other acts within the State of Florida, which independently of the actual intention of such person respecting his or her domicile might be taken to indicate that such person is or may intend to be or become domiciled in the State of Florida, and if such person desires to maintain or continue his or her domicile in such state other than the State of Florida, the person may manifest and evidence his or her permanent domicile and intention to permanently maintain and continue his or her domicile in such state other than the State of Florida, by filing in the office of the clerk of the circuit court in any county in the State of Florida in which the person may have a place of abode or in which the person may have done or performed such acts which independently may indicate that he or she is or may intend to be or become domiciled in the State of Florida, a sworn statement that the person's domicile is in such state other than the State of Florida, as the case may be, naming such state where he or she is domiciled and stating that he or she intends to permanently continue and maintain his or her domicile in such other state so named in said sworn statement. Such sworn statement shall also contain a declaration that the person making the same is at the time of the making of such statement a bona fide resident of such state other than the State of Florida, and shall set forth therein his or her place of abode within the State of Florida, if any. Such sworn statement may contain such other and further facts with reference to any acts done or performed by such person which such person desires or intends not to be construed as evidencing any intention to establish his or her domicile within the State of Florida.

(5) The sworn statement permitted by this section shall be signed under oath before an official authorized to take affidavits. Upon the filing of such declaration with the clerk of the circuit court, it shall be the duty of the clerk in whose office such declaration is filed to record the same in a book to be provided for that purpose. For the performance of the duties herein prescribed, the clerk of the circuit court shall collect a service charge for each declaration as provided in s. 28.24.

(6) It shall be the duty of the Department of Legal Affairs to prescribe a form for the declaration herein provided for, and to furnish the same to the several clerks of the circuit courts of the state.

(7) Nothing herein shall be construed to repeal or abrogate other existing methods of proving and evidencing domicile except as herein specifically provided.

Laws 1941, c. 20412, §§ 1 to 6; Laws 1951, c. 26896, § 1; Laws 1969, c. 69–106, §§ 11, 35; Laws 1970, c. 70–134, § 15. Amended by Laws 1995, c. 95–147, § 1204, eff. July 10, 1995.

Cross References

Clerk of circuit court's office, location, see § 28.07.
Falsification of official statements, punishment, see § 837.06.

222.18. Exempting disability income benefits from legal processes

Disability income benefits under any policy or contract of life, health, accident, or other insurance of whatever form, shall not in any case be liable to attachment, garnishment, or legal process in the state, in favor of any creditor or creditors of the recipient of such disability income benefits, unless such policy or contract of insurance was effected for the benefit of such creditor or creditors.

Laws 1941, c. 20741, § 1.

Exemptions from legal process,
  Damages recovered for injuries sustained while in hazardous occupation, see § 769.05.
  Fraternal benefit society funds, see § 632.619.
  Teachers' retirement benefits, see § 238.15.
  Unemployment compensation benefits, see § 443.051.
  Workers' compensation benefits, see § 440.22.

222.20. Nonavailability of federal bankruptcy exemptions

In accordance with the provision of s. 522(b) of the Bankruptcy Code of 1978 (11 U.S.C. s. 522(b)), residents of this state shall not be entitled to the federal exemptions provided in s. 522(d) of the Bankruptcy Code of 1978 (11 U.S.C. s. 522(d)). Nothing herein shall affect the exemptions given to residents of this state by the State Constitution and the Florida Statutes.
Laws 1979, c. 79–363, § 1.

222.201. Availability of federal bankruptcy exemptions

(1) Notwithstanding s. 222.20, an individual debtor under the federal Bankruptcy Reform Act of 1978 may exempt, in addition to any other exemptions allowed under state law, any property listed in subsection (d)(10) of s. 522 of that act.

(2) The provisions of this section apply to any bankruptcy action that is filed on or after October 1, 1987.
Laws 1987, c. 87–375, § 2.

222.21. Exemption of pension money and certain tax-exempt funds or accounts from legal processes

(1) Money received by any debtor as pensioner of the United States within 3 months next preceding the issuing of an execution, attachment, or garnishment process may not be applied to the payment of the debts of the pensioner when it is made to appear by the affidavit of the debtor or otherwise that the pension money is necessary for the maintenance of the debtor's support or a family supported wholly or in part by the pension money. The filing of the affidavit by the debtor, or the making of such proof by the debtor, is prima facie evidence; and it is the duty of the court in which the proceeding is pending to release all pension moneys held by such attachment or garnishment process, immediately, upon the filing of such affidavit or the making of such proof.

(2)(a) Except as provided in paragraph (d), any money or other assets payable to an owner, a participant, or a beneficiary from, or any interest of any owner, participant, or beneficiary in, a fund or account is exempt from all claims of creditors of the owner, beneficiary, or participant if the fund or account is:

1. Maintained in accordance with a master plan, volume submitter plan, prototype plan, or any other plan or governing instrument that has been preapproved by the Internal Revenue Service as exempt from taxation under s. 401(a), s. 403(a), s. 403(b), s. 408, s. 408A, s. 409, s. 414, s. 457(b), or s. 501(a) of the Internal Revenue Code of 1986,[1] as amended, unless it has been subsequently determined that the plan or governing instrument is not exempt from taxation in a proceeding that has become final and nonappealable;

2. Maintained in accordance with a plan or governing instrument that has been determined by the Internal Revenue Service to be exempt from taxation under s. 401(a), s. 403(a), s. 403(b), s. 408, s. 408A, s. 409, s. 414, s. 457(b), or s. 501(a) of the Internal Revenue Code of 1986,[1] as

amended, unless it has been subsequently determined that the plan or governing instrument is not exempt from taxation in a proceeding that has become final and nonappealable; or

3.   Not maintained in accordance with a plan or governing instrument described in subparagraph 1. or subparagraph 2. if the person claiming exemption under this paragraph proves by a preponderance of the evidence that the fund or account is maintained in accordance with a plan or governing instrument that:

a.   Is in substantial compliance with the applicable requirements for tax exemption under s. 401(a), s. 403(a), s. 403(b), s. 408, s. 408A, s. 409, s. 414, s. 457(b), or s. 501(a) of the Internal Revenue Code of 1986,[1] as amended; or

b.   Would have been in substantial compliance with the applicable requirements for tax exemption under s. 401(a), s. 403(a), s. 403(b), s. 408, s. 408A, s. 409, s. 414, s. 457(b), or s. 501(a) of the Internal Revenue Code of 1986,[1] as amended, but for the negligent or wrongful conduct of a person or persons other than the person who is claiming the exemption under this section.

(b) It is not necessary that a fund or account that is described in paragraph (a) be maintained in accordance with a plan or governing instrument that is covered by any part of the Employee Retirement Income Security Act for money or assets payable from or any interest in that fund or account to be exempt from claims of creditors under that paragraph.

(c) Any money or other assets or any interest in any fund or account that is exempt from claims of creditors of the owner, beneficiary, or participant under paragraph (a) does not cease to be exempt after the owner's death by reason of a direct transfer or eligible rollover that is excluded from gross income under the Internal Revenue Code of 1986, including, but not limited to, a direct transfer or eligible rollover to an inherited individual retirement account as defined in s. 408(d)(3) of the Internal Revenue Code of 1986,[2] as amended. This paragraph is intended to clarify existing law, is remedial in nature, and shall have retroactive application to all inherited individual retirement accounts without regard to the date an account was created.

(d) Any fund or account described in paragraph (a) is not exempt from the claims of an alternate payee under a qualified domestic relations order or from the claims of a surviving spouse pursuant to an order determining the amount of elective share and contribution as provided in part II of chapter 732. However, the interest of any alternate payee under a qualified domestic relations order is exempt from all claims of any creditor, other than the Department of Revenue, of the alternate payee. As used in this paragraph, the terms "alternate payee" and "qualified domestic relations order" have the meanings ascribed to them in s. 414(p) of the Internal Revenue Code of 1986.[3]

(e) This subsection applies to any proceeding that is filed on or after the effective date of this act.

Laws 1987, c. 87–375, § 1. Amended by Laws 1998, c. 98–159, § 1, eff. Jan. 1, 1999; Laws 1999, c. 99–8, § 25, eff. June 29, 1999; Laws 2005, c. 2005–82, § 5, eff. May 26, 2005; Laws 2005, c. 2005–101, § 1, eff. June 1, 2005; Laws 2007, c. 2007–74, § 1, eff. July 1, 2007; Laws 2011, c. 2011–84, § 1, eff. May 31, 2011.

[1] 26 U.S.C.A. §§ 401(a), 403(a), 403(b), 408, 408A, 409, 414, 457(b), and 501(a).

[2] 26 U.S.C.A. § 408(d)(3).

[3] 26 U.S.C.A. § 414(p).

Cross References

Florida Retirement System, benefits, see F.S.A. § 121.091.

222.22. **Exemption of assets in qualified tuition programs, medical savings accounts, Coverdell education savings accounts, and hurricane savings accounts from legal process**

(1) Moneys paid into or out of, the assets of, and the income of any validly existing qualified tuition program authorized by s. 529 of the Internal Revenue Code of 1986,[1] as amended, including, but not limited to, the Florida Prepaid College Trust Fund advance payment contracts under s. 1009.98 and Florida Prepaid College Trust Fund participation agreements under s. 1009.981, are not liable to attachment, levy, garnishment, or legal process in the state in favor of any creditor of or claimant against any program participant, purchaser, owner or contributor, or program beneficiary.

(2) Moneys paid into or out of, the assets of, and the income of a health savings account or medical savings account authorized under ss. 220 and 223 of the Internal Revenue Code of 1986,[2] as amended, are not liable to attachment, levy, garnishment, or legal process in this state in favor of any creditor of or claimant against any account participant, purchaser, owner or contributor, or account beneficiary.

(3) Moneys paid into or out of, the assets of, and the income of any Coverdell education savings account, also known as an educational IRA, established or existing in accordance with s. 530 of the Internal Revenue Code of 1986,[3] as amended, are not liable to attachment, levy, garnishment, or legal process in this state in favor of any creditor of or claimant against any account participant, purchaser, owner or contributor, or account beneficiary.

(4)(a) Moneys paid into or out of, the assets of, and the income of any hurricane savings account established by an insurance policyholder for residential property in this state equal to twice the deductible sum of such insurance to cover an insurance deductible or other uninsured portion of the risks of loss from a hurricane, rising flood waters, or other catastrophic windstorm event are not liable to attachment, levy, garnishment, or legal process in this state in favor of any creditor of or claimant against any account participant, purchaser, owner or contributor, or account beneficiary.

(b) As used in this subsection, the term "hurricane savings account" means an account established by the owner of residential real estate in this state, which meets the requirements of homestead exemption under s. 4, Art. X of the State Constitution, who specifies that the purpose of the account is to cover the amount of insurance deductibles and other uninsured portions of risks of loss from hurricanes, rising flood waters, or other catastrophic windstorm events.

(c) This subsection shall take effect only when the federal government provides tax-exempt or tax-deferred status to a hurricane savings account, disaster savings account, or other similar account created to cover an insurance deductible or other uninsured portion of the risks of loss from a hurricane, rising flood waters, or other catastrophic windstorm event.

(5) Except as provided in s. 1009.986(7), as it relates to any validly existing qualified ABLE program authorized by s. 529A of the Internal Revenue Code,[4] including, but not limited to, the Florida ABLE program participation agreements under s. 1009.986, moneys paid into or out of such a program, and the income and assets of such a program, are not liable to attachment,

levy, garnishment, or legal process in this state in favor of any creditor of or claimant against any designated beneficiary or other program participant.

Laws 1988, c. 88–313, § 2.   Amended by Laws 1998, c. 98–159, § 2, eff. Jan. 1, 1999; Laws 1998, c. 98–421, § 50, eff. July 1, 1998; Laws 1999, c. 99–220, § 2, eff. May 26, 1999; Laws 2002, c. 2002–387, § 926, eff. Jan. 7, 2003; Laws 2005, c. 2005–101, § 2, eff. June 1, 2005; Laws 2015, c. 2015–56, § 3, eff. May 21, 2015.

[1] 26 U.S.C.A. § 529.
[2] 26 U.S.C.A. §§ 220 and 223.
[3] 26 U.S.C.A. § 530.
[4] 26 U.S.C.A. § 529A.

222.25. Other individual property of natural persons exempt from legal process

The following property is exempt from attachment, garnishment, or other legal process:

(1) A debtor's interest, not to exceed $1,000 in value, in a single motor vehicle as defined in s. 320.01.

(2) A debtor's interest in any professionally prescribed health aids for the debtor or a dependent of the debtor.

(3) A debtor's interest in a refund or a credit received or to be received, or the traceable deposits in a financial institution of a debtor's interest in a refund or credit, pursuant to s. 32 of the Internal Revenue Code of 1986,[1] as amended. This exemption does not apply to a debt owed for child support or spousal support.

(4) A debtor's interest in personal property, not to exceed $4,000, if the debtor does not claim or receive the benefits of a homestead exemption under s. 4, Art. X of the State Constitution. This exemption does not apply to a debt owed for child support or spousal support.

Added by Laws 1993, c. 93–256, § 3, eff. Oct. 1, 1993.   Amended by Laws 2001, c. 2001–129, § 1, eff. June 1, 2001; Laws 2007, c. 2007–185, § 1, eff. July 1, 2007; Laws 2008, c. 2008–4, § 43, eff. July 1, 2008.

[1] 26 U.S.C.A. § 32.

222.29. No exemption for fraudulent transfers

An exemption from attachment, garnishment, or legal process provided by this chapter is not effective if it results from a fraudulent transfer or conveyance as provided in chapter 726. Added by Laws 1993, c. 93–256, § 4, eff. Oct. 1, 1993.

222.30. Fraudulent asset conversions

(1) As used in this section, "conversion" means every mode, direct or indirect, absolute or conditional, of changing or disposing of an asset, such that the products or proceeds of the asset become immune or exempt by law from claims of creditors of the debtor and the products or proceeds of the asset remain property of the debtor. The definitions of chapter 726 apply to this section unless the application of a definition would be unreasonable.

(2) Any conversion by a debtor of an asset that results in the proceeds of the asset becoming exempt by law from the claims of a creditor of the debtor is a fraudulent asset conversion as to the creditor, whether the creditor's claim to the asset arose before or after the conversion of the asset, if the debtor made the conversion with the intent to hinder, delay, or defraud the creditor.

(3) In an action for relief against a fraudulent asset conversion, a creditor may obtain:

(a) Avoidance of the fraudulent asset conversion to the extent necessary to satisfy the creditor's claim.

(b) An attachment or other provisional remedy against the asset converted in accordance with applicable law.

(c) Subject to applicable principles of equity and in accordance with applicable rules of civil procedure:

1. An injunction against further conversion by the debtor of the asset or of other property.

2. Any other relief the circumstances may require.

(4) If a creditor has obtained a judgment on a claim against the debtor, the creditor, if the court so orders, may levy execution on the asset converted or its proceeds.

(5) A cause of action with respect to a fraudulent asset conversion is extinguished unless an action is brought within 4 years after the fraudulent asset conversion was made.

(6) If an asset is converted and the converted asset is subsequently transferred to a third party, the provisions of chapter 726 apply to the transfer to the third party.

Added by Laws 1993, c. 93–256, § 5, eff. Oct. 1, 1993.

TITLE XXIX

PUBLIC HEALTH

CHAPTER 393

DEVELOPMENTAL DISABILITIES

Revision

Laws 1970, c. 70–343, repealed §§ 393.01 to 393.12, constituting all of the sections of Fla.St.1969, Chapter 393, and created a new Chapter 393, consisting of §§ 393.016 to 393.196 which was treated by the division of statutory revision as amendatory of Fla.St.1969, Chapter 393, and the provisions were reallocated or renumbered accordingly.

Cross References

Adult protective services, confidentiality of records, see § 415.107.
Agency for Persons with Disabilities, provision of services, see § 20.197(2).
Consumer protection, protected consumer report security freeze, see F.S.A. § 501.0051.
Corrections Mental Health Act, see § 945.40 et seq.
Criminal conflict and civil regional counsel offices, see § 27.511.
Florida Mental Health Act, see § 394.451 et seq.
Health facility and services planning, Agency for Health Care Administration duties and responsibilities, see F.S.A. § 408.034.
HIV and AIDS, education courses, health care facility employees and clients, see § 381.0035.
Human resource personnel, refingerprinting and rescreening exemption, see F.S.A. §§ 402.3057, 409.1757.
Medicaid enrollment, see F.S.A. § 409.972.
Medicaid managed care, mandatory and voluntary enrollment, see F.S.A. § 409.972.
Protection from abuse, neglect and exploitation, see § 415.101 et seq.
Public defenders and other court-appointed counsel, private court-appointed counsel, see § 27.5304.
Representation by public defender, see § 27.51(d).

393.063. Definitions

For the purposes of this chapter, the term:

(1) "Agency" means the Agency for Persons with Disabilities.

(2) "Adult day training" means training services which take place in a nonresidential setting, separate from the home or facility in which the client resides; are intended to support the

participation of clients in daily, meaningful, and valued routines of the community; and may include work-like settings that do not meet the definition of supported employment.

(3) "Autism" means a pervasive, neurologically based developmental disability of extended duration which causes severe learning, communication, and behavior disorders with age of onset during infancy or childhood. Individuals with autism exhibit impairment in reciprocal social interaction, impairment in verbal and nonverbal communication and imaginative ability, and a markedly restricted repertoire of activities and interests.

(4) "Cerebral palsy" means a group of disabling symptoms of extended duration which results from damage to the developing brain that may occur before, during, or after birth and that results in the loss or impairment of control over voluntary muscles. For the purposes of this definition, cerebral palsy does not include those symptoms or impairments resulting solely from a stroke.

(5) "Client" means any person determined eligible by the agency for services under this chapter.

(6) "Client advocate" means a friend or relative of the client, or of the client's immediate family, who advocates for the best interests of the client in any proceedings under this chapter in which the client or his or her family has the right or duty to participate.

(7) "Comprehensive assessment" means the process used to determine eligibility for services under this chapter.

(8) "Comprehensive transitional education program" means the program established in s. 393.18.

(9) "Developmental disability" means a disorder or syndrome that is attributable to intellectual disability, cerebral palsy, autism, spina bifida, or Prader-Willi syndrome; that manifests before the age of 18; and that constitutes a substantial handicap that can reasonably be expected to continue indefinitely.

(10) "Developmental disabilities center" means a state-owned and state-operated facility, formerly known as a "Sunland Center," providing for the care, habilitation, and rehabilitation of clients with developmental disabilities.

(11) "Direct service provider" means a person 18 years of age or older who has direct face-to-face contact with a client while providing services to the client or has access to a client's living areas or to a client's funds or personal property.

(12) "Domicile" means the place where a client legally resides, which place is his or her permanent home. Domicile may be established as provided in s. 222.17. Domicile may not be established in Florida by a minor who has no parent domiciled in Florida, or by a minor who has no legal guardian domiciled in Florida, or by any alien not classified as a resident alien.

(13) "Down syndrome" means a disorder caused by the presence of an extra chromosome 21.

(14) "Express and informed consent" means consent voluntarily given in writing with sufficient knowledge and comprehension of the subject matter to enable the person giving consent to make a knowing decision without any element of force, fraud, deceit, duress, or other form of constraint or coercion.

(15) "Family care program" means the program established in s. 393.068.

(16) "Foster care facility" means a residential facility licensed under this chapter which provides a family living environment including supervision and care necessary to meet the

physical, emotional, and social needs of its residents. The capacity of such a facility may not be more than three residents.

(17) "Group home facility" means a residential facility licensed under this chapter which provides a family living environment including supervision and care necessary to meet the physical, emotional, and social needs of its residents. The capacity of such a facility shall be at least 4 but not more than 15 residents.

(18) "Guardian advocate" means a person appointed by a written order of the court to represent a person with developmental disabilities under s. 393.12.

(19) "Habilitation" means the process by which a client is assisted to acquire and maintain those life skills which enable the client to cope more effectively with the demands of his or her condition and environment and to raise the level of his or her physical, mental, and social efficiency. It includes, but is not limited to, programs of formal structured education and treatment.

(20) "High-risk child" means, for the purposes of this chapter, a child from 3 to 5 years of age with one or more of the following characteristics:

(a) A developmental delay in cognition, language, or physical development.

(b) A child surviving a catastrophic infectious or traumatic illness known to be associated with developmental delay, when funds are specifically appropriated.

(c) A child with a parent or guardian with developmental disabilities who requires assistance in meeting the child's developmental needs.

(d) A child who has a physical or genetic anomaly associated with developmental disability.

(21) "Intellectual disability" means significantly subaverage general intellectual functioning existing concurrently with deficits in adaptive behavior which manifests before the age of 18 and can reasonably be expected to continue indefinitely. For the purposes of this definition, the term:

(a) "Adaptive behavior" means the effectiveness or degree with which an individual meets the standards of personal independence and social responsibility expected of his or her age, cultural group, and community.

(b) "Significantly subaverage general intellectual functioning" means performance that is two or more standard deviations from the mean score on a standardized intelligence test specified in the rules of the agency.

For purposes of the application of the criminal laws and procedural rules of this state to matters relating to pretrial, trial, sentencing, and any matters relating to the imposition and execution of the death penalty, the terms "intellectual disability" or "intellectually disabled" are interchangeable with and have the same meaning as the terms "mental retardation" or "retardation" and "mentally retarded" as defined in this section before July 1, 2013.

(22) "Intermediate care facility for the developmentally disabled" or "ICF/DD" means a residential facility licensed and certified under part VIII of chapter 400.

(23) "Medical/dental services" means medically necessary services that are provided or ordered for a client by a person licensed under chapter 458, chapter 459, or chapter 466. Such services may include, but are not limited to, prescription drugs, specialized therapies, nursing supervision, hospitalization, dietary services, prosthetic devices, surgery, specialized equipment and supplies, adaptive equipment, and other services as required to prevent or alleviate a medical or dental condition.

(24) "Personal care services" means individual assistance with or supervision of essential activities of daily living for self-care, including ambulation, bathing, dressing, eating, grooming, and toileting, and other similar services that are incidental to the care furnished and essential to the health, safety, and welfare of the client if no one else is available to perform those services.

(25) "Prader-Willi syndrome" means an inherited condition typified by neonatal hypotonia with failure to thrive, hyperphagia or an excessive drive to eat which leads to obesity usually at 18 to 36 months of age, mild to moderate intellectual disability, hypogonadism, short stature, mild facial dysmorphism, and a characteristic neurobehavior.

(26) "Relative" means an individual who is connected by affinity or consanguinity to the client and who is 18 years of age or older.

(27) "Resident" means a person who has a developmental disability and resides at a residential facility, whether or not such person is a client of the agency.

(28) "Residential facility" means a facility providing room and board and personal care for persons who have developmental disabilities.

(29) "Residential habilitation" means supervision and training with the acquisition, retention, or improvement in skills related to activities of daily living, such as personal hygiene skills, homemaking skills, and the social and adaptive skills necessary to enable the individual to reside in the community.

(30) "Residential habilitation center" means a community residential facility licensed under this chapter which provides habilitation services. The capacity of such a facility may not be fewer than nine residents. After October 1, 1989, new residential habilitation centers may not be licensed and the licensed capacity for any existing residential habilitation center may not be increased.

(31) "Respite service" means appropriate, short-term, temporary care that is provided to a person who has a developmental disability in order to meet the planned or emergency needs of the person or the family or other direct service provider.

(32) "Restraint" means a physical device, method, or drug used to control dangerous behavior.

(a) A physical restraint is any manual method or physical or mechanical device, material, or equipment attached or adjacent to an individual's body so that he or she cannot easily remove the restraint and which restricts freedom of movement or normal access to one's body.

(b) A drug used as a restraint is a medication used to control the person's behavior or to restrict his or her freedom of movement and is not a standard treatment for the person's medical or psychiatric condition. Physically holding a person during a procedure to forcibly administer psychotropic medication is a physical restraint.

(c) Restraint does not include physical devices, such as orthopedically prescribed appliances, surgical dressings and bandages, supportive body bands, or other physical holding necessary for routine physical examinations and tests; for purposes of orthopedic, surgical, or other similar medical treatment; to provide support for the achievement of functional body position or proper balance; or to protect a person from falling out of bed.

(33) "Seclusion" means the involuntary isolation of a person in a room or area from which the person is prevented from leaving. The prevention may be by physical barrier or by a staff member who is acting in a manner, or who is physically situated, so as to prevent the person from leaving the room or area. For the purposes of this chapter, the term does not mean isolation due to the medical condition or symptoms of the person.

(34) "Self-determination" means an individual's freedom to exercise the same rights as all other citizens, authority to exercise control over funds needed for one's own support, including prioritizing these funds when necessary, responsibility for the wise use of public funds, and self-advocacy to speak and advocate for oneself in order to gain independence and ensure that individuals with a developmental disability are treated equally.

(35) "Specialized therapies" means those treatments or activities prescribed by and provided by an appropriately trained, licensed, or certified professional or staff person and may include, but are not limited to, physical therapy, speech therapy, respiratory therapy, occupational therapy, behavior therapy, physical management services, and related specialized equipment and supplies.

(36) "Spina bifida" means, for purposes of this chapter, a person with a medical diagnosis of spina bifida cystica or myelomeningocele.

(37) "Support coordinator" means a person who is designated by the agency to assist individuals and families in identifying their capacities, needs, and resources, as well as finding and gaining access to necessary supports and services; coordinating the delivery of supports and services; advocating on behalf of the individual and family; maintaining relevant records; and monitoring and evaluating the delivery of supports and services to determine the extent to which they meet the needs and expectations identified by the individual, family, and others who participated in the development of the support plan.

(38) "Supported employment" means employment located or provided in an integrated work setting, with earnings paid on a commensurate wage basis, and for which continued support is needed for job maintenance.

(39) "Supported living" means a category of individually determined services designed and coordinated in such a manner as to provide assistance to adult clients who require ongoing supports to live as independently as possible in their own homes, to be integrated into the community, and to participate in community life to the fullest extent possible.

(40) "Training" means a planned approach to assisting a client to attain or maintain his or her maximum potential and includes services ranging from sensory stimulation to instruction in skills for independent living and employment.

(41) "Treatment" means the prevention, amelioration, or cure of a client's physical and mental disabilities or illnesses.

Laws 1977, c. 77–335, § 1; Laws 1979, c. 79–148, § 1; Laws 1979, c. 79–400, § 153; Laws 1981, c. 81–23, § 3; Laws 1985, c. 85–54, § 4; Laws 1985, c. 85–147, § 1; Laws 1987, c. 87–238, § 5; Laws 1988, c. 88–398, § 5; Laws 1989, c. 89–308, § 7; Laws 1989, c. 89–339, §§ 2, 4; Laws 1990, c. 90–306, § 27; Laws 1990, c. 90–333, § 1; Laws 1991, c. 91–158, § 17; Laws 1994, c. 94–154, § 3; Laws 1995, c. 95–148, § 1045; Laws 1995, c. 95–228, § 53; Laws 1995, c. 95–293, § 1; Laws 1996, c. 96–417, § 13. Amended by Laws 1998, c. 98–171, § 23, eff. July 1, 1998; Laws 1998, c. 98–403, § 140, eff. Oct. 1, 1998; Laws 1999, c. 99–8, § 80, eff. June 29, 1999; Laws 1999, c. 99–13, § 203, eff. June 29, 1999; Laws 2000, c. 2000–338, § 3, eff. June 20, 2000; Laws 2002, c. 2002–400, § 35, eff. June 7, 2002; Laws 2004, c. 2004–260, § 7, eff. July 1, 2004; Laws 2004, c. 2004–267, § 71, eff. July 1, 2004; Laws 2006, c. 2006–197, § 15, eff. July 1, 2006; Laws 2006, c. 2006–227, § 10, eff. July 1, 2006; Laws 2008, c. 2008–244, § 2, eff. July 1, 2008; Laws 2011, c. 2011–135, § 2, eff. July 1, 2011; Laws 2013, c. 2013–162, § 9, eff. July 1, 2013.

Cross References

Dependent children with special needs, appointment of attorneys, see F.S.A. § 39.01305.
Employers of persons with disabilities, limitation of liability, see F.S.A. § 768.0895.
Health facility and services planning, projects subject to review, exemptions, see F.S.A. § 408.036.

Home health agencies, registration of particular service providers exempt from licensure, see F.S.A. § 400.509.

Infant health care, prenatally diagnosed conditions, see F.S.A. § 383.141.

Juvenile delinquency, incompetency, retardation as under this section, see § 985.19.

Public K-12 specialized instruction for exceptional students, see § 1003.57.

Regional autism centers, establishment and services provided, see § 1004.55.

393.0657. Persons not required to be refingerprinted or rescreened

Persons who have undergone any portion of the background screening required under s. 393.0655 within the last 12 months are not required to repeat such screening in order to comply with the screening requirements if such persons have not been unemployed for more than 90 consecutive days since that screening occurred. Such persons are responsible for providing documentation of the screening and shall undergo screening for any remaining background screening requirements that have never been conducted or have not been completed within the last 12 months.

Laws 1987, c. 87–128, § 1; Laws 1987, c. 87–141, § 1; Laws 1993, c. 93–39, § 22; Laws 1994, c. 94–154, § 8. Amended by Laws 2002, c. 2002–219, § 8, eff. July 1, 2002; Laws 2002, c. 2002–387, § 979, eff. Jan. 7, 2003; Laws 2004, c. 2004–5, § 40, eff. June 29, 2004; Laws 2006, c. 2006–227, § 17, eff. July 1, 2006; Laws 2008, c. 2008–244, § 5, eff. July 1, 2008.

393.066. Community services and treatment

(1) The agency shall plan, develop, organize, and implement its programs of services and treatment for persons with developmental disabilities to allow clients to live as independently as possible in their own homes or communities and to achieve productive lives as close to normal as possible. All elements of community-based services shall be made available, and eligibility for these services shall be consistent across the state.

(2) All services needed shall be purchased instead of provided directly by the agency, when such arrangement is more cost-efficient than having those services provided directly. All purchased services must be approved by the agency.

(3) Community-based services that are medically necessary to prevent institutionalization shall, to the extent of available resources, include:

(a) Adult day training services.

(b) Family care services.

(c) Guardian advocate referral services.

(d) Medical/dental services, except that medical services shall not be provided to clients with spina bifida except as specifically appropriated by the Legislature.

(e) Parent training.

(f) Personal care services.

(g) Recreation.

(h) Residential facility services.

(i) Respite services.

(j) Social services.

(k) Specialized therapies.

(l) Supported employment.

(m) Supported living.

(n) Training, including behavioral analysis services.

(o) Transportation.

(p) Other habilitative and rehabilitative services as needed.

(4) The agency shall utilize the services of private businesses, not-for-profit organizations, and units of local government whenever such services are more cost-efficient than such services provided directly by the department, including arrangements for provision of residential facilities.

(5) In order to improve the potential for utilization of more cost-effective, community-based residential facilities, the agency shall promote the statewide development of day habilitation services for clients who live with a direct service provider in a community-based residential facility and who do not require 24-hour-a-day care in a hospital or other health care institution, but who may, in the absence of day habilitation services, require admission to a developmental disabilities center. Each day service facility shall provide a protective physical environment for clients, ensure that direct service providers meet minimum screening standards as required in s. 393.0655, make available to all day habilitation service participants at least one meal on each day of operation, provide facilities to enable participants to obtain needed rest while attending the program, as appropriate, and provide social and educational activities designed to stimulate interest and provide socialization skills.

(6) To promote independence and productivity, the agency shall provide supports and services, within available resources, to assist clients enrolled in Medicaid waivers who choose to pursue gainful employment.

(7) For the purpose of making needed community-based residential facilities available at the least possible cost to the state, the agency is authorized to lease privately owned residential facilities under long-term rental agreements, if such rental agreements are projected to be less costly to the state over the useful life of the facility than state purchase or state construction of such a facility.

(8) The agency may adopt rules providing definitions, eligibility criteria, and procedures for the purchase of services provided pursuant to this section.

Laws 1977, c. 77–335, § 1; Laws 1980, c. 80–174, § 2; Laws 1983, c. 83–218, § 43; Laws 1984, c. 84–226, § 15; Laws 1985, c. 85–54, § 6; Laws 1985, c. 85–147, § 2; Laws 1986, c. 86–220, § 10; Laws 1987, c. 87–238, § 7; Laws 1989, c. 89–308, § 11; Laws 1991, c. 91–158, § 18; Laws 1992, c. 92–174, § 4; Laws 1993, c. 93–143, §§ 2, 3; Laws 1993, c. 93–200, § 9; Laws 1993, c. 93–267, § 5; Laws 1994, c. 94–154, § 9. Amended by Laws 1998, c. 98–152, § 1, eff. May 22, 1998; Laws 1999, c. 99–8, § 83, eff. June 29, 1999; Laws 1999, c. 99–144, § 3, eff. May 7, 1999; Laws 2004, c. 2004–267, § 74, eff. July 1, 2004; Laws 2006, c. 2006–227, § 18, eff. July 1, 2006; Laws 2008, c. 2008–244, § 6, eff. July 1, 2008.

393.0661. Home and community-based services delivery system; comprehensive redesign

The Legislature finds that the home and community-based services delivery system for persons with developmental disabilities and the availability of appropriated funds are two of the critical elements in making services available. Therefore, it is the intent of the Legislature that the Agency for Persons with Disabilities shall develop and implement a comprehensive redesign of the system.

(1) The redesign of the home and community-based services system shall include, at a minimum, all actions necessary to achieve an appropriate rate structure, client choice within a specified service package, appropriate assessment strategies, an efficient billing process that contains reconciliation and monitoring components, and a redefined role for support coordinators that avoids potential conflicts of interest and ensures that family/client budgets are linked to levels of need.

(a) The agency shall use an assessment instrument that the agency deems to be reliable and valid, including, but not limited to, the Department of Children and Families' Individual Cost Guidelines or the agency's Questionnaire for Situational Information. The agency may contract with an external vendor or may use support coordinators to complete client assessments if it develops sufficient safeguards and training to ensure ongoing inter-rater reliability.

(b) The agency, with the concurrence of the Agency for Health Care Administration, may contract for the determination of medical necessity and establishment of individual budgets.

(2) A provider of services rendered to persons with developmental disabilities pursuant to a federally approved waiver shall be reimbursed according to a rate methodology based upon an analysis of the expenditure history and prospective costs of providers participating in the waiver program, or under any other methodology developed by the Agency for Health Care Administration, in consultation with the Agency for Persons with Disabilities, and approved by the Federal Government in accordance with the waiver.

(3) The Agency for Health Care Administration, in consultation with the agency, shall seek federal approval and implement a four-tiered waiver system to serve eligible clients through the developmental disabilities and family and supported living waivers. For the purpose of this waiver program, eligible clients shall include individuals with a diagnosis of Down syndrome or a developmental disability as defined in s. 393.063. The agency shall assign all clients receiving services through the developmental disabilities waiver to a tier based on the Department of Children and Families' Individual Cost Guidelines, the agency's Questionnaire for Situational Information, or another such assessment instrument deemed to be valid and reliable by the agency; client characteristics, including, but not limited to, age; and other appropriate assessment methods.

(a) Tier one is limited to clients who have service needs that cannot be met in tier two, three, or four for intensive medical or adaptive needs and that are essential for avoiding institutionalization, or who possess behavioral problems that are exceptional in intensity, duration, or frequency and present a substantial risk of harm to themselves or others. Total annual expenditures under tier one may not exceed $150,000 per client each year, provided that expenditures for clients in tier one with a documented medical necessity requiring intensive behavioral residential habilitation services, intensive behavioral residential habilitation services with medical needs, or special medical home care, as provided in the Developmental Disabilities Waiver Services Coverage and Limitations Handbook, are not subject to the $150,000 limit on annual expenditures.

(b) Tier two is limited to clients whose service needs include a licensed residential facility and who are authorized to receive a moderate level of support for standard residential habilitation services or a minimal level of support for behavior focus residential habilitation services, or clients in supported living who receive more than 6 hours a day of in-home support services. Total annual expenditures under tier two may not exceed $53,625 per client each year.

(c) Tier three includes, but is not limited to, clients requiring residential placements, clients in independent or supported living situations, and clients who live in their family home. Total annual expenditures under tier three may not exceed $34,125 per client each year.

(d) Tier four includes individuals who were enrolled in the family and supported living waiver on July 1, 2007, who shall be assigned to this tier without the assessments required by this section. Tier four also includes, but is not limited to, clients in independent or supported living situations and clients who live in their family home. Total annual expenditures under tier four may not exceed $14,422 per client each year.

(e) The Agency for Health Care Administration shall also seek federal approval to provide a consumer-directed option for persons with developmental disabilities which corresponds to the funding levels in each of the waiver tiers. The agency shall implement the four-tiered waiver system beginning with tiers one, three, and four and followed by tier two. The agency and the Agency for Health Care Administration may adopt rules necessary to administer this subsection.

(f) The agency shall seek federal waivers and amend contracts as necessary to make changes to services defined in federal waiver programs administered by the agency as follows:

1. Supported living coaching services may not exceed 20 hours per month for persons who also receive in-home support services.

2. Limited support coordination services are the only type of support coordination service that may be provided to persons under the age of 18 who live in the family home.

3. Personal care assistance services are limited to 180 hours per calendar month and may not include rate modifiers. Additional hours may be authorized for persons who have intensive physical, medical, or adaptive needs if such hours are essential for avoiding institutionalization.

4. Residential habilitation services are limited to 8 hours per day. Additional hours may be authorized for persons who have intensive medical or adaptive needs and if such hours are essential for avoiding institutionalization, or for persons who possess behavioral problems that are exceptional in intensity, duration, or frequency and present a substantial risk of harming themselves or others. This restriction shall be in effect until the four-tiered waiver system is fully implemented.

5. Chore services, nonresidential support services, and homemaker services are eliminated. The agency shall expand the definition of in-home support services to allow the service provider to include activities previously provided in these eliminated services.

6. Massage therapy, medication review, and psychological assessment services are eliminated.

7. The agency shall conduct supplemental cost plan reviews to verify the medical necessity of authorized services for plans that have increased by more than 8 percent during either of the 2 preceding fiscal years.

8. The agency shall implement a consolidated residential habilitation rate structure to increase savings to the state through a more cost-effective payment method and establish uniform rates for intensive behavioral residential habilitation services.

9. Pending federal approval, the agency may extend current support plans for clients receiving services under Medicaid waivers for 1 year beginning July 1, 2007, or from the date approved, whichever is later. Clients who have a substantial change in circumstances which threatens their health and safety may be reassessed during this year in order to determine the necessity for a change in their support plan.

10. The agency shall develop a plan to eliminate redundancies and duplications between in-home support services, companion services, personal care services, and supported living coaching by limiting or consolidating such services.

11. The agency shall develop a plan to reduce the intensity and frequency of supported employment services to clients in stable employment situations who have a documented history of at least 3 years' employment with the same company or in the same industry.

(4) The geographic differential for Miami-Dade, Broward, and Palm Beach Counties for residential habilitation services shall be 7.5 percent.

(5) The geographic differential for Monroe County for residential habilitation services shall be 20 percent.

(6) Effective January 1, 2010, and except as otherwise provided in this section, a client served by the home and community-based services waiver or the family and supported living waiver funded through the agency shall have his or her cost plan adjusted to reflect the amount of expenditures for the previous state fiscal year plus 5 percent if such amount is less than the client's existing cost plan. The agency shall use actual paid claims for services provided during the previous fiscal year that are submitted by October 31 to calculate the revised cost plan amount. If the client was not served for the entire previous state fiscal year or there was any single change in the cost plan amount of more than 5 percent during the previous state fiscal year, the agency shall set the cost plan amount at an estimated annualized expenditure amount plus 5 percent. The agency shall estimate the annualized expenditure amount by calculating the average of monthly expenditures, beginning in the fourth month after the client enrolled, interrupted services are resumed, or the cost plan was changed by more than 5 percent and ending on August 31, 2009, and multiplying the average by 12. In order to determine whether a client was not served for the entire year, the agency shall include any interruption of a waiver-funded service or services lasting at least 18 days. If at least 3 months of actual expenditure data are not available to estimate annualized expenditures, the agency may not rebase a cost plan pursuant to this subsection. The agency may not rebase the cost plan of any client who experiences a significant change in recipient condition or circumstance which results in a change of more than 5 percent to his or her cost plan between July 1 and the date that a rebased cost plan would take effect pursuant to this subsection.

(7) The agency shall collect premiums or cost sharing pursuant to s. 409.906(13)(d).

(8) This section or related rule does not prevent or limit the Agency for Health Care Administration, in consultation with the Agency for Persons with Disabilities, from adjusting fees, reimbursement rates, lengths of stay, number of visits, or number of services, or from limiting enrollment, or making any other adjustment necessary to comply with the availability of moneys and any limitations or directions provided in the General Appropriations Act.

(9) The Agency for Persons with Disabilities shall submit quarterly status reports to the Executive Office of the Governor, the chair of the Senate Ways and Means Committee or its successor, and the chair of the House Fiscal Council or its successor regarding the financial status of home and community-based services, including the number of enrolled individuals who are receiving services through one or more programs; the number of individuals who have requested services who are not enrolled but who are receiving services through one or more programs, with a description indicating the programs from which the individual is receiving services; the number of individuals who have refused an offer of services but who choose to remain on the list of individuals waiting for services; the number of individuals who have requested services but who are receiving no services; a frequency distribution indicating the length of time individuals have been waiting for services; and information concerning the actual and projected costs compared to the amount of the appropriation available to the program and any projected surpluses or deficits. If at any time an analysis by the agency, in consultation with the Agency for Health Care Administration, indicates that the cost of services is expected to exceed the amount appropriated, the agency shall submit a plan in accordance with subsection (8) to the Executive Office of the Governor, the chair of the Senate Ways and Means Committee or its successor, and the chair of the House Fiscal Council or its successor to remain within the amount appropriated. The agency shall work with the Agency for Health Care Administration to implement the plan so as to remain within the appropriation.

(10) Implementation of Medicaid waiver programs and services authorized under this chapter is limited by the funds appropriated for the individual budgets pursuant to s. 393.0662 and the four-tiered waiver system pursuant to subsection (3). Contracts with independent support coordinators and service providers must include provisions requiring compliance with agency cost containment initiatives. The agency shall implement monitoring and accounting procedures necessary to track actual expenditures and project future spending compared to available appropriations for Medicaid waiver programs. When necessary based on projected deficits, the agency must establish specific corrective action plans that incorporate corrective actions of contracted providers that are sufficient to align program expenditures with annual appropriations. If deficits continue during the 2012–2013 fiscal year, the agency in conjunction with the Agency for Health Care Administration shall develop a plan to redesign the waiver program and submit the plan to the President of the Senate and the Speaker of the House of Representatives by September 30, 2013. At a minimum, the plan must include the following elements:

(a) *Budget predictability.*—Agency budget recommendations must include specific steps to restrict spending to budgeted amounts based on alternatives to the iBudget and four-tiered Medicaid waiver models.

(b) *Services.*—The agency shall identify core services that are essential to provide for client health and safety and recommend elimination of coverage for other services that are not affordable based on available resources.

(c) *Flexibility.*—The redesign shall be responsive to individual needs and to the extent possible encourage client control over allocated resources for their needs.

(d) *Support coordination services.*—The plan shall modify the manner of providing support coordination services to improve management of service utilization and increase accountability and responsiveness to agency priorities.

(e) *Reporting.*—The agency shall provide monthly reports to the President of the Senate and the Speaker of the House of Representatives on plan progress and development on July 31, 2013, and August 31, 2013.

(f) *Implementation.*—The implementation of a redesigned program is subject to legislative approval and shall occur no later than July 1, 2014. The Agency for Health Care Administration shall seek federal waivers as needed to implement the redesigned plan approved by the Legislature.

Added by Laws 2002, c. 2002–400, § 39, eff. June 7, 2002. Amended by Laws 2004, c. 2004–267, § 75, eff. July 1, 2004; Laws 2005, c. 2005–60, § 1, eff. July 1, 2005; Laws 2005, c. 2005–133, § 15, eff. July 1, 2005; Laws 2006, c. 2006–15, § 2, eff. May 25, 2006; Laws 2007, c. 2007–64, § 1, eff. July 1, 2007; Laws 2007, c. 2007–331, § 1, eff. Oct. 26, 2007; Laws 2008, c. 2008–144, § 1, eff. July 1, 2008; Laws 2009, c. 2009–56, § 2, eff. July 1, 2009; Laws 2010, c. 2010–157, § 1, eff. July 1, 2010; Laws 2011, c. 2011–135, § 1, eff. July 1, 2011; Laws 2014, c. 2014–19, § 72, eff. July 1, 2014.

393.0662. Individual budgets for delivery of home and community-based services; iBudget system established

The Legislature finds that improved financial management of the existing home and community-based Medicaid waiver program is necessary to avoid deficits that impede the provision of services to individuals who are on the waiting list for enrollment in the program. The Legislature further finds that clients and their families should have greater flexibility to choose the services that best allow them to live in their community within the limits of an established budget. Therefore, the Legislature intends that the agency, in consultation with the Agency for Health Care Administration, develop and implement a comprehensive redesign of the service delivery system using individual budgets as the basis for allocating the funds appropriated for the home and community-based services Medicaid waiver program among eligible enrolled clients. The service delivery system that uses individual budgets shall be called the iBudget system.

(1) The agency shall establish an individual budget, referred to as an iBudget, for each individual served by the home and community-based services Medicaid waiver program. The funds appropriated to the agency shall be allocated through the iBudget system to eligible, Medicaid-enrolled clients. For the iBudget system, eligible clients shall include individuals with a diagnosis of Down syndrome or a developmental disability as defined in s. 393.063. The iBudget system shall be designed to provide for: enhanced client choice within a specified service package; appropriate assessment strategies; an efficient consumer budgeting and billing process that includes reconciliation and monitoring components; a redefined role for support coordinators that avoids potential conflicts of interest; a flexible and streamlined service review process; and a methodology and process that ensures the equitable allocation of available funds to each client based on the client's level of need, as determined by the variables in the allocation algorithm.

(a) In developing each client's iBudget, the agency shall use an allocation algorithm and methodology. The algorithm shall use variables that have been determined by the agency to have a statistically validated relationship to the client's level of need for services provided through the home and community-based services Medicaid waiver program. The algorithm and methodology may consider individual characteristics, including, but not limited to, a client's age and living situation, information from a formal assessment instrument that the agency determines is valid and reliable, and information from other assessment processes.

(b) The allocation methodology shall provide the algorithm that determines the amount of funds allocated to a client's iBudget. The agency may approve an increase in the amount of funds allocated, as determined by the algorithm, based on the client having one or more of the following needs that cannot be accommodated within the funding as determined by the algorithm and having no other resources, supports, or services available to meet the need:

1. An extraordinary need that would place the health and safety of the client, the client's caregiver, or the public in immediate, serious jeopardy unless the increase is approved. An extraordinary need may include, but is not limited to:

a. A documented history of significant, potentially life-threatening behaviors, such as recent attempts at suicide, arson, nonconsensual sexual behavior, or self-injurious behavior requiring medical attention;

b. A complex medical condition that requires active intervention by a licensed nurse on an ongoing basis that cannot be taught or delegated to a nonlicensed person;

c. A chronic comorbid condition. As used in this subparagraph, the term "comorbid condition" means a medical condition existing simultaneously but independently with another medical condition in a patient; or

d. A need for total physical assistance with activities such as eating, bathing, toileting, grooming, and personal hygiene.

However, the presence of an extraordinary need alone does not warrant an increase in the amount of funds allocated to a client's iBudget as determined by the algorithm.

2. A significant need for one-time or temporary support or services that, if not provided, would place the health and safety of the client, the client's caregiver, or the public in serious

jeopardy, unless the increase is approved. A significant need may include, but is not limited to, the provision of environmental modifications, durable medical equipment, services to address the temporary loss of support from a caregiver, or special services or treatment for a serious temporary condition when the service or treatment is expected to ameliorate the underlying condition. As used in this subparagraph, the term "temporary" means a period of fewer than 12 continuous months. However, the presence of such significant need for one-time or temporary supports or services alone does not warrant an increase in the amount of funds allocated to a client's iBudget as determined by the algorithm.

3. A significant increase in the need for services after the beginning of the service plan year that would place the health and safety of the client, the client's caregiver, or the public in serious jeopardy because of substantial changes in the client's circumstances, including, but not limited to, permanent or long-term loss or incapacity of a caregiver, loss of services authorized under the state Medicaid plan due to a change in age, or a significant change in medical or functional status which requires the provision of additional services on a permanent or long-term basis that cannot be accommodated within the client's current iBudget. As used in this subparagraph, the term "long-term" means a period of 12 or more continuous months. However, such significant increase in need for services of a permanent or long-term nature alone does not warrant an increase in the amount of funds allocated to a client's iBudget as determined by the algorithm.

The agency shall reserve portions of the appropriation for the home and community-based services Medicaid waiver program for adjustments required pursuant to this paragraph and may use the services of an independent actuary in determining the amount of the portions to be reserved.

(c) A client's iBudget shall be the total of the amount determined by the algorithm and any additional funding provided pursuant to paragraph (b). A client's annual expenditures for home and community-based services Medicaid waiver services may not exceed the limits of his or her iBudget. The total of all clients' projected annual iBudget expenditures may not exceed the agency's appropriation for waiver services.

(2) The Agency for Health Care Administration, in consultation with the agency, shall seek federal approval to amend current waivers, request a new waiver, and amend contracts as necessary to implement the iBudget system to serve eligible, enrolled clients through the home and community-based services Medicaid waiver program and the Consumer-Directed Care Plus Program.

(3) The agency shall transition all eligible, enrolled clients to the iBudget system. The agency may gradually phase in the iBudget system.

(a) While the agency phases in the iBudget system, the agency may continue to serve eligible, enrolled clients under the four-tiered waiver system established under s. 393.065 while those clients await transitioning to the iBudget system.

(b) The agency shall design the phase-in process to ensure that a client does not experience more than one-half of any expected overall increase or decrease to his or her existing annualized cost plan during the first year that the client is provided an iBudget due solely to the transition to the iBudget system.

(4) A client must use all available services authorized under the state Medicaid plan, school-based services, private insurance and other benefits, and any other resources that may be available to the client before using funds from his or her iBudget to pay for support and services.

(5) The service limitations in s. 393.0661(3)(f)1., 2., and 3. do not apply to the iBudget system.

(6) Rates for any or all services established under rules of the Agency for Health Care Administration shall be designated as the maximum rather than a fixed amount for individuals who receive an iBudget, except for services specifically identified in those rules that the agency determines are not appropriate for negotiation, which may include, but are not limited to, residential habilitation services.

(7) The agency shall ensure that clients and caregivers have access to training and education to inform them about the iBudget system and enhance their ability for self-direction. Such training shall be offered in a variety of formats and at a minimum shall address the policies and processes of the iBudget system; the roles and responsibilities of consumers, caregivers, waiver support coordinators, providers, and the agency; information available to help the client make decisions regarding the iBudget system; and examples of support and resources available in the community.

(8) The agency shall collect data to evaluate the implementation and outcomes of the iBudget system.

(9) The agency and the Agency for Health Care Administration may adopt rules specifying the allocation algorithm and methodology; criteria and processes for clients to access reserved funds for extraordinary needs, temporarily or permanently changed needs, and one-time needs; and processes and requirements for selection and review of services, development of support and cost plans, and management of the iBudget system as needed to administer this section.

Added by Laws 2010, c. 2010–157, § 2, eff. July 1, 2010. Amended by Laws 2011, c. 2011–135, § 31, eff. July 1, 2011.

393.11. Involuntary admission to residential services

(1) **Jurisdiction.**—If a person has an intellectual disability and requires involuntary admission to residential services provided by the agency, the circuit court of the county in which the person resides has jurisdiction to conduct a hearing and enter an order involuntarily admitting the person in order for the person to receive the care, treatment, habilitation, and rehabilitation that the person needs. For the purpose of identifying intellectual disability, diagnostic capability shall be established by the agency. Except as otherwise specified, the proceedings under this section are governed by the Florida Rules of Civil Procedure.

(2) **Petition.**—

(a) A petition for involuntary admission to residential services may be executed by a petitioning commission.

(b) The petitioning commission shall consist of three persons. One of these persons shall be a physician licensed and practicing under chapter 458 or chapter 459.

(c) The petition shall be verified and must:

1. State the name, age, and present address of the commissioners and their relationship to the person who has an intellectual disability or autism;

2. State the name, age, county of residence, and present address of the person who has an intellectual disability or autism;

3. Allege that the commission believes that the person needs involuntary residential services and specify the factual information on which the belief is based;

4. Allege that the person lacks sufficient capacity to give express and informed consent to a voluntary application for services and lacks the basic survival and self-care skills to provide for the person's well-being or is likely to physically injure others if allowed to remain at liberty; and

5. State which residential setting is the least restrictive and most appropriate alternative and specify the factual information on which the belief is based.

(d) The petition must be filed in the circuit court of the county in which the person who has the intellectual disability or autism resides.

(3) Notice.—

(a) Notice of the filing of the petition shall be given to the individual and his or her legal guardian. The notice shall be given both verbally and in writing in the language of the client, or in other modes of communication of the client, and in English. Notice shall also be given to such other persons as the court may direct. The petition for involuntary admission to residential services shall be served with the notice.

(b) If a motion or petition has been filed pursuant to s. 916.303 to dismiss criminal charges against a defendant who has an intellectual disability or autism, and a petition is filed to involuntarily admit the defendant to residential services under this section, the notice of the filing of the petition must also be given to the defendant's attorney, the state attorney of the circuit from which the defendant was committed, and the agency.

(c) The notice must state that a hearing shall be set to inquire into the need of the person who has an intellectual disability or autism for involuntary residential services. The notice must also state the date of the hearing on the petition.

(d) The notice must state that the individual who has an intellectual disability or autism has the right to be represented by counsel of his or her own choice and that, if the person cannot afford an attorney, the court shall appoint one.

(4) Agency participation.—

(a) Upon receiving the petition, the court shall immediately order the developmental services program of the agency to examine the person being considered for involuntary admission to residential services.

(b) Following examination, the agency shall file a written report with the court at least 10 working days before the date of the hearing. The report must be served on the petitioner, the person who has the intellectual disability, and the person's attorney at the time the report is filed with the court.

(c) The report must contain the findings of the agency's evaluation, any recommendations deemed appropriate, and a determination of whether the person is eligible for services under this chapter.

(5) Examining committee.—

(a) Upon receiving the petition, the court shall immediately appoint an examining committee to examine the person being considered for involuntary admission to residential services provided by the agency.

(b) The court shall appoint at least three disinterested experts who have demonstrated to the court an expertise in the diagnosis, evaluation, and treatment of persons who have intellectual disabilities. The committee must include at least one licensed and qualified physician, one licensed and qualified psychologist, and one qualified professional who, at a minimum, has a master's degree in social work, special education, or vocational rehabilitation counseling, to examine the person and to testify at the hearing on the involuntary admission to residential services.

(c) Counsel for the person who is being considered for involuntary admission to residential services and counsel for the petition commission has the right to challenge the qualifications of those appointed to the examining committee.

(d) Members of the committee may not be employees of the agency or be associated with each other in practice or in employer-employee relationships. Members of the committee may not have served as members of the petitioning commission. Members of the committee may not be employees of the members of the petitioning commission or be associated in practice with members of the commission.

(e) The committee shall prepare a written report for the court. The report must explicitly document the extent that the person meets the criteria for involuntary admission. The report, and expert testimony, must include, but not be limited to:

1. The degree of the person's intellectual disability and whether, using diagnostic capabilities established by the agency, the person is eligible for agency services;

2. Whether, because of the person's degree of intellectual disability, the person:

a. Lacks sufficient capacity to give express and informed consent to a voluntary application for services pursuant to s. 393.065;

b. Lacks basic survival and self-care skills to such a degree that close supervision and habilitation in a residential setting is necessary and if not provided would result in a real and present threat of substantial harm to the person's well-being; or

c. Is likely to physically injure others if allowed to remain at liberty.

3. The purpose to be served by residential care;

4. A recommendation on the type of residential placement which would be the most appropriate and least restrictive for the person; and

5. The appropriate care, habilitation, and treatment.

(f) The committee shall file the report with the court at least 10 working days before the date of the hearing. The report must be served on the petitioner, the person who has the intellectual disability, the person's attorney at the time the report is filed with the court, and the agency.

(g) Members of the examining committee shall receive a reasonable fee to be determined by the court. The fees shall be paid from the general revenue fund of the county in which the person who has the intellectual disability resided when the petition was filed.

(h) The agency shall develop and prescribe by rule one or more standard forms to be used as a guide for members of the examining committee.

(6) Counsel; guardian ad litem.—

(a) The person who has the intellectual disability must be represented by counsel at all stages of the judicial proceeding. If the person is indigent and cannot afford counsel, the court shall appoint a public defender at least 20 working days before the scheduled hearing. The person's counsel shall have full access to the records of the service provider and the agency. In all cases, the attorney shall represent the rights and legal interests of the person, regardless of who initiates the proceedings or pays the attorney's fee.

(b) If the attorney, during the course of his or her representation, reasonably believes that the person who has the intellectual disability cannot adequately act in his or her own interest, the attorney may seek the appointment of a guardian ad litem. A prior finding of incompetency is not required before a guardian ad litem is appointed pursuant to this section.

(7) Hearing.—

(a) The hearing for involuntary admission shall be conducted, and the order shall be entered, in the county in which the petition is filed. The hearing shall be conducted in a physical setting not likely to be injurious to the person's condition.

(b) A hearing on the petition must be held as soon as practicable after the petition is filed, but reasonable delay for the purpose of investigation, discovery, or procuring counsel or witnesses shall be granted.

(c) The court may appoint a general or special magistrate to preside. Except as otherwise specified, the magistrate's proceeding shall be governed by the Florida Rules of Civil Procedure.

(d) The person who has the intellectual disability must be physically present throughout the entire proceeding. If the person's attorney believes that the person's presence at the hearing is not in his or her best interest, the person's presence may be waived once the court has seen the person and the hearing has commenced.

(e) The person has the right to present evidence and to cross-examine all witnesses and other evidence alleging the appropriateness of the person's admission to residential care. Other relevant and material evidence regarding the appropriateness of the person's admission to residential services; the most appropriate, least restrictive residential placement; and the appropriate care, treatment, and habilitation of the person, including written or oral reports, may be introduced at the hearing by any interested person.

(f) The petitioning commission may be represented by counsel at the hearing. The petitioning commission shall have the right to call witnesses, present evidence, cross-examine witnesses, and present argument on behalf of the petitioning commission.

(g) All evidence shall be presented according to chapter 90. The burden of proof shall be on the party alleging the appropriateness of the person's admission to residential services. The burden of proof shall be by clear and convincing evidence.

(h) All stages of each proceeding shall be stenographically reported.

(8) Order.—

(a) In all cases, the court shall issue written findings of fact and conclusions of law to support its decision. The order must state the basis for the findings of fact.

(b) An order of involuntary admission to residential services may not be entered unless the court finds that:

1. The person is intellectually disabled or autistic;

2. Placement in a residential setting is the least restrictive and most appropriate alternative to meet the person's needs; and

3. Because of the person's degree of intellectual disability or autism, the person:

a. Lacks sufficient capacity to give express and informed consent to a voluntary application for services pursuant to s. 393.065 and lacks basic survival and self-care skills to such a degree that close supervision and habilitation in a residential setting is necessary and, if not provided, would result in a real and present threat of substantial harm to the person's well-being; or

b. Is likely to physically injure others if allowed to remain at liberty.

(c) If the evidence presented to the court is not sufficient to warrant involuntary admission to residential services, but the court feels that residential services would be beneficial, the court may recommend that the person seek voluntary admission.

(d) If an order of involuntary admission to residential services provided by the agency is entered by the court, a copy of the written order shall be served upon the person, the person's counsel, the agency, and the state attorney and the person's defense counsel, if applicable. The order of involuntary admission sent to the agency shall also be accompanied by a copy of the examining committee's report and other reports contained in the court file.

(e) Upon receiving the order, the agency shall, within 45 days, provide the court with a copy of the person's family or individual support plan and copies of all examinations and evaluations, outlining the treatment and rehabilitative programs. The agency shall document that the person has been placed in the most appropriate, least restrictive and cost-beneficial residential setting. A copy of the family or individual support plan and other examinations and evaluations shall be served upon the person and the person's counsel at the same time the documents are filed with the court.

(9) Effect of the order of involuntary admission to residential services.—

(a) An order authorizing an admission to residential care may not be considered an adjudication of mental incompetency. A person is not presumed incompetent solely by reason of the person's involuntary admission to residential services. A person may not be denied the full exercise of all legal rights guaranteed to citizens of this state and of the United States.

(b) Any minor involuntarily admitted to residential services shall, upon reaching majority, be given a hearing to determine the continued appropriateness of his or her involuntary admission.

(10) Competency.—

(a) The issue of competency is separate and distinct from a determination of the appropriateness of involuntary admission to residential services due to intellectual disability.

(b) The issue of the competency of a person who has an intellectual disability for purposes of assigning guardianship shall be determined in a separate proceeding according to the procedures and requirements of chapter 744. The issue of the competency of a person who has an intellectual disability or autism for purposes of determining whether the person is competent to proceed in a criminal trial shall be determined in accordance with chapter 916.

(11) Continuing jurisdiction.—The court which issues the initial order for involuntary admission to residential services under this section has continuing jurisdiction to enter further orders to ensure that the person is receiving adequate care, treatment, habilitation, and rehabilitation, including psychotropic medication and behavioral programming. Upon request, the court may transfer the continuing jurisdiction to the court where a client resides if it is different from where the original involuntary admission order was issued. A person may not be released from an order for involuntary admission to residential services except by the order of the court.

(12) Appeal.—

(a) Any party to the proceeding who is affected by an order of the court, including the agency, may appeal to the appropriate district court of appeal within the time and in the manner prescribed by the Florida Rules of Appellate Procedure.

(b) The filing of an appeal by the person who has an intellectual disability stays admission of the person into residential care. The stay remains in effect during the pendency of all review proceedings in Florida courts until a mandate issues.

(13) Habeas corpus.—At any time and without notice, any person involuntarily admitted into residential care, or the person's parent or legal guardian in his or her behalf, is entitled to file a petition for a writ of habeas corpus to question the cause, legality, and appropriateness of the person's involuntary admission. Each person, or the person's parent or legal guardian, shall receive specific written notice of the right to petition for a writ of habeas corpus at the time of his or her involuntary placement.

Laws 1925, c. 10272, § 4; Comp.Gen.Laws 1927, § 3677; Laws 1961, c. 61–426, § 1; Laws 1967, c. 67–65, § 5; Laws 1970, c. 70–343, § 1; Laws 1970, c. 70–439, § 1; Laws 1973, c. 73–308, § 4; Laws 1973, c. 73–334, § 25; Laws 1975, c. 75–259, § 8; Laws 1977, c. 77–147, § 197; Laws 1977, c. 77–335, § 2; Laws 1979, c. 79–400, § 155; Laws 1980, c. 80–174, § 3; Laws 1981, c. 81–290, § 5; Laws 1988, c. 88–398, § 8; Laws 1990, c. 90–333, § 2; Laws 1992, c. 92–58, § 7; Laws 1994, c. 95–154, § 14; Laws 1995, c. 95–143, § 95; Laws 1995, c. 95–148, § 1048. Amended by Laws 1998, c. 98–92, § 2, eff. Oct. 1, 1998; Laws 1999, c. 99–8, § 89, eff. June 29, 1999; Laws 1999, c. 99–240, § 5, eff. Oct. 1, 1999; Laws 2004, c. 2004–11, § 76, eff. Oct. 1, 2004; Laws 2004, c. 2004–267, § 78, eff. July 1, 2004; Laws 2006, c. 2006–227, § 27, eff. July 1, 2006; Laws 2013, c. 2013–162, § 10, eff. July 1, 2013.

Cross References

Adjudication of persons mentally or physically incompetent, see § 744.331.
Hospitalization of mentally ill persons, see §§ 394.4625, 394.467.

393.115. Discharge

(1) Discharge at the age of majority.—

(a) When any residential client reaches his or her 18th birthday, the agency shall give the resident or legal guardian the option to continue residential services or to be discharged from residential services.

(b) If the resident appears to meet the criteria for involuntary admission to residential services, as defined in s. 393.11, the agency shall file a petition to determine the appropriateness of continued residential placement on an involuntary basis. The agency shall file the petition for involuntary admission in the county in which the client resides. If the resident was originally involuntarily admitted to residential services pursuant to s. 393.11, then the agency shall file the petition in the court having continuing jurisdiction over the case.

(c) Nothing in this section shall in any way limit or restrict the resident's right to a writ of habeas corpus or the right of the agency to transfer a resident receiving residential care to a program of appropriate services provided by the agency when such program is the appropriate habilitative setting for the resident.

(2) Discharge after criminal or juvenile commitment.—Any person with developmental disabilities committed to the custody of the agency pursuant to the provisions of the applicable criminal or juvenile court law shall be discharged in accordance with the requirements of the applicable criminal or juvenile court law.

Laws 1919, c. 7887, § 7; Laws 1925, c. 10272, §§ 2, 3; Comp.Gen. Laws 1927, §§ 3669, 3675, 3676; Laws 1961, c. 61–426, § 1; Laws 1969, c. 69–106, §§ 19, 35; Laws 1970, c. 70–343, § 1; Laws 1970, c. 70–439, § 1; Laws 1973, c. 73–308, § 7; Laws 1977, c. 77–147, § 194; Laws 1977, c. 77–335, § 3; Fla.St.1977, § 393.05; Laws 1978, c. 78–95, § 19; Laws 1988, c. 88–398, § 9; Laws 1989, c. 89–308, § 16; Laws 1995, c. 95–148, § 702. Amended by Laws 2004, c. 2004–267, § 107, eff. July 1, 2004.

Cross References

Discharge of involuntary patients, see § 394.469.

393.12.   Capacity; appointment of guardian advocate

(1) Capacity.—

(a) A person with a developmental disability may not be presumed incapacitated solely by reason of his or her acceptance in nonresidential services or admission to residential care and may not be denied the full exercise of all legal rights guaranteed to citizens of this state and of the United States.

(b) The determination of incapacity of a person with a developmental disability and the appointment of a guardian must be conducted in a separate proceeding according to the procedures and requirements of chapter 744 and the Florida Probate Rules.

(2) Appointment of a guardian advocate.—

(a) A circuit court may appoint a guardian advocate, without an adjudication of incapacity, for a person with developmental disabilities, if the person lacks the decisionmaking ability to do some, but not all, of the decisionmaking tasks necessary to care for his or her person or property or if the person has voluntarily petitioned for the appointment of a guardian advocate. Except as otherwise specified, the proceeding shall be governed by the Florida Rules of Probate Procedure.

(b) A person who is being considered for appointment or is appointed as a guardian advocate need not be represented by an attorney unless required by the court or if the guardian advocate is delegated any rights regarding property other than the right to be the representative payee for government benefits. This paragraph applies only to proceedings relating to the appointment of a guardian advocate and the court's supervision of a guardian advocate and is not an exercise of the Legislature's authority pursuant to s. 2(a), Art. V of the State Constitution.

(c) If a petition is filed pursuant to this section requesting appointment of a guardian advocate for a minor who is the subject of any proceeding under chapter 39, the court division with jurisdiction over guardianship matters has jurisdiction over the proceedings pursuant to this section when the minor reaches the age of 17 years and 6 months or anytime thereafter. The minor shall be provided all the due process rights conferred upon an alleged developmentally disabled adult pursuant to this chapter. The order of appointment of a guardian advocate under this section shall issue upon the minor's 18th birthday or as soon thereafter as possible. Any proceeding pursuant to this paragraph shall be conducted separately from any other proceeding.

(3) Petition.—A petition to appoint a guardian advocate for a person with a developmental disability may be executed by an adult person who is a resident of this state. The petition must be verified and must:

(a) State the name, age, and present address of the petitioner and his or her relationship to the person with a developmental disability;

(b) State the name, age, county of residence, and present address of the person with a developmental disability;

(c) Allege that the petitioner believes that the person needs a guardian advocate and specify the factual information on which such belief is based;

(d) Specify the exact areas in which the person lacks the decisionmaking ability to make informed decisions about his or her care and treatment services or to meet the essential requirements for his or her physical health or safety;

(e) Specify the legal disabilities to which the person is subject; and

(f) State the name of the proposed guardian advocate, the relationship of that person to the person with a developmental disability; the relationship that the proposed guardian advocate had or has with a provider of health care services, residential services, or other services to the person with a developmental disability; and the reason why this person should be appointed. If a willing and qualified guardian advocate cannot be located, the petition shall so state.

(4) Notice.—

(a) Notice of the filing of the petition must be given to the person with a developmental disability, verbally and in writing in the language of the person and in English. Notice must also be given to the next of kin of the person with a developmental disability as defined in chapter 744, a health care surrogate designated pursuant to an advance directive under chapter 765, an agent under a durable power of attorney, and such other persons as the court may direct. A copy of the petition to appoint a guardian advocate must be served with the notice.

(b) The notice must state that a hearing will be held to inquire into the capacity of the person with a developmental disability to exercise the rights enumerated in the petition. The notice must also state the date of the hearing on the petition.

(c) The notice shall state that the person with a developmental disability has the right to be represented by counsel of his or her own choice and the court shall initially appoint counsel.

(5) Counsel.—Within 3 days after a petition has been filed, the court shall appoint an attorney to represent a person with a developmental disability who is the subject of a petition to appoint a guardian advocate. The person with a developmental disability may substitute his or her own attorney for the attorney appointed by the court.

(a) The court shall initially appoint a private attorney who shall be selected from the attorney registry compiled pursuant to s. 27.40. Such attorney must have completed a minimum of 8 hours of education in guardianship. The court may waive this requirement for an attorney who has served as a court-appointed attorney in guardian advocate proceedings or as an attorney of record for guardian advocates for at least 3 years.

(b) An attorney representing a person with a developmental disability may not also serve as the guardian advocate of the person, as counsel for the guardian advocate, or as counsel for the person petitioning for the appointment of a guardian advocate.

(6) Hearing.—

(a) Upon the filing of the petition to appoint a guardian advocate, the court shall set a date for holding a hearing on the petition. The hearing must be held as soon as practicable after the petition is filed, but reasonable delay for the purpose of investigation, discovery, or procuring counsel or witnesses may be granted.

(b) The hearing must be held at the time and place specified in the notice of hearing and must be conducted in a manner consistent with due process.

(c) The person with a developmental disability has the right to be present at the hearing and shall be present unless good cause to exclude the individual can be shown. The person has the right to remain silent, to present evidence, to call and cross-examine witnesses, and to have the hearing open or closed, as the person may choose.

(d) At the hearing, the court shall receive and consider all reports relevant to the person's disability, including, but not limited to, the person's current individual family or individual support plan, the individual education plan, and other professional reports documenting the condition and needs of the person.

(e) The Florida Evidence Code, chapter 90, applies at the hearing. The burden of proof must be by clear and convincing evidence.

(7) Advance directives for health care and durable power of attorney.—In each proceeding in which a guardian advocate is appointed under this section, the court shall determine whether the person with a developmental disability has executed any valid advance directive under chapter 765 or a durable power of attorney under chapter 709.

(a) If the person with a developmental disability has executed an advance directive or durable power of attorney, the court must consider and find whether the documents will sufficiently address the needs of the person with a developmental disability for whom the guardian advocate is sought. A guardian advocate may not be appointed if the court finds that the advance directive or durable power of attorney provides an alternative to the appointment of a guardian advocate which will sufficiently address the needs of the person with a developmental disability.

(b) If an interested person seeks to contest an advance directive or durable power of attorney executed by a person with a developmental disability, the interested person shall file a verified statement. The verified statement shall include the factual basis for the belief that the advance directive or durable power of attorney is invalid or does not sufficiently address the needs of the person for whom a guardian advocate is sought or that the person with authority under the advance directive or durable power of attorney is abusing his or her power.

(c) If an advance directive exists, the court shall specify in its order and letters of guardian advocacy what authority, if any, the guardian advocate shall exercise over the person's health care surrogate. Pursuant to the grounds listed in s. 765.105, the court, upon its own motion, may, with notice to the health care surrogate and any other appropriate parties, modify or revoke the authority of the health care surrogate to make health care decisions for the person with a developmental disability. For purposes of this section, the term "health care decision" has the same meaning as in s. 765.101.

(d) If any durable power of attorney exists, the court shall specify in its order and letters of guardian advocacy what powers of the agent, if any, are suspended and granted to the guardian advocate. The court, however, may not suspend any powers of the agent unless the court determines the durable power of attorney is invalid or there is an abuse by the agent of the powers granted.

(8) Court order.—If the court finds the person with a developmental disability requires the appointment of a guardian advocate, the court shall enter a written order appointing the guardian advocate and containing the findings of facts and conclusions of law on which the court made its decision, including:

(a) The nature and scope of the person's lack of decisionmaking ability;

(b) The exact areas in which the individual lacks decisionmaking ability to make informed decisions about care and treatment services or to meet the essential requirements for his or her physical health and safety;

(c) The specific legal disabilities to which the person with a developmental disability is subject;

(d) The name of the person selected as guardian advocate and the reasons for the court's selection; and

(e) The powers, duties, and responsibilities of the guardian advocate, including bonding of the guardian advocate, as provided in s. 744.351.

(9) Legal rights.—A person with a developmental disability for whom a guardian advocate has been appointed retains all legal rights except those that have been specifically granted to the guardian advocate.

(10) Powers and duties of guardian advocate.—A guardian advocate for a person with a developmental disability shall be a person or corporation qualified to act as guardian, with the same powers, duties, and responsibilities required of a guardian under chapter 744 or those defined by court order under this section. However, a guardian advocate may not be required to file an annual accounting under s. 744.3678 if the court determines that the person with a developmental disability receives income only from Social Security benefits and the guardian advocate is the person's representative payee for the benefits.

(11) Court costs.—In all proceedings under this section, court costs may not be charged against the agency.

(12) Suggestion of restoration of rights.—Any interested person, including the person with a developmental disability, may file a suggestion of restoration of rights with the court in which the guardian advocacy is pending. The suggestion must state that the person with a developmental disability is currently capable of exercising some or all of the rights that were delegated to the guardian advocate and provide evidentiary support for the filing of the suggestion. Evidentiary support includes, but is not limited to, a signed statement from a medical, psychological, or psychiatric practitioner by whom the person with a developmental disability was evaluated and which supports the suggestion for the restoration. If the petitioner is unable to provide evidentiary support due to the lack of access to such information or reports, the petitioner may state a good faith basis for the suggestion for the restoration of rights without attaching evidentiary support. The court shall immediately set a hearing if no evidentiary support is attached to inquire of the petitioner and guardian advocate as to the reason and enter such orders as are appropriate to secure the required documents. The person with a disability and the person's attorney shall be provided notice of the hearing.

(a) Within 3 days after the filing of the suggestion, counsel shall be appointed for the person with a developmental disability as set forth in subsection (5).

(b) The clerk of the court shall immediately send notice of the filing of the suggestion to the person with a developmental disability, the guardian advocate, the attorney for the person with a developmental disability, the attorney for the guardian advocate, if any, and any other interested person designated by the court. Formal notice shall be served on the guardian advocate. Informal notice may be served on other persons. Notice need not be served on the person who filed the suggestion.

(c) Any objections to the suggestion must be filed within 20 days after service of the notice. If an objection is timely filed, or if the evidentiary support suggests that restoration of rights is not appropriate, the court shall set the matter for hearing. The hearing shall be conducted as set forth in s. 744.1095. The court, at the hearing, shall consider all reports and testimony relevant to the person's decisionmaking abilities at the hearing, including, but not limited to, the person's current individual family plan or individual support plan, the individual education plan, and other professional reports that document the condition and needs of the person.

(d) Notice of the hearing and copies of the objections shall be served upon the person with a developmental disability, the attorney for the person with a developmental disability, the guardian advocate, the attorney for the guardian advocate, the next of kin of the person with a developmental disability, and any other interested person as directed by the court.

(e) If no objections are filed and the court is satisfied with the evidentiary support for restoration, the court shall enter an order of restoration of rights which were delegated to a guardian advocate and which the person with a developmental disability may now exercise.

(f) At the conclusion of a hearing, the court shall enter an order denying the suggestion or restoring all or some of the rights that were delegated to the guardian advocate. If only some rights are restored to the person with a developmental disability, the court shall enter amended letters of guardian advocacy.

(g) If only some rights are restored to the person with a developmental disability, the order must state which rights are restored and amended letters of guardian advocacy shall be issued by the court. The guardian advocate shall amend the current plan as required under chapter 744 if personal rights are restored to the person with a developmental disability. The guardian advocate shall file a final accounting as required under chapter 744 if all property rights are restored to the person with a developmental disability. The guardian advocate must file the amended plan or final accounting within 60 days after the order restoring rights and amended letters of guardian advocacy are issued. A copy of the reports shall be served upon the person with a developmental disability and the attorney for the person with a developmental disability.

Laws 1955, c. 29853, § 1; Laws 1961, c. 61–426, § 1; Laws 1963, c. 63–559, § 26; Laws 1970, c. 70–343, § 1; Laws 1973, c. 73–308, § 5; Laws 1973, c. 73–334, § 25; Laws 1977, c. 77–335, § 4; Laws 1980, c. 80–171, § 2; Laws 1988, c. 88–398, § 10; Laws 1989, c. 89–96, § 109; Laws 1994, c. 94–154, § 15; Laws 1995, c. 95–143, § 96; Laws 1995, c. 95–148, § 1049. Amended by Laws 2004, c. 2004–260, § 8, eff. July 1, 2004; Laws 2004, c. 2004–267, § 108, eff. July 1, 2004; Laws 2008, c. 2008–124, § 1, eff. July 1, 2008; Laws 2015, c. 2015–112, § 4, eff. July 1, 2015.

Cross References

Children,
    Continuing care for young adults, see F.S.A. § 39.6251.
    Judicial review, see F.S.A. § 39.701.
Criminal conflict and civil regional counsel offices, see § 27.511.

393.125. Hearing rights

(1) Review of agency decisions.—

(a) For Medicaid programs administered by the agency, any developmental services applicant or client, or his or her parent, guardian advocate, or authorized representative, may request a hearing in accordance with federal law and rules applicable to Medicaid cases and has the right to request an administrative hearing pursuant to ss. 120.569 and 120.57. These hearings shall be provided by the Department of Children and Families pursuant to s. 409.285 and shall follow procedures consistent with federal law and rules applicable to Medicaid cases.

(b) Any other developmental services applicant or client, or his or her parent, guardian, guardian advocate, or authorized representative, who has any substantial interest determined by the agency, has the right to request an administrative hearing pursuant to ss. 120.569 and 120.57, which shall be conducted pursuant to s. 120.57(1), (2), or (3).

(c) Notice of the right to an administrative hearing shall be given, both verbally and in writing, to the applicant or client, and his or her parent, guardian, guardian advocate, or authorized representative, at the same time that the agency gives the applicant or client notice of the agency's action. The notice shall be given, both verbally and in writing, in the language of the client or applicant and in English.

(d) A request for a hearing under this section shall be made to the agency, in writing, within 30 days after the applicant's or client's receipt of the notice.

(2) Review of provider decisions.—The agency shall adopt rules to establish uniform guidelines for the agency and service providers relevant to termination, suspension, or reduction of client services by the service provider. The rules shall ensure the due process rights of service providers and clients.

Laws 1989, c. 89–308, § 17; Laws 1995, c. 95–148, § 703; Laws 1996, c. 96–410, § 122. Amended by Laws 2004, c. 2004–267, § 109, eff. July 1, 2004; Laws 2010, c. 2010–157, § 3, eff. July 1, 2010; Laws 2014, c. 2014–19, § 74, eff. July 1, 2014.

TITLE XXXIII

REGULATION OF TRADE, COMMERCE, INVESTMENTS, AND SOLICITATIONS

CHAPTER 518

INVESTMENT OF FIDUCIARY FUNDS

Cross References

Guardians, powers and duties, see § 744.361.
Trust investments required to be in accordance with this chapter, see § 736.0901.
Trusts, duties of trustees, loyalty, see § 736.0802.
Veterans guardianship, see § 744.602 et seq.

518.01.   Investments of funds received from United States Department of Veterans Affairs

Subject to the conditions herein contained, and except as otherwise authorized by law, guardians holding funds received from, or currently in receipt of funds from, the United States Department of Veterans Affairs, to the extent of those funds alone, may invest such funds only in the following:

(1) United States government obligations.—In bonds or other obligations, either bearing interest or sold on a discount basis, of the United States, or the United States Treasury, or those for the payment of the principal and interest of which the faith and credit of the United States is pledged, including such bonds or obligations of the District of Columbia.

(2) Bonds and obligations of states and territories.—In bonds or other interest-bearing obligations of any state of the United States, or the Territory of Puerto Rico; provided such state or territory has not, within 10 years previous to the date of making such investment, defaulted for more than 90 days in the payment of any part of the principal or interest of any of its bonded indebtedness.

(3) Bonds and other obligations of political subdivisions within the state of Florida.—In bonds or other interest-bearing obligations of any incorporated county, city, town, school district, or road and bridge district located within the state and which has according to the federal census next preceding the date of making the investment, a population of not less than 2,000 inhabitants and for which the full faith and credit of such political subdivision has been pledged; provided, that such political subdivision or its successor through merger, consolidation, or otherwise, has not within 5 years previous to the making of such investment, defaulted for more than 6 months in the payment of any part of the principal or interest of its bonded indebtedness.

(4) Bonds and obligations of political subdivisions located outside the state of Florida.—In bonds or other interest-bearing obligations of any incorporated county, city, or town located outside of the state, but within another state of the United States, which county, city, or town has, according to the federal census next preceding the date of making the investment a population of not less than 40,000 inhabitants and the indebtedness of which does not exceed 7 percent of the last preceding valuation of property for the purposes of taxation; provided, that the full faith and credit of such political subdivision shall have been pledged for the payment of the principal and interest of such bonds or obligations, and provided further, that such political subdivision or its successor, through merger, consolidation, or otherwise, has not within 15 years previous to the making of such investment, defaulted for more than 90 days in the payment of any part of the principal or interest of its bonded indebtedness.

(5) Bonds or obligations of federal land banks and farm credit institutions.—In the bonds or other interest-bearing obligations of any federal land bank organized under any Act of Congress enacted prior to June 14, 1937, provided such bank is not in default in the payment of principal or interest on any of its obligations at the time of making the investment; and on any notes, bonds, debentures, or other similar obligations, consolidated or otherwise, issued by farm credit institutions pursuant to the Farm Credit Act of 1971, Pub. L. No. 92–181.[1]

(6) Bonds of railroad companies.—

(a) Bonds bearing a fixed rate of interest secured by first mortgage, general mortgage, refunding mortgage, or consolidated mortgage which is a lien on real estate, rights or interest therein, leaseholds, right-of-way, trackage, or other fixed assets; provided, that such bonds have been issued or assumed by a qualified railroad company or guaranteed as to principal and interest by indorsement by a qualified railroad company or guaranteed as to principal and interest by indorsement, which guaranty has been assumed by a qualified railroad company.

(b) In bonds secured by first mortgage upon terminal, depot, or tunnel property, including buildings and appurtenances used in the service or transportation by one or more qualified railroad companies; provided that such bonds have been issued or assumed by a qualified railroad company or guaranteed as to principal and interest by indorsement by a qualified railroad company, or guaranteed as to principal and interest by indorsement, which guaranty has been assumed by a qualified railroad company.

(c) As used in this subsection, the words "qualified railroad company" means a railroad corporation other than a street railroad corporation which, at the date of the investment by the fiduciary, meets the following requirements:

1. It shall be a railroad corporation incorporated under the laws of the United States or of any state or commonwealth thereof or of the District of Columbia.

2. It shall own and operate within the United States not less than 500 miles of standard gauge railroad lines, exclusive of sidings.

3. Its railroad operating revenues derived from the operation of all railroad lines operated by it, including leased lines and lines owned or leased by a subsidiary corporation, all of the voting stock of which, except directors' qualifying shares, is owned by it, for its fiscal year next preceding the date of the investment, shall have been not less than $10 million.

4. At no time during its fiscal year in which the investment is made, and its 5 fiscal years immediately prior thereto, shall it have been in default in the payment of any part of the principal or interest owing by it upon any part of its funded indebtedness.

5. In at least 4 of its 5 fiscal years immediately preceding the date of investment, its net income available for fixed charges shall have been at least equal to its fixed charges, and in its fiscal year immediately preceding the date of investment, its net income available for fixed charges shall have been not less than $1\frac{1}{4}$ times its fixed charges.

(d) As used in this subsection, the words "income available for fixed charges" mean the amount obtained by deducting from gross income all items deductible in ascertaining the net income other than contingent income interest and those constituting fixed charges as used in the accounting reports of common carriers as prescribed by the accounting regulations of the Interstate Commerce Commission.[2]

(e) As used in this subsection, the words "fixed charges" mean rent for leased roads, miscellaneous rents, funded debt interest, and amortization of discount on funded debt.

(7) Bonds of gas, water, or electric companies.—In bonds issued by, or guaranteed as to principal and interest by, or assumed by, any gas, water, or electric company, subject to the following conditions:

(a) Gas, water, or electric companies by which such bonds are issued, guaranteed, or assumed, shall be incorporated under the laws of the United States or any state or commonwealth thereof or of the District of Columbia.

(b) The company shall be an operating company transacting the business of supplying water, electrical energy, artificial gas, or natural gas for light, heat, power, and other purposes, and provided that at least 75 percent of its gross operating revenue shall be derived from such business and not more than 15 percent of its gross operating revenues shall be derived from any other one kind of business.

(c) The company shall be subject to regulation by a public service commission, a public utility commission, or any other similar regulatory body duly established by the laws of the United States or any state or commonwealth or of the District of Columbia in which such company operates.

(d) The company shall have all the franchises necessary to operate in the territory in which at least 75 percent of its gross revenues are obtained, which franchises shall either be indeterminate permits of, or agreements with, or subject to the jurisdiction of, a public service commission or other duly constituted regulatory body, or shall extend at least 5 years beyond the maturity of the bonds.

(e) The company shall have been in existence for a period of not less than 8 fiscal years, and at no time within the period of 8 fiscal years immediately preceding the date of such investment shall such company have failed to pay punctually and regularly the matured principal and interest of all its indebtedness, direct, assumed, or guaranteed, but the period of life of the company, together with the period of life of any predecessor company, or company from which a major portion of its property was acquired by consolidation, merger, or purchase, shall be considered together in determining such required period.

(f) For a period of 5 fiscal years immediately preceding the date of the investment, net earnings shall have averaged per year not less than 2 times the average annual interest charges on its entire funded debt, applicable to that period and for the last fiscal year preceding the date of investment, such net earnings shall have been not less than 2 times such interest charges for that year.

(g) The bonds of any such company must be part of an issue of not less than $1 million and must be mortgage bonds secured by a first or refunding mortgage upon property owned and operated by the company issuing or assuming them or must be underlying mortgage bonds secured by property owned and operated by the companies issuing or assuming them. The aggregate principal amount of bonds secured by such first or refunding mortgage, plus the principal amount of all the underlying outstanding bonds, shall not exceed 60 percent of the value of the physical property owned, which shall be book value less such reserves for depreciation or retirement, as the company may have established, and subject to the lien of such mortgage or mortgages securing the total mortgage debt. If such mortgage is a refunding mortgage, it must provide for the retirement on or before the date of maturity of all bonds secured by prior liens on the property.

(h) As used in this subsection, the words "gross operating revenues and expenses" mean, respectively, the total amount earned from the operation of, and the total expenses of maintaining and operating, all property owned and operated by, or leased and operated by, such companies, as determined by the system of accounts prescribed by the Public Service Commission or other similar regulatory body having jurisdiction.

(i) As used in this subsection, the words "net earnings" mean the balance obtained by deducting from its gross operating revenues, its operating and maintenance expenses, taxes, other than federal and state income taxes, rentals, and provisions for depreciation, renewals and retirements of the physical assets of the company, and by adding to such balance its income from securities and miscellaneous sources, but not, however, exceeding 15 percent of such balance.

(8) Bonds of telephone companies.—In bonds issued by, or guaranteed as to principal and interest by, or assumed by, any telephone company, subject to the following conditions:

(a) The telephone company by which such bonds are issued shall be incorporated under the laws of the United States or of any state or commonwealth thereof or of the District of Columbia and shall be engaged in the business of supplying telephone service in the United States and shall be subject to regulations by the Federal Communications Commission, a public service commission, a public utility commission, or any similar regulatory body duly established by the laws of the United States or of any state or commonwealth or of the District of Columbia in which such company operates.

(b) The company by which such bonds are issued, guaranteed, or assumed shall have been in existence for a period of not less than 8 fiscal years, and at no time within the period of 8 fiscal years immediately preceding the date of such investment shall such company have failed to pay punctually and regularly the matured principal and interest of all its indebtedness, direct, assumed, or guaranteed, but the period of life of the company, together with the period of life of any predecessor company, or company from which a major portion of its property was acquired by consolidation, merger, or purchase, shall be considered together in determining such required period. The company shall file with the Federal Communications Commission, or a public service commission or similar regulatory body having jurisdiction over it, and make public in each year a statement and a report giving the income account covering the previous fiscal year, and a balance sheet showing in reasonable detail the assets and liabilities at the end of the year.

(c) For a period of 5 fiscal years immediately preceding the investment, the net earnings of such telephone company shall have averaged per year not less than twice the average annual interest charges on its outstanding obligations applicable to that period, and for the last fiscal year preceding such investment, such net earnings shall have been not less than twice such interest charges for that year.

(d) The bonds must be part of an issue of not less than $5 million and must be mortgage bonds secured by a first or refunding mortgage upon property owned and operated by the company issuing or assuming them, or must be underlying mortgage bonds similarly secured. As of the close of the fiscal year preceding the date of the investment by the fiduciary, the aggregate principal amount of bonds secured by such first or refunding mortgage, plus the principal amount of all the underlying outstanding bonds, shall not exceed 60 percent of the value of the real estate and tangible personal property owned absolutely, which value shall be book value less such reserves for depreciation or retirement as the company may have established, and subject to the lien of such mortgage, or mortgages, securing the total mortgage debt. If such mortgage is a refunding mortgage, it must provide for the retirement, on or before the date of their maturity, of all bonds secured by prior liens on the property.

(e) As used in this subsection, the words "gross operating revenues and expenses" mean, respectively, the total amount earned from the operation of, and the total expenses of maintaining and operating all property owned and operated by, or leased and operated by, such company as determined by the system of accounts prescribed by the Federal Communications Commission, or any other similar federal or state regulatory body having jurisdiction in the matter.

(f) As used in this subsection, the words "net earnings" mean the balance obtained by deducting from the telephone company's gross operating revenues its operating and maintenance expenses, provision for depreciation of the physical assets of the company, taxes, other than federal and state income taxes, rentals, and miscellaneous charges, and by adding to such balance its income from securities and miscellaneous sources but not, however, to exceed 15 percent of such balance.

(9) First mortgages.—In mortgages signed by one or more individuals or corporations, subject to the following conditions:

(a) If the taking of the mortgages as an investment for any particular trust, estate, or guardianship will not result in more than 40 percent of the then value of the principal of such trust, estate, or guardianship being invested in mortgages.

(b) Within 30 days preceding the taking of a mortgage as an investment, the property encumbered or to be encumbered thereby shall be appraised by two or more reputable persons especially familiar with real estate values. The fair market value of the property as disclosed by the appraisal of such persons shall be set forth in a writing dated and signed by them and in such writing they shall certify that their valuation of the property was made after an inspection of the same, including all buildings and other improvements.

(c) The mortgage shall encumber improved real estate located in the state and in or within 5 miles of the corporate limits of a city or town having a population of 2,000 or more, according to the federal census next preceding the date of making any such investment.

(d) The mortgage shall be or become, through the recordation of documents simultaneously filed for record, a first lien upon the property described therein prior to all other liens, except taxes previously levied or assessed but not due and payable at the time the mortgage is taken as an investment.

(e) The mortgage shall secure no indebtedness other than that owing to the executor, administrator, trustee, or guardian taking the same as an investment.

(f) The amount of the indebtedness secured by the mortgage shall not exceed 60 percent of the fair market value, as determined in accordance with the provisions of paragraph (b), of the property encumbered or to be encumbered by said mortgage.

(g) If the amount of the indebtedness secured by the mortgage is in excess of 50 percent of the fair market value, as determined in accordance with the provisions of paragraph (b), of the property encumbered or to be encumbered by said mortgage, then the mortgage shall require principal payments, at annual or more frequent intervals, sufficient to reduce by or before the expiration of 3 years from the date the mortgage is taken as an investment, the unpaid principal balance secured thereby to an amount not in excess of 50 percent of the fair market value of said property, as determined in accordance with the provisions of paragraph (b).

(h) The mortgage shall contain a covenant of the mortgagor to keep insured at all times the improvements on the real estate encumbered by said mortgage, with loss payable to the mortgagee, against loss and damage by fire, in an amount not less than the unpaid principal secured by said mortgage.

(i) Provided, however, that the foregoing limitations and requirements shall not apply to notes or bonds secured by mortgage or trust deed insured by the Federal Housing Administrator, and that notes or bonds secured by mortgage or trust deed insured by the Federal Housing Administrator are declared to be eligible for investment under the provisions of this chapter.

(10) Life insurance.—Annuity or endowment contracts with any life insurance company which is qualified to do business in the state under the laws thereof.

(11) Savings and loan associations.—In savings share or investment share accounts of any federal savings and loan association chartered under the laws of the United States, and doing business in this state, and in the shares of any Florida building and loan association which is a member of the Federal Home Loan Bank System.

(12) Savings accounts, certificates of deposit; state and national banks.—In savings accounts and certificates of deposit in any bank chartered under the laws of the United States and doing business in this state, and in savings accounts and certificates of deposit in any bank chartered under the laws of this state.

(13) Savings share accounts, credit unions.—In savings share accounts of any credit union chartered under the laws of the United States and doing business in this state, and savings share accounts of any credit union chartered under the laws of this state, provided the credit union is insured under the federal share insurance program or an approved state share insurance program.

In determining the qualification of investments under the requirements of this section, published statements of corporations or statements of reliable companies engaged in the business of furnishing statistical information on bonds may be used.

Laws 1937, c. 17949, § 1; Comp.Gen.Laws Supp.1940, § 7100(9); Laws 1953, c. 28154, § 1; Laws 1963, c. 63–111, § 1; Laws 1973, c. 73–41, § 1; Laws 1974, c. 74–92, § 2; Laws 1993, c. 93–268, § 24.

[1] 12 U.S.C.A. § 2001 et seq.
[2] Abolished by Pub.L.No. 104-88, § 101.

Cross References

Agricultural cooperative marketing associations, see § 618.07.
Associations, see § 665.012 et seq.
Banks and trust companies,
    Common trust funds, see § 660.42 et seq.
    Investments generally, see § 658.67.
Deposits in banks designated as depositories of public money, see § 658.60.
Escheat of unclaimed funds, see § 716.02.
Fraternal benefit societies, funds and investments, see §§ 632.623, 632.624.
Guardians, investments by, see § 744.444.
Insurance companies, see § 625.301 et seq.
Insurers, investments in certain securities of federal agencies, see § 625.313.
Prudent investor rule, see § 518.11.
Trustees, investments by, see §§ 736.0703, 736.0816.

518.06. Investment of fiduciary funds in loans insured by Federal Housing Administrator

Banks, savings banks, trust companies, building and loan associations, insurance companies, and guardians holding funds received from or currently in receipt of funds from the United States Department of Veterans Affairs to the extent of those funds alone, may:

(1) Make such loans and advances of credit, and purchases of obligations representing loans and advances of credit, as are insured by the Federal Housing Administrator, and obtain such insurance;

(2) Make such loans secured by real property or leasehold as the Federal Housing Administrator insures or makes a commitment to insure, and obtain such insurance.

Laws 1935, c. 17130, § 1; Comp.Gen.Laws Supp.1936, § 7100(1); Laws 1937, c. 17980, § 1; Laws 1953, c. 28154, § 2; Laws 1993, c. 93–268, § 25.

518.07. Investment of fiduciary funds in bonds, etc., issued by Federal Housing Administrator

(1) Banks, savings banks, trust companies, building and loan associations, insurance companies, guardians holding funds received from or currently in receipt of funds from the United States Department of Veterans Affairs to the extent of those funds alone, the state and its political subdivisions, all institutions and agencies thereof, with the approval of the officials or boards having supervision or management of same, may invest their funds and moneys in their custody or possession, eligible for investment, in notes or bonds secured by mortgage or trust deed insured by the Federal Housing Administrator, in debentures issued by the Federal Housing Administrator, and in securities issued by national mortgage associations.

(2) Such notes, bonds, debentures, and securities made eligible for investment may be used wherever, by statute of this state, collateral is required as security for the deposit of public or other funds; or deposits are required to be made with any public official or departments, or an

investment of capital or surplus, or a reserve or other fund, is required to be maintained consisting of designated securities.

Laws 1935, c. 17130, § 2; Comp.Gen.Laws Supp.1936, § 7100(2); Laws 1937, c. 17980, § 2; Laws 1953, c. 28154, § 3; Laws 1993, c. 93–268, § 25.

518.08. Applicability of laws requiring security, etc.

No law of this state requiring security upon which loans or investments may be made, prescribing the nature, amount, or form of such security, prescribing or limiting interest rates upon loans or investments, limiting investments of capital or deposits, or prescribing or limiting the period for which loans or investments may be made, shall be deemed to apply to loans or investments made pursuant to ss. 518.06 and 518.07.

Laws 1935, c. 17130, § 3; Comp.Gen.Laws Supp.1936, § 7100(3).

518.09. Housing bonds legal investments and security

The state and all public officers, municipal corporations, political subdivisions, and public bodies, all banks, bankers, trust companies, savings banks and institutions, building and loan associations, savings and loan associations, investment companies, all insurance companies, insurance associations, and other persons carrying on an insurance business, and guardians holding funds received from or currently in receipt of funds from the United States Department of Veterans Affairs to the extent of those funds alone may legally invest any sinking funds, moneys, or other funds belonging to them or within their control in any bonds or other obligations issued by a housing authority pursuant to the Housing Authorities Law of this state (chapter 421), or issued by any public housing authority or agency in the United States, when such bonds or other obligations are secured by a pledge of annual contributions to be paid by the United States Government or any agency thereof, and such bonds and other obligations shall be authorized security for all public deposits; it being the purpose of this section to authorize any person, associations, political subdivisions, bodies, and officers, public or private, to use any funds owned or controlled by them, including, but not limited to, sinking, insurance, investment, retirement, compensation, pension, and trust funds, and funds held on deposit, for the purchase of any bonds or other obligations; provided, however, that nothing contained in this section shall be construed as relieving any person from any duty of exercising reasonable care in selecting securities.

Laws 1939, c. 19512, §§ 1 to 3; Comp.Gen.Laws Supp.1940, § 7100(3–nn); Laws 1953, c. 28154, § 4; Laws 1993, c. 93–268, § 27.

518.10. Fiduciary defined as used in ss. 518.11–518.14

For the purpose of ss. 518.11–518.14, a "fiduciary" is defined as an executor, administrator, trustee, guardian (except any guardian holding funds received from or currently in receipt of funds from the United States Department of Veterans Affairs, to the extent of those funds alone), or other person, whether individual or corporate, who by reason of a written agreement, will, court order, or other instrument has the responsibility for the acquisition, investment, reinvestment, exchange, retention, sale, or management of money or property of another.

Laws 1953, c. 28154, § 5; Laws 1993, c. 93–268, § 28.

518.11. Investments by fiduciaries; prudent investor rule

(1) A fiduciary has a duty to invest and manage investment assets as follows:

(a) The fiduciary has a duty to invest and manage investment assets as a prudent investor would considering the purposes, terms, distribution requirements, and other circumstances of the trust. This standard requires the exercise of reasonable care and caution and is to be applied to investments not in isolation, but in the context of the investment portfolio as a whole and as a part of an overall investment strategy that should incorporate risk and return objectives reasonably suitable to the trust, guardianship, or probate estate. If the fiduciary has special skills, or is named fiduciary on the basis of representations of special skills or expertise, the fiduciary is under a duty to use those skills.

(b) No specific investment or course of action is, taken alone, prudent or imprudent. The fiduciary may invest in every kind of property and type of investment, subject to this section. The fiduciary's investment decisions and actions are to be judged in terms of the fiduciary's reasonable business judgment regarding the anticipated effect on the investment portfolio as a whole under the facts and circumstances prevailing at the time of the decision or action. The prudent investor rule is a test of conduct and not of resulting performance.

(c) The fiduciary has a duty to diversify the investments unless, under the circumstances, the fiduciary believes reasonably it is in the interests of the beneficiaries and furthers the purposes of the trust, guardianship, or estate not to diversify.

(d) The fiduciary has a duty, within a reasonable time after acceptance of the trust, estate, or guardianship, to review the investment portfolio and to make and implement decisions concerning the retention and disposition of original preexisting investments in order to conform to the provisions of this section. The fiduciary's decision to retain or dispose of an asset may be influenced properly by the asset's special relationship or value to the purposes of the trust, estate, or guardianship, or to some or all of the beneficiaries, consistent with the trustee's duty of impartiality, or to the ward.

(e) The fiduciary has a duty to pursue an investment strategy that considers both the reasonable production of income and safety of capital, consistent with the fiduciary's duty of impartiality and the purposes of the trust, estate, or guardianship. Whether investments are underproductive or overproductive of income shall be judged by the portfolio as a whole and not as to any particular asset.

(f) The circumstances that the fiduciary may consider in making investment decisions include, without limitation, the general economic conditions, the possible effect of inflation, the expected tax consequences of investment decisions or strategies, the role each investment or course of action plays within the overall portfolio, the expected total return, including both income yield and appreciation of capital, and the duty to incur only reasonable and appropriate costs. The fiduciary may, but need not, consider related trusts, estates, and guardianships, and the income available from other sources to, and the assets of, beneficiaries when making investment decisions.

(2) The provisions of this section may be expanded, restricted, eliminated, or otherwise altered by express provisions of the governing instrument, whether the instrument was executed before or after the effective date of this section. An express provision need not refer specifically to this statute. The fiduciary is not liable to any person for the fiduciary's reasonable reliance on those express provisions.

(3) Nothing in this section abrogates or restricts the power of an appropriate court in proper cases:

(a) To direct or permit the trustee to deviate from the terms of the governing instrument; or

---

(b) To direct or permit the fiduciary to take, or to restrain the fiduciary from taking, any action regarding the making or retention of investments.

(4) The following terms or comparable language in the investment powers and related provisions of a governing instrument shall be construed as authorizing any investment or strategy permitted under this section: "investments permissible by law for investment of trust funds," "legal investments," "authorized investments," "using the judgment and care under the circumstances then prevailing that persons of prudence, discretion, and intelligence exercise in the management of their own affairs, not in regard to speculation but in regard to the permanent disposition of their funds, considering the probable income as well as the probable safety of their capital," "prudent trustee rule," "prudent person rule," and "prudent investor rule."

(5) This section applies to all existing and future fiduciary relationships subject to this section, but only as to acts or omissions occurring after October 1, 1993.

Laws 1953, c. 28154, § 6; Laws 1993, c. 93–257, § 2. Amended by Laws 1997, c. 97–98, § 26, eff. July 1, 1997; Laws 1997, c. 97–103, § 686, eff. July 1, 1997.

UNIFORM PRUDENT INVESTOR ACT

Table of Jurisdiction Wherein Act Has Been Adopted

For text of Uniform Act, and variation notes and annotation materials for adopting jurisdictions, see Uniform Laws Annotated, Master Edition, Volume 7B.

Jurisdiction	Laws	Effective Date	Statutory Citation
Alabama	2006, c. 216	1–1–2007	Code 1975, §§ 19–3B–901 to 19–3B–906.
Alaska	1998, c. 43	5–23–1998	AS §§ 13.36.225 to 13.36.290.
Arizona	2008, c. 247	1–1–2009	A.R.S. §§ 14–10901 to 14–10909.
Arkansas	2001, Act 151	2–8–2001	A.C.A. §§ 24–2–610 to 24–2–619.
California	1995, c. 63	1–1–1996	West's Ann. Cal. Probate Code, §§ 16045 to 16054.
Colorado	1995, S.B. 95–121	7–1–1995	West's C.R.S.A. §§ 15–1.1–101 to 15–1.1–115.
Connecticut	1997, P.A. 97–140	6–13–1997*	C.G.S.A. §§ 45a–541 to 45a–541l.
District of Columbia	2004, c. 15–104	3–10–2004	D.C. Official Code, 2001 Ed. §§ 19–1309.01 to 19–1309.06.
Florida	1993, c. 93–257	10–1–1993	West's F.S.A. §§ 518.11, 518.112.
Hawaii	1997, c. 26	4–14–1997	H.R.S. §§ 554C–1 to 554C–12.
Idaho	1997, c. 14	7–1–1997	I.C. §§ 68–501 to 68–514.
Illinois	1992, P.A. 87–715	1–1–1992	S.H.A. 760 ILCS 5/5, 5/5.1.
Indiana	1999, P.L. 137–1999	7–1–1999	West's A.I.C. §§ 30–4–3.5–1 to 30–4–3.5–13.
Iowa	1999, H.F. 663	7–1–2000	I.C.A. §§ 633A.4301 to 633A.4309.
Kansas	2000, c. 80	7–1–2000	K.S.A. 58–24a01 to 58–24a19.
Maine	2004, c. 618	7–1–2005	18–B M.R.S.A. §§ 901 to 908.
Massachusetts	1998, c. 398	12–4–1998*	M.G.L.A. c. 203C, §§ 1 to 11.
Michigan	1998, P.A. 386	4–1–2000	M.C.L.A. §§ 700.1501 to 700.1512.
Minnesota	1996, c. 314	1–1–1997	M.S.A. §§ 501B.151, 501B.152.
Mississippi	2006, c. 474	7–1–2006	Code 1972, §§ 91–9–601 to 91–9–627.
Missouri	2004, H.B. No. 1511	1–1–2005	V.A.M.S. §§ 469.900 to 469.913.
Montana	2013, ch. 264	10–1–2013	M.C.A. 72–38–901 to 72–38–906.
Nebraska	2003, LB 130	1–1–2005	R.R.S. 1943, §§ 30–3883 to 30–3889.
Nevada	2003, c. 355	10–1–2003	NRS 164.700 to 164.775.
New Hampshire	2004, c. 130	10–1–2004	RSA 564–B:9–901 to 564–B:9–907.

Jurisdiction	Laws	Effective Date	Statutory Citation
New Jersey	1997, c. 26	3–7–1997	N.J.S.A. 3B:20–11.1 to 3B:20–11.12.
New Mexico	1995, c. 210	7–1–1995	NMSA 1978, §§ 45–7–601 to 45–7–612.
New York	1994, c. 609	1–1–1995	McKinney's EPTL 11–2.3.
North Carolina	2005, c. 192	1–1–2006	G.S. §§ 36C–9–901 to 36C–9–907.
North Dakota	2007, c. 549	8–1–2007	NDCC 59–17–01 to 59–17–06.
Ohio	2006, H.B. 416	1–1–2007	R.C. §§ 5809.01 to 5809.08.
Oklahoma	1995, c. 351	11–1–1995	60 Okl.St.Ann. §§ 175.60 to 175.72.
Oregon	2005, c. 348	6–29–2005 *	ORS 130.750 to 130.775.
Pennsylvania	1999, c. 1999–28	6–25–1999*	20 Pa. C.S.A. §§ 7201 to 7214.
Rhode Island	1996, c. 276	8–6–1996*	Gen. Laws 1956, §§ 18–15–1 to 18–15–13.
South Carolina	2005, c. 66	1–1–2006	Code 1976, § 62–7–933.
Tennessee...........	2002, c. 696	7–1–2002	T.C.A. §§ 35–14–101 to 35–14–114.
Texas	2003, c. 1103	1–1–2004	V.T.C.A. Property Code §§ 117.001 to 117.012.
Utah................	2004, c. 89	7–1–2004	U.C.A. 1953, 75–7–901 to 75–7–907.
Vermont............	2009, P.A. 20	7–1–2009	14A V.S.A. §§ 901 to 908.
Virgin Islands	2004, No. 6678	8–12–2004 *	9 V.I.C. §§ 701 to 714.
Virginia	1999, c. 772	1–1–2000	Code 1950, §§ 64.2–780 to 64.2–791.
Washington	1995, S.S.B. 5333	7–23–1995	West's RCWA 11.100.010 to 11.100.140.
West Virginia	1996, S.B. 294	7–1–1996	Code, 44–6C–1 to 44–6C–15.
Wisconsin	2004, c. 283	4–30–2004	W.S.A. 881.01.
Wyoming	2003, c. 124	7–1–2003	Wyo.Stat.Ann. §§ 4–10–901 to 4–10–913.

* Date of approval.

Cross References

Family trust companies, investments, see F.S.A. § 662.132.
Florida Uniform Prudent Management of Institutional Funds Act, see F.S.A. § 617.2104.
Trust investments, prudent investor rule application, see F.S.A. § 736.0902.

518.112. Delegation of investment functions

(1) A fiduciary may delegate any part or all of the investment functions, with regard to acts constituting investment functions that a prudent investor of comparable skills might delegate under the circumstances, to an investment agent as provided in subsection (3), if the fiduciary exercises reasonable care, judgment, and caution in selecting the investment agent, in establishing the scope and specific terms of any delegation, and in reviewing periodically the agent's actions in order to monitor overall performance and compliance with the scope and specific terms of the delegation.

(2)(a) The requirements of subsection (1) notwithstanding, a fiduciary that administers an insurance contract on the life or lives of one or more persons may delegate without any continuing obligation to review the agent's actions, certain investment functions with respect to any such contract as provided in subsection (3), to any one or more of the following persons as investment agents:

1. The trust's settlor if the trust is one described in s. 733.707(3);

2. Beneficiaries of the trust or estate, regardless of the beneficiary's interest therein, whether vested or contingent;

3. The spouse, ancestor, or descendant of any person described in subparagraph 1. or subparagraph 2.;

4. Any person or entity nominated by a majority of the beneficiaries entitled to receive notice under paragraph (3)(b); or

5. An investment agent if the fiduciary exercises reasonable care, judgment, and caution in selecting the investment agent and in establishing the scope and specific terms of any delegation.

(b) The delegable investment functions under this subsection include:

1. A determination of whether the insurance contract was procured or effected in compliance with s. 627.404;

2. A determination of whether any insurance contract is or remains a proper investment;

3. The investigation of the financial strength of the life insurance company;

4. A determination of whether or not to exercise any policy option available under any insurance contracts;

5. A determination of whether or not to diversify such contracts relative to one another or to other assets, if any, administered by the fiduciary; or

6. An inquiry about changes in the health or financial condition of the insured or insureds relative to any such contract.

(c) Until the contract matures and the policy proceeds are received, a fiduciary that administers insurance contracts under this subsection is not obligated to diversify nor allocate other assets, if any, relative to such insurance contracts.

(3) A fiduciary may delegate investment functions to an investment agent under subsection (1) or subsection (2), if:

(a) In the case of a guardianship, the fiduciary has obtained court approval.

(b) In the case of a trust or estate, the fiduciary has given written notice, of its intention to begin delegating investment functions under this section, to all beneficiaries, or their legal representative, eligible to receive distributions from the trust or estate within 30 days of the delegation unless such notice is waived by the eligible beneficiaries entitled to receive such notice. This notice shall thereafter, until or unless the beneficiaries eligible to receive income from the trust or distributions from the estate at the time are notified to the contrary, authorize the trustee or legal representative to delegate investment functions pursuant to this subsection. This discretion to revoke the delegation does not imply under subsection (2) any continuing obligation to review the agent's actions.

1. Notice to beneficiaries eligible to receive distributions from the trust from the estate, or their legal representatives shall be sufficient notice to all persons who may join the eligible class of beneficiaries in the future.

2. Additionally, as used herein, legal representative includes one described in s. 731.303, without any requirement of a court order, an attorney-in-fact under a durable power of attorney sufficient to grant such authority, a legally appointed guardian, or equivalent under applicable law, any living, natural guardian of a minor child, or a guardian ad litem.

3. Written notice shall be given as provided in part III of chapter 731 as to an estate, and as provided in s. 736.0109 and part III of chapter 736 as to a trust.

(4) If all requirements of subsection (3) are satisfied, the fiduciary shall not be responsible otherwise for the investment decisions nor actions or omissions of the investment agent to which the investment functions are delegated.

(5) The investment agent shall, by virtue of acceptance of its appointment, be subject to the jurisdiction of the courts of this state.

(6) In performing a delegated function, the investment agent shall be subject to the same standards as the fiduciary.

Laws 1993, c. 93–257, § 3. Amended by Laws 1997, c. 97–240, § 8, eff. May 30, 1997; Laws 2010, c. 2010–172, § 2, eff. July 1, 2010.

Cross References

Family trust companies, powers, see F.S.A. § 662.130.
Power of attorney, agents, duties, see F.S.A. § 709.2114.
Trustees, delegation of powers and duties, see § 736.0807

518.115. Power of fiduciary or custodian to deposit securities in a central depository

(1)(a) Notwithstanding any other provision of law, any fiduciary, as defined in s. 518.10, holding securities, as defined in s. 678.102(1),[1] in its fiduciary capacity, and any bank or trust company holding securities as a custodian, managing agent, or custodian for a fiduciary, is authorized to deposit or arrange for the deposit of such securities in a clearing corporation, as defined in s. 678.102(3).[1] When such securities are so deposited, certificates representing securities of the same class of the same issuer may be merged and held in bulk in the name of the nominee of such clearing corporation with any other such securities deposited in such clearing corporation by any person, regardless of the ownership of such securities, and certificates of small denomination may be merged into one or more certificates of larger denomination.

(b) A bank or a trust company so depositing securities with a clearing corporation shall be subject to such rules and regulations with respect to the making and maintenance of such deposit as, in the case of state-chartered institutions, the Financial Services Commission and, in the case of national banking associations, the Comptroller of the Currency may from time to time issue.

(c) Notwithstanding any other provisions of law, ownership of, and other interests in, the securities credited to such account may be transferred by entries on the books of said clearing corporation without physical delivery of any securities. The records of such fiduciary and the records of such bank or trust company acting as custodian, managing agent, or custodian for a fiduciary shall at all times show the name of the party for whose account the securities are so deposited. A bank or trust company acting as custodian for a fiduciary shall, on demand by the fiduciary, certify in writing to the fiduciary the securities so deposited by such bank or trust company in such clearing corporation for the account of such fiduciary. A fiduciary shall, on demand by any party to a judicial proceeding for the settlement of such fiduciary's account or on demand by the attorney for such party, certify in writing to such party the securities deposited by such fiduciary in such clearing corporation for its account as such fiduciary.

(2) This section shall apply to any fiduciary holding securities in its fiduciary capacity, and to any bank or trust company holding securities as a custodian, managing agent, or custodian for a fiduciary, acting on June 18, 1974, or who thereafter may act regardless of the date of the agreement, instrument, or court order by which it is appointed and regardless of whether or not such fiduciary, custodian, managing agent, or custodian for a fiduciary owns capital stock of such clearing corporation.

Laws 1974, c. 74–224, § 1. Amended by Laws 2003, c. 2003–261, § 613, eff. June 26, 2003.

[1] Repealed by Laws 1998, c. 98–11, § 25.

518.116. Power of certain fiduciaries and custodians to deposit United States Government and agency securities with a Federal Reserve bank

(1)(a) Notwithstanding any other provision of law, any fiduciary, as defined in s. 518.10, which is a bank or trust company holding securities in its fiduciary capacity, and any bank or trust company holding securities as a custodian, managing agent, or custodian for a fiduciary, is authorized to deposit or arrange for the deposit with the Federal Reserve Bank in its district of any securities, the principal and interest of which the United States Government or any department, agency, or instrumentality thereof has agreed to pay or has guaranteed payment, to be credited to one or more accounts on the books of said Federal Reserve Bank in the name of such bank or trust company to be designated fiduciary or safekeeping accounts, to which account other similar securities may be credited.

(b) A bank or trust company so depositing securities with a Federal Reserve Bank shall be subject to such rules and regulations with respect to the making and maintenance of such deposits as, in the case of state-chartered institutions, the Financial Services Commission and, in the case of national banking associations, the Comptroller of the Currency may from time to time issue. The records of such bank or trust company shall at all times show the ownership of the securities held in such account.

(c) Notwithstanding any other provision of law, ownership of, and other interests in, the securities credited to such account may be transferred by entries on the books of said Federal Reserve Bank without physical delivery of any securities. The records of such fiduciary and the records of such bank or trust company acting as custodian, managing agent, or custodian for a fiduciary shall at all times show the name of the party for whose account the securities are so deposited. A bank or a trust company acting as custodian for a fiduciary shall, on demand by the fiduciary, certify in writing to the fiduciary the securities so deposited by such bank or trust company with such Federal Reserve Bank for the account of such fiduciary. A fiduciary shall, on demand by any party to a judicial proceeding for the settlement of such fiduciary's account or on demand by the attorney for such party, certify in writing to such party the securities deposited by such fiduciary with such Federal Reserve bank for its account as such fiduciary.

(2) This section shall apply to any fiduciary and to any bank or trust company holding securities as custodian, managing agent, or custodian for a fiduciary, acting on June 18, 1974, or who thereafter may act regardless of the date of the instrument or court order by which it is appointed.

Laws 1974, c. 74–224, § 2; Laws 1977, c. 77–174, § 1. Amended by Laws 2003, c. 2003–261, § 614, eff. June 26, 2003.

518.117. Permissible investments of fiduciary funds

A fiduciary that is authorized by lawful authority to engage in trust business as defined in s. 658.12(20) may invest fiduciary funds in accordance with s. 660.417 so long as the investment otherwise complies with this chapter.

Added by Laws 2006, c. 2006–217, § 15, eff. July 1, 2007.

518.12. Instrument creating or defining powers, duties of fiduciary not affected

Nothing contained in ss. 518.10–518.14 shall be construed as conferring a power of sale upon any fiduciary not possessing such power or as authorizing any departure from, or variation of, the express terms or limitations set forth in any will, agreement, court order, or other instrument creating or defining the fiduciary's duties and powers, but the terms "legal investment" or "authorized investment" or words of similar import, as used in any such instrument, shall be taken to mean any investment which is permitted by the terms of s. 518.11.

Laws 1953, c. 28154, § 7; Laws 1957, c. 57–120, § 1.

518.13. Authority of court to permit deviation from terms of instrument creating trust not affected

Nothing contained in ss. 518.10–518.14 shall be construed as restricting the power of a court of proper jurisdiction to permit a fiduciary to deviate from the terms of any will, agreement, or other instrument relating to the acquisition, investment, reinvestment, exchange, retention, sale, or management of fiduciary property.

Laws 1953, c. 28154, § 8.

518.14. Scope of ss. 518.10–518.13

The provisions of ss. 518.10–518.13 shall govern fiduciaries acting under wills, agreements, court orders, and other instruments now existing or hereafter made.

Laws 1953, c. 28154, § 9.

518.15. Bonds or motor vehicle tax anticipation certificates, legal investments and security

Notwithstanding any restrictions on investments contained in any law of this state, the state and all public officers, municipal corporations, political subdivisions, and public bodies, all banks, bankers, trust companies, savings banks, building and loan associations, savings and loan associations, investment companies, and all persons carrying on an insurance business, and all executors, administrators, guardians, trustees, and other fiduciaries may legally invest any sinking funds, moneys or other funds belonging to them or within their control in bonds or motor vehicle anticipation certificates issued under authority of s. 18, Art. XII of the State Constitution of 1885 as adopted by s. 9(d) of Art. XII, 1968 revised constitution, and the additional provisions of s. 9(d), and such bonds or certificates shall be authorized security for all public deposits, including, but not restricted to, deposits as authorized in s. 17.57, it being the purpose of this act to authorize any person, firm or corporation, association, political subdivision, body, and officer, public or private, to use any funds owned or controlled by them, including, but not limited to, sinking, insurance, investment, retirement, compensation, pension, and trust funds, and funds held on deposit, for the purchase of any such bonds or anticipation certificates, up to the amount as authorized by law to be invested in any type of security, including United States Government Bonds.

Laws 1953, c. 27990, § 1; Laws 1969, c. 69–216, § 31. Amended by Laws 2003, c. 2003–261, § 615, eff. June 26, 2003.

518.151. Higher education bonds or certificates, legal investments and security

Notwithstanding any restrictions on investments contained in any law of this state, the state and all public officers, municipal corporations, political subdivisions, and public bodies, all banks, bankers, trust companies, savings banks, building and loan associations, savings and loan associations, investment companies, and all persons carrying on an insurance business, and all executors, administrators, guardians, trustees, and other fiduciaries may legally invest any sinking funds, moneys or other funds belonging to them or within their control in higher education bonds or certificates issued under authority of s. 19, Art. XII of the State Constitution of 1885 or of s. 9(a), Art. XII of the constitution as revised in 1968, as amended, and such bonds or certificates shall be authorized security for all public deposits, including, but not restricted to, deposits as authorized in s. 17.57, it being the purpose of this act to authorize any person, firm or corporation, association, political subdivision, body, and officer, public or private, to use any funds owned or controlled by them, including, but not limited to, sinking, insurance, investment, retirement, compensation, pension, and trust funds, and funds held on deposit, for the purchase of any such bonds or certificates, up to the amount as authorized by law to be invested in any type of security, including United States Government Bonds.

Laws 1965, c. 65–443, § 1; Laws 1971, c. 71–355, § 140. Amended by Laws 2003, c. 2003–261, § 616, eff. June 26, 2003.

518.152.   Puerto Rican bonds or obligations, legal investments and securities

Notwithstanding any restrictions on investments contained in any law of this state, all public officers and public bodies of the state, counties, municipal corporations, and other political subdivisions; all banks, bankers, trust companies, savings banks, building and loan associations, savings and loan associations, investment companies, and other persons carrying on a banking business; all insurance companies, insurance associations and other persons carrying on an insurance business; all persons holding in trust any pension, health and welfare, and vacation funds; all administrators, executors, guardians, trustees, and other fiduciaries of any public, quasi-public, or private fund or estate; and all other persons authorized to invest in bonds or other obligations may legally invest any sinking funds, moneys, or other funds belonging to them or within their control in bonds or other obligations issued by the Commonwealth of Puerto Rico, its agencies, authorities, instrumentalities, municipalities, or political subdivisions, provided such agency, authority, instrumentality, municipality, or political subdivision has not, within 5 years prior to the making of such investment, defaulted for more than 90 days in the payment of any part of the principal or interest of its bonded indebtedness. Such bonds or obligations shall be authorized security for all public deposits, including, but not restricted to, deposits as authorized in s. 17.57, it being the purpose of this section to authorize any person, firm, corporation, association, political subdivision, body, and officer, public or private, to use any funds owned or controlled by them, including, but not limited to, sinking, insurance, investment, retirement, compensation, pension and trust funds, and funds held on deposit, for the purchase of any such bonds or obligations up to the amount as authorized by law to be invested in any type of security, including United States Government Bonds. However, nothing contained in this section shall be construed as relieving any person from any duty of exercising reasonable care in selecting securities.

Laws 1972, c. 72–136, § 1. Amended by Laws 2003, c. 2003–261, § 617, eff. June 26, 2003.

518.16.   Chapter cumulative

This chapter shall be cumulative to any other law providing for investments and security for public deposits.

Laws 1953, c. 27990, § 2; Laws 1953, c. 28154, § 11.

TITLE XXXVIII

BANKS AND BANKING

CHAPTER 655

FINANCIAL INSTITUTIONS GENERALLY

Cross References

Credit union powers, see § 657.031.
Savings Bank Act, see § 667.001 et seq.

655.769. Definitions of terms used in ss. 655.77–655.91

As used in ss. 655.77–655.91, the term:

(1) "Check" includes a share draft of a credit union.

(2) "Deposit" includes a share of a credit union.

(3) "Depositor" includes a member of a credit union.

(4) "Institution" means any state or national bank, state or federal association, or state or federal credit union.

Added by Laws 1992, c. 92–303, § 45, eff. July 3, 1992.

655.77. Deposits by minors

Deposits made by a minor, or made in the minor's name by other than a court-appointed guardian, may be withdrawn by the minor in the absence of an agreement to the contrary made between the institution and the depositor at the time the account is opened. In case of any such agreement, such moneys, until the minor's disabilities are removed, may be withdrawn by the person or persons designated in such agreement.

Added by Laws 1992, c. 92–303, § 46, eff. July 3, 1992. Amended by Laws 1997, c. 97–102, § 526, eff. July 1, 1997.

655.78. Deposit accounts in two or more names

(1) Unless otherwise expressly provided in a contract, agreement, or signature card executed in connection with the opening or maintenance of an account, including a certificate of deposit, a deposit account in the names of two or more persons may be paid to, or on the order of, either or any of such persons or to, or on the order of, the guardian of the property of any such person who is incompetent, whether the other or others are competent. The check or other order for payment to any such person or guardian is a valid and sufficient release and discharge of the obligation of the institution for funds transferred thereby.

(2) In the case of a credit union, a member may designate any person or persons to hold deposits with the member in joint tenancy with the right of survivorship; but a joint tenant, unless he or she is a member in his or her own right, may not be permitted to vote, obtain a loan, or hold office or be required to pay an entrance or membership fee.

Added by Laws 1992, c. 92–303, § 47, eff. July 3, 1992. Amended by Laws 1997, c. 97–102, § 527, eff. July 1, 1997.

655.79. Deposits and accounts in two or more names; presumption as to vesting on death

(1) Unless otherwise expressly provided in a contract, agreement, or signature card executed in connection with the opening or maintenance of an account, including a certificate of deposit, a deposit account in the names of two or more persons shall be presumed to have been intended by such persons to provide that, upon the death of any one of them, all rights, title, interest, and claim in, to, and in respect of such deposit account, less all proper setoffs and charges in favor of the institution, vest in the surviving person or persons. Any deposit or account made in the name of two persons who are husband and wife shall be considered a tenancy by the entirety unless otherwise specified in writing.

(2) The presumption created in this section may be overcome only by proof of fraud or undue influence or clear and convincing proof of a contrary intent. In the absence of such proof, all rights, title, interest, and claims in, to, and in respect of such deposits and account and the additions thereto, and the obligation of the institution created thereby, less all proper setoffs and charges in favor of the institution against any one or more of such persons, upon the death of any such person, vest in the surviving person or persons, notwithstanding the absence of proof of any donative intent or delivery, possession, dominion, control, or acceptance on the part of any person and notwithstanding that the provisions hereof may constitute or cause a vesting or disposition of property or rights or interests therein, testamentary in nature, which, except for the provisions of this section, would or might otherwise be void or voidable.

(3) This section does not abridge, impair, or affect the validity, effectiveness, or operation of any of the provisions of ss. 655.78 and 674.405 or the rights of institutions to make payments as therein provided.

Added by Laws 1992, c. 92–303, § 48, eff. July 3, 1992. Amended by Laws 2008, c. 2008–75, § 8, eff. Oct. 1, 2008.

655.80. Convenience accounts

(1) A convenience account is a deposit account, other than a certificate of deposit, in the name of one individual (principal), in which one or more other individuals have been designated as agents with the right to make deposits to and to withdraw funds from or draw checks on such account. The designation of agents, the substitution or removal of agents, or any other change in the contractual terms or provisions governing a convenience account may be made only by the principal. Except as otherwise provided in this section, the agency relationship created under this account is not affected by the subsequent death or incompetence of the principal.

(2) All rights, interests, and claims in, to, and in respect of, such deposits and convenience account and the additions thereto shall be those of the principal only.

(3) Any balance standing to the credit of a convenience account shall be paid to the guardian of the property of the principal, to any person designated in a court order entered pursuant to s. 735.206, to any person designated by letter or other writing as authorized by s. 735.301, or to the personal representative of the deceased principal's estate, upon presentation of effective written notice and, if applicable, proof of judicial appointment of such guardian or personal representative by a court of competent jurisdiction. No such court order or letter, written notice, or proof of judicial appointment is effective until it is served upon and received by an officer of the institution during regular banking hours and in such time and in such manner as to afford the institution a reasonable opportunity to act on it prior to the happening of any of the events described in s. 674.303. No other notice, knowledge, or other information shown to have been available to an institution affects its right to the protection provided by this section.

(4) Payment by an institution pursuant to this section is a valid and sufficient release and discharge to the institution from all claims for payments so paid.

(5) Without qualifying any other right to setoff or lien, and subject to any contractual provision, if the principal is indebted to the institution, the institution has a right to setoff against the account.

Added by Laws 1992, c. 92–303, § 49, eff. July 3, 1992.

655.82. Pay-on-death accounts

(1) As used in this section:

(a) "Account" means a contract of deposit between a depositor and an institution, including, but not limited to, a checking account, savings account, certificate of deposit, and share account.

(b) "Beneficiary" means a person named as one to whom sums on deposit in an account are payable on request after death of all parties or for whom a party is named as trustee.

(c) "Devisee" means any person designated in a will to receive a testamentary disposition of real or personal property.

(d) "Heirs" means those persons, including a surviving spouse, who are entitled, under the laws of this state regarding intestate succession, to the property of a decedent.

(e) "Multiple-party account" means an account payable on request to one or more of two or more parties, whether or not a right of survivorship is mentioned.

(f) "Party" means a person who, by the terms of an account, has a present right, subject to request, to payment from the account other than as a beneficiary.

(g) "Payment" means disbursement of sums on deposit, and includes withdrawal, payment to a party or third person pursuant to check or other request, and a pledge of sums on deposit by a party, or a setoff, reduction, or other disposition of all or part of an account pursuant to a pledge.

(h) "Pay-on-death designation" means the designation of:

1. A beneficiary in an account payable on request to one party during the party's lifetime and on the party's death to one or more beneficiaries, or to one or more parties during their lifetimes and on death of all of them to one or more beneficiaries; or

2. A beneficiary in an account in the name of one or more parties as trustee for one or more beneficiaries if the relationship is established by the terms of the account and there is no subject of the trust other than the sums on deposit in the account, whether or not payment to the beneficiary is mentioned.

(i) "Personal representative" means an executor, administrator, curator, successor personal representative, special administrator, or any other person who performs substantially the same function under the law governing their status.

(j) "Receive," as it relates to notice to an institution, means receipt in the office or branch office of the institution in which the account is established, but if the terms of the account require notice at a particular place, in the place required.

(k) "Request" means a request for payment complying with all terms of the account, including special requirements concerning necessary signatures and regulations of the institution; but, for purposes of this section, if terms of the account condition payment on advance notice, a request for payment is treated as immediately effective and a notice of intent to withdraw is treated as a request for payment.

(*l*) "Successor" means any person, other than a creditor, who is entitled to property of a decedent under the decedent's will or otherwise.

(m) "Sums on deposit" means the balance payable on an account, including interest and dividends earned, whether or not included in the current balance, and any deposit of life insurance proceeds added to the account by reason of death of a party.

(n) "Terms of the account" means the deposit agreement and other terms and conditions, including the form, of the contract of deposit.

(2) A beneficiary in an account having a pay-on-death designation has no right to sums on deposit during the lifetime of any party.

(3) In an account with a pay-on-death designation:

(a) On the death of one of two or more parties, sums on deposit in the account belong to the surviving party or parties.

(b) On the death of the sole party or the last survivor of two or more parties, sums on deposit belong to the surviving beneficiary or beneficiaries. If two or more beneficiaries survive, sums on deposit belong to them in equal and undivided shares, and, unless otherwise provided in a depository agreement written between December 31, 1994, and July 1, 2001, there is no right of survivorship in the event of death of a beneficiary thereafter. If no beneficiary survives, sums on deposit belong to the estate of the last surviving party.

(4) A pay-on-death designation in a multiple-party account without right of survivorship is ineffective. For purposes of this section, designation of an account as a tenancy in common establishes that the account is without right of survivorship.

(5) The ownership right of a surviving party or beneficiary, or of the decedent's estate, in sums on deposit is subject to requests for payment made by a party before the party's death,

whether paid by the institution before or after death, or unpaid. The surviving party or beneficiary, or the decedent's estate, is liable to the payee of an unpaid request for payment. The liability is limited to a proportionate share of the amount transferred under this section, to the extent necessary to discharge the request for payment.

(6) An institution, on request, may pay sums on deposit in an account with a pay-on-death designation to:

(a) One or more of the parties, whether or not another party is disabled, incapacitated, or deceased when the payment is requested and whether or not a party survives another party;

(b) The beneficiary or beneficiaries, if proof of death is presented to the institution showing that the beneficiary or beneficiaries survived all persons named as parties; or

(c) The personal representative, if any, or, if there is none, the heirs or devisees of a deceased party, if proof of death is presented to the institution showing that the deceased party was the survivor of all other persons named on the account either as a party or beneficiary.

(7) Payment made pursuant to this section discharges the institution from all claims for amounts so paid, whether or not the payment is consistent with the beneficial ownership of the account as between parties, beneficiaries, or their successors. Payment may be made whether or not a party or beneficiary is disabled, incapacitated, or deceased when payment is requested, received, or made.

(8) A beneficiary in an account at a credit union having a pay-on-death designation, unless the beneficiary is a member in her or his own right, may not be permitted to vote, obtain an extension of credit, or hold office or be required to pay an entrance or membership fee.

(9) The following is an example of the form of a contract of deposit that may be used to select a pay-on-death account for use by one or more parties:

SINGLE–PARTY ACCOUNT OR MULTIPLE–PARTY

ACCOUNT WITH PAY–ON–DEATH DESIGNATION

PARTIES (Name each party): _____   _____
OWNERSHIP (Select one and initial):
_____   SINGLE–PARTY ACCOUNT
_____   MULTIPLE–PARTY ACCOUNT
RIGHTS AT DEATH (Select one and initial):
_____   SINGLE–PARTY ACCOUNT
   At death of the party, ownership passes as part of the party's estate
_____   SINGLE–PARTY ACCOUNT WITH A PAY–ON–DEATH DESIGNATION
(Name one or more beneficiaries):

_____

At death of the party, ownership passes to the designated pay-on-death beneficiaries and is not part of the party's estate.
_____   MULTIPLE–PARTY ACCOUNT WITH RIGHT OF SURVIVORSHIP
At death of a party, ownership passes to the surviving party or parties.
_____   MULTIPLE–PARTY ACCOUNT WITH RIGHT OF SURVIVORSHIP AND A
              PAY–ON–DEATH DESIGNATION
(Name one or more beneficiaries):

_____

At death of the last surviving party, ownership passes to the designated pay-on-death beneficiaries and is not part of the last surviving party's estate.

Added by Laws 1994, c. 94–216, § 1, eff. Jan. 1, 1995. Amended by Laws 1997, c. 97–102, § 529, eff. July 1, 1997; Laws 2001, c. 2001–243, § 21, eff. June 15, 2001.

UNIFORM MULTIPLE-PERSON ACCOUNTS ACT

Table of Jurisdictions Wherein Act Has Been Adopted

For text of Uniform Act, and variation notes and annotation materials for adopting jurisdictions, see Uniform Laws Annotated, Master Edition, Volume 8B.

Jurisdiction	Laws	Effective Date	Statutory Citation
Alabama	1997, No. 97–644	3–1–1998	Code 1975, §§ 5–24–1 to 5–24–34.
Alaska	1996, c. 75	1–1–1997	AS 13.06.050, 13.33.201 to 13.33.227.
Arizona	1994, c. 290	After 12–31–1994	A.R.S. §§ 14–6102, 14–6201 to 14–6227.
Colorado	1990, S.B. 90–91	7–1–1990	West's C.R.S.A. §§ 15–10–201, 15–15–201 to 15–15–227.
District of Columbia	2001, D.C. Law 13–292	4–27–2001	D.C. Official Code, 2001 Ed. §§ 19–602.01 to 19–602.27.
Florida	1994, c. 94–216	1–1–1995	West's F.S.A. § 655.82.
Montana	1993, c. 494	10–1–1993	MCA §§ 72–1–103, 72–6–201 to 72–6–227.
Nebraska	1993, LB 250	5–6–1993 *	R.R.S. 1943, §§30–2209, 30–2716 to 30–2733.
New Mexico	1992, c. 66	7–1–1992	NMSA 1978, §§ 45–1–201, 45–6–201 to 45–6–227.
North Dakota	1991, c. 351	7–1–1991	NDCC 30.1–01–06, 30.1–31–02 to 30.1–31–20.
South Carolina	2013, No. 100	1–1–2014	Code 1976, §§ 35–6–101 to 35–6–113, 35–6–201.
Virgin Islands	2009, No. 7150	1–1–2011	15 V.I.C. § 6–201 to 15 V.I.C. § 6–227.

* Date of approval.

UNIFORM NONPROBATE TRANSFERS ON DEATH ACT

Table of Jurisdictions Wherein Act Has Been Adopted

For text of Uniform Act, and variation notes and annotation materials for adopting jurisdictions, see Uniform Laws Annotated, Master Edition, Volume 8B.

Jurisdiction	Laws	Effective Date	Statutory Citation
Alabama [3]	1997, Nos. 97–644, 97–703	Part 2 3–1–1998; Part 3 8–1–1997	Code 1975, §§ 5–24–1 to 5–24–34, 8–6–140 to 8–6–151.
Alaska	1996, c. 75	1–1–1997	AS 13.06.050, 13.33.101 to 13.33.310.
Arizona	1994, c. 290	After 12–31–1994	A.R.S. §§ 14–6101 to 14–6311.
Arkansas [2]	1993, No. 114	8–13–1993	A.C.A. §§ 28–14–101 to 28–14–112.
California [1]	1998, c. 242	1–1–1999	West's Ann.Cal. Probate Code, §§ 5000 to 5003, 5500 to 5512.
Colorado	1990, S.B. 90–91	7–1–1990	West's C.R.S.A. §§ 15–10–201, 15–15–101 to 15–15–311.
Connecticut [2]	1997, No. 97–42	5–14–1997 *	C.G.S.A. §§ 45a–468 to 45a–468m.

Jurisdiction	Laws	Effective Date	Statutory Citation
Delaware [2]	70 Del. Laws, c. 394	6–26–1996	12 Del. C. §§ 801 to 812.
District of Columbia ...	2001, D.C. Law 13–292	4–27–2001	D.C. Official Code, 2001 Ed. §§ 19–601.01 to 19–603.11.
Florida [3]	1994, c. 94–216	1–1–1995	West's F.S.A. §§ 655.82, 711.50 to 711.512.
Georgia [2]	1999, Act 392	7–1–1999	O.C.G.A. §§ 53–5–60 to 53–5–71.
Hawaii [2]	1998, c. 63	4–29–1998	HRS §§ 539–1 to 539–12.
Idaho [2]	1996, c. 303	7–1–1996	I.C. §§ 15–6–301 to 15–6–312.
Illinois [2]	1994, P.A. 88–577	1–1–1995	S.H.A. 815 ILCS 10/0.01 to 10/10.
Indiana [2]	2002, P.L. 2–2002	7–1–2002	West's A.I.C. 32–17–9–1 to 32–17–9–15.
Iowa [2]	1997, c. 178	7–1–1997	I.C.A. §§ 633D.1 to 633D.12.
Kansas [2]	1994, c. 44	7–1–1994	K.S.A. 17–49a01 to 17–49a12.
Kentucky [2]	1998, c. 407	8–1–1998	KRS 292.6501 to 292.6512.
Maine [2]	1997, c. 627	3–27–1998 *	18–A M.R.S.A. §§ 6–301 to 6–312.
Maryland [2]	1994, c. 644	10–1–1994	Code, Estates and Trusts, §§ 16–101 to 16–112.
Massachusetts [1]	2008, c. 521	3–31–2012	M.G.L.A. c. 190B, §§ 6–101 to 6–311.
Michigan [1]	1998, P.A. 386	4–1–2000	M.C.L.A. §§ 700.6101 to 700.6310.
Minnesota [2]	1992, c. 461	6–1–1992	M.S.A. §§ 524.6–301 to 524.6–311.
Mississippi [2]	1997, c. 413	3–24–1997	Code 1972, §§ 91–21–1 to 91–21–25.
Montana	1993, c. 494	10–1–1993	MCA §§ 72–1–103, 72–6–111 to 72–6–311.
Nebraska	1993, LB 250	5–6–1993*	R.R.S 1943, §§ 30–2209, 30–2715 to 30–2746.
New Hampshire [2]	1997, c. 231	1–1–1998	RSA 563–C:1 to 563–C:12.
New Jersey [2]	1995, c. 130	6–22–1995*	N.J.S.A. 3B:30–1 to 3B:30–12.
New Mexico	1992, c. 66	7–1–1992	NMSA 1978, §§ 45–1–201, 45–6–101 to 45–6–311.
New York [2]	2005, c. 325	1–1–2006	McKinney's EPTL 13–4.1 to 13–4.12.
North Carolina [2]	2005, c. 411	10–1–2005	G.S. §§ 41–40 to 41–51.
North Dakota	1991, c. 351	7–1–1991	NDCC 30.1–01–06, 30.1–31–01 to 30.1–31–30.
Ohio [2]	1993, H.B. 62	10–1–1993	R.C. §§ 1709.01 to 1709.11.
Oklahoma [2]	1994, c. 208	9–1–1994	71 Okl.St.Ann. §§ 901 to 913.
Oregon [2]	1991, c. 306	6–19–1991*	ORS 59.535 to 59.585.
Pennsylvania [2]	1996, P.L. 1118	12–18–1996*	20 Pa.C.S.A. §§ 6401 to 6413.
Rhode Island [2]	1998, c. 98–260	7–9–1998	Gen. Laws 1956, §§ 7–11.1–1 to 7–11.1–12.
South Carolina [2]	1997, No. 102	6–13–1997	Code 1976, §§ 35–6–10 to 35–6–100.
South Dakota [2]	1995, c. 168	Registrations of securities in beneficiary form by decedents dying on or after 7–1–1996	SDCL 29A–6–301 to 29A–6–311.
Tennessee [2]	1995, c. 471	7–1–1995	T.C.A. §§ 35–12–101 to 35–12–113.
Utah [2]	1995, c. 9	5–1–1995	U.C.A. 1953, 75–6–301 to 75–6–313.
Vermont [2]	1999, Act 23	5–17–1999*	9 V.S.A. §§ 4351 to 4360.
Virgin Islands [2]	2010, No. 7150	1–1–2011	15 V.I.C. §§ 6–301 to 6–311.
Virginia [2]	1994, c. 422		Code 1950, § 64.2–620.
Washington [2]	1993, c. 287	7–25–1993	West's RCWA 21.35.005 to 21.35.902.
West Virginia [2]	1994, c. 62	3–10–1994*	Code, 36–10–1 to 36–10–12.
Wisconsin [1]	1989, Act 331	5–11–1990	W.S.A. 705.20 to 705.30.
Wyoming [2]	1993, c. 171	7–1–1993	Wyo.Stat.Ann. §§ 2–16–101 to 2–16–112.

* Date of approval.
[1] Adopted only Parts 1 and 3 of the Act.
[2] Adopted only Part 3 of the Act.

[3] Adopted only Parts 2 and 3 of the Act.

UNIFORM PROBATE CODE ACT

Table of Jurisdictions Wherein Code Has Been Adopted

For text of Uniform Act, and variation notes and annotation materials for adopting jurisdictions, see Uniform Laws Annotated, Master Edition, Volumes 8, Pt. I, 8, Pt. II, and 8, Pt. III.

Jurisdiction	Laws	Effective Date	Statutory Citation
Alaska [2]	1972, c. 78	1–1–1973	AS 13.06.005 to 13.36.390.
Arizona [2]	1973, c. 75	1–1–1974	A.R.S. §§ 14–1101 to 14–7308.
Colorado [2]	1973, H.B. 1039	7–1–1974	West's C.R.S.A. §§ 15–10–101 to 15–17–103.
Florida [1]	1974, c. 74–106	7–1–1975	West's F.S.A. §§ 655.82, 711.50 to 711.512, 731.005 to 735.302.
Hawaii [5]	1976, c. 200	7–1–1976	HRS §§ 539–1 to 539–12; 560:1–101 to 560:8–101.
Idaho [4]	1971, c. 111	7–1–1972	I.C. §§ 15–1–101 to 15–7–308.
Maine [4]	1979, c. 540	1–1–1981	18–A M.R.S.A. §§ 1–101 to 8–401.
Massachusetts	2008, c. 521	1–15–2009 *	M.G.L.A. c. 190B, §§ 1–101 to 7–503.
Michigan [4]	1998, P.A. 386	4–1–2000	M.C.L.A. §§700.1101 to 700.8102.
Minnesota [3]	1974, c. 442	8–1–1975	M.S.A. §§ 524.1–101 to 524.8–103.
Montana [2]	1974, c. 365	7–1–1975	MCA 72–1–101 to 72–6–311.
Nebraska [1]	1974, L.B. 354	1–1–1977	R.R.S.1943, §§ 30–2201 to 30–2902.
New Jersey [6]	2004, c. 132	8–31–2004 *	N.J.S.A. 3B:1–1 to 3B:30–12, 17:16I–1 to 17:16I–17.
New Mexico [2]	1975, c. 257	7–1–1976	NMSA 1978, §§ 45–1–101 to 45–7–522.
North Dakota [2]	1973, c. 257	7–1–1975	NDCC 30.1–01–01 to 30.1–35–01.
South Carolina [4]	1986, Act 539	7–1–1987	Code 1976, §§ 35–6–10 to 35–6–100; 62–1–100 to 62–7–604.
South Dakota [5]	SL 1994, c. 232	7–1–1995	SDCL 29A–1–101 to 29A–8–101.
Utah [5]	1975, c. 150	7–1–1977	U.C.A.1953, 75–1–101 to 75–8–101.
Virgin Islands	Act 7174, sec. 12(b), amended by Act 7150, sec. 2	1–1–2011	15 V.I.C. 1-101 to 10-203.

* Approval date.
[1] Adopted 1989 Revision of Article VI.
[2] Adopted 1990 Revision of Article II and 1989 Revision of Article VI.
[3] Adopted 1990 Revision of Article II.
[4] Adopted Part 3 of 1989 Revision of Article VI.
[5] Adopted 1990 Revision of Article II and Part 3 of 1989 Revision of Article VI.
[6] Adopted 1990 Revision of Article II and Parts 2 and 3 of 1989 Revision of Article VI.

Cross References

Uniform Transfer-on-Death Security Registration Act, see § 711.50 et seq.

655.825. Deposits in trust; applicability of s. 655.82 in place of former s. 655.81

(1) Because deposits in trust are also accounts with a pay-on-death designation as described in s. 655.82, it is the intent of the Legislature that the provisions of s. 655.82 shall apply to and govern deposits in trust. References to s. 655.81 in any depository agreement shall be interpreted after the effective date of this act as references to s. 655.82.

(2) This section shall take effect July 1, 2001, and shall apply to deposits made to a depository account created after December 31, 1994.

Added by Laws 2001, c. 2001–243, § 3, eff. July 1, 2001.

For Annotative Materials, see West's Florida Statutes Annotated

131

655.93.   Definitions for ss. 655.93–655.94

As used in ss. 655.93–655.94, the term:

(1) "Lessee" means a person who contracts with a lessor for the use of a safe-deposit box.

(2) "Lessor" means a financial institution that rents safe-deposit facilities.

(3) "Safe-deposit box" means a safe-deposit box, vault, or other safe-deposit receptacle maintained by a lessor, and the rules relating thereto apply to property or documents kept in safekeeping in the financial institution's vault.

Added by Laws 1992, c. 92–303, § 60, eff. July 3, 1992.

655.931.   Authority to engage in safe-deposit business

A financial institution may maintain and lease safe-deposit boxes and may accept property or documents for safekeeping if, except in the case of property or documents accepted through night depositories, it issues a receipt therefor.

Added by Laws 1992, c. 92–303, § 61, eff. July 3, 1992.

655.932.   Lease to minor

A lessor may lease a safe-deposit box to, and in connection therewith deal with, a minor with the same effect as if leasing to and dealing with a person of full legal capacity.

Added by Laws 1992, c. 92–303, § 62, eff. July 3, 1992.

655.933.   Access by fiduciaries

If a safe-deposit box is made available by a lessor to one or more persons acting as fiduciaries, the lessor may, except as otherwise expressly provided in the lease or the writings pursuant to which such fiduciaries are acting, allow access thereto as follows:

(1) By any one or more of the persons acting as personal representatives.

(2) By any one or more of the persons otherwise acting as fiduciaries if authorized in writing, which writing is signed by all other persons so acting.

(3) By any agent authorized in writing, which writing is signed by all persons acting as fiduciaries.

Added by Laws 1992, c. 92–303, § 63, eff. July 3, 1992.

655.934.   Effect of lessee's death or incapacity

If a lessor without knowledge of the death or an order determining the incapacity of the lessee deals with the lessee's agent in accordance with a written power of attorney or a durable power of attorney signed by such lessee, the transaction binds the lessee's estate and the lessee.

Added by Laws 1992, c. 92–303, § 64, eff. July 3, 1992. Amended by Laws 2010, c. 2010–132, § 1, eff. Oct. 1, 2010.

655.935.   Search procedure on death of lessee

If satisfactory proof of the death of the lessee is presented, a lessor shall permit the person named in a court order for that purpose, or if no order has been served upon the lessor, the spouse, a parent, an adult descendant, or a person named as a personal representative in a copy of a purported will produced by such person, to open and examine the contents of a safe-deposit box leased or coleased by a decedent, or any documents delivered by a decedent for safekeeping, in the presence of an officer of the lessor.

---

(1) If requested by such person, the lessor shall remove and deliver only:

(a) Any writing purporting to be a will of the decedent, to the court having probate jurisdiction in the county in which the financial institution is located.

(b) Any writing purporting to be a deed to a burial plot or to give burial instructions, to the person making the request for a search.

(c) Any document purporting to be an insurance policy on the life of the decedent, to the beneficiary named therein.

(2) The officer of the lessor shall make a complete copy of any document removed and delivered pursuant to this section and place that copy, together with a memorandum of delivery identifying the name of the officer, the person to whom the document was delivered, the purported relationship of the person to whom the document was delivered, and the date of delivery, in the safe-deposit box leased or coleased by the decedent.

(3) The lessor may charge reasonable fees to cover costs incurred pursuant to this section.

(4) Access granted pursuant to this section is not considered the initial opening of the safe-deposit box pursuant to s. 733.6065.

Added by Laws 1992, c. 92–303, § 65, eff. July 3, 1992. Amended by Laws 2006, c. 2006–134, § 1, eff. July 1, 2006; Laws 2006, c. 2006–213, § 67, eff. Oct. 1, 2006; Laws 2010, c. 2010–132, § 2, eff. Oct. 1, 2010.

655.936. Delivery of safe-deposit box contents or property held in safekeeping to personal representative

(1) Subject to the provisions of subsection (3), the lessor shall immediately deliver to a personal representative appointed by a court in this state, upon presentation of a certified copy of his or her letters of authority, all property deposited with it by the decedent for safekeeping, and shall grant the personal representative access to any safe-deposit box in the decedent's name and permit him or her to remove from such box any part or all of the contents thereof.

(2) If a personal representative of a deceased lessee has been appointed by a court of any other state, a lessor may, at its discretion, after 3 months from the issuance to such personal representative of his or her letters of authority, deliver to such personal representative all properties deposited with it for safekeeping and the contents of any safe-deposit box in the name of the decedent if at such time the lessor has not received written notice of the appointment of a personal representative in this state, and such delivery is a valid discharge of the lessor for all property or contents so delivered. A personal representative appointed by a court of any other state shall furnish the lessor with an affidavit setting forth facts showing the domicile of the deceased lessee to be other than this state and stating that there are no unpaid creditors of the deceased lessee in this state, together with a certified copy of his or her letters of authority. A lessor making delivery pursuant to this subsection shall maintain in its files a receipt executed by such personal representative which itemizes in detail all property so delivered.

(3) Notwithstanding the provisions of subsection (1), after the death of a lessee of a safe-deposit box, the lessor shall permit the initial opening of the safe-deposit box and the removal of the contents of the safe-deposit box in accordance with s. 733.6065.

(4) A lessor is not liable for damages or penalty by reason of any delivery made pursuant to this section.

Added by Laws 1992, c. 92–303, § 66, eff. July 3, 1992. Amended by Laws 1997, c. 97–102, § 531, eff. July 1, 1997; Laws 1997, c. 97–240, § 12, eff. May 30, 1997; Laws 2001, c. 2001–226, § 3, eff. Jan. 1, 2002; Laws 2006, c. 2006–134, § 2, eff. July 1, 2006; Laws 2006, c. 2006–213, § 68, eff. Oct. 1, 2006.

Cross References

Probate, foreign personal representative, see § 734.101.

655.937. Access to safe-deposit boxes leased in two or more names

(1) Unless specifically provided in the lease or rental agreement to the contrary, if [1] a safe-deposit box is rented or leased in the names of two or more lessees, access to the safe-deposit box will be granted to:

(a) Either or any of such lessees, regardless of whether or not the other lessee or lessees or any of them are living or competent.

(b) Subject to s. 655.933, those persons named in s. 655.933.

(c) Subject to s. 655.935, those persons named in s. 655.935.

(d) Subject to s. 733.6065, the personal representative of the estate of either or any of such lessees who is deceased, or the guardian of the property of either or any of such lessees who is incapacitated.

(2) In all cases described in subsection (1), the signature on the safe-deposit entry or access record, or the receipt or acquittance, in the case of property or documents otherwise held for safekeeping, is a valid and sufficient release and discharge to the lessor for granting access to such safe-deposit box or for the delivery of such property or documents otherwise held for safekeeping.

(3) A lessor may not be held liable for damages or penalty by reason of any access granted or delivery made pursuant to this section.

(4) The right of access by a colessee is separate from the rights and responsibilities of other persons who may be granted access to a safe-deposit box after the death or incapacity of another colessee, and such right of access is not subject to the provisions of s. 655.935, s. 733.6065, or other requirements imposed upon personal representatives, guardians, or other fiduciaries.

(5) After the death of a colessee, the surviving colessee or any other person who is granted access to the safe-deposit box pursuant to this section may make a written inventory of the box, which must be conducted by the person making the request in the presence of one other person as specified in this subsection. Each person present shall verify the contents of the box by signing a copy of the inventory under penalty of perjury.

(a) If the person making the written inventory is a surviving colessee, the other person may be any other person granted access pursuant to this section, an employee of the institution where the box is located, or an attorney licensed in this state.

(b) If the person making the written inventory is not a surviving colessee, the other person may be a surviving colessee, an employee of the institution where the box is located, or an attorney licensed in this state.

Added by Laws 1992, c. 92–303, § 67, eff. July 3, 1992. Amended by Laws 2006, c. 2006–134, § 3, eff. July 1, 2006; Laws 2006, c. 2006–213, § 69, eff. Oct. 1, 2006.

[1] As amended by Laws 2006, c. 2006–213, § 69. The amendment by Laws 2006, c. 2006–134, § 3, used the word "when" rather than "if".

655.938. Adverse claims to contents of safe-deposit box

(1) An adverse claim to the contents of a safe-deposit box, or to property held in safekeeping, is not sufficient to require the lessor to deny access to its lessee unless:

(a) The lessor is directed to do so by a court order issued in an action in which the lessee is served with process and named as a party by a name which identifies the lessee with the name in which the safe-deposit box is leased or the property held; or

(b) The safe-deposit box is leased or the property is held in the name of a lessee with the addition of words indicating that the contents or property are held in a fiduciary capacity, and the adverse claim is supported by a written statement of facts disclosing that it is made by, or on behalf of, a beneficiary and that there is reason to know that the fiduciary will misappropriate the trust property.

(2) A claim is also an adverse claim if one of several lessees claims, contrary to the terms of the lease, an exclusive right of access, or if one or more persons claim a right of access as agents or officers of a lessee to the exclusion of others as agents or officers, or if it is claimed that a lessee is the same person as one using another name.

Added by Laws 1992, c. 92–303, § 68, eff. July 3, 1992.

655.939. Limiting right of access for failure to comply with security procedures

If any individual who has a right of access to a safe-deposit box is unwilling or unable for any reason or cause to comply with any of the lessor's normal requirements or procedures in connection with such access relating to security, safety, or protection, the lessor has the right to limit or deny access to the safe-deposit box by such individual unless all lessees of such safe-deposit box take such action as is necessary to ensure reasonable compliance with such security, safety, or protection requirements or procedures.

Added by Laws 1992, c. 92–303, § 69, eff. July 3, 1992.

655.94. Special remedies for nonpayment of rent

(1) If the rental due on a safe-deposit box has not been paid for 3 months, the lessor may send a notice by certified mail to the last known address of the lessee stating that the safe-deposit box will be opened and its contents stored at the expense of the lessee unless payment of the rental is made within 30 days. If the rental is not paid within 30 days from the mailing of the notice, the box may be opened in the presence of an officer of the lessor and of a notary public. The contents shall be sealed in a package by a notary public who shall write on the outside the name of the lessee and the date of the opening. The notary public shall execute a certificate reciting the name of the lessee, the date of the opening of the box, and a list of its contents. The certificate shall be included in the package, and a copy of the certificate shall be sent by certified mail to the last known address of the lessee. The package shall then be placed in the general vaults of the lessor at a rental not exceeding the rental previously charged for the box. The lessor has a lien on the package and its contents to the extent of any rental due and owing plus the actual, reasonable costs of removing the contents from the safe-deposit box.

(2) If the contents of the safe-deposit box have not been claimed within 1 year after the mailing of the certificate, the lessor may send a further notice to the last known address of the lessee stating that, unless the accumulated charges are paid within 30 days, the contents of the box will be sold at public auction at a specified time and place or, in the case of securities listed on a stock exchange, will be sold upon the exchange on or after a specified date and unsalable items will be destroyed. The time, place, and manner of sale shall also be posted conspicuously on the premises of the lessor and advertised once in a newspaper of general circulation in the community. If the articles are not claimed, they may then be sold in accordance with the notice. The balance of the proceeds, after deducting accumulated charges, including the expenses of advertising and conducting the sale, shall be deposited to the credit of the lessee in

any account maintained by the lessee, or, if none, shall be deemed a deposit account with the financial institution operating the safe-deposit facility, and shall be identified on the books of the financial institution as arising from the sale of contents of a safe-deposit box.

(3) Any documents or writings of a private nature, and having little or no apparent value, need not be offered for sale, but shall be retained, unless claimed by the owner, for the period specified for unclaimed contents, after which they may be destroyed.

Added by Laws 1992, c. 92–303, § 70, eff. July 3, 1992. Amended by Laws 2004, c. 2004–340, § 12, eff. July 1, 2004; Laws 2004, c. 2004–390, § 95, eff. July 1, 2004.

TITLE XL

REAL AND PERSONAL PROPERTY

CHAPTER 689

CONVEYANCES OF LAND AND DECLARATIONS OF TRUST

689.01. How real estate conveyed

No estate or interest of freehold, or for a term of more than 1 year, or any uncertain interest of, in or out of any messuages, lands, tenements or hereditaments shall be created, made,

---

granted, transferred or released in any other manner than by instrument in writing, signed in the presence of two subscribing witnesses by the party creating, making, granting, conveying, transferring or releasing such estate, interest, or term of more than 1 year, or by the party's lawfully authorized agent, unless by will and testament, or other testamentary appointment, duly made according to law; and no estate or interest, either of freehold, or of term of more than 1 year, or any uncertain interest of, in, to, or out of any messuages, lands, tenements or hereditaments, shall be assigned or surrendered unless it be by instrument signed in the presence of two subscribing witnesses by the party so assigning or surrendering, or by the party's lawfully authorized agent, or by the act and operation of law. No seal shall be necessary to give validity to any instrument executed in conformity with this section. Corporations may execute any and all conveyances in accordance with the provisions of this section or ss. 692.01 and 692.02.

Act Nov. 15, 1828, § 1; Rev.St.1892, § 1950; Gen.St.1906, § 2448; Rev.Gen.St.1920, § 3787; Comp.Gen. Laws 1927, § 5660; Laws 1941, c. 20954, § 4. Amended by Laws 1997, c. 97–102, § 751, eff. July 1, 1997; Laws 2008, c. 2008–35, § 2, eff. July 1, 2008.

Cross References

Acknowledgment of instruments, see § 695.03 et seq.
Adverse possession, color of title, see §§ 95.16, 95.18.
Certain conveyances made valid, see § 694.01 et seq.
Clouds on title, removing, see § 65.021 et seq.
Corporations, conveyances by, see § 692.01 et seq.
Dual contracts, prohibition, see § 877.10.
Ejectment, see § 66.011 et seq.
Estates by entireties, see § 689.11.
Fraudulent transfers, see § 726.101 et seq.
Future and life estates, rule in Shelley's case, abolishment, see § 689.17.
Leases of goods, statute of frauds, see § 680.201.
Limitation of actions, deeds and wills on record, see F.S.A. § 95.231.
Marketable record title, when, see § 712.01 et seq.
Married women's interest in real estate, conveyance of, see § 708.08.
Quieting title, see § 65.011.
Record of conveyances of real estate, see § 695.01 et seq.
Sale of goods, statute of frauds, see § 672.201.
Seal, necessity, see § 68.06.
Statute of frauds, see § 725.01 et seq.
Witnesses, lack of, instrument conveying title, quieting title, see § 65.061.

689.02. Form of warranty deed prescribed

(1) Warranty deeds of conveyance to land may be in the following form, viz.:

"This indenture, made this ___ day of ___ A.D.___, between _____, of the County of _____ in the State of _____, party of the first part, and _____, of the County of _____, in the State of ___, party of the second part, witnesseth: That the said party of the first part, for and in consideration of the sum of _____ dollars, to her or him in hand paid by the said party of the second part, the receipt whereof is hereby acknowledged, has granted, bargained and sold to the said party of the second part, her or his heirs and assigns forever, the following described land, to wit:

And the said party of the first part does hereby fully warrant the title to said land, and will defend the same against the lawful claims of all persons whomsoever."

(2) The form for warranty deeds of conveyance to land shall include a blank space for the property appraiser's parcel identification number describing the property conveyed, which number, if available, shall be entered on the deed before it is presented for recording. The failure to include such blank space or the parcel identification number, or the inclusion of an incorrect parcel identification number, does not affect the validity of the conveyance or the recordability of the deed. Such parcel identification number is not a part of the legal description of the property otherwise set forth in the deed and may not be used as a substitute for the legal description of the property being conveyed.

Laws 1891, c. 4038, § 1; Gen.St.1906, § 2449; Rev.Gen.St.1920, § 3788; Comp.Gen.Laws 1927, § 5661; Laws 1987, c. 87–66, § 1; Laws 1988, c. 88–176, § 17; Laws 1989, c. 89–356, § 60. Amended by Laws 1997, c. 97–102, § 752, eff. July 1, 1997; Laws 2013, c. 2013–241, § 1, eff. Oct. 1, 2013.

Cross References

Boundaries, settlement, see Civil Procedure Rule 1.010.
Form of deed by county, see § 125.411.

689.03. Effect of such deed

A conveyance executed substantially in the foregoing form shall be held to be a warranty deed with full common-law covenants, and shall just as effectually bind the grantor, and the grantor's heirs, as if said covenants were specifically set out therein. And this form of conveyance when signed by a married woman shall be held to convey whatever interest in the property conveyed which she may possess.

Laws 1891, c. 4038, § 2; Gen.St.1906, § 2450; Rev.Gen.St.1920, § 3789; Comp.Gen.Laws 1927, § 5662; Laws 1941, c. 20954, § 5. Amended by Laws 1997, c. 97–102, § 753, eff. July 1, 1997.

Cross References

Acknowledgment of deeds, see § 695.03 et seq.

689.04. How executed

Such deeds shall be executed and acknowledged as is now or may hereafter be provided by the law regulating conveyances of realty by deed.

Laws 1891, c. 4038, § 3; Gen.St.1906, § 2451; Rev.Gen.St.1920, § 3790; Comp.Gen.Laws 1927, § 5663.

Cross References

Acknowledgment of instruments, see § 695.03 et seq.

689.045. Conveyances to or by partnership

(1) Any estate in real property may be acquired in the name of a limited partnership. Title so acquired must be conveyed or encumbered in the partnership name. Unless otherwise provided in the certificate of limited partnership, a conveyance or encumbrance of real property held in the partnership name, and any other instrument affecting title to real property in which the partnership has an interest, must be executed in the partnership name by one of the general partners.

(2) Every conveyance to a limited partnership in its name recorded before January 1, 1972, as required by law while the limited partnership was in existence is validated and is deemed to convey the title to the real property described in the conveyance to the partnership named as grantee.

---

(3) When title to real property is held in the name of a limited partnership or a general partnership, one of the general partners may execute and record, in the public records of the county in which such partnership's real property is located, an affidavit stating the names of the general partners then existing and the authority of any general partner to execute a conveyance, encumbrance, or other instrument affecting such partnership's real property. The affidavit shall be conclusive as to the facts therein stated as to purchasers without notice.

Laws 1971, c. 71–9, § 2; Fla.St.1985, § 620.081; Laws 1986, c. 86–263, § 71. Amended by Laws 1995, c. 95–242, § 23, eff. Jan. 1, 1996.

689.05. How declarations of trust proved

All declarations and creations of trust and confidence of or in any messuages, lands, tenements or hereditaments shall be manifested and proved by some writing, signed by the party authorized by law to declare or create such trust or confidence, or by the party's last will and testament, or else they shall be utterly void and of none effect; provided, always, that where any conveyance shall be made of any lands, messuages or tenements by which a trust or confidence shall or may arise or result by the implication or construction of law, or be transferred or extinguished by the act and operation of law, then, and in every such case, such trust or confidence shall be of the like force and effect as the same would have been if this section had not been made, anything herein contained to the contrary in anywise notwithstanding.

Act Nov. 15, 1828, § 2; Rev.St.1892, § 1951; Gen.St.1906, § 2452; Rev.Gen.St.1920, § 3791; Comp.Gen. Laws 1927, § 5664. Amended by Laws 1997, c. 97–102, § 754, eff. July 1, 1997.

Cross References

Powers of trustee, see §§ 736.0703, 736.0816.

689.06. How trust estate conveyed

All grants, conveyances, or assignments of trust or confidence of or in any lands, tenements, or hereditaments, or of any estate or interest therein, shall be by deed signed and delivered, in the presence of two subscribing witnesses, by the party granting, conveying, or assigning, or by the party's attorney or agent thereunto lawfully authorized, or by last will and testament duly made and executed, or else the same shall be void and of no effect.

Act Nov. 15, 1828, § 3; Rev.St.1892, § 1952; Gen.St.1906, § 2453; Rev.Gen.St.1920, § 3792; Comp.Gen. Laws 1927, § 5665; Laws 1980, c. 80–219, § 1. Amended by Laws 1997, c. 97–102, § 755, eff. July 1, 1997.

689.07. "Trustee" or "as trustee" added to name of grantee, transferee, assignee, or mortgagee transfers interest or creates lien as if additional word or words not used

(1) Every deed or conveyance of real estate heretofore or hereafter made or executed in which the words "trustee" or "as trustee" are added to the name of the grantee, and in which no beneficiaries are named, the nature and purposes of the trust, if any, are not set forth, and the trust is not identified by title or date, shall grant and is hereby declared to have granted a fee simple estate with full power and authority in and to the grantee in such deed to sell, convey, and grant and encumber both the legal and beneficial interest in the real estate conveyed, unless a contrary intention shall appear in the deed or conveyance; provided, that there shall not appear of record among the public records of the county in which the real property is situate at the time of recording of such deed or conveyance, a declaration of trust by the grantee so described declaring the purposes of such trust, if any, declaring that the real estate is held other than for the benefit of the grantee.

(2) Every instrument heretofore or hereafter made or executed transferring or assigning an interest in real property in which the words "trustee" or "as trustee" are added to the name of the transferee or assignee, and in which no beneficiaries are named, the nature and purposes of the trust, if any, are not set forth, and the trust is not identified by title or date, shall transfer and assign, and is hereby declared to have transferred and assigned, the interest of the transferor or assign or to the transferee or assignee with full power and authority to transfer, assign, and encumber such interest, unless a contrary intention shall appear in the instrument; provided that there shall not appear of record among the public records of the county in which the real property is situate at the time of the recording of such instrument, a declaration of trust by the assignee or transferee so described declaring the purposes of such trust, if any, or declaring that the interest in real property is held other than for the benefit of the transferee or assignee.

(3) Every mortgage of any interest in real estate or assignment thereof heretofore or hereafter made or executed in which the words "trustee" or "as trustee" are added to the name of the mortgagee or assignee, and in which no beneficiaries are named, the nature and purposes of the trust, if any, are not set forth, and the trust is not identified by title or date, shall vest and is hereby declared to have vested full rights of ownership to such mortgage or assignment and the lien created thereby with full power in such mortgagee or assignee to assign, hypothecate, release, satisfy, or foreclose such mortgage unless a contrary intention shall appear in the mortgage or assignment; provided that there shall not appear of record among the public records of the county in which the property constituting security is situate at the time of recording of such mortgage or assignment, a declaration of trust by such mortgagee or assignee declaring the purposes of such trust, if any, or declaring that such mortgage is held other than for the benefit of the mortgagee or assignee.

(4) Nothing herein contained shall prevent any person from causing any declaration of trust to be recorded before or after the recordation of the instrument evidencing title or ownership of property in a trustee; nor shall this section be construed as preventing any beneficiary under an unrecorded declaration of trust from enforcing the terms thereof against the trustee; provided, however, that any grantee, transferee, assignee, or mortgagee, or person obtaining a release or satisfaction of mortgage from such trustee for value prior to the placing of record of such declaration of trust among the public records of the county in which such real property is situate, shall take such interest or hold such previously mortgaged property free and clear of the claims of the beneficiaries of such declaration of trust and of anyone claiming by, through or under such beneficiaries, and such person need not see to the application of funds furnished to obtain such transfer of interest in property or assignment or release or satisfaction of mortgage thereon.

(5) In all cases in which tangible personal property is or has been sold, transferred, or mortgaged in a transaction in conjunction with and subordinate to the transfer or mortgage of real property, and the personal property so transferred or mortgaged is physically located on and used in conjunction with such real property, the prior provisions of this section are applicable to the transfer or mortgage of such personal property, and, where the prior provisions of this section in fact apply to a transfer or mortgage of personal property, then any transferee or mortgagee of such tangible personal property shall take such personal property free and clear of the claims of the beneficiaries under such declaration of trust (if any), and of the claims of anyone claiming by, through, or under such beneficiaries, and the release or satisfaction of a mortgage on such personal property by such trustee shall release or satisfy such

personal property from the claims of the beneficiaries under such declaration of trust, if any, and from the claims of anyone claiming by, through, or under such beneficiaries.

Laws 1915, c. 6925, § 1; Laws 1919, c. 7838, § 10, subsec. 11; Rev.Gen.St.1920, § 3793; Comp.Gen.Laws 1927, § 5666; Laws 1959, c. 59–251, § 1. Amended by Laws 2004, c. 2004–19, § 1, eff. April 24, 2004.

Retroactivity

Section 2 of Laws 2004, c. 2004–19, provides:

"The amendments to section 689.07, Florida Statutes, provided by this act are intended to clarify existing law and shall apply retroactively."

Cross References

Nature of a mortgage, see § 697.02.
Racketeer Influenced and Corrupt Organization (RICO) Act, see § 895.01 et seq.
Record of conveyances of real estate, see § 695.01 et seq.

689.071. Florida Land Trust Act

(1) **Short title.**—This section may be cited as the "Florida Land Trust Act."

(2) **Definitions.**—As used in this section, the term:

(a) "Beneficial interest" means any interest, vested or contingent and regardless of how small or minimal such interest may be, in a land trust which is held by a beneficiary.

(b) "Beneficiary" means any person or entity having a beneficial interest in a land trust. A trustee may be a beneficiary of the land trust for which such trustee serves as trustee.

(c) "Land trust" means any express written agreement or arrangement by which a use, confidence, or trust is declared of any land, or of any charge upon land, under which the title to real property, including, but not limited to, a leasehold or mortgagee interest, is vested in a trustee by a recorded instrument that confers on the trustee the power and authority prescribed in s. 689.073(1) and under which the trustee has no duties other than the following:

1. The duty to convey, sell, lease, mortgage, or deal with the trust property, or to exercise such other powers concerning the trust property as may be provided in the recorded instrument, in each case as directed by the beneficiaries or by the holder of the power of direction;

2. The duty to sell or dispose of the trust property at the termination of the trust;

3. The duty to perform ministerial and administrative functions delegated to the trustee in the trust agreement or by the beneficiaries or the holder of the power of direction; or

4. The duties required of a trustee under chapter 721, if the trust is a timeshare estate trust complying with s. 721.08(2)(c)4. or a vacation club trust complying with s. 721.53(1)(e). However, the duties of the trustee of a land trust created before June 28, 2013, may exceed the limited duties listed in this paragraph to the extent authorized in subsection (12).

(d) "Power of direction" means the authority of a person, as provided in the trust agreement, to direct the trustee of a land trust to convey property or interests, execute a lease or mortgage, distribute proceeds of a sale or financing, and execute documents incidental to the administration of a land trust.

(e) "Recorded instrument" has the same meaning as provided in s. 689.073(1).

(f) "Trust agreement" means the written agreement governing a land trust or other trust, including any amendments.

(g) "Trust property" means any interest in real property, including, but not limited to, a leasehold or mortgagee interest, conveyed by a recorded instrument to a trustee of a land trust or other trust.

(h) "Trustee" means the person designated in a recorded instrument or trust agreement to hold title to the trust property of a land trust or other trust.

(3) Ownership vests in trustee.—Every recorded instrument transferring any interest in real property to the trustee of a land trust and conferring upon the trustee the power and authority prescribed in s. 689.073(1), whether or not reference is made in the recorded instrument to the beneficiaries of such land trust or to the trust agreement or any separate collateral unrecorded declarations or agreements, is effective to vest, and is hereby declared to have vested, in such trustee both legal and equitable title, and full rights of ownership, over the trust property or interest therein, with full power and authority as granted and provided in the recorded instrument to deal in and with the trust property or interest therein or any part thereof. The recorded instrument does not itself create an entity, regardless of whether the relationship among the beneficiaries and the trustee is deemed to be an entity under other applicable law.

(4) Statute of uses inapplicable.—Section 689.09 and the statute of uses do not execute a land trust or vest the trust property in the beneficiary or beneficiaries of the land trust, notwithstanding any lack of duties on the part of the trustee or the otherwise passive nature of the land trust.

(5) Doctrine of merger inapplicable.—The doctrine of merger does not extinguish a land trust or vest the trust property in the beneficiary or beneficiaries of the land trust, regardless of whether the trustee is the sole beneficiary of the land trust.

(6) Personal property.—In all cases in which the recorded instrument or the trust agreement, as hereinabove provided, contains a provision defining and declaring the interests of beneficiaries of a land trust to be personal property only, such provision is controlling for all purposes when such determination becomes an issue under the laws or in the courts of this state. If no such personal property designation appears in the recorded instrument or in the trust agreement, the interests of the land trust beneficiaries are real property.

(7) Trustee liability.—In addition to any other limitation on personal liability existing pursuant to statute or otherwise, the provisions of ss. 736.08125 and 736.1013 apply to the trustee of a land trust created pursuant to this section.

(8) Land trust beneficiaries.—

(a) Except as provided in this section, the beneficiaries of a land trust are not liable, solely by being beneficiaries, under a judgment, decree, or order of court or in any other manner for a debt, obligation, or liability of the land trust. Any beneficiary acting under the trust agreement of a land trust is not liable to the land trust's trustee or to any other beneficiary for the beneficiary's good faith reliance on the provisions of the trust agreement. A beneficiary's duties and liabilities under a land trust may be expanded or restricted in a trust agreement or beneficiary agreement.

(b) 1. If provided in the recorded instrument, in the trust agreement, or in a beneficiary agreement:

a. A particular beneficiary may own the beneficial interest in a particular portion or parcel of the trust property of a land trust;

b. A particular person may be the holder of the power of direction with respect to the trustee's actions concerning a particular portion or parcel of the trust property of a land trust; and

c. The beneficiaries may own specified proportions or percentages of the beneficial interest in the trust property or in particular portions or parcels of the trust property of a land trust.

2. Multiple beneficiaries may own a beneficial interest in a land trust as tenants in common, joint tenants with right of survivorship, or tenants by the entireties.

(c) If a beneficial interest in a land trust is determined to be personal property as provided in subsection (6), chapter 679 applies to the perfection of any security interest in that beneficial interest. If a beneficial interest in a land trust is determined to be real property as provided in subsection (6), then to perfect a lien or security interest against that beneficial interest, the mortgage, deed of trust, security agreement, or other similar security document must be recorded in the public records of the county that is specified for such security documents in the recorded instrument or in a declaration of trust or memorandum of such declaration of trust recorded in the public records of the same county as the recorded instrument. If no county is so specified for recording such security documents, the proper county for recording such a security document against a beneficiary's interest in any trust property is the county where the trust property is located. The perfection of a lien or security interest in a beneficial interest in a land trust does not affect, attach to, or encumber the legal or equitable title of the trustee in the trust property and does not impair or diminish the authority of the trustee under the recorded instrument, and parties dealing with the trustee are not required to inquire into the terms of the unrecorded trust agreement or any lien or security interest against a beneficial interest in the land trust.

(d) The trustee's legal and equitable title to the trust property of a land trust is separate and distinct from the beneficial interest of a beneficiary in the land trust and in the trust property. A lien, judgment, mortgage, security interest, or other encumbrance attaching to the trustee's legal and equitable title to the trust property of a land trust does not attach to the beneficial interest of any beneficiary; and any lien, judgment, mortgage, security interest, or other encumbrance against a beneficiary or beneficial interest does not attach to the legal or equitable title of the trustee to the trust property held under a land trust, unless the lien, judgment, mortgage, security interest, or other encumbrance by its terms or by operation of other law attaches to both the interest of the trustee and the interest of such beneficiary.

(e) Any subsequent document appearing of record in which a beneficiary of a land trust transfers or encumbers any beneficial interest in the land trust does not transfer or encumber the legal or equitable title of the trustee to the trust property and does not diminish or impair the authority of the trustee under the terms of the recorded instrument. Parties dealing with the trustee of a land trust are not required to inquire into the terms of the unrecorded trust agreement.

(f) The trust agreement for a land trust may provide that one or more persons have the power to direct the trustee to convey property or interests, execute a mortgage, distribute proceeds of a sale or financing, and execute documents incidental to administration of the land trust. The power of direction, unless provided otherwise in the trust agreement of the land trust, is conferred upon the holders of the power for the use and benefit of all holders of any beneficial interest in the land trust. In the absence of a provision in the trust agreement of a land trust to the contrary, the power of direction shall be in accordance with the percentage of individual ownership. In exercising the power of direction, the holders of the power of direction are presumed to act in a fiduciary capacity for the benefit of all holders of any beneficial interest in the land trust, unless otherwise provided in the trust agreement. A beneficial interest in a land trust is indefeasible, and the power of direction may not be exercised so as to alter, amend, revoke, terminate, defeat, or otherwise affect or change the enjoyment of any beneficial interest in a land trust.

(g) A land trust does not fail, and any use relating to the trust property may not be defeated, because beneficiaries are not specified by name in the recorded instrument to the trustee or because duties are not imposed upon the trustee. The power conferred by any recorded instrument on a trustee of a land trust to sell, lease, encumber, or otherwise dispose of property described in the recorded instrument is effective, and a person dealing with the trustee of a land trust is not required to inquire any further into the right of the trustee to act or the disposition of any proceeds.

(h) The principal residence of a beneficiary shall be entitled to the homestead tax exemption even if the homestead is held by a trustee in a land trust, provided the beneficiary qualifies for the homestead exemption under chapter 196.

(i) In a foreclosure against trust property or other litigation affecting the title to trust property of a land trust, the appointment of a guardian ad litem is not necessary to represent the interest of any beneficiary.

(9) Successor trustee.—

(a) If the recorded instrument and the unrecorded trust agreement are silent as to the appointment of a successor trustee of a land trust in the event of the death, incapacity, resignation, or termination due to dissolution of a trustee or if a trustee is unable to serve as trustee of a land trust, one or more persons having the power of direction may appoint a successor trustee or trustees of the land trust by filing a declaration of appointment of a successor trustee or trustees in the public records of the county in which the trust property is located. The declaration must be signed by a beneficiary or beneficiaries of the land trust and by the successor trustee or trustees, must be acknowledged in the manner provided for acknowledgment of deeds, and must contain:

1. The legal description of the trust property.

2. The name and address of the former trustee.

3. The name and address of the successor trustee or trustees.

4. A statement that one or more persons having the power of direction of the land trust appointed the successor trustee or trustees, together with an acceptance of appointment by the successor trustee or trustees.

(b) If the recorded instrument is silent as to the appointment of a successor trustee or trustees of a land trust but an unrecorded trust agreement provides for the appointment of a successor trustee or trustees in the event of the death, incapacity, resignation, or termination due to dissolution of the trustee of a land trust, then upon the appointment of any successor trustee pursuant to the terms of the unrecorded trust agreement, the successor trustee or trustees shall file a declaration of appointment of a successor trustee in the public records of the county in which the trust property is located. The declaration must be signed by both the former trustee and the successor trustee or trustees, must be acknowledged in the manner provided for acknowledgment of deeds, and must contain:

1. The legal description of the trust property.

2. The name and address of the former trustee.

3. The name and address of the successor trustee or trustees.

---

4. A statement of resignation by the former trustee and a statement of acceptance of appointment by the successor trustee or trustees.

5. A statement that the successor trustee or trustees were duly appointed under the terms of the unrecorded trust agreement.

If the appointment of any successor trustee of a land trust is due to the death or incapacity of the former trustee, the declaration need not be signed by the former trustee and a copy of the death certificate or a statement that the former trustee is incapacitated or unable to serve must be attached to or included in the declaration, as applicable.

(c) If the recorded instrument provides for the appointment of any successor trustee of a land trust and any successor trustee is appointed in accordance with the recorded instrument, no additional declarations of appointment of any successor trustee are required under this section.

(d) Each successor trustee appointed with respect to a land trust is fully vested with all the estate, properties, rights, powers, trusts, duties, and obligations of the predecessor trustee, except that any successor trustee of a land trust is not under any duty to inquire into the acts or omissions of a predecessor trustee and is not liable for any act or failure to act of a predecessor trustee. A person dealing with any successor trustee of a land trust pursuant to a declaration filed under this section is not obligated to inquire into or ascertain the authority of the successor trustee to act within or exercise the powers granted under the recorded instruments or any unrecorded trust agreement.

(e) A trust agreement may provide that the trustee of a land trust, when directed to do so by the holder of the power of direction or by the beneficiaries of the land trust or legal representatives of the beneficiaries, may convey the trust property directly to another trustee on behalf of the beneficiaries or to another representative named in such directive.

(10) Trustee as creditor.—

(a) If a debt is secured by a security interest or mortgage against a beneficial interest in a land trust or by a mortgage on trust property of a land trust, the validity or enforceability of the debt, security interest, or mortgage and the rights, remedies, powers, and duties of the creditor with respect to the debt or the security are not affected by the fact that the creditor and the trustee are the same person, and the creditor may extend credit, obtain any necessary security interest or mortgage, and acquire and deal with the property comprising the security as though the creditor were not the trustee.

(b) A trustee of a land trust does not breach a fiduciary duty to the beneficiaries, and it is not evidence of a breach of any fiduciary duty owed by the trustee to the beneficiaries for a trustee to be or become a secured or unsecured creditor of the land trust, the beneficiary of the land trust, or a third party whose debt to such creditor is guaranteed by a beneficiary of the land trust.

(11) Notices to trustee.—Any notice required to be given to a trustee of a land trust regarding trust property by a person who is not a party to the trust agreement must identify the trust property to which the notice pertains or include the name and date of the land trust to which the notice pertains, if such information is shown on the recorded instrument for such trust property.

(12) Determination of applicable law.—Except as otherwise provided in this section, chapter 736 does not apply to a land trust governed by this section.

(a) A trust is not a land trust governed by this section if there is no recorded instrument that confers on the trustee the power and authority prescribed in s. 689.073(1).

(b) For a trust created before June 28, 2013:

1. The trust is a land trust governed by this section if a recorded instrument confers on the trustee the power and authority described in s. 689.073(1) and if:

a. The recorded instrument or the trust agreement expressly provides that the trust is a land trust; or

b. The intent of the parties that the trust be a land trust is discerned from the trust agreement or the recorded instrument,

without regard to whether the trustee's duties under the trust agreement are greater than those limited duties described in paragraph (2)(c).

2. The trust is not a land trust governed by this section if:

a. The recorded instrument or the trust agreement expressly provides that the trust is to be governed by chapter 736, or by any predecessor trust code or other trust law other than this section; or

b. The intent of the parties that the trust be governed by chapter 736, or by any predecessor trust code or other trust law other than this section, is discerned from the trust agreement or the recorded instrument,

without regard to whether the trustee's duties under the trust agreement are greater than those limited duties listed in paragraph (2)(c), and without consideration of any references in the trust agreement to provisions of chapter 736 made applicable to the trust by chapter 721, if the trust is a timeshare estate trust complying with s. 721.08(2)(c)4. or a vacation club trust complying with s. 721.53(1)(e).

3. Solely for the purpose of determining the law governing a trust under subparagraph 1. or subparagraph 2., the determination shall be made without consideration of any amendment to the trust agreement made on or after June 28, 2013, except as provided in paragraph (d).

4. If the determination of whether a trust is a land trust governed by this section cannot be made under either subparagraph 1. or subparagraph 2., the determination shall be made under paragraph (c) as if the trust was created on or after June 28, 2013.

(c) If a recorded instrument confers on the trustee the power and authority described in s. 689.073(1) and the trust was created on or after June 28, 2013, the trust shall be determined to be a land trust governed by this section only if the trustee's duties under the trust agreement, including any amendment made on or after such date, are no greater than those limited duties described in paragraph (2)(c).

(d) If the trust agreement for a land trust created before June 28, 2013, is amended on or after such date to add to or increase the duties of the trustee beyond the duties provided in the trust agreement as of June 28, 2013, the trust shall remain a land trust governed by this section only if the additional or increased duties of the trustee implemented by the amendment are no greater than those limited duties described in paragraph (2)(c).

(13) Uniform Commercial Code transition rule.—This section does not render ineffective any effective Uniform Commercial Code financing statement filed before July 1, 2014, to perfect a security interest in a beneficial interest in a land trust that is determined to be real property as provided in subsection (6), but such a financing statement ceases to be effective at the earlier of July 1, 2019, or the time the financing statement would have ceased to be effective under the law of the jurisdiction in which it is filed, and the filing of a Uniform Commercial Code continuation statement after July 1, 2014, does not continue the effectiveness of such a financing statement. The recording of a mortgage, deed of trust, security agreement, or other similar security document against such a beneficial interest that is real property in the public records specified in paragraph (8)(c) continues the effectiveness and priority of a financing statement filed against such a beneficial interest before July 1, 2014, if:

(a) The recording of the security document in that county is effective to perfect a lien on such beneficial interest under paragraph (8)(c);

(b) The recorded security document identifies a financing statement filed before July 1, 2014, by indicating the office in which the financing statement was filed and providing the dates of filing and the file numbers, if any, of the financing statement and of the most recent continuation statement filed with respect to the financing statement; and

(c) The recorded security document indicates that such financing statement filed before July 1, 2014, remains effective.

If no original security document bearing the debtor's signature is readily available for recording in the public records, a secured party may proceed under this subsection with such financing statement filed before July 1, 2014, by recording a copy of a security document verified by the secured party as being a true and correct copy of an original authenticated by the debtor. This subsection does not apply to the perfection of a security interest in any beneficial interest in a land trust that is determined to be personal property under subsection (6).

(14) Remedial act.—This act is remedial in nature and shall be given a liberal interpretation to effectuate the intent and purposes hereinabove expressed.

(15) Exclusion.—This act does not apply to any deed, mortgage, or other instrument to which s. 689.07 applies.

Laws 1963, c. 63–468, §§ 1 to 6; Laws 1984, c. 84–31, § 1. Amended by Laws 2002, c. 2002–233, § 2, eff. May 6, 2002; Laws 2006, c. 2006–217, § 21, eff. July 1, 2007; Laws 2006, c. 2006–274, § 1, eff. Oct. 1, 2006; Laws 2007, c. 2007–153, § 7, eff. July 1, 2007; Laws 2013, c. 2013–240, §§ 1, 2, eff. June 28, 2013.

Cross References

Abolishment of dower and curtesy, see § 732.111.
Florida Trust Code, scope, see F.S.A. § 736.0102.
Racketeer Influenced and Corrupt Organization (RICO) Act, see § 895.01 et seq.

689.072. Real estate interests transferred to or by a custodian or trustee of an individual retirement account or qualified plan

(1)(a) A conveyance, deed, mortgage, lease assignment, or other recorded instrument that transfers an interest in real property in this state, including a leasehold or mortgagee interest, to a person who is qualified to act as a custodian or trustee for an individual retirement account under 26 U.S.C. s. 408(a)(2), as amended, in which instrument the transferee is designated "custodian," "as custodian," "trustee," or "as trustee" and the account owner or beneficiary of the custodianship in the individual retirement account is named, creates custodial property and transfers title to the custodian or trustee when an interest in real property is recorded in the name of the custodian or trustee, followed by the words "as custodian or trustee for the benefit of __(name of individual retirement account owner or beneficiary)__ individual retirement account."

(b) This section also applies to a qualified stock bonus, pension, or profit-sharing plan created under 26 U.S.C. s. 401(a), as amended, in which instrument a person is designated "custodian," "as custodian," "trustee," or "as trustee" and the plan, plan participant, or plan beneficiary of the custodianship in the plan also creates custodial property and transfers title to the custodian or trustee when an interest in real property is recorded in the name of the custodian or trustee, followed by the words "as custodian, or trustee of the ___(name of plan)___ for the benefit of ___(name of plan participant or beneficiary)___."

(2) A transfer to a custodian or trustee of an individual retirement account or qualified plan pursuant to this section incorporates the provisions of this section into the disposition and grants to the custodian or trustee the power to protect, conserve, sell, lease, encumber, or otherwise manage and dispose of the real property described in the recorded instrument without joinder of the named individual retirement account owner, plan participant, or beneficiary, except as provided in subsection (5).

(3) A person dealing with the custodian or trustee does not have a duty to inquire as to the qualifications of the custodian or trustee and may rely on the powers of the custodian or trustee for the custodial property created under this section regardless of whether such powers are specified in the recorded instrument. A grantee, mortgagee, lessee, transferee, assignee, or person obtaining a satisfaction or release or otherwise dealing with the custodian or trustee regarding such custodial property is not required to inquire into:

(a) The identification or status of any named individual retirement account owner, plan participant, or beneficiary of the individual retirement account or qualified plan or his or her heirs or assigns to whom a custodian or trustee may be accountable under the terms of the individual retirement account agreement or qualified plan document;

(b) The authority of the custodian or trustee to act within and exercise the powers granted under the individual retirement account agreement or qualified plan document;

(c) The adequacy or disposition or any consideration provided to the custodian or trustee in connection with any interest acquired from such custodian or trustee; or

(d) Any provision of an individual retirement account agreement or qualified plan document.

(4) A person dealing with the custodian or trustee under the recorded instrument takes any interest transferred by such custodian or trustee, within the authority provided under this section, free of claims of the named owner, plan participant, or beneficiary of the individual retirement account or qualified plan or of anyone claiming by, through, or under such owner, plan participant, or beneficiary.

(5) If notice of the revocation or termination of the individual retirement account agreement, qualified plan, or custodianship established under such individual retirement account agreement or qualified plan is recorded, any disposition or encumbrance of the custodial property must be by an instrument executed by the custodian or trustee or the successor and the respective owner, plan participant, or beneficiary of the individual retirement account or qualified plan.

(6) In dealing with custodial property created under this section, a custodian or trustee shall observe the standard of care of a prudent person dealing with property of another person. This section does not relieve the custodian or trustee from liability for breach of the individual retirement account agreement, custodial agreement, or qualified plan document.

(7) A provision of the recorded instrument that defines and declares the interest of the owner, plan participant, or beneficiary of the individual retirement account or qualified plan to be personal property controls only if a determination becomes an issue in any legal proceeding.

(8) As used in this section, the term "beneficiary" applies only when the individual retirement account owner or qualified plan participant is deceased.

(9)(a) This section does not apply to any deed, mortgage, or instrument to which s. 689.071 applies.

(b) Section 689.09 does not apply to transfers of real property interests to a custodian or trustee under this section.

(10) This section is remedial and shall be liberally construed to effectively carry out its purposes.

Added by Laws 2006, c. 2006–147, § 1, eff. July 1, 2006.

689.073. Powers conferred on trustee in recorded instrument

(1) **Ownership vests in trustee.**—Every conveyance, deed, mortgage, lease assignment, or other instrument heretofore or hereafter made, hereinafter referred to as the "recorded instrument," transferring any interest in real property, including, but not limited to, a leasehold or mortgagee interest, to any person or any corporation, bank, trust company, or other entity duly formed under the laws of its state of qualification, which recorded instrument designates the person, corporation, bank, trust company, or other entity "trustee" or "as trustee" and confers on the trustee the power and authority to protect, to conserve, to sell, to lease, to encumber, or otherwise to manage and dispose of the real property described in the recorded instrument, is effective to vest, and is declared to have vested, in such trustee full power and authority as granted and provided in the recorded instrument to deal in and with such property, or interest therein or any part thereof, held in trust under the recorded instrument.

(2) **No duty to inquire.**—Any grantee, mortgagee, lessee, transferee, assignee, or person obtaining satisfactions or releases or otherwise in any way dealing with the trustee with respect to the real property or any interest in such property held in trust under the recorded instrument, as hereinabove provided for, is not obligated to inquire into the identification or status of any named or unnamed beneficiaries, or their heirs or assigns to whom a trustee may be accountable under the terms of the recorded instrument, or under any unrecorded separate declarations or agreements collateral to the recorded instrument, whether or not such declarations or agreements are referred to therein; or to inquire into or ascertain the authority of such trustee to act within and exercise the powers granted under the recorded instrument; or to inquire into the adequacy or disposition of any consideration, if any is paid or delivered to such trustee in connection with any interest so acquired from such trustee; or to inquire into any of the provisions of any such unrecorded declarations or agreements.

(3) **Beneficiary claims.**—All persons dealing with the trustee under the recorded instrument as hereinabove provided take any interest transferred by the trustee thereunder, within the power and authority as granted and provided therein, free and clear of the claims of all the named or unnamed beneficiaries of such trust, and of any unrecorded declarations or agreements collateral thereto whether referred to in the recorded instrument or not, and of anyone claiming by, through, or under such beneficiaries. However, this section does not prevent a beneficiary of any such unrecorded collateral declarations or agreements from enforcing the terms thereof against the trustee.

(4) **Exclusion.**—This section does not apply to any deed, mortgage, or other instrument to which s. 689.07 applies.

(5) **Applicability.**—The section applies without regard to whether any reference is made in the recorded instrument to the beneficiaries of such trust or to any separate collateral unrecorded declarations or agreements, without regard to the provisions of any unrecorded trust agreement or declaration of trust, and without regard to whether the trust is governed by s. 689.071 or chapter 736. This section applies both to recorded instruments that are recorded after June 28, 2013, and to recorded instruments that were previously recorded and governed by similar

provisions contained in s. 689.071(3), Florida Statutes 2012, and any such recorded instrument purporting to confer power and authority on a trustee under such provisions of s. 689.071(3), Florida Statutes 2012, is valid and has the effect of vesting full power and authority in such trustee as provided in this section.

Laws 1963, c. 63–468, §§ 2, 3; Laws 1984, c. 84–31, § 1. Amended by Laws 2002, c. 2002–233, § 2, eff. May 6, 2002; Laws 2006, c. 2006–217, § 21, eff. July 1, 2007; Laws 2006, c. 2006–274, § 1, eff. Oct. 1, 2006; Laws 2007, c. 2007–153, § 7, eff. July 1, 2007. Renumbered from 689.071(4), (5) and amended Laws 2013, c. 2013–240, § 1, eff. June 28, 2013.

689.075. Inter vivos trusts; powers retained by settlor

(1) A trust which is otherwise valid and which complies with s. 736.0403, including, but not limited to, a trust the principal of which is composed of real property, intangible personal property, tangible personal property, the possible expectancy of receiving as a named beneficiary death benefits as described in s. 733.808, or any combination thereof, and which has been created by a written instrument shall not be held invalid or an attempted testamentary disposition for any one or more of the following reasons:

(a) Because the settlor or another person or both possess the power to revoke, amend, alter, or modify the trust in whole or in part;

(b) Because the settlor or another person or both possess the power to appoint by deed or will the persons and organizations to whom the income shall be paid or the principal distributed;

(c) Because the settlor or another person or both possess the power to add to, or withdraw from, the trust all or any part of the principal or income at one time or at different times;

(d) Because the settlor or another person or both possess the power to remove the trustee or trustees and appoint a successor trustee or trustees;

(e) Because the settlor or another person or both possess the power to control the trustee or trustees in the administration of the trust;

(f) Because the settlor has retained the right to receive all or part of the income of the trust during her or his life or for any part thereof; or

(g) Because the settlor is, at the time of the execution of the instrument, or thereafter becomes, sole trustee.

(2) Nothing contained herein shall affect the validity of those accounts, including but not limited to bank accounts, share accounts, deposits, certificates of deposit, savings certificates, and other similar arrangements, heretofore or hereafter established at any bank, savings and loan association, or credit union by one or more persons, in trust for one or more other persons, which arrangements are, by their terms, revocable by the person making the same until her or his death or incompetency.

(3) The fact that any one or more of the powers specified in subsection (1) are in fact exercised once, or more than once, shall not affect the validity of the trust or its nontestamentary character.

(4) This section shall be applicable to trusts executed before or after July 1, 1969, by persons who are living on or after said date.

(5) The amendment of this section, by chapter 75–74, Laws of Florida, is intended to clarify the legislative intent of this section at the time of its original enactment that it apply to all otherwise valid trusts which are created by written instrument and which are not expressly excluded by the terms of this section and that no such trust shall be declared invalid for any of

the reasons stated in subsections (1) and (3) regardless of whether the trust involves or relates to an interest in real property.

Laws 1969, c. 69–192, §§ 1, 2; Laws 1969, Ex. Sess., c. 69–1747, § 1; Laws 1971, c. 71–126, §§ 1, 2; Laws 1973, c. 73–333, § 169; Laws 1974, c. 74–78, § 1; Laws 1975, c. 75–74, §§ 1, 2. Amended by Laws 1995, c. 95–401, § 5, eff. July 1, 1995; Laws 1997, c. 97–102, § 756, eff. July 1, 1997; Laws 2006, c. 2006–217, § 22, eff. July 1, 2007.

689.08. Fines and common recoveries

Conveyance by fine or by common recovery shall never be used in this state.

Act Feb. 4, 1835, § 2; Rev.St.1892, § 1953; Gen.St.1906, § 2454; Rev.Gen.St.1920, § 3794; Comp.Gen. Laws 1927, § 5667.

689.09. Deeds under statute of uses

By deed of bargain and sale, or by deed of lease and release, or of covenant to stand seized to the use of any other person, or by deed operating by way of covenant to stand seized to the use of another person, of or in any lands or tenements in this state, the possession of the bargainor, releasor or covenantor shall be deemed and adjudged to be transferred to the bargainee, releasee or person entitled to the use as perfectly as if such bargainee, releasee or person entitled to the use had been enfeoffed by livery of seizin of the land conveyed by such deed of bargain and sale, release or covenant to stand seized; provided, that livery of seizin can be lawfully made of the lands or tenements at the time of the execution of the said deeds or any of them.

Act Nov. 15, 1828, § 12; Rev.St.1892, § 1954; Gen.St.1906, § 2455; Rev.Gen.St.1920, § 3795; Comp. Gen.Laws 1927, § 5668.

689.10. Words of limitation and the words "fee simple" dispensed with

Where any real estate has heretofore been conveyed or granted or shall hereafter be conveyed or granted without there being used in the said deed or conveyance or grant any words of limitation, such as heirs or successors, or similar words, such conveyance or grant, whether heretofore made or hereafter made, shall be construed to vest the fee simple title or other whole estate or interest which the grantor had power to dispose of at that time in the real estate conveyed or granted, unless a contrary intention shall appear in the deed, conveyance or grant.

Laws 1903, c. 5145, § 1; Gen.St.1906, § 2456; Rev.Gen.St.1920, § 3796; Laws 1925, c. 10170, § 1; Comp.Gen.Laws 1927, § 5669.

689.11. Conveyances between husband and wife direct; homestead

(1) A conveyance of real estate, including homestead, made by one spouse to the other shall convey the legal title to the grantee spouse in all cases in which it would be effectual if the parties were not married, and the grantee need not execute the conveyance. An estate by the entirety may be created by the action of the spouse holding title:

(a) Conveying to the other by a deed in which the purpose to create the estate is stated; or

(b) Conveying to both spouses.

(2) All deeds heretofore made by a husband direct to his wife or by a wife direct to her husband are hereby validated and made as effectual to convey the title as they would have been were the parties not married;

(3) Provided, that nothing herein shall be construed as validating any deed made for the purpose, or that operates to defraud any creditor or to avoid payment of any legal debt or claim; and

(4) Provided further that this section shall not apply to any conveyance heretofore made, the validity of which shall be contested by suit commenced within 1 year of the effective date of this law.

Laws 1903, c. 5147, § 1; Gen.St.1906, § 2457; Rev.Gen.St.1920, § 3797; Comp.Gen.Laws 1927, § 5670; Laws 1941, c. 20954, § 6; Laws 1947, c. 23964, § 1; Laws 1971, c. 71–54, § 1.

Cross References

Fraudulent transfers, see § 726.101 et seq.
Homestead and exemptions, see Const. Art. 10, § 4.
Married women's property, see § 708.08 et seq.; Const. Art. 10, § 5.
Quieting title, property conveyed without joining wife, see § 65.071.
Sale of property rights by guardian, see § 744.457.

689.111. Conveyances of homestead; power of attorney

(1) A deed or mortgage of homestead realty owned by an unmarried person may be executed by virtue of a power of attorney executed in the same manner as a deed.

(2) A deed or mortgage of homestead realty owned by a married person, or owned as an estate by the entirety, may be executed by virtue of a power of attorney executed solely by one spouse to the other, or solely by one spouse or both spouses to a third party, provided the power of attorney is executed in the same manner as a deed. Nothing in this section shall be construed as dispensing with the requirement that husband and wife join in the conveyance or mortgage of homestead realty, but the joinder may be accomplished through the exercise of a power of attorney.

Laws 1971, c. 71–27, § 1.

689.115. Estate by the entirety in mortgage made or assigned to husband and wife

Any mortgage encumbering real property, or any assignment of a mortgage encumbering real property, made to two persons who are husband and wife, heretofore or hereafter made, creates an estate by the entirety in such mortgage and the obligation secured thereby unless a contrary intention appears in such mortgage or assignment.

Laws 1986, c. 86–29, § 1; Laws 1991, c. 91–110, § 21.

689.12. How state lands conveyed for educational purposes

(1) The title to all lands granted to or held by the state for educational purposes shall be conveyed by deed executed by the members of the State Board of Education, with an impression of the seal of the Board of Trustees of the Internal Improvement Trust Fund of the state thereon and when so impressed by this seal deeds shall be entitled to be recorded in the public records and to be received in evidence in all courts and judicial proceedings.

(2) Lands held for any tuberculosis hospital and declared to be surplus to the needs of such hospital may be conveyed to the district school board in which said lands are located for educational purposes.

Laws 1901, c. 4999, § 1; Gen.St.1906, § 2458; Rev.Gen.St.1920, § 3798; Comp.Gen.Laws 1927, § 5671; Laws 1967, c. 67–191, §§ 1, 2; Laws 1969, c. 69–106, §§ 27, 35; Laws 1969, c. 69–300, § 1.

Cross References

Seal of department of agriculture and consumer services, see § 570.031.

689.13. Rule against perpetuities not applicable to dispositions of property for private cemeteries, etc.

No disposition of property, or the income thereof, hereafter made for the maintenance or care of any public or private burying ground, churchyard, or other place for the burial of the dead, or any portion thereof, or grave therein, or monument or other erection in or about the same, shall fail by reason of such disposition having been made in perpetuity; but such disposition shall be held to be made for a charitable purpose or purposes.

Laws 1931, c. 14655, § 1; Comp.Gen.Laws Supp.1936, § 5671(1).

Cross References

Cemeteries and grave space defined, see § 497.005.

689.14. Entailed estates

No property, real or personal, shall be entailed in this state. Any instrument purporting to create an estate tail, express or implied, shall be deemed to create an estate for life in the first taker with remainder per stirpes to the lineal descendants of the first taker in being at the time of her or his death. If the remainder fails for want of such remainderman, then it shall vest in any other remaindermen designated in such instrument, or, if there is no such designation, then it shall revert to the original donor or to her or his heirs.

Act Nov. 17, 1829, § 20; Rev.St.1892, § 1818; Gen.St.1906, § 2293; Rev.Gen.St.1920, § 3616; Comp. Gen.Laws 1927, § 5481; Laws 1941, c. 20954, § 2; Laws 1945, c. 23126, § 1. Amended by Laws 1997, c. 97–102, § 757, eff. July 1, 1997.

Cross References

Abolition of rule in Shelley's case, see § 689.17.

689.15. Estates by survivorship

The doctrine of the right of survivorship in cases of real estate and personal property held by joint tenants shall not prevail in this state; that is to say, except in cases of estates by entirety, a devise, transfer or conveyance heretofore or hereafter made to two or more shall create a tenancy in common, unless the instrument creating the estate shall expressly provide for the right of survivorship; and in cases of estates by entirety, the tenants, upon dissolution of marriage, shall become tenants in common.

Act Nov. 17, 1829, § 20; Rev.St.1892, § 1819; Gen.St.1906, § 2294; Rev.Gen.St.1920, § 3617; Comp. Gen.Laws 1927, § 5482; Laws 1941, c. 20954, § 3; Laws 1973, c. 73–300, § 1.

Cross References

Estates by entireties, creation, see § 689.11.
Married women's agreements with husband, see § 708.09.
Married women's property, effect on estate by entireties, see § 708.10.
Uniform Simultaneous Death Act, see § 732.601.

689.17. Rule in Shelley's Case abolished

The rule in Shelley's Case is hereby abolished. Any instrument purporting to create an estate for life in a person with remainder to her or his heirs, lawful heirs, heirs of her or his body or to her or his heirs described by words of similar import, shall be deemed to create an estate for life with remainder per stirpes to the life tenant's lineal descendants in being at the time said life estate commences, but said remainder shall be subject to open and to take in per stirpes other lineal descendants of the life tenant who come into being during the continuance of said life estate.

Laws 1945, c. 23126, § 2. Amended by Laws 1997, c. 97–102, § 758, eff. July 1, 1997.

Cross References

Order of succession, see § 732.103.
Per stirpes, inheritance by, see § 732.104.

689.175. Worthier title doctrine abolished

The doctrine of worthier title is abolished as a rule of law and as a rule of construction. Language in a governing instrument describing the beneficiaries of a disposition as the transferor's "heirs," "heirs at law," "next of kin," "distributees," "relatives," or "family," or language of similar import, does not create or presumptively create a reversionary interest in the transferor.

Added by Laws 2006, c. 2006–217, § 23, eff. July 1, 2007.

689.18. Reverter or forfeiture provisions, limitations; exceptions

(1) It is hereby declared by the Legislature of the state that reverter or forfeiture provisions of unlimited duration in the conveyance of real estate or any interest therein in the state constitute an unreasonable restraint on alienation and are contrary to the public policy of the state.

(2) All reverter or forfeiture provisions of unlimited duration embodied in any plat or deed executed more than 21 years prior to the passage of this law conveying real estate or any interest therein in the state, be and the same are hereby canceled and annulled and declared to be of no further force and effect.

(3) All reverter provisions in any conveyance of real estate or any interest therein in the state, now in force, shall cease and terminate and become null, void, and unenforceable 21 years from the date of the conveyance embodying such reverter or forfeiture provision.

(4) No reverter or forfeiture provision contained in any deed conveying real estate or any interest therein in the state, executed on and after July 1, 1951, shall be valid and binding more than 21 years from the date of such deed, and upon the expiration of such period of 21 years, the reverter or forfeiture provision shall become null, void, and unenforceable.

(5) Any and all conveyances of real property in this state heretofore or hereafter made to any governmental, educational, literary, scientific, religious, public utility, public transportation, charitable or nonprofit corporation or association are hereby excepted from the provisions of this section.

(6) Any holder of a possibility of reverter who claims title to any real property in the state, or any interest therein by reason of a reversion or forfeiture under the terms or provisions of any deed heretofore executed and delivered containing such reverter or forfeiture provision shall have 1 year from July 1, 1951, to institute suit in a court of competent jurisdiction in this state to establish or enforce such right, and failure to institute such action within said time shall be conclusive evidence of the abandonment of any such right, title, or interest, and all right of forfeiture or reversion shall thereupon cease and determine, and become null, void, and unenforceable.

(7) This section shall not vary, alter, or terminate the restrictions placed upon said real estate, contained either in restrictive covenants or reverter or forfeiture clauses, and all said restrictions may be enforced and violations thereof restrained by a court of competent jurisdiction whenever any one of said restrictions or conditions shall be violated, or threat to violate the same be made by owners or parties in possession or control of said real estate, by an injunction which may be issued upon petition of any person adversely affected, mandatorily requiring the abatement of such violations or threatened violation and restraining any future violation of said restrictions and conditions.

Laws 1951, c. 26927, §§ 1 to 7; Laws 1955, c. 29615, § 7; Laws 1977, c. 77–104, § 218.

689.19. Variances of names in recorded instruments

(1) The word "instrument" as used in this section shall be construed to mean and include not only instruments voluntarily executed but also papers filed or issued in or in connection with actions and other proceedings in court and orders, judgments and decrees entered therein and transcripts of such judgments and proceedings in foreclosure of mortgage or other liens.

(2) Variances between any two instruments affecting the title to the same real property both of which shall have been spread on the record for the period of more than 10 years among the public records of the county in which such real property is situated, with respect to the names of persons named in the respective instruments or in acknowledgments thereto arising from the full Christian name appearing in one and only the initial letter of that Christian name appearing in the other or from a full middle name appearing in one and only the initial letter of that middle name appearing in the other or from the initial letter of a middle name appearing in one and not appearing in the other, irrespective of which one of the two instruments in which any such variance occurred was prior in point of time to the other and irrespective of whether the instruments were executed or originated before or after August 5, 1953, shall not destroy or impair the presumption that the person so named in one of said instruments was the same person as the one so named in the other of said instruments which would exist if the names in the two instruments were identical; and, in spite of any such variance, the person so named in one of said instruments shall be presumed to be the same person as the one so named in the other until such time as the contrary appears and, until such time, either or both of such instruments or the record thereof or certified copy or copies of the record thereof shall be admissible in evidence in the same manner as though the names in the two instruments were identical.

Laws 1953, c. 28208, § 1.

Cross References

Marketable record title, see § 712.01 et seq.
Recordation of conveyances, see § 695.01 et seq.

689.20. Limitation on use of word "minerals"

Whenever the word "minerals" is hereafter used in any deed, lease, or other contract in writing, said word or term shall not include any of the following: topsoil, muck, peat, humus, sand, and common clay, unless expressly provided in said deed, lease, or other contract in writing.

Laws 1959, c. 59–375, § 1.

Cross References

Assessment of oil, mineral, and other subsurface rights, see § 193.481.
Exploration for minerals by surface owner, see § 715.06.

689.225. Statutory rule against perpetuities

(1) Short title.—This section may be cited as the "Florida Uniform Statutory Rule Against Perpetuities."

(2) Statement of the rule.—

(a) A nonvested property interest in real or personal property is invalid unless:

1. When the interest is created, it is certain to vest or terminate no later than 21 years after the death of an individual then alive; or

2. The interest either vests or terminates within 90 years after its creation.

(b) A general power of appointment not presently exercisable because of a condition precedent is invalid unless:

1. When the power is created, the condition precedent is certain to be satisfied or become impossible to satisfy no later than 21 years after the death of an individual then alive; or

2. The condition precedent either is satisfied or becomes impossible to satisfy within 90 years after its creation.

(c) A nongeneral power of appointment or a general testamentary power of appointment is invalid unless:

1. When the power is created, it is certain to be irrevocably exercised or otherwise to terminate no later than 21 years after the death of an individual then alive; or

2. The power is irrevocably exercised or otherwise terminates within 90 years after its creation.

(d) In determining whether a nonvested property interest or a power of appointment is valid under subparagraph (a)1., subparagraph (b)1., or subparagraph (c)1., the possibility that a child will be born to an individual after the individual's death is disregarded.

(e) If, in measuring a period from the creation of a trust or other property arrangement, language in a governing instrument (i) seeks to disallow the vesting or termination of any interest or trust beyond, (ii) seeks to postpone the vesting or termination of any interest or trust until, or (iii) seeks to operate in effect in any similar fashion upon, the later of:

1. The expiration of a period of time not exceeding 21 years after the death of a specified life or the survivor of specified lives, or upon the death of a specified life or the death of the survivor of specified lives in being at the creation of the trust or other property arrangement, or

2. The expiration of a period of time that exceeds or might exceed 21 years after the death of the survivor of lives in being at the creation of the trust or other property arrangement,

that language is inoperative to the extent it produces a period of time that exceeds 21 years after the death of the survivor of the specified lives.

(f) As to any trust created after December 31, 2000, this section shall apply to a nonvested property interest or power of appointment contained in a trust by substituting 360 years in place of "90 years" in each place such term appears in this section unless the terms of the trust require that all beneficial interests in the trust vest or terminate within a lesser period.

(3) When nonvested property interest or power of appointment created.—

(a) Except as provided in paragraphs (b), (d), and (e) of this subsection and in paragraph (a) of subsection (6), the time of creation of a nonvested property interest or a power of appointment is determined under general principles of property law.

(b) For purposes of this section, if there is a person who alone can exercise a power created by a governing instrument to become the unqualified beneficial owner of a nonvested property interest or a property interest subject to a power of appointment described in paragraph (b) or paragraph (c) of subsection (2), the nonvested property interest or power of appointment is created when the power to become the unqualified beneficial owner terminates.

(c) For purposes of this section, a joint power with respect to community property or to marital property under the Uniform Marital Property Act held by individuals married to each other is a power exercisable by one person alone.

(d) For purposes of this section, a nonvested property interest or a power of appointment arising from a transfer of property to a previously funded trust or other existing property arrangement is created when the nonvested property interest or power of appointment in the original contribution was created.

(e) For purposes of this section, if a nongeneral or testamentary power of appointment is exercised to create another nongeneral or testamentary power of appointment, every nonvested property interest or power of appointment created through the exercise of such other nongeneral or testamentary power is considered to have been created at the time of the creation of the first nongeneral or testamentary power of appointment.

(4) Reformation.—Upon the petition of an interested person, a court shall reform a disposition in the manner that most closely approximates the transferor's manifested plan of distribution and is within the 90 years allowed by subparagraph (2)(a)2., subparagraph (2)(b)2., or subparagraph (2)(c)2. if:

(a) A nonvested property interest or a power of appointment becomes invalid under subsection (2);

(b) A class gift is not but might become invalid under subsection (2) and the time has arrived when the share of any class member is to take effect in possession or enjoyment; or

(c) A nonvested property interest that is not validated by subparagraph (2)(a)1. can vest but not within 90 years after its creation.

(5) Exclusions from statutory rule against perpetuities.—Subsection (2) does not apply to:

(a) A nonvested property interest or a power of appointment arising out of a nondonative transfer, except a nonvested property interest or a power of appointment arising out of:

1.   A premarital or postmarital agreement;

2.   A separation or divorce settlement;

3.   A spouse's election;

4.   A similar arrangement arising out of a prospective, existing, or previous marital relationship between the parties;

5.   A contract to make or not to revoke a will or trust;

6.   A contract to exercise or not to exercise a power of appointment;

7.   A transfer in satisfaction of a duty of support; or

8.   A reciprocal transfer;

(b) A fiduciary's power relating to the administration or management of assets, including the power of a fiduciary to sell, lease, or mortgage property, and the power of a fiduciary to determine principal and income;

(c) A power to appoint a fiduciary;

(d) A discretionary power of a trustee to distribute principal before termination of a trust to a beneficiary having an indefeasibly vested interest in the income and principal;

(e) A nonvested property interest held by a charity, government, or governmental agency or subdivision, if the nonvested property interest is preceded by an interest held by another charity, government, or governmental agency or subdivision;

(f) A nonvested property interest in, or a power of appointment with respect to, a trust or other property arrangement forming part of a pension, profit-sharing, stock bonus, health, disability, death benefit, income deferral, or other current or deferred benefit plan for one or more employees, independent contractors, or their beneficiaries or spouses, to which contributions are made for the purpose of distributing to or for the benefit of the participants, or their beneficiaries or spouses, the property, income, or principal in the trust or other property arrangement, except a nonvested property interest or a power of appointment that is created by an election of a participant or a beneficiary or spouse; or

(g) A property interest, power of appointment, or arrangement that was not subject to the common-law rule against perpetuities or is excluded by another statute of this state.

(6) Application.—

(a) Except as extended by paragraph (c), this section applies to a nonvested property interest or a power of appointment that is created on or after October 1, 1988. For purposes of this subsection, a nonvested property interest or a power of appointment created by the exercise of a power of appointment is created when the power is irrevocably exercised or when a revocable exercise becomes irrevocable.

(b) This section also applies to a power of appointment that was created before October 1, 1988, but only to the extent that it remains unexercised on October 1, 1988.

(c) If a nonvested property interest or a power of appointment was created before October 1, 1988, and is determined in a judicial proceeding commenced on or after October 1, 1988, to violate this state's rule against perpetuities as that rule existed before October 1, 1988, a court, upon the petition of an interested person, may reform the disposition in the manner that most closely approximates the transferor's manifested plan of distribution and is within the limits of the rule against perpetuities applicable when the nonvested property interest or power of appointment was created.

(7) Rule of construction.—With respect to any matter relating to the validity of an interest within the rule against perpetuities, unless a contrary intent appears, it shall be presumed that the transferor of the interest intended that the interest be valid. This section is the sole expression of any rule against perpetuities or remoteness in vesting in this state. No common-law rule against perpetuities or remoteness in vesting shall exist with respect to any interest or power regardless of whether such interest or power is governed by this section.

(8) Uniformity of application and construction.—This section shall be applied and construed to effectuate its general purpose to make uniform the law with respect to the subject of this act among states enacting it.

Laws 1988, c. 88–40, § 1. Amended by Laws 1997, c. 97–240, § 1, eff. May 30, 1997; Laws 2000, c. 2000–245, § 1, eff. Dec. 31, 2000.

UNIFORM STATUTORY RULE AGAINST PERPETUITIES

Table of Jurisdictions Wherein Act Has Been Adopted

For text of Uniform Act, and variation notes and annotation materials for adopting jurisdictions, see Uniform Laws Annotated, Master Edition, Volume 8B.

Jurisdiction	Laws	Effective Date	Statutory Citation
Alabama	2011-532	1–1–2012	Ala. Code 1975 §§ 35–4A–1 to 35–4A–8.
Alaska	1994, c. 82	1–1–1996	AS §§ 34.27.050 to 34.27.100.
Arizona	1994, c. 290	After 12–31–1994	A.R.S. §§ 14–2901 to 14–2906.
Arkansas	2007, c. 240	3–9–2007	A.C.A. §§ 18–3–101 to 18–3–109.
California	1991, c. 156	7–22–1991 *	West's Ann.Cal.Probate Code, §§ 21200 to 21231.
Colorado	1991, c. 315	5–31–1991	West's C.R.S.A. §§ 15–11–1101 to 15–11–1107.
Connecticut	1989, P.A. No. 89–44	5–2–1989 *	C.G.S.A. §§ 45a–490 to 45a–496.
District of Columbia . . .	2001, D.C. Law 13–292	4–27–2001	D.C. Official Code, 2001 Ed. §§ 19–901 to 19–907.
Florida	1988, c. 88–40	10–1–1988	West's F.S.A. § 689.225.
Georgia	1990, p. 1837	5–1–1990	O.C.G.A. §§ 44–6–200 to 44–6–206.
Hawaii	1992, Act 262	6–18–1992	HRS §§ 525–1 to 525–6.
Indiana	2002, P.L. 2–2002	7–1–2002	West's A.I.C. §§ 32–17–8–1 to 32–17–8–6.
Kansas	1992, c. 302	5–22–1992 *	K.S.A. §§ 59–3401 to 59–3408.
Massachusetts	2010, c. 409	1–2–2012	M.G.L.A. c. 190B, §§ 2–901 2–906.
Michigan	1988, P.A. 418	12–24–1988	M.C.L.A. §§ 554.71 to 554.78.
Minnesota	1987, c. 60	1–1–1991	M.S.A. §§ 501A.01 to 501A.07.
Montana	1989, c. 250	10–1–1989	MCA §§ 72–2–1001 to 72–2–1007.
Nebraska	1989, LB377	8–25–1989	R.R.S. 1943, §§ 76–2001 to 76–2008.
Nevada	1987, c. 25	10–1–1987	N.R.S. §§ 111.103 to 111.1039.
New Mexico	1992, c. 66	7–1–1992	NMSA 1978, §§ 45–2–901 to 45–2–906.
North Carolina	1995, c. 190	10–1–1995	G.S. §§ 41–15 to 41–23.
North Dakota	1991, c. 484	7–1–1991	NDCC §§ 47–02–27.1 to 47–02–27.5.
Oregon	1989, c. 208	1–1–1990	ORS §§ 105.950 to 105.975.
South Carolina	1987, No. 12	3–12–1987	Code 1976, §§ 27–6–10 to 27–6–80.
Tennessee	1994, c. 654	7–1–1994	T.C.A. §§ 66–1–201 to 66–1–208.
Virgin Islands	2010, c. 7150	1–1–2011	15 V.I.C. §§ 2–901 to 2–906.
Virginia	2000, c. 714	7–1–2000	Code 1950, §§ 55–12.1 to 55–12.6.
West Virginia	1992, c. 74	90 days from 2–10–1992	Code, §§ 36–1A–1 to 36–1A–8.

* Date of approval.

Cross References

Irrevocable trusts,
Nonjudicial modification, see § 736.0412.
Judicial modification, best interest of beneficiaries, see § 736.04115.
Trustee's power to invade principal in trust, see § 736.04117.

689.25. Failure to disclose homicide, suicide, deaths, or diagnosis of HIV or AIDS infection in an occupant of real property

(1)(a) The fact that an occupant of real property is infected or has been infected with human immunodeficiency virus or diagnosed with acquired immune deficiency syndrome is not a material fact that must be disclosed in a real estate transaction.

(b) The fact that a property was, or was at any time suspected to have been, the site of a homicide, suicide, or death is not a material fact that must be disclosed in a real estate transaction.

(2) A cause of action shall not arise against an owner of real property, his or her agent, an agent of a transferee of real property, or a person licensed under chapter 475 for the failure to disclose to the transferee that the property was or was suspected to have been the site of a homicide, suicide, or death or that an occupant of that property was infected with human immunodeficiency virus or diagnosed with acquired immune deficiency syndrome.

Laws 1988, c. 88–380, § 46. Amended by Laws 2003, c. 2003–164, § 51, eff. July 1, 2003.

689.261. Sale of residential property; disclosure of ad valorem taxes to prospective purchaser

(1) A prospective purchaser of residential property must be presented a disclosure summary at or before execution of the contract for sale. Unless a substantially similar disclosure summary is included in the contract for sale, a separate disclosure summary must be attached to the contract for sale. The disclosure summary, whether separate or included in the contract, must be in a form substantially similar to the following:

PROPERTY TAX

DISCLOSURE SUMMARY

BUYER SHOULD NOT RELY ON THE SELLER'S CURRENT PROPERTY TAXES AS THE AMOUNT OF PROPERTY TAXES THAT THE BUYER MAY BE OBLIGATED TO PAY IN THE YEAR SUBSEQUENT TO PURCHASE. A CHANGE OF OWNERSHIP OR PROPERTY IMPROVEMENTS TRIGGERS REASSESSMENTS OF THE PROPERTY THAT COULD RESULT IN HIGHER PROPERTY TAXES. IF YOU HAVE ANY QUESTIONS CONCERNING VALUATION, CONTACT THE COUNTY PROPERTY APPRAISER'S OFFICE FOR INFORMATION.

(2) Unless included in the contract, the disclosure summary must be provided by the seller. If the disclosure summary is not included in the contract for sale, the contract for sale must refer to and incorporate by reference the disclosure summary and include, in prominent language, a statement that the potential purchaser should not execute the contract until he or she has read the disclosure summary required by this section.

Added by Laws 2004, c. 2004–349, § 5, eff. Jan. 1, 2005.

689.27. Termination by servicemember of agreement to purchase real property

(1) Notwithstanding any other provisions of law and for the purposes of this section:

(a) "Closing" means the finalizing of the sale of property, upon which title to the property is transferred from the seller to the buyer.

(b) "Contract" means an instrument purporting to contain an agreement to purchase real property.

(c) "Property" means a house, condominium, or mobile home that a servicemember intends to purchase to serve as his or her primary residence.

(d) "Servicemember" shall have the same meaning as provided in s. 250.01.

(2) Any servicemember may terminate a contract to purchase property, prior to closing on such property, by providing the seller or mortgagor of the property with a written notice of termination to be effective immediately, if any of the following criteria are met:

(a) The servicemember is required, pursuant to permanent change of station orders received after entering into a contract for the property and prior to closing, to move 35 miles or more from the location of the property;

(b) The servicemember is released from active duty or state active duty after having agreed to purchase the property and prior to closing while serving on active duty or state active duty status, and the property is 35 miles or more from the servicemember's home of record prior to entering active duty or state active duty;

(c) Prior to closing, the servicemember receives military orders requiring him or her to move into government quarters or the servicemember becomes eligible to live in and opts to move into government quarters; or

(d) Prior to closing, the servicemember receives temporary duty orders, temporary change of station orders, or active duty or state active duty orders to an area 35 miles or more from the location of the property, provided such orders are for a period exceeding 90 days.

(3) The notice to the seller or mortgagor canceling the contract must be accompanied by either a copy of the official military orders or a written verification signed by the servicemember's commanding officer.

(4) Upon termination of a contract under this section, the seller or mortgagor or his or her agent shall refund any funds provided by the servicemember under the contract within 7 days. The servicemember is not liable for any other fees due to the termination of the contract as provided for in this section.

(5) The provisions of this section may not be waived or modified by the agreement of the parties under any circumstances.

Added by Laws 2003, c. 2003–72, § 19, eff. June 2, 2003.

689.28. Prohibition against transfer fee covenants

(1) **Intent.**—The Legislature finds and declares that the public policy of this state favors the marketability of real property and the transferability of interests in real property free of title defects or unreasonable restraints on alienation. The Legislature further finds and declares that transfer fee covenants violate this public policy by impairing the marketability and transferability of real property and by constituting an unreasonable restraint on alienation regardless of the duration of such covenants or the amount of such transfer fees, and do not run with the title to the property or bind subsequent owners of the property under common law or equitable principles.

(2) **Definitions.**—As used in this section, the term:

(a) "Environmental covenant" means a covenant or servitude that imposes limitations on the use of real property pursuant to an environmental remediation project pertaining to the property. An environmental covenant is not a transfer fee covenant.

(b) "Transfer" means the sale, gift, conveyance, assignment, inheritance, or other transfer of an ownership interest in real property located in this state.

(c) "Transfer fee" means a fee or charge required by a transfer fee covenant and payable upon the transfer of an interest in real property, or payable for the right to make or accept such transfer, regardless of whether the fee or charge is a fixed amount or is determined as a percentage of the value of the property, the purchase price, or other consideration given for the transfer. The following are not transfer fees for purposes of this section:

1. Any consideration payable by the grantee to the grantor for the interest in real property being transferred, including any subsequent additional consideration for the property payable by the grantee based upon any subsequent appreciation, development, or sale of the property. For

the purposes of this subparagraph, an interest in real property may include a separate mineral estate and its appurtenant surface access rights.

2. Any commission payable to a licensed real estate broker for the transfer of real property pursuant to an agreement between the broker and the grantor or the grantee, including any subsequent additional commission for that transfer payable by the grantor or the grantee based upon any subsequent appreciation, development, or sale of the property.

3. Any interest, charges, fees, or other amounts payable by a borrower to a lender pursuant to a loan secured by a mortgage against real property, including, but not limited to, any fee payable to the lender for consenting to an assumption of the loan or a transfer of the real property subject to the mortgage, any fees or charges payable to the lender for estoppel letters or certificates, and any shared appreciation interest or profit participation or other consideration described in s. 687.03(4) and payable to the lender in connection with the loan.

4. Any rent, reimbursement, charge, fee, or other amount payable by a lessee to a lessor under a lease, including, but not limited to, any fee payable to the lessor for consenting to an assignment, subletting, encumbrance, or transfer of the lease.

5. Any consideration payable to the holder of an option to purchase an interest in real property or the holder of a right of first refusal or first offer to purchase an interest in real property for waiving, releasing, or not exercising the option or right upon the transfer of the property to another person.

6. Any tax, fee, charge, assessment, fine, or other amount payable to or imposed by a governmental authority.

7. Any fee, charge, assessment, fine, or other amount payable to a homeowners', condominium, cooperative, mobile home, or property owners' association pursuant to a declaration or covenant or law applicable to such association, including, but not limited to, fees or charges payable for estoppel letters or certificates issued by the association or its authorized agent.

8. Any fee, charge, assessment, dues, contribution, or other amount imposed by a declaration or covenant encumbering four or more parcels in a community, as defined in s. 720.301, and payable to a nonprofit or charitable organization for the purpose of supporting cultural, educational, charitable, recreational, environmental, conservation, or other similar activities benefiting the community that is subject to the declaration or covenant.

9. Any fee, charge, assessment, dues, contribution, or other amount pertaining to the purchase or transfer of a club membership relating to real property owned by the member, including, but not limited to, any amount determined by reference to the value, purchase price, or other consideration given for the transfer of the real property.

10. Any payment required pursuant to an environmental covenant.

(d) "Transfer fee covenant" means a declaration or covenant recorded against the title to real property which requires or purports to require the payment of a transfer fee to the declarant or other person specified in the declaration or covenant or to their successors or assigns upon a subsequent transfer of an interest in the real property.

(3) **Prohibition.**—A transfer fee covenant recorded in this state on or after July 1, 2008, does not run with the title to real property and is not binding on or enforceable at law or in equity against any subsequent owner, purchaser, or mortgagee of any interest in real property as an equitable servitude or otherwise. Any liens purporting to secure the payment of a transfer fee under a transfer fee covenant that is recorded in this state on or after July 1, 2008, are void and

unenforceable. This subsection does not mean that transfer fee covenants or liens recorded in this state before July 1, 2008, are presumed valid and enforceable.

Added by Laws 2008, c. 2008–35, § 1, eff. July 1, 2008.

689.29. Disclosure of subsurface rights to prospective purchaser

(1) A seller must provide a prospective purchaser of residential property with a disclosure summary at or before the execution of a contract if the seller or an affiliated or related entity has previously severed or retained or will sever or retain any of the subsurface rights or right of entry. The disclosure summary must be conspicuous, in boldface type, and in a form substantially similar to the following:

SUBSURFACE RIGHTS DISCLOSURE SUMMARY

SUBSURFACE RIGHTS HAVE BEEN OR WILL BE SEVERED FROM THE TITLE TO REAL PROPERTY BY CONVEYANCE (DEED) OF THE SUBSURFACE RIGHTS FROM THE SELLER OR AN AFFILIATED OR RELATED ENTITY OR BY RESERVATION OF THE SUBSURFACE RIGHTS BY THE SELLER OR AN AFFILIATED OR RELATED ENTITY. WHEN SUBSURFACE RIGHTS ARE SEVERED FROM THE PROPERTY, THE OWNER OF THOSE RIGHTS MAY HAVE THE PERPETUAL RIGHT TO DRILL, MINE, EXPLORE, OR REMOVE ANY OF THE SUBSURFACE RESOURCES ON OR FROM THE PROPERTY EITHER DIRECTLY FROM THE SURFACE OF THE PROPERTY OR FROM A NEARBY LOCATION. SUBSURFACE RIGHTS MAY HAVE A MONETARY VALUE.

(Purchaser's Initials)

(2) If the disclosure summary is not included in the contract for sale, the contract for sale must refer to and incorporate by reference the disclosure summary and must include, in prominent language, a statement that the potential purchaser should not execute the contract until he or she has read the disclosure summary required under this section.

(3) As used in this section, the term:

(a) "Seller" means a seller of real property which, at the time of sale, is zoned for residential use and is property upon which a new dwelling is being constructed or will be constructed pursuant to the contract for sale with the seller or has been constructed since the last transfer of the property.

(b) "Subsurface rights" means the rights to all minerals, mineral fuels, and other resources, including, but not limited to, oil, gas, coal, oil shale, uranium, metals, and phosphate, whether or not they are mixed with any other substance found or located beneath the surface of the earth.

Added by Laws 2014, c. 2014–34, § 1, eff. Oct. 1, 2014.

CHAPTER 695

RECORD OF CONVEYANCES OF REAL ESTATE

For Annotative Materials, see West's Florida Statutes Annotated

695.25. Short form of acknowledgment

The forms of acknowledgment set forth in this section may be used, and are sufficient for their respective purposes, under any law of this state. The forms shall be known as "Statutory Short Forms of Acknowledgment" and may be referred to by that name. The authorization of the forms in this section does not preclude the use of other forms.

(1) For an individual acting in his or her own right:

STATE OF ___

COUNTY OF ___

The foregoing instrument was acknowledged before me this __(date)__ by __(name of person acknowledging)__ , who is personally known to me or who has produced __(type of identification)__ as identification.

> (Signature of person taking acknowledgment)
> (Name typed, printed or stamped)
> (Title or rank)
> (Serial number, if any)

(2) For a corporation:

STATE OF ___

COUNTY OF ___

The foregoing instrument was acknowledged before me this __(date)__ by __(name of officer or agent, title of officer or agent)__ of __(name of corporation acknowledging)__ , a __(state or place of incorporation)__ corporation, on behalf of the corporation. He/she is personally known to me or has produced __(type of identification)__ as identification.

> (Signature of person taking acknowledgment)
>
> (Name typed, printed or stamped)
> (Title or rank)
> (Serial number, if any)

(3) For a partnership:

STATE OF _____

COUNTY OF _____

The foregoing instrument was acknowledged before me this __(date)__ by __(name of acknowledging partner or agent)__ , partner (or agent) on behalf of __(name of partnership)__ , a partnership. He/she is personally known to me or has produced __(type of identification)__ as identification.

> (Signature of person taking acknowledgment)
>
> (Name typed, printed or stamped)
> (Title or rank)
> (Serial number, if any)

(4) For an individual acting as principal by an attorney in fact:

STATE OF _____

COUNTY OF _____

The foregoing instrument was acknowledged before me this _(date)_ by _(name of attorney in fact)_ as attorney in fact, who is personally known to me or who has produced _(type of identification)_ as identification on behalf of _(name of principal)_ .

_____
(Signature of person taking acknowledgment)
_____
(Name typed, printed or stamped)
(Title or rank)
(Serial number, if any)

(5) By any public officer, trustee, or personal representative:

STATE OF _____

COUNTY OF _____

The foregoing instrument was acknowledged before me this _(date)_ by _(name and title of position)_ , who is personally known to me or who has produced _(type of identification)_ as identification.

_____
(Signature of person taking acknowledgment)
_____
(Name typed, printed or stamped)
(Title or rank)
(Serial number, if any) .

Laws 1973, c. 73–62, § 1; Laws 1991, c. 91–291, § 10; Laws 1993, c. 93–62, § 7. Amended by Laws 1997, c. 97–102, § 772, eff. July 1, 1997.

695.26. Requirements for recording instruments affecting real property

(1) No instrument by which the title to real property or any interest therein is conveyed, assigned, encumbered, or otherwise disposed of shall be recorded by the clerk of the circuit court unless:

(a) The name of each person who executed such instrument is legibly printed, typewritten, or stamped upon such instrument immediately beneath the signature of such person and the post-office address of each such person is legibly printed, typewritten, or stamped upon such instrument;

(b) The name and post-office address of the natural person who prepared the instrument or under whose supervision it was prepared are legibly printed, typewritten, or stamped upon such instrument;

(c) The name of each witness to the instrument is legibly printed, typewritten, or stamped upon such instrument immediately beneath the signature of such witness;

(d) The name of any notary public or other officer authorized to take acknowledgments or proofs whose signature appears upon the instrument is legibly printed, typewritten, or stamped upon such instrument immediately beneath the signature of such notary public or other officer authorized to take acknowledgment or proofs;

(e) A 3–inch by 3–inch space at the top right-hand corner on the first page and a 1–inch by 3–inch space at the top right-hand corner on each subsequent page are reserved for use by the clerk of the court; and

(f) In any instrument other than a mortgage conveying or purporting to convey any interest in real property, the name and post-office address of each grantee in such instrument are legibly printed, typewritten, or stamped upon such instrument.

(2) If a name or address is printed, typewritten, or stamped on an instrument in a position other than the position required by subsection (1), the clerk of the circuit court may, in her or his discretion, accept the instrument for recordation if she or he determines that the connection between the signature and the name or the name and the address is apparent.

(3) This section does not apply to:

(a) An instrument executed before July 1, 1991.

(b) A decree, order, judgment, or writ of any court.

(c) An instrument executed, acknowledged, or proved outside of this state.

(d) A will.

(e) A plat.

(f) An instrument prepared or executed by any public officer other than a notary public.

(4) The failure of the clerk of the circuit court to comply with this section does not impair the validity of the recordation or of the constructive notice imparted by recordation.

Laws 1990, c. 90–183, § 1; Laws 1994, c. 94–348, §§ 8, 22. Amended by Laws 1997, c. 97–102, § 773, eff. July 1, 1997.

695.27. Uniform Real Property Electronic Recording Act

(1) **Short title.**—This section may be cited as the "Uniform Real Property Electronic Recording Act."

(2) **Definitions.**—As used in this section:

(a) "Document" means information that is:

1. Inscribed on a tangible medium or that is stored in an electronic or other medium and is retrievable in perceivable form; and

2. Eligible to be recorded in the Official Records, as defined in s. 28.222, and maintained by a county recorder.

(b) "Electronic" means relating to technology having electrical, digital, magnetic, wireless, optical, electromagnetic, or similar capabilities.

(c) "Electronic document" means a document that is received by a county recorder in an electronic form.

(d) "Electronic signature" means an electronic sound, symbol, or process that is executed or adopted by a person with the intent to sign the document and is attached to or logically associated with a document such that, when recorded, it is assigned the same document number or a consecutive page number immediately following such document.

(e) "Person" means an individual, corporation, business trust, estate, trust, partnership, limited liability company, association, joint venture, public corporation, government or governmental subdivision, agency, instrumentality, or any other legal or commercial entity.

(f) "State" means a state of the United States, the District of Columbia, Puerto Rico, the United States Virgin Islands, or any territory or insular possession subject to the jurisdiction of the United States.

(3) Validity of electronic documents.—

(a) If a law requires, as a condition for recording, that a document be an original, be on paper or another tangible medium, or be in writing, the requirement is satisfied by an electronic document satisfying the requirements of this section.

(b) If a law requires, as a condition for recording, that a document be signed, the requirement is satisfied by an electronic signature.

(c) A requirement that a document or a signature associated with a document be notarized, acknowledged, verified, witnessed, or made under oath is satisfied if the electronic signature of the person authorized to perform that act, and all other information required to be included, is attached to or logically associated with the document or signature. A physical or electronic image of a stamp, impression, or seal need not accompany an electronic signature.

(4) Recording of documents.—

(a) In this subsection, the term "paper document" means a document that is received by the county recorder in a form that is not electronic.

(b) A county recorder:

1.   Who implements any of the functions listed in this section shall do so in compliance with standards established by rule by the Department of State.

2.   May receive, index, store, archive, and transmit electronic documents.

3.   May provide for access to, and for search and retrieval of, documents and information by electronic means.

4.   Who accepts electronic documents for recording shall continue to accept paper documents as authorized by state law and shall place entries for both types of documents in the same index.

5.   May convert paper documents accepted for recording into electronic form.

6.   May convert into electronic form information recorded before the county recorder began to record electronic documents.

7.   May agree with other officials of a state or a political subdivision thereof, or of the United States, on procedures or processes to facilitate the electronic satisfaction of prior approvals and conditions precedent to recording.

(5) Administration and standards.—

(a) The Department of State, by rule pursuant to ss. 120.536(1) and 120.54, shall prescribe standards to implement this section in consultation with the Electronic Recording Advisory Committee, which is hereby created. The Florida Association of Court Clerks and Comptrollers shall provide administrative support to the committee and technical support to the Department of State and the committee at no charge. The committee shall consist of nine members, as follows:

1.   Five members appointed by the Florida Association of Court Clerks and Comptrollers, one of whom must be an official from a large urban charter county where the duty to maintain official records exists in a county office other than the clerk of court or comptroller.

2. One attorney appointed by the Real Property, Probate and Trust Law Section of The Florida Bar Association.

3. Two members appointed by the Florida Land Title Association.

4. One member appointed by the Florida Bankers Association.

(b) Appointed members shall serve a 1–year term. All initial terms shall commence on the effective date of this act. Members shall serve until their successors are appointed. An appointing authority may reappoint a member for successive terms. A vacancy on the committee shall be filled in the same manner in which the original appointment was made, and the term shall be for the balance of the unexpired term.

(c) The first meeting of the committee shall be within 60 days of the effective date of this act. Thereafter, the committee shall meet at the call of the chair, but at least annually.

(d) The members of the committee shall serve without compensation and shall not claim per diem and travel expenses from the Secretary of State.

(e) To keep the standards and practices of county recorders in this state in harmony with the standards and practices of recording offices in other jurisdictions that enact substantially this section and to keep the technology used by county recorders in this state compatible with technology used by recording offices in other jurisdictions that enact substantially this section, the Department of State, in consultation with the committee, so far as is consistent with the purposes, policies, and provisions of this section, in adopting, amending, and repealing standards, shall consider:

1. Standards and practices of other jurisdictions.

2. The most recent standards adopted by national standard-setting bodies, such as the Property Records Industry Association.

3. The views of interested persons and governmental officials and entities.

4. The needs of counties of varying size, population, and resources.

5. Standards requiring adequate information security protection to ensure that electronic documents are accurate, authentic, adequately preserved, and resistant to tampering.

(f) The committee shall terminate on July 1, 2010.

(6) **Uniformity of application and construction.**—In applying and construing this section, consideration must be given to the need to promote uniformity of the law with respect to its subject matter among states that enact it.

(7) **Relation to Electronic Signatures in Global and National Commerce Act.**—This section modifies, limits, and supersedes the federal Electronic Signatures in Global and National Commerce Act, 15 U.S.C. ss. 7001 et seq., but this section does not modify, limit, or supersede s. 101(c) of that act, 15 U.S.C. s. 7001(c), or authorize electronic delivery of any of the notices described in s. 103(b) of that act, 15 U.S.C. s. 7003(b).

Added by Laws 2007, c. 2007–233, § 1, eff. June 27, 2007.

UNIFORM REAL PROPERTY ELECTRONIC RECORDING ACT

Table of Jurisdictions Wherein Act Has Been Adopted

For text of Uniform Act, and variation notes and annotation materials for adopting jurisdictions, see Uniform Laws Annotated, Master Edition, Volume 7B.

For Annotative Materials, see West's Florida Statutes Annotated

Jurisdiction	Laws	Effective Date	Statutory Citation
Alabama	2009–510	1–1–2010	Code, 1975, §§ 35–4–120 to 35–4–127.
Arizona	2005, c. 109	1–1–2006	A.R.S. §§ 11–487 to 11–487.06.
Arkansas	2007, c. 734	7–31–2007	A.C.A. §§ 14–2–301 to 14–2–308.
Connecticut	2008, P.A. 08–56	10–1–2009	C.G.S.A. §§ 7–35aa to 7–35gg.
Delaware	2005, c. 23	1–1–2006	25 Del.C. §§ 180 to 184.
District of Columbia	D.C Law 16–25	10–18–2005	D.C. Official Code, 2001 Ed. §§ 42–1231 to 42–1235.
Florida	2007, c. 233	6–27–2007	West's F.S.A. § 695.27.
Georgia	2009, c. 140	5–5–2009	O.C.G.A. §§ 44–2–35 to 44–2–39.2.
Hawaii	2009, c. 102	7–1–2009	H.R.S. §§ 502–121 to 502–125.
Idaho	2007, c. 63	7–1–2007	I.C. §§ 31–2901 to 31–2907.
Illinois	2007, P.A. 95–472	8–27–2007	S.H.A. 765 ILCS 33/1 to 33/99.
Kansas	2006, c. 145	4–19–2006 *	K.S.A. 58–4401 to 58–4407.
Michigan	2010, No. 123	7–19–2010	M.C.L.A. §§ 565.841 to 565.847.
Minnesota	2008, c. 238	7–1–2008	M.S.A. §§ 507.0941 to 507.0949.
Mississippi	2011, c. 364	7–1–2011	Miss. Code Ann. §§ 89–5–101 to 89–5–113.
Nevada	2007, c. 57	10–1–2007	N.R.S. 111.366 to 111.3697.
New Mexico	2007, c. 261	7–1–2007	NMSA 1978, §§ 14–9A–1 to 14–9A–7.
New York	2011, c. 549	9–22–2012	NY Real Prop. §§ 290, 291–I, 317.
North Carolina	2005, c. 391	9–13–2005	G.S. §§ 47–16.1 to 47–16.7.
Oklahoma	2008, c. 295	11–1–2008	16 Okl.St.Ann. §§ 86.1 to 86.7.
Pennsylvania	2012, c. 100	7–5–2012	21 P.S. §§ 483.1 to 483.9.
South Carolina	2008, Act 210	5–13–2008	Code 1976, §§ 30–6–10 to 30–6–70.
South Dakota	2014, ch. 47	7–1–2014	SDCL, §§ 7–9A–1 to 7–9A–10.
Tennessee	2007, c. 420	7–1–2007	T.C.A. §§ 66–24–201 to 66–24–206.
Texas	2005, c. 699	9–1–2005	V.T.C.A., Property Code §§ 15.001 to 15.008.
Utah	2014, c. 89	7–1–2015	U.C.A. §§ 17–21a–101 to 17–21a–403.
Virgin Islands	2010, c. 7142	10–1–2010	28 V.I.C. §§ 151 to 157.
Virginia	2005, c. 744	7–1–2005	Code 1950, §§ 55–142.10 to 55–142.15.
Washington	2008, c. 57	6–12–2008	West's RCWA 65.24.010 to 65.24.901.
Wisconsin	2006, c. 421	6–3–2006	W.S.A. 706.25.

* Date of approval.

695.28. Validity of recorded electronic documents

(1) A document that is otherwise entitled to be recorded and that was or is submitted to the clerk of the court or county recorder by electronic means and accepted for recordation is deemed validly recorded and provides notice to all persons notwithstanding:

(a) That the document was received and accepted for recordation before the Department of State adopted standards implementing s. 695.27; or

(b) Any defects in, deviations from, or the inability to demonstrate strict compliance with any statute, rule, or procedure to submit or record an electronic document in effect at the time the electronic document was submitted for recording.

(2) This section does not alter the duty of the clerk or recorder to comply with s. 695.27 or rules adopted pursuant to that section.

Added by Laws 2011, c. 2011–173, § 1, eff. June 17, 2011.

Applicability

Laws 2011, c. 2011–173, § 2, provides:

"This act is intended to clarify existing law and applies prospectively and retroactively."

CHAPTER 709

POWERS OF ATTORNEY AND SIMILAR INSTRUMENTS

PART I. POWERS OF APPOINTMENT

PART II. POWERS OF ATTORNEY

Cross References

Family trust companies, prohibitions, see F.S.A. § 662.131.
Fiduciary lawyer-client privilege, see F.S.A. § 90.5021.
Health care surrogates, capacity of principal, see F.S.A. § 765.204.
Tax exemption for deployed servicemembers, see F.S.A. § 196.173.

PART I. POWERS OF APPOINTMENT

709.02. Power of appointment; method of release

Powers of appointment over any property, real, personal, intangible or mixed, may be released, in whole or in part, by a written instrument signed by the donee or donees of such powers. Such written releases shall be signed in the presence of two witnesses but need not be sealed, acknowledged or recorded in order to be valid, nor shall it be necessary to the validity of such releases for spouses of married donees to join such donees in the execution of releases, in whole or part, of powers of appointment.

Laws 1945, c. 23007, § 1. Amended by Laws 1997, c. 97–102, § 795, eff. July 1, 1997.

709.03. Power of appointment; property held in trust

If property subject to a power of appointment is held in trust by a person, firm or corporation other than the donee or donees of the power, a written release, in whole or in part, of a power to appoint the same shall be delivered to such trustee or trustees before the written release becomes legally effective. In no other instance shall a delivery of a release, in whole or in part, of a power of appointment be necessary to the validity of such release.

Laws 1945, c. 23007, § 2.

709.04. Power of appointment; effect of release

Any power of appointment wholly released by a written instrument signed by the donee or donees of such power shall be, in legal effect, completely revoked, and shall not, after such release, be subject to being exercised in any manner whatsoever. Any power of appointment partially released by a written instrument signed by the donee or donees of such power shall be, in legal effect, as to such released part, completely revoked, and shall not after such release be subject to being exercised in any manner whatsoever as to such released part.

Laws 1945, c. 23007, § 3.

709.05. Powers of appointment; validation of prior releases

All releases, in whole or in part, of powers of appointment heretofore executed in a manner that conforms with the provisions of this law be and they are hereby validated and shall be given the same force and effect as if executed subsequently to the effective date of this law.

Laws 1945, c. 23007, § 4.

709.06. Powers of appointment included in law

Powers of appointment referred to in this law shall include not only those recognized as such by general law but also those designated as such under the tax law of the United States.

Laws 1945, c. 23007, § 5.

709.07. Power of appointment; effect of release on title to property

No such release, in whole or in part, of a power of appointment shall affect the title to property of any bona fide purchaser for value who does not have notice or knowledge of such release.

Laws 1945, c. 23007, § 7.

PART II. POWERS OF ATTORNEY

UNIFORM DURABLE POWER OF ATTORNEY ACT

Table of Jurisdictions Wherein Act Has Been Adopted

For text of Uniform Act, and variation notes and annotation materials for adopting jurisdictions, see Uniform Laws Annotated, Master Edition, Volume 8A.

Jurisdiction	Laws	Effective Date	Statutory Citation
Alabama	1981, No. 81–98 p. 117	3–4–1981	Code 1975, § 26–1–2.
Arizona	1973, c. 75	1–1–1974	A.R.S. §§ 14–5501 to 14–5503.
California	1981, c. 511	9–16–1981*	West's Ann.Cal.Probate Code, §§ 4124 to 4128, 4206, 4304, and 4305.
Colorado	1973, H.B. 1039	7–1–1974	West's C.R.S.A. §§ 15–14–500.3 to 15–14–502.
Delaware	1982 [63 Del. Laws], c. 267	6–21–1982*	12 Del.C. §§ 4901 to 4906.
District of Columbia	1987, D.C. Law 6–204		D.C. Official Code, 2001 Ed. §§ 21–2081 to 21–2085.
Florida	1974, c. 74–245		West's F.S.A. §§ 709.2101 to 709.2402.
Idaho	1982, c. 138		I.C. §§ 15–5–501 to 15–5–507.
Kentucky	1972, c. 168		KRS 386.093.
Michigan	1998, P.A. 386	4–1–2000	M.C.L.A. §§ 700.5501 to 700.5505.
Minnesota	1984, c. 603	8–1–1984	M.S.A. §§ 523.07 to 523.08.
Mississippi	1994, c. 336	7–1–1994	Code 1972, §§ 87–3–101 to 87–3–113.
Missouri	1989, H.B.No. 145	8–28–1989	V.A.M.S. §§ 404.700 to 404.735
Montana	1985, c. 283		MCA 72–5–501, 72–5–502.
New Hampshire	2001, c. 257:1	1–1–2002	RSA 506:6.
New Jersey	2000, c. 109:1	9–8–2000*	N.J.S.A. 46:2B–8.1 to 46:2B–8.14.
New Mexico	1995, c. 210	7–1–1995	NMSA 1978, §§ 45–5–501 to 45–5–505.
North Carolina	1983, c. 626		GS §§ 32A–8 to 32A–14.
North Dakota	1985, c. 370		NDCC 30.1–30–01 to 30.1–30–06.
Oklahoma	1988, c. 293	11–1–1988	58 Okl.St.Ann. §§ 1071 to 1077.
Pennsylvania	1982, P.L. 45, No. 26, § 9	2–18–1982	20 Pa.C.S.A. §§ 5604 to 5606.
South Carolina	1986, Act 539	7–1–1987	Code 1976, §§ 62–5–501 to 62–5–505.
Tennessee	1983, c. 299	7–1–1983	T.C.A. §§ 34–6–101 to 34–6–111.
Utah	1975, c. 150	7–1–1977	U.C.A. 1953, 75–5–501 to 75–5–504.
Vermont	2001, No. 135	6–13–2002	14 V.S.A. § 3508.
Virgin Islands	1991, No. 5718	9–23–1991	15 V.I.C. §§ 1261 to 1267.
Washington	1985, c. 30		West's RCWA 11.94.010 to 11.94.901.

* Date of approval.

709.2101. Short title

This part may be cited as the "Florida Power of Attorney Act."
Added by Laws 2011, c. 2011–210, § 3, eff. Oct. 1, 2011.

709.2102. Definitions

As used in this part, the term:

(1) "Agent" means a person granted authority to act for a principal under a power of attorney, whether denominated an agent, attorney in fact, or otherwise. The term includes an original agent, co-agent, and successor agent.

(2) "Another state" means a state of the United States, the District of Columbia, Puerto Rico, the United States Virgin Islands, or any territory or insular possession subject to the jurisdiction of the United States.

(3) "Broker-dealer" means a broker-dealer registered with the United States Securities and Exchange Commission or the Commodity Futures Trading Commission if the broker-dealer is acting in that capacity.

(4) "Durable" means, with respect to a power of attorney, not terminated by the principal's incapacity.

(5) "Electronic" means technology having electrical, digital, magnetic, wireless, optical, electromagnetic, or similar capabilities.

(6) "Financial institution" has the same meaning as in s. 655.005.

(7) "Incapacity" means the inability of an individual to take those actions necessary to obtain, administer, and dispose of real and personal property, intangible property, business property, benefits, and income.

(8) "Knowledge" means a person has actual knowledge of the fact, has received a notice or notification of the fact, or has reason to know the fact from all other facts and circumstances known to the person at the time in question. An organization that conducts activities through employees has notice or knowledge of a fact involving a power of attorney only from the time information was received by an employee having responsibility to act on matters involving the power of attorney, or would have had if brought to the employee's attention if the organization had exercised reasonable diligence. An organization exercises reasonable diligence if the organization maintains reasonable routines for communicating significant information to the employee having responsibility to act on matters involving the power of attorney and there is reasonable compliance with the routines. Reasonable diligence does not require an employee to communicate information unless the communication is part of the individual's regular duties or the individual knows that a matter involving the power of attorney would be materially affected by the information.

(9) "Power of attorney" means a writing that grants authority to an agent to act in the place of the principal, whether or not the term is used in that writing.

(10) "Presently exercisable general power of appointment" means, with respect to property or a property interest subject to a power of appointment, power exercisable at the time in question to vest absolute ownership in the principal individually, the principal's estate, the principal's creditors, or the creditors of the principal's estate. The term includes a power of appointment not exercisable until the occurrence of a specified event, the satisfaction of an ascertainable standard, or the passage of a specified period only after the occurrence of the specified event, the satisfaction of the ascertainable standard, or the passage of the specified period. The term does not include a power exercisable in a fiduciary capacity or only by will.

(11) "Principal" means an individual who grants authority to an agent in a power of attorney.

(12) "Property" means anything that may be the subject of ownership, whether real or personal, legal or equitable, or any interest or right therein.

(13) "Record" means information that is inscribed on a tangible medium or that is stored in an electronic or other medium and is retrievable in perceivable form.

(14) "Sign" means having present intent to authenticate or adopt a record to:

(a) Execute by signature or mark; or

(b) Attach to, or logically associate with the record an electronic sound, symbol, or process.

(15) "Third person" means any person other than the principal, or the agent in the agent's capacity as agent.

Added by Laws 2011, c. 2011–210, § 4, eff. Oct. 1, 2011. Amended by Laws 2013, c. 2013–90, § 1, eff. May 30, 2013.

709.2103. Applicability

This part applies to all powers of attorney except:

(1) A proxy or other delegation to exercise voting rights or management rights with respect to an entity;

(2) A power created on a form prescribed by a government or governmental subdivision, agency, or instrumentality for a governmental purpose;

(3) A power to the extent it is coupled with an interest in the subject of the power, including a power given to or for the benefit of a creditor in connection with a credit transaction;

(4) A power created by a person other than an individual;

(5) A power given to a transfer agent to facilitate a specific transfer or disposition of one or more identified stocks, bonds, or other financial instruments;

(6) A power authorizing a financial institution or broker-dealer, or an employee of the financial institution or broker-dealer, to act as agent for the account owner in executing trades or transfers of cash, securities, commodities, or other financial assets in the regular course of business; and

(7) A delegation of powers by a trustee in accordance with s. 736.0807.

Added by Laws 2011, c. 2011–210, § 5, eff. Oct. 1, 2011. Amended by Laws 2013, c. 2013–90, § 2, eff. May 30, 2013.

709.2104. Durable power of attorney

Except as otherwise provided under this part, a power of attorney is durable if it contains the words: "This durable power of attorney is not terminated by subsequent incapacity of the principal except as provided in chapter 709, Florida Statutes," or similar words that show the principal's intent that the authority conferred is exercisable notwithstanding the principal's subsequent incapacity.

Added by Laws 2011, c. 2011–210, § 6, eff. Oct. 1, 2011.

709.2105. Qualifications of agent; execution of power of attorney

(1) The agent must be a natural person who is 18 years of age or older or a financial institution that has trust powers, has a place of business in this state, and is authorized to conduct trust business in this state.

(2) A power of attorney must be signed by the principal and by two subscribing witnesses and be acknowledged by the principal before a notary public or as otherwise provided in s. 695.03.

(3) If the principal is physically unable to sign the power of attorney, the notary public before whom the principal's oath or acknowledgment is made may sign the principal's name on the power of attorney pursuant to s. 117.05(14).

Added by Laws 2011, c. 2011–210, § 7, eff. Oct. 1, 2011. Amended by Laws 2013, c. 2013–90, § 3, eff. May 30, 2013.

709.2106. Validity of power of attorney

(1) A power of attorney executed on or after October 1, 2011, is valid if its execution complies with s. 709.2105.

(2) A power of attorney executed before October 1, 2011, is valid if its execution complied with the law of this state at the time of execution.

(3) A power of attorney executed in another state which does not comply with the execution requirements of this part is valid in this state if, when the power of attorney was executed, the power of attorney and its execution complied with the law of the state of execution. A third person who is requested to accept a power of attorney that is valid in this state solely because of this subsection may in good faith request, and rely upon, without further investigation, an opinion of counsel as to any matter of law concerning the power of attorney, including the due execution and validity of the power of attorney. An opinion of counsel requested under this subsection must be provided at the principal's expense. A third person may reject a power of attorney that is valid in this state solely because of this subsection if the agent does not provide the requested opinion of counsel, and in such case, a third person has no liability for rejecting the power of attorney. This subsection does not affect any other rights of a third person who is requested to accept the power of attorney under this part, or any other provisions of applicable law.

(4) A military power of attorney is valid if it is executed in accordance with 10 U.S.C. s. 1044b, as amended. A deployment-contingent power of attorney may be signed in advance, is effective upon the deployment of the principal, and shall be afforded full force and effect by the courts of this state.

(5) Except as otherwise provided in the power of attorney, a photocopy or electronically transmitted copy of an original power of attorney has the same effect as the original. Notwithstanding this subsection, an original power of attorney that is relied upon to affect the title to real property may be required for recording in the official records.

(6) An original of a properly executed power of attorney may be presented to the clerk of the circuit court for recording in the official records as provided under s. 28.222 upon payment of the service charge as provided under s. 28.24.

Added by Laws 2011, c. 2011–210, § 8, eff. Oct. 1, 2011. Amended by Laws 2013, c. 2013–90, § 4, eff. May 30, 2013.

709.2107. Meaning and effectiveness of power of attorney

The meaning and effectiveness of a power of attorney is governed by this part if the power of attorney:

(1) Is used in this state; or

(2) States that it is to be governed by the laws of this state.

Added by Laws 2011, c. 2011–210, § 9, eff. Oct. 1, 2011.

709.2108. When power of attorney is effective

(1) Except as provided in this section, a power of attorney is exercisable when executed.

(2) If a power of attorney executed before October 1, 2011, is conditioned on the principal's lack of capacity and the power of attorney has not become exercisable before that date, the power of attorney is exercisable upon the delivery of the affidavit of a physician who has primary responsibility for the treatment and care of the principal and who is licensed to practice

medicine or osteopathic medicine pursuant to chapter 458 or chapter 459 as of the date of the affidavit. The affidavit executed by the physician must state that the physician is licensed to practice medicine or osteopathic medicine pursuant to chapter 458 or chapter 459, that the physician is the primary physician who has responsibility for the treatment and care of the principal, and that the physician believes that the principal lacks the capacity to manage property.

(3) Except as provided in subsection (2) and s. 709.2106(4), a power of attorney is ineffective if the power of attorney provides that it is to become effective at a future date or upon the occurrence of a future event or contingency.

Added by Laws 2011, c. 2011–210, § 10, eff. Oct. 1, 2011.

709.2109. Termination or suspension of power of attorney or agent's authority

(1) A power of attorney terminates when:

(a) The principal dies;

(b) The principal becomes incapacitated, if the power of attorney is not durable;

(c) The principal is adjudicated totally or partially incapacitated by a court, unless the court determines that certain authority granted by the power of attorney is to be exercisable by the agent;

(d) The principal revokes the power of attorney;

(e) The power of attorney provides that it terminates;

(f) The purpose of the power of attorney is accomplished; or

(g) The agent's authority terminates and the power of attorney does not provide for another agent to act under the power of attorney.

(2) An agent's authority is exercisable until the authority terminates. An agent's authority terminates when:

(a) The agent dies, becomes incapacitated, resigns, or is removed by a court;

(b) An action is filed for the dissolution or annulment of the agent's marriage to the principal or for their legal separation, unless the power of attorney otherwise provides; or

(c) The power of attorney terminates.

(3) If any person initiates judicial proceedings to determine the principal's incapacity or for the appointment of a guardian advocate, the authority granted under the power of attorney is suspended until the petition is dismissed or withdrawn or the court enters an order authorizing the agent to exercise one or more powers granted under the power of attorney. However, if the agent named in the power of attorney is the principal's parent, spouse, child, or grandchild, the authority under the power of attorney is not suspended unless a verified motion in accordance with s. 744.3203 is also filed.

(a) If an emergency arises after initiation of proceedings to determine incapacity and before adjudication regarding the principal's capacity, the agent may petition the court in which the proceeding is pending for authorization to exercise a power granted under the power of attorney. The petition must set forth the nature of the emergency, the property or matter involved, and the power to be exercised by the agent.

(b) Notwithstanding the provisions of this section, unless otherwise ordered by the court, a proceeding to determine incapacity does not affect the authority of the agent to make health care decisions for the principal, including, but not limited to, those provided in chapter 765. If the principal has executed a health care advance directive designating a health care surrogate, the terms of the directive control if the directive and the power of attorney are in conflict unless the power of attorney is later executed and expressly states otherwise.

(4) Termination or suspension of an agent's authority or of a power of attorney is not effective as to an agent who, without knowledge of the termination or suspension, acts in good faith under the power of attorney. An act so performed, unless otherwise invalid or unenforceable, binds the principal and the principal's successors in interest.

Added by Laws 2011, c. 2011–210, § 11, eff. Oct. 1, 2011. Amended by Laws 2015, c. 2015–83, § 1, eff. July 1, 2015.

Applicability

Laws 2015, c. 2015–83, § 20, provides:

"Sections 709.2109 and 744.3203, Florida Statutes, as created by this act, apply to all proceedings filed on or after July 1, 2015. The amendments made by this act to ss. 744.107, 744.1075, 744.108, 744.3025, 744.3031, 744.309, 744.3115, 744.312, 744.331, 744.344, 744.345, 744.359, 744.361, 744.367, 744.369, 744.3715, and 744.464, Florida Statutes, apply to all proceedings pending on July 1, 2015."

709.2110. Revocation of power of attorney

(1) A principal may revoke a power of attorney by expressing the revocation in a subsequently executed power of attorney or other writing signed by the principal. The principal may give notice of the revocation to an agent who has accepted authority under the revoked power of attorney.

(2) Except as provided in subsection (1), the execution of a power of attorney does not revoke a power of attorney previously executed by the principal.

Added by Laws 2011, c. 2011–210, § 12, eff. Oct. 1, 2011.

709.2111. Co-agents and successor agents

(1) A principal may designate two or more persons to act as co-agents. Unless the power of attorney otherwise provides, each co-agent may exercise its authority independently.

(2) A principal may designate one or more successor agents to act if an agent resigns, dies, becomes incapacitated, is not qualified to serve, or declines to serve. Unless the power of attorney otherwise provides, a successor agent:

(a) Has the same authority as that granted to the original agent; and

(b) May not act until the predecessor agents have resigned, have died, have become incapacitated, are no longer qualified to serve, or have declined to serve.

(3) Except as otherwise provided in the power of attorney and subsection (4), an agent who does not participate in or conceal a breach of fiduciary duty committed by another agent, including a predecessor agent, is not liable for the actions or omissions of the other agent.

(4) An agent who has actual knowledge of a breach or imminent breach of fiduciary duty by another agent, including a predecessor agent, must take any action reasonably appropriate in the circumstances to safeguard the principal's best interests. If the agent in good faith believes that the principal is not incapacitated, giving notice to the principal is a sufficient action. An agent who fails to take action as required by this subsection is liable to the principal for the

principal's reasonably foreseeable damages that could have been avoided if the agent had taken such action.

(5) A successor agent does not have a duty to review the conduct or decisions of a predecessor agent. Except as provided in subsection (4), a successor agent does not have a duty to institute any proceeding against a predecessor agent, or to file any claim against a predecessor agent's estate, for any of the predecessor agent's actions or omissions as agent.

(6) If a power of attorney requires that two or more persons act together as co-agents, notwithstanding the requirement that they act together, one or more of the agents may delegate to a co-agent the authority to conduct banking transactions as provided in s. 709.2208(1), whether the authority to conduct banking transactions is specifically enumerated or incorporated by reference to that section in the power of attorney.

Added by Laws 2011, c. 2011–210, § 13, eff. Oct. 1, 2011.

709.2112. Reimbursement and compensation of agent

(1) Unless the power of attorney otherwise provides, an agent is entitled to reimbursement of expenses reasonably incurred on behalf of the principal.

(2) Unless the power of attorney otherwise provides, a qualified agent is entitled to compensation that is reasonable under the circumstances.

(3) Notwithstanding any provision in the power of attorney, an agent may not be paid compensation unless the agent is a qualified agent.

(4) For purposes of this section, the term "qualified agent" means an agent who is the spouse of the principal, an heir of the principal within the meaning of s. 732.103, a financial institution that has trust powers and a place of business in this state, an attorney or certified public accountant who is licensed in this state, or a natural person who is a resident of this state and who has never been an agent for more than three principals at the same time.

Added by Laws 2011, c. 2011–210, § 14, eff. Oct. 1, 2011.

709.2113. Agent's acceptance of appointment

Except as otherwise provided in the power of attorney, a person accepts appointment as an agent by exercising authority or performing duties as an agent or by any other assertion or conduct indicating acceptance. The scope of an agent's acceptance is limited to those aspects of the power of attorney for which the agent's assertions or conduct reasonably manifests acceptance.

Added by Laws 2011, c. 2011–210, § 15, eff. Oct. 1, 2011.

709.2114. Agent's duties

(1) An agent is a fiduciary. Notwithstanding the provisions in the power of attorney, an agent who has accepted appointment:

(a) Must act only within the scope of authority granted in the power of attorney. In exercising that authority, the agent:

1. May not act contrary to the principal's reasonable expectations actually known by the agent;

2. Must act in good faith;

3. May not act in a manner that is contrary to the principal's best interest, except as provided in paragraph (2)(d) and s. 709.2202; and

4. Must attempt to preserve the principal's estate plan, to the extent actually known by the agent, if preserving the plan is consistent with the principal's best interest based on all relevant factors, including:

   a. The value and nature of the principal's property;

   b. The principal's foreseeable obligations and need for maintenance;

   c. Minimization of taxes, including income, estate, inheritance, generation-skipping transfer, and gift taxes;

   d. Eligibility for a benefit, a program, or assistance under a statute or rule; and

   e. The principal's personal history of making or joining in making gifts;

(b) May not delegate authority to a third person except as authorized under s. 518.112 or this part or by executing a power of attorney on a form prescribed by a government or governmental subdivision, agency, or instrumentality for a governmental purpose;

(c) Must keep a record of all receipts, disbursements, and transactions made on behalf of the principal; and

(d) Must create and maintain an accurate inventory each time the agent accesses the principal's safe-deposit box, if the power of attorney authorizes the agent to access the box.

(2) Except as otherwise provided in the power of attorney, an agent who has accepted appointment shall:

(a) Act loyally for the sole benefit of the principal;

(b) Act so as not to create a conflict of interest that impairs the agent's ability to act impartially in the principal's best interest;

(c) Act with the care, competence, and diligence ordinarily exercised by agents in similar circumstances; and

(d) Cooperate with a person who has authority to make health care decisions for the principal in order to carry out the principal's reasonable expectations to the extent actually known by the agent and, otherwise, act in the principal's best interest.

(3) An agent who acts in good faith is not liable to any beneficiary of the principal's estate plan for failure to preserve the plan.

(4) If an agent is selected by the principal because of special skills or expertise possessed by the agent or in reliance on the agent's representation that the agent has special skills or expertise, the special skills or expertise must be considered in determining whether the agent has acted with care, competence, and diligence under the circumstances.

(5) Absent a breach of duty to the principal, an agent is not liable if the value of the principal's property declines.

(6) Except as otherwise provided in the power of attorney, an agent is not required to disclose receipts, disbursements, transactions conducted on behalf of the principal, or safe-deposit box inventories, unless ordered by a court or requested by the principal, a court-appointed guardian, another fiduciary acting for the principal, a governmental agency having authority to protect the welfare of the principal, or, upon the death of the principal, by the personal representative or successor in interest of the principal's estate. If requested, the agent must comply with the

request within 60 days or provide a writing or other record substantiating why additional time is needed and comply with the request within an additional 60 days.

Added by Laws 2011, c. 2011–210, § 16, eff. Oct. 1, 2011. Amended by Laws 2013, c. 2013–90, § 5, eff. May 30, 2013.

709.2115. Exoneration of agent

A power of attorney may provide that the agent is not liable for any acts or decisions made by the agent in good faith and under the power of attorney, except to the extent the provision:

(1) Relieves the agent of liability for breach of a duty committed dishonestly, with improper motive, or with reckless indifference to the purposes of the power of attorney or the best interest of the principal; or

(2) Was inserted as a result of an abuse of a confidential or fiduciary relationship with the principal.

Added by Laws 2011, c. 2011–210, § 17, eff. Oct. 1, 2011.

709.2116. Judicial relief; conflicts of interests

(1) A court may construe or enforce a power of attorney, review the agent's conduct, terminate the agent's authority, remove the agent, and grant other appropriate relief.

(2) The following persons may petition the court:

(a) The principal or the agent, including any nominated successor agent.

(b) A guardian, conservator, trustee, or other fiduciary acting for the principal or the principal's estate.

(c) A person authorized to make health care decisions for the principal if the health care of the principal is affected by the actions of the agent.

(d) Any other interested person if the person demonstrates to the court's satisfaction that the person is interested in the welfare of the principal and has a good faith belief that the court's intervention is necessary.

(e) A governmental agency having regulatory authority to protect the welfare of the principal.

(f) A person asked to honor the power of attorney.

(3) In any proceeding commenced by filing a petition under this section, including, but not limited to, the unreasonable refusal of a third person to allow an agent to act pursuant to the power of attorney, and in challenges to the proper exercise of authority by the agent, the court shall award reasonable attorney fees and costs as in chancery actions.

(4) If an agent's exercise of a power is challenged in a judicial proceeding brought by or on behalf of the principal on the grounds that the exercise of the power was affected by a conflict of interest, and evidence is presented that the agent or an affiliate of the agent had a personal interest in the exercise of the power, the agent or affiliate has the burden of proving, by clear and convincing evidence that the agent acted:

(a) Solely in the interest of the principal; or

(b) In good faith in the principal's best interest, and the conflict of interest was expressly authorized in the power of attorney.

(5) For purposes of subsection (4):

(a) A provision authorizing an agent to engage in a transaction affected by a conflict of interest which is inserted into a power of attorney as the result of the abuse of a fiduciary or confidential relationship with the principal by the agent or the agent's affiliate is invalid.

(b) Affiliates of an agent include:

1. The agent's spouse;

2. The agent's descendants, siblings, parents, or their spouses;

3. A corporation or other entity in which the agent, or a person who owns a significant interest in the agent, has an interest that might affect the agent's best judgment;

4. A person or entity that owns a significant interest in the agent; or

5. The agent acting in a fiduciary capacity for someone other than the principal.

Added by Laws 2011, c. 2011–210, § 18, eff. Oct. 1, 2011. Amended by Laws 2013, c. 2013–90, § 6, eff. May 30, 2013.

709.2117. Agent's liability

An agent who violates this part is liable to the principal or the principal's successors in interest for the amount required to:

(1) Restore the value of the principal's property to what it would have been had the violation not occurred; and

(2) Reimburse the principal or the principal's successors in interest for the attorney's fees and costs paid from the principal's funds on the agent's behalf in defense of the agent's actions.
Added by Laws 2011, c. 2011–210, § 19, eff. Oct. 1, 2011.

709.2118. Agent's resignation

Unless the power of attorney provides a different method for an agent's resignation, an agent may resign by giving notice to the principal, to the guardian if the principal is incapacitated and one has been appointed for the principal, and to any co-agent, or if none, the next successor agent.
Added by Laws 2011, c. 2011–210, § 20, eff. Oct. 1, 2011.

709.2119. Acceptance of and reliance upon power of attorney

(1)(a) A third person who in good faith accepts a power of attorney that appears to be executed in the manner required by law at the time of its execution may rely upon the power of attorney and the actions of the agent which are reasonably within the scope of the agent's authority and may enforce any obligation created by the actions of the agent as if:

1. The power of attorney were genuine, valid, and still in effect;

2. The agent's authority were genuine, valid, and still in effect; and

3. The authority of the officer executing for or on behalf of a financial institution that has trust powers and acting as agent is genuine, valid, and still in effect.

(b) For purposes of this subsection, and without limiting what constitutes good faith, a third person does not accept a power of attorney in good faith if the third person has notice that:

1. The power of attorney is void, invalid, or terminated; or

2. The purported agent's authority is void, invalid, suspended, or terminated.

(2) A third person may require:

(a) An agent to execute an affidavit stating where the principal is domiciled; that the principal is not deceased; that there has been no revocation, or partial or complete termination by adjudication of incapacity or by the occurrence of an event referenced in the power of attorney; that there has been no suspension by initiation of proceedings to determine incapacity, or to appoint a guardian, of the principal; that the agent's authority has not been terminated by the filing of an action for dissolution or annulment of marriage or legal separation of the agent and principal; and, if the affiant is a successor agent, the reasons for the unavailability of the predecessor agents, if any, at the time the authority is exercised.

(b) An officer of a financial institution acting as agent to execute a separate affidavit, or include in the form of the affidavit, the officer's title and a statement that the officer has full authority to perform all acts and enter into all transactions authorized by the power of attorney for and on behalf of the financial institution in its capacity as agent.

(c) A written affidavit executed by the agent under this subsection may, but need not, be in the following form:

STATE OF_____

COUNTY OF_____

Before me, the undersigned authority, personally appeared (agent) ("Affiant"), who swore or affirmed that:

1. Affiant is the agent named in the Power of Attorney executed by (principal) ("Principal") on (date) .

2. This Power of Attorney is currently exercisable by Affiant. The principal is domiciled in (insert name of state, territory, or foreign country) .

3. To the best of Affiant's knowledge after diligent search and inquiry:

a. The Principal is not deceased;

b. Affiant's authority has not been suspended by initiation of proceedings to determine incapacity or to appoint a guardian or a guardian advocate;

c. Affiant's authority has not been terminated by the filing of an action for dissolution or annulment of Affiant's marriage to the principal, or their legal separation; and

d. There has been no revocation, or partial or complete termination, of the power of attorney or of Affiant's authority.

4. Affiant is acting within the scope of authority granted in the power of attorney.

5. Affiant is the successor to (insert name of predecessor agent) , who has resigned, died, become incapacitated, is no longer qualified to serve, has declined to serve as agent, or is otherwise unable to act, if applicable.

6. Affiant agrees not to exercise any powers granted by the Power of Attorney if Affiant attains knowledge that the power of attorney has been revoked, has been partially or completely terminated or suspended, or is no longer valid because of the death or adjudication of incapacity of the Principal.

_____
(Affiant)

Sworn to (or affirmed) and subscribed before me this ___ day of (month) , (year) , by (name of person making statement)

 (Signature of Notary Public-State of Florida)

(Print, Type, or Stamp Commissioned Name of Notary Public)

Personally Known OR Produced Identification

(Type of Identification Produced)

(3) A third person who is asked to accept a power of attorney that appears to be executed in accordance with s. 709.2105 may in good faith request, and rely upon, without further investigation:

(a) A certified English translation of the power of attorney if the power of attorney contains, in whole or in part, language other than English;

(b) An opinion of counsel as to any matter of law concerning the power of attorney if the third person making the request provides in a writing or other record the reason for the request; or

(c) The affidavit described in subsection (2).

(4) An English translation or an opinion of counsel requested under this section must be provided at the principal's expense unless the request is made after the time specified in s. 709.2120(1) for acceptance or rejection of the power of attorney.

(5) Third persons who act in reliance upon the authority granted to an agent and in accordance with the instructions of the agent shall be held harmless by the principal from any loss suffered or liability incurred as a result of actions taken before the receipt of notice as provided in s. 709.2121. A third person who acts in good faith upon any representation, direction, decision, or act of the agent is not liable to the principal or the principal's estate, beneficiaries, or joint owners for those acts.

(6) The acts of an agent under a power of attorney are as valid and binding on the principal or the principal's estate as if the principal were alive and competent if, in connection with any activity pertaining to hostilities in which the United States is then engaged, the principal is officially listed or reported by a branch of the United States Armed Forces in a missing status as defined in 37 U.S.C. s. 551 or 5 U.S.C. s. 5561, regardless of whether the principal is dead, alive, or incompetent. Homestead property held as tenants by the entireties may not be conveyed by a power of attorney regulated under this provision until 1 year after the first official report or listing of the principal as missing or missing in action. An affidavit of an officer of the Armed Forces having maintenance and control of the records pertaining to those missing or missing in action that the principal has been in that status for a given period is conclusive presumption of the fact.

Added by Laws 2011, c. 2011–210, § 21, eff. Oct. 1, 2011. Amended by Laws 2013, c. 2013–90, § 7, eff. May 30, 2013.

709.2120.   Rejecting power of attorney

(1) A third person must accept or reject a power of attorney within a reasonable time. Four days, excluding Saturdays, Sundays, and legal holidays, are presumed to be a reasonable time for a financial institution or broker-dealer to accept or reject a power of attorney with respect to:

(a) A banking transaction, if the power of attorney expressly contains authority to conduct banking transactions pursuant to s. 709.2208(1); or

(b) An investment transaction, if the power of attorney expressly contains authority to conduct investment transactions pursuant to s. 709.2208(2).

(2) A third person may not require an additional or different form of power of attorney for authority granted in the power of attorney presented.

(3) A third person who rejects a power of attorney for any reason other than as provided in paragraph (4)(a) must state in writing the reason for the rejection.

(4) A third person is not required to accept a power of attorney if:

(a) The third person is not otherwise required to engage in a transaction with the principal in the same circumstances;

(b) The third person has knowledge of the termination or suspension of the agent's authority or of the power of attorney before exercising the power;

(c) A timely request by the third person for an affidavit, English translation, or opinion of counsel under s. 709.2119(4) is refused by the agent;

(d) Except as provided in paragraph (b), the third person believes in good faith that the power is not valid or that the agent does not have authority to perform the act requested; or

(e) The third person makes, or has knowledge that another person has made, a report to the local adult protective services office stating a good faith belief that the principal may be subject to physical or financial abuse, neglect, exploitation, or abandonment by the agent or a person acting for or with the agent.

(5) A third person who, in violation of this section, rejects a power of attorney is subject to:

(a) A court order mandating acceptance of the power of attorney; and

(b) Liability for damages, including reasonable attorney fees and costs, incurred in any action or proceeding that confirms, for the purpose tendered, the validity of the power of attorney or mandates acceptance of the power of attorney.

Added by Laws 2011, c. 2011–210, § 22, eff. Oct. 1, 2011. Amended by Laws 2013, c. 2013–90, § 8, eff. May 30, 2013.

709.2121. Notice

(1) A notice, including a notice of revocation, notice of partial or complete termination by adjudication of incapacity or by the occurrence of an event referenced in the power of attorney, notice of death of the principal, notice of suspension by initiation of proceedings to determine incapacity or to appoint a guardian, or other notice, is not effective until written notice is provided to the agent or any third persons relying upon a power of attorney.

(2) Notice must be in writing and must be accomplished in a manner reasonably suitable under the circumstances and likely to result in receipt of the notice or document. Permissible methods of notice or for sending a document include first-class mail, personal delivery, delivery to the person's last known place of residence or place of business, or a properly directed facsimile or other electronic message.

(3) Notice to a financial institution or broker-dealer must contain the principal's name and address and the last four digits of the principal's taxpayer identification number and be directed to an officer or a manager of the financial institution or broker-dealer in this state.

(4) Notice is effective when given, except that notice upon a financial institution, brokerage company, or title insurance company is not effective until 5 days, excluding Saturdays, Sundays, and legal holidays, after it is received.

Added by Laws 2011, c. 2011–210, § 23, eff. Oct. 1, 2011. Amended by Laws 2013, c. 2013–90, § 9, eff. May 30, 2013.

709.2201. Authority of agent

(1) Except as provided in this section or other applicable law, an agent may only exercise authority specifically granted to the agent in the power of attorney and any authority reasonably necessary to give effect to that express grant of specific authority. General provisions in a power of attorney which do not identify the specific authority granted, such as provisions purporting to give the agent authority to do all acts that the principal can do, are not express grants of specific authority and do not grant any authority to the agent. Court approval is not required for any action of the agent in furtherance of an express grant of specific authority.

(2) As a confirmation of the law in effect in this state when this part became effective, such authorization may include, without limitation, authority to:

(a) Execute stock powers or similar documents on behalf of the principal and delegate to a transfer agent or similar person the authority to register any stocks, bonds, or other securities into or out of the principal's or nominee's name.

(b) Convey or mortgage homestead property. However, if the principal is married, the agent may not mortgage or convey homestead property without joinder of the principal's spouse or the spouse's guardian. Joinder by a spouse may be accomplished by the exercise of authority in a power of attorney executed by the joining spouse, and either spouse may appoint the other as his or her agent.

(c) If such authority is specifically granted in a durable power of attorney, make all health care decisions on behalf of the principal, including, but not limited to, those set forth in chapter 765.

(3) Notwithstanding the provisions of this section, an agent may not:

(a) Perform duties under a contract that requires the exercise of personal services of the principal;

(b) Make any affidavit as to the personal knowledge of the principal;

(c) Vote in any public election on behalf of the principal;

(d) Execute or revoke any will or codicil for the principal; or

(e) Exercise powers and authority granted to the principal as trustee or as court-appointed fiduciary.

(4) Subject to s. 709.2202, if the subjects over which authority is granted in a power of attorney are similar or overlap, the broadest authority controls.

(5) Authority granted in a power of attorney is exercisable with respect to property that the principal has when the power of attorney is executed and to property that the principal acquires later, whether or not the property is located in this state and whether or not the authority is exercised or the power of attorney is executed in this state.

(6) An act performed by an agent pursuant to a power of attorney has the same effect and inures to the benefit of and binds the principal and the principal's successors in interest as if the principal had performed the act.

Added by Laws 2011, c. 2011–210, § 24, eff. Oct. 1, 2011.

709.2202. Authority that requires separate signed enumeration

(1) Notwithstanding s. 709.2201, an agent may exercise the following authority only if the principal signed or initialed next to each specific enumeration of the authority, the exercise of

the authority is consistent with the agent's duties under s. 709.2114, and the exercise is not otherwise prohibited by another agreement or instrument:

(a) Create an inter vivos trust;

(b) With respect to a trust created by or on behalf of the principal, amend, modify, revoke, or terminate the trust, but only if the trust instrument explicitly provides for amendment, modification, revocation, or termination by the settlor's agent;

(c) Make a gift, subject to subsection (4);

(d) Create or change rights of survivorship;

(e) Create or change a beneficiary designation;

(f) Waive the principal's right to be a beneficiary of a joint and survivor annuity, including a survivor benefit under a retirement plan; or

(g) Disclaim property and powers of appointment.

(2) In addition to signing the power of attorney on behalf of the principal pursuant to s. 709.2105(3), if the principal is physically unable to sign or initial next to any enumerated authority for which subsection (1) requires the principal to sign or initial, the notary public before whom the principal's oath or acknowledgment is made may sign the principal's name or initials if:

(a) The principal directs the notary to sign the principal's name or initials on the power of attorney next to any enumerated authority for which subsection (1) requires the principal to sign or initial;

(b) The signing or initialling by the notary is done in the presence of the principal and witnessed by two disinterested subscribing witnesses; and

(c) The notary writes the statement "Signature or initials affixed by the notary pursuant to s. 709.2202(2), Florida Statutes," below each signature or initial that the notary writes on behalf of the principal.

Only one notarial certificate in substantially the same form as those described in s. 117.05(14), which states the circumstances of all signatures and initials written by the notary public, is required to be completed by the notary public.

(3) Notwithstanding a grant of authority to do an act described in subsection (1), unless the power of attorney otherwise provides, an agent who is not an ancestor, spouse, or descendant of the principal may not exercise authority to create in the agent, or in an individual to whom the agent owes a legal obligation of support, an interest in the principal's property, whether by gift, right of survivorship, beneficiary designation, disclaimer, or otherwise.

(4) Unless the power of attorney otherwise provides, a provision in a power of attorney granting general authority with respect to gifts authorizes the agent to only:

(a) Make outright to, or for the benefit of, a person a gift of any of the principal's property, including by the exercise of a presently exercisable general power of appointment held by the principal, in an amount per donee per calendar year not to exceed the annual dollar limits of the federal gift tax exclusion under 26 U.S.C. s. 2503(b), as amended, without regard to whether the federal gift tax exclusion applies to the gift, or if the principal's spouse agrees to consent to a split gift pursuant to 26 U.S.C. s. 2513, as amended, in an amount per donee per calendar year not to exceed twice the annual federal gift tax exclusion limit; and

(b) Consent, pursuant to 26 U.S.C. s. 2513, as amended, to the splitting of a gift made by the principal's spouse in an amount per donee per calendar year not to exceed the aggregate annual gift tax exclusions for both spouses.

(5) Notwithstanding subsection (1), if a power of attorney is otherwise sufficient to grant an agent authority to conduct banking transactions, as provided in s. 709.2208(1), conduct investment transactions as provided in s. 709.2208(2), or otherwise make additions to or withdrawals from an account of the principal, making a deposit to or withdrawal from an insurance policy, retirement account, individual retirement account, benefit plan, bank account, or any other account held jointly or otherwise held in survivorship or payable on death, is not considered to be a change to the survivorship feature or beneficiary designation, and no further specific authority is required for the agent to exercise such authority. A financial institution or broker-dealer does not have a duty to inquire as to the appropriateness of the agent's exercise of that authority and is not liable to the principal or any other person for actions taken in good faith reliance on the appropriateness of the agent's actions. This subsection does not eliminate the agent's fiduciary duties to the principal with respect to any exercise of the power of attorney.

(6) This section does not apply to a power of attorney executed before October 1, 2011.

Added by Laws 2011, c. 2011–210, § 25, eff. Oct. 1, 2011. Amended by Laws 2013, c. 2013–90, § 10, eff. May 30, 2013.

709.2208. Banks and other financial institutions

(1) A power of attorney that includes the statement that the agent has "authority to conduct banking transactions as provided in section 709.2208(1), Florida Statutes" grants general authority to the agent to engage in the following transactions with financial institutions without additional specific enumeration in the power of attorney:

(a) Establish, continue, modify, or terminate an account or other banking arrangement with a financial institution.

(b) Contract for services available from a financial institution, including renting a safe-deposit box or space in a vault.

(c) Withdraw, by check, order, electronic funds transfer, or otherwise, money or property of the principal deposited with or left in the custody of a financial institution.

(d) Receive statements of account, vouchers, notices, and similar documents from a financial institution and act with respect to them.

(e) Purchase cashier's checks, official checks, counter checks, bank drafts, money orders, and similar instruments.

(f) Endorse and negotiate checks, cashier's checks, official checks, drafts, and other negotiable paper of the principal or payable to the principal or the principal's order, transfer money, receive the cash or other proceeds of those transactions, and accept a draft drawn by a person upon the principal and pay it when due.

(g) Apply for, receive, and use debit cards, electronic transaction authorizations, and traveler's checks from a financial institution.

(h) Use, charge, or draw upon any line of credit, credit card, or other credit established by the principal with a financial institution.

(i) Consent to an extension of the time of payment with respect to commercial paper or a financial transaction with a financial institution.

(2) A power of attorney that specifically includes the statement that the agent has "authority to conduct investment transactions as provided in section 709.2208(2), Florida Statutes" grants general authority to the agent with respect to securities held by financial institutions or broker-dealers to take the following actions without additional specific enumeration in the power of attorney:

(a) Buy, sell, and exchange investment instruments.

(b) Establish, continue, modify, or terminate an account with respect to investment instruments.

(c) Pledge investment instruments as security to borrow, pay, renew, or extend the time of payment of a debt of the principal.

(d) Receive certificates and other evidences of ownership with respect to investment instruments.

(e) Exercise voting rights with respect to investment instruments in person or by proxy, enter into voting trusts, and consent to limitations on the right to vote.

(f) Sell commodity futures contracts and call and put options on stocks and stock indexes.

For purposes of this subsection, the term "investment instruments" means stocks, bonds, mutual funds, and all other types of securities and financial instruments, whether held directly, indirectly, or in any other manner, including shares or interests in a private investment fund, including, but not limited to, a private investment fund organized as a limited partnership, a limited liability company, a statutory or common law business trust, a statutory trust, or a real estate investment trust, joint venture, or any other general or limited partnership; derivatives or other interests of any nature in securities such as options, options on futures, and variable forward contracts; mutual funds; common trust funds; money market funds; hedge funds; private equity or venture capital funds; insurance contracts; and other entities or vehicles investing in securities or interests in securities whether registered or otherwise, except commodity futures contracts and call and put options on stocks and stock indexes.

Added by Laws 2011, c. 2011–210, § 26, eff. Oct. 1, 2011. Amended by Laws 2013, c. 2013–90, § 11, eff. May 30, 2013.

709.2301. Principles of law and equity

The common law of agency and principles of equity supplement this part, except as modified by this part or other state law.

Added by Laws 2011, c. 2011–210, § 27, eff. Oct. 1, 2011.

709.2302. Laws applicable to financial institutions and entities

This part does not supersede any other law applicable to financial institutions or other entities, and that law controls if inconsistent with this part.

Added by Laws 2011, c. 2011–210, § 28, eff. Oct. 1, 2011.

709.2303. Remedies under other law

The remedies under this part are not exclusive and do not abrogate any right or remedy under any other law other than this part.

Added by Laws 2011, c. 2011–210, § 29, eff. Oct. 1, 2011.

709.2401. Relation to electronic signatures in federal law

This part modifies, limits, and supersedes the federal Electronic Signatures in Global and National Commerce Act, 15 U.S.C. s. 7001 et seq., but does not modify, limit, or supersede s. 101(c) of that act,[1] or authorize electronic delivery of any of the notices described in s. 103(b) of that act.[2]

Added by Laws 2011, c. 2011–210, § 30, eff. Oct. 1, 2011.

[1] 15 U.S.C.A. § 7001(c).
[2] 15 U.S.C.A. § 7003(b).

709.2402. Effect on existing powers of attorney

Except as otherwise provided in this part:

(1) With respect to formalities of execution, this part applies to a power of attorney created on or after October 1, 2011.

(2) With respect to all matters other than formalities of execution, this part applies to a power of attorney regardless of the date of creation.

(3) With respect to a power of attorney existing on October 1, 2011, this part does not invalidate such power of attorney and it shall remain in effect. If a right was acquired under any other law before October 1, 2011, that law continues to apply to the right even if it has been repealed or superseded.

(4) An act of an agent occurring before October 1, 2011, is not affected by this part.

Added by Laws 2011, c. 2011–210, § 31, eff. Oct. 1, 2011.

CHAPTER 710

TRANSFERS TO MINORS

TRANSFERS TO MINORS

Former Provisions

Laws 1985, c. 85–95, § 2, provides for the repeal of §§ 710.01 through 710.10 containing the "Florida Gifts to Minors Act". Section 1 of the 1985 Law enacted § 710.101 et seq., creating the "Florida Uniform Transfers to Minors Act".

UNIFORM TRANSFERS TO MINORS ACT

Table of Jurisdictions Wherein Act Has Been Adopted

For text of Uniform Act, and variation notes and annotation materials for adopting jurisdictions, see Uniform Laws Annotated, Master Edition, Volume 8C.

Jurisdiction	Laws	Effective Date	Statutory Citation
Alabama	1986, No. 86–453	10–1–1986	Code 1975, §§ 35–5A–1 to 35–5A–24.
Alaska	1990, c. 11	1–1–1991	AS 13.46.010 to 13.46.999.
Arizona	1988, c. 81	5–16–1988 *	A.R.S. §§ 14–7651 to 14–7671.
Arkansas	1985, No. 476	3–21–1985	A.C.A. §§ 9–26–201 to 9–26–227.
California	1984, c. 243	6–24–1984 *	West's Ann.Cal.Prob.Code, §§ 3900 to 3925.
Colorado	1984, p. 383	7–1–1984	West's C.R.S.A. §§ 11–50–101 to 11–50–126.
Connecticut	1995, P.A. 95–117	10–1–1995	C.G.S.A. §§ 45a–557 to 45a–560b.
Delaware	70 Del. Laws, c. 393	6–26–1996	12 Del. C. §§4501 to 4523.
District of Columbia	1986, D.C. Law 6–87	3–12–1986	D.C. Official Code, 2001 Ed. §§ 21–301 to 21–324.
Florida	1985, c. 85–95	10–1–1985	West's F.S.A. §§ 710.101 to 710.126.
Georgia	1990, p. 667	7–1–1990	O.C.G.A. §§ 44–5–110 to 44–5–134.
Hawaii	1985, No. 91	7–1–1985	HRS §§ 553A–1 to 553A–24.
Idaho	1984, c. 152	7–1–1984	I.C. §§ 68–801 to 68–825.
Illinois	1985, P.A. 84–915	7–1–1986	S.H.A. 760 ILCS 20/1 to 20/24.
Indiana	1989, P.L. 267–1989	5–4–1989 *	West's A.I.C. 30–2–8.5–1 to 30–2–8.5–40.
Iowa	1986, H.F. 2381	4–7–1986 *	I.C.A. §§ 565B.1 to 565B.25.
Kansas	1985, c. 143	4–4–1985 *	K.S.A. 38–1701 to 38–1726.
Kentucky	1986, c. 182	3–28–1986 *	KRS 385.012 to 385.252.
Louisiana	1987, No. 469	1–1–1988	LSA–R.S. 9:751 to 9:773.
Maine	1987, c. 734	4–19–1988 *	33 M.R.S.A. §§ 1651 to 1674.
Maryland	1989, c. 638	7–1–1989	Code, Estates and Trusts, §§ 13–301 to 13–324.
Massachusetts	1986, c. 362	1–30–1987	M.G.L.A. c. 201A, §§ 1 to 24.
Michigan	1998, P.A. 433	12–30–1998	M.C.L.A. §§ 554.521 to 554.552.
Minnesota	1985, c. 221	1–1–1986	M.S.A. §§ 527.21 to 527.44.
Mississippi	1994, c. 416	1–1–1995	Code 1972, §§ 91–20–1 to 91–20–49.
Missouri	1985, S.B. 35, 17, 18, 84, 206, 259, 278	7–30–1985 *	V.A.M.S. §§ 404.005 to 404.094.
Montana	1985, c. 102		MCA 72–26–501 to 72–26–803.
Nebraska	1992, LB 907	2–28–1992 *	R.R.S.1943, §§ 43–2701 to 43–2724.
Nevada	1985, c. 51	3–28–1985 *	N.R.S. 167.010 to 167.100.

For Annotative Materials, see West's Florida Statutes Annotated

Jurisdiction	Laws	Effective Date	Statutory Citation
New Hampshire	1985, No. 197:1	7–30–1985	RSA 463–A:1 to 463–A:26.
New Jersey [1]	1987, c. 18	7–1–1987	N.J.S.A. 46:38A–1 to 46:38A–57.
New Mexico	1989, c. 357	7–1–1989	NMSA 1978, §§ 46–7–11 to 46–7–34.
New York	1996, c. 304	7–10–1996	McKinney's EPTL, 7–6.1 to 7–6.26.
North Carolina	1987, c. 563	10–1–1987	G.S. §§ 33A–1 to 33A–24.
North Dakota	1985, c. 508		NDCC 47–24.1–01 to 47–24.1–22.
Ohio	2006, H.B. 416	1–1–2007	R.C. §§ 5814.01 to 5814.09.
Oklahoma	1986, c. 261	11–1–1986	58 Okl.St.Ann. §§ 1201 to 1225.
Oregon	1985, c. 665	1–1–1986	ORS 126.805 to 126.886.
Pennsylvania	1992, Act 152	12–16–1992	20 Pa.C.S.A., §§ 5301 to 5321.
Rhode Island	1985, c. 389	6–28–1985	Gen.Laws 1956, §§ 18–7–1 to 18–7–26.
South Dakota	SL 1986, c. 409		SDCL 55–10A–1 to 55–10A–26.
Tennessee...........	1992, c. 664	10–1–1992	T.C.A. §§ 35–7–101 to 35–7–126.
Texas	1995, c. 1043	9–1–1995	V.T.C.A. Property Code, §§ 141.001 to 141.025.
Utah...............	1990, c. 272	7–1–1990	U.C.A.1953, 75–5a–101 to 75–5a–123.
Virgin Islands	2001, No. 6423	8–2–2001 *	15 V.I.C. §§ 1251a to 1251x.
Virginia	1988, c. 516		Code 1950, §§ 64.2–1900 to 64.2–1922.
Washington	1991, c. 193	7–1–1991	West's RCWA 11.114.010 to 11.114.904.
West Virginia	1986, c. 169	7–1–1986	Code 36–7–1 to 36–7–24.
Wisconsin	1987–89, c. 191	4–8–1988	W.S.A. 54.854 to 54.898.
Wyoming	1987, c. 201	5–22–1987	Wyo.Stat.Ann. §§ 34–13–114 to 34–13–137.

* Date of approval.
[1] Repealed Gifts to Minors Act of 1966, effective July 1, 2007. Transfers to Minors Act adopted, effective July 1, 1987.

710.101. Short title

This act may be cited as the "Florida Uniform Transfers to Minors Act."

Laws 1985, c. 85–95, § 1.

710.102. Definitions

As used in this act, the term:

(1) "Adult" means an individual who has attained the age of 21 years.

(2) "Benefit plan" means a retirement plan and may include, but is not limited to, any pension, profit-sharing, stock-bonus, or stock-ownership plan or individual retirement account.

(3) "Broker" means a person lawfully engaged in the business of effecting transactions in securities or commodities for the person's own account or for the account of others.

(4) "Conservator" means a person appointed or qualified by a court to act as general, limited, or temporary guardian of a minor's property or a person legally authorized to perform substantially the same functions.

(5) "Court" means the circuit court.

(6) "Custodial property" means any interest in property transferred to a custodian under this act and the income from and proceeds of that interest in property.

(7) "Custodian" means a person so designated under s. 710.111 or a successor or substitute custodian designated under s. 710.121.

(8) "Financial institution" means a bank, trust company, savings institution, or credit union, chartered and supervised under state or federal law.

(9) "General power of appointment" means a power of appointment as defined in s. 732.2025(3).

(10) "Legal representative" means an individual's personal representative or conservator.

(11) "Member of the minor's family" means the minor's parent, stepparent, spouse, grandparent, brother, sister, uncle, or aunt, whether of the whole or half blood or by adoption.

(12) "Minor" means an individual who has not attained the age of 21 years.

(13) "Person" means an individual, corporation, organization, or other legal entity.

(14) "Personal representative" means an executor, administrator, successor personal representative, or special administrator of a decedent's estate or a person legally authorized to perform substantially the same functions.

(15) "Qualified minor's trust" means a trust that meets the requirements of s. 2503(c) of the Internal Revenue Code of 1986,[1] as amended.

(16) "State" includes any state of the United States, the District of Columbia, the Commonwealth of Puerto Rico, and any territory or possession subject to the legislative authority of the United States.

(17) "Transfer" means a transaction that creates custodial property under s. 710.111.

(18) "Transferor" means a person who makes a transfer under this act.

(19) "Trust company" means a financial institution, corporation, or other legal entity, authorized to exercise general trust powers.

Laws 1985, c. 85–95, § 1. Amended by Laws 2005, c. 2005–101, § 3, eff. June 1, 2005; Laws 2015, c. 2015–140, § 1, eff. July 1, 2015.

[1] 26 U.S.C.A. § 2503(c).

Cross References

Fiduciary lawyer-client privilege, see F.S.A. § 90.5021.
Guardianship, natural guardians, see F.S.A. § 744.301.
Minor, definition, see § 1.01.
Rights, privileges and obligations of persons 18 years of age or older, see § 743.07.

710.103. Scope and jurisdiction

(1) This act applies to a transfer that refers to this act in the designation under s. 710.111(1) by which the transfer is made if at the time of the transfer, the transferor, the minor, or the custodian is a resident of this state or the custodial property is located in this state. The custodianship so created remains subject to this act despite a subsequent change in residence of a transferor, the minor, or the custodian, or the removal of custodial property from this state.

(2) A person designated as custodian under this act is subject to personal jurisdiction in this state with respect to any matter relating to the custodianship.

(3) A transfer that purports to be made and which is valid under the Uniform Transfers to Minors Act, the Uniform Gifts to Minors Act, or a substantially similar act, of another state is governed by the law of the designated state and may be executed and is enforceable in this state if, at the time of the transfer, the transferor, the minor, or the custodian is a resident of the designated state or the custodial property is located in the designated state.

Laws 1985, c. 85–95, § 1.

710.104. Nomination of custodian

(1) A person having the right to designate the recipient of property transferable upon the occurrence of a future event may revocably nominate a custodian to receive the property for a

minor beneficiary upon the occurrence of the event by naming the custodian followed in substance by the words: "as custodian for (name of minor) under the Florida Uniform Transfers to Minors Act." The nomination may name one or more persons as substitute custodians to whom the property must be transferred, in the order named, if the first nominated custodian dies before the transfer or is unable, declines, or is ineligible to serve. The nomination may be made in a will, a trust, a deed, an instrument exercising a power of appointment, or in a writing designating a beneficiary of contractual rights, including, but not limited to, the right to a benefit plan, which is registered with or delivered to the payor, issuer, or other obligor of the contractual rights.

(2) A custodian nominated under this section must be a person to whom a transfer of property of that kind may be made under s. 710.111(1).

(3) The nomination of a custodian under this section does not create custodial property until the nominating instrument becomes irrevocable or a transfer to the nominated custodian is completed under s. 710.111. Unless the nomination of a custodian has been revoked, upon the occurrence of the future event the custodianship becomes effective and the custodian shall enforce a transfer of the custodial property pursuant to s. 710.111.

Laws 1985, c. 85–95, § 1. Amended by Laws 2005, c. 2005–101, § 4, eff. June 1, 2005.

710.105. Transfer by gift or exercise of power of appointment

A person may make a transfer by irrevocable gift to, or the irrevocable exercise of a power of appointment in favor of, a custodian for the benefit of a minor pursuant to s. 710.111. Notwithstanding s. 710.106, a transfer by irrevocable gift from a trust over which the grantor has at the time of transfer a right of revocation, as defined in s. 733.707(3)(e), shall be treated for all purposes under this act as a transfer made directly by the grantor of the trust.

Laws 1985, c. 85–95, § 1. Amended by Laws 2015, c. 2015–140, § 2, eff. July 1, 2015.

710.106. Transfer authorized by will or trust

(1) A personal representative or trustee may make an irrevocable transfer pursuant to s. 710.111 to a custodian for the benefit of a minor as authorized in the governing will or trust.

(2) If the testator or settlor has nominated a custodian under s. 710.104 to receive the custodial property, the transfer must be made to that person.

(3) If the testator or settlor has not nominated a custodian under s. 710.104, or all persons so nominated as custodian die before the transfer or are unable, decline, or are ineligible to serve, the personal representative or the trustee, as the case may be, shall designate the custodian from among those eligible to serve as custodian for property of that kind under s. 710.111(1).

Laws 1985, c. 85–95, § 1.

710.107. Other transfer by fiduciary

(1) Subject to subsection (3), a personal representative or trustee may make an irrevocable transfer to another adult or trust company as custodian for the benefit of a minor pursuant to s. 710.111, in the absence of a will or under a will or trust that does not contain an authorization to do so.

(2) Subject to subsection (3), a conservator may make an irrevocable transfer to another adult or trust company as custodian for the benefit of the minor pursuant to s. 710.111.

(3) A transfer under subsection (1) or subsection (2) may be made only if:

(a) The personal representative, trustee, or conservator considers the transfer to be in the best interest of the minor;

(b) The transfer is not prohibited by or inconsistent with provisions of the applicable will, trust agreement, or other governing instrument; and

(c) The transfer is authorized by the court if it exceeds $10,000 in value.
Laws 1985, c. 85–95, § 1.

710.108.   Transfer by obligor

(1) Subject to subsections (2) and (3), a person not subject to s. 710.106 or s. 710.107 who holds property, including, but not limited to, a benefit plan, of a minor not having a conservator, or who owes a liquidated debt to a minor not having a conservator, may make an irrevocable transfer to a custodian for the benefit of the minor pursuant to s. 710.111.

(2) If a person having the right to do so under s. 710.104 has nominated a custodian under that section to receive the custodial property, the transfer must be made to that person.

(3) If no custodian has been nominated under s. 710.104, or all persons so nominated as custodian die before the transfer or are unable, decline, or are ineligible to serve, a transfer under this section may be made to an adult member of the minor's family or to a trust company unless the property exceeds $15,000 in value.
Laws 1985, c. 85–95, § 1; Laws 1987, c. 87–226, § 61. Amended by Laws 2005, c. 2005–101, § 5, eff. June 1, 2005.

710.109.   Receipt for custodial property

A written acknowledgment of delivery by a custodian constitutes a sufficient receipt and discharge for custodial property transferred to the custodian pursuant to this act.
Laws 1985, c. 85–95, § 1.

710.111.   Manner of creating custodial property and effecting transfer; designation of initial custodian; control

(1) Custodial property is created and a transfer is made whenever:

(a) An uncertificated security or a certificated security in registered form is either:

1. Registered in the name of the transferor, an adult other than the transferor, or a trust company, followed in substance by the words: "as custodian for ___(name of minor)___ under the Florida Uniform Transfers to Minors Act"; or

2. Delivered if in certificated form, or any document necessary for the transfer of an uncertificated security is delivered, together with any necessary endorsement to an adult other than the transferor or to a trust company as custodian, accompanied by an instrument in substantially the form set forth in subsection (2);

(b) Money is paid or delivered to a broker or financial institution for credit to an account in the name of the transferor, an adult other than the transferor, or a trust company, followed in substance by the words: "as custodian for ___(name of minor)___ under the Florida Uniform Transfers to Minors Act";

(c) The ownership of a life or endowment insurance policy or annuity contract is either:

1. Registered with the issuer in the name of the transferor, an adult other than the transferor, or a trust company, followed in substance by the words: "as custodian for ___(name of minor)___ under the Florida Uniform Transfers to Minors Act"; or

2. Assigned in a writing delivered to an adult other than the transferor or to a trust company whose name in the assignment is followed in substance by the words: "as custodian for ___(name of minor)___ under the Florida Uniform Transfers to Minors Act";

(d) An irrevocable exercise of a power of appointment or an irrevocable present right to future payment under a contract is the subject of a written notification delivered to the payor, issuer, or other obligor that the right is transferred to the transferor, an adult other than the transferor, or a trust company, whose name in the notification is followed in substance by the words: "as custodian for ___(name of minor)___ under the Florida Uniform Transfers to Minors Act";

(e) An interest in real property is recorded in the name of the transferor, an adult other than the transferor, or a trust company, followed in substance by the words: "as custodian for ___(name of minor)___ under the Florida Uniform Transfers to Minors Act";

(f) A certificate of title issued by a department or agency of a state or of the United States which evidences title to tangible personal property is either:

1. Issued in the name of the transferor, an adult other than the transferor, or a trust company, followed in substance by the words: "as custodian for ___(name of minor)___ under the Florida Uniform Transfers to Minors Act"; or

2. Delivered to an adult other than the transferor or to a trust company, endorsed to that person followed in substance by the words: "as custodian for ___(name of minor)___ under the Florida Uniform Transfers to Minors Act"; or

(g) An interest in any property not described in paragraphs (a)–(f) is transferred to an adult other than the transferor or to a trust company by a written instrument in substantially the form set forth in subsection (2).

(2) An instrument in the following form satisfies the requirements of subparagraph (1)(a)2. and paragraph (1)(g):

"TRANSFER UNDER THE FLORIDA UNIFORM TRANSFERS TO MINORS ACT

I, ___(name of transferor or name and representative capacity if a fiduciary)___ hereby transfer to ___(name of custodian)___, as custodian for ___(name of minor)___ under the Florida Uniform Transfers to Minors Act, the following: ___(insert a description of the custodial property sufficient to identify it)___.

Dated: _____

___(signature)___

___(name of custodian)___ acknowledges receipt of the property described above as custodian for the minor named above under the Florida Uniform Transfers to Minors Act.

Dated: _____

___(signature of custodian)___."

(3) A transferor shall place the custodian in control of the custodial property as soon as practicable.

Laws 1985, c. 85–95, § 1.

710.112. Single custodianship

A transfer may be made only for one minor, and only one person may be the custodian. All custodial property held under this act by the same custodian for the benefit of the same minor constitutes a single custodianship.

Laws 1985, c. 85–95, § 1.

710.113. Validity and effect of transfer

(1) The validity of a transfer made in a manner prescribed in this act is not affected by:

(a) Failure of the transferor to comply with s. 710.111(3) concerning possession and control;

(b) Designation of an ineligible custodian, except designation of the transferor in the case of property for which the transferor is ineligible to serve as custodian under s. 710.111(1); or

(c) Death or incapacity of a person nominated under s. 710.104 or designated under s. 710.111 as custodian or the disclaimer of the office by that person.

(2) A transfer made pursuant to s. 710.111 is irrevocable, and the custodial property is indefeasibly vested in the minor, but the custodian has all the rights, powers, duties, and authority provided in this act, and neither the minor nor the minor's legal representative has any right, power, duty, or authority with respect to the custodial property except as provided in this act.

(3) By making a transfer, the transferor incorporates in the disposition all the provisions of this act and grants to the custodian, and to any third person dealing with a person designated as custodian, the respective powers, rights, and immunities provided in this act.

Laws 1985, c. 85–95, § 1.

710.114. Care of custodial property

(1) A custodian shall:

(a) Take control of custodial property;

(b) Register or record title to custodial property if appropriate; and

(c) Collect, hold, manage, invest, and reinvest custodial property.

(2) In dealing with custodial property, a custodian shall observe the standard of care that would be observed by a prudent person dealing with property of another and is not limited by any other statute restricting investments by fiduciaries. If a custodian has a special skill or expertise or is named custodian on the basis of representations of a special skill or expertise, the custodian shall use that skill or expertise. However, a custodian, in the custodian's discretion and without liability to the minor or the minor's estate, may retain any custodial property received from a transferor.

(3) A custodian may invest in or pay premiums on life insurance or endowment policies on the life of the minor only if the minor or the minor's estate is the sole beneficiary, or on the life of another person in whom the minor has an insurable interest only to the extent that the minor, the minor's estate, or the custodian in the capacity of custodian is the irrevocable beneficiary.

(4) A custodian at all times shall keep custodial property separate and distinct from all other property in a manner sufficient to identify it clearly as custodial property of the minor. Custodial property consisting of an undivided interest is so identified if the minor's interest is held as a tenant in common and is fixed. Custodial property subject to recordation is so identified if it is recorded, and custodial property subject to registration is so identified if it is

either registered, or held in an account designated, in the name of the custodian, followed in substance by the words: "as a custodian for ___(name of minor)___ under the Florida Uniform Transfers to Minors Act."

(5) A custodian shall keep records of all transactions with respect to custodial property, including information necessary for the preparation of the minor's tax returns, and shall make them available for inspection at reasonable intervals by a parent or legal representative of the minor or by the minor if the minor has attained the age of 14 years.

Laws 1985, c. 85–95, § 1.

710.115. Powers of custodian

(1) A custodian, acting in a custodial capacity, has all the rights, powers, and authority over custodial property that unmarried adult owners have over their own property, but a custodian may exercise those rights, powers, and authority in that capacity only.

(2) This section does not relieve a custodian from liability for breach of s. 710.114.

Laws 1985, c. 85–95, § 1.

710.116. Use of custodial property

(1) A custodian may deliver or pay to the minor or expend for the minor's benefit so much of the custodial property as the custodian considers advisable for the use and benefit of the minor, without court order and without regard to the duty or ability of the custodian personally or of any other person to support the minor, or to any other income or property of the minor which may be applicable or available for that purpose.

(2) A custodian may, without court order, transfer all or part of the custodial property to a qualified minor's trust. A transfer of property pursuant to this subsection terminates the custodianship to the extent of the property transferred.

(3) On petition of an interested person or the minor if the minor has attained the age of 14 years, the court may order the custodian to deliver or pay to the minor or expend for the minor's benefit so much of the custodial property as the court considers advisable for the use and benefit of the minor.

(4) A delivery, payment, or expenditure under this section is in addition to, not in substitution for, and does not affect any obligation of a person to support the minor.

Laws 1985, c. 85–95, § 1. Amended by Laws 2005, c. 2005–101, § 6, eff. June 1, 2005.

710.117. Custodian's expenses, compensation, and bond

(1) A custodian is entitled to reimbursement from custodial property for reasonable expenses incurred in the performance of the custodian's duties.

(2) Except for one who is a transferor under s. 710.105, a custodian has a noncumulative election during each calendar year to charge reasonable compensation for services performed during that year.

(3) Except as provided in s. 710.121(6), a custodian need not give a bond.

Laws 1985, c. 85–95, § 1.

710.118. Exemption of third person from liability

A third person in good faith and without court order may act on the instructions of or otherwise deal with any person purporting to make a transfer or purporting to act in the capacity of a custodian and, in the absence of knowledge, is not responsible for determining:

(1) The validity of the purported custodian's designation;

(2) The propriety of, or the authority under this act for, any act of the purported custodian;

(3) The validity or propriety under this act of any instrument or instructions executed or given either by the person purporting to make a transfer or by the purported custodian; or

(4) The propriety of the application of any property of the minor delivered to the purported custodian.

Laws 1985, c. 85–95, § 1.

710.119. Liability to third persons

(1) A claim based on:

(a) A contract entered into by a custodian acting in a custodial capacity;

(b) An obligation arising from the ownership or control of custodial property; or

(c) A tort committed during the custodianship,

may be asserted against the custodial property by proceeding against the custodian in the custodial capacity, whether or not the custodian or the minor is personally liable therefor.

(2) A custodian is not personally liable:

(a) On a contract properly entered into in the custodial capacity unless the custodian fails to reveal that capacity and to identify the custodianship in the contract; or

(b) For an obligation arising from control of custodial property or for a tort committed during the custodianship unless the custodian is personally at fault.

(3) A minor is not personally liable for an obligation arising from ownership of custodial property or for a tort committed during the custodianship unless the minor is personally at fault.

Laws 1985, c. 85–95, § 1.

710.121. Renunciation, resignation, death, or removal of custodian; designation of successor custodian

(1) A person nominated under s. 710.104 or designated under s. 710.111 as custodian may decline to serve by delivering a valid disclaimer under chapter 739 to the person who made the nomination or to the transferor or the transferor's legal representative. If the event giving rise to a transfer has not occurred and no substitute custodian able, willing, and eligible to serve was nominated under s. 710.104, the person who made the nomination may nominate a substitute custodian under s. 710.104; otherwise, the transferor or the transferor's legal representative shall designate a substitute custodian at the time of the transfer, in either case from among the persons eligible to serve as custodian for that kind of property under s. 710.111(1). The custodian so designated has the rights of a successor custodian.

(2) A custodian at any time may designate a trust company or an adult other than a transferor under s. 710.105 as successor custodian by executing and dating an instrument of designation before a subscribing witness other than the successor. If the instrument of designation does not contain or is not accompanied by the resignation of the custodian, the designation of the successor does not take effect until the custodian resigns, dies, becomes incapacitated, or is removed.

(3) A custodian may resign at any time by delivering written notice to the minor if the minor has attained the age of 14 years and to the successor custodian and by delivering the custodial property to the successor custodian.

(4) If a custodian is ineligible, dies, or becomes incapacitated without having effectively designated a successor and the minor has attained the age of 14 years, the minor may designate as successor custodian, in the manner prescribed in subsection (2), an adult member of the minor's family, a conservator of the minor, or a trust company. If the minor has not attained the age of 14 years or fails to act within 60 days after the ineligibility, death, or incapacity, the conservator of the minor becomes successor custodian. If the minor has no conservator or the conservator declines to act, the transferor, the legal representative of the transferor or of the custodian, an adult member of the minor's family, or any other interested person may petition the court to designate a successor custodian.

(5) A custodian who declines to serve under subsection (1) or resigns under subsection (3), or the legal representative of a deceased or incapacitated custodian, as soon as practicable, shall put the custodial property and records in the possession and control of the successor custodian. The successor custodian by action may enforce the obligation to deliver custodial property and records and becomes responsible for each item as received.

(6) A transferor, the legal representative of a transferor, an adult member of the minor's family, a guardian of the person of the minor, the conservator of the minor, or the minor if the minor has attained the age of 14 years may petition the court to remove the custodian for cause and designate a successor custodian other than a transferor under s. 710.105 or to require the custodian to give appropriate bond.

Laws 1985, c. 85–95, § 1. Amended by Laws 2005, c. 2005–108, § 4, eff. July 1, 2005.

710.122. Accounting by and determination of liability of custodian

(1) A minor who has attained the age of 14 years, the minor's guardian of the person or legal representative, an adult member of the minor's family, a transferor, or a transferor's legal representative may petition the court for an accounting by the custodian or the custodian's legal representative or for a determination of responsibility, as between the custodial property and the custodian personally, for claims against the custodial property unless the responsibility has been adjudicated in an action under s. 710.119 to which the minor or the minor's legal representative was a party.

(2) A successor custodian may petition the court for an accounting by the predecessor custodian.

(3) The court, in a proceeding under this act or in any other proceeding, may require or permit the custodian or the custodian's legal representative to account.

(4) If a custodian is removed under s. 710.121(6), the court shall require an accounting and order delivery of the custodial property and records to the successor custodian and the execution of all instruments required for transfer of the custodial property.

Laws 1985, c. 85–95, § 1.

710.123. Termination of custodianship

(1) The custodian shall transfer in an appropriate manner the custodial property to the minor or to the minor's estate upon the earlier of:

(a) The minor's attainment of 21 years of age with respect to custodial property transferred under s. 710.105 or s. 710.106. However, a transferor can, with respect to such custodial property, create the custodianship so that it terminates when the minor attains 25 years of age;

(b) The minor's attainment of 18 years of age with respect to custodial property transferred under s. 710.107 or s. 710.108; or

(c) The minor's death.

(2) If the transferor of a custodianship under paragraph (1)(a) creates the custodianship to terminate when the minor attains 25 years of age, in the case of a custodianship created by irrevocable gift or by irrevocable inter vivos exercise of a general power of appointment, the minor nevertheless has the absolute right to compel immediate distribution of the entire custodial property when the minor attains 21 years of age.

(3) As to a custodianship described in subsection (2), a transferor may provide, by delivery of a written instrument to the custodian upon the creation of such custodianship, that the minor's right to compel immediate distribution of the entire custodial property will terminate upon the expiration of a fixed period that begins with the custodian's delivery of a written notice to the minor of the existence of such right. To be effective to terminate the minor's right to compel an immediate distribution of the entire custodial property when the minor attains 21 years of age, the custodian's written notice must be delivered at least 30 days before, and not later than 30 days after, the date upon which the minor attains 21 years of age, and the fixed period specified in the notice for the termination of such right cannot expire before the later of 30 days after the minor attains 21 years of age or 30 days after the custodian delivers such notice.

(4) Notwithstanding the definition of the term "minor" as provided in s. 710.102, if the transferor creates the custodianship to terminate when the minor attains 25 years of age, solely for purposes of the application of the termination provisions of this section, the term "minor" means an individual who has not attained 25 years of age.

(5) A financial institution has no liability to a custodian or minor for distribution of custodial property to, or for the benefit of, the minor in a custodianship created by irrevocable gift or by irrevocable exercise of a general power of appointment when the minor attains 21 years of age.
Laws 1985, c. 85–95, § 1. Amended by Laws 2015, c. 2015–140, § 3, eff. July 1, 2015.

Cross References

Minor, definitions, see § 1.01.
Rights, privileges and obligations of persons 18 years of age or older, see § 743.07.

710.124. Applicability

This act applies to a transfer within the scope of s. 710.103 made after October 1, 1985, if:

(1) The transfer purports to have been made under the Florida Gifts to Minors Act (former ss. 710.01–710.10); or

(2) The instrument by which the transfer purports to have been made uses in substance the designation "as custodian under the Uniform Gifts to Minors Act" or "as custodian under the Uniform Transfers to Minors Act" of any other state, and the application of this act is necessary to validate the transfer.
Laws 1985, c. 85–95, § 1; Laws 1987, c. 87–226, § 62.

710.125. Effect on existing custodianships

(1) Any transfer of custodial property as now defined in this act made before October 1, 1985, is validated notwithstanding that there was no specific authority in the Florida Gifts to Minors Act for the coverage of custodial property of that kind or for a transfer from that source at the time the transfer was made.

(2) This act applies to all transfers made before October 1, 1985, in a manner and form prescribed in the Florida Gifts to Minors Act, except insofar as the application impairs

constitutionally vested rights or extends the duration of custodianships in existence on October 1, 1985.

(3) Sections 710.102–710.123 with respect to the age of a minor for whom custodial property is held under this act do not apply to custodial property held in a custodianship that terminated because of the minor's attainment of the age of 18 after January 1, 1975, and before October 1, 1985.

Laws 1985, c. 85–95, § 1.

710.126. Uniformity of application and construction

This act shall be applied and construed to effectuate its general purpose to make uniform the law with respect to the subject of this act among states enacting it.

Laws 1985, c. 85–95, § 1.

CHAPTER 711

FLORIDA UNIFORM TRANSFER-ON-DEATH
SECURITY REGISTRATION ACT

UNIFORM NONPROBATE TRANSFERS ON DEATH ACT

Table of Jurisdictions Wherein Act Has Been Adopted

For text of Uniform Act, and variation notes and annotation materials for adopting jurisdictions, see Uniform Laws Annotated, Master Edition, Volume 8B.

Jurisdiction	Laws	Effective Date	Statutory Citation
Alabama [3]	1997, Nos. 97–644, 97–703	Part 2 3–1–1998; Part 3 8–1–1997	Code 1975, §§ 5–24–1 to 5–24–34, 8–6–140 to 8–6–151.
Alaska	1996, c. 75	1–1–1997	AS 13.06.050, 13.33.101 to 13.33.310.
Arizona	1994, c. 290	After 12–31–1994	A.R.S. §§ 14–6101 to 14–6311.
Arkansas [2]	1993, No. 114	8–13–1993	A.C.A. §§ 28–14–101 to 28–14–112.
California [1]	1998, c. 242	1–1–1999	West's Ann.Cal. Probate Code, §§ 5000 to 5003, 5500 to 5512.
Colorado	1990, S.B. 90–91	7–1–1990	West's C.R.S.A. §§ 15–10–201, 15–15–101 to 15–15–311.

Jurisdiction	Laws	Effective Date	Statutory Citation
Connecticut [2]	1997, No. 97–42	5–14–1997 *	C.G.S.A. §§ 45a–468 to 45a–468m.
Delaware [2]	70 Del. Laws, c. 394	6–26–1996	12 Del. C. §§ 801 to 812.
District of Columbia	2001, D.C. Law 13–292	4–27–2001	D.C. Official Code, 2001 Ed. §§ 19–601.01 to 19–603.11.
Florida [3]	1994, c. 94–216	1–1–1995	West's F.S.A. §§ 655.82, 711.50 to 711.512.
Georgia [2]	1999, Act 392	7–1–1999	O.C.G.A. §§ 53–5–60 to 53–5–71.
Hawaii [2]	1998, c. 63	4–29–1998	HRS §§ 539–1 to 539–12.
Idaho [2]	1996, c. 303	7–1–1996	I.C. §§ 15–6–301 to 15–6–312.
Illinois [2]	1994, P.A. 88–577	1–1–1995	S.H.A. 815 ILCS 10/0.01 to 10/10.
Indiana [2]	2002, P.L. 2–2002	7–1–2002	West's A.I.C. 32–17–9–1 to 32–17–9–15.
Iowa [2]	1997, c. 178	7–1–1997	I.C.A. §§ 633D.1 to 633D.12.
Kansas [2]	1994, c. 44	7–1–1994	K.S.A. 17–49a01 to 17–49a12.
Kentucky [2]	1998, c. 407	8–1–1998	KRS 292.6501 to 292.6512.
Maine [2]	1997, c. 627	3–27–1998 *	18–A M.R.S.A. §§ 6–301 to 6–312.
Maryland [2]	1994, c. 644	10–1–1994	Code, Estates and Trusts, §§ 16–101 to 16–112.
Massachusetts [1]	2008, c. 521	3–31–2012	M.G.L.A. c. 190B, §§ 6–101 to 6–311.
Michigan [1]	1998, P.A. 386	4–1–2000	M.C.L.A. §§ 700.6101 to 700.6310.
Minnesota [2]	1992, c. 461	6–1–1992	M.S.A. §§ 524.6–301 to 524.6–311.
Mississippi [2]	1997, c. 413	3–24–1997	Code 1972, §§ 91–21–1 to 91–21–25.
Montana	1993, c. 494	10–1–1993	MCA §§ 72–1–103, 72–6–111 to 72–6–311.
Nebraska	1993, LB 250	5–6–1993*	R.R.S 1943, §§ 30–2209, 30–2715 to 30–2746.
New Hampshire [2]	1997, c. 231	1–1–1998	RSA 563–C:1 to 563–C:12.
New Jersey [2]	1995, c. 130	6–22–1995*	N.J.S.A. 3B:30–1 to 3B:30–12.
New Mexico	1992, c. 66	7–1–1992	NMSA 1978, §§ 45–1–201, 45–6–101 to 45–6–311.
New York [2]	2005, c. 325	1–1–2006	McKinney's EPTL 13–4.1 to 13–4.12.
North Carolina [2]	2005, c. 411	10–1–2005	G.S. §§ 41–40 to 41–51.
North Dakota	1991, c. 351	7–1–1991	NDCC 30.1–01–06, 30.1–31–01 to 30.1–31–30.
Ohio [2]	1993, H.B. 62	10–1–1993	R.C. §§ 1709.01 to 1709.11.
Oklahoma [2]	1994, c. 208	9–1–1994	71 Okl.St.Ann. §§ 901 to 913.
Oregon [2]	1991, c. 306	6–19–1991*	ORS 59.535 to 59.585.
Pennsylvania [2]	1996, P.L. 1118	12–18–1996*	20 Pa.C.S.A. §§ 6401 to 6413.
Rhode Island [2]	1998, c. 98–260	7–9–1998	Gen. Laws 1956, §§ 7–11.1–1 to 7–11.1–12.
South Carolina [2]	1997, No. 102	6–13–1997	Code 1976, §§ 35–6–10 to 35–6–100.
South Dakota [2]	1995, c. 168	Registrations of securities in beneficiary form by decedents dying on or after 7–1–1996	SDCL 29A–6–301 to 29A–6–311.
Tennessee [2]	1995, c. 471	7–1–1995	T.C.A. §§ 35–12–101 to 35–12–113.
Utah [2]	1995, c. 9	5–1–1995	U.C.A. 1953, 75–6–301 to 75–6–313.
Vermont [2]	1999, Act 23	5–17–1999*	9 V.S.A. §§ 4351 to 4360.
Virgin Islands [2]	2010, No. 7150	1–1–2011	15 V.I.C. §§ 6–301 to 6–311.
Virginia [2]	1994, c. 422		Code 1950, § 64.2–620.
Washington [2]	1993, c. 287	7–25–1993	West's RCWA 21.35.005 to 21.35.902.
West Virginia [2]	1994, c. 62	3–10–1994*	Code, 36–10–1 to 36–10–12.
Wisconsin [1]	1989, Act 331	5–11–1990	W.S.A. 705.20 to 705.30.
Wyoming [2]	1993, c. 171	7–1–1993	Wyo.Stat.Ann. §§ 2–16–101 to 2–16–112.

* Date of approval.

For Annotative Materials, see West's Florida Statutes Annotated

[1] Adopted only Parts 1 and 3 of the Act.
[2] Adopted only Part 3 of the Act.
[3] Adopted only Parts 2 and 3 of the Act.

UNIFORM TOD SECURITY REGISTRATION

Table of Jurisdictions Wherein Act Has Been Adopted

For text of Uniform Act, and variation notes and annotation materials for adopting jurisdictions, see Uniform Laws Annotated, Master Edition, Volume 8B.

Jurisdiction	Laws	Effective Date	Statutory Citation
Alabama	1997, No. 97–703	8–1–1997	Code 1975, §§ 8–6–140 to 8–6–151.
Alaska	1996, c. 75	1–1–1997	AS 13.06.050, 13.33.301 to 13.33.310.
Arizona	1994, c. 290	After 12–31–1994	A.R.S. §§ 14–6301 to 14–6311.
Arkansas	1993, No. 114	8–13–1993	A.C.A. §§ 28–14–101 to 28–14–112.
California	1998, c. 242	1–1–1999	West's Ann.Cal. Probate Code, §§ 5500 to 5512.
Colorado	1990, S.B. 90–91	7–1–1990	West's C.R.S.A. §§ 15–10–201, 15–15–301 to 15–15–311.
Connecticut	1997, No. 97–42	5–14–1997 *	C.G.S.A. §§ 45a–468 to 45a–468m.
Delaware	70 Del. Laws, c. 394	6–26–1996	12 Del. C. §§ 801 to 812.
District of Columbia	2001, D.C. Law 13–292	4–27–2001	D.C. Official Code, 2001 Ed. §§ 19–603.01 to 19–603.11.
Florida	1994, c. 94–216	1–1–1995	West's F.S.A. §§ 711.50 to 711.512.
Georgia	1999, Act 392	7–1–1999	O.C.G.A. §§ 53–5–60 to 53–5–71.
Hawaii	1998, c. 63	4–29–1998	HRS §§ 539–1 to 539–12.
Idaho	1996, c. 303	7–1–1996	I.C. §§ 15–6–301 to 15–6–312.
Illinois	1994, P.A. 88–577	1–1–1995	S.H.A. 815 ILCS 10/0.01 to 10/12.
Indiana	2002, P.L. 2–2002	7–1–2002	West's A.I.C. 32–17–9–1 to 32–17–9–15.
Iowa	1997, c. 178	7–1–1997	I.C.A. §§ 633D.1 to 633D.12.
Kansas	1994, c. 44	7–1–1994	K.S.A. 17–49a01 to 17–49a12.
Kentucky	1998, c. 407	8–1–1998	KRS 292.6501 to 292.6512.
Maine	1997, c. 627	3–27–1998 *	18–A M.R.S.A. §§ 6–301 to 6–312.
Maryland	1994, c. 644	10–1–1994	Code, Estates and Trusts, §§ 16–101 to 16–112.
Massachusetts	2008, c. 521	3–31–2012	M.G.L.A. c. 190B, §§ 6-301 to 6-311.
Michigan	1998, P.A. 386	4–1–2000	M.C.L.A. §§ 700.6301 to 700.6310.
Minnesota	1992, c. 461	6–1–1992	M.S.A. §§ 524.6–301 to 524.6–311.
Mississippi	1997, c. 413	3–24–1997	Code 1972, §§ 91–21–1 to 91–21–25.
Montana	1993, c. 494	10–1–1993	MCA §§ 72–1–103, 72–6–301 to 72–6–311.
Nebraska	1993, LB 250	5–6–1993*	R.R.S. 1943, §§ 30–2209, 30–2734 to 30–2746.
Nevada	2011, c. 270	10–1–2011	N.R.S. 111.480 to 111.650.
New Hampshire	1997, c. 231	1–1–1998	RSA 563–C:1 to 563–C:12.
New Jersey	1995, c. 130	6–22–1995*	N.J.S.A. 3B:30–1 to 3B:30–12.
New Mexico	1992, c. 66	7–1–1992	NMSA 1978, §§ 45–1–201, 45–6–301 to 45–6–311.
New York	2005, c. 325	1–1–2006	McKinney's EPTL 13–4.1 to 13–4.12.
North Carolina	2005, c. 411	10–1–2005	G.S. §§ 41–40 to 41–51.
North Dakota	1991, c. 351	7–1–1991	NDCC 30.1–01–06, 30.1–31–21 to 30.1–31–30.
Ohio	1993, H.B. 62	10–1–1993	R.C. §§ 1709.01 to 1709.11.
Oklahoma	1994, c. 208	9–1–1994	71 Okl.St.Ann. §§ 901 to 913.
Oregon	1991, c. 306	6–19–1991 *	ORS 59.535 to 59.585.

Jurisdiction	Laws	Effective Date	Statutory Citation
Pennsylvania	1996, P.L. 1118	12–18–1996 *	20 Pa.C.S.A. §§ 6401 to 6413.
Rhode Island	1998, c. 98–260	7–9–1998	Gen. Laws 1956, §§ 7–11.1–1 to 7–11.1–12.
South Carolina	1997, No. 102	6–13–1997	Code 1976, §§ 35–6–10 to 35–6–100.
South Dakota	1995, c. 168	Registrations of securities in beneficiary form by decedents dying on or after 7–1–1996.	SDCL 29A–6–301 to 29A–6–311.
Tennessee	1995, c. 471	7–1–1995	T.C.A. §§ 35–12–101 to 35–12–113.
Utah	1995, c. 9	5–1–1995	U.C.A. 1953, 75–6–301 to 75–6–313.
Vermont	1999, P.A. 23	5–17–1999 *	9 V.S.A. §§ 4351 to 4360.
Virgin Islands	2009, No. 7150	1–1–2011	15 V.I.C. §§ 6–301 to 6–311.
Virginia	1994, c. 422		Code 1950, §§ 64.2–612 to 64.2–619.
Washington	1993, c. 287	7–25–1993	West's RCWA 21.35.005 to 21.35.902.
West Virginia	1994, c. 62	3–10–1994*	Code, 36–10–1 to 36–10–12.
Wisconsin	1989, Act 331	5–11–1990	W.S.A. 705.21 to 705.30.
Wyoming	1993, c. 171	7–1–1993	Wyo.Stat.Ann. §§ 2–16–101 to 2–16–112.

* Date of approval.

UNIFORM PROBATE CODE ACT

Table of Jurisdictions Wherein Code Has Been Adopted

For text of Uniform Act, and variation notes and annotation materials for adopting jurisdictions, see Uniform Laws Annotated, Master Edition, Volumes 8, Pt. I, 8, Pt. II, and 8, Pt. III.

Jurisdiction	Laws	Effective Date	Statutory Citation
Alaska [2]	1972, c. 78	1–1–1973	AS 13.06.005 to 13.36.390.
Arizona [2]	1973, c. 75	1–1–1974	A.R.S. §§ 14–1101 to 14–7308.
Colorado [2]	1973, H.B. 1039	7–1–1974	West's C.R.S.A. §§ 15–10–101 to 15–17–103.
Florida [1]	1974, c. 74–106	7–1–1975	West's F.S.A. §§ 655.82, 711.50 to 711.512, 731.005 to 735.302.
Hawaii [5]	1976, c. 200	7–1–1976	HRS §§ 539–1 to 539–12; 560:1–101 to 560:8–101.
Idaho [4]	1971, c. 111	7–1–1972	I.C. §§ 15–1–101 to 15–7–308.
Maine [4]	1979, c. 540	1–1–1981	18–A M.R.S.A. §§ 1–101 to 8–401.
Massachusetts	2008, c. 521	1–15–2009 *	M.G.L.A. c. 190B, §§ 1–101 to 7–503.
Michigan [4]	1998, P.A. 386	4–1–2000	M.C.L.A. §§700.1101 to 700.8102.
Minnesota [3]	1974, c. 442	8–1–1975	M.S.A. §§ 524.1–101 to 524.8–103.
Montana [2]	1974, c. 365	7–1–1975	MCA 72–1–101 to 72–6–311.
Nebraska [1]	1974, L.B. 354	1–1–1977	R.R.S.1943, §§ 30–2201 to 30–2902.
New Jersey [6]	2004, c. 132	8–31–2004 *	N.J.S.A. 3B:1–1 to 3B:30–12, 17:16I–1 to 17:16I–17.
New Mexico [2]	1975, c. 257	7–1–1976	NMSA 1978, §§ 45–1–101 to 45–7–522.
North Dakota [2]	1973, c. 257	7–1–1975	NDCC 30.1–01–01 to 30.1–35–01.
South Carolina [4]	1986, Act 539	7–1–1987	Code 1976, §§ 35–6–10 to 35–6–100; 62–1–100 to 62–7–604.
South Dakota [5]	SL 1994, c. 232	7–1–1995	SDCL 29A–1–101 to 29A–8–101.
Utah [5]	1975, c. 150	7–1–1977	U.C.A.1953, 75–1–101 to 75–8–101.
Virgin Islands	Act 7174, sec. 12(b), amended by	1–1–2011	15 V.I.C. 1-101 to 10-203.

Jurisdiction	Laws	Effective Date	Statutory Citation
	Act 7150, sec. 2		

* Approval date.
[1] Adopted 1989 Revision of Article VI.
[2] Adopted 1990 Revision of Article II and 1989 Revision of Article VI.
[3] Adopted 1990 Revision of Article II.
[4] Adopted Part 3 of 1989 Revision of Article VI.
[5] Adopted 1990 Revision of Article II and Part 3 of 1989 Revision of Article VI.
[6] Adopted 1990 Revision of Article II and Parts 2 and 3 of 1989 Revision of Article VI.

Cross References

Financial transactions, pay-on-death accounts, see § 655.82.

711.50. Short title

Sections 711.50–711.512 may be cited as the "Florida Uniform Transfer-on-Death Security Registration Act."

Added by Laws 1994, c. 94–216, § 3, eff. Jan. 1, 1995.

711.501. Definitions

In ss. 711.50–711.512, unless the context otherwise requires, the term:

(1) "Beneficiary form" means a registration of a security which indicates the present owner of the security and the intention of the owner regarding the person who will become the owner of the security upon the death of the owner.

(2) "Devisee" means any person designated in a will to receive a disposition of real or personal property.

(3) "Heirs" means those persons, including the surviving spouse, who are entitled under the statutes of intestate succession to the property of a decedent.

(4) "Person" means an individual, a corporation, an organization, or other legal entity.

(5) "Personal representative" includes an executor, administrator, successor personal representative, special administrator, and persons who perform substantially the same function under the law governing their status.

(6) "Property" includes both real and personal property or any interest therein and means anything that may be the subject of ownership.

(7) "Register," including its derivatives, means to issue a certificate showing the ownership of a certificated security or, in the case of an uncertificated security, to initiate or transfer an account showing ownership of securities.

(8) "Registering entity" means a person who originates or transfers a security title by registration, and includes a broker maintaining security accounts for customers and a transfer agent or other person acting for or as an issuer of securities.

(9) "Security" means a share, participation, or other interest in property, in a business, or in an obligation of an enterprise or other issuer, and includes a certificated security, an uncertificated security, and a security account.

(10) "Security account" means:

(a) A reinvestment account associated with a security, a securities account with a broker, a cash balance in a brokerage account, cash, interest, earnings, or dividends earned or declared on a security in an account, a reinvestment account, or a brokerage account, whether or not credited to the account before the owner's death;

(b) An investment management account, investment advisory account, investment agency account, custody account, or any other type of account with a bank or trust company, including the securities in the account, the cash balance in the account, and cash equivalents, and any interest, earnings, or dividends earned or declared on a security in the account, whether or not credited to the account before the owner's death; or

(c) A cash balance or other property held for or due to the owner of a security as a replacement for or product of an account security, whether or not credited to the account before the owner's death.

(11) "State" includes any state of the United States, the District of Columbia, the Commonwealth of Puerto Rico, and any territory or possession subject to the legislative authority of the United States.

Added by Laws 1994, c. 94–216, § 3, eff. Jan. 1, 1995. Amended by Laws 2005, c. 2005–85, § 1, eff. July 1, 2005.

711.502. Registration in beneficiary form; sole or joint tenancy ownership

Only individuals whose registration of a security shows sole ownership by one individual or multiple ownership by two or more with right of survivorship, rather than as tenants in common, may obtain registration in beneficiary form. Multiple owners of a security registered in beneficiary form hold as joint tenants with right of survivorship, as tenants by the entireties, or as owners of community property held in survivorship form, and not as tenants in common.

Added by Laws 1994, c. 94–216, § 3, eff. Jan. 1, 1995.

711.503. Registration in beneficiary form; applicable law

A security may be registered in beneficiary form if the form is authorized by this or a similar statute of the state of organization of the issuer or registering entity, the location of the registering entity's principal office, the office of its transfer agent or its office making the registration, or by this or a similar statute of the law of the state listed as the owner's address at the time of registration. A registration governed by the law of a jurisdiction in which this or similar legislation is not in force or was not in force when a registration in beneficiary form was made is nevertheless presumed to be valid and authorized as a matter of contract law.

Added by Laws 1994, c. 94–216, § 3, eff. Jan. 1, 1995.

711.504. Origination of registration in beneficiary form

A security, whether evidenced by certificate or account, is registered in beneficiary form when the registration includes a designation of a beneficiary to take the ownership at the death of the owner or the deaths of all multiple owners.

Added by Laws 1994, c. 94–216, § 3, eff. Jan. 1, 1995.

711.505. Form of registration in beneficiary form

Registration in beneficiary form may be shown by the words "transfer on death" or the abbreviation "TOD," or by the words "pay on death" or the abbreviation "POD," after the name of the registered owner and before the name of a beneficiary.

Added by Laws 1994, c. 94–216, § 3, eff. Jan. 1, 1995.

711.506. Effect of registration in beneficiary form

The designation of a transfer-on-death beneficiary on a registration in beneficiary form has no effect on ownership until the owner's death. A registration of a security in beneficiary form may be canceled or changed at any time by the sole owner or all then-surviving owners without the consent of the beneficiary.

Added by Laws 1994, c. 94–216, § 3, eff. Jan. 1, 1995.

711.507. Ownership on death of owner

On death of a sole owner or the last to die of all multiple owners, ownership of securities registered in beneficiary form passes to the beneficiary or beneficiaries who survive all owners. On proof of death of all owners and compliance with any applicable requirements of the registering entity, a security registered in beneficiary form may be reregistered in the name of the beneficiary or beneficiaries who survived the death of all owners. Until division of the security after the death of all owners, multiple beneficiaries surviving the death of all owners hold their interests as tenants in common. If no beneficiary survives the death of all owners, the security belongs to the estate of the deceased sole owner or the estate of the last to die of all multiple owners.

Added by Laws 1994, c. 94–216, § 3, eff. Jan. 1, 1995.

711.508. Protection of registering entity

(1) A registering entity is not required to offer or to accept a request for security registration in beneficiary form. If a registration in beneficiary form is offered by a registering entity, the owner requesting registration in beneficiary form assents to the protections given to the registering entity by ss. 711.50–711.512.

(2) By accepting a request for registration of a security in beneficiary form, the registering entity agrees that the registration will be implemented on death of the deceased owner as provided in ss. 711.50–711.512.

(3) A registering entity is discharged from all claims to a security by the estate, creditors, heirs, or devisees of a deceased owner if it registers a transfer of the security in accordance with s. 711.507 and does so in good faith reliance on the registration, on ss. 711.50–711.512, and on information provided to it by affidavit of the personal representative of the deceased owner, or by the surviving beneficiary or by the surviving beneficiary's representatives, or other information available to the registering entity. The protections of ss. 711.50–711.512 do not extend to a reregistration or payment made after a registering entity has received written notice from any claimant to any interest in the security objecting to implementation of a registration in beneficiary form. No other notice or other information available to the registering entity affects its right to protection under ss. 711.50–711.512.

(4) The protection provided by ss. 711.50–711.512 to the registering entity of a security does not affect the rights of beneficiaries in disputes between themselves and other claimants to ownership of the security transferred or its value or proceeds.

Added by Laws 1994, c. 94–216, § 3, eff. Jan. 1, 1995.

711.509. Nontestamentary transfer on death

(1) A transfer on death resulting from a registration in beneficiary form is effective by reason of the contract regarding the registration between the owner and the registering entity and ss. 711.50–711.512 and is not testamentary.

(2) Sections 711.50–711.512 do not limit the rights of creditors of security owners against beneficiaries and other transferees under other laws of this state.

Added by Laws 1994, c. 94–216, § 3, eff. Jan. 1, 1995.

711.51. Terms, conditions, and forms for registration

(1) A registering entity offering to accept registrations in beneficiary form may establish the terms and conditions under which it will receive requests for registrations in beneficiary form, and requests for implementation of registrations in beneficiary form, including requests for cancellation of previously registered transfer-on-death beneficiary designations and requests for reregistration to effect a change of beneficiary. The terms and conditions so established may provide for proving death, avoiding or resolving any problems concerning fractional shares, designating primary and contingent beneficiaries, and substituting a named beneficiary's descendants to take in the place of the named beneficiary in the event of the beneficiary's death. Substitution may be indicated by appending to the name of the primary beneficiary the letters "LDPS," standing for "lineal descendants per stirpes." This designation substitutes a deceased beneficiary's descendants who survive the owner for a beneficiary who fails to so survive, the descendants to be identified and to share in accordance with the law of the beneficiary's domicile at the owner's death governing inheritance by descendants of an intestate. Other forms of identifying beneficiaries who are to take on one or more contingencies, and rules for providing proofs and assurances needed to satisfy reasonable concerns by registering entities regarding conditions and identities relevant to accurate implementation of registrations in beneficiary form, may be contained in a registering entity's terms and conditions.

(2) The following are illustrations of registrations in beneficiary form which a registering entity may authorize:

(a) Sole owner-sole beneficiary: John S Brown TOD (or POD) John S Brown Jr.

(b) Multiple owners-sole beneficiary: John S Brown Mary B Brown JT TEN TOD John S Brown Jr.

(c) Multiple owners-primary and secondary (substituted) beneficiaries:

1. John S Brown Mary B Brown JT TEN TOD John S Brown Jr SUB BENE Peter Q Brown; or

2. John S Brown Mary B Brown JT TEN TOD John S Brown Jr LDPS.

Added by Laws 1994, c. 94–216, § 3, eff. Jan. 1, 1995.

711.511. Rules of construction

(1) Sections 711.50–711.512 shall be liberally construed and applied to promote their underlying purposes and policy and to make uniform the laws with respect to the subject of these sections among states enacting them.

(2) Unless displaced by the particular provisions of ss. 711.50–711.512, the principles of law and equity supplement the provisions of these sections.

Added by Laws 1994, c. 94–216, § 3, eff. Jan. 1, 1995.

711.512. Application of ss. 711.50–711.512

Sections 711.50–711.512 apply to registrations of securities in beneficiary form made before, on, or after January 1, 1995, by decedents dying on or after January 1, 1995.

Added by Laws 1994, c. 94–216, § 3, eff. Jan. 1, 1995.

CHAPTER 716

ESCHEATS

Section
716.01. Declaration of policy.
716.02. Escheat of funds in the possession of federal agencies.
716.03. Department to institute proceedings to recover escheated property.
716.04. Jurisdiction.
716.05. Money recovered to be paid into State Treasury.
716.06. Public records.
716.07. Recovery of escheated property by claimant.

Cross References

Disposition of Unclaimed Property Act, provisions as supplemental to other remedies, see § 717.1401.

716.01. Declaration of policy

It is hereby declared to be the policy of the state, while protecting the interests of the owners thereof, to possess all unclaimed and abandoned money and property for the benefit of all the people of the state, and this law shall be liberally construed to accomplish such purpose.
Laws 1947, c. 24333, § 1.

Cross References

Decedent's estates, see §§ 732.107, 733.816.
Disposition of Unclaimed Property Act, see § 717.001 et seq.

716.02. Escheat of funds in the possession of federal agencies

All property within the provisions of subsections (1), (2), (3), (4) and (5), are declared to have escheated, or to escheat, including all principal and interest accruing thereon, and to have become the property of the state.

(1) All money or other property which has remained in, or has been deposited in the custody of, or under the control of, any court of the United States, in and for any district within this state, or which has been deposited with and is in the custody of any depository, registry, clerk or other officer of such court, or the United States treasury, which money or other property the rightful owner or owners thereof, either:

(a) Has been unknown for a period of 5 or more consecutive years; or,

(b) Has died, without having disposed thereof, and without having left heirs, next of kin or distributees, or

(c) Has made no demand for such money or other property for 5 years;

are declared to have escheated, or to escheat, together with all interest accrued thereon, and to have become the property of the state.

(2) After June 16, 1947, all money or other property which has remained in, or has been deposited in the custody of, or under the control of, any court of the United States, in and for any district within this state, for a period of 4 years, the rightful owner or owners of which, either:

(a) Shall have been unknown for a period of 4 years; or,

(b) Shall have died without having disposed thereof, and without having left or without leaving heirs, next of kin or distributees; or,

(c) Shall have failed within 4 years to demand the payment or delivery of such funds or other property;

is hereby declared to have escheated, or to escheat, together with all interest accrued thereon, and to have become the property of the state.

(3) All money or other property which has remained in, or has been deposited in the custody of, or under the control of any officer, department or agency of the United States for 5 or more consecutive years, which money or other property had its situs or source in this state, except as hereinafter provided in subsection (4), the sender of which is unknown, or who sent the money or other property for an unknown purpose, or money which is credited as "unknown," and which said governmental agency is unable to credit to any particular account, or the sender of which has been unknown for a period of 5 or more consecutive years; or when known, has died without having disposed thereof, and without leaving heirs, next of kin or distributees, or for any reason is unclaimed from such governmental agency.

(4) In the event any money is due to any resident of this state as a refund, rebate or tax rebate from the United States Commissioner of Internal Revenue, the United States Treasurer, or other governmental agency or department, which said resident will, or is likely to have her or his rights to apply for and secure such refund or rebate barred by any statute of limitations or, in any event, has failed for a period of 1 year after said resident could have filed a claim for said refund or rebate, the Department of Financial Services is appointed agent of such resident to demand, file and apply for said refund or rebate, and is appointed to do any act which a natural person could do to recover such money, and it is hereby declared that when the department files such application or any other proceeding to secure such refund or rebate, its agency is coupled with an interest in the money sought and money recovered.

(5) It is the purpose of this chapter to include all funds or other property in the possession of the government of the United States, and of its departments, officers, and agencies, which property has its situs in this state or belonged to a resident thereof, and not to limit the application of this chapter by the naming of any particular agency. This chapter shall include all funds held in the United States Department of Veterans Affairs, Comptroller of Currency, United States Treasury, Department of Internal Revenue, federal courts, registry of federal courts, and such evidences of indebtedness as adjusted service bonds, old matured debts issued prior to 1917, unclaimed and interest thereon, postal savings bonds, liberty bonds, victory notes, treasury bonds, treasury notes, certificates of indebtedness, treasury bills, treasurer's savings certificates, bonuses and adjusted compensation, allotments, and all unclaimed refunds or rebates of whatever kind or nature, which are subjects of escheat, under the terms of this chapter. Provided, however, that nothing in this chapter shall be construed to mean that any refunds due ratepayers under order of any court of the United States shall become the property of the state.

Laws 1947, c. 24333, § 2; Laws 1949, c. 25035, § 11; Laws 1969, c. 69–106, §§ 12, 35; Laws 1970, c. 70–405, § 1. Amended by Laws 1993, c. 93–268, § 36, eff. June 3, 1993; Laws 1997, c. 97–102, § 847, eff. July 1, 1997; Laws 2003, c. 2003–261, § 1881, eff. June 26, 2003.

716.03. Department to institute proceedings to recover escheated property

When there exists, or may exist, escheated funds or property under this chapter, the Department of Financial Services shall demand or institute proceedings in the name of the state for an adjudication that an escheat to the state of such funds or property has occurred; and shall take appropriate action to recover such funds or property.

Laws 1947, c. 24333, § 3; Laws 1949, c. 25035, § 11; Laws 1969, c. 69–106, §§ 12, 35. Amended by Laws 2003, c. 2003–261, § 1882, eff. June 26, 2003.

716.04. Jurisdiction

Whenever the Department of Financial Services is of the opinion an escheat has occurred, or shall occur, of any money or other property deposited in the custody of, or under the control of, any court of the United States, in and for any district within the state, or in the custody of any depository, registry or clerk or other officer of such court, or the treasury of the United States, it shall cause to be filed a complaint in the Circuit Court of Leon County, or in any other court of competent jurisdiction, to ascertain if any escheat has occurred, and to cause said court to enter a judgment or decree of escheat in favor of the state, with costs, disbursements, and attorney fee.

Laws 1947, c. 24333, § 4; Laws 1969, c. 69–106, §§ 12, 35. Amended by Laws 2003, c. 2003–261, § 1883, eff. June 26, 2003.

716.05. Money recovered to be paid into State Treasury

When any funds or property which has escheated within the meaning of this chapter has been recovered by the Department of Financial Services, the department shall first pay all costs incident to the collection and recovery of such funds or property and shall promptly deposit the remaining balance of such funds or property with the Chief Financial Officer, to be distributed in accordance with law.

Laws 1947, c. 24333, § 5; Laws 1969, c. 69–106, §§ 12, 35; Laws 1983, c. 83–216, § 153. Amended by Laws 2003, c. 2003–261, § 1884, eff. June 26, 2003.

716.06. Public records

All records in the office of the Chief Financial Officer or the Department of Financial Services relating to federal funds, pursuant to this chapter, shall be public records.

Laws 1947, c. 24333, § 6; Laws 1969, c. 69–106, §§ 12, 35. Amended by Laws 2003, c. 2003–261, § 1885, eff. June 26, 2003.

716.07. Recovery of escheated property by claimant

(1) Any person who claims any property, funds, or money delivered to the Treasurer or Chief Financial Officer under this chapter, shall, within 5 years from the date of receipt of such property, funds, or money, file a verified claim with the Chief Financial Officer, setting forth the facts upon which such party claims to be entitled to recover such money or property.   All claims made for recovery of property, funds, or money, not filed within 5 years from the date that such property, funds, or money is received by the Chief Financial Officer, shall be forever barred, and the Chief Financial Officer shall be without power to consider or determine any claims so made by any claimant after 5 years from the date that the property, funds, or money was received by the Chief Financial Officer.

(2) The Chief Financial Officer shall approve or disapprove the claim. If the claim is approved, the funds, money, or property of the claimant, less any expenses and costs which shall have been incurred by the state in securing the possession of said property, as provided by this chapter, shall be delivered to the claimant by the Chief Financial Officer upon warrant issued according to law and her or his receipt taken therefor. If the court finds, upon any judicial review, that the claimant is entitled to the property, money, or funds claimed, and shall render judgment in her or his or its favor, declaring that the claimant is entitled to such property,

funds, or money, then upon presentation of said judgment or a certified copy thereof to the Chief Financial Officer, the Chief Financial Officer shall draw her or his warrant for the amount of money stated in such judgment, without interest or cost to the state, less any sum paid by the state as costs or expenses in securing possession of such property, funds, or money. When payment has been made to any claimant, no action thereafter shall be maintained by any other claimant against the state or any officer thereof, for or on account of such money, property, or funds.

Laws 1947, c. 24333, § 7; Laws 1963, c. 63–559, § 30; Laws 1969, c. 69–106, §§ 12, 35; Laws 1978, c. 78–95, § 7. Amended by Laws 1997, c. 97–102, § 848, eff. July 1, 1997; Laws 2003, c. 2003–261, § 1886, eff. June 26, 2003.

CHAPTER 717

DISPOSITION OF UNCLAIMED PROPERTY

Former Provisions

Laws 1987, c. 87–105, § 42, eff. July 1, 1987, repealed §§ 717.01 to 717.25 and §§ 717.27 to 717.30, which comprised Fla.St.1985, Chapter 717, "Disposition of Unclaimed Property". Prior to the 1987 law, § 717.26 was repealed by Laws 1971, c. 71–377, § 280. Laws 1987, c. 87–105, §§ 1 to 41, enacted §§ 717.001 to 717.1401 which comprises Fla.St.1987, Chapter 717, Disposition of Unclaimed Property.

UNIFORM UNCLAIMED PROPERTY ACT (1981 ACT)

Tables of Jurisdictions Wherein Act Has Been Adopted

For text of Uniform Act, and variation notes and annotation materials for adopting jurisdictions, see Uniform Laws Annotated, Master Edition, Volume 8C.

Jurisdiction	Laws	Effective Date	Statutory Citation
Alaska	1986, c. 133	9–19–1986	AS 34.45.110 to 34.45.780.
Colorado	1987, c. 274	7–1–1987	West's C.R.S.A. §§ 38–13–101 to 38–13–134.
District of Columbia ...	1981, D.C.Law 3–160		D.C. Official Code, 2001 Ed. §§ 41–101 to 41–142.
Florida	1987, c. 87–105	7–1–1987	West's F.S.A. §§ 717.001 to 717.1401.
Georgia	1990, p. 1506	7–1–1990	O.C.G.A. §§ 44–12–190 to 44–12–236.
Idaho	1983, c. 209	7–1–1983	I.C. §§ 14–501 to 14–543.
Iowa[1]	1967, c. 391	7–1–1967	I.C.A. §§ 556.1 to 556.29.
Maryland[2]	1966, c. 611	6–1–1966	Code, Commercial Law, §§ 17–101 to 17–326.
Minnesota[3]	1969, c. 725	7–1–1969	M.S.A. §§ 345.31 to 345.60.
New Hampshire	1986, c. 204.1	1–1–1987	RSA 471–C:1 to 471–C:43.
New Jersey	1989, c. 58	4–14–1989	N.J.S.A. §§ 46:30B–1 to 46:30B–109.
North Dakota	1985, c. 510		NDCC 47–30.1–01 to 47–30.1–38.
Oklahoma	1991, c. 331	9–1–1991	60 Okl.St.Ann. §§ 651 to 688.
Oregon[4]	1957, c. 670	8–20–1957	ORS 98.302 to 98.436.
Rhode Island	P.L.1986, c. 500	7–1–1987	Gen.Laws 1956, §§ 33–21.1–1 to 33–21.1–41.
South Carolina	1988, Act No. 658, Pt. II, § 34A	7–1–1988	Code 1976, §§ 27–18–10 to 27–18–400.
South Dakota	1992, c. 312	7–1–1993	SDCL 43–41B–1 to 43–41B–42.
Tennessee[5]	1978, c. 561	3–6–1978	T.C.A. §§ 66–29–101 to 66–29–154.
Utah[6]	1983, c. 164	7–1–1983	U.C.A.1953, 67–4a–101 to 67–4a–902.
Virginia	1984, c. 121		Code 1950, §§ 55–210.1 to 55–210.30.
Washington	1983, c. 179	6–30–1983	West's RCWA 63.29.010 to 63.29.905.
Wisconsin	1983, Act 408	12–31–1984	W.S.A. 177.01 to 177.41.
Wyoming	1993, c. 213	3–11–1993*	Wyo.Stat.Ann. §§ 34–24–101 to 34–24–140.

* Date of approval.

[1] The Iowa act, as amended by L.1984, H.F. 2522, retains the basic format and many of the provisions of the Uniform Disposition of Unclaimed Property Act of 1966, but now also contains many of the major provisions of the Uniform Unclaimed Property Act of 1981. Accordingly, the citation of the Iowa act is set forth in the tables for both acts.

[2] The Maryland act, as amended by L.1985, c. 602, retains the basic format and many of the provisions of the Uniform Disposition of Unclaimed Property Act of 1954, but now also contains certain provisions of the Uniform Unclaimed Property Act of 1981. Accordingly, the citation of the Maryland act is set forth in the table for both acts.

[3] The Minnesota act, as amended, retains the basic format and many of the provisions of the Uniform Disposition of Unclaimed Property Act of 1966, but now also contains many of the major provisions of the Uniform Unclaimed Property Act of 1981. Accordingly, the citation of the Minnesota act is set forth in the tables for both acts.

[4] The Oregon act, as amended by L.1983, c. 716, now contains the basic format and many of the provisions of the Uniform Disposition of Unclaimed Property Act of 1966, but now also contains many of the major provisions of the Uniform Unclaimed Property Act of 1981. Accordingly, the citation of the Oregon act is set forth in the tables for both acts.

[5] The Tennessee act, as amended by L.1984, c. 544, retains the basic format and many of the provisions of the Uniform Disposition of Unclaimed Property Act of 1966, but now also contains many of the provisions of the Uniform Unclaimed Property Act of 1981. Accordingly, the citation of the Tennessee act is set forth in tables for both acts.

[6] Original 1983 adoption repealed in 1995. New provisions enacted in 1995 substantially retaining major provisions of Uniform Act.

Cross References

Decedent's estates, see § 732.107.

Unclaimed property held by personal representative, disposition, see § 733.816.

Disposition of unclaimed trust funds, see § 402.17.

Federal agencies, funds in possession, escheat, see § 716.02.

Mail-in secondhand precious metals dealers, transactions, see § 538.32.

Pari-mutuel pools, abandoned interest, escheat to state, see § 550.1645.

Timeshare estates, trustee foreclosure procedure for assessment liens, see F.S.A. § 721.855.

Timeshare estates, trustee foreclosure procedure for mortgage liens, see F.S.A. § 721.856.

Unclaimed articles, see § 550.1645.

717.001. Short title

This chapter may be cited as the "Florida Disposition of Unclaimed Property Act."

Laws 1987, c. 87–105, § 1.

717.101. Definitions

As used in this chapter, unless the context otherwise requires:

(1) "Aggregate" means the amounts reported for owners of unclaimed property of less than $50 or where there is no name for the individual or entity listed on the holder's records, regardless of the amount to be reported.

(2) "Apparent owner" means the person whose name appears on the records of the holder as the person entitled to property held, issued, or owing by the holder.

(3) "Banking organization" means any state or national bank, international banking entity or similar entity, trust company, savings bank, industrial savings bank, land bank, safe-deposit company, private bank, or any organization otherwise defined by law as a bank or banking organization.

(4) "Business association" means any corporation (other than a public corporation), joint stock company, investment company, business trust, partnership, or association for business purposes of two or more individuals, whether or not for profit, including a banking organization, financial organization, insurance company, dissolved pension plan, or utility.

(5) "Claimant" means the person on whose behalf a claim is filed.

(6) "Credit balance" means an account balance in the customer's favor.

(7) "Department" means the Department of Financial Services.

(8) "Domicile" means the state of incorporation, in the case of a corporation incorporated under the laws of a state, and the state of the principal place of business, in the case of a person not incorporated under the laws of a state.

(9) "Due diligence" means the use of reasonable and prudent methods under particular circumstances to locate apparent owners of inactive accounts using the taxpayer identification number or social security number, if known, which may include, but are not limited to, using a nationwide database, cross-indexing with other records of the holder, mailing to the last known address unless the last known address is known to be inaccurate, or engaging a licensed agency or company capable of conducting such search and providing updated addresses.

(10) "Financial organization" means a state or federal savings association, savings and loan association, bank, trust company, international bank agency, cooperative bank, building and loan association, or credit union.

(11) "Health care provider" means any state-licensed entity that provides and receives payment for health care services. These entities include, but are not limited to, hospitals, outpatient centers, physician practices, and skilled nursing facilities.

(12) "Holder" means a person, wherever organized or domiciled, who is:

(a) In possession of property belonging to another;

(b) A trustee in case of a trust; or

(c) Indebted to another on an obligation.

(13) "Insurance company" means an association, corporation, or fraternal or mutual benefit organization, whether or not for profit, which is engaged in providing insurance coverage, including, by way of illustration and not limitation, accident, burial, casualty, credit life, contract performance, dental, fidelity, fire, health, hospitalization, illness, life (including endowments and annuities), malpractice, marine, mortgage, surety, and wage protection insurance.

(14) "Intangible property" includes, by way of illustration and not limitation:

(a) Moneys, checks, drafts, deposits, interest, dividends, and income.

(b) Credit balances, customer overpayments, security deposits and other instruments as defined by chapter 679, refunds, unpaid wages, unused airline tickets, and unidentified remittances.

(c) Stocks, and other intangible ownership interests in business associations.

(d) Moneys deposited to redeem stocks, bonds, bearer bonds, original issue discount bonds, coupons, and other securities, or to make distributions.

(e) Amounts due and payable under the terms of insurance policies.

(f) Amounts distributable from a trust or custodial fund established under a plan to provide any health, welfare, pension, vacation, severance, retirement, death, stock purchase, profit sharing, employee savings, supplemental unemployment insurance, or similar benefit.

(15) "Last known address" means a description of the location of the apparent owner sufficient for the purpose of the delivery of mail. For the purposes of identifying, reporting, and remitting property to the department which is presumed to be unclaimed, "last known address" includes any partial description of the location of the apparent owner sufficient to establish the apparent owner was a resident of this state at the time of last contact with the apparent owner or at the time the property became due and payable.

(16) "Lawful charges" means charges against dormant accounts that are authorized by statute for the purpose of offsetting the costs of maintaining the dormant account.

(17) "Managed care payor" means a health care plan that has a defined system of selecting and limiting health care providers as evidenced by a managed care contract with the health care providers. These plans include, but are not limited to, managed care health insurance companies and health maintenance organizations.

(18) "Owner" means a depositor in the case of a deposit, a beneficiary in the case of a trust or a deposit in trust, or a payee in the case of other intangible property, or a person having a legal or equitable interest in property subject to this chapter or his or her legal representative.

(19) "Public corporation" means a corporation created by the state, founded and owned in the public interest, supported by public funds, and governed by those deriving their power from the state.

(20) "Reportable period" means the calendar year ending December 31 of each year.

(21) "State," when applied to a part of the United States, includes any state, district, commonwealth, territory, insular possession, and any other area subject to the legislative authority of the United States.

(22) "Trust instrument" means a trust instrument as defined in s. 736.0103.

(23) "Ultimate equitable owner" means a natural person who, directly or indirectly, owns or controls an ownership interest in a corporation, a foreign corporation, an alien business organization, or any other form of business organization, regardless of whether such natural person owns or controls such ownership interest through one or more natural persons or one or

more proxies, powers of attorney, nominees, corporations, associations, partnerships, trusts, joint stock companies, or other entities or devices, or any combination thereof.

(24) "Utility" means a person who owns or operates, for public use, any plant, equipment, property, franchise, or license for the transmission of communications or the production, storage, transmission, sale, delivery, or furnishing of electricity, water, steam, or gas.

Laws 1987, c. 87–105, § 2. Amended by Laws 1991, c. 91–110, § 23; Laws 1996, c. 96–301, § 1, eff. Dec. 1, 1996; Laws 1997, c. 97–102, § 1770, eff. July 1, 1997; Laws 2001, c. 2001–36, § 1, eff. Oct. 1, 2001; Laws 2003, c. 2003–21, § 1, eff. May 21, 2003; Laws 2003, c. 2003–261, § 1887, eff. June 26, 2003; Laws 2004, c. 2004–390, § 110, eff. July 1, 2004; Laws 2005, c. 2005–163, § 1, eff. June 8, 2005; Laws 2013, c. 2013–172, § 2, eff. Oct. 1, 2013.

717.102. Property presumed unclaimed; general rule

(1) All intangible property, including any income or increment thereon less any lawful charges, that is held, issued, or owing in the ordinary course of the holder's business and the owner fails to claim such property for more than 5 years after the property becomes payable or distributable is presumed unclaimed, except as otherwise provided by this chapter.

(2) Property is payable or distributable for the purpose of this chapter notwithstanding the owner's failure to make demand or to present any instrument or document required to receive payment.

Laws 1987, c. 87–105, § 3. Amended by Laws 2001, c. 2001–36, § 2, eff. Oct. 1, 2001.

717.103. General rules for taking custody of intangible unclaimed property

Unless otherwise provided in this chapter or by other statute of this state, intangible property is subject to the custody of the department as unclaimed property if the conditions leading to a presumption that the property is unclaimed as described in ss. 717.102 and 717.105–717.116 are satisfied and:

(1) The last known address, as shown on the records of the holder, of the apparent owner is in this state;

(2) The records of the holder do not reflect the identity of the person entitled to the property, and it is established that the last known address of the person entitled to the property is in this state;

(3) The records of the holder do not reflect the last known address of the apparent owner, and it is established that:

(a) The last known address of the person entitled to the property is in this state; or

(b) The holder is a domiciliary or a government or governmental subdivision or agency of this state and has not previously paid the property to the state of the last known address of the apparent owner or other person entitled to the property;

(4) The last known address, as shown on the records of the holder, of the apparent owner or other person entitled to the property is in a state that does not provide by law for the escheat or custodial taking of the property, or its escheat or unclaimed property law is not applicable to the property, and the holder is a domiciliary or a government or governmental subdivision or agency of this state;

(5) The last known address, as shown on the records of the holder, of the apparent owner is in a foreign nation and the holder is a domiciliary or a government or governmental subdivision or agency of this state; or

(6) The transaction out of which the property arose occurred in this state, and;

(a)1. The last known address of the apparent owner or other person entitled to the property is unknown; or

2. The last known address of the apparent owner or other person entitled to the property is in a state that does not provide by law for the escheat or custodial taking of the property, or its escheat or unclaimed property law is not applicable to the property; and

(b) The holder is a domiciliary of a state that does not provide by law for the escheat or custodial taking of the property, or its escheat or unclaimed property law is not applicable to the property.

Laws 1987, c. 87–105, § 4. Amended by Laws 2001, c. 2001–36, § 3, eff. Oct. 1, 2001.

717.1035. Property originated or issued by this state, any political subdivision of this state, or any entity incorporated, organized, created, or otherwise located in the state

(1) All intangible property, including, but not limited to, any interest, dividend, or other earnings thereon, less any lawful charges, held by a business association, federal, state, or local government or governmental subdivision, agency, or entity, or any other person or entity, regardless of where the holder may be found, if the owner has not claimed or corresponded in writing concerning the property within 3 years after the date prescribed for payment or delivery, is presumed to be unclaimed property and subject to the custody of this state as such if:

(a) The last known address of the owner is unknown; and

(b) The person or entity originating or issuing the intangible property is this state or any political subdivision of this state, or the person or entity is incorporated, organized, created, or otherwise located in this state.

(2) The provisions of subsection (1) shall not apply to property which is or may be presumed unclaimed and subject to the custody of this state pursuant to any other provision of law containing a dormancy period different than that prescribed in subsection (1).

(3) The provisions of subsection (1) shall apply to all property held at the time of enactment, or at any time thereafter, regardless of when such property became or becomes presumptively unclaimed.

Added by Laws 1990, c. 90–113, § 1, eff. Oct. 1, 1990. Amended by Laws 1992, c. 92–169, § 2, eff. April 9, 1992; Laws 2001, c. 2001–36, § 4, eff. Oct. 1, 2001.

717.104. Traveler's checks and money orders

(1) Subject to subsection (4), any sum payable on a traveler's check that has been outstanding for more than 15 years after its issuance is presumed unclaimed unless the owner, within 15 years, has communicated in writing with the issuer concerning it or otherwise indicated an interest as evidenced by a memorandum or other record on file with the issuer.

(2) Subject to subsection (4), any sum payable on a money order or similar written instrument, other than a third party bank check, that has been outstanding for more than 7 years after its issuance is presumed unclaimed unless the owner, within 7 years, has communicated in writing with the issuer concerning it or otherwise indicated an interest as evidenced by a memorandum or other record on file with the issuer.

(3) No holder may deduct from the amount of any traveler's check or money order any charges imposed by reason of the failure to present those instruments for payment unless there is a valid and enforceable written contract between the issuer and the owner of the property pursuant to which the issuer may impose those charges and the issuer regularly imposes those

charges and does not regularly reverse or otherwise cancel those charges with respect to the property.

(4) No sum payable on a traveler's check, money order, or similar written instrument, other than a third party bank check, described in subsections (1) and (2) may be subjected to the custody of this state as unclaimed property unless:

(a) The records of the issuer show that the traveler's check, money order, or similar written instrument was purchased in this state;

(b) The issuer has its principal place of business in this state and the records of the issuer do not show the state in which the traveler's check, money order, or similar written instrument was purchased; or

(c) The issuer has its principal place of business in this state; the records of the issuer show the state in which the traveler's check, money order, or similar written instrument was purchased; and the laws of the state of purchase do not provide for the escheat or custodial taking of the property, or its escheat or unclaimed property law is not applicable to the property.

(5) Notwithstanding any other provision of this chapter, subsection (4) applies to sums payable on traveler's checks, money orders, and similar written instruments presumed unclaimed on or after February 1, 1965, except to the extent that those sums have been paid over to a state prior to January 1, 1974.

Laws 1987, c. 87–105, § 5. Amended by Laws 2001, c. 2001–36, § 5, eff. Oct. 1, 2001.

717.1045. Gift certificates and similar credit items

Notwithstanding s. 717.117, an unredeemed gift certificate or credit memo as defined in s. 501.95 is not required to be reported as unclaimed property.

(1) The consideration paid for an unredeemed gift certificate or credit memo is the property of the issuer of the unredeemed gift certificate or credit memo.

(2) An unredeemed gift certificate or credit memo is subject only to any rights of a purchaser or owner thereof and is not subject to a claim made by any state acting on behalf of a purchaser or owner.

(3) It is the intent of the Legislature that this section apply to the custodial holding of unredeemed gift certificates and credit memos.

(4) However, a gift certificate or credit memo described in s. 501.95(2)(b) shall be reported as unclaimed property. The consideration paid for such a gift certificate or credit memo is the property of the owner of the gift certificate or credit memo.

Added by Laws 2007, c. 2007–256, § 2, eff. June 28, 2007.

717.105. Checks, drafts, and similar instruments issued or certified by banking and financial organizations

(1) Any sum payable on a check, draft, or similar instrument, except those subject to ss. 717.104 and 717.115, on which a banking or financial organization is directly liable, including, but not limited to, a cashier's check or a certified check, which has been outstanding for more than 5 years after it was payable or after its issuance if payable on demand, is presumed unclaimed unless the owner, within 5 years, has communicated in writing with the banking or financial organization concerning it or otherwise indicated an interest as evidenced by a memorandum or other record on file with the banking or financial organization.

(2) No holder may deduct from the amount of any instrument subject to this section any charges imposed by reason of the failure to present the instrument for encashment unless there is a valid and enforceable written contract between the holder and the owner of the instrument pursuant to which the holder may impose those charges and does not regularly reverse or otherwise cancel those charges with respect to the instrument.

Laws 1987, c. 87–105, § 6. Amended by Laws 1996, c. 96–301, § 2, eff. Dec. 1, 1996; Laws 2001, c. 2001–36, § 6, eff. Oct. 1, 2001.

717.106. Bank deposits and funds in financial organizations

(1) Any demand, savings, or matured time deposit with a banking or financial organization, including deposits that are automatically renewable, and any funds paid toward the purchase of shares, a mutual investment certificate, or any other interest in a banking or financial organization is presumed unclaimed unless the owner has, within 5 years:

(a) Increased or decreased the amount of the deposit or presented the passbook or other similar evidence of the deposit for the crediting of interest;

(b) Communicated in writing or by documented telephone contact with the banking or financial organization concerning the property;

(c) Otherwise indicated an interest in the property as evidenced by a memorandum or other record on file with the banking or financial organization;

(d) Owned other property to which paragraph (a), paragraph (b), or paragraph (c) is applicable and if the banking or financial organization communicates in writing with the owner with regard to the property that would otherwise be presumed unclaimed under this subsection at the address to which communications regarding the other property regularly are sent; or

(e) Had another relationship with the banking or financial organization concerning which the owner has:

1. Communicated in writing with the banking or financial organization; or

2. Otherwise indicated an interest as evidenced by a memorandum or other record on file with the banking or financial organization and if the banking or financial organization communicates in writing with the owner with regard to the property that would otherwise be unclaimed under this subsection at the address to which communications regarding the other relationship regularly are sent.

(2) For purpose of paragraph (1)(a), property includes any interest or dividends thereon.

(3) No holder may impose with respect to property described in subsection (1) any charges due to dormancy or inactivity or cease payment of interest unless:

(a) There is an enforceable written contract between the holder and the owner of the property pursuant to which the holder may impose those charges or cease payment of interest.

(b) For property in excess of $2, the holder, no more than 3 months prior to the initial imposition of those charges or cessation of interest, has given written notice to the owner of the amount of those charges at the last known address of the owner stating that those charges shall be imposed or that interest shall cease, but the notice provided in this section need not be given with respect to charges imposed or interest ceased before July 1, 1987.

(c) The holder regularly imposes those charges or ceases payment of interest and does not regularly reverse or otherwise cancel those charges or retroactively credit interest with respect to such property.

---

(4) Any property described in subsection (1) that is automatically renewable is matured for purposes of subsection (1) upon the expiration of its initial time period except that, in the case of any renewal to which the owner consents at or about the time of renewal by communicating in writing with the banking or financial organization or otherwise indicating consent as evidenced by a memorandum or other record on file prepared by an employee of the organization, the property is matured upon the expiration of the last time period for which consent was given. If, at the time provided for delivery in s. 717.119, a penalty or forfeiture in the payment of interest would result from the delivery of the property, the time for delivery is extended until the time when no penalty or forfeiture would result.

(5) If the documents establishing a deposit described in subsection (1) state the address of a beneficiary of the deposit, and the account has a value of at least $50, notice shall be given to the beneficiary as provided for notice to the apparent owner under s. 717.117(4). This subsection shall apply to accounts opened on or after October 1, 1990.

Laws 1987, c. 87–105, § 7. Amended by Laws 1990, c. 90–113, § 2, eff. Oct. 1, 1990; Laws 1991, c. 91–110, § 63; Laws 1996, c. 96–301, § 3, eff. Dec. 1, 1996; Laws 2001, c. 2001–36, § 7, eff. Oct. 1, 2001; Laws 2004, c. 2004–390, § 111, eff. July 1, 2004; Laws 2005, c. 2005–163, § 2, eff. June 8, 2005.

717.107. Funds owing under life insurance policies

(1) Funds held or owing under any life or endowment insurance policy or annuity contract which has matured or terminated are presumed unclaimed if unclaimed for more than 5 years after the funds became due and payable as established from the records of the insurance company holding or owing the funds, but property described in paragraph (3)(b) is presumed unclaimed if such property is not claimed for more than 2 years. The amount presumed unclaimed shall include any amount due and payable under s. 627.4615.

(2) If a person other than the insured or annuitant is entitled to the funds and no address of the person is known to the company or it is not definite and certain from the records of the company who is entitled to the funds, it is presumed that the last known address of the person entitled to the funds is the same as the last known address of the insured or annuitant according to the records of the company.

(3) For purposes of this chapter, a life or endowment insurance policy or annuity contract not matured by actual proof of the death of the insured or annuitant according to the records of the company is deemed matured and the proceeds due and payable if:

(a) The company knows that the insured or annuitant has died; or

(b)1. The insured has attained, or would have attained if he or she were living, the limiting age under the mortality table on which the reserve is based;

2. The policy was in force at the time the insured attained, or would have attained, the limiting age specified in subparagraph 1.; and

3. Neither the insured nor any other person appearing to have an interest in the policy within the preceding 2 years, according to the records of the company, has assigned, readjusted, or paid premiums on the policy; subjected the policy to a loan; corresponded in writing with the company concerning the policy; or otherwise indicated an interest as evidenced by a memorandum or other record on file prepared by an employee of the company.

(4) For purposes of this chapter, the application of an automatic premium loan provision or other nonforfeiture provision contained in an insurance policy does not prevent the policy from being matured or terminated under subsection (1) if the insured has died or the insured or the

beneficiaries of the policy otherwise have become entitled to the proceeds thereof before the depletion of the cash surrender value of a policy by the application of those provisions.

(5) If the laws of this state or the terms of the life insurance policy require the company to give notice to the insured or owner that an automatic premium loan provision or other nonforfeiture provision has been exercised and the notice, given to an insured or owner whose last known address according to the records of the company is in this state, is undeliverable, the company shall make a reasonable search to ascertain the policyholder's correct address to which the notice must be mailed.

(6) Notwithstanding any other provision of law, if the company learns of the death of the insured or annuitant and the beneficiary has not communicated with the insurer within 4 months after the death, the company shall take reasonable steps to pay the proceeds to the beneficiary.

(7) Commencing 2 years after July 1, 1987, every change of beneficiary form issued by an insurance company under any life or endowment insurance policy or annuity contract to an insured or owner who is a resident of this state must request the following information:

(a) The name of each beneficiary, or if a class of beneficiaries is named, the name of each current beneficiary in the class.

(b) The address of each beneficiary.

(c) The relationship of each beneficiary to the insured.

Laws 1987, c. 87–105, § 8. Amended by Laws 1997, c. 97–102, § 849, eff. July 1, 1997; Laws 2001, c. 2001–36, § 8, eff. Oct. 1, 2001; Laws 2004, c. 2004–390, § 112, eff. July 1, 2004.

717.1071. Lost owners of unclaimed demutualization, rehabilitation, or related reorganization proceeds [1]

(1) Property distributable in the course of a demutualization, rehabilitation, or related reorganization of an insurance company is deemed abandoned 2 years after the date the property is first distributable if, at the time of the first distribution, the last known address of the owner on the books and records of the holder is known to be incorrect or the distribution or statements are returned by the post office as undeliverable; and the owner has not communicated in writing with the holder or its agent regarding the interest or otherwise communicated with the holder regarding the interest as evidenced by a memorandum or other record on file with the holder or its agent.

(2) Property distributable in the course of demutualization, rehabilitation, or related reorganization of a mutual insurance company that is not subject to subsection (1) shall be reportable as otherwise provided by this chapter.

(3) Property subject to this section shall be reported and delivered no later than May 1 as of the preceding December 31; however, the initial report under this section shall be filed no later than November 1, 2003, as of December 31, 2002.

Added by Laws 2003, c. 2003–21, § 2, eff. May 21, 2003; Laws 2003, c. 2003–281, § 75, eff. July 11, 2003.

[1] Reviser's Note—2003: As enacted by s. 75, ch. 2003–281. For a description of multiple acts in the same session affecting a statutory provision, *see* preface to the *Florida Statutes*, "Statutory Construction." Section 717.1071 was also enacted by s. 2, ch. 2003–21, and the version reads:

"717.1071. Unclaimed demutualization proceeds.—Unclaimed property payable or distributable in the course of a demutualization of an insurance company is presumed unclaimed 5 years after the earlier of the date of last contact with the policyholder or the date the property became payable or distributable."

717.108. Deposits held by utilities

Any deposit, including any interest thereon, made by a subscriber with a utility to secure payment or any sum paid in advance for utility services to be furnished, less any lawful charges, that remains unclaimed by the owner for more than 1 year after termination of the services for which the deposit or advance payment was made is presumed unclaimed.

Laws 1987, c. 87–105, § 9. Amended by Laws 1996, c. 96–301, § 4, eff. Dec. 1, 1996; Laws 2001, c. 2001–36, § 9, eff. Oct. 1, 2001.

717.109. Refunds held by business associations

Except as otherwise provided by law, any sum that a business association has been ordered to refund by a court or administrative agency which has been unclaimed by the owner for more than 1 year after it became payable in accordance with the final determination or order providing for the refund, regardless of whether the final determination or order requires any person entitled to a refund to make a claim for it, is presumed unclaimed.

Laws 1987, c. 87–105, § 10. Amended by Laws 2001, c. 2001–36, § 10, eff. Oct. 1, 2001; Laws 2004, c. 2004–390, § 113, eff. July 1, 2004.

717.1101. Unclaimed equity and debt of business associations

(1)(a) Stock or other equity interest in a business association is presumed unclaimed 3 years after the earliest of:

1. The date of the most recent dividend, stock split, or other distribution unclaimed by the apparent owner;

2. The date of a statement of account or other notification or communication that was returned as undeliverable; or

3. The date the holder discontinued mailings, notifications, or communications to the apparent owner.

(b) Unmatured or unredeemed debt, other than a bearer bond or an original issue discount bond, is presumed unclaimed 3 years after the date of the most recent interest payment unclaimed by the owner.

(c) Matured or redeemed debt is presumed unclaimed 3 years after the date of maturity or redemption.

(d) At the time property is presumed unclaimed under paragraph (a) or paragraph (b), any other property right accrued or accruing to the owner as a result of the property interest and not previously presumed unclaimed is also presumed unclaimed.

(2) The running of such 3–year period ceases if the person:

(a) 1. Communicates in writing with the association or its agent regarding the interest or a dividend, distribution, or other sum payable as a result of the interest; or

2. Otherwise communicates with the association regarding the interest or a dividend, distribution, or other sum payable as a result of the interest, as evidenced by a memorandum or other record on file with the association or its agent.

(b) Presents an instrument issued to pay interest or a dividend or other cash distribution. If any future dividend, distribution, or other sum payable to the owner as a result of the interest is subsequently not claimed by the owner, a new period in which the property is presumed unclaimed commences and relates back only to the time a subsequent dividend, distribution, or other sum became due and payable.

(3) At the same time any interest is presumed unclaimed under this section, any dividend, distribution, or other sum then held for or owing to the owner as a result of the interest, is presumed unclaimed.

(4) Any dividend, profit, distribution, interest redemption, payment on principal, or other sum held or owing by a business association for or to a shareholder, certificateholder, member, bondholder, or other security holder, who has not claimed such amount or corresponded in writing with the business association concerning such amount, within 3 years after the date prescribed for payment or delivery, is presumed unclaimed.

Laws 1987, c. 87–105, § 11. Amended by Laws 1996, c. 96–301, § 5, eff. Dec. 1, 1996; Laws 2001, c. 2001–36, § 11, eff. Oct. 1, 2001; Laws 2003, c. 2003–21, § 3, eff. May 21, 2003; Laws 2005, c. 2005–163, § 3, eff. June 8, 2005.

717.111. Property of business associations held in course of dissolution

All intangible property distributable in the course of a voluntary or involuntary dissolution of a business association which is not claimed by the owner for more than 6 months after the date specified for final distribution is presumed unclaimed.

Laws 1987, c. 87–105, § 12. Amended by Laws 2001, c. 2001–36, § 12, eff. Oct. 1, 2001.

717.112. Property held by agents and fiduciaries

(1) Except as provided in ss. 717.1125 and 733.816, all intangible property and any income or increment thereon held in a fiduciary capacity for the benefit of another person is presumed unclaimed unless the owner has within 5 years after it has become payable or distributable increased or decreased the principal, accepted payment of principal or income, communicated concerning the property, or otherwise indicated an interest as evidenced by a memorandum or other record on file with the fiduciary.

(2) Funds in an individual retirement account or a retirement plan for self-employed individuals or similar account or plan established pursuant to the Internal Revenue laws of the United States are not payable or distributable within the meaning of subsection (1) unless, under the terms of the account or plan, distribution of all or part of the funds would then be mandatory.

(3) For the purpose of this section, a person who holds property as an agent for a business association is deemed to hold the property in a fiduciary capacity for that business association alone, unless the agreement between said person and the business association provides otherwise.

(4) For the purposes of this chapter, a person who is deemed to hold property in a fiduciary capacity for a business association alone is the holder of the property only insofar as the interest of the business association in the property is concerned, and the business association is the holder of the property insofar as the interest of any other person in the property is concerned.

(5) All intangible property, and any income or increment thereon, issued by a government or governmental subdivision or agency, public corporation, or public authority and held in an agency capacity for the governmental subdivision, agency, public corporation, or public authority for the benefit of the owner of record, is presumed unclaimed unless the owner has, within 1 year after such property has become payable or distributable, increased or decreased the principal, accepted payment of the principal or income, communicated concerning the property,

or otherwise indicated an interest in the property as evidenced by a memorandum or other record on file with the fiduciary.

Laws 1987, c. 87–105, § 13. Amended by Laws 1996, c. 96–301, § 6, eff. Dec. 1, 1996; Laws 2001, c. 2001–36, § 13, eff. Oct. 1, 2001; Laws 2013, c. 2013–172, § 3, eff. Oct. 1, 2013.

717.1125. Property held by fiduciaries under trust instruments

All intangible property and any income or increment thereon held in a fiduciary capacity for the benefit of another person under a trust instrument is presumed unclaimed unless the owner has, within 2 years after it has become payable or distributable, increased or decreased the principal, accepted payment of principal or income, communicated concerning the property, or otherwise indicated an interest as evidenced by a memorandum or other record on file with the fiduciary.

Added by Laws 2013, c. 2013–172, § 4, eff. Oct. 1, 2013.

717.113. Property held by courts and public agencies

All intangible property held for the owner by any court, government or governmental subdivision or agency, public corporation, or public authority that has not been claimed by the owner for more than 1 year after it became payable or distributable is presumed unclaimed. Notwithstanding the provisions of this section, funds deposited in the Minerals Trust Fund pursuant to s. 377.247 are presumed unclaimed only if the funds have not been claimed by the owner for more than 5 years after the date of first production from the well.

Laws 1987, c. 87–105, § 14. Amended by Laws 1994, c. 94–193, § 4, eff. Oct. 1, 1994; Laws 1996, c. 96–321, § 71, eff. July 1, 1996; Laws 2001, c. 2001–36, § 14, eff. Oct. 1, 2001.

Cross References

Tax sales, distribution of proceeds, see F.S.A. § 197.582.

717.115. Wages

Unpaid wages, including wages represented by unpresented payroll checks, owing in the ordinary course of the holder's business that have not been claimed by the owner for more than 1 year after becoming payable are presumed unclaimed.

Laws 1987, c. 87–105, § 16, eff. July 1, 1987. Amended by Laws 2001, c. 2001–36, § 15, eff. Oct. 1, 2001.

717.116. Contents of safe-deposit box or other safekeeping repository

All tangible and intangible property held by a banking or financial organization in a safe-deposit box or any other safekeeping repository in this state in the ordinary course of the holder's business, and proceeds resulting from the sale of the property permitted by law, that has not been claimed by the owner for more than 3 years after the lease or rental period on the box or other repository has expired are presumed unclaimed.

Laws 1987, c. 87–105, § 17. Amended by Laws 1996, c. 96–301, § 8, eff. Dec. 1, 1996; Laws 2001, c. 2001–36, § 16, eff. Oct. 1, 2001; Laws 2004, c. 2004–390, § 114, eff. July 1, 2004.

717.117. Report of unclaimed property

(1) Every person holding funds or other property, tangible or intangible, presumed unclaimed and subject to custody as unclaimed property under this chapter shall report to the department on such forms as the department may prescribe by rule. In lieu of forms, a report identifying 25 or more different apparent owners must be submitted by the holder via electronic medium as the department may prescribe by rule. The report must include:

(a) Except for traveler's checks and money orders, the name, social security number or taxpayer identification number, and date of birth, if known, and last known address, if any, of each person appearing from the records of the holder to be the owner of any property which is presumed unclaimed and which has a value of $50 or more.

(b) For unclaimed funds which have a value of $50 or more held or owing under any life or endowment insurance policy or annuity contract, the full name, taxpayer identification number or social security number, date of birth, if known, and last known address of the insured or annuitant and of the beneficiary according to records of the insurance company holding or owing the funds.

(c) For all tangible property held in a safe-deposit box or other safekeeping repository, a description of the property and the place where the property is held and may be inspected by the department, and any amounts owing to the holder. Contents of a safe-deposit box or other safekeeping repository which consist of documents or writings of a private nature and which have little or no apparent value shall not be presumed unclaimed.

(d) The nature and identifying number, if any, or description of the property and the amount appearing from the records to be due. Items of value under $50 each may be reported in the aggregate.

(e) The date the property became payable, demandable, or returnable, and the date of the last transaction with the apparent owner with respect to the property.

(f) Any person or business association or public corporation holding funds presumed unclaimed and having a total value of $10 or less may file a zero balance report for that reporting period. The balance brought forward to the new reporting period is zero.

(g) Such other information as the department may prescribe by rule as necessary for the administration of this chapter.

(h) Credit balances, customer overpayments, security deposits, and refunds having a value of less than $10 shall not be presumed unclaimed.

(2) If the holder of property presumed unclaimed and subject to custody as unclaimed property is a successor holder or if the holder has changed the holder's name while in possession of the property, the holder shall file with the holder's report all known names and addresses of each prior holder of the property. Compliance with this subsection means the holder exercises reasonable and prudent efforts to determine the names of all prior holders.

(3) The report must be filed before May 1 of each year. The report shall apply to the preceding calendar year. The department may impose and collect a penalty of $10 per day up to a maximum of $500 for the failure to timely report or the failure to include in a report information required by this chapter. The penalty shall be remitted to the department within 30 days after the date of the notification to the holder that the penalty is due and owing. As necessary for proper administration of this chapter, the department may waive any penalty due with appropriate justification. On written request by any person required to file a report and upon a showing of good cause, the department may postpone the reporting date. The department must provide information contained in a report filed with the department to any person requesting a copy of the report or information contained in a report, to the extent the information requested is not confidential, within 45 days after the report has been processed and added to the unclaimed property database subsequent to a determination that the report is accurate and that the reported property is the same as the remitted property.

(4) Holders of inactive accounts having a value of $50 or more shall use due diligence to locate apparent owners. Not more than 120 days and not less than 60 days prior to filing the report required by this section, the holder in possession of property presumed unclaimed and subject to custody as unclaimed property under this chapter shall send written notice to the apparent owner at the apparent owner's last known address informing the apparent owner that the holder is in possession of property subject to this chapter, if the holder has in its records an address for the apparent owner which the holder's records do not disclose to be inaccurate.

(5) Any holder of intangible property may file with the department a petition for determination that the property is unclaimed requesting the department to accept custody of the property. The petition shall state any special circumstances that exist, contain the information required by subsection (2), and show that a diligent search has been made to locate the owner. If the department finds that the proof of diligent search is satisfactory, it shall give notice as provided in s. 717.118 and accept custody of the property.

(6) Upon written request by any entity or person required to file a report, stating such entity's or person's justification for such action, the department may place that entity or person in an inactive status as an unclaimed property "holder."

(7)(a) This section does not apply to the unclaimed patronage refunds as provided for by contract or through bylaw provisions of entities organized under chapter 425.

(b) This section does not apply to intangible property held, issued, or owing by a business association subject to the jurisdiction of the United States Surface Transportation Board or its successor federal agency if the apparent owner of such intangible property is a business association. The holder of such property does not have any obligation to report, to pay, or to deliver such property to the department.

(c) This section does not apply to credit balances, overpayments, refunds, or outstanding checks owed by a health care provider to a managed care payor with whom the health care provider has a managed care contract, provided that the credit balances, overpayments, refunds, or outstanding checks become due and owing pursuant to the managed care contract.

(8)(a) As used in this subsection, the term "property identifier" means the descriptor used by the holder to identify the unclaimed property.

(b) Social security numbers and property identifiers contained in reports required under this section, held by the department, are confidential and exempt from s. 119.07(1) and s. 24(a), Art. I of the State Constitution.

(c) This exemption applies to social security numbers and property identifiers held by the department before, on, or after the effective date of this exemption.

(d) This subsection is subject to the Open Government Sunset Review Act in accordance with s. 119.15, and shall stand repealed October 2, 2017, unless reviewed and saved from repeal through reenactment by the Legislature.

Laws 1987, c. 87–105, § 18. Amended by Laws 1992, c. 92–169, § 1, eff. April 9, 1992; Laws 1992, c. 92–319, § 30, eff. July 8, 1992; Laws 1993, c. 93–280, § 1, eff. Oct. 1, 1993; Laws 1996, c. 96–301, § 9, eff. Dec. 1, 1996; Laws 1997, c. 97–102, § 1771, eff. July 1, 1997; Laws 2001, c. 2001–36, § 17, eff. Oct. 1, 2001; Laws 2002, c. 2002–64, § 1, eff. April 22, 2002; Laws 2003, c. 2003–261, § 1888, eff. June 26, 2003; Laws 2004, c. 2004–390, § 115, eff. July 1, 2004; Laws 2005, c. 2005–163, § 4, eff. June 8, 2005; Laws 2007, c. 2007–69, § 1, eff. Oct. 1, 2007; Laws 2012, c. 2012–227, § 1, eff. May 4, 2012.

Repeal

Subsection (8) is repealed by its own terms on October 2, 2017, unless reviewed and saved from repeal by the Legislature.

Financial institutions, check-clearing functions, unclaimed credit balances, see § 655.851.

Tax sales, distribution of proceeds, see F.S.A. § 197.582.

717.118. Notification of apparent owners of unclaimed property

(1) It is specifically recognized that the state has an obligation to make an effort to notify owners of unclaimed property in a cost-effective manner. In order to provide all the citizens of this state an effective and efficient program for the recovery of unclaimed property, the department shall use cost-effective means to make at least one active attempt to notify owners of unclaimed property accounts valued at more than $250 with a reported address or taxpayer identification number. Such active attempt to notify apparent owners shall include any attempt by the department to directly contact the owner. Other means of notification, such as publication of the names of owners in the newspaper, on television, on the Internet, or through other promotional efforts and items in which the department does not directly attempt to contact the owner are expressly declared to be passive attempts. Nothing in this subsection precludes other agencies or entities of state government from notifying owners of the existence of unclaimed property or attempting to notify apparent owners of unclaimed property.

(2) Notification provided directly to individual apparent owners shall consist of a description of the property and information regarding recovery of unclaimed property from the department.

(3) This section is not applicable to sums payable on traveler's checks, money orders, and other written instruments presumed unclaimed under s. 717.104.

Laws 1987, c. 87–105, § 19. Amended by Laws 1996, c. 96–301, § 10, eff. Dec. 1, 1996; Laws 2001, c. 2001–36, § 18, eff. Oct. 1, 2001; Laws 2004, c. 2004–390, § 116, eff. July 1, 2004; Laws 2005, c. 2005–163, § 5, eff. June 8, 2005.

717.119. Payment or delivery of unclaimed property

(1) Every person who is required to file a report under s. 717.117 shall simultaneously pay or deliver to the department all unclaimed property required to be reported. Such payment or delivery shall accompany the report as required in this chapter for the preceding calendar year.

(2) Payment of unclaimed funds may be made to the department by electronic funds transfer.

(3) If the owner establishes the right to receive the unclaimed property to the satisfaction of the holder before the property has been delivered to the department or it appears that for some other reason the presumption that the property is unclaimed is erroneous, the holder need not pay or deliver the property to the department. In lieu of delivery, the holder shall file a verified written explanation of the proof of claim or of the error in the presumption that the property was unclaimed.

(4) All stock or other intangible ownership interest reported under this chapter on the annual report filing required in s. 717.117 shall be remitted to the department with the report. Upon delivery of the stock or other intangible ownership interest to the department, the holder and any transfer agent, registrar, or other person acting for or on behalf of a holder is relieved of all liability of every kind in accordance with the provisions of s. 717.1201 to every person for any losses or damages resulting to the person by the delivery to the department of the stock or other intangible ownership interest.

(5) All intangible and tangible property held in a safe-deposit box or any other safekeeping repository reported under s. 717.117 shall not be delivered to the department until 120 days after the report due date. The delivery of the property, through the United States mail or any

other carrier, shall be insured by the holder at an amount equal to the estimated value of the property. Each package shall be clearly marked on the outside "Deliver Unopened." A holder's safe-deposit box contents shall be delivered to the department in a single shipment. In lieu of a single shipment, holders may provide the department with a single detailed shipping schedule that includes package tracking information for all packages being sent pursuant to this section.

(a) Holders may remit the value of cash and coins found in unclaimed safe-deposit boxes to the department by cashier's check or by electronic funds transfer, unless the cash or coins have a value above face value. The department shall identify by rule those cash and coin items having a numismatic value. Cash and coin items identified as having a numismatic value shall be remitted to the department in their original form.

(b) Any firearm or ammunition found in an unclaimed safe-deposit box or any other safekeeping repository shall be delivered by the holder to a law enforcement agency for disposal pursuant to s. 705.103(2)(b) with the balance of the proceeds deposited into the State School Fund if the firearm is sold. However, the department is authorized to make a reasonable attempt to ascertain the historical value to collectors of any firearm that has been delivered to the department. Any firearm appearing to have historical value to collectors may be sold by the department pursuant to s. 717.122 to a person having a federal firearms license. Any firearm which is not sold pursuant to s. 717.122 shall be delivered by the department to a law enforcement agency in this state for disposal pursuant to s. 705.103(2)(b) with the balance of the proceeds deposited into the State School Fund if the firearm is sold. The department shall not be administratively, civilly, or criminally liable for any firearm delivered by the department to a law enforcement agency in this state for disposal.

(c) If such property is not paid or delivered to the department on or before the applicable payment or delivery date, the holder shall pay to the department a penalty for each safe-deposit box shipment received late. The penalty shall be $100 for a safe-deposit box shipment container that is late 30 days or less. Thereafter, the penalty shall be $500 for a safe-deposit box shipment container that is late for each additional successive 30–day period. The penalty assessed against a holder for a late safe-deposit box shipment container shall not exceed $4,000 annually. The penalty shall be remitted to the department within 30 days after the date of the notification to the holder that the penalty is due and owing.

(d) The department may waive any penalty due with appropriate justification, as provided by rule.

(6) Any holder may request an extension in writing of up to 60 days for the delivery of property if extenuating circumstances exist for the late delivery of the property. Any such extension the department may grant shall be in writing.

Laws 1987, c. 87–105, § 20. Amended by Laws 1996, c. 96–301, § 11, eff. Dec. 1, 1996; Laws 2001, c. 2001–36, § 19, eff. Oct. 1, 2001; Laws 2003, c. 2003–21, § 4, eff. May 21, 2003; Laws 2004, c. 2004–390, § 117, eff. July 1, 2004; Laws 2005, c. 2005–163, § 6, eff. June 8, 2005.

717.1201.   **Custody by state; holder relieved from liability; reimbursement of holder paying claim; reclaiming for owner; defense of holder; payment of safe-deposit box or repository charges**

(1) Upon the payment or delivery of property to the department, the state assumes custody and responsibility for the safekeeping of property. Any person who pays or delivers property to the department in good faith is relieved of all liability to the extent of the value of the property

---

paid or delivered for any claim then existing or which thereafter may arise or be made in respect to the property.

(2) Any holder who has paid money to the department pursuant to this chapter may make payment to any person appearing to be entitled to payment and, upon filing proof that the payee is entitled thereto, the department shall forthwith repay the holder without deduction of any fee or other charges. If repayment is sought for a payment made on a negotiable instrument, including a traveler's check or money order, the holder must be repaid under this subsection upon filing proof that the instrument was duly presented and that the payee is entitled to payment. The holder shall be repaid for payment made under this subsection even if the payment was made to a person whose claim was barred under s. 717.129(1).

(3) Any holder who has delivered property, including a certificate of any interest in a business association, other than money to the department pursuant to this chapter may reclaim the property if still in the possession of the department, without payment of any fee or other charges, upon filing proof that the owner has claimed the property from the holder.

(4) The department may accept an affidavit of the holder stating the facts that entitle the holder to recover money and property under this section as sufficient proof.

(5) If the holder pays or delivers property to the department in good faith and thereafter any other person claims the property from the holder paying or delivering, or another state claims the money or property under that state's laws relating to escheat or abandoned or unclaimed property, the department, upon written notice of the claim, shall defend the holder against the claim and indemnify the holder against any liability on the claim.

(6) For the purposes of this section, "good faith" means that:

(a) Payment or delivery was made in a reasonable attempt to comply with this chapter.

(b) The person delivering the property was not a fiduciary then in breach of trust in respect to the property and had a reasonable basis for believing, based on the facts then known to that person, that the property was unclaimed for the purposes of this chapter.

(c) There is no showing that the records pursuant to which the delivery was made did not meet reasonable commercial standards of practice in the industry.

(7) Property removed from a safe-deposit box or other safekeeping repository is received by the department subject to the holder's right under this subsection to be reimbursed for the actual cost of the opening and to any valid lien or contract providing for the holder to be reimbursed for unpaid rent or storage charges. The department shall make the reimbursement to the holder out of the proceeds remaining after the deduction of the department's selling cost.

Laws 1987, c. 87–105, § 21. Amended by Laws 2001, c. 2001–36, § 20, eff. Oct. 1, 2001; Laws 2004, c. 2004–390, § 118, eff. July 1, 2004.

717.121. Crediting of dividends, interest, or increments to owner's account

Whenever property other than money is paid or delivered to the department under this chapter, the owner is entitled to receive from the department any dividends, interest, or other increments realized or accruing on the property at or before liquidation or conversion thereof into money.

Laws 1987, c. 87–105, § 22.

717.122. Public sale of unclaimed property

(1) Except as provided in paragraph (2)(a), the department after the receipt of unclaimed property shall sell it to the highest bidder at public sale on the Internet or at a specified physical location wherever in the judgment of the department the most favorable market for the property involved exists. The department may decline the highest bid and reoffer the property for sale if in the judgment of the department the bid is insufficient. The department shall have the discretion to withhold from sale any unclaimed property that the department deems to be of benefit to the people of the state. If in the judgment of the department the probable cost of sale exceeds the value of the property, it need not be offered for sale and may be disposed of as the department determines appropriate. Any sale at a specified physical location held under this section must be preceded by a single publication of notice, at least 3 weeks in advance of sale, in a newspaper of general circulation in the county in which the property is to be sold. The department shall proportionately deduct auction fees, preparation costs, and expenses from the amount posted to the owner's account when safe-deposit box contents are sold. No action or proceeding may be maintained against the department for or on account of any decision to decline the highest bid or withhold any unclaimed property from sale.

(2)(a) Securities listed on an established stock exchange must be sold at prices prevailing at the time of sale on the exchange. Other securities may be sold over the counter at prices prevailing at the time of sale or by any other method the department deems advisable. The department may authorize the agent or broker acting on behalf of the department to deduct fees from the proceeds of these sales at a rate agreed upon in advance by the agent or broker and the department. The department shall reimburse owners' accounts for these brokerage fees from the State School Fund unless the securities are sold at the owner's request.

(b) Unless the department deems it to be in the public interest to do otherwise, all securities presumed unclaimed and delivered to the department may be sold upon receipt. Any person making a claim pursuant to this chapter is entitled to receive either the securities delivered to the department by the holder, if they still remain in the hands of the department, or the proceeds received from sale, but no person has any claim under this chapter against the state, the holder, any transfer agent, any registrar, or any other person acting for or on behalf of a holder for any appreciation in the value of the property occurring after delivery by the holder to the state.

(c) Certificates for unclaimed stock or other equity interest of business associations that cannot be canceled and registered in the department's name or that cannot be readily liquidated and converted into the currency of the United States may be sold for the value of the certificate, if any, in accordance with subsection (1) or may be destroyed in accordance with s. 717.128.

(3) The purchaser of property at any sale conducted by the department pursuant to this chapter is entitled to ownership of the property purchased free from all claims of the owner or previous holder thereof and of all persons claiming through or under them. The department shall execute all documents necessary to complete the transfer of ownership.

(4) The sale of unclaimed tangible personal property is not subject to tax under chapter 212 when such property is sold by or on behalf of the department pursuant to this section.

Laws 1987, c. 87–105, § 23. Amended by Laws 1990, c. 90–113, § 3, eff. Oct. 1, 1990; Laws 1996, c. 96–301, § 12, eff. Dec. 1, 1996; Laws 2001, c. 2001–36, § 21, eff. Oct. 1, 2001; Laws 2004, c. 2004–390, § 119, eff. July 1, 2004; Laws 2005, c. 2005–163, § 7, eff. June 8, 2005.

717.123. Deposit of funds

(1) All funds received under this chapter, including the proceeds from the sale of unclaimed property under s. 717.122, shall forthwith be deposited by the department in the Unclaimed Property Trust Fund. The department shall retain, from funds received under this chapter, an amount not exceeding $15 million from which the department shall make prompt payment of claims allowed by the department and shall pay the costs incurred by the department in administering and enforcing this chapter. All remaining funds received by the department under this chapter shall be deposited by the department into the State School Fund.

(2) The department shall record the name and last known address of each person appearing from the holder's reports to be entitled to the unclaimed property in the total amounts of $5 or greater; the name and the last known address of each insured person or annuitant; and with respect to each policy or contract listed in the report of an insurance corporation, its number, the name of the corporation, and the amount due.

Laws 1987, c. 87–105, § 24. Amended by Laws 1996, c. 96–301, § 13, eff. Dec. 1, 1996; Laws 2001, c. 2001–36, § 22, eff. Oct. 1, 2001; Laws 2004, c. 2004–390, § 120, eff. July 1, 2004.

717.124. Unclaimed property claims

(1) Any person, excluding another state, claiming an interest in any property paid or delivered to the department under this chapter may file with the department a claim on a form prescribed by the department and verified by the claimant or the claimant's representative. The claimant's representative must be an attorney licensed to practice law in this state, a licensed Florida-certified public accountant, or a private investigator licensed under chapter 493. The claimant's representative must be registered with the department under this chapter. The claimant, or the claimant's representative, shall provide the department with a legible copy of a valid driver license of the claimant at the time the original claim form is filed. If the claimant has not been issued a valid driver license at the time the original claim form is filed, the department shall be provided with a legible copy of a photographic identification of the claimant issued by the United States, a state or territory of the United States, a foreign nation, or a political subdivision or agency thereof or other evidence deemed acceptable by the department by rule. In lieu of photographic identification, a notarized sworn statement by the claimant may be provided which affirms the claimant's identity and states the claimant's full name and address. The claimant must produce to the notary photographic identification of the claimant issued by the United States, a state or territory of the United States, a foreign nation, or a political subdivision or agency thereof or other evidence deemed acceptable by the department by rule. The notary shall indicate the notary's full address on the notarized sworn statement. Any claim filed without the required identification or the sworn statement with the original claim form and the original power of attorney or purchase agreement, if applicable, is void.

(a) Within 90 days after receipt of a claim, the department may return any claim that provides for the receipt of fees and costs greater than that permitted under this chapter or that contains any apparent errors or omissions. The department may also request that the claimant or the claimant's representative provide additional information. The department shall retain a copy or electronic image of the claim.

(b) A claimant or the claimant's representative shall be deemed to have withdrawn a claim if no response to the department's request for additional information is received by the department within 60 days after the notification of any apparent errors or omissions.

(c) Within 90 days after receipt of the claim, or the response of the claimant or the claimant's representative to the department's request for additional information, whichever is later, the department shall determine each claim. Such determination shall contain a notice of rights provided by ss. 120.569 and 120.57. The 90–day period shall be extended by 60 days if the department has good cause to need additional time or if the unclaimed property:

1. Is owned by a person who has been a debtor in bankruptcy;

2. Was reported with an address outside of the United States;

3. Is being claimed by a person outside of the United States; or

4. Contains documents filed in support of the claim that are not in the English language and have not been accompanied by an English language translation.

(d) The department shall deny any claim under which the claimant's representative has refused to authorize the department to reduce the fees and costs to the maximum permitted under this chapter.

(2) A claim for a cashier's check or a stock certificate without the original instrument may require an indemnity bond equal to the value of the claim to be provided prior to issue of the stock or payment of the claim by the department.

(3) The department may require an affidavit swearing to the authenticity of the claim, lack of documentation, and an agreement to allow the department to provide the name and address of the claimant to subsequent claimants coming forward with substantiated proof to claim the account. This shall apply to claims equal to or less than $250. The exclusive remedy of a subsequent claimant to the property shall be against the person who received the property from the department.

(4)(a) Except as otherwise provided in this chapter, if a claim is determined in favor of the claimant, the department shall deliver or pay over to the claimant the property or the amount the department actually received or the proceeds if it has been sold by the department, together with any additional amount required by s. 717.121.

(b) If an owner authorizes an attorney licensed to practice law in this state, Florida-certified public accountant, or private investigator licensed under chapter 493, and registered with the department under this chapter, to claim the unclaimed property on the owner's behalf, the department is authorized to make distribution of the property or money in accordance with such power of attorney. The original power of attorney must be executed by the owner and must be filed with the department.

(c) 1. Payments of approved claims for unclaimed cash accounts shall be made to the owner after deducting any fees and costs authorized pursuant to a written power of attorney. The contents of a safe-deposit box shall be delivered directly to the claimant notwithstanding any power of attorney or agreement to the contrary.

2. Payments of fees and costs authorized pursuant to a written power of attorney for approved claims shall be made or issued to the law firm of the designated attorney licensed to practice law in this state, the public accountancy firm of the licensed Florida-certified public accountant, or the designated employing private investigative agency licensed by this state. Such payments shall be made by electronic funds transfer and may be made on such periodic schedule as the department may define by rule, provided the payment intervals do not exceed 31 days. Payment made to an attorney licensed in this state, a Florida-certified public accountant, or a private investigator licensed under chapter 493, operating individually or as a sole practitioner, shall be to the attorney, certified public accountant, or private investigator.

(5) The department shall not be administratively, civilly, or criminally liable for any property or funds distributed pursuant to this section, provided such distribution is made in good faith.

(6) This section does not supersede the licensing requirements of chapter 493.

(7) The department may allow an apparent owner to electronically submit a claim for unclaimed property to the department. If a claim is submitted electronically for $1,000 or less, the department may use a method of identity verification other than a copy of a valid driver license, other government-issued photographic identification, or a sworn notarized statement. The department may adopt rules to implement this subsection.

(8) This section applies to all unclaimed property reported and remitted to the Chief Financial Officer, including, but not limited to, property reported pursuant to ss. 43.19, 45.032, 732.107, 733.816, and 744.534.

Laws 1987, c. 87–105, § 25. Amended by Laws 1989, c. 89–291, § 3, eff. July 5, 1989; Laws 1989, c. 89–299, § 8, eff. July 5, 1989; Laws 1990, c. 90–113, § 4, eff. Oct. 1, 1990; Laws 1996, c. 96–301, § 14, eff. Dec. 1, 1996; Laws 1996, c. 96–410, § 295, eff. Oct. 1, 1996; Laws 1997, c. 97–93, § 31, eff. July 1, 1997; Laws 1997, c. 97–102, § 1772, eff. July 1, 1997; Laws 2001, c. 2001–36, § 23, eff. Oct. 1, 2001; Laws 2004, c. 2004–390, § 121, eff. July 1, 2004; Laws 2005, c. 2005–163, § 8, eff. June 8, 2005; Laws 2013, c. 2013–34, § 1, eff. July 1, 2013.

717.12403. Unclaimed demand, savings, or checking account in a financial institution held in the name of more than one person

(1)(a) If an unclaimed demand, savings, or checking account in a financial institution is reported as an "and" account in the name of two or more persons who are not beneficiaries, it is presumed that each person must claim the account in order for the claim to be approved by the department. This presumption may be rebutted by showing that entitlement to the account has been transferred to another person or by clear and convincing evidence demonstrating that the account should have been reported by the financial institution as an "or" account.

(b) If an unclaimed demand, savings, or checking account in a financial institution is reported as an "and" account and one of the persons on the account is deceased, it is presumed that the account is a survivorship account. This presumption may be rebutted by showing that entitlement to the account has been transferred to another person or by clear and convincing evidence demonstrating that the account is not a survivorship account.

(2) If an unclaimed demand, savings, or checking account in a financial institution is reported as an "or" account in the name of two or more persons who are not beneficiaries, it is presumed that either person listed on the account may claim the entire amount held in the account. This presumption may be rebutted by showing that entitlement to the account has been transferred to another person or by clear and convincing evidence demonstrating that the account should have been reported by the financial institution as an "and" account.

(3) If an unclaimed demand, savings, or checking account in a financial institution is reported in the name of two or more persons who are not beneficiaries without identifying whether the account is an "and" account or an "or" account, it is presumed that the account is an "or" account. This presumption may be rebutted by showing that entitlement to the account has been transferred to another person or by clear and convincing evidence demonstrating that the account should have been reported by the financial institution as an "and" account.

(4) The department shall be deemed to have made a distribution in good faith if the department remits funds consistent with this section.

Added by Laws 2004, c. 2004–390, § 122, eff. July 1, 2004.

717.12404.   Claims on behalf of a business entity or trust

(1)(a) Claims on behalf of an active or dissolved corporation, for which the last annual report is not available from the Department of State through the Internet, must be accompanied by a microfiche copy of the records on file with the Department of State or, if the corporation has not made a corporate filing with the Department of State, the claim must be accompanied by a uniform resource locator for the address of a free Internet site operated by the state of incorporation of the corporation that provides access to the last corporate filing identifying the officers and directors of the corporation. If available, the claim must be accompanied by a printout of the officers and directors from the Department of State Internet site or the free Internet site operated by the state of incorporation of the corporation. If the free Internet site is not available, the claim must be accompanied by an authenticated copy of the last corporate filing identifying the officers and directors from the appropriate authorized official of the state of incorporation.

(b) A claim on behalf of a corporation must be made by an officer or director identified on the last corporate filing.

(2) Claims on behalf of a dissolved corporation, a business entity other than an active corporation, or a trust must include a legible copy of a valid driver license of the person acting on behalf of the dissolved corporation, business entity other than an active corporation, or trust. If the person has not been issued a valid driver license, the department shall be provided with a legible copy of a photographic identification of the person issued by the United States, a foreign nation, or a political subdivision or agency thereof. In lieu of photographic identification, a notarized sworn statement by the person may be provided which affirms the person's identity and states the person's full name and address. The person must produce his or her photographic identification issued by the United States, a state or territory of the United States, a foreign nation, or a political subdivision or agency thereof or other evidence deemed acceptable by the department by rule. The notary shall indicate the notary's full address on the notarized sworn statement. Any claim filed without the required identification or the sworn statement with the original claim form and the original power of attorney, if applicable, is void.

Added by Laws 2004, c. 2004–390, § 123, eff. July 1, 2004. Amended by Laws 2005, c. 2005–163, § 9, eff. June 8, 2005.

717.12405.   Claims by estates

An estate or any person representing an estate or acting on behalf of an estate may claim unclaimed property only after the heir or legatee of the decedent entitled to the property has been located. Any estate, or any person representing an estate or acting on behalf of an estate, that receives unclaimed property before the heir or legatee of the decedent entitled to the property has been located, is personally liable for the unclaimed property and must immediately return the full amount of the unclaimed property or the value thereof to the department in accordance with s. 717.1341.

Added by Laws 2004, c. 2004–390, § 124, eff. July 1, 2004.

717.12406.   Joint ownership of unclaimed securities or dividends

For the purpose of determining joint ownership of unclaimed securities or dividends, the term:

(1) ''TEN COM'' means tenants in common.

(2) ''TEN ENT'' means tenants by the entireties.

(3) "JT TEN" or "JT" means joint tenants with the right of survivorship and not as tenants in common.

(4) "And" means tenants in common with each person entitled to an equal pro rata share.

(5) "Or" means that each person listed on the account is entitled to all of the funds.

Added by Laws 2005, c. 2005–163, § 10, eff. June 8, 2005.

717.1241. Conflicting claims

(1) When conflicting claims have been received by the department for the same unclaimed property account or accounts, the property shall be remitted in accordance with the claim filed by the person as follows, notwithstanding the withdrawal of a claim:

(a) To the person submitting the first claim received by the Bureau of Unclaimed Property of the department that is complete or made complete.

(b) If a claimant's claim and a claimant's representative's claim are received by the Bureau of Unclaimed Property of the department on the same day and both claims are complete, to the claimant.

(c) If a buyer's claim and a claimant's claim or a claimant's representative's claim are received by the Bureau of Unclaimed Property of the department on the same day and the claims are complete, to the buyer.

(d) As between two or more claimant's representative's claims received by the Bureau of Unclaimed Property of the department that are complete or made complete on the same day, to the claimant's representative who has agreed to receive the lowest fee. If the two or more claimant's representatives whose claims received by the Bureau of Unclaimed Property of the department were complete or made complete on the same day are charging the same lowest fee, the fee shall be divided equally between the claimant's representatives.

(e) If more than one buyer's claim received by the Bureau of Unclaimed Property of the department is complete or made complete on the same day, the department shall remit the unclaimed property to the buyer who paid the highest amount to the seller. If the buyers paid the same amount to the seller, the department shall remit the unclaimed property to the buyers divided in equal amounts.

(2) The purpose of this section is solely to provide guidance to the department regarding to whom it should remit the unclaimed property and is not intended to extinguish or affect any private cause of action that any person may have against another person for breach of contract or other statutory or common-law remedy. A buyer's sole remedy, if any, shall be against the claimant's representative or the seller, or both. A claimant's representative's sole remedy, if any, shall be against the buyer or the seller, or both. A claimant's or seller's sole remedy, if any, shall be against the buyer or the claimant's representative, or both. Nothing in this section forecloses the right of a person to challenge the department's determination of completeness in a proceeding under ss. 120.569 and 120.57.

(3) A claim is complete when entitlement to the unclaimed property has been established.

Added by Laws 1996, c. 96–301, § 15, eff. Dec. 1, 1996. Amended by Laws 2001, c. 2001–36, § 24, eff. Oct. 1, 2001; Laws 2004, c. 2004–390, § 125, eff. July 1, 2004; Laws 2005, c. 2005–163, § 11, eff. June 8, 2005.

717.1242. Restatement of jurisdiction of the circuit court sitting in probate and the department

(1) It is and has been the intent of the Legislature that, pursuant to s. 26.012(2)(b), circuit courts have jurisdiction of proceedings relating to the settlement of the estates of decedents and other jurisdiction usually pertaining to courts of probate. It is and has been the intent of the Legislature that, pursuant to s. 717.124, the department determines the merits of claims for property paid or delivered to the department under this chapter. Consistent with this legislative intent, any estate or beneficiary, as defined in s. 731.201, of an estate seeking to obtain property paid or delivered to the department under this chapter must file a claim with the department as provided in s. 717.124.

(2) If any estate or heir of an estate seeks or obtains an order from a circuit court sitting in probate directing the department to pay or deliver to any person property paid or delivered to the department under this chapter, the estate or heir shall be ordered to pay the department reasonable costs and attorney's fees in any proceeding brought by the department to oppose, appeal, or collaterally attack the order if the department is the prevailing party in any such proceeding.

Added by Laws 1996, c. 96–301, § 16, eff. Dec. 1, 1996. Amended by Laws 2004, c. 2004–390, § 126, eff. July 1, 2004; Laws 2005, c. 2005–163, § 12, eff. June 8, 2005.

717.1243. Small estate accounts

(1) A claim for unclaimed property made by a beneficiary, as defined in s. 731.201, of a deceased owner need not be accompanied by an order of a probate court if the claimant files with the department an affidavit, signed by all beneficiaries, stating that all the beneficiaries have amicably agreed among themselves upon a division of the estate and that all funeral expenses, expenses of the last illness, and any other lawful claims have been paid, and any additional information reasonably necessary to make a determination of entitlement. If the owner died testate, the claim shall be accompanied by a copy of the will.

(2) Each person receiving property under this section shall be personally liable for all lawful claims against the estate of the owner, but only to the extent of the value of the property received by such person under this section, exclusive of the property exempt from claims of creditors under the constitution and laws of this state.

(3) Any heir or devisee of the owner, who was lawfully entitled to share in the property but did not receive his or her share of the property, may enforce his or her rights in appropriate proceedings against those who received the property and shall be awarded taxable costs as in chancery actions, including attorney's fees.

(4) This section only applies if all of the unclaimed property held by the department on behalf of the owner has an aggregate value of $5,000 or less and no probate proceeding is pending.

(5) Nothing in this section shall be interpreted as precluding the use of live testimony in order to establish entitlement.

Added by Laws 1996, c. 96–301, § 17, eff. Dec. 1, 1996. Amended by Laws 2001, c. 2001–36, § 25, eff. Oct. 1, 2001; Laws 2003, c. 2003–154, § 23, eff. June 12, 2003; Laws 2005, c. 2005–163, § 13, eff. June 8, 2005.

717.1244. Determinations of unclaimed property claims

In rendering a determination regarding the merits of an unclaimed property claim, the department shall rely on the applicable statutory, regulatory, common, and case law. Agency statements applying the statutory, regulatory, common, and case law to unclaimed property claims are not agency statements subject to s. 120.56(4).

Added by Laws 2004, c. 2004–390, § 127, eff. July 1, 2004.

717.1245. Garnishment of unclaimed property

If any person files a petition for writ of garnishment seeking to obtain property paid or delivered to the department under this chapter, the petitioner shall be ordered to pay the department reasonable costs and attorney's fees in any proceeding brought by the department to oppose, appeal, or collaterally attack the petition or writ if the department is the prevailing party in any such proceeding.

Added by Laws 2005, c. 2005–163, § 14, eff. June 8, 2005.

717.125. Claim of another state to recover property; procedure

(1) At any time after property has been paid or delivered to the department under this chapter, another state may recover the property if:

(a) The property was subjected to custody by this state because the records of the holder did not reflect the last known address of the apparent owner when the property was presumed unclaimed under this chapter, and the other state establishes that the last known address of the apparent owner or other person entitled to the property was in that state and under the laws of that state the property escheated to or was subject to a claim of abandonment or being unclaimed by that state;

(b) The last known address of the apparent owner or other person entitled to the property, as reflected by the records of the holder, is in the other state and under the laws of that state the property has escheated to or become subject to a claim of abandonment by that state;

(c) The records of the holder were erroneous in that they did not accurately reflect the actual owner of the property and the last known address of the actual owner is in the other state and under laws of that state the property escheated to or was subject to a claim of abandonment by that state;

(d) The property was subject to custody by this state under s. 717.103(6) and under the laws of the state of domicile of the holder the property has escheated to or become subject to a claim of abandonment by that state; or

(e) The property is the sum payable on a traveler's check, money order, or other similar instrument that was subjected to custody by this state under s. 717.104, and the instrument was purchased in the other state, and under the laws of that state the property escheated to or became subject to a claim of abandonment by that state.

(2) The claim of another state to recover escheated or unclaimed property under this section must be presented in a form prescribed by the department, and the department shall determine the claim within 90 days after it is presented. Such determination shall contain a notice of rights provided by ss. 120.569 and 120.57.

(3) The department shall require a state, prior to recovery of property under this section, to indemnify this state and its officers and employees against any liability on a claim for the property.

Laws 1987, c. 87–105, § 26. Amended by Laws 1996, c. 96–410, § 296, eff. Oct. 1, 1996; Laws 2001, c. 2001–36, § 26, eff. Oct. 1, 2001.

717.126. Administrative hearing; burden of proof; proof of entitlement; venue

(1) Any person aggrieved by a decision of the department may petition for a hearing as provided in ss. 120.569 and 120.57. In any proceeding for determination of a claim to property paid or delivered to the department under this chapter, the burden shall be upon the claimant to establish entitlement to the property by a preponderance of evidence. Having the same name as that reported to the department is not sufficient, in the absence of other evidence, to prove entitlement to unclaimed property.

(2) Unless otherwise agreed by the parties, venue shall be in Tallahassee, Leon County, Florida. However, upon the request of a party, the presiding officer may, in the presiding officer's discretion, conduct the hearing at an alternative remote video location.

Laws 1987, c. 87–105, § 27. Amended by Laws 1996, c. 96–410, § 297, eff. Oct. 1, 1996; Laws 2004, c. 2004–390, § 128, eff. July 1, 2004.

717.1261. Death certificates

Any person who claims entitlement to unclaimed property by means of the death of one or more persons shall file a copy of the death certificate of the decedent or decedents that has been certified as being authentic by the issuing governmental agency.

Added by Laws 2004, c. 2004–390, § 129, eff. July 1, 2004.

717.1262. Court documents

Any person who claims entitlement to unclaimed property by reason of a court document shall file a certified copy of the court document with the department.

Added by Laws 2004, c. 2004–390, § 130, eff. July 1, 2004.

717.127. Election to take payment or delivery

The department may decline to receive any property reported under this chapter that the department considers to have a value less than the expense of giving notice and of sale. If the department elects not to receive custody of the property, the holder shall be notified within 120 days after filing the report required under s. 717.117 or remitting the property required under s. 717.119.

Laws 1987, c. 87–105, § 28. Amended by Laws 1996, c. 96–301, § 18, eff. Dec. 1, 1996.

717.128. Destruction or disposition of property having insubstantial commercial value; immunity from liability

If the department after investigation finds that any property delivered under this chapter has insubstantial commercial value, the department may destroy or otherwise dispose of the property. No action or proceeding may be maintained against the state or any officer or against the holder for or on account of any action taken by the department pursuant to this section with respect to the property.

Laws 1987, c. 87–105, § 29.

717.129. Periods of limitation

(1) The expiration before or after July 1, 1987, of any period of time specified by contract, statute, or court order, during which a claim for money or property may be made or during which an action or proceeding may be commenced or enforced to obtain payment of a claim for money or to recover property, does not prevent the money or property from being presumed

unclaimed or affect any duty to file a report or to pay or deliver unclaimed property to the department as required by this chapter.

(2) No action or proceeding may be commenced by the department with respect to any duty of a holder under this chapter more than 10 years after the duty arose.

Laws 1987, c. 87–105, § 30. Amended by Laws 2001, c. 2001–36, § 27, eff. Oct. 1, 2001.

717.1301. Investigations; examinations; subpoenas

(1) The department may make investigations and examinations within or outside this state of claims, reports, and other records as it deems necessary to administer and enforce the provisions of this chapter. In such investigations and examinations the department may administer oaths, examine witnesses, issue subpoenas, and otherwise gather evidence. The department may request any person who has not filed a report under s. 717.117 to file a verified report stating whether or not the person is holding any unclaimed property reportable or deliverable under this chapter.

(2) Subpoenas for witnesses whose evidence is deemed material to any investigation or examination under this section may be issued by the department under seal of the department, or by any court of competent jurisdiction, commanding such witnesses to appear before the department at a time and place named and to bring such books, records, and documents as may be specified or to submit such books, records, and documents to inspection. Such subpoenas may be served by an authorized representative of the department.

(3) If any person shall refuse to testify, produce books, records, and documents, or otherwise refuse to obey a subpoena issued under this section, the department may present its petition to a court of competent jurisdiction in or for the county in which such person resides or has its principal place of business, whereupon the court shall issue its rule nisi requiring such person to obey forthwith the subpoena issued by the department or show cause for failing to obey said subpoena. Unless said person shows sufficient cause for failing to obey the subpoena, the court shall forthwith direct such person to obey the same subject to such punishment as the court may direct including, but not limited to, the restraint, by injunction or by appointment of a receiver, of any transfer, pledge, assignment, or other disposition of such person's assets or any concealment, alteration, destruction, or other disposition of subpoenaed books, records, or documents as the court deems appropriate, until such person has fully complied with such subpoena and the department has completed its investigation or examination. The department is entitled to the summary procedure provided in s. 51.011, and the court shall advance the cause on its calendar. Costs incurred by the department to obtain an order granting, in whole or in part, its petition shall be taxed against the subpoenaed person, and failure to comply with such order shall be a contempt of court.

(4) Witnesses shall be entitled to the same fees and mileage as they may be entitled by law for attending as witnesses in the circuit court, except where such examination or investigation is held at the place of business or residence of the witness.

(5) The material compiled by the department in an investigation or examination under this chapter is confidential until the investigation or examination is complete. The material compiled by the department in an investigation or examination under this chapter remains confidential after the department's investigation or examination is complete if the department has submitted the material or any part of it to any law enforcement agency or other administrative agency for further investigation or for the filing of a criminal or civil prosecution and such investigation has not been completed or become inactive.

(6) If an investigation or an examination of the records of any person results in the disclosure of property reportable and deliverable under this chapter, the department may assess the cost of investigation or the examination against the holder at the rate of $100 per 8–hour day for each investigator or examiner. Such fee shall be calculated on an hourly basis and shall be rounded to the nearest hour. The person shall also pay the travel expense and per diem subsistence allowance provided for state employees in s. 112.061. The person shall not be required to pay a per diem fee and expenses of an examination or investigation which shall consume more than 30 worker-days in any one year unless such examination or investigation is due to fraudulent practices of the person, in which case such person shall be required to pay the entire cost regardless of time consumed. The fee shall be remitted to the department within 30 days after the date of the notification that the fee is due and owing. Any person who fails to pay the fee within 30 days after the date of the notification that the fee is due and owing shall pay to the department interest at the rate of 12 percent per annum on such fee from the date of the notification.

Laws 1987, c. 87–105, § 31. Amended by Laws 2004, c. 2004–390, § 131, eff. July 1, 2004.

717.1311. Retention of records

(1) Every holder required to file a report under s. 717.117 shall maintain a record of the specific type of property, amount, name, and last known address of the owner for 5 years after the property becomes reportable, except to the extent that a shorter time is provided in subsection (2) or by rule of the department.

(2) Any business association that sells in this state its traveler's checks, money orders, or other similar written instruments, other than third-party bank checks on which the business association is directly responsible, or that provides such instruments to others for sale in this state, shall maintain a record of those instruments while they remain outstanding, indicating the state and date of issue for 3 years after the date the property is reportable.

Laws 1987, c. 87–105, § 32. Amended by Laws 1991, c. 91–110, § 24; Laws 1996, c. 96–301, § 19, eff. Dec. 1, 1996; Laws 2005, c. 2005–163, § 15, eff. June 8, 2005.

717.1315. Retention of records by claimant's representatives and buyers of unclaimed property

(1) Every claimant's representative and buyer of unclaimed property shall keep and use in his or her business such books, accounts, and records of the business conducted under this chapter to enable the department to determine whether such person is complying with this chapter and the rules adopted by the department under this chapter. Every claimant's representative and buyer of unclaimed property shall preserve such books, accounts, and records, including every power of attorney or agreement between the owner and such claimant's representative or buyer, for at least 3 years after the date of the initial power of attorney or agreement.

(2) A claimant's representative or buyer of unclaimed property, operating at two or more places of business in this state, may maintain the books, accounts, and records of all such offices at any one of such offices, or at any other office maintained by such claimant's representative or buyer of unclaimed property, upon the filing of a written notice with the department designating in the written notice the office at which such records are maintained.

(3) A claimant's representative or buyer of unclaimed property shall make all books, accounts, and records available at a convenient location in this state upon request of the department.

Added by Laws 2001, c. 2001–36, § 28, eff. Oct. 1, 2001. Amended by Laws 2004, c. 2004–390, § 132, eff. July 1, 2004; Laws 2005, c. 2005–163, § 16, eff. June 8, 2005.

717.132. Enforcement; cease and desist orders; fines

(1) The department may bring an action in any court of competent jurisdiction to enforce or administer any provision of this chapter, any rule or order promulgated under this chapter, or any written agreement entered into with the department.

(2) In addition to any other powers conferred upon it to enforce and administer the provisions of this chapter, the department may issue and serve upon a person an order to cease and desist and to take corrective action whenever the department finds that such person is violating, has violated, or is about to violate any provision of this chapter, any rule or order promulgated under this chapter, or any written agreement entered into with the department. For purposes of this subsection, the term "corrective action" includes refunding excessive charges, requiring a person to return unclaimed property, requiring a holder to remit unclaimed property, and requiring a holder to correct a report that contains errors or omissions. Any such order shall contain a notice of rights provided by ss. 120.569 and 120.57.

(3) In addition to any other powers conferred upon it to enforce and administer the provisions of this chapter, the department or a court of competent jurisdiction may impose fines against any person found to have violated any provision of this chapter, any rule or order promulgated under this chapter, or any written agreement entered into with the department in an amount not to exceed $2,000 for each violation. All fines collected under this subsection shall be deposited as received in the Unclaimed Property Trust Fund.

Laws 1987, c. 87–105, § 33. Amended by Laws 1993, c. 93–280, § 4, eff. Oct. 1, 1993; Laws 1996, c. 96–301, § 20, eff. Dec. 1, 1996; Laws 1996, c. 96–410, § 298, eff. Oct. 1, 1996; Laws 2001, c. 2001–36, § 29, eff. Oct. 1, 2001; Laws 2004, c. 2004–390, § 133, eff. July 1, 2004; Laws 2005, c. 2005–163, § 17, eff. June 8, 2005.

717.1322. Administrative and civil enforcement

(1) The following acts are violations of this chapter and constitute grounds for an administrative enforcement action by the department in accordance with the requirements of chapter 120 and for civil enforcement by the department in a court of competent jurisdiction:

(a) Failure to comply with any provision of this chapter, any rule or order adopted under this chapter, or any written agreement entered into with the department.

(b) Fraud, misrepresentation, deceit, or gross negligence in any matter within the scope of this chapter.

(c) Fraudulent misrepresentation, circumvention, or concealment of any matter required to be stated or furnished to an owner or apparent owner under this chapter, regardless of reliance by or damage to the owner or apparent owner.

(d) Willful imposition of illegal or excessive charges in any unclaimed property transaction.

(e) False, deceptive, or misleading solicitation or advertising within the scope of this chapter.

(f) Failure to maintain, preserve, and keep available for examination all books, accounts, or other documents required by this chapter, by any rule or order adopted under this chapter, or by any agreement entered into with the department under this chapter.

(g) Refusal to permit inspection of books and records in an investigation or examination by the department or refusal to comply with a subpoena issued by the department under this chapter.

(h) Criminal conduct in the course of a person's business.

(i) Failure to timely pay any fine imposed or assessed under this chapter or any rule adopted under this chapter.

(j) Requesting or receiving compensation for notifying a person of his or her unclaimed property or assisting another person in filing a claim for unclaimed property, unless the person is an attorney licensed to practice law in this state, a Florida-certified public accountant, or a private investigator licensed under chapter 493, or entering into, or making a solicitation to enter into, a power of attorney to file a claim for unclaimed property owned by another, or a contract or agreement to purchase unclaimed property, unless such person is registered with the department pursuant to this chapter and an attorney licensed to practice law in this state in the regular practice of her or his profession, a Florida-certified public accountant who is acting within the scope of the practice of public accounting as defined in chapter 473, or a private investigator licensed under chapter 493. This subsection does not apply to a person who has been granted a durable power of attorney to convey and receive all of the real and personal property of the owner, is the court-appointed guardian of the owner, has been employed as an attorney or qualified representative to contest the department's denial of a claim, or has been employed as an attorney to probate the estate of the owner or an heir or legatee of the owner.

(k) Failure to authorize the release of records in the possession of a third party after being requested to do so by the department regarding a pending examination or investigation.

(*l*) Receipt or solicitation of consideration to be paid in advance of the approval of a claim under this chapter.

(2) Upon a finding by the department that any person has committed any of the acts set forth in subsection (1), the department may enter an order:

(a) Revoking for a minimum of 5 years or suspending for a maximum of 5 years a registration previously granted under this chapter during which time the registrant may not reapply for a registration under this chapter;

(b) Placing a registrant or an applicant for a registration on probation for a period of time and subject to such conditions as the department may specify;

(c) Placing permanent restrictions or conditions upon issuance or maintenance of a registration under this chapter;

(d) Issuing a reprimand;

(e) Imposing an administrative fine not to exceed $2,000 for each such act; or

(f) Prohibiting any person from being a director, officer, agent, employee, or ultimate equitable owner of a 10–percent or greater interest in an employer of a registrant.

(3) A registrant is subject to civil enforcement and the disciplinary actions specified in subsection (2) for violations of subsection (1) by an agent or employee of the registrant's employer if the registrant knew or should have known that such agent or employee was violating any provision of this chapter.

(4)(a) The department shall adopt, by rule, and periodically review the disciplinary guidelines applicable to each ground for disciplinary action which may be imposed by the department under this chapter.

(b) The disciplinary guidelines shall specify a meaningful range of designated penalties based upon the severity or repetition of specific offenses, or both. It is the legislative intent that minor violations be distinguished from more serious violations; that such guidelines consider the amount of the claim involved, the complexity of locating the owner, the steps taken to ensure the accuracy of the claim by the person filing the claim, the acts of commission and omission of the ultimate owners in establishing themselves as rightful owners of the funds, the acts of commission or omission of the agent or employee of an employer in the filing of the claim, the actual knowledge of the agent, employee, employer, or owner in the filing of the claim, the departure, if any, by the agent or employee from the internal controls and procedures established by the employer with regard to the filing of a claim, the number of defective claims previously filed by the agent, employee, employer, or owner; that such guidelines provide reasonable and meaningful notice of likely penalties that may be imposed for proscribed conduct; and that such penalties be consistently applied by the department.

(c) A specific finding of mitigating or aggravating circumstances shall allow the department to impose a penalty other than that provided for in such guidelines. The department shall adopt by rule disciplinary guidelines to designate possible mitigating and aggravating circumstances and the variation and range of penalties permitted for such circumstances. Such mitigating and aggravating circumstances shall also provide for consideration of, and be consistent with, the legislative intent expressed in paragraph (b).

(d) In any proceeding brought under this chapter, the administrative law judge, in recommending penalties in any recommended order, shall follow the penalty guidelines established by the department and shall state in writing any mitigating or aggravating circumstances upon which the recommended penalty is based.

(5) The department may seek any appropriate civil legal remedy available to it by filing a civil action in a court of competent jurisdiction against any person who has, directly or through a claimant's representative, wrongfully submitted a claim as the ultimate owner of property and improperly received funds from the department in violation of this chapter.

Added by Laws 2004, c. 2004–390, § 134, eff. July 1, 2004. Amended by Laws 2005, c. 2005–163, § 18, eff. June 8, 2005.

717.1323. Prohibited practice

No person may knowingly enter false information onto the Internet website of the Bureau of Unclaimed Property.

Added by Laws 2005, c. 2005–163, § 19, eff. June 8, 2005.

717.133. Interstate agreements and cooperation; joint and reciprocal actions with other states

(1) The department may enter into agreements with other states to exchange information needed to enable this or another state to audit or otherwise determine unclaimed property that it or another state may be entitled to subject to a claim of custody. The department may require the reporting of information needed to enable compliance with agreements made pursuant to this section and prescribe the form.

(2) The department may join with other states to seek enforcement of this chapter against any person.

(3) At the request of another state, the department may bring an action in the name of the other state in any court of competent jurisdiction to enforce the unclaimed property laws of the other state against a holder in this state of property subject to escheat or a claim of abandonment by the other state, if the other state has agreed to pay expenses incurred in bringing the action.

(4) The department may request that the attorney general of another state or any other person bring an action in the name of the department in the other state. The department may pay all expenses including attorneys' fees in any action under this subsection.

(5) As necessary for proper administration of this chapter, the department may enter into contracts for the location or collection of property subject to payment or delivery to the department under this chapter.

Laws 1987, c. 87–105, § 34.

717.1331. Actions against holders

The department may initiate, or cause to be initiated, an action against a holder to enforce a subpoena or recover unclaimed property. If the department prevails in a civil or administrative action to enforce a subpoena or recover unclaimed property initiated by or on behalf of the department, the holder shall be ordered to pay the department reasonable costs and attorney's fees.

Added by Laws 2004, c. 2004–390, § 135, eff. July 1, 2004. Amended by Laws 2005, c. 2005–163, § 20, eff. June 8, 2005.

717.1333. Evidence; estimations; audit reports, examiner's worksheets, investigative reports, other related documents

(1) In any proceeding involving a holder under ss. 120.569 and 120.57 in which an auditor, examiner, or investigator acting under authority of this chapter is available for cross-examination, any official written report, worksheet, or other related paper, or copy thereof, compiled, prepared, drafted, or otherwise made or received by the auditor, examiner, or investigator, after being duly authenticated by the auditor, examiner, or investigator, may be admitted as competent evidence upon the oath of the auditor, examiner, or investigator that the report, worksheet, or related paper was prepared or received as a result of an audit, examination, or investigation of the books and records of the person audited, examined, or investigated, or the agent thereof.

(2) If the records of the holder that are available for the periods subject to this chapter are insufficient to permit the preparation of a report of the unclaimed property due and owing by a holder, the amount due may be reasonably estimated.

Added by Laws 2004, c. 2004–390, § 136, eff. July 1, 2004. Amended by Laws 2005, c. 2005–163, § 21, eff. June 8, 2005.

717.134. Penalties and interest

(1) The department may impose and collect a penalty of $500 per day up to a maximum of $5,000 and 25 percent of the value of property not reported until a report is rendered for any person who willfully fails to render any report required under this chapter. Upon a holder's showing of good cause, the department may waive said penalty or any portion thereof. If the holder acted in good faith and without negligence, the department shall waive the penalty provided herein.

(2) The department may impose and collect a penalty of $500 per day up to a maximum of $5,000 and 25 percent of the value of property not paid or delivered until the property is paid or delivered for any person who willfully refuses to pay or deliver abandoned property to the department as required under this chapter.

(3) Any person who willfully or fraudulently conceals, destroys, damages, or makes unlawful disposition of any property or of the books, records, or accounts pertaining to property which is

subject to the provisions of this chapter is guilty of a misdemeanor of the second degree, punishable as provided in s. 775.082 or s. 775.083.

(4) In addition to any damages, penalties, or fines for which a person may be liable under any other provision of law, any person who fails to report or pay or deliver unclaimed property within the time prescribed by this chapter shall pay to the department interest at the rate of 12 percent per annum on such property, or value thereof, from the date such property shall have been paid or delivered. The department may waive any penalty due under this subsection with appropriate justification.

(5) The department may impose and collect a penalty of $500 per day up to a maximum of $5,000 and 25 percent of the value of property willfully not reported with all of the information required by this chapter. Upon a holder's showing of good cause, the department may waive the penalty or any portion thereof. If the holder acted in good faith and without negligence, the department shall waive the penalty provided herein.

Laws 1987, c. 87–105, § 35. Amended by Laws 1996, c. 96–301, § 21, eff. Dec. 1, 1996; Laws 2004, c. 2004–390, § 137, eff. July 1, 2004.

717.1341. Invalid claims, recovery of property, interest and penalties

(1)(a) No person shall receive unclaimed property that the person is not entitled to receive. Any person who receives, or assists another person to receive, unclaimed property that the person is not entitled to receive is strictly, jointly, personally, and severally liable for the unclaimed property and shall immediately return the property, or the reasonable value of the property if the property has been damaged or disposed of, to the department plus interest at the rate set in accordance with s. 55.03(1). Assisting another person to receive unclaimed property includes executing a claim form on the person's behalf.

(b) 1. In the case of stocks or bonds which have been sold, the proceeds from the sale shall be returned to the department plus any dividends or interest received thereon plus an amount equal to the brokerage fee plus interest at a rate set in accordance with s. 55.03(1) on the proceeds from the sale of the stocks or bonds, the dividends or interest received, and the brokerage fee.

2. In the case of stocks or bonds which have not been sold, the stocks or bonds and any dividends or interest received thereon shall be returned to the department, together with interest on the dividends or interest received, at a rate set in accordance with s. 55.03(1) of the value of the property.

(2) The department may maintain a civil or administrative action:

(a) To recover unclaimed property that was paid or remitted to a person who was not entitled to the unclaimed property or to offset amounts owed to the department against amounts owed to an owner representative;

(b) Against a person who assists another person in receiving, or attempting to receive, unclaimed property that the person is not entitled to receive; or

(c) Against a person who attempts to receive unclaimed property that the person is not entitled to receive.

(3) If the department prevails in any proceeding under subsection (2), a fine not to exceed three times the value of the property received or sought to be received may be imposed on any person who knowingly, or with reckless disregard or deliberate ignorance of the truth, violated this section. If the department prevails in a civil or administrative proceeding under subsection

(2), the person who violated subsection (1) shall be ordered to pay the department reasonable costs and attorney's fees.

(4) No person shall knowingly file, knowingly conspire to file, or knowingly assist in filing, a claim for unclaimed property the person is not entitled to receive. Any person who violates this subsection regarding unclaimed property of an aggregate value:

(a) Greater than $50,000, is guilty of a felony of the first degree, punishable as provided in s. 775.082, s. 775.083, or s. 775.084;

(b) Greater than $10,000 up to $50,000, is guilty of a felony of the second degree, punishable as provided in s. 775.082, s. 775.083, or s. 775.084;

(c) Greater than $250 up to $10,000, is guilty of a felony of the third degree, punishable as provided in s. 775.082, s. 775.083, or s. 775.084;

(d) Greater than $50 up to $250, is guilty of a misdemeanor of the first degree, punishable as provided in s. 775.082 or s. 775.083; or

(e) Up to $50, is guilty of a misdemeanor of the second degree, punishable as provided in s. 775.082 or s. 775.083.

Added by Laws 2004, c. 2004–390, § 138, eff. July 1, 2004. Amended by Laws 2011, c. 2011–169, § 2, eff. July 1, 2011.

717.135. Power of attorney to recover reported property in the custody of the department

(1) A power of attorney executed by a claimant to a claimant's representative for compensation to recover or assist in the recovery of property reported to the department under s. 717.117 shall be in 10–point type or greater.

(2) A power of attorney described in subsection (1) must:

(a) Limit the fees and costs for services to 20 percent per unclaimed property account held by the department. Fees and costs for cash accounts shall be based on the value of the property at the time the power of attorney is signed by the claimant. Fees and costs for accounts containing securities or other intangible ownership interests, which securities or interests are not converted to cash, shall be based on the purchase price of the security as quoted on a national exchange or other market on which the property is regularly traded at the time the securities or other ownership interest is remitted to the claimant or the claimant's representative. Fees and costs for tangible property or safe-deposit box accounts shall be based on the value of the tangible property or contents of the safe-deposit box at the time the ownership interest is transferred or remitted to the claimant. Total fees and costs on any single account owned by a natural person residing in this country must not exceed $1,000; or

(b) Fully disclose that the property is held by the Bureau of Unclaimed Property of the Department of Financial Services pursuant to this chapter, the mailing address of the bureau, the Internet address of the bureau, the person or name of the entity that held the property prior to the property becoming unclaimed, the date of the holder's last contact with the owner, if known, and the approximate value of the property, and identify which of the following categories of unclaimed property the claimant's representative is seeking to recover, as reported by the holder:

1. Cash accounts.

2. Stale dated checks.

3. Life insurance or annuity contract assets.

4. Utility deposits.

5. Securities or other interests in business associations.

6. Wages.

7. Accounts receivable.

8. Contents of safe-deposit boxes.

This subsection shall not apply if probate proceedings must be initiated on behalf of the claimant for an estate that has never been probated or if the unclaimed property is being claimed by a person outside of the United States.

(3)(a) A power of attorney described in paragraph (2)(b) must state in 12–point type or greater in the order indicated with the blank spaces accurately completed:

FULL DISCLOSURE STATEMENT

The property is currently held by the State of Florida Department of Financial Services, Bureau of Unclaimed Property, pursuant to chapter 717, Florida Statutes. The mailing address of the Bureau of Unclaimed Property is_____. The Internet address of the Bureau of Unclaimed Property is_____.

The property was Remitted by:_____.

Date of last contact:_____.

Property category:_____.

(b) Immediately above the signature line for the claimant, a power of attorney described in paragraph (2)(b) must state in 12–point type or greater:

Claimant agrees, by signing below, that the FULL DISCLOSURE STATEMENT has been read and fully understood.

(4)(a) Powers of attorney for recovery of cash accounts shall state the value of the unclaimed property, the unclaimed property account number, and the percentage value of the unclaimed property account to be paid to the claimant and shall also state the percentage value of compensation to be paid to the claimant's representative, if applicable.

(b) Powers of attorney for recovery of accounts containing securities, safe-deposit box accounts, other intangible or tangible ownership interests, or other types of accounts, except cash accounts, shall state the unclaimed property account number, the number of shares of stock, if applicable, the approximate value of the unclaimed property, and the percentage value of compensation to be paid to the claimant's representative, if applicable.

(c) All powers of attorney shall include:

1. The name and professional license number of the claimant's representative.

2. The name, address, and telephone number of the claimant's representative's firm or employer.

3. The name, address, and telephone number of the claimant.

4. If applicable, the taxpayer identification number or social security number, address, and telephone number of the claimant.

5. The name and address to whom the warrant is to be issued, if different than the claimant's name and address.

(d) The original of all such disclosures and powers of attorney shall be signed and dated by the claimant of the property and shall be filed with the claim form.

(e) All powers of attorney executed by a claimant to a claimant's representative for compensation to recover or assist in the recovery of property reported to the department under s. 717.117 must use the following form on 8 and ½–inch by 11–inch paper or on 8 and ½–inch by 14–inch paper with all of the text on one side of the paper and with the other side of the paper left blank. The power of attorney must be accurately completed and executed. The title of the power of attorney shall be in bold 14–point type or greater and underlined. Except as otherwise provided in this section, the rest of the power of attorney shall be in 10–point type or greater. All unclaimed property accounts claimed must be identified on the power of attorney by account number. The power of attorney must state in bold 12–point type or greater at the top of the power of attorney in the order indicated:

LIMITED POWER OF ATTORNEY

$_____ = Approximate Dollar Value of the Property

_____ = Number of Shares of Stock to be Recovered (If Applicable)

_____ Percent to be Paid as Compensation to the Claimant's Representative

$_____ = Amount to be Paid to Claimant's Representative

$_____ = Net Amount to be Paid to Claimant

Property Account Numbers:_____

(f) All fees, whether expressed as a percentage or as a flat fee, are subject to the limitations and requirements of subsection (2).

(g) This section does not prohibit the:

1. Use of bolding, italics, print of different colors, and text borders as a means of highlighting or stressing certain selected items within the text.

2. Placement of the name, address, and telephone number of the representative's firm or company in the top margin above the words "POWER OF ATTORNEY." No additional writing of any kind may be placed in the top margin including, but not limited to, logos, license numbers, Internet addresses, or slogans.

3. Placement of the word "pending" prior to the words "NET AMOUNT TO BE PAID TO CLAIMANT," if it is not yet possible to determine the percentage interest of an heir or legatee prior to a determination on the issue by the probate court.

4. Deletion of the words "Number of Shares of Stock (If Applicable)" if the agreement does not relate to the recovery of securities.

5. Deletion of the words "Percent to Be Paid as Compensation to Claimant's Representative" if the power of attorney provides for a flat fee to be paid as compensation to the claimant's representative.

(5) As used in this section, "claimant" means the person on whose behalf a claim is filed.

(6) This section does not supersede the licensing requirements of chapter 493.

Laws 1987, c. 87–105, § 36. Amended by Laws 1991, c. 91–261, § 1, eff. May 30, 1991; Laws 1994, c. 94–191, § 2, eff. May 14, 1994; Laws 1996, c. 96–301, § 22, eff. Dec. 1, 1996; Laws 2001, c. 2001–36, § 30, eff. Oct. 1, 2001; Laws 2003, c. 2003–261, § 1889, eff. June 26, 2003; Laws 2004, c. 2004–390, § 139, eff. July 1, 2004; Laws 2005, c. 2005–163, § 22, eff. June 8, 2005.

717.1351. Acquisition of unclaimed property

(1) A person desiring to acquire ownership of or entitlement to property reported to the department under s. 717.117 must be an attorney licensed to practice law in this state, a licensed Florida-certified public accountant, a private investigator licensed under chapter 493, or an employer of a licensed private investigator which employer possesses a Class "A" license under chapter 493 and must be registered with the department under this chapter.

(2) All contracts to acquire ownership of or entitlement to unclaimed property from the person or persons entitled to the unclaimed property must be in 10–point type or greater and must:

(a) Have a purchase price that discounts the value of the unclaimed property at the time the agreement is executed by the seller at no greater than 20 percent per account held by the department. An unclaimed property account must not be discounted in excess of $1,000. However, the $1,000 discount limitation does not apply if probate proceedings must be initiated on behalf of the seller for an estate that has never been probated or if the seller of the unclaimed property is not a natural person or is a person outside the United States; or

(b) Fully disclose that the property is held by the Bureau of Unclaimed Property of the Department of Financial Services pursuant to this chapter, the mailing address of the bureau, the Internet address of the bureau, the person or name of the entity that held the property prior to the property becoming unclaimed, the date of the holder's last contact with the owner, if known, and the approximate value of the property, and identify which of the following categories of unclaimed property the buyer is seeking to purchase as reported by the holder:

1. Cash accounts.

2. Stale dated checks.

3. Life insurance or annuity contract assets.

4. Utility deposits.

5. Securities or other interests in business associations.

6. Wages.

7. Accounts receivable.

8. Contents of safe-deposit boxes.

The purchase agreement described in this paragraph must state in 12–point type or greater in the order indicated with the blank spaces accurately completed:

FULL DISCLOSURE STATEMENT

The property is currently held by the State of Florida Department of Financial Services, Bureau of Unclaimed Property, pursuant to chapter 717, Florida Statutes. The mailing address of the Bureau of Unclaimed Property is_____. The Internet address of the Bureau of Unclaimed Property is_____.

The property was remitted by:_____.

Date of last contact:_____.

Property category:_____.

Immediately above the signature line for the seller, the purchase agreement described in this paragraph must state in 12–point type or greater:

Seller agrees, by signing below, that the FULL DISCLOSURE STATEMENT has been read and fully understood.

(3) The originals of all such disclosures and agreements to transfer ownership of or entitlement to unclaimed property shall be signed and dated by the seller and shall be filed with the claim form. The claimant shall provide the department with a legible copy of a valid driver license of the seller at the time the original claim form is filed. If a seller has not been issued a valid driver license at the time the original claim form is filed, the department shall be provided with a legible copy of a photographic identification of the seller issued by the United States or a foreign nation, a state or territory of the United States or a foreign nation, or a political subdivision or agency thereof. In lieu of photographic identification, a notarized sworn statement by the seller may be provided which affirms the seller's identity and states the seller's full name and address. The seller must produce to the notary his or her photographic identification issued by the United States, a state or territory of the United States, a foreign nation, or a political subdivision or agency thereof or other evidence deemed acceptable by department rule. The notary shall indicate the notary's full address on the notarized sworn statement. If a claim is filed without the required identification or the sworn statement with the original claim form and the original agreement to acquire ownership of or entitlement to the unclaimed property, the claim is void.

(4) Any contract to acquire ownership of or entitlement to unclaimed property from the person or persons entitled to the unclaimed property must provide for the purchase price to be remitted to the seller or sellers within 10 days after the execution of the contract by the seller or sellers. The contract must specify the unclaimed property account number, the name of the holder who reported the property to the department, the category of unclaimed property, the value of the unclaimed property account, and the number of shares of stock, if applicable. Proof of payment by check must be filed with the department with the claim.

(5) All agreements to purchase unclaimed property from an owner must use the following form on 8 and ½–inch by 11–inch paper or on 8 and ½–inch by 14–inch paper with all of the text on one side of the paper and with the other side of the paper left blank. The agreement must be accurately completed and executed. The title of the agreement shall be in bold 14–point type or greater and underlined. Except as otherwise provided in this section, the rest of the agreement shall be in 10–point type or greater. All unclaimed property accounts to be purchased must be identified on the agreement by account number. The agreement must state, in bold 12–point type or greater at the top of the agreement in the order indicated:

PURCHASE AGREEMENT

$_____ = Approximate Dollar Value of the Property

_____ = Number of Shares of Stock (If Applicable)

_____ = Percent of Property to be Paid to the Buyer

$_____ = Amount to be Paid to Buyer

$_____ = Net Amount to be Paid to Seller

Property Account Number(s):_____

(6) All agreements shall include:

(a) The name and professional license number of the registrant.

(b) The name, address, and telephone number of the registrant's firm or employer.

(c) The name, address, and telephone number of the seller.

(d) The taxpayer identification number or social security number of the seller, if available.

(e) The name and address to whom the warrant is to be issued if it is different from the seller's name and address.

(f) The original signature of the registrant and the date signed by the registrant.

(7) This section does not prohibit the:

(a) Use of bolding, italics, print of different colors, or text borders as a means of highlighting or stressing certain selected items within the text.

(b) Placement of the name, address, and telephone number of the registrant's firm or company in the top margin above the words "PURCHASE AGREEMENT." No additional writing of any kind may be placed in the top margin, including, but not limited to, logos, license numbers, Internet addresses, or slogans.

(c) Deletion of the words "Number of Shares of Stock (If Applicable)" if the agreement does not relate to the recovery of securities.

(d) Deletion of the words "Percent of Property to be Paid to Buyer," if the purchase agreement provides for a flat fee to be paid as compensation to the buyer.

(8) This section does not supersede the licensing requirements of chapter 493.

Added by Laws 2004, c. 2004–390, § 140, eff. July 1, 2004. Amended by Laws 2005, c. 2005–163, § 23, eff. June 8, 2005.

717.1355. Theme park and entertainment complex tickets

This chapter does not apply to any tickets for admission to a theme park or entertainment complex as defined in s. 509.013(9), or to any tickets to a permanent exhibition or recreational activity within such theme park or entertainment complex.

Added by Laws 1996, c. 96–301, § 23, eff. Dec. 1, 1996.

Cross References

Consumer protection, gift certificates and credit memos, see § 501.95.

717.136. Foreign transactions

This chapter does not apply to any property held, due, and owing in a foreign country and arising out of foreign transaction.

Laws 1987, c. 87–105, § 37.

717.138. Rulemaking authority

The department shall administer and provide for the enforcement of this chapter. The department has authority to adopt rules pursuant to ss. 120.536(1) and 120.54 to implement the provisions of this chapter. The department may adopt rules to allow for electronic filing of fees, forms, and reports required by this chapter.

Laws 1987, c. 87–105, § 39. Amended by Laws 1998, c. 98–200, § 220, eff. July 1, 1998; Laws 2001, c. 2001–36, § 31, eff. Oct. 1, 2001; Laws 2003, c. 2003–261, § 1890, eff. June 26, 2003.

717.1381. Void unclaimed property powers of attorney and purchase agreements

(1) Protecting the interests of owners of unclaimed property is declared to be the public policy of this state. It is in the best interests of the owners of unclaimed property that they have the

opportunity to receive the full amount of the unclaimed property returned to them without deduction of any fees. Further, it is specifically recognized that the Legislature has mandated and the state has an obligation to make a meaningful and active effort to notify owners concerning their unclaimed property. The state recognizes that this policy and obligation cannot be fulfilled without providing the state with the first opportunity to notify the owners of unclaimed property that they may file a claim for their property with the department. In furtherance of this policy and obligation:

(a) Any oral or written agreement or power of attorney for compensation or gain or in the expectation of compensation or gain, that includes an unclaimed property account valued at more than $250 which was made on or before 45 days after the holder or examination report was processed and added to the unclaimed property database, subsequent to a determination that the report was accurate and that the reported property was the same as the remitted property, is void as contrary to public policy.

(b) Any oral or written purchase agreement that includes an unclaimed property account valued at more than $250, owned by another and made on or before 45 days after the holder or examination report was processed and added to the unclaimed property database, subsequent to a determination that the report was accurate and that the reported property was the same as the remitted property, is void as contrary to public policy.

(2) A person may not enter into a power of attorney or an agreement, or make a solicitation to enter into a power of attorney or an agreement, that is void under this section.

Added by Laws 2005, c. 2005–163, § 24, eff. June 8, 2005.

717.1382. United States savings bond; unclaimed property; escheatment; procedure

(1) Notwithstanding any other provision of law, a United States savings bond in possession of the department or registered to a person with a last known address in the state, including a bond that is lost, stolen, or destroyed, is presumed abandoned and unclaimed 5 years after the bond reaches maturity and no longer earns interest and shall be reported and remitted to the department by the financial institution or other holder in accordance with ss. 717.117(1) and (3) and 717.119, if the department is not in possession of the bond.

(2)(a) After a United States savings bond is abandoned and unclaimed in accordance with subsection (1), the department may commence a civil action in a court of competent jurisdiction in Leon County for a determination that the bond shall escheat to the state. Upon determination of escheatment, all property rights to the bond or proceeds from the bond, including all rights, powers, and privileges of survivorship of an owner, coowner, or beneficiary, shall vest solely in the state.

(b) Service of process by publication may be made on a party in a civil action pursuant to this section. A notice of action shall state the name of any known owner of the bond, the nature of the action or proceeding in short and simple terms, the name of the court in which the action or proceeding is instituted, and an abbreviated title of the case.

(c) The notice of action shall require a person claiming an interest in the bond to file a written defense with the clerk of the court and serve a copy of the defense by the date fixed in the notice. The date must not be less than 28 or more than 60 days after the first publication of the notice.

(d) The notice of action shall be published once a week for 4 consecutive weeks in a newspaper of general circulation published in Leon County. Proof of publication shall be placed in the court file.

(e) 1. If no person files a claim with the court for the bond and if the department has substantially complied with the provisions of this section, the court shall enter a default judgment that the bond, or proceeds from such bond, has escheated to the state.

2. If a person files a claim for one or more bonds and, after notice and hearing, the court determines that the claimant is not entitled to the bonds claimed by such claimant, the court shall enter a judgment that such bonds, or proceeds from such bonds, have escheated to the state.

3. If a person files a claim for one or more bonds and, after notice and hearing, the court determines that the claimant is entitled to the bonds claimed by such claimant, the court shall enter a judgment in favor of the claimant.

(3) The department may redeem a United States savings bond escheated to the state pursuant to this section or, in the event that the department is not in possession of the bond, seek to obtain the proceeds from such bond. Proceeds received by the department shall be deposited in accordance with s. 717.123.

Added by Laws 2015, c. 2015–152, § 1, eff. July 1, 2015.

717.1383. United States savings bond; claim for bond

A person claiming a United States savings bond escheated to the state under s. 717.1382, or for the proceeds from such bond, may file a claim with the department. The department may approve the claim if the person is able to provide sufficient proof of the validity of the person's claim. Once a bond, or the proceeds from such bond, are remitted to a claimant, no action thereafter may be maintained by any other person against the department, the state, or any officer thereof, for or on account of such funds. The person's sole remedy, if any, shall be against the claimant who received the bond or the proceeds from such bond.

Added by Laws 2015, c. 2015–152, § 2, eff. July 1, 2015.

717.139. Uniformity of application and construction

This chapter shall be applied and construed as to effectuate its general purpose of protecting the interest of missing owners of property, while providing that the benefit of all unclaimed and abandoned property shall go to all the people of the state, and to make uniform the law with respect to the subject of this chapter among states enacting it.

Laws 1987, c. 87–105, § 40.

717.1400. Registration

(1) In order to file claims as a claimant's representative, acquire ownership of or entitlement to unclaimed property, receive a distribution of fees and costs from the department, and obtain unclaimed property dollar amounts, numbers of reported shares of stock, and social security numbers held by the department, a private investigator holding a Class "C" individual license under chapter 493 must register with the department on such form as the department shall prescribe by rule, and must be verified by the applicant. To register with the department, a private investigator must provide:

(a) A legible copy of the applicant's Class "A" business license under chapter 493 or that of the applicant's firm or employer which holds a Class "A" business license under chapter 493.

(b) A legible copy of the applicant's Class "C" individual license issued under chapter 493.

(c) The business address and telephone number of the applicant's private investigative firm or employer.

(d) The names of agents or employees, if any, who are designated to act on behalf of the private investigator, together with a legible copy of their photo identification issued by an agency of the United States, or a state, or a political subdivision thereof.

(e) Sufficient information to enable the department to disburse funds by electronic funds transfer.

(f) The tax identification number of the private investigator's firm or employer which holds a Class "A" business license under chapter 493.

(2) In order to file claims as a claimant's representative, acquire ownership of or entitlement to unclaimed property, receive a distribution of fees and costs from the department, and obtain unclaimed property dollar amounts, numbers of reported shares of stock, and social security numbers held by the department, a Florida-certified public accountant must register with the department on such form as the department shall prescribe by rule, and must be verified by the applicant. To register with the department a Florida-certified public accountant must provide:

(a) The applicant's Florida Board of Accountancy number.

(b) A legible copy of the applicant's current driver license showing the full name and current address of such person. If a current driver license is not available, another form of identification showing the full name and current address of such person or persons shall be filed with the department.

(c) The business address and telephone number of the applicant's public accounting firm or employer.

(d) The names of agents or employees, if any, who are designated to act on behalf of the Florida-certified public accountant, together with a legible copy of their photo identification issued by an agency of the United States, or a state, or a political subdivision thereof.

(e) Sufficient information to enable the department to disburse funds by electronic funds transfer.

(f) The tax identification number of the accountant's public accounting firm employer.

(3) In order to file claims as a claimant's representative, acquire ownership of or entitlement to unclaimed property, receive a distribution of fees and costs from the department, and obtain unclaimed property dollar amounts, numbers of reported shares of stock, and social security numbers held by the department, an attorney licensed to practice in this state must register with the department on such form as the department shall prescribe by rule, and must be verified by the applicant. To register with the department, such attorney must provide:

(a) The applicant's Florida Bar number.

(b) A legible copy of the applicant's current driver license showing the full name and current address of such person. If a current driver license is not available, another form of identification showing the full name and current address of such person or persons shall be filed with the department.

(c) The business address and telephone number of the applicant's firm or employer.

(d) The names of agents or employees, if any, who are designated to act on behalf of the attorney, together with a legible copy of their photo identification issued by an agency of the United States, or a state, or a political subdivision thereof.

(e) Sufficient information to enable the department to disburse funds by electronic funds transfer.

(f) The tax identification number of the attorney's firm or employer.

(4) Information and documents already on file with the department prior to the effective date of this provision need not be resubmitted in order to complete the registration.

(5) If a material change in the status of a registration occurs, a registrant must, within 30 days, provide the department with the updated documentation and information in writing. Material changes include, but are not limited to: a designated agent or employee ceasing to act on behalf of the designating person, a surrender, suspension, or revocation of a license, or a license renewal.

(a) If a designated agent or employee ceases to act on behalf of the person who has designated the agent or employee to act on such person's behalf, the designating person must, within 30 days, inform the Bureau of Unclaimed Property in writing of the termination of agency or employment.

(b) If a registrant surrenders the registrant's license or the license is suspended or revoked, the registrant must, within 30 days, inform the bureau in writing of the surrender, suspension, or revocation.

(c) If a private investigator's Class "C" individual license under chapter 493 or a private investigator's employer's Class "A" business license under chapter 493 is renewed, the private investigator must provide a copy of the renewed license to the department within 30 days after the receipt of the renewed license by the private investigator or the private investigator's employer.

(6) A registrant's firm or employer may not have a name that might lead another person to conclude that the registrant's firm or employer is affiliated or associated with the United States, or an agency thereof, or a state or an agency or political subdivision of a state. The department shall deny an application for registration or revoke a registration if the applicant's or registrant's firm or employer has a name that might lead another person to conclude that the firm or employer is affiliated or associated with the United States, or an agency thereof, or a state or an agency or political subdivision of a state. Names that might lead another person to conclude that the firm or employer is affiliated or associated with the United States, or an agency thereof, or a state or an agency or political subdivision of a state, include, but are not limited to, the words United States, Florida, state, bureau, division, department, or government.

(7) The licensing and other requirements of this section must be maintained as a condition of registration with the department.

Added by Laws 2004, c. 2004–390, § 141, eff. July 1, 2004. Amended by Laws 2005, c. 2005–2, § 133, eff. July 5, 2005; Laws 2005, c. 2005–163, § 25, eff. June 8, 2005.

717.1401. Repeal

This chapter shall not repeal, but shall be additional and supplemental to the existing provisions of ss. 43.18, 43.19, and 402.17 and chapter 716.

Laws 1987, c. 87–105, § 41. Amended by Laws 1992, c. 92–348, § 62, eff. Dec. 16, 1992.

TITLE XLI

STATUTE OF FRAUDS, FRAUDULENT TRANSFERS, AND GENERAL ASSIGNMENTS

CHAPTER 725

UNENFORCEABLE CONTRACTS

725.01. Promise to pay another's debt, etc.

No action shall be brought whereby to charge any executor or administrator upon any special promise to answer or pay any debt or damages out of her or his own estate, or whereby to charge the defendant upon any special promise to answer for the debt, default or miscarriage of another person or to charge any person upon any agreement made upon consideration of marriage, or upon any contract for the sale of lands, tenements or hereditaments, or of any uncertain interest in or concerning them, or for any lease thereof for a period longer than 1 year, or upon any agreement that is not to be performed within the space of 1 year from the making thereof, or whereby to charge any health care provider upon any guarantee, warranty, or assurance as to the results of any medical, surgical, or diagnostic procedure performed by any physician licensed under chapter 458, osteopathic physician licensed under chapter 459, chiropractic physician licensed under chapter 460, podiatric physician licensed under chapter 461, or dentist licensed under chapter 466, unless the agreement or promise upon which such action shall be brought, or some note or memorandum thereof shall be in writing and signed by the party to be charged therewith or by some other person by her or him thereunto lawfully authorized.

Act Nov. 15, 1828, § 10; Rev.St.1892, § 1995; Gen.St.1906, § 2517; Rev.Gen.St.1920, § 3872; Comp. Gen.Laws 1927, § 5779; Laws 1975, c. 75–9, § 10. Amended by Laws 1997, c. 97–102, § 933, eff. July 1, 1997; Laws 1997, c. 97–264, § 60, eff. July 1, 1997; Laws 1998, c. 98–166, §§ 227, 294, eff. July 1, 1998.

Cross References

Conveyance of real estate, see § 689.01.
Crimes, human trafficking, see F.S.A. § 787.06.
Leases of goods, statute of frauds, see § 680.201.
Letters of credit, see § 675.104.
Promise to pay debts barred by statute of limitations, necessity of writing, see § 95.04.
Real estate, necessity of writing, see § 689.01.
Statute of frauds, see § 672.201.
Trust declaration, necessity of writing, see § 689.05.
Wills, necessity of writing, see § 732.701.

725.03. Newspaper subscription

No person shall be liable to pay for any newspaper, periodical or other like matter, unless the person shall subscribe for or order the same in writing.

Laws 1851, c. 379, § 1; Rev.St.1892, § 1997; Gen.St.1906, § 2519; Rev.Gen.St.1920, § 3874; Comp.Gen. Laws 1927, § 5781. Amended by Laws 1997, c. 97–102, § 934, eff. July 1, 1997.

725.04. Voluntary payment; pleading

When a suit is instituted by a party to a contract to recover a payment made pursuant to the contract and by the terms of the contract there was no enforceable obligation to make the payment or the making of the payment was excused, the defense of voluntary payment may not be interposed by the person receiving payment to defeat recovery of the payment.

Laws 1943, c. 21902, §§ 1, 2; Laws 1955, c. 29737, § 1; Fla.St.1965, § 52.24; Laws 1967, c. 67–254, § 41.

725.05. Satisfaction for less than amount due

When the amount of any debt or obligation is liquidated, the parties may satisfy the debt by a written instrument other than by endorsement on a check for less than the full amount due.

Laws 1971, c. 71–94, § 1.

725.06. Construction contracts; limitation on indemnification

(1) Any portion of any agreement or contract for or in connection with, or any guarantee of or in connection with, any construction, alteration, repair, or demolition of a building, structure, appurtenance, or appliance, including moving and excavating associated therewith, between an owner of real property and an architect, engineer, general contractor, subcontractor, sub-subcontractor, or materialman or any combination thereof wherein any party referred to herein promises to indemnify or hold harmless the other party to the agreement, contract, or guarantee for liability for damages to persons or property caused in whole or in part by any act, omission, or default of the indemnitee arising from the contract or its performance, shall be void and unenforceable unless the contract contains a monetary limitation on the extent of the indemnification that bears a reasonable commercial relationship to the contract and is part of the project specifications or bid documents, if any. Notwithstanding the foregoing, the monetary limitation on the extent of the indemnification provided to the owner of real property by any party in privity of contract with such owner shall not be less than $1 million per occurrence, unless otherwise agreed by the parties. Indemnification provisions in any such agreements, contracts, or guarantees may not require that the indemnitor indemnify the indemnitee for damages to persons or property caused in whole or in part by any act, omission, or default of a party other than:

(a) The indemnitor;

(b) Any of the indemnitor's contractors, subcontractors, sub-subcontractors, materialmen, or agents of any tier or their respective employees; or

(c) The indemnitee or its officers, directors, agents, or employees. However, such indemnification shall not include claims of, or damages resulting from, gross negligence, or willful, wanton or intentional misconduct of the indemnitee or its officers, directors, agents or employees, or for statutory violation or punitive damages except and to the extent the statutory violation or punitive damages are caused by or result from the acts or omissions of the indemnitor or any of the indemnitor's contractors, subcontractors, sub-subcontractors, material-men, or agents of any tier or their respective employees.

(2) A construction contract for a public agency or in connection with a public agency's project may require a party to that contract to indemnify and hold harmless the other party to the contract, their officers and employees, from liabilities, damages, losses and costs, including, but not limited to, reasonable attorney's fees, to the extent caused by the negligence, recklessness, or intentional wrongful misconduct of the indemnifying party and persons employed or utilized by the indemnifying party in the performance of the construction contract.

(3) Except as specifically provided in subsection (2), a construction contract for a public agency or in connection with a public agency's project may not require one party to indemnify, defend, or hold harmless the other party, its employees, officers, directors, or agents from any liability, damage, loss, claim, action, or proceeding, and any such contract provision is void as against public policy of this state.

(4) This section does not affect any contracts, agreements, or guarantees entered into before the effective date of this section or any renewals thereof.

Laws 1972, c. 72–52, § 1; Fla.St.1972 Supp., § 768.085. Amended by Laws 1997, c. 97–102, § 935, eff. July 1, 1997; Laws 2000, c. 2000–372, § 31, eff. July 1, 2000; Laws 2001, c. 2001–211, § 10, eff. July 1, 2001.

725.07. Discrimination on basis of sex, marital status, or race forbidden

(1) No person, as defined in s. 1.01(3) shall discriminate against any person based on sex, marital status, or race in the areas of loaning money, granting credit, or providing equal pay for equal services performed.

(2) Any violation of this section may be brought in the courts of this state by the individual upon whom the discrimination has been perpetrated in a civil action, and said individual shall be entitled to collect, not only compensatory damages, but, in addition thereto, punitive damages and reasonable attorney fees for a violation of this section.

Laws 1973, c. 73–251, §§ 1, 2.

Cross References

Applicability of this section to employers subject to federal Fair Labor Standards Act, see § 448.07.
Civil Rights Act, see § 760.01 et seq.
Trade practices, discrimination, see § 542.34.
Wage rate discrimination on account of sex, see § 448.07.

725.08. Design professional contracts; limitation in indemnification

(1) Notwithstanding the provisions of s. 725.06, if a design professional provides professional services to or for a public agency, the agency may require in a professional services contract with the design professional that the design professional indemnify and hold harmless the agency, and its officers and employees, from liabilities, damages, losses, and costs, including, but not limited to, reasonable attorneys' fees, to the extent caused by the negligence, reckless-ness, or intentionally wrongful conduct of the design professional and other persons employed or utilized by the design professional in the performance of the contract.

(2) Except as specifically provided in subsection (1), a professional services contract entered into with a public agency may not require that the design professional defend, indemnify, or hold harmless the agency, its employees, officers, directors, or agents from any liability, damage,

loss, claim, action, or proceeding, and any such contract provision shall be void as against the public policy of this state.

(3) "Professional services contract" means a written or oral agreement relating to the planning, design, construction, administration, study, evaluation, consulting, or other professional and technical support services furnished in connection with any actual or proposed construction, improvement, alteration, repair, maintenance, operation, management, relocation, demolition, excavation, or other facility, land, air, water, or utility development or improvement.

(4) "Design professional" means an individual or entity licensed by the state who holds a current certificate of registration under chapter 481 to practice architecture or landscape architecture, under chapter 472 to practice land surveying and mapping, or under chapter 471 to practice engineering, and who enters into a professional services contract.

(5) This section does not affect contracts or agreements entered into before the effective date of this section.

Added by Laws 2000, c. 2000–162, § 1, eff. May 25, 2000. Amended by Laws 2001, c. 2001–211, § 11, eff. July 1, 2001.

TITLE XLII

ESTATES AND TRUSTS

CHAPTER 731

PROBATE CODE: GENERAL PROVISIONS

PART I. SHORT TITLE; CONSTRUCTION

Enactment

Laws 1974, c. 74–106, § 3, repealed the sections contained in Fla.St.1973, Chapter 731, Florida Probate Law, First Part, and, by Section 1 of that law, created the Florida Probate Code contained in Fla.St.1974, Supp. Chapters 731 to 735, effective July 1, 1975. Laws 1975, c. 75–220, substantially amended provisions of the Probate Code enacted by Laws 1974, c. 74–106, and, by operation of § 113 of the 1975 law, the probate code as enacted in 1974 and amended in 1975 became effective January 1, 1976.

UNIFORM PROBATE CODE

Table of Jurisdictions Wherein Act Has Been Adopted

For text of Uniform Act, and variation notes and annotation materials for adopting jurisdictions, see Uniform Laws Annotated, Master Edition, Volumes 8, Pt. I, 8, Pt. II, and 8, Pt. III.

Jurisdiction	Laws	Effective Date	Statutory Citation
Alaska [2]	1972, c. 78	1–1–1973	AS 13.06.005 to 13.36.390.

Jurisdiction	Laws	Effective Date	Statutory Citation
Arizona [2]	1973, c. 75	1–1–1974	A.R.S. §§ 14–1101 to 14–7308.
Colorado [2]	1973, H.B. 1039	7–1–1974	West's C.R.S.A. §§ 15–10–101 to 15–17–103.
Florida [1]	1974, c. 74–106	7–1–1975	West's F.S.A. §§ 655.82, 711.50 to 711.512, 731.005 to 735.302.
Hawaii [5]	1976, c. 200	7–1–1976	HRS §§ 539–1 to 539–12; 560:1–101 to 560:8–101.
Idaho [4]	1971, c. 111	7–1–1972	I.C. §§ 15–1–101 to 15–7–308.
Maine [4]	1979, c. 540	1–1–1981	18–A M.R.S.A. §§ 1–101 to 8–401.
Massachusetts	2008, c. 521	1–15–2009 *	M.G.L.A. c. 190B, §§ 1–101 to 7–503.
Michigan [4]	1998, P.A. 386	4–1–2000	M.C.L.A. §§700.1101 to 700.8102.
Minnesota [3]	1974, c. 442	8–1–1975	M.S.A. §§ 524.1–101 to 524.8–103.
Montana [2]	1974, c. 365	7–1–1975	MCA 72–1–101 to 72–6–311.
Nebraska [1]	1974, L.B. 354	1–1–1977	R.R.S.1943, §§ 30–2201 to 30–2902.
New Jersey [6]	2004, c. 132	8–31–2004 *	N.J.S.A. 3B:1–1 to 3B:30–12, 17:16I–1 to 17:16I–17.
New Mexico [2]	1975, c. 257	7–1–1976	NMSA 1978, §§ 45–1–101 to 45–7–522.
North Dakota [2]	1973, c. 257	7–1–1975	NDCC 30.1–01–01 to 30.1–35–01.
South Carolina [4]	1986, Act 539	7–1–1987	Code 1976, §§ 35–6–10 to 35–6–100; 62–1–100 to 62–7–604.
South Dakota [5]	SL 1994, c. 232	7–1–1995	SDCL 29A–1–101 to 29A–8–101.
Utah [5]	1975, c. 150	7–1–1977	U.C.A.1953, 75–1–101 to 75–8–101.
Virgin Islands	Act 7174, sec. 12(b), amended by Act 7150, sec. 2	1–1–2011	15 V.I.C. 1-101 to 10-203.

* Approval date.
[1] Adopted 1989 Revision of Article VI.
[2] Adopted 1990 Revision of Article II and 1989 Revision of Article VI.
[3] Adopted 1990 Revision of Article II.
[4] Adopted Part 3 of 1989 Revision of Article VI.
[5] Adopted 1990 Revision of Article II and Part 3 of 1989 Revision of Article VI.
[6] Adopted 1990 Revision of Article II and Parts 2 and 3 of 1989 Revision of Article VI.

PART I. SHORT TITLE; CONSTRUCTION

731.005. Short title

Chapters 731–735 shall be known and may be cited as the Florida Probate Code and referred to as the "code."

Laws 1974, c. 74–106, § 1; Laws 1975, c. 75–220, § 1. Amended by Laws 2001, c. 2001–226, § 4, eff. Jan. 1, 2002.

731.011. Determination of substantive rights; procedures

The code became effective on January 1, 1976. The substantive rights of all persons that vested prior to January 1, 1976, shall be determined as provided in former chapters 731–737 and 744–746. The procedures for the enforcement of vested substantive rights shall be as provided in the Florida Probate Rules.

Laws 1974, c. 74–106, § 4; Laws 1975, c. 75–220, §§ 2, 113. Amended by Laws 2001, c. 2001–226, § 5, eff. Jan. 1, 2002.

Cross References

Killer not entitled to receive property or other benefits by reason of victim's death, see § 732.802.
Scope and application of rules of probate and guardianship, see Probate Rule 5.010.

Vesting of devises, see § 732.514.

731.102. Construction against implied repeal

This code is intended as unified coverage of its subject matter. No part of it shall be impliedly repealed by subsequent legislation if that construction can reasonably be avoided.
Laws 1974, c. 74–106, § 1; Laws 1975, c. 75–220, § 2.

731.103. Evidence as to death or status

In proceedings under this code and under chapter 736, the following additional rules relating to determination of death and status are applicable:

(1) An authenticated copy of a death certificate issued by an official or agency of the place where the death purportedly occurred is prima facie proof of the fact, place, date, and time of death and the identity of the decedent.

(2) A copy of any record or report of a governmental agency, domestic or foreign, that a person is alive, missing, detained, or, from the facts related, presumed dead is prima facie evidence of the status and of the dates, circumstances, and places disclosed by the record or report.

(3) A person who is absent from the place of his or her last known domicile for a continuous period of 5 years and whose absence is not satisfactorily explained after diligent search and inquiry is presumed to be dead. The person's death is presumed to have occurred at the end of the period unless there is evidence establishing that death occurred earlier. Evidence showing that the absent person was exposed to a specific peril of death may be a sufficient basis for the court determining at any time after such exposure that he or she died less than 5 years after the date on which his or her absence commenced. A petition for this determination shall be filed in the county in Florida where the decedent maintained his or her domicile or in any county of this state if the decedent was not a resident of Florida at the time his or her absence commenced.

(4) This section does not preclude the establishment of death by direct or circumstantial evidence prior to expiration of the 5-year time period set forth in subsection (3).
Laws 1974, c. 74–106, § 1; Laws 1975, c. 75–220, § 2. Amended by Laws 1997, c. 97–102, § 946, eff. July 1, 1997; Laws 2003, c. 2003–154, § 1, eff. June 12, 2003; Laws 2006, c. 2006–217, § 27, eff. July 1, 2007.

Cross References

Burden of proof, will in contests, see § 733.107.
Estates of missing persons, see § 733.209.
Evidence as to death or status, see Probate Rule 5.170.
Evidence of death, see Probate Rule 5.171.
Filing evidence of death, see Probate Rule 5.205.

731.1035. Applicable rules of evidence

In proceedings under this code, the rules of evidence in civil actions are applicable unless specifically changed by the code.
Added by Laws 2006, c. 2006–217, § 28, eff. July 1, 2007.

731.104. Verification of documents

When verification of a document is required in this code or by rule, the document filed shall include an oath or affirmation as provided in the Florida Probate Rules. Any person who willfully includes a false statement in the document shall be guilty of perjury.
Laws 1974, c. 74–106, § 1; Laws 1975, c. 75–220, § 2. Amended by Laws 2001, c. 2001–226, § 6, eff. Jan. 1, 2002.

Cross References

Burden of proof, will contests, see § 733.107.
Execution of wills, see § 732.502.
Oaths and affirmations,
    Proof of wills, see § 733.201.
    Self-proof, see § 732.503.
Perjury, see § 837.011 et seq.
Verification of documents, see Probate Rule 5.020.

731.105. In rem proceeding

Probate proceedings are in rem proceedings.

Laws 1975, c. 75–220, § 3.

731.106. Assets of nondomiciliaries

(1) A debt in favor of a nondomiciliary, other than one evidenced by investment or commercial paper or other instrument, is located in the county where the debtor resides or, if the debtor is not an individual, at the place where the debtor has its principal office. Commercial paper, investment paper, and other instruments are located where the instrument is at the time of death.

(2) When a nonresident decedent, whether or not a citizen of the United States, provides by will that the testamentary disposition of tangible or intangible personal property having a situs within this state, or of real property in this state, shall be construed and regulated by the laws of this state, the validity and effect of the dispositions shall be determined by Florida law. The court may, and in the case of a decedent who was at the time of death a resident of a foreign country the court shall, direct the personal representative appointed in this state to make distribution directly to those designated by the decedent's will as beneficiaries of the tangible or intangible property or to the persons entitled to receive the decedent's personal estate under the laws of the decedent's domicile.

Laws 1975, c. 75–220, § 3; Laws 1977, c. 77–174, § 1. Amended by Laws 1997, c. 97–102, § 947, eff. July 1, 1997; Laws 2001, c. 2001–226, § 7, eff. Jan. 1, 2002.

Cross References

Ancillary administration, see § 734.102.
Venue of probate proceedings, nondomiciliaries, see § 733.101.

731.109. Seal of the court

For the purposes of this code, the seal of the clerk of the circuit court is the seal of the court.

Laws 1975, c. 75–220, § 3.

Cross References

Clerk's seal, see § 28.071.

731.110. Caveat; proceedings

(1) Any interested person who is apprehensive that an estate, either testate or intestate, will be administered or that a will may be admitted to probate without that person's knowledge may file a caveat with the court. The caveat of the interested person, other than a creditor, may be filed before or after the death of the person for whom the estate will be, or is being, administered. The caveat of a creditor may be filed only after the person's death.

(2) If the caveator is a nonresident and is not represented by an attorney admitted to practice in this state who has signed the caveat, the caveator must designate some person residing in the county in which the caveat is filed as the agent of the caveator, upon whom service may be made; however, if the caveator is represented by an attorney admitted to practice in this state who has signed the caveat, it is not necessary to designate a resident agent.

(3) If a caveat has been filed by an interested person other than a creditor, the court may not admit a will of the decedent to probate or appoint a personal representative until formal notice of the petition for administration has been served on the caveator or the caveator's designated agent and the caveator has had the opportunity to participate in proceedings on the petition, as provided by the Florida Probate Rules. This subsection does not require a caveator to be served with formal notice of its own petition for administration.

(4) A caveat filed before the death of the person for whom the estate will be administered expires 2 years after filing.

Laws 1975, c. 75–220, § 3; Laws 1977, c. 77–87, § 2; Laws 1985, c. 85–79, § 1; Laws 1992, c. 92–200, § 2. Amended by Laws 1997, c. 97–102, § 948, eff. July 1, 1997; Laws 2001, c. 2001–226, § 9, eff. Jan. 1, 2002; Laws 2007, c. 2007–74, § 2, eff. July 1, 2007; Laws 2010, c. 2010–132, § 3, eff. Oct. 1, 2010; Laws 2013, c. 2013–172, § 5, eff. Oct. 1, 2013.

Cross References

Caveat, proceeding, see Probate Rule 5.260.
Limitation on presentation of claims, see § 733.702.

731.155. Applicability

This act shall take effect January 1, 2002. The substantive rights of all persons that have vested prior to January 1, 2002, shall be determined as provided in former chapters 63, 215, 409, 660, and 731–737 as they existed prior to January 1, 2002. The procedures for the enforcement of substantive rights which have vested prior to January 1, 2002, shall be as provided in this act, except that any Family Administration filed before January 1, 2002, may be completed as a Family Administration.

Added by Laws 2001, c. 2001–226, § 195, eff. Jan. 1, 2002.

PART II. DEFINITIONS

731.201. General definitions

Subject to additional definitions in subsequent chapters that are applicable to specific chapters or parts, and unless the context otherwise requires, in this code, in s. 409.9101, and in chapters 736, 738, 739, and 744, the term:

(1) "Authenticated," when referring to copies of documents or judicial proceedings required to be filed with the court under this code, means a certified copy or a copy authenticated according to the Federal Rules of Civil Procedure.

(2) "Beneficiary" means heir at law in an intestate estate and devisee in a testate estate. The term "beneficiary" does not apply to an heir at law or a devisee after that person's interest in the estate has been satisfied. In the case of a devise to an existing trust or trustee, or to a trust or trustee described by will, the trustee is a beneficiary of the estate. Except as otherwise provided in this subsection, the beneficiary of the trust is not a beneficiary of the estate of which that trust or the trustee of that trust is a beneficiary. However, if each trustee is also a personal

representative of the estate, each qualified beneficiary of the trust as defined in s. 736.0103 shall be regarded as a beneficiary of the estate.

(3) "Child" includes a person entitled to take as a child under this code by intestate succession from the parent whose relationship is involved, and excludes any person who is only a stepchild, a foster child, a grandchild, or a more remote descendant.

(4) "Claim" means a liability of the decedent, whether arising in contract, tort, or otherwise, and funeral expense. The term does not include an expense of administration or estate, inheritance, succession, or other death taxes.

(5) "Clerk" means the clerk or deputy clerk of the court.

(6) "Collateral heir" means an heir who is related to the decedent through a common ancestor but who is not an ancestor or descendant of the decedent.

(7) "Court" means the circuit court.

(8) "Curator" means a person appointed by the court to take charge of the estate of a decedent until letters are issued.

(9) "Descendant" means a person in any generational level down the applicable individual's descending line and includes children, grandchildren, and more remote descendants. The term "descendant" is synonymous with the terms "lineal descendant" and "issue" but excludes collateral heirs.

(10) "Devise," when used as a noun, means a testamentary disposition of real or personal property and, when used as a verb, means to dispose of real or personal property by will or trust. The term includes "gift," "give," "bequeath," "bequest," and "legacy." A devise is subject to charges for debts, expenses, and taxes as provided in this code, the will, or the trust.

(11) "Devisee" means a person designated in a will or trust to receive a devise. Except as otherwise provided in this subsection, in the case of a devise to an existing trust or trustee, or to a trust or trustee of a trust described by will, the trust or trustee, rather than the beneficiaries of the trust, is the devisee. However, if each trustee is also a personal representative of the estate, each qualified beneficiary of the trust as defined in s. 736.0103 shall be regarded as a devisee.

(12) "Distributee" means a person who has received estate property from a personal representative or other fiduciary other than as a creditor or purchaser. A testamentary trustee is a distributee only to the extent of distributed assets or increments to them remaining in the trustee's hands. A beneficiary of a testamentary trust to whom the trustee has distributed property received from a personal representative is a distributee. For purposes of this provision, "testamentary trustee" includes a trustee to whom assets are transferred by will, to the extent of the devised assets.

(13) "Domicile" means a person's usual place of dwelling and shall be synonymous with residence.

(14) "Estate" means the property of a decedent that is the subject of administration.

(15) "Exempt property" means the property of a decedent's estate which is described in s. 732.402.

(16) "File" means to file with the court or clerk.

(17) "Foreign personal representative" means a personal representative of another state or a foreign country.

(18) "Formal notice" means a form of notice that is described in and served by a method of service provided under rule 5.040(a) of the Florida Probate Rules.

---

(19) "Grantor" means one who creates or adds to a trust and includes "settlor" or "trustor" and a testator who creates or adds to a trust.

(20) "Heirs" or "heirs at law" means those persons, including the surviving spouse, who are entitled under the statutes of intestate succession to the property of a decedent.

(21) "Incapacitated" means a judicial determination that a person lacks the capacity to manage at least some of the person's property or to meet at least some of the person's essential health and safety requirements. A minor shall be treated as being incapacitated.

(22) "Informal notice" or "notice" means a method of service for pleadings or papers as provided under rule 5.040(b) of the Florida Probate Rules.

(23) "Interested person" means any person who may reasonably be expected to be affected by the outcome of the particular proceeding involved. In any proceeding affecting the estate or the rights of a beneficiary in the estate, the personal representative of the estate shall be deemed to be an interested person. In any proceeding affecting the expenses of the administration and obligations of a decedent's estate, or any claims described in s. 733.702(1), the trustee of a trust described in s. 733.707(3) is an interested person in the administration of the grantor's estate. The term does not include a beneficiary who has received complete distribution. The meaning, as it relates to particular persons, may vary from time to time and must be determined according to the particular purpose of, and matter involved in, any proceedings.

(24) "Letters" means authority granted by the court to the personal representative to act on behalf of the estate of the decedent and refers to what has been known as letters testamentary and letters of administration. All letters shall be designated "letters of administration."

(25) "Minor" means a person under 18 years of age whose disabilities have not been removed by marriage or otherwise.

(26) "Other state" means any state of the United States other than Florida and includes the District of Columbia, the Commonwealth of Puerto Rico, and any territory or possession subject to the legislative authority of the United States.

(27) "Parent" excludes any person who is only a stepparent, foster parent, or grandparent.

(28) "Personal representative" means the fiduciary appointed by the court to administer the estate and refers to what has been known as an administrator, administrator cum testamento annexo, administrator de bonis non, ancillary administrator, ancillary executor, or executor.

(29) "Petition" means a written request to the court for an order.

(30) "Power of appointment" means an authority, other than as an incident of the beneficial ownership of property, to designate recipients of beneficial interests in property.

(31) "Probate of will" means all steps necessary to establish the validity of a will and to admit a will to probate.

(32) "Property" means both real and personal property or any interest in it and anything that may be the subject of ownership.

(33) "Protected homestead" means the property described in s. 4(a)(1), Art. X of the State Constitution on which at the death of the owner the exemption inures to the owner's surviving spouse or heirs under s. 4(b), Art. X of the State Constitution. For purposes of the code, real property owned in tenancy by the entireties or in joint tenancy with rights of survivorship is not protected homestead.

(34) "Residence" means a person's place of dwelling.

(35) "Residuary devise" means a devise of the assets of the estate which remain after the provision for any devise which is to be satisfied by reference to a specific property or type of property, fund, sum, or statutory amount. If the will contains no devise which is to be satisfied by reference to a specific property or type of property, fund, sum, or statutory amount, "residuary devise" or "residue" means a devise of all assets remaining after satisfying the obligations of the estate.

(36) "Security" means a security as defined in s. 517.021.

(37) "Security interest" means a security interest as defined in s. 671.201.

(38) "Trust" means an express trust, private or charitable, with additions to it, wherever and however created. It also includes a trust created or determined by a judgment or decree under which the trust is to be administered in the manner of an express trust. "Trust" excludes other constructive trusts, and it excludes resulting trusts; conservatorships; custodial arrangements pursuant to the Florida Uniform Transfers to Minors Act;[1] business trusts providing for certificates to be issued to beneficiaries; common trust funds; land trusts under s. 689.071, except to the extent provided in s. 689.071(7); trusts created by the form of the account or by the deposit agreement at a financial institution; voting trusts; security arrangements; liquidation trusts; trusts for the primary purpose of paying debts, dividends, interest, salaries, wages, profits, pensions, or employee benefits of any kind; and any arrangement under which a person is nominee or escrowee for another.

(39) "Trustee" includes an original, additional, surviving, or successor trustee, whether or not appointed or confirmed by court.

(40) "Will" means an instrument, including a codicil, executed by a person in the manner prescribed by this code, which disposes of the person's property on or after his or her death and includes an instrument which merely appoints a personal representative or revokes or revises another will.

Laws 1974, c. 74–106, § 1; Laws 1975, c. 75–220, § 4; Laws 1977, c. 77–174, § 1; Laws 1985, c. 85–79, § 2; Laws 1987, c. 87–226, § 66; Laws 1988, c. 88–340, § 1; Laws 1993, c. 93–257, § 7. Amended by Laws 1995, c. 95–401, § 6, eff. July 1, 1995; Laws 1997, c. 97–102, § 949, eff. July 1, 1997; Laws 1998, c. 98–421, § 52, eff. July 1, 1998; Laws 2001, c. 2001–226, § 11, eff. Jan. 1, 2002; Laws 2002, c. 2002–1, § 106, eff. May 21, 2002; Laws 2003, c. 2003–154, § 2, eff. June 12, 2003; Laws 2005, c. 2005–108, § 2, eff. July 1, 2005; Laws 2006, c. 2006–217, § 29, eff. July 1, 2007; Laws 2007, c. 2007–74, § 3, eff. July 1, 2007; Laws 2007, c. 2007–153, § 8, eff. July 1, 2007; Laws 2009, c. 2009–115, § 1, eff. July 1, 2009; Laws 2010, c. 2010–132, § 4, eff. Oct. 1, 2010; Laws 2012, c. 2012–109, § 1, eff. July 1, 2012; Laws 2013, c. 2013–172, § 16, eff. Oct. 1, 2013.

[1] See § 710.101 et seq.

Applicability

The introductory language to § 1 of Laws 2012, c. 2012–109, provides:

"Effective July 1, 2012, and applicable to proceedings pending before or commenced on or after July 1, 2012, subsection (33) of section 731.201, Florida Statutes, is amended to read:"

Cross References

Anatomical gifts, see § 765.510 et seq.
Definitions, see Probate Rule 5.015.
Fiduciary lawyer-client privilege, see F.S.A. § 90.5021.
Homestead property, inter vivos transfers, see F.S.A. § 732.4017.
Investment of fiduciary funds in investment instruments, permissible activity under certain circumstances, see § 660.417.

Notice as meaning informal notice, see Probate Rule 5.040.

PART III. NOTICE AND REPRESENTATION

731.301. Notice

(1) If notice to an interested person of a petition or other proceeding is required, the notice shall be given to the interested person or that person's attorney as provided in the code or the Florida Probate Rules.

(2) In a probate proceeding, formal notice is sufficient to acquire jurisdiction over the person receiving formal notice to the extent of the person's interest in the estate or in the decedent's protected homestead.

(3) Persons given proper notice of a proceeding are bound by all orders entered in that proceeding.

Laws 1974, c. 74–106, § 1; Laws 1975, c. 75–220, § 5; Laws 1977, c. 77–87, § 3; Laws 1977, c. 77–174, § 1; Laws 1993, c. 93–257, § 1. Amended by Laws 1995, c. 95–211, § 64, eff. July 10, 1995; Laws 1997, c. 97–102, § 950, eff. July 1, 1997; Laws 2001, c. 2001–226, § 12, eff. Jan. 1, 2002; Laws 2010, c. 2010–132, § 5, eff. Oct. 1, 2010.

Cross References

Bonds, waiver, see § 733.403.
Claims against estate, notice, see § 733.701.
Constructive service of process,
　　Generally, see § 49.011 et seq.
　　Mailing notice of action, see § 49.12.
　　Publication, see § 49.011.
Notice, method and time, proof, see Probate Rule 5.040.
Process generally, see Civil Procedure Rule 1.070.
Proof, notice of action, see §§ 49.10, 49.11.
Recordation of probate records, see § 28.223.
Registered mail as including certified mail with return receipt requested, see § 1.01.
Request for notice and copies of pleadings, see Probate Rule 5.060.
Rights under will, waiver, see § 732.702.
Service of pleadings and papers, see Civil Procedure Rule 1.080.
Service of pleadings and papers in probate proceedings, see Probate Rule 5.041.
Waiver and consent, notice, see Probate Rule 5.180.

731.302. Waiver and consent by interested person

Subsequent to the filing of a petition for administration, an interested person, including a guardian ad litem, administrator ad litem, guardian of the property, personal representative, trustee, or other fiduciary, or a sole holder or all coholders of a power of revocation or a power of appointment, may waive, to the extent of that person's interest or the interest which that person represents, subject to the provisions of ss. 731.303 and 733.604, any right or notice or the filing of any document, exhibit, or schedule required to be filed and may consent to any action or proceeding which may be required or permitted by this code.

Laws 1974, c. 74–106, § 1; Laws 1975, c. 75–220, § 6; Laws 1977, c. 77–87, § 4; Laws 1979, c. 79–400, § 267; Laws 1984, c. 84–106, § 3. Amended by Laws 2003, c. 2003–154, § 25, eff. June 12, 2003.

Cross References

Notice, see Probate Rule 5.040.
Waiver and consent, notice, see Fla. Prob. R. Rule 5.040, 5.180.

Waiver of right to elect and other rights, see § 732.702.

731.303. Representation

In the administration of or in judicial proceedings involving estates of decedents, the following apply:

(1) Persons are bound by orders binding others in the following cases:

(a) 1. Orders binding the sole holder or all coholders of a power of revocation or a general, special, or limited power of appointment, including one in the form of a power of amendment or revocation to the extent that the power has not become unexercisable in fact, bind all persons to the extent that their interests, as persons who may take by virtue of the exercise or nonexercise of the power, are subject to the power.

2. Subparagraph 1. does not apply to:

a. Any matter determined by the court to involve fraud or bad faith by the trustee;

b. A power of a trustee to distribute trust property; or

c. A power of appointment held by a person while the person is the sole trustee.

(b) To the extent there is no conflict of interest between them or among the persons represented:

1. Orders binding a guardian of the property bind the ward.

2. Orders binding a trustee bind beneficiaries of the trust in proceedings to probate a will, in establishing or adding to a trust, in reviewing the acts or accounts of a prior fiduciary, and in proceedings involving creditors or other third parties. However, for purposes of this section, a conflict of interest shall be deemed to exist when each trustee of a trust that is a beneficiary of the estate is also a personal representative of the estate.

3. Orders binding a personal representative bind persons interested in the undistributed assets of a decedent's estate, in actions or proceedings by or against the estate.

(c) An unborn or unascertained person, or a minor or any other person under a legal disability, who is not otherwise represented is bound by an order to the extent that person's interest is represented by another party having the same or greater quality of interest in the proceeding.

(2) Orders binding a guardian of the person shall not bind the ward.

(3) In proceedings involving the administration of estates, notice is required as follows:

(a) Notice as prescribed by law shall be given to every interested person, or to one who can bind the interested person as described in paragraph (1)(a) or paragraph (1)(b). Notice may be given both to the interested person and to another who can bind him or her.

(b) Notice is given to unborn or unascertained persons who are not represented pursuant to paragraph (1)(a) or paragraph (1)(b) by giving notice to all known persons whose interests in the proceedings are the same as, or of a greater quality than, those of the unborn or unascertained persons.

(4) If the court determines that representation of the interest would otherwise be inadequate, the court may, at any time, appoint a guardian ad litem to represent the interests of an incapacitated person, an unborn or unascertained person, a minor or any other person otherwise under a legal disability, or a person whose identity or address is unknown. If not

precluded by conflict of interest, a guardian ad litem may be appointed to represent several persons or interests.

(5) The holder of a power of appointment over property not held in trust may represent and bind persons whose interests, as permissible appointees, takers in default, or otherwise, are subject to the power. Representation under this subsection does not apply to:

(a) Any matter determined by the court to involve fraud or bad faith by the trustee;

(b) A power of a trustee to distribute trust property; or

(c) A power of appointment held by a person while the person is the sole trustee.

Laws 1974, c. 74–106, § 1; Laws 1975, c. 75–220, § 7; Laws 1977, c. 77–87, § 5; Laws 1977, c. 77–174, § 1; Laws 1988, c. 88–217, § 1; Laws 1992, c. 92–200, § 3. Amended by Laws 1997, c. 97–102, § 951, eff. July 1, 1997; Laws 2001, c. 2001–226, § 13, eff. Jan. 1, 2002; Laws 2002, c. 2002–82, § 3, eff. April 23, 2002; Laws 2003, c. 2003–154, § 3, eff. June 12, 2003; Laws 2006, c. 2006–217, § 30, eff. July 1, 2007; Laws 2007, c. 2007–153, § 9, eff. July 1, 2007.

Cross References

Conflict of interest, personal representatives, see § 733.610.
Estoppel, improper distribution of estate, see § 733.812.
Formal notice defined, see § 731.201.
Guardian ad litem, appointment, see Probate Rule 5.120.
Waiver and consent, notice, see Fla. Prob. R. Rule 5.040, 5.180.

731.401. Arbitration of disputes

(1) A provision in a will or trust requiring the arbitration of disputes, other than disputes of the validity of all or a part of a will or trust, between or among the beneficiaries and a fiduciary under the will or trust, or any combination of such persons or entities, is enforceable.

(2) Unless otherwise specified in the will or trust, a will or trust provision requiring arbitration shall be presumed to require binding arbitration under chapter 682, the Revised Florida Arbitration Code. If an arbitration enforceable under this section is governed under chapter 682, the arbitration provision in the will or trust shall be treated as an agreement for the purposes of applying chapter 682.

Added by Laws 2007, c. 2007–74, § 4, eff. July 1, 2007. Amended by Laws 2013, c. 2013–232, § 37, eff. July 1, 2013.

CHAPTER 732

PROBATE CODE: INTESTATE SUCCESSION AND WILLS

PART I. INTESTATE SUCCESSION

INTESTATE SUCCESSION & WILLS

Enactment

Laws 1974, c. 74–106, § 3, repealed the sections contained in Fla.St.1973, Chapter 732, Florida Probate Law, Second Part, and, by Section 1 of that law, created the Florida Probate Code contained in Fla.St.1974, Supp. Chapters 731 to 735, effective July 1, 1975. Laws 1975, c. 75–220, substantially amended provisions of the Probate Code enacted by Laws 1974, c. 74–106; and, by operation of § 113 of the 1975 law, the probate code as enacted in 1974 and amended in 1975 became effective January 1, 1976.

Cross References

Inventories and accountings, public records exemptions, see § 733.604.

PART I.   INTESTATE SUCCESSION

732.101.   Intestate estate

(1) Any part of the estate of a decedent not effectively disposed of by will passes to the decedent's heirs as prescribed in the following sections of this code.

(2) The decedent's death is the event that vests the heirs' right to the decedent's intestate property.

Laws 1974, c. 74–106, § 1; Laws 1975, c. 75–220, § 8. Amended by Laws 2001, c. 2001–226, § 14, eff. Jan. 1, 2002.

Cross References

Killer not entitled to receive property or other benefits by reason of victim's death, see § 732.802.

732.102.   Spouse's share of intestate estate

The intestate share of the surviving spouse is:

(1) If there is no surviving descendant of the decedent, the entire intestate estate.

(2) If the decedent is survived by one or more descendants, all of whom are also descendants of the surviving spouse, and the surviving spouse has no other descendant, the entire intestate estate.

(3) If there are one or more surviving descendants of the decedent who are not lineal descendants of the surviving spouse, one-half of the intestate estate.

(4) If there are one or more surviving descendants of the decedent, all of whom are also descendants of the surviving spouse, and the surviving spouse has one or more descendants who are not descendants of the decedent, one-half of the intestate estate.

Laws 1974, c. 74–106, § 1; Laws 1975, c. 75–220, § 8. Amended by Laws 2001, c. 2001–226, § 15, eff. Jan. 1, 2002; Laws 2007, c. 2007–74, § 5, eff. July 1, 2007; Laws 2011, c. 2011–183, § 2, eff. Oct. 1, 2011.

Retroactivity

Laws 2012, c. 2012–109, § 2, provides:

"Notwithstanding section 2 or section 14 of chapter 2011–183, Laws of Florida, the amendments to section 732.102, Florida Statutes, made by section 2 of that act apply only to the estates of decedents dying on or after October 1, 2011."

Cross References

Elective share of spouse, see § 732.201.

732.103.   Share of other heirs

The part of the intestate estate not passing to the surviving spouse under s. 732.102, or the entire intestate estate if there is no surviving spouse, descends as follows:

(1) To the descendants of the decedent.

(2) If there is no descendant, to the decedent's father and mother equally, or to the survivor of them.

---

(3) If there is none of the foregoing, to the decedent's brothers and sisters and the descendants of deceased brothers and sisters.

(4) If there is none of the foregoing, the estate shall be divided, one-half of which shall go to the decedent's paternal, and the other half to the decedent's maternal, kindred in the following order:

(a) To the grandfather and grandmother equally, or to the survivor of them.

(b) If there is no grandfather or grandmother, to uncles and aunts and descendants of deceased uncles and aunts of the decedent.

(c) If there is either no paternal kindred or no maternal kindred, the estate shall go to the other kindred who survive, in the order stated above.

(5) If there is no kindred of either part, the whole of the property shall go to the kindred of the last deceased spouse of the decedent as if the deceased spouse had survived the decedent and then died intestate entitled to the estate.

(6) If none of the foregoing, and if any of the descendants of the decedent's great-grandparents were Holocaust victims as defined in s. 626.9543(3)(a), including such victims in countries cooperating with the discriminatory policies of Nazi Germany, then to the descendants of the great-grandparents. The court shall allow any such descendant to meet a reasonable, not unduly restrictive, standard of proof to substantiate his or her lineage. This subsection only applies to escheated property and shall cease to be effective for proceedings filed after December 31, 2004.

Laws 1974, c. 74–106, § 1; Laws 1975, c. 75–220, § 8; Laws 1977, c. 77–174, § 1. Amended by Laws 2001, c. 2001–226, § 16, eff. Jan. 1, 2002; Laws 2004, c. 2004–390, § 145, eff. July 1, 2004; Laws 2006, c. 2006–1, § 102, eff. July 4, 2006; Laws 2007, c. 2007–74, § 6, eff. July 1, 2007.

Cross References

Legacies and distributive shares,
  Distribution, see § 733.811.
  Proceedings for payment, see § 733.802.
  Time for delivery, see § 733.801.
Married man conveying property as single where separated 30 years or more, quieting title as against heirs, see
  § 65.071.
Power of attorney, agents, reimbursement and compensation, see F.S.A. § 709.2112.

732.104. Inheritance per stirpes

Descent shall be per stirpes, whether to descendants or to collateral heirs.

Laws 1974, c. 74–106, § 1; Laws 1975, c. 75–220, § 9. Amended by Laws 2007, c. 2007–74, § 7, eff. July 1, 2007.

Cross References

Devises to be per stirpes, see § 732.611.

732.105. Half blood

When property descends to the collateral kindred of the intestate and part of the collateral kindred are of the whole blood to the intestate and the other part of the half blood, those of the half blood shall inherit only half as much as those of the whole blood; but if all are of the half blood they shall have whole parts.

Laws 1974, c. 74–106, § 1; Laws 1975, c. 75–220, § 10.

732.106. Afterborn heirs

Heirs of the decedent conceived before his or her death, but born thereafter, inherit intestate property as if they had been born in the decedent's lifetime.

Laws 1974, c. 74–106, § 1; Laws 1975, c. 75–220, § 10; Laws 1977, c. 77–87, § 6. Amended by Laws 1997, c. 97–102, § 952, eff. July 1, 1997.

Cross References

Persons bound by orders binding others, see § 731.303.

732.107. Escheat

(1) When a person dies leaving an estate without being survived by any person entitled to a part of it, that part shall escheat to the state.

(2) Property that escheats shall be sold as provided in the Florida Probate Rules and the proceeds paid to the Chief Financial Officer of the state and deposited in the State School Fund.

(3) At any time within 10 years after the payment to the Chief Financial Officer, a person claiming to be entitled to the proceeds may reopen the administration to assert entitlement to the proceeds. If no claim is timely asserted, the state's rights to the proceeds shall become absolute.

(4) The Department of Legal Affairs shall represent the state in all proceedings concerning escheated estates.

(5)(a) If a person entitled to the proceeds assigns the rights to receive payment to an attorney, Florida-certified public accountant, or private investigative agency which is duly licensed to do business in this state pursuant to a written agreement with that person, the Department of Financial Services is authorized to make distribution in accordance with the assignment.

(b) Payments made to an attorney, Florida-certified public accountant, or private investigative agency shall be promptly deposited into a trust or escrow account which is regularly maintained by the attorney, Florida-certified public accountant, or private investigative agency in a financial institution authorized to accept such deposits and located in this state.

(c) Distribution by the attorney, Florida-certified public accountant, or private investigative agency to the person entitled to the proceeds shall be made within 10 days following final credit of the deposit into the trust or escrow account at the financial institution, unless a party to the agreement protests the distribution in writing before it is made.

(d) The department shall not be civilly or criminally liable for any proceeds distributed pursuant to this subsection, provided such distribution is made in good faith.

Laws 1974, c. 74–106, § 1; Laws 1975, c. 75–220, § 10; Laws 1989, c. 89–291, § 4; Laws 1989, c. 89–299, § 9. Amended by Laws 1997, c. 97–102, § 953, eff. July 1, 1997; Laws 2001, c. 2001–36, § 32, eff. Oct. 1, 2001; Laws 2001, c. 2001–226, § 17, eff. Jan. 1, 2002; Laws 2003, c. 2003–261, § 1896, eff. June 26, 2003.

Cross References

Computation of time, limitation of actions, see § 95.031.
Death of person served by publication, limitation of actions, see § 95.111.
Determination of beneficiaries, see § 733.105.
Disposition of unclaimed property, see § 717.001 et seq.
Escheat, see Probate Rule 5.386.
Escheats, see § 716.01 et seq.
Recovery of escheated property by claimant, see § 716.07.
Tolling of limitations period, see § 95.051.

732.108. Adopted persons and persons born out of wedlock

(1) For the purpose of intestate succession by or from an adopted person, the adopted person is a descendant of the adopting parent and is one of the natural kindred of all members of the adopting parent's family, and is not a descendant of his or her natural parents, nor is he or she one of the kindred of any member of the natural parent's family or any prior adoptive parent's family, except that:

(a) Adoption of a child by the spouse of a natural parent has no effect on the relationship between the child and the natural parent or the natural parent's family.

(b) Adoption of a child by a natural parent's spouse who married the natural parent after the death of the other natural parent has no effect on the relationship between the child and the family of the deceased natural parent.

(c) Adoption of a child by a close relative, as defined in s. 63.172(2), has no effect on the relationship between the child and the families of the deceased natural parents.

(2) For the purpose of intestate succession in cases not covered by subsection (1), a person born out of wedlock is a descendant of his or her mother and is one of the natural kindred of all members of the mother's family. The person is also a descendant of his or her father and is one of the natural kindred of all members of the father's family, if:

(a) The natural parents participated in a marriage ceremony before or after the birth of the person born out of wedlock, even though the attempted marriage is void.

(b) The paternity of the father is established by an adjudication before or after the death of the father. Chapter 95 shall not apply in determining heirs in a probate proceeding under this paragraph.

(c) The paternity of the father is acknowledged in writing by the father.

Laws 1974, c. 74–106, § 1; Laws 1975, c. 75–220, § 11; Laws 1977, c. 77–87, § 7; Laws 1977, c. 77–174, § 1; Laws 1987, c. 87–27, § 2. Amended by Laws 1997, c. 97–102, § 954, eff. July 1, 1997; Laws 2007, c. 2007–74, § 8, eff. July 1, 2007; Laws 2009, c. 2009–115, § 2, eff. July 1, 2009.

Cross References

Adoption, see § 63.012 et seq.
Adoption judgment, effect on inheritance, see § 63.172.
Class gifts, adopted and illegitimate children, see § 732.608.
Marriage of parents, illegitimate children, see § 742.091.
Paternity, see § 742.011 et seq.
Special or local law legitimizing children, see Const. Art. 3, § 11.
Void marriages, see §§ 741.21, 741.211.

732.1081. Termination of parental rights

For the purpose of intestate succession by a natural or adoptive parent, a natural or adoptive parent is barred from inheriting from or through a child if the natural or adoptive parent's parental rights were terminated pursuant to chapter 39 prior to the death of the child, and the natural or adoptive parent shall be treated as if the parent predeceased the child.

Added by Laws 2012, c. 2012–109, § 4, eff. July 1, 2012.

732.109. Debts to decedent

A debt owed to the decedent shall not be charged against the intestate share of any person except the debtor. If the debtor does not survive the decedent, the debt shall not be taken into account in computing the intestate share of the debtor's heirs.

Laws 1974, c. 74–106, § 1; Laws 1975, c. 75–220, § 11.

732.1101. Aliens

Aliens shall have the same rights of inheritance as citizens.

Laws 1974, c. 74–106, § 1; Laws 1975, c. 75–220, § 12. Amended by Laws 1997, c. 97–102, § 955, eff. July 1, 1997; Laws 2001, c. 2001–226, § 18, eff. Jan. 1, 2002.

Cross References

Disposition of unclaimed property, see § 717.001 et seq.
Rights of inheritance by aliens, regulation by law permitted, see Const. Art. 1, § 2.

732.111. Dower and curtesy abolished

Dower and curtesy are abolished.

Laws 1974, c. 74–106, § 1; Laws 1975, c. 75–220, § 12.

PART II. ELECTIVE SHARE OF SURVIVING SPOUSE; RIGHTS IN COMMUNITY PROPERTY

Cross References

Pension money and certain tax-exempt funds or accounts from legal process, exemption, see § 222.21.

732.201. Right to elective share

The surviving spouse of a person who dies domiciled in Florida has the right to a share of the elective estate of the decedent as provided in this part, to be designated the elective share.

Laws 1974, c, 74–106, § 1; Laws 1975, c. 75–220, § 13. Amended by Laws 1999, c. 99–343, § 1, eff. Oct. 1, 1999.

Cross References

Duty to pay elective share, see Probate Rule 5.360.
Intestate share of spouse, see § 732.102.
Killer not entitled to receive property or other benefits by reason of victim's death, see § 732.802.

732.2025. Definitions

As used in ss. 732.2025–732.2155, the term:

(1) "Direct recipient" means the decedent's probate estate and any other person who receives property included in the elective estate by transfer from the decedent, including transfers described in s. 732.2035(8), by right of survivorship, or by beneficiary designation under a governing instrument. For this purpose, a beneficiary of an insurance policy on the decedent's life, the net cash surrender value of which is included in the elective estate, is treated as having received property included in the elective estate. In the case of property held in trust, "direct recipient" includes the trustee but excludes the beneficiaries of the trust.

(2) "Elective share trust" means a trust under which:

(a) The surviving spouse is entitled for life to the use of the property or to all of the income payable at least as often as annually;

(b) The surviving spouse has the right under the terms of the trust or state law to require the trustee either to make the property productive or to convert it within a reasonable time; and

(c) During the spouse's life, no person other than the spouse has the power to distribute income or principal to anyone other than the spouse.

As used in this subsection, the term "income" has the same meaning as that provided in s. 643(b) of the Internal Revenue Code,[1] as amended, and regulations adopted under that section.

(3) "General power of appointment" means a power of appointment under which the holder of the power, whether or not the holder has the capacity to exercise it, has the power to create a present or future interest in the holder, the holder's estate, or the creditors of either. The term includes a power to consume or invade the principal of a trust, but only if the power is not limited by an ascertainable standard relating to the holder's health, education, support, or maintenance.

(4) "Governing instrument" means a deed; will; trust; insurance or annuity policy; account with payable-on-death designation; security registered in beneficiary form (TOD); pension, profit-sharing, retirement, or similar benefit plan; an instrument creating or exercising a power of appointment or a power of attorney; or a dispositive, appointive, or nominative instrument of any similar type.

(5) "Payor" means an insurer, business entity, employer, government, governmental agency or subdivision, or any other person, other than the decedent's personal representative or a trustee of a trust created by the decedent, authorized or obligated by law or a governing instrument to make payments.

(6) "Person" includes an individual, trust, estate, partnership, association, company, or corporation.

(7) "Probate estate" means all property wherever located that is subject to estate administration in any state of the United States or in the District of Columbia.

(8) "Qualifying special needs trust" or "supplemental needs trust" means a trust established for an ill or disabled surviving spouse with court approval before or after a decedent's death, if, commencing on the decedent's death:

(a) The income and principal are distributable to or for the benefit of the spouse for life in the discretion of one or more trustees less than half of whom are ineligible family trustees. For purposes of this paragraph, ineligible family trustees include the decedent's grandparents and any descendants of the decedent's grandparents who are not also descendants of the surviving spouse; and

(b) During the spouse's life, no person other than the spouse has the power to distribute income or principal to anyone other than the spouse.

The requirement for court approval shall not apply if the aggregate value of all property in all qualifying special needs trusts for the spouse is less than $100,000. For purposes of this subsection, value is determined on the "applicable valuation date" as defined in s. 732.2095(1)(a).

(9) "Revocable trust" means a trust that is includable in the elective estate under s. 732.2035(4).

(10) "Transfer in satisfaction of the elective share" means an irrevocable transfer by the decedent during life to an elective share trust.

(11) "Transfer tax value" means the value the interest would have for purposes of the United States estate and gift tax laws if it passed without consideration to an unrelated person on the applicable valuation date.

Added by Laws 1999, c. 99–343, § 2, eff. Oct. 1, 1999. Amended by Laws 2001, c. 2001–226, § 19, eff. Oct. 1, 2001; Laws 2002, c. 2002–82, § 2, eff. April 23, 2002; Laws 2004, c. 2004–5, § 151, eff. June 29, 2004; Laws 2007, c. 2007–74, § 9, eff. July 1, 2007; Laws 2009, c. 2009–115, § 3, eff. July 1, 2009.

[1] 26 U.S.C.A. § 643(b).

732.2035. Property entering into elective estate

Except as provided in s. 732.2045, the elective estate consists of the sum of the values as determined under s. 732.2055 of the following property interests:

(1) The decedent's probate estate.

(2) The decedent's ownership interest in accounts or securities registered in "Pay On Death," "Transfer On Death," "In Trust For," or coownership with right of survivorship form. For this purpose, "decedent's ownership interest" means, in the case of accounts or securities held in tenancy by the entirety, one-half of the value of the account or security, and in all other cases, that portion of the accounts or securities which the decedent had, immediately before death, the right to withdraw or use without the duty to account to any person.

(3) The decedent's fractional interest in property, other than property described in subsection (2) or subsection (7), held by the decedent in joint tenancy with right of survivorship or in tenancy by the entirety. For this purpose, "decedent's fractional interest in property" means the value of the property divided by the number of tenants.

(4) That portion of property, other than property described in subsection (2), transferred by the decedent to the extent that at the time of the decedent's death the transfer was revocable by the decedent alone or in conjunction with any other person. This subsection does not apply to a transfer that is revocable by the decedent only with the consent of all persons having a beneficial interest in the property.

(5)(a) That portion of property, other than property described in subsection (3), subsection (4), or subsection (7), transferred by the decedent to the extent that at the time of the decedent's death:

1. The decedent possessed the right to, or in fact enjoyed the possession or use of, the income or principal of the property; or

2. The principal of the property could, in the discretion of any person other than the spouse of the decedent, be distributed or appointed to or for the benefit of the decedent.

In the application of this subsection, a right to payments under a commercial or private annuity, an annuity trust, a unitrust, or a similar arrangement shall be treated as a right to that portion of the income of the property necessary to equal the annuity, unitrust, or other payment.

(b) The amount included under this subsection is:

1. With respect to subparagraph (a)1., the value of the portion of the property to which the decedent's right or enjoyment related, to the extent the portion passed to or for the benefit of any person other than the decedent's probate estate; and

2. With respect to subparagraph (a)2., the value of the portion subject to the discretion, to the extent the portion passed to or for the benefit of any person other than the decedent's probate estate.

(c) This subsection does not apply to any property if the decedent's only interests in the property are that:

1. The property could be distributed to or for the benefit of the decedent only with the consent of all persons having a beneficial interest in the property; or

2. The income or principal of the property could be distributed to or for the benefit of the decedent only through the exercise or in default of an exercise of a general power of appointment held by any person other than the decedent; or

3. The income or principal of the property is or could be distributed in satisfaction of the decedent's obligation of support; or

4. The decedent had a contingent right to receive principal, other than at the discretion of any person, which contingency was beyond the control of the decedent and which had not in fact occurred at the decedent's death.

(6) The decedent's beneficial interest in the net cash surrender value immediately before death of any policy of insurance on the decedent's life.

(7) The value of amounts payable to or for the benefit of any person by reason of surviving the decedent under any public or private pension, retirement, or deferred compensation plan, or any similar arrangement, other than benefits payable under the federal Railroad Retirement Act [1] or the federal Social Security System. In the case of a defined contribution plan as defined in s. 414(i) of the Internal Revenue Code of 1986,[2] as amended, this subsection shall not apply to the excess of the proceeds of any insurance policy on the decedent's life over the net cash surrender value of the policy immediately before the decedent's death.

(8) Property that was transferred during the 1–year period preceding the decedent's death as a result of a transfer by the decedent if the transfer was either of the following types:

(a) Any property transferred as a result of the termination of a right or interest in, or power over, property that would have been included in the elective estate under subsection (4) or subsection (5) if the right, interest, or power had not terminated until the decedent's death.

(b) Any transfer of property to the extent not otherwise included in the elective estate, made to or for the benefit of any person, except:

1. Any transfer of property for medical or educational expenses to the extent it qualifies for exclusion from the United States gift tax under s. 2503(e) of the Internal Revenue Code,[3] as amended; and

2. After the application of subparagraph 1., the first annual exclusion amount of property transferred to or for the benefit of each donee during the 1–year period, but only to the extent the transfer qualifies for exclusion from the United States gift tax under s. 2503(b) or (c) of the Internal Revenue Code,[4] as amended. For purposes of this subparagraph, the term "annual exclusion amount" means the amount of one annual exclusion under s. 2503(b) or (c) of the Internal Revenue Code,[4] as amended.

(c) Except as provided in paragraph (d), for purposes of this subsection:

1. A "termination" with respect to a right or interest in property occurs when the decedent transfers or relinquishes the right or interest, and, with respect to a power over property, a termination occurs when the power terminates by exercise, release, lapse, default, or otherwise.

2. A distribution from a trust the income or principal of which is subject to subsection (4), subsection (5), or subsection (9) shall be treated as a transfer of property by the decedent and not as a termination of a right or interest in, or a power over, property.

(d) Notwithstanding anything in paragraph (c) to the contrary:

1. A "termination" with respect to a right or interest in property does not occur when the right or interest terminates by the terms of the governing instrument unless the termination is determined by reference to the death of the decedent and the court finds that a principal purpose for the terms of the instrument relating to the termination was avoidance of the elective share.

2. A distribution from a trust is not subject to this subsection if the distribution is required by the terms of the governing instrument unless the event triggering the distribution is determined by reference to the death of the decedent and the court finds that a principal purpose of the terms of the governing instrument relating to the distribution is avoidance of the elective share.

(9) Property transferred in satisfaction of the elective share.

Fla.St.1997, § 732.206; Laws 1975, c. 75–220, § 15. Renumbered as 732.2035 and amended by Laws 1999, c. 99–343, § 3, eff. Oct. 1, 1999. Amended by Laws 2001, c. 2001–226, § 20, eff. Oct. 1, 2001; Laws 2007, c. 2007–74, § 10, eff. July 1, 2007.

[1] 45 U.S.C.A. § 231 et seq.
[2] 26 U.S.C.A. § 414(i).
[3] 26 U.S.C.A. § 2503(e).
[4] 26 U.S.C.A. § 2503(b) or (c).

732.2045. Exclusions and overlapping application

(1) **Exclusions.**—Section 732.2035 does not apply to:

(a) Except as provided in s. 732.2155(4), any transfer of property by the decedent to the extent the transfer is irrevocable before the effective date of this subsection or after that date but before the date of the decedent's marriage to the surviving spouse.

(b) Any transfer of property by the decedent to the extent the decedent received adequate consideration in money or money's worth for the transfer.

(c) Any transfer of property by the decedent made with the written consent of the decedent's spouse. For this purpose, spousal consent to split-gift treatment under the United States gift tax laws does not constitute written consent to the transfer by the decedent.

(d) The proceeds of any policy of insurance on the decedent's life in excess of the net cash surrender value of the policy whether payable to the decedent's estate, a trust, or in any other manner.

(e) Any policy of insurance on the decedent's life maintained pursuant to a court order.

(f) The decedent's one-half of the property to which ss. 732.216–732.228, or any similar provisions of law of another state, apply and real property that is community property under the laws of the jurisdiction where it is located.

(g) Property held in a qualifying special needs trust on the date of the decedent's death.

(h) Property included in the gross estate of the decedent for federal estate tax purposes solely because the decedent possessed a general power of appointment.

(i) Property which constitutes the protected homestead of the decedent whether held by the decedent or by a trust at the decedent's death.

(2) **Overlapping application.**—If s. 732.2035(1) and any other subsection of s. 732.2035 apply to the same property interest, the amount included in the elective estate under other subsections is reduced by the amount included under subsection (1). In all other cases, if more than one subsection of s. 732.2035 applies to a property interest, only the subsection resulting in the largest elective estate shall apply.

Added by Laws 1999, c. 99–343, § 4, eff. Oct. 1, 1999. Amended by Laws 2001, c. 2001–226, § 21, eff. Oct. 1, 2001; Laws 2009, c. 2009–115, § 4, eff. July 1, 2009.

732.2055. Valuation of the elective estate

For purposes of s. 732.2035, "value" means:

---

(1) In the case of any policy of insurance on the decedent's life includable under s. 732.2035(4), (5), or (6), the net cash surrender value of the policy immediately before the decedent's death.

(2) In the case of any policy of insurance on the decedent's life includable under s. 732.2035(8), the net cash surrender value of the policy on the date of the termination or transfer.

(3) In the case of amounts includable under s. 732.2035(7), the transfer tax value of the amounts on the date of the decedent's death.

(4) In the case of other property included under s. 732.2035(8), the fair market value of the property on the date of the termination or transfer, computed after deducting any mortgages, liens, or security interests on the property as of that date.

(5) In the case of all other property, the fair market value of the property on the date of the decedent's death, computed after deducting from the total value of the property:

(a) All claims paid or payable from the elective estate; and

(b) To the extent they are not deducted under paragraph (a), all mortgages, liens, or security interests on the property.

Added by Laws 1999, c. 99–343, § 5, eff. Oct. 1, 1999. Amended by Laws 2001, c. 2001–226, § 22, eff. Oct. 1, 2001.

732.2065. Amount of the elective share

The elective share is an amount equal to 30 percent of the elective estate.

Laws 1975, c. 75–220, § 15; Laws 1981, c. 81–27, § 1. Renumbered from 732.207 and amended by Laws 1999, c. 99–343, § 6, eff. Oct. 1, 1999.

732.2075. Sources from which elective share payable; abatement

(1) Unless otherwise provided in the decedent's will or, in the absence of a provision in the decedent's will, in a trust referred to in the decedent's will, the following are applied first to satisfy the elective share:

(a) Property interests included in the elective estate that pass or have passed to or for the benefit of the surviving spouse, including interests that are contingent upon making the election, but only to the extent that such contingent interests do not diminish other property interests that would be applied to satisfy the elective share in the absence of the contingent interests.

(b) To the extent paid to or for the benefit of the surviving spouse, amounts payable under any plan or arrangement described in s. 732.2035(7).

(c) To the extent paid to or for the benefit of the surviving spouse, the decedent's one-half of any property described in s. 732.2045(1)(f).

(d) To the extent paid to or for the benefit of the surviving spouse, the proceeds of any term or other policy of insurance on the decedent's life if, at the time of decedent's death, the policy was owned by any person other than the surviving spouse.

(e) Property held for the benefit of the surviving spouse in a qualifying special needs trust.

(f) Property interests that would have satisfied the elective share under any preceding paragraph of this subsection but were disclaimed.

(2) If, after the application of subsection (1), the elective share is not fully satisfied, the unsatisfied balance shall be allocated entirely to one class of direct recipients of the remaining elective estate and apportioned among those recipients, and if the elective share amount is not

fully satisfied, to the next class of direct recipients, in the following order of priority, until the elective share amount is satisfied:

(a) *Class 1.*—The decedent's probate estate and revocable trusts.

(b) *Class 2.*—Recipients of property interests, other than protected charitable interests, included in the elective estate under s. 732.2035(2), (3), or (6) and, to the extent the decedent had at the time of death the power to designate the recipient of the property, property interests, other than protected charitable interests, included under s. 732.2035(5) and (7).

(c) *Class 3.*—Recipients of all other property interests, other than protected charitable interests, included in the elective estate.

For purposes of this subsection, a protected charitable interest is any interest for which a charitable deduction with respect to the transfer of the property was allowed or allowable to the decedent or the decedent's spouse under the United States gift or income tax laws.

(3) If, after the application of subsections (1) and (2), the elective share amount is not fully satisfied, the additional amount due to the surviving spouse shall be determined and satisfied as follows:

(a) The remaining unsatisfied balance shall be satisfied from property described in paragraphs (1)(a) and (b) which passes or which has passed in a trust in which the surviving spouse has a beneficial interest, other than an elective share trust or a qualified special needs trust.

(b) In determining the amount of the remaining unsatisfied balance, the effect, if any, of any change caused by the operation of this subsection in the value of the spouse's beneficial interests in property described in paragraphs (1)(a) and (b) shall be taken into account, including, if necessary, further recalculations of the value of those beneficial interests.

(c) If there is more than one trust to which this subsection could apply, unless otherwise provided in the decedent's will or, in the absence of a provision in the decedent's will, in a trust referred to in the decedent's will, the unsatisfied balance shall be apportioned pro rata to all such trusts in proportion to the value, as determined under s. 732.2095(2)(d), of the surviving spouse's beneficial interests in the trusts.

(4) If, after the application of subsections (1), (2), and (3), the elective share is not fully satisfied, any remaining unsatisfied balance shall be satisfied from direct recipients of protected charitable lead interests, but only to the extent and at such times that contribution is permitted without disqualifying the charitable interest in that property for a deduction under the United States gift tax laws. For purposes of this subsection, a protected charitable lead interest is a protected charitable interest as defined in subsection (2) in which one or more deductible interests in charity precede some other nondeductible interest or interests in the property.

(5) The contribution required of the decedent's probate estate and revocable trusts may be made in cash or in kind. In the application of this subsection, subsections (6) and (7) are to be applied to charge contribution for the elective share to the beneficiaries of the probate estate and revocable trusts as if all beneficiaries were taking under a common governing instrument.

(6) Unless otherwise provided in the decedent's will or, in the absence of a provision in the decedent's will, in a trust referred to in the decedent's will, any amount to be satisfied from the decedent's probate estate, other than from property passing to an inter vivos trust, shall be paid from the assets of the probate estate in the order prescribed in s. 733.805.

(7) Unless otherwise provided in the trust instrument or, in the decedent's will if there is no provision in the trust instrument, any amount to be satisfied from trust property shall be paid

from the assets of the trust in the order provided for claims under s. 736.05053(2) and (3). A direction in the decedent's will is effective only for revocable trusts.

Laws 1975, c. 75–220, § 15. Renumbered from 732.209 and amended by Laws 1999, c. 99–343, § 7, eff. Oct. 1, 1999. Amended by Laws 2001, c. 2001–226, § 23, eff. Oct. 1, 2001; Laws 2002, c. 2002–82, § 4, eff. April 23, 2002; Laws 2006, c. 2006–217, § 31, eff. July 1, 2007; Laws 2007, c. 2007–74, § 11, eff. July 1, 2007; Laws 2009, c. 2009–115, § 5, eff. July 1, 2009.

732.2085. Liability of direct recipients and beneficiaries

(1) Only direct recipients of property included in the elective estate and the beneficiaries of the decedent's probate estate or of any trust that is a direct recipient, are liable to contribute toward satisfaction of the elective share.

(a) Within each of the classes described in s. 732.2075(2)(b) and (c), each direct recipient is liable in an amount equal to the value, as determined under s. 732.2055, of the proportional part of the liability for all members of the class.

(b) Trust and probate estate beneficiaries who receive a distribution of principal after the decedent's death are liable in an amount equal to the value of the principal distributed to them multiplied by the contribution percentage of the distributing trust or estate. For this purpose, "contribution percentage" means the remaining unsatisfied balance of the trust or estate at the time of the distribution divided by the value of the trust or estate as determined under s. 732.2055. "Remaining unsatisfied balance" means the amount of liability initially apportioned to the trust or estate reduced by amounts or property previously contributed by any person in satisfaction of that liability.

(2) In lieu of paying the amount for which they are liable, beneficiaries who have received a distribution of property included in the elective estate and direct recipients other than the decedent's probate estate or revocable trusts, may:

(a) Contribute a proportional part of all property received; or

(b) With respect to any property interest received before the date of the court's order of contribution:

1. Contribute all of the property; or

2. If the property has been sold or exchanged prior to the date on which the spouse's election is filed, pay an amount equal to the value of the property, less reasonable costs of sale, on the date it was sold or exchanged.

In the application of paragraph (a), the "proportional part of all property received" is determined separately for each class of priority under s. 732.2075(2).

(3) If a person pays the value of the property on the date of a sale or exchange or contributes all of the property received, as provided in paragraph (2)(b):

(a) No further contribution toward satisfaction of the elective share shall be required with respect to that property.

(b) Any unsatisfied contribution is treated as additional unsatisfied balance and reapportioned to other recipients as provided in s. 732.2075 and this section.

(4) If any part of s. 732.2035 or s. 732.2075 is preempted by federal law with respect to a payment, an item of property, or any other benefit included in the elective estate, a person who, not for value, receives the payment, item of property, or any other benefit is obligated to return the payment, item of property, or benefit, or is personally liable for the amount of the payment or the value of that item of property or benefit, as provided in ss. 732.2035 and 732.2075, to the

person who would have been entitled to it were that section or part of that section not preempted.

Added by Laws 1999, c. 99–343, § 8, eff. Oct. 1, 1999. Amended by Laws 2001, c. 2001–226, § 24, eff. Oct. 1, 2001; Laws 2009, c. 2009–115, § 6, eff. July 1, 2009.

732.2095. Valuation of property used to satisfy elective share

(1) **Definitions.**—As used in this section, the term:

(a) "Applicable valuation date" means:

1. In the case of transfers in satisfaction of the elective share, the date of the decedent's death.

2. In the case of property held in a qualifying special needs trust on the date of the decedent's death, the date of the decedent's death.

3. In the case of other property irrevocably transferred to or for the benefit of the surviving spouse during the decedent's life, the date of the transfer.

4. In the case of property distributed to the surviving spouse by the personal representative, the date of distribution.

5. Except as provided in subparagraphs 1., 2., and 3., in the case of property passing in trust for the surviving spouse, the date or dates the trust is funded in satisfaction of the elective share.

6. In the case of property described in s. 732.2035(2) or (3), the date of the decedent's death.

7. In the case of proceeds of any policy of insurance payable to the surviving spouse, the date of the decedent's death.

8. In the case of amounts payable to the surviving spouse under any plan or arrangement described in s. 732.2035(7), the date of the decedent's death.

9. In all other cases, the date of the decedent's death or the date the surviving spouse first comes into possession of the property, whichever occurs later.

(b) "Qualifying power of appointment" means a general power of appointment that is exercisable alone and in all events by the decedent's spouse in favor of the spouse or the spouse's estate. For this purpose, a general power to appoint by will is a qualifying power of appointment if the power may be exercised by the spouse in favor of the spouse's estate without the consent of any other person.

(c) "Qualifying invasion power" means a power held by the surviving spouse or the trustee of an elective share trust to invade trust principal for the health, support, and maintenance of the spouse. The power may, but need not, provide that the other resources of the spouse are to be taken into account in any exercise of the power.

(2) Except as provided in this subsection, the value of property for purposes of s. 732.2075 is the fair market value of the property on the applicable valuation date.

(a) If the surviving spouse has a life interest in property not in trust that entitles the spouse to the use of the property for life, the value of the spouse's interest is one-half of the value of the property on the applicable valuation date.

(b) If the surviving spouse has an interest in a trust, or portion of a trust, which meets the requirements of an elective share trust, the value of the spouse's interest is a percentage of the value of the principal of the trust, or trust portion, on the applicable valuation date as follows:

1. One hundred percent if the trust instrument includes both a qualifying invasion power and a qualifying power of appointment.

2. Eighty percent if the trust instrument includes a qualifying invasion power but no qualifying power of appointment.

3. Fifty percent in all other cases.

(c) If the surviving spouse is a beneficiary of a trust, or portion of a trust, which meets the requirements of a qualifying special needs trust, the value of the principal of the trust, or trust portion, on the applicable valuation date.

(d) If the surviving spouse has an interest in a trust that does not meet the requirements of either an elective share trust or a qualifying special needs trust, the value of the spouse's interest is the transfer tax value of the interest on the applicable valuation date; however, the aggregate value of all of the spouse's interests in the trust shall not exceed one-half of the value of the trust principal on the applicable valuation date.

(e) In the case of any policy of insurance on the decedent's life the proceeds of which are payable outright or to a trust described in paragraph (b), paragraph (c), or paragraph (d), the value of the policy for purposes of s. 732.2075 and paragraphs (b), (c), and (d) is the net proceeds.

(f) In the case of a right to one or more payments from an annuity or under a similar contractual arrangement or under any plan or arrangement described in s. 732.2035(7), the value of the right to payments for purposes of s. 732.2075 and paragraphs (b), (c), and (d) is the transfer tax value of the right on the applicable valuation date.

Added by Laws 1999, c. 99–343, § 9, eff. Oct. 1, 1999. Amended by Laws 2001, c. 2001–226, § 25, eff. Oct. 1, 2001.

732.2105. Effect of election on other interests

The elective share shall be in addition to homestead, exempt property, and allowances as provided in part IV.

Laws 1975, c. 75–220, § 15. Renumbered from 732.208 and amended by Laws 1999, c. 99–343, § 10, eff. Oct. 1, 1999. Amended by Laws 2001, c. 2001–226, § 26, eff. Oct. 1, 2001.

Cross References

Exempt property, see § 732.402.

732.2115. Protection of payors and other third parties

Although a property interest is included in the decedent's elective estate under s. 732.2035(2)–(8), a payor or other third party is not liable for paying, distributing, or transferring the property to a beneficiary designated in a governing instrument, or for taking any other action in good faith reliance on the validity of a governing instrument.

Added by Laws 1999, c. 99–343, § 11, eff. Oct. 1, 1999.

732.2125. Right of election; by whom exercisable

The right of election may be exercised:

(1) By the surviving spouse.

(2) With approval of the court having jurisdiction of the probate proceeding by an attorney in fact or a guardian of the property of the surviving spouse. Before approving the election, the court shall determine that the election is in the best interests of the surviving spouse during the spouse's probable lifetime.

Laws 1975, c. 75–220, § 15. Renumbered from 732.210 and amended by Laws 1999, c. 99–343, § 12, eff. Oct. 1, 1999. Amended by Laws 2001, c. 2001–226, § 27, eff. Oct. 1, 2001; Laws. 2010, c. 2010–132, § 6, eff. Oct. 1, 2010.

732.2135. Time of election; extensions; withdrawal

(1) Except as provided in subsection (2), the election must be filed on or before the earlier of the date that is 6 months after the date of service of a copy of the notice of administration on the surviving spouse, or an attorney in fact or guardian of the property of the surviving spouse, or the date that is 2 years after the date of the decedent's death.

(2) Within the period provided in subsection (1), the surviving spouse or an attorney in fact or guardian of the property of the surviving spouse may petition the court for an extension of time for making an election. For good cause shown, the court may extend the time for election. If the court grants the petition for an extension, the election must be filed within the time allowed by the extension.

(3) The surviving spouse or an attorney in fact, guardian of the property, or personal representative of the surviving spouse may withdraw an election at any time within 8 months after the decedent's death and before the court's order of contribution.

(4) A petition for an extension of the time for making the election or for approval to make the election shall toll the time for making the election.

(5) If the court determines that an election is made or pursued in bad faith, the court may assess attorney's fees and costs against the surviving spouse or the surviving spouse's estate.

Laws 1975, c. 75–220, § 15.   Renumbered from 732.212 and amended by Laws 1999, c. 99–343, § 13, eff. Oct. 1, 1999.   Amended by Laws 2001, c. 2001–226, § 28, eff. Oct. 1, 2001; Laws 2006, c. 2006–134, § 4, eff. July 1, 2006; Laws 2009, c. 2009–115, § 7, eff. July 1, 2009.

732.2145. Order of contribution; personal representative's duty to collect contribution

(1) The court shall determine the elective share and contribution. Contributions shall bear interest at the statutory rate beginning 90 days after the order of contribution. The order is prima facie correct in proceedings in any court or jurisdiction.

(2) Except as provided in subsection (3), the personal representative shall collect contribution from the recipients of the elective estate as provided in the court's order of contribution.

(a) If property within the possession or control of the personal representative is distributable to a beneficiary or trustee who is required to contribute in satisfaction of the elective share, the personal representative shall withhold from the distribution the contribution required of the beneficiary or trustee.

(b) If, after the order of contribution, the personal representative brings an action to collect contribution from property not within the personal representative's control, the judgment shall include the personal representative's costs and reasonable attorney's fees. The personal representative is not required to seek collection of any portion of the elective share from property not within the personal representative's control until after the entry of the order of contribution.

(3) A personal representative who has the duty under this section of enforcing contribution may be relieved of that duty by an order of the court finding that it is impracticable to enforce contribution in view of the improbability of obtaining a judgment or the improbability of collection under any judgment that might be obtained, or otherwise. The personal representative shall not be liable for failure to attempt collection if the attempt would have been economically impracticable.

(4) Nothing in this section limits the independent right of the surviving spouse to collect the elective share as provided in the order of contribution, and that right is hereby conferred. If the

surviving spouse brings an action to enforce the order, the judgment shall include the surviving spouse's costs and reasonable attorney's fees.

Added by Laws 1999, c. 99–343, § 14, eff. Oct. 1, 1999. Amended by Laws 2001, c. 2001–226, § 29, eff. Oct. 1, 2001.

732.2155. Effective date; effect of prior waivers; transition rules

(1) Sections 732.201–732.2155 are effective on October 1, 1999, for all decedents dying on or after October 1, 2001. The law in effect prior to October 1, 1999, applies to decedents dying before October 1, 2001.

(2) Nothing in ss. 732.201–732.2155 modifies or applies to the rights of spouses under chapter 61.

(3) A waiver of elective share rights before the effective date of this section which is otherwise in compliance with the requirements of s. 732.702 is a waiver of all rights under ss. 732.201–732.2145.

(4) Notwithstanding anything in s. 732.2045(1)(a) to the contrary, any trust created by the decedent before the effective date of ss. 732.201–732.2145 that meets the requirements of an elective share trust is treated as if the decedent created the trust after the effective date of these sections and in satisfaction of the elective share.

(5) Sections 732.201–732.2155 do not affect any interest in contracts entered into for adequate consideration in money or money's worth before October 1, 1999, to the extent that the contract was irrevocable at all times from October 1, 1999, until the date of the decedent's death.

(6) Sections 732.201—732.2155 do not affect any interest in property held, as of the decedent's death, in a trust, whether revocable or irrevocable, if:

(a) The property was an asset of the trust at all times between October 1, 1999, and the date of the decedent's death;

(b) The decedent was not married to the decedent's surviving spouse when the property was transferred to the trust; and

(c) The property was a nonmarital asset as defined in s. 61.075 immediately prior to the decedent's death.

Added by Laws 1999, c. 99–343, § 15, eff. Oct. 1, 1999. Amended by Laws 2001, c. 2001–226, § 30, eff. Oct. 1, 2001.

732.216. Short title

Sections 732.216–732.228 may be cited as the "Florida Uniform Disposition of Community Property Rights at Death Act."

Laws 1992, c. 92–200, § 4.

UNIFORM DISPOSITION OF COMMUNITY PROPERTY RIGHTS AT DEATH ACT

Table of Jurisdictions Wherein Act Has Been Adopted

For text of Uniform Act, and variation notes and annotation materials for adopting jurisdictions, see Uniform Laws Annotated, Master Edition Volume 8A.

Jurisdiction	Laws	Effective Date	Statutory Citation
Alaska	1984, c. 47	8–8–1984	AS 13.41.005 to 13.41.055.

Jurisdiction	Laws	Effective Date	Statutory Citation
Arkansas	1981, No. 660	10–1–1981	A.C.A. §§ 28–12–101 to 28–12–113.
Colorado	1973, c. 452	7–1–1973	West's C.R.S.A. §§ 15–20–101 to 15–20–111.
Connecticut	1985, No. 85–340	6–16–1985 *	C.G.S.A. §§ 45a–458 to 45a–466.
Florida	1992, c. 92–200	10–1–1992	West's F.S.A. §§ 732.216 to 732.228.
Hawaii	1973, c. 132		HRS §§ 510–21 to 510–30.
Kentucky	1974, c. 328	6–21–1974	KRS 391.210 to 391.260.
Michigan	1975, P.A. 289	12–10–1975 *	M.C.L.A. §§ 557.261 to 557.271.
Minnesota	2013, c. 24	8–1–2013	M.S.A. §§ 519A.01 to 519A.11.
Montana	1989, c. 395	10–1–1989	MCA §§ 72–9–101 to 72–9–120.
New York	1981, c. 187	9–1–1981	McKinney's EPTL 6–6.1 to 6–6.7.
North Carolina	1981, c. 882	7–8–1981	G.S. §§ 31C–1 to 31C–12.
Oregon	1973, c. 205	10–5–1973	ORS 112.705 to 112.775.
Utah	2012, c. 132	5–8–2012	U.C.A. §§ 75–2b–101 to 75–2b–111.
Virginia	1982, c. 456		Code 1950, §§ 64.2–315 to 64.2–324.
Wyoming	1985, c. 16	5–23–1985	Wyo.Stat.Ann. §§ 2–7–720 to 2–7–729.

* Date of approval.

732.217. Application

Sections 732.216–732.228 apply to the disposition at death of the following property acquired by a married person:

(1) Personal property, wherever located, which:

(a) Was acquired as, or became and remained, community property under the laws of another jurisdiction;

(b) Was acquired with the rents, issues, or income of, or the proceeds from, or in exchange for, community property; or

(c) Is traceable to that community property.

(2) Real property, except real property held as tenants by the entirety, which is located in this state, and which:

(a) Was acquired with the rents, issues, or income of, the proceeds from, or in exchange for, property acquired as, or which became and remained, community property under the laws of another jurisdiction; or

(b) Is traceable to that community property.

Laws 1992, c. 92–200, § 5. Amended by Laws 2003, c. 2003–154, § 4, eff. June 12, 2003.

732.218. Rebuttable presumptions

In determining whether ss. 732.216–732.228 apply to specific property, the following rebuttable presumptions apply:

(1) Property acquired during marriage by a spouse of that marriage while domiciled in a jurisdiction under whose laws property could then be acquired as community property is presumed to have been acquired as, or to have become and remained, property to which these sections apply.

(2) Real property located in this state, other than homestead and real property held as tenants by the entirety, and personal property wherever located acquired by a married person while domiciled in a jurisdiction under whose laws property could not then be acquired as community

property and title to which was taken in a form which created rights of survivorship are presumed to be property to which these sections do not apply.

Laws 1992, c. 92–200, § 6. Amended by Laws 2001, c. 2001–226, § 31, eff. Jan. 1, 2002.

732.219. Disposition upon death

Upon the death of a married person, one-half of the property to which ss. 732.216–732.228 apply is the property of the surviving spouse and is not subject to testamentary disposition by the decedent or distribution under the laws of succession of this state. One-half of that property is the property of the decedent and is subject to testamentary disposition or distribution under the laws of succession of this state. The decedent's one-half of that property is not in the elective estate.

Laws 1992, c. 92–200, § 7. Amended by Laws 2001, c. 2001–226, § 32, eff. Jan. 1, 2002; Laws 2002, c. 2002–1, § 107, eff. May 21, 2002.

732.221. Perfection of title of personal representative or beneficiary

If the title to any property to which ss. 732.216–732.228 apply is held by the surviving spouse at the time of the decedent's death, the personal representative or a beneficiary of the decedent may institute an action to perfect title to the property. The personal representative has no duty to discover whether any property held by the surviving spouse is property to which ss. 732.216–732.228 apply, unless a written demand is made by a beneficiary within 3 months after service of a copy of the notice of administration on the beneficiary or by a creditor within 3 months after the first publication of the notice to creditors.

Laws 1992, c. 92–200, § 8. Amended by Laws 2001, c. 2001–226, § 33, eff. Jan. 1, 2002.

732.222. Purchaser for value or lender

(1) If a surviving spouse has apparent title to property to which ss. 732.216–732.228 apply, a purchaser for value or a lender taking a security interest in the property takes the interest in the property free of any rights of the personal representative or a beneficiary of the decedent.

(2) If a personal representative or a beneficiary of the decedent has apparent title to property to which ss. 732.216–732.228 apply, a purchaser for value or a lender taking a security interest in the property takes that interest in the property free of any rights of the surviving spouse.

(3) A purchaser for value or a lender need not inquire whether a vendor or borrower acted properly.

(4) The proceeds of a sale or creation of a security interest must be treated as the property transferred to the purchaser for value or a lender.

Laws 1992, c. 92–200, § 9. Amended by Laws 1997, c. 97–102, § 956, eff. July 1, 1997; Laws 2001, c. 2001–226, § 34, eff. Jan. 1, 2002.

732.223. Perfection of title of surviving spouse

If the title to any property to which ss. 732.216–732.228 apply was held by the decedent at the time of the decedent's death, title of the surviving spouse may be perfected by an order of the probate court or by execution of an instrument by the personal representative or the beneficiaries of the decedent with the approval of the probate court. The probate court in which the decedent's estate is being administered has no duty to discover whether property held by the decedent is property to which ss. 732.216–732.228 apply. The personal representative has no duty to discover whether property held by the decedent is property to which ss. 732.216–732.228 apply unless a written demand is made by the surviving spouse or the spouse's successor in interest within 3 months after service of a copy of the notice of administration on the surviving spouse or the spouse's successor in interest.

Laws 1992, c. 92–200, § 10. Amended by Laws 1997, c. 97–102, § 957, eff. July 1, 1997; Laws 2001, c. 2001–226, § 35, eff. Jan. 1, 2002.

732.224. Creditor's rights

Sections 732.216–732.228 do not affect rights of creditors with respect to property to which ss. 732.216–732.228 apply.

Laws 1992, c. 92–200, § 11.

732.225. Acts of married persons

Sections 732.216–732.228 do not prevent married persons from severing or altering their interests in property to which these sections apply. The reinvestment of any property to which these sections apply in real property located in this state which is or becomes homestead property creates a conclusive presumption that the spouses have agreed to terminate the community property attribute of the property reinvested.

Laws 1992, c. 92–200, § 12.

732.226. Limitations on testamentary disposition

Sections 732.216–732.228 do not authorize a person to dispose of property by will if it is held under limitations imposed by law preventing testamentary disposition by that person.

Laws 1992, c. 92–200, § 13.

732.227. Homestead defined

For purposes of ss. 732.216–732.228, the term "homestead" refers only to property the descent and devise of which is restricted by s. 4(c), Art. X of the State Constitution.

Laws 1992, c. 92–200, § 14.

732.228. Uniformity of application and construction

Sections 732.216–732.228 are to be so applied and construed as to effectuate their general purpose to make uniform the law with respect to the subject of these sections among those states which enact them.

Laws 1992, c. 92–200, § 15.

PART III. PRETERMITTED SPOUSE AND CHILDREN

732.301. Pretermitted spouse

When a person marries after making a will and the spouse survives the testator, the surviving spouse shall receive a share in the estate of the testator equal in value to that which the surviving spouse would have received if the testator had died intestate, unless:

(1) Provision has been made for, or waived by, the spouse by prenuptial or postnuptial agreement;

(2) The spouse is provided for in the will; or

(3) The will discloses an intention not to make provision for the spouse.

The share of the estate that is assigned to the pretermitted spouse shall be obtained in accordance with s. 733.805.

Laws 1974, c. 74–106, § 1; Laws 1975, c. 75–220, § 16; Laws 1977, c. 77–87, § 9.

Cross References

Effect of subsequent marriage, birth, or dissolution of marriage, see § 732.507.

732.302. Pretermitted children

When a testator omits to provide by will for any of his or her children born or adopted after making the will and the child has not received a part of the testator's property equivalent to a child's part by way of advancement, the child shall receive a share of the estate equal in value to that which the child would have received if the testator had died intestate, unless:

(1) It appears from the will that the omission was intentional; or

(2) The testator had one or more children when the will was executed and devised substantially all the estate to the other parent of the pretermitted child and that other parent survived the testator and is entitled to take under the will.

The share of the estate that is assigned to the pretermitted child shall be obtained in accordance with s. 733.805.

Laws 1974, c. 74–106, § 1; Laws 1975, c. 75–220, § 16. Amended by Laws 1997, c. 97–102, § 958, eff. July 1, 1997; Laws 2001, c. 2001–226, § 36, eff. Jan. 1, 2002.

Cross References

Effect of subsequent marriage, birth, or dissolution of marriage, see § 732.507.

PART IV. EXEMPT PROPERTY AND ALLOWANCES

732.401. Descent of homestead

(1) If not devised as authorized by law and the constitution, the homestead shall descend in the same manner as other intestate property; but if the decedent is survived by a spouse and one or more descendants, the surviving spouse shall take a life estate in the homestead, with a vested remainder to the descendants in being at the time of the decedent's death per stirpes.

(2) In lieu of a life estate under subsection (1), the surviving spouse may elect to take an undivided one-half interest in the homestead as a tenant in common, with the remaining undivided one-half interest vesting in the decedent's descendants in being at the time of the decedent's death, per stirpes.

(a) The right of election may be exercised:

1. By the surviving spouse; or

2. With the approval of a court having jurisdiction of the real property, by an attorney in fact or guardian of the property of the surviving spouse. Before approving the election, the court shall determine that the election is in the best interests of the surviving spouse during the spouse's probable lifetime.

(b) The election must be made within 6 months after the decedent's death and during the surviving spouse's lifetime. The time for making the election may not be extended except as provided in paragraph (c).

(c) A petition by an attorney in fact or by a guardian of the property of the surviving spouse for approval to make the election must be filed within 6 months after the decedent's death and during the surviving spouse's lifetime. If the petition is timely filed, the time for making the election shall be extended for at least 30 days after the rendition of the order allowing the election.

(d) Once made, the election is irrevocable.

(e) The election shall be made by filing a notice of election containing the legal description of the homestead property for recording in the official record books of the county or counties where the homestead property is located. The notice must be in substantially the following form:

ELECTION OF SURVIVING SPOUSE TO TAKE A ONE–HALF INTEREST OF DECEDENT'S INTEREST IN HOMESTEAD PROPERTY

STATE OF_____

COUNTY OF_____

1. The decedent, _____, died on _____ On the date of the decedent's death, The decedent was married to _____, who survived the decedent.

2. At the time of the decedent's death, the decedent owned an interest in real property that the affiant believes to be homestead property described in s. 4, Article X of the State Constitution, which real property being in _____ County, Florida, and described as: (description of homestead property)

3. Affiant elects to take one-half of decedent's interest in the homestead as a tenant in common in lieu of a life estate.

4. If affiant is not the surviving spouse, affiant is the surviving spouse's attorney in fact or guardian of the property, and an order has been rendered by a court having jurisdiction of the real property authorizing the undersigned to make this election.

_____

(Affiant)

Sworn to (or affirmed) and subscribed before me this __ day of (month) , (year) , by (affiant)

(Signature of Notary Public-State of Florida)

(Print, Type, or Stamp Commissioned Name of Notary Public)

Personally Known OR Produced Identification

(Type of Identification Produced)

(3) Unless and until an election is made under subsection (2), expenses relating to the ownership of the homestead shall be allocated between the surviving spouse, as life tenant, and the decedent's descendants, as remaindermen, in accordance with chapter 738. If an election is made, expenses relating to the ownership of the homestead shall be allocated between the surviving spouse and the descendants as tenants in common in proportion to their respective shares, effective as of the date the election is filed for recording.

(4) If the surviving spouse's life estate created in subsection (1) is disclaimed pursuant to chapter 739, the interests of the decedent's descendants may not be divested.

(5) This section does not apply to property that the decedent owned in tenancy by the entireties or in joint tenancy with rights of survivorship.

Laws 1974, c. 74–106, § 1; Laws 1975, c. 75–220, § 17. Amended by Laws 2001, c. 2001–226, § 37, eff. Jan. 1, 2002; Laws 2007, c. 2007–74, § 12, eff. July 1, 2007; Laws 2010, c. 2010–132, § 7, eff. Oct. 1, 2010; Laws 2012, c. 2012–109, § 3, eff. July 1, 2012.

Cross References

Homestead, right of surviving spouse, see Const. Art. 10, § 4.
Homestead assessments, see F.S.A. § 193.155.
Property interests, disclaimer of rights of survivorship in jointly held property, see § 739.202.
Tax apportionment, life estate, see § 733.817.

732.4015. Devise of homestead

(1) As provided by the Florida Constitution, the homestead shall not be subject to devise if the owner is survived by a spouse or a minor child or minor children, except that the homestead may be devised to the owner's spouse if there is no minor child or minor children.

(2) For the purposes of subsection (1), the term:

(a) "Owner" includes the grantor of a trust described in s. 733.707(3) that is evidenced by a written instrument which is in existence at the time of the grantor's death as if the interest held in trust was owned by the grantor.

(b) "Devise" includes a disposition by trust of that portion of the trust estate which, if titled in the name of the grantor of the trust, would be the grantor's homestead.

(3) If an interest in homestead has been devised to the surviving spouse as authorized by law and the constitution, and the surviving spouse's interest is disclaimed, the disclaimed interest shall pass in accordance with chapter 739.

Laws 1974, c. 74–106, § 1; Fla.St.1974, Supp. § 732.516; Laws 1975, c. 75–220, §§ 18, 30; Laws 1992, c. 92–200, § 16. Amended by Laws 1997, c. 97–102, § 959, eff. July 1, 1997; Laws 2001, c. 2001–226, § 38, eff. Jan. 1, 2002; Laws 2007, c. 2007–74, § 13, eff. July 1, 2007; Laws 2010, c. 2010–132, § 8, eff. Oct. 1, 2010.

Cross References

Homestead real property, proceedings to determine, see Probate Rule 5.405.
Property interests, disclaimer of rights of survivorship in jointly held property, see § 739.202.
Waiver of rights by spouse, see § 732.702.

732.4017. Inter vivos transfer of homestead property

(1) If the owner of homestead property transfers an interest in that property, including a transfer in trust, with or without consideration, to one or more persons during the owner's lifetime, the transfer is not a devise for purposes of s. 731.201(10) or s. 732.4015, and the interest transferred does not descend as provided in s. 732.401 if the transferor fails to retain a power, held in any capacity, acting alone or in conjunction with any other person, to revoke or revest that interest in the transferor.

(2) As used in this section, the term "transfer in trust" refers to a trust under which the transferor of the homestead property, alone or in conjunction with another person, does not possess a right of revocation as that term is defined in s. 733.707(3)(e). A power possessed by the transferor which is exercisable during the transferor's lifetime to alter the beneficial use and enjoyment of the interest within a class of beneficiaries identified only in the trust instrument is not a right of revocation if the power may not be exercised in favor of the transferor, the transferor's creditors, the transferor's estate, or the creditors of the transferor's estate or exercised to discharge the transferor's legal obligations. This subsection does not create an inference that a power not described in this subsection is a power to revoke or revest an interest in the transferor.

(3) The transfer of an interest in homestead property described in subsection (1) may not be treated as a devise of that interest even if:

(a) The transferor retains a separate legal or equitable interest in the homestead property, directly or indirectly through a trust or other arrangement such as a term of years, life estate, reversion, possibility of reverter, or fractional fee interest;

(b) The interest transferred does not become a possessory interest until a date certain or upon a specified event, the occurrence or nonoccurrence of which does not constitute a power held by the transferor to revoke or revest the interest in the transferor, including, without limitation, the death of the transferor; or

(c) The interest transferred is subject to divestment, expiration, or lapse upon a date certain or upon a specified event, the occurrence or nonoccurrence of which does not constitute a power held by the transferor to revoke or revest the interest in the transferor, including, without limitation, survival of the transferor.

(4) It is the intent of the Legislature that this section clarify existing law.
Added by Laws 2010, c. 2010–132, § 9, eff. Oct. 1, 2010.

732.402. Exempt property

(1) If a decedent was domiciled in this state at the time of death, the surviving spouse, or, if there is no surviving spouse, the children of the decedent shall have the right to a share of the estate of the decedent as provided in this section, to be designated "exempt property."

(2) Exempt property shall consist of:

(a) Household furniture, furnishings, and appliances in the decedent's usual place of abode up to a net value of $20,000 as of the date of death.

(b) Two motor vehicles as defined in s. 316.003(21), which do not, individually as to either such motor vehicle, have a gross vehicle weight in excess of 15,000 pounds, held in the decedent's name and regularly used by the decedent or members of the decedent's immediate family as their personal motor vehicles.

(c) All qualified tuition programs authorized by s. 529 of the Internal Revenue Code of 1986, as amended, including, but not limited to, the Florida Prepaid College Trust Fund advance payment contracts under s. 1009.98 and the Florida Prepaid College Trust Fund participation agreements under s. 1009.981.

(d) All benefits paid pursuant to s. 112.1915.

(3) Exempt property shall be exempt from all claims against the estate except perfected security interests thereon.

(4) Exempt property shall be in addition to protected homestead, statutory entitlements, and property passing under the decedent's will or by intestate succession.

(5) Property specifically or demonstratively devised by the decedent's will to any devisee shall not be included in exempt property. However, persons to whom property has been specifically or demonstratively devised and who would otherwise be entitled to it as exempt property under this section may have the court determine the property to be exempt from claims, except for perfected security interests thereon, after complying with the provisions of subsection (6).

(6) Persons entitled to exempt property shall be deemed to have waived their rights under this section unless a petition for determination of exempt property is filed by or on behalf of the persons entitled to the exempt property on or before the later of the date that is 4 months after

the date of service of the notice of administration or the date that is 40 days after the date of termination of any proceeding involving the construction, admission to probate, or validity of the will or involving any other matter affecting any part of the estate subject to this section.

(7) Property determined as exempt under this section shall be excluded from the value of the estate before residuary, intestate, or pretermitted or elective shares are determined.

Laws 1974, c. 74–106, § 1; Laws 1975, c. 75–220, § 19; Laws 1977, c. 77–87, § 10; Laws 1977, c. 77–174, § 1; Laws 1981, c. 81–238, § 1; Laws 1985, c. 85–79, § 3; Laws 1987, c. 87–226, § 67. Amended by Laws 1998, c. 98–421, § 51, eff. July 1, 1998; Laws 1999, c. 99–220, § 3, eff. May 26, 1999; Laws 2001, c. 2001–180, § 3, eff. June 7, 2001; Laws 2001, c. 2001–226, § 39, eff. Jan. 1, 2002; Laws 2002, c. 2002–387, § 1036, eff. Jan. 7, 2003; Laws 2006, c. 2006–134, § 5, eff. July 1, 2006; Laws 2006, c. 2006–303, § 5, eff. July 1, 2006; Laws 2009, c. 2009–115, § 8, eff. July 1, 2009.

Cross References

Distribution without administration, exempt personal property, see Probate Rule 5.420.

Effect of election on other interests, see § 732.2105.

Exempt property defined, see § 731.201.

Exemption of homestead from forced sale,

    Designation of homestead after levy, see § 222.02.

    Designation of homestead before levy, see § 222.01 et seq.

    Injunction, see § 222.09.

    Jurisdiction, see §§ 222.08, 222.10.

    Personal property, exemption, see § 222.061.

    Selection of exempt personal property, see § 222.07.

Proceedings to determine exempt property, see Probate Rule 5.406.

Wages and unemployment compensation not subject to administration, see § 222.16.

732.403. Family allowance

In addition to protected homestead and statutory entitlements, if the decedent was domiciled in Florida at the time of death, the surviving spouse and the decedent's lineal heirs the decedent was supporting or was obligated to support are entitled to a reasonable allowance in money out of the estate for their maintenance during administration. The court may order this allowance to be paid as a lump sum or in periodic installments. The allowance shall not exceed a total of $18,000. It shall be paid to the surviving spouse, if living, for the use of the spouse and dependent lineal heirs. If the surviving spouse is not living, it shall be paid to the lineal heirs or to the persons having their care and custody. If any lineal heir is not living with the surviving spouse, the allowance may be made partly to the lineal heir or guardian or other person having the heir's care and custody and partly to the surviving spouse, as the needs of the dependent heir and the surviving spouse appear. The family allowance is not chargeable against any benefit or share otherwise passing to the surviving spouse or to the dependent lineal heirs, unless the will otherwise provides. The death of any person entitled to a family allowance terminates the right to that part of the allowance not paid. For purposes of this section, the term "lineal heir" or "lineal heirs" means lineal ascendants and lineal descendants of the decedent.

Laws 1974, c. 74–106, § 1; Laws 1975, c. 75–220, § 19. Amended by Laws 1997, c. 97–102, § 960, eff. July 1, 1997; Laws 2001, c. 2001–226, § 40, eff. Jan. 1, 2002.

Cross References

Estate assets, order of appropriation, see § 733.805.

Family allowance determination proceedings, see Probate Rule 5.407.

Order of payment of expenses and claims, see § 733.707.

Payment of family allowance, see § 733.608.

Priorities and preferences,
    Claims against estate, see § 733.707.
    Order of payment, see § 733.805.
Waiver of rights, family allowance, see § 732.702.

PART V. WILLS

732.501. Who may make a will

Any person who is of sound mind and who is either 18 or more years of age or an emancipated minor may make a will.

Laws 1974, c. 74–106, § 1; Laws 1975, c. 75–220, § 20. Amended by Laws 2001, c. 2001–226, § 41, eff. Jan. 1, 2002.

Cross References

Conveyance by will generally, see § 689.01.
Married minors, removal of disabilities of nonage, see § 743.01 et seq.
Rule against perpetuities, see § 689.225.

732.502. Execution of wills

Every will must be in writing and executed as follows:

(1)(a) *Testator's signature.*—

1. The testator must sign the will at the end; or

2. The testator's name must be subscribed at the end of the will by some other person in the testator's presence and by the testator's direction.

(b) *Witnesses.*—The testator's:

1. Signing, or

2. Acknowledgment:

a. That he or she has previously signed the will, or

b. That another person has subscribed the testator's name to it,

must be in the presence of at least two attesting witnesses.

(c) *Witnesses' signatures.*—The attesting witnesses must sign the will in the presence of the testator and in the presence of each other.

(2) Any will, other than a holographic or nuncupative will, executed by a nonresident of Florida, either before or after this law takes effect, is valid as a will in this state if valid under the laws of the state or country where the will was executed. A will in the testator's handwriting that has been executed in accordance with subsection (1) shall not be considered a holographic will.

(3) Any will executed as a military testamentary instrument in accordance with 10 U.S.C. s. 1044d, Chapter 53, by a person who is eligible for military legal assistance is valid as a will in this state.

(4) No particular form of words is necessary to the validity of a will if it is executed with the formalities required by law.

(5) A codicil shall be executed with the same formalities as a will.

Laws 1974, c. 74–106, § 1; Laws 1975, c. 75–220, § 21; Laws 1977, c. 77–87, § 11. Amended by Laws 1997, c. 97–102, § 961, eff. July 1, 1997; Laws 2001, c. 2001–226, § 42, eff. Jan. 1, 2002; Laws 2003, c. 2003–154, § 5, eff. June 12, 2003.

Cross References

Killer not entitled to receive property or other benefits from death of victim, see § 732.802.

Rule against perpetuities, see § 689.225.

Verification of documents, see § 731.104.

Vital statistics, certified copies of vital records, see F.S.A. § 382.025.

732.503. Self-proof of will

(1) A will or codicil executed in conformity with s. 732.502 may be made self-proved at the time of its execution or at any subsequent date by the acknowledgment of it by the testator and the affidavits of the witnesses, made before an officer authorized to administer oaths and evidenced by the officer's certificate attached to or following the will, in substantially the following form:

STATE OF FLORIDA

COUNTY OF _____

I, _____, declare to the officer taking my acknowledgment of this instrument, and to the subscribing witnesses, that I signed this instrument as my will.

_____

Testator

We, _____ and _____, have been sworn by the officer signing below, and declare to that officer on our oaths that the testator declared the instrument to be the testator's will and signed it in our presence and that we each signed the instrument as a witness in the presence of the testator and of each other.

_____

Witness

_____

Witness

Acknowledged and subscribed before me by the testator, (type or print testator's name), who is personally known to me or who has produced (state type of identification—see s. 117.05(5)(b)2.) as identification, and sworn to and subscribed before me by the witnesses, (type or print name of first witness) who is personally known to me or who has produced (state type of identification—see s. 117.05(5)(b)2.) as identification and (type or print name of second witness) who is personally known to me or who has produced (state type of identification—see s. 117.05(5)(b)2.) as identification, and subscribed by me in the presence of the testator and the subscribing witnesses, all on (date).

_____(Signature of Officer)_____

(Print, type, or stamp commissioned name and affix official seal)

(2) A will or codicil made self-proved under former law, or executed in another state and made self-proved under the laws of that state, shall be considered as self-proved under this section.

Laws 1974, c. 74–106, § 1; Laws 1975, c. 75–220, § 21; Laws 1977, c. 77–87, § 12; Laws 1993, c. 93–62, § 8. Amended by Laws 1997, c. 97–102, § 962, eff. July 1, 1997; Laws 1998, c. 98–246, § 18, eff. Jan. 1, 1999; Laws 2001, c. 2001–226, § 43, eff. Jan. 1, 2002.

Cross References

Nursing home records, copies of care and treatment records, see F.S.A. § 400.145.
Perjury, see § 837.011 et seq.
Proof of wills, see § 733.201.
Verification of documents, see § 731.104.
Will contests, burden of proof, see F.S.A. § 733.107.

732.504. Who may witness

(1) Any person competent to be a witness may act as a witness to a will.

(2) A will or codicil, or any part of either, is not invalid because the will or codicil is signed by an interested witness.

Laws 1974, c. 74–106, § 1; Laws 1975, c. 75–220, § 22; Laws 1977, c. 77–174, § 1; Laws 1979, c. 79–400, § 268.

Cross References

Anatomical gifts, attestation, see § 765.514.

732.505. Revocation by writing

A will or codicil, or any part of either, is revoked:

(1) By a subsequent inconsistent will or codicil, even though the subsequent inconsistent will or codicil does not expressly revoke all previous wills or codicils, but the revocation extends only so far as the inconsistency.

(2) By a subsequent will, codicil, or other writing executed with the same formalities required for the execution of wills declaring the revocation.

Laws 1974, c. 74–106, § 1; Laws 1975, c. 75–220, § 23; Laws 1977, c. 77–87, § 13; Laws 1979, c. 79–400, § 269. Amended by Laws 2001, c. 2001–226, § 44, eff. Jan. 1, 2002.

Cross References

Burden of proof in will contests, see § 733.107.
Discovery of later will, see § 733.208.

732.506. Revocation by act

A will or codicil is revoked by the testator, or some other person in the testator's presence and at the testator's direction, by burning, tearing, canceling, defacing, obliterating, or destroying it with the intent, and for the purpose, of revocation.

Laws 1974, c. 74–106, § 1; Laws 1975, c. 75–220, § 23. Amended by Laws 1997, c. 97–102, § 963, eff. July 1, 1997.

Cross References

Burden of proof in will contests, see § 733.107.

732.507. Effect of subsequent marriage, birth, adoption, or dissolution of marriage

(1) Neither subsequent marriage, birth, nor adoption of descendants shall revoke the prior will of any person, but the pretermitted child or spouse shall inherit as set forth in ss. 732.301 and 732.302, regardless of the prior will.

(2) Any provision of a will executed by a married person that affects the spouse of that person shall become void upon the divorce of that person or upon the dissolution or annulment of the marriage. After the dissolution, divorce, or annulment, the will shall be administered and construed as if the former spouse had died at the time of the dissolution, divorce, or annulment of the marriage, unless the will or the dissolution or divorce judgment expressly provides otherwise.

Laws 1974, c. 74–106, § 1; Laws 1975, c. 75–220, § 24; Laws 1990, c. 90–23, § 3. Amended by Laws 2001, c. 2001–226, § 45, eff. Jan. 1, 2002; Laws 2007, c. 2007–74, § 14, eff. July 1, 2007.

Cross References

Pretermitted children, see § 732.302.
Pretermitted spouse, see § 732.301.
Unborn persons, when bound by others, see § 731.303.

732.508. Revival by revocation

(1) The revocation by the testator of a will that revokes a former will shall not revive the former will, even though the former will is in existence at the date of the revocation of the subsequent will.

(2) The revocation of a codicil to a will does not revoke the will, and, in the absence of evidence to the contrary, it shall be presumed that in revoking the codicil the testator intended to reinstate the provisions of a will or codicil that were changed or revoked by the revoked codicil, as if the revoked codicil had never been executed.

Laws 1974, c. 74–106, § 1; Laws 1975, c. 75–220, § 25.

732.509. Revocation of codicil

The revocation of a will revokes all codicils to that will.

Laws 1974, c. 74–106, § 1; Laws 1975, c. 75–220, § 26.

732.5105. Republication of wills by codicil

The execution of a codicil referring to a previous will has the effect of republishing the will as modified by the codicil.

Laws 1974, c. 74–106, § 1; Laws 1975, c. 75–220, § 26.

732.511. Republication of wills by reexecution

If a will has been revoked or if it is invalid for any other reason, it may be republished and made valid by its reexecution or the execution of a codicil republishing it with the formalities required by this law for the execution of wills.

Laws 1974, c. 74–106, § 1; Laws 1975, c. 75–220, § 26.

732.512. Incorporation by reference

(1) A writing in existence when a will is executed may be incorporated by reference if the language of the will manifests this intent and describes the writing sufficiently to permit its identification.

(2) A will may dispose of property by reference to acts and events which have significance apart from their effect upon the dispositions made by the will, whether they occur before or after the execution of the will or before or after the testator's death. The execution or revocation of a will or trust by another person is such an event.

Laws 1974, c. 74–106, § 1; Laws 1975, c. 75–220, § 27.

732.513. Devises to trustee

(1) A valid devise may be made to the trustee of a trust that is evidenced by a written instrument in existence at the time of making the will, or by a written instrument subscribed concurrently with making of the will, if the written instrument is identified in the will.

(2) The devise shall not be invalid for any or all of the following reasons:

(a) Because the trust is amendable or revocable, or both, by any person.

(b) Because the trust has been amended or revoked in part after execution of the will or a codicil to it.

(c) Because the only res of the trust is the possible expectancy of receiving, as a named beneficiary, a devise under a will or death benefits as described in s. 733.808, and even though the testator or other person has reserved any or all rights of ownership in the death benefit policy, contract, or plan, including the right to change the beneficiary.

(d) Because of any of the provisions of s. 689.075.

(3) The devise shall dispose of property under the terms of the instrument that created the trust as previously or subsequently amended.

(4) An entire revocation of the trust by an instrument in writing before the testator's death shall invalidate the devise or bequest.

(5) Unless the will provides otherwise, the property devised shall not be held under a testamentary trust of the testator but shall become a part of the principal of the trust to which it is devised.

Laws 1974, c. 74–106, § 1; Laws 1975, c. 75–74, § 3; Laws 1975, c. 75–220, § 28; Laws 1988, c. 88–340, § 2. Amended by Laws 2001, c. 2001–226, § 46, eff. Jan. 1, 2002; Laws 2006, c. 2006–217, § 32, eff. July 1, 2007.

UNIFORM TESTAMENTARY ADDITIONS TO TRUSTS ACT (1960)

Table of Jurisdictions Wherein Act Has Been Adopted

For text of Uniform Act, and variation notes and annotation materials for adopting jurisdictions, see Uniform Laws Annotated, Master Edition, Volume 8B.

Jurisdiction	Laws	Effective Date	Statutory Citation
California	1965, p. 3734	9–17–1965	West's Ann.Cal.Prob.Code, §§ 6300 to 6303.
District of Columbia ...	P.L. 89–183, 79 Stat. 688	1–1–1966	D.C. Official Code, 2001 Ed. § 18–306.
Florida..............	1961, c. 61–427	8–1–1961	West's F.S.A. § 732.513.
Illinois	1955, p. 47, § 1	7–1–1955	S.H.A. 755 ILCS 5/4–4.
Indiana	1953, c. 112	1–1–1954	West's A.I.C. 29–1–5–9.
Iowa................	1963, c. 326	1–1–1964	I.C.A. §§ 633.275, 633.277.
Kansas	1968, c. 203	7–1–1968	K.S.A. 59–3101 to 59–3105.
Maine...............	1963, c. 34	9–21–1963	18–A M.R.S.A. § 2–511.
Maryland	1959, c. 612	6–1–1959	Code, Estates and Trusts, §§ 4–411, 4–412.

Jurisdiction	Laws	Effective Date	Statutory Citation
Mississippi	1958, c. 240	5–6–1958	Code 1972, § 91–5–11.
Nevada	1967, c. 260	4–5–1967	N.R.S. 163.220 to 163.250.
New Jersey	1962, c. 241	2–28–1963	N.J.S.A. 3B:4–1 to 3B:4–6.
New York	1966, c. 952	9–1–1967	McKinney's EPTL 3–3.7.
Oklahoma	1961, p. 637	10–27–1961	84 Okl.St.Ann. §§ 301 to 304.
Oregon	1969, c. 591	7–1–1970	ORS 112.265.
Pennsylvania	1957, P.L. 793	7–11–1957	20 Pa.C.S.A. § 2515.
South Carolina	1961, p. 223	4–14–1961	Code 1976, § 62–2–510.
Tennessee	1961, c. 303	3–17–1961	T.C.A. § 32–3–106.
Vermont	1961, No. 208	7–11–1961	14 V.S.A. § 2329.
Washington	1965, c. 145	7–1–1967	West's RCWA 11.12.250.
Wyoming	1957, c. 180	2–20–1957 *	Wyo.Stat.Ann. § 2–6–103.

* Date of approval.

Cross References

Inter vivos trusts, powers retained by settlor, see § 689.075.
Trustee defined, see § 731.201.

732.514. Vesting of devises

The death of the testator is the event that vests the right to devises unless the testator in the will has provided that some other event must happen before a devise vests.

Laws 1974, c. 74–106, § 1; Laws 1975, c. 75–220, § 28. Amended by Laws 1997, c. 97–102, § 964, eff. July 1, 1997; Laws 2001, c. 2001–226, § 47, eff. Jan. 1, 2002.

Cross References

Rule against perpetuities, see § 689.225.
Vesting of rights under the probate code, see § 731.011.

732.515. Separate writing identifying devises of tangible property

A written statement or list referred to in the decedent's will shall dispose of items of tangible personal property, other than property used in trade or business, not otherwise specifically disposed of by the will. To be admissible under this section as evidence of the intended disposition, the writing must be signed by the testator and must describe the items and the devisees with reasonable certainty. The writing may be prepared before or after the execution of the will. It may be altered by the testator after its preparation. It may be a writing that has no significance apart from its effect upon the dispositions made by the will. If more than one otherwise effective writing exists, then, to the extent of any conflict among the writings, the provisions of the most recent writing revoke the inconsistent provisions of each prior writing.

Laws 1974, c. 74–106, § 1; Laws 1975, c. 75–220, § 29. Amended by Laws 2001, c. 2001–226, § 48, eff. Jan. 1, 2002.

732.5165. Effect of fraud, duress, mistake, and undue influence

A will is void if the execution is procured by fraud, duress, mistake, or undue influence. Any part of the will is void if so procured, but the remainder of the will not so procured shall be valid if it is not invalid for other reasons. If the revocation of a will, or any part thereof, is procured by fraud, duress, mistake, or undue influence, such revocation is void.

Laws 1975, c. 75–220, § 31. Amended by Laws 2011, c. 2011–183, § 6, eff. June 21, 2011.

Cross References

Killer not entitled to benefits accruing from death of victim, see § 732.802.

732.517. Penalty clause for contest

A provision in a will purporting to penalize any interested person for contesting the will or instituting other proceedings relating to the estate is unenforceable.

Laws 1974, c. 74–106, § 1; Laws 1975, c. 75–220, § 32.

Cross References

Costs, see § 733.106.
Individual liability of personal representative, see § 733.619.

732.518. Will contests

An action to contest the validity of all or part of a will or the revocation of all or part of a will may not be commenced before the death of the testator.

Laws 1992, c. 92–200, § 17. Amended by Laws 2011, c. 2011–183, § 7, eff. June 21, 2011.

PART VI.   RULES OF CONSTRUCTION

732.6005.   Rules of construction and intention

(1) The intention of the testator as expressed in the will controls the legal effect of the testator's dispositions. The rules of construction expressed in this part shall apply unless a contrary intention is indicated by the will.

(2) Subject to the foregoing, a will is construed to pass all property which the testator owns at death, including property acquired after the execution of the will.

Laws 1974, c. 74–106, § 1; Fla.St.1974, Supp. § 732.602; Laws 1975, c. 75–220, §§ 33, 35. Amended by Laws 1997, c. 97–102, § 965, eff. July 1, 1997; Laws 2001, c. 2001–226, § 49, eff. Jan. 1, 2002.

Cross References

Burden of proof in will contests, see § 733.107.
Rule in Shelley's case, abolition, see § 689.17.

732.601. Simultaneous Death Law

Unless a contrary intention appears in the governing instrument:

(1) When title to property or its devolution depends on priority of death and there is insufficient evidence that the persons have died otherwise than simultaneously, the property of each person shall be disposed of as if that person survived.

(2) When two or more beneficiaries are designated to take successively by reason of survivorship under another person's disposition of property and there is insufficient evidence that the beneficiaries died otherwise than simultaneously, the property thus disposed of shall be divided into as many equal parts as there are successive beneficiaries and the parts shall be distributed to those who would have taken if each designated beneficiary had survived.

(3) When there is insufficient evidence that two joint tenants or tenants by the entirety died otherwise than simultaneously, the property so held shall be distributed one-half as if one had survived and one-half as if the other had survived. If there are more than two joint tenants and

all of them so died, the property thus distributed shall be in the proportion that one bears to the number of joint tenants.

(4) When the insured and the beneficiary in a policy of life or accident insurance have died and there is insufficient evidence that they died otherwise than simultaneously, the proceeds of the policy shall be distributed as if the insured had survived the beneficiary.

Laws 1974, c. 74–106, § 1; Laws 1975, c. 75–220, § 34. Amended by Laws 1997, c. 97–102, § 966, eff. July 1, 1997; Laws 2001, c. 2001–226, § 50, eff. Jan. 1, 2002.

Uniform Simultaneous Death Act (1940)

Table of Jurisdictions Wherein Act Has Been Adopted

For text of Uniform Act, and variation notes and annotation materials for adopting jurisdictions, see Uniform Laws Annotated, Master Edition, Volume 8B.

Jurisdiction	Laws	Effective Date	Statutory Citation
Alabama	1949, p. 852	9–7–1949	Code 1975, §§ 43–7–1 to 43–7–8.
California	1945, p. 1885	9–15–1945	West's Ann.Cal.Prob.Code, §§ 220 to 234.
Connecticut	1943, c. 266, p. 272	10–1–1943	C.G.S.A. § 45a–440.
Delaware	1945, c. 234	4–18–1945 *	12 Del.C. §§ 701 to 707.
Florida	1941, c. 20884	6–12–1941	West's F.S.A. § 732.601.
Georgia	1996, p. 504	1–1–1998	O.C.G.A. §§ 53–10–1 to 53–10–6.
Idaho	1943, c. 83	2–23–1943 *	I.C. § 15–2–613.
Illinois	1941, vol. 1, p. 6	7–16–1941	S.H.A. 755 ILCS 5/3–1, 5/3–2.
Indiana	1941, c. 49	2–24–1941 *	West's A.I.C. 29–2–14–1 to 29–2–14–8.
Iowa	1963, c. 326	1–1–1964	I.C.A. §§ 633.523 to 633.528.
Maine	1941, c. 111	3–29–1941	18–A M.R.S.A. § 2–805.
Maryland	1941, c. 191	6–1–1941	Code, Courts and Judicial Proceedings, §§ 10–801 to 10–807.
Minnesota	1943, c. 248	4–2–1943 *	M.S.A. § 524.2–702.
Mississippi	1956, c. 214	7–1–1956	Code 1972, §§ 91–3–1 to 91–3–15.
Missouri	1947, Vol. 1, p. 13	9–10–1947	V.A.M.S. §§ 471.010 to 471.080.
Nebraska	1947, c. 112	3–8–1947	R.R.S.1943, §§ 30–121 to 30–128.
Nevada	1949, c. 44	3–9–1949 *	N.R.S. 135.010 to 135.090.
New Jersey	1947, c. 384	7–3–1947	N.J.S.A. 3B:6–1 to 3B:6–7.
Oklahoma	1959, c. 385	10–2–1959	58 Okl.St.Ann. §§ 1001 to 1008.
Pennsylvania	1972, No. 164	7–1–1972	20 Pa.C.S.A. §§ 8501 to 8505.
Rhode Island	1947, c. 1871	4–28–1947	Gen.Laws 1956, §§ 33–2–1 to 33–2–9.
Tennessee	1941, c. 59	2–10–1941	T.C.A. §§ 31–3–101 to 31–3–120.
Vermont	1941, No. 41	3–21–1941	14 V.S.A. §§ 621 to 627.
West Virginia	1953, c. 66	2–18–1953	Code, 42–5–1 to 42–5–10.
Wyoming	1941, c. 94	2–21–1941	Wyo.Stat.Ann. §§ 2–13–101 to 2–13–107.

* Date of approval.

[1] Repeals this act and enacts the Uniform Simultaneous Death Act (1993) effective July 1, 2011.

Cross References

Killer not entitled to benefits accruing from death of victim, see § 732.802.

732.603. Antilapse; deceased devisee; class gifts

(1) Unless a contrary intent appears in the will, if a devisee who is a grandparent, or a descendant of a grandparent, of the testator:

(a) Is dead at the time of the execution of the will;

(b) Fails to survive the testator; or

(c) Is required by the will or by operation of law to be treated as having predeceased the testator,

a substitute gift is created in the devisee's surviving descendants who take per stirpes the property to which the devisee would have been entitled had the devisee survived the testator.

(2) When a power of appointment is exercised by will, unless a contrary intent appears in the document creating the power of appointment or in the testator's will, if an appointee who is a grandparent, or a descendant of a grandparent, of the donor of the power:

(a) Is dead at the time of the execution of the will or the creation of the power;

(b) Fails to survive the testator; or

(c) Is required by the will, the document creating the power, or by operation of law to be treated as having predeceased the testator,

a substitute gift is created in the appointee's surviving descendants who take per stirpes the property to which the appointee would have been entitled had the appointee survived the testator. Unless the language creating a power of appointment expressly excludes the substitution of the descendants of an object of a power for the object, a surviving descendant of a deceased object of a power of appointment may be substituted for the object whether or not the descendant is an object of the power.

(3) In the application of this section:

(a) Words of survivorship in a devise or appointment to an individual, such as "if he survives me," or to "my surviving children," are a sufficient indication of an intent contrary to the application of subsections (1) and (2). Words of survivorship used by the donor of the power in a power to appoint to an individual, such as the term "if he survives the donee," or in a power to appoint to the donee's "then surviving children," are a sufficient indication of an intent contrary to the application of subsection (2).

(b) The term:

1. "Appointment" includes an alternative appointment and an appointment in the form of a class gift.

2. "Appointee" includes:

a. A class member if the appointment is in the form of a class gift.

b. An individual or class member who was deceased at the time the testator executed his or her will as well as an individual or class member who was then living but who failed to survive the testator.

3. "Devise" also includes an alternative devise and a devise in the form of a class gift.

4. "Devisee" also includes:

a. A class member if the devise is in the form of a class gift.

b. An individual or class member who was deceased at the time the testator executed his or her will as well as an individual or class member who was then living but who failed to survive the testator.

(4) This section applies only to outright devises and appointments. Devises and appointments in trust, including to a testamentary trust, are subject to s. 736.1106.

Laws 1974, c. 74–106, § 1; Laws 1975, c. 75–220, § 36. Amended by Laws 1997, c. 97–102, § 967, eff. July 1, 1997; Laws 2001, c. 2001–226, § 51, eff. Jan. 1, 2002; Laws 2003, c. 2003–154, § 6, eff. June 12, 2003; Laws 2006, c. 2006–217, § 33, eff. July 1, 2007.

Cross References

Antilapse, survivorship with respect to future interests under terms of inter vivos and testamentary trusts, substitute
   takers, see § 736.1106.
Rule against perpetuities, see § 689.225.

732.604. Failure of testamentary provision

(1) Except as provided in s. 732.603, if a devise other than a residuary devise fails for any
reason, it becomes a part of the residue.

(2) Except as provided in s. 732.603, if the residue is devised to two or more persons, the
share of a residuary devisee that fails for any reason passes to the other residuary devisee, or to
the other residuary devisees in proportion to the interests of each in the remaining part of the
residue.

Laws 1974, c. 74–106, § 1; Laws 1975, c. 75–220, § 37. Amended by Laws 1997, c. 97–102, § 968, eff.
July 1, 1997; Laws 2001, c. 2001–226, § 52, eff. Jan. 1, 2002; Laws 2003, c. 2003–154, § 29, eff. June 12,
2003; Laws 2006, c. 2006–217, § 34, eff. July 1, 2007.

Cross References

Antilapse, survivorship with respect to future interests under terms of inter vivos and testamentary trusts, substitute
   takers, see § 736.1106.

732.605. Change in securities; accessions; nonademption

(1) If the testator intended a specific devise of certain securities rather than their equivalent
value, the specific devisee is entitled only to:

(a) As much of the devised securities as is a part of the estate at the time of the testator's
death.

(b) Any additional or other securities of the same entity owned by the testator because of
action initiated by the entity, excluding any acquired by exercise of purchase options.

(c) Securities of another entity owned by the testator as a result of a merger, consolidation,
reorganization, or other similar action initiated by the entity.

(d) Securities of the same entity acquired as a result of a plan of reinvestment.

(2) Distributions before death with respect to a specifically devised security, whether in cash
or otherwise, which are not provided for in subsection (1) are not part of the specific devise.

Laws 1974, c. 74–106, § 1; Laws 1975, c. 75–220, § 37. Amended by Laws 2001, c. 2001–226, § 53, eff.
Jan. 1, 2002.

Cross References

Ademption by satisfaction, see § 732.609.
Securities defined, see § 731.201.
Securities transactions, definitions, see § 517.021.
Valuation, securities, see § 733.810.

732.606. Nonademption of specific devises in certain cases; sale by guardian of the property; unpaid proceeds of sale, condemnation, or insurance

(1) If specifically devised property is sold by a guardian of the property or if a condemnation
award or insurance proceeds are paid to a guardian of the property, the specific devisee has the
right to a general pecuniary devise equal to the net sale price, the condemnation award, or the

insurance proceeds. This subsection does not apply if, subsequent to the sale, condemnation, or casualty, it is adjudicated that the disability of the testator has ceased and the testator survives the adjudication by 1 year. The right of the specific devisee under this subsection is reduced by any right described in subsection (2).

(2) A specific devisee has the right to the remaining specifically devised property and:

(a) Any balance of the purchase price owing from a purchaser to the testator at death because of sale of the property plus any security interest.

(b) Any amount of a condemnation award for the taking of the property unpaid at death.

(c) Any proceeds unpaid at death on fire or casualty insurance on the property.

(d) Property owned by the testator at death as a result of foreclosure, or obtained instead of foreclosure, of the security for the specifically devised obligation.

Laws 1974, c. 74–106, § 1; Laws 1975, c. 75–220, § 38. Amended by Laws 1997, c. 97–102, § 969, eff. July 1, 1997; Laws 2001, c. 2001–226, § 54, eff. Jan. 1, 2002.

732.607. Exercise of power of appointment

A general residuary clause in a will, or a will making general disposition of all the testator's property, does not exercise a power of appointment held by the testator unless specific reference is made to the power or there is some other indication of intent to include the property subject to the power.

Laws 1974, c. 74–106, § 1; Laws 1975, c. 75–220, § 38.

Cross References

Rule against perpetuities, see § 689.225.

732.608. Construction of terms

The laws used to determine paternity and relationships for the purposes of intestate succession apply when determining whether class gift terminology and terms of relationship include adopted persons and persons born out of wedlock.

Laws 1974, c. 74–106, § 1; Laws 1975, c. 75–220, § 38. Amended by Laws 2010, c. 2010–132, § 10, eff. Oct. 1, 2010.

Cross References

Adoption, see § 63.012 et seq.
Adoption judgment, effect on inheritance, see § 63.172.
Intestate succession, illegitimate and adopted children, see § 732.108.
Marriage of parents, illegitimate children, see § 742.091.
Paternity, see § 742.011 et seq.
Special or local laws legitimizing children, see Const. Art. 3, § 11.
Void marriages, see §§ 741.21, 741.211.

732.609. Ademption by satisfaction

Property that a testator gave to a person in the testator's lifetime is treated as a satisfaction of a devise to that person, in whole or in part, only if the will provides for deduction of the lifetime gift, the testator declares in a contemporaneous writing that the gift is to be deducted from the devise or is in satisfaction of the devise, or the devisee acknowledges in writing that the gift is in satisfaction. For purposes of part satisfaction, property given during the testator's lifetime is valued at the time the devisee came into possession or enjoyment of the property or at the time of the death of the testator, whichever occurs first.

Laws 1974, c. 74–106, § 1; Laws 1975, c. 75–220, § 38.

Cross References

Abatement and contribution, see § 733.805.
Advancement, see § 733.806.
Securities, nonademption, see § 732.605.
Valuation, distribution of estate, see § 733.810.

732.611.　Devises to multigeneration classes to be per stirpes

Unless the will provides otherwise, all devises to descendants, issue, and other multigeneration classes shall be per stirpes.

Laws 1974, c. 74–106, § 1; Laws 1975, c. 75–220, § 38.　Amended by Laws 2006, c. 2006–217, § 35, eff. July 1, 2007.

Cross References

Intestate succession, inheritance per stirpes, see § 732.104.

732.615.　Reformation to correct mistakes

Upon application of any interested person, the court may reform the terms of a will, even if unambiguous, to conform the terms to the testator's intent if it is proved by clear and convincing evidence that both the accomplishment of the testator's intent and the terms of the will were affected by a mistake of fact or law, whether in expression or inducement.　In determining the testator's original intent, the court may consider evidence relevant to the testator's intent even though the evidence contradicts an apparent plain meaning of the will.

Added by Laws 2011, c. 2011–183, § 3, eff. July 1, 2011.

Cross References

Fees and costs of will reformation, see F.S.A. § 733.1061.

732.616.　Modification to achieve testator's tax objectives

Upon application of any interested person, to achieve the testator's tax objectives the court may modify the terms of a will in a manner that is not contrary to the testator's probable intent. The court may provide that the modification has retroactive effect.

Added by Laws 2011, c. 2011–183, § 4, eff. July 1, 2011.

Cross References

Fees and costs of will modification, see F.S.A. § 733.1061.

PART VII.　CONTRACTUAL ARRANGEMENTS RELATING TO DEATH

732.701.　Agreements concerning succession

(1) No agreement to make a will, to give a devise, not to revoke a will, not to revoke a devise, not to make a will, or not to make a devise shall be binding or enforceable unless the agreement is in writing and signed by the agreeing party in the presence of two attesting witnesses.　Such an agreement executed by a nonresident of Florida, either before or after this law takes effect, is valid in this state if valid when executed under the laws of the state or country where the agreement was executed, whether or not the agreeing party is a Florida resident at the time of death.

(2) The execution of a joint will or mutual wills neither creates a presumption of a contract to make a will nor creates a presumption of a contract not to revoke the will or wills.

Laws 1974, c. 74–106, § 1; Laws 1975, c. 75–220, § 39. Amended by Laws 2001, c. 2001–226, § 55, eff. Jan. 1, 2002.

Cross References

Execution of wills, see § 732.502.
Premarital agreements, see § 61.079.
Revocation of wills, see §§ 732.505, 732.506.
Rule against perpetuities, see § 689.225.

732.702. Waiver of spousal rights

(1) The rights of a surviving spouse to an elective share, intestate share, pretermitted share, homestead, exempt property, family allowance, and preference in appointment as personal representative of an intestate estate or any of those rights, may be waived, wholly or partly, before or after marriage, by a written contract, agreement, or waiver, signed by the waiving party in the presence of two subscribing witnesses. The requirement of witnesses shall be applicable only to contracts, agreements, or waivers signed by Florida residents after the effective date of this law. Any contract, agreement, or waiver executed by a nonresident of Florida, either before or after this law takes effect, is valid in this state if valid when executed under the laws of the state or country where it was executed, whether or not he or she is a Florida resident at the time of death. Unless the waiver provides to the contrary, a waiver of "all rights," or equivalent language, in the property or estate of a present or prospective spouse, or a complete property settlement entered into after, or in anticipation of, separation, dissolution of marriage, or divorce, is a waiver of all rights to elective share, intestate share, pretermitted share, homestead, exempt property, family allowance, and preference in appointment as personal representative of an intestate estate, by the waiving party in the property of the other and a renunciation by the waiving party of all benefits that would otherwise pass to the waiving party from the other by intestate succession or by the provisions of any will executed before the written contract, agreement, or waiver.

(2) Each spouse shall make a fair disclosure to the other of that spouse's estate if the agreement, contract, or waiver is executed after marriage. No disclosure shall be required for an agreement, contract, or waiver executed before marriage.

(3) No consideration other than the execution of the agreement, contract, or waiver shall be necessary to its validity, whether executed before or after marriage.

Laws 1974, c. 74–106, § 1; Laws 1975, c. 75–220, § 39; Laws 1977, c. 77–87, § 14. Amended by Laws 2001, c. 2001–226, § 56, eff. Jan. 1, 2002.

Cross References

Notice of waiver, see § 731.302.
Premarital agreements, see § 61.079.

732.703. Effect of divorce, dissolution, or invalidity of marriage on disposition of certain assets at death

(1) As used in this section, unless the context requires otherwise, the term:

(a) "Asset," when not modified by other words or phrases, means an asset described in subsection (3), except as provided in paragraph (4)(j).

(b) "Beneficiary" means any person designated in a governing instrument to receive an interest in an asset upon the death of the decedent.

(c) "Death certificate" means a certified copy of a death certificate issued by an official or agency for the place where the decedent's death occurred.

(d) "Employee benefit plan" means any funded or unfunded plan, program, or fund established by an employer to provide an employee's beneficiaries with benefits that may be payable on the employee's death.

(e) "Governing instrument" means any writing or contract governing the disposition of all or any part of an asset upon the death of the decedent.

(f) "Payor" means any person obligated to make payment of the decedent's interest in an asset upon the death of the decedent, and any other person who is in control or possession of an asset.

(g) "Primary beneficiary" means a beneficiary designated under the governing instrument to receive an interest in an asset upon the death of the decedent who is not a secondary beneficiary. A person who receives an interest in the asset upon the death of the decedent due to the death of another beneficiary prior to the decedent's death is also a primary beneficiary.

(h) "Secondary beneficiary" means a beneficiary designated under the governing instrument who will receive an interest in an asset if the designation of the primary beneficiary is revoked or otherwise cannot be given effect.

(2) A designation made by or on behalf of the decedent providing for the payment or transfer at death of an interest in an asset to or for the benefit of the decedent's former spouse is void as of the time the decedent's marriage was judicially dissolved or declared invalid by court order prior to the decedent's death, if the designation was made prior to the dissolution or court order. The decedent's interest in the asset shall pass as if the decedent's former spouse predeceased the decedent. An individual retirement account described in s. 408 or s. 408A of the Internal Revenue Code of 1986,[1] or an employee benefit plan, may not be treated as a trust for purposes of this section.

(3) Subsection (2) applies to the following assets in which a resident of this state has an interest at the time of the resident's death:

(a) A life insurance policy, qualified annuity, or other similar tax-deferred contract held within an employee benefit plan.

(b) An employee benefit plan.

(c) An individual retirement account described in s. 408 or s. 408A of the Internal Revenue Code of 1986,[1] including an individual retirement annuity described in s. 408(b) of the Internal Revenue Code of 1986. [2]

(d) A payable-on-death account.

(e) A security or other account registered in a transfer-on-death form.

(f) A life insurance policy, annuity, or other similar contract that is not held within an employee benefit plan or a tax-qualified retirement account.

(4) Subsection (2) does not apply:

(a) To the extent that controlling federal law provides otherwise;

(b) If the governing instrument is signed by the decedent, or on behalf of the decedent, after the order of dissolution or order declaring the marriage invalid and such governing instrument expressly provides that benefits will be payable to the decedent's former spouse;

(c) To the extent a will or trust governs the disposition of the assets and s. 732.507(2) or s. 736.1105 applies;

(d) If the order of dissolution or order declaring the marriage invalid requires that the decedent acquire or maintain the asset for the benefit of a former spouse or children of the marriage, payable upon the death of the decedent either outright or in trust, only if other assets of the decedent fulfilling such a requirement for the benefit of the former spouse or children of the marriage do not exist upon the death of the decedent;

(e) If, under the terms of the order of dissolution or order declaring the marriage invalid, the decedent could not have unilaterally terminated or modified the ownership of the asset, or its disposition upon the death of the decedent;

(f) If the designation of the decedent's former spouse as a beneficiary is irrevocable under applicable law;

(g) If the governing instrument is governed by the laws of a state other than this state;

(h) To an asset held in two or more names as to which the death of one coowner vests ownership of the asset in the surviving coowner or coowners;

(i) If the decedent remarries the person whose interest would otherwise have been revoked under this section and the decedent and that person are married to one another at the time of the decedent's death; or

(j) To state-administered retirement plans under chapter 121.

(5) In the case of an asset described in paragraph (3)(a), paragraph (3)(b), or paragraph (3)(c), unless payment or transfer would violate a court order directed to, and served as required by law on, the payor:

(a) If the governing instrument does not explicitly specify the relationship of the beneficiary to the decedent or if the governing instrument explicitly provides that the beneficiary is not the decedent's spouse, the payor is not liable for making any payment on account of, or transferring any interest in, the asset to the beneficiary.

(b) As to any portion of the asset required by the governing instrument to be paid after the decedent's death to a primary beneficiary explicitly designated in the governing instrument as the decedent's spouse:

1. If the death certificate states that the decedent was married at the time of his or her death to that spouse, the payor is not liable for making a payment on account of, or for transferring an interest in, that portion of the asset to such primary beneficiary.

2. If the death certificate states that the decedent was not married at the time of his or her death, or if the death certificate states that the decedent was married to a person other than the spouse designated as the primary beneficiary at the time of his or her death, the payor is not liable for making a payment on account of, or for transferring an interest in, that portion of the asset to a secondary beneficiary under the governing instrument.

3. If the death certificate is silent as to the decedent's marital status at the time of his or her death, the payor is not liable for making a payment on account of, or for transferring an interest in, that portion of the asset to the primary beneficiary upon delivery to the payor of an affidavit validly executed by the primary beneficiary in substantially the following form:

STATE OF _____

COUNTY OF _____

Before me, the undersigned authority, personally appeared   (type or print Affiant's name) ("Affiant"), who swore or affirmed that:

1.   (Type or print name of Decedent)   ("Decedent") died on   (type or print the date of the Decedent's death) .

2.   Affiant is a "primary beneficiary" as that term is defined in Section 732.703, Florida Statutes. Affiant and Decedent were married on   (type or print the date of marriage) , and were legally married to one another on the date of the Decedent's death.

_____

(Affiant)

Sworn to or affirmed before me by the affiant who is personally known to me or who has produced   (state type of identification)   as identification this __ day of   (month) , (year)

  (Signature of Officer)

  (Print, Type, or Stamp Commissioned name of Notary Public)

4.   If the death certificate is silent as to the decedent's marital status at the time of his or her death, the payor is not liable for making a payment on account of, or for transferring an interest in, that portion of the asset to the secondary beneficiary upon delivery to the payor of an affidavit validly executed by the secondary beneficiary affidavit in substantially the following form:

STATE OF _____

COUNTY OF _____

Before me, the undersigned authority, personally appeared   (type or print Affiant's name) ("Affiant"), who swore or affirmed that:

1.   (Type or print name of Decedent)   ("Decedent") died on   (type or print the date of the Decedent's death) .

2.   Affiant is a "secondary beneficiary" as that term is defined in Section 732.703, Florida Statutes. On the date of the Decedent's death, the Decedent was not legally married to the spouse designated as the "primary beneficiary" as that term is defined in Section 732.703, Florida Statutes.

Sworn to or affirmed before me by the affiant who is personally known to me or who has produced   (state type of identification)   as identification this __ day of   (month) , (year)

  (Signature of Officer)

  (Print, Type, or Stamp Commissioned name of Notary Public)

(6) In the case of an asset described in paragraph (3)(d), paragraph (3)(e), or paragraph (3)(f), the payor is not liable for making any payment on account of, or transferring any interest in, the asset to any beneficiary.

(7) Subsections (5) and (6) apply notwithstanding the payor's knowledge that the person to whom the asset is transferred is different from the person who would own the interest pursuant to subsection (2).

(8) This section does not affect the ownership of an interest in an asset as between the former spouse and any other person entitled to such interest by operation of this section, the rights of

any purchaser for value of any such interest, the rights of any creditor of the former spouse or any other person entitled to such interest, or the rights and duties of any insurance company, financial institution, trustee, administrator, or other third party.

(9) This section applies to all designations made by or on behalf of decedents dying on or after July 1, 2012, regardless of when the designation was made.

Added by Laws 2012, c. 2012–148, § 1, eff. July 1, 2012. Amended by Laws 2013, c. 2013–172, § 6, eff. Oct. 1, 2013.

¹ 26 U.S.C.A. §§ 408, 408A.
² 26 U.S.C.A. § 408(b).

PART VIII. GENERAL PROVISIONS

732.802. Killer not entitled to receive property or other benefits by reason of victim's death

(1) A surviving person who unlawfully and intentionally kills or participates in procuring the death of the decedent is not entitled to any benefits under the will or under the Florida Probate Code, and the estate of the decedent passes as if the killer had predeceased the decedent. Property appointed by the will of the decedent to or for the benefit of the killer passes as if the killer had predeceased the decedent.

(2) Any joint tenant who unlawfully and intentionally kills another joint tenant thereby effects a severance of the interest of the decedent so that the share of the decedent passes as the decedent's property and the killer has no rights by survivorship. This provision applies to joint tenancies with right of survivorship and tenancies by the entirety in real and personal property; joint and multiple-party accounts in banks, savings and loan associations, credit unions, and other institutions; and any other form of coownership with survivorship incidents.

(3) A named beneficiary of a bond, life insurance policy, or other contractual arrangement who unlawfully and intentionally kills the principal obligee or the person upon whose life the policy is issued is not entitled to any benefit under the bond, policy, or other contractual arrangement; and it becomes payable as though the killer had predeceased the decedent.

(4) Any other acquisition of property or interest by the killer, including a life estate in homestead property, shall be treated in accordance with the principles of this section.

(5) A final judgment of conviction of murder in any degree is conclusive for purposes of this section. In the absence of a conviction of murder in any degree, the court may determine by the greater weight of the evidence whether the killing was unlawful and intentional for purposes of this section.

(6) This section does not affect the rights of any person who, before rights under this section have been adjudicated, purchases from the killer for value and without notice property which the killer would have acquired except for this section, but the killer is liable for the amount of the proceeds or the value of the property. Any insurance company, bank, or other obligor making payment according to the terms of its policy or obligation is not liable by reason of this section unless prior to payment it has received at its home office or principal address written notice of a claim under this section.

Laws 1974, c. 74–106, § 1; Laws 1975, c. 75–220, § 41; Laws 1982, c. 82–71, § 1.

Cross References

Murder, see § 782.04.

732.804. Provisions relating to disposition of the body

Before issuance of letters, any person may carry out written instructions of the decedent relating to the decedent's body and funeral and burial arrangements. The fact that cremation occurred pursuant to a written direction signed by the decedent that the body be cremated is a complete defense to a cause of action against any person acting or relying on that direction.

Laws 1974, c. 74–106, § 1; Laws 1975, c. 75–220, § 43. Amended by Laws 1997, c. 97–102, § 971, eff. July 1, 1997; Laws 2001, c. 2001–226, § 58, eff. Jan. 1, 2002.

Cross References

Offenses pertaining to cremation, see § 872.03.

732.805. Spousal rights procured by fraud, duress, or undue influence

(1) A surviving spouse who is found to have procured a marriage to the decedent by fraud, duress, or undue influence is not entitled to any of the following rights or benefits that inure solely by virtue of the marriage or the person's status as surviving spouse of the decedent unless the decedent and the surviving spouse voluntarily cohabited as husband and wife with full knowledge of the facts constituting the fraud, duress, or undue influence or both spouses otherwise subsequently ratified the marriage:

(a) Any rights or benefits under the Florida Probate Code, including, but not limited to, entitlement to elective share or family allowance; preference in appointment as personal representative; inheritance by intestacy, homestead, or exempt property; or inheritance as a pretermitted spouse.

(b) Any rights or benefits under a bond, life insurance policy, or other contractual arrangement if the decedent is the principal obligee or the person upon whose life the policy is issued, unless the surviving spouse is provided for by name, whether or not designated as the spouse, in the bond, life insurance policy, or other contractual arrangement.

(c) Any rights or benefits under a will, trust, or power of appointment, unless the surviving spouse is provided for by name, whether or not designated as the spouse, in the will, trust, or power of appointment.

(d) Any immunity from the presumption of undue influence that a surviving spouse may have under state law.

(2) Any of the rights or benefits listed in paragraphs (1)(a)–(c) which would have passed solely by virtue of the marriage to a surviving spouse who is found to have procured the marriage by fraud, duress, or undue influence shall pass as if the spouse had predeceased the decedent.

(3) A challenge to a surviving spouse's rights under this section may be maintained as a defense, objection, or cause of action by any interested person after the death of the decedent in any proceeding in which the fact of marriage may be directly or indirectly material.

(4) The contestant has the burden of establishing, by a preponderance of the evidence, that the marriage was procured by fraud, duress, or undue influence. If ratification of the marriage is raised as a defense, the surviving spouse has the burden of establishing, by a preponderance of the evidence, the subsequent ratification by both spouses.

(5) In all actions brought under this section, the court shall award taxable costs as in chancery actions, including attorney's fees. When awarding taxable costs and attorney's fees, the court may direct payment from a party's interest, if any, in the estate, or enter a judgment that may be satisfied from other property of the party, or both.

(6) An insurance company, financial institution, or other obligor making payment according to the terms of its policy or obligation is not liable by reason of this section unless, before payment, it received written notice of a claim pursuant to this section.

(a) The notice required by this subsection must be in writing and must be accomplished in a manner reasonably suitable under the circumstances and likely to result in receipt of the notice. Permissible methods of notice include first-class mail, personal delivery, delivery to the person's last known place of residence or place of business, or a properly directed facsimile or other electronic message.

(b) To be effective, notice to a financial institution or insurance company must contain the name, address, and the taxpayer identification number, or the account or policy number, of the principal obligee or person whose life is insured and shall be directed to an officer or a manager of the financial institution or insurance company in this state. If the financial institution or insurance company has no offices in this state, the notice shall be directed to the principal office of the financial institution or insurance company.

(c) Notice shall be effective when given, except that notice to a financial institution or insurance company is not effective until 5 business days after being given.

(7) The rights and remedies granted in this section are in addition to any other rights or remedies a person may have at law or equity.

(8) Unless sooner barred by adjudication, estoppel, or a provision of the Florida Probate Code or Florida Probate Rules, an interested person is barred from bringing an action under this section unless the action is commenced within 4 years after the decedent's date of death. A cause of action under this section accrues on the decedent's date of death.

Added by Laws 2010, c. 2010–132, § 11, eff. Oct. 1, 2010.

732.806. Gifts to lawyers and other disqualified persons

(1) Any part of a written instrument which makes a gift to a lawyer or a person related to the lawyer is void if the lawyer prepared or supervised the execution of the written instrument, or solicited the gift, unless the lawyer or other recipient of the gift is related to the person making the gift.

(2) This section is not applicable to a provision in a written instrument appointing a lawyer, or a person related to the lawyer, as a fiduciary.

(3) A provision in a written instrument purporting to waive the application of this section is unenforceable.

(4) If property distributed in kind, or a security interest in that property, is acquired by a purchaser or lender for value from a person who has received a gift in violation of this section, the purchaser or lender takes title free of any claims arising under this section and incurs no personal liability by reason of this section, whether or not the gift is void under this section.

(5) In all actions brought under this section, the court must award taxable costs as in chancery actions, including attorney fees. When awarding taxable costs and attorney fees under this section, the court may direct payment from a party's interest in the estate or trust, or enter a judgment that may be satisfied from other property of the party, or both. Attorney fees and costs may not be awarded against a party who, in good faith, initiates an action under this section to declare a gift void.

(6) If a part of a written instrument is invalid by reason of this section, the invalid part is severable and may not affect any other part of the written instrument which can be given effect,

including a term that makes an alternate or substitute gift. In the case of a power of appointment, this section does not affect the power to appoint in favor of persons other than the lawyer or a person related to the lawyer.

(7) For purposes of this section:

(a) A lawyer is deemed to have prepared, or supervised the execution of, a written instrument if the preparation, or supervision of the execution, of the written instrument was performed by an employee or lawyer employed by the same firm as the lawyer.

(b) A person is "related" to an individual if, at the time the lawyer prepared or supervised the execution of the written instrument or solicited the gift, the person is:

1. A spouse of the individual;

2. A lineal ascendant or descendant of the individual;

3. A sibling of the individual;

4. A relative of the individual or of the individual's spouse with whom the lawyer maintains a close, familial relationship;

5. A spouse of a person described in subparagraph 2., subparagraph 3., or subparagraph 4.; or

6. A person who cohabitates with the individual.

(c) The term "written instrument" includes, but is not limited to, a will, a trust, a deed, a document exercising a power of appointment, or a beneficiary designation under a life insurance contract or any other contractual arrangement that creates an ownership interest or permits the naming of a beneficiary.

(d) The term "gift" includes an inter vivos gift, a testamentary transfer of real or personal property or any interest therein, and the power to make such a transfer regardless of whether the gift is outright or in trust; regardless of when the transfer is to take effect; and regardless of whether the power is held in a fiduciary or nonfiduciary capacity.

(8) The rights and remedies granted in this section are in addition to any other rights or remedies a person may have at law or in equity.

(9) This section applies only to written instruments executed on or after October 1, 2013.

Added by Laws 2013, c. 2013–172, § 7, eff. Oct. 1, 2013. Amended by Laws 2014, c. 2014–127, § 1, eff. July 1, 2014.

PART IX. PRODUCTION OF WILLS

732.901. Production of wills

(1) The custodian of a will must deposit the will with the clerk of the court having venue of the estate of the decedent within 10 days after receiving information that the testator is dead. The custodian must supply the testator's date of death or the last four digits of the testator's social security number to the clerk upon deposit.

(2) Upon petition and notice, the custodian of any will may be compelled to produce and deposit the will. All costs, damages, and a reasonable attorney's fee shall be adjudged to petitioner against the delinquent custodian if the court finds that the custodian had no just or reasonable cause for failing to deposit the will.

(3) An original will submitted to the clerk with a petition or other pleading is deemed to have been deposited with the clerk.

(4) Upon receipt, the clerk shall retain and preserve the original will in its original form for at least 20 years. If the probate of a will is initiated, the original will may be maintained by the clerk with the other pleadings during the pendency of the proceedings, but the will must at all times be retained in its original form for the remainder of the 20–year period whether or not the will is admitted to probate or the proceedings are terminated. Transforming and storing a will on film, microfilm, magnetic, electronic, optical, or other substitute media or recording a will onto an electronic recordkeeping system, whether or not in accordance with the standards adopted by the Supreme Court of Florida, or permanently recording a will does not eliminate the requirement to preserve the original will.

(5) For purposes of this section, the term "will" includes a separate writing as described in s. 732.515.

Laws 1974, c. 74–106, § 1; Laws 1975, c. 75–220, § 44; Laws 1992, c. 92–200, § 18. Amended by Laws 1997, c. 97–102, § 972, eff. July 1, 1997; Laws 2001, c. 2001–226, § 59, eff. Jan. 1, 2002; Laws 2013, c. 2013–172, § 8, eff. Oct. 1, 2013.

Cross References

Discovery of later will, see § 733.208.
Notice, method and time, see § 731.301.

CHAPTER 733

PROBATE CODE: ADMINISTRATION OF ESTATES

PART I. GENERAL PROVISIONS

PART II. COMMENCING ADMINISTRATION

ADMINISTRATION OF ESTATES

Enactment

Laws 1974, c. 74–106, § 3, repealed the sections contained in Fla.St.1973, Chapter 733, Florida Probate Law, Third Part, and, by Section 1 of that law, created the Florida Probate Code contained in Fla.St.1974, Supp., Chapters 731 to 735, effective July 1, 1975. Laws 1975, c. 75–220, substantially amended provisions of the Probate Code enacted by Laws 1974, c. 74–106; and, by operation of § 113 of the 1975 law, the probate code as enacted in 1974 and amended in 1975 became effective January 1, 1976.

For the text of Probate Rules promulgated by the Supreme Court of Florida, see Appendix I following the text of this title.

PART I. GENERAL PROVISIONS

733.101. Venue of probate proceedings

(1) The venue for probate of wills and granting letters shall be:

(a) In the county in this state where the decedent was domiciled.

(b) If the decedent had no domicile in this state, then in any county where the decedent's property is located.

(c) If the decedent had no domicile in this state and possessed no property in this state, then in the county where any debtor of the decedent resides.

(2) For the purpose of this section, a married woman whose husband is an alien or a nonresident of Florida may establish or designate a separate domicile in this state.

(3) Whenever a proceeding is filed laying venue in an improper county, the court may transfer the action in the same manner as provided in the Florida Rules of Civil Procedure. Any action taken by the court or the parties before the transfer is not affected by the improper venue.
Laws 1974, c. 74–106, § 1; Laws 1975, c. 75–220, § 46. Amended by Laws 1997, c. 97–102, § 981, eff. July 1, 1997; Laws 2001, c. 2001–226, § 78, eff. Jan. 1, 2002.

Cross References

Aliens, rights of inheritance, regulation by law, see Const. Art. 1, § 2.
Change of venue, see § 47.091 et seq.
Intestate succession, aliens, see § 732.1101.
Transfers of actions, wrong venue, see Civil Procedure Rule 1.060.
Venue generally, see § 47.011 et seq.
Venue of probate proceedings, see Probate Rule 5.050.

733.103. Effect of probate

(1) Until admitted to probate in this state or in the state where the decedent was domiciled, the will shall be ineffective to prove title to, or the right to possession of, property of the testator.

(2) In any collateral action or proceeding relating to devised property, the probate of a will in Florida shall be conclusive of its due execution; that it was executed by a competent testator, free of fraud, duress, mistake, and undue influence; and that the will was unrevoked on the testator's death.
Laws 1974, c. 74–106, § 1; Laws 1975, c. 75–220, § 48; Laws 1977, c. 77–87, § 17; Laws 1977, c. 77–174, § 1. Amended by Laws 2001, c. 2001–226, § 79, eff. Jan. 1, 2002.

Cross References

Discovery of later will, see § 733.208.

733.104. Suspension of statutes of limitation in favor of the personal representative

(1) If a person entitled to bring an action dies before the expiration of the time limited for the commencement of the action and the cause of action survives, the action may be commenced by that person's personal representative before the later of the expiration of the time limited for the commencement of the action or 12 months after the decedent's death.

(2) If a person against whom a cause of action exists dies before the expiration of the time limited for commencement of the action and the cause of action survives, if a claim is timely filed, the expiration of the time limited for commencement of the action shall not apply.
Laws 1974, c. 74–106, § 1; Laws 1975, c. 75–220, § 48; Laws 1977, c. 77–174, § 1. Amended by Laws 1997, c. 97–102, § 982, eff. July 1, 1997; Laws 2001, c. 2001–226, § 80, eff. Jan. 1, 2002.

Claims, limitations on presenting, see § 733.702.
Claims of remaining heirs, limitation, see § 95.22.
Death of person served by publication, limitations, see § 95.111.
Limitations of actions generally, see § 95.011 et seq.
Recordation of will, commencement of limitations, see § 95.231.

733.105. Determination of beneficiaries

(1) When property passes by intestate succession or the will is unclear and there is doubt about:

(a) Who is entitled to receive any part of the property, or

(b) The shares and amounts that any person is entitled to receive,

any interested person may petition the court to determine beneficiaries or their shares.

(2) Any personal representative who makes distribution or takes any other action pursuant to an order determining beneficiaries shall be fully protected.

(3) A separate civil action to determine beneficiaries may be brought when an estate has not been administered.

Laws 1974, c. 74–106, § 1; Laws 1975, c. 75–220, § 48; Laws 1977, c. 77–104, § 226; Laws 1977, c. 77–174, § 1. Amended by Laws 1997, c. 97–102, § 983, eff. July 1, 1997; Laws 2001, c. 2001–226, § 81, eff. Jan. 1, 2002.

Cross References

Definition of beneficiaries, see § 731.201.
Determination of beneficiaries and shares, see Probate Rule 5.385.
Parties bound by orders of the court, see § 731.303.

733.1051. Limited judicial construction of will with federal tax provisions

(1) Upon the application of a personal representative or a person who is or may be a beneficiary who is affected by the outcome of the construction, a court at any time may construe the terms of a will to define the respective shares or determine beneficiaries, in accordance with the intention of a testator, if a disposition occurs during the applicable period and the will contains a provision that:

(a) Includes a disposition formula referring to the terms "unified credit," "estate tax exemption," "applicable exemption amount," "applicable credit amount," "applicable exclusion amount," "generation-skipping transfer tax exemption," "GST exemption," "marital deduction," "maximum marital deduction," "unlimited marital deduction," or "maximum charitable deduction";

(b) Measures a share of an estate based on the amount that may pass free of federal estate tax or the amount that may pass free of federal generation-skipping transfer tax;

(c) Otherwise makes a disposition referring to a charitable deduction, marital deduction, or another provision of federal estate tax or generation-skipping transfer tax law; or

(d) Appears to be intended to reduce or minimize the federal estate tax or generation-skipping transfer tax.

(2) For purposes of this section:

(a) The term "applicable period" means a period beginning January 1, 2010, and ending on the end of the day on the earlier of December 31, 2010, or the day before the date that an act becomes law that repeals or otherwise modifies or has the effect of repealing or modifying s. 901 of the Economic Growth and Tax Relief Reconciliation Act of 2001.

(b) A "disposition occurs" when the testator dies.

(3) In construing the will, the court shall consider the terms and purposes of the will, the facts and circumstances surrounding the creation of the will, and the testator's probable intent. In determining the testator's probable intent, the court may consider evidence relevant to the testator's intent even though the evidence contradicts an apparent plain meaning of the will.

(4) This section does not apply to a disposition that is specifically conditioned upon no federal estate or generation-skipping transfer tax being imposed.

(5)(a) Unless otherwise ordered by the court, during the applicable period and without court order, the personal representative administering a will containing one or more provisions described in subsection (1) may:

1. Delay or refrain from making any distribution.

2. Incur and pay fees and costs reasonably necessary to determine its duties and obligations, including compliance with provisions of existing and reasonably anticipated future federal tax laws.

3. Establish and maintain reserves for the payment of these fees and costs and federal taxes.

(b) The personal representative shall not be liable for its actions as provided in this subsection made or taken in good faith.

(6) The provisions of this section are in addition to, and not in derogation of, rights under the common law to construe a will.

(7) This section is remedial in nature and intended to provide a new or modified legal remedy. This section shall operate retroactively to January 1, 2010.
Added by Laws 2010, c. 2010–132, § 12, eff. May 27, 2010.

733.106. Costs and attorney fees

(1) In all probate proceedings, costs may be awarded as in chancery actions.

(2) A person nominated as personal representative, or any proponent of a will if the person so nominated does not act within a reasonable time, if in good faith justified in offering the will in due form for probate, shall receive costs and attorney fees from the estate even though probate is denied or revoked.

(3) Any attorney who has rendered services to an estate may be awarded reasonable compensation from the estate.

(4) If costs and attorney fees are to be paid from the estate under this section, s. 733.6171(4), s. 736.1005, or s. 736.1006, the court, in its discretion, may direct from what part of the estate they shall be paid.

(a) If the court directs an assessment against a person's part of the estate and such part is insufficient to fully pay the assessment, the court may direct payment from the person's part of a trust, if any, if a pour-over will is involved and the matter is interrelated with the trust.

(b) All or any part of the costs and attorney fees to be paid from the estate may be assessed against one or more persons' part of the estate in such proportions as the court finds to be just and proper.

(c) In the exercise of its discretion, the court may consider the following factors:

1. The relative impact of an assessment on the estimated value of each person's part of the estate.

2. The amount of costs and attorney fees to be assessed against a person's part of the estate.

3. The extent to which a person whose part of the estate is to be assessed, individually or through counsel, actively participated in the proceeding.

4. The potential benefit or detriment to a person's part of the estate expected from the outcome of the proceeding.

5. The relative strength or weakness of the merits of the claims, defenses, or objections, if any, asserted by a person whose part of the estate is to be assessed.

6. Whether a person whose part of the estate is to be assessed was a prevailing party with respect to one or more claims, defenses, or objections.

7. Whether a person whose part of the estate is to be assessed unjustly caused an increase in the amount of costs and attorney fees incurred by the personal representative or another interested person in connection with the proceeding.

8. Any other relevant fact, circumstance, or equity.

(d) The court may assess a person's part of the estate without finding that the person engaged in bad faith, wrongdoing, or frivolousness.

Laws 1974, c. 74–106, § 1; Laws 1975, c. 75–220, § 49. Amended by Laws 1997, c. 97–102, § 984, eff. July 1, 1997; Laws 2001, c. 2001–226, § 82, eff. Jan. 1, 2002; Laws 2015, c. 2015–27, § 1, eff. July 1, 2015.

Applicability

Laws 2015, c. 2015–27, § 11, provides:

"The amendments made by this act to ss. 733.106, 736.1005, and 736.1006, Florida Statutes, apply to proceedings commenced on or after July 1, 2015. The law in effect before July 1, 2015, applies to proceedings commenced before that date."

Cross References

Compensation of personal representatives, see § 733.617.
Contesting wills, penalty clause, see § 732.517.
Court costs generally, see § 57.011 et seq.
Production of wills, costs, see § 732.901.

733.1061. Fees and costs; will reformation and modification

(1) In a proceeding arising under s. 732.615 or s. 732.616, the court shall award taxable costs as in chancery actions, including attorney's fees and guardian ad litem fees.

(2) When awarding taxable costs, including attorney's fees and guardian ad litem fees, under this section, the court in its discretion may direct payment from a party's interest, if any, in the estate or enter a judgment which may be satisfied from other property of the party, or both.

Added by Laws 2011, c. 2011–183, § 5, eff. July 1, 2011.

733.107. Burden of proof in contests; presumption of undue influence

(1) In all proceedings contesting the validity of a will, the burden shall be upon the proponent of the will to establish prima facie its formal execution and attestation. A self-proving affidavit executed in accordance with s. 732.503 or an oath of an attesting witness executed as required

in s. 733.201(2) is admissible and establishes prima facie the formal execution and attestation of the will. Thereafter, the contestant shall have the burden of establishing the grounds on which the probate of the will is opposed or revocation is sought.

(2) In any transaction or event to which the presumption of undue influence applies, the presumption implements public policy against abuse of fiduciary or confidential relationships and is therefore a presumption shifting the burden of proof under ss. 90.301–90.304.

Laws 1974, c. 74–106, § 1; Laws 1975, c. 75–220, § 50. Amended by Laws 2001, c. 2001–226, § 83, eff. Jan. 1, 2002; Laws 2002, c. 2002–82, § 5, eff. April 23, 2002; Laws 2010, c. 2010–132, § 13, eff. Oct. 1, 2010; Laws 2014, c. 2014–127, § 3, eff. July 1, 2014.

Cross References

Burden of proof in will contests, see Probate Rule 5.275.
Lost or destroyed wills, see § 733.207.
Penalty clauses for contesting wills, see § 732.517.
Presumptions,
    Death, see § 731.103.
    Joint wills, see § 732.701.
Proof of wills, see § 733.201.
Revocation of wills, see §§ 732.505, 732.506.
Self-proof of wills, see § 732.503.
Verification of documents, see § 731.104.

733.109. Revocation of probate

(1) A proceeding to revoke the probate of a will shall be brought in the court having jurisdiction over the administration. Any interested person, including a beneficiary under a prior will, unless barred under s. 733.212 or s. 733.2123, may commence the proceeding before final discharge of the personal representative.

(2) Pending the determination of any petition for revocation of probate, the personal representative shall proceed with the administration of the estate as if no revocation proceeding had been commenced, except that no distribution may be made to beneficiaries in contravention of the rights of those who, but for the will, would be entitled to the property disposed of.

(3) Revocation of probate of a will shall not affect or impair the title to property purchased in good faith for value from the personal representative prior to an order of revocation.

Laws 1974, c. 74–106, § 1; Laws 1975, c. 75–220, § 50; Laws 1977, c. 77–87, § 18; Laws 1977, c. 77–104, § 227. Amended by Laws 2001, c. 2001–226, § 84, eff. Jan. 1, 2002.

Cross References

Procedure in adversary proceedings, see Probate Rule 5.025.
Revocation of probate, see Probate Rule 5.270.
Revocation of wills,
    Generally, see §§ 732.505, 732.506.
    Agreements not to revoke, see § 732.701.
    Codicils, see § 732.509.
    Revival by revocation, see § 732.508.

PART II. COMMENCING ADMINISTRATION

733.201. Proof of wills

(1) Self-proved wills executed in accordance with this code may be admitted to probate without further proof.

---

(2) A will may be admitted to probate upon the oath of any attesting witness taken before any circuit judge, commissioner appointed by the court, or clerk.

(3) If it appears to the court that the attesting witnesses cannot be found or that they have become incapacitated after the execution of the will or their testimony cannot be obtained within a reasonable time, a will may be admitted to probate upon the oath of the personal representative nominated by the will as provided in subsection (2), whether or not the nominated personal representative is interested in the estate, or upon the oath of any person having no interest in the estate under the will stating that the person believes the writing exhibited to be the true last will of the decedent.

Laws 1974, c. 74–106, § 1; Laws 1975, c. 75–220, § 51. Amended by Laws 1997, c. 97–102, § 985, eff. July 1, 1997; Laws 2001, c. 2001–226, § 85, eff. Jan. 1, 2002; Laws 2009, c. 2009–115, § 9, eff. July 1, 2009.

Cross References

Burden of proof in will contests, see § 733.107.
Perjury, see § 837.011 et seq.
Proof of wills, see Probate Rule 5.210.
Self-proof of wills, see § 732.503.
Verification of documents, see § 731.104.

733.202. Petition

Any interested person may petition for administration.

Laws 1974, c. 74–106, § 1; Laws 1975, c. 75–220, § 52; Laws 1977, c. 77–87, § 19; Laws 1992, c. 92–200, § 19. Amended by Laws 1997, c. 97–102, § 986, eff. July 1, 1997; Laws 2001, c. 2001–226, § 86, eff. Jan. 1, 2002.

Cross References

Petition for administration, see Probate Rule 5.200.
Petitions defined, see § 731.201.
Preference in appointment, see § 733.301.
Removal of personal representative, see § 733.504 et seq.
Venue, see § 47.011 et seq.

733.204. Probate of a will written in a foreign language

(1) No will written in a foreign language shall be admitted to probate unless it is accompanied by a true and complete English translation.

(2) No personal representative who complies in good faith with the English translation of the will as established by the court shall be liable for doing so.

Laws 1974, c. 74–106, § 1; Laws 1975, c. 75–220, § 54; Laws 1977, c. 77–174, § 1. Amended by Laws 2001, c. 2001–226, § 88, eff. Jan. 1, 2002.

Cross References

Probate of will written in foreign language, see Probate Rule 5.210.
Probate of wills, in general, see Probate Rule 5.210.

733.205. Probate of notarial will

(1) When a copy of a notarial will in the possession of a notary entitled to its custody in a foreign state or country, the laws of which state or country require that the will remain in the

custody of the notary, duly authenticated by the notary, whose official position, signature, and seal of office are further authenticated by an American consul, vice consul, or other American consular officer within whose jurisdiction the notary is a resident, or whose official position, signature, and seal of office have been authenticated according to the requirements of the Hague Convention of 1961, is presented to the court, it may be admitted to probate if the original could have been admitted to probate in this state.

(2) The duly authenticated copy shall be prima facie evidence of its purported execution and of the facts stated in the certificate in compliance with subsection (1).

(3) Any interested person may oppose the probate of such a notarial will or may petition for revocation of probate of such a notarial will, as in the original probate of a will in this state.
Laws 1974, c. 74–106, § 1; Laws 1975, c. 75–220, § 55. Amended by Laws 2001, c. 2001–226, § 89, eff. Jan. 1, 2002; Laws 2003, c. 2003–154, § 7, eff. June 12, 2003.

Cross References

Probate of notarial will, see Probate Rule 5.210.
Probate of wills, generally, see Probate Rule 5.210.

733.206. Probate of will of resident after foreign probate

(1) If a will of any person who dies a resident of this state is admitted to probate in any other state or country through inadvertence, error, or omission before probate in this state, the will may be admitted to probate in this state if the original could have been admitted to probate in this state.

(2) An authenticated copy of the will, foreign proof of the will, the foreign order of probate, and any letters issued shall be filed instead of the original will and shall be prima facie evidence of its execution and admission to foreign probate.

(3) Any interested person may oppose the probate of the will or may petition for revocation of the probate of the will, as in the original probate of a will in this state.
Laws 1974, c. 74–106, § 1; Laws 1975, c. 75–220, § 56. Amended by Laws 2001, c. 2001–226, § 90, eff. Jan. 1, 2002.

Cross References

Probate of will of resident after foreign probate, see Probate Rule 5.210.
Revocation of probate, see § 733.109.

733.207. Establishment and probate of lost or destroyed will

Any interested person may establish the full and precise terms of a lost or destroyed will and offer the will for probate. The specific content of the will must be proved by the testimony of two disinterested witnesses, or, if a correct copy is provided, it shall be proved by one disinterested witness.
Laws 1974, c. 74–106, § 1; Laws 1975, c. 75–220, § 57. Amended by Laws 2001, c. 2001–226, § 91, eff. Jan. 1, 2002.

Cross References

Lost or destroyed will, establishment and probate, see Probate Rule 5.510.
Revocation of will,
    Acts, see § 732.506.
    Later writings, see § 732.505.

Revocation of will—Cont'd
Revival by revocation, see § 732.508.

733.208. Discovery of later will

On the discovery of a later will or codicil, any interested person may petition to revoke the probate of the earlier will or to probate the later will or codicil. No will or codicil may be offered after the testate or intestate estate has been completely administered and the personal representative discharged.

Laws 1974, c. 74–106, § 1; Laws 1975, c. 75–220, § 58. Amended by Laws 2001, c. 2001–226, § 92, eff. Jan. 1, 2002.

Cross References

Revocation of appointment of representative upon later discovery of will, see § 733.301.

733.209. Estates of missing persons

Any interested person may petition to administer the estate of a missing person; however, no personal representative shall be appointed until the court determines the missing person is dead.

Laws 1974, c. 74–106, § 1; Laws 1975, c. 75–220, § 59. Amended by Laws 2001, c. 2001–226, § 93, eff. Jan. 1, 2002.

Cross References

Presumption of death, absented persons, see § 731.103.

733.212. Notice of administration; filing of objections

(1) The personal representative shall promptly serve a copy of the notice of administration on the following persons who are known to the personal representative:

(a) The decedent's surviving spouse;

(b) Beneficiaries;

(c) The trustee of any trust described in s. 733.707(3) and each qualified beneficiary of the trust as defined in s. 736.0103, if each trustee is also a personal representative of the estate; and

(d) Persons who may be entitled to exempt property

in the manner provided for service of formal notice, unless served under s. 733.2123. The personal representative may similarly serve a copy of the notice on any devisees under a known prior will or heirs or others who claim or may claim an interest in the estate.

(2) The notice shall state:

(a) The name of the decedent, the file number of the estate, the designation and address of the court in which the proceedings are pending, whether the estate is testate or intestate, and, if testate, the date of the will and any codicils.

(b) The name and address of the personal representative and the name and address of the personal representative's attorney, and that the fiduciary lawyer-client privilege in s. 90.5021 applies with respect to the personal representative and any attorney employed by the personal representative.

(c) That any interested person on whom a copy of the notice of administration is served must file on or before the date that is 3 months after the date of service of a copy of the notice of administration on that person any objection that challenges the validity of the will, the venue, or the jurisdiction of the court. The 3–month time period may only be extended for estoppel based upon a misstatement by the personal representative regarding the time period within which an objection must be filed. The time period may not be extended for any other reason, including affirmative representation, failure to disclose information, or misconduct by the personal representative or any other person. Unless sooner barred by subsection (3), all objections to the validity of a will, venue, or the jurisdiction of the court must be filed no later than the earlier of the entry of an order of final discharge of the personal representative or 1 year after service of the notice of administration.

(d) That persons who may be entitled to exempt property under s. 732.402 will be deemed to have waived their rights to claim that property as exempt property unless a petition for determination of exempt property is filed by such persons or on their behalf on or before the later of the date that is 4 months after the date of service of a copy of the notice of administration on such persons or the date that is 40 days after the date of termination of any proceeding involving the construction, admission to probate, or validity of the will or involving any other matter affecting any part of the exempt property.

(e) That an election to take an elective share must be filed on or before the earlier of the date that is 6 months after the date of service of a copy of the notice of administration on the surviving spouse, or an attorney in fact or a guardian of the property of the surviving spouse, or the date that is 2 years after the date of the decedent's death.

(3) Any interested person on whom a copy of the notice of administration is served must object to the validity of the will, the venue, or the jurisdiction of the court by filing a petition or other pleading requesting relief in accordance with the Florida Probate Rules on or before the date that is 3 months after the date of service of a copy of the notice of administration on the objecting person, or those objections are forever barred. The 3–month time period may only be extended for estoppel based upon a misstatement by the personal representative regarding the time period within which an objection must be filed. The time period may not be extended for any other reason, including affirmative representation, failure to disclose information, or misconduct by the personal representative or any other person. Unless sooner barred by this subsection, all objections to the validity of a will, venue, or the jurisdiction of the court must be filed no later than the earlier of the entry of an order of final discharge of the personal representative or 1 year after service of the notice of administration.

(4) The appointment of a personal representative or a successor personal representative shall not extend or renew the period for filing objections under this section, unless a new will or codicil is admitted.

(5) The personal representative is not individually liable to any person for giving notice under this section, regardless of whether it is later determined that notice was not required by this section. The service of notice in accordance with this section shall not be construed as conferring any right.

(6) If the personal representative in good faith fails to give notice required by this section, the personal representative is not liable to any person for the failure. Liability, if any, for the failure is on the estate.

(7) If a will or codicil is subsequently admitted to probate, the personal representative shall promptly serve a copy of a new notice of administration as required for an initial will admission.

(8) For the purpose of determining deadlines established by reference to the date of service of a copy of the notice of administration in cases in which such service has been waived, service shall be deemed to occur on the date the waiver is filed.

Laws 1974, c. 74–106, § 1; Laws 1975, c. 75–220, § 60; Laws 1977, c. 77–104, § 227; Laws 1988, c. 88–340, § 3; Laws 1989, c. 89–340, § 2; Laws 1990, c. 90–23, § 2; Laws 1993, c. 93–257, § 8. Amended by Laws 1995, c. 95–401, § 7, eff. Oct. 1, 1995; Laws 1999, c. 99–397, § 191, eff. July 1, 1999; Laws 2001, c. 2001–226, § 94, eff. Jan. 1, 2002; Laws 2003, c. 2003–154, § 8, eff. June 12, 2003; Laws 2006, c. 2006–134, § 6, eff. July 1, 2006; Laws 2006, c. 2006–217, § 36, eff. July 1, 2007; Laws 2011, c. 2011–183, § 8, eff. June 21, 2011; Laws 2013, c. 2013–172, § 17, eff. Oct. 1, 2013; Laws 2015, c. 2015–27, § 2, eff. July 1, 2015.

Applicability

Laws 2015, c. 2015–27, § 9, provides:

"The amendments made by this act to ss. 733.212, 733.2123, 733.3101, and 733.504, Florida Statutes, apply to proceedings commenced on or after July 1, 2015. The law in effect before July 1, 2015, applies to proceedings commenced before that date."

Cross References

Computation of time, see Civil Procedure Rule 1.090.
Death of person served by publication, limitation of actions, see § 95.111.
Legal and official advertisements, see § 50.011 et seq.
Limitation of actions, computation of time, see § 95.031.
Notice of administration, filing of objections and claims, see Probate Rule 5.240.
Proof of publication, see §§ 50.041, 50.051.
Recordation of will, commencement of limitations period, see § 95.231.
Remaining heirs, claims, limitation of actions, see § 95.22.
Tolling of limitations period, see § 95.051.

733.2121. Notice to creditors; filing of claims

(1) Unless creditors' claims are otherwise barred by s. 733.710, the personal representative shall promptly publish a notice to creditors. The notice shall contain the name of the decedent, the file number of the estate, the designation and address of the court in which the proceedings are pending, the name and address of the personal representative, the name and address of the personal representative's attorney, and the date of first publication. The notice shall state that creditors must file claims against the estate with the court during the time periods set forth in s. 733.702, or be forever barred.

(2) Publication shall be once a week for 2 consecutive weeks, in a newspaper published in the county where the estate is administered or, if there is no newspaper published in the county, in a newspaper of general circulation in that county.

(3)(a) The personal representative shall promptly make a diligent search to determine the names and addresses of creditors of the decedent who are reasonably ascertainable, even if the claims are unmatured, contingent, or unliquidated, and shall promptly serve a copy of the notice on those creditors. Impracticable and extended searches are not required. Service is not required on any creditor who has filed a claim as provided in this part, whose claim has been paid in full, or whose claim is listed in a personal representative's timely filed proof of claim.

(b) The personal representative is not individually liable to any person for giving notice under this section, even if it is later determined that notice was not required. The service of notice to creditors in accordance with this section shall not be construed as admitting the validity or enforceability of a claim.

(c) If the personal representative in good faith fails to give notice required by this section, the personal representative is not liable to any person for the failure. Liability, if any, for the failure is on the estate.

(d) If a decedent at the time of death was 55 years of age or older, the personal representative shall promptly serve a copy of the notice to creditors and provide a copy of the death certificate on the Agency for Health Care Administration within 3 months after the first publication of the notice to creditors, unless the agency has already filed a statement of claim in the estate proceedings.

(e) If the Department of Revenue has not previously been served with a copy of the notice to creditors, then service of the inventory on the Department of Revenue shall be the equivalent of service of a copy of the notice to creditors.

(4) Claims are barred as provided in ss. 733.702 and 733.710.

Added by Laws 2001, c. 2001–226, § 95, eff. Jan. 1, 2002. Amended by Laws 2003, c. 2003–154, § 9, eff. June 12, 2003; Laws 2005, c. 2005–140, § 4, eff. July 1, 2005.

733.2123. Adjudication before issuance of letters

A petitioner may serve formal notice of the petition for administration on interested persons. A person who is served with such notice before the issuance of letters or who has waived notice may not challenge the validity of the will, testacy of the decedent, venue, or jurisdiction of the court, except in the proceedings before issuance of letters.

Laws 1975, c. 75–220, § 60; Laws 1981, c. 81–27, § 2. Amended by Laws 1997, c. 97–102, § 987, eff. July 1, 1997; Laws 2001, c. 2001–226, § 96, eff. Jan. 1, 2002; Laws 2010, c. 2010–132, § 14, eff. Oct. 1, 2010; Laws 2015, c. 2015–27, § 3, eff. July 1, 2015.

Applicability

Laws 2015, c. 2015–27, § 9, provides:

"The amendments made by this act to ss. 733.212, 733.2123, 733.3101, and 733.504, Florida Statutes, apply to proceedings commenced on or after July 1, 2015. The law in effect before July 1, 2015, applies to proceedings commenced before that date."

Cross References

Waiver and consent, notice, see § 731.302.

733.213. Probate as prerequisite to judicial construction of will

A will may not be construed until it has been admitted to probate.

Laws 1974, c. 74–106, § 1; Laws 1975, c. 75–220, § 61. Amended by Laws 2001, c. 2001–226, § 97, eff. Jan. 1, 2002.

PART III. PREFERENCE IN APPOINTMENT AND QUALIFICATIONS OF PERSONAL REPRESENTATIVE

733.301. Preference in appointment of personal representative

(1) In granting letters of administration, the following order of preference shall be observed:

(a) In testate estates:

1. The personal representative, or his or her successor, nominated by the will or pursuant to a power conferred in the will.

2. The person selected by a majority in interest of the persons entitled to the estate.

3. A devisee under the will. If more than one devisee applies, the court may select the one best qualified.

(b) In intestate estates:

1. The surviving spouse.

2. The person selected by a majority in interest of the heirs.

3. The heir nearest in degree. If more than one applies, the court may select the one best qualified.

(2) A guardian of the property of a ward who if competent would be entitled to appointment as, or to select, the personal representative may exercise the right to select the personal representative.

(3) In either a testate or an intestate estate, if no application is made by any of the persons described in subsection (1), the court shall appoint a capable person; but no person may be appointed under this subsection:

(a) Who works for, or holds public office under, the court.

(b) Who is employed by, or holds office under, any judge exercising probate jurisdiction.

(4) After letters have been granted in either a testate or an intestate estate, if a person who was entitled to, and has not waived, preference over the person appointed at the time of the appointment and on whom formal notice was not served seeks the appointment, the letters granted may be revoked and the person entitled to preference may have letters granted after formal notice and hearing.

(5) After letters have been granted in either a testate or an intestate estate, if any will is subsequently admitted to probate, the letters shall be revoked and new letters granted.

Laws 1974, c. 74–106, § 1; Laws 1975, c. 75–220, § 62; Laws 1977, c. 77–87, § 21; Laws 1977, c. 77–174, § 1. Amended by Laws 1997, c. 97–102, § 988, eff. July 1, 1997; Laws 2001, c. 2001–226, § 98, eff. Jan. 1, 2002.

Cross References

Later discovered wills, see § 733.208.

733.302. Who may be appointed personal representative

Subject to the limitations in this part, any person who is sui juris and is a resident of Florida at the time of the death of the person whose estate is to be administered is qualified to act as personal representative in Florida.

Laws 1974, c. 74–106, § 1; Laws 1975, c. 75–220, § 63; Laws 1979, c. 79–343, § 5. Amended by Laws 1997, c. 97–102, § 989, eff. July 1, 1997; Laws 2001, c. 2001–226, § 99, eff. Jan. 1, 2002.

Cross References

Disqualification of personal representative, notice to procure order approving resignation, see Probate Rule 5.310.
Felonies defined, see § 775.08.
Removal of personal representative, see § 733.504 et seq.

733.303. Persons not qualified

(1) A person is not qualified to act as a personal representative if the person:

(a) Has been convicted of a felony.

(b) Is mentally or physically unable to perform the duties.

(c) Is under the age of 18 years.

(2) If the person named as personal representative in the will is not qualified, letters shall be granted as provided in s. 733.301.

Laws 1974, c. 74–106, § 1; Laws 1975, c. 75–220, § 63; Laws 1977, c. 77–87, § 22. Amended by Laws 1997, c. 97–102, § 990, eff. July 1, 1997.

Cross References

Disabilities of nonage, removal, see § 743.01 et seq.
Disqualification of personal representative, see Probate Rule 5.310.
Minor, definition, see § 1.01.
Rights, privileges and obligations of persons 18 years of age or older, see § 743.07.

733.304. Nonresidents

A person who is not domiciled in the state cannot qualify as personal representative unless the person is:

(1) A legally adopted child or adoptive parent of the decedent;

(2) Related by lineal consanguinity to the decedent;

(3) A spouse or a brother, sister, uncle, aunt, nephew, or niece of the decedent, or someone related by lineal consanguinity to any such person; or

(4) The spouse of a person otherwise qualified under this section.

Laws 1974, c. 74–106, § 1; Laws 1975, c. 75–220, § 63; Laws 1979, c. 79–343, § 6.

733.305. Trust companies and other corporations and associations

(1) All trust companies incorporated under the laws of Florida, all state banking corporations and state savings associations authorized and qualified to exercise fiduciary powers in Florida, and all national banking associations and federal savings and loan associations authorized and qualified to exercise fiduciary powers in Florida shall be entitled to act as personal representatives and curators of estates.

(2) When a qualified corporation has been named as a personal representative in a will and subsequently transfers its business and assets to, consolidates or merges with, or is in any manner provided by law succeeded by, another qualified corporation, on the death of the testator, the successor corporation may qualify as personal representative unless the will provides otherwise.

(3) A corporation authorized and qualified to act as a personal representative as a result of merger or consolidation shall succeed to the rights and duties of all predecessor corporations as the personal representative of estates upon filing proof in the court, and without a new appointment. A purchase of substantially all the assets and the assumption of substantially all the liabilities shall be deemed a merger for the purpose of this section.

Laws 1974, c. 74–106, § 1; Laws 1975, c. 75–220, § 63; Laws 1977, c. 77–174, § 1; Laws 1981, c. 81–27, § 3. Amended by Laws 2001, c. 2001–226, § 100, eff. Jan. 1, 2002.

Cross References

Trust companies, powers, see § 660.34.

733.306. Effect of appointment of debtor

The appointment of a debtor as personal representative shall not extinguish the debt due the decedent.

Laws 1974, c. 74–106, § 1; Laws 1975, c. 75–220, § 63. Amended by Laws 2001, c. 2001–226, § 101, eff. Jan. 1, 2002.

733.307. Succession of administration

The personal representative of the estate of a deceased personal representative is not authorized to administer the estate of the first decedent. On the death of a sole or surviving personal representative, the court shall appoint a successor personal representative to complete the administration of the estate.

Laws 1974, c. 74–106, § 1; Laws 1975, c. 75–220, § 64. Amended by Laws 2001, c. 2001–226, § 102, eff. Jan. 1, 2002.

733.308. Administrator ad litem

When an estate must be represented and the personal representative is unable to do so, the court shall appoint an administrator ad litem without bond to represent the estate in that proceeding. The fact that the personal representative is seeking reimbursement for claims against the decedent does not require appointment of an administrator ad litem.

Laws 1974, c. 74–106, § 1; Laws 1975, c. 75–220, § 65. Amended by Laws 2001, c. 2001–226, § 103, eff. Jan. 1, 2002.

Cross References

Administrator ad litem and guardian ad litem, see Probate Rule 5.120.
Fiduciary lawyer-client privilege, see F.S.A. § 90.5021.

733.309. Executor de son tort

No person shall be liable to a creditor of a decedent as executor de son tort, but any person taking, converting, or intermeddling with the property of a decedent shall be liable to the personal representative or curator, when appointed, for the value of all the property so taken or converted and for all damages to the estate caused by the wrongful action. This section shall not be construed to prevent a creditor of a decedent from suing anyone in possession of property fraudulently conveyed by the decedent to set aside the fraudulent conveyance.

Laws 1974, c. 74–106, § 1; Laws 1975, c. 75–220, § 65. Amended by Laws 1997, c. 97–102, § 991, eff. July 1, 1997; Laws 2001, c. 2001–226, § 104, eff. Jan. 1, 2002.

733.3101. Personal representative not qualified

(1) A personal representative shall resign immediately if the personal representative knows that he or she was not qualified to act at the time of appointment.

(2) Any time a personal representative, who was qualified to act at the time of appointment, knows that he or she would not be qualified for appointment if application for appointment were then made, the personal representative shall promptly file and serve a notice setting forth the reasons. The personal representative's notice shall state that any interested person may petition to remove the personal representative. An interested person on whom a copy of the personal representative's notice is served may file a petition requesting the personal representative's removal within 30 days after the date on which such notice is served.

(3) A personal representative who fails to comply with this section shall be personally liable for costs, including attorney fees, incurred in any removal proceeding if the personal representative is removed. This liability extends to a personal representative who does not know, but should have known, of the facts that would have required him or her to resign under subsection (1) or to file and serve notice under subsection (2). This liability shall be cumulative to any other provided by law.

(4) As used in this section, the term "qualified" means that the personal representative is qualified under ss. 733.302–733.305.

Added by Laws 2001, c. 2001–226, § 105, eff. Jan. 1, 2002. Amended by Laws 2015, c. 2015–27, § 4, eff. July 1, 2015.

Applicability

Laws 2015, c. 2015–27, § 9, provides:

"The amendments made by this act to ss. 733.212, 733.2123, 733.3101, and 733.504, Florida Statutes, apply to proceedings commenced on or after July 1, 2015. The law in effect before July 1, 2015, applies to proceedings commenced before that date."

PART IV. FIDUCIARY BONDS

733.402. Bond of fiduciary; when required; form

(1) Unless the bond requirement has been waived by the will or by the court, every fiduciary to whom letters are granted shall execute and file a bond with surety, as defined in s. 45.011, to be approved by the clerk without a service fee. The bond shall be payable to the Governor and the Governor's successors in office, conditioned on the performance of all duties as personal representative according to law. The bond must be joint and several.

(2) No bond shall be void or invalid because of an informality in it or an informality or illegality in the appointment of the fiduciary. The bond shall have the same force as if the appointment had been legally made and the bond executed in proper form.

(3) The requirements of this section shall not apply to banks and trust companies authorized by law to act as personal representative.

(4) On petition by any interested person or on the court's own motion, the court may waive the requirement of filing a bond, require a bond, increase or decrease the bond, or require additional surety.

Laws 1974, c. 74–106, § 1; Laws 1975, c. 75–220, § 67; Laws 1977, c. 77–87, § 24; Laws 1977, c. 77–174, § 1. Amended by Laws 1997, c. 97–102, § 992, eff. July 1, 1997; Laws 2001, c. 2001–226, § 107, eff. Jan. 1, 2002.

Cross References

Bond with surety, definition, see § 45.011.
Trust companies, powers, see § 660.34.

733.403. Amount of bond

All bonds required by this part shall be in the penal sum that the court deems sufficient after consideration of the gross value of the estate, the relationship of the personal representative to the beneficiaries, exempt property and any family allowance, the type and nature of assets, known creditors, and liens and encumbrances on the assets.

Laws 1974, c. 74–106, § 1; Laws 1975, c. 75–220, § 67. Amended by Laws 2001, c. 2001–226, § 108, eff. Jan. 1, 2002.

Cross References

Issuance of letters, bond, see Probate Rule 5.235.

733.404. Liability of surety

No surety for any personal representative or curator shall be charged beyond the value of the assets of an estate because of any omission or mistake in pleading or of false pleading of the personal representative or curator.

Laws 1974, c. 74–106, § 1; Laws 1975, c. 75–220, § 68. Amended by Laws 2001, c. 2001–226, § 109, eff. Jan. 1, 2002.

733.405. Release of surety

(1) Subject to the limitations of this section, on the petition of any interested person, the surety is entitled to be released from liability for the future acts and omissions of the fiduciary.

(2) Pending the hearing of the petition, the court may restrain the fiduciary from acting, except to preserve the estate.

(3) On hearing, the court shall enter an order prescribing the amount of the new bond for the fiduciary and the date when the bond shall be filed. If the fiduciary fails to give the new bond, the fiduciary shall be removed at once, and further proceedings shall be had as in cases of removal.

(4) The original surety shall remain liable in accordance with the terms of its original bond for all acts and omissions of the fiduciary that occur prior to the approval of the new surety and filing and approval of the bond. The new surety shall be liable on its bond only after the filing and approval of the new bond.

Laws 1974, c. 74–106, § 1; Laws 1975, c. 75–220, § 68. Amended by Laws 1997, c. 97–102, § 993, eff. July 1, 1997; Laws 2001, c. 2001–226, § 110, eff. Jan. 1, 2002.

733.406. Bond premium allowable as expense of administration

A personal representative or other fiduciary required to give bond shall pay the reasonable premium as an expense of administration.

Laws 1899, c. 4716, § 1; Gen.St.1906, § 2789; Rev.Gen.St.1920, § 4336; Comp.Gen. Laws 1927, § 6299; Laws 1945, c. 22858, § 7; Fla.St.1957, § 648.05; Laws 1959, c. 59–205, § 613; Fla.St.1969, § 627.0902; Fla.St.1981, § 627.753; Laws 1982, c. 82–243, § 566. Amended by Laws 1997, c. 97–102, § 994, eff. July 1, 1997; Laws 2001, c. 2001–226, § 111, eff. Jan. 1, 2002.

PART V. CURATORS; RESIGNATION AND REMOVAL OF PERSONAL REPRESENTATIVES

733.501. Curators

(1) When it is necessary, the court may appoint a curator after formal notice to the person apparently entitled to letters of administration. The curator may be authorized to perform any duty or function of a personal representative. If there is great danger that any of the decedent's property is likely to be wasted, destroyed, or removed beyond the jurisdiction of the court and if the appointment of a curator would be delayed by giving notice, the court may appoint a curator without giving notice.

(2) Bond shall be required of the curator as the court deems necessary. No bond shall be required of banks and trust companies as curators.

(3) Curators shall be allowed reasonable compensation for their services, and the court may consider the provisions of s. 733.617.

(4) Curators shall be subject to removal and surcharge.

Laws 1974, c. 74–106, § 1; Laws 1975, c. 75–220, § 69; Laws 1977, c. 77–174, § 1. Amended by Laws 1997, c. 97–102, § 995, eff. July 1, 1997; Laws 2001, c. 2001–226, § 112, eff. Jan. 1, 2002; Laws 2002, c. 2002–1, § 108, eff. May 21, 2002.

Cross References

Bond,
   Extent of liability, see § 733.404.
   Filing, see § 733.402.
   Waiver, see § 733.403.
Curator defined, see § 731.201.
Curators, see Probate Rule 5.122.
Fiduciary lawyer-client privilege, see F.S.A. § 90.5021.
Inventory, see § 733.604.

733.502. Resignation of personal representative

A personal representative may resign. After notice to all interested persons, the court may accept the resignation and then revoke the letters of the resigning personal representative if the interests of the estate are not jeopardized by the resignation. The acceptance of the resignation shall not exonerate the personal representative or the surety from liability.

Laws 1974, c. 74–106, § 1; Laws 1975, c. 75–220, § 69; Laws 1977, c. 77–87, § 25. Amended by Laws 1997, c. 97–102, § 996, eff. July 1, 1997; Laws 2001, c. 2001–226, § 113, eff. Jan. 1, 2002.

Cross References

Appointment of successor, see Probate Rule 5.430.
Disqualification of personal representative, notice to procure order approving resignation, see Probate Rule 5.310.
Execution by personal representative, see Probate Rule 5.330.
Fiduciary accounting, see Probate Rule 5.346.
Resignation of personal representative, see Probate Rule 5.430.

733.503. Appointment of successor upon resignation

When the personal representative's resignation is accepted, the court shall appoint a personal representative or shall appoint a curator to serve until a successor personal representative is appointed.

Laws 1974, c. 74–106, § 1; Laws 1975, c. 75–220, § 69. Amended by Laws 1997, c. 97–102, § 997, eff. July 1, 1997; Laws 2001, c. 2001–226, § 114, eff. Jan. 1, 2002.

733.5035. Surrender of assets after resignation

When the resignation has been accepted by the court, all estate assets, records, documents, papers, and other property of or concerning the estate in the resigning personal representative's possession or control shall immediately be surrendered to the successor fiduciary. The court may establish the conditions and specify the assets and records, if any, that the resigning personal representative may retain until the final accounting of the resigning personal representative has been approved.

Added by Laws 2001, c. 2001–226, § 115, eff. Jan. 1, 2002.

733.5036. Accounting and discharge following resignation

(1) A resigning personal representative shall file and serve a final accounting of the personal representative's administration.

---

(2) After determination and satisfaction of the liability, if any, of the resigning personal representative, after compensation of the personal representative and the attorney and other persons employed by the personal representative, and upon receipt of evidence that undistributed estate assets have been delivered to the successor fiduciary, the personal representative shall be discharged, the bond released, and the surety discharged.

Added by Laws 2001, c. 2001–226, § 116, eff. Jan. 1, 2002.

733.504. Removal of personal representative; causes for removal

A personal representative shall be removed and the letters revoked if he or she was not qualified to act at the time of appointment. A personal representative may be removed and the letters revoked for any of the following causes:

(1) Adjudication that the personal representative is incapacitated.

(2) Physical or mental incapacity rendering the personal representative incapable of the discharge of his or her duties.

(3) Failure to comply with any order of the court, unless the order has been superseded on appeal.

(4) Failure to account for the sale of property or to produce and exhibit the assets of the estate when so required.

(5) Wasting or maladministration of the estate.

(6) Failure to give bond or security for any purpose.

(7) Conviction of a felony.

(8) Insolvency of, or the appointment of a receiver or liquidator for, any corporate personal representative.

(9) Holding or acquiring conflicting or adverse interests against the estate that will or may interfere with the administration of the estate as a whole. This cause of removal shall not apply to the surviving spouse because of the exercise of the right to the elective share, family allowance, or exemptions, as provided elsewhere in this code.

(10) Revocation of the probate of the decedent's will that authorized or designated the appointment of the personal representative.

(11) Removal of domicile from Florida, if domicile was a requirement of initial appointment.

(12) The personal representative was qualified to act at the time of appointment but is not now entitled to appointment.

Removal under this section is in addition to any penalties prescribed by law.

Laws 1974, c. 74–106, § 1; Laws 1975, c. 75–220, § 69; Laws 1977, c. 77–174, § 1. Amended by Laws 1997, c. 97–102, § 998, eff. July 1, 1997; Laws 2001, c. 2001–226, § 117, eff. Jan. 1, 2002; Laws 2009, c. 2009–115, § 10, eff. July 1, 2009; Laws 2015, c. 2015–27, § 5, eff. July 1, 2015.

Applicability

Laws 2015, c. 2015–27, § 9, provides:

"The amendments made by this act to ss. 733.212, 733.2123, 733.3101, and 733.504, Florida Statutes, apply to proceedings commenced on or after July 1, 2015. The law in effect before July 1, 2015, applies to proceedings commenced before that date."

Cross References

Disqualification of personal representative, notice to procure order approving resignation, see Probate Rule 5.310.
Felony defined, see § 775.08.

733.505. Jurisdiction in removal proceedings

A petition for removal shall be filed in the court having jurisdiction of the administration.

Laws 1974, c. 74–106, § 1; Laws 1975, c. 75–220, § 70. Amended by Laws 2001, c. 2001–226, § 118, eff. Jan. 1, 2002.

Cross References

Disqualification of personal representative, notice to procure order approving resignation, see Probate Rule 5.310.
Proceedings for removal, see Probate Rule 5.440.

733.506. Proceedings for removal

Proceedings for removal of a personal representative may be commenced by the court or upon the petition of an interested person. The court shall revoke the letters of a removed personal representative. The removal of a personal representative shall not exonerate the removed personal representative or the removed personal representative's surety from any liability.

Laws 1974, c. 74–106, § 1; Laws 1975, c. 75–220, § 71. Amended by Laws 2001, c. 2001–226, § 119, eff. Jan. 1, 2002.

Cross References

Proceedings for removal, see Probate Rule 5.440.

733.5061. Appointment of successor upon removal

When a personal representative is removed, the court shall appoint a personal representative or shall appoint a curator to serve until a successor personal representative is appointed.

Added by Laws 2001, c. 2001–226, § 120, eff. Jan. 1, 2002.

733.508. Accounting and discharge of removed personal representatives upon removal

(1) A removed personal representative shall file and serve a final accounting of that personal representative's administration.

(2) After determination and satisfaction of the liability, if any, of the removed personal representative, after compensation of that personal representative and the attorney and other persons employed by that personal representative, and upon receipt of evidence that the estate assets have been delivered to the successor fiduciary, the removed personal representative shall be discharged, the bond released, and the surety discharged.

Laws 1974, c. 74–106, § 1; Laws 1975, c. 75–220, § 72. Amended by Laws 1997, c. 97–102, § 999, eff. July 1, 1997; Laws 2001, c. 2001–226, § 122, eff. Jan. 1, 2002.

Cross References

Fiduciary accounting, see Probate Rule 5.346.
Proceedings for removal, see Probate Rule 5.440.

733.509. Surrender of assets upon removal

Upon entry of an order removing a personal representative, the removed personal representative shall immediately deliver all estate assets, records, documents, papers, and other property of or concerning the estate in the removed personal representative's possession or control to the remaining personal representative or successor fiduciary.

Laws 1974, c. 74–106, § 1; Laws 1975, c. 75–220, § 73. Amended by Laws 2001, c. 2001–226, § 123, eff. Jan. 1, 2002.

Cross References

Proceedings for removal of personal representative, see Probate Rule 5.440.

PART VI. DUTIES AND POWERS OF PERSONAL REPRESENTATIVE

733.601. Time of accrual of duties and powers

The duties and powers of a personal representative commence upon appointment. The powers of a personal representative relate back in time to give acts by the person appointed, occurring before appointment and beneficial to the estate, the same effect as those occurring after appointment. A personal representative may ratify and accept acts on behalf of the estate done by others when the acts would have been proper for a personal representative.

Laws 1974, c. 74–106, § 1; Laws 1975, c. 75–220, § 74. Amended by Laws 1997, c. 97–102, § 1000, eff. July 1, 1997; Laws 2001, c. 2001–226, § 124, eff. Jan. 1, 2002.

733.602. General duties

(1) A personal representative is a fiduciary who shall observe the standards of care applicable to trustees. A personal representative is under a duty to settle and distribute the estate of the decedent in accordance with the terms of the decedent's will and this code as expeditiously and efficiently as is consistent with the best interests of the estate. A personal representative shall use the authority conferred by this code, the authority in the will, if any, and the authority of any order of the court, for the best interests of interested persons, including creditors.

(2) A personal representative shall not be liable for any act of administration or distribution if the act was authorized at the time. Subject to other obligations of administration, a probated will is authority to administer and distribute the estate according to its terms. An order of appointment of a personal representative is authority to distribute apparently intestate assets to the heirs of the decedent if, at the time of distribution, the personal representative is not aware of a proceeding challenging intestacy or a proceeding questioning the appointment or fitness to continue. Nothing in this section affects the duty of the personal representative to administer and distribute the estate in accordance with the rights of interested persons.

Laws 1974, c. 74–106, § 1; Laws 1975, c. 75–220, § 74; Laws 1977, c. 77–87, § 27; Laws 1977, c. 77–174, § 1; Laws 1979, c. 79–400, § 270; Laws 1989, c. 89–340, § 3. Amended by Laws 1997, c. 97–102, § 1001, eff. July 1, 1997; Laws 2001, c. 2001–226, § 125, eff. Jan. 1, 2002; Laws 2006, c. 2006–217, § 37, eff. July 1, 2007; Laws 2009, c. 2009–115, § 11, eff. July 1, 2009.

733.603. Personal representative to proceed without court order

A personal representative shall proceed expeditiously with the settlement and distribution of a decedent's estate and, except as otherwise specified by this code or ordered by the court, shall do so without adjudication, order, or direction of the court. A personal representative may invoke the jurisdiction of the court to resolve questions concerning the estate or its administration.

Laws 1974, c. 74–106, § 1; Laws 1975, c. 75–220, § 75. Amended by Laws 1997, c. 97–102, § 1002, eff. July 1, 1997; Laws 2001, c. 2001–226, § 126, eff. Jan. 1, 2002.

733.604. Inventories and accountings; public records exemptions

(1)(a) Unless an inventory has been previously filed, a personal representative shall file a verified inventory of property of the estate, listing it with reasonable detail and including for each listed item its estimated fair market value at the date of the decedent's death.

(b) 1. Any inventory of an estate, whether initial, amended, or supplementary, filed with the clerk of the court in conjunction with the administration of an estate is confidential and exempt from s. 119.07(1) and s. 24(a), Art. I of the State Constitution.

2. Any inventory of an elective estate, whether initial, amended, or supplementary, filed with the clerk of the court in conjunction with an election made in accordance with part II of chapter 732 is confidential and exempt from s. 119.07(1) and s. 24(a), Art. I of the State Constitution.

3. Any accounting, whether interim, final, amended, or supplementary, filed with the clerk of court in an estate proceeding is confidential and exempt from s. 119.07(1) and s. 24(a), Art. I of the State Constitution.

4. Any inventory or accounting made confidential and exempt by subparagraph 1., subparagraph 2., or subparagraph 3. shall be disclosed by the custodian for inspection or copying:

a. To the personal representative;

b. To the personal representative's attorney;

c. To an interested person as defined in s. 731.201; or

d. By court order upon a showing of good cause.

5. These exemptions apply to any inventory or accounting filed before, on, or after July 1, 2009.

(2) If the personal representative learns of any property not included in the original inventory, or learns that the estimated value or description indicated in the original inventory for any item is erroneous or misleading, the personal representative shall file a verified amended or supplementary inventory showing any new items and their estimated value at the date of the decedent's death, or the revised estimated value or description.

(3) Upon written request to the personal representative, a beneficiary shall be furnished a written explanation of how the inventory value for an asset was determined, or, if an appraisal was obtained, a copy of the appraisal, as follows:

(a) To a residuary beneficiary or heir in an intestate estate, regarding all inventoried assets.

(b) To any other beneficiary, regarding all assets distributed or proposed to be distributed to that beneficiary.

The personal representative must notify each beneficiary of that beneficiary's rights under this subsection. Neither a request nor the failure to request information under this subsection affects any rights of a beneficiary in subsequent proceedings concerning any accounting of the personal representative or the propriety of any action of the personal representative.

Laws 1974, c. 74–106, § 1; Laws 1975, c. 75–220, § 76; Laws 1980, c. 80–127, § 1; Laws 1984, c. 84–106, § 4; Laws 1985, c. 85–72, § 1; Laws 1985, c. 85–342, § 29; Laws 1987, c. 87–266, § 68. Amended by Laws 1995, c. 95–401, § 28, eff. July 1, 1995; Laws 1997, c. 97–102, § 1003, eff. July 1, 1997; Laws 1997, c. 97–240, § 13, eff. May 30, 1997; Laws 2001, c. 2001–226, § 127, eff. Jan. 1, 2002; Laws 2009, c. 2009–230, § 1, eff. July 1, 2009; Laws 2014, c. 2014–82, § 1, eff. July 1, 2014.

Cross References

Execution by personal representative, see Probate Rule 5.330.
Inventory, see Probate Rule 5.340.

733.6065. Opening safe-deposit box

(1) Subject to the provisions of s. 655.936(2), the initial opening of a safe-deposit box that is leased or coleased by the decedent shall be conducted in the presence of any two of the following persons: an employee of the institution where the box is located, the personal representative, or the personal representative's attorney of record. Each person who is present must verify the contents of the box by signing a copy of the inventory under penalties of perjury. The personal representative shall file the safe-deposit box inventory, together with a copy of the box entry record from a date which is 6 months prior to the date of death to the date of inventory, with the court within 10 days after the box is opened. Unless otherwise ordered by the court, this inventory and the attached box entry record is subject to inspection only by persons entitled to inspect an inventory under s. 733.604(1). The personal representative may remove the contents of the box.

(2) The right to open and examine the contents of a safe-deposit box leased by a decedent, or any documents delivered by a decedent for safekeeping, and to receive items as provided for in s. 655.935 is separate from the rights provided for in subsection (1).

Added by Laws 2001, c. 2001–226, § 129, eff. Jan. 1, 2002. Amended by Laws 2006, c. 2006–134, § 7, eff. July 1, 2006; Laws 2006, c. 2006–213, § 71, eff. Oct. 1, 2006.

Cross References

Access to safe-deposit boxes leased in two or more names, see § 655.937.
Safe-deposit boxes,
    Access to safe-deposit boxes leased in two or more names, § 655.937.
    Death of lessee, search procedure, see § 655.936.
Search procedures upon death of safe-deposit box lessees, see § 655.935.

733.607. Possession of estate

(1) Except as otherwise provided by a decedent's will, every personal representative has a right to, and shall take possession or control of, the decedent's property, except the protected homestead, but any real property or tangible personal property may be left with, or surrendered to, the person presumptively entitled to it unless possession of the property by the personal representative will be necessary for purposes of administration. The request by a personal representative for delivery of any property possessed by a beneficiary is conclusive evidence that the possession of the property by the personal representative is necessary for the purposes of administration, in any action against the beneficiary for possession of it. The personal representative shall take all steps reasonably necessary for the management, protection, and preservation of the estate until distribution and may maintain an action to recover possession of property or to determine the title to it.

(2) If, after providing for statutory entitlements and all devises other than residuary devises, the assets of the decedent's estate are insufficient to pay the expenses of the administration and obligations of the decedent's estate, the personal representative is entitled to payment from the trustee of a trust described in s. 733.707(3), in the amount the personal representative certifies in writing to be required to satisfy the insufficiency, subject to the exclusions and preferences under s. 736.05053. The provisions of s. 733.805 shall apply in determining the amount of any payment required by this section.

Laws 1974, c. 74–106, § 1; Laws 1975, c. 75–220, § 77; Laws 1977, c. 77–87, § 28; Laws 1993, c. 93–257, § 9. Amended by Laws 1995, c. 95–401, § 9, eff. Oct. 1, 1995; Laws 1997, c. 97–102, § 1005, eff. July 1, 1997; Laws 2001, c. 2001–226, § 130, eff. Jan. 1, 2002; Laws 2010, c. 2010–122, § 1, eff. July 1, 2010.

Cross References
Advancement, see § 733.806.
Homestead real property, proceedings to determine, see Probate Rule 5.405.
Trusts,
    Notice of trust, see § 736.05055.
    Proceedings against certain trustees, limitations, see § 736.1014.

733.608. General power of the personal representative

(1) All real and personal property of the decedent, except the protected homestead, within this state and the rents, income, issues, and profits from it shall be assets in the hands of the personal representative:

(a) For the payment of devises, family allowance, elective share, estate and inheritance taxes, claims, charges, and expenses of the administration and obligations of the decedent's estate.

(b) To enforce contribution and equalize advancement.

(c) For distribution.

(2) If property that reasonably appears to the personal representative to be protected homestead is not occupied by a person who appears to have an interest in the property, the personal representative is authorized, but not required, to take possession of that property for the limited purpose of preserving, insuring, and protecting it for the person having an interest in the property, pending a determination of its homestead status. If the personal representative takes possession of that property, any rents and revenues may be collected by the personal representative for the account of the heir or devisee, but the personal representative shall have no duty to rent or otherwise make the property productive.

(3) If the personal representative expends funds or incurs obligations to preserve, maintain, insure, or protect the property referenced in subsection (2), the personal representative shall be entitled to a lien on that property and its revenues to secure repayment of those expenditures and obligations incurred. These expenditures and obligations incurred, including, but not limited to, fees and costs, shall constitute a debt owed to the personal representative that is charged against and which may be secured by a lien on the protected homestead, as provided in this section.   The debt shall include any amounts paid for these purposes after the decedent's death and prior to the personal representative's appointment to the extent later ratified by the personal representative in the court proceeding provided for in this section.

(a) On the petition of the personal representative or any interested person, the court having jurisdiction of the administration of the decedent's estate shall adjudicate the amount of the debt after formal notice to the persons appearing to have an interest in the property.

(b) The persons having an interest in the protected homestead shall have no personal liability for the repayment of the above noted debt. The personal representative may enforce payment of the debt through any of the following methods:

1.   By foreclosure of the lien as provided in this section;

2.   By offset of the debt against any other property in the personal representative's possession that otherwise would be distributable to any person having an interest in the protected homestead, but only to the extent of the fraction of the total debt owed to the personal representative the numerator of which is the value of that person's interest in the protected homestead and the denominator of which is the total value of the protected homestead; or

3. By offset of the debt against the revenues from the protected homestead received by the personal representative.

(4) The personal representative's lien shall attach to the property and take priority as of the date and time a notice of that lien is recorded in the official records of the county where that property is located, and the lien may secure expenditures and obligations incurred, including, but not limited to, fees and costs made before or after recording the notice. The notice of lien may be recorded before adjudicating the amount of the debt. The notice of lien shall also be filed in the probate proceeding, but failure to do so does not affect the validity of the lien. A copy of the notice of lien shall be served in the manner provided for service of formal notice upon each person appearing to have an interest in the property. The notice of lien must state:

(a) The name and address of the personal representative and the personal representative's attorney;

(b) The legal description of the property;

(c) The name of the decedent and also, to the extent known to the personal representative, the name and address of each person appearing to have an interest in the property; and

(d) That the personal representative has expended or is obligated to expend funds to preserve, maintain, insure, and protect the property and that the lien stands as security for recovery of those expenditures and obligations incurred, including, but not limited to, fees and costs. Substantial compliance with the foregoing provisions renders the notice in comportment with this section.

(5) The lien shall terminate upon the earliest of:

(a) Recording a satisfaction or release signed by the personal representative in the official records of the county where the property is located;

(b) The discharge of the personal representative when the estate administration is complete;

(c) One year from the recording of the lien in the official records unless a proceeding to determine the debt or enforce the lien has been filed; or

(d) The entry of an order releasing the lien.

(6) Within 14 days after receipt of the written request of any interested person, the personal representative shall deliver to the requesting person at a place designated in the written request an estoppel letter setting forth the unpaid balance of the debt secured by the lien referred to in this section. After complete satisfaction of the debt secured by the lien, the personal representative shall record within 30 days after complete payment, a satisfaction of the lien in the official records of the county where the property is located. If a judicial proceeding is necessary to compel compliance with the provisions of this subsection, the prevailing party shall be entitled to an award of attorney's fees and costs.

(7) The lien created by this section may be foreclosed in the manner of foreclosing a mortgage under the provisions of chapter 702.

(8) In any action for enforcement of the debt described in this section, the court shall award taxable costs as in chancery actions, including reasonable attorney's fees.

(9) A personal representative entitled to recover a debt for expenditures and obligations incurred, including, but not limited to, fees and costs, under this section may be relieved of the duty to enforce collection by an order of the court finding:

(a) That the estimated court costs and attorney's fees in collecting the debt will approximate or exceed the amount of the recovery; or

(b) That it is impracticable to enforce collection in view of the improbability of collection.

(10) A personal representative shall not be liable for failure to attempt to enforce collection of the debt if the personal representative reasonably believes it would have been economically impracticable.

(11) The personal representative shall not be liable for failure to take possession of the protected homestead or to expend funds on its behalf. In the event that the property is determined by the court not to be protected homestead, subsections (2)–(10) shall not apply and any liens previously filed shall be deemed released upon recording of the order in the official records of the county where the property is located.

(12) Upon the petition of an interested party to accommodate a sale or the encumbrance of the protected homestead, the court may transfer the lien provided for in this section from the property to the proceeds of the sale or encumbrance by requiring the deposit of the proceeds into a restricted account subject to the lien. The court shall have continuing jurisdiction over the funds deposited. The transferred lien shall attach only to the amount asserted by the personal representative, and any proceeds in excess of that amount shall not be subject to the lien or otherwise restricted under this section. Alternatively, the personal representative and the apparent owners of the protected homestead may agree to retain in escrow the amount demanded as reimbursement by the personal representative, to be held there under the continuing jurisdiction of the court pending a final determination of the amount properly reimbursable to the personal representative under this section.

(13) This act shall apply to estates of decedents dying after the date on which this act becomes a law.

Laws 1974, c. 74–106, § 1; Laws 1975, c. 75–220, § 77; Laws 1977, c. 77–87, § 29. Amended by Laws 2001, c. 2001–226, § 131, eff. Jan. 1, 2002; Laws 2003, c. 2003–154, § 10, eff. June 12, 2003; Laws 2010, c. 2010–132, § 15, eff. Oct. 1, 2010.

Cross References

Homestead real property, proceedings to determine, see Probate Rule 5.405.

733.609. Improper exercise of power; breach of fiduciary duty

(1) A personal representative's fiduciary duty is the same as the fiduciary duty of a trustee of an express trust, and a personal representative is liable to interested persons for damage or loss resulting from the breach of this duty. In all actions for breach of fiduciary duty or challenging the exercise of or failure to exercise a personal representative's powers, the court shall award taxable costs as in chancery actions, including attorney's fees.

(2) When awarding taxable costs, including attorney's fees, under this section, the court in its discretion may direct payment from a party's interest, if any, in the estate or enter a judgment which may be satisfied from other property of the party, or both.

(3) This section shall apply to all proceedings commenced hereunder after the effective date, without regard to the date of the decedent's death.

Laws 1974, c. 74–106, § 1; Laws 1975, c. 75–220, § 78. Amended by Laws 1997, c. 97–102, § 1006, eff. July 1, 1997; Laws 2001, c. 2001–226, § 132, eff. Jan. 1, 2002; Laws 2003, c. 2003–154, § 11, eff. June 12, 2003.

Cross References

Execution by personal representative, see Probate Rule 5.330.

733.610. **Sale, encumbrance, or transaction involving conflict of interest**

Any sale or encumbrance to the personal representative or the personal representative's spouse, agent, or attorney, or any corporation or trust in which the personal representative has a substantial beneficial interest, or any transaction that is affected by a conflict of interest on the part of the personal representative, is voidable by any interested person except one who has consented after fair disclosure, unless:

(1) The will or a contract entered into by the decedent expressly authorized the transaction; or

(2) The transaction is approved by the court after notice to interested persons.

Laws 1974, c. 74–106, § 1; Laws 1975, c. 75–220, § 78. Amended by Laws 1997, c. 97–102, § 1007, eff. July 1, 1997; Laws 2001, c. 2001–226, § 133, eff. Jan. 1, 2002.

Cross References

Informal notice, see § 731.301.

733.611. **Persons dealing with the personal representative; protection**

Except as provided in s. 733.613(1), a person who in good faith either assists or deals for value with a personal representative is protected as if the personal representative acted properly. The fact that a person knowingly deals with the personal representative does not require the person to inquire into the authority of the personal representative. A person is not bound to see to the proper application of estate assets paid or delivered to the personal representative. This protection extends to instances in which a procedural irregularity or jurisdictional defect occurred in proceedings leading to the issuance of letters, including a case in which the alleged decedent is alive. This protection is in addition to any protection afforded by comparable provisions of the laws relating to commercial transactions and laws simplifying transfers of securities by fiduciaries.

Laws 1974, c. 74–106, § 1; Laws 1975, c. 75–220, § 78; Laws 1977, c. 77–87, § 30; Laws 1977, c. 77–174, § 1. Amended by Laws 1997, c. 97–102, § 1008, eff. July 1, 1997; Laws 2001, c. 2001–226, § 134, eff. Jan. 1, 2002.

Cross References

Securities transactions, definitions, see § 517.021.

733.612. **Transactions authorized for the personal representative; exceptions**

Except as otherwise provided by the will or court order, and subject to the priorities stated in s. 733.805, without court order, a personal representative, acting reasonably for the benefit of the interested persons, may properly:

(1) Retain assets owned by the decedent, pending distribution or liquidation, including those in which the personal representative is personally interested or that are otherwise improper for fiduciary investments.

(2) Perform or compromise, or, when proper, refuse to perform, the decedent's contracts. In performing the decedent's enforceable contracts to convey or lease real property, among other possible courses of action, the personal representative may:

(a) Convey the real property for cash payment of all sums remaining due or for the purchaser's note for the sum remaining due, secured by a mortgage on the property.

(b) Deliver a deed in escrow, with directions that the proceeds, when paid in accordance with the escrow agreement, be paid as provided in the escrow agreement.

(3) Receive assets from fiduciaries or other sources.

(4) Invest funds as provided in ss. 518.10–518.14, considering the amount to be invested, liquidity needs of the estate, and the time until distribution will be made.

(5) Acquire or dispose of an asset, excluding real property in this or another state, for cash or on credit and at public or private sale, and manage, develop, improve, exchange, partition, or change the character of an estate asset.

(6) Make ordinary or extraordinary repairs or alterations in buildings or other structures; demolish improvements; or erect new party walls or buildings.

(7) Enter into a lease, as lessor or lessee, for a term within, or extending beyond, the period of administration, with or without an option to renew.

(8) Enter into a lease or arrangement for exploration and removal of minerals or other natural resources or enter into a pooling or unitization agreement.

(9) Abandon property when it is valueless or so encumbered, or in a condition, that it is of no benefit to the estate.

(10) Vote, or refrain from voting, stocks or other securities in person or by general or limited proxy.

(11) Pay calls, assessments, and other sums chargeable or accruing against, or on account of, securities, unless barred by the provisions relating to claims.

(12) Hold property in the name of a nominee or in other form without disclosure of the interest of the estate, but the personal representative is liable for any act of the nominee in connection with the property so held.

(13) Insure the assets of the estate against damage or loss and insure against personal and fiduciary liability to third persons.

(14) Borrow money, with or without security, to be repaid from the estate assets or otherwise, other than real property, and advance money for the protection of the estate.

(15) Extend, renew, or in any manner modify any obligation owing to the estate. If the personal representative holds a mortgage, security interest, or other lien upon property of another person, he or she may accept a conveyance or transfer of encumbered assets from the owner in satisfaction of the indebtedness secured by its lien instead of foreclosure.

(16) Pay taxes, assessments, and other expenses incident to the administration of the estate.

(17) Sell or exercise stock subscription or conversion rights or consent, directly or through a committee or other agent, to the reorganization, consolidation, merger, dissolution, or liquidation of a corporation or other business enterprise.

(18) Allocate items of income or expense to either estate income or principal, as permitted or provided by law.

(19) Employ persons, including, but not limited to, attorneys, accountants, auditors, appraisers, investment advisers, and others, even if they are one and the same as the personal representative or are associated with the personal representative, to advise or assist the personal representative in the performance of administrative duties; act upon the recommendations of those employed persons without independent investigation; and, instead of acting personally, employ one or more agents to perform any act of administration, whether or not discretionary.

Any fees and compensation paid to a person who is the same as, associated with, or employed by, the personal representative shall be taken into consideration in determining the personal representative's compensation.

(20) Prosecute or defend claims or proceedings in any jurisdiction for the protection of the estate and of the personal representative.

(21) Sell, mortgage, or lease any personal property of the estate or any interest in it for cash, credit, or for part cash or part credit, and with or without security for the unpaid balance.

(22) Continue any unincorporated business or venture in which the decedent was engaged at the time of death:

(a) In the same business form for a period of not more than 4 months from the date of appointment, if continuation is a reasonable means of preserving the value of the business, including good will.

(b) In the same business form for any additional period of time that may be approved by court order.

(23) Provide for exoneration of the personal representative from personal liability in any contract entered into on behalf of the estate.

(24) Satisfy and settle claims and distribute the estate as provided in this code.

(25) Enter into agreements with the proper officer or department head, commissioner, or agent of any department of the government of the United States, waiving the statute of limitations concerning the assessment and collection of any federal tax or any deficiency in a federal tax.

(26) Make partial distribution to the beneficiaries of any part of the estate not necessary to satisfy claims, expenses of administration, taxes, family allowance, exempt property, and an elective share, in accordance with the decedent's will or as authorized by operation of law.

(27) Execute any instruments necessary in the exercise of the personal representative's powers.

Laws 1974, c. 74–106, § 1; Laws 1975, c. 75–220, § 78; Laws 1976, c. 76–172, § 3; Laws 1977, c. 77–87, § 31; Laws 1977, c. 77–174, § 1; Laws 1979, c. 79–400, § 271. Amended by Laws 1997, c. 97–102, § 1009, eff. July 1, 1997; Laws 2001, c. 2001–226, § 135, eff. Jan. 1, 2002.

Cross References

Compromise of claims, see § 733.708.

Continuance of business of decedent, see Probate Rule 5.350.

Execution by personal representative, see Probate Rule 5.330.

Sales of real property where power not conferred, see Probate Rule 5.370.

733.6121. Personal representative; powers as to environmental issues relating to property subject to administration; liability

(1) Except as otherwise provided by the will or by court order, and subject to s. 733.805, the personal representative has, without court authorization, the powers specified in subsection (2).

(2) A personal representative has the power, acting reasonably and for the benefit of the interested persons:

(a) To inspect or investigate, or cause to be inspected or investigated, property subject to administration, including interests in sole proprietorships, partnerships, or corporations and any assets owned by such a business entity for the purpose of determining compliance with an environmental law affecting that property or to respond to an actual or threatened violation of an environmental law affecting that property;

(b) To take, on behalf of the estate, any action necessary to prevent, abate, or otherwise remedy an actual or potential violation of an environmental law affecting property subject to administration, either before or after initiation of an enforcement action by a governmental body;

(c) To settle or compromise at any time any claim against the estate or the personal representative that may be asserted by a governmental body or private party which involves the alleged violation of an environmental law affecting property subject to administration over which the personal representative has responsibility;

(d) To disclaim any power granted by any document, statute, or rule of law which, in the sole judgment of the personal representative, could cause the personal representative to incur personal liability, or the estate to incur liability, under any environmental law;

(e) To decline to serve as a personal representative, or having undertaken to serve, to resign at any time, if the personal representative believes that there is or could be a conflict of interest because of potential claims or liabilities that could be asserted on behalf of the estate by reason of the type or condition of the assets held; or

(f) To charge against the assets of the estate the cost of any inspection, investigation, review, abatement, response, cleanup, or remedial action considered reasonable by the personal representative; and, in the event of the closing or termination of the estate or the transfer of the estate property to another personal representative, to hold moneys sufficient to cover the cost of cleaning up any known environmental problem.

(3) A personal representative is not personally liable to any beneficiary or any other party for a decrease in value of assets in an estate by reason of the personal representative's compliance or efforts to comply with an environmental law, specifically including any reporting requirement under that law.

(4) A personal representative who acquires ownership or control of a vessel or other property without having owned, operated, or materially participated in the management of that vessel or property before assuming ownership or control as personal representative is not considered an owner or operator for purposes of liability under chapter 376, chapter 403, or any other environmental law. A personal representative who willfully, knowingly, or recklessly causes or exacerbates a release or threatened release of a hazardous substance is personally liable for the cost of the response, to the extent that the release or threatened release is attributable to the personal representative's activities. This subsection does not preclude the filing of claims against the assets that constitute the estate held by the personal representative or the filing of actions against the personal representative as representative of the estate. In such an action, an award or judgment against the personal representative must be satisfied only from the assets of the estate.

(5) Neither the acceptance by the personal representative of the property or a failure by the personal representative to inspect or investigate the property creates any inference of liability under an environmental law with respect to that property.

(6) For the purposes of this section, the term "environmental law" means a federal, state, or local law, rule, regulation, or ordinance that relates to protection of the environment or human health, and the term "hazardous substance" means a substance, material, or waste defined as

hazardous or toxic, or any contaminant, pollutant, or constituent thereof, or otherwise regulated by an environmental law.

(7) This section applies to any estate admitted to probate on or after July 1, 1995.

Added by Laws 1995, c. 95–401, § 18, eff. July 1, 1995. Amended by Laws 1997, c. 97–102, § 1010, eff. July 1, 1997; Laws 2001, c. 2001–226, § 136, eff. Jan. 1, 2002.

733.613. Personal representative's right to sell real property

(1) When a personal representative of an intestate estate, or whose testator has not conferred a power of sale or whose testator has granted a power of sale but the power is so limited by the will or by operation of law that it cannot be conveniently exercised, shall consider that it is for the best interest of the estate and of those interested in it that real property be sold, the personal representative may sell it at public or private sale. No title shall pass until the court authorizes or confirms the sale. No bona fide purchaser shall be required to examine any proceedings before the order of sale.

(2) When a decedent's will confers specific power to sell or mortgage real property or a general power to sell any asset of the estate, the personal representative may sell, mortgage, or lease, without authorization or confirmation of court, any real property of the estate or any interest therein for cash or credit, or for part cash and part credit, and with or without security for unpaid balances. The sale, mortgage, or lease need not be justified by a showing of necessity, and the sale pursuant to power of sale shall be valid.

(3) In a sale or mortgage which occurs under a specific power to sell or mortgage real property, or under a court order authorizing or confirming that act, the purchaser or lender takes title free of claims of creditors of the estate and entitlements of estate beneficiaries, except existing mortgages or other liens against real property are not affected.

Laws 1974, c. 74–106, § 1; Laws 1975, c. 75–220, § 78. Amended by Laws 1997, c. 97–102, § 1011, eff. July 1, 1997; Laws 2001, c. 2001–226, § 137, eff. Jan. 1, 2002.

Cross References

Execution by personal representative, see Probate Rule 5.330.
Sales of real property where no power conferred, see Probate Rule 5.370.

733.614. Powers and duties of successor personal representative

A successor personal representative has the same power and duty as the original personal representative to complete the administration and distribution of the estate as expeditiously as possible, but shall not exercise any power made personal to the personal representative named in the will without court approval.

Laws 1974, c. 74–106, § 1; Laws 1975, c. 75–220, § 78. Amended by Laws 1997, c. 97–102, § 1012, eff. July 1, 1997; Laws 2001, c. 2001–226, § 138, eff. Jan. 1, 2002.

733.615. Joint personal representatives; when joint action required

(1) If two or more persons are appointed joint personal representatives, and unless the will provides otherwise, the concurrence of all joint personal representatives appointed pursuant to a will or codicil executed prior to October 1, 1987, or appointed to administer an intestate estate of a decedent who died prior to October 1, 1987, or of a majority of joint personal representatives appointed pursuant to a will or codicil executed on or after October 1, 1987, or appointed to administer an intestate estate of a decedent dying on or after October 1, 1987, is required on all acts connected with the administration and distribution of the estate. This restriction does

not apply when any joint personal representative receives and receipts for property due the estate, when the concurrence required under this subsection cannot readily be obtained in the time reasonably available for emergency action necessary to preserve the estate, or when a joint personal representative has been delegated to act for the others.

(2) Where action by a majority of the joint personal representatives appointed is authorized, a joint personal representative who has not joined in exercising a power is not liable to the beneficiaries or to others for the consequences of the exercise, and a dissenting joint personal representative is not liable for the consequences of an action in which the dissenting personal representative joins at the direction of the majority of the joint personal representatives, if the dissent is expressed in writing to the other joint personal representatives at or before the time of the action.

(3) A person dealing with a joint personal representative without actual knowledge that joint personal representatives have been appointed, or if advised by a joint personal representative that the joint personal representative has authority to act alone for any of the reasons mentioned in subsection (1), is as fully protected in dealing with that joint personal representative as if that joint personal representative possessed and properly exercised the power.

Laws 1974, c. 74–106, § 1; Laws 1975, c. 75–220, § 79; Laws 1987, c. 87–317, § 1; Laws 1988, c. 88–340, § 4. Amended by Laws 1997, c. 97–102, § 1013, eff. July 1, 1997; Laws 2001, c. 2001–226, § 139, eff. Jan. 1, 2002.

733.616. Powers of surviving personal representatives

Unless otherwise provided by the terms of the will or a court order, every power exercisable by joint personal representatives may be exercised by the one or more remaining after the appointment of one or more is terminated. If one or more, but not all, nominated as joint personal representatives are not appointed, those appointed may exercise all powers granted to those nominated.

Laws 1974, c. 74–106, § 1; Laws 1975, c. 75–220, § 79. Amended by Laws 2001, c. 2001–226, § 140, eff. Jan. 1, 2002.

733.617. Compensation of personal representative

(1) A personal representative shall be entitled to a commission payable from the estate assets without court order as compensation for ordinary services. The commission shall be based on the compensable value of the estate, which is the inventory value of the probate estate assets and the income earned by the estate during administration.

(2) A commission computed on the compensable value of the estate is presumed to be reasonable compensation for a personal representative in formal administration as follows:

(a) At the rate of 3 percent for the first $1 million.

(b) At the rate of 2.5 percent for all above $1 million and not exceeding $5 million.

(c) At the rate of 2 percent for all above $5 million and not exceeding $10 million.

(d) At the rate of 1.5 percent for all above $10 million.

(3) In addition to the previously described commission, a personal representative shall be allowed further compensation as is reasonable for any extraordinary services including, but not limited to:

(a) The sale of real or personal property.

(b) The conduct of litigation on behalf of or against the estate.

(c) Involvement in proceedings for the adjustment or payment of any taxes.

(d) The carrying on of the decedent's business.

(e) Dealing with protected homestead.

(f) Any other special services which may be necessary for the personal representative to perform.

(4) If the will provides that a personal representative's compensation shall be based upon specific criteria, other than a general reference to commissions allowed by law or words of similar import, including, but not limited to, rates, amounts, commissions, or reference to the personal representative's regularly published schedule of fees in effect at the decedent's date of death, or words of similar import, then a personal representative shall be entitled to compensation in accordance with that provision. However, except for references in the will to the personal representative's regularly published schedule of fees in effect at the decedent's date of death, or words of similar import, if there is no written contract with the decedent regarding compensation, a personal representative may renounce the provisions contained in the will and be entitled to compensation under this section. A personal representative may also renounce the right to all or any part of the compensation.

(5) If the probate estate's compensable value is $100,000 or more, and there are two representatives, each personal representative is entitled to the full commission allowed to a sole personal representative. If there are more than two personal representatives and the probate estate's compensable value is $100,000 or more, the compensation to which two would be entitled must be apportioned among the personal representatives. The basis for apportionment shall be one full commission allowed to the personal representative who has possession of and primary responsibility for administration of the assets and one full commission among the remaining personal representatives according to the services rendered by each of them respectively. If the probate estate's compensable value is less than $100,000 and there is more than one personal representative, then one full commission must be apportioned among the personal representatives according to the services rendered by each of them respectively.

(6) If the personal representative is a member of The Florida Bar and has rendered legal services in connection with the administration of the estate, then in addition to a fee as personal representative, there also shall be allowed a fee for the legal services rendered.

(7) Upon petition of any interested person, the court may increase or decrease the compensation for ordinary services of the personal representative or award compensation for extraordinary services if the facts and circumstances of the particular administration warrant. In determining reasonable compensation, the court shall consider all of the following factors, giving weight to each as it determines to be appropriate:

(a) The promptness, efficiency, and skill with which the administration was handled by the personal representative;

(b) The responsibilities assumed by and the potential liabilities of the personal representative;

(c) The nature and value of the assets that are affected by the decedent's death;

(d) The benefits or detriments resulting to the estate or interested persons from the personal representative's services;

(e) The complexity or simplicity of the administration and the novelty of the issues presented;

(f) The personal representative's participation in tax planning for the estate and the estate's beneficiaries and in tax return preparation, review, or approval;

(g) The nature of the probate, nonprobate, and exempt assets, the expenses of administration, the liabilities of the decedent, and the compensation paid to other professionals and fiduciaries;

(h) Any delay in payment of the compensation after the services were furnished; and

(i) Any other relevant factors.

Laws 1974, c. 74–106, § 1; Laws 1975, c. 75–220, § 80; Laws 1976, c. 76–172, § 1; Laws 1988, c. 88–340, § 5; Laws 1990, c. 90–129, § 1; Laws 1993, c. 93–257, § 10. Amended by Laws 1995, c. 95–401, § 1, eff. Jan. 1, 1996; Laws 2001, c. 2001–226, § 141, eff. Jan. 1, 2002; Laws 2002, c. 2002–1, § 109, eff. May 21, 2002.

Cross References

Costs and attorneys fees, see § 733.106.
Trusts, attorneys' fees of trustees, see § 736.1007.

733.6171. Compensation of attorney for the personal representative

(1) Attorneys for personal representatives shall be entitled to reasonable compensation payable from the estate assets without court order.

(2) The attorney, the personal representative, and persons bearing the impact of the compensation may agree to compensation determined in a different manner than provided in this section. Compensation may also be determined in a different manner than provided in this section if the manner is disclosed to the parties bearing the impact of the compensation and if no objection is made as provided for in the Florida Probate Rules.

(3) Compensation for ordinary services of attorneys in formal estate administration is presumed to be reasonable if based on the compensable value of the estate, which is the inventory value of the probate estate assets and the income earned by the estate during the administration as provided in the following schedule:

(a) One thousand five hundred dollars for estates having a value of $40,000 or less.

(b) An additional $750 for estates having a value of more than $40,000 and not exceeding $70,000.

(c) An additional $750 for estates having a value of more than $70,000 and not exceeding $100,000.

(d) For estates having a value in excess of $100,000, at the rate of 3 percent on the next $900,000.

(e) At the rate of 2.5 percent for all above $1 million and not exceeding $3 million.

(f) At the rate of 2 percent for all above $3 million and not exceeding $5 million.

(g) At the rate of 1.5 percent for all above $5 million and not exceeding $10 million.

(h) At the rate of 1 percent for all above $10 million.

(4) In addition to fees for ordinary services, the attorney for the personal representative shall be allowed further reasonable compensation for any extraordinary service. What is an extraordinary service may vary depending on many factors, including the size of the estate. Extraordinary services may include, but are not limited to:

(a) Involvement in a will contest, will construction, a proceeding for determination of beneficiaries, a contested claim, elective share proceeding, apportionment of estate taxes, or any adversarial proceeding or litigation by or against the estate.

(b) Representation of the personal representative in audit or any proceeding for adjustment, determination, or collection of any taxes.

(c) Tax advice on postmortem tax planning, including, but not limited to, disclaimer, renunciation of fiduciary commission, alternate valuation date, allocation of administrative expenses between tax returns, the QTIP or reverse QTIP election, allocation of GST exemption, qualification for Internal Revenue Code ss. 6166 and 303 privileges, deduction of last illness expenses, fiscal year planning, distribution planning, asset basis considerations, handling income or deductions in respect of a decedent, valuation discounts, special use and other valuation, handling employee benefit or retirement proceeds, prompt assessment request, or request for release of personal liability for payment of tax.

(d) Review of estate tax return and preparation or review of other tax returns required to be filed by the personal representative.

(e) Preparation of the estate's federal estate tax return. If this return is prepared by the attorney, a fee of one-half of 1 percent up to a value of $10 million and one-fourth of 1 percent on the value in excess of $10 million of the gross estate as finally determined for federal estate tax purposes, is presumed to be reasonable compensation for the attorney for this service. These fees shall include services for routine audit of the return, not beyond the examining agent level, if required.

(f) Purchase, sale, lease, or encumbrance of real property by the personal representative or involvement in zoning, land use, environmental, or other similar matters.

(g) Legal advice regarding carrying on of the decedent's business or conducting other commercial activity by the personal representative.

(h) Legal advice regarding claims for damage to the environment or related procedures.

(i) Legal advice regarding homestead status of real property or proceedings involving that status and services related to protected homestead.

(j) Involvement in fiduciary, employee, or attorney compensation disputes.

(k) Proceedings involving ancillary administration of assets not subject to administration in this state.

(5) Upon petition of any interested person, the court may increase or decrease the compensation for ordinary services of the attorney or award compensation for extraordinary services if the facts and circumstances of the particular administration warrant. In determining reasonable compensation, the court shall consider all of the following factors, giving weight to each as it determines to be appropriate:

(a) The promptness, efficiency, and skill with which the administration was handled by the attorney.

(b) The responsibilities assumed by and the potential liabilities of the attorney.

(c) The nature and value of the assets that are affected by the decedent's death.

(d) The benefits or detriments resulting to the estate or interested persons from the attorney's services.

(e) The complexity or simplicity of the administration and the novelty of issues presented.

(f) The attorney's participation in tax planning for the estate and the estate's beneficiaries and tax return preparation, review, or approval.

(g) The nature of the probate, nonprobate, and exempt assets, the expenses of administration, the liabilities of the decedent, and the compensation paid to other professionals and fiduciaries.

(h) Any delay in payment of the compensation after the services were furnished.

(i) Any other relevant factors.

(6) If a separate written agreement regarding compensation exists between the attorney and the decedent, the attorney shall furnish a copy to the personal representative prior to commencement of employment, and, if employed, shall promptly file and serve a copy on all interested persons. Neither a separate agreement nor a provision in the will suggesting or directing that the personal representative retain a specific attorney will obligate the personal representative to employ the attorney or obligate the attorney to accept the representation, but if the attorney who is a party to the agreement or who drafted the will is employed, the compensation paid shall not exceed the compensation provided in the agreement or in the will.

Laws 1993, c. 93–257, § 4. Amended by Laws 1995, c. 95–401, § 2, eff. July 1, 1995; Laws 2001, c. 2001–226, § 142, eff. Jan. 1, 2002.

733.6175. Proceedings for review of employment of agents and compensation of personal representatives and employees of estate

(1) The court may review the propriety of the employment of any person employed by the personal representative and the reasonableness of any compensation paid to that person or to the personal representative.

(2) Court proceedings to determine reasonable compensation of the personal representative or any person employed by the personal representative, if required, are a part of the estate administration process, and the costs, including attorneys' fees, of the person assuming the burden of proof of propriety of the employment and reasonableness of the compensation shall be determined by the court and paid from the assets of the estate unless the court finds the requested compensation to be substantially unreasonable. The court shall direct from which part of the estate the compensation shall be paid.

(3) The burden of proof of propriety of the employment and the reasonableness of the compensation shall be upon the personal representative and the person employed. Any person who is determined to have received excessive compensation from an estate for services rendered may be ordered to make appropriate refunds.

(4) The court may determine reasonable compensation for the personal representative or any person employed by the personal representative without receiving expert testimony. Any party may offer expert testimony after notice to interested persons. If expert testimony is offered, a reasonable expert witness fee shall be awarded by the court and paid from the assets of the estate. The court shall direct from what part of the estate the fee shall be paid.

Laws 1976, c. 76–172, § 2. Amended by Laws 1997, c. 97–102, § 1014, eff. July 1, 1997; Laws 2001, c. 2001–226, § 143, eff. Jan. 1, 2002.

Cross References

Discharge or final accounting, objections, see Probate Rule 5.401.
Related court rule provision, see Probate Rule 5.355.

733.619. Individual liability of personal representative

(1) Unless otherwise provided in the contract, a personal representative is not individually liable on a contract, except a contract for attorney's fee, properly entered into as fiduciary

unless the personal representative fails to reveal that representative capacity and identify the estate in the contract.

(2) A personal representative is individually liable for obligations arising from ownership or control of the estate or for torts committed in the course of administration of the estate only if personally at fault.

(3) Claims based on contracts, except a contract for attorney's fee, entered into by a personal representative as a fiduciary, on obligations arising from ownership or control of the estate, or on torts committed in the course of estate administration, may be asserted against the estate by proceeding against the personal representative in that capacity, whether or not the personal representative is individually liable.

(4) Issues of liability as between the estate and the personal representative individually may be determined in a proceeding for accounting, surcharge, or indemnification, or other appropriate proceeding.

Laws 1975, c. 75–220, § 82; Laws 1977, c. 77–87, § 32; Laws 1977, c. 77–104, § 228. Amended by Laws 1997, c. 97–102, § 1015, eff. July 1, 1997; Laws 2001, c. 2001–226, § 144, eff. Jan. 1, 2002.

Cross References

Penalty for contesting will, see § 732.517.

733.620. Exculpation of personal representative

(1) A term of a will relieving a personal representative of liability to a beneficiary for breach of fiduciary duty is unenforceable to the extent that the term:

(a) Relieves the personal representative of liability for breach of fiduciary duty committed in bad faith or with reckless indifference to the purposes of the will or the interests of interested persons; or

(b) Was inserted into the will as the result of an abuse by the personal representative of a fiduciary or confidential relationship with the testator.

(2) An exculpatory term drafted or caused to be drafted by the personal representative is invalid as an abuse of a fiduciary or confidential relationship unless:

(a) The personal representative proves that the exculpatory term is fair under the circumstances.

(b) The term's existence and contents were adequately communicated directly to the testator or to the independent attorney of the testator. This paragraph applies only to wills created on or after July 1, 2007.

Added by Laws 2007, c. 2007–74, § 15, eff. July 1, 2007.

PART VII. CREDITORS' CLAIMS

Cross References

Trusts, proceedings against certain trustees, limitations, see § 736.1014.

733.701. Notifying creditors

Unless creditors' claims are otherwise barred by s. 733.710, every personal representative shall cause notice to creditors to be published and served under s. 733.2121.

Laws 1974, c. 74–106, § 1; Laws 1975, c. 75–220, § 83; Laws 1977, c. 77–87, § 33; Laws 1989, c. 89–340, § 4. Amended by Laws 2001, c. 2001–226, § 145, eff. Jan. 1, 2002; Laws 2003, c. 2003–154, § 31, eff. June 12, 2003.

Cross References

Computation of time, limitation of actions, see § 95.031.
Death of person served by publication, limitations, see § 95.111.
Notice generally, see § 731.301 et seq.
Recordation of will, commencement of limitations period, see § 95.231.
Remaining heirs, claims, limitation of actions, see § 95.22.
Tolling of limitations period, see § 95.051.
Will on record, limitations, see § 95.231.

733.702. Limitations on presentation of claims

(1) If not barred by s. 733.710, no claim or demand against the decedent's estate that arose before the death of the decedent, including claims of the state and any of its political subdivisions, even if the claims are unmatured, contingent, or unliquidated; no claim for funeral or burial expenses; no claim for personal property in the possession of the personal representative; and no claim for damages, including, but not limited to, an action founded on fraud or another wrongful act or omission of the decedent, is binding on the estate, on the personal representative, or on any beneficiary unless filed in the probate proceeding on or before the later of the date that is 3 months after the time of the first publication of the notice to creditors or, as to any creditor required to be served with a copy of the notice to creditors, 30 days after the date of service on the creditor, even though the personal representative has recognized the claim or demand by paying a part of it or interest on it or otherwise. The personal representative may settle in full any claim without the necessity of the claim being filed when the settlement has been approved by the interested persons.

(2) No cause of action, including, but not limited to, an action founded upon fraud or other wrongful act or omission, shall survive the death of the person against whom the claim may be made, whether or not an action is pending at the death of the person, unless a claim is filed within the time periods set forth in this part.

(3) Any claim not timely filed as provided in this section is barred even though no objection to the claim is filed unless the court extends the time in which the claim may be filed. An extension may be granted only upon grounds of fraud, estoppel, or insufficient notice of the claims period. No independent action or declaratory action may be brought upon a claim which was not timely filed unless an extension has been granted by the court. If the personal representative or any other interested person serves on the creditor a notice to file a petition for an extension, the creditor shall be limited to a period of 30 days from the date of service of the notice in which to file a petition for extension.

(4) Nothing in this section affects or prevents:

(a) A proceeding to enforce any mortgage, security interest, or other lien on property of the decedent.

(b) To the limits of casualty insurance protection only, any proceeding to establish liability that is protected by the casualty insurance.

(c) The filing of a cross-claim or counterclaim against the estate in an action instituted by the estate; however, no recovery on a cross-claim or counterclaim shall exceed the estate's recovery in that action.

(5) Nothing in this section shall extend the limitations period set forth in s. 733.710.

Laws 1974, c. 74–106, § 1; Laws 1975, c. 75–220, § 84; Laws 1980, c. 80–127, § 2; Laws 1981, c. 81–27, § 4; Laws 1983, c. 83–216, § 160; Laws 1984, c. 84–106, § 5; Laws 1985, c. 85–79, § 4; Laws 1988, c. 88–340, § 6; Laws 1989, c. 89–340, § 5; Laws 1990, c. 90–23, § 4. Amended by Laws 1997, c. 97–102, § 1016, eff. July 1, 1997; Laws 2001, c. 2001–226, § 146, eff. Jan. 1, 2002; Laws 2002, c. 2002–82, § 6, eff. April 23, 2002; Laws 2006, c. 2006–312, § 26, eff. Jan. 1, 2009; Laws 2010, c. 2010–4, § 21, eff. June 29, 2010.

Cross References

Computation of time, limitation of actions, see § 95.031.
Death of person served by publication, limitation of actions, see § 95.111.
Recordation of will, commencement of limitations period, see § 95.231.
Remaining heirs, claims, limitation of actions, see § 95.22.
Tolling of limitations period, see § 95.051.
Will on record, limitation of actions, see § 95.231.

733.703. Form and manner of presenting claim

(1) A creditor shall file a written statement of the claim. No additional charge may be imposed by a claimant who files a claim against the estate.

(2) Within the time allowed by s. 733.702, the personal representative may file a proof of claim of all claims he or she has paid or intends to pay. A claimant whose claim is listed in a personal representative's proof of claim shall be deemed to have filed a statement of the claim listed. Except as provided otherwise in this part, the claim shall be treated as if the claimant had filed it.

Laws 1974, c. 74–106, § 1; Laws 1975, c. 75–220, § 84; Laws 1981, c. 81–27, § 5; Laws 1985, c. 85–79, § 5; Laws 1989, c. 89–340, § 6. Amended by Laws 2001, c. 2001–226, § 147, eff. Jan. 1, 2002.

Cross References

Form and manner of presenting claims, see Probate Rule 5.490.

733.704. Amendment of claims

If a bona fide attempt to file a claim is made but the claim is defective as to form, the court may permit the amendment of the claim at any time.

Laws 1974, c. 74–106, § 1; Laws 1975, c. 75–220, § 85; Laws 1977, c. 77–174, § 1. Amended by Laws 2001, c. 2001–226, § 148, eff. Jan. 1, 2002.

Cross References

Amending claims, see Probate Rule 5.490.

733.705. Payment of and objection to claims

(1) The personal representative shall pay all claims within 1 year from the date of first publication of notice to creditors, provided that the time shall be extended with respect to claims in litigation, unmatured claims, and contingent claims for the period necessary to dispose of those claims pursuant to subsections (5), (6), (7), and (8). The court may extend the time for payment of any claim upon a showing of good cause. No personal representative shall be compelled to pay the debts of the decedent until after the expiration of 5 months from the first publication of notice to creditors. If any person brings an action against a personal representative within the 5 months on any claim to which the personal representative has not filed an

objection, the plaintiff shall not receive any costs or attorneys' fees, nor shall the judgment change the class of the claim for payment under this code.

(2) On or before the expiration of 4 months from the first publication of notice to creditors or within 30 days from the timely filing or amendment of a claim, whichever occurs later, a personal representative or other interested person may file a written objection to a claim. If an objection is filed, the person filing it shall serve a copy of the objection as provided by the Florida Probate Rules. The failure to serve a copy of the objection constitutes an abandonment of the objection. For good cause, the court may extend the time for filing or serving an objection to any claim. Objection to a claim constitutes an objection to an amendment of that claim unless the objection is withdrawn.

(3) If the objection is filed by a person other than the personal representative, the personal representative may apply to the court for an order relieving him or her from the obligation to defend the estate in an independent action or for the appointment of the objector as administrator ad litem to defend the action. Fees for the attorney for the administrator ad litem may be awarded as provided in s. 733.106(3). If costs or attorney's fees are awarded from or against the estate, the probate court may charge or apportion that award as provided in s. 733.106(4).

(4) An objection by an interested person to a personal representative's proof of claim shall state the particular item or items to which the interested person objects and shall be filed and served as provided in subsection (2). Issues of liability as between the estate and the personal representative individually for items listed in a personal representative's proof of claim shall be determined in the estate administration, in a proceeding for accounting or surcharge, or in another appropriate proceeding, whether or not an objection has been filed. If an objection to an item listed as to be paid in a personal representative's proof of claim is filed and served, and the personal representative has not paid the item, the other subsections of this section shall apply as if a claim for the item had been filed by the claimant; but if the personal representative has paid the claim after listing it as to be paid, issues of liability as between the estate and the personal representative individually shall be determined in the manner provided for an item listed as paid.

(5) The claimant is limited to a period of 30 days from the date of service of an objection within which to bring an independent action upon the claim, or a declaratory action to establish the validity and amount of an unmatured claim which is not yet due but which is certain to become due in the future, or a declaratory action to establish the validity of a contingent claim upon which no cause of action has accrued on the date of service of an objection and that may or may not become due in the future, unless an extension of this time is agreed to by the personal representative in writing before it expires. For good cause, the court may extend the time for filing an action or proceeding after objection is filed. No action or proceeding on the claim may be brought against the personal representative after the time limited above, and the claim is barred without court order. If an objection is filed to the claim of any creditor and the creditor brings an action to establish the claim, a judgment establishing the claim shall give it no priority over claims of the same class to which it belongs.

(6) A claimant may bring an independent action or declaratory action upon a claim which was not timely filed pursuant to s. 733.702(1) only if the claimant has been granted an extension of time to file the claim pursuant to s. 733.702(3).

(7) If an unmatured claim has not become due before the time for distribution of an estate, the personal representative may prepay the full amount of principal plus accrued interest due on the claim, without discount and without penalty, regardless of any prohibition against prepay-

ment or provision for penalty in any instrument on which the claim is founded. If the claim is not prepaid, no order of discharge may be entered until the creditor and personal representative have filed an agreement disposing of the claim, or in the absence of an agreement until the court provides for payment by one of the following methods:

(a) Requiring the personal representative to reserve such assets as the court determines to be adequate to pay the claim when it becomes due; in fixing the amount to be reserved, the court may determine the value of any security or collateral to which the creditor may resort for payment of the claim and may direct the reservation, if necessary, of sufficient assets to pay the claim or to pay the difference between the value of any security or collateral and the amount necessary to pay the claim. If the estate is insolvent, the court may direct a proportionate amount to be reserved. The court shall direct that the amount reserved be retained by the personal representative until the time that the claim becomes due, and that so much of the reserved amount as is not used for payment be distributed according to law;

(b) Requiring that the claim be adequately secured by a mortgage, pledge, bond, trust, guaranty, or other security, as may be determined by the court, the security to remain in effect until the time the claim becomes due, and so much of the security or collateral as is not needed for payment be distributed according to law; or

(c) Making provisions for the disposition or satisfaction of the claim as are equitable, and in a manner so as not to delay unreasonably the closing of the estate.

(8) If no cause of action has accrued on a contingent claim before the time for distribution of an estate, no order of discharge may be entered until the creditor and the personal representative have filed an agreement disposing of the claim or, in the absence of an agreement, until:

(a) The court determines that the claim is adequately secured or that it has no value,

(b) Three months from the date on which a cause of action accrues upon the claim, provided that no action on the claim is then pending,

(c) Five years from the date of first publication of notice to creditors, or

(d) The court provides for payment of the claim upon the happening of the contingency by one of the methods described in paragraph (a), paragraph (b), or paragraph (c) of subsection (7),

whichever occurs first. No action or proceeding on the claim may be brought against the personal representative after the time limited above, and the claim is barred without court order. If an objection is filed to the claim of any creditor and the creditor brings an action to establish the claim, a judgment establishing the claim shall give it no priority over claims of the same class to which it belongs.

(9) Interest shall be paid by the personal representative on written obligations of the decedent providing for the payment of interest. On all other claims, interest shall be allowed and paid beginning 5 months from the first publication of the notice to creditors.

(10) The court may determine all issues concerning claims or matters not requiring trial by jury.

(11) An order for extension of time authorized under this section may be entered only in the estate administration proceeding.

Laws 1974, c. 74–106, § 1; Laws 1975, c. 75–220, § 86; Laws 1977, c. 77–87, § 34; Laws 1977, c. 77–174, § 1; Laws 1984, c. 84–25, § 1; Laws 1986, c. 86–249, § 1; Laws 1988, c. 88–340, § 7; Laws 1989, c. 89–340, § 7; Laws 1991, c. 91–61, § 2. Amended by Laws 1997, c. 97–102, § 1017, eff. July 1, 1997; Laws 2001, c. 2001–226, § 149, eff. Jan. 1, 2002.

Cross References

Computation of time, see Civil Procedure Rule 1.090.
Objections to claims, form and manner, see Probate Rule 5.496.
Registered mail defined to include certified mail with return receipt requested, see § 1.01.

733.706. Executions and levies

Except upon approval by the court, no execution or other process shall issue on or be levied against property of the estate. An order approving execution or other process to be levied against property of the estate may be entered only in the estate administration proceeding. Claims on all judgments against a decedent shall be filed in the same manner as other claims against estates of decedents. This section shall not be construed to prevent the enforcement of mortgages, security interests, or liens encumbering specific property.

Laws 1974, c. 74–106, § 1; Laws 1975, c. 75–220, § 86; Laws 1989, c. 89–340, § 8.

733.707. Order of payment of expenses and obligations

(1) The personal representative shall pay the expenses of the administration and obligations of the decedent's estate in the following order:

(a) *Class 1.*—Costs, expenses of administration, and compensation of personal representatives and their attorneys fees and attorneys fees awarded under s. 733.106(3).

(b) *Class 2.*—Reasonable funeral, interment, and grave marker expenses, whether paid by a guardian, the personal representative, or any other person, not to exceed the aggregate of $6,000.

(c) *Class 3.*—Debts and taxes with preference under federal law, claims pursuant to ss. 409.9101 and 414.28, and claims in favor of the state for unpaid court costs, fees, or fines.

(d) *Class 4.*—Reasonable and necessary medical and hospital expenses of the last 60 days of the last illness of the decedent, including compensation of persons attending the decedent.

(e) *Class 5.*—Family allowance.

(f) *Class 6.*—Arrearage from court-ordered child support.

(g) *Class 7.*—Debts acquired after death by the continuation of the decedent's business, in accordance with s. 733.612(22), but only to the extent of the assets of that business.

(h) *Class 8.*—All other claims, including those founded on judgments or decrees rendered against the decedent during the decedent's lifetime, and any excess over the sums allowed in paragraphs (b) and (d).

(2) After paying any preceding class, if the estate is insufficient to pay all of the next succeeding class, the creditors of the latter class shall be paid ratably in proportion to their respective claims.

(3) Any portion of a trust with respect to which a decedent who is the grantor has at the decedent's death a right of revocation, as defined in paragraph (e), either alone or in conjunction with any other person, is liable for the expenses of the administration and obligations of the decedent's estate to the extent the decedent's estate is insufficient to pay them as provided in ss. 733.607(2) and 736.05053.

(a) For purposes of this subsection, any trusts established as part of, and all payments from, either an employee annuity described in s. 403 of the Internal Revenue Code of 1986,[1] as amended, an Individual Retirement Account, as described in s. 408 of the Internal Revenue Code of 1986,[2] as amended, a Keogh (HR–10) Plan, or a retirement or other plan established by a corporation which is qualified under s. 401 of the Internal Revenue Code of 1986,[3] as amended, shall not be considered a trust over which the decedent has a right of revocation.

(b) For purposes of this subsection, any trust described in s. 664 of the Internal Revenue Code of 1986,[4] as amended, shall not be considered a trust over which the decedent has a right of revocation.

(c) This subsection shall not impair any rights an individual has under a qualified domestic relations order as that term is defined in s. 414(p) of the Internal Revenue Code of 1986,[5] as amended.

(d) For purposes of this subsection, property held or received by a trust to the extent that the property would not have been subject to claims against the decedent's estate if it had been paid directly to a trust created under the decedent's will or other than to the decedent's estate, or assets received from any trust other than a trust described in this subsection, shall not be deemed assets of the trust available to the decedent's estate.

(e) For purposes of this subsection, a "right of revocation" is a power retained by the decedent, held in any capacity, to:

1. Amend or revoke the trust and revest the principal of the trust in the decedent; or

2. Withdraw or appoint the principal of the trust to or for the decedent's benefit.

Laws 1974, c. 74–106, § 1; Laws 1975, c. 75–220, § 86; Laws 1977, c. 77–87, § 35; Laws 1985, c. 85–79, § 7; Laws 1987, c. 87–226, § 69; Laws 1993, c. 93–208, § 20; Laws 1993, c. 93–257, § 11. Amended by Laws 1995, c. 95–401, § 10, eff. July 1, 1995; Laws 1997, c. 97–102, § 1018, eff. July 1, 1997; Laws 1997, c. 97–240, § 3, eff. May 30, 1997; Laws 2001, c. 2001–226, § 150, eff. Jan. 1, 2002; Laws 2010, c. 2010–122, § 2, eff. July 1, 2010; Laws 2012, c. 2012–100, § 17, eff. July 1, 2012.

[1] 26 U.S.C.A. § 403.
[2] 26 U.S.C.A. § 408.
[3] 26 U.S.C.A. § 401.
[4] 26 U.S.C.A. § 664.
[5] 26 U.S.C.A. § 414(p).

Cross References

Family allowance, see § 732.403.
Homestead property, inter vivos transfers, see F.S.A. § 732.4017.
Legacies and distributive shares, delivery, see § 733.801.
Notice of trustee duties, proceedings for payment, see § 733.802.
Property interests, disclaimer, see § 739.201.
Property, transfers to minors, transfers by gift or exercise of power of appointment, see F.S.A. § 710.105.
Trusts,
    Notice of trust, see § 736.05055.
    Proceedings against certain trustees, limitations, see § 736.1014.
    Settlor's estate expenses and obligations, payment by trustee, see § 736.05053.

733.708. Compromise

When a proposal is made to compromise any claim, whether in suit or not, by or against the estate of a decedent or to compromise any question concerning the distribution of a decedent's estate, the court may enter an order authorizing the compromise if satisfied that the compromise will be for the best interest of the interested persons. The order shall relieve the personal representative of liability or responsibility for the compromise. Claims against the estate may not be compromised until after the time for filing objections to claims has expired.

Laws 1974, c. 74–106, § 1; Laws 1975, c. 75–220, § 86. Amended by Laws 2001, c. 2001–226, § 151, eff. Jan. 1, 2002.

Cross References

Power of personal representative to compromise claims, see § 733.612.

733.710.   Limitations on claims against estates

(1) Notwithstanding any other provision of the code, 2 years after the death of a person, neither the decedent's estate, the personal representative, if any, nor the beneficiaries shall be liable for any claim or cause of action against the decedent, whether or not letters of administration have been issued, except as provided in this section.

(2) This section shall not apply to a creditor who has filed a claim pursuant to s. 733.702 within 2 years after the person's death, and whose claim has not been paid or otherwise disposed of pursuant to s. 733.705.

(3) This section shall not affect the lien of any duly recorded mortgage or security interest or the lien of any person in possession of personal property or the right to foreclose and enforce the mortgage or lien.

Laws 1974, c. 74–106, § 1; Fla.St.1974, Supp. § 733.108; Laws 1975, c. 75–220, § 50; Laws 1977, c. 77–87, § 36; Laws 1989, c. 89–340, § 9. Amended by Laws 2001, c. 2001–226, § 152, eff. Jan. 1, 2002.

Cross References

Computation of time, limitation of actions, see § 95.031.
Death of person served by publication, limitations, see § 95.111.
Deed or will on record, limitations, see § 95.231.
Limitation of actions generally, see § 95.011 et seq.
Limitations where deed or will on record, see § 95.231.
Public assistance, discharge of debt, see § 414.28.
Recordation of deed or will, commencement of limitations, see § 95.231.
Remaining heirs, claims, limitation of actions, see § 95.22.
Tolling of limitations period, see § 95.051.

PART VIII.   SPECIAL PROVISIONS FOR DISTRIBUTION

Cross References

Distribution and discharge, see Probate Rule 5.400.

733.801.   Delivery of devises and distributive shares

(1) No personal representative shall be required to pay or deliver any devise or distributive share or to surrender possession of any land to any beneficiary until the expiration of 5 months from the granting of letters.

(2) Except as otherwise provided in the will, the personal representative shall pay as an expense of administration the reasonable expenses of storage, insurance, packing, and delivery of tangible personal property to a beneficiary.

Laws 1974, c. 74–106, § 1; Laws 1975, c. 75–220, § 86. Amended by Laws 2001, c. 2001–226, § 153, eff. Jan. 1, 2002.

Cross References

Computation of time, see Civil Procedure Rule 1.090.

733.802.   Proceedings for compulsory payment of devises or distributive interest

(1) Before final distribution, no personal representative shall be compelled:

(a) To pay a devise in money before the final settlement of the personal representative's accounts,

(b) To deliver specific personal property devised, unless the personal property is exempt personal property,

(c) To pay all or any part of a distributive share in the personal estate of a decedent, or

(d) To surrender land to any beneficiary,

unless the beneficiary establishes that the property will not be required for the payment of debts, family allowance, estate and inheritance taxes, claims, elective share of the surviving spouse, charges, or expenses of administration or to provide funds for contribution or to enforce equalization in case of advancements.

(2) An order directing the surrender of real property or the delivery of personal property by the personal representative to the beneficiary shall be conclusive in favor of bona fide purchasers for value from the beneficiary or distributee as against the personal representative and all other persons claiming by, through, under, or against the decedent or the decedent's estate.

(3) If the administration of the estate has not been completed before the entry of an order of partial distribution, the court may require the person entitled to distribution to give a bond with sureties as prescribed in s. 45.011, conditioned on the making of due contribution for the payment of devises, family allowance, estate and inheritance taxes, claims, elective share of the spouse, charges, expenses of administration, and equalization in case of advancements, plus any interest on them.

Laws 1974, c. 74–106, § 1; Laws 1975, c. 75–220, § 86; Laws 1977, c. 77–87, § 37; Laws 1977, c. 77–174, § 1; Laws 1979, c. 79–400, § 272. Amended by Laws 1997, c. 97–102, § 1019, eff. July 1, 1997; Laws 2001, c. 2001–226, § 154, eff. Jan. 1, 2002.

Cross References

Proceedings for payment of devises or distributive interest, see Probate Rule 5.380.

733.803. Encumbered property; liability for payment

The specific devisee of any encumbered property shall be entitled to have the encumbrance on devised property paid at the expense of the residue of the estate only when the will shows that intent. A general direction in the will to pay debts does not show that intent.

Laws 1974, c. 74–106, § 1; Laws 1975, c. 75–220, § 86. Amended by Laws 2001, c. 2001–226, § 155, eff. Jan. 1, 2002.

733.805. Order in which assets abate

(1) Funds or property designated by the will shall be used to pay debts, family allowance, exempt property, elective share charges, expenses of administration, and devises, to the extent the funds or property is sufficient. If no provision is made or the designated fund or property is insufficient, the funds and property of the estate shall be used for these purposes, and to raise the shares of a pretermitted spouse and children, except as otherwise provided in subsections (3) and (4), in the following order:

(a) Property passing by intestacy.

(b) Property devised to the residuary devisee or devisees.

(c) Property not specifically or demonstratively devised.

(d) Property specifically or demonstratively devised.

(2) Demonstrative devises shall be classed as general devises upon the failure or insufficiency of funds or property out of which payment should be made, to the extent of the insufficiency. Devises to the decedent's surviving spouse, given in satisfaction of, or instead of, the surviving spouse's statutory rights in the estate, shall not abate until other devises of the same class are exhausted. Devises given for a valuable consideration shall abate with other devises of the same class only to the extent of the excess over the amount of value of the consideration until all others of the same class are exhausted. Except as herein provided, devises shall abate equally and ratably and without preference or priority as between real and personal property. When property that has been specifically devised or charged with a devise is sold or used by the personal representative, other devisees shall contribute according to their respective interests to the devisee whose devise has been sold or used. The amounts of the respective contributions shall be determined by the court and shall be paid or withheld before distribution is made.

(3) Section 733.817 shall be applied before this section is applied.

(4) In determining the contribution required under s. 733.607(2), subsections (1)–(3) of this section and s. 736.05053(2) shall be applied as if the beneficiaries of the estate and the beneficiaries of a trust described in s. 733.707(3), other than the estate or trust itself, were taking under a common instrument.

Laws 1974, c. 74–106, § 1; Laws 1975, c. 75–220, § 88; Laws 1977, c. 77–174, § 1. Amended by Laws 1997, c. 97–102, § 1020, eff. July 1, 1997; Laws 2001, c. 2001–226, § 156, eff. Jan. 1, 2002; Laws 2006, c. 2006–217, § 38, eff. July 1, 2007.

Cross References

Accessions, change in securities, see § 732.605.
Ademption by satisfaction, see § 732.609.

733.806. Advancement

If a person dies intestate, property that the decedent gave during lifetime to an heir is treated as an advancement against the heir's share of the estate only if declared in a contemporaneous writing by the decedent or acknowledged in writing by the heir. The property advanced shall be valued at the time the heir came into possession or enjoyment of the property or at the time of the death of the decedent, whichever first occurs. If the recipient of the property does not survive the decedent, the property shall not be taken into account in computing the intestate share to be received by the recipient's descendants unless the declaration or acknowledgment provides otherwise.

Laws 1974, c. 74–106, § 1; Laws 1975, c. 75–220, § 89. Amended by Laws 1997, c. 97–102, § 1021, eff. July 1, 1997; Laws 2001, c. 2001–226, § 157, eff. Jan. 1, 2002.

Cross References

Ademption by satisfaction, see § 732.609.

733.808. Death benefits; disposition of proceeds

(1) Death benefits of any kind, including, but not limited to, proceeds of:

(a) An individual life insurance policy;

(b) A group life insurance policy;

(c) A benefit plan as defined by s. 710.102;

(d) An annuity or endowment contract; and

(e) A health or accident policy,

may be made payable to the trustee under a trust agreement or declaration of trust in existence at the time of the death of the insured, employee, or annuitant or the owner of or participant in the benefit plan. The death benefits shall be held and disposed of by the trustee in accordance with the terms of the trust as they appear in writing on the date of the death of the insured, employee, annuitant, owner, or participant. It shall not be necessary to the validity of the trust agreement or declaration of trust, whether revocable or irrevocable, that it have a trust corpus other than the right of the trustee to receive death benefits.

(2) Death benefits of any kind, including, but not limited to, proceeds of:

(a) An individual life insurance policy;

(b) A group life insurance policy;

(c) A benefit plan as defined in s. 710.102;

(d) An annuity or endowment contract; and

(e) A health or accident policy,

may be made payable to the trustee named, or to be named, in a written instrument that is admitted to probate as the last will of the insured, the owner of the policy, the employee, owner, or participant covered by the plan or contract, or any other person, whether or not the will is in existence at the time of designation. Upon the admission of the will to probate, the death benefits shall be paid to the trustee, to be held, administered, and disposed of in accordance with the terms of the trust or trusts created by the will.

(3) In the event no trustee makes proper claim to the proceeds from the insurance company or other obligor within a period of 6 months after the date of the death of the insured, employee, annuitant, owner, or participant, or if satisfactory evidence is furnished to the insurance company or obligor within that period that there is, or will be, no trustee to receive the proceeds, payment shall be made by the insurance company or obligor to the personal representative of the person making the designation, unless otherwise provided by agreement with the insurer or obligor during the lifetime of the insured, employee, annuitant, owner, or participant.

(4) Unless the trust agreement, declaration of trust, or will expressly refers to this subsection and directs that it does not apply, death benefits payable as provided in subsection (1), subsection (2), or subsection (3), unless paid to a personal representative under the provisions of subsection (3), shall not be deemed to be part of the decedent's estate and shall not be subject to any obligation to pay the expenses of the administration and obligations of the decedent's estate or for contribution required from a trust under s. 733.607(2) to any greater extent than if the proceeds were payable directly to the beneficiaries named in the trust.

(5) The death benefits held in trust may be commingled with any other assets that may properly come into the trust.

(6) This section does not affect the validity of any designation of a beneficiary of proceeds previously made that designates as beneficiary the trustee of any trust established under a trust agreement or declaration of trust or by will.

Laws 1974, c. 74–106, § 1; Laws 1975, c. 75–220, § 91; Laws 1977, c. 77–87, § 38. Amended by Laws 2001, c. 2001–226, § 158, eff. Jan. 1, 2002; Laws 2005, c. 2005–101, § 7, eff. June 1, 2005; Laws 2014, c. 2014–127, § 5, eff. July 1, 2014.

733.809. Right of retainer

The amount of a noncontingent indebtedness due from a beneficiary to the estate or its present value, if not due, may be offset against that beneficiary's interest. However, that beneficiary shall have the benefit of any defense that would be available in a direct proceeding for recovery of the debt.

Laws 1974, c. 74–106, § 1; Laws 1975, c. 75–220, § 91; Laws 1977, c. 77–87, § 39. Amended by Laws 1997, c. 97–102, § 1022, eff. July 1, 1997; Laws 2001, c. 2001–226, § 159, eff. Jan. 1, 2002.

733.810. Distribution in kind; valuation

(1) Assets shall be distributed in kind unless:

(a) A general power of sale is conferred;

(b) A contrary intention is indicated by the will or trust; or

(c) Disposition is made otherwise under the provisions of this code.

(2) Any pecuniary devise, family allowance, or other pecuniary share of the estate or trust may be satisfied in kind if:

(a) The person entitled to payment has not demanded cash;

(b) The property is distributed at fair market value as of its distribution date; and

(c) No residuary devisee has requested that the asset remain a part of the residuary estate.

(3) When not practicable to distribute undivided interests in a residuary asset, the asset may be sold.

(4) When the fiduciary under a will or trust is required, or has an option, to satisfy a pecuniary devise or transfer in trust, to or for the benefit of the surviving spouse, with an in-kind distribution, at values as finally determined for federal estate tax purposes, the fiduciary shall, unless the governing instrument otherwise provides, satisfy the devise or transfer in trust by distribution of assets, including cash, fairly representative of the appreciated or depreciated value of all property available for that distribution, taking into consideration any gains and losses realized from a prior sale of any property not devised specifically, generally, or demonstratively.

(5) A personal representative or a trustee is authorized to distribute any distributable assets, non-pro rata among the beneficiaries subject to the fiduciary's duty of impartiality.

Laws 1974, c. 74–106, § 1; Laws 1975, c. 75–220, § 92; Laws 1977, c. 77–87, § 40. Amended by Laws 2001, c. 2001–226, § 160, eff. Jan. 1, 2002.

Cross References

Ademption by satisfaction, see § 732.609.
Securities, accession and nonademption, see § 732.605.

733.811. Distribution; right or title of distributee

If a distributee receives from a fiduciary an instrument transferring assets in kind, payment in distribution, or possession of specific property, the distributee has succeeded to the estate's interest in the assets as against all persons interested in the estate. However, the fiduciary may recover the assets or their value if the distribution was improper.

Laws 1974, c. 74–106, § 1; Laws 1975, c. 75–220, § 93. Amended by Laws 2001, c. 2001–226, § 161, eff. Jan. 1, 2002.

733.812. Improper distribution or payment; liability of distributee or payee

A distributee or a claimant who was paid improperly must return the assets or funds received, and the income from those assets or interest on the funds since distribution or payment, unless the distribution or payment cannot be questioned because of adjudication, estoppel, or limitations. If the distributee or claimant does not have the property, its value at the date of disposition, income thereon, and gain received by the distributee or claimant must be returned.
Laws 1974, c. 74–106, § 1; Laws 1975, c. 75–220, § 92. Amended by Laws 1997, c. 97–102, § 1023, eff. July 1, 1997; Laws 2001, c. 2001–226, § 162, eff. Jan. 1, 2002.

Cross References

Orders binding interests of others, see § 731.303.

733.813. Purchasers from distributees protected

If property distributed in kind, or a security interest in that property, is acquired by a purchaser or lender for value from a distributee, the purchaser or lender takes title free of any claims of the estate and incurs no personal liability to the estate, whether or not the distribution was proper. The purchaser or lender need not inquire whether a personal representative acted properly in making the distribution in kind.
Laws 1974, c. 74–106, § 1; Laws 1975, c. 75–220, § 93. Amended by Laws 2001, c. 2001–226, § 163, eff. Jan. 1, 2002.

733.814. Partition for purpose of distribution

When two or more beneficiaries are entitled to distribution of undivided interests in any property, the personal representative or any beneficiary may petition the court before the estate is closed to partition the property in the same manner as provided by law for civil actions of partition. The court may direct the personal representative to sell any property that cannot be partitioned without prejudice to the owners and that cannot be allotted equitably and conveniently.
Laws 1974, c. 74–106, § 1; Laws 1975, c. 75–220, § 93. Amended by Laws 2001, c. 2001–226, § 164, eff. Jan. 1, 2002.

Cross References

Estates by survivorship, see § 689.15.
Partition of property, see § 64.011 et seq.
Powers of personal representatives, see § 733.612.

733.815. Private contracts among interested persons

Subject to the rights of creditors and taxing authorities, interested persons may agree among themselves to alter the interests, shares, or amounts to which they are entitled in a written contract executed by them. The personal representative shall abide by the terms of the contract, subject to the personal representative's obligation to administer the estate for the benefit of interested persons who are not parties to the contract, and to pay costs of administration. Trustees of a testamentary trust are interested persons for the purposes of this section. Nothing in this section relieves trustees of any duties owed to beneficiaries of trusts.
Laws 1974, c. 74–106, § 1; Laws 1975, c. 75–220, § 94. Amended by Laws 1997, c. 97–102, § 1024, eff. July 1, 1997; Laws 2001, c. 2001–226, § 165, eff. Jan. 1, 2002.

Cross References
Penalty for contesting will, see § 732.517.

733.816. Disposition of unclaimed property held by personal representatives

(1) In all cases in which there is unclaimed property in the hands of a personal representative that cannot be distributed or paid because of the inability to find the lawful owner or because no lawful owner is known or because the lawful owner refuses to accept the property after a reasonable attempt to distribute it and after notice to that lawful owner, the court shall order the personal representative to sell the property and deposit the proceeds and cash already in hand, after retaining those amounts provided for in subsection (4), with the clerk and receive a receipt, and the clerk shall deposit the funds in the registry of the court to be disposed of as follows:

(a) If the value of the funds is $500 or less, the clerk shall post a notice for 30 days at the courthouse door giving the amount involved, the name of the personal representative, and the other pertinent information that will put interested persons on notice.

(b) If the value of the funds is over $500, the clerk shall publish the notice once a month for 2 consecutive months in a newspaper of general circulation in the county.

After the expiration of 6 months from the posting or first publication, the clerk shall deposit the funds with the Chief Financial Officer after deducting the clerk's fees and the costs of publication.

(2) Upon receipt of the funds, the Chief Financial Officer shall deposit them to the credit of the State School Fund, to become a part of the school fund. All interest and all income that may accrue from the money while so deposited shall belong to the fund. The funds so deposited shall constitute and be a permanent appropriation for payments by the Chief Financial Officer in obedience to court orders entered as provided by subsection (3).

(3) Within 10 years from the date of deposit with the Chief Financial Officer, on written petition to the court that directed the deposit of the funds and informal notice to the Department of Legal Affairs, and after proof of entitlement, any person entitled to the funds before or after payment to the Chief Financial Officer and deposit as provided by subsection (1) may obtain a court order directing the payment of the funds to that person. All funds deposited with the Chief Financial Officer and not claimed within 10 years from the date of deposit shall escheat to the state for the benefit of the State School Fund.

(4) The personal representative depositing assets with the clerk is permitted to retain from the funds a sufficient amount to pay final costs of administration chargeable to the assets accruing between the deposit of the funds with the clerk of the court and the order of discharge. Any funds so retained which are surplus shall be deposited with the clerk prior to discharge of the personal representative.

(5)(a) If a person entitled to the funds assigns the right to receive payment or part payment to an attorney or private investigative agency which is duly licensed to do business in this state pursuant to a written agreement with that person, the Department of Financial Services is authorized to make distribution in accordance with the assignment.

(b) Payments made to an attorney or private investigative agency shall be promptly deposited into a trust or escrow account which is regularly maintained by the attorney or private investigative agency in a financial institution located in this state and authorized to accept these deposits.

(c) Distribution by the attorney or private investigative agency to the person entitled to the funds shall be made within 10 days following final credit of the deposit into the trust or escrow account at the financial institution, unless a party to the agreement protests the distribution in writing before it is made.

(d) The department shall not be civilly or criminally liable for any funds distributed pursuant to this subsection, provided the distribution is made in good faith.

Laws 1974, c. 74–106, § 1; Laws 1975, c. 75–220, § 95; Laws 1985, c. 85–79, § 6; Laws 1989, c. 89–291, § 5; Laws 1989, c. 89–299, § 10. Amended by Laws 1995, c. 95–401, § 21, eff. July 1, 1995; Laws 1997, c. 97–102, § 1025, eff. July 1, 1997; Laws 2001, c. 2001–226, § 166, eff. Jan. 1, 2002; Laws 2003, c. 2003–261, § 1897, eff. June 26, 2003.

Cross References

Computation of period of limitations, see § 95.031.
Computation of time, see Civil Procedure Rule 1.090.
Death of person served by publication, limitation of actions, see § 95.111.
Escheats, see § 716.01 et seq.
Recovery of escheated property by claimant, see § 716.07.
Tolling of limitations period, see § 95.051.
Unclaimed property disposition, property held by agents and fiduciaries, see F.S.A. § 717.112.

733.817. Apportionment of estate taxes

(1) **Definitions.**—As used in this section, the term:

(a) "Fiduciary" means a person, other than the personal representative in possession of property included in the measure of the tax, who is liable to the applicable taxing authority for payment of the entire tax to the extent of the value of the property in possession.

(b) "Generation-skipping transfer tax" means the generation-skipping transfer tax imposed by chapter 13 of the Internal Revenue Code [1] on direct skips of interests includable in the federal gross estate or a corresponding tax imposed by any state or country or political subdivision of the foregoing. The term does not include the generation-skipping transfer tax on taxable distributions, taxable terminations, or any other generation-skipping transfer. The terms "direct skip," "taxable distribution," and "taxable termination" have the same meanings as provided in s. 2612 of the Internal Revenue Code.[2]

(c) "Governing instrument" means a will, trust instrument, or any other document that controls the transfer of property on the occurrence of the event with respect to which the tax is being levied.

(d) "Gross estate" means the gross estate, as determined by the Internal Revenue Code [3] with respect to the federal estate tax and the Florida estate tax, and as that concept is otherwise determined by the estate, inheritance, or death tax laws of the particular state, country, or political subdivision whose tax is being apportioned.

(e) "Included in the measure of the tax" means for each separate tax that an interest may incur, only interests included in the measure of that particular tax are considered. As used in this section, the term does not include:

1. Any interest, whether passing under the will or not, to the extent the interest is initially deductible from the gross estate, without regard to any subsequent reduction of the deduction by reason of the charge of any part of the applicable tax to the interest. If an election is required for deductibility, an interest is not initially deductible unless the election for deductibility is allowed.

2. Interests or amounts that are not included in the gross estate but are included in the amount upon which the applicable tax is computed, such as adjusted taxable gifts pursuant to s. 2001 of the Internal Revenue Code.[4]

3. Gift taxes included in the gross estate pursuant to s. 2035 of the Internal Revenue Code [5] and the portion of any inter vivos transfer included in the gross estate pursuant to s. 529 of the Internal Revenue Code,[6] notwithstanding inclusion in the gross estate.

(f) "Internal Revenue Code" means the Internal Revenue Code of 1986,[3] as amended.

(g) "Net tax" means the net tax payable to the particular state, country, or political subdivision whose tax is being apportioned, after taking into account all credits against the applicable tax except as provided in this section. With respect to the federal estate tax, net tax is determined after taking into account all credits against the tax except for the credit for foreign death taxes and except for the credit or deduction for state taxes imposed by states other than this state.

(h) "Nonresiduary devise" means any devise that is not a residuary devise.

(i) "Nonresiduary interest," in connection with a trust, means any interest in a trust which is not a residuary interest.

(j) "Recipient" means, with respect to property or an interest in property included in the gross estate, an heir at law in an intestate estate; devisee in a testate estate; beneficiary of a trust; beneficiary of a life insurance policy, annuity, or other contractual right; surviving tenant; taker as a result of the exercise or in default of the exercise of a general power of appointment; person who receives or is to receive the property or an interest in the property; or person in possession of the property, other than a creditor.

(k) "Residuary devise" has the meaning in s. 731.201.

(*l*) "Residuary interest," in connection with a trust, means an interest in the assets of a trust which remain after provision for any distribution that is to be satisfied by reference to a specific property or type of property, fund, sum, or statutory amount.

(m) "Revocable trust" means a trust as described in s. 733.707(3).

(n) "Section 2044 interest" means an interest included in the measure of the tax by reason of s. 2044 of the Internal Revenue Code.[7]

(*o*) "State" means any state, territory, or possession of the United States, the District of Columbia, or the Commonwealth of Puerto Rico.

(p) "Tax" means any estate tax, inheritance tax, generation-skipping transfer tax, or other tax levied or assessed under the laws of this or any other state, the United States, any other country, or any political subdivision of the foregoing, as finally determined, which is imposed as a result of the death of the decedent. The term also includes any interest or penalties imposed in addition to the tax. Unless the context indicates otherwise, the term means each separate tax. The term does not include any additional estate tax imposed by s. 2032A(c) or s. 2057(f) of the Internal Revenue Code [8] or a corresponding tax imposed by any state or country or political subdivision of the foregoing. The additional estate tax imposed shall be apportioned as provided in s. 2032A or s. 2057 of the Internal Revenue Code.[9]

(q) "Temporary interest" means an interest in income or an estate for a specific period of time, for life, or for some other period controlled by reference to extrinsic events, whether or not in trust.

(r) "Tentative Florida tax" with respect to any property means the net Florida estate tax that would have been attributable to that property if no tax were payable to any other state in respect of that property.

(s) "Value" means the pecuniary worth of the interest involved as finally determined for purposes of the applicable tax after deducting any debt, expense, or other deduction chargeable to it for which a deduction was allowed in determining the amount of the applicable tax. A lien or other encumbrance is not regarded as chargeable to a particular interest to the extent that it will be paid from other interests. The value of an interest is not reduced by reason of the charge against it of any part of the tax, except as provided in paragraph (3)(a).

(2) Allocation of tax.—Except as effectively directed in the governing instrument pursuant to subsection (4), the net tax attributable to the interests included in the measure of each tax shall be determined by the proportion that the value of each interest included in the measure of the tax bears to the total value of all interests included in the measure of the tax. Notwithstanding the foregoing provision of this subsection and except as effectively directed in the governing instrument:

(a) The net tax attributable to section 2044 interests [10] shall be determined in the manner provided for the federal estate tax in s. 2207A of the Internal Revenue Code,[11] and the amount so determined shall be deducted from the tax to determine the net tax attributable to all other interests included in the measure of the tax.

(b) The foreign tax credit allowed with respect to the federal estate tax shall be allocated among the recipients of interests finally charged with the payment of the foreign tax in reduction of any federal estate tax chargeable to the recipients of the foreign interests, whether or not any federal estate tax is attributable to the foreign interests. Any excess of the foreign tax credit shall be applied to reduce proportionately the net amount of federal estate tax chargeable to the remaining recipients of the interests included in the measure of the federal estate tax.

(c) The reduction in the net tax attributable to the deduction for state death taxes allowed by s. 2058 of the Internal Revenue Code [12] shall be allocated to the recipients of the interests that produced the deduction. For this purpose, the reduction in the net tax shall be calculated in the manner provided for interests other than those described in paragraph (a).

(d) The reduction in the Florida tax, if one is imposed, on the estate of a Florida resident for tax paid to another state shall be allocated as follows:

1. If the net tax paid to another state is greater than or equal to the tentative Florida tax attributable to the property subject to tax in the other state, none of the Florida tax shall be attributable to that property.

2. If the net tax paid to another state is less than the tentative Florida tax attributable to the property subject to tax in the other state, the net Florida tax attributable to the property subject to tax in the other state shall be the excess of the amount of the tentative Florida tax attributable to the property over the net tax payable to the other state with respect to the property.

3. Any remaining net Florida tax shall be attributable to property included in the measure of the Florida tax exclusive of the property subject to tax in another state.

4. The net federal tax attributable to the property subject to tax in the other state shall be determined as if the property were located in that state.

(e) The net tax attributable to a temporary interest, if any, is regarded as attributable to the principal that supports the temporary interest.

---

(3) Apportionment of tax.—Except as otherwise effectively directed in the governing instrument pursuant to subsection (4), the net tax attributable to each interest shall be apportioned as follows:

(a) *Generation-skipping transfer tax.*—Any federal or state generation-skipping transfer tax shall be apportioned as provided in s. 2603 of the Internal Revenue Code [13] after the application of the remaining provisions of this subsection to taxes other than the generation-skipping transfer tax.

(b) *Section 2044 interests.*[10]—The net tax attributable to section 2044 interests shall be apportioned among the recipients of the section 2044 interests in the proportion that the value of each section 2044 interest bears to the total of all section 2044 interests. The net tax apportioned by this paragraph to section 2044 interests that pass in the manner described in paragraph (c) or paragraph (d) shall be apportioned to the section 2044 interests in the manner described in those paragraphs before the apportionment of the net tax attributable to the other interests passing as provided in those paragraphs. The net tax attributable to the interests other than the section 2044 interests which pass in the manner described in paragraph (c) or paragraph (d) shall be apportioned only to such other interests pursuant to those paragraphs.

(c) *Wills.*—The net tax attributable to property passing under the decedent's will shall be apportioned in the following order of priority:

1. The net tax attributable to nonresiduary devises shall be charged to and paid from the residuary estate, whether or not all interests in the residuary estate are included in the measure of the tax. If the residuary estate is insufficient to pay the net tax attributable to all nonresiduary devises, the balance of the net tax attributable to nonresiduary devises shall be apportioned among the recipients of the nonresiduary devises in the proportion that the value of each nonresiduary devise included in the measure of the tax bears to the total of all nonresiduary devises included in the measure of the tax.

2. The net tax attributable to residuary devises shall be apportioned among the recipients of the residuary devises included in the measure of the tax in the proportion that the value of each residuary devise included in the measure of the tax bears to the total of all residuary devises included in the measure of the tax. If the residuary estate is insufficient to pay the net tax attributable to all residuary devises, the balance of the net tax attributable to residuary devises shall be apportioned among the recipients of the nonresiduary devises in the proportion that the value of each nonresiduary devise included in the measure of the tax bears to the total of all nonresiduary devises included in the measure of the tax.

(d) *Trusts.*—The net tax attributable to property passing under the terms of any trust other than a trust created in the decedent's will shall be apportioned in the following order of priority:

1. The net tax attributable to nonresiduary interests of the trust shall be charged to and paid from the residuary portion of the trust, whether or not all interests in the residuary portion are included in the measure of the tax. If the residuary portion is insufficient to pay the net tax attributable to all nonresiduary interests, the balance of the net tax attributable to nonresiduary interests shall be apportioned among the recipients of the nonresiduary interests in the proportion that the value of each nonresiduary interest included in the measure of the tax bears to the total of all nonresiduary interests included in the measure of the tax.

2. The net tax attributable to residuary interests of the trust shall be apportioned among the recipients of the residuary interests of the trust included in the measure of the tax in the proportion that the value of each residuary interest included in the measure of the tax bears to the total of all residuary interests of the trust included in the measure of the tax. If the

residuary portion is insufficient to pay the net tax attributable to all residuary interests, the balance of the net tax attributable to residuary interests shall be apportioned among the recipients of the nonresiduary interests in the proportion that the value of each nonresiduary interest included in the measure of the tax bears to the total of all nonresiduary interests included in the measure of the tax.

Except as provided in paragraph (g), this paragraph applies separately for each trust.

(e) *Protected homestead, exempt property, and family allowance.*—

1. The net tax attributable to an interest in protected homestead, exempt property, and the family allowance determined under s. 732.403 shall be apportioned against the recipients of other interests in the estate or passing under any revocable trust in the following order of priority:

a. Class I.—Recipients of interests passing by intestacy that are included in the measure of the federal estate tax.

b. Class II.—Recipients of residuary devises, residuary interests, and pretermitted shares under ss. 732.301 and 732.302 that are included in the measure of the federal estate tax.

c. Class III.—Recipients of nonresiduary devises and nonresiduary interests that are included in the measure of the federal estate tax.

2. Any net tax apportioned to a class pursuant to this paragraph shall be apportioned among each recipient in the class in the proportion that the value of the interest of each bears to the total value of all interests included in that class. A tax may not be apportioned under this paragraph to the portion of any interest applied in satisfaction of the elective share whether or not included in the measure of the tax. For purposes of this paragraph, if the value of the interests described in s. 732.2075(1) exceeds the amount of the elective share, the elective share shall be treated as satisfied first from interests other than those described in classes I, II, and III, and to the extent that those interests are insufficient to satisfy the elective share, from the interests passing to or for the benefit of the surviving spouse described in classes I, II, and III, beginning with those described in class I, until the elective share is satisfied. This paragraph has priority over paragraphs (a) and (h).

3. The balance of the net tax attributable to any interest in protected homestead, exempt property, and the family allowance determined under s. 732.403 which is not apportioned under the preceding provisions of this paragraph shall be apportioned to the recipients of those interests included in the measure of the tax in the proportion that the value of each bears to the total value of those interests included in the measure of the tax.

(f) *Construction.*—For purposes of this subsection:

1. If the decedent's estate is the beneficiary of a life insurance policy, annuity, or contractual right included in the decedent's gross estate, or is the taker as a result of the exercise or default in exercise of a general power of appointment held by the decedent, that interest shall be regarded as passing under the terms of the decedent's will for the purposes of paragraph (c) or by intestacy if not disposed of by will. Additionally, any interest included in the measure of the tax by reason of s. 2041 of the Internal Revenue Code [14] passing to the decedent's creditors or the creditors of the decedent's estate shall be regarded as passing to the decedent's estate for the purpose of this subparagraph.

2. If a trust is the beneficiary of a life insurance policy, annuity, or contractual right included in the decedent's gross estate, or is the taker as a result of the exercise or default in exercise of a

general power of appointment held by the decedent, that interest shall be regarded as passing under the trust for purposes of paragraph (d).

(g) *Common instrument construction.*—In the application of this subsection, paragraphs (b)–(f) shall be applied to apportion the net tax to the recipients under certain governing instruments as if all recipients under those instruments, other than the estate or revocable trust itself, were taking under a common instrument. This construction applies to the following:

1. The decedent's will and revocable trust if the estate is a beneficiary of the revocable trust or if the revocable trust is a beneficiary of the estate.

2. A revocable trust of the decedent and another revocable trust of the decedent if either trust is the beneficiary of the other trust.

(h) *Other interests.*—The net tax that is not apportioned to interests under paragraphs (b)–(g), including, but not limited to, the net tax attributable to interests passing by intestacy, interests applied in satisfaction of the elective share pursuant to s. 732.2075(2), interests passing by reason of the exercise or nonexercise of a general power of appointment, jointly held interests passing by survivorship, life insurance, properties in which the decedent held a reversionary or revocable interest, annuities, and contractual rights, shall be apportioned among the recipients of the remaining interests included in the measure of the tax in the proportion that the value of each such interest bears to the total value of all remaining interests included in the measure of the tax.

(i) *Assessment of liability by court.*—If the court finds that:

1. It is inequitable to apportion interest or penalties, or both, in the manner provided in paragraphs (a)–(h), the court may assess liability for the payment thereof in the manner that the court finds equitable.

2. The payment of any tax was not effectively directed in the governing instrument pursuant to subsection (4) and that such tax is not apportioned by this subsection, the court may assess liability for the payment of such tax in the manner that the court finds equitable.

(4) Direction against apportionment.—

(a) Except as provided in this subsection, a governing instrument may not direct that taxes be paid from property other than that passing under the governing instrument.

(b) For a direction in a governing instrument to be effective to direct payment of taxes attributable to property passing under the governing instrument in a manner different from that provided in this section, the direction must be express.

(c) For a direction in a governing instrument to be effective to direct payment of taxes attributable to property not passing under the governing instrument from property passing under the governing instrument, the governing instrument must expressly direct that the property passing under the governing instrument bear the burden of taxation for property not passing under the governing instrument. Except as provided in paragraph (d), a direction in the governing instrument to the effect that all taxes are to be paid from property passing under the governing instrument whether attributable to property passing under the governing instrument or otherwise shall be effective to direct payment from property passing under the governing instrument of taxes attributable to property not passing under the governing instrument.

(d) In addition to satisfying the other provisions of this subsection:

1. a. For a direction in the decedent's will or revocable trust to be effective in waiving the right of recovery provided in s. 2207A of the Internal Revenue Code [11] for the tax attributable to section 2044 interests,[10] and for any tax imposed by Florida based upon such section 2044 interests,[10] the direction must expressly waive that right of recovery. An express direction that property passing under the will or revocable trust bear the tax imposed by s. 2044 of the Internal Revenue Code [7] is deemed an express waiver of the right of recovery provided in s. 2207A of the Internal Revenue Code.[11] A reference to "qualified terminable interest property," "QTIP," or property in which the decedent had a "qualifying income interest for life" is deemed to be a reference to property upon which tax is imposed by s. 2044 of the Internal Revenue Code [7] which is subject to the right of recovery provided in s. 2207A of the Internal Revenue Code.[11]

b. If property is included in the gross estate pursuant to ss. 2041 and 2044 of the Internal Revenue Code [15], the property is deemed included under s. 2044,[7] and not s. 2041,[14] for purposes of allocation and apportionment of the tax.

2. For a direction in the decedent's will or revocable trust to be effective in waiving the right of recovery provided in s. 2207B of the Internal Revenue Code [16] for tax imposed by reason of s. 2036 of the Internal Revenue Code,[17] and any tax imposed by Florida based upon s. 2036 of the Internal Revenue Code,[17] the direction must expressly waive that right of recovery. An express direction that property passing under the will or revocable trust bear the tax imposed by s. 2036 of the Internal Revenue Code [17] is deemed an express waiver of the right of recovery provided in s. 2207B of the Internal Revenue Code.[16] If property is included in the gross estate pursuant to ss. 2036 and 2038 of the Internal Revenue Code,[18] the property is deemed included under s. 2038,[19] not s. 2036,[17] for purposes of allocation and apportionment of the tax, and there is no right of recovery under s. 2207B of the Internal Revenue Code.[16]

3. A general statement in the decedent's will or revocable trust waiving all rights of reimbursement or recovery under the Internal Revenue Code is not an express waiver of the rights of recovery provided in s. 2207A or s. 2207B of the Internal Revenue Code.[20]

4. For a direction in a governing instrument to be effective to direct payment of generation-skipping transfer tax in a manner other than as provided in s. 2603 of the Internal Revenue Code,[13] and any tax imposed by Florida based on s. 2601 of the Internal Revenue Code,[21] the direction must specifically reference the tax imposed by s. 2601 of the Internal Revenue Code.[21] A reference to the generation-skipping transfer tax or s. 2603 of the Internal Revenue Code [13] is deemed to be a reference to property upon which tax is imposed by reason of s. 2601 of the Internal Revenue Code.[21]

(e) If the decedent expressly directs by will, the net tax attributable to property over which the decedent held a general power of appointment may be determined in a manner other than as provided in subsection (2) if the net tax attributable to that property does not exceed the difference between the total net tax determined pursuant to subsection (2), determined without regard to this paragraph, and the total net tax that would have been payable if the value of the property subject to such power of appointment had not been included in the decedent's gross estate. If tax is attributable to one or more section 2044 interests [10] pursuant to subsection (2), the net tax attributable to the section 2044 interests [10] shall be calculated before the application of this paragraph unless the decedent expressly directs otherwise by will.

(f) If the decedent's will expressly provides that the tax is to be apportioned as provided in the decedent's revocable trust by specific reference to the revocable trust, an express direction in the revocable trust is deemed to be a direction contained in the will as well as the revocable trust.

(g) An express direction in the decedent's will to pay tax from the decedent's revocable trust by specific reference to the revocable trust is effective unless a contrary express direction is contained in the revocable trust.

(h) If governing instruments contain effective directions that conflict as to payment of taxes, the most recently executed tax apportionment provision controls to the extent of the conflict. For the purpose of this subsection, if a will or other governing instrument is amended, the date of the codicil to the will or amendment to the governing instrument is regarded as the date of the will or other governing instrument only if the codicil or amendment contains an express tax apportionment provision or an express modification of the tax apportionment provision. A general statement ratifying or republishing all provisions not otherwise amended does not meet this condition. If the decedent's will and another governing instrument were executed on the same date, the will is deemed executed after the other governing instrument. The earlier conflicting governing instrument controls as to any tax remaining unpaid after the application of the later conflicting governing instrument.

(i) A grant of permission or authority in a governing instrument to request payment of tax from property passing under another governing instrument is not a direction apportioning the tax to the property passing under the other governing instrument. A grant of permission or authority in a governing instrument to pay tax attributable to property not passing under the governing instrument is not a direction apportioning the tax to property passing under the governing instrument.

(j) This section applies to any tax remaining to be paid after the application of any effective express directions. An effective express direction for payment of tax on specific property or a type of property in a manner different from that provided in this section is not effective as an express direction for payment of tax on other property or other types of property included in the measure of the tax.

(5) Transfer of property.—A personal representative or fiduciary shall not be required to transfer to a recipient any property reasonably anticipated to be necessary for the payment of taxes. Further, the personal representative or fiduciary is not required to transfer any property to the recipient until the amount of the tax due from the recipient is paid by the recipient. If property is transferred before final apportionment of the tax, the recipient shall provide a bond or other security for his or her apportioned liability in the amount and form prescribed by the personal representative or fiduciary.

(6) Order of apportionment.—

(a) The personal representative may petition at any time for an order of apportionment. If administration of the decedent's estate has not commenced at any time after 90 days from the decedent's death, any fiduciary may petition for an order of apportionment in the court in which venue would be proper for administration of the decedent's estate. Notice of the petition for order of apportionment must be served on all interested persons in the manner provided for service of formal notice. At any time after 6 months from the decedent's death, any recipient may petition the court for an order of apportionment.

(b) The court shall determine all issues concerning apportionment. If the tax to be apportioned has not been finally determined, the court shall determine the probable tax due or to become due from all interested persons, apportion the probable tax, and retain jurisdiction over the parties and issues to modify the order of apportionment as appropriate until after the tax is finally determined.

(7) Deficiency.—

(a) If the personal representative or fiduciary does not have possession of sufficient property otherwise distributable to the recipient to pay the tax apportioned to the recipient, whether under this section, the Internal Revenue Code,[3] or the governing instrument, if applicable, the personal representative or fiduciary shall recover the deficiency in tax so apportioned to the recipient:

1. From the fiduciary in possession of the property to which the tax is apportioned, if any; and

2. To the extent of any deficiency in collection from the fiduciary, or to the extent collection from the fiduciary is excused pursuant to subsection (8) and in all other cases, from the recipient of the property to which the tax is apportioned, unless relieved of this duty as provided in subsection (8).

(b) In any action to recover the tax apportioned, the order of apportionment is prima facie correct.

(c) In any action for the enforcement of an order of apportionment, the court shall award taxable costs as in chancery actions, including reasonable attorney fees, and may award penalties and interest on the unpaid tax in accordance with equitable principles.

(d) This subsection does not authorize the recovery of any tax from a company issuing life insurance included in the gross estate, or from a bank, trust company, savings and loan association, or similar institution with respect to any account in the name of the decedent and any other person which passed by operation of law at the decedent's death.

(8) Relief from duty.—

(a) A personal representative or fiduciary who has the duty under this section of collecting the apportioned tax from recipients may be relieved of the duty to collect the tax by an order of the court finding that:

1. The estimated court costs and attorney fees in collecting the apportioned tax from a person against whom the tax has been apportioned will approximate or exceed the amount of the recovery;

2. The person against whom the tax has been apportioned is a resident of a foreign country other than Canada and refuses to pay the apportioned tax on demand; or

3. It is impracticable to enforce contribution of the apportioned tax against a person against whom the tax has been apportioned in view of the improbability of obtaining a judgment or the improbability of collection under any judgment that might be obtained, or otherwise.

(b) A personal representative or fiduciary is not liable for failure to attempt to enforce collection if the personal representative or fiduciary reasonably believes that collection would have been economically impracticable.

(9) Uncollected tax.—Any apportioned tax that is not collected shall be reapportioned in accordance with this section as if the portion of the property to which the uncollected tax had been apportioned had been exempt.

(10) Contribution.—This section does not limit the right of any person who has paid more than the amount of the tax apportionable to that person, calculated as if all apportioned amounts would be collected, to obtain contribution from those who have not paid the full amount of the tax apportionable to them, calculated as if all apportioned amounts would be collected, and that right is hereby conferred. In any action to enforce contribution, the court shall award taxable costs as in chancery actions, including reasonable attorney fees.

(11) Foreign tax.—This section does not require the personal representative or fiduciary to pay any tax levied or assessed by a foreign country unless specific directions to that effect are contained in the will or other instrument under which the personal representative or fiduciary is acting.

Laws 1974, c. 74–106, § 1; Laws 1975, c. 75–220, § 95; Laws 1977, c. 77–87, § 41; Laws 1979, c. 79–400, § 273; Laws 1992, c. 92–200, § 20. Amended by Laws 1997, c. 97–102, § 1026, eff. July 1, 1997. Laws 1997, c. 97–240, § 9, eff. Oct. 1, 1998; Laws 2000, c. 2000–159, § 13, eff. July 4, 2000; Laws 2001, c. 2001–226, § 167, eff. Jan. 1, 2002; Laws 2006, c. 2006–217, § 39, eff. July 1, 2007; Laws 2010, c. 2010–5, § 122, eff. June 29, 2010; Laws 2015, c. 2015–27, § 6, eff. July 1, 2015.

[1] 26 U.S.C.A. § 2601 et seq.
[2] 26 U.S.C.A. § 2612.
[3] 26 U.S.C.A. § 1 et seq.
[4] 26 U.S.C.A. § 2001 et seq.
[5] 26 U.S.C.A. § 2035.
[6] 26 U.S.C.A. § 529.
[7] 26 U.S.C.A. § 2044.
[8] 26 U.S.C.A. §§ 2032A(c); 2057(f).
[9] 26 U.S.C.A. §§ 2032A; 2057.
[10] See 26 U.S.C.A. § 2044.
[11] 26 U.S.C.A. § 2207A.
[12] 26 U.S.C.A. § 2058.
[13] 26 U.S.C.A. § 2603.
[14] 26 U.S.C.A. § 2041.
[15] 26 U.S.C.A. §§ 2041 and 2044.
[16] 26 U.S.C.A. § 2207B.
[17] 26 U.S.C.A. § 2036.
[18] 26 U.S.C.A. §§ 2036 and 2038.
[19] 26 U.S.C.A. § 2038.
[20] 26 U.S.C.A. §§ 2207A; 2207B.
[21] 26 U.S.C.A. § 2601.

Applicability

Laws 2015, c. 2015–27, § 10, provides:

"(1) The amendment made by this act to s. 733.817(1)(g) and (2)(c), Florida Statutes, is remedial in nature, is intended to clarify existing law, and applies retroactively to all proceedings pending or commenced on or after July 1, 2015, in which the apportionment of taxes has not been finally determined or agreed for the estates of decedents who die after December 31, 2004.

"(2) The amendment made by this act to s. 733.817(1)(e)3., (3)(e), (3)(g), (4)(b), (4)(c), (4)(d)1.b., (4)(e), (4)(h), and (6), Florida Statutes, applies to the estates of decedents who die on or after July 1, 2015.

"(3) Except as provided in subsections (1) and (2), the amendment made by this act to s. 733.817, Florida Statutes, is remedial in nature, is intended to clarify existing law, and applies retroactively to all proceedings pending or commenced on or after July 1, 2015, in which the apportionment of taxes has not been finally determined or agreed and without regard to the date of the decedent's death."

Cross References

Estates and trusts, apportionment of receipts and disbursements when decedent dies or income interest begins, see F.S.A. § 738.302.

Homestead, life estate, see § 732.401.

No discharge of personal representative until tax is paid, see § 198.26.
State taxation of estates, see § 198.01 et seq.

PART IX. CLOSING ESTATES

733.901. Final discharge

(1) After administration has been completed, the personal representative shall be discharged.

(2) The discharge of the personal representative shall release the personal representative and shall bar any action against the personal representative, as such or individually, and the surety.

Laws 1974, c. 74–106, § 1; Laws 1975, c. 75–220, § 96; Laws 1977, c. 77–87, § 42; Laws 1977, c. 77–174, § 1; Laws 1981, c. 81–27, § 6. Amended by Laws 1995, c. 95–401, § 29, eff. July 1, 1995; Laws 1997, c. 97–102, § 1027, eff. July 1, 1997; Laws 2001, c. 2001–226, § 168, eff. Jan. 1, 2002.

Cross References

Computation of time, see Civil Procedure Rule 1.090.
Discharge or final accounting, objections, see Probate Rule 5.401.
Execution by personal representative, see Probate Rule 5.330.
Federal estate tax return, notice, see Probate Rule 5.395.
Final settlement and discharge, see Probate Rule 5.400.
Interim accountings, see Probate Rule 5.345.
Order requiring accounting, see Probate Rule 5.150.

733.903. Subsequent administration

The final settlement of an estate and the discharge of the personal representative shall not prevent further administration. The order of discharge may not be revoked based upon the discovery of a will or later will.

Laws 1974, c. 74–106, § 1; Laws 1975, c. 75–220, § 96; Laws 1988, c. 88–110, § 1. Amended by Laws 2001, c. 2001–226, § 169, eff. Jan. 1, 2002.

Cross References

Subsequent administration, see Probate Rule 5.460.

CHAPTER 734

PROBATE CODE: FOREIGN PERSONAL REPRESENTATIVES; ANCILLARY ADMINISTRATION

PART I. GENERAL PROVISIONS

Enactment

Laws 1974, c. 74–106, § 3, repealed the sections contained in Fla.St.1973, Chapter 734, Florida Probate Law, Fourth Part, and, by Section 1 of that law, created the Florida Probate Code contained in Fla.St.1974, Supp. Chapters 731 to 735, effective July 1, 1975. Laws 1975, c. 75–220, substantially amended provisions of the Probate Code enacted by Laws 1974, c. 74–106; and, by operation of § 113 of the 1975 law, the probate code as enacted in 1974 and amended in 1975 became effective January 1, 1976.

PART I. GENERAL PROVISIONS

734.101. Foreign personal representative

(1) Personal representatives who produce authenticated copies of probated wills or letters of administration duly obtained in any state or territory of the United States may maintain actions in the courts of this state.

(2) Personal representatives appointed in any state or country may be sued in this state concerning property in this state and may defend actions or proceedings brought in this state.

(3) Debtors who have not received a written demand for payment from a personal representative or curator appointed in this state within 90 days after appointment of a personal representative in any other state or country, and whose property in Florida is subject to a mortgage or other lien securing the debt held by the foreign personal representative, may pay the foreign personal representative after the expiration of 90 days from the date of appointment of the foreign personal representative. Thereafter, a satisfaction of the mortgage or lien executed by the foreign personal representative, with an authenticated copy of the letters or other evidence of authority attached, may be recorded in the public records. The satisfaction shall be an effective discharge of the mortgage or lien, irrespective of whether the debtor making payment had received a written demand before paying the debt.

(4) Except as provided in s. 655.936, all persons indebted to the estate of a decedent, or having possession of personal property belonging to the estate, who have received no written demand from a personal representative or curator appointed in this state for payment of the debt or the delivery of the property are authorized to pay the debt or to deliver the personal property to the foreign personal representative after the expiration of 90 days from the date of appointment of the foreign personal representative.

Laws 1974, c. 74–106, § 1; Laws 1975, c. 75–220, § 98. Amended by Laws 1997, c. 97–102, § 1028, eff. July 1, 1997; Laws 2001, c. 2001–226, § 170, eff. Jan. 1, 2002; Laws 2002, c. 2002–1, § 110, eff. May 21, 2002; Laws 2007, c. 2007–74, § 16, eff. July 1, 2007.

Cross References

Effect of probate, see § 733.103.
Nonresidents, see § 733.304.
Probate of wills of residents after foreign probate, see § 733.206.

734.102. Ancillary administration

(1) If a nonresident of this state dies leaving assets in this state, credits due from residents in this state, or liens on property in this state, a personal representative specifically designated in the decedent's will to administer the Florida property shall be entitled to have ancillary letters issued, if qualified to act in Florida. Otherwise, the foreign personal representative of the decedent's estate shall be entitled to have letters issued, if qualified to act in Florida. If the

foreign personal representative is not qualified to act in Florida and the will names an alternate or successor who is qualified to act in Florida, the alternate or successor shall be entitled to have letters issued. Otherwise, those entitled to a majority interest of the Florida property may have letters issued to a personal representative selected by them who is qualified to act in Florida. If the decedent dies intestate and the foreign personal representative is not qualified to act in Florida, the order of preference for appointment of a personal representative as prescribed in this code shall apply. If ancillary letters are applied for by other than the domiciliary personal representative, prior notice shall be given to any domiciliary personal representative.

(2) Ancillary administration shall be commenced as provided by the Florida Probate Rules.

(3) If the will and any codicils are executed as required by the code, they shall be admitted to probate.

(4) The ancillary personal representative shall give bond as do personal representatives generally. All proceedings for appointment and administration of the estate shall be as similar to those in original administrations as possible.

(5) Unless creditors' claims are otherwise barred by s. 733.710, the ancillary personal representative shall cause a notice to creditors to be served and published according to the requirements of chapter 733. Claims not filed in accordance with chapter 733 shall be barred as provided in s. 733.702.

(6) After the payment of all expenses of administration and claims against the estate, the court may order the remaining property held by the ancillary personal representative transferred to the foreign personal representative or distributed to the beneficiaries.

(7) Ancillary personal representatives shall have the same rights, powers, and authority as other personal representatives in Florida to manage and settle estates; to sell, lease, or mortgage local property; and to raise funds for the payment of debts, claims, and devises in the domiciliary jurisdiction. No property shall be sold, leased, or mortgaged to pay a debt or claim that is barred by any statute of limitation or of nonclaim of this state.

Laws 1974, c. 74–106, § 1; Laws 1975, c. 75–220, § 98; Laws 1977, c. 77–87, § 43; Laws 1977, c. 77–174, § 1. Amended by Laws 1997, c. 97–102, § 1029, eff. July 1, 1997; Laws 2001, c. 2001–226, § 171, eff. Jan. 1, 2002.

Cross References

Ancillary administration, see Probate Rule 5.470.
Foreign probate,
    Effect, see § 733.103.
    Subsequent domestic probate, see § 733.206.
Personal representatives, qualifications, nonresidents, see § 733.304.
Short form, ancillary administration, see Probate Rule 5.475.

734.1025. Nonresident decedent's testate estate with property not exceeding $50,000 in this state; determination of claims

(1) When a nonresident decedent dies testate and leaves property subject to administration in this state the gross value of which does not exceed $50,000 at the date of death, the foreign personal representative of the estate before the expiration of 2 years after the decedent's death may file in the circuit court of the county where any property is located an authenticated transcript of so much of the foreign proceedings as will show the will and beneficiaries of the estate, as provided in the Florida Probate Rules. The court shall admit the will and any codicils to probate if they comply with s. 732.502(1), (2), or (3).

(2) The foreign personal representative may cause a notice to creditors to be served and published according to the relevant requirements of chapter 733. Claims not filed in accordance with chapter 733 shall be barred as provided in s. 733.702. If any claim is filed, a personal representative shall be appointed as provided in the Florida Probate Rules.

Laws 1980, c. 80–203, § 1; Laws 1989, c. 89–340, § 10. Amended by Laws 1997, c. 97–102, § 1030, eff. July 1, 1997; Laws 1999, c. 99–3, § 79, eff. June 29, 1999; Laws 2001, c. 2001–226, § 172, eff. Jan. 1, 2002; Laws 2003, c. 2003–154, § 12, eff. June 12, 2003.

734.104. Foreign wills; admission to record; effect on title

(1) An authenticated copy of the will of a nonresident that devises real property in this state, or any right, title, or interest in the property, may be admitted to record in any county of this state where the property is located at any time after 2 years from the death of the decedent or at any time after the domiciliary personal representative has been discharged if there has been no proceeding to administer the estate of the decedent in this state, provided:

(a) The will was executed as required by chapter 732; and

(b) The will has been admitted to probate in the proper court of any other state, territory, or country.

(2) A petition to admit a foreign will to record may be filed by any person and shall be accompanied by authenticated copies of the foreign will, the petition for probate, and the order admitting the will to probate. If no petition is required as a prerequisite to the probate of a will in the jurisdiction where the will of the nonresident was probated, upon proof by affidavit or certificate that no petition is required, an authenticated copy of the will may be admitted to record without an authenticated copy of a petition for probate, and the order admitting the will to record in this state shall recite that no petition was required in the jurisdiction of original probate.

(3) If the court finds that the requirements of this section have been met, it shall enter an order admitting the foreign will to record.

(4) When admitted to record, the foreign will shall be as valid and effectual to pass title to real property and any right, title, or interest therein as if the will had been admitted to probate in this state.

Laws 1974, c. 74–106, § 1; Laws 1975, c. 75–220, § 98; Laws 1977, c. 77–87, § 45; Laws 1977, c. 77–104, § 229; Laws 1979, c. 79–221, § 15; Laws 1979, c. 79–400, § 274; Laws 1989, c. 89–340, § 11. Amended by Laws 2001, c. 2001–226, § 173, eff. Jan. 1, 2002.

Cross References

Computation of time, limitation of actions, see § 95.031.
Death of person served by publication, limitations, see § 95.111.
Notarial wills, see § 733.205.
Probate of resident's will after foreign probate, see § 733.206.
Recordation of will, commencement of limitations period, see § 95.231.
Remaining heirs, claims, limitation of actions, see § 95.22.
Tolling of limitations period, see § 95.051.
Venue of probate proceedings, see § 733.101.
Will on record, limitation of actions, see § 95.231.

PART II. JURISDICTION OVER FOREIGN PERSONAL REPRESENTATIVES

734.201. Jurisdiction by act of foreign personal representative

A foreign personal representative submits personally to the jurisdiction of the courts of this state in any proceeding concerning the estate by:

(1) Filing authenticated copies of the domiciliary proceedings under s. 734.104;

(2) Receiving payment of money or taking delivery of personal property, under s. 734.101; or

(3) Doing any act as a personal representative in this state that would have given the state jurisdiction over that person as an individual.

Laws 1974, c. 74–106, § 1; Laws 1975, c. 75–220, § 99. Amended by Laws 1997, c. 97–102, § 1031, eff. July 1, 1997; Laws 2001, c. 2001–226, § 174, eff. Jan. 1, 2002.

734.202. Jurisdiction by act of decedent

In addition to jurisdiction conferred by s. 734.201, a foreign personal representative is subject to the jurisdiction of the courts of this state to the same extent that the decedent was subject to jurisdiction immediately before death.

Laws 1974, c. 74–106, § 1; Laws 1975, c. 75–220, § 100. Amended by Laws 1997, c. 97–102, § 1032, eff. July 1, 1997; Laws 2001, c. 2001–226, § 175, eff. Jan. 1, 2002.

CHAPTER 735

PROBATE CODE: SMALL ESTATES

PART I. SUMMARY ADMINISTRATION

PART II. DISPOSITION OF PERSONAL PROPERTY WITHOUT ADMINISTRATION

Enactment

Laws 1974, c. 74–106, § 3, repealed the sections contained in Fla.St.1973, Chapter 735, Small Estates; Administration Unnecessary, and, by Section 1 of that law, created the Florida Probate Code contained in Fla.St.1974, Supp. Chapters 731 to 735, effective July 1, 1975. Laws 1975, c. 75–220, substantially amended provisions of the Probate Code enacted by Laws 1974, c. 74–106; and, by operation of § 113 of the 1975 law, the probate code as enacted in 1974 and amended in 1975 became effective January 1, 1976.

PART I.　SUMMARY ADMINISTRATION

735.201.　Summary administration; nature of proceedings

Summary administration may be had in the administration of either a resident or nonresident decedent's estate, when it appears:

(1) In a testate estate, that the decedent's will does not direct administration as required by chapter 733.

(2) That the value of the entire estate subject to administration in this state, less the value of property exempt from the claims of creditors, does not exceed $75,000 or that the decedent has been dead for more than 2 years.

Laws 1974, c. 74–106, § 1; Laws 1975, c. 75–220, § 105; Laws 1980, c. 80–203, § 2; Laws 1989, c. 89–340, § 13.　Amended by Laws 2001, c. 2001–226, § 179, eff. Jan. 1, 2002.

Cross References

Evidence as to death or status, see § 731.103.
Summary administration, petition, hearing and distribution, see Probate Rule 5.530.
Valuation, see § 733.810.

735.202.　May be administered in the same manner as other estates

The estate may be administered in the same manner as the administration of any other estate, or it may be administered as provided in this part.

Laws 1974, c. 74–106, § 1; Laws 1975, c. 75–220, § 106.

Cross References

Summary administration, petition, hearing and distribution, see Probate Rule 5.530.

735.203.　Petition for summary administration

(1) A petition for summary administration may be filed by any beneficiary or person nominated as personal representative in the decedent's will offered for probate.　The petition must be signed and verified by the surviving spouse, if any, and any beneficiaries except that the joinder in a petition for summary administration is not required of a beneficiary who will receive a full distributive share under the proposed distribution.　However, formal notice of the petition must be served on a beneficiary not joining in the petition.

(2) If a person named in subsection (1) has died, is incapacitated, or is a minor, or has conveyed or transferred all interest in the property of the estate, then, as to that person, the petition must be signed and verified by:

(a) The personal representative, if any, of a deceased person or, if none, the surviving spouse, if any, and the beneficiaries;

(b) The guardian of an incapacitated person or a minor; or

(c) The grantee or transferee of any of them shall be authorized to sign and verify the petition instead of the beneficiary or surviving spouse.

(3) If each trustee of a trust that is a beneficiary of the estate of the deceased person is also a petitioner, formal notice of the petition for summary administration shall be served on each qualified beneficiary of the trust as defined in s. 736.0103 unless joinder in, or consent to, the petition is obtained from each qualified beneficiary of the trust.

Laws 1974, c. 74–106, § 1; Laws 1975, c. 75–220, § 107; Laws 1977, c. 77–174, § 1.　Amended by Laws 2001, c. 2001–226, § 180, eff. Jan. 1, 2002; Laws 2009, c. 2009–115, § 12, eff. July 1, 2009; Laws 2010, c. 2010–132, § 16, eff. Oct. 1, 2010.

Cross References

Summary administration, petition, hearing and distribution, see Probate Rule 5.530.
Valuation, see § 733.810.

735.2055. Filing of petition

The petition for summary administration may be filed at any stage of the administration of an estate if it appears that at the time of filing the estate would qualify.
Laws 1977, c. 77–87, § 47.

735.206. Summary administration distribution

(1) Upon the filing of the petition for summary administration, the will, if any, shall be proved in accordance with chapter 733 and be admitted to probate.

(2) Prior to entry of the order of summary administration, the petitioner shall make a diligent search and reasonable inquiry for any known or reasonably ascertainable creditors, serve a copy of the petition on those creditors, and make provision for payment for those creditors to the extent that assets are available.

(3) The court may enter an order of summary administration allowing immediate distribution of the assets to the persons entitled to them.

(4) The order of summary administration and distribution so entered shall have the following effect:

(a) Those to whom specified parts of the decedent's estate, including exempt property, are assigned by the order shall be entitled to receive and collect the parts and to have the parts transferred to them. They may maintain actions to enforce the right.

(b) Debtors of the decedent, those holding property of the decedent, and those with whom securities or other property of the decedent are registered are authorized and empowered to comply with the order by paying, delivering, or transferring to those specified in the order the parts of the decedent's estate assigned to them by the order, and the persons so paying, delivering, or transferring shall not be accountable to anyone else for the property.

(c) After the entry of the order, bona fide purchasers for value from those to whom property of the decedent may be assigned by the order shall take the property free of all claims of creditors of the decedent and all rights of the surviving spouse and all other beneficiaries.

(d) Property of the decedent that is not exempt from claims of creditors and that remains in the hands of those to whom it may be assigned by the order shall continue to be liable for claims against the decedent until barred as provided in the code. Any known or reasonably ascertainable creditor who did not receive notice and for whom provision for payment was not made may enforce the claim and, if the creditor prevails, shall be awarded reasonable attorney's fees as an element of costs against those who joined in the petition.

(e) The recipients of the decedent's property under the order of summary administration shall be personally liable for a pro rata share of all lawful claims against the estate of the decedent, but only to the extent of the value of the estate of the decedent actually received by each recipient, exclusive of the property exempt from claims of creditors under the constitution and statutes of Florida.

(f) After 2 years from the death of the decedent, neither the decedent's estate nor those to whom it may be assigned shall be liable for any claim against the decedent, unless proceedings have been taken for the enforcement of the claim.

(g) Any heir or devisee of the decedent who was lawfully entitled to share in the estate but who was not included in the order of summary administration and distribution may enforce all rights in appropriate proceedings against those who procured the order and, if successful, shall be awarded reasonable attorney's fees as an element of costs.

Laws 1974, c. 74–106, § 1; Laws 1975, c. 75–220, § 108; Laws 1977, c. 77–87, § 48; Laws 1977, c. 77–174, § 1; Laws 1989, c. 89–340, § 14. Amended by Laws 1997, c. 97–102, § 1035, eff. July 1, 1997; Laws 2001, c. 2001–226, § 181, eff. Jan. 1, 2002.

Cross References

Summary administration, petition, hearing and distribution, see Probate Rule 5.530.

735.2063. Notice to creditors

(1) Any person who has obtained an order of summary administration may publish a notice to creditors according to the relevant requirements of s. 733.2121, notifying all persons having claims or demands against the estate of the decedent that an order of summary administration has been entered by the court. The notice shall specify the total value of the estate and the names and addresses of those to whom it has been assigned by the order.

(2) If proof of publication of the notice is filed with the court, all claims and demands of creditors against the estate of the decedent who are not known or are not reasonably ascertainable shall be forever barred unless the claims and demands are filed with the court within 3 months after the first publication of the notice.

Laws 1980, c. 80–203, § 3. Amended by Laws 2001, c. 2001–226, § 182, eff. Jan. 1, 2002; Laws 2003, c. 2003–154, § 13, eff. June 12, 2003.

PART II. DISPOSITION OF PERSONAL PROPERTY WITHOUT ADMINISTRATION

735.301. Disposition without administration

(1) No administration shall be required or formal proceedings instituted upon the estate of a decedent leaving only personal property exempt under the provisions of s. 732.402, personal property exempt from the claims of creditors under the Constitution of Florida, and nonexempt personal property the value of which does not exceed the sum of the amount of preferred funeral expenses and reasonable and necessary medical and hospital expenses of the last 60 days of the last illness.

(2) Upon informal application by affidavit, letter, or otherwise by any interested party, and if the court is satisfied that subsection (1) is applicable, the court, by letter or other writing under the seal of the court, may authorize the payment, transfer, or disposition of the personal property, tangible or intangible, belonging to the decedent to those persons entitled.

(3) Any person, firm, or corporation paying, delivering, or transferring property under the authorization shall be forever discharged from liability thereon.

Laws 1974, c. 74–106, § 1; Laws 1975, c. 75–220, § 111; Laws 1977, c. 77–87, § 50; Laws 1977, c. 77–174, § 1; Laws 1979, c. 79–400, § 275. Amended by Laws 1998, c. 98–421, § 52, eff. July 1, 1998; Laws 2001, c. 2001–226, § 184, eff. Jan. 1, 2002.

Cross References

Disposition without administration, see Probate Rule 5.420.

735.302. Income tax refunds in certain cases

(1) In any case when the United States Treasury Department determines that an overpayment of federal income tax exists and the person in whose favor the overpayment is determined is dead at the time the overpayment of tax is to be refunded, and irrespective of whether the decedent had filed a joint and several or separate income tax return, the amount of the overpayment, if not in excess of $2,500, may be refunded as follows:

(a) Directly to the surviving spouse on his or her verified application; or

(b) If there is no surviving spouse, to one of the decedent's children who is designated in a verified application purporting to be executed by all of the decedent's children over the age of 14 years.

In either event, the application must show that the decedent was not indebted, that provision has been made for the payment of the decedent's debts, or that the entire estate is exempt from the claims of creditors under the constitution and statutes of the state, and that no administration of the estate, including summary administration, has been initiated and that none is planned, to the knowledge of the applicant.

(2) If a refund is made to the surviving spouse or designated child pursuant to the application, the refund shall operate as a complete discharge to the United States from liability from any action, claim, or demand by any beneficiary of the decedent or other person. This section shall be construed as establishing the ownership or rights of the payee in the refund.

Laws 1974, c. 74–106, § 1; Laws 1975, c. 75–220, § 112; Laws 1977, c. 77–87, § 51; Laws 1977, c. 77–174, § 1. Amended by Laws 2001, c. 2001–226, § 185, eff. Jan. 1, 2002.

CHAPTER 736

FLORIDA TRUST CODE

PART I. GENERAL PROVISIONS AND DEFINITIONS

PART II. JUDICIAL PROCEEDINGS

FLORIDA TRUST CODE

For Annotative Materials, see West's Florida Statutes Annotated

Effective Date

Chapter 736, Florida Trust Code, was added by Laws 2006, c. 2006–217, effective July 1, 2007.

Former Provisions

Laws 1974, c. 74–106, § 3, repealed the sections contained in Fla.St.1973, Chapter 736, Miscellaneous Probate Provisions, and, by Section 1 of that law, created the Florida Probate Code contained in Fla.St.1974, Supp. Chapters 731 to 735, effective July 1, 1975.

Laws 1975, c. 75–220, substantially amended provisions of the Probate Code enacted by Laws 1974, c. 74–106; and, by operation of § 113 of the 1975 law, the probate code as enacted in 1974 and amended in 1975 became effective January 1, 1976.

UNIFORM TRUST CODE (2000)

(Last Revised or Amended in 2004 and 2005)

Table of Jurisdictions Wherein Act Has Been Adopted

For text of Uniform Act, and variation notes and annotation materials for adopting jurisdictions, see Uniform Laws Annotated, Master Edition Volume 7C.

Jurisdiction	Laws	Effective Date	Statutory Citation
Alabama	2006, c. 216	1–1–2007	Code 1975, §§ 19–3B–101 to 19–3B–1305.
Arizona	2008, c. 247	1–1–2009	A.R.S. §§ 14–10101 to 14–11102.
Arkansas	2005, c. 1031	8–12–2005	A.C.A. §§ 28–73–101 to 28–73–1105.
District of Columbia	2004, c. 15–104	3–10–2004	D.C. Official Code, 2001 Ed. §§ 19–1301.01 to 19–1311.03.
Florida[1]	2006, c. 217	7–1–2007	West's F.S.A. §§ 736.0101 to 736.1303.
Kansas	2002, c. 133	1–1–2003	K.S.A. 58a–101 to 58a–1107.
Kentucky	2014, Ch. 25	7–15–2014	KRS §§ 386B.1–010 to 386B.11–050.
Maine	2004, c. 618	7–1–2005	18–B M.R.S.A. §§ 101 to 1104.
Maryland	2014, Ch. 585	1–1–2015	MD Code, Estates and Trusts §§ 14.5–101 to 14.5–1006.
Massachusetts	2012, c. 140	7–8–2012	M.G.L.A. 203E, §§ 101 to 1013.
Michigan	2009, No. 46	4–1–2010	M.C.L.A. §§ 700.7101 to 700.8206.
Mississippi	2014, Ch. 421	7–1–2014	Miss. Code Ann. §§ 91–8–101 to 91–8–1206.
Missouri	2004, H.B. No. 1511	1–1–2005	V.A.M.S. §§ 456.1–101 to 456.11–1106.
Montana	2013, Ch. 264	10–1–2013	MCA §§ 72–38–101 to 72–38–1102.
Nebraska[2]	2003, LB 130	1–1–2005	R.R.S. 1943, §§ 30–3801 to 30–38,110.
New Hampshire	2004, c. 130	10–1–2004	RSA 564–B:1–101 to 564–B:12–1206.
New Mexico	2003, c. 122	7–1–2003	NMSA 1978, §§ 46A–1–101 to 46A–11–1105.
North Carolina	2005, c. 192	1–1–2006	G.S. §§ 36C–1–101 to 36C–11–1104.
North Dakota	2007, c. 549	8–1–2007	NDCC 59–09–01 to 59–19–02.
Ohio	2006, H.B. 416	1–1–2007	R.C. §§ 5801.01 to 5811.03.
Oregon	2005, c. 348	6–29–2005 *	ORS 130.001 to 130.910.
Pennsylvania	2006, c. 98	11–6–2006	20 Pa.C.S.A. §§ 7701 to 7799.3.
South Carolina	2005, c. 66	1–1–2006	Code 1976, §§ 62–7–101 to 62–7–1106.
Tennessee	2004, c. 537	7–1–2004	T.C.A. §§ 35–15–101 to 35–15–1103.
Utah	2004, c. 89	7–1–2004	U.C.A. 1953, 75–7–101 to 75–7–1201.
Vermont	2009, P.A. 20	7–1–2009	14A V.S.A. §§ 101 to 1204.
Virginia	2005, c. 935	7–1–2006	Code 1950, §§ 64.2–700 to 64.2–808.
West Virginia	2011, c. 66	6–10–2011	W. Va. Code §§ 44D–1–101 to 44D–11–1105.
Wisconsin	2013, Act 92	7–1–2014	W.S.A. §§ 701.0101 to 701.1013.
Wyoming	2003, c. 124	7–1–2003	Wyo.Stat.Ann. §§ 4–10–101 to 4–10–1103.

* Approval date.

[1] Enacts the Uniform Trust Code and repeals the Uniform Trustees' Powers Act effective July 1, 2007.

[2] Repealed the Uniform Prudent Investor Act (R.R.S. 1943, §§ 8–2201 to 8–2213) and the Uniform Trustees' Powers Act (R.R.S. 1943, §§ 30–2819 to 30–2826), and enacted the Uniform Trust Code (R.R.S. 1943, §§ 30–3801 to 30–38,110) by L.2003, LB 130, operative January 1, 2005.

Cross References

Family trust companies,
    Investments, see F.S.A. § 662.132.
    Powers, see F.S.A. § 662.130.
Florida Land Trust Act, see F.S.A. § 689.071.

Probate, death or status evidence, see § 731.103.

Trust business, substitution of fiduciaries, see § 660.46.

PART I. GENERAL PROVISIONS AND DEFINITIONS

736.0101. Short title

This chapter may be cited as the "Florida Trust Code" and for purposes of this chapter is referred to as the "code."

Added by Laws 2006, c. 2006–217, § 1, eff. July 1, 2007.

736.0102. Scope

(1) Except as otherwise provided in this section, this code applies to express trusts, charitable or noncharitable, and trusts created pursuant to a law, judgment, or decree that requires the trust to be administered in the manner of an express trust.

(2) This code does not apply to constructive or resulting trusts; conservatorships; custodial arrangements pursuant to the Florida Uniform Transfers to Minors Act;[1] business trusts providing for certificates to be issued to beneficiaries; common trust funds; trusts created by the form of the account or by the deposit agreement at a financial institution; voting trusts; security arrangements; liquidation trusts; trusts for the primary purpose of paying debts, dividends, interest, salaries, wages, profits, pensions, or employee benefits of any kind; and any arrangement under which a person is nominee or escrowee for another.

(3) This code does not apply to any land trust under s. 689.071, except to the extent provided in s. 689.071(7), s. 721.08(2)(c)4., or s. 721.53(1)(e). A trust governed at its creation by this chapter, former chapter 737, or any prior trust statute superseded or replaced by any provision of former chapter 737, is not a land trust regardless of any amendment or modification of the trust, any change in the assets held in the trust, or any continuing trust resulting from the distribution or retention in further trust of assets from the trust.

Added by Laws 2006, c. 2006–217, § 1, eff. July 1, 2007. Amended by Laws 2007, c. 2007–153, § 10, eff. July 1, 2007; Laws 2013, c. 2013–240, § 3, eff. June 28, 2013.

[1] F.S.A. § 710.101 et seq.

736.0103. Definitions

Unless the context otherwise requires, in this code:

(1) "Action," with respect to an act of a trustee, includes a failure to act.

(2) "Affiliate" means any person or entity that directly or indirectly through one or more intermediaries owns or controls, is owned or controlled by, or is under common control or ownership with, the fiduciary. An affiliate may include, but is not limited to, an investment adviser, administrator, broker, transfer agent, placement agent, servicing agent, registrar, custodian, underwriter, sponsor, distributor, or manager.

(3) "Ascertainable standard" means a standard relating to an individual's health, education, support, or maintenance within the meaning of s. 2041(b)(1)(A) or s. 2514(c)(1) of the Internal Revenue Code of 1986, as amended.[1]

(4) "Beneficiary" means a person who has a present or future beneficial interest in a trust, vested or contingent, or who holds a power of appointment over trust property in a capacity other than that of trustee. An interest as a permissible appointee of a power of appointment, held by a person in a capacity other than that of trustee, is not a beneficial interest for purposes

of this subsection. Upon an irrevocable exercise of a power of appointment, the interest of a person in whose favor the appointment is made shall be considered a present or future beneficial interest in a trust in the same manner as if the interest had been included in the trust instrument.

(5) "Charitable trust" means a trust, or portion of a trust, created for a charitable purpose as described in s. 736.0405(1).

(6) "Distributee" means a beneficiary who is currently entitled to receive a distribution.

(7) "Environmental law" means a federal, state, or local law, rule, regulation, or ordinance that relates to protection of the environment or human health.

(8) "General power of appointment" means a power of appointment exercisable in favor of the holder of the power, the power holder's creditors, the power holder's estate, or the creditors of the power holder's estate.

(9) "Guardian of the person" means a person appointed by the court to make decisions regarding the support, care, education, health, and welfare of a minor or an incapacitated adult. The term does not include a guardian ad litem.

(10) "Guardian of the property" means a person appointed by the court to administer the estate of a minor or incapacitated adult.

(11) "Interests of the beneficiaries" means the beneficial interests provided in the terms of the trust.

(12) "Jurisdiction" with respect to a geographic area, includes a state or country.

(13) "Permissible distributee" means a beneficiary who is currently eligible to receive a distribution.

(14) "Power of withdrawal" means a presently exercisable general power of appointment other than a power:

(a) Exercisable by a trustee and limited by an ascertainable standard; or

(b) Exercisable by another person only upon consent of the trustee or a person holding an adverse interest.

(15) "Property" means anything that may be the subject of ownership, real or personal, legal or equitable, or any interest therein.

(16) "Qualified beneficiary" means a living beneficiary who, on the date the beneficiary's qualification is determined:

(a) Is a distributee or permissible distributee of trust income or principal;

(b) Would be a distributee or permissible distributee of trust income or principal if the interests of the distributees described in paragraph (a) terminated on that date without causing the trust to terminate; or

(c) Would be a distributee or permissible distributee of trust income or principal if the trust terminated in accordance with its terms on that date.

(17) "Revocable," as applied to a trust, means revocable by the settlor without the consent of the trustee or a person holding an adverse interest.

(18) "Settlor" means a person, including a testator, who creates or contributes property to a trust. If more than one person creates or contributes property to a trust, each person is a settlor of the portion of the trust property attributable to that person's contribution except to the extent another person has the power to revoke or withdraw that portion.

(19) "Spendthrift provision" means a term of a trust that restrains both voluntary and involuntary transfer of a beneficiary's interest.

(20) "State" means any state of the United States and includes the District of Columbia, the Commonwealth of Puerto Rico, and any territory or possession subject to the legislative authority of the United States.

(21) "Terms of a trust" means the manifestation of the settlor's intent regarding a trust's provisions as expressed in the trust instrument or as may be established by other evidence that would be admissible in a judicial proceeding.

(22) "Trust instrument" means an instrument executed by a settlor that contains terms of the trust, including any amendments to the trust.

(23) "Trustee" means the original trustee and includes any additional trustee, any successor trustee, and any cotrustee.

Added by Laws 2006, c. 2006–217, § 1, eff. July 1, 2007. Amended by Laws 2009, c. 2009–117, § 1, eff. July 1, 2009; Laws 2013, c. 2013–172, § 9, eff. Oct. 1, 2013.

[1] 26 U.S.C.A. § 2041(b)(1)(A) or § 2514(c)(1).

Cross References

Corporations, directors, qualifications, see § 607.0802.
Fiduciary lawyer-client privilege, see F.S.A. § 90.5021.
Petition for summary administration, see § 735.203.
Principal and income, trustees' power to adjust, see § 738.104.
Property interests, disclaimer, see § 739.201.

736.0104. Knowledge

(1) Subject to subsection (2), a person has knowledge of a fact if the person:

(a) Has actual knowledge of the fact;

(b) Has received a notice or notification of the fact; or

(c) Has reason to know the fact from all the other facts and circumstances known to the person at the time in question.

(2) An organization that conducts activities through employees has notice or knowledge of a fact involving a trust only from the time the information was received by an employee having responsibility to act on matters involving the trust, or would have been brought to the employee's attention if the organization had exercised reasonable diligence. An organization exercises reasonable diligence if the organization maintains reasonable routines for communicating significant information to the employee having responsibility to act on matters involving the trust and there is reasonable compliance with the routines. Reasonable diligence does not require an employee of the organization to communicate information unless the communication is part of the individual's regular duties or the individual knows a matter involving the trust would be materially affected by the information.

Added by Laws 2006, c. 2006–217, § 1, eff. July 1, 2007.

736.0105. Default and mandatory rules

(1) Except as otherwise provided in the terms of the trust, this code governs the duties and powers of a trustee, relations among trustees, and the rights and interests of a beneficiary.

(2) The terms of a trust prevail over any provision of this code except:

(a) The requirements for creating a trust.

(b) The duty of the trustee to act in good faith and in accordance with the terms and purposes of the trust and the interests of the beneficiaries.

(c) The requirement that a trust and its terms be for the benefit of the trust's beneficiaries, and that the trust have a purpose that is lawful, not contrary to public policy, and possible to achieve.

(d) The periods of limitation for commencing a judicial proceeding.

(e) The power of the court to take such action and exercise such jurisdiction as may be necessary in the interests of justice.

(f) The requirements under s. 736.0108(1) for the designation of a principal place of administration of the trust and the requirements under s. 736.0107 for the designation of a jurisdiction the law of which determines the meaning and effect of the terms of a trust.

(g) The jurisdiction and venue provisions in ss. 736.0202, 736.0203, and 736.0204.

(h) The restrictions on the designation of representative under s. 736.0306.

(i) The formalities required under s. 736.0403(2) for the execution of a trust.

(j) The power of the court to modify or terminate a trust under ss. 736.0410–736.04115, except as provided in s. 736.04115(3)(b), and under ss. 736.0413, 736.0415, and 736.0416.

(k) The ability to modify a trust under s. 736.0412, except as provided in s. 736.0412(4)(b).

(*l*) The effect of a spendthrift provision and the rights of certain creditors and assignees to reach a trust as provided in part V.

(m) The trustee's duty under s. 736.05053 to pay expenses and obligations of the settlor's estate.

(n) The trustee's duty under s. 736.05055 to file a notice of trust at the settlor's death.

(o) The right of a trustee under s. 736.0701 to decline a trusteeship and the right of a trustee under s. 736.0705 to resign a trusteeship.

(p) The power of the court under s. 736.0702 to require, dispense with, modify, or terminate a bond.

(q) The power of the court under s. 736.0708(2) to adjust a trustee's compensation specified in the terms of the trust that is unreasonably low or high.

(r) The duty under s. 736.0813(1)(a) and (b) to notify qualified beneficiaries of an irrevocable trust of the existence of the trust, of the identity of the trustee, and of their rights to trust accountings.

(s) The duty under s. 736.0813(1)(c) and (d) to provide a complete copy of the trust instrument and to account to qualified beneficiaries.

(t) The duty under s. 736.0813(1)(e) to respond to the request of a qualified beneficiary of an irrevocable trust for relevant information about the assets and liabilities of the trust and the particulars relating to trust administration.

(u) The effect of an exculpatory term under s. 736.1011.

(v) The rights under ss. 736.1013–736.1017 of a person other than a trustee or beneficiary.

(w) The effect of a penalty clause for contesting a trust under s. 736.1108.

Added by Laws 2006, c. 2006–217, § 1, eff. July 1, 2007. Amended by Laws 2009, c. 2009–117, § 2, eff. July 1, 2009.

736.0106. Common law of trusts; principles of equity

The common law of trusts and principles of equity supplement this code, except to the extent modified by this code or another law of this state.

Added by Laws 2006, c. 2006–217, § 1, eff. July 1, 2007.

736.0107. Governing law

The meaning and effect of the terms of a trust are determined by:

(1) The law of the jurisdiction designated in the terms of the trust, provided there is a sufficient nexus to the designated jurisdiction at the time of the creation of the trust or during the trust administration, including, but not limited to, the location of real property held by the trust or the residence or location of an office of the settlor, trustee, or any beneficiary; or

(2) In the absence of a controlling designation in the terms of the trust, the law of the jurisdiction where the settlor resides at the time the trust is first created.

Notwithstanding subsection (1) or subsection (2), a designation in the terms of a trust is not controlling as to any matter for which the designation would be contrary to a strong public policy of this state.

Added by Laws 2006, c. 2006–217, § 1, eff. July 1, 2007.

736.0108. Principal place of administration

(1) Terms of a trust designating the principal place of administration of the trust are valid only if there is a sufficient connection with the designated jurisdiction. Without precluding other means for establishing a sufficient connection, terms of a trust designating the principal place of administration are valid and controlling if:

(a) A trustee's principal place of business is located in or a trustee is a resident of the designated jurisdiction; or

(b) All or part of the administration occurs in the designated jurisdiction.

(2) Unless otherwise validly designated in the trust instrument, the principal place of administration of a trust is the trustee's usual place of business where the records pertaining to the trust are kept or, if the trustee has no place of business, the trustee's residence. In the case of cotrustees, the principal place of administration is:

(a) The usual place of business of the corporate trustee, if there is only one corporate cotrustee;

(b) The usual place of business or residence of the individual trustee who is a professional fiduciary, if there is only one such person and no corporate cotrustee; or otherwise

(c) The usual place of business or residence of any of the cotrustees as agreed on by the cotrustees.

(3) Notwithstanding any other provision of this section, the principal place of administration of a trust, for which a bank, association, or trust company organized under the laws of this state or bank or savings association organized under the laws of the United States with its main office in this state has been appointed trustee, shall not be moved or otherwise affected solely because the trustee engaged in an interstate merger transaction with an out-of-state bank pursuant to s. 658.2953 in which the out-of-state bank is the resulting bank.

(4) A trustee is under a continuing duty to administer the trust at a place appropriate to its purposes and its administration.

(5) Without precluding the right of the court to order, approve, or disapprove a transfer, the trustee, in furtherance of the duty prescribed by subsection (4), may transfer the trust's principal place of administration to another state or to a jurisdiction outside of the United States.

(6) The trustee shall notify the qualified beneficiaries of a proposed transfer of a trust's principal place of administration not less than 60 days before initiating the transfer. The notice of proposed transfer must include:

(a) The name of the jurisdiction to which the principal place of administration is to be transferred.

(b) The address and telephone number at the new location at which the trustee can be contacted.

(c) An explanation of the reasons for the proposed transfer.

(d) The date on which the proposed transfer is anticipated to occur.

(e) The date, not less than 60 days after the notice is provided, by which the qualified beneficiary must notify the trustee of an objection to the proposed transfer.

(7) The authority of a trustee to act under this section without court approval to transfer a trust's principal place of administration is suspended if a qualified beneficiary files a lawsuit objecting to the proposed transfer on or before the date specified in the notice. The suspension is effective until the lawsuit is dismissed or withdrawn.

(8) In connection with a transfer of the trust's principal place of administration, the trustee may transfer any of the trust property to a successor trustee designated in the terms of the trust or appointed pursuant to s. 736.0704.

Added by Laws 2006, c. 2006–217, § 1, eff. July 1, 2007.

736.0109. Methods and waiver of notice

(1) Notice to a person under this code or the sending of a document to a person under this code must be accomplished in a manner reasonably suitable under the circumstances and likely to result in receipt of the notice or document. Permissible methods of notice or for sending a document include first-class mail, personal delivery, delivery to the person's last known place of residence or place of business, or a properly directed facsimile or other electronic message.

(2) Notice otherwise required under this code or a document otherwise required to be sent under this code need not be provided to a person whose identity or location is unknown to and not reasonably ascertainable by the trustee.

(3) In addition to the methods listed in subsection (1) for sending a document, a sender may post a document to a secure electronic account or website where the document can be accessed.

(a) Before a document may be posted to an electronic account or website, the recipient must sign a separate written authorization solely for the purpose of authorizing the sender to post documents on an electronic account or website. The written authorization must:

1. Enumerate the documents that may be posted in this manner.

2. Contain specific instructions for accessing the electronic account or website, including the security procedures required to access the electronic account or website, such as a username and password.

3. Advise the recipient that a separate notice will be sent when a document is posted to the electronic account or website and the manner in which the separate notice will be sent.

4. Advise the recipient that the authorization to receive documents by electronic posting may be amended or revoked at any time and include specific instructions for revoking or amending the authorization, including the address designated for the purpose of receiving notice of the revocation or amendment.

5. Advise the recipient that posting a document on the electronic account or website may commence a limitations period as short as 6 months even if the recipient never actually accesses the electronic account, electronic website, or the document.

(b) Once the recipient signs the written authorization, the sender must provide a separate notice to the recipient when a document is posted to the electronic account or website. As used in this subsection, the term "separate notice" means a notice sent to the recipient by means other than electronic posting, which identifies each document posted to the electronic account or website and provides instructions for accessing the posted document. The separate notice requirement is satisfied if the recipient accesses the document on the electronic account or website.

(c) A document sent by electronic posting is deemed received by the recipient on the earlier of the date that the separate notice is received or the date that the recipient accesses the document on the electronic account or website.

(d) At least annually after a recipient signs a written authorization, a sender shall send a notice advising recipients who have authorized one or more documents to be posted to an electronic account or website that such posting may commence a limitations period as short as 6 months even if the recipient never accesses the electronic account or website or the document and that authority to receive documents by electronic posting may be amended or revoked at any time. This notice must be given by means other than electronic posting and may not be accompanied by any other written communication. Failure to provide such notice within 380 days after the last notice is deemed to automatically revoke the authorization to receive documents in the manner permitted under this subsection 380 days after the last notice is sent.

(e) The notice required in paragraph (d) may be in substantially the following form: "You have authorized the receipt of documents through posting to an electronic account or website where the documents can be accessed. This notice is being sent to advise you that a limitations period, which may be as short as 6 months, may be running as to matters disclosed in a trust accounting or other written report of a trustee posted to the electronic account or website even if you never actually access the electronic account or website or the documents. You may amend or revoke the authorization to receive documents by electronic posting at any time. If you have any questions, please consult your attorney."

(f) A sender may rely on the recipient's authorization until the recipient amends or revokes the authorization by sending a notice to the address designated for that purpose in the authorization. The recipient, at any time, may amend or revoke an authorization to have documents posted on the electronic account or website.

(g) A document provided to a recipient solely through electronic posting must remain accessible to the recipient on the electronic account or website for at least 4 years after the date that the document is deemed received by the recipient. The electronic account or website must allow the recipient to download or print the document. This subsection does not affect or alter the duties of a trustee to keep clear, distinct, and accurate records pursuant to s. 736.0810 or affect or alter the time periods for which the trustee must maintain those records.

(h) To be effective, the posting of a document to an electronic account or website must be done in accordance with this subsection. The sender has the burden of establishing compliance with this subsection.

(i) This subsection does not preclude the sending of a document by other means.

(4) Notice to a person under this code, or the sending of a document to a person under this code by electronic message, is complete when the document is sent.

(a) An electronic message is presumed received on the date that the message is sent.

(b) If the sender has knowledge that an electronic message did not reach the recipient, the electronic message is deemed to have not been received. The sender has the burden to prove that another copy of the notice or document was sent by electronic message or by other means authorized by this section.

(5) Notice under this code or the sending of a document under this code may be waived by the person to be notified or to whom the document is to be sent.

(6) Notice and service of documents in a judicial proceeding are governed by the Florida Rules of Civil Procedure.

Added by Laws 2006, c. 2006–217, § 1, eff. July 1, 2007. Amended by Laws 2015, c. 2015–176, § 1, eff. July 1, 2015.

Cross References

Fiduciary fund investment, investment functions delegation, see F.S.A. § 518.112.

736.0110. Others treated as qualified beneficiaries

(1) A charitable organization expressly designated to receive distributions under the terms of a charitable trust has the rights of a qualified beneficiary under this code if the charitable organization, on the date the charitable organization's qualification is being determined:

(a) Is a distributee or permissible distributee of trust income or principal;

(b) Would be a distributee or permissible distributee of trust income or principal on termination of the interests of other distributees or permissible distributees then receiving or eligible to receive distributions; or

(c) Would be a distributee or permissible distributee of trust income or principal if the trust terminated on that date.

(2) A person appointed to enforce a trust created for the care of an animal or another noncharitable purpose as provided in s. 736.0408 or s. 736.0409 has the rights of a qualified beneficiary under this code.

(3) The Attorney General may assert the rights of a qualified beneficiary with respect to a charitable trust having its principal place of administration in this state.

Added by Laws 2006, c. 2006–217, § 1, eff. July 1, 2007.

736.0111. Nonjudicial settlement agreements

(1) For purposes of this section, the term "interested persons" means persons whose interest would be affected by a settlement agreement.

(2) Except as otherwise provided in subsection (3), interested persons may enter into a binding nonjudicial settlement agreement with respect to any matter involving a trust.

(3) A nonjudicial settlement agreement among the trustee and trust beneficiaries is valid only to the extent the terms and conditions could be properly approved by the court. A nonjudicial settlement may not be used to produce a result not authorized by other provisions of this code, including, but not limited to, terminating or modifying a trust in an impermissible manner.

(4) Matters that may be resolved by a nonjudicial settlement agreement include:

(a) The interpretation or construction of the terms of the trust.

(b) The approval of a trustee's report or accounting.

(c) The direction to a trustee to refrain from performing a particular act or the grant to a trustee of any necessary or desirable power.

(d) The resignation or appointment of a trustee and the determination of a trustee's compensation.

(e) The transfer of a trust's principal place of administration.

(f) The liability of a trustee for an action relating to the trust.

(5) Any interested person may request the court to approve or disapprove a nonjudicial settlement agreement.

Added by Laws 2006, c. 2006–217, § 1, eff. July 1, 2007.

736.0112. Qualification of foreign trustee

Unless otherwise doing business in this state, local qualification by a foreign trustee is not required for the trustee to receive distribution from a local estate. Nothing in this chapter shall affect the provisions of s. 660.41.

Added by Laws 2006, c. 2006–217, § 1, eff. July 1, 2007.

PART II. JUDICIAL PROCEEDINGS

736.0201. Role of court in trust proceedings

(1) Except as provided in subsections (5) and (6) and s. 736.0206, judicial proceedings concerning trusts shall be commenced by filing a complaint and shall be governed by the Florida Rules of Civil Procedure.

(2) The court may intervene in the administration of a trust to the extent the court's jurisdiction is invoked by an interested person or as provided by law.

(3) A trust is not subject to continuing judicial supervision unless ordered by the court.

(4) A judicial proceeding involving a trust may relate to the validity, administration, or distribution of a trust, including proceedings to:

(a) Determine the validity of all or part of a trust;

(b) Appoint or remove a trustee;

(c) Review trustees' fees;

(d) Review and settle interim or final accounts;

(e) Ascertain beneficiaries; determine any question arising in the administration or distribution of any trust, including questions of construction of trust instruments; instruct trustees; and determine the existence or nonexistence of any immunity, power, privilege, duty, or right;

(f) Obtain a declaration of rights; or

(g) Determine any other matters involving trustees and beneficiaries.

(5) A proceeding for the construction of a testamentary trust may be filed in the probate proceeding for the testator's estate. The proceeding shall be governed by the Florida Probate Rules.

(6) Rule 1.525, Florida Rules of Civil Procedure, shall apply to judicial proceedings concerning trusts, except that the following do not constitute taxation of costs or attorney's fees even if the payment is for services rendered or costs incurred in a judicial proceeding:

(a) A trustee's payment of compensation or reimbursement of costs to persons employed by the trustee from assets of the trust.

(b) A determination by the court directing from what part of the trust fees or costs shall be paid, unless the determination is made under s. 736.1004 in an action for breach of fiduciary duty or challenging the exercise of, or failure to exercise, a trustee's powers.

Added by Laws 2006, c. 2006–217, § 2, eff. July 1, 2007. Amended by Laws 2011, c. 2011–183, § 13, eff. June 21, 2011.

736.0202. Jurisdiction over trustee and beneficiary

(1) In rem jurisdiction.—Any beneficiary of a trust having its principal place of administration in this state is subject to the jurisdiction of the courts of this state to the extent of the beneficiary's interest in the trust.

(2) Personal jurisdiction.—

(a) Any trustee, trust beneficiary, or other person, whether or not a citizen or resident of this state, who personally or through an agent does any of the following acts related to a trust, submits to the jurisdiction of the courts of this state involving that trust:

1. Accepts trusteeship of a trust having its principal place of administration in this state at the time of acceptance.

2. Moves the principal place of administration of a trust to this state.

3. Serves as trustee of a trust created by a settlor who was a resident of this state at the time of creation of the trust or serves as trustee of a trust having its principal place of administration in this state.

4. Accepts or exercises a delegation of powers or duties from the trustee of a trust having its principal place of administration in this state.

5. Commits a breach of trust in this state, or commits a breach of trust with respect to a trust having its principal place of administration in this state at the time of the breach.

6. Accepts compensation from a trust having its principal place of administration in this state.

7. Performs any act or service for a trust having its principal place of administration in this state.

8. Accepts a distribution from a trust having its principal place of administration in this state with respect to any matter involving the distribution.

(b) A court of this state may exercise personal jurisdiction over a trustee, trust beneficiary, or other person, whether found within or outside the state, to the maximum extent permitted by the State Constitution or the Federal Constitution.

Added by Laws 2006, c. 2006–217, § 2, eff. July 1, 2007. Amended by Laws 2013, c. 2013–172, § 10, eff. Oct. 1, 2013.

736.02025. Service of process

(1) Except as otherwise provided in this section, service of process upon any person may be made as provided in chapter 48.

(2) Where only in rem or quasi in rem relief is sought against a person in a matter involving a trust, service of process on that person may be made by sending a copy of the summons and complaint by any commercial delivery service requiring a signed receipt or by any form of mail requiring a signed receipt. Service under this subsection shall be complete upon signing of a receipt by the addressee or by any person authorized to receive service of a summons on behalf of the addressee as provided in chapter 48. Proof of service shall be by verified statement of the person serving the summons, to which must be attached the signed receipt or other evidence satisfactory to the court that delivery was made to the addressee or other authorized person.

(3) Under any of the following circumstances, service of original process pursuant to subsection (2) may be made by first-class mail:

(a) If registered or certified mail service to the addressee is unavailable and if delivery by commercial delivery service is also unavailable.

(b) If delivery is attempted and is refused by the addressee.

(c) If delivery by mail requiring a signed receipt is unclaimed after notice to the addressee by the delivering entity.

(4) If service of process is obtained under subsection (3), proof of service shall be made by verified statement of the person serving the summons. The verified statement must state the basis for service by first-class mail, the date of mailing, and the address to which the mail was sent.

Added by Laws 2013, c. 2013–172, § 11, eff. Oct. 1, 2013.

736.0203. Subject matter jurisdiction

The circuit court has original jurisdiction in this state of all proceedings arising under this code.

Added by Laws 2006, c. 2006–217, § 2, eff. July 1, 2007.

736.0204. Venue

Venue for actions and proceedings concerning trusts, including those under s. 736.0201, may be laid in:

(1) Any county where the venue is proper under chapter 47;

(2) Any county where the beneficiary suing or being sued resides or has its principal place of business; or

(3) The county where the trust has its principal place of administration.

Added by Laws 2006, c. 2006–217, § 2, eff. July 1, 2007.

736.0206. Proceedings for review of employment of agents and review of compensation of trustee and employees of trust

(1) The court may review the propriety of the employment by a trustee of any person, including any attorney, auditor, investment adviser, or other specialized agent or assistant, and the reasonableness of any compensation paid to that person or to the trustee.

(2) If the settlor's estate is being probated, and the settlor's trust or the trustee of the settlor's trust is a beneficiary under the settlor's will, the trustee, any person employed by the trustee, or

any interested person may have the propriety of employment and the reasonableness of the compensation of the trustee or any person employed by the trustee determined in the probate proceeding.

(3) The burden of proof of the propriety of the employment and the reasonableness of the compensation shall be on the trustee and the person employed by the trustee. Any person who is determined to have received excessive compensation from a trust for services rendered may be ordered to make appropriate refunds.

(4) Court proceedings to determine reasonable compensation of a trustee or any person employed by a trustee, if required, are a part of the trust administration process. The costs, including attorney's fees, of the person assuming the burden of proof of propriety of the employment and reasonableness of the compensation shall be determined by the court and paid from the assets of the trust unless the court finds the compensation paid or requested to be substantially unreasonable. The court shall direct from which part of the trust assets the compensation shall be paid.

(5) The court may determine reasonable compensation for a trustee or any person employed by a trustee without receiving expert testimony. Any party may offer expert testimony after notice to interested persons. If expert testimony is offered, a reasonable expert witness fee may be awarded by the court and paid from the assets of the trust unless the court finds that the expert testimony did not assist the court. The court shall direct from which part of the trust assets the fee shall be paid.

(6) In a proceeding pursuant to subsection (2), the petitioner may serve formal notice as provided in the Florida Probate Rules, and such notice shall be sufficient for the court to acquire jurisdiction over the person receiving the notice to the extent of the person's interest in the trust.

Added by Laws 2006, c. 2006–217, § 2, eff. July 1, 2007. Amended by Laws 2010, c. 2010–122, § 3, eff. July 1, 2010.

736.0207. Trust contests

(1) In an action to contest the validity or revocation of all or part of a trust, the contestant has the burden of establishing the grounds for invalidity.

(2) An action to contest the validity of all or part of a revocable trust, or the revocation of part of a revocable trust, may not be commenced until the trust becomes irrevocable by its terms or by the settlor's death. If all of a revocable trust has been revoked, an action to contest the revocation may not be commenced until after the settlor's death. This section does not prohibit such action by the guardian of the property of an incapacitated settlor.

Added by Laws 2006, c. 2006–217, § 2, eff. July 1, 2007. Amended by Laws 2011, c. 2011–183, § 9, eff. June 21, 2011; Laws 2014, c. 2014–127, § 7, eff. July 1, 2014.

Cross References

Guardians, powers upon court approval, see § 744.441.
Trust business, substitution of fiduciaries, see § 660.46.

PART III.   REPRESENTATION

Cross References

Trust business, substitution of fiduciaries, see § 660.46.

736.0301. Representation; basic effect

(1) Notice, information, accountings, or reports given to a person who may represent and bind another person under this part may serve as a substitute for and have the same effect as notice, information, accountings, or reports given directly to the other person.

(2) Actions taken by a person who represents the interests of another person under this part are binding on the person whose interests are represented to the same extent as if the actions had been taken by the person whose interests are represented.

(3) Except as otherwise provided in s. 736.0602, a person under this part who represents a settlor lacking capacity may receive notice and give a binding consent on the settlor's behalf.

(4) A trustee is not liable for giving notice, information, accountings, or reports to a beneficiary who is represented by another person under this part, and nothing in this part prohibits the trustee from giving notice, information, accountings, or reports to the person represented.

Added by Laws 2006, c. 2006–217, § 3, eff. July 1, 2007.

Cross References

Fiduciary fund investment, investment functions delegation, see F.S.A. § 518.112.

736.0302. Representation by holder of power of appointment

(1) The holder of a power of appointment may represent and bind persons whose interests, as permissible appointees, takers in default, or otherwise, are subject to the power.

(2) The takers in default of the exercise of a power of appointment may represent and bind persons whose interests, as permissible appointees, are subject to the power.

(3) Subsection (1) does not apply to:

(a) Any matter determined by the court to involve fraud or bad faith by the trustee; or

(b) A power of appointment held by a person while the person is the sole trustee.

(4) As used in this section, the term "power of appointment" does not include a power of a trustee to make discretionary distributions of trust property.

Added by Laws 2006, c. 2006–217, § 3, eff. July 1, 2007. Amended by Laws 2009, c. 2009–117, § 3, eff. July 1, 2009.

736.0303. Representation by fiduciaries and parents

To the extent there is no conflict of interest between the representative and the person represented or among those being represented with respect to a particular question or dispute:

(1) A guardian of the property may represent and bind the estate that the guardian of the property controls.

(2) An agent having authority to act with respect to the particular question or dispute may represent and bind the principal.

(3) A trustee may represent and bind the beneficiaries of the trust.

(4) A personal representative of a decedent's estate may represent and bind persons interested in the estate.

(5) A parent may represent and bind the parent's unborn child, or the parent's minor child if a guardian of the property for the minor child has not been appointed.

Added by Laws 2006, c. 2006–217, § 3, eff. July 1, 2007.

736.0304. Representation by person having substantially identical interest

Unless otherwise represented, a minor, incapacitated, or unborn individual, or a person whose identity or location is unknown and not reasonably ascertainable, may be represented by and bound by another person having a substantially identical interest with respect to the particular question or dispute, but only to the extent there is no conflict of interest between the representative and the person represented.

Added by Laws 2006, c. 2006–217, § 3, eff. July 1, 2007.

736.0305. Appointment of representative

(1) If the court determines that an interest is not represented under this part, or that the otherwise available representation might be inadequate, the court may appoint a representative to receive notice, give consent, and otherwise represent, bind, and act on behalf of a minor, incapacitated, or unborn individual, or a person whose identity or location is unknown. If not precluded by a conflict of interest, a representative may be appointed to represent several persons or interests.

(2) A representative may act on behalf of the individual represented with respect to any matter arising under this code, whether or not a judicial proceeding concerning the trust is pending.

(3) In making decisions, a representative may consider general benefits accruing to the living members of the represented individual's family.

Added by Laws 2006, c. 2006–217, § 3, eff. July 1, 2007.

736.0306. Designated representative

(1) If specifically nominated in the trust instrument, one or more persons may be designated to represent and bind a beneficiary and receive any notice, information, accounting, or report. The trust instrument may also authorize any person or persons, other than a trustee of the trust, to designate one or more persons to represent and bind a beneficiary and receive any notice, information, accounting, or report.

(2) Except as otherwise provided in this code, a person designated, as provided in subsection (1) may not represent and bind a beneficiary while that person is serving as trustee.

(3) Except as otherwise provided in this code, a person designated, as provided in subsection (1) may not represent and bind another beneficiary if the person designated also is a beneficiary, unless:

(a) That person was named by the settlor; or

(b) That person is the beneficiary's spouse or a grandparent or descendant of a grandparent of the beneficiary or the beneficiary's spouse.

(4) No person designated, as provided in subsection (1), is liable to the beneficiary whose interests are represented, or to anyone claiming through that beneficiary, for any actions or omissions to act made in good faith.

Added by Laws 2006, c. 2006–217, § 3, eff. July 1, 2007. Amended by Laws 2009, c. 2009–117, § 4, eff. July 1, 2009.

PART IV.   CREATION, VALIDITY, MODIFICATION, AND TERMINATION

736.0401.   Methods of creating trust

A trust may be created by:

(1) Transfer of property to another person as trustee during the settlor's lifetime or by will or other disposition taking effect on the settlor's death;

(2) Declaration by the owner of property that the owner holds identifiable property as trustee; or

(3) Exercise of a power of appointment in favor of a trustee.

Added by Laws 2006, c. 2006–217, § 4, eff. July 1, 2007.

736.0402.   Requirements for creation

(1) A trust is created only if:

(a) The settlor has capacity to create a trust.

(b) The settlor indicates an intent to create the trust.

(c) The trust has a definite beneficiary or is:

1.   A charitable trust;

2.   A trust for the care of an animal, as provided in s. 736.0408; or

3.   A trust for a noncharitable purpose, as provided in s. 736.0409.

(d) The trustee has duties to perform.

(e) The same person is not the sole trustee and sole beneficiary.

(2) A beneficiary is definite if the beneficiary can be ascertained now or in the future, subject to any applicable rule against perpetuities.

(3) A power of a trustee to select a beneficiary from an indefinite class is valid.   If the power is not exercised within a reasonable time, the power fails and the property subject to the power passes to the persons who would have taken the property had the power not been conferred.

Added by Laws 2006, c. 2006–217, § 4, eff. July 1, 2007.

736.0403.   Trusts created in other jurisdictions; formalities required for revocable trusts

(1) A trust not created by will is validly created if the creation of the trust complies with the law of the jurisdiction in which the trust instrument was executed or the law of the jurisdiction in which, at the time of creation, the settlor was domiciled.

(2) Notwithstanding subsection (1):

(a) No trust or confidence of or in any messuages, lands, tenements, or hereditaments shall arise or result unless the trust complies with the provisions of s. 689.05.

(b) The testamentary aspects of a revocable trust, executed by a settlor who is a domiciliary of this state at the time of execution, are invalid unless the trust instrument is executed by the settlor with the formalities required for the execution of a will in this state.   For purposes of this subsection, the term "testamentary aspects" means those provisions of the trust instrument that dispose of the trust property on or after the death of the settlor other than to the settlor's estate.

(3) Paragraph (2)(b) does not apply to trusts established as part of an employee annuity described in s. 403 of the Internal Revenue Code of 1986, as amended,[1] an individual retirement account as described in s. 408 of the Internal Revenue Code of 1986, as amended,[2] a Keogh

(HR–10) Plan, or a retirement or other plan that is qualified under s. 401 of the Internal Revenue Code of 1986, as amended.[3]

(4) Paragraph (2)(b) applies to trusts created on or after the effective date of this code.[4] Section 737.111, as in effect prior to the effective date of this code,[4] continues to apply to trusts created before the effective date of this code.[4]

Added by Laws 2006, c. 2006–217, § 4, eff. July 1, 2007.

[1] 26 U.S.C.A. § 403.
[2] 26 U.S.C.A. § 408.
[3] 26 U.S.C.A. § 401.
[4] July 1, 2007.

Cross References

Land conveyances, inter vivos trusts, see § 689.075.

736.0404. Trust purposes

A trust may be created only to the extent the purposes of the trust are lawful, not contrary to public policy, and possible to achieve. A trust and its terms must be for the benefit of its beneficiaries.

Added by Laws 2006, c. 2006–217, § 4, eff. July 1, 2007.

736.0405. Charitable purposes; enforcement

(1) A trust may be created for charitable purposes. Charitable purposes include, but are not limited to, the relief of poverty; the advancement of arts, sciences, education, or religion; and the promotion of health, governmental, or municipal purposes.

(2) If the terms of a charitable trust do not indicate a particular charitable purpose or beneficiary, the court may select one or more charitable purposes or beneficiaries. The selection must be consistent with the settlor's intent to the extent such intent can be ascertained.

(3) The settlor of a charitable trust, among others, has standing to enforce the trust.

Added by Laws 2006, c. 2006–217, § 4, eff. July 1, 2007.

736.0406. Effect of fraud, duress, mistake, or undue influence

If the creation, amendment, or restatement of a trust is procured by fraud, duress, mistake, or undue influence, the trust or any part so procured is void. The remainder of the trust not procured by such means is valid if the remainder is not invalid for other reasons. If the revocation of a trust, or any part thereof, is procured by fraud, duress, mistake, or undue influence, such revocation is void.

Added by Laws 2006, c. 2006–217, § 4, eff. July 1, 2007. Amended by Laws 2011, c. 2011–183, § 10, eff. June 21, 2011.

736.0407. Evidence of oral trust

Except as required by s. 736.0403 or a law other than this code, a trust need not be evidenced by a trust instrument but the creation of an oral trust and its terms may be established only by clear and convincing evidence.

Added by Laws 2006, c. 2006–217, § 4, eff. July 1, 2007.

736.0408. Trust for care of an animal

(1) A trust may be created to provide for the care of an animal alive during the settlor's lifetime. The trust terminates on the death of the animal or, if the trust was created to provide for the care of more than one animal alive during the settlor's lifetime, on the death of the last surviving animal.

(2) A trust authorized by this section may be enforced by a person appointed in the terms of the trust or, if no person is appointed, by a person appointed by the court. A person having an interest in the welfare of the animal may request the court to appoint a person to enforce the trust or to remove a person appointed.

(3) Property of a trust authorized by this section may be applied only to the intended use of the property, except to the extent the court determines that the value of the trust property exceeds the amount required for the intended use. Except as otherwise provided in the terms of the trust, property not required for the intended use must be distributed to the settlor, if then living, otherwise as part of the settlor's estate.

Added by Laws 2006, c. 2006–217, § 4, eff. July 1, 2007.

736.0409. Noncharitable trust without ascertainable beneficiary

Except as otherwise provided in s. 736.0408 or by another provision of law, the following rules apply:

(1) A trust may be created for a noncharitable purpose without a definite or definitely ascertainable beneficiary or for a noncharitable but otherwise valid purpose to be selected by the trustee. The trust may not be enforced for more than 21 years.

(2) A trust authorized by this section may be enforced by a person appointed in the terms of the trust or, if no person is appointed, by a person appointed by the court.

(3) Property of a trust authorized by this section may be applied only to the intended use of the property, except to the extent the court determines that the value of the trust property exceeds the amount required for the intended use. Except as otherwise provided in the terms of the trust, property not required for the intended use must be distributed to the settlor, if then living, otherwise as part of the settlor's estate.

Added by Laws 2006, c. 2006–217, § 4, eff. July 1, 2007.

736.0410. Modification or termination of trust; proceedings for disapproval of nonjudicial acts

(1) In addition to the methods of termination prescribed by ss. 736.04113–736.0414, a trust terminates to the extent the trust expires or is revoked or is properly distributed pursuant to the terms of the trust.

(2) A proceeding to disapprove a proposed modification or termination under s. 736.0412 or a trust combination or division under s. 736.0417 may be commenced by any beneficiary.

(3) A proceeding to disapprove a proposed termination under s. 736.0414(1) may be commenced by any qualified beneficiary.

Added by Laws 2006, c. 2006–217, § 4, eff. July 1, 2007.

736.04113. Judicial modification of irrevocable trust when modification is not inconsistent with settlor's purpose

(1) Upon the application of a trustee of the trust or any qualified beneficiary, a court at any time may modify the terms of a trust that is not then revocable in the manner provided in subsection (2), if:

(a) The purposes of the trust have been fulfilled or have become illegal, impossible, wasteful, or impracticable to fulfill;

(b) Because of circumstances not anticipated by the settlor, compliance with the terms of the trust would defeat or substantially impair the accomplishment of a material purpose of the trust; or

(c) A material purpose of the trust no longer exists.

(2) In modifying a trust under this section, a court may:

(a) Amend or change the terms of the trust, including terms governing distribution of the trust income or principal or terms governing administration of the trust;

(b) Terminate the trust in whole or in part;

(c) Direct or permit the trustee to do acts that are not authorized or that are prohibited by the terms of the trust; or

(d) Prohibit the trustee from performing acts that are permitted or required by the terms of the trust.

(3) In exercising discretion to modify a trust under this section:

(a) The court shall consider the terms and purposes of the trust, the facts and circumstances surrounding the creation of the trust, and extrinsic evidence relevant to the proposed modification.

(b) The court shall consider spendthrift provisions as a factor in making a decision, but the court is not precluded from modifying a trust because the trust contains spendthrift provisions.

(4) The provisions of this section are in addition to, and not in derogation of, rights under the common law to modify, amend, terminate, or revoke trusts.

Added by Laws 2006, c. 2006–217, § 4, eff. July 1, 2007.

736.04114. Limited judicial construction of irrevocable trust with federal tax provisions

(1) Upon the application of a trustee or any qualified beneficiary of a trust, a court at any time may construe the terms of a trust that is not then revocable to define the respective shares or determine beneficiaries, in accordance with the intention of the settlor, if a disposition occurs during the applicable period and the trust contains a provision that:

(a) Includes a formula disposition referring to the "unified credit," "estate tax exemption," "applicable exemption amount," "applicable credit amount," "applicable exclusion amount," "generation-skipping transfer tax exemption," "GST exemption," "marital deduction," "maximum marital deduction," "unlimited marital deduction," or "maximum charitable deduction";

(b) Measures a share of a trust based on the amount that can pass free of federal estate tax or the amount that can pass free of federal generation-skipping transfer tax;

(c) Otherwise makes a disposition referring to a charitable deduction, marital deduction, or another provision of federal estate tax or generation-skipping transfer tax law; or

(d) Appears to be intended to reduce or minimize federal estate tax or generation-skipping transfer tax.

(2) For the purpose of this section:

(a) "Applicable period" means a period beginning January 1, 2010, and ending on the end of the day on the earlier of:

1.　December 31, 2010; or

2.　The day before the date that an act becomes law which repeals or otherwise modifies or has the effect of repealing or modifying s. 901 of the Economic Growth and Tax Relief Reconciliation Act of 2001.

(b) A "disposition occurs" when an interest takes effect in possession or enjoyment.

(3) In construing the trust, the court shall consider the terms and purposes of the trust, the facts and circumstances surrounding the creation of the trust, and the settlor's probable intent. In determining the settlor's probable intent, the court may consider evidence relevant to the settlor's intent even though the evidence contradicts an apparent plain meaning of the trust instrument.

(4) This section does not apply to a disposition that is specifically conditioned upon no federal estate or generation-skipping transfer tax being imposed.

(5) Unless otherwise ordered by the court, during the applicable period and without court order, the trustee administering a trust containing one or more provisions described in subsection (1) may:

(a) Delay or refrain from making any distribution;

(b) Incur and pay fees and costs reasonably necessary to determine its duties and obligations, including compliance with provisions of existing and reasonably anticipated future federal tax laws; and

(c) Establish and maintain reserves for the payment of these fees and costs and federal taxes.

The trustee is not liable for its actions as provided in this subsection which are made or taken in good faith.

(6) The provisions of this section are in addition to, and not in derogation of, rights under this code or the common law to construe a trust.

(7) This section is remedial in order to provide a new or modified legal remedy. This section applies retroactively and is effective as of January 1, 2010.

Added by Laws 2010, c. 2010–122, § 4, eff. May 27, 2010.

Retroactivity

Subsection (7) provides that this section applies retroactively and is effective as of January 1, 2010.

736.04115.　Judicial modification of irrevocable trust when modification is in best interests of beneficiaries

(1) Without regard to the reasons for modification provided in s. 736.04113, if compliance with the terms of a trust is not in the best interests of the beneficiaries, upon the application of a trustee or any qualified beneficiary, a court may at any time modify a trust that is not then revocable as provided in s. 736.04113(2).

(2) In exercising discretion to modify a trust under this section:

(a) The court shall exercise discretion in a manner that conforms to the extent possible with the intent of the settlor, taking into account the current circumstances and best interests of the beneficiaries.

(b) The court shall consider the terms and purposes of the trust, the facts and circumstances surrounding the creation of the trust, and extrinsic evidence relevant to the proposed modification.

(c) The court shall consider spendthrift provisions as a factor in making a decision, but the court is not precluded from modifying a trust because the trust contains spendthrift provisions.

(3) This section shall not apply to:

(a) Any trust created prior to January 1, 2001.

(b) Any trust created after December 31, 2000, if:

1. Under the terms of the trust, all beneficial interests in the trust must vest or terminate within the period prescribed by the rule against perpetuities in s. 689.225(2), notwithstanding s. 689.225(2)(f).

2. The terms of the trust expressly prohibit judicial modification.

(4) For purposes of subsection (3), a revocable trust shall be treated as created when the right of revocation terminates.

(5) The provisions of this section are in addition to, and not in derogation of, rights under the common law to modify, amend, terminate, or revoke trusts.

Added by Laws 2006, c. 2006–217, § 4, eff. July 1, 2007.

736.04117. Trustee's power to invade principal in trust

(1)(a) Unless the trust instrument expressly provides otherwise, a trustee who has absolute power under the terms of a trust to invade the principal of the trust, referred to in this section as the "first trust," to make distributions to or for the benefit of one or more persons may instead exercise the power by appointing all or part of the principal of the trust subject to the power in favor of a trustee of another trust, referred to in this section as the "second trust," for the current benefit of one or more of such persons under the same trust instrument or under a different trust instrument; provided:

1. The beneficiaries of the second trust may include only beneficiaries of the first trust;

2. The second trust may not reduce any fixed income, annuity, or unitrust interest in the assets of the first trust; and

3. If any contribution to the first trust qualified for a marital or charitable deduction for federal income, gift, or estate tax purposes under the Internal Revenue Code of 1986, as amended,[1] the second trust shall not contain any provision which, if included in the first trust, would have prevented the first trust from qualifying for such a deduction or would have reduced the amount of such deduction.

(b) For purposes of this subsection, an absolute power to invade principal shall include a power to invade principal that is not limited to specific or ascertainable purposes, such as health, education, maintenance, and support, whether or not the term "absolute" is used. A power to invade principal for purposes such as best interests, welfare, comfort, or happiness shall constitute an absolute power not limited to specific or ascertainable purposes.

(2) The exercise of a power to invade principal under subsection (1) shall be by an instrument in writing, signed and acknowledged by the trustee, and filed with the records of the first trust.

(3) The exercise of a power to invade principal under subsection (1) shall be considered the exercise of a power of appointment, other than a power to appoint to the trustee, the trustee's creditors, the trustee's estate, or the creditors of the trustee's estate, and shall be subject to the provisions of s. 689.225 covering the time at which the permissible period of the rule against perpetuities begins and the law that determines the permissible period of the rule against perpetuities of the first trust.

(4) The trustee shall notify all qualified beneficiaries of the first trust, in writing, at least 60 days prior to the effective date of the trustee's exercise of the trustee's power to invade principal pursuant to subsection (1), of the manner in which the trustee intends to exercise the power. A copy of the proposed instrument exercising the power shall satisfy the trustee's notice obligation under this subsection. If all qualified beneficiaries waive the notice period by signed written instrument delivered to the trustee, the trustee's power to invade principal shall be exercisable immediately. The trustee's notice under this subsection shall not limit the right of any beneficiary to object to the exercise of the trustee's power to invade principal except as provided in other applicable provisions of this code.

(5) The exercise of the power to invade principal under subsection (1) is not prohibited by a spendthrift clause or by a provision in the trust instrument that prohibits amendment or revocation of the trust.

(6) Nothing in this section is intended to create or imply a duty to exercise a power to invade principal, and no inference of impropriety shall be made as a result of a trustee not exercising the power to invade principal conferred under subsection (1).

(7) The provisions of this section shall not be construed to abridge the right of any trustee who has a power of invasion to appoint property in further trust that arises under the terms of the first trust or under any other section of this code or under another provision of law or under common law.

Added by Laws 2007, c. 2007–153, § 2, eff. July 1, 2007.

[1] 26 U.S.C.A. § 1 et seq.

736.0412. Nonjudicial modification of irrevocable trust

(1) After the settlor's death, a trust may be modified at any time as provided in s. 736.04113(2) upon the unanimous agreement of the trustee and all qualified beneficiaries.

(2) Modification of a trust as authorized in this section is not prohibited by a spendthrift clause or by a provision in the trust instrument that prohibits amendment or revocation of the trust.

(3) An agreement to modify a trust under this section is binding on a beneficiary whose interest is represented by another person under part III of this code.

(4) This section shall not apply to:

(a) Any trust created prior to January 1, 2001.

(b) Any trust created after December 31, 2000, if, under the terms of the trust, all beneficial interests in the trust must vest or terminate within the period prescribed by the rule against perpetuities in s. 689.225(2), notwithstanding s. 689.225(2)(f), unless the terms of the trust expressly authorize nonjudicial modification.

(c) Any trust for which a charitable deduction is allowed or allowable under the Internal Revenue Code until the termination of all charitable interests in the trust.

(5) For purposes of subsection (4), a revocable trust shall be treated as created when the right of revocation terminates.

(6) The provisions of this section are in addition to, and not in derogation of, rights under the common law to modify, amend, terminate, or revoke trusts.

Added by Laws 2006, c. 2006–217, § 4, eff. July 1, 2007.

736.0413.   Cy pres

(1) If a particular charitable purpose becomes unlawful, impracticable, impossible to achieve, or wasteful, the court may apply the doctrine of cy pres to modify or terminate the trust by directing that the trust property be applied or distributed, in whole or in part, in a manner consistent with the settlor's charitable purposes.

(2) A proceeding to modify or terminate a trust under this section may be commenced by a settlor, a trustee, or any qualified beneficiary.

Added by Laws 2006, c. 2006–217, § 4, eff. July 1, 2007.

736.0414.   Modification or termination of uneconomic trust

(1) After notice to the qualified beneficiaries, the trustee of a trust consisting of trust property having a total value less than $50,000 may terminate the trust if the trustee concludes that the value of the trust property is insufficient to justify the cost of administration.

(2) Upon application of a trustee or any qualified beneficiary, the court may modify or terminate a trust or remove the trustee and appoint a different trustee if the court determines that the value of the trust property is insufficient to justify the cost of administration.

(3) Upon termination of a trust under this section, the trustee shall distribute the trust property in a manner consistent with the purposes of the trust. The trustee may enter into agreements or make such other provisions that the trustee deems necessary or appropriate to protect the interests of the beneficiaries and the trustee and to carry out the intent and purposes of the trust.

(4) The existence of a spendthrift provision in the trust does not make this section inapplicable unless the trust instrument expressly provides that the trustee may not terminate the trust pursuant to this section.

(5) This section does not apply to an easement for conservation or preservation.

Added by Laws 2006, c. 2006–217, § 4, eff. July 1, 2007.

736.0415.   Reformation to correct mistakes

Upon application of a settlor or any interested person, the court may reform the terms of a trust, even if unambiguous, to conform the terms to the settlor's intent if it is proved by clear and convincing evidence that both the accomplishment of the settlor's intent and the terms of the trust were affected by a mistake of fact or law, whether in expression or inducement. In determining the settlor's original intent, the court may consider evidence relevant to the settlor's intent even though the evidence contradicts an apparent plain meaning of the trust instrument.

Added by Laws 2006, c. 2006–217, § 4, eff. July 1, 2007.

736.0416. Modification to achieve settlor's tax objectives

Upon application of any interested person, to achieve the settlor's tax objectives the court may modify the terms of a trust in a manner that is not contrary to the settlor's probable intent. The court may provide that the modification has retroactive effect.

Added by Laws 2006, c. 2006–217, § 4, eff. July 1, 2007.

736.0417. Combination and division of trusts

(1) After notice to the qualified beneficiaries, a trustee may combine two or more trusts into a single trust or divide a trust into two or more separate trusts, if the result does not impair rights of any beneficiary or adversely affect achievement of the purposes of the trusts or trust, respectively.

(2) Subject to the terms of the trust, the trustee may take into consideration differences in federal tax attributes and other pertinent factors in administering the trust property of any separate account or trust, in making applicable tax elections, and in making distributions. A separate trust created by severance must be treated as a separate trust for all purposes from the date on which the severance is effective. The effective date of the severance may be retroactive to a date before the date on which the trustee exercises such power.

Added by Laws 2006, c. 2006–217, § 4, eff. July 1, 2007.

PART V. CREDITORS' CLAIMS; SPENDTHRIFT AND DISCRETIONARY TRUSTS

736.0501. Rights of beneficiary's creditor or assignee

Except as provided in s. 736.0504, to the extent a beneficiary's interest is not subject to a spendthrift provision, the court may authorize a creditor or assignee of the beneficiary to reach the beneficiary's interest by attachment of present or future distributions to or for the benefit of the beneficiary or by other means. The court may limit the award to such relief as is appropriate under the circumstances.

Added by Laws 2006, c. 2006–217, § 5, eff. July 1, 2007. Amended by Laws 2007, c. 2007–153, § 11, eff. July 1, 2007.

736.0502. Spendthrift provision

(1) A spendthrift provision is valid only if the provision restrains both voluntary and involuntary transfer of a beneficiary's interest. This subsection does not apply to any trust the terms of which are included in an instrument executed before the effective date of this code.

(2) A term of a trust providing that the interest of a beneficiary is held subject to a spendthrift trust, or words of similar import, is sufficient to restrain both voluntary and involuntary transfer of the beneficiary's interest.

(3) A beneficiary may not transfer an interest in a trust in violation of a valid spendthrift provision and, except as otherwise provided in this part, a creditor or assignee of the beneficiary may not reach the interest or a distribution by the trustee before receipt of the interest or distribution by the beneficiary.

(4) A valid spendthrift provision does not prevent the appointment of interests through the exercise of a power of appointment.

Added by Laws 2006, c. 2006–217, § 5, eff. July 1, 2007. Amended by Laws 2007, c. 2007–153, § 12, eff. July 1, 2007.

736.0503. Exceptions to spendthrift provision

(1) As used in this section, the term "child" includes any person for whom an order or judgment for child support has been entered in this or any other state.

(2) To the extent provided in subsection (3), a spendthrift provision is unenforceable against:

(a) A beneficiary's child, spouse, or former spouse who has a judgment or court order against the beneficiary for support or maintenance.

(b) A judgment creditor who has provided services for the protection of a beneficiary's interest in the trust.

(c) A claim of this state or the United States to the extent a law of this state or a federal law so provides.

(3) Except as otherwise provided in this subsection and in s. 736.0504, a claimant against which a spendthrift provision may not be enforced may obtain from a court, or pursuant to the Uniform Interstate Family Support Act, [1] an order attaching present or future distributions to or for the benefit of the beneficiary. The court may limit the award to such relief as is appropriate under the circumstances. Notwithstanding this subsection, the remedies provided in this subsection apply to a claim by a beneficiary's child, spouse, former spouse, or a judgment creditor described in paragraph (2)(a) or paragraph (2)(b) only as a last resort upon an initial showing that traditional methods of enforcing the claim are insufficient.

Added by Laws 2006, c. 2006–217, § 5, eff. July 1, 2007. Amended by Laws 2007, c. 2007–153, § 13, eff. July 1, 2007.

[1] Section 88.0011 et seq.

736.0504. Discretionary trusts; effect of standard

(1) As used in this section, the term "discretionary distribution" means a distribution that is subject to the trustee's discretion whether or not the discretion is expressed in the form of a standard of distribution and whether or not the trustee has abused the discretion.

(2) Whether or not a trust contains a spendthrift provision, if a trustee may make discretionary distributions to or for the benefit of a beneficiary, a creditor of the beneficiary, including a creditor as described in s. 736.0503(2), may not:

(a) Compel a distribution that is subject to the trustee's discretion; or

(b) Attach or otherwise reach the interest, if any, which the beneficiary might have as a result of the trustee's authority to make discretionary distributions to or for the benefit of the beneficiary.

(3) If the trustee's discretion to make distributions for the trustee's own benefit is limited by an ascertainable standard, a creditor may not reach or compel distribution of the beneficial interest except to the extent the interest would be subject to the creditor's claim were the beneficiary not acting as trustee.

(4) This section does not limit the right of a beneficiary to maintain a judicial proceeding against a trustee for an abuse of discretion or failure to comply with a standard for distribution.

Added by Laws 2006, c. 2006–217, § 5, eff. July 1, 2007. Amended by Laws 2007, c. 2007–153, § 14, eff. July 1, 2007.

736.0505. Creditors' claims against settlor

(1) Whether or not the terms of a trust contain a spendthrift provision, the following rules apply:

(a) The property of a revocable trust is subject to the claims of the settlor's creditors during the settlor's lifetime to the extent the property would not otherwise be exempt by law if owned directly by the settlor.

(b) With respect to an irrevocable trust, a creditor or assignee of the settlor may reach the maximum amount that can be distributed to or for the settlor's benefit. If a trust has more than one settlor, the amount the creditor or assignee of a particular settlor may reach may not exceed the settlor's interest in the portion of the trust attributable to that settlor's contribution.

(c) Notwithstanding the provisions of paragraph (b), the assets of an irrevocable trust may not be subject to the claims of an existing or subsequent creditor or assignee of the settlor, in whole or in part, solely because of the existence of a discretionary power granted to the trustee by the terms of the trust, or any other provision of law, to pay directly to the taxing authorities or to reimburse the settlor for any tax on trust income or principal which is payable by the settlor under the law imposing such tax.

(2) For purposes of this section:

(a) During the period the power may be exercised, the holder of a power of withdrawal is treated in the same manner as the settlor of a revocable trust to the extent of the property subject to the power.

(b) Upon the lapse, release, or waiver of the power, the holder is treated as the settlor of the trust only to the extent the value of the property affected by the lapse, release, or waiver exceeds the greater of the amount specified in:

1. Section 2041(b)(2) [1] or s. 2514(e); [2] or

2. Section 2503(b) [3] and, if the donor was married at the time of the transfer to which the power of withdrawal applies, twice the amount specified in s. 2503(b), [3]

of the Internal Revenue Code of 1986, as amended.

(3) Subject to the provisions of s. 726.105, for purposes of this section, the assets in:

(a) A trust described in s. 2523(e) of the Internal Revenue Code of 1986, [4] as amended, or a trust for which the election described in s. 2523(f) of the Internal Revenue Code of 1986, [5] as amended, has been made; and

(b) Another trust, to the extent that the assets in the other trust are attributable to a trust described in paragraph (a),

shall, after the death of the settlor's spouse, be deemed to have been contributed by the settlor's spouse and not by the settlor.

Added by Laws 2006, c. 2006–217, § 5, eff. July 1, 2007. Amended by Laws 2010, c. 2010–122, § 5, eff. July 1, 2010.

[1] 26 U.S.C.A. § 2041(b)(2).
[2] 26 U.S.C.A. § 2514(e).
[3] 26 U.S.C.A. § 2503(b).
[4] 26 U.S.C.A. § 2523(e).
[5] 26 U.S.C.A. § 2523(f).

736.05053.   Trustee's duty to pay expenses and obligations of settlor's estate

(1) A trustee of a trust described in s. 733.707(3) shall pay to the personal representative of a settlor's estate any amounts that the personal representative certifies in writing to the trustee are required to pay the expenses of the administration and obligations of the settlor's estate. Payments made by a trustee, unless otherwise provided in the trust instrument, must be charged as expenses of the trust without a contribution from anyone. The interests of all beneficiaries of such a trust are subject to the provisions of this subsection; however, the payments must be made from assets, property, or the proceeds of the assets or property that are included in the settlor's gross estate for federal estate tax purposes and may not be made from assets proscribed in s. 733.707(3) or death benefits described in s. 733.808(4) unless the trust instrument expressly refers to s. 733.808(4) and directs that it does not apply.

(2) Unless a settlor provides by will, or designates in a trust described in s. 733.707(3) funds or property passing under the trust to be used as designated, the expenses of the administration and obligations of the settlor's estate must be paid from the trust in the following order:

(a) Property of the residue of the trust remaining after all distributions that are to be satisfied by reference to a specific property or type of property, fund, or sum.

(b) Property that is not to be distributed from specified or identified property or a specified or identified item of property.

(c) Property that is to be distributed from specified or identified property or a specified or identified item of property.

(3) Trust distributions that are to be satisfied from specified or identified property must be classed as distributions to be satisfied from the general assets of the trust and not otherwise disposed of in the trust instrument on the failure or insufficiency of funds or property from which payment should be made, to the extent of the insufficiency. Trust distributions given for valuable consideration abate with other distributions of the same class only to the extent of the excess over the value of the consideration until all others of the same class are exhausted. Except as provided in this section, trust distributions abate equally and ratably and without preference or priority between real and personal property. When a specified or identified item of property that has been designated for distribution in the trust instrument or that is charged with a distribution is sold or taken by the trustee, other beneficiaries shall contribute according to their respective interests to the beneficiary whose property has been sold or taken.   Before distribution, the trustee shall determine the amounts of the respective contributions and such amounts must be paid or withheld before distribution is made.

(4) The trustee shall pay the expenses of trust administration, including compensation of trustees and attorneys of the trustees, before and in preference to the expenses of the administration and obligations of the settlor's estate.

(5) Nonresiduary trust dispositions shall abate pro rata with nonresiduary devises pursuant to the priorities specified in this section and s. 733.805, determined as if the beneficiaries of the will and trust, other than the estate or trust itself, were taking under a common instrument.

Added by Laws 2006, c. 2006–217, § 5, eff. July 1, 2007. Amended by Laws 2010, c. 2010–122, § 6, eff. July 1, 2010; Laws 2014, c. 2014–127, § 9, eff. July 1, 2014.

Cross References

Probate,
    Distribution, order in which assets abate, see § 733.805.
    Elective share of surviving spouse, sources of payment, see § 732.2075.

736.05055. Notice of trust

(1) Upon the death of a settlor of a trust described in s. 733.707(3), the trustee must file a notice of trust with the court of the county of the settlor's domicile and the court having jurisdiction of the settlor's estate.

(2) The notice of trust must contain the name of the settlor, the settlor's date of death, the title of the trust, if any, the date of the trust, and the name and address of the trustee.

(3) If the settlor's probate proceeding has been commenced, the clerk shall notify the trustee in writing of the date of the commencement of the probate proceeding and the file number.

(4) The clerk shall file and index the notice of trust in the same manner as a caveat unless there exists a probate proceeding for the settlor's estate, in which case the notice of trust must be filed in the probate proceeding and the clerk shall send a copy to the personal representative.

(5) The clerk shall send a copy of any caveat filed regarding the settlor to the trustee, and the notice of trust to any caveator, unless there is a probate proceeding pending and the personal representative and the trustee are the same.

(6) Any proceeding affecting the expenses of the administration or obligations of the settlor's estate prior to the trustee filing a notice of trust are binding on the trustee.

(7) The trustee's failure to file the notice of trust does not affect the trustee's obligation to pay expenses of administration and obligations of the settlor's estate as provided in s. 733.607(2).
Added by Laws 2006, c. 2006–217, § 5, eff. July 1, 2007.

736.0506. Overdue distribution

(1) As used in this section, the term "mandatory distribution" means a distribution of income or principal the trustee is required to make to a beneficiary under the terms of the trust, including a distribution on termination of the trust. The term does not include a distribution subject to the exercise of the trustee's discretion, even if:

(a) The discretion is expressed in the form of a standard of distribution; or

(b) The terms of the trust authorizing a distribution couple language of discretion with language of direction.

(2) A creditor or assignee of a beneficiary may reach a mandatory distribution of income or principal, including a distribution upon termination of the trust, if the trustee has not made the distribution to the beneficiary within a reasonable time after the designated distribution date, whether or not a trust contains a spendthrift provision.
Added by Laws 2006, c. 2006–217, § 5, eff. July 1, 2007.

736.0507. Personal obligations of trustee

Except to the extent of the trustee's interest in the trust other than as a trustee, trust property is not subject to personal obligations of the trustee, even if the trustee becomes insolvent or bankrupt.
Added by Laws 2006, c. 2006–217, § 5, eff. July 1, 2007.

PART VI.   REVOCABLE TRUSTS

736.0601. Capacity of settlor of revocable trust

The capacity required to create, amend, revoke, or add property to a revocable trust, or to direct the actions of the trustee of a revocable trust, is the same as that required to make a will.
Added by Laws 2006, c. 2006–217, § 6, eff. July 1, 2007.

736.0602. **Revocation or amendment of revocable trust**

(1) Unless the terms of a trust expressly provide that the trust is irrevocable, the settlor may revoke or amend the trust. This subsection does not apply to a trust created under an instrument executed before the effective date of this code.

(2) If a revocable trust is created or funded by more than one settlor:

(a) To the extent the trust consists of community property, the trust may be revoked by either spouse acting alone but may be amended only by joint action of both spouses.

(b) To the extent the trust consists of property other than community property, each settlor may revoke or amend the trust with regard to the portion of the trust property attributable to that settlor's contribution.

(c) Upon the revocation or amendment of the trust by fewer than all of the settlors, the trustee shall promptly notify the other settlors of the revocation or amendment.

(3) Subject to s. 736.0403(2), the settlor may revoke or amend a revocable trust:

(a) By substantial compliance with a method provided in the terms of the trust; or

(b) If the terms of the trust do not provide a method, by:

1. A later will or codicil that expressly refers to the trust or specifically devises property that would otherwise have passed according to the terms of the trust; or

2. Any other method manifesting clear and convincing evidence of the settlor's intent.

(4) Upon revocation of a revocable trust, the trustee shall deliver the trust property as the settlor directs.

(5) A settlor's powers with respect to revocation, amendment, or distribution of trust property may be exercised by an agent under a power of attorney only as authorized by s. 709.2202.

(6) A guardian of the property of the settlor may exercise a settlor's powers with respect to revocation, amendment, or distribution of trust property only as provided in s. 744.441.

(7) A trustee who does not know that a trust has been revoked or amended is not liable for distributions made and other actions taken on the assumption that the trust had not been amended or revoked.

Added by Laws 2006, c. 2006–217, § 6, eff. July 1, 2007. Amended by Laws 2011, c. 2011–210, § 32, eff. Oct. 1, 2011.

736.0603. **Settlor's powers; powers of withdrawal**

(1) While a trust is revocable, the duties of the trustee are owed exclusively to the settlor.

(2) During the period the power may be exercised, the holder of a power of withdrawal has the rights of a settlor of a revocable trust under this section to the extent of the property subject to the power.

Added by Laws 2006, c. 2006–217, § 6, eff. July 1, 2007.

736.0604. **Limitation on action contesting validity of revocable trust**

An action to contest the validity of a trust that was revocable at the settlor's death is barred, if not commenced within the earlier of:

(1) The time as provided in chapter 95; or

(2) Six months after the trustee sent the person a copy of the trust instrument and a notice informing the person of the trust's existence, of the trustee's name and address, and of the time allowed for commencing a proceeding.

Added by Laws 2006, c. 2006–217, § 6, eff. July 1, 2007.

PART VII.   OFFICE OF TRUSTEE

736.0701.   Accepting or declining trusteeship

(1) Except as otherwise provided in subsection (3), a person designated as trustee accepts the trusteeship:

(a) By substantially complying with a method of acceptance provided in the terms of the trust; or

(b) If the terms of the trust do not provide a method or the method provided in the terms is not expressly made exclusive, by accepting delivery of the trust property, exercising powers or performing duties as trustee, or otherwise indicating acceptance of the trusteeship.

(2) A person designated as trustee who has not accepted the trusteeship may decline the trusteeship. A designated trustee who does not accept the trusteeship within a reasonable time after knowing of the designation is deemed to have declined the trusteeship.

(3) A person designated as trustee may, without accepting the trusteeship:

(a) Act to preserve the trust property if, within a reasonable time after acting, the person sends to a qualified beneficiary a written statement declining the trusteeship.

(b) Inspect or investigate trust property to determine potential liability under environmental or other law or for any other purpose.

Added by Laws 2006, c. 2006–217, § 7, eff. July 1, 2007.

736.0702.   Trustee's bond

(1) A trustee shall give bond to secure performance of the trustee's duties only if the court finds that a bond is needed to protect the interests of the beneficiaries or is required by the terms of the trust and the court has not dispensed with the requirement.

(2) The court may specify the amount of a bond, the trustee's liabilities under the bond, and whether sureties are necessary. The court may modify or terminate a bond at any time.

Added by Laws 2006, c. 2006–217, § 7, eff. July 1, 2007.

736.0703.   Cotrustees

(1) Cotrustees who are unable to reach a unanimous decision may act by majority decision.

(2) If a vacancy occurs in a cotrusteeship, the remaining cotrustees or a majority of the remaining cotrustees may act for the trust.

(3) A cotrustee must participate in the performance of a trustee's function unless the cotrustee is unavailable to perform the function because of absence, illness, disqualification under other provision of law, or other temporary incapacity or the cotrustee has properly delegated the performance of the function to another cotrustee.

(4) If a cotrustee is unavailable to perform duties because of absence, illness, disqualification under other law, or other temporary incapacity, and prompt action is necessary to achieve the purposes of the trust or to avoid injury to the trust property, the remaining cotrustee or a majority of the remaining cotrustees may act for the trust.

(5) A cotrustee may not delegate to another cotrustee the performance of a function the settlor reasonably expected the cotrustees to perform jointly, except that a cotrustee may delegate investment functions to a cotrustee pursuant to and in compliance with s. 518.112. A cotrustee may revoke a delegation previously made.

(6) Except as otherwise provided in subsection (7), a cotrustee who does not join in an action of another cotrustee is not liable for the action.

(7) Except as otherwise provided in subsection (9), each cotrustee shall exercise reasonable care to:

(a) Prevent a cotrustee from committing a breach of trust.

(b) Compel a cotrustee to redress a breach of trust.

(8) A dissenting cotrustee who joins in an action at the direction of the majority of the cotrustees and who notifies any cotrustee of the dissent at or before the time of the action is not liable for the action.

(9) If the terms of a trust provide for the appointment of more than one trustee but confer upon one or more of the trustees, to the exclusion of the others, the power to direct or prevent specified actions of the trustees, the excluded trustees shall act in accordance with the exercise of the power. Except in cases of willful misconduct on the part of the excluded trustee, an excluded trustee is not liable, individually or as a fiduciary, for any consequence that results from compliance with the exercise of the power. An excluded trustee does not have a duty or an obligation to review, inquire, investigate, or make recommendations or evaluations with respect to the exercise of the power. The trustee or trustees having the power to direct or prevent actions of the excluded trustees shall be liable to the beneficiaries with respect to the exercise of the power as if the excluded trustees were not in office and shall have the exclusive obligation to account to and to defend any action brought by the beneficiaries with respect to the exercise of the power. The provisions of s. 736.0808(2) do not apply if the person entrusted with the power to direct the actions of the excluded trustee is also a cotrustee.

Added by Laws 2006, c. 2006–217, § 7, eff. July 1, 2007. Amended by Laws 2008, c. 2008–76, § 1, eff. July 1, 2008; Laws 2009, c. 2009–117, § 5, eff. July 1, 2009; Laws 2014, c. 2014–115, § 1, eff. July 1, 2014.

736.0704. Vacancy in trusteeship; appointment of successor

(1) A vacancy in a trusteeship occurs if:

(a) A person designated as trustee declines the trusteeship;

(b) A person designated as trustee cannot be identified or does not exist;

(c) A trustee resigns;

(d) A trustee is disqualified or removed;

(e) A trustee dies; or

(f) A trustee is adjudicated to be incapacitated.

(2) If one or more cotrustees remain in office, a vacancy in a trusteeship need not be filled. A vacancy in a trusteeship must be filled if the trust has no remaining trustee.

(3) A vacancy in a trusteeship of a noncharitable trust that is required to be filled must be filled in the following order of priority:

(a) By a person named or designated pursuant to the terms of the trust to act as successor trustee.

(b) By a person appointed by unanimous agreement of the qualified beneficiaries.

(c) By a person appointed by the court.

(4) A vacancy in a trusteeship of a charitable trust that is required to be filled must be filled in the following order of priority:

(a) By a person named or designated pursuant to the terms of the trust to act as successor trustee.

(b) By a person selected by unanimous agreement of the charitable organizations expressly designated to receive distributions under the terms of the trust.

(c) By a person appointed by the court.

(5) The court may appoint an additional trustee or special fiduciary whenever the court considers the appointment necessary for the administration of the trust, whether or not a vacancy in a trusteeship exists or is required to be filled.

Added by Laws 2006, c. 2006–217, § 7, eff. July 1, 2007.

736.0705. Resignation of trustee

(1) A trustee may resign:

(a) Upon at least 30 days' notice to the qualified beneficiaries, the settlor, if living, and all cotrustees; or

(b) With the approval of the court.

(2) In approving a resignation, the court may issue orders and impose conditions reasonably necessary for the protection of the trust property.

(3) Any liability of a resigning trustee or of any sureties on the trustee's bond for acts or omissions of the trustee is not discharged or affected by the trustee's resignation.

Added by Laws 2006, c. 2006–217, § 7, eff. July 1, 2007.

736.0706. Removal of trustee

(1) The settlor, a cotrustee, or a beneficiary may request the court to remove a trustee, or a trustee may be removed by the court on the court's own initiative.

(2) The court may remove a trustee if:

(a) The trustee has committed a serious breach of trust;

(b) The lack of cooperation among cotrustees substantially impairs the administration of the trust;

(c) Due to the unfitness, unwillingness, or persistent failure of the trustee to administer the trust effectively, the court determines that removal of the trustee best serves the interests of the beneficiaries; or

(d) There has been a substantial change of circumstances or removal is requested by all of the qualified beneficiaries, the court finds that removal of the trustee best serves the interests of all of the beneficiaries and is not inconsistent with a material purpose of the trust, and a suitable cotrustee or successor trustee is available.

(3) Pending a final decision on a request to remove a trustee, or in lieu of or in addition to removing a trustee, the court may order such appropriate relief under s. 736.1001(2) as may be necessary to protect the trust property or the interests of the beneficiaries.

Added by Laws 2006, c. 2006–217, § 7, eff. July 1, 2007.

736.0707. Delivery of property by former trustee

(1) Unless a cotrustee remains in office or the court otherwise orders and until the trust property is delivered to a successor trustee or other person entitled to the property, a trustee who has resigned or been removed has the duties of a trustee and the powers necessary to protect the trust property.

(2) A trustee who has resigned or been removed shall within a reasonable time deliver the trust property within the trustee's possession to the cotrustee, successor trustee, or other person entitled to the property, subject to the right of the trustee to retain a reasonable reserve for the payment of debts, expenses, and taxes. The provisions of this subsection are in addition to and are not in derogation of the rights of a removed or resigning trustee under the common law.
Added by Laws 2006, c. 2006–217, § 7, eff. July 1, 2007.

736.0708. Compensation of trustee

(1) If the terms of a trust do not specify the trustee's compensation, a trustee is entitled to compensation that is reasonable under the circumstances.

(2) If the terms of a trust specify the trustee's compensation, the trustee is entitled to be compensated as specified, but the court may allow more or less compensation if:

(a) The duties of the trustee are substantially different from those contemplated when the trust was created; or

(b) The compensation specified by the terms of the trust would be unreasonably low or high.

(3) If the trustee has rendered other services in connection with the administration of the trust, the trustee shall also be allowed reasonable compensation for the other services rendered in addition to reasonable compensation as trustee.
Added by Laws 2006, c. 2006–217, § 7, eff. July 1, 2007.

736.0709. Reimbursement of expenses

(1) A trustee is entitled to be reimbursed out of the trust property, with interest as appropriate, for reasonable expenses that were properly incurred in the administration of the trust.

(2) An advance by the trustee of money for the protection of the trust gives rise to a lien against trust property to secure reimbursement with reasonable interest.
Added by Laws 2006, c. 2006–217, § 7, eff. July 1, 2007.

PART VIII. DUTIES AND POWERS OF TRUSTEE

Cross References

Funeral, cemetery, and consumer services, preneed sales, disposition of proceeds received on contracts, see § 497.458.
Personal representatives, general duties, see § 733.602.

736.0801. Duty to administer trust

Upon acceptance of a trusteeship, the trustee shall administer the trust in good faith, in accordance with its terms and purposes and the interests of the beneficiaries, and in accordance with this code.
Added by Laws 2006, c. 2006–217, § 8, eff. July 1, 2007.

736.0802. Duty of loyalty

(1) As between a trustee and the beneficiaries, a trustee shall administer the trust solely in the interests of the beneficiaries.

(2) Subject to the rights of persons dealing with or assisting the trustee as provided in s. 736.1016, a sale, encumbrance, or other transaction involving the investment or management of trust property entered into by the trustee for the trustee's own personal account or which is otherwise affected by a conflict between the trustee's fiduciary and personal interests is voidable by a beneficiary affected by the transaction unless:

(a) The transaction was authorized by the terms of the trust;

(b) The transaction was approved by the court;

(c) The beneficiary did not commence a judicial proceeding within the time allowed by s. 736.1008;

(d) The beneficiary consented to the trustee's conduct, ratified the transaction, or released the trustee in compliance with s. 736.1012;

(e) The transaction involves a contract entered into or claim acquired by the trustee when that person had not become or contemplated becoming trustee;

(f) The transaction was consented to in writing by a settlor of the trust while the trust was revocable;

(g) The transaction is one by a corporate trustee that involves a money market mutual fund, mutual fund, or a common trust fund described in s. 736.0816(3); or

(h) With regard to a trust that is administered by a family trust company, licensed family trust company, or foreign licensed family trust company operating under chapter 662, the transaction is authorized by s. 662.132(4)–(8).

(3)(a) A sale, encumbrance, or other transaction involving the investment or management of trust property is presumed to be affected by a conflict between personal and fiduciary interests if the sale, encumbrance, or other transaction is entered into by the trustee with:

1. The trustee's spouse;

2. The trustee's descendants, siblings, parents, or their spouses;

3. An officer, director, employee, agent, or attorney of the trustee; or

4. A corporation or other person or enterprise in which the trustee, or a person that owns a significant interest in the trustee, has an interest that might affect the trustee's best judgment.

(b) This subsection does not apply to a trust being administered by a family trust company, licensed family trust company, or foreign licensed family trust company operating under chapter 662 if the sale, encumbrance, or other transaction is authorized by s. 662.132(4)–(8).

(4) A transaction not concerning trust property in which the trustee engages in the trustee's individual capacity involves a conflict between personal and fiduciary interests if the transaction concerns an opportunity properly belonging to the trust.

(5)(a) An investment by a trustee authorized by lawful authority to engage in trust business, as defined in s. 658.12(20), in investment instruments, as defined in s. 660.25(6), that are owned or controlled by the trustee or its affiliate, or from which the trustee or its affiliate receives compensation for providing services in a capacity other than as trustee, is not presumed to be affected by a conflict between personal and fiduciary interests provided the investment otherwise complies with chapters 518 and 660 and the trustee complies with the requirements of this subsection.

(b) A trustee who, pursuant to this subsection, invests trust funds in investment instruments that are owned or controlled by the trustee or its affiliate shall disclose the following to all qualified beneficiaries:

1. Notice that the trustee has invested trust funds in investment instruments owned or controlled by the trustee or its affiliate.

2. The identity of the investment instruments.

3. The identity and relationship to the trustee of any affiliate that owns or controls the investment instruments.

(c) A trustee who, pursuant to this subsection, invests trust funds in investment instruments with respect to which the trustee or its affiliate receives compensation for providing services in a capacity other than as trustee shall disclose to all qualified beneficiaries, the nature of the services provided by the trustee or its affiliate, and all compensation, including, but not limited to, fees or commissions paid or to be paid by the account and received or to be received by an affiliate arising from such affiliated investment.

(d) Disclosure required by this subsection shall be made at least annually unless there has been no change in the method or increase in the rate at which such compensation is calculated since the most recent disclosure. The disclosure may be given in a trust disclosure document as defined in s. 736.1008, in a copy of the prospectus for the investment instrument, in any other written disclosure prepared for the investment instrument under applicable federal or state law, or in a written summary that includes all compensation received or to be received by the trustee and any affiliate of the trustee and an explanation of the manner in which such compensation is calculated, either as a percentage of the assets invested or by some other method.

(e) This subsection shall apply as follows:

1. This subsection does not apply to qualified investment instruments or to a trust for which a right of revocation exists.

2. For investment instruments other than qualified investment instruments, paragraphs (a), (b), (c), and (d) shall apply to irrevocable trusts created on or after July 1, 2007, which expressly authorize the trustee, by specific reference to this subsection, to invest in investment instruments owned or controlled by the trustee or its affiliate.

3. For investment instruments other than qualified investment instruments, paragraphs (a), (b), (c), and (d) shall apply to irrevocable trusts created on or after July 1, 2007, that are not described in subparagraph 2. and to irrevocable trusts created prior to July 1, 2007, only as follows:

a. Such paragraphs shall not apply until the statement required in paragraph (f) is provided and a majority of the qualified beneficiaries have provided written consent. All consents must be obtained within 90 days after the date of delivery of the written request. Once given, consent shall be valid as to all investment instruments acquired pursuant to the consent prior to the date of any withdrawal of the consent.

(I) Any qualified beneficiary may petition the court for an order to prohibit, limit, or restrict a trustee's authority to make investments under this subsection. The burden shall be upon the petitioning beneficiary to show good cause for the relief sought.

(II) The court may award costs and attorney's fees relating to any petition under this subparagraph in the same manner as in chancery actions. When costs and attorney's fees are to be paid out of the trust, the court, in its discretion, may direct from which part of the trust such costs and fees shall be paid.

b.   The consent of a majority of the qualified beneficiaries under this subparagraph may be withdrawn prospectively by written notice of a majority of any one of the class or classes of the qualified beneficiaries.

(f) 1.   The trustee of a trust as defined in s. 731.201 may request authority to invest in investment instruments described in this subsection other than a qualified investment instrument, by providing to all qualified beneficiaries a written request containing the following:

a.   The name, telephone number, street address, and mailing address of the trustee and of any individuals who may be contacted for further information.

b.   A statement that the investment or investments cannot be made without the consent of a majority of each class of the qualified beneficiaries.

c.   A statement that, if a majority of each class of qualified beneficiaries consent, the trustee will have the right to make investments in investment instruments, as defined in s. 660.25(6), which are owned or controlled by the trustee or its affiliate, or from which the trustee or its affiliate receives compensation for providing services in a capacity other than as trustee, that such investment instruments may include investment instruments sold primarily to trust accounts, and that the trustee or its affiliate may receive fees in addition to the trustee's compensation for administering the trust.

d.   A statement that the consent may be withdrawn prospectively at any time by written notice given by a majority of any class of the qualified beneficiaries.

A statement by the trustee is not delivered if the statement is accompanied by another written communication other than a written communication by the trustee that refers only to the statement.

2.   For purposes of paragraph (e) and this paragraph:

a.   "Majority of the qualified beneficiaries" means:

(I) If at the time the determination is made there are one or more beneficiaries as described in s. 736.0103(16)(c), at least a majority in interest of the beneficiaries described in s. 736.0103(16)(a), at least a majority in interest of the beneficiaries described in s. 736.0103(16)(b), and at least a majority in interest of the beneficiaries described in s. 736.0103(16)(c), if the interests of the beneficiaries are reasonably ascertainable; otherwise, a majority in number of each such class; or

(II) If there is no beneficiary as described in s. 736.0103(16)(c), at least a majority in interest of the beneficiaries described in s. 736.0103(16)(a) and at least a majority in interest of the beneficiaries described in s. 736.0103(16)(b), if the interests of the beneficiaries are reasonably ascertainable; otherwise, a majority in number of each such class.

b.   "Qualified investment instrument" means a mutual fund, common trust fund, or money market fund described in and governed by s. 736.0816(3).

c.   An irrevocable trust is created upon execution of the trust instrument.   If a trust that was revocable when created thereafter becomes irrevocable, the irrevocable trust is created when the right of revocation terminates.

(g) Nothing in this chapter is intended to create or imply a duty for the trustee to seek the application of this subsection to invest in investment instruments described in paragraph (a), and no inference of impropriety may be made as a result of a trustee electing not to invest trust assets in investment instruments described in paragraph (a).

(h) This subsection is not the exclusive authority under this code for investing in investment instruments described in paragraph (a). A trustee who invests trust funds in investment instruments described in paragraph (a) is not required to comply with paragraph (b), paragraph (c), or paragraph (f) if the trustee is permitted to invest in such investment instruments pursuant to subsection (2).

(i) This subsection does not apply to a trust administered by a family trust company, licensed family trust company, or foreign licensed family trust company operating under chapter 662.

(6) In voting shares of stock or in exercising powers of control over similar interests in other forms of enterprise, the trustee shall act in the best interests of the beneficiaries. If the trust is the sole owner of a corporation or other form of enterprise, the trustee shall elect or appoint directors or other managers who will manage the corporation or enterprise in the best interests of the beneficiaries.

(7) This section does not preclude the following transactions, if fair to the beneficiaries:

(a) An agreement between a trustee and a beneficiary relating to the appointment or compensation of the trustee;

(b) A payment of reasonable compensation to the trustee;

(c) A transaction between a trust and another trust, the decedent's estate, or a guardian of the property of which the trustee is a fiduciary or in which a beneficiary has an interest;

(d) A deposit of trust money in a regulated financial service institution operated by the trustee; or

(e) An advance by the trustee of money for the protection of the trust.

(8) This section does not preclude the employment of persons, including, but not limited to, attorneys, accountants, investment advisers, or agents, even if they are the trustee, an affiliate of the trustee, or otherwise associated with the trustee, to advise or assist the trustee in the exercise of any of the trustee's powers and to pay reasonable compensation and costs incurred in connection with such employment from the assets of the trust; to act without independent investigation on their recommendations; and, instead of acting personally, to employ one or more agents to perform any act of administration, whether or not discretionary.

(9) The court may appoint a special fiduciary to act with respect to any proposed transaction that might violate this section if entered into by the trustee.

(10) Payment of costs or attorney's fees incurred in any proceeding from the assets of the trust may be made by the trustee without the approval of any person and without court authorization, unless the court orders otherwise as provided in paragraph (b).

(a) If a claim or defense based upon a breach of trust is made against a trustee in a proceeding, the trustee shall provide written notice to each qualified beneficiary of the trust whose share of the trust may be affected by the payment of attorney's fees and costs of the intention to pay costs or attorney's fees incurred in the proceeding from the trust prior to making payment. The written notice shall be delivered by sending a copy by any commercial delivery service requiring a signed receipt, by any form of mail requiring a signed receipt, or as provided in the Florida Rules of Civil Procedure for service of process. The written notice shall inform each qualified beneficiary of the trust whose share of the trust may be affected by the payment of attorney's fees and costs of the right to apply to the court for an order prohibiting the trustee from paying attorney's fees or costs from trust assets. If a trustee is served with a motion for an order prohibiting the trustee from paying attorney's fees or costs in the proceeding and the trustee pays attorney's fees or costs before an order is entered on the motion, the trustee and the trustee's attorneys who have been paid attorney's fees or costs from trust assets to defend against the claim or defense are subject to the remedies in paragraphs (b) and (c).

(b) If a claim or defense based upon breach of trust is made against a trustee in a proceeding, a party must obtain a court order to prohibit the trustee from paying costs or attorney's fees from trust assets. To obtain an order prohibiting payment of costs or attorney's fees from trust assets, a party must make a reasonable showing by evidence in the record or by proffering evidence that provides a reasonable basis for a court to conclude that there has been a breach of trust. The trustee may proffer evidence to rebut the evidence submitted by a party. The court in its discretion may defer ruling on the motion, pending discovery to be taken by the parties. If the court finds that there is a reasonable basis to conclude that there has been a breach of trust, unless the court finds good cause, the court shall enter an order prohibiting the payment of further attorney's fees and costs from the assets of the trust and shall order attorney's fees or costs previously paid from assets of the trust to be refunded. An order entered under this paragraph shall not limit a trustee's right to seek an order permitting the payment of some or all of the attorney's fees or costs incurred in the proceeding from trust assets, including any fees required to be refunded, after the claim or defense is finally determined by the court. If a claim or defense based upon a breach of trust is withdrawn, dismissed, or resolved without a determination by the court that the trustee committed a breach of trust after the entry of an order prohibiting payment of attorney's fees and costs pursuant to this paragraph, the trustee may pay costs or attorney's fees incurred in the proceeding from the assets of the trust without further court authorization.

(c) If the court orders a refund under paragraph (b), the court may enter such sanctions as are appropriate if a refund is not made as directed by the court, including, but not limited to, striking defenses or pleadings filed by the trustee. Nothing in this subsection limits other remedies and sanctions the court may employ for the failure to refund timely.

(d) Nothing in this subsection limits the power of the court to review fees and costs or the right of any interested persons to challenge fees and costs after payment, after an accounting, or after conclusion of the litigation.

(e) Notice under paragraph (a) is not required if the action or defense is later withdrawn or dismissed by the party that is alleging a breach of trust or resolved without a determination by the court that the trustee has committed a breach of trust.

Added by Laws 2006, c. 2006–217, § 8, eff. July 1, 2007. Amended by Laws 2007, c. 2007–153, § 3, eff. July 1, 2007; Laws 2008, c. 2008–4, § 159, eff. July 1, 2008; Laws 2008, c. 2008–76, § 2, eff. July 1, 2008; Laws 2009, c. 2009–115, § 20, eff. July 1, 2009; Laws 2013, c. 2013–172, § 18, eff. Oct. 1, 2013; Laws 2014, c. 2014–97, § 38, eff. Oct. 1, 2015.

Cross References

Family trust companies, investments, see F.S.A. § 662.132.

736.0803. Impartiality

If a trust has two or more beneficiaries, the trustee shall act impartially in administering the trust property, giving due regard to the beneficiaries' respective interests.

Added by Laws 2006, c. 2006–217, § 8, eff. July 1, 2007.

736.0804. Prudent administration

A trustee shall administer the trust as a prudent person would, by considering the purposes, terms, distribution requirements, and other circumstances of the trust. In satisfying this standard, the trustee shall exercise reasonable care, skill, and caution.

Added by Laws 2006, c. 2006–217, § 8, eff. July 1, 2007.

736.0805. Expenses of administration

In administering a trust, the trustee shall only incur expenses that are reasonable in relation to the trust property, the purposes of the trust, and the skills of the trustee.

Added by Laws 2006, c. 2006–217, § 8, eff. July 1, 2007.

736.0806. Trustee's skills

A trustee who has special skills or expertise, or is named trustee in reliance on the trustee's representation that the trustee has special skills or expertise, shall use those special skills or expertise.

Added by Laws 2006, c. 2006–217, § 8, eff. July 1, 2007.

736.0807. Delegation by trustee

(1) A trustee may delegate duties and powers that a prudent trustee of comparable skills could properly delegate under the circumstances, including investment functions pursuant to s. 518.112. The trustee shall exercise reasonable care, skill, and caution in:

(a) Selecting an agent.

(b) Establishing the scope and terms of the delegation, consistent with the purposes and terms of the trust.

(c) Reviewing the agent's actions periodically, in order to monitor the agent's performance and compliance with the terms of the delegation.

(2) In performing a delegated function, an agent owes a duty to the trust to exercise reasonable care to comply with the terms of the delegation.

(3) A trustee who complies with subsection (1) and, when investment functions are delegated, s. 518.112 is not liable to the beneficiaries or to the trust for an action of the agent to whom the function was delegated.

Added by Laws 2006, c. 2006–217, § 8, eff. July 1, 2007. Amended by Laws 2009, c. 2009–117, § 6, eff. July 1, 2009; Laws 2013, c. 2013–172, § 13, eff. Oct. 1, 2013.

736.0808. Powers to direct

(1) Subject to ss. 736.0403(2) and 736.0602(3)(a), the trustee may follow a direction of the settlor that is contrary to the terms of the trust while a trust is revocable.

(2) If the terms of a trust confer on a person other than the settlor of a revocable trust the power to direct certain actions of the trustee, the trustee shall act in accordance with an exercise of the power unless the attempted exercise is manifestly contrary to the terms of the trust or the trustee knows the attempted exercise would constitute a serious breach of a fiduciary duty that the person holding the power owes to the beneficiaries of the trust.

(3) The terms of a trust may confer on a trustee or other person a power to direct the modification or termination of the trust.

(4) A person, other than a beneficiary, who holds a power to direct is presumptively a fiduciary who, as such, is required to act in good faith with regard to the purposes of the trust and the interests of the beneficiaries. The holder of a power to direct is liable for any loss that results from breach of a fiduciary duty.

Added by Laws 2006, c. 2006–217, § 8, eff. July 1, 2007.

736.0809. Control and protection of trust property

A trustee shall take reasonable steps to take control of and protect the trust property.

Added by Laws 2006, c. 2006–217, § 8, eff. July 1, 2007.

736.0810. Recordkeeping and identification of trust property

(1) A trustee shall keep clear, distinct, and accurate records of the administration of the trust.

(2) A trustee shall keep trust property separate from the trustee's own property.

(3) Except as otherwise provided in subsection (4), a trustee shall cause the trust property to be designated so that the interest of the trust, to the extent feasible, appears in records maintained by a party other than a trustee or beneficiary.

(4) If the trustee maintains records clearly indicating the respective interests, a trustee may invest as a whole the property of two or more separate trusts.

Added by Laws 2006, c. 2006–217, § 8, eff. July 1, 2007.

736.08105. Duty to ascertain marketable title of trust real property

A trustee holding title to real property received from a settlor or estate shall not be required to obtain title insurance or proof of marketable title until a marketable title is required for a sale or conveyance of the real property.

Added by Laws 2006, c. 2006–217, § 8, eff. July 1, 2007.

736.0811. Enforcement and defense of claims

A trustee shall take reasonable steps to enforce claims of the trust and to defend claims against the trust.

Added by Laws 2006, c. 2006–217, § 8, eff. July 1, 2007.

736.0812. Collecting trust property

A trustee shall take reasonable steps to compel a former trustee or other person to deliver trust property to the trustee and, except as provided in s. 736.08125, to redress a breach of trust known to the trustee to have been committed by a former trustee.

Added by Laws 2006, c. 2006–217, § 8, eff. July 1, 2007.

736.08125. Protection of successor trustees

(1) A successor trustee is not personally liable for actions taken by any prior trustee, nor does any successor trustee have a duty to institute any proceeding against any prior trustee, or file any claim against any prior trustee's estate, for any of the prior trustee's actions as trustee under any of the following circumstances:

(a) As to a successor trustee who succeeds a trustee who was also the settlor of a trust that was revocable during the time that the settlor served as trustee;

(b) As to any beneficiary who has waived any accounting required by s. 736.0813, but only as to the periods included in the waiver;

(c) As to any beneficiary who has released the successor trustee from the duty to institute any proceeding or file any claim;

(d) As to any person who is not an eligible beneficiary; or

(e) As to any eligible beneficiary:

1. If a super majority of the eligible beneficiaries have released the successor trustee;

2. If the eligible beneficiary has not delivered a written request to the successor trustee to institute an action or file a claim against the prior trustee within 6 months after the date of the successor trustee's acceptance of the trust, if the successor trustee has notified the eligible beneficiary in writing of acceptance by the successor trustee in accordance with s. 736.0813(1)(a) and that writing advises the beneficiary that, unless the beneficiary delivers the written request within 6 months after the date of acceptance, the right to proceed against the successor trustee will be barred pursuant to this section; or

3. For any action or claim that the eligible beneficiary is barred from bringing against the prior trustee.

(2) For the purposes of this section, the term:

(a) "Eligible beneficiaries" means:

1. At the time the determination is made, if there are one or more beneficiaries as described in s. 736.0103(16)(c), the beneficiaries described in s. 736.0103(16)(a) and (c); or

2. If there is no beneficiary as described in s. 736.0103(16)(c), the beneficiaries described in s. 736.0103(16)(a) and (b).

(b) "Super majority of eligible beneficiaries" means at least two-thirds in interest of the eligible beneficiaries if the interests of the eligible beneficiaries are reasonably ascertainable, otherwise, at least two-thirds in number of the eligible beneficiaries.

(3) Nothing in this section affects any liability of the prior trustee or the right of the successor trustee or any beneficiary to pursue an action or claim against the prior trustee.

Added by Laws 2006, c. 2006–217, § 8, eff. July 1, 2007. Amended by Laws 2013, c. 2013–172, § 19, eff. Oct. 1, 2013.

Cross References

Timeshare plans,
   Subordination instruments, see § 721.53
   Trusts, see § 721.08.

736.0813. Duty to inform and account

The trustee shall keep the qualified beneficiaries of the trust reasonably informed of the trust and its administration.

(1) The trustee's duty to inform and account includes, but is not limited to, the following:

(a) Within 60 days after acceptance of the trust, the trustee shall give notice to the qualified beneficiaries of the acceptance of the trust, the full name and address of the trustee, and that the fiduciary lawyer-client privilege in s. 90.5021 applies with respect to the trustee and any attorney employed by the trustee.

(b) Within 60 days after the date the trustee acquires knowledge of the creation of an irrevocable trust, or the date the trustee acquires knowledge that a formerly revocable trust has become irrevocable, whether by the death of the settlor or otherwise, the trustee shall give notice to the qualified beneficiaries of the trust's existence, the identity of the settlor or settlors, the right to request a copy of the trust instrument, the right to accountings under this section, and that the fiduciary lawyer-client privilege in s. 90.5021 applies with respect to the trustee and any attorney employed by the trustee.

(c) Upon reasonable request, the trustee shall provide a qualified beneficiary with a complete copy of the trust instrument.

(d) A trustee of an irrevocable trust shall provide a trust accounting, as set forth in s. 736.08135, from the date of the last accounting or, if none, from the date on which the trustee became accountable, to each qualified beneficiary at least annually and on termination of the trust or on change of the trustee.

(e) Upon reasonable request, the trustee shall provide a qualified beneficiary with relevant information about the assets and liabilities of the trust and the particulars relating to administration.

Paragraphs (a) and (b) do not apply to an irrevocable trust created before the effective date of this code, or to a revocable trust that becomes irrevocable before the effective date of this code. Paragraph (a) does not apply to a trustee who accepts a trusteeship before the effective date of this code.

(2) A qualified beneficiary may waive the trustee's duty to account under paragraph (1)(d). A qualified beneficiary may withdraw a waiver previously given. Waivers and withdrawals of prior waivers under this subsection must be in writing. Withdrawals of prior waivers are effective only with respect to accountings for future periods.

(3) The representation provisions of part III apply with respect to all rights of a qualified beneficiary under this section.

(4) As provided in s. 736.0603(1), the trustee's duties under this section extend only to the settlor while a trust is revocable.

(5) This section applies to trust accountings rendered for accounting periods beginning on or after July 1, 2007.

Added by Laws 2006, c. 2006–217, § 8, eff. July 1, 2007. Amended by Laws 2007, c. 2007–153, § 15, eff. July 1, 2007; Laws 2011, c. 2011–183, § 11, eff. June 21, 2011; Laws 2013, c. 2013–172, § 14, eff. Oct. 1, 2013.

Cross References

Trust business, fiduciary fund investment, syndicate securities, see § 660.418.

736.08135. Trust accountings

(1) A trust accounting must be a reasonably understandable report from the date of the last accounting or, if none, from the date on which the trustee became accountable, that adequately discloses the information required in subsection (2).

(2)(a) The accounting must begin with a statement identifying the trust, the trustee furnishing the accounting, and the time period covered by the accounting.

(b) The accounting must show all cash and property transactions and all significant transactions affecting administration during the accounting period, including compensation paid to the trustee and the trustee's agents. Gains and losses realized during the accounting period and all receipts and disbursements must be shown.

(c) To the extent feasible, the accounting must identify and value trust assets on hand at the close of the accounting period. For each asset or class of assets reasonably capable of valuation, the accounting shall contain two values, the asset acquisition value or carrying value and the estimated current value. The accounting must identify each known noncontingent liability with an estimated current amount of the liability if known.

(d) To the extent feasible, the accounting must show significant transactions that do not affect the amount for which the trustee is accountable, including name changes in investment holdings, adjustments to carrying value, a change of custodial institutions, and stock splits.

(e) The accounting must reflect the allocation of receipts, disbursements, accruals, or allowances between income and principal when the allocation affects the interest of any beneficiary of the trust.

(f) The trustee shall include in the final accounting a plan of distribution for any undistributed assets shown on the final accounting.

(3) This section applies to all trust accountings rendered for any accounting periods beginning on or after January 1, 2003.

Added by Laws 2006, c. 2006–217, § 8, eff. July 1, 2007.

736.0814. Discretionary powers; tax savings

(1) Notwithstanding the breadth of discretion granted to a trustee in the terms of the trust, including the use of such terms as "absolute," "sole," or "uncontrolled," the trustee shall exercise a discretionary power in good faith and in accordance with the terms and purposes of the trust and the interests of the beneficiaries. A court shall not determine that a trustee abused its discretion merely because the court would have exercised the discretion in a different manner or would not have exercised the discretion.

(2) Subject to subsection (3) and unless the terms of the trust expressly indicate that a rule in this subsection does not apply, a person who is a beneficiary and a trustee may not:

(a) Make discretionary distributions of either principal or income to or for the benefit of that trustee, except to provide for that trustee's health, education, maintenance, or support as described under ss. 2041 and 2514 of the Internal Revenue Code;[1]

(b) Make discretionary allocations of receipts or expenses as between principal and income, unless the trustee acts in a fiduciary capacity whereby the trustee has no power to enlarge or shift any beneficial interest except as an incidental consequence of the discharge of the trustee's fiduciary duties;

(c) Make discretionary distributions of either principal or income to satisfy any of the trustee's legal support obligations; or

(d) Exercise any other power, including, but not limited to, the right to remove or to replace any trustee, so as to cause the powers enumerated in paragraph (a), paragraph (b), or paragraph (c) to be exercised on behalf of, or for the benefit of, a beneficiary who is also a trustee.

(3) Subsection (2) does not apply to:

(a) A power held by the settlor of the trust;

(b) A power held by the settlor's spouse who is the trustee of a trust for which a marital deduction, as defined in s. 2056(a) or s. 2523(a) of the Internal Revenue Code of 1986, as amended,[2] was previously allowed;

(c) Any trust during any period that the trust may be revoked or amended by its settlor; or

(d) A trust if contributions to the trust qualify for the annual exclusion under s. 2503(c) of the Internal Revenue Code of 1986, as amended.[3]

(4) A power whose exercise is limited or prohibited by subsection (2) may be exercised by the remaining trustees whose exercise of the power is not so limited or prohibited. If there is no trustee qualified to exercise the power, on petition by any qualified beneficiary, the court may appoint an independent trustee with authority to exercise the power.

(5) A person who has the right to remove or to replace a trustee does not possess nor may that person be deemed to possess, by virtue of having that right, the powers of the trustee that is subject to removal or to replacement.

Added by Laws 2006, c. 2006–217, § 8, eff. July 1, 2007.

[1] 26 U.S.C.A. §§ 2041 and 2514.
[2] 26 U.S.C.A. § 2056(a) or § 2523(a).
[3] 26 U.S.C.A. § 2503(c).

736.08147.   Duty to distribute trust income

If a will or trust instrument granting income to the settlor's or testator's spouse for life is silent as to the time of distribution of income and the frequency of distributions, the trustee shall distribute all net income, as defined in chapter 738, to the spouse no less frequently than annually. This provision shall apply to any trust established before, on, or after July 1, 2007, unless the trust instrument expressly directs or permits net income to be distributed less frequently than annually.

Added by Laws 2006, c. 2006–217, § 8, eff. July 1, 2007.

736.0815.   General powers of trustee

(1) A trustee, without authorization by the court, may, except as limited or restricted by this code, exercise:

(a) Powers conferred by the terms of the trust.

(b) Except as limited by the terms of the trust:

1. All powers over the trust property that an unmarried competent owner has over individually owned property.

2. Any other powers appropriate to achieve the proper investment, management, and distribution of the trust property.

3. Any other powers conferred by this code.

(2) The exercise of a power is subject to the fiduciary duties prescribed by this code.

Added by Laws 2006, c. 2006–217, § 8, eff. July 1, 2007.

736.0816.   Specific powers of trustee

Except as limited or restricted by this code, a trustee may:

(1) Collect trust property and accept or reject additions to the trust property from a settlor, including an asset in which the trustee is personally interested, and hold property in the name of a nominee or in other form without disclosure of the trust so that title to the property may pass by delivery but the trustee is liable for any act of the nominee in connection with the property so held.

(2) Acquire or sell property, for cash or on credit, at public or private sale.

(3) Acquire an undivided interest in a trust asset, including, but not limited to, a money market mutual fund, mutual fund, or common trust fund, in which asset the trustee holds an undivided interest in any trust capacity, including any money market or other mutual fund from which the trustee or any affiliate or associate of the trustee is entitled to receive reasonable compensation for providing necessary services as an investment adviser, portfolio manager, or servicing agent. A trustee or affiliate or associate of the trustee may receive compensation for such services in addition to fees received for administering the trust provided such compensation is fully disclosed in writing to all qualified beneficiaries. As used in this subsection, the term "mutual fund" includes an open-end or closed-end management investment company or investment trust registered under the Investment Company Act of 1940, 15 U.S.C. ss. 80a–1 et seq., as amended.

(4) Exchange, partition, or otherwise change the character of trust property.

(5) Deposit trust money in an account in a regulated financial service institution.

(6) Borrow money, with or without security, and mortgage or pledge trust property for a period within or extending beyond the duration of the trust and advance money for the protection of the trust.

(7) With respect to an interest in a proprietorship, partnership, limited liability company, business trust, corporation, or other form of business or enterprise, continue the business or other enterprise and take any action that may be taken by shareholders, members, or property owners, including, but not limited to, merging, dissolving, or otherwise changing the form of business organization or contributing additional capital.

(8) With respect to stocks or other securities, exercise the rights of an absolute owner, including, but not limited to, the right to:

(a) Vote, or give proxies to vote, with or without power of substitution, or enter into or continue a voting trust agreement.

(b) Hold a security in the name of a nominee or in other form without disclosure of the trust so that title may pass by delivery.

(c) Pay calls, assessments, and other sums chargeable or accruing against the securities, and sell or exercise stock subscription or conversion rights.

(d) Deposit the securities with a depositary or other regulated financial service institution.

(9) With respect to an interest in real property, construct, or make ordinary or extraordinary repairs to, alterations to, or improvements in, buildings or other structures, demolish improvements, raze existing or erect new party walls or buildings, subdivide or develop land, dedicate land to public use or grant public or private easements, and make or vacate plats and adjust boundaries.

(10) Enter into a lease for any purpose as lessor or lessee, including a lease or other arrangement for exploration and removal of natural resources, with or without the option to purchase or renew, for a period within or extending beyond the duration of the trust.

(11) Grant an option involving a sale, lease, or other disposition of trust property or acquire an option for the acquisition of property, including an option exercisable beyond the duration of the trust, and exercise an option so acquired.

(12) Insure the property of the trust against damage or loss and insure the trustee, trustee's agents, and beneficiaries against liability arising from the administration of the trust.

(13) Abandon or decline to administer property of no value or of insufficient value to justify the collection or continued administration of such property.

(14) Pay or contest any claim, settle a claim by or against the trust, and release, in whole or in part, a claim belonging to the trust.

(15) Pay taxes, assessments, compensation of the trustee and of employees and agents of the trust, and other expenses incurred in the administration of the trust.

(16) Allocate items of income or expense to trust income or principal, as provided by law.

(17) Exercise elections with respect to federal, state, and local taxes.

(18) Select a mode of payment under any employee benefit or retirement plan, annuity, or life insurance payable to the trustee, exercise rights under such plan, annuity, or insurance, including exercise of the right to indemnification for expenses and against liabilities, and take appropriate action to collect the proceeds.

(19) Make loans out of trust property, including, but not limited to, loans to a beneficiary on terms and conditions that are fair and reasonable under the circumstances, and the trustee has a lien on future distributions for repayment of those loans.

(20) Employ persons, including, but not limited to, attorneys, accountants, investment advisers, or agents, even if they are the trustee, an affiliate of the trustee, or otherwise associated with the trustee, to advise or assist the trustee in the exercise of any of the trustee's powers and pay reasonable compensation and costs incurred in connection with such employment from the assets of the trust and act without independent investigation on the recommendations of such persons.

(21) Pay an amount distributable to a beneficiary who is under a legal disability or who the trustee reasonably believes is incapacitated, by paying the amount directly to the beneficiary or applying the amount for the beneficiary's benefit, or by:

(a) Paying the amount to the beneficiary's guardian of the property or, if the beneficiary does not have a guardian of the property, the beneficiary's guardian of the person;

(b) Paying the amount to the beneficiary's custodian under a Uniform Transfers to Minors Act [1] or custodial trustee under a Uniform Custodial Trust Act, and, for that purpose, creating a custodianship or custodial trust;

(c) Paying the amount to an adult relative or other person having legal or physical care or custody of the beneficiary, to be expended on the beneficiary's behalf, if the trustee does not know of a guardian of the property, guardian of the person, custodian, or custodial trustee; or

(d) Managing the amount as a separate fund on the beneficiary's behalf, subject to the beneficiary's continuing right to withdraw the distribution.

(22) On distribution of trust property or the division or termination of a trust, make distributions in divided or undivided interests, allocate particular assets in proportionate or disproportionate shares, value the trust property for those purposes, and adjust for resulting differences in valuation.

(23) Prosecute or defend, including appeals, an action, claim, or judicial proceeding in any jurisdiction to protect trust property or the trustee in the performance of the trustee's duties.

(24) Sign and deliver contracts and other instruments that are useful to achieve or facilitate the exercise of the trustee's powers.

(25) On termination of the trust, exercise the powers appropriate to wind up the administration of the trust and distribute the trust property to the persons entitled to the property, subject

to the right of the trustee to retain a reasonable reserve for the payment of debts, expenses, and taxes.

Added by Laws 2006, c. 2006–217, § 8, eff. July 1, 2007. Amended by Laws 2007, c. 2007–153, § 4, eff. July 1, 2007.

[1] See F.S.A. § 710.101 et seq.

736.08163. Powers of trustees relating to environmental or human health laws or to trust property contaminated with hazardous or toxic substances; liability

(1) From the creation of a trust until final distribution of the assets from the trust, the trustee has, without court authorization, the powers specified in subsection (2).

(2) Unless otherwise provided in the trust instrument, a trustee has the power, acting reasonably, to:

(a) Inspect or investigate, or cause to be inspected or investigated, property held by the trustee, including interests in sole proprietorships, partnerships, or corporations and any assets owned by any such business entity for the purpose of determining compliance with an environmental law affecting that property or to respond to an actual or threatened violation of an environmental law affecting that property;

(b) Take, on behalf of the trust, any action necessary to prevent, abate, or otherwise remedy an actual or potential violation of an environmental law affecting property held by the trustee, before or after initiation of an enforcement action by a governmental body;

(c) Refuse to accept property in trust if the trustee determines that any property to be donated or conveyed to the trustee is contaminated with a hazardous substance or is being used or has been used for an activity directly or indirectly involving a hazardous substance, which circumstance could result in liability to the trust or trustee or otherwise impair the value of the assets to be held;

(d) Settle or compromise at any time any claim against the trust or trustee that may be asserted by a governmental body or private party that involves the alleged violation of an environmental law affecting property of any trust over which the trustee has responsibility;

(e) Disclaim any power granted by any document, law, or rule of law that, in the sole judgment of the trustee, may cause the trustee to incur personal liability, or the trust to incur liability, under any environmental law;

(f) Decline to serve as a trustee, or having undertaken to serve as a trustee, resign at any time, if the trustee believes there is or may be a conflict of interest in its fiduciary capacity and in its individual capacity because of potential claims or liabilities that may be asserted against the trustee on behalf of the trust by reason of the type or condition of the assets held; or

(g) Charge against the income and principal of the trust the cost of any inspection, investigation, review, abatement, response, cleanup, or remedial action that this section authorizes the trustee to take and, if the trust terminates or closes or the trust property is transferred to another trustee, hold assets sufficient to cover the cost of cleaning up any known environmental problem.

(3) A trustee is not personally liable to any beneficiary or any other person for a decrease in value of assets in a trust by reason of the trustee's compliance or efforts to comply with an environmental law, specifically including any reporting requirement under that law.

(4) A trustee that acquires ownership or control of a vessel or other property, without having owned, operated, or materially participated in the management of that vessel or property before

assuming ownership or control as trustee, is not considered an owner or operator for purposes of liability under chapter 376, chapter 403, or any other environmental law. A trustee that willfully, knowingly, or recklessly causes or exacerbates a release or threatened release of a hazardous substance is personally liable for the cost of the response, to the extent that the release or threatened release is attributable to the trustee's activities. This subsection does not preclude the filing of claims against the assets that constitute the trust held by the trustee or the filing of actions against the trustee in its representative capacity and in any such action, an award or judgment against the trustee must be satisfied only from the assets of the trust.

(5) The acceptance by the trustee of the property or a failure by the trustee to inspect or investigate the property does not create any inference as to whether there is liability under an environmental law with respect to that property.

(6) For the purposes of this section, the term "hazardous substance" means a substance defined as hazardous or toxic, or any contaminant, pollutant, or constituent thereof, or otherwise regulated, by an environmental law.

(7) This section does not apply to any trust created under a document executed before July 1, 1995, unless the trust is amendable and the settlor amends the trust at any time to incorporate the provisions of this section.

Added by Laws 2006, c. 2006–217, § 8, eff. July 1, 2007.

Cross References

Timeshare plans,
   Subordination instruments, see § 721.53
   Trusts, see § 721.08.

736.08165. Administration pending outcome of contest or other proceeding

(1) Pending the outcome of a proceeding filed to determine the validity of all or part of a trust or the beneficiaries of all or part of a trust, the trustee shall proceed with the administration of the trust as if no proceeding had been commenced, except no action may be taken and no distribution may be made to a beneficiary in contravention of the rights of those persons who may be affected by the outcome of the proceeding.

(2) Upon motion of a party and after notice to interested persons, a court, on good cause shown, may make an exception to the prohibition under subsection (1) and authorize the trustee to act or to distribute trust assets to a beneficiary subject to any conditions the court, in the court's discretion, may impose, including the posting of bond by the beneficiary.

Added by Laws 2006, c. 2006–217, § 8, eff. July 1, 2007.

736.0817. Distribution on termination

Upon the occurrence of an event terminating or partially terminating a trust, the trustee shall proceed expeditiously to distribute the trust property to the persons entitled to the property, subject to the right of the trustee to retain a reasonable reserve for the payment of debts, expenses, and taxes. The provisions of this section are in addition to and are not in derogation of the rights of a trustee under the common law with respect to final distribution of a trust.

Added by Laws 2006, c. 2006–217, § 8, eff. July 1, 2007.

PART IX. TRUST INVESTMENTS

736.0901. Applicability of chapter 518

A trustee shall invest trust property in accordance with chapter 518.
Added by Laws 2006, c. 2006–217, § 9, eff. July 1, 2007.

Cross References

Durable power of attorney, see § 709.2104.

736.0902. Nonapplication of prudent investor rule

(1) Notwithstanding the provisions of s. 518.11 or s. 736.0804, with respect to any contract for life insurance acquired or retained on the life of a qualified person, a trustee has no duty to:

(a) Determine whether the contract of life insurance is or was procured or effected in compliance with s. 627.404;

(b) Determine whether any contract of life insurance is, or remains, a proper investment;

(c) Investigate the financial strength of the life insurance company;

(d) Determine whether to exercise any policy option available under the contract for life insurance;

(e) Diversify any such contract for life insurance or the assets of the trust with respect to the contract for life insurance; or

(f) Inquire about or investigate the health or financial condition of any insureds.

(2) For purposes of this section, a "qualified person" is a person who is insured or a proposed insured, or the spouse of that person, who has provided the trustee with the funds used to acquire or pay premiums with respect to a policy of insurance on the life of that person or the spouse of that person, or on the lives of that person and the spouse of that person.

(3) The trustee is not liable to the beneficiaries of the trust or any other person for any loss sustained with respect to a contract for life insurance to which this section applies.

(4) Unless otherwise provided in the trust instrument, paragraph (1)(a) applies to any contract for life insurance on the life of a qualified person.

(5) Unless otherwise provided in the trust instrument, paragraphs (1)(b)–(f) apply if:

(a) The trust instrument, by reference to this section, makes this section applicable to contracts for life insurance held by the trust; or

(b) The trustee gives notice that this section applies to a contract for life insurance held by the trust.

1. The notice of the application of this section shall be given to the qualified beneficiaries and shall contain a copy or restatement of this section.

2. Notice given pursuant to any of the provisions of part III of this chapter to a person who represents the interests of any of the persons set forth in subparagraph 1. shall be treated as notice to the person so represented.

3. Notice shall be given in the manner provided in s. 736.0109.

4. If any person notified pursuant to this paragraph delivers a written objection to the application of this section to the trustee within 30 days after the date on which the objector received such notice, paragraphs (1)(b)–(f) shall not apply until the objection is withdrawn.

5. There shall exist a rebuttable presumption that any notice sent by United States mail is received 3 days after depositing the notice in the United States mail system with proper postage prepaid.

(6) This section does not apply to any contract for life insurance purchased from any affiliate of the trustee, or with respect to which the trustee or any affiliate of the trustee receives any commission unless the duties have been delegated to another person in accordance with s. 518.112. For purposes of this subsection, an "affiliate" is any person who controls, is controlled by, or is under common control with the trustee.

(7) Paragraph (1)(a) does not apply if the trustee applied for or accepted ownership of a contract of life insurance and the trustee had knowledge that:

(a) The benefits were not payable to a person specified in s. 627.404 when the contract of life insurance was issued; or

(b) The contract of life insurance is or was purchased with resources or guarantees directly or indirectly provided by a person who, at the time of the inception of such contract, did not have an insurable interest in the insured as defined by s. 627.404, and, at the time of the inception of such contract, there is a verbal or written arrangement, agreement, or plan with a third party to transfer ownership of the policy or policy benefits in a manner that would be in violation of state law.

(8) A trustee who performs fiduciary or advisory services related to a policy of life insurance to which subsection (1) applies shall not be compensated for performing the applicable service to which subsection (1) applies.

Added by Laws 2010, c. 2010–172, § 1, eff. July 1, 2010.

PART X. LIABILITY OF TRUSTEE AND RIGHTS
OF PERSONS DEALING WITH TRUSTEE

736.1001. Remedies for breach of trust

(1) A violation by a trustee of a duty the trustee owes to a beneficiary is a breach of trust.

(2) To remedy a breach of trust that has occurred or may occur, the court may:

(a) Compel the trustee to perform the trustee's duties;

(b) Enjoin the trustee from committing a breach of trust;

(c) Compel the trustee to redress a breach of trust by paying money or restoring property or by other means;

(d) Order a trustee to account;

(e) Appoint a special fiduciary to take possession of the trust property and administer the trust;

(f) Suspend the trustee;

(g) Remove the trustee as provided in s. 736.0706;

(h) Reduce or deny compensation to the trustee;

(i) Subject to s. 736.1016, void an act of the trustee, impose a lien or a constructive trust on trust property, or trace trust property wrongfully disposed of and recover the property or its proceeds; or

(j) Order any other appropriate relief.

(3) As an illustration of the remedies available to the court and without limiting the court's discretion as provided in subsection (2), if a breach of trust results in the favoring of any beneficiary to the detriment of any other beneficiary or consists of an abuse of the trustee's discretion:

(a) To the extent the breach of trust has resulted in no distribution to a beneficiary or a distribution that is too small, the court may require the trustee to pay from the trust to the beneficiary an amount the court determines will restore the beneficiary, in whole or in part, to his or her appropriate position.

(b) To the extent the breach of trust has resulted in a distribution to a beneficiary that is too large, the court may restore the beneficiaries, the trust, or both, in whole or in part, to their appropriate positions by requiring the trustee to withhold an amount from one or more future distributions to the beneficiary who received the distribution that was too large or by requiring that beneficiary to return some or all of the distribution to the trust.

Added by Laws 2006, c. 2006–217, § 10, eff. July 1, 2007. Amended by Laws 2007, c. 2007–5, § 147, eff. July 3, 2007; Laws 2007, c. 2007–153, § 19, eff. July 1, 2007.

736.1002. Damages for breach of trust

(1) A trustee who commits a breach of trust is liable for the greater of:

(a) The amount required to restore the value of the trust property and trust distributions to what they would have been if the breach had not occurred, including lost income, capital gain, or appreciation that would have resulted from proper administration; or

(b) The profit the trustee made by reason of the breach.

(2) Except as otherwise provided in this subsection, if more than one person, including a trustee or trustees, is liable to the beneficiaries for a breach of trust, each liable person is entitled to pro rata contribution from the other person or persons. A person is not entitled to contribution if the person committed the breach of trust in bad faith. A person who received a benefit from the breach of trust is not entitled to contribution from another person to the extent of the benefit received.

(3) In determining the pro rata shares of liable persons in the entire liability for a breach of trust:

(a) Their relative degrees of fault shall be the basis for allocation of liability.

(b) If equity requires, the collective liability of some as a group shall constitute a single share.

(c) Principles of equity applicable to contribution generally shall apply.

(4) The right of contribution shall be enforced as follows:

(a) Contribution may be enforced by separate action, whether or not judgment has been entered in an action against two or more liable persons for the same breach of trust.

(b) When a judgment has been entered in an action against two or more liable persons for the same breach of trust, contribution may be enforced in that action by judgment in favor of one judgment defendant against any other judgment defendants by motion upon notice to all parties to the action.

(c) If there is a judgment for breach of trust against the liable person seeking contribution, any separate action by that person to enforce contribution must be commenced within 1 year after the judgment has become final by lapse of time for appeal or after appellate review.

(d) If there is no judgment for the breach of trust against the liable person seeking contribution, the person's right of contribution is barred unless the person has:

1. Discharged by payment the common liability within the period of the statute of limitations applicable to the beneficiary's right of action against the liable person and the person has commenced an action for contribution within 1 year after payment, or

2. Agreed, while action is pending against the liable person, to discharge the common liability and has within 1 year after the agreement paid the liability and commenced the person's action for contribution.

(5) The beneficiary's recovery of a judgment for breach of trust against one liable person does not of itself discharge other liable persons from liability for the breach of trust unless the judgment is satisfied. The satisfaction of the judgment does not impair any right of contribution.

(6) The judgment of the court in determining the liability of several defendants to the beneficiary for breach of trust is binding upon such defendants in determining the right of such defendants to contribution.

(7) Subsection (2) applies to all causes of action for breach of trust pending on July 1, 2007, under which causes of action the right of contribution among persons jointly and severally liable is involved and to all causes of action filed after July 1, 2007.

Added by Laws 2006, c. 2006–217, § 10, eff. July 1, 2007.

736.1003. Damages in absence of breach

Absent a breach of trust, a trustee is not liable to a beneficiary for a loss or depreciation in the value of trust property or for not having made a profit.

Added by Laws 2006, c. 2006–217, § 10, eff. July 1, 2007.

736.1004. Attorney's fees and costs

(1)(a) In all actions for breach of fiduciary duty or challenging the exercise of, or failure to exercise, a trustee's powers; and

(b) In proceedings arising under ss. 736.0410–736.0417,

the court shall award taxable costs as in chancery actions, including attorney fees and guardian ad litem fees.

(2) When awarding taxable costs under this section, including attorney fees and guardian ad litem fees, the court, in its discretion, may direct payment from a party's interest, if any, in the trust or enter a judgment that may be satisfied from other property of the party, or both.

Added by Laws 2006, c. 2006–217, § 10, eff. July 1, 2007.

736.1005. Attorney fees for services to the trust

(1) Any attorney who has rendered services to a trust may be awarded reasonable compensation from the trust. The attorney may apply to the court for an order awarding attorney fees and, after notice and service on the trustee and all beneficiaries entitled to an accounting under s. 736.0813, the court shall enter an order on the fee application.

(2) If attorney fees are to be paid from the trust under subsection (1), s. 736.1007(5)(a), or s. 733.106(4)(a), the court, in its discretion, may direct from what part of the trust the fees shall be paid.

(a) All or any part of the attorney fees to be paid from the trust may be assessed against one or more persons' part of the trust in such proportions as the court finds to be just and proper.

(b) In the exercise of its discretion, the court may consider the following factors:

1. The relative impact of an assessment on the estimated value of each person's part of the trust.

2. The amount of attorney fees to be assessed against a person's part of the trust.

3. The extent to which a person whose part of the trust is to be assessed, individually or through counsel, actively participated in the proceeding.

4. The potential benefit or detriment to a person's part of the trust expected from the outcome of the proceeding.

5. The relative strength or weakness of the merits of the claims, defenses, or objections, if any, asserted by a person whose part of the trust is to be assessed.

6. Whether a person whose part of the trust is to be assessed was a prevailing party with respect to one or more claims, defenses, or objections.

7. Whether a person whose part of the trust is to be assessed unjustly caused an increase in the amount of attorney fees incurred by the trustee or another person in connection with the proceeding.

8. Any other relevant fact, circumstance, or equity.

(c) The court may assess a person's part of the trust without finding that the person engaged in bad faith, wrongdoing, or frivolousness.

(3) Except when a trustee's interest may be adverse in a particular matter, the attorney shall give reasonable notice in writing to the trustee of the attorney's retention by an interested person and the attorney's entitlement to fees pursuant to this section. A court may reduce any fee award for services rendered by the attorney prior to the date of actual notice to the trustee, if the actual notice date is later than a date of reasonable notice. In exercising this discretion, the court may exclude compensation for services rendered after the reasonable notice date but before the date of actual notice.

Added by Laws 2006, c. 2006–217, § 10, eff. July 1, 2007. Amended by Laws 2015, c. 2015–27, § 7, eff. July 1, 2015.

Applicability

Laws 2015, c. 2015–27, § 11, provides:

"The amendments made by this act to ss. 733.106, 736.1005, and 736.1006, Florida Statutes, apply to proceedings commenced on or after July 1, 2015. The law in effect before July 1, 2015, applies to proceedings commenced before that date."

Cross References

Wills, effect of dissolved and invalid marriages on disposition of assets, see F.S.A. § 732.703.

736.1006. Costs in trust proceedings

(1) In all trust proceedings, costs may be awarded as in chancery actions.

(2) If costs are to be paid from the trust under subsection (1) or s. 733.106(4)(a), the court, in its discretion, may direct from what part of the trust the costs shall be paid. All or any part of the costs to be paid from the trust may be assessed against one or more persons' part of the trust

in such proportions as the court finds to be just and proper. In the exercise of its discretion, the court may consider the factors set forth in s. 736.1005(2).

Added by Laws 2006, c. 2006–217, § 10, eff. July 1, 2007. Amended by Laws 2015, c. 2015–27, § 8, eff. July 1, 2015.

Applicability

Laws 2015, c. 2015–27, § 11, provides:

"The amendments made by this act to ss. 733.106, 736.1005, and 736.1006, Florida Statutes, apply to proceedings commenced on or after July 1, 2015. The law in effect before July 1, 2015, applies to proceedings commenced before that date."

736.1007. Trustee's attorney's fees

(1) If the trustee of a revocable trust retains an attorney to render legal services in connection with the initial administration of the trust, the attorney is entitled to reasonable compensation for those legal services, payable from the assets of the trust without court order. The trustee and the attorney may agree to compensation that is determined in a manner or amount other than the manner or amount provided in this section. The agreement is not binding on a person who bears the impact of the compensation unless that person is a party to or otherwise consents to be bound by the agreement. The agreement may provide that the trustee is not individually liable for the attorney's fees and costs.

(2) Unless otherwise agreed, compensation based on the value of the trust assets immediately following the settlor's death and the income earned by the trust during initial administration at the rate of 75 percent of the schedule provided in s. 733.6171(3)(a)–(h) is presumed to be reasonable total compensation for ordinary services of all attorneys employed generally to advise a trustee concerning the trustee's duties in initial trust administration.

(3) An attorney who is retained to render only limited and specifically defined legal services shall be compensated as provided in the retaining agreement. If the amount or method of determining compensation is not provided in the agreement, the attorney is entitled to a reasonable fee, taking into account the factors set forth in subsection (6).

(4) Ordinary services of the attorney in an initial trust administration include legal advice and representation concerning the trustee's duties relating to:

(a) Review of the trust instrument and each amendment for legal sufficiency and interpretation.

(b) Implementation of substitution of the successor trustee.

(c) Persons who must or should be served with required notices and the method and timing of such service.

(d) The obligation of a successor to require a former trustee to provide an accounting.

(e) The trustee's duty to protect, insure, and manage trust assets and the trustee's liability relating to these duties.

(f) The trustee's duty regarding investments imposed by the prudent investor rule.

(g) The trustee's obligation to inform and account to beneficiaries and the method of satisfaction of such obligations, the liability of the trust and trustee to the settlor's creditors, and the advisability or necessity for probate proceedings to bar creditors.

(h) Contributions due to the personal representative of the settlor's estate for payment of expenses of administration and obligations of the settlor's estate.

(i) Identifying tax returns required to be filed by the trustee, the trustee's liability for payment of taxes, and the due date of returns.

(j) Filing a nontaxable affidavit, if not filed by a personal representative.

(k) Order of payment of expenses of administration of the trust and order and priority of abatement of trust distributions.

(*l*) Distribution of income or principal to beneficiaries or funding of further trusts provided in the governing instrument.

(m) Preparation of any legal documents required to effect distribution.

(n) Fiduciary duties, avoidance of self-dealing, conflicts of interest, duty of impartiality, and obligations to beneficiaries.

(*o*) If there is a conflict of interest between a trustee who is a beneficiary and other beneficiaries of the trust, advice to the trustee on limitations of certain authority of the trustee regarding discretionary distributions or exercise of certain powers and alternatives for appointment of an independent trustee and appropriate procedures.

(p) Procedures for the trustee's discharge from liability for administration of the trust on termination or resignation.

(5) In addition to the attorney's fees for ordinary services, the attorney for the trustee shall be allowed further reasonable compensation for any extraordinary service. What constitutes an extraordinary service may vary depending on many factors, including the size of the trust. Extraordinary services may include, but are not limited to:

(a) Involvement in a trust contest, trust construction, a proceeding for determination of beneficiaries, a contested claim, elective share proceedings, apportionment of estate taxes, or other adversary proceedings or litigation by or against the trust.

(b) Representation of the trustee in an audit or any proceeding for adjustment, determination, or collection of any taxes.

(c) Tax advice on postmortem tax planning, including, but not limited to, disclaimer, renunciation of fiduciary commission, alternate valuation date, allocation of administrative expenses between tax returns, the QTIP or reverse QTIP election, allocation of GST exemption, qualification for Internal Revenue Code ss. 303 and 6166 privileges,[1] deduction of last illness expenses, distribution planning, asset basis considerations, throwback rules, handling income or deductions in respect of a decedent, valuation discounts, special use and other valuation, handling employee benefit or retirement proceeds, prompt assessment request, or request for release from personal liability for payment of tax.

(d) Review of an estate tax return and preparation or review of other tax returns required to be filed by the trustee.

(e) Preparation of decedent's federal estate tax return. If this return is prepared by the attorney, a fee of one-half of 1 percent up to a value of $10 million and one-fourth of 1 percent on the value in excess of $10 million, of the gross estate as finally determined for federal estate tax purposes, is presumed to be reasonable compensation for the attorney for this service. These fees shall include services for routine audit of the return, not beyond the examining agent level, if required.

(f) Purchase, sale, lease, or encumbrance of real property by the trustee or involvement in zoning, land use, environmental, or other similar matters.

(g) Legal advice regarding carrying on of decedent's business or conducting other commercial activity by the trustee.

(h) Legal advice regarding claims for damage to the environment or related procedures.

(i) Legal advice regarding homestead status of trust real property or proceedings involving the status.

(j) Involvement in fiduciary, employee, or attorney compensation disputes.

(k) Considerations of special valuation of trust assets, including discounts for blockage, minority interests, lack of marketability, and environmental liability.

(6) Upon petition of any interested person in a proceeding to review the compensation paid or to be paid to the attorney for the trustee, the court may increase or decrease the compensation for ordinary services of the attorney for the trustee or award compensation for extraordinary services if the facts and circumstances of the particular administration warrant. In determining reasonable compensation, the court shall consider all of the following factors giving such weight to each as the court may determine to be appropriate:

(a) The promptness, efficiency, and skill with which the initial administration was handled by the attorney.

(b) The responsibilities assumed by, and potential liabilities of, the attorney.

(c) The nature and value of the assets that are affected by the decedent's death.

(d) The benefits or detriments resulting to the trust or the trust's beneficiaries from the attorney's services.

(e) The complexity or simplicity of the administration and the novelty of issues presented.

(f) The attorney's participation in tax planning for the estate, the trust, and the trust's beneficiaries and tax return preparation or review and approval.

(g) The nature of the trust assets, the expenses of administration, and the claims payable by the trust and the compensation paid to other professionals and fiduciaries.

(h) Any delay in payment of the compensation after the services were furnished.

(i) Any other relevant factors.

(7) If a separate written agreement regarding compensation exists between the attorney and the settlor, the attorney shall furnish a copy to the trustee prior to commencement of employment and, if employed, shall promptly file and serve a copy on all interested persons. A separate agreement or a provision in the trust suggesting or directing the trustee to retain a specific attorney does not obligate the trustee to employ the attorney or obligate the attorney to accept the representation but, if the attorney who is a party to the agreement or who drafted the trust is employed, the compensation paid shall not exceed the compensation provided in the agreement.

(8) As used in this section, the term "initial trust administration" means administration of a revocable trust during the period that begins with the death of the settlor and ends on the final distribution of trust assets outright or to continuing trusts created under the trust agreement but, if an estate tax return is required, not until after issuance of an estate tax closing letter or

other evidence of termination of the estate tax proceeding.   This initial period is not intended to include continued regular administration of the trust.

Added by Laws 2006, c. 2006–217, § 10, eff. July 1, 2007.   Amended by Laws 2010, c. 2010–122, § 7, eff. July 1, 2010.

[1] See 26 U.S.C.A. §§ 303 and 6166.

736.1008.   Limitations on proceedings against trustees

(1) Except as provided in subsection (2), all claims by a beneficiary against a trustee for breach of trust are barred as provided in chapter 95 as to:

(a) All matters adequately disclosed in a trust disclosure document issued by the trustee, with the limitations period beginning on the date of receipt of adequate disclosure.

(b) All matters not adequately disclosed in a trust disclosure document if the trustee has issued a final trust accounting and has given written notice to the beneficiary of the availability of the trust records for examination and that any claims with respect to matters not adequately disclosed may be barred unless an action is commenced within the applicable limitations period provided in chapter 95.   The limitations period begins on the date of receipt of the final trust accounting and notice.

(2) Unless sooner barred by adjudication, consent, or limitations, a beneficiary is barred from bringing an action against a trustee for breach of trust with respect to a matter that was adequately disclosed in a trust disclosure document unless a proceeding to assert the claim is commenced within 6 months after receipt from the trustee of the trust disclosure document or a limitation notice that applies to that disclosure document, whichever is received later.

(3) When a trustee has not issued a final trust accounting or has not given written notice to the beneficiary of the availability of the trust records for examination and that claims with respect to matters not adequately disclosed may be barred, a claim against the trustee for breach of trust based on a matter not adequately disclosed in a trust disclosure document is barred as provided in chapter 95 and accrues when the beneficiary has actual knowledge of:

(a) The facts upon which the claim is based if such actual knowledge is established by clear and convincing evidence; or

(b) The trustee's repudiation of the trust or adverse possession of trust assets.

Paragraph (a) applies to claims based upon acts or omissions occurring on or after July 1, 2008.

(4) As used in this section, the term:

(a) "Trust disclosure document" means a trust accounting or any other written report of the trustee.   A trust disclosure document adequately discloses a matter if the document provides sufficient information so that a beneficiary knows of a claim or reasonably should have inquired into the existence of a claim with respect to that matter.

(b) "Trust accounting" means an accounting that adequately discloses the information required by and that substantially complies with the standards set forth in s. 736.08135.

(c) "Limitation notice" means a written statement of the trustee that an action by a beneficiary against the trustee for breach of trust based on any matter adequately disclosed in a trust disclosure document may be barred unless the action is commenced within 6 months after receipt of the trust disclosure document or receipt of a limitation notice that applies to that trust disclosure document, whichever is later.   A limitation notice may but is not required to be in the following form: "An action for breach of trust based on matters disclosed in a trust accounting or other written report of the trustee may be subject to a 6-month statute of limitations from the receipt of the trust accounting or other written report. If you have questions, please consult your attorney."

(5) For purposes of this section, a limitation notice applies to a trust disclosure document when the limitation notice is:

(a) Contained as a part of the trust disclosure document or as a part of another trust disclosure document received within 1 year prior to the receipt of the latter trust disclosure document;

(b) Accompanied concurrently by the trust disclosure document or by another trust disclosure document that was received within 1 year prior to the receipt of the latter trust disclosure document;

(c) Delivered separately within 10 days after the delivery of the trust disclosure document or of another trust disclosure document that was received within 1 year prior to the receipt of the latter trust disclosure document. For purposes of this paragraph, a limitation notice is not delivered separately if the notice is accompanied by another written communication, other than a written communication that refers only to the limitation notice; or

(d) Received more than 10 days after the delivery of the trust disclosure document, but only if the limitation notice references that trust disclosure document and:

1. Offers to provide to the beneficiary on request another copy of that trust disclosure document if the document was received by the beneficiary within 1 year prior to receipt of the limitation notice; or

2. Is accompanied by another copy of that trust disclosure document if the trust disclosure document was received by the beneficiary 1 year or more prior to the receipt of the limitation notice.

(6)(a) Notwithstanding subsections (1), (2), and (3), all claims by a beneficiary against a trustee are barred:

1. Upon the later of:

a. Ten years after the date the trust terminates, the trustee resigns, or the fiduciary relationship between the trustee and the beneficiary otherwise ends if the beneficiary had actual knowledge of the existence of the trust and the beneficiary's status as a beneficiary throughout the 10–year period; or

b. Twenty years after the date of the act or omission of the trustee that is complained of if the beneficiary had actual knowledge of the existence of the trust and the beneficiary's status as a beneficiary throughout the 20–year period; or

2. Forty years after the date the trust terminates, the trustee resigns, or the fiduciary relationship between the trustee and the beneficiary otherwise ends.

(b) When a beneficiary shows by clear and convincing evidence that a trustee actively concealed facts supporting a cause of action, any existing applicable statute of repose shall be extended by 30 years.

(c) For purposes of sub-subparagraph (a)1.b., the failure of the trustee to take corrective action is not a separate act or omission and does not extend the period of repose established by this subsection.

(d) This subsection applies to claims based upon acts or omissions occurring on or after July 1, 2008.

(7) This section applies to trust accountings for accounting periods beginning on or after July 1, 2007, and to written reports, other than trust accountings, received by a beneficiary on or after July 1, 2007.

Added by Laws 2006, c. 2006–217, § 10, eff. July 1, 2007. Amended by Laws 2007, c. 2007–153, § 5, eff. July 1, 2007; Laws 2008, c. 2008–76, § 3, eff. July 1, 2008.

Cross References

Payments from deferred compensation plans, annuities, and retirement plans or accounts, see § 738.602.
Principal and income,
    Distribution to residuary and remainder beneficiaries, see § 738.202.
    Total return unitrusts, see § 738.1041.
Trust business, substitution of fiduciaries, see § 660.46.

736.1009. Reliance on trust instrument

A trustee who acts in reasonable reliance on the terms of the trust as expressed in the trust instrument is not liable to a beneficiary for a breach of trust to the extent the breach resulted from the reliance.

Added by Laws 2006, c. 2006–217, § 10, eff. July 1, 2007.

736.1010. Event affecting administration or distribution

If the happening of an event, including marriage, divorce, performance of educational requirements, or death, affects the administration or distribution of a trust, a trustee who has exercised reasonable care to ascertain the happening of the event is not liable for a loss resulting from the trustee's lack of knowledge.

Added by Laws 2006, c. 2006–217, § 10, eff. July 1, 2007.

736.1011. Exculpation of trustee

(1) A term of a trust relieving a trustee of liability for breach of trust is unenforceable to the extent that the term:

(a) Relieves the trustee of liability for breach of trust committed in bad faith or with reckless indifference to the purposes of the trust or the interests of the beneficiaries; or

(b) Was inserted into the trust instrument as the result of an abuse by the trustee of a fiduciary or confidential relationship with the settlor.

(2) An exculpatory term drafted or caused to be drafted by the trustee is invalid as an abuse of a fiduciary or confidential relationship unless:

(a) The trustee proves that the exculpatory term is fair under the circumstances.

(b) The term's existence and contents were adequately communicated directly to the settlor or the independent attorney of the settlor. This paragraph applies only to trusts created on or after July 1, 2007.

Added by Laws 2006, c. 2006–217, § 10, eff. July 1, 2007. Amended by Laws 2007, c. 2007–153, § 6, eff. July 1, 2007.

736.1012. Beneficiary's consent, release, or ratification

A trustee is not liable to a beneficiary for breach of trust if the beneficiary consented to the conduct constituting the breach, released the trustee from liability for the breach, or ratified the transaction constituting the breach, unless:

(1) The consent, release, or ratification of the beneficiary was induced by improper conduct of the trustee; or

(2) At the time of the consent, release, or ratification, the beneficiary did not know of the beneficiary's rights or of the material facts relating to the breach.

Added by Laws 2006, c. 2006–217, § 10, eff. July 1, 2007.

736.1013. Limitation on personal liability of trustee

(1) Except as otherwise provided in the contract, a trustee is not personally liable on a contract properly entered into in the trustee's fiduciary capacity in the course of administering the trust if the trustee in the contract disclosed the fiduciary capacity.

(2) A trustee is personally liable for torts committed in the course of administering a trust or for obligations arising from ownership or control of trust property only if the trustee is personally at fault.

(3) A claim based on a contract entered into by a trustee in the trustee's fiduciary capacity, on an obligation arising from ownership or control of trust property, or on a tort committed in the course of administering a trust may be asserted in a judicial proceeding against the trustee in the trustee's fiduciary capacity, whether or not the trustee is personally liable for the claim.

(4) Issues of liability between the trust estate and the trustee individually may be determined in a proceeding for accounting, surcharge, or indemnification or in any other appropriate proceeding.

Added by Laws 2006, c. 2006–217, § 10, eff. July 1, 2007.

Cross References

Land conveyances, land trusts transferring interest in real estate, see § 689.071.
Timeshare plans,
    Subordination instruments, see § 721.53
    Trusts, see § 721.08.

736.1014. Limitations on actions against certain trusts

(1) After the death of a settlor, no creditor of the settlor may bring, maintain, or continue any direct action against a trust described in s. 733.707(3), the trustee of the trust, or any beneficiary of the trust that is dependent on the individual liability of the settlor. Such claims and causes of action against the settlor shall be presented and enforced against the settlor's estate as provided in part VII of chapter 733, and the personal representative of the settlor's estate may obtain payment from the trustee of a trust described in s. 733.707(3) as provided in ss. 733.607(2), 733.707(3), and 736.05053.

(2) This section does not preclude a direct action against a trust described in s. 733.707(3), the trustee of the trust, or a beneficiary of the trust that is not dependent on the individual liability of the settlor.

(3) This section does not affect the lien of any duly recorded mortgage or security interest or the lien of any person in possession of personal property or the right to foreclose and enforce the mortgage or lien.

Added by Laws 2006, c. 2006–217, § 10, eff. July 1, 2007.

736.1015. Interest as general partner

(1) Unless personal liability is imposed in the contract, a trustee who holds an interest as a general partner in a general or limited partnership is not personally liable on a contract entered

into by the partnership after the trust's acquisition of the interest if the fiduciary capacity was disclosed in the contract or in a statement previously filed pursuant to a Uniform Partnership Act [1] or Uniform Limited Partnership Act.[2]

(2) A trustee who holds an interest as a general partner is not personally liable for torts committed by the partnership or for obligations arising from ownership or control of the interest unless the trustee is personally at fault.

(3) If the trustee of a revocable trust holds an interest as a general partner, the settlor is personally liable for contracts and other obligations of the partnership as if the settlor were a general partner.

Added by Laws 2006, c. 2006–217, § 10, eff. July 1, 2007.

[1] See F.S.A. § 620.081001 et seq.
[2] See F.S.A. § 620.1101 et seq.

Cross References

Timeshare plans,
    Subordination instruments, see § 721.53
    Trusts, see § 721.08.

736.1016. Protection of person dealing with trustee

(1) A person other than a beneficiary who in good faith assists a trustee or who in good faith and for value deals with a trustee, without knowledge that the trustee is exceeding or improperly exercising the trustee's powers, is protected from liability as if the trustee properly exercised the power.

(2) A person other than a beneficiary who in good faith deals with a trustee is not required to inquire into the extent of the trustee's powers or the propriety of their exercise.

(3) A person who in good faith delivers assets to a trustee need not ensure their proper application.

(4) A person other than a beneficiary who in good faith assists a former trustee or who in good faith and for value deals with a former trustee, without knowledge that the trusteeship has terminated, is protected from liability as if the former trustee were still a trustee.

(5) Comparable protective provisions of other laws relating to commercial transactions or transfer of securities by fiduciaries prevail over the protection provided by this section.

Added by Laws 2006, c. 2006–217, § 10, eff. July 1, 2007.

736.1017. Certification of trust

(1) Instead of furnishing a copy of the trust instrument to a person other than a beneficiary, the trustee may furnish to the person a certification of trust containing the following information:

(a) The trust exists and the date the trust instrument was executed.

(b) The identity of the settlor.

(c) The identity and address of the currently acting trustee.

(d) The powers of the trustee.

(e) The revocability or irrevocability of the trust and the identity of any person holding a power to revoke the trust.

(f) The authority of cotrustees to sign or otherwise authenticate and whether all or less than all are required in order to exercise powers of the trustee.

(g) The manner of taking title to trust property.

(2) A certification of trust may be signed or otherwise authenticated by any trustee.

(3) A certification of trust must state that the trust has not been revoked, modified, or amended in any manner that would cause the representations contained in the certification of trust to be incorrect.

(4) A certification of trust need not contain the dispositive terms of a trust.

(5) A recipient of a certification of trust may require the trustee to furnish copies of any excerpts from the original trust instrument and later amendments that designate the trustee and confer upon the trustee the power to act in the pending transaction.

(6) A person who acts in reliance on a certification of trust without knowledge that the representations contained in the certification are incorrect is not liable to any person for so acting and may assume without inquiry the existence of the facts contained in the certification. Knowledge of the terms of the trust may not be inferred solely from the fact that a copy of all or part of the trust instrument is held by the person relying on the certification.

(7) A person who in good faith enters into a transaction in reliance on a certification of trust may enforce the transaction against the trust property as if the representations contained in the certification were correct.

(8) This section does not limit the right of a person to obtain a copy of the trust instrument when required to be furnished by law or in a judicial proceeding concerning the trust.

Added by Laws 2006, c. 2006–217, § 10, eff. July 1, 2007.

736.1018. Improper distribution or payment; liability of distributee

Any person who received a distribution or was paid improperly from a trust shall return the assets or funds received and the income from those assets or interest on the funds from the date of distribution or payment unless the distribution or payment cannot be questioned because of adjudication, estoppel, or limitations. If the person does not have the assets or funds, the value of the assets or funds at the date of disposition, income from the assets or funds, and gain received by the person from the assets or funds shall be returned.

Added by Laws 2006, c. 2006–217, § 10, eff. July 1, 2007.

PART XI.   RULES OF CONSTRUCTION

736.1101.   Rules of construction; general provisions

Except as provided in s. 736.0105(2):

(1) The intent of the settlor as expressed in the terms of the trust controls the legal effect of the dispositions made in the trust.

(2) The rules of construction as expressed in this part shall apply unless a contrary intent is indicated by the terms of the trust.

Added by Laws 2006, c. 2006–217, § 11, eff. July 1, 2007.

736.1102. Construction of terms

The laws used to determine paternity and relationships for the purposes of intestate succession apply when determining whether class gift terminology and terms of relationship include adopted persons and persons born out of wedlock.

Added by Laws 2006, c. 2006–217, § 11, eff. July 1, 2007. Amended by Laws 2010, c. 2010–132, § 17, eff. Oct. 1, 2010.

736.1103. Gifts to multigeneration classes to be per stirpes

Class gifts to descendants, issue, and other multigeneration classes shall be per stirpes.

Added by Laws 2006, c. 2006–217, § 11, eff. July 1, 2007.

736.1104. Killer not entitled to receive property or other benefits by reason of victim's death

(1) A beneficiary of a trust who unlawfully and intentionally kills or unlawfully and intentionally participates in procuring the death of the settlor or another person on whose death such beneficiary's interest depends, is not entitled to any trust interest, including homestead, dependent on the victim's death, and such interest shall devolve as though the killer had predeceased the victim.

(2) A final judgment of conviction of murder in any degree is conclusive for the purposes of this section. In the absence of a murder conviction in any degree, the court may determine by the greater weight of the evidence whether the killing was unlawful and intentional for purposes of this section.

Added by Laws 2006, c. 2006–217, § 11, eff. July 1, 2007.

736.1105. Dissolution of marriage; effect on revocable trust

Unless the trust instrument or the judgment for dissolution of marriage or divorce expressly provides otherwise, if a revocable trust is executed by a husband or wife as settlor prior to annulment of the marriage or entry of a judgment for dissolution of marriage or divorce of the settlor from the settlor's spouse, any provision of the trust that affects the settlor's spouse will become void upon annulment of the marriage or entry of the judgment of dissolution of marriage or divorce and any such trust shall be administered and construed as if the settlor's spouse had died on the date of the annulment or on entry of the judgment for dissolution of marriage or divorce.

Added by Laws 2006, c. 2006–217, § 11, eff. July 1, 2007.

736.1106. Antilapse; survivorship with respect to future interests under terms of inter vivos and testamentary trusts; substitute takers

(1) As used in this section, the term:

(a) "Beneficiary" means the beneficiary of a future interest and includes a class member if the future interest is in the form of a class gift.

(b) "Distribution date," with respect to a future interest, means the time when the future interest is to take effect. The distribution date need not occur at the beginning or end of a calendar day, but can occur at a time during the course of a day. The distribution date refers to the time that the right to possession or enjoyment arises and is not necessarily the time that any benefit of the right is realized.

(c) "Future interest" includes an alternative future interest and a future interest in the form of a class gift.

(d) "Future interest under the terms of a trust" means a future interest created by an inter vivos or testamentary transfer to an existing trust or creating a trust or by an exercise of a power of appointment to an existing trust directing the continuance of an existing trust, designating a beneficiary of an existing trust, or creating a trust.

(e) "Surviving beneficiary" or "surviving descendant" means a beneficiary or a descendant who did not predecease the distribution date or is not deemed to have predeceased the distribution date by operation of law.

(2) A future interest under the terms of a trust is contingent upon the beneficiary surviving the distribution date. Unless a contrary intent appears in the trust instrument, if a beneficiary of a future interest under the terms of a trust fails to survive the distribution date, and the deceased beneficiary leaves surviving descendants, a substitute gift is created in the beneficiary's surviving descendants. They take per stirpes the property to which the beneficiary would have been entitled if the beneficiary had survived the distribution date.

(3) In the application of this section:

(a) Words of survivorship attached to a future interest are a sufficient indication of an intent contrary to the application of this section.

(b) A residuary clause in a will is not a sufficient indication of an intent contrary to the application of this section, whether or not the will specifically provides that lapsed or failed devises are to pass under the residuary clause.

(4) If, after the application of subsections (2) and (3), there is no surviving taker, the property passes in the following order:

(a) If the future interest was created by the exercise of a power of appointment, the property passes under the donor's gift-in-default clause, if any, which clause is treated as creating a future interest under the terms of a trust.

(b) If no taker is produced by the application of paragraph (a) and the trust was created in a nonresiduary devise or appointment in the transferor's will, the property passes under the residuary clause in the transferor's will. For purposes of this section, the residuary clause is treated as creating a future interest under the terms of a trust.

(c) If no taker is produced by the application of paragraph (a) or paragraph (b), the property passes to those persons, including the state, and in such shares as would succeed to the transferor's intestate estate under the intestate succession law of the transferor's domicile if the transferor died when the disposition is to take effect in possession or enjoyment.

For purposes of paragraphs (b) and (c), the term "transferor" with respect to a future interest created by the exercise of a power of appointment, means the donor if the power was a nongeneral power and the donee if the power was a general power.

(5) Unless a contrary intent appears in the trust instrument, subsections (2)–(4) do not apply to an outright devise that vests upon the death of the settlor unless the beneficiary is a grandparent, or a lineal descendant of a grandparent, of the settlor or testator and the beneficiary:

(a) Is dead at the time of the execution of the revocable trust or will;

(b) Fails to survive the settlor or testator; or

(c) Is required by the inter vivos trust or by operation of law to be treated as having predeceased the settlor or testator.

A devise in a revocable trust or a testamentary trust that is to take effect at the death of the settlor or testator does not vest until the death of the settlor or testator.

(6) Subsections (1)–(4) apply to all trusts other than trusts that were irrevocable before the effective date of this code. Sections 732.603, 732.604, and 737.6035, as they exist on June 30, 2007, continue to apply to other trusts executed on or after June 12, 2003. Subsection (5) applies to those trusts that become irrevocable after June 30, 2014.

Added by Laws 2006, c. 2006–217, § 11, eff. July 1, 2007. Amended by Laws 2007, c. 2007–153, § 16, eff. July 1, 2007; Laws 2009, c. 2009–117, § 7, eff. July 1, 2009; Laws 2014, c. 2014–127, § 11, eff. July 1, 2014.

Cross References

Probate, deceased devisees and appointees, substitute gifts, see § 732.603.

736.1107. Change in securities; accessions; nonademption

A gift of specific securities, rather than their equivalent value, entitles the beneficiary only to:

(1) As much of the gifted securities of the same issuer held by the trust estate at the time of the occurrence of the event entitling the beneficiary to distribution.

(2) Any additional or other securities of the same issuer held by the trust estate because of action initiated by the issuer, excluding any acquired by exercise of purchase options.

(3) Securities of another issuer held by the trust estate as a result of a merger, consolidation, reorganization, or other similar action initiated by the original issuer.

Added by Laws 2006, c. 2006–217, § 11, eff. July 1, 2007.

736.1108. Penalty clause for contest

(1) A provision in a trust instrument purporting to penalize any interested person for contesting the trust instrument or instituting other proceedings relating to a trust estate or trust assets is unenforceable.

(2) This section applies to trusts created on or after October 1, 1993. For purposes of this subsection, a revocable trust shall be treated as created when the right of revocation terminates.

Added by Laws 2006, c. 2006–217, § 11, eff. July 1, 2007.

PART XII. CHARITABLE TRUSTS

736.1201. Definitions

As used in this part:

(1) "Charitable organization" means an organization described in s. 501(c)(3) of the Internal Revenue Code[1] and exempt from tax under s. 501(a) of the Internal Revenue Code.[2]

(2) "Internal Revenue Code" means the Internal Revenue Code of 1986, as amended.[3]

(3) "Private foundation trust" means a trust, including a trust described in s. 4947(a)(1) of the Internal Revenue Code,[4] as defined in s. 509(a) of the Internal Revenue Code.[5]

(4) "Split interest trust" means a trust for individual and charitable beneficiaries that is subject to the provisions of s. 4947(a)(2) of the Internal Revenue Code.[6]

(5) "State attorney" means the state attorney for the judicial circuit of the principal place of administration of the trust pursuant to s. 736.0108.

Added by Laws 2006, c. 2006–217, § 12, eff. July 1, 2007.

[1] 26 U.S.C.A. § 501(c)(3).
[2] 26 U.S.C.A. § 501(a).
[3] 26 U.S.C.A. § 1 et seq.
[4] 26 U.S.C.A. § 4947(a)(1).
[5] 26 U.S.C.A. § 509(a).
[6] 26 U.S.C.A. § 4947(a)(2).

Cross References

Guardians, powers upon court approval, see § 744.441.

736.1202. Application of this part

Except as otherwise provided in the trust, the provisions of this part apply to all private foundation trusts and split interest trusts, whether created or established before or after November 1, 1971, and to all trust assets acquired by the trustee before or after November 1, 1971.

Added by Laws 2006, c. 2006–217, § 12, eff. July 1, 2007.

736.1203. Trustee of a private foundation trust or a split interest trust

Except as provided in s. 736.1205, the trustee of a private foundation trust or a split interest trust has the duties and powers conferred on the trustee by this part.

Added by Laws 2006, c. 2006–217, § 12, eff. July 1, 2007.

736.1204. Powers and duties of trustee of a private foundation trust or a split interest trust

(1) In the exercise of a trustee's powers, including the powers granted by this part, a trustee has a duty to act with due regard to the trustee's obligation as a fiduciary, including a duty not to exercise any power in such a way as to:

(a) Deprive the trust of an otherwise available tax exemption, deduction, or credit for tax purposes;

(b) Deprive a donor of a trust asset or tax deduction or credit; or

(c) Operate to impose a tax on a donor, trust, or other person.

For purposes of this subsection, the term "tax" includes, but is not limited to, any federal, state, or local excise, income, gift, estate, or inheritance tax.

(2) Except as provided in s. 736.1205, a trustee of a private foundation trust shall make distributions at such time and in such manner as not to subject the trust to tax under s. 4942 of the Internal Revenue Code.[1]

(3) Except as provided in subsection (4) and in s. 736.1205, a trustee of a private foundation trust, or a split interest trust to the extent that the split interest trust is subject to the provisions of s. 4947(a)(2) of the Internal Revenue Code,[2] in the exercise of the trustee's powers shall not:

(a) Engage in any act of self-dealing as defined in s. 4941(d) of the Internal Revenue Code;[3]

(b) Retain any excess business holdings as defined in s. 4943(c) of the Internal Revenue Code;[4]

(c) Make any investments in a manner that subjects the foundation to tax under s. 4944 of the Internal Revenue Code;[5] or

(d) Make any taxable expenditures as defined in s. 4945(d) of the Internal Revenue Code.[6]

(4) Paragraphs (3)(b) and (c) shall not apply to a split interest trust if:

(a) All the income interest, and none of the remainder interest, of the trust is devoted solely to one or more of the purposes described in s. 170(c)(2)(B) of the Internal Revenue Code,[7] and all amounts in the trust for which a deduction was allowed under s. 170, s. 545(b)(2), s. 556(b)(2), s. 642(c), s. 2055, s. 2106(a)(2), or s. 2522 of the Internal Revenue Code[8] have an aggregate fair market value of not more than 60 percent of the aggregate fair market value of all amounts in the trust; or

(b) A deduction was allowed under s. 170, s. 545(b)(2), s. 556(b)(2), s. 642(c), s. 2055, s. 2106(a)(2), or s. 2522 of the Internal Revenue Code[8] for amounts payable under the terms of the trust to every remainder beneficiary but not to any income beneficiary.

Added by Laws 2006, c. 2006–217, § 12, eff. July 1, 2007. Amended by Laws 2007, c. 2007–153, § 17, eff. July 1, 2007.

[1] 26 U.S.C.A. § 4942.
[2] 26 U.S.C.A. § 4947(a)(2).
[3] 26 U.S.C.A. § 4941(d).
[4] 26 U.S.C.A. § 4943(c).
[5] 26 U.S.C.A. § 4944.
[6] 26 U.S.C.A. § 4945(d).
[7] 26 U.S.C.A. § 170(c)(2)(B).
[8] 26 U.S.C.A. § 170, § 545(b)(2), § 556(b)(2), § 642(c), § 2055, § 2106, or § 2522.

736.1205. Notice that this part does not apply

In the case of a power to make distributions, if the trustee determines that the governing instrument contains provisions that are more restrictive than s. 736.1204(2), or if the trust contains other powers, inconsistent with the provisions of s. 736.1204(3) that specifically direct acts by the trustee, the trustee shall notify the state attorney when the trust becomes subject to this part. Section 736.1204 does not apply to any trust for which notice has been given pursuant to this section unless the trust is amended to comply with the terms of this part.

Added by Laws 2006, c. 2006–217, § 12, eff. July 1, 2007.

736.1206. Power to amend trust instrument

(1) In the case of a trust that is solely for a named charitable organization or organizations and for which the trustee does not possess any discretion concerning the distribution of income or principal among two or more such organizations, the trustee may amend the governing instrument to comply with the provisions of s. 736.1204(2) with the consent of the named charitable organization or organizations.

(2) In the case of a charitable trust that is not subject to the provisions of subsection (1), the trustee may amend the governing instrument to comply with the provisions of s. 736.1204(2) with the consent of the state attorney.

Added by Laws 2006, c. 2006–217, § 12, eff. July 1, 2007.

736.1207. Power of court to permit deviation

This part does not affect the power of a court to relieve a trustee from any restrictions on the powers and duties that are placed on the trustee by the governing instrument or applicable law for cause shown and on complaint of the trustee, state attorney, or an affected beneficiary and notice to the affected parties.

Added by Laws 2006, c. 2006–217, § 12, eff. July 1, 2007.

736.1208. Release; property and persons affected; manner of effecting

(1) The trustee of a trust, all of the unexpired interests in which are devoted to one or more charitable purposes, may release a power to select charitable donees unless the creating instrument provides otherwise.

(2) The release of a power to select charitable donees may apply to all or any part of the property subject to the power and may reduce or limit the charitable organizations, or classes of charitable organizations, in whose favor the power is exercisable.

(3) A release shall be effected by a duly acknowledged written instrument signed by the trustee and delivered as provided in subsection (4).

(4) Delivery of a release shall be accomplished as follows:

(a) If the release is accomplished by specifying a charitable organization or organizations as beneficiary or beneficiaries of the trust, by delivery of a copy of the release to each designated charitable organization.

(b) If the release is accomplished by reducing the class of permissible charitable organizations, by delivery of a copy of the release to the state attorney.

(5) If a release is accomplished by specifying a public charitable organization or organizations as beneficiary or beneficiaries of the trust, the trust at all times thereafter shall be operated exclusively for the benefit of, and be supervised by, the specified public charitable organization or organizations.

Added by Laws 2006, c. 2006–217, § 12, eff. July 1, 2007.

736.1209. Election to come under this part

With the consent of that organization or organizations, a trustee of a trust for the benefit of a public charitable organization or organizations may come under s. 736.1208(5) by filing with the state attorney an election, accompanied by the proof of required consent. Thereafter the trust shall be subject to s. 736.1208(5).

Added by Laws 2006, c. 2006–217, § 12, eff. July 1, 2007. Amended by Laws 2007, c. 2007–5, § 148, eff. July 3, 2007; Laws 2007, c. 2007–153, § 18, eff. July 1, 2007.

736.1210. Interpretation

This part shall be interpreted to effectuate the intent of the state to preserve, foster, and encourage gifts to, or for the benefit of, charitable organizations.

Added by Laws 2006, c. 2006–217, § 12, eff. July 1, 2007.

736.1211. Protections afforded to certain charitable trusts and organizations

(1) A charitable organization, private foundation trust, split interest trust, or a private foundation as defined in s. 509(a) of the Internal Revenue Code [1] may not be required by a state agency or a local government to disclose the race, religion, gender, national origin, socioeconomic status, age, ethnicity, disability, marital status, sexual orientation, or political party registration of its employees, officers, directors, trustees, members, or owners, without the prior written consent of the individual or individuals in question.

(2) A private foundation as defined in s. 509(a) of the Internal Revenue Code,[1] a private foundation trust, a split interest trust, or a grant-making organization may not be required by the state or any local government to disclose the race, religion, gender, national origin, socioeconomic status, age, ethnicity, disability, marital status, sexual orientation, or political party registration of any person, or of the employees, officers, directors, trustees, members, or owners of any entity that has received monetary or in-kind contributions from or contracted with the organization, trust, or foundation, without the prior written consent of the individual or individuals in question. For purposes of this subsection, a "grant-making organization" is an organization that makes grants to charitable organizations but is not a private foundation, private foundation trust, or split interest trust.

(3) A state agency or a local government may not require that the governing board or officers of a charitable organization, private foundation trust, split interest trust, or a private foundation as defined in s. 509(a) of the Internal Revenue Code [1] include an individual or individuals of any particular race, religion, gender, national origin, socioeconomic status, age, ethnicity, disability, marital status, sexual orientation, or political party registration. Further, a state agency or a local government may not prohibit service as a board member or officer by an individual or individuals based upon their familial relationship to each other or to a donor or require that the governing board or officers include one or more individuals who do not share a familial relationship with each other or with a donor.

(4) A charitable organization, private foundation trust, split interest trust, or any private foundation as defined in s. 509(a) of the Internal Revenue Code [1] may not be required by a state agency or a local government to distribute its funds to or contract with any person or entity based upon the race, religion, gender, national origin, socioeconomic status, age, ethnicity, disability, marital status, sexual orientation, or political party registration of the person or of the employees, officers, directors, trustees, members, or owners of the entity, or based upon the populations, locales, or communities served by the person or entity, except as a lawful condition on the expenditure of particular funds imposed by the donor of such funds.
Added by Laws 2010, c. 2010–122, § 8, eff. July 1, 2010.

[1] 26 U.S.C.A. § 509(a).

PART XIII. MISCELLANEOUS

736.1301. Electronic records and signatures

Any provisions of this code governing the legal effect, validity, or enforceability of electronic records or electronic signatures, and of contracts formed or performed with the use of such records or signatures, are deemed to conform to the requirements of s. 102 of the Electronic Signatures in Global and National Commerce Act, 15 U.S.C. s. 7002, and supersede, modify, and limit the requirements of the Electronic Signatures in Global and National Commerce Act.[1]
Added by Laws 2006, c. 2006–217, § 13, eff. July 1, 2007.

[1] 15 U.S.C.A. § 7001 et seq.

736.1302. Severability clause

If any provision of this code or its application to any person or circumstances is held invalid, the invalidity does not affect other provisions or applications of this code that can be given effect without the invalid provision or application, and to this end the provisions of this code are severable.
Added by Laws 2006, c. 2006–217, § 13, eff. July 1, 2007.

736.1303.   Application to existing relationships

(1) Except as otherwise provided in this code, on July 1, 2007:

(a) This code applies to all trusts created before, on, or after such date.

(b) This code applies to all judicial proceedings concerning trusts commenced on or after such date.

(c) This code applies to judicial proceedings concerning trusts commenced before such date, unless the court finds that application of a particular provision of this code would substantially interfere with the effective conduct of the judicial proceedings or prejudice the rights of the parties, in which case the particular provision of this code does not apply and the superseded law applies.

(d) Any rule of construction or presumption provided in this code applies to trust instruments executed before the effective date of this code unless there is a clear indication of a contrary intent in the terms of the trust.

(e) An act done before such date is not affected by this code.

(2) If a right is acquired, extinguished, or barred on the expiration of a prescribed period that has commenced to run under any other law before July 1, 2007, that law continues to apply to the right even if it has been repealed or superseded.

Added by Laws 2006, c. 2006–217, § 13, eff. July 1, 2007.

CHAPTER 737

TRUST ADMINISTRATION [REPEALED]

Repeal of Chapter

Chapter 737, Trust Administration, consisting of §§ 737.101, 737.105, 737.106, 737.111, 737.115, 737.116, 737.201, 737.202, 737.203, 737.2035, 737.204, 737.2041, 737.205, 737.206, 737.2065, 737.207, 737.208, 737.209, 737.301, 737.302, 737.303, 737.3035, 737.304, 737.305, 737.3053, 737.3054, 737.3055, 737.306, 737.3061, 737.307, 737.308, 737.309, 737.401, 737.402, 737.4025, 737.403, 737.4031, 737.4032, 737.4033, 737.404, 737.405, 737.406, 737.501, 737.502, 737.503, 737.504, 737.505, 737.506, 737.507, 737.508, 737.509, 737.510, 737.511, 737.512, 737.6035, 737.621, 737.622, 737.623, 737.624, 737.625, 737.626, and 737.627, was repealed by Laws 2006, c. 2006–217, effective July 1, 2007 and Laws 2008, c. 2008–5, § 16, eff. July 1, 2008.

See, now, Chapter 736, Florida Trust Code.

CHAPTER 738

PRINCIPAL AND INCOME

PRINCIPAL AND INCOME

Revision

Laws 1974, c. 74–106, § 3, repealed the provisions of Fla.St.1973, Chapters 690, 691, and 737, pertaining to the Uniform Principal and Income Law, Trust Administration Law, and Trust Accounting Law, respectively. Laws 1974, c. 74–106, § 1, enacted Fla.St.1974, Supp., Chapter 737, Trust Administration, which superseded the provisions of the repealed chapters, effective July 1, 1975.

Laws 1975, c. 75–220, § 112 changed the effective date of Laws 1974, c. 74–106 to January 1, 1976. Laws 1975, c. 75–221, effective January 1, 1976, rewrote provisions contained in Chapter 737 as enacted by Laws 1974, c. 74–106, and renumbered provisions contained in Chapter 737, part VI, to Chapter 738.

For the effect of prior laws on vested substantive rights, see § 731.011.

UNIFORM PRINCIPAL AND INCOME ACT (1997)

Table of Jurisdictions Wherein 1997 Act Has Been Adopted

For text of Uniform Act, and variation notes and annotation materials for adopting jurisdictions, see Uniform Laws Annotated, Master Edition, Volume 7A, Part III.

Jurisdiction	Laws	Effective Date	Statutory Citation
Alabama	2000, Act 675	1–1–2001	Code 1975, §§ 19–3A–101 to 19–3A–608.
Alaska	2003, c. 145	9–1–2003	AS §§ 13.38.200 to 13.38.990.
Arizona	2001, c. 176	1–1–2002	A.R.S. §§ 14–7401 to 14–7431.
Arkansas	1999, Act 647	1–1–2000	A.C.A. §§ 28–70–101 to 28–70–606.
California	1999, c. 145	1–1–2000	West's Ann.Cal.Probate Code §§ 16320 to 16375.
Colorado	2000, c. 257	7–1–2001	West's C.R.S.A. §§ 15–1–401 to 15–1–436.
Connecticut	1999, P.A. 99–164	1–1–2000	C.G.S.A. §§ 45a–542 to 45a–542ff.
District of Columbia	2001, D.C. Law 13–292	4–27–2001	D.C. Official Code, 2001 Ed. §§ 28–4801.01 to 28–4806.03.
Florida	2002, c. 42	1–1–2003	West's F.S.A. §§ 738.101 to 738.804.
Georgia	2010, c. 506	7–1–2010	O.C.G.A. §§ 53–12–380 to 53–12–431.
Hawaii	2000, c. 191	7–1–2000	HRS §§ 557A–101 to 557A–506.
Idaho	2001, c. 261	7–1–2001	I.C. §§ 68–10–101 to 68–10–605.
Indiana	2002, c. 84	1–1–2003	West's A.I.C. §§ 30–2–14–1 to 30–2–14–44.
Iowa	1999, H.F. 584	7–1–1999	I.C.A. §§ 637.101 to 637.701.
Kansas	2000, c. 61	7–1–2000	K.S.A. §§ 58–9–101 to 58–9–603.
Kentucky	2004, c. 158	1–1–2005	KRS 386.450 to 386.504.
Maine	2002, c. 544	1–1–2003	18–A M.R.S.A. §§ 7–701 to 7–773.
Maryland	2000, c. 292	10–1–2000	Code, Estates and Trusts, §§ 15–501 to 15–530.
Massachusetts	2005, c. 129	1–1–2006	M.G.L.A. c. 203D, §§ 1 to 29.
Michigan	2004, c. 159	9–1–2004	M.C.L.A. §§ 555.501 to 555.1006.
Minnesota[1]	1969, c. 1006	1–1–1970	M.S.A. §§ 501B.59 to 501B.76.
Mississippi	2012, c. 351	1–1–2013	Miss. Code Ann. §§ 91–17–101 to 91–17–604.
Missouri	2001, H.B. 241	7–10–2001 *	V.A.M.S. §§ 469.401 to 469.467.
Montana	2003, c. 506	4–25–2003 *	MCA §§ 72–34–421 to 72–34–453.
Nebraska	2001, LB 56	9–1–2001	R.R.S.1943, §§ 30–3116 to 30–3149.
Nevada	2003, c. 355	10–1–2003	NRS 164.780 to 164.925.
New Hampshire	2006, c. 320	1–1–2007	RSA 564–C:1–101 to 564–C:6–602.
New Jersey	2001, c. 212	1–1–2002	N.J.S.A. 3B:19B–1 to 3B:19B–31.
New Mexico	2001, c. 113	7–1–2001	NMSA 1978, §§ 46–3A–101 to 46–3A–603.
New York	2001, c. 243	1–1–2002	McKinney's EPTL 11–A–1.1 to 11–A–6.4.
North Carolina	2003, c. 232	1–1–2004	G.S. §§ 37A–1–101 to 37A–6–602.
North Dakota	1999, c. 532	8–1–1999	NDCC 59–04.2–01 to 59–04.2–30.
Ohio	2006, H.B. 416	1–1–2007	R.C. §§ 5812.01 to 5812.52.
Oklahoma	1998, c. 115	11–1–1998	60 Okl.St.Ann. §§ 175.101 to 175.603.
Oregon	2003, c. 279	1–1–2004	ORS 116.007, 129.200 to 129.450.
Pennsylvania	2002, c. 50	5–16–2002 *	20 Pa.C.S.A. §§ 8101 to 8191.
South Carolina	2005, c. 66	1–1–2006	Code 1976, §§ 62–7–901 to 62–7–932.
South Dakota[2]	2007, c. 282	7–1–2007	SDCL 55–13A–101 to 55–13A–602.
Tennessee	2000, c. 829	7–1–2000	T.C.A. §§ 35–6–101 to 35–6–602.
Texas	2003, c. 659	1–1–2004	V.T.C.A. Property Code §§ 116.001 to 116.206.
Utah	2004, c. 285	5–3–2004	U.C.A. 1953, §§ 22–3–101 to 22–3–604.
Vermont	2011, c. 114	7–1–2012	14 V.S.A. §§ 3321 to 3376.
Virginia	1999, c. 975	1–1–2000	Code 1950, §§ 64.2–1000 to 64.2–1032.
Washington	2002, c. 345	1–1–2003	West's RCWA 11.104A.001 to 11.104A.907.
West Virginia	2000, c. 273	7–1–2000	Code, 44B–1–101 to 44B–6–606.
Wisconsin	2005, c. 10	5–17–2005	W.S.A. 701.1101 to 701.1136.
Wyoming	2001, c. 11	7–1–2001	Wyo.Stat.Ann. §§ 2–3–801 to 2–3–834.

* Approval date.

[1] Minnesota's act remains a substantial adoption of the provisions of the Uniform Principal and Income Act (1962), but various amendments and newly enacted sections have adopted several provisions of the Uniform Principal and Income Act (1997). Therefore, Minnesota will be carried in the Table of Adopting Jurisdictions for both acts.

[2] Enacted the Uniform Principal and Income Act (1997) without repealing the Uniform Principal and Income Act (1962).

Cross References

Trusts, duties of trustees, distribution of trust income, see § 736.08147.

738.101. Short title

This chapter may be cited as the "Florida Uniform Principal and Income Act."

Added by Laws 2002, c. 2002–42, § 1, eff. Jan. 1, 2003.

738.102. Definitions

As used in this chapter, the term:

(1) "Accounting period" means a calendar year unless another 12–month period is selected by a fiduciary. The term includes a portion of a calendar year or other 12–month period that begins when an income interest begins or ends when an income interest ends.

(2) "Beneficiary" means, in the case of a decedent's estate, an heir or devisee and, in the case of a trust, an income beneficiary or a remainder beneficiary.

(3) "Carrying value" means the fair market value at the time the assets are received by the fiduciary. For the estates of decedents and trusts described in s. 733.707(3), after the grantor's death, the assets are considered received as of the date of death. If there is a change in fiduciaries, a majority of the continuing fiduciaries may elect to adjust the carrying values to reflect the fair market value of the assets at the beginning of their administration. If such election is made, it must be reflected on the first accounting filed after the election. For assets acquired during the administration of the estate or trust, the carrying value is equal to the acquisition costs of the asset.

(4) "Fiduciary" means a personal representative or a trustee. The term includes an executor, administrator, successor personal representative, special administrator, or a person performing substantially the same function.

(5) "Income" means money or property that a fiduciary receives as current return from a principal asset. The term includes a portion of receipts from a sale, exchange, or liquidation of a principal asset, to the extent provided in ss. 738.401–738.403 and s. 738.503.

(6) "Income beneficiary" means a person to whom net income of a trust is or may be payable.

(7) "Income interest" means the right of an income beneficiary to receive all or part of net income, whether the terms of the trust require the net income to be distributed or authorize the net income to be distributed in the trustee's discretion.

(8) "Mandatory income interest" means the right of an income beneficiary to receive net income that the terms of the trust require the fiduciary to distribute.

(9) "Net income" means the total receipts allocated to income during an accounting period minus the disbursements made from income during the period, plus or minus transfers under this chapter to or from income during the period.

(10) "Person" means an individual, corporation, business trust, estate, trust, partnership, limited liability company, association, joint venture, public corporation, or any other legal or commercial entity or a government or governmental subdivision, agency, or instrumentality.

(11) "Principal" means property held in trust for distribution to a remainder beneficiary when the trust terminates.

(12) "Remainder beneficiary" means a person entitled to receive principal when an income interest ends.

(13) "Terms of a trust" means the manifestation of the intent of a grantor or decedent with respect to the trust, expressed in a manner that admits of its proof in a judicial proceeding, whether by written or spoken words or by conduct.

(14) "Trustee" includes an original, additional, or successor trustee, whether or not appointed or confirmed by a court.

Added by Laws 2002, c. 2002–42, § 1, eff. Jan. 1, 2003. Amended by Laws 2012, c. 2012–49, § 2, eff. Jan. 1, 2013.

738.103. Fiduciary duties; general principles

(1) In allocating receipts and disbursements to or between principal and income, and with respect to any matter within the scope of ss. 738.201 and 738.202 and ss. 738.301–738.303, a fiduciary:

(a) Shall administer a trust or estate in accordance with the terms of the trust or the will, even if there is a different provision in this chapter.

(b) May administer a trust or estate by the exercise of a discretionary power of administration given to the fiduciary by the terms of the trust or the will, even if the exercise of the power produces a result different from a result required or permitted by this chapter.

(c) Shall administer a trust or estate in accordance with this chapter if the terms of the trust or the will do not contain a different provision or do not give the fiduciary a discretionary power of administration.

(d) Shall add a receipt or charge a disbursement to principal to the extent the terms of the trust and this chapter do not provide a rule for allocating the receipt or disbursement to or between principal and income.

(2) In exercising the power to adjust under s. 738.104(1) or a discretionary power of administration regarding a matter within the scope of this chapter, whether granted by the terms of a trust, a will, or this chapter, a fiduciary shall administer a trust or estate impartially, based on what is fair and reasonable to all of the beneficiaries, except to the extent the terms of the trust or the will clearly manifest an intention that the fiduciary shall or may favor one or more of the beneficiaries. A determination in accordance with this chapter is presumed to be fair and reasonable to all of the beneficiaries.

(3) Except as provided in s. 738.1041(9), this chapter pertains to the administration of a trust and is applicable to any trust that is administered in this state or under its law. This chapter also applies to any estate that is administered in this state unless the provision is limited in application to a trustee, rather than a fiduciary.

Added by Laws 2002, c. 2002–42, § 1, eff. Jan. 1, 2003. Amended by Laws 2012, c. 2012–49, § 3, eff. Jan. 1, 2013.

738.104. Trustee's power to adjust

(1) A trustee may adjust between principal and income to the extent the trustee considers necessary if the trustee invests and manages trust assets as a prudent investor, the terms of the trust describe the amount that may or shall be distributed to a beneficiary by referring to the trust's income, and the trustee determines, after applying the rules in s. 738.103(1), that the trustee is unable to comply with s. 738.103(2).

(2) In deciding whether and to what extent to exercise the power conferred by subsection (1), a trustee shall consider all factors relevant to the trust and its beneficiaries, including the following factors to the extent they are relevant:

(a) The nature, purpose, and expected duration of the trust.

(b) The intent of the grantor.

(c) The identity and circumstances of the beneficiaries.

(d) The needs for liquidity, regularity of income, and preservation and appreciation of capital.

(e) The assets held in the trust; the extent to which the assets consist of financial assets, interests in closely held enterprises, tangible and intangible personal property, or real property; the extent to which an asset is used by a beneficiary; and whether an asset was purchased by the trustee or received from the grantor.

(f) The net amount allocated to income under the other sections of this chapter and the increases or decreases in the value of the principal assets, which the trustee may estimate as to assets for which market values are not readily available.

(g) Whether and to what extent the terms of the trust give the trustee the power to invade principal or accumulate income or prohibit the trustee from invading principal or accumulating income and the extent to which the trustee has exercised a power from time to time to invade principal or accumulate income.

(h) The actual and anticipated effect of economic conditions on principal and income and effects of inflation and deflation.

(i) The anticipated tax consequences of an adjustment.

(3) A trustee may not make an adjustment:

(a) That reduces the actuarial value of the income interest in a trust to which a person transfers property with the intent to qualify for a gift tax exclusion;

(b) That changes the amount payable to a beneficiary as a fixed annuity or a fixed fraction of the value of the trust assets;

(c) From any amount that is permanently set aside for charitable purposes under a will or the terms of a trust unless both income and principal are so set aside;

(d) If possessing or exercising the power to adjust causes an individual to be treated as the owner of all or part of the trust for income tax purposes and the individual would not be treated as the owner if the trustee did not possess the power to adjust;

(e) If possessing or exercising the power to adjust causes all or part of the trust assets to be included for estate tax purposes in the estate of an individual who has the power to remove a trustee or appoint a trustee, or both, and the assets would not be included in the estate of the individual if the trustee did not possess the power to adjust;

(f) If the trustee is a beneficiary of the trust; or

(g) If the trustee is not a beneficiary of the trust but the adjustment would benefit the trustee directly or indirectly, except that in the case of a trustee whose compensation for acting as trustee is based upon the value of trust assets, an adjustment that affects the value of trust assets shall not be deemed to benefit the trustee.

(4) If paragraph (3)(d), paragraph (3)(e), paragraph (3)(f), or paragraph (3)(g) applies to a trustee and there is more than one trustee, a cotrustee to whom the provision does not apply may make the adjustment unless the exercise of the power by the remaining trustee is not permitted by the terms of the trust.

(5) A trustee may release the entire power to adjust conferred by subsection (1) or may release only the power to adjust from income to principal or the power to adjust from principal to

income if the trustee is uncertain about whether possessing or exercising the power will cause a result described in paragraphs (3)(a)–(e) or paragraph (3)(g) or if the trustee determines that possessing or exercising the power will or may deprive the trust of a tax benefit or impose a tax burden not described in subsection (3). A release under this subsection may be permanent or for a specified period, including a period measured by the life of an individual.

(6) Terms of a trust that limit a trustee's power to adjust between principal and income do not affect the application of this section unless it is clear from the terms of the trust that the terms are intended to deny the trustee the power to adjust conferred by subsection (1).

(7) Nothing in this chapter is intended to create or imply a duty to make an adjustment and no inference of impropriety shall be made as a result of a trustee not exercising the power to adjust conferred by subsection (1).

(8) With respect to a trust in existence on January 1, 2003:

(a) A trustee shall not have the power to adjust under this section until the statement required in subsection (9) is provided and either no objection is made or any objection which is made has been terminated.

1. An objection is made if, within 60 days after the date of the statement required in subsection (9), a super majority of the eligible beneficiaries deliver to the trustee a written objection to the application of this section to such trust. An objection shall be deemed to be delivered to the trustee on the date the objection is mailed to the mailing address listed in the notice provided in subsection (9).

2. An objection is terminated upon the earlier of the receipt of consent from a super majority of eligible beneficiaries of the class that made the objection, or the resolution of the objection pursuant to paragraph (c).

(b) An objection or consent under this section may be executed by a legal representative or natural guardian of a beneficiary without the filing of any proceeding or approval of any court.

(c) If an objection is delivered to the trustee, then the trustee may petition the circuit court for an order quashing the objection and vesting in such trustee the power to adjust under this section. The burden will be on the objecting beneficiaries to prove that the power to adjust would be inequitable, illegal, or otherwise in contravention of the grantor's intent. The court may award costs and attorney's fees relating to the trustee's petition in the same manner as in chancery actions. When costs and attorney's fees are to be paid out of the trust, the court may, in its discretion, direct from which part of the trust they shall be paid.

(d) If no timely objection is made or if the trustee is vested with the power to adjust by court order, the trustee may thereafter exercise the power to adjust without providing notice of its intent to do so unless, in vesting the trustee with the power to adjust, the court determines that unusual circumstances require otherwise.

(e) 1. If a trustee makes a good faith effort to comply with the notice provisions of subsection (9), but fails to deliver notice to one or more beneficiaries entitled to such notice, neither the validity of the notice required under this subsection nor the trustee's power to adjust under this section shall be affected until the trustee has actual notice that one or more beneficiaries entitled to notice were not notified. Until the trustee has actual notice of the notice deficiency, the trustee shall have all of the powers and protections granted a trustee with the power to adjust under this chapter.

2. When the trustee has actual notice that one or more beneficiaries entitled to notice under subsection (9) were not notified, the trustee's power to adjust under this section shall cease until

all beneficiaries who are entitled to such notice, including those who were previously provided with such notice, are notified and given the opportunity to object as provided for under this subsection.

(f) The objection of a super majority of eligible beneficiaries under this subsection shall be valid for a period of 1 year after the date of the notice set forth in subsection (9). Upon expiration of the objection, the trustee may thereafter give a new notice under subsection (9).

(g) Nothing in this section is intended to create or imply a duty of the trustee of a trust existing on January 1, 2003, to seek a power to adjust pursuant to this subsection or to give the notice described in subsection (9) if the trustee does not desire to have a power to adjust under this section, and no inference of impropriety shall be made as the result of a trustee not seeking a power to adjust pursuant to this subsection.

(9)(a) A trustee of a trust in existence on January 1, 2003, that is not prohibited under subsection (3) from exercising the power to adjust shall, any time prior to initially exercising the power, provide to all eligible beneficiaries a statement containing the following:

1. The name, telephone number, street address, and mailing address of the trustee and of any individuals who may be contacted for further information;

2. A statement that unless a super majority of the eligible beneficiaries objects to the application of this section to the trust within 60 days after the date the statement pursuant to this subsection was served, this section shall apply to the trust; and

3. A statement that, if this section applies to the trust, the trustee will have the power to adjust between income and principal and that such a power may have an effect on the distributions to such beneficiary from the trust.

(b) The statement may contain information regarding a trustee's fiduciary obligations with respect to the power to adjust between income and principal under this section.

(c) The statement referred to in this subsection shall be served informally, in the manner provided in the Florida Rules of Civil Procedure relating to service of pleadings subsequent to the initial pleading. The statement may be served on a legal representative or natural guardian of a beneficiary without the filing of any proceeding or approval of any court.

(d) For purposes of subsection (8) and this subsection, the term:

1. "Eligible beneficiaries" means:

a. If at the time the determination is made there are one or more beneficiaries described in s. 736.0103(16)(c), the beneficiaries described in s. 736.0103(16)(a) and (c); or

b. If there is no beneficiary described in s. 736.0103(16)(c), the beneficiaries described in s. 736.0103(16)(a) and (b).

2. "Super majority of the eligible beneficiaries" means:

a. If at the time the determination is made there are one or more beneficiaries described in s. 736.0103(16)(c), at least two-thirds in interest of the beneficiaries described in s. 736.0103(16)(a) or two-thirds in interest of the beneficiaries described in s. 736.0103(16)(c), if the interests of the beneficiaries are reasonably ascertainable; otherwise, it means two-thirds in number of either such class; or

b. If there is no beneficiary described in s. 736.0103(16)(c), at least two-thirds in interest of the beneficiaries described in s. 736.0103(16)(a) or two-thirds in interest of the beneficiaries described in s. 736.0103(16)(b), if the interests of the beneficiaries are reasonably ascertainable, otherwise, two-thirds in number of either such class.

(10) A trust exists on January 1, 2003, if it is not revocable on January 1, 2003. A trust is revocable if revocable by the grantor alone or in conjunction with any other person. A trust is not revocable for purposes of this section if revocable by the grantor only with the consent of all persons having a beneficial interest in the property.

Added by Laws 2002, c. 2002–42, § 1, eff. Jan. 1, 2003. Amended by Laws 2003, c. 2003–43, § 1, eff. May 23, 2003; Laws 2005, c. 2005–85, § 5, eff. July 1, 2005; Laws 2006, c. 2006–217, § 40, eff. July 1, 2007; Laws 2012, c. 2012–49, § 4, eff. Jan. 1, 2013; Laws 2013, c. 2013–172, § 20, eff. Oct. 1, 2013.

738.1041. Total return unitrust

(1) For purposes of this section, the term:

(a) "Average fair market value" means the average of the fair market values of assets held by the trust at the beginning of the current and each of the 2 preceding years, or for the entire term of the trust if there are less than 2 preceding years, and adjusted as follows:

1. If assets have been added to the trust during the years used to determine the average, the amount of each addition is added to all years in which such addition was not included.

2. If assets have been distributed from the trust during the years used to determine the average, other than in satisfaction of the unitrust amount, the amount of each distribution is subtracted from all years in which such distribution was not included.

(b) "Disinterested person" means a person who is not a related or subordinate party with respect to the person acting as trustee of the trust and excludes the grantor and any interested trustee.

(c) "Fair market value" means the fair market value of the assets held by the trust as otherwise determined under this chapter, reduced by all known noncontingent liabilities.

(d) "Income trust" means a trust, created by an inter vivos or a testamentary instrument, which directs or permits the trustee to distribute the net income of the trust to one or more persons, in fixed proportions or in amounts or proportions determined by the trustee and regardless of whether the trust directs or permits the trustee to distribute the principal of the trust to one or more such persons.

(e) "Interested distributee" means a person to whom distributions of income or principal can currently be made and who has the power to remove the existing trustee and designate as successor a person who may be a related or subordinate party with respect to such distributee.

(f) "Interested trustee" means an individual trustee to whom the net income or principal of the trust can currently be distributed or would be distributed if the trust were then to terminate and be distributed, any trustee whom an interested distributee has the power to remove and replace with a related or subordinate party, or an individual trustee whose legal obligation to support a beneficiary may be satisfied by distributions of income and principal of the trust.

(g) "Related or subordinate party" has the same meaning as provided in the Internal Revenue Code, 26 U.S.C. s. 672(c) or any successor provision thereof.

(h) "Unitrust amount" means the amount determined by multiplying the average fair market value of the assets as calculated in paragraph (a) by the percentage calculated under paragraph (2)(b).

(2) A trustee may, without court approval, convert an income trust to a total return unitrust, reconvert a total return unitrust to an income trust, or change the percentage used to calculate the unitrust amount or the method used to determine the fair market value of the trust if:

(a) The trustee adopts a written statement regarding trust distributions which provides:

1. In the case of a trust being administered as an income trust, that future distributions from the trust will be unitrust amounts rather than net income, and indicates the manner in which the unitrust amount will be calculated and the method in which the fair market value of the trust will be determined.

2. In the case of a trust being administered as a total return unitrust, that:

a. Future distributions from the trust will be net income rather than unitrust amounts; or

b. The percentage used to calculate the unitrust amount or the method used to determine the fair market value of the trust will be changed, and indicates the manner in which the new unitrust amount will be calculated and the method in which the new fair market value of the trust will be determined;

(b) The trustee determines the terms of the unitrust under one of the following methods:

1. A disinterested trustee determines, or if there is no trustee other than an interested trustee, the interested trustee appoints a disinterested person who, in its sole discretion but acting in a fiduciary capacity, determines for the interested trustee:

a. The percentage to be used to calculate the unitrust amount, provided the percentage used is not greater than 5 percent nor less than 3 percent;

b. The method to be used in determining the fair market value of the trust; and

c. Which assets, if any, are to be excluded in determining the unitrust amount; or

2. The interested trustee or disinterested trustee administers the trust such that:

a. The percentage used to calculate the unitrust amount is 50 percent of the rate as defined in the Internal Revenue Code, 26 U.S.C. s. 7520, in effect for the month the conversion under this section becomes effective and for each January thereafter; however, if the percentage calculated exceeds 5 percent, the unitrust percentage is 5 percent and if the percentage calculated is less than 3 percent, the unitrust percentage is 3 percent; and

b. The fair market value of the trust shall be determined at least annually on an asset-by-asset basis, reasonably and in good faith, in accordance with s. 738.202(5), except the following property shall not be included in determining the value of the trust:

(I) Any residential property or any tangible personal property that, as of the first business day of the current valuation year, one or more current beneficiaries of the trust have or have had the right to occupy, or have or have had the right to possess or control, other than in his or her capacity as trustee of the trust, and instead the right of occupancy or the right to possession and control is the unitrust amount with respect to such property; however, the unitrust amount must be adjusted to take into account partial distributions from or receipt into the trust of such property during the valuation year;

(II) Any asset specifically given to a beneficiary and the return on investment on such property, which return on investment shall be distributable to the beneficiary; or

(III) Any asset while held in a decedent's estate;

(c) The trustee sends written notice of its intention to take such action, along with copies of the written statement regarding trust distributions and this section, and, if applicable, the determinations of the trustee or the disinterested person to:

1. The grantor of the trust, if living.

2. All living persons who are currently receiving or eligible to receive distributions of income from the trust.

3. All living persons who would receive distributions of principal of the trust if the trust were to terminate at the time of giving such notice without regard to the exercise of any power of appointment, or, if the trust does not provide for its termination, all living persons who would receive or be eligible to receive distributions of income or principal of the trust if the persons identified in subparagraph 2. were deceased.

4. All persons acting as advisers or protectors of the trust.

Notice under this paragraph shall be served informally in the manner provided in the Florida Rules of Civil Procedure relating to service of pleadings subsequent to the initial pleading. Notice may be served on a legal representative or natural guardian of a person without filing any proceeding or approval of any court;

(d) At least one person receiving notice under each of subparagraphs (c)2. and 3. is legally competent; and

(e) No person receiving such notice objects, by written instrument delivered to the trustee, to the proposed action of the trustee or the determinations of the disinterested person within 60 days after service of such notice. An objection may be executed by a legal representative or natural guardian of a person without filing any proceeding or approval of any court.

(3) If a trustee desires to convert an income trust to a total return unitrust, reconvert a total return unitrust to an income trust, or change the percentage used to calculate the unitrust amount or the method used to determine a fair market value of the trust but does not have the ability to or elects not to do it under subsection (2), the trustee may petition the circuit court for such order as the trustee deems appropriate. In that event, the court, in its own discretion or on the petition of such trustee or any person having an income or remainder interest in the trust, may appoint a disinterested person who, acting in a fiduciary capacity, shall present such information to the court as is necessary for the court to make a determination hereunder.

(4) Following the conversion of an income trust to a total return unitrust, the trustee:

(a) Shall treat the unitrust amount as if it were net income of the trust for purposes of determining the amount available, from time to time, for distribution from the trust.

(b) May allocate to trust income for each taxable year of the trust, or portion thereof:

1. Net short-term capital gain described in the Internal Revenue Code, 26 U.S.C. s. 1222(5), for such year, or portion thereof, but only to the extent that the amount so allocated together with all other amounts allocated to trust income, as determined under the provisions of this chapter without regard to this section and s. 738.104, for such year, or portion thereof, does not exceed the unitrust amount for such year, or portion thereof.

2. Net long-term capital gain described in the Internal Revenue Code, 26 U.S.C. s. 1222(7), for such year, or portion thereof, but only to the extent that the amount so allocated together with all other amounts, including amounts described in subparagraph 1., allocated to trust income for such year, or portion thereof, does not exceed the unitrust amount for such year, or portion thereof.

(5) In administering a total return unitrust, the trustee may, in its sole discretion but subject to the provisions of the governing instrument, determine:

(a) The effective date of the conversion.

(b) The timing of distributions, including provisions for prorating a distribution for a short year in which a beneficiary's right to payments commences or ceases.

(c) Whether distributions are to be made in cash or in kind or partly in cash and partly in kind.

(d) If the trust is reconverted to an income trust, the effective date of such reconversion.

(e) Such other administrative issues as may be necessary or appropriate to carry out the purposes of this section.

(6) Conversion to a total return unitrust under this section does not affect any other provision of the governing instrument, if any, regarding distributions of principal.

(7) Any trustee or disinterested person who in good faith takes or fails to take any action under this section is not liable to any person affected by such action or inaction, regardless of whether such person received written notice as provided in this section or such person was under a legal disability at the time of the delivery of such notice. Such person's exclusive remedy is to obtain, under subsection (8), an order of the court directing the trustee to convert an income trust to a total return unitrust, to reconvert from a total return unitrust to an income trust, or to change the percentage used to calculate the unitrust amount. If a court determines that the trustee or disinterested person has not acted in good faith in taking or failing to take any action under this section, s. 738.105(3) applies.

(8) If a majority in interest of the income or remainder beneficiaries of an income trust has delivered to the trustee a written objection to the amount of the income distributions of the trust, and, if the trustee has failed to resolve the objection to the satisfaction of the objecting beneficiaries within 6 months after receipt of such written objection, the objecting beneficiaries may petition the court in accordance with subsection (3).

(9) This section pertains to the administration of a trust and is applicable to any trust that is administered in this state or under Florida law unless:

(a) The governing instrument reflects an intention that the current beneficiary or beneficiaries are to receive an amount other than a reasonable current return from the trust;

(b) The trust is a trust described in the Internal Revenue Code, 26 U.S.C. s. 170(f)(2)(B), s. 642(c)(5), s. 664(d), s. 2702(a)(3), or s. 2702(b);

(c) One or more persons to whom the trustee could distribute income have a power of withdrawal over the trust:

1. That is not subject to an ascertainable standard under the Internal Revenue Code, 26 U.S.C. s. 2041 or s. 2514, and exceeds in any calendar year the amount set forth in the Internal Revenue Code, 26 U.S.C. s. 2041(b)(2) or s. 2514(e); or

2. A power of withdrawal over the trust that can be exercised to discharge a duty of support he or she possesses; or

(d) The governing instrument expressly prohibits use of this section by specific reference to the section. A provision in the governing instrument that, "The provisions of section 738.1041, Florida Statutes, as amended, or any corresponding provision of future law, may not be used in the administration of this trust," or similar words reflecting such intent are sufficient to preclude the use of this section.

(10) The grantor of a trust may create an express total return unitrust that will be effective as provided in the trust instrument without requiring a conversion under this section.

(a) An express total return unitrust created by the grantor of the trust is treated as a unitrust only if the terms of the trust instrument contain all of the following provisions:

1. That distributions from the trust will be unitrust amounts and the manner in which the unitrust amount will be calculated; and

2. The percentage to be used to calculate the unitrust amount, provided the percentage used is not greater than 5 percent nor less than 3 percent.

(b) The trust instrument may also contain provisions specifying:

1. The method to be used in determining the fair market value of the trust, including whether to use an average fair market value or the fair market value of the assets held by the trust at the beginning of the current year; or

2. Which assets, if any, are to be excluded in determining the unitrust amount.

(c) This section establishes the method of determining the fair market value of the trust if the trust instrument is silent as to subparagraph (b)1., and to specify those assets, if any, which are to be excluded in determining the unitrust amount if the trust instrument is silent as to subparagraph (b)2.

Added by Laws 2002, c. 2002–42, § 1, eff. Jan. 1, 2003. Amended by Laws 2003, c. 2003–43, § 2, eff. May 23, 2003; Laws 2005, c. 2005–85, § 6, eff. July 1, 2005; Laws 2006, c. 2006–217, § 41, eff. July 1, 2007; Laws 2012, c. 2012–49, § 5, eff. Jan. 1, 2013.

738.105. Judicial control of discretionary powers

(1) A court may not change a trustee's decision to exercise or not to exercise a discretionary power conferred by this chapter unless the court determines that the decision was an abuse of the trustee's discretion. A court may not determine that a trustee abused its discretion merely because the court would have exercised the discretion in a different manner or would not have exercised the discretion.

(2) The decisions to which subsection (1) applies include:

(a) A determination under s. 738.104(1) of whether and to what extent an amount should be transferred from principal to income or from income to principal.

(b) A determination of the factors that are relevant to the trust and trust beneficiaries, the extent to which such factors are relevant, and the weight, if any, to be given to the relevant factors, in deciding whether and to what extent to exercise the power conferred by s. 738.104(1).

(3) If a court determines that a trustee has abused its discretion, the remedy is to restore the income and remainder beneficiaries to the positions they would have occupied if the trustee had not abused its discretion, in accordance with the following:

(a) To the extent the abuse of discretion has resulted in no distribution to a beneficiary or a distribution that is too small, the court shall require the trustee to distribute from the trust to the beneficiary an amount the court determines will restore the beneficiary, in whole or in part, to his or her appropriate position.

(b) To the extent the abuse of discretion has resulted in a distribution to a beneficiary that is too large, the court shall restore the beneficiaries, the trust, or both, in whole or in part, to their appropriate positions by requiring the trustee to withhold an amount from one or more future distributions to the beneficiary who received the distribution that was too large or requiring that beneficiary to return some or all of the distribution to the trust.

(c) To the extent the court is unable, after applying paragraphs (a) and (b), to restore the beneficiaries or the trust, or both, to the positions they would have occupied if the trustee had not abused its discretion, the court may require the trustee to pay an appropriate amount from its own funds to one or more of the beneficiaries or the trust or both.

(4) Upon the filing of a petition by the trustee, the court having jurisdiction over the trust shall determine whether a proposed exercise or nonexercise by the trustee of a discretionary power conferred by this chapter will result in an abuse of the trustee's discretion. If the petition describes the proposed exercise or nonexercise of the power and contains sufficient information to inform the beneficiaries of the reasons for the proposal, the facts upon which the trustee relies, and an explanation of how the income and remainder beneficiaries will be affected by the proposed exercise or nonexercise of the power, a beneficiary who challenges the proposed exercise or nonexercise has the burden of establishing that such exercise or nonexercise will result in an abuse of discretion.

(5) If an action is instituted alleging an abuse of discretion in the exercise or nonexercise of the power of adjustment conferred by s. 738.104(1) and the court determines that no abuse of discretion has occurred, the trustee's costs and attorney's fees incurred in defending the action shall be paid from the trust assets.

Added by Laws 2002, c. 2002–42, § 1, eff. Jan. 1, 2003. Amended by Laws 2012, c. 2012–49, § 6, eff. Jan. 1, 2013.

738.201. Determination and distribution of net income

After a decedent dies, in the case of an estate, or after an income interest in a trust ends, the following rules apply:

(1) A fiduciary of an estate or of a terminating income interest shall determine the amount of net income and net principal receipts received from property specifically given to a beneficiary under ss. 738.301–738.706 and subsection (5). The fiduciary shall distribute the net income and net principal receipts to the beneficiary who is to receive the specific property.

(2) A fiduciary shall determine the remaining net income of a decedent's estate or a terminating income interest under ss. 738.301–738.706 and by:

(a) Including in net income all income from property used to discharge liabilities.

(b) Paying from income or principal, in the fiduciary's discretion, fees of attorneys, accountants, and fiduciaries; court costs and other expenses of administration; and interest on death taxes. The fiduciary may pay those expenses from income of property passing to a trust for which the fiduciary claims an estate tax marital or charitable deduction under the Internal Revenue Code [1] or comparable law of any state only to the extent the payment of those expenses from income will not cause the reduction or loss of the deduction.

(c) Paying from principal all other disbursements made or incurred in connection with the settlement of a decedent's estate or the winding up of a terminating income interest, including debts, funeral expenses, disposition of remains, family allowances, and death taxes and related penalties that are apportioned to the estate or terminating income interest by the will, the terms of the trust, or applicable law.

(3) If a beneficiary who receives a pecuniary devise outright is also entitled to receive interest or any other amount on the devise under the terms of the will or trust, the fiduciary shall distribute the interest or other amount from net income determined under subsection (2) or from principal to the extent net income is insufficient.

(4) A fiduciary shall distribute the net income remaining after distributions required under subsections (1)–(3) in the manner described in s. 738.202 to all other beneficiaries, including a beneficiary who receives a pecuniary amount in trust, even if the beneficiary holds an unqualified power to withdraw assets from the trust or other presently exercisable general power of appointment over the trust.

(5) A fiduciary may not reduce principal or income receipts from property described in subsection (1) because of a payment described in s. 738.701 or s. 738.702 to the extent the will, the terms of the trust, or applicable law requires the fiduciary to make the payment from assets other than the property or to the extent the fiduciary recovers or expects to recover the payment from a third party. The net income and principal receipts from the property are determined by including all of the amounts the fiduciary receives or pays with respect to the property, whether those amounts accrued or became due before, on, or after the date of a decedent's death or an income interest's terminating event, and by making a reasonable provision for amounts the fiduciary believes the estate or terminating income interest may become obligated to pay after the property is distributed.

Added by Laws 2002, c. 2002–42, § 1, eff. Jan. 1, 2003. Amended by Laws 2012, c. 2012–49, § 7, eff. Jan. 1, 2013.

[1] 26 U.S.C.A. § 1 et seq.

738.202. Distribution to residuary and remainder beneficiaries

(1) Each beneficiary described in s. 738.201(4) is entitled to receive a portion of the net income remaining after the application of s. 738.201(1)–(3), which is equal to the beneficiary's fractional interest in undistributed principal assets, using carrying values as of the distribution date. If a fiduciary makes more than one distribution of assets to beneficiaries to whom this section applies, each beneficiary, including one who does not receive part of the distribution, is entitled, as of each distribution date, to the net income the fiduciary received after the date of death or terminating event or earlier distribution date but has not distributed as of the current distribution date.

(2) In determining a beneficiary's share of net income, the following applies:

(a) The beneficiary is entitled to receive a portion of the net income equal to the beneficiary's fractional interest in the carrying value of the undistributed principal assets immediately before the distribution date, excluding the amount of unpaid liabilities.

(b) The beneficiary's fractional interest in the undistributed principal assets shall be calculated:

1. At the time the interest began and adjusted for any disproportionate distributions since the interest began;

2. By excluding any liabilities of the estate or trust from the calculation;

3. By also excluding property specifically given to a beneficiary and property required to pay pecuniary amounts not in trust; and

4. On the basis of the aggregate carrying value of those assets determined under subsection (1) as of the distribution date.

(c) If a disproportionate distribution of principal is made to any beneficiary, the respective fractional interests of all beneficiaries in the remaining underlying assets shall be recomputed by:

1. Adjusting the carrying value of the principal assets to their fair market value before the distribution;

2. Reducing the fractional interest of the recipient of the disproportionate distribution in the remaining principal assets by the fair market value of the principal distribution; and

3. Recomputing the fractional interests of all beneficiaries in the remaining principal assets based upon the now restated carrying values.

(3) If a fiduciary does not distribute all of the collected but undistributed net income to each person as of a distribution date, the fiduciary shall maintain appropriate records showing the interest of each beneficiary in that net income.

(4) A fiduciary may apply the provisions of this section, to the extent the fiduciary considers appropriate, to net gain or loss realized after the date of death or terminating event or earlier distribution date from the disposition of a principal asset if this section applies to the income from the asset.

(5) The carrying value or fair market value of trust assets shall be determined on an asset-by-asset basis and is conclusive if reasonable and determined in good faith. Determinations of fair market value based on appraisals performed within 2 years before or after the valuation date are presumed reasonable. The values of trust assets are conclusively presumed to be reasonable and determined in good faith unless proven otherwise in a proceeding commenced by or on behalf of a person interested in the trust within the time provided in s. 736.1008.

(6) All distributions to a beneficiary shall be valued based on their fair market value on the date of distribution.

Added by Laws 2002, c. 2002–42, § 1, eff. Jan. 1, 2003. Amended by Laws 2003, c. 2003–43, § 3, eff. May 23, 2003; Laws 2006, c. 2006–217, § 42, eff. July 1, 2007; Laws 2012, c. 2012–49, § 8, eff. Jan. 1, 2013.

738.301. When right to income begins and ends

An income beneficiary is entitled to net income from the date on which the income interest begins.

(1) An income interest begins on the date specified in the terms of the trust or, if no date is specified, on the date an asset becomes subject to a trust or successive income interest.

(2) An asset becomes subject to a trust:

(a) On the date the asset is transferred to the trust in the case of an asset that is transferred to a trust during the transferor's life;

(b) On the date of a testator's death in the case of an asset that becomes subject to a trust by reason of a will, even if there is an intervening period of administration of the testator's estate; or

(c) On the date of an individual's death in the case of an asset that is transferred to a fiduciary by a third party because of the individual's death.

(3) An asset becomes subject to a successive income interest on the day after the preceding income interest ends, as determined under subsection (4), even if there is an intervening period of administration to wind up the preceding income interest.

(4) An income interest ends on the day before an income beneficiary dies or another terminating event occurs, or on the last day of a period during which there is no beneficiary to whom a fiduciary may distribute income.

Added by Laws 2002, c. 2002–42, § 1, eff. Jan. 1, 2003. Amended by Laws 2012, c. 2012–49, § 9, eff. Jan. 1, 2013.

738.302. Apportionment of receipts and disbursements when decedent dies or income interest begins

(1) A fiduciary shall allocate an income receipt or disbursement other than one to which s. 738.201(1) applies to principal if the due date of the receipt or disbursement occurs before a decedent dies in the case of an estate or before an income interest begins in the case of a trust or successive income interest.

(2) A fiduciary shall allocate an income receipt or disbursement to income if the due date of the receipt or disbursement occurs on or after the date on which a decedent dies or an income interest begins and the due date is a periodic due date. An income receipt or disbursement shall be treated as accruing from day to day if the due date of the receipt or disbursement is not periodic or the receipt or disbursement has no due date. The portion of the receipt or disbursement accruing before the date on which a decedent dies or an income interest begins shall be allocated to principal and the balance shall be allocated to income.

(3) An item of income or an obligation is due on the date the payor is required to make a payment. If a payment date is not stated, there is no due date for the purposes of this chapter. Distributions to shareholders or other owners from an entity to which s. 738.401 applies are deemed to be due on the date fixed by the entity for determining who is entitled to receive the distribution or, if no date is fixed, on the declaration date for the distribution. A due date is periodic for receipts or disbursements that shall be paid at regular intervals under a lease or an obligation to pay interest or if an entity customarily makes distributions at regular intervals.

(4) Nothing in this section shall prevent the application of s. 733.817 to apportion tax to the income recipient under this section.

Added by Laws 2002, c. 2002–42, § 1, eff. Jan. 1, 2003. Amended by Laws 2012, c. 2012–49, § 10, eff. Jan. 1, 2013.

738.303. Apportionment when income interest ends

(1) For purposes of this section, "undistributed income" means net income received on or before the date on which an income interest ends. The term does not include an item of income or expense that is due or accrued or net income that has been added or is required to be added to principal under the terms of the trust. In the case of a trust being administered as a unitrust under s. 738.1041, the term "undistributed income" means the prorated unitrust amount computed on a daily basis through the date on which the income interest ends.

(2) When a mandatory income interest ends, the fiduciary shall pay to a mandatory income beneficiary who survives that date, or the estate of a deceased mandatory income beneficiary whose death causes the interest to end, the beneficiary's share of the undistributed income that is not disposed of under the terms of the trust unless the beneficiary has an unqualified power to revoke more than 5 percent of the trust immediately before the income interest ends. In the latter case, the undistributed income from the portion of the trust that may be revoked shall be added to principal.

(3) When a fiduciary's obligation to pay a fixed annuity or a fixed fraction of the value of the trust's assets ends, the fiduciary shall prorate the final payment if and to the extent required by applicable law to accomplish a purpose of the trust or its grantor relating to income, gift, estate, or other tax requirements.

Added by Laws 2002, c. 2002–42, § 1, eff. Jan. 1, 2003. Amended by Laws 2005, c. 2005–85, § 7, eff. July 1, 2005; Laws 2012, c. 2012–49, § 11, eff. Jan. 1, 2013.

738.401. Character of receipts

(1) For purposes of this section, the term "entity" means a corporation, partnership, limited liability company, regulated investment company, real estate investment trust, common trust fund, or any other organization in which a fiduciary has an interest other than a trust or estate to which s. 738.402 applies, a business or activity to which s. 738.403 applies, or an asset-backed security to which s. 738.608 applies.

(2) Except as otherwise provided in this section, a fiduciary shall allocate to income money received from an entity.

(3) Except as otherwise provided in this section, a fiduciary shall allocate the following receipts from an entity to principal:

(a) Property other than money.

(b) Money received in one distribution or a series of related distributions in exchange for part or all of a trust's or estate's interest in the entity.

(c) Money received in total or partial liquidation of the entity.

(d) Money received from an entity that is a regulated investment company or a real estate investment trust if the money received represents short-term or long-term capital gain realized within the entity.

(e) Money received from an entity listed on a public stock exchange during any year of the trust or estate which exceeds 10 percent of the fair market value of the trust's or estate's interest in the entity on the first day of that year. The amount to be allocated to principal must be reduced to the extent that the cumulative distributions from the entity to the trust or estate allocated to income do not exceed a cumulative annual return of 3 percent of the fair market value of the interest in the entity at the beginning of each year or portion of a year for the number of years or portion of years in the period that the interest in the entity has been held by the trust or estate. If a trustee has exercised a power to adjust under s. 738.104 during any period the interest in the entity has been held by the trust, the trustee, in determining the total income distributions from that entity, must take into account the extent to which the exercise of that power resulted in income to the trust from that entity for that period. If the income of the trust for any period has been computed under s. 738.1041, the trustee, in determining the total income distributions from that entity for that period, must take into account the portion of the unitrust amount paid as a result of the ownership of the trust's interest in the entity for that period.

(4) If a fiduciary elects, or continues an election made by its predecessor, to reinvest dividends in shares of stock of a distributing corporation or fund, whether evidenced by new certificates or entries on the books of the distributing entity, the new shares retain their character as income.

(5) Money is received in partial liquidation:

(a) To the extent the entity, at or near the time of a distribution, indicates that such money is a distribution in partial liquidation; or

(b) To the extent the total amount of money and property received in a distribution or series of related distributions from an entity that is not listed on a public stock exchange exceeds 20 percent of the trust's or estate's pro rata share of the entity's gross assets, as shown by the entity's year-end financial statements immediately preceding the initial receipt.

This subsection does not apply to an entity to which subsection (7) applies.

---

(6) Money may not be taken into account in determining any excess under paragraph (5)(b), to the extent that the cumulative distributions from the entity to the trust or the estate allocated to income do not exceed the greater of:

(a) A cumulative annual return of 3 percent of the entity's carrying value computed at the beginning of each period for the number of years or portion of years that the entity was held by the fiduciary. If a trustee has exercised a power to adjust under s. 738.104 during any period the interest in the entity has been held by the trust, the trustee, in determining the total income distributions from that entity, must take into account the extent to which exercise of the power resulted in income to the trust from that entity for that period. If the income of a trust for any period has been computed pursuant to s. 738.1041, the trustee, in determining the total income distributions from the entity for that period, must take into account the portion of the unitrust amount paid as a result of the ownership of the trust's interest in the entity for that period; or

(b) If the entity is treated as a partnership, subchapter S corporation, or a disregarded entity pursuant to the Internal Revenue Code of 1986,[1] as amended, the amount of income tax attributable to the trust's or estate's ownership share of the entity, based on its pro rata share of the taxable income of the entity that distributes the money, for the number of years or portion of years that the interest in the entity was held by the fiduciary, calculated as if all of that tax was incurred by the fiduciary.

(7) The following applies to money or property received by a private trustee as a distribution from an investment entity described in this subsection:

(a) The trustee shall first treat as income of the trust all of the money or property received from the investment entity in the current year which would be considered income under this chapter if the trustee had directly held the trust's pro rata share of the assets of the investment entity. For this purpose, all distributions received in the current year must be aggregated.

(b) The trustee shall next treat as income of the trust any additional money or property received in the current year which would have been considered income in the prior 2 years under paragraph (a) if additional money or property had been received from the investment entity in any of those prior 2 years. The amount to be treated as income shall be reduced by any distributions of money or property made by the investment entity to the trust during the current and prior 2 years which were treated as income under this paragraph.

(c) The remainder of the distribution, if any, is treated as principal.

(d) As used in this subsection, the term:

1. "Investment entity" means an entity, other than a business activity conducted by the trustee described in s. 738.403 or an entity that is listed on a public stock exchange, which is treated as a partnership, subchapter S corporation, or disregarded entity pursuant to the Internal Revenue Code of 1986, as amended, and which normally derives 50 percent or more of its annual cumulative net income from interest, dividends, annuities, royalties, rental activity, or other passive investments, including income from the sale or exchange of such passive investments.

2. "Private trustee" means a trustee who is a natural person, but only if the trustee is unable to use the power to adjust between income and principal with respect to receipts from entities described in this subsection pursuant to s. 738.104. A bank, trust company, or other commercial trustee is not considered a private trustee.

(8) This section shall be applied before ss. 738.705 and 738.706 and does not modify or change any of the provisions of those sections.

Added by Laws 2002, c. 2002–42, § 1, eff. Jan. 1, 2003. Amended by Laws 2003, c. 2003–43, § 4, eff. May 23, 2003; Laws 2005, c. 2005–85, § 8, eff. July 1, 2005; Laws 2012, c. 2012–49, § 12, eff. Jan. 1, 2013.

[1] 26 U.S.C.A. § 1 et seq.

738.402. Distribution from trust or estate

A fiduciary shall allocate to income an amount received as a distribution of income from a trust or an estate in which the trust has an interest other than a purchased interest and allocate to principal an amount received as a distribution of principal from such a trust or estate. If a fiduciary purchases an interest in a trust that is an investment entity, or a decedent or donor transfers an interest in such a trust to a fiduciary, s. 738.401 or s. 738.608 applies to a receipt from the trust.

Added by Laws 2002, c. 2002–42, § 1, eff. Jan. 1, 2003. Amended by Laws 2012, c. 2012–49, § 13, eff. Jan. 1, 2013.

738.403. Business and other activities conducted by fiduciary

(1) If a fiduciary who conducts a business or other activity determines that it is in the best interest of all the beneficiaries to account separately for the business or activity instead of accounting for the business or activity as part of the trust's or estate's general accounting records, the fiduciary may maintain separate accounting records for the transactions of the business or other activity, whether or not the assets of such business or activity are segregated from other trust or estate assets.

(2) A fiduciary who accounts separately for a business or other activity may determine the extent to which the net cash receipts of the business or activity must be retained for working capital, the acquisition or replacement of fixed assets, and other reasonably foreseeable needs of the business or activity, and the extent to which the remaining net cash receipts are accounted for as principal or income in the trust's or estate's general accounting records. If a fiduciary sells assets of the business or other activity, other than in the ordinary course of the business or activity, the fiduciary must account for the net amount received as principal in the trust's or estate's general accounting records to the extent the fiduciary determines that the amount received is no longer required in the conduct of the business.

(3) Activities for which a fiduciary may maintain separate accounting records include:

(a) Retail, manufacturing, service, and other traditional business activities.

(b) Farming.

(c) Raising and selling livestock and other animals.

(d) Management of rental properties.

(e) Extraction of minerals and other natural resources.

(f) Timber operations.

(g) Activities to which s. 738.607 applies.

Added by Laws 2002, c. 2002–42, § 1, eff. Jan. 1, 2003. Amended by Laws 2012, c. 2012–49, § 14, eff. Jan. 1, 2013.

738.501. Principal receipts

A fiduciary shall allocate to principal:

(1) To the extent not allocated to income under this chapter, assets received from a donor during the donor's lifetime, a decedent's estate, a trust with a terminating income interest, or a payor under a contract naming the trust, estate, or fiduciary as beneficiary.

(2) Money or other property received from the sale, exchange, liquidation, or change in form of a principal asset, including realized profit, subject to this section.

(3) Amounts recovered from third parties to reimburse the trust or estate because of disbursements described in s. 738.702(1)(g) or for other reasons to the extent not based on the loss of income.

(4) Proceeds of property taken by eminent domain; however, a separate award made for the loss of income with respect to an accounting period during which a current income beneficiary had a mandatory income interest is income.

(5) Net income received in an accounting period during which there is no beneficiary to whom a fiduciary may or shall distribute income.

(6) Other receipts as provided in ss. 738.601–738.608.

Added by Laws 2002, c. 2002–42, § 1, eff. Jan. 1, 2003. Amended by Laws 2012, c. 2012–49, § 15, eff. Jan. 1, 2013.

738.502. Rental property

If a fiduciary accounts for receipts from rental property pursuant to this section, the fiduciary shall allocate to income an amount received as rent of real or personal property, including an amount received for cancellation or renewal of a lease. An amount received as a refundable deposit, including a security deposit or a deposit that is to be applied as rent for future periods, must be added to principal and held subject to the terms of the lease and is not available for distribution to a beneficiary until the fiduciary's contractual obligations have been satisfied with respect to that amount.

Added by Laws 2002, c. 2002–42, § 1, eff. Jan. 1, 2003. Amended by Laws 2012, c. 2012–49, § 16, eff. Jan. 1, 2013.

738.503. Obligation to pay money

(1) An amount received as interest, whether determined at a fixed, variable, or floating rate, on an obligation to pay money to the fiduciary, including an amount received as consideration for prepaying principal, shall be allocated to income without any provision for amortization of premium.

(2) Except as otherwise provided herein, a fiduciary shall allocate to principal an amount received from the sale, redemption, or other disposition of an obligation to pay money to the fiduciary.

(3) The increment in value of a bond or other obligation for the payment of money bearing no stated interest but payable at a future time in excess of the price at which it was issued or purchased, if purchased after issuance, is distributable as income. If the increment in value accrues and becomes payable pursuant to a fixed schedule of appreciation, it may be distributed to the beneficiary who was the income beneficiary at the time of increment from the first principal cash available or, if none is available, when the increment is realized by sale, redemption, or other disposition. If unrealized increment is distributed as income but out of principal, the principal must be reimbursed for the increment when realized. If, in the reasonable judgment of the fiduciary, exercised in good faith, the ultimate payment of the bond

principal is in doubt, the fiduciary may withhold the payment of incremental interest to the income beneficiary.

(4) This section does not apply to an obligation to which s. 738.602, s. 738.603, s. 738.604, s. 738.605, s. 738.607, or s. 738.608 applies.

Added by Laws 2002, c. 2002–42, § 1, eff. Jan. 1, 2003. Amended by Laws 2012, c. 2012–49, § 17, eff. Jan. 1, 2013.

738.504. Insurance policies and similar contracts

(1) Except as otherwise provided in subsection (2), a fiduciary shall allocate to principal the proceeds of a life insurance policy or other contract in which the trust, estate, or fiduciary is named as beneficiary, including a contract that insures the trust, estate, or fiduciary against loss for damage to, destruction of, or loss of title to a trust or estate asset. The fiduciary shall allocate dividends on an insurance policy to income if the premiums on the policy are paid from income and to principal if the premiums are paid from principal.

(2) A fiduciary shall allocate to income the proceeds of a contract that insures the fiduciary against loss of occupancy or other use by an income beneficiary, loss of income, or, subject to s. 738.403, loss of profits from a business.

(3) This section does not apply to a contract to which s. 738.602 applies.

Added by Laws 2002, c. 2002–42, § 1, eff. Jan. 1, 2003. Amended by Laws 2012, c. 2012–49, § 18, eff. Jan. 1, 2013.

738.601. Insubstantial allocations not required

If a fiduciary determines that an allocation between principal and income required by s. 738.602, s. 738.603, s. 738.604, s. 738.605, or s. 738.608 is insubstantial, the fiduciary may allocate the entire amount to principal unless one of the circumstances described in s. 738.104(3) applies to the allocation. This power may be exercised by a cofiduciary under the circumstances described in s. 738.104(4) and may be released for the reasons and in the manner described in s. 738.104(5). An allocation is presumed to be insubstantial if:

(1) The amount of the allocation would increase or decrease net income in an accounting period, as determined before the allocation, by less than 10 percent; or

(2) The value of the asset producing the receipt for which the allocation would be made is less than 10 percent of the total value of the trust or estate assets at the beginning of the accounting period.

Added by Laws 2002, c. 2002–42, § 1, eff. Jan. 1, 2003. Amended by Laws 2012, c. 2012–49, § 19, eff. Jan. 1, 2013.

738.602. Payments from deferred compensation plans, annuities, and retirement plans or accounts

(1) As used in this section, the term:

(a) "Fund" means a private or commercial annuity, an individual retirement account, an individual retirement annuity, a deferred compensation plan, a pension plan, a profit-sharing plan, a stock-bonus plan, an employee stock-ownership plan, or another similar arrangement in which federal income tax is deferred.

(b) "Income of the fund" means income that is determined according to subsection (2) or subsection (3).

(c) "Nonseparate account" means a fund for which the value of the participant's or account owner's right to receive benefits can be determined only by the occurrence of a date or event as defined in the instrument governing the fund.

(d) "Payment" means a distribution from a fund that a fiduciary may receive over a fixed number of years or during the life of one or more individuals because of services rendered or property transferred to the payor in exchange for future payments. The term includes a distribution made in money or property from the payor's general assets or from a fund created by the payor or payee.

(e) "Separate account" means a fund holding assets exclusively for the benefit of a participant or account owner and:

1. The value of such assets or the value of the separate account is ascertainable at any time; or

2. The administrator of the fund maintains records that show receipts and disbursements associated with such assets.

(2)(a) For a fund that is a separate account, income of the fund shall be determined:

1. As if the fund were a trust subject to the provisions of ss. 738.401–738.706; or

2. As a unitrust amount calculated by multiplying the fair market value of the fund as of the first day of the first accounting period and, thereafter, as of the last day of the accounting period that immediately precedes the accounting period during which a payment is received by the percentage determined in accordance with s. 738.1041(2)(b)2.a. The fiduciary shall determine such percentage as of the first month that the fiduciary's election to treat the income of the fund as a unitrust amount becomes effective. For purposes of this subparagraph, "fair market value" means the fair market value of the assets held in the fund as of the applicable valuation date determined as provided in this subparagraph. The fiduciary is not liable for good faith reliance upon any valuation supplied by the person or persons in possession of the fund. If the fiduciary makes or terminates an election under this subparagraph, the fiduciary shall make such disclosure in a trust disclosure document that satisfies the requirements of s. 736.1008(4)(a).

(b) The fiduciary may elect the method of determining the income of the fund pursuant to this subsection and may change the method of determining income of the fund for any future accounting period.

(3) For a fund that is a nonseparate account, income of the fund is a unitrust amount determined by calculating the present value of the right to receive the remaining payments under the Internal Revenue Code, 26 U.S.C. s. 7520, as of the first day of the accounting period and multiplying it by the percentage determined in accordance with s. 738.1041(2)(b)2.a. The fiduciary shall determine the unitrust amount as of the first month that the fiduciary's election to treat the income of the fund as a unitrust amount becomes effective.

(4) Except for those trusts described in subsection (5), the fiduciary shall allocate to income the lesser of the payment received from a fund or the income determined under subsection (2) or subsection (3). Any remaining amount of the payment shall be allocated to principal.

(5) For a trust that, in order to qualify for the estate or gift tax marital deduction under the Internal Revenue Code [1] or comparable law of any state, entitles the spouse to all of the income of the trust, and the terms of the trust are silent as to the time and frequency for distribution of the income of the fund:

(a) For a fund that is a separate account, unless the spouse directs the fiduciary to leave the income of the fund in the fund, the fiduciary shall withdraw and pay to the spouse, at least annually:

1. All of the income of the fund determined in accordance with subparagraph (2)(a)1.; or

2. The income of the fund as a unitrust amount determined in accordance with subparagraph (2)(a)2.

(b) For a fund that is a nonseparate account, the fiduciary shall withdraw and pay to the spouse, at least annually, the income of the fund as a unitrust amount determined in accordance with subsection (3).

(6) This section does not apply to payments to which s. 738.603 applies.

Added by Laws 2002, c. 2002–42, § 1, eff. Jan. 1, 2003. Amended by Laws 2009, c. 2009–207, § 1, eff. July 1, 2009; Laws 2012, c. 2012–49, § 20, eff. Jan. 1, 2013.

[1] 26 U.S.C.A. § 1 et seq.

738.603. Liquidating asset

(1) For purposes of this section, the term "liquidating asset" means an asset the value of which will diminish or terminate because the asset is expected to produce receipts for a period of limited duration. The term includes a leasehold, patent, copyright, royalty right, and right to receive payments for more than 1 year under an arrangement that does not provide for the payment of interest on the unpaid balance. The term does not include a payment subject to s. 738.602, resources subject to s. 738.604, timber subject to s. 738.605, an activity subject to s. 738.607, an asset subject to s. 738.608, or any asset for which the fiduciary establishes a reserve for depreciation under s. 738.703.

(2) A fiduciary shall allocate to income 5 percent of the receipts from the carrying value of a liquidating asset and the balance to principal. Amounts allocated to principal shall reduce the carrying value of the liquidating asset, but not below zero. Amounts received in excess of the remaining carrying value must be allocated to principal.

Added by Laws 2002, c. 2002–42, § 1, eff. Jan. 1, 2003. Amended by Laws 2012, c. 2012–49, § 21, eff. Jan. 1, 2013.

738.604. Minerals, water, and other natural resources

(1) If a fiduciary accounts for receipts from an interest in minerals or other natural resources pursuant to this section, the fiduciary shall allocate such receipts as follows:

(a) If received as nominal delay rental or nominal annual rent on a lease, a receipt shall be allocated to income.

(b) If received from a production payment, a receipt shall be allocated to income if and to the extent the agreement creating the production payment provides a factor for interest or its equivalent. The balance shall be allocated to principal.

(c) If an amount received as a royalty, shut-in-well payment, take-or-pay payment, bonus, or delay rental is more than nominal, 90 percent shall be allocated to principal and the balance to income.

(d) If an amount is received from a working interest or any other interest not provided for in paragraph (a), paragraph (b), or paragraph (c), 90 percent of the net amount received shall be allocated to principal and the balance to income.

(2) An amount received on account of an interest in water that is renewable shall be allocated to income. If the water is not renewable, 90 percent of the amount shall be allocated to principal and the balance to income.

(3) This chapter applies whether or not a decedent or donor was extracting minerals, water, or other natural resources before the interest became subject to the trust or estate.

(4) If a trust or estate owns an interest in minerals, water, or other natural resources on January 1, 2003, the fiduciary may allocate receipts from the interest as provided in this chapter or in the manner used by the fiduciary before January 1, 2003. If the trust or estate acquires an interest in minerals, water, or other natural resources after January 1, 2003, the fiduciary shall allocate receipts from the interest as provided in this chapter.

Added by Laws 2002, c. 2002–42, § 1, eff. Jan. 1, 2003. Amended by Laws 2012, c. 2012–49, § 22, eff. Jan. 1, 2013.

738.605. Timber

(1) If a fiduciary accounts for receipts from the sale of timber and related products pursuant to this section, the fiduciary shall allocate such net receipts as follows:

(a) To income to the extent the amount of timber removed from the land does not exceed the rate of growth of the timber during the accounting periods in which a beneficiary has a mandatory income interest;

(b) To principal to the extent the amount of timber removed from the land exceeds the rate of growth of the timber or the net receipts are from the sale of standing timber;

(c) To or between income and principal if the net receipts are from the lease of timberland or from a contract to cut timber from land owned by a trust or estate by determining the amount of timber removed from the land under the lease or contract and applying the rules in paragraphs (a) and (b); or

(d) To principal to the extent advance payments, bonuses, and other payments are not allocated pursuant to paragraph (a), paragraph (b), or paragraph (c).

(2) In determining net receipts to be allocated pursuant to subsection (1), a fiduciary shall deduct and transfer to principal a reasonable amount for depletion.

(3) This chapter applies whether or not a decedent or donor was harvesting timber from the property before the property became subject to the trust or estate.

(4) If a trust or estate owns an interest in timberland on January 1, 2003, the fiduciary may allocate net receipts from the sale of timber and related products as provided in this chapter or in the manner used by the fiduciary before January 1, 2003. If the trust or estate acquires an interest in timberland after January 1, 2003, the fiduciary shall allocate net receipts from the sale of timber and related products as provided in this chapter.

Added by Laws 2002, c. 2002–42, § 1, eff. Jan. 1, 2003. Amended by Laws 2012, c. 2012–49, § 23, eff. Jan. 1, 2013.

738.606. Property not productive of income

(1) If a marital deduction under the Internal Revenue Code [1] or comparable law of any state is allowed for all or part of a trust the income of which must be distributed to the grantor's spouse and the assets of which consist substantially of property that does not provide the spouse with sufficient income from or use of the trust assets, and if the amounts the trustee transfers from principal to income under s. 738.104 and distributes to the spouse from principal pursuant to the terms of the trust are insufficient to provide the spouse with the beneficial enjoyment

required to obtain the marital deduction, the spouse may require the trustee to make property productive of income, convert property within a reasonable time, or exercise the power conferred by ss. 738.104 and 738.1041. The trustee may decide which action or combination of actions to take.

(2) In cases not governed by subsection (1), proceeds from the sale or other disposition of an asset are principal without regard to the amount of income the asset produces during any accounting period.

Added by Laws 2002, c. 2002–42, § 1, eff. Jan. 1, 2003. Amended by Laws 2012, c. 2012–49, § 24, eff. Jan. 1, 2013.

[1] 26 U.S.C.A. § 1 et seq.

738.607. Derivatives and options

(1) For purposes of this section, "derivative" means a contract or financial instrument or a combination of contracts and financial instruments which gives a trust the right or obligation to participate in some or all changes in the price of a tangible or intangible asset or group of assets, or changes in a rate, an index of prices or rates, or other market indicator for an asset or a group of assets.

(2) To the extent a fiduciary does not account under s. 738.403 for transactions in derivatives, the fiduciary shall allocate to principal receipts from and disbursements made in connection with those transactions.

(3) If a fiduciary grants an option to buy property from the trust or estate whether or not the trust or estate owns the property when the option is granted, grants an option that permits another person to sell property to the trust or estate, or acquires an option to buy property for the trust or estate or an option to sell an asset owned by the trust or estate, and the fiduciary or other owner of the asset is required to deliver the asset if the option is exercised, an amount received for granting the option shall be allocated to principal. An amount paid to acquire the option shall be paid from principal. A gain or loss realized upon the exercise of an option, including an option granted to a grantor of the trust or estate for services rendered, shall be allocated to principal.

Added by Laws 2002, c. 2002–42, § 1, eff. Jan. 1, 2003. Amended by Laws 2012, c. 2012–49, § 25, eff. Jan. 1, 2013.

738.608. Asset-backed securities

(1) For purposes of this section, "asset-backed security" means an asset the value of which is based upon the right given the owner to receive distributions from the proceeds of financial assets that provide collateral for the security. The term includes an asset that gives the owner the right to receive from the collateral financial assets only the interest or other current return or only the proceeds other than interest or current return. The term does not include an asset to which s. 738.401 or s. 738.602 applies.

(2) If a trust or estate receives a payment from interest or other current return and from other proceeds of the collateral financial assets, the fiduciary shall allocate to income the portion of the payment which the payor identifies as being from interest or other current return and allocate the balance of the payment to principal.

(3) If a trust or estate receives one or more payments in exchange for the trust's or estate's entire interest in an asset-backed security during a single accounting period, the fiduciary shall allocate the payments to principal. If a payment is one of a series of payments that will result in

the liquidation of the trust's or estate's interest in the security over more than a single accounting period, the fiduciary shall allocate 10 percent of the payment to income and the balance to principal.

Added by Laws 2002, c. 2002–42, § 1, eff. Jan. 1, 2003. Amended by Laws 2012, c. 2012–49, § 26, eff. Jan. 1, 2013.

738.701. Disbursements from income

A fiduciary shall make the following disbursements from income to the extent they are not disbursements to which s. 738.201(2) applies:

(1) One-half of the regular compensation of the fiduciary and of any person providing investment advisory or custodial services to the fiduciary.

(2) One-half of all expenses for accountings, judicial proceedings, or other matters that involve both the income and remainder interests.

(3) All of the other ordinary expenses incurred in connection with the administration, management, or preservation of trust property and the distribution of income, including interest, ordinary repairs, regularly recurring taxes assessed against principal, and expenses of a proceeding or other matter that concerns primarily the income interest.

(4) Recurring premiums on insurance covering the loss of a principal asset or the loss of income from or use of the asset.

Added by Laws 2002, c. 2002–42, § 1, eff. Jan. 1, 2003. Amended by Laws 2012, c. 2012–49, § 27, eff. Jan. 1, 2013.

738.702. Disbursements from principal

(1) A fiduciary shall make the following disbursements from principal:

(a) The remaining one-half of the disbursements described in s. 738.701(1) and (2).

(b) All of the trustee's compensation calculated on principal as a fee for acceptance, distribution, or termination and disbursements made to prepare property for sale.

(c) Payments on the principal of a trust debt.

(d) Expenses of a proceeding that concerns primarily principal, including a proceeding to construe the trust or will, or to protect the trust, estate, or its property.

(e) Premiums paid on a policy of insurance not described in s. 738.701(4) of which the trust or estate is the owner and beneficiary.

(f) Estate, inheritance, and other transfer taxes, including penalties, apportioned to the trust.

(g) Disbursements related to environmental matters, including reclamation, assessing environmental conditions, remedying and removing environmental contamination, monitoring remedial activities and the release of substances, preventing future releases of substances, collecting amounts from persons liable or potentially liable for the costs of such activities, penalties imposed under environmental laws or regulations and other payments made to comply with those laws or regulations, statutory or common law claims by third parties, and defending claims based on environmental matters.

(h) Payments representing extraordinary repairs or expenses incurred in making a capital improvement to principal, including special assessments; however, a fiduciary may establish an allowance for depreciation out of income to the extent permitted by s. 738.703.

(2) If a principal asset is encumbered with an obligation that requires income from that asset to be paid directly to the creditor, the trustee shall transfer from principal to income an amount equal to the income paid to the creditor in reduction of the principal balance of the obligation. Added by Laws 2002, c. 2002–42, § 1, eff. Jan. 1, 2003. Amended by Laws 2012, c. 2012–49, § 28, eff. Jan. 1, 2013.

738.703. Transfers from income to principal for depreciation

(1) For purposes of this section, "depreciation" means a reduction in value due to wear, tear, decay, corrosion, or gradual obsolescence of a fixed asset having a useful life of more than 1 year.

(2) A fiduciary may transfer to principal a reasonable amount of the net cash receipts from a principal asset that is subject to depreciation but may not transfer any amount for depreciation:

(a) Of that portion of real property used or available for use by a beneficiary as a residence or of tangible personal property held or made available for the personal use or enjoyment of a beneficiary;

(b) During the administration of a decedent's estate; or

(c) Under this section if the fiduciary is accounting under s. 738.403 for the business or activity in which the asset is used.

(3) The amount of depreciation taken for tax purposes with respect to an asset shall be presumed to be a reasonable amount of depreciation. An amount taken for depreciation shall not be considered unreasonable solely because it is greater or less than the amount taken for tax purposes.

(4) An amount transferred to principal need not be held as a separate fund.

Added by Laws 2002, c. 2002–42, § 1, eff. Jan. 1, 2003. Amended by Laws 2012, c. 2012–49, § 29, eff. Jan. 1, 2013.

738.704. Transfers from income to reimburse principal

(1) If a fiduciary makes or expects to make a principal disbursement described in this section, the fiduciary may transfer an appropriate amount from income to principal in one or more accounting periods to reimburse principal or to provide a reserve for future principal disbursements.

(2) Principal disbursements to which subsection (1) applies include the following, but only to the extent the fiduciary has not been and does not expect to be reimbursed by a third party:

(a) An amount chargeable to income but paid from principal because the amount is unusually large.

(b) Disbursements made to prepare property for rental, including tenant allowances, leasehold improvements, and broker's commissions.

(c) Disbursements described in s. 738.702(1)(g).

(3) If the asset the ownership of which gives rise to the disbursements becomes subject to a successive income interest after an income interest ends, a fiduciary may continue to transfer amounts from income to principal as provided in subsection (1).

(4) To the extent principal cash is not sufficient to pay the principal balance of payments due on mortgaged property, income may be applied to such payment in order to avoid a default on any mortgage or security interest securing the property. Income shall be reimbursed for such payments out of the first available principal cash. If the asset the ownership of which gives rise

to the disbursements described in this subsection becomes subject to a successive income interest after an income interest ends, all rights of the initial income interest shall lapse, and amounts remaining due from principal shall not be a lien on the assets of the trust.

Added by Laws 2002, c. 2002–42, § 1, eff. Jan. 1, 2003. Amended by Laws 2012, c. 2012–49, § 30, eff. Jan. 1, 2013.

738.705. Income taxes

(1) A tax required to be paid by a fiduciary based on receipts allocated to income shall be paid from income.

(2) A tax required to be paid by a fiduciary based on receipts allocated to principal shall be paid from principal, even if the tax is called an income tax by the taxing authority.

(3) A tax required to be paid by a fiduciary on the trust's or estate's share of an entity's taxable income shall be paid proportionately:

(a) From income to the extent receipts from the entity are allocated to income.

(b) From principal to the extent receipts from the entity are allocated to principal.

(c) From principal to the extent that the income taxes payable by the trust or estate exceed the total receipts from the entity.

(4) After applying subsections (1)–(3), the fiduciary shall adjust income or principal receipts to the extent that the trust's or estate's income taxes are reduced, but not eliminated, because the trust or estate receives a deduction for payments made to a beneficiary. The amount distributable to that beneficiary as income as a result of this adjustment shall be equal to the cash received by the trust or estate, reduced, but not below zero, by the entity's taxable income allocable to the trust or estate multiplied by the trust's or estate's income tax rate. The reduced amount shall be divided by the difference between 1 and the trust's or estate's income tax rate in order to determine the amount distributable to that beneficiary as income before giving effect to other receipts or disbursements allocable to that beneficiary's interest.

Added by Laws 2002, c. 2002–42, § 1, eff. Jan. 1, 2003. Amended by Laws 2012, c. 2012–49, § 31, eff. Jan. 1, 2013.

738.706. Adjustments between principal and income because of taxes

(1) A fiduciary may make adjustments between principal and income to offset the shifting of economic interests or tax benefits between income beneficiaries and remainder beneficiaries which arise from:

(a) Elections and decisions, other than those described in paragraph (b), that the fiduciary makes from time to time regarding tax matters;

(b) An income tax or any other tax that is imposed upon the fiduciary or a beneficiary as a result of a transaction involving or a distribution from the estate or trust; or

(c) The ownership by an estate or trust of an interest in an entity whose taxable income, whether or not distributed, is includable in the taxable income of the estate, trust, or a beneficiary.

(2) If the amount of an estate tax marital deduction or charitable contribution deduction is reduced because a fiduciary deducts an amount paid from principal for income tax purposes instead of deducting such amount for estate tax purposes, and as a result estate taxes paid from principal are increased and income taxes paid by an estate, trust, or beneficiary are decreased, each estate, trust, or beneficiary that benefits from the decrease in income tax shall reimburse

the principal from which the increase in estate tax is paid. The total reimbursement shall equal the increase in the estate tax to the extent the principal used to pay the increase would have qualified for a marital deduction or charitable contribution deduction but for the payment. The proportionate share of the reimbursement for each estate, trust, or beneficiary whose income taxes are reduced shall be the same as such estate's, trust's, or beneficiary's proportionate share of the total decrease in income tax. An estate or trust shall reimburse principal from income. Added by Laws 2002, c. 2002–42, § 1, eff. Jan. 1, 2003.

738.801. Apportionment of expenses; improvements

(1) For purposes of this section, the term:

(a) "Remainderman" means the holder of the remainder interests after the expiration of a tenant's estate in property.

(b) "Tenant" means the holder of an estate for life or term of years in real property or personal property, or both.

(2) If a trust has not been created, expenses shall be apportioned between the tenant and remainderman as follows:

(a) The following expenses are allocated to and shall be paid by the tenant:

1. All ordinary expenses incurred in connection with the administration, management, or preservation of the property, including interest, ordinary repairs, regularly recurring taxes assessed against the property, and expenses of a proceeding or other matter that concerns primarily the tenant's estate or use of the property.

2. Recurring premiums on insurance covering the loss of the property or the loss of income from or use of the property.

3. Any of the expenses described in subparagraph (b)3. which are attributable to the use of the property by the tenant.

(b) The following expenses are allocated to and shall be paid by the remainderman:

1. Payments on the principal of a debt secured by the property, except to the extent the debt is for expenses allocated to the tenant.

2. Expenses of a proceeding or other matter that concerns primarily the title to the property, other than title to the tenant's estate.

3. Except as provided in subparagraph (a)3., expenses related to environmental matters, including reclamation, assessing environmental conditions, remedying and removing environmental contamination, monitoring remedial activities and the release of substances, preventing future releases of substances, collecting amounts from persons liable or potentially liable for the costs of such activities, penalties imposed under environmental laws or regulations and other payments made to comply with those laws or regulations, statutory or common law claims by third parties, and defending claims based on environmental matters.

4. Extraordinary repairs.

(c) If the tenant or remainderman incurred an expense for the benefit of his or her own estate without consent or agreement of the other, he or she must pay such expense in full.

(d) Except as provided in paragraph (c), the cost of, or special taxes or assessments for, an improvement representing an addition of value to property forming part of the principal shall be paid by the tenant if the improvement is not reasonably expected to outlast the estate of the tenant. In all other cases, only a part shall be paid by the tenant while the remainder shall be paid by the remainderman. The part payable by the tenant is ascertainable by taking that percentage of the total that is found by dividing the present value of the tenant's estate by the present value of an estate of the same form as that of the tenant, except that it is limited for a period corresponding to the reasonably expected duration of the improvement. The computation of present values of the estates shall be made by using the rate defined in 26 U.S.C. s. 7520, then in effect and, in the case of an estate for life, the official mortality tables then in effect under 26 U.S.C. s. 7520. Other evidence of duration or expectancy may not be considered.

(3) This section does not apply to the extent it is inconsistent with the instrument creating the estates, the agreement of the parties, or the specific direction of the taxing or other statutes.

(4) The common law applicable to tenants and remaindermen supplements this section, except as modified by this section or other laws.

Added by Laws 2002, c. 2002–42, § 1, eff. Jan. 1, 2003. Amended by Laws 2012, c. 2012–49, § 32, eff. Jan. 1, 2013.

738.802. Uniformity of application and construction

In applying and construing this act, consideration shall be given to the need to promote uniformity of the law with respect to the act's subject matter among states that enact such act.

Added by Laws 2002, c. 2002–42, § 1, eff. Jan. 1, 2003.

738.803. Severability

If any provision of this chapter or its application to any person or circumstance is held invalid, the invalidity shall not affect other provisions or applications of this chapter which can be given effect without the invalid provision or application, and to this end the provisions of this chapter are severable.

Added by Laws 2002, c. 2002–42, § 1, eff. Jan. 1, 2003.

738.804. Application

Except as provided in the trust instrument, the will, or this chapter, this chapter shall apply to any receipt or expense received or incurred and any disbursement made after January 1, 2003, by any trust or decedent's estate, whether established before or after January 1, 2003, and whether the asset involved was acquired by the trustee or personal representative before or after January 1, 2003. Receipts or expenses received or incurred and disbursements made before January 1, 2003, shall be governed by the law of this state in effect at the time of the event, except as otherwise expressly provided in the will or terms of the trust or in this chapter.

Added by Laws 2002, c. 2002–42, § 1, eff. Jan. 1, 2003.

CHAPTER 739

FLORIDA UNIFORM DISCLAIMER OF PROPERTY INTERESTS ACT

UNIFORM DISCLAIMER OF PROPERTY INTERESTS ACT (1999)

Table of Jurisdictions Wherein Act Has Been Adopted

For text of Uniform Act, and variation notes and annotation materials for adopting jurisdictions, see Uniform Laws Annotated, Master Edition Volume 8A.

Jurisdiction	Laws	Effective Date	Statutory Citation
Alaska	2010, c. 63	9–7–2010	AS 13.70.010 to 13.70.195.
Arizona	2005, c. 195	8–12–2005	A.R.S. §§ 14–10001 to 14–10018.
Arkansas	2003, c. 610	9–1–2003	A.C.A. §§ 28–2–201 to 28–2–220.
Colorado	2011, c. 203	8–10–2011	West's C.R.S.A. §§ 15–11–1201 to 15–11–1218.
Delaware	2006, c. 302	6–27–2006	12 Del.C. §§ 601 to 617.
District of Columbia	2006, D.C. Law 16–205	3–2–2007	D.C. Official Code, 2001 Ed. §§ 19–1501 to 19–1518.
Florida	2005, c. 108	7–1–2005	F.S.A. §§ 739.101 to 739.701.
Hawaii	2000, c. 43	7–1–2000	HRS §§ 526–1 to 526–16.
Indiana	2003, c. 5	7–1–2003	West's A.I.C. 32–17.5–1–1 to 32–17.5–10–1.
Iowa	2004, c. 1015	3–29–2004 *	I.C.A. §§ 633E.1 to 633E.17.
Maryland	2004, c. 465	10–1–2004	Code, Estates and Trusts, §§ 9–201 to 9–216.
Massachusetts	2008, c. 521	7–1–2011	M.G.L.A. c. 190B, § 2–801.
Minnesota	2009, c. 67	1–1–2010	M.S.A. §§ 524.2–1101 to 524.2–1116.
Nevada	2007, c. 102	10–1–2007	N.R.S. 120.100 to 120.350.
New Mexico	2001, c. 290	7–1–2001	NMSA 1978 §§ 46–10–1 to 46–10–17.
North Dakota	2001, c. 301	8–1–2001	NDCC 30.1–10.1–01 to 30.1–10.1–12.
Oregon	2001, c. 245	1–1–2002	ORS 105.623 to 105.649.
Virgin Islands	2009, No. 7150	1–1–2011	15 V.I.C. §§ 2–1101 to 2–1119.
Virginia	2003, c. 253	3–16–2003 *	Code 1950, §§ 64.2–2600 to 64.2–2614.
West Virginia	2002, c. 317	7–1–2002	Code, 42–6–1 to 42–6–19.

* Date of approval.

Cross References

Florida Retirement System, benefits payable, see § 121.091.
Homesteads, devise, see F.S.A. § 732.4015.
Transfers to minors, custodians, declining to serve, see § 710.121.

739.101. Short title

This chapter may be cited as the "Florida Uniform Disclaimer of Property Interests Act."
Added by Laws 2005, c. 2005–108, § 1, eff. July 1, 2005.

739.102. Definitions

As used in this chapter, the term:

(1) "Benefactor" means the creator of the interest that is subject to a disclaimer.

(2) "Beneficiary designation" means an instrument, other than an instrument creating or amending a trust, naming the beneficiary of:

(a) An annuity or insurance policy;

(b) An account with a designation for payment on death;

(c) A security registered in beneficiary form;

(d) A pension, profit-sharing, retirement, or other employment-related benefit plan; or

(e) Any other nonprobate transfer at death.

(3) "Disclaimant" means the person to whom a disclaimed interest or power would have passed had the disclaimer not been made.

(4) "Disclaimed interest" means the interest that would have passed to the disclaimant had the disclaimer not been made.

(5) "Disclaimer" means the refusal to accept an interest in or power over property. The term includes a renunciation.

(6) "Fiduciary" means a personal representative, trustee, agent acting under a power of attorney, guardian, or other person authorized to act as a fiduciary with respect to the property of another person.

(7) "Future interest" means an interest that takes effect in possession or enjoyment, if at all, later than the time of its creation.

(8) "Insolvent" means, solely for purposes of this chapter, that the sum of a person's debts is greater than all of the person's assets at fair valuation and that the person is generally not paying his or her debts as they become due. For purposes of this subsection, the term "assets" has the same meaning as that provided in s. 726.102.

(9) "Jointly held property" means property held in the names of two or more persons under an arrangement in which all holders have concurrent interests and under which the last surviving holder is entitled to the whole of the property. Jointly held property does not include property held as tenants by the entirety.

(10) "Person" includes individuals, ascertained and unascertained, living or not living, whether entitled to an interest by right of intestacy or otherwise; a government, governmental subdivision, agency, or instrumentality; and a public corporation.

(11) "Time of distribution" means the time when a disclaimed interest would have taken effect in possession or enjoyment.

(12) "Trust" means:

(a) An express trust (including an honorary trust or a trust under s. 736.0408), charitable or noncharitable, with additions thereto, whenever and however created; and

(b) A trust created pursuant to a statute, judgment, or decree which requires the trust be administered in the manner of an express trust.

As used in this chapter, the term "trust" does not include a constructive trust or a resulting trust.

Added by Laws 2005, c. 2005–108, § 1, eff. July 1, 2005. Amended by Laws 2006, c. 2006–217, § 43, eff. July 1, 2007; Laws 2009, c. 2009–115, § 13, eff. July 1, 2009.

739.103. Scope

This chapter applies to disclaimers of any interest in or power over property, whenever created. Except as provided in s. 739.701, this chapter is the exclusive means by which a disclaimer may be made under Florida law.

Added by Laws 2005, c. 2005–108, § 1, eff. July 1, 2005.

739.104. Power to disclaim; general requirements; when irrevocable

(1) A person may disclaim, in whole or in part, conditionally or unconditionally, any interest in or power over property, including a power of appointment. A person may disclaim the interest or power even if its creator imposed a spendthrift provision or similar restriction on transfer or a restriction or limitation on the right to disclaim. A disclaimer shall be unconditional unless the disclaimant explicitly provides otherwise in the disclaimer.

(2) With court approval, a fiduciary may disclaim, in whole or part, any interest in or power over property, including a power of appointment, except that a disclaimer of a power arising under s. 739.201(4) does not require court approval. Without court approval, a fiduciary may disclaim, in whole or in part, any interest in or power over property, including a power of appointment, if and to the extent that the instrument creating the fiduciary relationship explicitly grants the fiduciary the right to disclaim. In the absence of a court-appointed guardian, notwithstanding anything in chapter 744 to the contrary, without court approval, a natural guardian under s. 744.301 may disclaim on behalf of a minor child of the natural guardian, in whole or in part, any interest in or power over property, including a power of appointment, which the minor child is to receive solely as a result of another disclaimer, but only if the disclaimed interest or power does not pass to or for the benefit of the natural guardian as a result of the disclaimer.

(3) To be effective, a disclaimer must be in writing, declare the writing as a disclaimer, describe the interest or power disclaimed, and be signed by the person making the disclaimer and witnessed and acknowledged in the manner provided for deeds of real estate to be recorded in this state. In addition, for a disclaimer to be effective, an original of the disclaimer must be delivered or filed in the manner provided in s. 739.301.

(4) A partial disclaimer may be expressed as a fraction, percentage, monetary amount, term of years, limitation of a power, or any other interest or estate in the property.

(5) A disclaimer becomes irrevocable when any conditions to which the disclaimant has made the disclaimer subject are satisfied and when the disclaimer is delivered or filed pursuant to s. 739.301 or it becomes effective as provided in ss. 739.201–739.207, whichever occurs later.

(6) A disclaimer made under this chapter is not a transfer, assignment, or release.

Added by Laws 2005, c. 2005–108, § 1, eff. July 1, 2005. Amended by Laws 2006, c. 2006–1, § 103, eff. July 4, 2006; Laws 2009, c. 2009–115, § 14, eff. July 1, 2009.

739.201. Disclaimer of interest in property

Except for a disclaimer governed by s. 739.202, s. 739.203, or s. 739.204, the following rules apply to a disclaimer of an interest in property:

(1) The disclaimer takes effect as of the time the instrument creating the interest becomes irrevocable or, if the interest arose under the law of intestate succession, as of the time of the intestate's death.

(2) The disclaimed interest passes according to any provision in the instrument creating the interest providing explicitly for the disposition of the interest, should it be disclaimed, or of disclaimed interests in general.

(3) If the instrument does not contain a provision described in subsection (2), the following rules apply:

(a) If the disclaimant is an individual, the disclaimed interest passes as if the disclaimant had died immediately before the interest was created, unless under the governing instrument or other applicable law the disclaimed interest is contingent on surviving to the time of distribution, in which case the disclaimed interest passes as if the disclaimant had died immediately before the time for distribution. However, if, by law or under the governing instrument, the descendants of the disclaimant would share in the disclaimed interest by any method of representation had the disclaimant died before the time of distribution, the disclaimed interest passes only to the descendants of the disclaimant who survive the time of distribution. For purposes of this subsection, a disclaimed interest is created at the death of the benefactor or such earlier time, if any, that the benefactor's transfer of the interest is a completed gift for federal gift tax purposes. Also for purposes of this subsection, a disclaimed interest in a trust described in s. 733.707(3) shall pass as if the interest had been created under a will.

(b) If the disclaimant is not an individual, the disclaimed interest passes as if the disclaimant did not exist.

(c) Upon the disclaimer of a preceding interest, a future interest held by a person other than the disclaimant takes effect as if the disclaimant had died or ceased to exist immediately before the time of distribution, but a future interest held by the disclaimant is not accelerated in possession or enjoyment as a result of the disclaimer.

(4) In the case of a disclaimer of property over which the disclaimant has a power, in a fiduciary or nonfiduciary capacity, to direct the beneficial enjoyment of the disclaimed property, unless the disclaimer specifically provides to the contrary with reference to this subsection, the disclaimant shall also be deemed to have disclaimed that power unless the power is limited by an ascertainable standard, as defined in s. 736.0103, as in effect when the disclaimer becomes irrevocable.

Added by Laws 2005, c. 2005–108, § 1, eff. July 1, 2005. Amended by Laws 2009, c. 2009–115, § 15, eff. July 1, 2009.

739.202. Disclaimer of rights of survivorship in jointly held property

(1) Upon the death of a holder of jointly held property:

(a) If, during the deceased holder's lifetime, the deceased holder could have unilaterally regained a portion of the property attributable to the deceased holder's contributions without the consent of any other holder, another holder may disclaim, in whole or in part, a fractional share of that portion of the property attributable to the deceased holder's contributions determined by dividing the number one by the number of joint holders alive immediately after the death of the holder to whose death the disclaimer relates.

(b) For all other jointly held property, another holder may disclaim, in whole or in part, a fraction of the whole of the property the numerator of which is one and the denominator of which is the product of the number of joint holders alive immediately before the death of the holder to whose death the disclaimer relates multiplied by the number of joint holders alive immediately after the death of the holder to whose death the disclaimer relates.

(2) A disclaimer under subsection (1) takes effect as of the death of the holder of jointly held property to whose death the disclaimer relates.

(3) An interest in jointly held property disclaimed by a surviving holder of the property passes as if the disclaimant predeceased the holder to whose death the disclaimer relates.

Added by Laws 2005, c. 2005–108, § 1, eff. July 1, 2005.

739.203. Disclaimer of property held as tenancy by the entirety

(1) The survivorship interest in property held as a tenancy by the entirety to which the survivor succeeds by operation of law upon the death of the cotenant may be disclaimed as provided in this chapter. For purposes of this chapter only, the deceased tenant's interest in property held as a tenancy by the entirety shall be deemed to be an undivided one-half interest.

(2) A disclaimer under subsection (1) takes effect as of the death of the deceased tenant to whose death the disclaimer relates.

(3) The survivorship interest in property held as a tenancy by the entirety disclaimed by the surviving tenant passes as if the disclaimant had predeceased the tenant to whose death the disclaimer relates.

(4) A disclaimer of an interest in real property held as tenants by the entirety does not cause the disclaimed interest to be homestead property for purposes of descent and distribution under ss. 732.401 and 732.4015.

Added by Laws 2005, c. 2005–108, § 1, eff. July 1, 2005.

739.204. Disclaimer of interest by trustee

If a trustee having the power to disclaim under the instrument creating the fiduciary relationship or pursuant to court order disclaims an interest in property that otherwise would have become trust property, the interest does not become trust property.

Added by Laws 2005, c. 2005–108, § 1, eff. July 1, 2005.

739.205. Disclaimer of power of appointment or other power not held in a fiduciary capacity

If a holder disclaims a power of appointment or other power not held in a fiduciary capacity, the following rules apply:

(1) If the holder has not exercised the power, the disclaimer takes effect as of the time the instrument creating the power becomes irrevocable.

(2) If the holder has exercised the power and the disclaimer is of a power other than a presently exercisable general power of appointment, the disclaimer takes effect immediately after the last exercise of the power.

(3) The instrument creating the power is construed as if the power expired when the disclaimer became effective.

Added by Laws 2005, c. 2005–108, § 1, eff. July 1, 2005.

739.206. Disclaimer by appointee, object, or taker in default of exercise of power of appointment

(1) A disclaimer of an interest in property by an appointee of a power of appointment takes effect as of the time the instrument by which the holder exercises the power becomes irrevocable.

(2) A disclaimer of an interest in property by an object, or taker in default of an exercise of a power of appointment, takes effect as of the time the instrument creating the power becomes irrevocable.

Added by Laws 2005, c. 2005–108, § 1, eff. July 1, 2005.

739.207. Disclaimer of power held in fiduciary capacity

(1) If a fiduciary disclaims a power held in a fiduciary capacity which has not been exercised, the disclaimer takes effect as of the time the instrument creating the power becomes irrevocable.

(2) If a fiduciary disclaims a power held in a fiduciary capacity which has been exercised, the disclaimer takes effect immediately after the last exercise of the power.

(3) A disclaimer under this section is effective as to another fiduciary if the disclaimer so provides and the fiduciary disclaiming has the authority to bind the estate, trust, or other person for whom the fiduciary is acting, except that a disclaimer of a fiduciary power arising under s. 739.201(4) shall bind only the disclaiming fiduciary.

Added by Laws 2005, c. 2005–108, § 1, eff. July 1, 2005. Amended by Laws 2009, c. 2009–115, § 16, eff. July 1, 2009.

739.301. Delivery or filing

(1) Subject to subsections (2) through (12), delivery of a disclaimer may be effected by personal delivery, first-class mail, or any other method that results in its receipt. A disclaimer sent by first-class mail shall be deemed to have been delivered on the date it is postmarked. Delivery by any other method shall be effective upon receipt by the person to whom the disclaimer is to be delivered under this section.

(2) In the case of a disclaimer of an interest created under the law of intestate succession or an interest created by will, other than an interest in a testamentary trust:

(a) The disclaimer must be delivered to the personal representative of the decedent's estate; or

(b) If no personal representative is serving when the disclaimer is sought to be delivered, the disclaimer must be filed with the clerk of the court in any county where venue of administration would be proper.

(3) In the case of a disclaimer of an interest in a testamentary trust:

(a) The disclaimer must be delivered to the trustee serving when the disclaimer is delivered or, if no trustee is then serving, to the personal representative of the decedent's estate; or

(b) If no personal representative is serving when the disclaimer is sought to be delivered, the disclaimer must be filed with the clerk of the court in any county where venue of administration of the decedent's estate would be proper.

(4) In the case of a disclaimer of an interest in an inter vivos trust:

(a) The disclaimer must be delivered to the trustee serving when the disclaimer is delivered;

(b) If no trustee is then serving, it must be filed with the clerk of the court in any county where the filing of a notice of trust would be proper; or

(c) If the disclaimer is made before the time the instrument creating the trust becomes irrevocable, the disclaimer must be delivered to the grantor of the revocable trust or the transferor of the interest or to such person's legal representative.

(5) In the case of a disclaimer of an interest created by a beneficiary designation made before the time the designation becomes irrevocable, the disclaimer must be delivered to the person making the beneficiary designation or to such person's legal representative.

(6) In the case of a disclaimer of an interest created by a beneficiary designation made after the time the designation becomes irrevocable, the disclaimer must be delivered to the person obligated to distribute the interest.

(7) In the case of a disclaimer by a surviving holder of jointly held property, or by the surviving tenant in property held as a tenancy by the entirety, the disclaimer must be delivered to the person to whom the disclaimed interest passes or, if such person cannot reasonably be located by the disclaimant, the disclaimer must be delivered as provided in subsection (2).

(8) In the case of a disclaimer by an object, or taker in default of exercise, of a power of appointment at any time after the power was created:

(a) The disclaimer must be delivered to the holder of the power or to the fiduciary acting under the instrument that created the power; or

(b) If no fiduciary is serving when the disclaimer is sought to be delivered, the disclaimer must be filed with a court having authority to appoint the fiduciary.

(9) In the case of a disclaimer by an appointee of a nonfiduciary power of appointment:

(a) The disclaimer must be delivered to the holder, the personal representative of the holder's estate, or the fiduciary under the instrument that created the power; or

(b) If no fiduciary is serving when the disclaimer is sought to be delivered, the disclaimer must be filed with a court having authority to appoint the fiduciary.

(10) In the case of a disclaimer by a fiduciary of a power over a trust or estate, the disclaimer must be delivered as provided in subsection (2), subsection (3), or subsection (4) as if the power disclaimed were an interest in property.

(11) In the case of a disclaimer of a power exercisable by an agent, other than a power exercisable by a fiduciary over a trust or estate, the disclaimer must be delivered to the principal or the principal's representative.

(12) Notwithstanding subsection (1), delivery of a disclaimer of an interest in or relating to real estate shall be presumed upon the recording of the disclaimer in the office of the clerk of the court of the county or counties where the real estate is located.

(13) A fiduciary or other person having custody of the disclaimed interest is not liable for any otherwise proper distribution or other disposition made without actual notice of the disclaimer or, if the disclaimer is barred under s. 739.402, for any otherwise proper distribution or other disposition made in reliance on the disclaimer, if the distribution or disposition is made without actual knowledge of the facts constituting the bar of the right to disclaim.

Added by Laws 2005, c. 2005–108, § 1, eff. July 1, 2005.

739.401. When disclaimer is permitted

A disclaimer may be made at any time unless barred under s. 739.402.

Added by Laws 2005, c. 2005–108, § 1, eff. July 1, 2005.

739.402. When disclaimer is barred or limited

(1) A disclaimer is barred by a written waiver of the right to disclaim.

(2) A disclaimer of an interest in property is barred if any of the following events occur before the disclaimer becomes effective:

(a) The disclaimant accepts the interest sought to be disclaimed;

(b) The disclaimant voluntarily assigns, conveys, encumbers, pledges, or transfers the interest sought to be disclaimed or contracts to do so;

(c) The interest sought to be disclaimed is sold pursuant to a judicial sale; or

(d) The disclaimant is insolvent when the disclaimer becomes irrevocable.

(3) A disclaimer, in whole or in part, of the future exercise of a power held in a fiduciary capacity is not barred by its previous exercise.

(4) A disclaimer, in whole or in part, of the future exercise of a power not held in a fiduciary capacity is not barred by its previous exercise unless the power is exercisable in favor of the disclaimant.

(5) A disclaimer of an interest in, or a power over, property which is barred by this section is ineffective.

Added by Laws 2005, c. 2005–108, § 1, eff. July 1, 2005. Amended by Laws 2009, c. 2009–115, § 17, eff. July 1, 2009.

739.501. Tax-qualified disclaimer

Notwithstanding any provision of this chapter other than s. 739.402, if, as a result of a disclaimer or transfer, the disclaimed or transferred interest is treated pursuant to the provisions of s. 2518 of the Internal Revenue Code of 1986 [1] as never having been transferred to the disclaimant, the disclaimer or transfer is effective as a disclaimer under this chapter.

Added by Laws 2005, c. 2005–108, § 1, eff. July 1, 2005. Amended by Laws 2009, c. 2009–115, § 18, eff. July 1, 2009.

[1] 26 U.S.C.A. § 2518.

739.601. Recording of disclaimer relating to real estate

(1) A disclaimer of an interest in or relating to real estate does not provide constructive notice to all persons unless the disclaimer contains a legal description of the real estate to which the disclaimer relates and unless the disclaimer is filed for recording in the office of the clerk of the court in the county or counties where the real estate is located.

(2) An effective disclaimer meeting the requirements of subsection (1) constitutes constructive notice to all persons from the time of filing. Failure to record the disclaimer does not affect its validity as between the disclaimant and persons to whom the property interest or power passes by reason of the disclaimer.

Added by Laws 2005, c. 2005–108, § 1, eff. July 1, 2005.

739.701. Application to existing relationships

Except as otherwise provided in s. 739.402, an interest in or power over property existing on July 1, 2005, as to which the time for delivering or filing a disclaimer under laws superseded by this chapter has not expired, may be disclaimed after July 1, 2005.

Added by Laws 2005, c. 2005–108, § 1, eff. July 1, 2005.

TITLE XLIII

DOMESTIC RELATIONS

CHAPTER 744

GUARDIANSHIP

PART I. GENERAL PROVISIONS

PART II. VENUE

PART III. TYPES OF GUARDIANSHIP

PART IV. GUARDIANS

GUARDIANSHIP

For Annotative Materials, see West's Florida Statutes Annotated

Revision

Fla.St.1941, Chapter 744, Guardian and Ward, comprised of §§ 744.01 to 744.44, was repealed by Laws 1945, c. 22750, enacting a revised guardianship law. The provisions of the revised law appeared as Fla.St.1949, in Chapters 744 to 746. Chapter 744, Florida Guardianship Law, First Part, was comprised of §§ 744.01 to 744.67.

Fla.St.1949, Chapter 744, Florida Guardianship Law, First Part, as amended, containing §§ 744.01 to 744.73, was repealed by Laws 1974, c. 74–106, § 3, effective July 1, 1975. Laws 1974, c. 74–106, § 1, enacted Fla.St.1974, Supp., Chapter 744, Guardianship, §§ 744.101 to 744.507, effective on the same date. Laws 1975, c. 75–220, § 113, changed the effective date to January 1, 1976, and Laws 1975, c. 75–222, substantially amended and renumbered Chapter 744 as contained in Fla.St.1975, effective on the same date.

Cross References

Child placement,
    Permanent guardianship of dependent children, see § 39.6221.
    Relative Caregiver Program, see § 39.5085.
Children,
    Continuing care for young adults, see F.S.A. § 39.6251.
    Judicial review, see F.S.A. § 39.701.
Consumer protection, protected consumer report security freeze, see F.S.A. § 501.0051.
Criminal conflict and civil regional counsel offices, see § 27.511.
Durable power of attorney, see § 709.2104.

Property interests, power to disclaim, see § 739.104.

Public defenders and other court-appointed counsel, private court-appointed counsel, see F.S.A. § 27.5304.

Unlawful possession of the personal identification information of another person, see F.S.A. § 817.5685.

PART I. GENERAL PROVISIONS

744.101. Short title

This chapter may be cited as the "Florida Guardianship Law."

Laws 1974, c. 74–106, § 1; Laws 1975, c. 75–222, § 1; Laws 1989, c. 89–96, § 1.

744.1012. Legislative intent

The Legislature finds that adjudicating a person totally incapacitated and in need of a guardian deprives such person of all her or his civil and legal rights and that such deprivation may be unnecessary. The Legislature further finds that it is desirable to make available the least restrictive form of guardianship to assist persons who are only partially incapable of caring for their needs. Recognizing that every individual has unique needs and differing abilities, the Legislature declares that it is the purpose of this act to promote the public welfare by establishing a system that permits incapacitated persons to participate as fully as possible in all decisions affecting them; that assists such persons in meeting the essential requirements for their physical health and safety, in protecting their rights, in managing their financial resources, and in developing or regaining their abilities to the maximum extent possible; and that accomplishes these objectives through providing, in each case, the form of assistance that least interferes with the legal capacity of a person to act in her or his own behalf. This act shall be liberally construed to accomplish this purpose.

Laws 1989, c. 89–96, § 3; Laws 1990, c. 90–271, § 1. Amended by Laws 1997, c. 97–102, § 1067, eff. July 1, 1997.

744.102. Definitions

As used in this chapter, the term:

(1) "Attorney for the alleged incapacitated person" means an attorney who represents the alleged incapacitated person. The attorney shall represent the expressed wishes of the alleged incapacitated person to the extent it is consistent with the rules regulating The Florida Bar.

(2) "Audit" means a systematic review of financial and all other documents to ensure compliance with s. 744.368, rules of court, and local procedures using generally accepted accounting principles. The term includes various practices that meet professional standards, such as verifications, reviews of substantiating papers and accounts, interviews, inspections, and investigations.

(3) "Clerk" means the clerk or deputy clerk of the court.

(4) "Corporate guardian" means a corporation authorized to exercise fiduciary or guardianship powers in this state and includes a nonprofit corporate guardian.

(5) "Court" means the circuit court.

(6) "Court monitor" means a person appointed by the court under s. 744.107 to provide the court with information concerning a ward.

(7) "Estate" means the property of a ward subject to administration.

(8) "Foreign guardian" means a guardian appointed in another state or country.

(9) "Guardian" means a person who has been appointed by the court to act on behalf of a ward's person or property, or both.

(a) "Limited guardian" means a guardian who has been appointed by the court to exercise the legal rights and powers specifically designated by court order entered after the court has found that the ward lacks the capacity to do some, but not all, of the tasks necessary to care for his or her person or property, or after the person has voluntarily petitioned for appointment of a limited guardian.

(b) "Plenary guardian" means a person who has been appointed by the court to exercise all delegable legal rights and powers of the ward after the court has found that the ward lacks the capacity to perform all of the tasks necessary to care for his or her person or property.

(10) "Guardian ad litem" means a person who is appointed by the court having jurisdiction of the guardianship or a court in which a particular legal matter is pending to represent a ward in that proceeding.

(11) "Guardian advocate" means a person appointed by a written order of the court to represent a person with developmental disabilities under s. 393.12. As used in this chapter, the term does not apply to a guardian advocate appointed for a person determined incompetent to consent to treatment under s. 394.4598.

(12) "Incapacitated person" means a person who has been judicially determined to lack the capacity to manage at least some of the property or to meet at least some of the essential health and safety requirements of the person.

(a) To "manage property" means to take those actions necessary to obtain, administer, and dispose of real and personal property, intangible property, business property, benefits, and income.

(b) To "meet essential requirements for health or safety" means to take those actions necessary to provide the health care, food, shelter, clothing, personal hygiene, or other care without which serious and imminent physical injury or illness is more likely than not to occur.

(13) "Minor" means a person under 18 years of age whose disabilities have not been removed by marriage or otherwise.

(14) "Next of kin" means those persons who would be heirs at law of the ward or alleged incapacitated person if the person were deceased and includes the lineal descendants of the ward or alleged incapacitated person.

(15) "Nonprofit corporate guardian" means a nonprofit corporation organized for religious or charitable purposes and existing under the laws of this state.

(16) "Preneed guardian" means a person named in a written declaration to serve as guardian in the event of the incapacity of the declarant as provided in s. 744.3045.

(17) "Professional guardian" means any guardian who has at any time rendered services to three or more wards as their guardian. A person serving as a guardian for two or more relatives as defined in s. 744.309(2) is not considered a professional guardian. A public guardian shall be considered a professional guardian for purposes of regulation, education, and registration.

(18) "Property" means both real and personal property or any interest in it and anything that may be the subject of ownership.

(19) "Standby guardian" means a person empowered to assume the duties of guardianship upon the death or adjudication of incapacity of the last surviving natural or appointed guardian.

(20) "Surrogate guardian" means a guardian designated according to s. 744.442.

(21) "Totally incapacitated" means incapable of exercising any of the rights enumerated in s. 744.3215(2) and (3).

(22) "Ward" means a person for whom a guardian has been appointed.

Laws 1974, c. 74–106, § 1; Laws 1975, c. 75–222, § 2; Laws 1977, c. 77–104, § 231; Laws 1979, c. 79–221, § 1; Laws 1980, c. 80–171, § 3; Laws 1989, c. 89–96, § 4; Laws 1990, c. 90–271, § 2; Laws 1996, c. 96–354, § 1. Amended by Laws 1997, c. 97–102, § 1780, eff. July 1, 1997; Laws 2003, c. 2003–57, § 6, eff. May 30, 2003; Laws 2004, c. 2004–260, § 9, eff. July 1, 2004; Laws 2006, c. 2006–178, § 1, eff. July 1, 2006; Laws 2014, c. 2014–124, § 1, eff. July 1, 2014.

Cross References

Capacity determination, appointment of guardian advocate, see § 393.12.

Definitions, see Probate Rule 5.015.

Durable power of attorney, see § 709.2101 et seq.

Fiduciary lawyer-client privilege, see F.S.A. § 90.5021.

Florida Retirement System, benefits, see § 121.091.

Florida Retirement System Investment Plan, see F.S.A. § 121.4501.

Guardianship law rules, definitions, see Probate Rule 5.540.

Probate code, definitions, see § 731.201.

744.1025. Additional definitions

The definitions contained in the Florida Probate Code shall be applicable to the Florida Guardianship Law, unless the context requires otherwise, insofar as such definitions do not conflict with definitions contained in this law.

Laws 1979, c. 79–221, § 2; Laws 1989, c. 89–96, § 5.

Cross References

Probate Code, definitions, see § 731.201.

744.104. Verification of documents

When verification of a document is required in this chapter or by rule, the document filed shall include an oath or affirmation or the following statement: "Under penalties of perjury, I declare that I have read the foregoing, and the facts alleged are true to the best of my knowledge and belief." Any person who shall willfully include a false statement in the document shall be guilty of perjury and upon conviction shall be punished accordingly.

Laws 1974, c. 74–106, § 1; Laws 1975, c. 75–222, § 2; Laws 1989, c. 89–96, § 7.

Cross References

Pleadings, verification, motions, see Probate Rule 5.020.

744.105. Costs

In all guardianship proceedings, costs may be awarded. When the costs are to be paid out of the property of the ward, the court may direct from what part of the property the costs shall be paid.

Laws 1974, c. 74–106, § 1; Laws 1975, c. 75–222, § 3; Laws 1989, c. 89–96, § 8; Laws 1990, c. 90–271, § 3.

744.106. Notice

The requirements for notice under this chapter are those provided for in the Florida Probate Rules except as provided in s. 744.331(1).

Laws 1975, c. 75–222, § 4; Laws 1989, c. 89–96, § 9; Laws 1995, c. 95–211, § 65.

Cross References

Waiver of notice, see Probate Rule 5.180.

744.107. Court monitors

(1) The court may, upon inquiry from any interested person or upon its own motion in any proceeding over which it has jurisdiction, appoint a monitor. The court shall not appoint as a monitor a family member or any person with a personal interest in the proceedings. The order of appointment shall be served upon the guardian, the ward, and such other persons as the court may determine.

(2) The monitor may investigate, seek information, examine documents, or interview the ward and shall report to the court his or her findings. The report shall be verified and shall be served on the guardian, the ward, and such other persons as the court may determine.

(3) If it appears from the monitor's report that further action by the court to protect the interests of the ward is necessary, the court shall, after a hearing with notice, enter any order necessary to protect the ward or the ward's estate, including amending the plan, requiring an accounting, ordering production of assets, freezing assets, suspending a guardian, or initiating proceedings to remove a guardian.

(4) Unless otherwise prohibited by law, a monitor may be allowed a reasonable fee as determined by the court and paid from the property of the ward. No full-time state, county, or municipal employee or officer shall be paid a fee for such investigation and report. If the court finds the motion for court monitor to have been filed in bad faith, the costs of the proceeding, including attorney's fees, may be assessed against the movant.

(5) The court may appoint the office of criminal conflict and civil regional counsel as monitor if the ward is indigent.

Laws 1975, c. 75–222, §§ 18, 26; Laws 1989, c. 89–96, § 10; Laws 1990, c. 90–271, § 4. Amended by Laws 1997, c. 97–102, § 1068, eff. July 1, 1997; Laws 2006, c. 2006–77, § 2, eff. June 6, 2006; Laws 2015, c. 2015–83, § 2, eff. July 1, 2015.

Applicability

Laws 2015, c. 2015–83, § 20, provides:

"*Sections 709.2109 and 744.3203, Florida Statutes, as created by this act, apply to all proceedings filed on or after July 1, 2015. The amendments made by this act to ss. 744.107, 744.1075, 744.108, 744.3025, 744.3031, 744.309, 744.3115, 744.312, 744.331, 744.344, 744.345, 744.359, 744.361, 744.367, 744.369, 744.3715, and 744.464, Florida Statutes, apply to all proceedings pending on July 1, 2015.*"

744.1075. Emergency court monitor

(1)(a) A court, upon inquiry from any interested person or upon its own motion, in any proceeding over which the court has jurisdiction, may appoint a court monitor on an emergency basis without notice. The court must specifically find that there appears to be imminent danger that the physical or mental health or safety of the ward will be seriously impaired or that the ward's property is in danger of being wasted, misappropriated, or lost unless immediate action is taken. The scope of the matters to be investigated and the powers and duties of the monitor must be specifically enumerated by court order.

(b) The authority of a monitor appointed under this section expires 60 days after the date of appointment or upon a finding of no probable cause, whichever occurs first. The authority of the monitor may be extended for an additional 30 days upon a showing that the emergency conditions still exist.

(2) Within 15 days after the entry of the order of appointment, the monitor shall file his or her report of findings and recommendations to the court. The report shall be verified and may be supported by documents or other evidence.

(3) Upon review of the report, the court shall determine whether there is probable cause to take further action to protect the person or property of the ward. If the court finds no probable cause, the court shall issue an order finding no probable cause and discharging the monitor.

(4)(a) If the court finds probable cause, the court shall issue an order to show cause directed to the guardian or other respondent stating the essential facts constituting the conduct charged and requiring the respondent to appear before the court to show cause why the court should not take further action. The order shall specify the time and place of the hearing with a reasonable time to allow for the preparation of a defense after service of the order.

(b) At any time prior to the hearing on the order to show cause, the court may issue a temporary injunction, a restraining order, or an order freezing assets; may suspend the guardian or appoint a guardian ad litem; or may issue any other appropriate order to protect the physical or mental health or safety or property of the ward. A copy of all such orders or injunctions shall be transmitted by the court or under its direction to all parties at the time of entry of the order or injunction.

(c) Following a hearing on the order to show cause, the court may impose sanctions on the guardian or his or her attorney or other respondent or take any other action authorized by law, including entering a judgment of contempt; ordering an accounting; freezing assets; referring the case to local law enforcement agencies or the state attorney; filing an abuse, neglect, or exploitation complaint with the Department of Children and Families; or initiating proceedings to remove the guardian.

Nothing in this subsection shall be construed to preclude the mandatory reporting requirements of chapter 39.

(5) Unless otherwise prohibited by law, a monitor may be allowed a reasonable fee as determined by the court and paid from the property of the ward. No full-time state, county, or municipal employee or officer shall be paid a fee for such investigation and report. If the court finds the motion for a court monitor to have been filed in bad faith, the costs of the proceeding, including attorney's fees, may be assessed against the movant.

(6) The court may appoint the office of criminal conflict and civil regional counsel as monitor if the ward is indigent.

Added by Laws 2006, c. 2006–77, § 3, eff. June 6, 2006. Amended by Laws 2014, c. 2014–19, § 291, eff. July 1, 2014; Laws 2015, c. 2015–83, § 3, eff. July 1, 2015.

Applicability

Laws 2015, c. 2015–83, § 20, provides:

"*Sections 709.2109 and 744.3203, Florida Statutes, as created by this act, apply to all proceedings filed on or after July 1, 2015. The amendments made by this act to ss. 744.107, 744.1075, 744.108, 744.3025, 744.3031, 744.309, 744.3115, 744.312, 744.331, 744.344, 744.345, 744.359, 744.361, 744.367, 744.369, 744.3715, and 744.464, Florida Statutes, apply to all proceedings pending on July 1, 2015.*"

744.1076. Court orders appointing court monitors and emergency court monitors; reports of court monitors; orders finding no probable cause; public records exemptions

(1)(a) The order of any court appointing a court monitor pursuant to s. 744.107 or an emergency court monitor pursuant to s. 744.1075 is exempt from s. 24(a), Art. I of the State Constitution.

(b) The reports of an appointed court monitor or emergency court monitor relating to the medical condition, financial affairs, or mental health of the ward are confidential and exempt from s. 24(a), Art. I of the State Constitution. Such reports may be subject to inspection as determined by the court or upon a showing of good cause.

(c) The public records exemptions provided in this subsection expire if a court makes a finding of probable cause, except that information otherwise made confidential or exempt shall retain its confidential or exempt status.

(2) Court orders finding no probable cause pursuant to s. 744.107 or s. 744.1075 are confidential and exempt from s. 24(a), Art. I of the State Constitution; however, such orders may be subject to inspection as determined by the court or upon a showing of good cause.

Added by Laws 2006, c. 2006–129, § 1, eff. June 6, 2006. Amended by Laws 2008, c. 2008–4, § 161, eff. July 1, 2008; Laws 2011, c. 2011–204, § 1, eff. Oct. 1, 2011.

744.108. Guardian and attorney fees and expenses

(1) A guardian, or an attorney who has rendered services to the ward or to the guardian on the ward's behalf, is entitled to a reasonable fee for services rendered and reimbursement for costs incurred on behalf of the ward.

(2) When fees for a guardian or an attorney are submitted to the court for determination, the court shall consider the following criteria:

(a) The time and labor required;

(b) The novelty and difficulty of the questions involved and the skill required to perform the services properly;

(c) The likelihood that the acceptance of the particular employment will preclude other employment of the person;

(d) The fee customarily charged in the locality for similar services;

(e) The nature and value of the incapacitated person's property, the amount of income earned by the estate, and the responsibilities and potential liabilities assumed by the person;

(f) The results obtained;

(g) The time limits imposed by the circumstances;

(h) The nature and length of the relationship with the incapacitated person; and

(i) The experience, reputation, diligence, and ability of the person performing the service.

(3) In awarding fees to attorney guardians, the court must clearly distinguish between fees and expenses for legal services and fees and expenses for guardian services and must have determined that no conflict of interest exists.

(4) Fees for legal services may include customary and reasonable charges for work performed by legal assistants employed by and working under the direction of the attorney.

(5) All petitions for guardian and attorney fees and expenses must be accompanied by an itemized description of the services performed for the fees and expenses sought to be recovered.

(6) A petition for fees or expenses may not be approved without prior notice to the guardian and to the ward, unless the ward is a minor or is totally incapacitated.

(7) A petition for fees shall include the period covered and the total amount of all prior fees paid or costs awarded to the petitioner in the guardianship proceeding currently before the court.

(8) When court proceedings are instituted to review or determine a guardian's or an attorney's fees under subsection (2), such proceedings are part of the guardianship administration process and the costs, including costs and attorney fees for the guardian's attorney, an attorney appointed under s. 744.331(2), or an attorney who has rendered services to the ward, shall be determined by the court and paid from the assets of the guardianship estate unless the court finds the requested compensation under subsection (2) to be substantially unreasonable.

(9) The court may determine that a request for compensation by the guardian, the guardian's attorney, a person employed by the guardian, an attorney appointed under s. 744.331(2), or an attorney who has rendered services to the ward, is reasonable without receiving expert testimony. A person or party may offer expert testimony for or against a request for compensation after giving notice to interested persons. Reasonable expert witness fees shall be awarded by the court and paid from the assets of the guardianship estate using the standards in subsection (8).

Laws 1975, c. 75–222, §§ 18, 26; Laws 1989, c. 89–86, § 11; Laws 1990, c. 90–271, § 5; Laws 1996, c. 96–354, § 2. Amended by Laws 2003, c. 2003–57, § 7, eff. May 30, 2003; Laws 2015, c. 2015–83, § 4, eff. July 1, 2015.

Applicability

Laws 2015, c. 2015–83, § 20, provides:

"Sections 709.2109 and 744.3203, Florida Statutes, as created by this act, apply to all proceedings filed on or after July 1, 2015. The amendments made by this act to ss. 744.107, 744.1075, 744.108, 744.3025, 744.3031, 744.309, 744.3115, 744.312, 744.331, 744.344, 744.345, 744.359, 744.361, 744.367, 744.369, 744.3715, and 744.464, Florida Statutes, apply to all proceedings pending on July 1, 2015."

Cross References

Criminal conflict and civil regional counsel offices, see § 27.511.

744.1083. Professional guardian registration

(1) A professional guardian must register with the Statewide Public Guardianship Office established in part IX of this chapter.

(2) Annual registration shall be made on forms furnished by the Statewide Public Guardianship Office and accompanied by the applicable registration fee as determined by rule. The fee may not exceed $100.

(3) Registration must include the following:

(a) Sufficient information to identify the professional guardian, as follows:

1. If the professional guardian is a natural person, the name, address, date of birth, and employer identification or social security number of the person.

2. If the professional guardian is a partnership or association, the name, address, and employer identification number of the entity.

(b) Documentation that the bonding and educational requirements of s. 744.1085 have been met.

(c) Sufficient information to distinguish a guardian providing guardianship services as a public guardian, individually, through partnership, corporation, or any other business organization.

(4) Prior to registering a professional guardian, the Statewide Public Guardianship Office must receive and review copies of the credit and criminal investigations conducted under s. 744.3135. The credit and criminal investigations must have been completed within the previous 2 years.

(5) The executive director of the office may deny registration to a professional guardian if the executive director determines that the guardian's proposed registration, including the guardian's credit or criminal investigations, indicates that registering the professional guardian would violate any provision of this chapter. If a guardian who is currently registered with the office violates a provision of this chapter, the executive director of the office may suspend or revoke the guardian's registration. If the executive director denies registration to a professional guardian or suspends or revokes a professional guardian's registration, the Statewide Public Guardianship Office must send written notification of the denial, suspension, or revocation to the chief judge of each judicial circuit in which the guardian was serving on the day of the office's decision to deny, suspend, or revoke the registration.

(6) The Department of Elderly Affairs may adopt rules necessary to administer this section.

(7) A trust company, a state banking corporation or state savings association authorized and qualified to exercise fiduciary powers in this state, or a national banking association or federal savings and loan association authorized and qualified to exercise fiduciary powers in this state, may, but is not required to, register as a professional guardian under this section. If a trust company, state banking corporation, state savings association, national banking association, or federal savings and loan association described in this subsection elects to register as a professional guardian under this subsection, the requirements of subsections (3) and (4) do not apply and the registration must include only the name, address, and employer identification number of the registrant, the name and address of its registered agent, if any, and the documentation described in paragraph (3)(b).

(8) The Department of Elderly Affairs may contract with the Florida Guardianship Foundation or other not-for-profit entity to register professional guardians.

(9) The department or its contractor shall ensure that the clerks of the court and the chief judge of each judicial circuit receive information about each registered professional guardian.

(10) A state college or university or an independent college or university that is located and chartered in Florida, that is accredited by the Commission on Colleges of the Southern Association of Colleges and Schools or the Accrediting Council for Independent Colleges and Schools, and that confers degrees as defined in s. 1005.02(7) may, but is not required to, register as a professional guardian under this section. If a state college or university or independent

college or university elects to register as a professional guardian under this subsection, the requirements of subsections (3) and (4) do not apply and the registration must include only the name, address, and employer identification number of the registrant.

Added by Laws 2002, c. 2002–195, § 3, eff. April 29, 2002. Amended by Laws 2003, c. 2003–57, § 8, eff. May 30, 2003; Laws 2004, c. 2004–260, § 10, eff. July 1, 2004; Laws 2006, c. 2006–178, § 2, eff. July 1, 2006; Laws 2009, c. 2009–175, § 2, eff. July 1, 2009.

744.1085. Regulation of professional guardians; application; bond required; educational requirements

(1) The provisions of this section are in addition to and supplemental to any other provision of the Florida Guardianship Law, except s. 744.3145.

(2) Each professional guardian who files a petition for appointment after October 1, 1997, shall post a blanket fiduciary bond with the clerk of the circuit court in the county in which the guardian's primary place of business is located. The guardian shall provide proof of the fiduciary bond to the clerks of each additional circuit court in which he or she is serving as a professional guardian. The bond shall be maintained by the guardian in an amount not less than $50,000. The bond must cover all wards for whom the guardian has been appointed at any given time. The liability of the provider of the bond is limited to the face amount of the bond, regardless of the number of wards for whom the professional guardian has been appointed. The act or omissions of each employee of a professional guardian who has direct contact with the ward or access to the ward's assets is covered by the terms of such bond. The bond must be payable to the Governor of the State of Florida and his or her successors in office and conditioned on the faithful performance of all duties by the guardian. In form, the bond must be joint and several. The bond is in addition to any bonds required under s. 744.351. This subsection does not apply to any attorney who is licensed to practice law in this state and who is in good standing, to any financial institution as defined in s. 744.309(4), or a public guardian. The expenses incurred to satisfy the bonding requirements prescribed in this section may not be paid with the assets of any ward.

(3) Each professional guardian defined in s. 744.102(17) and public guardian must receive a minimum of 40 hours of instruction and training. Each professional guardian must receive a minimum of 16 hours of continuing education every 2 calendar years after the year in which the initial 40–hour educational requirement is met. The instruction and education must be completed through a course approved or offered by the Statewide Public Guardianship Office. The expenses incurred to satisfy the educational requirements prescribed in this section may not be paid with the assets of any ward. This subsection does not apply to any attorney who is licensed to practice law in this state.

(4) Each professional guardian must allow, at the guardian's expense, an investigation of the guardian's credit history, and the credit history of employees of the guardian, in a manner prescribed by the Department of Elderly Affairs.

(5) As required in s. 744.3135, each professional guardian shall allow a level 2 background screening of the guardian and employees of the guardian in accordance with the provisions of s. 435.04.

(6) After July 1, 2005, each professional guardian shall be required to demonstrate competency to act as a professional guardian by taking an examination approved by the Department of Elderly Affairs.

(a) The Department of Elderly Affairs shall determine the minimum examination score necessary for passage of guardianship examinations.

(b) The Department of Elderly Affairs shall determine the procedure for administration of the examination.

(c) The Department of Elderly Affairs or its contractor shall charge an examination fee for the actual costs of the development and the administration of the examination, not to exceed $500.

(d) The Department of Elderly Affairs may recognize passage of a national guardianship examination in lieu of all or part of the examination approved by the Department of Elderly Affairs, except that all professional guardians must take and pass an approved examination section related to Florida law and procedure.

(7) The Department of Elderly Affairs shall set the minimum score necessary to demonstrate professional guardianship competency.

(8) The Department of Elderly Affairs shall waive the examination requirement in subsection (6) if a professional guardian can provide:

(a) Proof that the guardian has actively acted as a professional guardian for 5 years or more; and

(b) A letter from a circuit judge before whom the professional guardian practiced at least 1 year which states that the professional guardian had demonstrated to the court competency as a professional guardian.

(9) After July 1, 2004, the court shall not appoint any professional guardian who has not met the requirements of this section and s. 744.1083.

(10) This section does not apply to a professional guardian or the employees of that professional guardian when that guardian is a trust company, a state banking corporation, state savings association authorized and qualified to exercise fiduciary powers in this state, or a national banking association or federal savings and loan association authorized and qualified to exercise fiduciary powers in this state.

Added by Laws 1997, c. 97–161, § 1, eff. Oct. 1, 1997. Amended by Laws 1999, c. 99–277, § 9, eff. Oct. 1, 1999; Laws 2003, c. 2003–57, § 9, eff. May 30, 2003; Laws 2004, c. 2004–260, § 17, eff. July 1, 2004; Laws 2004, c. 2004–267, § 62, eff. July 1, 2004; Laws 2006, c. 2006–178, § 32, eff. July 1, 2006.

744.109. Records

(1) All hearings on appointment of a guardian; adjudication of incapacity; modification, termination, or revocation of the adjudication of incapacity; or restoration of capacity must be electronically or stenographically recorded.

(2) If an appeal is taken from any of these proceedings, a transcript must be furnished to an indigent ward at public expense.

Laws 1989, c. 89–96, § 12.

744.1095. Hearings

At any hearing under this chapter, the alleged incapacitated person or the adjudicated ward has the right to:

(1) Remain silent and refuse to testify at the hearing. The person may not be held in contempt of court or otherwise penalized for refusing to testify. Refusal to testify may not be used as evidence of incapacity;

(2) Testify;

(3) Present evidence;

(4) Call witnesses;

(5) Confront and cross-examine all witnesses; and

(6) Have the hearing open or closed as she or he may choose.

Laws 1989, c. 89–96, § 13; Laws 1990, c. 90–271, § 6. Amended by Laws 1997, c. 97–102, § 1069, eff. July 1, 1997.

PART II. VENUE

744.201. Domicile of ward

The domicile of a resident ward is the county where the ward resides.

Laws 1974, c. 74–106, § 1; Laws 1975, c. 75–222, § 5; Laws 1989, c. 89–96, § 14.

744.202. Venue

(1) The venue in proceedings for declaration of incapacity shall be where the alleged incapacitated person resides or is found. The provisions of this section do not apply to veterans.

(2) The venue in proceedings for the appointment of a guardian shall be:

(a) If the incapacitated person is a resident of this state, in the county where the incapacitated person resides.

(b) If the incapacitated person is not a resident of this state, in any county in this state where property of the incapacitated person is located.

(c) If the incapacitated person is not a resident of this state and owns no property in this state, in the county where any debtor of the incapacitated person resides.

(3) When the residence of an incapacitated person is changed to another county, the guardian shall petition to have the venue of the guardianship changed to the county of the acquired residence, except as provided in s. 744.2025.

(4) If an incapacitated person is a resident of this state and is found in a county other than the county of residence, the venue for declaration of incapacity and for the appointment of a guardian may be the county where the incapacitated person is found. Upon transfer of the incapacitated person to the county of residence, the guardian may have the venue of the guardianship changed to the county of residence and a successor guardian may be appointed.

Laws 1974, c. 74–106, § 1; Laws 1975, c. 75–222, § 5; Laws 1989, c. 89–96, § 15; Laws 1990, c. 90–271, § 7; Laws 1995, c. 95–401, § 33; Laws 1996, c. 96–354, § 3.

Cross References

Domicile change of incompetent, related court rule provision, see Probate Rule 5.050.

744.2025. Change of ward's residence

(1) **Prior court approval required.**—A guardian who has power pursuant to this chapter to determine the residence of the ward may not, without court approval, change the residence of the ward from this state to another, or from one county of this state to another county of this state, unless such county is adjacent to the county of the ward's current residence. Any guardian who wishes to remove the ward from the ward's current county of residence to another county which is not adjacent to the ward's current county of residence must obtain court approval prior to removal of the ward. In granting its approval, the court shall, at a minimum, consider the reason for such relocation and the longevity of such relocation.

(2) Immediate court notification required.—Any guardian who wishes to remove the ward from the ward's current county of residence to another county adjacent to the ward's county of residence shall notify the court having jurisdiction of the guardianship within 15 days after relocation of the ward. Such notice shall state the compelling reasons for relocation of the ward and how long the guardian expects the ward to remain in such other county.

Laws 1989, c. 89–96, § 16; Laws 1990, c. 90–271, § 8; Laws 1996, c. 96–354, § 4.

PART III.   TYPES OF GUARDIANSHIP

744.301.   Natural guardians

(1) The parents jointly are the natural guardians of their own children and of their adopted children, during minority, unless the parents' parental rights have been terminated pursuant to chapter 39. If a child is the subject of any proceeding under chapter 39, the parents may act as natural guardians under this section unless the court division with jurisdiction over guardianship matters finds that it is not in the child's best interests. If one parent dies, the surviving parent remains the sole natural guardian even if he or she remarries. If the marriage between the parents is dissolved, the natural guardianship belongs to the parent to whom sole parental responsibility has been granted, or if the parents have been granted shared parental responsibility, both continue as natural guardians. If the marriage is dissolved and neither parent is given parental responsibility for the child, neither may act as natural guardian of the child. The mother of a child born out of wedlock is the natural guardian of the child and is entitled to primary residential care and custody of the child unless the court enters an order stating otherwise.

(2) Except as otherwise provided in this chapter, on behalf of any of their minor children, and without appointment, authority, or bond if the amounts received in the aggregate do not exceed $15,000, natural guardians may:

(a) Settle and consummate a settlement of any claim or cause of action accruing to any of their minor children for damages to the person or property of any minor children;

(b) Collect, receive, manage, and dispose of the proceeds of any settlement;

(c) Collect, receive, manage, and dispose of any real or personal property distributed from an estate or trust;

(d) Collect, receive, manage, and dispose of and make elections regarding the proceeds from a life insurance policy or annuity contract payable to, or otherwise accruing to the benefit of, the child; and

(e) Collect, receive, manage, dispose of, and make elections regarding the proceeds of any benefit plan as defined in s. 710.102, of which the minor is a beneficiary, participant, or owner.

(3) In addition to the authority granted in subsection (2), natural guardians are authorized, on behalf of any of their minor children, to waive and release, in advance, any claim or cause of action against a commercial activity provider, or its owners, affiliates, employees, or agents, which would accrue to a minor child for personal injury, including death, and property damage resulting from an inherent risk in the activity.

(a) As used in this subsection, the term "inherent risk" means those dangers or conditions, known or unknown, which are characteristic of, intrinsic to, or an integral part of the activity and which are not eliminated even if the activity provider acts with due care in a reasonably prudent manner. The term includes, but is not limited to:

1. The failure by the activity provider to warn the natural guardian or minor child of an inherent risk; and

2. The risk that the minor child or another participant in the activity may act in a negligent or intentional manner and contribute to the injury or death of the minor child. A participant does not include the activity provider or its owners, affiliates, employees, or agents.

(b) To be enforceable, a waiver or release executed under this subsection must, at a minimum, include the following statement in uppercase type that is at least 5 points larger than, and clearly distinguishable from, the rest of the text of the waiver or release:

NOTICE TO THE MINOR CHILD'S NATURAL GUARDIAN

READ THIS FORM COMPLETELY AND CAREFULLY. YOU ARE AGREEING TO LET YOUR MINOR CHILD ENGAGE IN A POTENTIALLY DANGEROUS ACTIVITY. YOU ARE AGREEING THAT, EVEN IF __(name of released party or parties)__ USES REASONABLE CARE IN PROVIDING THIS ACTIVITY, THERE IS A CHANCE YOUR CHILD MAY BE SERIOUSLY INJURED OR KILLED BY PARTICIPATING IN THIS ACTIVITY BECAUSE THERE ARE CERTAIN DANGERS INHERENT IN THE ACTIVITY WHICH CANNOT BE AVOIDED OR ELIMINATED. BY SIGNING THIS FORM YOU ARE GIVING UP YOUR CHILD'S RIGHT AND YOUR RIGHT TO RECOVER FROM __(name of released party or parties)__ IN A LAWSUIT FOR ANY PERSONAL INJURY, INCLUDING DEATH, TO YOUR CHILD OR ANY PROPERTY DAMAGE THAT RESULTS FROM THE RISKS THAT ARE A NATURAL PART OF THE ACTIVITY. YOU HAVE THE RIGHT TO REFUSE TO SIGN THIS FORM, AND __(name of released party or parties)__ HAS THE RIGHT TO REFUSE TO LET YOUR CHILD PARTICIPATE IF YOU DO NOT SIGN THIS FORM.

(c) If a waiver or release complies with paragraph (b) and waives no more than allowed under this subsection, there is a rebuttable presumption that the waiver or release is valid and that any injury or damage to the minor child arose from the inherent risk involved in the activity.

1. To rebut the presumption that the waiver or release is valid, a claimant must demonstrate by a preponderance of the evidence that the waiver or release does not comply with this subsection.

2. To rebut the presumption that the injury or damage to the minor child arose from an inherent risk involved in the activity, a claimant must demonstrate by clear and convincing evidence that the conduct, condition, or other cause resulting in the injury or damage was not an inherent risk of the activity.

3. If a presumption under this paragraph is rebutted, liability and compensatory damages must be established by a preponderance of the evidence.

(d) Nothing in this subsection limits the ability of natural guardians, on behalf of any of their minor children, to waive and release, in advance, any claim or cause of action against a noncommercial activity provider, or its owners, affiliates, employees, or agents, to the extent authorized by common law.

(4) All instruments executed by a natural guardian for the benefit of the ward under the powers specified in this section are binding on the ward. The natural guardian may not,

without a court order, use the property of the ward for the guardian's benefit or to satisfy the guardian's support obligation to the ward.

Laws 1974, c. 74–106, § 1; Laws 1975, c. 75–166, § 8; Laws 1975, c. 75–222, § 7; Laws 1977, c. 77–190, § 1; Laws 1979, c. 79–221, § 3; Laws 1989, c. 89–96, § 17; Laws 1992, c. 92–200, § 22; Laws 1995, c. 95–211, § 66. Amended by Laws 1997, c. 97–170, § 73, eff. July 1, 1997; Laws 2002, c. 2002–195, § 11, eff. April 29, 2002; Laws 2005, c. 2005–101, § 8, eff. June 1, 2005; Laws 2006, c. 2006–178, § 3, eff. July 1, 2006; Laws 2010, c. 2010–27, § 2, eff. April 27, 2010; Laws 2012, c. 2012–48, § 1, eff. July 1, 2012; Laws 2015, c. 2015–112, § 5, eff. July 1, 2015.

Cross References

Custody and support of children, see § 61.13.
Health care surrogates for minors, designation form, see F.S.A. § 765.2038.
Health care surrogates for minors, designation, see F.S.A. § 765.2035.
Married minors, removal of nonage disabilities, see § 743.01 et seq.
Motorsport nonspectator liability releases, see F.S.A. § 549.09.
Property interests, power to disclaim, see § 739.104.

744.3021. Guardians of minors

(1) Except as provided in subsection (4), upon petition of a parent, brother, sister, next of kin, or other person interested in the welfare of a minor, a guardian for a minor may be appointed by the court without the necessity of adjudication pursuant to s. 744.331. A guardian appointed for a minor, whether of the person or property, has the authority of a plenary guardian.

(2) A minor is not required to attend the hearing on the petition for appointment of a guardian, unless otherwise directed by the court.

(3) In its discretion, the court may appoint an attorney to represent the interests of a minor at the hearing on the petition for appointment of a guardian.

(4) If a petition is filed pursuant to this section requesting appointment of a guardian for a minor who is the subject of any proceeding under chapter 39 and who is aged 17 years and 6 months or older, the court division with jurisdiction over guardianship matters has jurisdiction over the proceedings under s. 744.331. The alleged incapacitated minor under this subsection shall be provided all the due process rights conferred upon an alleged incapacitated adult pursuant to this chapter and applicable court rules. The order of adjudication under s. 744.331 and the letters of limited or plenary guardianship may issue upon the minor's 18th birthday or as soon thereafter as possible. Any proceeding pursuant to this subsection shall be conducted separately from any other proceeding.

Laws 1990, c. 90–271, § 9. Amended by Laws 2015, c. 2015–112, § 6, eff. July 1, 2015.

744.3025. Claims of minors

(1)(a) The court may appoint a guardian ad litem to represent the minor's interest before approving a settlement of the minor's portion of the claim in a case in which a minor has a claim for personal injury, property damage, wrongful death, or other cause of action in which the gross settlement of the claim exceeds $15,000 if the court believes a guardian ad litem is necessary to protect the minor's interest.

(b) Except as provided in paragraph (e), the court shall appoint a guardian ad litem to represent the minor's interest before approving a settlement of the minor's claim in a case in which the gross settlement involving a minor equals or exceeds $50,000.

(c) The appointment of the guardian ad litem must be without the necessity of bond or notice.

(d) The duty of the guardian ad litem is to protect the minor's interests as described in the Florida Probate Rules.

(e) A court need not appoint a guardian ad litem for the minor if a guardian of the minor has previously been appointed and that guardian has no potential adverse interest to the minor.

(2) Unless waived, the court shall award reasonable fees and costs to the guardian ad litem to be paid out of the gross proceeds of the settlement.

(3) A settlement of a claim pursuant to this section is subject to the confidentiality provisions of this chapter.

Added by Laws 2006, c. 2006–178, § 4, eff. July 1, 2006. Amended by Laws 2015, c. 2015–83, § 5, eff. July 1, 2015.

Applicability

Laws 2015, c. 2015–83, § 20, provides:

"Sections 709.2109 and 744.3203, Florida Statutes, as created by this act, apply to all proceedings filed on or after July 1, 2015. The amendments made by this act to ss. 744.107, 744.1075, 744.108, 744.3025, 744.3031, 744.309, 744.3115, 744.312, 744.331, 744.344, 744.345, 744.359, 744.361, 744.367, 744.369, 744.3715, and 744.464, Florida Statutes, apply to all proceedings pending on July 1, 2015."

744.3031. Emergency temporary guardianship

(1) A court, prior to appointment of a guardian but after a petition for determination of incapacity has been filed pursuant to this chapter, may appoint an emergency temporary guardian for the person or property, or both, of an alleged incapacitated person. The court must specifically find that there appears to be imminent danger that the physical or mental health or safety of the person will be seriously impaired or that the person's property is in danger of being wasted, misappropriated, or lost unless immediate action is taken. The subject of the proceeding or any adult interested in the welfare of that person may apply to the court in which the proceeding is pending for the emergency appointment of a temporary guardian. The powers and duties of the emergency temporary guardian must be specifically enumerated by court order. The court shall appoint counsel to represent the alleged incapacitated person during any such summary proceedings, and such appointed counsel may request that the proceeding be recorded and transcribed.

(2) Notice of filing of the petition for appointment of an emergency temporary guardian and a hearing on the petition must be served on the alleged incapacitated person and on the alleged incapacitated person's attorney at least 24 hours before the hearing on the petition is commenced, unless the petitioner demonstrates that substantial harm to the alleged incapacitated person would occur if the 24–hour notice is given.

(3) The court may appoint an emergency temporary guardian on its own motion if no petition for appointment of guardian has been filed at the time of entry of an order determining incapacity.

(4) The authority of an emergency temporary guardian expires 90 days after the date of appointment or when a guardian is appointed, whichever occurs first. The authority of the emergency temporary guardian may be extended for an additional 90 days upon a showing that the emergency conditions still exist.

(5) The court may issue an injunction, restraining order, or other appropriate writ to protect the physical or mental health or safety of the person who is the ward of the emergency temporary guardianship.

(6) The emergency temporary guardian shall take an oath to faithfully perform the duties of a guardian before letters of emergency temporary guardianship are issued.

(7) Before exercising authority as guardian, the emergency temporary guardian of the property may be required to file a bond in accordance with s. 744.351.

(8) An emergency temporary guardian's authority and responsibility begins upon issuance of letters of emergency temporary guardianship in accordance with s. 744.345.

(9)(a) An emergency temporary guardian shall file a final report no later than 30 days after the expiration of the emergency temporary guardianship.

(b) A court may not authorize any payment of the emergency temporary guardian's final fees or the final fees of his or her attorney until the final report is filed.

(c) If an emergency temporary guardian is a guardian for the property, the final report must consist of a verified inventory of the property, as provided in s. 744.365, as of the date the letters of emergency temporary guardianship were issued, a final accounting that gives a full and correct account of the receipts and disbursements of all the property of the ward over which the guardian had control, and a statement of the property of the ward on hand at the end of the emergency temporary guardianship. If the emergency temporary guardian becomes the successor guardian of the property, the final report must satisfy the requirements of the initial guardianship report for the guardian of the property as provided in s. 744.362.

(d) If the emergency temporary guardian is a guardian of the person, the final report must summarize the activities of the temporary guardian with regard to residential placement, medical condition, mental health and rehabilitative services, and the social condition of the ward to the extent of the authority granted to the temporary guardian in the letters of guardianship. If the emergency temporary guardian becomes the successor guardian of the person, the report must satisfy the requirements of the initial report for a guardian of the person as stated in s. 744.362.

(e) A copy of the final report of the emergency temporary guardianship shall be served on the successor guardian and the ward.

Laws 1989, c. 89–96, § 19; Laws 1990, c. 90–271, § 10. Amended by Laws 1997, c. 97–102, § 1070, eff. July 1, 1997; Laws 2006, c. 2006–178, § 5, eff. July 1, 2006; Laws 2015, c. 2015–83, § 6, eff. July 1, 2015.

Applicability

Laws 2015, c. 2015–83, § 20, provides:

"Sections 709.2109 and 744.3203, Florida Statutes, as created by this act, apply to all proceedings filed on or after July 1, 2015. The amendments made by this act to ss. 744.107, 744.1075, 744.108, 744.3025, 744.3031, 744.309, 744.3115, 744.312, 744.331, 744.344, 744.345, 744.359, 744.361, 744.367, 744.369, 744.3715, and 744.464, Florida Statutes, apply to all proceedings pending on July 1, 2015."

744.304. Standby guardianship

(1) Upon a petition by the natural guardians or a guardian appointed under s. 744.3021, the court may appoint a standby guardian of the person or property of a minor. The court may also

appoint an alternate to the guardian to act if the standby guardian does not serve or ceases to serve after appointment. Notice of a hearing on the petition must be served on the parents, natural or adoptive, and on any guardian currently serving unless the notice is waived in writing by them or waived by the court for good cause shown.

(2) Upon petition of a currently serving guardian, a standby guardian of the person or property of an incapacitated person may be appointed by the court. Notice of the hearing shall be served on the ward's next of kin.

(3) The standby guardian or alternate shall be empowered to assume the duties of guardianship immediately on the death, removal, or resignation of the guardian of a minor, or on the death or adjudication of incapacity of the last surviving natural guardian of a minor, or upon the death, removal, or resignation of the guardian for an adult. The guardian of the ward's property may not be empowered to deal with the ward's property, other than to safeguard it, before issuance of letters of guardianship. If the ward is over the age of 18 years, the court shall conduct a hearing as provided in s. 744.331 before confirming the appointment of the standby guardian, unless the ward has previously been found to be incapacitated.

(4) Within 20 days after assumption of duties as guardian, a standby guardian shall petition for confirmation of appointment. If the court finds the standby guardian to be qualified to serve as guardian under ss. 744.309 and 744.312, appointment of the guardian must be confirmed. Each guardian so confirmed shall file an oath in accordance with s. 744.347, shall file a bond, and shall submit to a credit and a criminal history record check as set forth in s. 744.3135, if required. Letters of guardianship must then be issued in the manner provided in s. 744.345.

(5) After the assumption of duties by a standby guardian, the court shall have jurisdiction over the guardian and the ward.

Laws 1974, c. 74–106, § 1; Laws 1975, c. 75–222, § 7; Laws 1977, c. 77–174, § 1; Laws 1989, c. 89–96, § 20; Laws 1990, c. 90–271, § 11. Amended by Laws 1997, c. 97–102, § 1071, eff. July 1, 1997; Laws 2006, c. 2006–178, § 6, eff. July 1, 2006.

744.3045. Preneed guardian

(1) A competent adult may name a preneed guardian by making a written declaration that names such guardian to serve in the event of the declarant's incapacity.

(2) The written declaration must reasonably identify the declarant and preneed guardian and be signed by the declarant in the presence of at least two attesting witnesses present at the same time.

(3) The declarant may file the declaration with the clerk of the court. When a petition for incapacity is filed, the clerk shall produce the declaration.

(4) Production of the declaration in a proceeding for incapacity shall constitute a rebuttable presumption that the preneed guardian is entitled to serve as guardian. The court shall not be bound to appoint the preneed guardian if the preneed guardian is found to be unqualified to serve as guardian.

(5) The preneed guardian shall assume the duties of guardian immediately upon an adjudication of incapacity.

(6) If the preneed guardian refuses to serve, a written declaration appointing an alternate preneed guardian constitutes a rebuttable presumption that such preneed guardian is entitled to serve as guardian. The court is not bound to appoint the alternate preneed guardian if the alternate preneed guardian is found to be unqualified to serve as guardian.

(7) Within 20 days after assumption of duties as guardian, a preneed guardian shall petition for confirmation of appointment. If the court finds the preneed guardian to be qualified to serve as guardian pursuant to ss. 744.309 and 744.312, appointment of the guardian must be confirmed. Each guardian so confirmed shall file an oath in accordance with s. 744.347 and shall file a bond, if required. Letters of guardianship must then be issued in the manner provided in s. 744.345.

Laws 1989, c. 89–96, § 21; Laws 1990, c. 90–271, § 12.

744.3046. Preneed guardian for minor

(1) Both parents, natural or adoptive, if living, or the surviving parent, may nominate a preneed guardian of the person or property or both of the parent's minor child by making a written declaration that names such guardian to serve if the minor's last surviving parent becomes incapacitated or dies. The declarant or declarants may also name an alternate to the guardian to act if the designated preneed guardian refuses to serve, renounces the appointment, dies, or becomes incapacitated after the death of the last surviving parent of the minor.

(2) The written declaration must reasonably identify the declarant or declarants and the designated preneed guardian and must be signed by the declarant or declarants in the presence of at least two attesting witnesses present at the same time. The written declaration must also provide the following information for each minor child named in such declaration: the full name as it appears on the birth certificate or as ordered by a court, date of birth, and social security number, if any.

(3) The declarant must file the declaration with the clerk of the court. When a petition for incapacity of the last surviving parent or the appointment of a guardian upon the death of the last surviving parent is filed, the clerk shall produce the declaration.

(4) Production of the declaration in a proceeding to determine incapacity of the last surviving parent, or in a proceeding to appoint a guardian upon the death of the last surviving parent, constitutes a rebuttable presumption that the designated preneed guardian is entitled to serve as guardian. The court is not bound to appoint the designated preneed guardian if the designated preneed guardian is found to be unqualified to serve as guardian.

(5) The preneed guardian shall assume the duties of guardian immediately upon an adjudication of incapacity of the last surviving parent or the death of the last surviving parent.

(6) If the preneed guardian refuses to serve, a written declaration appointing an alternate preneed guardian constitutes a rebuttable presumption that the alternate preneed guardian is entitled to serve as guardian. The court is not bound to appoint the alternate preneed guardian if the alternate preneed guardian is found to be unqualified to serve as guardian.

(7) Within 20 days after assumption of duties as guardian, a preneed guardian shall petition for confirmation of appointment. If the court finds the preneed guardian to be qualified to serve as guardian, appointment of the guardian must be confirmed. Each guardian so confirmed shall file an oath in accordance with s. 744.347 and shall file a bond, if the court requires a bond. Letters of guardianship must then be issued in the manner provided in s. 744.345.

(8) The clerk shall maintain all declarations filed pursuant to this section until:

(a) A petition for incapacity of the last surviving parent is filed or petition for the appointment of a guardian upon the death of the last surviving parent is filed as provided in subsection (3); or

(b) All minor children named in the declaration have reached the age of majority.

The clerk may dispose of such written declaration in accordance with law.

Laws 1992, c. 92–200, § 23.

744.306. Foreign guardians

(1) When the residence of a ward of a foreign guardian is moved to this state, the guardian shall, within 60 days after such change of residence, file the authenticated order of her or his appointment with the clerk of the court in the county where the ward resides. Such order shall be recognized and given full faith and credit in the courts of this state. The guardian and the ward are subject to this chapter.

(2) A guardian appointed in any state, territory, or country may maintain or defend any action in this state as a representative of her or his ward.

(3) Debtors who have received no written demand for payment from a guardian appointed in this state within 60 days after the appointment of a guardian, curator, conservator, or committee in any state, territory, or country other than this state, and whose property in this state is subject to a mortgage or other lien securing the debt held by the foreign guardian, curator, conservator, or committee, may pay the debt to the foreign guardian, curator, conservator, or committee after the expiration of 60 days from the date of her or his appointment. A satisfaction of the mortgage or lien, executed after the 60 days have expired by the foreign guardian, curator, conservator, or committee, with an authenticated copy of the letters or other evidence of authority of the foreign guardian, curator, conservator, or committee attached, may be recorded in the public records of this state and shall constitute an effective discharge of the mortgage or lien, irrespective of whether the debtor had received written demand before paying the debt.

(4) All persons indebted to a ward, or having possession of personal property belonging to a ward, who have received no written demand for payment of the indebtedness or the delivery of the property from a guardian appointed in this state are authorized to pay the indebtedness or to deliver the personal property to the foreign guardian, curator, conservator, or committee after the expiration of the 60 days from the date of her or his appointment.

Laws 1974, c. 74–106, § 1; Laws 1975, c. 75–222, § 7; Laws 1989, c. 89–96, § 23. Amended by Laws 1997, c. 97–102, § 1072, eff. July 1, 1997.

744.307. Foreign guardian may manage the property of nonresident ward

(1) A guardian of the property of a nonresident ward, duly appointed by a court of another state, territory, or country, who desires to manage any part or all of the property of the ward located in this state, may file a petition showing his or her appointment, describing the property, stating its estimated value, and showing the indebtedness, if any, existing against the ward in this state, to the best of the guardian's knowledge and belief.

(2) The guardian shall designate a resident agent as required by the Florida Probate Rules.

(3) The guardian shall file authenticated copies of his or her letters of guardianship or other authority and of his or her bond or other security. The court shall determine if the foreign bond or other security is sufficient to guarantee the faithful management of the ward's property in this state. The court may require a new guardian's bond in this state in the amount it deems necessary and conditioned for the proper management and application of the property of the ward coming into the custody of the guardian in this state.

---

(4) Thereafter, the guardianship shall be governed by the law concerning guardianships.

Laws 1974, c. 74–106, § 1; Laws 1975, c. 75–222, § 7; Laws 1989, c. 89–96, § 24; Laws 1995, c. 95–211, § 67. Amended by Laws 1997, c. 97–102, § 1073, eff. July 1, 1997.

744.308. Resident guardian of the property of nonresident ward

(1) The court may appoint a person qualified under s. 744.309 as guardian of a nonresident ward's property upon the petition of a foreign guardian, next of kin, or creditor of the ward, regardless of whether he or she has a foreign guardian or not.

(2) The petition for the appointment of a guardian for the property of a nonresident ward shall be in writing and shall be prepared in accordance with the requirements of s. 744.334.

(3) If it is alleged that the incapacity is due to mental or physical incapacity, the petition shall be accompanied by an authenticated copy of the adjudication of incapacity from the qualified authorities in the state, territory, or country where the incapacitated person is domiciled and shall state whether the incapacitated person is in the custody of any person or institution and, if so, the name and post office address of the custodian. The adjudication shall constitute prima facie proof of the incapacity.

(4) If the question about the mental or physical incapacity of a nonresident is presented while the nonresident is temporarily residing in this state and he or she is not under an adjudication of incapacity made in some other state, territory, or country, the procedure for the appointment of a guardian of the nonresident's property shall be the same as though he or she were a resident of this state.

(5) When the ground for the appointment of a guardian is incapacity for which the person has been adjudicated in another state, territory, or country, notice of the hearing shall be served personally or by registered mail on the ward and the ward's next of kin and legal custodian, if any, at least 20 days before the hearing.

(6) In the appointment of the guardian, the court shall be governed by s. 744.312.

(7) The duties, powers, and liabilities for the custody, control, management, and disposition of the ward's property and removal, accounting, and discharge shall be governed by the law applicable to guardians of property of resident wards.

Laws 1974, c. 74–106, § 1; Laws 1975, c. 75–222, § 7; Laws 1977, c. 77–174, § 1; Laws 1989, c. 89–96, § 25; Laws 1990, c. 90–271, § 13. Amended by Laws 1997, c. 97–102, § 1074, eff. July 1, 1997.

744.3085. Guardian advocates

A circuit court may appoint a guardian advocate, without an adjudication of incapacity, for a person with developmental disabilities if the person lacks the capacity to do some, but not all, of the tasks necessary to care for his or her person, property, or estate, or if the person has voluntarily petitioned for the appointment of a guardian advocate. Unless otherwise specified, the proceeding shall be governed by the Florida Probate Rules. In accordance with the legislative intent of this chapter, courts are encouraged to consider appointing a guardian advocate, when appropriate, as a less restrictive form of guardianship.

Added by Laws 2004, c. 2004–260, § 11, eff. July 1, 2004.

PART IV. GUARDIANS

744.309. Who may be appointed guardian of a resident ward

(1) **Resident.—**

(a) Any resident of this state who is sui juris and is 18 years of age or older is qualified to act as guardian of a ward.

(b) No judge shall act as guardian after this law becomes effective, except when he or she is related to the ward by blood, marriage, or adoption, or has maintained a close relationship with the ward or the ward's family, and serves without compensation.

(2) Nonresident.—A nonresident of the state may serve as guardian of a resident ward if he or she is:

(a) Related by lineal consanguinity to the ward;

(b) A legally adopted child or adoptive parent of the ward;

(c) A spouse, brother, sister, uncle, aunt, niece, or nephew of the ward, or someone related by lineal consanguinity to any such person; or

(d) The spouse of a person otherwise qualified under this section.

(3) Disqualified persons.—No person who has been convicted of a felony or who, from any incapacity or illness, is incapable of discharging the duties of a guardian, or who is otherwise unsuitable to perform the duties of a guardian, shall be appointed to act as guardian. Further, no person who has been judicially determined to have committed abuse, abandonment, or neglect against a child as defined in s. 39.01 or s. 984.03(1), (2), and (37), or who has been found guilty of, regardless of adjudication, or entered a plea of nolo contendere or guilty to, any offense prohibited under s. 435.04 or similar statute of another jurisdiction, shall be appointed to act as a guardian. Except as provided in subsection (5) or subsection (6), a person who provides substantial services to the proposed ward in a professional or business capacity, or a creditor of the proposed ward, may not be appointed guardian and retain that previous professional or business relationship. A person may not be appointed a guardian if he or she is in the employ of any person, agency, government, or corporation that provides service to the proposed ward in a professional or business capacity, except that a person so employed may be appointed if he or she is the spouse, adult child, parent, or sibling of the proposed ward or the court determines that the potential conflict of interest is insubstantial and that the appointment would clearly be in the proposed ward's best interest. The court may not appoint a guardian in any other circumstance in which a conflict of interest may occur.

(4) Trust company, state bank or savings association, or national bank or federal savings and loan association.—A trust company, a state banking corporation or state savings association authorized and qualified to exercise fiduciary powers in this state, or a national banking association or federal savings and loan association authorized and qualified to exercise fiduciary powers in this state may act as guardian of the property of the ward.

(5) Nonprofit corporate guardian.—A nonprofit corporation organized for religious or charitable purposes and existing under the laws of this state may be appointed guardian for a ward. If the nonprofit corporate guardian charges fees against the assets or property of the ward for its services, the corporation must employ at least one professional guardian.

(6) Health care provider.—A provider of health care services to the ward, whether direct or indirect, may not be appointed the guardian of the ward, unless the court specifically finds that there is no conflict of interest with the ward's best interests.

(7) For-profit corporate guardian.—A for-profit corporate guardian existing under the laws of this state is qualified to act as guardian of a ward if the entity is qualified to do business in the state, is wholly owned by the person who is the circuit's public guardian in the circuit where the corporate guardian is appointed, has met the registration requirements of s. 744.1083, and posts and maintains a bond or insurance policy under paragraph (a).

(a) The for-profit corporate guardian must meet one of the following requirements:

1. Post and maintain a blanket fiduciary bond of at least $250,000 with the clerk of the circuit court in the county in which the corporate guardian has its principal place of business. The corporate guardian shall provide proof of the fiduciary bond to the clerks of each additional circuit court in which he or she is serving as a guardian. The bond must cover all wards for whom the corporation has been appointed as a guardian at any given time. The liability of the provider of the bond is limited to the face value of the bond, regardless of the number of wards for whom the corporation is acting as a guardian. The terms of the bond must cover the acts or omissions of each agent or employee of the corporation who has direct contact with the ward or access to the assets of the guardianship. The bond must be payable to the Governor and his or her successors in office and be conditioned on the faithful performance of all duties of a guardian under this chapter. The bond is in lieu of and not in addition to the bond required under s. 744.1085 but is in addition to any bonds required under s. 744.351. The expenses incurred to satisfy the bonding requirements of this section may not be paid with the assets of any ward; or

2. Maintain a liability insurance policy that covers any losses sustained by the guardianship caused by errors, omissions, or any intentional misconduct committed by the corporation's officers or agents. The policy must cover all wards for whom the corporation is acting as a guardian for losses up to $250,000. The terms of the policy must cover acts or omissions of each agent or employee of the corporation who has direct contact with the ward or access to the assets of the guardianship. The corporate guardian shall provide proof of the policy to the clerk of each circuit court in which he or she is serving as a guardian.

(b) A for-profit corporation appointed as guardian before July 1, 2015, is also qualified to serve as a guardian in the particular guardianships in which the corporation has already been appointed as guardian.

Laws 1974, c. 74–106, § 1; Laws 1975, c. 75–222, § 8; Laws 1979, c. 79–221, § 4; Laws 1981, c. 81–27, § 7; Laws 1983, c. 83–139, § 2; Laws 1989, c. 89–96, § 26; Laws 1990, c. 90–271, § 14; Laws 1996, c. 96–184, § 1; Laws 1996, c. 96–354, § 5. Amended by Laws 1997, c. 97–102, § 1781, eff. July 1, 1997; Laws 1998, c. 98–280, § 48, eff. June 30, 1998; Laws 1998, c. 98–403, § 159, eff. Oct. 1, 1998; Laws 2000, c. 2000–135, § 8, eff. July 1, 2000; Laws 2000, c. 2000–349, § 110, eff. Sept. 1, 2000; Laws 2002, c. 2002–195, § 4, eff. April 29, 2002; Laws 2004, c. 2004–267, § 31, eff. July 1, 2004; Laws 2010, c. 2010–114, § 53, eff. Aug. 1, 2010; Laws 2015, c. 2015–83, § 7, eff. July 1, 2015.

Applicability

Laws 2015, c. 2015–83, § 20, provides:

"Sections 709.2109 and 744.3203, Florida Statutes, as created by this act, apply to all proceedings filed on or after July 1, 2015. The amendments made by this act to ss. 744.107, 744.1075, 744.108, 744.3025, 744.3031, 744.309, 744.3115, 744.312, 744.331, 744.344, 744.345, 744.359, 744.361, 744.367, 744.369, 744.3715, and 744.464, Florida Statutes, apply to all proceedings pending on July 1, 2015."

Cross References

Termination of guardianship on change of domicile of resident ward, see Probate Rules 5.670, 5.680.
Termination of guardianship upon removal of ward's incapacity, or death, see Probate Rule 5.680.

744.3115. Advance directives for health care

In each proceeding in which a guardian is appointed under this chapter, the court shall determine whether the ward, prior to incapacity, has executed any valid advance directive under chapter 765. If any advance directive exists, the court shall specify in its order and letters of guardianship what authority, if any, the guardian shall exercise over the ward with regard to health care decisions and what authority, if any, the surrogate shall continue to exercise over the ward with regard to health care decisions. Pursuant to the grounds listed in s. 765.105, the court, upon its own motion, may, with notice to the surrogate and any other appropriate parties, modify or revoke the authority of the surrogate to make health care decisions for the ward. Any order revoking or modifying the authority of the surrogate must be supported by specific written findings of fact. If the court order provides that the guardian is responsible for making health care decisions for the ward, the guardian shall assume the responsibilities of the surrogate which are provided in s. 765.205. For purposes of this section, the term "health care decision" has the same meaning as in s. 765.101.

Laws 1992, c. 92–199, § 6; Laws 1994, c. 94–183, § 1. Amended by Laws 2006, c. 2006–178, § 7, eff. July 1, 2006; Laws 2015, c. 2015–83, § 8, eff. July 1, 2015.

Applicability

Laws 2015, c. 2015–83, § 20, provides:

"Sections 709.2109 and 744.3203, Florida Statutes, as created by this act, apply to all proceedings filed on or after July 1, 2015. The amendments made by this act to ss. 744.107, 744.1075, 744.108, 744.3025, 744.3031, 744.309, 744.3115, 744.312, 744.331, 744.344, 744.345, 744.359, 744.361, 744.367, 744.369, 744.3715, and 744.464, Florida Statutes, apply to all proceedings pending on July 1, 2015."

Cross References

Surrogates, modification or revocation of authority under this section, see § 765.205.

744.312. Considerations in appointment of guardian

(1) If the person designated is qualified to serve pursuant to s. 744.309, the court shall appoint any standby guardian or preneed guardian, unless the court determines that appointing such person is contrary to the best interests of the ward.

(2) If a guardian cannot be appointed under subsection (1), the court may appoint any person who is fit and proper and qualified to act as guardian, whether related to the ward or not. The court shall give preference to the appointment of a person who:

(a) Is related by blood or marriage to the ward;

(b) Has educational, professional, or business experience relevant to the nature of the services sought to be provided;

(c) Has the capacity to manage the financial resources involved; or

(d) Has the ability to meet the requirements of the law and the unique needs of the individual case.

(3) The court shall also:

(a) Consider the wishes expressed by an incapacitated person as to who shall be appointed guardian.

(b) Consider the preference of a minor who is age 14 or over as to who should be appointed guardian.

(c) Consider any person designated as guardian in any will in which the ward is a beneficiary.

(d) Consider the wishes of the ward's next of kin, when the ward cannot express a preference.

(4) Except when a standby guardian or a preneed guardian is appointed by the court:

(a) In each case when a court appoints a professional guardian and does not use a rotation system for such appointment, the court must make specific findings of fact stating why the person was selected as guardian in the particular matter involved. The findings must reference each of the factors listed in subsections (2) and (3).

(b) An emergency temporary guardian who is a professional guardian may not be appointed as the permanent guardian of a ward unless one of the next of kin of the alleged incapacitated person or the ward requests that the professional guardian be appointed as permanent guardian. The court may waive the limitations of this paragraph if the special requirements of the guardianship demand that the court appoint a guardian because he or she has special talent or specific prior experience. The court must make specific findings of fact that justify waiving the limitations of this paragraph.

(5) The court may not give preference to the appointment of a person under subsection (2) based solely on the fact that such person was appointed by the court to serve as an emergency temporary guardian.

Laws 1974, c. 74–106, § 1; Laws 1975, c. 75–222, § 12; Laws 1977, c. 77–174, § 1; Laws 1979, c. 79–221, § 5; Laws 1989, c. 89–96, § 27; Laws 1990, c. 90–271, § 15. Amended by Laws 2015, c. 2015–83, § 9, eff. July 1, 2015.

Applicability

Laws 2015, c. 2015–83, § 20, provides:

"Sections 709.2109 and 744.3203, Florida Statutes, as created by this act, apply to all proceedings filed on or after July 1, 2015. The amendments made by this act to ss. 744.107, 744.1075, 744.108, 744.3025, 744.3031, 744.309, 744.3115, 744.312, 744.331, 744.344, 744.345, 744.359, 744.361, 744.367, 744.369, 744.3715, and 744.464, Florida Statutes, apply to all proceedings pending on July 1, 2015."

Cross References

Petition for appointment of guardian, see Probate Rule 5.560.

744.3125. Application for appointment

(1) Every prospective guardian must complete an application for appointment as guardian. The application must list the person's qualifications to serve as a guardian.

(2) A person may not be appointed a guardian unless the person discloses in the application form the names of all wards for whom the person is currently acting as a guardian. The application must identify each ward by court file number and circuit court in which the case is pending and must state whether the person is acting as the limited or plenary guardian of the person or property or both.

(3) This section does not apply to corporate guardians other than nonprofit corporate guardians or to public guardians.

(4) Nonprofit corporate guardians must file quarterly with the clerk of court disclosure statements that contain the information required under subsections (1) and (2), rather than filing a guardianship application with each petition to be appointed guardian.

Laws 1989, c. 89–96, § 29; Laws 1990, c. 90–271, § 16. Amended by Laws 1997, c. 97–102, § 1075, eff. July 1, 1997.

Cross References

Application for appointment, see Probate Rule 5.590.

744.3135. Credit and criminal investigation

(1) The court shall require all guardians who are seeking appointment by the court, other than a corporate guardian as described in s. 744.309(4), and all employees of a professional guardian, other than a corporate guardian as described in s. 744.309(4), who have a fiduciary responsibility to a ward, to submit, at their own expense, to a credit history investigation and to undergo level 2 background screening as required under s. 435.04. On petition by any interested person or on the court's own motion, the court may waive the requirement of a credit history investigation or a level 2 background screening, or both. If appointed, a nonprofessional guardian may petition the court for reimbursement of the reasonable expenses of the credit history investigation and background screening. The court must consider the results of any investigation before appointing a guardian. At any time, the court may require a guardian or the guardian's employees to submit to an investigation of the person's credit history and complete a level 1 or level 2 background screening pursuant to s. 435.03. The court shall consider the results of any investigation in determining whether to reappoint a guardian. The clerk of the court shall maintain a file on each guardian appointed by the court and retain in the file documentation of the result of any investigation conducted under this section. A professional guardian shall pay the clerk of the court a fee of up to $7.50 for handling and processing professional guardian files.·

(2) For nonprofessional guardians, the court shall accept the satisfactory completion of a criminal history record check as described in this subsection. A nonprofessional guardian satisfies the requirements of this section by undergoing a state and national criminal history record check using fingerprints. Any nonprofessional guardian who is so required shall have his or her fingerprints taken and forward them along with the necessary fee to the Department of Law Enforcement for processing. The results of the fingerprint criminal history record check shall be forwarded to the clerk of the court, who shall maintain the results in the nonprofessional guardian's file and make the results available to the court.

(3) For professional guardians, the court and the Statewide Public Guardianship Office shall accept the satisfactory completion of a criminal history record check by any method described in this subsection. A professional guardian satisfies the requirements of this section by undergoing an electronic fingerprint criminal history record check. A professional guardian may use any electronic fingerprinting equipment used for criminal history record checks. The Statewide Public Guardianship Office shall adopt a rule detailing the acceptable methods for completing an electronic fingerprint criminal history record check under this section. The professional guardian shall pay the actual costs incurred by the Federal Bureau of Investigation and the Department of Law Enforcement for the criminal history record check. The entity completing the record check must immediately send the results of the criminal history record check to the clerk of the court and the Statewide Public Guardianship Office. The clerk of the

court shall maintain the results in the professional guardian's file and shall make the results available to the court.

(4)(a) A professional guardian, and each employee of a professional guardian who has a fiduciary responsibility to a ward, must complete, at his or her own expense, a level 2 background screening as set forth in s. 435.04 before and at least once every 5 years after the date the guardian is registered. A professional guardian, and each employee of a professional guardian who has a fiduciary responsibility to a ward, must complete, at his or her own expense, a level 1 background screening as set forth in s. 435.03 at least once every 2 years after the date the guardian is registered. However, a professional guardian is not required to resubmit fingerprints for a criminal history record check if he or she has been screened using electronic fingerprinting equipment and the fingerprints are retained by the Department of Law Enforcement in order to notify the clerk of the court of any crime charged against the person in this state or elsewhere, as appropriate.

(b) All fingerprints electronically submitted to the Department of Law Enforcement under this section shall be retained by the Department of Law Enforcement in a manner provided by rule and entered in the statewide automated biometric identification system authorized by s. 943.05(2)(b). The fingerprints shall thereafter be available for all purposes and uses authorized for arrest fingerprints entered in the Criminal Justice Information Program under s. 943.051.

(c) The Department of Law Enforcement shall search all arrest fingerprints received under s. 943.051 against the fingerprints retained in the statewide automated biometric identification system under paragraph (b). Any arrest record that is identified with the fingerprints of a person described in this paragraph must be reported to the clerk of court. The clerk of court must forward any arrest record received for a professional guardian to the Statewide Public Guardianship Office within 5 days. Each professional guardian who elects to submit fingerprint information electronically shall participate in this search process by paying an annual fee to the Statewide Public Guardianship Office of the Department of Elderly Affairs and by informing the clerk of court and the Statewide Public Guardianship Office of any change in the status of his or her guardianship appointment. The amount of the annual fee to be imposed for performing these searches and the procedures for the retention of professional guardian fingerprints and the dissemination of search results shall be established by rule of the Department of Law Enforcement. At least once every 5 years, the Statewide Public Guardianship Office must request that the Department of Law Enforcement forward the fingerprints maintained under this section to the Federal Bureau of Investigation.

(5)(a) A professional guardian, and each employee of a professional guardian who has a fiduciary responsibility to a ward, must complete, at his or her own expense, an investigation of his or her credit history before and at least once every 2 years after the date of the guardian's registration with the Statewide Public Guardianship Office.

(b) The Statewide Public Guardianship Office shall adopt a rule detailing the acceptable methods for completing a credit investigation under this section. If appropriate, the Statewide Public Guardianship Office may administer credit investigations. If the office chooses to administer the credit investigation, the office may adopt a rule setting a fee, not to exceed $25, to reimburse the costs associated with the administration of a credit investigation.

(6) The Statewide Public Guardianship Office may inspect at any time the results of any credit or criminal history record check of a public or professional guardian conducted under this section. The office shall maintain copies of the credit or criminal history record check results in the guardian's registration file. If the results of a credit or criminal investigation of a public or

professional guardian have not been forwarded to the Statewide Public Guardianship Office by the investigating agency, the clerk of the court shall forward copies of the results of the investigations to the office upon receiving them.

(7) The requirements of this section do not apply to a professional guardian, or to the employees of a professional guardian, that is a trust company, a state banking corporation or state savings association authorized and qualified to exercise fiduciary powers in this state, or a national banking association or federal savings and loan association authorized and qualified to exercise fiduciary powers in this state.

Laws 1989, c. 89–96, § 30. Amended by Laws 1997, c. 97–102, § 1076, eff. July 1, 1997; Laws 1997, c. 97–161, § 2, eff. Oct. 1, 1997; Laws 1999, c. 99–277, § 10, eff. Oct. 1, 1999; Laws 2002, c. 2002–195, § 5, eff. April 29, 2002; Laws 2003, c. 2003–57, § 10, eff. May 30, 2003; Laws 2003, c. 2003–402, § 114, eff. July 1, 2004; Laws 2004, c. 2004–260, § 12, eff. July 1, 2004; Laws 2004, c. 2004–267, § 22, eff. July 1, 2004; Laws 2006, c. 2006–178, § 8, eff. July 1, 2006; Laws 2007, c. 2007–127, § 1, eff. July 1, 2007; Laws 2013, c. 2013–116, § 58, eff. July 1, 2013; Laws 2014, c. 2014–124, § 2, eff. July 1, 2014.

744.3145. Guardian education requirements

(1) Each ward is entitled to a guardian competent to perform the duties of a guardian necessary to protect the interests of the ward.

(2) Each person appointed by the court to be a guardian, other than a parent who is the guardian of the property of a minor child, must receive a minimum of 8 hours of instruction and training which covers:

(a) The legal duties and responsibilities of the guardian;

(b) The rights of the ward;

(c) The availability of local resources to aid the ward; and

(d) The preparation of habilitation plans and annual guardianship reports, including financial accounting for the ward's property.

(3) Each person appointed by the court to be the guardian of the property of his or her minor child must receive a minimum of 4 hours of instruction and training that covers:

(a) The legal duties and responsibilities of the guardian of the property;

(b) The preparation of the initial inventory and annual guardianship accountings for the ward's property; and

(c) Use of guardianship assets.

(4) Each person appointed by the court to be a guardian must complete the required number of hours of instruction and education within 4 months after his or her appointment as guardian. The instruction and education must be completed through a course approved by the chief judge of the circuit court and taught by a court-approved organization. Court-approved organizations may include, but are not limited to, community or junior colleges, guardianship organizations, and the local bar association or The Florida Bar.

(5) Expenses incurred by the guardian to satisfy the education requirement may be paid from the ward's estate, unless the court directs that such expenses be paid by the guardian individually.

(6) The court may, in its discretion, waive some or all of the requirements of this section or impose additional requirements. The court shall make its decision on a case-by-case basis and, in making its decision, shall consider the experience and education of the guardian, the duties assigned to the guardian, and the needs of the ward.

---

(7) The provisions of this section do not apply to professional guardians.

Laws 1989, c. 89–96, § 31; Laws 1990, c. 90–271, § 17. Amended by Laws 1997, c. 97–102, § 1077, eff. July 1, 1997; Laws 1997, c. 97–161, § 3, eff. Oct. 1, 1997; Laws 2003, c. 2003–57, § 11, eff. May 30, 2003; Laws 2006, c. 2006–178, § 9, eff. July 1, 2006.

PART V. ADJUDICATION OF INCAPACITY AND APPOINTMENT OF GUARDIANS

744.3201. Petition to determine incapacity

(1) A petition to determine incapacity of a person may be executed by an adult person.

(2) The petition must be verified and must:

(a) State the name, age, and present address of the petitioner and his or her relationship to the alleged incapacitated person;

(b) State the name, age, county of residence, and present address of the alleged incapacitated person;

(c) Specify the primary language spoken by the alleged incapacitated person, if known;

(d) Allege that the petitioner believes the alleged incapacitated person to be incapacitated and specify the factual information on which such belief is based and the names and addresses of all persons known to the petitioner who have knowledge of such facts through personal observations;

(e) State the name and address of the alleged incapacitated person's attending or family physician, if known;

(f) State which rights enumerated in s. 744.3215 the alleged incapacitated person is incapable of exercising, to the best of petitioner's knowledge. If the petitioner has insufficient experience to make such judgments, the petition must so state; and

(g) State the names, relationships, and addresses of the next of kin of the alleged incapacitated person, so far as are known, specifying the dates of birth of any who are minors.

(3) A copy of any petition for appointment of guardian or emergency temporary guardian, if applicable, shall be filed with the petition to determine incapacity.

Laws 1989, c. 89–96, § 33; Laws 1990, c. 90–271, § 18; Laws 1995, c. 95–401, § 22. Amended by Laws 1997, c. 97–102, § 1078, eff. July 1, 1997.

Cross References

Adult protective services, protective services intervention when capacity to consent is lacking, see F.S.A. § 415.1051.

744.3203. Suspension of power of attorney before incapacity determination

(1) At any time during proceedings to determine incapacity but before the entry of an order determining incapacity, the authority granted under an alleged incapacitated person's power of attorney to a parent, spouse, child, or grandchild is suspended when the petitioner files a motion stating that a specific power of attorney should be suspended for any of the following grounds:

(a) The agent's decisions are not in accord with the alleged incapacitated person's known desires.

(b) The power of attorney is invalid.

(c) The agent has failed to discharge his or her duties or incapacity or illness renders the agent incapable of discharging duties.

(d) The agent has abused powers.

(e) There is a danger that the property of the alleged incapacitated person may be wasted, misappropriated, or lost unless the authority under the power of attorney is suspended.

Grounds for suspending a power of attorney do not include the existence of a dispute between the agent and the petitioner which is more appropriate for resolution in some other forum or a legal proceeding other than a guardianship proceeding.

(2) The motion must:

(a) Identify one or more of the grounds in subsection (1);

(b) Include specific statements of fact showing that grounds exist to justify the relief sought; and

(c) Include the following statement: "Under penalties of perjury, I declare that I have read the foregoing motion and that the facts stated in it are true to the best of my knowledge and belief," followed by the signature of the petitioner.

(3) Upon the filing of a response to the motion by the agent under the power of attorney, the court shall schedule the motion for an expedited hearing. Unless an emergency arises and the agent's response sets forth the nature of the emergency, the property or matter involved, and the power to be exercised by the agent, notice must be given to all interested persons, the alleged incapacitated person, and the alleged incapacitated person's attorney. The court order following the hearing must set forth what powers the agent is permitted to exercise, if any, pending the outcome of the petition to determine incapacity.

(4) In addition to any other remedy authorized by law, a court may award reasonable attorney fees and costs to an agent who successfully challenges the suspension of the power of attorney if the petitioner's motion was made in bad faith.

(5) The suspension of authority granted to persons other than a parent, spouse, child, or grandchild shall be as provided in s. 709.2109.

Added by Laws 2015, c. 2015–83, § 10, eff. July 1, 2015.

Applicability

Laws 2015, c. 2015–83, § 20, provides:

"Sections 709.2109 and 744.3203, Florida Statutes, as created by this act, apply to all proceedings filed on or after July 1, 2015. The amendments made by this act to ss. 744.107, 744.1075, 744.108, 744.3025, 744.3031, 744.309, 744.3115, 744.312, 744.331, 744.344, 744.345, 744.359, 744.361, 744.367, 744.369, 744.3715, and 744.464, Florida Statutes, apply to all proceedings pending on July 1, 2015."

744.3215. Rights of persons determined incapacitated

(1) A person who has been determined to be incapacitated retains the right:

(a) To have an annual review of the guardianship report and plan.

(b) To have continuing review of the need for restriction of his or her rights.

(c) To be restored to capacity at the earliest possible time.

(d) To be treated humanely, with dignity and respect, and to be protected against abuse, neglect, and exploitation.

(e) To have a qualified guardian.

(f) To remain as independent as possible, including having his or her preference as to place and standard of living honored, either as he or she expressed or demonstrated his or her preference prior to the determination of his or her incapacity or as he or she currently expresses his or her preference, insofar as such request is reasonable.

(g) To be properly educated.

(h) To receive prudent financial management for his or her property and to be informed how his or her property is being managed, if he or she has lost the right to manage property.

(i) To receive services and rehabilitation necessary to maximize the quality of life.

(j) To be free from discrimination because of his or her incapacity.

(k) To have access to the courts.

(l) To counsel.

(m) To receive visitors and communicate with others.

(n) To notice of all proceedings related to determination of capacity and guardianship, unless the court finds the incapacitated person lacks the ability to comprehend the notice.

(o) To privacy.

(2) Rights that may be removed from a person by an order determining incapacity but not delegated to a guardian include the right:

(a) To marry. If the right to enter into a contract has been removed, the right to marry is subject to court approval.

(b) To vote.

(c) To personally apply for government benefits.

(d) To have a driver license.

(e) To travel.

(f) To seek or retain employment.

(3) Rights that may be removed from a person by an order determining incapacity and which may be delegated to the guardian include the right:

(a) To contract.

(b) To sue and defend lawsuits.

(c) To apply for government benefits.

(d) To manage property or to make any gift or disposition of property.

(e) To determine his or her residence.

(f) To consent to medical and mental health treatment.

(g) To make decisions about his or her social environment or other social aspects of his or her life.

(4) Without first obtaining specific authority from the court, as described in s. 744.3725, a guardian may not:

(a) Commit the ward to a facility, institution, or licensed service provider without formal placement proceeding, pursuant to chapter 393, chapter 394, or chapter 397.

(b) Consent on behalf of the ward to the performance on the ward of any experimental biomedical or behavioral procedure or to the participation by the ward in any biomedical or behavioral experiment. The court may permit such performance or participation only if:

1. It is of direct benefit to, and is intended to preserve the life of or prevent serious impairment to the mental or physical health of the ward; or

2. It is intended to assist the ward to develop or regain his or her abilities.

(c) Initiate a petition for dissolution of marriage for the ward.

(d) Consent on behalf of the ward to termination of the ward's parental rights.

(e) Consent on behalf of the ward to the performance of a sterilization or abortion procedure on the ward.

Laws 1989, c. 89–96, § 34; Laws 1990, c. 90–271, § 19; Laws 1993, c. 93–39, § 36; Laws 1994, c. 94–183, § 13; Laws 1996, c. 96–169, § 44; Laws 1996, c. 96–354, § 6. Amended by Laws 1997, c. 97–102, § 1782, eff. July 1, 1997; Laws 2006, c. 2006–178, § 10, eff. July 1, 2006.

744.331. Procedures to determine incapacity

(1) Notice of petition to determine incapacity.—Notice of the filing of a petition to determine incapacity and a petition for the appointment of a guardian if any and copies of the petitions must be served on and read to the alleged incapacitated person. The notice and copies of the petitions must also be given to the attorney for the alleged incapacitated person, and served upon all next of kin identified in the petition. The notice must state the time and place of the hearing to inquire into the capacity of the alleged incapacitated person and that an attorney has been appointed to represent the person and that, if she or he is determined to be incapable of exercising certain rights, a guardian will be appointed to exercise those rights on her or his behalf.

(2) Attorney for the alleged incapacitated person.—

(a) When a court appoints an attorney for an alleged incapacitated person, the court must appoint the office of criminal conflict and civil regional counsel or a private attorney as prescribed in s. 27.511(6). A private attorney must be one who is included in the attorney registry compiled pursuant to s. 27.40. Appointments of private attorneys must be made on a rotating basis, taking into consideration conflicts arising under this chapter.

(b) The court shall appoint an attorney for each person alleged to be incapacitated in all cases involving a petition for adjudication of incapacity. The alleged incapacitated person may substitute her or his own attorney for the attorney appointed by the court.

(c) Any attorney representing an alleged incapacitated person may not serve as guardian of the alleged incapacitated person or as counsel for the guardian of the alleged incapacitated person or the petitioner.

(d) Effective January 1, 2007, an attorney seeking to be appointed by a court for incapacity and guardianship proceedings must have completed a minimum of 8 hours of education in guardianship. A court may waive the initial training requirement for an attorney who has served as a court-appointed attorney in incapacity proceedings or as an attorney of record for guardians for not less than 3 years. The education requirement of this paragraph does not apply to the office of criminal conflict and civil regional counsel until July 1, 2008.

(3) Examining committee.—

(a) Within 5 days after a petition for determination of incapacity has been filed, the court shall appoint an examining committee consisting of three members. One member must be a psychiatrist or other physician. The remaining members must be either a psychologist, gerontologist, another psychiatrist, or other physician, a registered nurse, nurse practitioner, licensed social worker, a person with an advanced degree in gerontology from an accredited institution of higher education, or other person who by knowledge, skill, experience, training, or education may, in the court's discretion, advise the court in the form of an expert opinion. One of three members of the committee must have knowledge of the type of incapacity alleged in the petition. Unless good cause is shown, the attending or family physician may not be appointed to the committee. If the attending or family physician is available for consultation, the committee must consult with the physician. Members of the examining committee may not be related to or associated with one another, with the petitioner, with counsel for the petitioner or the proposed guardian, or with the person alleged to be totally or partially incapacitated. A member may not be employed by any private or governmental agency that has custody of, or furnishes, services or subsidies, directly or indirectly, to the person or the family of the person alleged to be incapacitated or for whom a guardianship is sought. A petitioner may not serve as a member of the examining committee. Members of the examining committee must be able to communicate, either directly or through an interpreter, in the language that the alleged incapacitated person speaks or to communicate in a medium understandable to the alleged incapacitated person if she or he is able to communicate. The clerk of the court shall send notice of the appointment to each person appointed no later than 3 days after the court's appointment.

(b) A person who has been appointed to serve as a member of an examining committee to examine an alleged incapacitated person may not thereafter be appointed as a guardian for the person who was the subject of the examination.

(c) Each person appointed to an examining committee must file an affidavit with the court stating that he or she has completed the required courses or will do so no later than 4 months after his or her initial appointment. Each year, the chief judge of the circuit must prepare a list of persons qualified to be members of an examining committee.

(d) A member of an examining committee must complete a minimum of 4 hours of initial training. The person must complete 2 hours of continuing education during each 2–year period after the initial training. The initial training and continuing education program must be developed under the supervision of the Statewide Public Guardianship Office, in consultation with the Florida Conference of Circuit Court Judges; the Elder Law and the Real Property, Probate and Trust Law sections of The Florida Bar; the Florida State Guardianship Association; and the Florida Guardianship Foundation. The court may waive the initial training requirement for a person who has served for not less than 5 years on examining committees. If a person wishes to obtain his or her continuing education on the Internet or by watching a video course, the person must first obtain the approval of the chief judge before taking an Internet or video course.

(e) Each member of the examining committee shall examine the person. Each examining committee member must determine the alleged incapacitated person's ability to exercise those rights specified in s. 744.3215. In addition to the examination, each examining committee member must have access to, and may consider, previous examinations of the person, including, but not limited to, habilitation plans, school records, and psychological and psychosocial reports voluntarily offered for use by the alleged incapacitated person. Each member of the examining committee must submit a report within 15 days after appointment.

(f) The examination of the alleged incapacitated person must include a comprehensive examination, a report of which shall be filed by each examining committee member as part of his or her written report. The comprehensive examination report should be an essential element, but not necessarily the only element, used in making a capacity and guardianship decision. The comprehensive examination must include, if indicated:

1. A physical examination;

2. A mental health examination; and

3. A functional assessment.

If any of these three aspects of the examination is not indicated or cannot be accomplished for any reason, the written report must explain the reasons for its omission.

(g) Each committee member's written report must include:

1. To the extent possible, a diagnosis, prognosis, and recommended course of treatment.

2. An evaluation of the alleged incapacitated person's ability to retain her or his rights, including, without limitation, the rights to marry; vote; contract; manage or dispose of property; have a driver license; determine her or his residence; consent to medical treatment; and make decisions affecting her or his social environment.

3. The results of the comprehensive examination and the committee member's assessment of information provided by the attending or family physician, if any.

4. A description of any matters with respect to which the person lacks the capacity to exercise rights, the extent of that incapacity, and the factual basis for the determination that the person lacks that capacity.

5. The names of all persons present during the time the committee member conducted his or her examination. If a person other than the person who is the subject of the examination supplies answers posed to the alleged incapacitated person, the report must include the response and the name of the person supplying the answer.

6. The signature of the committee member and the date and time the member conducted his or her examination.

(h) A copy of each committee member's report must be served on the petitioner and on the attorney for the alleged incapacitated person within 3 days after the report is filed and at least 5 days before the hearing on the petition.

(4) Dismissal of petition.—If a majority of the examining committee members conclude that the alleged incapacitated person is not incapacitated in any respect, the court shall dismiss the petition.

(5) Adjudicatory hearing.—

(a) Upon appointment of the examining committee, the court shall set the date upon which the petition will be heard. The date for the adjudicatory hearing must be set no more than 14 days after the filing of the reports of the examining committee members, unless good cause is shown. The adjudicatory hearing must be conducted at the time and place specified in the notice of hearing and in a manner consistent with due process.

(b) The alleged incapacitated person must be present at the adjudicatory hearing, unless waived by the alleged incapacitated person or the person's attorney or unless good cause can be shown for her or his absence. Determination of good cause rests in the sound discretion of the court.

(c) In the adjudicatory hearing on a petition alleging incapacity, the partial or total incapacity of the person must be established by clear and convincing evidence.

(6) Order determining incapacity.—If, after making findings of fact on the basis of clear and convincing evidence, the court finds that a person is incapacitated with respect to the exercise of a particular right, or all rights, the court shall enter a written order determining such incapacity. In determining incapacity, the court shall consider the person's unique needs and abilities and may only remove those rights that the court finds the person does not have the capacity to exercise. A person is determined to be incapacitated only with respect to those rights specified in the order.

(a) The court shall make the following findings:

1. The exact nature and scope of the person's incapacities;

2. The exact areas in which the person lacks capacity to make informed decisions about care and treatment services or to meet the essential requirements for her or his physical or mental health or safety;

3. The specific legal disabilities to which the person is subject; and

4. The specific rights that the person is incapable of exercising.

(b) When an order determines that a person is incapable of exercising delegable rights, the court must consider and find whether there is an alternative to guardianship that will sufficiently address the problems of the incapacitated person. A guardian may not be appointed if the court finds there is an alternative to guardianship which will sufficiently address the problems of the incapacitated person. If the court finds there is not an alternative to guardianship that sufficiently addresses the problems of the incapacitated person, a guardian must be appointed to exercise the incapacitated person's delegable rights.

(c) In determining that a person is totally incapacitated, the order must contain findings of fact demonstrating that the individual is totally without capacity to care for herself or himself or her or his property.

(d) An order adjudicating a person to be incapacitated constitutes proof of such incapacity until further order of the court.

(e) After the order determining that the person is incapacitated has been filed with the clerk, it must be served on the incapacitated person. The person is deemed incapacitated only to the extent of the findings of the court. The filing of the order is notice of the incapacity. An incapacitated person retains all rights not specifically removed by the court.

(f) Upon the filing of a verified statement by an interested person stating:

1. That he or she has a good faith belief that the alleged incapacitated person's trust, trust amendment, or durable power of attorney is invalid; and

2. A reasonable factual basis for that belief,

the trust, trust amendment, or durable power of attorney shall not be deemed to be an alternative to the appointment of a guardian. The appointment of a guardian does not limit the court's power to determine that certain authority granted by a durable power of attorney is to remain exercisable by the agent.

(7) Fees.—

(a) The examining committee and any attorney appointed under subsection (2) are entitled to reasonable fees to be determined by the court.

(b) The fees awarded under paragraph (a) shall be paid by the guardian from the property of the ward or, if the ward is indigent, by the state. The state shall have a creditor's claim against the guardianship property for any amounts paid under this section. The state may file its claim within 90 days after the entry of an order awarding attorney ad litem fees. If the state does not file its claim within the 90–day period, the state is thereafter barred from asserting the claim. Upon petition by the state for payment of the claim, the court shall enter an order authorizing immediate payment out of the property of the ward. The state shall keep a record of the payments.

(c) If the petition is dismissed or denied:

1. The fees of the examining committee shall be paid upon court order as expert witness fees under s. 29.004(6).

2. Costs and attorney fees of the proceeding may be assessed against the petitioner if the court finds the petition to have been filed in bad faith. The petitioner shall also reimburse the state courts system for any amounts paid under subparagraph 1. upon such a finding.

Laws 1975, c. 75–222, § 9, 26; Laws 1977, c. 77–328, § 4; Laws 1978, c. 78–342, § 1; Laws 1979, c. 79–221, § 6; Laws 1989, c. 89–96, § 35; Laws 1990, c. 90–271, § 20; Laws 1991, c. 91–303, § 4; Laws 1991, c. 91–306, § 5; Laws 1996, c. 96–354, § 7. Amended by Laws 1997, c. 97–102, § 1783, eff. July 1, 1997; Laws 2004, c. 2004–265, § 76, eff. July 1, 2004; Laws 2006, c. 2006–77, § 4, eff. June 6, 2006; Laws 2006, c. 2006–178, § 11, eff. July 1, 2006; Laws 2006, c. 2006–217, § 44, eff. July 1, 2007; Laws 2007, c. 2007–62, § 28, eff. Oct. 1, 2007; Laws 2015, c. 2015–83, § 11, eff. July 1, 2015.

Applicability

Laws 2015, c. 2015–83, § 20, provides:

"*Sections 709.2109 and 744.3203, Florida Statutes, as created by this act, apply to all proceedings filed on or after July 1, 2015. The amendments made by this act to ss. 744.107, 744.1075, 744.108, 744.3025, 744.3031, 744.309, 744.3115, 744.312, 744.331, 744.344, 744.345, 744.359, 744.361, 744.367, 744.369, 744.3715, and 744.464, Florida Statutes, apply to all proceedings pending on July 1, 2015.*"

Cross References

Capacity determination, appointment of guardian advocate, see § 393.12.
Concealed weapons and firearms, licenses to carry, see F.S.A. § 790.06.
Dissolution of marriage, incapacitation as under this section, see § 61.052.
Driver's licenses, forwarding licenses of persons adjudicated incapacitated under this section, see § 322.2505.
Driving under the influence, penalties, see F.S.A. § 316.193.
Firearms, sale and delivery, see § 790.065.
Parole, adjudication of incapacitation under this section, see § 947.16.
Petition to determine incapacity, see Probate Rule 5.550.

744.334. Petition for appointment of guardian or professional guardian; contents

(1) Every petition for the appointment of a guardian shall be verified by the petitioner and shall contain statements, to the best of petitioner's knowledge and belief, showing the name, age, residence, and post office address of the alleged incapacitated person or minor; the nature of her or his incapacity, if any; the extent of guardianship desired, either plenary or limited; the residence and post office address of the petitioner; the names and addresses of the next of kin of the incapacitated person or minor, if known to the petitioner; the name of the proposed guardian; the relationship and previous relationship of the proposed guardian to the ward; the nature and value of property subject to the guardianship; and the reasons why this person should be appointed guardian. If a willing and qualified guardian cannot be located, the petition must so state.

(2) The petition for appointment of a professional guardian must comply with the provisions of subsection (1), and must state that the petitioner is a professional guardian.

Laws 1975, c. 75–222, §§ 11, 26; Laws 1979, c. 79–221, § 7; Laws 1989, c. 89–96, § 36; Laws 1990, c. 90–271, § 21; Laws 1996, c. 96–354, § 8. Amended by Laws 1997, c. 97–102, § 1784, eff. July 1, 1997.

Cross References

Capacity determination, appointment of guardian advocate, see § 393.12.
Petition for appointment of guardian, see Probate Rule 5.560.

744.3371. Notice of petition for appointment of guardian and hearing

(1) When the petition for appointment of a guardian for an incapacitated person is heard upon the conclusion of the hearing in which the person is determined to be incapacitated, the court shall hear the petition without further notice. If the petition is heard on a later date, reasonable notice of the hearing must be served on the incapacitated person, the person's attorney, if any, any guardian then serving, the person's next of kin, and such other interested persons as the court may direct.

(2) When a petition for appointment of a guardian for a minor is filed, formal notice must be served on the minor's parents. If the petitioner has custody of the minor and the petition alleges that, after diligent search, the parents cannot be found, the parents may be served by informal notice, delivered to their last known address or addresses. When a parent petitions for appointment as guardian for his or her minor child, no notice is necessary unless the other parent is living and does not consent to the appointment.

Laws 1990, c. 90–271, § 22. Amended by Laws 1997, c. 97–102, § 1079, eff. July 1, 1997.

Cross References

Capacity, determinations, developmentally disabled persons, appointment of guardian advocate, see § 393.12.

744.341. Voluntary guardianship

(1) Without adjudication of incapacity, the court shall appoint a guardian of the property of a resident or nonresident person who, though mentally competent, is incapable of the care, custody, and management of his or her estate by reason of age or physical infirmity and who has voluntarily petitioned for the appointment. The petition shall be accompanied by a certificate of a licensed physician specifying that he or she has examined the petitioner and that the petitioner is competent to understand the nature of the guardianship and his or her delegation of authority. Notice of hearing on any petition for appointment and for authority to act shall be given to the petitioner and to any person to whom the petitioner requests that notice be given. Such request may be made in the petition for appointment of guardian or in a subsequent written request for notice signed by the petitioner.

(2) If requested in the petition for appointment of a guardian brought under this section, the court may direct the guardian to take possession of less than all of the ward's property and of the rents, income, issues, and profits from it. In such case, the court shall specify in its order the property to be included in the guardianship estate, and the duties and responsibilities of the guardian appointed under this section will extend only to such property.

(3) Unless the voluntary guardianship is limited pursuant to subsection (2), any guardian appointed under this section has the same duties and responsibilities as are provided by law for plenary guardians of the property, generally.

(4) A guardian must include in the annual report filed with the court a certificate from a licensed physician who examined the ward not more than 90 days before the annual report is filed with the court. The certificate must certify that the ward is competent to understand the nature of the guardianship and of the ward's authority to delegate powers to the voluntary guardian.

(5) A voluntary guardianship may be terminated by the ward by filing a notice with the court that the voluntary guardianship is terminated. A copy of the notice must be served on all interested persons.

Laws 1975, c. 75–222, §§ 11, 26; Laws 1979, c. 79–221, § 9; Laws 1984, c. 84–31, § 4; Laws 1989, c. 89–96, § 38; Laws 1990, c. 90–271, § 23. Amended by Laws 1997, c. 97–102, § 1080, eff. July 1, 1997; Laws 2006, c. 2006–178, § 12, eff. July 1, 2006.

744.342. Minors; guardianship

Upon petition, the court may appoint a guardian for a minor without appointing an examining committee or conducting an adjudicatory hearing pursuant to s. 744.331.

Laws 1990, c. 90–271, § 71.

744.344. Order of appointment

(1) The court may hear testimony on the question of who is entitled to preference in the appointment of a guardian. Any interested person may intervene in the proceedings. The order appointing a guardian must state the nature of the guardianship as either plenary or limited. If limited, the order must state that the guardian may exercise only those delegable rights which have been removed from the incapacitated person and specifically delegated to the guardian. The order shall state the specific powers and duties of the guardian.

(2) The order appointing a guardian must be consistent with the incapacitated person's welfare and safety, must be the least restrictive appropriate alternative, and must reserve to the incapacitated person the right to make decisions in all matters commensurate with the person's ability to do so.

(3) If a petition for appointment of guardian has been filed, an order appointing a guardian must be issued contemporaneously with the order adjudicating the person incapacitated. The order must specify the amount of the bond to be given by the guardian and must state specifically whether the guardian must place all, or part, of the property of the ward in a restricted account in a financial institution designated pursuant to s. 69.031.

(4) If a petition for the appointment of a guardian has not been filed or ruled upon at the time of the hearing on the petition to determine capacity, the court may appoint an emergency temporary guardian in the manner and for the purposes specified in s. 744.3031.

(5) A plenary guardian shall exercise all delegable rights and powers of the incapacitated person.

(6) A person for whom a limited guardian has been appointed retains all legal rights except those which have been specifically granted to the guardian in the court's written order.

Laws 1974, c. 74–106, § 1; Fla.St.1974 Supp. § 744.311; Laws 1975, c. 75–222, §§ 12, 26; Laws 1989, c. 89–96, § 39; Laws 1990, c. 90–271, § 24. Amended by Laws 1997, c. 97–102, § 1081, eff. July 1, 1997; Laws 2015, c. 2015–83, § 12, eff. July 1, 2015.

Applicability

Laws 2015, c. 2015–83, § 20, provides:

"Sections 709.2109 and 744.3203, Florida Statutes, as created by this act, apply to all proceedings filed on or after July 1, 2015. The amendments made by this act to ss.

744.107, 744.1075, 744.108, 744.3025, 744.3031, 744.309, 744.3115, 744.312, 744.331, 744.344, 744.345, 744.359, 744.361, 744.367, 744.369, 744.3715, and 744.464, Florida Statutes, apply to all proceedings pending on July 1, 2015."

744.345. Letters of guardianship

Letters of guardianship shall be issued to the guardian and shall specify whether the guardianship pertains to the person, or the property, or both, of the ward. The letters must state whether the guardianship is plenary or limited, and, if limited, the letters must state the powers and duties of the guardian. The letters shall state whether or not and to what extent the guardian is authorized to act on behalf of the ward with regard to any advance directive previously executed by the ward.

Laws 1974, c. 74–106, § 1; Laws 1975, c. 75–222, § 12; Fla.St. 1987, § 744.313; Laws 1989, c. 89–96, § 28; Laws 1990, c. 90–271, § 25; Laws 1992, c. 92–199, § 7; Laws 1994, c. 94–183, § 2. Amended by Laws 2015, c. 2015–83, § 13, eff. July 1, 2015.

Applicability

Laws 2015, c. 2015–83, § 20, provides:

"Sections 709.2109 and 744.3203, Florida Statutes, as created by this act, apply to all proceedings filed on or after July 1, 2015. The amendments made by this act to ss. 744.107, 744.1075, 744.108, 744.3025, 744.3031, 744.309, 744.3115, 744.312, 744.331, 744.344, 744.345, 744.359, 744.361, 744.367, 744.369, 744.3715, and 744.464, Florida Statutes, apply to all proceedings pending on July 1, 2015."

744.347. Oath of guardian

Before exercising his or her authority as guardian, every guardian shall take an oath that he or she will faithfully perform his or her duties as guardian. This oath is not jurisdictional.

Laws 1974, c. 74–106, § 1; Fla.St.1974, Supp. § 744.401; Laws 1975, c. 75–222, §§ 19, 26; Laws 1989, c. 89–96, § 40. Amended by Laws 1997, c. 97–102, § 1082, eff. July 1, 1997.

Cross References

Oath of guardian, see Probate Rule 5.600.

744.351. Bond of guardian

(1) Before exercising his or her authority as guardian, every person appointed a guardian of the property of a ward in this state shall file a bond with surety as prescribed in s. 45.011 to be approved by the clerk. The bond shall be payable to the Governor of the state and the Governor's successors in office, conditioned on the faithful performance of all duties by the guardian. In form the bond shall be joint and several. When the petitioner or guardian presents compelling reasons, the court may waive a bond or require the use of a designated financial institution as defined in s. 655.005(1).

(2) When the sureties on a bond are natural persons, the guardian shall be required to file with the annual guardianship report proof satisfactory to the court that the sureties are alive and solvent.

(3) The penal sum of a guardian's bond shall be fixed by the court, and it must be in an amount not less than the full amount of the cash on hand and on deposit belonging to the ward and subject to the control of the guardian, plus the value of the notes and bonds owned by the

ward that are payable to bearer, and plus the value of all other intangible personal property, in whatever form, owned by the ward which has a market value which readily can be fixed and which intangible personal property readily can be traded for cash or its equivalent.

(4) For good cause, the court may require, or increase or reduce the amount of, bond or change or release the surety.

(5) Financial institutions as defined in s. 744.309(4), other than a trust company operating under chapter 662 which is not a licensed family trust company or foreign licensed family trust company, and public guardians authorized by law to be guardians are not required to file bonds.

(6) When it is expedient in the judgment of any court having jurisdiction of any guardianship property, because the size of the bond required of the guardian is burdensome, or for other cause, the court may order, in lieu of a bond or in addition to a lesser bond, that the guardian place all or part of the property of the ward in a designated financial institution under the same conditions and limitations as are contained in s. 69.031. A designated financial institution shall also include a dealer, as defined in s. 517.021(6), if the dealer is a member of the Security Investment Protection Corporation and is doing business in the state.

Laws 1974, c. 74–106, § 1; Fla.St.1974, Supp. § 744.402; Laws 1975, c. 75–222, §§ 19, 26; Laws 1977, c. 77–174, § 1; Laws 1978, c. 78–342, § 2; Laws 1986, c. 86–120, § 2; Laws 1989, c. 89–96, § 41; Laws 1990, c. 90–271, § 26; Laws 1995, c. 95–401, § 30; Laws 1996, c. 96–354, § 9. Amended by Laws 1997, c. 97–102, § 1785, eff. July 1, 1997; Laws 2014, c. 2014–97, § 39, eff. Oct. 1, 2015.

744.354. Validity of bond

No bond executed by any guardian shall be invalid because of an informality in it or because of an informality or illegality in the appointment of the guardian. The bond shall have the same force and effect as if the bond had been executed in proper form and the appointment had been legally made.

Laws 1974, c. 74–106, § 1; Fla.St.1974, Supp. § 744.403; Laws 1975, c. 75–222, §§ 19, 26; Laws 1989, c. 89–96, § 42.

744.357. Liability of surety

No surety for a guardian shall be charged beyond the property of the ward.

Laws 1974, c. 74–106, § 1; Fla.St.1974, Supp. § 744.404; Laws 1975, c. 75–222, §§ 19, 26; Laws 1989, c. 89–96, § 43; Laws 1990, c. 90–271, § 27.

744.358. Liability of a guardian

(1) A guardian is not liable, solely because of the guardianship, for the debts, contracts, or torts of her or his ward.

(2) In dealing with the ward's property, a guardian is subject to the standards set forth in s. 518.11.

Laws 1989, c. 89–96, § 44; Laws 1990, c. 90–271, § 28. Amended by Laws 1997, c. 97–102, § 1083, eff. July 1, 1997.

744.359. Abuse, neglect, or exploitation by a guardian

(1) A guardian may not abuse, neglect, or exploit a ward.

(2) A guardian has committed exploitation when the guardian:

(a) Commits fraud in obtaining appointment as a guardian;

(b) Abuses his or her powers; or

(c) Wastes, embezzles, or intentionally mismanages the assets of the ward.

(3) A person who believes that a guardian is abusing, neglecting, or exploiting a ward shall report the incident to the central abuse hotline of the Department of Children and Families.

(4) This section shall be interpreted in conformity with s. 825.103.

Added by Laws 2015, c. 2015–83, § 14, eff. July 1, 2015.

Applicability

Laws 2015, c. 2015–83, § 20, provides:

"Sections 709.2109 and 744.3203, Florida Statutes, as created by this act, apply to all proceedings filed on or after July 1, 2015. The amendments made by this act to ss. 744.107, 744.1075, 744.108, 744.3025, 744.3031, 744.309, 744.3115, 744.312, 744.331, 744.344, 744.345, 744.359, 744.361, 744.367, 744.369, 744.3715, and 744.464, Florida Statutes, apply to all proceedings pending on July 1, 2015."

PART VI. POWERS AND DUTIES

744.361. Powers and duties of guardian

(1) The guardian of an incapacitated person is a fiduciary and may exercise only those rights that have been removed from the ward and delegated to the guardian. The guardian of a minor shall exercise the powers of a plenary guardian.

(2) The guardian shall act within the scope of the authority granted by the court and as provided by law.

(3) The guardian shall act in good faith.

(4) A guardian may not act in a manner that is contrary to the ward's best interests under the circumstances.

(5) A guardian who has special skills or expertise, or is appointed in reliance upon the guardian's representation that the guardian has special skills or expertise, shall use those special skills or expertise when acting on behalf of the ward.

(6) The guardian shall file an initial guardianship report in accordance with s. 744.362.

(7) The guardian shall file a guardianship report annually in accordance with s. 744.367.

(8) The guardian of the person shall implement the guardianship plan.

(9) When two or more guardians have been appointed, the guardians shall consult with each other.

(10) A guardian who is given authority over any property of the ward shall:

(a) Protect and preserve the property and invest it prudently as provided in chapter 518, apply it as provided in s. 744.397, and keep clear, distinct, and accurate records of the administration of the ward's property.

(b) Perform all other duties required of him or her by law.

(c) At the termination of the guardianship, deliver the property of the ward to the person lawfully entitled to it.

(11) The guardian shall observe the standards in dealing with the guardianship property that would be observed by a prudent person dealing with the property of another.

(12) The guardian, if authorized by the court, shall take possession of all of the ward's property and of the rents, income, issues, and profits from it, whether accruing before or after the guardian's appointment, and of the proceeds arising from the sale, lease, or mortgage of the property or of any part. All of the property and the rents, income, issues, and profits from it are assets in the hands of the guardian for the payment of debts, taxes, claims, charges, and expenses of the guardianship and for the care, support, maintenance, and education of the ward or the ward's dependents, as provided for under the terms of the guardianship plan or by law.

(13) Recognizing that every individual has unique needs and abilities, a guardian who is given authority over a ward's person shall, as appropriate under the circumstances:

(a) Consider the expressed desires of the ward as known by the guardian when making decisions that affect the ward.

(b) Allow the ward to maintain contact with family and friends unless the guardian believes that such contact may cause harm to the ward.

(c) Not restrict the physical liberty of the ward more than reasonably necessary to protect the ward or another person from serious physical injury, illness, or disease.

(d) Assist the ward in developing or regaining capacity, if medically possible.

(e) Notify the court if the guardian believes that the ward has regained capacity and that one or more of the rights that have been removed should be restored to the ward.

(f) To the extent applicable, make provision for the medical, mental, rehabilitative, or personal care services for the welfare of the ward.

(g) To the extent applicable, acquire a clear understanding of the risks and benefits of a recommended course of health care treatment before making a health care decision.

(h) Evaluate the ward's medical and health care options, financial resources, and desires when making residential decisions that are best suited for the current needs of the ward.

(i) Advocate on behalf of the ward in institutional and other residential settings and regarding access to home and community-based services.

(j) When not inconsistent with the person's goals, needs, and preferences, acquire an understanding of the available residential options and give priority to home and other community-based services and settings.

(14) A professional guardian must ensure that each of the guardian's wards is personally visited by the guardian or one of the guardian's professional staff at least once each calendar quarter. During the personal visit, the guardian or the guardian's professional staff person shall assess:

(a) The ward's physical appearance and condition.

(b) The appropriateness of the ward's current living situation.

(c) The need for any additional services and the necessity for continuation of existing services, taking into consideration all aspects of social, psychological, educational, direct service, health, and personal care needs.

(d) The nature and extent of visitation and communication with the ward's family and friends.

This subsection does not apply to a professional guardian who has been appointed only as guardian of the property.

Laws 1974, c. 74–106, § 1; Fla.St.1974, Supp. § 744.203; Laws 1975, c. 75–222, §§ 6, 26; Laws 1989, c. 89–96, § 45; Laws 1990, c. 90–271, § 29. Amended by Laws 1997, c. 97–102, § 1084, eff. July 1, 1997; Laws 2006, c. 2006–178, § 13, eff. July 1, 2006; Laws 2006, c. 2006–217, § 45, eff. July 1, 2007; Laws 2015, c. 2015–83, § 15, eff. July 1, 2015.

Applicability

Laws 2015, c. 2015–83, § 20, provides:

"Sections 709.2109 and 744.3203, Florida Statutes, as created by this act, apply to all proceedings filed on or after July 1, 2015. The amendments made by this act to ss. 744.107, 744.1075, 744.108, 744.3025, 744.3031, 744.309, 744.3115, 744.312, 744.331, 744.344, 744.345, 744.359, 744.361, 744.367, 744.369, 744.3715, and 744.464, Florida Statutes, apply to all proceedings pending on July 1, 2015."

744.362. Initial guardianship report

(1) Each guardian shall file with the court an initial guardianship report within 60 days after her or his letters of guardianship are signed. The initial guardianship report for a guardian of the property must consist of a verified inventory. The initial report for a guardian of the person must consist of an initial guardianship plan. The initial report shall be served on the ward, unless the ward is a minor under the age of 14 years or is totally incapacitated, and the attorney for the ward. Either the ward or the ward's attorney may request a hearing concerning the adequacy of the report.

(2) Review of the initial guardianship report and representation of the ward during an objection thereto, if any, shall be the appointed attorney's final official action on behalf of the ward. Thereafter, the court-appointed attorney is no longer obligated to represent the ward.

Laws 1989, c. 89–96, § 46; Laws 1990, c. 90–271, § 30; Laws 1992, c. 92–200, § 24; Laws 1995, c. 95–401, § 23. Amended by Laws 1997, c. 97–102, § 1085, eff. July 1, 1997.

744.363. Initial guardianship plan

(1) The initial guardianship plan shall include the following:

(a) The provision of medical, mental, or personal care services for the welfare of the ward;

(b) The provision of social and personal services for the welfare of the ward;

(c) The place and kind of residential setting best suited for the needs of the ward;

(d) The application of health and accident insurance and any other private or governmental benefits to which the ward may be entitled to meet any part of the costs of medical, mental health, or related services provided to the ward; and

(e) Any physical and mental examinations necessary to determine the ward's medical and mental health treatment needs.

(2) The initial guardianship plan for an incapacitated person must be based on the recommendations of the examining committee's examination, as incorporated into the order determining incapacity.

(3) Unless the ward has been found to be totally incapacitated or is a minor under the age of 14 years, the initial guardianship plan must contain an attestation that the guardian has consulted with the ward and, to the extent reasonable, has honored the ward's wishes consistent

with the rights retained by the ward under the plan. To the maximum extent reasonable, the plan must be in accordance with the wishes of the ward.

(4) The guardianship plan may not restrict the physical liberty of the ward more than reasonably necessary to protect the ward or others from serious physical injury, illness, or disease and to provide the ward with medical care and mental health treatment for the ward's physical and mental health.

(5) An initial guardianship plan continues in effect until it is amended or replaced by the approval of an annual guardianship plan, until the restoration of capacity or death of the ward, or until the ward, if a minor, reaches the age of 18 years. If there are significant changes in the capacity of the ward to meet the essential requirements for his or her health or safety, the guardian may file a petition to modify the guardianship plan and shall serve notice on all persons who received notice of the plan. At the hearing on such petition, the court may modify the guardianship plan and specify the effective date of such amendment.

(6) In exercising his or her powers, the guardian shall recognize any rights retained by the ward.

Laws 1989, c. 89–96, § 47; Laws 1990, c. 90–271, § 31. Amended by Laws 1997, c. 97–102, § 1086, eff. July 1, 1997.

744.365. Verified inventory

(1) **Filing.**—A guardian of the property shall file a verified inventory of the ward's property.

(2) **Contents.**—The verified inventory must include the following:

(a) All property of the ward, real and personal, that has come into the guardian's possession or knowledge, including a statement of all encumbrances, liens, and other secured claims on any item, any claims against the property, any cause of action accruing to the ward, and any trusts of which the ward is a beneficiary.

(b) The location of the real and personal property in sufficient detail so that it may be clearly identified or located.

(c) A description of all sources of income, including, without limitation, social security benefits and pensions.

(3) **Cash assets.**—Along with the verified inventory, the guardian must file a copy of the most current statement of all of the ward's cash assets from all institutions where the cash is on deposit.

(4) **Safe-deposit box.**—

(a) The initial opening of any safe-deposit box of the ward must be conducted in the presence of an employee of the institution where the box is located. The inventory of the contents of the box also must be conducted in the presence of the employee, who must verify the contents of the box by signing a copy of the inventory. This safe-deposit box inventory shall be filed with the court within 10 days after the box is opened.

(b) The guardian shall provide the ward with a copy of each signed safe-deposit box inventory unless the ward is a minor or has been adjudicated totally incapacitated or unless the order appointing the guardian states otherwise.

(c) Nothing may be removed from the ward's safe-deposit box without specific court approval.

(5) **Records retention.**—

(a) The guardian shall maintain substantiating papers and records sufficient to demonstrate the accuracy of the initial inventory for a period of 3 years after her or his discharge. The substantiating papers need not be filed with the court but must be made available for inspection and review at such time and place and before such persons as the court may order.

(b) As part of the substantiating papers, the guardian must identify by name, address, and occupation, the witness or witnesses, if any, who were present during the initial inventory of the ward's personal property.

(6) Audit fee.—

(a) Where the value of the ward's property exceeds $25,000, a guardian shall pay from the ward's property to the clerk of the circuit court a fee of up to $85, upon the filing of the verified inventory, for the auditing of the inventory. Upon petition by the guardian, the court may waive the auditing fee upon a showing of insufficient funds in the ward's estate. Any guardian unable to pay the auditing fee may petition the court for waiver of the fee. The court may waive the fee after it has reviewed the documentation filed by the guardian in support of the waiver.

(b) An audit fee may not be charged to any ward whose property has a value of less than $25,000.

Laws 1989, c. 89–96, § 49; Laws 1990, c. 90–271, § 32. Amended by Laws 1997, c. 97–102, § 1087, eff. July 1, 1997; Laws 2003, c. 2003–402, § 115, eff. July 1, 2004; Laws 2004, c. 2004–265, § 77, eff. July 1, 2004; Laws 2006, c. 2006–178, § 14, eff. July 1, 2006; Laws 2008, c. 2008–111, § 40, eff. July 1, 2008.

Cross References

Initial guardianship report of verified inventory and initial guardianship plan, see Probate Rule 5.620.

744.367. Duty to file annual guardianship report

(1) Unless the court requires filing on a calendar-year basis, each guardian of the person shall file with the court an annual guardianship plan at least 60 days, but no more than 90 days, before the last day of the anniversary month that the letters of guardianship were signed, and the plan must cover the coming fiscal year, ending on the last day in such anniversary month. If the court requires calendar-year filing, the guardianship plan for the forthcoming calendar year must be filed on or after September 1 but no later than December 1 of the current year.

(2) Unless the court requires or authorizes filing on a fiscal-year basis, each guardian of the property shall file with the court an annual accounting on or before April 1 of each year. The annual accounting must cover the preceding calendar year. If the court authorizes or directs filing on a fiscal-year basis, the annual accounting must be filed on or before the first day of the fourth month after the end of the fiscal year.

(3) The annual guardianship report of a guardian of the property must consist of an annual accounting, and the annual report of a guardian of the person must consist of an annual guardianship plan. The annual report shall be served on the ward, unless the ward is a minor or is totally incapacitated, and on the attorney for the ward, if any. The guardian shall provide a copy to any other person as the court may direct.

(4) Unless the ward is a minor or has been determined to be totally incapacitated, the guardian shall review a copy of the annual report with the ward, to the extent possible. Within 30 days after the annual report has been filed, any interested person, including the ward, may file written objections to any element of the report, specifying the nature of the objection.

(5) If the guardian fails to timely file the annual guardianship report, the judge may impose sanctions which may include contempt, removal of the guardian, or other sanctions provided by law in s. 744.3685.

(6) Notwithstanding any other requirement of this section or unless otherwise directed by the court, the guardian of the property may file the first annual accounting on either a fiscal-year or calendar-year basis. Unless the court directs otherwise, the guardian shall notify the court as to the guardian's filing intention within 30 days from the date the guardian was issued the letter of guardianship. All subsequent annual accountings must be filed on the same accounting period as the first annual accounting unless the court authorizes or directs otherwise. The first accounting period must end within 1 year after the end of the month in which the letters of guardianship were issued to the guardian of the property.

Laws 1974, c. 74–106, § 1; Fla.St.1974, Supp. § 744.205; Laws 1975, c. 75–222, §§ 6, 26; Laws 1989, c. 89–96, § 50; Laws 1990, c. 90–271, § 33; Laws 1992, c. 92–200, § 25; Laws 1995, c. 95–211, § 68; Laws 1995, c. 95–401, § 24; Laws 1996, c. 96–354, § 10. Amended by Laws 2006, c. 2006–178, § 15, eff. July 1, 2006; Laws 2015, c. 2015–83, § 16, eff. July 1, 2015.

Applicability

Laws 2015, c. 2015–83, § 20, provides:

"Sections 709.2109 and 744.3203, Florida Statutes, as created by this act, apply to all proceedings filed on or after July 1, 2015. The amendments made by this act to ss. 744.107, 744.1075, 744.108, 744.3025, 744.3031, 744.309, 744.3115, 744.312, 744.331, 744.344, 744.345, 744.359, 744.361, 744.367, 744.369, 744.3715, and 744.464, Florida Statutes, apply to all proceedings pending on July 1, 2015."

Cross References

Initial guardianship reports, see Probate Rule 5.690.

744.3675. Annual guardianship plan

Each guardian of the person must file with the court an annual guardianship plan which updates information about the condition of the ward. The annual plan must specify the current needs of the ward and how those needs are proposed to be met in the coming year.

(1) Each plan for an adult ward must, if applicable, include:

(a) Information concerning the residence of the ward, including:

1. The ward's address at the time of filing the plan.

2. The name and address of each place where the ward was maintained during the preceding year.

3. The length of stay of the ward at each place.

4. A statement of whether the current residential setting is best suited for the current needs of the ward.

5. Plans for ensuring during the coming year that the ward is in the best residential setting to meet his or her needs.

(b) Information concerning the medical and mental health conditions and treatment and rehabilitation needs of the ward, including:

1. A resume of any professional medical treatment given to the ward during the preceding year.

---

2. The report of a physician who examined the ward no more than 90 days before the beginning of the applicable reporting period. The report must contain an evaluation of the ward's condition and a statement of the current level of capacity of the ward.

3. The plan for providing medical, mental health, and rehabilitative services in the coming year.

(c) Information concerning the social condition of the ward, including:

1. The social and personal services currently used by the ward.

2. The social skills of the ward, including a statement of how well the ward communicates and maintains interpersonal relationships.

3. The social needs of the ward.

(2) Each plan filed by the legal guardian of a minor must include:

(a) Information concerning the residence of the minor, including:

1. The minor's address at the time of filing the plan.

2. The name and address of each place the minor lived during the preceding year.

(b) Information concerning the medical and mental health conditions and treatment and rehabilitation needs of the minor, including:

1. A resume of any professional medical treatment given to the minor during the preceding year.

2. A report from the physician who examined the minor no more than 180 days before the beginning of the applicable reporting period that contains an evaluation of the minor's physical and mental conditions.

3. The plan for providing medical services in the coming year.

(c) Information concerning the education of the minor, including:

1. A summary of the school progress report.

2. The social development of the minor, including a statement of how well the minor communicates and maintains interpersonal relationships.

3. The social needs of the minor.

(3) Each plan for an adult ward must address the issue of restoration of rights to the ward and include:

(a) A summary of activities during the preceding year that were designed to enhance the capacity of the ward.

(b) A statement of whether the ward can have any rights restored.

(c) A statement of whether restoration of any rights will be sought.

(4) The court, in its discretion, may require reexamination of the ward by a physician at any time.

Laws 1989, c. 89–96, § 51; Laws 1990, c. 90–271, § 34; Laws 1996, c. 96–354, § 11. Amended by Laws 1997, c. 97–102, § 1786, eff. July 1, 1997; Laws 1997, c. 97–161, § 4, eff. Oct. 1, 1997; Laws 2006, c. 2006–178, § 16, eff. July 1, 2006.

Cross References

Initial guardianship reports, see Probate Rule 5.690.
Initial guardianship report of verified inventory and initial guardianship plan, see Probate Rule 5.620.

744.3678. Annual accounting

(1) Each guardian of the property must file an annual accounting with the court.

(2) The annual accounting must include:

(a) A full and correct account of the receipts and disbursements of all of the ward's property over which the guardian has control and a statement of the ward's property on hand at the end of the accounting period. This paragraph does not apply to any property or any trust of which the ward is a beneficiary but which is not under the control or administration of the guardian.

(b) A copy of the annual or year-end statement of all of the ward's cash accounts from each of the institutions where the cash is deposited.

(3) The guardian must obtain a receipt, canceled check, or other proof of payment for all expenditures and disbursements made on behalf of the ward. The guardian must preserve all evidence of payment, along with other substantiating papers, for a period of 3 years after his or her discharge. The receipts, proofs of payment, and substantiating papers need not be filed with the court but shall be made available for inspection and review at the time and place and before the persons as the court may order.

(4) The guardian shall pay from the ward's estate to the clerk of the circuit court a fee based upon the following graduated fee schedule, upon the filing of the annual financial return, for the auditing of the return:

(a) For estates with a value of $25,000 or less the clerk of the court may charge a fee of up to $20.

(b) For estates with a value of more than $25,000 up to and including $100,000 the clerk of the court may charge a fee of up to $85.

(c) For estates with a value of more than $100,000 up to and including $500,000 the clerk of the court may charge a fee of up to $170.

(d) For estates with a value in excess of $500,000 the clerk of the court may charge a fee of up to $250.

Upon petition by the guardian, the court may waive the auditing fee upon a showing of insufficient funds in the ward's estate. Any guardian unable to pay the auditing fee may petition the court for a waiver of the fee. The court may waive the fee after it has reviewed the documentation filed by the guardian in support of the waiver.

(5) This section does not apply if the court determines that the ward receives income only from social security benefits and the guardian is the ward's representative payee for the benefits.

Laws 1989, c. 89–96, § 52; Laws 1990, c. 90–271, §§ 35, 72. Amended by Laws 1997, c. 97–102, § 1088, eff. July 1, 1997; Laws 2003, c. 2003–402, § 116, eff. July 1, 2004; Laws 2004, c. 2004–260, § 13, eff. July 1, 2004; Laws 2004, c. 2004–265, § 78, eff. July 1, 2004; Laws 2005, c. 2005–2, § 139, eff. July 5, 2005; Laws 2006, c. 2006–178, § 17, eff. July 1, 2006; Laws 2008, c. 2008–111, § 41, eff. July 1, 2008.

Cross References

Developmental disabilities, guardian advocate appointment, see § 393.12.
Initial guardianship reports, see Probate Rule 5.690.

744.3679. Simplified accounting procedures in certain cases

(1) In a guardianship of property, when all assets of the estate are in designated depositories under s. 69.031 and the only transactions that occur in that account are interest accrual, deposits from a settlement, or financial institution service charges, the guardian may elect to file an accounting consisting of:

(a) The original or a certified copy of the year-end statement of the ward's account from the financial institution; and

(b) A statement by the guardian under penalty of perjury that the guardian has custody and control of the ward's property as shown in the year-end statement.

(2) The accounting allowed by subsection (1) is in lieu of the accounting and auditing procedures under s. 744.3678(2). However, any interested party may seek judicial review as provided in s. 744.3685.

(3) The guardian need not be represented by an attorney in order to file the annual accounting allowed by subsection (1).

Laws 1993, c. 93–102, § 1. Amended by Laws 2006, c. 2006–178, § 18, eff. July 1, 2006.

744.368. Responsibilities of the clerk of the circuit court

(1) In addition to the duty to serve as the custodian of the guardianship files, the clerk shall review each initial and annual guardianship report to ensure that it contains information about the ward addressing, as appropriate:

(a) Physical and mental health care;

(b) Personal and social services;

(c) The residential setting;

(d) The application of insurance, private benefits, and government benefits;

(e) The physical and mental health examinations; and

(f) The initial verified inventory or the annual accounting.

(2) The clerk shall, within 30 days after the date of filing of the initial or annual report of the guardian of the person, complete his or her review of the report.

(3) Within 90 days after the filing of the verified inventory and accountings by a guardian of the property, the clerk shall audit the verified inventory and the accountings. The clerk shall advise the court of the results of the audit.

(4) The clerk shall report to the court when a report is not timely filed.

(5) If the clerk has reason to believe further review is appropriate, the clerk may request and review records and documents that reasonably impact guardianship assets, including, but not limited to, the beginning inventory balance and any fees charged to the guardianship.

(6) If a guardian fails to produce records and documents to the clerk upon request, the clerk may request the court to enter an order pursuant to s. 744.3685(2) by filing an affidavit that identifies the records and documents requested and shows good cause as to why the documents and records requested are needed to complete the audit.

(7) Upon application to the court supported by an affidavit pursuant to subsection (6), the clerk may issue subpoenas to nonparties to compel production of books, papers, and other documentary evidence. Before issuance of a subpoena by affidavit, the clerk must serve notice on the guardian and the ward, unless the ward is a minor or totally incapacitated, of the intent to serve subpoenas to nonparties.

(a) The clerk must attach the affidavit and the proposed subpoena to the notice to the guardian and, if appropriate, to the ward, and must:

1. State the time, place, and method for production of the documents or items, and the name and address of the person who is to produce the documents or items, if known, or, if not known,

a general description sufficient to identify the person or the particular class or group to which the person belongs.

2.   Include a designation of the items to be produced.

3.   State that the person who will be asked to produce the documents or items has the right to object to the production under this section and that the person is not required to surrender the documents or items.

(b) A copy of the notice and proposed subpoena may not be furnished to the person upon whom the subpoena is to be served.

(c) If the guardian or ward serves an objection to production under this subsection within 10 days after service of the notice, the documents or items may not be required to be produced until resolution of the objection. If an objection is not made within 10 days after service of the notice, the clerk may issue the subpoena to the nonparty. The court may shorten the period within which a guardian or ward is required to file an objection upon a showing by the clerk by affidavit that the ward's property is in imminent danger of being wasted, misappropriated, or lost unless immediate action is taken.

Laws 1989, c. 89–96, § 53; Laws 1990, c. 90–271, § 36. Amended by Laws 1997, c. 97–102, § 1089, eff. July 1, 1997; Laws 2006, c. 2006–178, § 19, eff. July 1, 2006; Laws 2014, c. 2014–124, § 3, eff. July 1, 2014.

744.3685. Order requiring guardianship report; contempt

(1) If a guardian fails to file the guardianship report, the court shall order the guardian to file the report within 15 days after the service of the order upon her or him or show cause why she or he may not be compelled to do so.

(2) If a guardian fails to comply with the submission of records and documents requested by the clerk during the audit, upon a showing of good cause by affidavit of the clerk which shows the reasons the records must be produced, the court may order the guardian to produce the records and documents within a period specified by the court unless the guardian shows good cause as to why the guardian may not be compelled to do so before the deadline specified by the court. The affidavit of the clerk shall be served with the order.

(3) A copy of an order entered pursuant to subsection (1) or subsection (2) shall be served on the guardian or on the guardian's resident agent. If the guardian fails to comply with the order within the time specified by the order without good cause, the court may cite the guardian for contempt of court and may fine her or him. The fine may not be paid out of the ward's property.

Laws 1974, c. 74–106, § 1; Fla.St. 1974, Supp. § 744.326; Laws 1975, c. 75–222, §§ 17, 26; Fla.St. 1987, § 744.431; Laws 1989, c. 89–96, § 70; Laws 1990, c. 90–271, § 37. Amended by Laws 1997, c. 97–102, § 1090, eff. July 1, 1997; Laws 2014, c. 2014–124, § 4, eff. July 1, 2014.

744.369. Judicial review of guardianship reports

(1) The court shall review the initial guardianship report within 60 days after the filing of the clerk's report of findings to the court. The court shall review the annual guardianship report within 30 days after the filing of the clerk's report of findings to the court.

(2) The court may appoint a general or special magistrate to assist the court in its review function. The court may require the general or special magistrate to conduct random field audits.

(3) If an initial or annual report is not timely filed, the court shall order the guardian to file the report or to show cause why the report has not been filed within the prescribed time. Service of the order and subsequent proceedings shall be governed by s. 744.3685.

(4) The court must review the initial and annual guardianship report to determine that the report:

(a) Meets the needs of the ward;

(b) Authorizes the guardian to act only in areas in which an adult ward has been declared incapacitated; and

(c) Conforms to all other requirements of the law.

(5) Upon examining the initial or annual guardianship report, the court shall enter an order approving or disapproving the report. If the court disapproves the report, the court shall order the guardian to provide a revised report or proof of any item in the report to the court. The guardian shall do so within a reasonable amount of time set by court.

(6) If the guardian fails to comply with the court order entered pursuant to subsection (5), the court shall take immediate action to compel compliance or to sanction the guardian after a hearing with appropriate notice to the ward, the ward's counsel, if any, the guardian, and the ward's next of kin.

(7) If an objection has been filed to a report, the court shall set the matter for hearing and shall conduct the hearing within 30 days after the filing of the objection. After the hearing, the court shall enter a written order either approving, or ordering modifications to, the report. If an objection is found to be without merit, the court may assess costs and attorney's fees against the person who made the objection.

(8) The approved report constitutes the authority for the guardian to act in the forthcoming year. The powers of the guardian are limited by the terms of the report. The annual report may not grant additional authority to the guardian without a hearing, as provided for in s. 744.331, to determine that the ward is incapacitated to act in that matter. Unless the court orders otherwise, the guardian may continue to act under authority of the last-approved report until the forthcoming year's report is approved.

Laws 1989, c. 89–96, § 54; Laws 1990, c. 90–271, § 38. Amended by Laws 1999, c. 99–277, § 1, eff. Oct. 1, 1999; Laws 2004, c. 2004–11, § 96, eff. Oct. 1, 2004; Laws 2015, c. 2015–83, § 17, eff. July 1, 2015.

Applicability

Laws 2015, c. 2015–83, § 20, provides:

"Sections 709.2109 and 744.3203, Florida Statutes, as created by this act, apply to all proceedings filed on or after July 1, 2015. The amendments made by this act to ss. 744.107, 744.1075, 744.108, 744.3025, 744.3031, 744.309, 744.3115, 744.312, 744.331, 744.344, 744.345, 744.359, 744.361, 744.367, 744.369, 744.3715, and 744.464, Florida Statutes, apply to all proceedings pending on July 1, 2015."

744.3701. Confidentiality

(1) Unless otherwise ordered by the court, upon a showing of good cause, an initial, annual, or final guardianship report or amendment thereto, or a court record relating to the settlement of a claim, is subject to inspection only by the court, the clerk or the clerk's representative, the guardian and the guardian's attorney, the guardian ad litem with regard to the settlement of the claim, the ward if he or she is at least 14 years of age and has not been determined to be totally

incapacitated, the ward's attorney, the minor if he or she is at least 14 years of age, or the attorney representing the minor with regard to the minor's claim, or as otherwise provided by this chapter.

(2) The court may direct disclosure and recording of parts of an initial, annual, or final report or amendment thereto, or a court record relating to the settlement of a claim, including a petition for approval of a settlement on behalf of a ward or minor, a report of a guardian ad litem relating to a pending settlement, or an order approving a settlement on behalf of a ward or minor, in connection with a real property transaction or for such other purpose as the court allows.

(3) A court record relating to the settlement of a ward's or minor's claim, including a petition for approval of a settlement on behalf of a ward or minor, a report of a guardian ad litem relating to a pending settlement, or an order approving a settlement on behalf of a ward or minor, is confidential and exempt from the provisions of s. 119.07(1) and s. 24(a), Art. I of the State Constitution and may not be disclosed except as specifically authorized.

Laws 1990, c. 90–271, § 39. Amended by Laws 1997, c. 97–102, § 1091, eff. July 1, 1997; Laws 2015, c. 2015–84, § 1, eff. July 1, 2015.

744.371. Relief to be granted

If it appears from the annual guardianship report that:

(1) The condition of the ward requires further examination;

(2) Any change in the proposed care, maintenance, or treatment is needed;

(3) The ward is qualified for restoration of some or all rights;

(4) The condition or maintenance of the ward requires the performance or doing of any other thing for the best interest of the ward which is not indicated in the plan; or

(5) There is any other matter necessary to protect the interests of the ward,

the court shall, after a hearing with appropriate notice, amend the plan or enter any other order necessary to protect the ward.

Laws 1974, c. 74–106, § 1; Fla.St.1974, Supp. § 744.206; Laws 1975, c. 75–222, §§ 6, 26; Laws 1989, c. 89–96, § 55; Laws 1990, c. 90–271, § 40.

744.3715. Petition for interim judicial review

(1) At any time, any interested person, including the ward, may petition the court for review alleging that the guardian is not complying with the guardianship plan, is exceeding his or her authority under the guardianship plan, is acting in a manner contrary to s. 744.361, is denying visitation between the ward and his or her relatives in violation of s. 744.361(13), or is not acting in the best interest of the ward. The petition for review must state the nature of the objection to the guardian's action or proposed action. Upon the filing of any such petition, the court shall review the petition and act upon it expeditiously.

(2) If the petition for review is found to be without merit, the court may assess costs and attorney's fees against the petitioner.

Laws 1989, c. 89–96, § 56; Laws 1990, c. 90–271, § 41. Amended by Laws 1997, c. 97–102, § 1092, eff. July 1, 1997; Laws 2015, c. 2015–83, § 18, eff. July 1, 2015.

Applicability

Laws 2015, c. 2015–83, § 20, provides:

"Sections 709.2109 and 744.3203, Florida Statutes, as created by this act, apply to all proceedings filed on or after July 1, 2015. The amendments made by this act to ss.

744.107, 744.1075, 744.108, 744.3025, 744.3031, 744.309, 744.3115, 744.312, 744.331, 744.344, 744.345, 744.359, 744.361, 744.367, 744.369, 744.3715, and 744.464, Florida Statutes, apply to all proceedings pending on July 1, 2015."

744.372. Judicial review of guardianships

The court retains jurisdiction over all guardianships. The court shall review the appropriateness and extent of a guardianship annually and:

(1) If an objection to the terms of the guardianship report has been filed pursuant to s. 744.367;

(2) If interim review has been requested under s. 744.3715;

(3) If a person, including the ward, has filed a suggestion of increased capacity; or

(4) If the guardianship report has not been received and the guardian has failed to respond to a show cause order.

Laws 1989, c. 89–96, § 57; Laws 1990, c. 90–271, § 42.

744.3725. Procedure for extraordinary authority

Before the court may grant authority to a guardian to exercise any of the rights specified in s. 744.3215(4), the court must:

(1) Appoint an independent attorney to act on the incapacitated person's behalf, and the attorney must have the opportunity to meet with the person and to present evidence and cross-examine witnesses at any hearing on the petition for authority to act;

(2) Receive as evidence independent medical, psychological, and social evaluations with respect to the incapacitated person by competent professionals or appoint its own experts to assist in the evaluations;

(3) Personally meet with the incapacitated person to obtain its own impression of the person's capacity, so as to afford the incapacitated person the full opportunity to express his or her personal views or desires with respect to the judicial proceeding and issue before the court;

(4) Find by clear and convincing evidence that the person lacks the capacity to make a decision about the issue before the court and that the incapacitated person's capacity is not likely to change in the foreseeable future;

(5) Be persuaded by clear and convincing evidence that the authority being requested is in the best interests of the incapacitated person; and

(6) In the case of dissolution of marriage, find that the ward's spouse has consented to the dissolution.

The provisions of this section and s. 744.3215(4) are procedural and do not establish any new or independent right to or authority over the termination of parental rights, dissolution of marriage, sterilization, abortion, or the termination of life support systems.

Laws 1989, c. 89–96, § 58; Laws 1990, c. 90–271, § 43; Laws 1995, c. 95–401, § 25. Amended by Laws 1997, c. 97–102, § 1093, eff. July 1, 1997.

744.373. Production of property

On the petition of a creditor or other interested person, including the ward, or on its own motion, the court may require a guardian of the property to produce satisfactory evidence that the property of the ward for which the guardian is responsible is in the guardian's possession or under her or his control. If it deems it necessary or proper, the court may order the guardian to produce the property for the inspection of the creditor, another interested person, the ward, or the court.

Laws 1974, c. 74–106, § 1; Fla.St. 1974, Supp. § 744.327; Laws 1975, c. 75–222, §§ 17, 26; Fla.St. 1987, § 744.434; Laws 1989, c. 89–96, § 71; Laws 1990, c. 90–271, § 44. Amended by Laws 1997, c. 97–102, § 1094, eff. July 1, 1997.

744.3735. Annual appearance of the guardian

The court may require the guardian to appear before the court at the time the guardian files the annual guardianship report or at such other time as the court determines, in order for the court to inquire as to any matter relating to the well-being of the ward.

Laws 1974, c. 74–106, § 1; Fla.St. 1974, Supp. § 744.328; Laws 1975, c. 75–222, §§ 17, 26; Laws 1979, c. 79–221, § 11; Fla.St. 1987, § 744.437; Laws 1989, c. 89–96, § 72.

Cross References

Annual guardianship reports, see Probate Rule 5.695.

744.374. Payments to guardian

If there is more than one guardian, either guardian may petition for an order directing the guardian of the property to pay to the guardian of the person periodic amounts for the support, care, maintenance, education, and other needs of the ward if not otherwise provided for in the guardianship plan. The amount may be increased or decreased from time to time. If an order is entered, the receipt of the guardian for payments made shall be a sufficient discharge of the guardian who makes the payments. The guardian shall not be bound to see to the application of the payments.

Laws 1974, c. 74–106, § 1; Fla.St.1974, Supp. § 744.207; Laws 1975, c. 75–222, §§ 6, 26; Laws 1989, c. 89–96, § 59; Laws 1990, c. 90–271, § 45. Amended by Laws 1997, c. 97–102, § 1095, eff. July 1, 1997.

744.381. Appraisals

When the court deems it necessary, appraisers may be appointed to appraise the property of the ward that is subject to the guardianship.

Laws 1974, c. 74–106, § 1; Fla.St.1974, Supp. § 744.3155; Laws 1975, c. 75–222, §§ 13, 26; Laws 1989, c. 89–96, § 61; Laws 1990, c. 90–271, § 46.

Cross References

Inventory, see Probate Rule 5.620.

744.384. Subsequently discovered or acquired property

(1) If a plenary guardian of the property of the ward learns of any property that is not included in previous inventories, the property shall be inventoried within 30 days after the discovery or acquisition.

(2) If a limited guardian of the property of the ward learns of any property that was not known to the court at the time of his or her appointment, he or she shall file a report of such property with the court. Upon petition by the guardian, ward, or other interested person, the court, after hearing with appropriate notice, may direct the guardian to take custody and control of such property, without further adjudicatory proceeding under s. 744.331.

Laws 1974, c. 74–106, § 1; Fla.St.1974, Supp. § 744.316; Laws 1975, c. 75–222, §§ 14, 26; Laws 1989, c. 89–96, § 62; Laws 1990, c. 90–271, § 47. Amended by Laws 1997, c. 97–102, § 1096, eff. July 1, 1997.

Cross References

Inventory, see Probate Rule 5.620.

744.387. Settlement of claims

(1) When a settlement of any claim by or against the guardian, whether arising as a result of personal injury or otherwise, and whether arising before or after appointment of a guardian, is proposed, but before an action to enforce it is begun, on petition by the guardian of the property stating the facts of the claim, question, or dispute and the proposed settlement, and on any evidence that is introduced, the court may enter an order authorizing the settlement if satisfied that the settlement will be for the best interest of the ward. The order shall relieve the guardian from any further responsibility in connection with the claim or dispute when the settlement has been made in accordance with the order. The order authorizing the settlement may also determine whether an additional bond is required and, if so, shall fix the amount of it.

(2) In the same manner as provided in subsection (1) or as authorized by s. 744.301, the natural guardians or guardian of a minor may settle any claim by or on behalf of a minor that does not exceed $15,000 without bond. A legal guardianship shall be required when the amount of the net settlement to the ward exceeds $15,000.

(3)(a) No settlement after an action has been commenced by or on behalf of a ward shall be effective unless approved by the court having jurisdiction of the action.

(b) In the event of settlement or judgment in favor of the ward or minor, the court may authorize the natural guardians or guardian, or a guardian of the property appointed by a court of competent jurisdiction, to collect the amount of the settlement or judgment and to execute a release or satisfaction. When the amount of net settlement to the ward or judgment exceeds $15,000 and no guardian has been appointed, the court shall require the appointment of a guardian for the property.

(4) In making a settlement under court order as provided in this section, the guardian is authorized to execute any instrument that may be necessary to effect the settlement. When executed, the instrument shall be a complete release of the person making the settlement.

Laws 1974, c. 74–106, § 1; Fla.St.1974, Supp. § 744.317; Laws 1975, c. 75–222, §§ 14, 26; Laws 1978, c. 78–342, § 3; Laws 1979, c. 79–221, § 10; Laws 1989, c. 89–96, § 63; Laws 1990, c. 90–271, § 48. Amended by Laws 2002, c. 2002–195, § 10, eff. April 29, 2002.

744.391. Actions by and against guardian or ward

If an action is brought by the guardian against the ward, or vice versa, or if the interest of the guardian is adverse to that of his or her ward, a guardian ad litem shall be appointed to represent the ward in that particular litigation. In any litigation between the guardian and the ward, a guardian ad litem shall be appointed to represent the ward. If there is a conflict of interest between the guardian and the ward, the guardian ad litem shall petition the court for removal of the guardian. Judgments in favor of the ward shall become the property of the ward without the necessity for any assignment by the guardian or receipt by the ward upon termination of guardianship. The guardian may receive payment and satisfy any judgment in behalf of the ward without joinder by the ward.

Laws 1974, c. 74–106, § 1; Fla.St.1974, Supp. § 744.318; Laws 1975, c. 75–222, §§ 15, 26; Laws 1989, c. 89–96, § 64. Amended by Laws 1997, c. 97–102, § 1097, eff. July 1, 1997.

Cross References

Guardian ad litem, appointment, see Probate Rule 5.120.

744.394. Suspension of statutes of limitations in favor of guardian

If a person entitled to bring an action is declared incapacitated before the expiration of the time limited for the commencement of it and the cause of the action survives, the action may be commenced by the guardian of the property after such expiration and within 1 year from the date of the order appointing the guardian or the time otherwise limited by law, whichever is longer.

Laws 1974, c. 74–106, § 1; Fla.St.1974, Supp. § 744.319; Laws 1975, c. 75–222, §§ 16, 26; Laws 1989, c. 89–96, § 65; Laws 1990, c. 90–271, § 49. Amended by Laws 1997, c. 97–102, § 1098, eff. July 1, 1997.

744.397. Application of income of property of ward

(1) The court may authorize the guardian of the property to apply the ward's income, first to the ward's care, support, education, and maintenance, and then for the care, support, education, maintenance, cost of final illness, and cost of funeral and burial or cremation of the parent, spouse, or dependents, if any, of the ward, to the extent necessary. If the income is not sufficient for these purposes, the court may authorize the expenditure of part of the principal for such purposes from time to time.

(2) The word "dependents," as used in subsection (1) means, in addition to those persons who are legal dependents of a ward under existing law, the person or persons whom the ward is morally or equitably obligated to aid, assist, maintain, or care for, including, but not limited to, such persons as the indigent spouse of the ward, based upon the showing of an existing need and an ability of the estate of the ward to pay for, provide, or furnish the aid, assistance, maintenance, or care without unreasonably jeopardizing the care, support, and maintenance of the ward.

(3) If the ward is a minor and the ward's parents are able to care for him or her and to support, maintain, and educate him or her, the guardian of the minor shall not so use his or her ward's property unless directed or authorized to do so by the court.

Laws 1974, c. 74–106, § 1; Fla.St.1974, Supp. § 744.3205; Laws 1975, c. 75–222, §§ 16, 26; Laws 1989, c. 89–96, § 66; Laws 1990, c. 90–271, § 50. Amended by Laws 1997, c. 97–102, § 1099, eff. July 1, 1997.

744.421. Petition for support of ward's dependents

Any person dependent on the ward for support may petition for an order directing the guardian of the property to contribute to the support of the dependent person from the property of the ward. The court may enter an order for suitable support and education of the dependent person out of the ward's property that is subject to the guardianship. The grant or denial of an order for support shall not preclude a further petition for increase, decrease, modification, or termination of allowance for support by either the petitioner or the guardian. The order for support shall be valid for payments made pursuant to it, but no valid payments can be made after the termination of the guardianship. The receipt of the petitioner shall be a sufficient release of the guardian for payments made pursuant to the order. If the property of the ward is derived in whole or in part from payments of compensation, adjusted compensation, pension, insurance, or other benefits made directly to the guardian by the United States Department of Veterans Affairs, notice of the petition for support shall be given by the petitioner to the office of the United States Department of Veterans Affairs having jurisdiction over the area in which the court is located and the chief attorney for the Department of Veterans' Affairs in this state at least 15 days before the hearing on the petition. The court may not authorize payments from the ward's property unless the ward has been adjudicated incapacitated to handle such property in accordance with s. 744.331; except in a voluntary guardianship, in which case such petition may be granted only upon the written consent of the ward.

Laws 1974, c. 74–106, § 1; Fla.St.1974, Supp. § 744.321; Laws 1975, c. 75–222, §§ 16, 26; Laws 1977, c. 77–174, § 1; Laws 1978, c. 78–305, § 1; Laws 1981, c. 81–167, § 80; Laws 1983, c. 83–55, § 84; Laws 1988, c. 88–290, § 30; Laws 1989, c. 89–96, § 67; Laws 1990, c. 90–271, § 51; Laws 1993, c. 93–268, § 37.

744.441. Powers of guardian upon court approval

After obtaining approval of the court pursuant to a petition for authorization to act, a plenary guardian of the property, or a limited guardian of the property within the powers granted by the order appointing the guardian or an approved annual or amended guardianship report, may:

(1) Perform, compromise, or refuse performance of a ward's contracts that continue as obligations of the estate, as he or she may determine under the circumstances.

(2) Execute, exercise, or release any powers as trustee, personal representative, custodian for minors, conservator, or donee of any power of appointment or other power that the ward might have lawfully exercised, consummated, or executed if not incapacitated, if the best interest of the ward requires such execution, exercise, or release.

(3) Make ordinary or extraordinary repairs or alterations in buildings or other structures; demolish any improvements; or raze existing, or erect new, party walls or buildings.

(4) Subdivide, develop, or dedicate land to public use; make or obtain the vacation of plats and adjust boundaries; adjust differences in valuation on exchange or partition by giving or receiving consideration; or dedicate easements to public use without consideration.

(5) Enter into a lease as lessor or lessee for any purpose, with or without option to purchase or renew, for a term within, or extending beyond, the period of guardianship.

(6) Enter into a lease or arrangement for exploration and removal of minerals or other natural resources or enter into a pooling or unitization agreement.

(7) Abandon property when, in the opinion of the guardian, it is valueless or is so encumbered or in such condition that it is of no benefit to the estate.

(8) Pay calls, assessments, and other sums chargeable or accruing against, or on account of, securities.

(9) Borrow money, with or without security, to be repaid from the property or otherwise and advance money for the protection of the estate.

(10) Effect a fair and reasonable compromise with any debtor or obligor or extend, renew, or in any manner modify the terms of any obligation owing to the estate.

(11) Prosecute or defend claims or proceedings in any jurisdiction for the protection of the estate and of the guardian in the performance of his or her duties. Before authorizing a guardian to bring an action described in s. 736.0207, the court shall first find that the action appears to be in the ward's best interests during the ward's probable lifetime. There shall be a rebuttable presumption that an action challenging the ward's revocation of all or part of a trust is not in the ward's best interests if the revocation relates solely to a devise. This subsection does not preclude a challenge after the ward's death. If the court denies a request that a guardian be authorized to bring an action described in s. 736.0207, the court shall review the continued need for a guardian and the extent of the need for delegation of the ward's rights.

(12) Sell, mortgage, or lease any real or personal property of the estate, including homestead property, or any interest therein for cash or credit, or for part cash and part credit, and with or without security for unpaid balances.

(13) Continue any unincorporated business or venture in which the ward was engaged.

(14) Purchase the entire fee simple title to real estate in this state in which the guardian has no interest, but the purchase may be made only for a home for the ward, to protect the home of the ward or the ward's interest, or as a home for the ward's dependent family. If the ward is a married person and the home of the ward or of the dependent family of the ward is owned by the ward and spouse as an estate by the entirety and the home is sold pursuant to the authority of subsection (12), the court may authorize the investment of any part or all of the proceeds from the sale toward the purchase of a fee simple title to real estate in this state for a home for the ward or the dependent family of the ward as an estate by the entirety owned by the ward and spouse. If the guardian is authorized to acquire title to real estate for the ward or dependent family of the ward as an estate by the entirety in accordance with the preceding provisions, the conveyance shall be in the name of the ward and spouse and shall be effective to create an estate by the entirety in the ward and spouse.

(15) Exercise any option contained in any policy of insurance payable to, or inuring to the benefit of, the ward.

(16) Pay reasonable funeral, interment, and grave marker expenses for the ward from the ward's estate, up to a maximum of $6,000.

(17) Make gifts of the ward's property to members of the ward's family in estate and income tax planning procedures.

(18) When the ward's will evinces an objective to obtain a United States estate tax charitable deduction by use of a split interest trust (as that term is defined in s. 736.1201), but the maximum charitable deduction otherwise allowable will not be achieved in whole or in part, execute a codicil on the ward's behalf amending said will to obtain the maximum charitable deduction allowable without diminishing the aggregate value of the benefits of any beneficiary under such will.

(19) Create or amend revocable trusts or create irrevocable trusts of property of the ward's estate which may extend beyond the disability or life of the ward in connection with estate, gift, income, or other tax planning or in connection with estate planning. The court shall retain oversight of the assets transferred to a trust, unless otherwise ordered by the court.

(20) Renounce or disclaim any interest by testate or intestate succession or by inter vivos transfer.

(21) Enter into contracts that are appropriate for, and in the best interest of, the ward.

(22) As to a minor ward, pay expenses of the ward's support, health, maintenance, and education, if the ward's parents, or either of them, are alive.

Laws 1974, c. 74–106, § 1; Fla.St.1974, Supp. § 744.501; Laws 1975, c. 75–222, §§ 22, 26; Laws 1977, c. 77–174, § 1; Laws 1977, c. 77–328, § 2; Laws 1979, c. 79–400, § 281; Laws 1980, c. 80–203, § 4; Laws 1986, c. 86–120, § 3; Laws 1987, c. 87–317, § 2; Laws 1989, c. 89–96, § 73; Laws 1990, c. 90–271, § 52. Amended by Laws 1997, c. 97–102, § 1100, eff. July 1, 1997; Laws 1997, c. 97–240, § 11, eff. May 30, 1997; Laws 2006, c. 2006–77, § 5, eff. June 6, 2006; Laws 2006, c. 2006–178, § 20, eff. July 1, 2006; Laws 2006, c. 2006–217, § 46, eff. July 1, 2007; Laws 2011, c. 2011–183, § 12, eff. June 21, 2011.

Cross References

Approval of acts, petition and notice, see Probate Rule 5.630.

Continuance of business of ward, see Probate Rule 5.640.
Estates and trusts, payment of funeral expenses by guardian, see § 733.707.
Execution by guardian, see Probate Rule 5.610.
Investment of fiduciary funds, see § 518.01 et seq.
Revocable trusts, revocation or amendment, see § 736.0602.

744.442. Delegation of authority

(1) A guardian may designate a surrogate guardian to exercise the powers of the guardian if the guardian is unavailable to act. A person designated as a surrogate guardian under this section must be a professional guardian.

(2)(a) A guardian must file a petition with the court requesting permission to designate a surrogate guardian.

(b) If the court approves the designation, the order must specify the name and business address of the surrogate guardian and the duration of appointment, which may not exceed 30 days. The court may extend the appointment for good cause shown. The surrogate guardian may exercise all powers of the guardian unless limited by order of the court. The surrogate guardian must file with the court an oath swearing or affirming that he or she will faithfully perform the duties delegated. The court may require the surrogate guardian to post a bond.

(3) This section does not limit the responsibility of the guardian to the ward and to the court. The guardian is liable for the acts of the surrogate guardian. The guardian may terminate the authority of the surrogate guardian by filing a written notice of the termination with the court.

(4) The surrogate guardian is subject to the jurisdiction of the court as if appointed to serve as guardian.
Added by Laws 2006, c. 2006–178, § 21, eff. July 1, 2006.

744.444. Power of guardian without court approval

Without obtaining court approval, a plenary guardian of the property, or a limited guardian of the property within the powers granted by the order appointing the guardian or an approved annual or amended guardianship report, may:

(1) Retain assets owned by the ward.

(2) Receive assets from fiduciaries or other sources.

(3) Vote stocks or other securities in person or by general or limited proxy or not vote stocks or other securities.

(4) Insure the assets of the estate against damage, loss, and liability and insure himself or herself against liability as to third persons.

(5) Execute and deliver in his or her name as guardian any instrument necessary or proper to carry out and give effect to this section.

(6) Pay taxes and assessments on the ward's property.

(7) Pay valid encumbrances against the ward's property in accordance with their terms, but no prepayment may be made without prior court approval.

(8) Pay reasonable living expenses for the ward, taking into consideration the accustomed standard of living, age, health, and financial condition of the ward. This subsection does not authorize the guardian of a minor to expend funds for the ward's living expenses if one or both of the ward's parents are alive.

(9) Elect to dissent from a will under s. 732.2125(2), seek approval to make an election in accordance with s. 732.401, or assert any other right or choice available to a surviving spouse in the administration of a decedent's estate.

(10) Deposit or invest liquid assets of the estate, including moneys received from the sale of other assets, in federally insured interest-bearing accounts, readily marketable secured loan arrangements, money market mutual funds, or other prudent investments. The guardian may redeem or sell such deposits or investments to pay the reasonable living expenses of the ward as provided herein.

(11) Pay incidental expenses in the administration of the estate.

(12) Sell or exercise stock subscription or conversion rights and consent, directly or through a committee or other agent, to the reorganization, consolidation, merger, dissolution, or liquidation of a corporation or other business enterprise.

(13) When reasonably necessary, employ persons, including attorneys, auditors, investment advisers, care managers, or agents, even if they are associated with the guardian, to advise or assist the guardian in the performance of his or her duties.

(14) Execute and deliver in his or her name as guardian any instrument that is necessary or proper to carry out the orders of the court.

(15) Hold a security in the name of a nominee or in other form without disclosure of the interest of the ward, but the guardian is liable for any act of the nominee in connection with the security so held.

(16) Pay or reimburse costs incurred and reasonable fees or compensation to persons, including attorneys, employed by the guardian pursuant to subsection (13) from the assets of the guardianship estate, subject to obtaining court approval of the annual accounting.

(17) Provide confidential information about a ward that is related to an investigation arising under part I of chapter 400 to a local or state ombudsman council member conducting such an investigation. Any such ombudsman shall have a duty to maintain the confidentiality of such information.

Laws 1974, c. 74–106, § 1; Fla.St.1974, Supp. § 744.502; Laws 1975, c. 75–222, §§ 23, 26; Laws 1977, c. 77–328, § 3; Laws 1979, c. 79–400, § 282; Laws 1984, c. 84–31, § 5; Laws 1989, c. 89–96, § 74; Laws 1990, c. 90–271, § 53. Amended by Laws 1997, c. 97–102, § 1101, eff. July 1, 1997; Laws 2000, c. 2000–155, § 8, eff. July 4, 2000; Laws 2003, c. 2003–57, § 12, eff. May 30, 2003; Laws 2010, c. 2010–132, § 18, eff. Oct. 1, 2010.

744.446. Conflicts of interest; prohibited activities; court approval; breach of fiduciary duty

(1) It is essential to the proper conduct and management of a guardianship that the guardian be independent and impartial. The fiduciary relationship which exists between the guardian and the ward may not be used for the private gain of the guardian other than the remuneration for fees and expenses provided by law. The guardian may not incur any obligation on behalf of the guardianship which conflicts with the proper discharge of the guardian's duties.

(2) Unless prior approval is obtained by court order, or unless such relationship existed prior to appointment of the guardian and is disclosed to the court in the petition for appointment of guardian, a guardian may not:

(a) Have any interest, financial or otherwise, direct or indirect, in any business transaction or activity with the guardianship;

(b) Acquire an ownership, possessory, security, or other pecuniary interest adverse to the ward;

(c) Be designated as a beneficiary on any life insurance policy, pension, or benefit plan of the ward unless such designation was validly made by the ward prior to adjudication of incapacity of the ward; and

(d) Directly or indirectly purchase, rent, lease, or sell any property or services from or to any business entity of which the guardian or the guardian's spouse or any of the guardian's lineal descendants, or collateral kindred, is an officer, partner, director, shareholder, or proprietor, or has any financial interest.

(3) Any activity prohibited by this section is voidable during the term of the guardianship or by the personal representative of the ward's estate, and the guardian is subject to removal and to imposition of personal liability through a proceeding for surcharge, in addition to any other remedies otherwise available.

(4) In the event of a breach by the guardian of the guardian's fiduciary duty, the court shall take those necessary actions to protect the ward and the ward's assets.

Laws 1989, c. 89–96, § 75; Laws 1990, c. 90–271, § 54. Amended by Laws 1997, c. 97–102, § 1102, eff. July 1, 1997; Laws 2002, c. 2002–195, § 6, eff. April 29, 2002.

744.447. Petition for authorization to act

(1) Application for authorization to perform, or confirmation of, any acts under s. 744.441 or s. 744.446 shall be by petition stating the facts showing the expediency or necessity for the action; a description of any property involved; and the price and terms of a sale, mortgage, or other contract. The application must state whether it conforms to the general terms of the guardianship report and whether the ward has been adjudicated incapacitated to act with respect to the rights to be exercised.

(2) No notice of a petition to authorize a sale of perishable personal property or of property rapidly deteriorating shall be required. Notice of a petition to perform any other acts under s. 744.441 or s. 744.446 shall be given to the ward, to the next of kin, if any, and to those interested persons who have filed requests for notices and copies of pleadings, as provided in the Florida Probate Rules, unless waived by the court. Notice need not be given to a ward who is under 14 years of age or who has been determined to be totally incapacitated.

Laws 1974, c. 74–106, § 1; Fla.St.1974, Supp. § 744.503; Laws 1975, c. 75–222, §§ 24, 26; Laws 1979, c. 79–221, § 12; Laws 1989, c. 89–96, § 76; Laws 1990, c. 90–271, § 55.

Cross References

Execution by guardian, see Probate Rule 5.610.
Petition and notice for approval of acts, see Probate Rule 5.630.

744.451. Order

(1) If a sale or mortgage is authorized, the order shall describe the property, and

(a) If the property is authorized for sale at private sale, the order shall fix the price and the terms of sale.

(b) If the sale is to be public, the order shall state that the sale shall be made to the highest bidder and the court reserves the right to reject all bids.

(2) An order for any other act permitted under s. 744.441 or s. 744.446 shall describe the permitted act and authorize the guardian to perform it.

Laws 1974, c. 74–106, § 1; Fla.St.1974, Supp. § 744.504; Laws 1975, c. 75–222, §§ 24, 26; Laws 1989, c. 89–96, § 77.

Petition and notice for approval of acts, see Probate Rule 5.630.

744.454. Guardian forbidden to borrow or purchase; exceptions

A professional guardian may not purchase property or borrow money from his or her ward. A guardian who is not a professional guardian may do so if:

(1) A court by written order authorizes the sale or loan after a hearing to which interested persons were given notice; or

(2) The property is sold at public sale and the guardian is a spouse, parent, child, brother, or sister of the ward or a cotenant of the ward in the property to be sold.

Laws 1974, c. 74–106, § 1; Fla.St.1974, Supp. § 744.506; Laws 1975, c. 75–222, §§ 24, 26; Laws 1977, c. 77–174, § 1; Laws 1989, c. 89–96, § 78; Laws 1996, c. 96–184, § 2; Laws 1996, c. 96–354, § 12. Amended by Laws 1997, c. 97–102, § 1787, eff. July 1, 1997; Laws 1997, c. 97–161, § 5, eff. Oct. 1, 1997.

744.457. Conveyance of various property rights by guardians of the property

(1)(a) All legal or equitable interests in property owned as an estate by the entirety by an incapacitated person for whom a guardian of the property has been appointed may be sold, transferred, conveyed, or mortgaged in accordance with s. 744.447, if the spouse who is not incapacitated joins in the sale, transfer, conveyance, or mortgage of the property. When both spouses are incapacitated, the sale, transfer, conveyance, or mortgage shall be by the guardians only. The sale, transfer, conveyance, or mortgage may be accomplished by one instrument or by separate instruments.

(b) In ordering or approving the sale and conveyance of the real or personal property owned by the ward and the ward's spouse as an estate by the entirety or as joint tenants with right of survivorship, the court may provide that one-half of the net proceeds of the sale shall go to the guardian of the ward and the other one-half to the ward's spouse, or the court may provide for the proceeds of the sale to retain the same character as to survivorship as the original asset.

(c) The guardian of the property shall collect all payments coming due on intangible property, such as notes and mortgages and other securities, and shall retain one-half of all principal and interest payments so collected and shall pay the other one-half of the collections to the spouse who is not incapacitated. If both spouses are incapacitated, the guardian of either shall collect the payments, retain one-half of the principal and interest payments, and pay the other one-half to the guardian of the other spouse.

(d) The spouse of the incapacitated person shall collect all payments of rents on real estate held as an estate by the entirety and, after paying all charges against the property, such as taxes, insurance, maintenance, and repairs, shall retain one-half of the net rents so collected and pay the other one-half to the guardian of the spouse who is incapacitated. If both spouses are incapacitated, the guardian of the property of either may collect the rent, pay the charges, retain one-half of the net rent, and pay the other one-half to the guardian of the other spouse.

(2) In determining the value of life estates or remainder interests, the American Experience Mortality Tables may be used.

(3) Nothing in this section shall prohibit the court in its discretion from appointing a sole guardian to serve as guardian for both spouses.

(4) Any contingent or expectant interest in property, including marital property rights and any right of survivorship incident to joint tenancy or tenancy by the entirety, may be conveyed or released in accordance with s. 744.447.

Laws 1974, c. 74–106, § 1; Fla.St.1974, Supp. § 744.506; Laws 1975, c. 75–222, §§ 24, 26; Laws 1979, c. 79–221, § 13; Laws 1987, c. 87–317, § 3; Laws 1989, c. 89–96, § 79; Laws 1990, c. 90–271, § 56. Amended by Laws 1997, c. 97–102, § 1103, eff. July 1, 1997.

744.461. Purchasers and lenders protected

No person purchasing or leasing from, or taking a mortgage, pledge, or other lien from, a guardian shall be bound to see that the money or other things of value paid to the guardian are actually needed or properly applied. The person is not otherwise bound as to the proprieties or expediencies of the acts of the guardian.

Laws 1974, c. 74–106, § 1; Fla.St.1974, Supp. § 744.507; Laws 1975, c. 75–222, §§ 24, 26; Laws 1989, c. 89–96, § 80.

744.462. Determination regarding alternatives to guardianship

Any judicial determination concerning the validity of the ward's durable power of attorney, trust, or trust amendment shall be promptly reported in the guardianship proceeding by the guardian of the property. If the instrument has been judicially determined to be valid or if, after the appointment of a guardian, a petition is filed alleging that there is an alternative to guardianship which will sufficiently address the problems of the ward, the court shall review the continued need for a guardian and the extent of the need for delegation of the ward's rights.

Added by Laws 2006, c. 2006–77, § 6, eff. June 6, 2006; Laws 2006, c. 2006–217, § 47, eff. July 1, 2007.

PART VII. TERMINATION

744.464. Restoration to capacity

(1) **Venue.**—A suggestion of capacity must be filed with the court in which the guardianship is pending.

(2) **Suggestion of capacity.—**

(a) Any interested person, including the ward, may file a suggestion of capacity. The suggestion of capacity must state that the ward is currently capable of exercising some or all of the rights which were removed.

(b) Upon the filing of the suggestion of capacity, the court shall immediately appoint a physician to examine the ward. The physician must examine the ward and file his or her report with the court within 20 days after the appointment.

(c) The court shall immediately send notice of the filing of the suggestion of capacity to the ward, the guardian, the attorney for the ward, if any, and any other interested persons designated by the court. Formal notice must be served on the guardian. Informal notice may be served on other persons. Notice need not be served on the person who filed the suggestion of capacity.

(d) Any objections to the suggestion of capacity must be filed within 20 days after service of the notice.

(e) If an objection is timely filed, or if the medical examination suggests that full restoration is not appropriate, the court shall set the matter for hearing. If the ward does not have an attorney, the court shall appoint one to represent the ward.

(f) Notice of the hearing and copies of the objections and medical examination reports shall be served upon the ward, the ward's attorney, the guardian, the ward's next of kin, and any other interested persons as directed by the court.

(3) Order of restoration.—

(a) If no objections are filed, and the court is satisfied that the medical examination establishes by a preponderance of the evidence that restoration of all or some of the ward's rights is appropriate, the court shall enter an order of restoration of capacity, restoring all or some of the rights which were removed from the ward in accordance with those findings.

(b) At the conclusion of a hearing, conducted pursuant to s. 744.1095, the court shall make specific findings of fact and, based on a preponderance of the evidence, enter an order either denying the suggestion of capacity or restoring all or some of the rights which were removed from the ward. The ward has the burden of proving by a preponderance of the evidence that the restoration of capacity is warranted.

(c) If only some rights are restored to the ward, the order must state which rights are restored, and the guardian shall prepare a new guardianship report which addresses only the remaining rights retained by the guardian. The guardian must file a copy of the new report with the court within 60 days after the entry of the order.

(4) Timeliness of hearing.—The court shall give priority to any suggestion of capacity and shall advance the cause on the calendar.

Laws 1975, c. 75–222, §§ 10, 26; Laws 1977, c. 77–174, § 1; Laws 1989, c. 89–96, § 81; Laws 1990, c. 90–271, § 57. Amended by Laws 1997, c. 97–102, § 1104, eff. July 1, 1997; Laws 2006, c. 2006–178, § 22, eff. July 1, 2006; Laws 2015, c. 2015–83, § 19, eff. July 1, 2015.

Applicability

Laws 2015, c. 2015–83, § 20, provides:

"Sections 709.2109 and 744.3203, Florida Statutes, as created by this act, apply to all proceedings filed on or after July 1, 2015. The amendments made by this act to ss. 744.107, 744.1075, 744.108, 744.3025, 744.3031, 744.309, 744.3115, 744.312, 744.331, 744.344, 744.345, 744.359, 744.361, 744.367, 744.369, 744.3715, and 744.464, Florida Statutes, apply to all proceedings pending on July 1, 2015."

744.467. Resignation of guardian

A guardian may resign and be relieved of his or her duties after the notice that the court may require and notice to the surety on his or her bond. Before entering an order discharging a guardian of the property, the court shall require the guardian to file a true and correct final report of his or her guardianship and to deliver to the successor guardian all property of the ward, all records concerning the property of the ward or of the guardianship, and all money due to the ward from him or her. A guardian of the person must deliver to the successor guardian copies of all records of medical or personal care, prior to being discharged. Before entering the order, the court shall be satisfied that the interest of the ward will not be placed in jeopardy by the resignation. The acceptance of the resignation shall not exonerate the guardian or the guardian's surety from any liability previously incurred.

Laws 1974, c. 74–106, § 1; Fla.St.1974, Supp. § 744.405; Laws 1975, c. 75–222, §§ 19, 26; Laws 1977, c. 77–174, § 1; Laws 1989, c. 89–96, § 82; Laws 1990, c. 90–271, § 58. Amended by Laws 1997, c. 97–102, § 1105, eff. July 1, 1997.

Cross References

Execution by guardian, see Probate Rule 5.610.
Resignation or disqualification of guardian, see Probate Rule 5.650.

744.471. Appointment of successor

A successor guardian must be appointed and duly qualified before a guardian shall be relieved of his or her duties and obligations as provided in s. 744.467. A successor guardian shall be appointed if a guardian dies, becomes incapacitated, or is removed. Successor guardians are governed by the laws concerning guardianships.

Laws 1974, c. 74–106, § 1; Fla.St.1974, Supp. § 744.406; Laws 1975, c. 75–222, §§ 20, 26; Laws 1989, c. 89–96, § 83; Laws 1995, c. 95–401, § 26. Amended by Laws 1997, c. 97–102, § 1106, eff. July 1, 1997.

Cross References

Appointment of successor, see Probate Rule 5.650.

744.474. Reasons for removal of guardian

A guardian may be removed for any of the following reasons, and the removal shall be in addition to any other penalties prescribed by law:

(1) Fraud in obtaining her or his appointment.

(2) Failure to discharge her or his duties.

(3) Abuse of her or his powers.

(4) An incapacity or illness, including substance abuse, which renders the guardian incapable of discharging her or his duties.

(5) Failure to comply with any order of the court.

(6) Failure to return schedules of property sold or accounts of sales of property or to produce and exhibit the ward's assets when so required.

(7) The wasting, embezzlement, or other mismanagement of the ward's property.

(8) Failure to give bond or security for any purpose when required by the court or failure to file with the annual guardianship plan the evidence required by s. 744.351 that the sureties on her or his bond are alive and solvent.

(9) Conviction of a felony.

(10) Appointment of a receiver, trustee in bankruptcy, or liquidator for any corporate guardian.

(11) Development of a conflict of interest between the ward and the guardian.

(12) Having been found guilty of, regardless of adjudication, or entered a plea of nolo contendere or guilty to, any offense prohibited under s. 435.04 or similar statute of another jurisdiction.

(13) A material failure to comply with the guardianship report by the guardian.

(14) A failure to comply with the rules for timely filing the initial and annual guardianship reports.

(15) A failure to fulfill the guardianship education requirements.

(16) The improper management of the ward's assets.

(17) A material change in the ward's financial circumstances such that the guardian is no longer qualified to manage the finances of the ward, or the previous degree of management is no longer required.

(18) After appointment, the guardian becomes a disqualified person as set forth in s. 744.309(3).

(19) Upon a showing by a person who did not receive notice of the petition for adjudication of incapacity, when such notice is required, or who is related to the ward within the relationships specified for nonresident relatives in ss. 744.309(2) and 744.312(2) and who has not previously been rejected by the court as a guardian that the current guardian is not a family member and subsection (20) applies.

(20) Upon a showing that removal of the current guardian is in the best interest of the ward. In determining whether a guardian who is related by blood or marriage to the ward is to be removed, there shall be a rebuttable presumption that the guardian is acting in the best interests of the ward.

(21) A bad faith failure to submit guardianship records during the audit pursuant to s. 744.368.

Laws 1974, c. 74–106, § 1; Fla.St.1974, Supp. § 744.407; Laws 1975, c. 75–222, §§ 21, 26; Laws 1989, c. 89–96, § 84; Laws 1995, c. 95–418, § 138; Laws 1996, c. 96–354, § 13. Amended by Laws 1997, c. 97–102, § 1788, eff. July 1, 1997; Laws 1999, c. 99–8, § 283, eff. June 29, 1999; Laws 1999, c. 99–277, § 2, eff. June 8, 1999; Laws 2000, c. 2000–349, § 111, eff. Sept. 1, 2000; Laws 2004, c. 2004–267, § 32, eff. July 1, 2004; Laws 2006, c. 2006–178, § 23, eff. July 1, 2006; Laws 2010, c. 2010–114, § 54, eff. Aug. 1, 2010; Laws 2014, c. 2014–124, § 5, eff. July 1, 2014.

Cross References

Proceedings for removal, see Probate Rule 5.660.
Resignation or disqualification of guardian, appointment of successor, see Probate Rule 5.650.

744.477. Proceedings for removal of a guardian

Proceedings for removal of a guardian may be instituted by the court, by any surety or other interested person, or by the ward. Reasonable notice shall be given to the guardian. On the hearing, the court may enter an order that is proper considering the pleadings and the evidence.

Laws 1974, c. 74–106, § 1; Fla.St.1974, Supp. § 744.408; Laws 1975, c. 75–222, §§ 21, 26; Laws 1989, c. 89–96, § 85; Laws 1990, c. 90–271, § 59.

Cross References

Proceedings for removal of guardian, see Probate Rule 5.660.
Resignation or disqualification of guardian, appointment of successor, see Probate Rule 5.650.

744.511. Accounting upon removal

A removed guardian shall file with the court a true, complete, and final report of his or her guardianship within 20 days after removal and shall serve a copy on the successor guardian and the ward, unless the ward is a minor or has been determined to be totally incapacitated.

Laws 1974, c. 74–106, § 1; Fla.St.1974, Supp. § 744.409; Laws 1975, c. 75–222, §§ 21, 26; Laws 1989, c. 89–96, § 86; Laws 1990, c. 90–271, § 60. Amended by Laws 1997, c. 97–102, § 1107, eff. July 1, 1997; Laws 2006, c. 2006–178, § 24, eff. July 1, 2006.

Cross References

Order requiring accounting, see Probate Rule 5.150.

Proceedings for removal of guardian, see Probate Rule 5.660.

744.514. Surrender of property upon removal

The successor guardian shall demand of the removed guardian or her or his heirs, personal representative, or surety all the property of the ward and copies of all records of the ward. The removed guardian or her or his heirs, personal representative, or surety shall turn over the items to her or his duly qualified successor.

Laws 1974, c. 74–106, § 1; Fla.St.1974, Supp. § 744.4105; Laws 1975, c. 75–222, §§ 21, 26; Laws 1989, c. 89–96, § 87; Laws 1990, c. 90–271, § 61. Amended by Laws 1997, c. 97–102, § 1108, eff. July 1, 1997.

Cross References

Proceedings for removal of guardian, see Probate Rule 5.660.

744.517. Proceedings for contempt

If a removed guardian of the property fails to file a true, complete, and final accounting of his or her guardianship; to turn over to his or her successor or to the ward all the property of his or her ward and copies of all records that are in his or her control and that concern the ward; or to pay over to the successor guardian of the property or to the ward all money due the ward by him or her, the court shall issue a show cause order. If cause is shown for the default, the court shall set a reasonable time within which to comply, and, on failure to comply with this or any subsequent order, the removed guardian may be held in contempt. Proceedings for contempt may be instituted by the court, by any interested person, including the ward, or by a successor guardian.

Laws 1974, c. 74–106, § 1; Fla.St.1974, Supp. § 744.411; Laws 1975, c. 75–222, §§ 21, 26; Laws 1989, c. 89–96, § 88; Laws 1990, c. 90–271, § 62. Amended by Laws 1997, c. 97–102, § 1109, eff. July 1, 1997.

Cross References

Proceedings for removal of guardian, see Probate Rule 5.660.

744.521. Termination of guardianship

When a ward becomes sui juris or is restored to capacity, when the guardian has been unable to locate the ward through diligent search, or, for a guardian of the property, when the property subject to the guardianship has been exhausted, the guardian shall file a final report and receive his or her discharge. A guardian of the person is discharged without further proceeding upon filing a certified copy of the ward's death certificate. The court may require proof of the removal of incapacity.

Laws 1974, c. 74–106, § 1; Fla.St.1974, Supp. § 744.412; Laws 1975, c. 75–222, §§ 21, 26; Laws 1986, c. 86–120, § 4; Laws 1989, c. 89–96, § 89; Laws 1990, c. 90–271, § 63. Amended by Laws 1997, c. 97–102, § 1110, eff. July 1, 1997.

Cross References

Termination of guardianship upon removal of ward's incapacity, death, or exhaustion of assets, see Probate Rule 5.680.

744.524. Termination of guardianship on change of domicile of resident ward

When the domicile of a resident ward has changed as provided in s. 744.2025, and the foreign court having jurisdiction over the ward at the ward's new domicile has appointed a guardian and that guardian has qualified and posted a bond in an amount required by the foreign court, the guardian in this state may file her or his final report and close the guardianship in this state. The guardian of the property in this state shall cause a notice to be published once a week for 2 consecutive weeks, in a newspaper of general circulation published in the county, that she or he has filed her or his accounting and will apply for discharge on a day certain and that jurisdiction of the ward will be transferred to the state of foreign jurisdiction. If an objection is filed to the termination of the guardianship in this state, the court shall hear the objection and enter an order either sustaining or overruling the objection. Upon the disposition of all objections filed, or if no objection is filed, final settlement shall be made by the Florida guardian. On proof that the remaining property in the guardianship has been received by the foreign guardian, the guardian of the property in this state shall be discharged. The entry of the order terminating the guardianship in this state shall not exonerate the guardian or the guardian's surety from any liability previously incurred.

Laws 1974, c. 74–106, § 1; Fla.St.1974, Supp. § 744.413; Laws 1975, c. 75–222, §§ 21, 26; Laws 1989, c. 89–96, § 90; Laws 1990, c. 90–271, § 64. Amended by Laws 1997, c. 97–102, § 1111, eff. July 1, 1997.

Cross References

Termination of guardianship on change of domicile of resident ward, see Probate Rule 5.670.

744.527. Final reports and application for discharge; hearing

(1) When the court terminates the guardianship for any of the reasons set forth in s. 744.521, the guardian shall promptly file his or her final report. If the ward has died, the guardian must file a final report with the court no later than 45 days after he or she has been served with letters of administration or letters of curatorship. If no objections are filed and if it appears that the guardian has made full and complete distribution to the person entitled and has otherwise faithfully discharged his or her duties, the court shall approve the final report. If objections are filed, the court shall conduct a hearing in the same manner as provided for a hearing on objections to annual guardianship reports.

(2) The guardian applying for discharge may retain from the funds in his or her possession a sufficient amount to pay the final costs of administration, including guardian and attorney's fees regardless of the death of the ward, accruing between the filing of his or her final returns and the order of discharge.

Laws 1974, c. 74–106, § 1; Fla.St.1974, Supp. § 744.414; Laws 1975, c. 75–222, §§ 21, 26; Laws 1989, c. 89–96, § 91; Laws 1990, c. 90–271, § 65. Amended by Laws 1997, c. 97–102, § 1112, eff. July 1, 1997; Laws 2006, c. 2006–178, § 25, eff. July 1, 2006.

Cross References

Order requiring accounting, see Probate Rule 5.150.
Termination of guardianship upon removal of incapacity, death or exhaustion of assets, see Probate Rule 5.680.

744.528. Discharge of guardian named as personal representative

(1) A guardian authorized to manage property, who is subsequently appointed personal representative, must serve a copy of the guardian's final report and petition for discharge upon the beneficiaries of the ward's estate who will be affected by the report.

(2) All such beneficiaries shall have 30 days to file objections to the final report and petition for discharge.

(3) Any interested person may file a notice of a hearing on any objections filed by the beneficiaries. Notice of the hearing must be served upon the guardian, beneficiaries of the

ward's estate, and any other person to whom the court directs service. If a notice of hearing on the objections is not served within 90 days after filing of the objections, the objections are deemed abandoned.

(4) The guardian may not be discharged until:

(a) All objections have been judicially resolved;

(b) The report of the guardian is approved by the court; and

(c) In the case of a guardian of the property, all property has been distributed to the ward's estate or the persons entitled to it.

Laws 1989, c. 89–96, § 92; Laws 1990, c. 90–271, § 66. Amended by Laws 2006, c. 2006–178, § 26, eff. July 1, 2006.

744.531. Order of discharge

If the court is satisfied that the guardian has faithfully discharged her or his duties, has rendered a complete and accurate final report, and, in the case of a guardian of the property, has delivered the property of the ward to the person entitled, and that the interest of the ward is protected, the court shall enter an order of discharge. The discharge shall operate as a release from the duties of the guardianship and as a bar to any action against the guardian or the guardian's surety unless the action is commenced within 3 years after the date of the order.

Laws 1974, c. 74–106, § 1; Fla.St.1974, Supp. § 744.415; Laws 1975, c. 75–222, §§ 21, 26; Laws 1989, c. 89–96, § 93; Laws 1990, c. 90–271, § 67. Amended by Laws 1997, c. 97–102, § 1113, eff. July 1, 1997.

Cross References

Termination of guardianship upon removal of incapacity, death or exhaustion of assets, see Probate Rule 5.680.

744.534. Disposition of unclaimed funds held by guardian

(1) In all cases in which it is appropriate for the guardianship to terminate due to the ward's death and in which property in the hands of the guardian cannot be distributed because no estate proceeding has been instituted, the guardian of the property shall be considered an interested person pursuant to s. 733.202 and may, after a reasonable time, institute such a proceeding. In the alternative, the guardian may follow the procedures set forth in subsection (2).

(2)(a) In those cases in which it is appropriate for the guardianship to terminate pursuant to s. 744.521 and in which property in the hands of a guardian cannot be distributed to the ward or the ward's estate solely because the guardian is unable to locate the ward through diligent search, the court shall order the guardian of the property to sell the property of the ward and deposit the proceeds and cash already on hand after retaining those amounts provided for in paragraph (e) with the clerk of the court exercising jurisdiction over the guardianship and receive a receipt. The clerk shall deposit the funds in the registry of the court, to be disposed of as follows:

1. If the value of the funds is $50 or less, the clerk shall post a notice for 30 days at the courthouse door giving the amount involved, the name of the ward, and other pertinent information that will put interested persons on notice.

2. If the value of the funds is over $50, the clerk shall publish the notice once a month for 2 consecutive months in a newspaper of general circulation in the county.

3. After the expiration of 6 months from the posting or first publication, the clerk shall deposit the funds with the Chief Financial Officer after deducting his or her fees and the costs of publication.

(b) Upon receipt of the funds, the Chief Financial Officer shall deposit them to the credit of public guardianship. All interest and all income that may accrue from the money while so deposited shall belong to the fund. The funds so deposited shall constitute and be a permanent appropriation for payments by the Chief Financial Officer in obedience to court orders entered as provided by paragraph (c).

(c) Within 5 years from the date of deposit with the Chief Financial Officer, on written petition to the court that directed the deposit of the funds and informal notice to the Department of Legal Affairs, and after proof of his or her right to them, any person entitled to the funds, before or after payment to the Chief Financial Officer and deposit as provided for in paragraph (a), may obtain a court order directing the payment of the funds to him or her. All funds deposited with the Chief Financial Officer and not claimed within 5 years from the date of deposit shall escheat to the state to be deposited in the Department of Elderly Affairs Administrative Trust Fund to be used solely for the benefit of public guardianship as determined by the Secretary of Elderly Affairs.

(d) Upon depositing the funds with the clerk, the guardian of the property may proceed with the filing of his or her final return and application for discharge under s. 744.527.

(e) The guardian depositing assets with the clerk is permitted to retain from the funds in his or her possession a sufficient amount to pay the final costs of administration, including guardian and attorney's fees accruing between the deposit of the funds with the clerk of the court and the order of discharge. Any surplus funds so retained must be deposited with the clerk prior to discharge of the guardian of the property.

Laws 1986, c. 86–120, § 5; Laws 1989, c. 89–96, § 94; Laws 1990, c. 90–271, § 68. Amended by Laws 1997, c. 97–102, § 1114, eff. July 1, 1997; Laws 2002, c. 2002–195, § 7, eff. April 29, 2002; Laws 2003, c. 2003–57, § 13, eff. May 30, 2003; Laws 2003, c. 2003–261, § 1898, eff. June 26, 2003.

Cross References

Elderly Affairs department, trust fund, see § 20.415.

PART VIII. VETERANS' GUARDIANSHIP

744.602. Short title; scope of part

(1) This part shall be known and may be cited as the "Veterans' Guardianship Law."

(2) The application of this part is limited to veterans and other persons who are entitled to receive benefits from the United States Department of Veterans Affairs. This part is not intended to replace the general law relating to guardianship except insofar as this part is inconsistent with the general law relating to guardianship; in which event, this part and the general law relating to guardianship shall be read together, with any conflict between this part and the general law of guardianship to be resolved by giving effect to this part.

Laws 1929, Ex.Sess., c. 14579, § 18; Comp.Gen.Laws Supp.1936, § 2146(1); Fla.St.1983, § 293.01; Laws 1984, c. 84–62, § 1; Laws 1993, c. 93–268, § 38.

Cross References

Veterans, general provisions, see § 295.01 et seq.

744.604. Definitions

As used in this part, the term:

(1) "Adjudication by a court of competent jurisdiction" means a judicial decision or finding that a person is or is not incapacitated as provided in s. 744.331.

(2) "Adjudication by the United States Department of Veterans Affairs" means a determination or finding that a person is competent or incompetent on examination in accordance with the laws and regulations governing the United States Department of Veterans Affairs.

(3) "Secretary" means the Secretary of Veterans Affairs as head of the United States Department of Veterans Affairs or her or his successor.

(4) "Benefits" means arrears of pay, bonus, pension, compensation, insurance, and all other moneys paid or payable by the United States through the United States Department of Veterans Affairs by reason of service in the Armed Forces of the United States.

(5) "Estate" means income on hand and assets acquired in whole or in part with income.

(6) "Guardian" means any person acting as a fiduciary for a ward's person or the ward's estate, or both.

(7) "Income" means moneys received from the United States Department of Veterans Affairs as benefits, and revenue or profit from any property acquired in whole or in part with such moneys.

(8) "Person" means an individual, a partnership, a corporation, or an association.

(9) "United States Department of Veterans Affairs" means the United States Department of Veterans Affairs or its predecessors or successors.

(10) "Ward" means a beneficiary of the United States Department of Veterans Affairs.

Laws 1929, Ex.Sess., c. 14579, § 1; Comp.Gen. Laws Supp.1936, § 2146(2); Laws 1973, c. 73–304, § 1; Fla.St.1983, § 293.02; Laws 1984, c. 84–62, § 2; Laws 1989, c. 89–96, § 95; Laws 1993, c. 93–268, § 39. Amended by Laws 1997, c. 97–102, § 1115, eff. July 1, 1997.

744.607. Secretary of Veterans Affairs as party in interest

The Secretary of Veterans Affairs shall be a party in interest in any proceeding for the appointment or removal of a guardian or for the removal of the disability of minority or mental incapacity of a ward, and in any suit or other proceeding affecting in any manner the administration by the guardian of the estate of any present or former ward whose estate includes assets derived in whole or in part from benefits heretofore or hereafter paid by the United States Department of Veterans Affairs. Not less than 15 days prior to hearing in such matter, notice in writing of the time and place thereof shall be given by mail (unless waived in writing) to the office of the United States Department of Veterans Affairs having jurisdiction over the area in which any such suit or any such proceeding is pending.

Laws 1943, c. 21795, § 3; Fla.St.1983, § 293.20; Laws 1984, c. 84–62, § 3; Laws 1993, c. 93–268, § 40.

744.609. Procedure for commitment of veteran to United States Department of Veterans Affairs hospital

The procedure for the placement into a United States Department of Veterans Affairs hospital of a ward hereunder shall be the procedure prescribed in s. 394.4672.

Laws 1984, c. 84–62, § 22; Laws 1993, c. 93–268, § 41.

744.613. Appointment of guardian for ward authorized

(1) Whenever, pursuant to any law of the United States or regulation of the United States Department of Veterans Affairs, the secretary requires, prior to the payment of benefits, that a guardian be appointed for a ward, the appointment may be made in the manner hereinafter provided.

(2) When a petition is filed for the appointment of a guardian of a minor ward, a certificate of the secretary or the secretary's authorized representative setting forth the age of such minor, as shown by the records of the United States Department of Veterans Affairs, and a statement that the appointment of a guardian is a condition precedent to the payment of any moneys due to the minor by the United States Department of Veterans Affairs are prima facie evidence of the necessity for such appointment.

(3) When a petition is filed for the appointment of a guardian of a mentally incompetent ward, a certificate of the secretary or the secretary's authorized representative, setting forth the fact that the person has been found incompetent and has been rated incompetent by the United States Department of Veterans Affairs, on examination in accordance with the laws and regulations governing the United States Department of Veterans Affairs, and that the appointment of a guardian is a condition precedent to the payment of any moneys due to such person by the United States Department of Veterans Affairs, is prima facie evidence of the necessity for such appointment.

Laws 1929, Ex.Sess., c. 14579, §§ 2, 5, 6; Comp.Gen.Laws Supp.1936, §§ 2146(3), (6), (7); Laws 1973, c. 73–304, § 1; Fla.St.1983, §§ 293.03, 293.06, 293.07; Laws 1984, c. 84–62, § 5; Laws 1993, c. 93–268, § 42. Amended by Laws 1997, c. 97–102, § 1116, eff. July 1, 1997.

744.616. Petition for appointment of guardian

(1) A petition for the appointment of a guardian may be filed in any court of competent jurisdiction by, or on behalf of, any person who under existing law is entitled to priority of appointment. If no person is so entitled, or if the person so entitled neglects or refuses to file such a petition within 30 days after the mailing of notice by the United States Department of Veterans Affairs to the last known address of such person, indicating the necessity for filing the petition, a petition for such appointment may be filed in any court of competent jurisdiction by, or on behalf of, any responsible person residing in this state.

(2)(a) The petition for appointment shall set forth:

1.   The name, age, and place of residence of the ward;

2.   The names and places of residence of the nearest relative, if known;

3.   The fact that the ward is entitled to receive moneys payable by or through the United States Department of Veterans Affairs;

4.   The amount of moneys then due and the amount of probable future payments;

5.   The name and address of the person or institution, if any, having actual custody of the ward; and

6.   The name, age, relationship, if any, occupation, and address of the proposed guardian.

(b) In the case of a mentally incompetent ward, the petition shall show that the ward has been found incompetent and has been rated incompetent on examination by the United States

Department of Veterans Affairs, in accordance with the laws and regulations governing the United States Department of Veterans Affairs.

Laws 1929, Ex.Sess., c. 14579, § 4; Comp.Gen.Laws Supp.1936, § 2146(5); Laws 1973, c. 73–304, § 1; Fla.St.1983, § 293.05; Laws 1984, c. 84–62, § 6; Laws 1993, c. 93–268, § 43.

744.617. Notice by court of petition filed for appointment of guardian

(1) When a petition for the appointment of a guardian has been filed pursuant to s. 744.616, the court shall cause such notice to be given as provided by the general guardianship law. In addition, notice of the petition shall be given to the office of the United States Department of Veterans Affairs having jurisdiction over the area in which the court is located.

(2) A copy of the petition provided for in s. 744.616 shall be mailed by the clerk of the court to the person or persons for whom a guardian is to be appointed, the clerk of court mailing the copy of the petition to the last known address of such person or persons not less than 5 days prior to the date set for the hearing of the petition by the court.

Laws 1927, c. 11906, § 2; Comp.Gen.Laws 1927, § 2134; Laws 1929, Ex.Sess., c. 14579, § 7; Comp.Gen. Laws Supp.1936, § 2146(8); Fla.St.1983, §§ 293.08, 294.03; Laws 1984, c. 84–62, § 7; Laws 1993, c. 93–268, § 44;

744.618. Persons who may be appointed guardian

(1) Notwithstanding any law with respect to priority of persons entitled to appointment, or nomination in the petition, the court may appoint some other individual or a bank or trust company as guardian if the court determines that the appointment of the other individual or bank or trust company would be in the best interest of the ward.

(2) It is unlawful for a circuit judge to appoint either herself or himself, or a member of her or his family, as guardian for any person entitled to the benefits provided for in 38 U.S.C., as amended, except in a case when the person entitled to such benefits is a member of the family of the circuit judge involved.

Laws 1927, c. 11906, § 4; Comp.Gen.Laws 1927, § 2136; Laws 1973, c. 73–334, § 24; Fla.St.1983, § 294.04; Laws 1984, c. 84–62, § 6. Amended by Laws 1997, c. 97–102, § 1117, eff. July 1, 1997.

744.619. Bond of guardian

When the appointment of a guardian is made, the guardian shall execute and file a bond to be approved by the court in an amount not less than the sum of the amount of moneys then due to the ward and the amount of moneys estimated to become payable during the ensuing year. The bond shall be in the form, and shall be conditioned, as required of guardians appointed under the general guardianship laws of this state. The court has the power to require, from time to time, the guardian to file an additional bond.

Laws 1929, Ex.Sess., c. 14579, § 8; Comp.Gen.Laws Supp.1936, § 2146(9); Fla.St.1983, § 293.09; Laws 1984, c. 84–62, § 7.

744.621. Inventory of ward's property; guardian's failure to file inventory; discharge; forfeiture of commissions

Every guardian shall, within 30 days after his or her qualification and whenever subsequently required by the circuit judge, file in the circuit court a complete inventory of all the ward's personal property in his or her hands and, also, a schedule of all real estate in the state belonging to his or her ward, describing it and its quality, whether it is improved or not, and, if it is improved, in what manner, and the appraised value of same. The failure on the part of the guardian to conform to the requirements of this section is a ground for the discharge of the guardian, in which case the guardian shall forfeit all commissions.

Laws 1927, c. 11906, § 6; Comp.Gen.Laws 1927, § 2138; Laws 1973, c. 73–334, § 24; Fla.St.1983, § 294.06; Laws 1984, c. 84–62, § 10. Amended by Laws 1997, c. 97–102, § 1118, eff. July 1, 1997.

744.622. Guardian empowered to receive moneys due ward from the United States Government

A guardian appointed under the provisions of s. 744.616 may receive income and benefits payable by the United States through the United States Department of Veterans Affairs and also has the right to receive for the account of the ward any moneys due from the United States Government in the way of arrears of pay, bonus, compensation or insurance, or other sums due by reason of his or her service (or the service of the person through whom the ward claims) in the Armed Forces of the United States and any other moneys due from the United States Government, payable through its agencies or entities, together with the income derived from investments of these moneys.

Laws 1927, c. 11906, § 6; Comp.Gen.Laws 1927, § 2138; Fla.St.1983, § 294.05; Laws 1984, c. 84–62, § 8; Laws 1993, c. 93–268, § 45. Amended by Laws 1997, c. 97–102, § 1119, eff. July 1, 1997.

744.624. Guardian's application of estate funds for support and maintenance of person other than ward

A guardian shall not apply any portion of the estate of her or his ward to the support and maintenance of any person other than her or his ward, except upon order of the court after a hearing, notice of which has been given to the proper office of the United States Department of Veterans Affairs as provided in s. 744.625.

Laws 1929, Ex.Sess., c. 14579, § 13; Comp.Gen.Laws Supp.1936, § 2146(14); Laws 1973, c. 73–304, § 1; Fla.St.1983, § 293.14; Laws 1984, c. 84–62, § 10; Laws 1993, c. 93–268, § 46. Amended by Laws 1997, c. 97–102, § 1120, eff. July 1, 1997.

744.625. Petition for support, or support and education, of ward's dependents; payments of apportioned benefits prohibit contempt action against veteran

(1) Any person who is dependent on a ward for support may petition a court of competent jurisdiction for an order directing the guardian of the ward's estate to contribute from the estate of the ward to the support, or support and education, of the dependent person, when the estate of the ward is derived in whole or in part from payments of compensation, adjusted compensation, pension, insurance, or other benefits made directly to the guardian of the ward by the United States Department of Veterans Affairs. A notice of the application for support, or support and education, shall be given by the applicant to the office of the United States Department of Veterans Affairs having jurisdiction over the area in which the court is located at least 15 days before the hearing on the application.

(2) The grant or denial of an order for support, or support and education, does not preclude a further petition for an increase, decrease, modification, or termination of the allowance for such support, or support and education, by either the petitioner or the guardian.

(3) The order for the support, or support and education, of the petitioner is valid for any payment made pursuant to the order, but no valid payment can be made after the termination of the guardianship. The receipt of the petitioner shall be a sufficient release of the guardian for payments made pursuant to the order.

---

(4) When a claim for apportionment of benefits filed with the United States Department of Veterans Affairs on behalf of a dependent or dependents of a disabled veteran is approved by the United States Department of Veterans Affairs, subsequent payments of such apportioned benefits by the United States Department of Veterans Affairs prohibit an action for contempt from being instituted against the veteran.

Laws 1984, c. 84–62, § 9; Laws 1993, c. 93–268, § 47.

744.626. Exemption of benefits from claims of creditors

Except as provided by federal law, payments of benefits from the United States Department of Veterans Affairs or the Social Security Administration to or for the benefit of a disabled veteran or the veteran's surviving spouse or dependents are exempt from the claims of creditors and shall not be liable to attachment, levy, or seizure by or under any legal or equitable process whatever, either before or after the receipt of the payments by the guardian or the beneficiary.

Laws 1984, c. 84–62, § 9; Laws 1993, c. 93–268, § 48. Amended by Laws 1997, c. 97–102, § 1121, eff. July 1, 1997.

744.627. Investment of funds of estate by guardian

Every guardian shall invest the funds of the estate in such manner or in such securities, in which the guardian has no interest, as allowed by chapter 518.

Laws 1929, Ex.Sess., c. 14579, § 12; Laws 1935, c. 17473, § 1; Comp.Gen.Laws Supp.1936, § 2146(13); Fla.St.1983, § 293.13; Laws 1984, c. 84–62, § 10.

744.631. Guardian's petition for authority to sell ward's real estate; notice by publication; penalties

(1) When a guardian of the estate of a minor or an incompetent ward, which guardian has the control or management of any real estate that is the property of such minor or incompetent, deems it necessary or expedient to sell all or part of the real estate, the guardian shall apply, either in term time or in vacation by petition to the judge of the circuit court for the county in which the real estate is situated, for authority to sell all or part of the real estate. If the prayer of the petition appears to the judge to be reasonable and just and financially beneficial to the estate of the ward, the judge may authorize the guardian to sell the real estate described in the petition under such conditions as the interest of the minor or incompetent may, in the opinion of the judge, seem to require.

(2) The authority to sell the real estate described in the petition shall not be granted unless the guardian has given previous notice, published once a week for 4 successive weeks in a newspaper published in the county where the application is made, of his or her intention to make application to the judge for authority to sell such real estate, the guardian setting forth in the notice the time and place and to what judge the application will be made. If the lands lie in more than one county, the application for such authority shall be made in each county in which the lands lie.

(3) The failure on the part of the guardian to comply with the provisions of this section makes the guardian and the guardian's bond agents individually responsible for any loss that may accrue to the estate of the ward involved, and is a ground for the immediate removal of such guardian as to his or her functions, but does not discharge the guardian as to his or her liability or discharge the liabilities of his or her sureties.

Laws 1927, c. 11906, § 9; Comp.Gen.Laws 1927, § 2141; Laws 1973, c. 73–334, § 24; Fla.St.1983, § 294.10; Laws 1984, c. 84–62, § 11. Amended by Laws 1997, c. 97–102, § 1122, eff. July 1, 1997.

744.634. Guardian's accounts, filing with court and certification to United States Department of Veterans Affairs; notice and hearing on accounts; failure to account

(1) Every guardian who receives on account of his or her ward any moneys from the United States Department of Veterans Affairs shall annually file with the court on the anniversary date of the appointment, in addition to such other accounts as may be required by the court, a full, true, and accurate account under oath, which account is an account of all moneys so received by him or her and of all disbursements from such moneys, and which account shows the balance of the moneys in his or her hands at the date of such filing and shows how the moneys are invested. A certified copy of each of such accounts filed with the court shall be sent by the guardian to the office of the United States Department of Veterans Affairs having jurisdiction over the area in which such court is located. If the requirement of certification is waived in writing by the United States Department of Veterans Affairs, an uncertified copy of each of such accounts shall be sent.

(2) The court, at its discretion or upon the petition of an interested party, shall fix a time and place for the hearing on such account; and notice of the hearing shall be given by the court to the United States Department of Veterans Affairs not less than 15 days prior to the date fixed for the hearing.

(3) The court need not appoint a guardian ad litem to represent the ward at the hearing provided for in subsection (2). If the residence of the next kin of the ward is known, notice by registered mail shall be sent to such relative. Notice also shall be served on the ward; or, if the ward is mentally incapable of understanding the matter at issue, the notice may be served on the person in charge of the institution where the ward is detained, or on the person having charge or custody of the ward.

(4) When a hearing on an account is required by the court or requested in the petition of an interested party as provided in subsection (2), the judge of the court on the day of the hearing as provided for in subsection (2) shall carefully examine the vouchers and audit and state the account between the guardian and ward. Proper evidence shall be required in support of any voucher or item of the account that may appear to the court not to be just and proper, such evidence to be taken by affidavit or by any other legal mode. If any voucher is rejected, the item or items covered by the disapproval of any voucher or vouchers shall be taxed against the guardian personally. After such examination, the court shall render a decree upon the account, which shall be entered on the record, and the account and vouchers shall be filed. Such partial settlement shall be taken and presumed as correct on final settlement of the guardianship.

(5) If a guardian fails to file any account of the moneys received by him or her from the United States Department of Veterans Affairs on account of his or her ward within 30 days after such account is required by either the court or the United States Department of Veterans Affairs, or fails to furnish the United States Department of Veterans Affairs a copy of his or her accounts as required by subsection (1), such failure shall be a ground for the removal of the guardian.
Laws 1927, c. 11906, §§ 7, 8; Comp.Gen.Laws 1927, §§ 2139, 2140; Laws 1929, Ex.Sess., c. 14579, §§ 9, 10; Comp.Gen.Laws Supp.1936, § 2146(10), (11); Laws 1973, c. 73–304, § 1; Fla.St.1983, §§ 293.10, 293.11, 294.08, 294.09; Laws 1984, c. 84–62, § 12; Laws 1993, c. 93–268, § 49. Amended by Laws 1997, c. 97–102, § 1123, eff. July 1, 1997.

744.637. Certified copies of public records made available

When a copy of any public record is required by the United States Department of Veterans Affairs to be used in determining the eligibility of any person to participate in benefits made available by the United States Department of Veterans Affairs, the official charged with the custody of such public record shall, without charge, provide to the applicant for such benefits or any person acting on her or his behalf, or to the authorized representative of the United States Department of Veterans Affairs, a certified copy of such record. For each and every certified copy so furnished by the official, the official shall be paid by the board of county commissioners the fee provided by law for copies.

Laws 1929, Ex.Sess., c. 14579, § 14; Comp.Gen.Laws Supp.1936, § 2146(15); Laws 1955, c. 29749, § 7; Laws 1973, c. 73–304, § 1; Fla.St.1983, § 293.15; Laws 1984, c. 84–62, § 13; Laws 1993, c. 93–268, § 50. Amended by Laws 1997, c. 97–102, § 1124, eff. July 1, 1997.

744.638.   Clerk of the circuit court; fees; duties

Upon the filing of the petition for guardianship, granting of same, and entering decree thereon, the clerk of the circuit court is entitled to the service charge as provided by law, which shall include the cost of recording the petition, bond, and decree and the issuing of letters of guardianship. The certificate of the secretary or the secretary's authorized representative provided for in s. 744.613 need not be recorded but must be kept in the file. Upon issuing letters of guardianship or letters appointing a guardian for the estate of a minor or incompetent, the clerk of the circuit court shall send to the regional office of the United States Department of Veterans Affairs having jurisdiction in this state two certified copies of the letters and two certified copies of the bond approved by the court, without charge or expense to the estate involved. The clerk of the circuit court shall also send a certified copy of such letters to the property appraiser and to the tax collector in each county in which the ward owns real property.

Laws 1927, c. 11906, § 10; Comp.Gen.Laws 1927, § 2142; Laws 1973, c. 73–304, § 1; Laws 1973, c. 73–334, § 24; Fla.St.1983, § 294.11; Laws 1987, c. 87–145, § 11; Laws 1993, c. 93–268, § 51; Laws 1984, c. 84–62, § 7. Amended by Laws 1997, c. 97–102, § 1125, eff. July 1, 1997.

744.639.   Attorney's fee

The fee for the attorney filing the petition and conducting the proceedings shall be fixed by the court in an amount as small as reasonably possible, not to exceed $250. However, this section is not to be interpreted to exclude a petition for extraordinary attorney's fees, properly filed, and if approved by the United States Department of Veterans Affairs, does not necessitate a hearing before the court for approval, but the court shall enter its order for withdrawal of said attorney's fees from the ward's guardianship account accordingly.

Laws 1927, c. 11906, § 10; Comp.Gen.Laws 1927, § 2142; Laws 1973, c. 73–304, § 1; Laws 1973, c. 73–334, § 24; Fla.St.1983, § 294.11; Laws 1984, c. 84–62, § 7; Laws 1995, c. 95–401, § 31. Amended by Laws 1997, c. 97–93, § 16, eff. July 1, 1997.

744.641.   Guardian's compensation; bond premiums

The amount of compensation payable to a guardian shall not exceed 5 percent of the income of the ward during any year and may be taken, by the guardian, on a monthly basis. In the event of extraordinary services rendered by such guardian, the court may, upon petition and after hearing on the petition, authorize additional compensation for the extraordinary services, payable from the estate of the ward. Provided that extraordinary services approved by the United States Department of Veteran's Affairs do not require a court hearing for approval of the fees, but shall require an order authorizing the guardian to withdraw the amount from the guardianship account. No compensation shall be allowed on the corpus of an estate received from a preceding guardian. The guardian may be allowed from the estate of her or his ward reasonable premiums paid by the guardian to any corporate surety upon the guardian's bond.

Laws 1929, Ex.Sess., c. 14579, § 11; Comp.Gen.Laws Supp.1936, § 2146(12); Laws 1973, c. 73–304, § 1; Fla.St.1983, § 293.12; Laws 1984, c. 84–62, § 14; Laws 1985, c. 85–62, § 63; Laws 1993, c. 93–268, § 52; Laws 1995, c. 95–401, § 32. Amended by Laws 1997, c. 97–102, § 1126, eff. July 1, 1997; Laws 1999, c. 99–3, § 85, eff. June 29, 1999.

744.643. Discharge of guardian of minor or incompetent ward

When a minor ward, for whom a guardian has been appointed under the provisions of this part or other laws of this state, attains his or her majority and, if such minor ward has been incompetent, is declared competent by the United States Department of Veterans Affairs and the court, or when an incompetent ward who is not a minor is declared competent by the United States Department of Veterans Affairs and the court, the guardian shall, upon making a satisfactory accounting, be discharged upon a petition filed for that purpose.

Laws 1929, Ex.Sess., c. 14579, § 16; Comp.Gen.Laws Supp.1936, § 2146(17); Laws 1973, c. 73–304, § 1; Fla.St.1983, § 293.17; Laws 1984, c. 84–62, § 15; Laws 1993, c. 93–268, § 53. Amended by Laws 1997, c. 97–102, § 1127, eff. July 1, 1997.

744.646. Final settlement of guardianship; notice required; guardian ad litem fee; papers required by United States Department of Veterans Affairs

On the final settlement of the guardianship, the notice provided herein for partial settlement must be given and the other proceedings conducted as in the case of partial settlement, except that a guardian ad litem may be appointed to represent the ward, the fee of which guardian ad litem shall in no case exceed $150. However, if the ward has been pronounced competent, is shown to be mentally sound, appears in court, and is 18 years of age, the settlement may be had between the guardian and the ward under the direction of the court without notice to the next of kin, or the appointment of a guardian ad litem. A certified copy of the final settlement so made in every case must be filed with the United States Department of Veterans Affairs by the clerk of the court.

Laws 1927, c. 11906, § 11; Comp.Gen.Laws 1927, § 2143; Laws 1973, c. 73–304, § 1; Laws 1977, c. 77–121, § 13; Fla.St.1983, § 294.12; Laws 1984, c. 84–62, § 16; Laws 1993, c. 93–268, § 54.

744.649. Notice of appointment of general guardian; closing of veteran's guardianship; transfer of responsibilities and penalties to general guardian

When the appointment of a general guardian has been made in the proper court and such guardian has qualified and taken charge of the other property of the ward, the general guardian shall file notice of such appointment in the court in which the veteran's guardianship is pending and have the veteran's guardianship settled up and closed so that the general guardian may take charge of the moneys referred to and described in ss. 744.613(2) and (3) and 744.622. When the appointment of a general guardian, whether for an incompetent or minor child or another beneficiary entitled to the benefits provided in 38 U.S.C., as amended, has been confirmed by the court having jurisdiction, such general guardian is responsible and is subject to the provisions and penalties contained in 38 U.S.C., as amended, as well as the requirements pertaining to guardians as set forth in this part.

Laws 1927, c. 11906, § 6; Comp.Gen.Laws 1927, § 2138; Fla.St.1983, § 294.07; Laws 1984, c. 84–62, § 17.

744.652. Construction and application of part

This part shall be construed liberally to secure the beneficial intents and purposes of this part and applies only to beneficiaries of the United States Department of Veterans Affairs. It shall be so interpreted and construed as to effectuate its general purpose of making the welfare of such beneficiaries the primary concern of their guardians and of the court.

Laws 1929, Ex.Sess., c. 14579, §§ 17, 19; Comp.Gen.Laws Supp.1936, § 2146(18); Laws 1973, c. 73–304, § 1; Fla.St.1983, § 293.18; Laws 1984, c. 84–62, § 18; Laws 1993, c. 93–268, § 55.

744.653. Annual guardianship report

Guardians appointed under the Veterans' Guardianship Law shall not be required to comply with the provisions of s. 744.367.

Laws 1991, c. 91–306, § 6.

PART IX. PUBLIC GUARDIANSHIP

744.701. Short title

This act shall be known and may be cited as the "Public Guardianship Act."

Laws 1986, c. 86–120, § 1; Laws 1989, c. 89–96, § 96.

744.702. Legislative intent

The Legislature finds that private guardianship is inadequate where there is no willing and responsible family member or friend, other person, bank, or corporation available to serve as guardian for an incapacitated person, and such person does not have adequate income or wealth for the compensation of a private guardian. The Legislature intends through this act to establish the Statewide Public Guardianship Office, and permit the establishment of offices of public guardian for the purpose of providing guardianship services for incapacitated persons when no private guardian is available. The Legislature further finds that alternatives to guardianship and less intrusive means of assistance should always be explored, including, but not limited to, guardian advocates, before an individual's rights are removed through an adjudication of incapacity. The purpose of this legislation is to provide a public guardian only to those persons whose needs cannot be met through less drastic means of intervention.

Laws 1986, c. 86–120, § 1; Laws 1989, c. 89–96, § 97. Amended by Laws 1999, c. 99–277, § 3, eff. Oct. 1, 1999.

744.7021. Statewide Public Guardianship Office

There is hereby created the Statewide Public Guardianship Office within the Department of Elderly Affairs.

(1) The Secretary of Elderly Affairs shall appoint the executive director, who shall be the head of the Statewide Public Guardianship Office. The executive director must be a member of The Florida Bar, knowledgeable of guardianship law and of the social services available to meet the needs of incapacitated persons, shall serve on a full-time basis, and shall personally, or through representatives of the office, carry out the purposes and functions of the Statewide Public Guardianship Office in accordance with state and federal law. The executive director shall serve at the pleasure of and report to the secretary.

(2) The executive director shall, within available resources, have oversight responsibilities for all public guardians.

(a) The executive director shall review the current public guardian programs in Florida and other states.

(b) The executive director, in consultation with local guardianship offices, shall develop statewide performance measures and standards.

(c) The executive director shall review the various methods of funding guardianship programs, the kinds of services being provided by such programs, and the demographics of the wards. In addition, the executive director shall review and make recommendations regarding the feasibility of recovering a portion or all of the costs of providing public guardianship services from the assets or income of the wards.

(d) By January 1 of each year, the executive director shall provide a status report and provide further recommendations to the secretary that address the need for public guardianship services and related issues.

(e) The executive director may provide assistance to local governments or entities in pursuing grant opportunities. The executive director shall review and make recommendations in the annual report on the availability and efficacy of seeking Medicaid matching funds. The executive director shall diligently seek ways to use existing programs and services to meet the needs of public wards.

(f) The executive director, in consultation with the Florida Guardianship Foundation, shall develop a guardianship training program curriculum that may be offered to all guardians whether public or private.

(3) The executive director may conduct or contract for demonstration projects authorized by the Department of Elderly Affairs, within funds appropriated or through gifts, grants, or contributions for such purposes, to determine the feasibility or desirability of new concepts of organization, administration, financing, or service delivery designed to preserve the civil and constitutional rights of persons of marginal or diminished capacity. Any gifts, grants, or contributions for such purposes shall be deposited in the Department of Elderly Affairs Administrative Trust Fund.

Added by Laws 1999, c. 99–277, § 4, eff. Oct. 1, 1999. Amended by Laws 2003, c. 2003–57, § 14, eff. May 30, 2003; Laws 2003, c. 2003–262, § 5, eff. July 1, 2003; Laws 2005, c. 2005–2, § 140, eff. July 5, 2005; Laws 2013, c. 2013–18, § 107, eff. July 2, 2013.

Cross References

Elderly Affairs department, trust fund, see § 20.415.

744.703. Office of public guardian; appointment, notification

(1) The executive director of the Statewide Public Guardianship Office, after consultation with the chief judge and other circuit judges within the judicial circuit and with appropriate advocacy groups and individuals and organizations who are knowledgeable about the needs of incapacitated persons, may establish, within a county in the judicial circuit or within the judicial circuit, one or more offices of public guardian and if so established, shall create a list of persons best qualified to serve as the public guardian, who have been investigated pursuant to s. 744.3135. The public guardian must have knowledge of the legal process and knowledge of social services available to meet the needs of incapacitated persons. The public guardian shall maintain a staff or contract with professionally qualified individuals to carry out the guardianship functions, including an attorney who has experience in probate areas and another person who has a master's degree in social work, or a gerontologist, psychologist, registered nurse, or

nurse practitioner. A public guardian that is a nonprofit corporate guardian under s. 744.309(5) must receive tax-exempt status from the United States Internal Revenue Service.

(2) The executive director shall appoint or contract with a public guardian from the list of candidates described in subsection (1). A public guardian must meet the qualifications for a guardian as prescribed in s. 744.309(1)(a). Upon appointment of the public guardian, the executive director shall notify the chief judge of the judicial circuit and the Chief Justice of the Supreme Court of Florida, in writing, of the appointment.

(3) If the needs of the county or circuit do not require a full-time public guardian, a part-time public guardian may be appointed at reduced compensation.

(4) A public guardian, whether full-time or part-time, may not hold any position that would create a conflict of interest.

(5) The public guardian is to be appointed for a term of 4 years, after which her or his appointment must be reviewed by the executive director, and may be reappointed for a term of up to 4 years. The executive director may suspend a public guardian with or without the request of the chief judge. If a public guardian is suspended, the executive director shall appoint an acting public guardian as soon as possible to serve until such time as a permanent replacement is selected. A public guardian may be removed from office during the term of office only by the executive director who must consult with the chief judge prior to said removal. A recommendation of removal made by the chief judge must be considered by the executive director.

(6) Public guardians who have been previously appointed by a chief judge prior to the effective date of this act pursuant to this section may continue in their positions until the expiration of their term pursuant to their agreement. However, oversight of all public guardians shall transfer to the Statewide Public Guardianship Office upon the effective date of this act. The executive director of the Statewide Public Guardianship Office shall be responsible for all future appointments of public guardians pursuant to this act.

Laws 1986, c. 86–120, § 1; Laws 1989, c. 89–96, § 98; Laws 1995, c. 95–211, § 69; Laws 1995, c. 95–401, § 27; Laws 1996, c. 96–354, § 16. Amended by Laws 1997, c. 97–102, § 1789, eff. July 1, 1997; Laws 1999, c. 99–277, § 5, eff. Oct. 1, 1999; Laws 2002, c. 2002–195, § 8, eff. April 29, 2002.

Cross References

Notice, appointment of public guardian, see Probate Rule 5.560.

744.704. Powers and duties

(1) A public guardian may serve as a guardian of a person adjudicated incapacitated under this chapter if there is no family member or friend, other person, bank, or corporation willing and qualified to serve as guardian.

(2) The public guardian shall be vested with all the powers and duties of a guardian under this chapter, except as otherwise provided by law.

(3) The public guardian shall primarily serve incapacitated persons who are of limited financial means, as defined by contract or rule of the Department of Elderly Affairs. The public guardian may serve incapacitated persons of greater financial means to the extent the Department of Elderly Affairs determines to be appropriate.

(4) The public guardian shall be authorized to employ sufficient staff to carry out the duties of his or her office.

(5) The public guardian may delegate to assistants and other members of his or her staff the powers and duties of the office of public guardian, except as otherwise limited by law. The public guardian shall retain ultimate responsibility for the discharge of his or her duties and responsibilities.

(6) The public guardian, when appointed guardian of an incapacitated person, shall seek a family member or friend, other person, bank, or corporation who is qualified and willing to serve as guardian. Upon determining that there is someone qualified and willing to serve as guardian, either the public guardian or the qualified person shall petition the court for appointment of a successor guardian.

(7) A public guardian shall not commit a ward to a mental health treatment facility, as defined in s. 394.455(32), without an involuntary placement proceeding as provided by law.

(8) When a person is appointed successor public guardian, he or she immediately succeeds to all·rights, duties, responsibilities, and powers of the preceding public guardian.

(9) When the position of public guardian is vacant, subordinate personnel employed under subsection (4) shall continue to act as if the position of public guardian were filled.

Laws 1986, c. 86–120, § 1; Laws 1989, c. 89–96, § 99; Laws 1996, c. 96–169, § 45. Amended by Laws 1997, c. 97–102, § 1790, eff. July 1, 1997; Laws 1999, c. 99–3, § 86, eff. June 29, 1999; Laws 2003, c. 2003–57, § 15, eff. May 30, 2003; Laws 2006, c. 2006–227, § 71, eff. July 1, 2006.

744.705. Costs of public guardian

(1) All costs of administration, including filing fees, shall be paid from the budget of the office of public guardian. No costs of administration, including filing fees, shall be recovered from the assets or the income of the ward.

(2) In any proceeding for appointment of a public guardian, or in any proceeding involving the estate of a ward for whom a public guardian has been appointed guardian, the court may waive any court costs or filing fees.

Laws 1986, c. 86–120, § 1; Laws 1989, c. 89–96, § 100.

744.706. Preparation of budget

Each public guardian, whether funded in whole or in part by money raised through local efforts, grants, or any other source or whether funded in whole or in part by the state, shall prepare a budget for the operation of the office of public guardian to be submitted to the Statewide Public Guardianship Office. As appropriate, the Statewide Public Guardianship Office will include such budgetary information in the Department of Elderly Affairs' legislative budget request. The office of public guardian shall be operated within the limitations of the General Appropriations Act and any other funds appropriated by the Legislature to that particular judicial circuit, subject to the provisions of chapter 216. The Department of Elderly Affairs shall make a separate and distinct request for an appropriation for the Statewide Public Guardianship Office. However, this section shall not be construed to preclude the financing of any operations of the office of the public guardian by moneys raised through local effort or through the efforts of the Statewide Public Guardianship Office.

Laws 1986, c. 86–120, § 1; Laws 1989, c. 89–96, § 101. Amended by Laws 1999, c. 99–277, § 6, eff. Oct. 1, 1999.

744.707. Procedures and rules

The public guardian, subject to the oversight of the Statewide Public Guardianship Office, is authorized to:

(1) Formulate and adopt necessary procedures to assure the efficient conduct of the affairs of the ward and general administration of the office and staff.

(2) Contract for services necessary to discharge the duties of the office.

(3) Accept the services of volunteer persons or organizations and provide reimbursement for proper and necessary expenses.

Laws 1986, c. 86–120, § 1; Laws 1989, c. 89–96, § 102. Amended by Laws 1999, c. 99–277, § 7, eff. Oct. 1, 1999.

744.708. Reports and standards

(1) The public guardian shall keep and maintain proper financial, case control, and statistical records on all matters in which the public guardian serves as guardian.

(2) No report or disclosure of the ward's personal and medical records shall be made, except as authorized by law.

(3) A public guardian shall file an annual report on the operations of the office of public guardian, in writing, by September 1 for the preceding fiscal year with the Statewide Public Guardianship Office which shall have responsibility for supervision of the operations of the office of public guardian.

(4) Within 6 months of his or her appointment as guardian of a ward, the public guardian shall submit to the clerk of the court for placement in the ward's guardianship file and to the executive director of the Statewide Public Guardianship Office a report on his or her efforts to locate a family member or friend, other person, bank, or corporation to act as guardian of the ward and a report on the ward's potential to be restored to capacity.

(5)(a) Each office of public guardian shall undergo an independent audit by a qualified certified public accountant at least once every 2 years. A copy of the audit report shall be submitted to the Statewide Public Guardianship Office.

(b) In addition to regular monitoring activities, the Statewide Public Guardianship Office shall conduct an investigation into the practices of each office of public guardian related to the managing of each ward's personal affairs and property. If feasible, the investigation shall be conducted in conjunction with the financial audit of each office of public guardian under paragraph (a).

(6) A public guardian shall ensure that each of the guardian's wards is personally visited by the public guardian or by one of the guardian's professional staff at least once each calendar quarter. During this personal visit, the public guardian or the professional staff person shall assess:

(a) The ward's physical appearance and condition.

(b) The appropriateness of the ward's current living situation.

(c) The need for any additional services and the necessity for continuation of existing services, taking into consideration all aspects of social, psychological, educational, direct service, health, and personal care needs.

(7) The ratio for professional staff to wards shall be 1 professional to 40 wards. The Statewide Public Guardianship Office may increase or decrease the ratio after consultation with

the local public guardian and the chief judge of the circuit court. The basis for the decision to increase or decrease the prescribed ratio must be included in the annual report to the secretary.

Laws 1986, c. 86–120, § 1; Laws 1989, c. 89–96, § 103; Laws 1996, c. 96–354, § 17. Amended by Laws 1997, c. 97–102, § 1791, eff. July 1, 1997; Laws 1999, c. 99–277, § 8, eff. Oct. 1, 1999; Laws 2001, c. 2001–266, § 127, eff. July 1, 2001; Laws 2006, c. 2006–178, § 27, eff. July 1, 2006; Laws 2010, c. 2010–102, § 159, eff. May 26, 2010.

Cross References

Report of public guardian, see Probate Rule 5.710.

744.7081. Access to records by Statewide Public Guardianship Office; confidentiality

Notwithstanding any other provision of law to the contrary, any medical, financial, or mental health records held by an agency, or the court and its agencies, which are necessary to evaluate the public guardianship system, to assess the need for additional public guardianship, or to develop required reports, shall be provided to the Statewide Public Guardianship Office upon that office's request. Any confidential or exempt information provided to the Statewide Public Guardianship Office shall continue to be held confidential or exempt as otherwise provided by law. All records held by the Statewide Public Guardianship Office relating to the medical, financial, or mental health of vulnerable adults as defined in chapter 415, persons with a developmental disability as defined in chapter 393, or persons with a mental illness as defined in chapter 394, shall be confidential and exempt from s. 119.07(1) and s. 24(a), Art. I of the State Constitution.

Added by Laws 1999, c. 99–278, § 1, eff. Oct. 1, 1999. Amended by Laws 2000, c. 2000–349, § 112, eff. Sept. 1, 2000; Laws 2004, c. 2004–361, § 1, eff. Oct. 1, 2004.

744.7082. Direct-support organization; definition; use of property; board of directors; audit; dissolution

(1) **Definition.**—As used in this section, the term "direct-support organization" means an organization whose sole purpose is to support the Statewide Public Guardianship Office and is:

(a) A not-for-profit corporation incorporated under chapter 617 and approved by the Department of State;

(b) Organized and operated to conduct programs and activities; to raise funds; to request and receive grants, gifts, and bequests of moneys; to acquire, receive, hold, invest, and administer, in its own name, securities, funds, objects of value, or other property, real or personal; and to make expenditures to or for the direct or indirect benefit of the Statewide Public Guardianship Office; and

(c) Determined by the Statewide Public Guardianship Office to be consistent with the goals of the office, in the best interests of the state, and in accordance with the adopted goals and mission of the Department of Elderly Affairs and the Statewide Public Guardianship Office.

(2) **Contract.**—The direct-support organization shall operate under a written contract with the Statewide Public Guardianship Office. The written contract must provide for:

(a) Certification by the Statewide Public Guardianship Office that the direct-support organization is complying with the terms of the contract and is doing so consistent with the goals and purposes of the office and in the best interests of the state. This certification must be made annually and reported in the official minutes of a meeting of the direct-support organization.

(b) The reversion of moneys and property held in trust by the direct-support organization:

1. To the Statewide Public Guardianship Office if the direct-support organization is no longer approved to operate for the office;

2. To the Statewide Public Guardianship Office if the direct-support organization ceases to exist;

3. To the Department of Elderly Affairs if the Statewide Public Guardianship Office ceases to exist; or

4. To the state if the Department of Elderly Affairs ceases to exist.

The fiscal year of the direct-support organization shall begin on July 1 of each year and end on June 30 of the following year.

(c) The disclosure of the material provisions of the contract, and the distinction between the Statewide Public Guardianship Office and the direct-support organization, to donors of gifts, contributions, or bequests, including such disclosure on all promotional and fundraising publications.

(3) Board of directors.—The Secretary of Elderly Affairs shall appoint a board of directors for the direct-support organization from a list of nominees submitted by the executive director of the Statewide Public Guardianship Office.

(4) Use of property.—The Department of Elderly Affairs may permit, without charge, appropriate use of fixed property and facilities of the department or the Statewide Public Guardianship Office by the direct-support organization. The department may prescribe any condition with which the direct-support organization must comply in order to use fixed property or facilities of the department or the Statewide Public Guardianship Office.

(5) Moneys.—Any moneys may be held in a separate depository account in the name of the direct-support organization and subject to the provisions of the written contract with the Statewide Public Guardianship Office. Expenditures of the direct-support organization shall be expressly used to support the Statewide Public Guardianship Office. The expenditures of the direct-support organization may not be used for the purpose of lobbying as defined in s. 11.045.

(6) Public records.—Personal identifying information of a donor or prospective donor to the direct-support organization who desires to remain anonymous is confidential and exempt from s. 119.07(1) and s. 24(a), Art. I of the State Constitution.

(7) Audit.—The direct-support organization shall provide for an annual financial audit in accordance with s. 215.981.

(8) Dissolution.—After July 1, 2004, any not-for-profit corporation incorporated under chapter 617 that is determined by a circuit court to be representing itself as a direct-support organization created under this section, but that does not have a written contract with the Statewide Public Guardianship Office in compliance with this section, is considered to meet the grounds for a judicial dissolution described in s. 617.1430(1)(a). The Statewide Public Guardianship Office shall be the recipient for all assets held by the dissolved corporation which accrued during the period that the dissolved corporation represented itself as a direct-support organization created under this section.

(9) Repeal.—This section is repealed October 1, 2018, unless reviewed and saved from repeal by the Legislature.

Added by Laws 2002, c. 2002–195, § 9, eff. April 29, 2002. Amended by Laws 2004, c. 2004–260, § 14, eff. May 28, 2004. Amended by Laws 2006, c. 2006–179, § 1, eff. July 1, 2006; Laws 2011, c. 2011–228, § 1, eff. Oct. 1, 2011; Laws 2014, c. 2014–96, § 25, eff. June 13, 2014.

Repeal

This section is repealed by its own terms on October 1, 2018, unless reviewed and saved from repeal by the Legislature.

744.709. Surety bond

Upon taking office, a public guardian shall file a bond with surety as prescribed in s. 45.011 to be approved by the clerk. The bond shall be payable to the Governor and the Governor's successors in office, in the penal sum of not less than $5,000 nor more than $25,000, conditioned on the faithful performance of all duties by the guardian. The amount of the bond shall be fixed by the majority of the judges within the judicial circuit. In form the bond shall be joint and several. The bond shall be purchased from the funds of the local office of public guardian.

Laws 1986, c. 86–120, § 1; Laws 1989, c. 89–96, § 104. Amended by Laws 1997, c. 97–102, § 1128, eff. July 1, 1997; Laws 1999, c. 99–277, § 11, eff. Oct. 1, 1999.

744.7101. Short title

Sections 744.7101–744.715 may be cited as the "Joining Forces for Public Guardianship Act."

Added by Laws 2004, c. 2004–260, § 1, eff. July 1, 2004.

744.711. Legislative findings and intent

The Legislature finds that public guardianship programs are necessary to ensure that the rights and best interests of Florida's vulnerable indigent and incapacitated residents are protected. In addition, the Legislature finds that the best solution to this problem is to encourage each county to establish, through the Statewide Public Guardianship Office, a local office of public guardian for the purpose of providing guardianship services to incapacitated persons when a private guardian is not available. Therefore, the Legislature intends to establish the Joining Forces for Public Guardianship matching grant program for the purpose of assisting counties to establish and fund community-supported public guardianship programs.

Added by Laws 2004, c. 2004–260, § 2, eff. July 1, 2004.

744.712. Joining Forces for Public Guardianship grant program; purpose

The Joining Forces for Public Guardianship matching grant program shall be established and administered by the Statewide Public Guardianship Office within the Department of Elderly Affairs. The purpose of the program is to provide startup funding to encourage communities to develop and administer locally funded and supported public guardianship programs to address the needs of indigent and incapacitated residents.

(1) The Statewide Public Guardianship Office may distribute the grant funds as follows:

(a) As initial startup funding to encourage counties that have no office of public guardian to establish an office, or as initial startup funding to open an additional office of public guardian within a county whose public guardianship needs require more than one office of public guardian.

(b) As support funding to operational offices of public guardian that demonstrate a necessity for funds to meet the public guardianship needs of a particular geographic area in the state which the office serves.

(c) To assist counties that have an operating public guardianship program but that propose to expand the geographic area or population of persons they serve, or to develop and administer innovative programs to increase access to public guardianship in this state.

Notwithstanding this subsection, the executive director of the office may award emergency grants if he or she determines that the award is in the best interests of public guardianship in this state. Before making an emergency grant, the executive director must obtain the written approval of the Secretary of Elderly Affairs. Subsections (2), (3), and (4) do not apply to the distribution of emergency grant funds.

(2) One or more grants may be awarded within a county. However, a county may not receive an award that equals, or multiple awards that cumulatively equal, more than 20 percent of the total amount of grant funds appropriated during any fiscal year.

(3) If an applicant is eligible and meets the requirements to receive grant funds more than once, the Statewide Public Guardianship Office shall award funds to prior awardees in the following manner:

(a) In the second year that grant funds are awarded, the cumulative sum of the award provided to one or more applicants within the same county may not exceed 75 percent of the total amount of grant funds awarded within that county in year one.

(b) In the third year that grant funds are awarded, the cumulative sum of the award provided to one or more applicants within the same county may not exceed 60 percent of the total amount of grant funds awarded within that county in year one.

(c) In the fourth year that grant funds are awarded, the cumulative sum of the award provided to one or more applicants within the same county may not exceed 45 percent of the total amount of grant funds awarded within that county in year one.

(d) In the fifth year that grant funds are awarded, the cumulative sum of the award provided to one or more applicants within the same county may not exceed 30 percent of the total amount of grant funds awarded within that county in year one.

(e) In the sixth year that grant funds are awarded, the cumulative sum of the award provided to one or more applicants within the same county may not exceed 15 percent of the total amount of grant funds awarded within that county in year one.

The Statewide Public Guardianship Office may not award grant funds to any applicant within a county that has received grant funds for more than 6 years.

(4) Grant funds shall be used only to provide direct services to indigent wards, except that up to 10 percent of the grant funds may be retained by the awardee for administrative expenses.

(5) Implementation of the program is subject to a specific appropriation by the Legislature in the General Appropriations Act.

Added by Laws 2004, c. 2004-260, § 3, eff. July 1, 2004.

744.713. Program administration; duties of the Statewide Public Guardianship Office

The Statewide Public Guardianship Office shall administer the grant program. The office shall:

(1) Publicize the availability of grant funds to entities that may be eligible for the funds.

(2) Establish an application process for submitting a grant proposal.

(3) Request, receive, and review proposals from applicants seeking grant funds.

(4) Determine the amount of grant funds each awardee may receive and award grant funds to applicants.

(5) Develop a monitoring process to evaluate grant awardees, which may include an annual monitoring visit to each awardee's local office.

(6) Ensure that persons or organizations awarded grant funds meet and adhere to the requirements of this act.

Added by Laws 2004, c. 2004–260, § 4, eff. July 1, 2004. Amended by Laws 2013, c. 2013–18, § 108, eff. July 2, 2013.

744.714. Eligibility

(1) Any person or organization that has not been awarded a grant must meet all of the following conditions to be eligible to receive a grant:

(a) The applicant must meet or directly employ staff that meet the minimum qualifications for a public guardian under this chapter.

(b) The applicant must have already been appointed by, or is pending appointment by, the Statewide Public Guardianship Office to become an office of public guardian in this state.

(2) Any person or organization that has been awarded a grant must meet all of the following conditions to be eligible to receive another grant:

(a) The applicant must meet or directly employ staff that meet the minimum qualifications for a public guardian under this chapter.

(b) The applicant must have been appointed by, or is pending reappointment by, the Statewide Public Guardianship Office to be an office of public guardian in this state.

(c) The applicant must have achieved a satisfactory monitoring score during the applicant's most recent evaluation.

Added by Laws 2004, c. 2004–260, § 5, eff. July 1, 2004.

744.715. Grant application requirements; review criteria; awards process

Grant applications must be submitted to the Statewide Public Guardianship Office for review and approval.

(1) A grant application must contain:

(a) The specific amount of funds being requested.

(b) The proposed annual budget for the office of public guardian for which the applicant is applying on behalf of, including all sources of funding, and a detailed report of proposed expenditures, including administrative costs.

(c) The total number of wards the applicant intends to serve during the grant period.

(d) Evidence that the applicant has:

1. Attempted to procure funds and has exhausted all possible other sources of funding; or

2. Procured funds from local sources, but the total amount of the funds collected or pledged is not sufficient to meet the need for public guardianship in the geographic area that the applicant intends to serve.

(e) An agreement or confirmation from a local funding source, such as a county, municipality, or any other public or private organization, that the local funding source will contribute matching funds to the public guardianship program totaling not less than $1 for every $1 of grant funds awarded. For purposes of this section, an applicant may provide evidence of agreements or confirmations from multiple local funding sources showing that the local funding sources will pool their contributed matching funds to the public guardianship program for a combined total of not less than $1 for every $1 of grant funds awarded. In–kind contributions, such as materials, commodities, office space, or other types of facilities, personnel services, or other items as determined by rule shall be considered by the office and may be counted as part or all of the local matching funds.

(f) A detailed plan describing how the office of public guardian for which the applicant is applying on behalf of will be funded in future years.

(g) Any other information determined by rule as necessary to assist in evaluating grant applicants.

(2) If the Statewide Public Guardianship Office determines that an applicant meets the requirements for an award of grant funds, the office may award the applicant any amount of grant funds the executive director deems appropriate, if the amount awarded meets the requirements of this act. The office may adopt a rule allocating the maximum allowable amount of grant funds which may be expended on any ward.

(3) A grant awardee must submit a new grant application for each year of additional funding.

(4)(a) In the first year of the Joining Forces for Public Guardianship program's existence, the Statewide Public Guardianship Office shall give priority in awarding grant funds to those entities that:

1. Are operating as appointed offices of public guardians in this state;

2. Meet all of the requirements for being awarded a grant under this act; and

3. Demonstrate a need for grant funds during the current fiscal year due to a loss of local funding formerly raised through court filing fees.

(b) In each fiscal year after the first year that grant funds are distributed, the Statewide Public Guardianship Office may give priority to awarding grant funds to those entities that:

1. Meet all of the requirements of this act for being awarded grant funds; and

2. Submit with their application an agreement or confirmation from a local funding source, such as a county, municipality, or any other public or private organization, that the local funding source will contribute matching funds totaling an amount equal to or exceeding $2 for every $1 of grant funds awarded by the office. An entity may submit with its application agreements or confirmations from multiple local funding sources showing that the local funding sources will pool their contributed matching funds to the public guardianship program for a combined total of not less than $2 for every $1 of grant funds awarded. In-kind contributions allowable under this section shall be evaluated by the Statewide Public Guardianship Office and may be counted as part or all of the local matching funds.

Added by Laws 2004, c. 2004–260, § 6, eff. July 1, 2004.

CHAPTER 747

CONSERVATORSHIP

Section
747.01.   Who are absentees under this law.
747.011.   Absentee incompetent for certain purposes.
747.02.   Jurisdiction.

Section

Cross References

Trial and appellate proceedings, filing fees, see § 28.241.

747.01.   Who are absentees under this law

(1) Any person serving in or with the Armed Forces of the United States, in or with the Red Cross, in or with the Merchant Marine or otherwise, during any period of time when a state of hostilities exists between the United States and any other power and for 1 year thereafter, who has been reported or listed as missing in action, interned in a neutral country, beleaguered, besieged or captured by the enemy, shall be an "absentee" within the meaning of this law; and,

(2) Any resident of this state, or any person owning property herein, who disappears under circumstances indicating that he or she may have died, either naturally, accidentally or at the hand of another, or may have disappeared as the result of mental derangement, amnesia or other mental cause, shall also be an "absentee" within the meaning of this law.

Laws 1945, c. 22888, § 1; Laws 1967, c. 67–458, § 1. Amended by Laws 1997, c. 97–102, § 1129, eff. July 1, 1997.

747.011.   Absentee incompetent for certain purposes

An "absentee" as defined in s. 747.01 is considered incompetent for the purposes of s. 4, Art. X of the State Constitution.

Laws 1971, c. 71–103, § 1.

Cross References

Homestead exemptions, see Const. Art. 10, § 4.

747.02.   Jurisdiction

The circuit court has jurisdiction to appoint a conservator of the estate of an absentee as defined in s. 747.01 upon a showing that:

(1)(a)1.   The absentee has an interest in any form of property in this state; or

2.   The absentee is a legal resident of this state; or

3.   The spouse or next of kin of the absentee is a legal resident of this state; and

(b) The absentee has not provided an adequate power of attorney authorizing another to act in his or her behalf with regard to such property or interest or the term of any such power of attorney has expired; and

(2) A necessity exists for providing care for the property or estate of the absentee or care for or judgments concerning the absentee's spouse and children or, if he or she has no spouse and children, the absentee's mother or father.

Laws 1945, c. 22888, § 2; Laws 1971, c. 71–103, § 2.   Amended by Laws 1997, c. 97–102, § 1130, eff. July 1, 1997.

747.03.   Petition

(1) The jurisdiction of the court shall be invoked by the filing of a petition by any person who would have an interest in the property or estate of the absentee were such absentee deceased or any person who is dependent on said absentee for his or her maintenance or support.

(2) The petition shall be sworn to by the petitioner and shall state:

(a) The names, addresses, and ages of the spouse, children, mother, father, brothers, and sisters, or, if none of these is living, the next of kin, of the absentee;

(b) The name, address, and age of any other person who would have an interest in the property or the estate of the absentee if he or she were deceased;

(c) The exact circumstances which cause the person missing to be an absentee under s. 747.01 including the date he or she was first known to be missing, interned, beleaguered, etc.;

(d) The necessity for establishing a conservatorship;

(e) Whether or not the person alleged to be an absentee has a will and the whereabouts of said will; and

(f) A statement of all property constituting an asset of the alleged absentee's estate or in which he or she has any interest and the approximate value of same.

Laws 1945, c. 22888, § 3; Laws 1971, c. 71–103, § 5.   Amended by Laws 1997, c. 97–102, § 1131, eff. July 1, 1997.

747.031.   Notice; hearing

(1) Notice of the hearing on the petition to appoint a conservator shall be given to all persons named in the petition by registered mail or certified mail with return receipt requested.

(2) The judge shall hear evidence on the question of whether the person alleged to be missing, interned, beleaguered, etc., is an absentee as defined by s. 747.01 and on the question of who is entitled to appointment as conservator.   Any person interested in such proceedings may intervene with leave of the court.

(3) The court may in its discretion appoint a guardian ad litem to represent the alleged absentee at the hearing.

Laws 1971, c. 71–103, § 6.

747.032.   Order of appointment

(1) If, after hearing, the court is satisfied that the person alleged to be an absentee is an absentee as defined in s. 747.01 and that it is necessary that a conservatorship be established, she or he shall appoint a conservator of the estate and property of said absentee to take charge of the absentee's estate and property under the supervision, and subject to the further orders, of the court.

(2) In the appointment of a conservator, the court shall give due consideration to the appointment of one of the next of kin of the absentee if such next of kin is a fit and proper person and is qualified to act.

Laws 1971, c. 71–103, § 7. Amended by Laws 1997, c. 97–102, § 1132, eff. July 1, 1997.

747.033. Oath

Every conservator, before exercising his or her authority as conservator, shall take oath that he or she will faithfully perform his or her duties as conservator and will render true accounts whenever required according to law, which oath may be administered by any officer authorized to administer oaths under the laws of this state. Such oath shall be filed with the court.

Laws 1971, c. 71–103, § 8. Amended by Laws 1997, c. 97–102, § 1133, eff. July 1, 1997.

747.034. Bond

The court may require the conservator to post a bond as required for a guardian under ss. 744.38 and 744.39.[1] All provisions of chapter 744 which are applicable to bonds are applicable to the bond of the conservator required under this chapter.

Laws 1971, c. 71–103, § 9.

[1] Sections 744.38 and 744.39 were repealed by Laws 1974, c. 74–106, § 3.

747.035. Rights, powers, and duties of conservator

(1) The conservator shall have all the rights, powers, and duties of a guardian of the property as established in chapter 744 and an absentee and an absentee's dependents shall be entitled to all benefits accruing to a ward or a ward's dependents under said chapter.

(2) The circuit court shall have the same responsibility as to a conservatorship as it has with respect to the guardianship of the property under said chapter.

Laws 1971, c. 71–103, § 10; Laws 1973, c. 73–334, § 32; Laws 1995, c. 95–211, § 70.

747.036. Resignation or removal of conservator

The provision for resignation and removal of a guardian of the property in chapter 746 [1] shall apply in the circuit court to resignation and removal of a conservator.

Laws 1971, c. 71–103, § 11.

[1] Chapter 746 was repealed by Laws 1974, c. 74–106, § 3.

747.04. Termination of conservatorship

(1) At any time upon petition signed by the absentee, or on petition of an attorney in fact acting under an adequate power of attorney granted by the absentee, the court shall direct the termination of the conservatorship and the transfer of all property held thereunder to the absentee or to the designated attorney in fact.

(2) Likewise, if at any time subsequent to the appointment of a conservator it shall appear that the absentee has died and an executor or administrator has been appointed for her or his estate, the court shall direct the termination of the conservatorship and the transfer of all property of the deceased absentee held thereunder to such executor or administrator.

(3) When the need for a conservatorship terminates, the conservator shall promptly file her or his final returns and application for discharge with the court. If it appears to the court that the returns are correct and that the conservator has made full and complete transfer of the

absentee's assets as directed, the court may approve the returns and discharge the conservator. If objections to the returns are filed, the circuit judge shall conduct a hearing under the same conditions for a hearing on objections to annual returns.

(4) Such discharge shall operate as a release from the duties of the conservatorship and as a bar to any suit against said conservator or her or his surety, unless such suit is commenced within 1 year from the date of discharge.

Laws 1945, c. 22888, § 4; Laws 1971, c. 71–103, § 12. Amended by Laws 1997, c. 97–102, § 1134, eff. July 1, 1997.

Cross References

Proceedings related to children, rulemaking authority, see § 39.0121.

747.051. Summary procedure

(1) If the wife of any person defined as an absentee in s. 747.01(1), or his next of kin if said absentee has no wife, shall wish to sell or transfer any property of the absentee which has a gross value of less than $5,000, or shall require the consent of the absentee in any matter regarding the absentee's children or in any other matter in which the gross value of the subject matter is less than $5,000, she may apply to the circuit court for an order authorizing said sale, transfer, or consent without opening a full conservatorship proceeding as provided by this chapter. She may make the application without the assistance of an attorney. Said application shall be made by petition on the following form, which form shall be made readily available to the applicant by the clerk of the circuit court:

In the Circuit Court

In re: __(Absentee)__ , case number _____.

PETITION FOR SUMMARY RELIEF

Petitioner,   __(Name)__ , whose residence is   __(Street & number)__ ,   __(City or town)__ , and   __(County)__ , Florida, and who is the   __(Describe relationship to absentee)__   of the absentee,   __(Name)__ , states that the absentee has been   __(Imprisoned or missing in action)__   since   __(Date)__   when   __(Describe details)__ . Petitioner desires to sell/transfer   __(Describe property)__   of the value of   __(Value)__   because   __(Give reasons)__ . The terms of sale/transfer are   __(Give reasons)__ . Petitioner requires the consent of the absentee for the purpose of _____.

__(Petitioner)__

State of Florida

County of_____

Sworn to (or affirmed) and subscribed before me this __ day of _____, __(year)__ , by __(name of person making statement)__ .

__(Signature of Notary Public—State of Florida)__

__(Print, Type, or Stamp Commissioned Name of Notary Public)__

Personally Known _____ OR Produced Identification _____

Type of Identification Produced_____

---

(2) The court shall, without hearing or notice, enter an order on said petition if it deems the relief requested in said petition necessary to protect the best interests of the absentee or her or his dependents.

(3) Such order shall be prima facie evidence of the validity of the proceedings and the authority of the petitioner to make a conveyance or transfer of the property or to give the absentee's consent in any matter prescribed by subsection (1).

Laws 1971, c. 71–103, § 3; Laws 1973, c. 73–334, § 32. Amended by Laws 1997, c. 97–102, § 1135, eff. July 1, 1997; Laws 1998, c. 98–246, § 19, eff. Jan. 1, 1999.

747.052. Procedure for order authorizing action by spouse or next of kin

(1) If the spouse, or the next of kin if there is no spouse, of any person defined as an absentee under s. 747.01(1), shall wish to sell, lease, or mortgage specific property having a gross value of $5,000 or more owned by the absentee or in which the absentee had an interest, or take specific action with respect to the absentee's interest having a gross value of $5,000 or more, he or she may petition the circuit court for an order authorizing the action with respect to such property or interest.

(2) The petition shall be sworn to by the petitioner and shall state:

(a) The names, addresses, and ages of the spouse, children, mother, father, brothers, and sisters, or, if none of these is living, the next of kin, of the absentee;

(b) The name, address, and age of any other person who would have an interest in the property or the estate of the absentee if she or he were deceased;

(c) The exact circumstances which cause the person missing to be an absentee under s. 747.01, including the date she or he was first known to be missing, interned, beleaguered, etc.;

(d) The reasons for the action for which the petition seeks authorization;

(e) Whether or not the person alleged to be an absentee has a will and the whereabouts of said will and contents if known; and

(f) A statement of all property constituting an asset of the alleged absentee's estate or in which she or he has any interest and the approximate value of same.

(3) Notice of the hearing on the petition shall be given to all persons named in the petition by registered mail or certified mail with return receipt requested.

(4) The judge shall hear evidence on the question of whether the person alleged to be missing, interned, beleaguered, etc., is an absentee as defined by s. 747.01 and on the question of whether the action in question should be authorized. Any person interested in such proceedings may intervene with leave of the court.

(5) The court may in its discretion appoint a guardian ad litem to represent the alleged absentee at the hearing.

(6) If, after hearing, the court is satisfied that the person alleged to be an absentee is an absentee as defined in s. 747.01, that the action in question should be authorized, and that there is no necessity for a full conservatorship as provided by s. 747.03, the court shall enter an order appointing the petitioner as conservator for the purposes of the action which is the subject of the petition and authorizing the conservator to take the action requested in the petition. The court shall require the conservator to account for the proceeds of the sale, lease, or other action, but the conservator shall not be required to subject the other property of the absentee to a conservatorship proceeding. The court may retain jurisdiction of the proceeding to make such further orders as it deems proper.

Laws 1971, c. 71–103, § 4. Amended by Laws 1997, c. 97–102, § 1136, eff. July 1, 1997.

TITLE XLIV

CIVIL RIGHTS

CHAPTER 765

HEALTH CARE ADVANCE DIRECTIVES

PART I.   GENERAL PROVISIONS

PART II.   HEALTH CARE SURROGATE

PART III.   LIFE–PROLONGING PROCEDURES

PART IV.   ABSENCE OF ADVANCE DIRECTIVE

For Annotative Materials, see West's Florida Statutes Annotated

Cross References

Anatomical Gift Act, see § 765.510 et seq.
Health care licensing, applicability, see § 408.802.
Health care licensure, denial, suspension, and revocation of license, registration, certificate, or application, see
     § 408.831.
Power of attorney,
     Agents, authority, see F.S.A. § 709.2201.
     Agent's authority, termination or suspension, see F.S.A. § 709.2109.

PART I. GENERAL PROVISIONS

765.101. Definitions

As used in this chapter:

(1) "Advance directive" means a witnessed written document or oral statement in which instructions are given by a principal or in which the principal's desires are expressed concerning any aspect of the principal's health care or health information, and includes, but is not limited to, the designation of a health care surrogate, a living will, or an anatomical gift made pursuant to part V of this chapter.

(2) "Attending physician" means the physician who has primary responsibility for the treatment and care of the patient while the patient receives such treatment or care in a hospital as defined in s. 395.002(12).

(3) "Close personal friend" means any person 18 years of age or older who has exhibited special care and concern for the patient, and who presents an affidavit to the health care facility

or to the primary physician stating that he or she is a friend of the patient; is willing and able to become involved in the patient's health care; and has maintained such regular contact with the patient so as to be familiar with the patient's activities, health, and religious or moral beliefs.

(4) "End-stage condition" means an irreversible condition that is caused by injury, disease, or illness which has resulted in progressively severe and permanent deterioration, and which, to a reasonable degree of medical probability, treatment of the condition would be ineffective.

(5) "Health care" means care, services, or supplies related to the health of an individual and includes, but is not limited to, preventive, diagnostic, therapeutic, rehabilitative, maintenance, or palliative care, and counseling, service, assessment, or procedure with respect to the individual's physical or mental condition or functional status or that affect the structure or function of the individual's body.

(6) "Health care decision" means:

(a) Informed consent, refusal of consent, or withdrawal of consent to any and all health care, including life-prolonging procedures and mental health treatment, unless otherwise stated in the advance directives.

(b) The decision to apply for private, public, government, or veterans' benefits to defray the cost of health care.

(c) The right of access to health information of the principal reasonably necessary for a health care surrogate or proxy to make decisions involving health care and to apply for benefits.

(d) The decision to make an anatomical gift pursuant to part V of this chapter.

(7) "Health care facility" means a hospital, nursing home, hospice, home health agency, or health maintenance organization licensed in this state, or any facility subject to part I of chapter 394.

(8) "Health care provider" or "provider" means any person licensed, certified, or otherwise authorized by law to administer health care in the ordinary course of business or practice of a profession.

(9) "Health information" means any information, whether oral or recorded in any form or medium, as defined in 45 C.F.R. s. 160.103 and the Health Insurance Portability and Accountability Act of 1996, 42 U.S.C. s. 1320d, as amended, that:

(a) Is created or received by a health care provider, health care facility, health plan, public health authority, employer, life insurer, school or university, or health care clearinghouse; and

(b) Relates to the past, present, or future physical or mental health or condition of the principal; the provision of health care to the principal; or the past, present, or future payment for the provision of health care to the principal.

(10) "Incapacity" or "incompetent" means the patient is physically or mentally unable to communicate a willful and knowing health care decision. For the purposes of making an anatomical gift, the term also includes a patient who is deceased.

(11) "Informed consent" means consent voluntarily given by a person after a sufficient explanation and disclosure of the subject matter involved to enable that person to have a general understanding of the treatment or procedure and the medically acceptable alternatives, including the substantial risks and hazards inherent in the proposed treatment or procedures, and to make a knowing health care decision without coercion or undue influence.

(12) "Life-prolonging procedure" means any medical procedure, treatment, or intervention, including artificially provided sustenance and hydration, which sustains, restores, or supplants a

spontaneous vital function. The term does not include the administration of medication or performance of medical procedure, when such medication or procedure is deemed necessary to provide comfort care or to alleviate pain.

(13) "Living will" or "declaration" means:

(a) A witnessed document in writing, voluntarily executed by the principal in accordance with s. 765.302; or

(b) A witnessed oral statement made by the principal expressing the principal's instructions concerning life-prolonging procedures.

(14) "Minor's principal" means a principal who is a natural guardian as defined in s. 744.301(1); legal custodian; or, subject to chapter 744, legal guardian of the person of a minor.

(15) "Persistent vegetative state" means a permanent and irreversible condition of unconsciousness in which there is:

(a) The absence of voluntary action or cognitive behavior of any kind.

(b) An inability to communicate or interact purposefully with the environment.

(16) "Physician" means a person licensed pursuant to chapter 458 or chapter 459.

(17) "Primary physician" means a physician designated by an individual or the individual's surrogate, proxy, or agent under a durable power of attorney as provided in chapter 709, to have primary responsibility for the individual's health care or, in the absence of a designation or if the designated physician is not reasonably available, a physician who undertakes the responsibility.

(18) "Principal" means a competent adult executing an advance directive and on whose behalf health care decisions are to be made or health care information is to be received, or both.

(19) "Proxy" means a competent adult who has not been expressly designated to make health care decisions for a particular incapacitated individual, but who, nevertheless, is authorized pursuant to s. 765.401 to make health care decisions for such individual.

(20) "Reasonably available" means readily able to be contacted without undue effort and willing and able to act in a timely manner considering the urgency of the patient's health care needs.

(21) "Surrogate" means any competent adult expressly designated by a principal to make health care decisions and to receive health information. The principal may stipulate whether the authority of the surrogate to make health care decisions or to receive health information is exercisable immediately without the necessity for a determination of incapacity or only upon the principal's incapacity as provided in s. 765.204.

(22) "Terminal condition" means a condition caused by injury, disease, or illness from which there is no reasonable medical probability of recovery and which, without treatment, can be expected to cause death.

Laws 1992, c. 92–199, § 2; Laws 1994, c. 94–183, § 3; Laws 1996, c. 96–169, § 46. Amended by Laws 1999, c. 99–331, § 16, eff. Oct. 1, 1999; Laws 2001, c. 2001–250, § 3, eff. July 15, 2001; Laws 2001, c. 2001–277, § 131, eff. July 1, 2001; Laws 2006, c. 2006–1, § 104, eff. July 4, 2006; Laws 2006, c. 2006–178, § 28, eff. July 1, 2006; Laws 2015, c. 2015–153, § 2, eff. Oct. 1, 2015.

Cross References

Developmental disabilities, capacity, appointment of guardian advocate, see § 393.12.

765.102. Legislative findings and intent

(1) The Legislature finds that every competent adult has the fundamental right of self-determination regarding decisions pertaining to his or her own health, including the right to choose or refuse medical treatment. This right is subject to certain interests of society, such as the protection of human life and the preservation of ethical standards in the medical profession.

(2) To ensure that such right is not lost or diminished by virtue of later physical or mental incapacity, the Legislature intends that a procedure be established to allow a person to plan for incapacity by executing a document or orally designating another person to direct the course of his or her health care or receive his or her health information, or both, upon his or her incapacity. Such procedure should be less expensive and less restrictive than guardianship and permit a previously incapacitated person to exercise his or her full right to make health care decisions as soon as the capacity to make such decisions has been regained.

(3) The Legislature also recognizes that some competent adults may want to receive immediate assistance in making health care decisions or accessing health information, or both, without a determination of incapacity. The Legislature intends that a procedure be established to allow a person to designate a surrogate to make health care decisions or receive health information, or both, without the necessity for a determination of incapacity under this chapter.

(4) The Legislature recognizes that for some the administration of life-prolonging medical procedures may result in only a precarious and burdensome existence. In order to ensure that the rights and intentions of a person may be respected even after he or she is no longer able to participate actively in decisions concerning himself or herself, and to encourage communication among such patient, his or her family, and his or her physician, the Legislature declares that the laws of this state recognize the right of a competent adult to make an advance directive instructing his or her physician to provide, withhold, or withdraw life-prolonging procedures or to designate another to make the health care decision for him or her in the event that such person should become incapacitated and unable to personally direct his or her health care.

(5) The Legislature recognizes the need for all health care professionals to rapidly increase their understanding of end-of-life and palliative care. Therefore, the Legislature encourages the professional regulatory boards to adopt appropriate standards and guidelines regarding end-of-life care and pain management and encourages educational institutions established to train health care professionals and allied health professionals to implement curricula to train such professionals to provide end-of-life care, including pain management and palliative care.

(6) For purposes of this chapter:

(a) Palliative care is the comprehensive management of the physical, psychological, social, spiritual, and existential needs of patients. Palliative care is especially suited to the care of persons who have incurable, progressive illnesses.

(b) Palliative care must include:

1. An opportunity to discuss and plan for end-of-life care.

2. Assurance that physical and mental suffering will be carefully attended to.

3. Assurance that preferences for withholding and withdrawing life-sustaining interventions will be honored.

4. Assurance that the personal goals of the dying person will be addressed.

5. Assurance that the dignity of the dying person will be a priority.

6. Assurance that health care providers will not abandon the dying person.

7. Assurance that the burden to family and others will be addressed.

8. Assurance that advance directives for care will be respected regardless of the location of care.

9. Assurance that organizational mechanisms are in place to evaluate the availability and quality of end-of-life, palliative, and hospice care services, including the evaluation of administrative and regulatory barriers.

10. Assurance that necessary health care services will be provided and that relevant reimbursement policies are available.

11. Assurance that the goals expressed in subparagraphs 1.–10. will be accomplished in a culturally appropriate manner.

(7) The Department of Elderly Affairs, the Agency for Health Care Administration, and the Department of Health shall jointly create a campaign on end-of-life care for purposes of educating the public. This campaign should include culturally sensitive programs to improve understanding of end-of-life care issues in minority communities.

Laws 1992, c. 92–199, § 2. Amended by Laws 1997, c. 97–102, § 1144, eff. July 1, 1997; Laws 1999, c. 99–331, § 17, eff. Oct. 1, 1999; Laws 2000, c. 2000–295, § 7, eff. June 15, 2000; Laws 2001, c. 2001–250, § 4, eff. July 15, 2001; Laws 2001, c. 2001–277, §§ 132, 133, eff. July 1, 2001; Laws 2015, c. 2015–153, § 3, eff. Oct. 1, 2015.

765.103. Existing advance directives

Any advance directive made prior to October 1, 1999, shall be given effect as executed, provided such directive was legally effective when written.

Laws 1992, c. 92–199, § 2. Amended by Laws 1999, c. 99–331, § 18, eff. Oct. 1, 1999.

765.104. Amendment or revocation

(1) An advance directive may be amended or revoked at any time by a competent principal:

(a) By means of a signed, dated writing;

(b) By means of the physical cancellation or destruction of the advance directive by the principal or by another in the principal's presence and at the principal's direction;

(c) By means of an oral expression of intent to amend or revoke; or

(d) By means of a subsequently executed advance directive that is materially different from a previously executed advance directive.

(2) Unless otherwise provided in the advance directive or in an order of dissolution or annulment of marriage, the dissolution or annulment of marriage of the principal revokes the designation of the principal's former spouse as a surrogate.

(3) Any such amendment or revocation will be effective when it is communicated to the surrogate, health care provider, or health care facility. No civil or criminal liability shall be imposed upon any person for a failure to act upon an amendment or revocation unless that person has actual knowledge of such amendment or revocation.

(4) Any patient for whom a medical proxy has been recognized under s. 765.401 and for whom any previous legal disability that precluded the patient's ability to consent is removed may amend or revoke the recognition of the medical proxy and any uncompleted decision made by that proxy. The amendment or revocation takes effect when it is communicated to the proxy,

the health care provider, or the health care facility in writing or, if communicated orally, in the presence of a third person.

Laws 1992, c. 92–199, § 2; Laws 1996, c. 96–169, § 47. Amended by Laws 1999, c. 99–331, § 19, eff. Oct. 1, 1999; Laws 2002, c. 2002–195, § 12, eff. April 29, 2002; Laws 2015, c. 2015–153, § 4, eff. Oct. 1, 2015.

765.105. Review of surrogate or proxy's decision

(1) The patient's family, the health care facility, or the primary physician, or any other interested person who may reasonably be expected to be directly affected by the surrogate or proxy's decision concerning any health care decision may seek expedited judicial intervention pursuant to rule 5.900 of the Florida Probate Rules, if that person believes:

(a) The surrogate or proxy's decision is not in accord with the patient's known desires or this chapter;

(b) The advance directive is ambiguous, or the patient has changed his or her mind after execution of the advance directive;

(c) The surrogate or proxy was improperly designated or appointed, or the designation of the surrogate is no longer effective or has been revoked;

(d) The surrogate or proxy has failed to discharge duties, or incapacity or illness renders the surrogate or proxy incapable of discharging duties;

(e) The surrogate or proxy has abused his or her powers; or

(f) The patient has sufficient capacity to make his or her own health care decisions.

(2) This section does not apply to a patient who is not incapacitated and who has designated a surrogate who has immediate authority to make health care decisions or [1] receive health information, or both, on behalf of the patient.

Laws 1992, c. 92–199, § 2; Laws 1994, c. 94–183, § 4. Amended by Laws 2015, c. 2015–153, § 5, eff. Oct. 1, 2015.

[1] The word "or" was substituted for the word "and" by the Division of Law Revision and Information.

Cross References

Surrogates, modification or revocation of authority, see § 744.3115.

765.106. Preservation of existing rights

The provisions of this chapter are cumulative to the existing law regarding an individual's right to consent, or refuse to consent, to medical treatment and do not impair any existing rights or responsibilities which a health care provider, a patient, including a minor, competent or incompetent person, or a patient's family may have under the common law, Federal Constitution, State Constitution, or statutes of this state.

Laws 1992, c. 92–199, § 2; Laws 1994, c. 94–183, § 5.

765.107. Construction

(1) This chapter shall not be construed to repeal by implication any provision of s. 766.103, the Florida Medical Consent Law. For all purposes, the Florida Medical Consent Law shall be considered an alternative to provisions of this section.

(2) Procedures provided in this chapter permitting the withholding or withdrawal of life-prolonging procedures do not apply to a person who never had capacity to designate a health care surrogate or execute a living will.

Laws 1992, c. 92–199, § 2. Amended by Laws 1999, c. 99–331, § 20, eff. Oct. 1, 1999.

765.108.   Effect with respect to insurance

The making of an advance directive pursuant to the provisions of this chapter shall not affect the sale, procurement, or issuance of any policy of life insurance, nor shall such making of an advance directive be deemed to modify the terms of an existing policy of life insurance. No policy of life insurance will be legally impaired or invalidated by the withholding or withdrawal of life-prolonging procedures from an insured patient in accordance with the provisions of this chapter, nor by any other treatment decision made according to this chapter, notwithstanding any term of the policy to the contrary. A person shall not be required to make an advance directive as a condition for being insured for, or receiving, health care services.

Laws 1992, c. 92–199, § 2.

765.109.   Immunity from liability;   weight of proof;   presumption

(1) A health care facility, provider, or other person who acts under the direction of a health care facility or provider is not subject to criminal prosecution or civil liability, and will not be deemed to have engaged in unprofessional conduct, as a result of carrying out a health care decision made in accordance with the provisions of this chapter. The surrogate or proxy who makes a health care decision on a patient's behalf, pursuant to this chapter, is not subject to criminal prosecution or civil liability for such action.

(2) The provisions of this section shall apply unless it is shown by a preponderance of the evidence that the person authorizing or effectuating a health care decision did not, in good faith, comply with the provisions of this chapter.

Laws 1992, c. 92–199, § 2.

765.110.   Health care facilities and providers;   discipline

(1) A health care facility, pursuant to Pub. L. No. 101–508, ss. 4206 and 4751,[1] shall provide to each patient written information concerning the individual's rights concerning advance directives and the health care facility's policies respecting the implementation of such rights, and shall document in the patient's medical records whether or not the individual has executed an advance directive.

(2) A health care provider or health care facility may not require a patient to execute an advance directive or to execute a new advance directive using the facility's or provider's forms. The patient's advance directives shall travel with the patient as part of the patient's medical record.

(3) A health care provider or health care facility shall be subject to professional discipline and revocation of license or certification, and a fine of not more than $1,000 per incident, or both, if the health care provider or health care facility, as a condition of treatment or admission, requires an individual to execute or waive an advance directive.

(4) The Department of Elderly Affairs for hospices and, in consultation with the Department of Elderly Affairs, the Department of Health for health care providers; the Agency for Health Care Administration for hospitals, nursing homes, home health agencies, and health maintenance organizations; and the Department of Children and Families for facilities subject to part I of chapter 394 shall adopt rules to implement the provisions of the section.

Laws 1992, c. 92–199, § 2;   Laws 1994, c. 94–183, § 6;   Laws 1994, c. 94–218, § 243;   Laws 1996, c. 96–169, § 48.   Amended by Laws 1999, c. 99–8, § 284, eff. June 29, 1999;   Laws 1999, c. 99–331, § 21, eff. Oct. 1, 1999;   Laws 2014, c. 2014–19, § 293, eff. July 1, 2014.

[1] See 42 U.S.C.A. §§ 1395i–3, 1395cc, 1395bbb, 1396a and 1396r.

765.1103. Pain management and palliative care

(1) A patient shall be given information concerning pain management and palliative care when he or she discusses with the primary physician, or such physician's designee, the diagnosis, planned course of treatment, alternatives, risks, or prognosis for his or her illness. If the patient is incapacitated, the information shall be given to the patient's health care surrogate or proxy, court-appointed guardian as provided in chapter 744, or attorney in fact under a durable power of attorney as provided in chapter 709. The court-appointed guardian or attorney in fact must have been delegated authority to make health care decisions on behalf of the patient.

(2) Health care providers and practitioners regulated under chapter 458, chapter 459, or chapter 464 must, as appropriate, comply with a request for pain management or palliative care from a patient under their care or, for an incapacitated patient under their care, from a surrogate, proxy, guardian, or other representative permitted to make health care decisions for the incapacitated patient. Facilities regulated under chapter 395, chapter 400, or chapter 429 must comply with the pain management or palliative care measures ordered by the patient's physician.

Added by Laws 2000, c. 2000–295, § 8, eff. June 15, 2000. Amended by Laws 2001, c. 2001–250, § 5, eff. July 15, 2001; Laws 2001, c. 2001–277, § 134, eff. July 1, 2001; Laws 2006, c. 2006–197, § 105, eff. July 1, 2006; Laws 2015, c. 2015–153, § 6, eff. Oct. 1, 2015.

765.1105. Transfer of a patient

(1) A health care provider or facility that refuses to comply with a patient's advance directive, or the treatment decision of his or her surrogate or proxy, shall make reasonable efforts to transfer the patient to another health care provider or facility that will comply with the directive or treatment decision. This chapter does not require a health care provider or facility to commit any act which is contrary to the provider's or facility's moral or ethical beliefs, if the patient:

(a) Is not in an emergency condition; and

(b) Has received written information upon admission informing the patient of the policies of the health care provider or facility regarding such moral or ethical beliefs.

(2) A health care provider or facility that is unwilling to carry out the wishes of the patient or the treatment decision of his or her surrogate or proxy because of moral or ethical beliefs must within 7 days either:

(a) Transfer the patient to another health care provider or facility. The health care provider or facility shall pay the costs for transporting the patient to another health care provider or facility; or

(b) If the patient has not been transferred, carry out the wishes of the patient or the patient's surrogate or proxy, unless s. 765.105 applies.

Laws 1992, c. 92–199, § 4; Laws 1994, c. 94–183, § 11. Amended by Laws 1997, c. 97–102, § 1148, eff. July 1, 1997. Renumbered as § 765.1105 and amended by Laws 1999, c. 99–331, § 30, eff. Oct. 1, 1999. Amended by Laws 2015, c. 2015–153, § 7, eff. Oct. 1, 2015.

765.1115. Falsification, forgery, or willful concealment, cancellation, or destruction of directive or revocation or amendment; penalties

(1) Any person who willfully conceals, cancels, defaces, obliterates, or damages an advance directive without the principal's consent or who falsifies or forges the revocation or amendment

of an advance directive of another, and who thereby causes life-prolonging procedures to be utilized in contravention of the previously expressed intent of the principal, commits a felony of the third degree, punishable as provided in s. 775.082, s. 775.083, or s. 775.084.

(2) Any person who falsifies or forges the advance directive of another or who willfully conceals or withholds personal knowledge of the revocation of an advance directive, with the intent to cause a withholding or withdrawal of life-prolonging procedures contrary to the wishes of the principal, and who thereby because of such act directly causes life-prolonging procedures to be withheld or withdrawn and death to be hastened, commits a felony of the second degree, punishable as provided in s. 775.082, s. 775.083, or s. 775.084.

Laws 1992, c. 92–199, § 4. Renumbered from 765.13 and amended by Laws 1999, c. 99–331, § 31, eff. Oct. 1, 1999.

765.112. Recognition of advance directive executed in another state

An advance directive executed in another state in compliance with the law of that state or of this state is validly executed for the purposes of this chapter.

Laws 1992, c. 92–199, § 2.

765.113. Restrictions on providing consent

Unless the principal expressly delegates such authority to the surrogate in writing, or a surrogate or proxy has sought and received court approval pursuant to rule 5.900 of the Florida Probate Rules, a surrogate or proxy may not provide consent for:

(1) Abortion, sterilization, electroshock therapy, psychosurgery, experimental treatments that have not been approved by a federally approved institutional review board in accordance with 45 C.F.R. part 46 or 21 C.F.R. part 56, or voluntary admission to a mental health facility.

(2) Withholding or withdrawing life-prolonging procedures from a pregnant patient prior to viability as defined in s. 390.0111(4).

Laws 1992, c. 92–199, § 2; Laws 1994, c. 94–183, § 7. Amended by Laws 1999, c. 99–3, § 87, eff. June 29, 1999.

PART II. HEALTH CARE SURROGATE

765.201. Short title

Sections 765.202–765.205 may be cited as the "Florida Health Care Surrogate Act."

Laws 1992, c. 92–199, § 3.

765.202. Designation of a health care surrogate

(1) A written document designating a surrogate to make health care decisions for a principal or receive health information on behalf of a principal, or both, shall be signed by the principal in the presence of two subscribing adult witnesses. A principal unable to sign the instrument may, in the presence of witnesses, direct that another person sign the principal's name as required herein. An exact copy of the instrument shall be provided to the surrogate.

(2) The person designated as surrogate shall not act as witness to the execution of the document designating the health care surrogate. At least one person who acts as a witness shall be neither the principal's spouse nor blood relative.

(3) A document designating a health care surrogate may also designate an alternate surrogate provided the designation is explicit. The alternate surrogate may assume his or her duties as

surrogate for the principal if the original surrogate is not willing, able, or reasonably available to perform his or her duties. The principal's failure to designate an alternate surrogate shall not invalidate the designation of a surrogate.

(4) If neither the designated surrogate nor the designated alternate surrogate is willing, able, or reasonably available to make health care decisions on behalf of the principal and in accordance with the principal's instructions, the health care facility may seek the appointment of a proxy pursuant to part IV.

(5) A principal may designate a separate surrogate to consent to mental health treatment in the event that the principal is determined by a court to be incompetent to consent to mental health treatment and a guardian advocate is appointed as provided under s. 394.4598. However, unless the document designating the health care surrogate expressly states otherwise, the court shall assume that the health care surrogate authorized to make health care decisions under this chapter is also the principal's choice to make decisions regarding mental health treatment.

(6) A principal may stipulate in the document that the authority of the surrogate to receive health information or make health care decisions, or both, is exercisable immediately without the necessity for a determination of incapacity as provided in s. 765.204.

(7) Unless the document states a time of termination, the designation shall remain in effect until revoked by the principal.

(8) A written designation of a health care surrogate executed pursuant to this section establishes a rebuttable presumption of clear and convincing evidence of the principal's designation of the surrogate.

Laws 1992, c. 92–199, § 3; Laws 1994, c. 94–183, § 8; Laws 1996, c. 96–169, § 49. Amended by Laws 1997, c. 97–102, § 1797, eff. July 1, 1997; Laws 2015, c. 2015–153, § 8, eff. Oct. 1, 2015.

Cross References

Autopsies, consent of health care surrogate, see § 872.04.

765.203. Suggested form of designation

A written designation of a health care surrogate executed pursuant to this chapter may, but need not be, in the following form:

DESIGNATION OF HEALTH CARE SURROGATE

I,   (name) , designate as my health care surrogate under s. 765.202, Florida Statutes:

Name: (name of health care surrogate)

Address: (address)

Phone: (telephone)

If my health care surrogate is not willing, able, or reasonably available to perform his or her duties, I designate as my alternate health care surrogate:

Name: (name of alternate health care surrogate)

Address: (address)

Phone: (telephone)

INSTRUCTIONS FOR HEALTH CARE

I authorize my health care surrogate to:

 (Initial here) Receive any of my health information, whether oral or recorded in any form or medium, that:

1. Is created or received by a health care provider, health care facility, health plan, public health authority, employer, life insurer, school or university, or health care clearinghouse; and

2. Relates to my past, present, or future physical or mental health or condition; the provision of health care to me; or the past, present, or future payment for the provision of health care to me.

I further authorize my health care surrogate to:

 (Initial here) Make all health care decisions for me, which means he or she has the authority to:

1. Provide informed consent, refusal of consent, or withdrawal of consent to any and all of my health care, including life-prolonging procedures.

2. Apply on my behalf for private, public, government, or veterans' benefits to defray the cost of health care.

3. Access my health information reasonably necessary for the health care surrogate to make decisions involving my health care and to apply for benefits for me.

4. Decide to make an anatomical gift pursuant to part V of chapter 765, Florida Statutes.

 (Initial here) Specific instructions and restrictions: _____

_____

_____

While I have decisionmaking capacity, my wishes are controlling and my physicians and health care providers must clearly communicate to me the treatment plan or any change to the treatment plan prior to its implementation.

To the extent I am capable of understanding, my health care surrogate shall keep me reasonably informed of all decisions that he or she has made on my behalf and matters concerning me.

THIS HEALTH CARE SURROGATE DESIGNATION IS NOT AFFECTED BY MY SUBSE-QUENT INCAPACITY EXCEPT AS PROVIDED IN CHAPTER 765, FLORIDA STATUTES.

PURSUANT TO SECTION 765.104, FLORIDA STATUTES, I UNDERSTAND THAT I MAY, AT ANY TIME WHILE I RETAIN MY CAPACITY, REVOKE OR AMEND THIS DESIGNATION BY:

 (1) SIGNING A WRITTEN AND DATED INSTRUMENT WHICH EXPRESSES MY INTENT TO AMEND OR REVOKE THIS DESIGNATION;

 (2) PHYSICALLY DESTROYING THIS DESIGNATION THROUGH MY OWN ACTION OR BY THAT OF ANOTHER PERSON IN MY PRESENCE AND UNDER MY DIRECTION;

 (3) VERBALLY EXPRESSING MY INTENTION TO AMEND OR REVOKE THIS DESIGNA-TION; OR

 (4) SIGNING A NEW DESIGNATION THAT IS MATERIALLY DIFFERENT FROM THIS DESIGNATION.

MY HEALTH CARE SURROGATE'S AUTHORITY BECOMES EFFECTIVE WHEN MY PRI-MARY PHYSICIAN DETERMINES THAT I AM UNABLE TO MAKE MY OWN HEALTH CARE DECISIONS UNLESS I INITIAL EITHER OR BOTH OF THE FOLLOWING BOXES:

IF I INITIAL THIS BOX [____], MY HEALTH CARE SURROGATE'S AUTHORITY TO RECEIVE MY HEALTH INFORMATION TAKES EFFECT IMMEDIATELY.

IF I INITIAL THIS BOX [____], MY HEALTH CARE SURROGATE'S AUTHORITY TO MAKE HEALTH CARE DECISIONS FOR ME TAKES EFFECT IMMEDIATELY. PURSUANT TO SECTION 765.204(3), FLORIDA STATUTES, ANY INSTRUCTIONS OR HEALTH CARE DECISIONS I MAKE, EITHER VERBALLY OR IN WRITING, WHILE I POSSESS CAPACITY SHALL SUPERSEDE ANY INSTRUCTIONS OR HEALTH CARE DECISIONS MADE BY MY SURROGATE THAT ARE IN MATERIAL CONFLICT WITH THOSE MADE BY ME.

SIGNATURES: Sign and date the form here:

      (date)   (sign your name)
      (address)   (print your name)
      (city)   (state)

SIGNATURES OF WITNESSES:

First witness   Second witness
  (print name)   (print name)
  (address)   (address)
  (city)   (state)   (city)   (state)
  (signature of witness)   (signature of witness)
  (date)   (date)

Laws 1992, c. 92–199, § 3. Amended by Laws 1997, c. 97–102, § 1145, eff. July 1, 1997; Laws 2000, c. 2000–295, § 9, eff. June 15, 2000; Laws 2008, c. 2008–223, § 1, eff. July 1, 2008; Laws 2015, c. 2015–153, § 9, eff. Oct. 1, 2015.

765.2035. Designation of a health care surrogate for a minor

(1) A natural guardian as defined in s. 744.301(1), legal custodian, or legal guardian of the person of a minor may designate a competent adult to serve as a surrogate to make health care decisions for the minor. Such designation shall be made by a written document signed by the minor's principal in the presence of two subscribing adult witnesses. If a minor's principal is unable to sign the instrument, the principal may, in the presence of witnesses, direct that another person sign the minor's principal's name as required by this subsection. An exact copy of the instrument shall be provided to the surrogate.

(2) The person designated as surrogate may not act as witness to the execution of the document designating the health care surrogate.

(3) A document designating a health care surrogate may also designate an alternate surrogate; however, such designation must be explicit. The alternate surrogate may assume his or her duties as surrogate if the original surrogate is not willing, able, or reasonably available to perform his or her duties. The minor's principal's failure to designate an alternate surrogate does not invalidate the designation.

(4) If neither the designated surrogate or the designated alternate surrogate is willing, able, or reasonably available to make health care decisions for the minor on behalf of the minor's principal and in accordance with the minor's principal's instructions, s. 743.0645(2) shall apply as if no surrogate had been designated.

(5) A natural guardian as defined in s. 744.301(1), legal custodian, or legal guardian of the person of a minor may designate a separate surrogate to consent to mental health treatment for

the minor. However, unless the document designating the health care surrogate expressly states otherwise, the court shall assume that the health care surrogate authorized to make health care decisions for a minor under this chapter is also the minor's principal's choice to make decisions regarding mental health treatment for the minor.

(6) Unless the document states a time of termination, the designation shall remain in effect until revoked by the minor's principal. An otherwise valid designation of a surrogate for a minor shall not be invalid solely because it was made before the birth of the minor.

(7) A written designation of a health care surrogate executed pursuant to this section establishes a rebuttable presumption of clear and convincing evidence of the minor's principal's designation of the surrogate and becomes effective pursuant to s. 743.0645(2)(a).

Added by Laws 2015, c. 2015–153, § 10, eff. Oct. 1, 2015.

765.2038. Designation of health care surrogate for a minor; suggested form

A written designation of a health care surrogate for a minor executed pursuant to this chapter may, but need not [1] be, in the following form:

DESIGNATION OF HEALTH CARE SURROGATE

FOR MINOR

I/We, __(name/names)__ , the [___] natural guardian(s) as defined in s. 744.301(1), Florida Statutes; [___] legal custodian(s); [___] legal guardian(s) [check one] of the following minor(s):

_____ ;

_____ ;

_____ ,

pursuant to s. 765.2035, Florida Statutes, designate the following person to act as my/our surrogate for health care decisions for such minor(s) in the event that I/we am/are not able or reasonably available to provide consent for medical treatment and surgical and diagnostic procedures:

Name: __(name)__

Address: __(address)__

Zip Code: __(zip code)__

Phone: __(telephone)__

If my/our designated health care surrogate for a minor is not willing, able, or reasonably available to perform his or her duties, I/we designate the following person as my/our alternate health care surrogate for a minor:

Name: __(name)__

Address: __(address)__

Zip Code: __(zip code)__

Phone: __(telephone)__

I/We authorize and request all physicians, hospitals, or other providers of medical services to follow the instructions of my/our surrogate or alternate surrogate, as the case may be, at any time and under any circumstances whatsoever, with regard to medical treatment and surgical and diagnostic procedures for a minor, provided the medical care and treatment of any minor is on the advice of a licensed physician.

I/We fully understand that this designation will permit my/our designee to make health care decisions for a minor and to provide, withhold, or withdraw consent on my/our behalf, to apply for public benefits to defray the cost of health care, and to authorize the admission or transfer of a minor to or from a health care facility.

I/We will notify and send a copy of this document to the following person(s) other than my/our surrogate, so that they may know the identity of my/our surrogate:

Name: ___(name)___

Name: ___(name)___

Signed: ___(signature)___

Date: ___(date)___

WITNESSES:

1. ___(witness)___

2. ___(witness)___

Added by Laws 2015, c. 2015–153, § 11, eff. Oct. 1, 2015.

[1] The word "not" was substituted for the word "to" by the Division of Law Revision and Information.

765.204. Capacity of principal; procedure

(1) A principal is presumed to be capable of making health care decisions for herself or himself unless she or he is determined to be incapacitated. While a principal has decisionmaking capacity, the principal's wishes are controlling. Each physician or health care provider must clearly communicate to a principal with decisionmaking capacity the treatment plan and any change to the treatment plan prior to implementation of the plan or the change to the plan. Incapacity may not be inferred from the person's voluntary or involuntary hospitalization for mental illness or from her or his intellectual disability.

(2) If a principal's capacity to make health care decisions for herself or himself or provide informed consent is in question, the primary or attending physician shall evaluate the principal's capacity and, if the evaluating physician concludes that the principal lacks capacity, enter that evaluation in the principal's medical record. If the evaluating physician has a question as to whether the principal lacks capacity, another physician shall also evaluate the principal's capacity, and if the second physician agrees that the principal lacks the capacity to make health care decisions or provide informed consent, the health care facility shall enter both physician's evaluations in the principal's medical record. If the principal has designated a health care surrogate or has delegated authority to make health care decisions to an attorney in fact under a durable power of attorney, the health care facility shall notify such surrogate or attorney in fact in writing that her or his authority under the instrument has commenced, as provided in chapter 709 or s. 765.203. If an attending physician determines that the principal lacks capacity, the hospital in which the attending physician made such a determination shall notify the principal's primary physician of the determination.

(3) The surrogate's authority commences either upon a determination under subsection (2) that the principal lacks capacity or upon a stipulation of such authority pursuant to s. 765.101(21). Such authority remains in effect until a determination that the principal has regained such capacity, if the authority commenced as a result of incapacity, or until the

authority is revoked, if the authority commenced immediately pursuant to s. 765.101(21). Upon commencement of the surrogate's authority, a surrogate who is not the principal's spouse shall notify the principal's spouse or adult children of the principal's designation of the surrogate. Except if the principal provided immediately exercisable authority to the surrogate pursuant to s. 765.101(21), in the event that the primary or attending physician determines that the principal has regained capacity, the authority of the surrogate shall cease, but recommences if the principal subsequently loses capacity as determined pursuant to this section. A health care provider is not liable for relying upon health care decisions made by a surrogate while the principal lacks capacity. At any time when a principal lacks capacity, a health care decision made on the principal's behalf by a surrogate is effective to the same extent as a decision made by the principal. If a principal possesses capacity, health care decisions of the principal take precedence over decisions made by the surrogate that present a material conflict.

(4) Notwithstanding subsections (2) and (3), if the principal has designated a health care surrogate and has stipulated that the authority of the surrogate is to take effect immediately, or has appointed an agent under a durable power of attorney as provided in chapter 709 to make health care decisions for the principal, the health care facility shall notify such surrogate or agent in writing when a determination of incapacity has been entered into the principal's medical record.

(5) A determination made pursuant to this section that a principal lacks capacity to make health care decisions shall not be construed as a finding that a principal lacks capacity for any other purpose.

(6) If the surrogate is required to consent to withholding or withdrawing life-prolonging procedures, part III applies.

Laws 1992, c. 92–199, § 3. Amended by Laws 1997, c. 97–102, § 1146, eff. July 1, 1997; Laws 1999, c. 99–331, § 22, eff. Oct. 1, 1999; Laws 2000, c. 2000–295, § 10, eff. June 15, 2000; Laws 2013, c. 2013–162, § 23, eff. July 1, 2013; Laws 2015, c. 2015–153, § 12, eff. Oct. 1, 2015.

765.205. Responsibility of the surrogate

(1) The surrogate, in accordance with the principal's instructions, unless such authority has been expressly limited by the principal, shall:

(a) Have authority to act for the principal and to make all health care decisions for the principal during the principal's incapacity.

(b) Consult expeditiously with appropriate health care providers to provide informed consent, and make only health care decisions for the principal which he or she believes the principal would have made under the circumstances if the principal were capable of making such decisions. If there is no indication of what the principal would have chosen, the surrogate may consider the patient's best interest in deciding that proposed treatments are to be withheld or that treatments currently in effect are to be withdrawn.

(c) Provide written consent using an appropriate form whenever consent is required, including a physician's order not to resuscitate.

(d) Be provided access to the appropriate health information of the principal.

(e) Apply for public benefits, such as Medicare and Medicaid, for the principal and have access to information regarding the principal's income and assets and banking and financial records to the extent required to make application. A health care provider or facility may not, however, make such application a condition of continued care if the principal, if capable, would have refused to apply.

(2) The surrogate may authorize the release of health information to appropriate persons to ensure the continuity of the principal's health care and may authorize the admission, discharge, or transfer of the principal to or from a health care facility or other facility or program licensed under chapter 400 or chapter 429.

(3) If, after the appointment of a surrogate, a court appoints a guardian, the surrogate shall continue to make health care decisions for the principal, unless the court has modified or revoked the authority of the surrogate pursuant to s. 744.3115. The surrogate may be directed by the court to report the principal's health care status to the guardian.

Laws 1992, c. 92–199, § 3; Laws 1994, c. 94–183, § 9; Laws 1996, c. 96–169, § 50. Amended by Laws 1999, c. 99–331, § 23, eff. Oct. 1, 1999; Laws 2000, c. 2000–295, § 11, eff. June 15, 2000; Laws 2001, c. 2001–250, § 6, eff. July 15, 2001; Laws 2001, c. 2001–277, § 135, eff. July 1, 2001; Laws 2006, c. 2006–197, § 106, eff. July 1, 2006; Laws 2015, c. 2015–153, § 13, eff. Oct. 1, 2015.

Cross References

Guardianship, advance directives for health care, see F.S.A. § 744.3115.

PART III. LIFE–PROLONGING PROCEDURES

765.301. Short title

Sections 765.302–765.309 may be cited as the "Life-Prolonging Procedure Act of Florida."
Laws 1992, c. 92–199, § 4. Amended by Laws 1999, c. 99–331, § 24, eff. Oct. 1, 1999.

765.302. Procedure for making a living will; notice to physician

(1) Any competent adult may, at any time, make a living will or written declaration and direct the providing, withholding, or withdrawal of life-prolonging procedures in the event that such person has a terminal condition, has an end-stage condition, or is in a persistent vegetative state. A living will must be signed by the principal in the presence of two subscribing witnesses, one of whom is neither a spouse nor a blood relative of the principal. If the principal is physically unable to sign the living will, one of the witnesses must subscribe the principal's signature in the principal's presence and at the principal's direction.

(2) It is the responsibility of the principal to provide for notification to her or his primary physician that the living will has been made. In the event the principal is physically or mentally incapacitated at the time the principal is admitted to a health care facility, any other person may notify the physician or health care facility of the existence of the living will. A primary physician or health care facility which is so notified shall promptly make the living will or a copy thereof a part of the principal's medical records.

(3) A living will, executed pursuant to this section, establishes a rebuttable presumption of clear and convincing evidence of the principal's wishes.

Laws 1992, c. 92–199, § 4. Amended by Laws 1997, c. 97–102, § 1147, eff. July 1, 1997; Laws 1999, c. 99–331, § 25, eff. Oct. 1, 1999; Laws 2015, c. 2015–153, § 14, eff. Oct. 1, 2015.

765.303. Suggested form of a living will

(1) A living will may, BUT NEED NOT, be in the following form:

Living Will

Declaration made this ____ day of ____, (year) , I, _____, willfully and voluntarily make known my desire that my dying not be artificially prolonged under the circumstances set forth below, and I do hereby declare that, if at any time I am incapacitated and __(initial)__ I have a terminal condition

or __(initial)__ I have an end-stage condition

or __(initial)__ I am in a persistent vegetative state

and if my primary physician and another consulting physician have determined that there is no reasonable medical probability of my recovery from such condition, I direct that life-prolonging procedures be withheld or withdrawn when the application of such procedures would serve only to prolong artificially the process of dying, and that I be permitted to die naturally with only the administration of medication or the performance of any medical procedure deemed necessary to provide me with comfort care or to alleviate pain.

It is my intention that this declaration be honored by my family and physician as the final expression of my legal right to refuse medical or surgical treatment and to accept the consequences for such refusal.

In the event that I have been determined to be unable to provide express and informed consent regarding the withholding, withdrawal, or continuation of life-prolonging procedures, I wish to designate, as my surrogate to carry out the provisions of this declaration:

Name:_____

Address:_____

_____   Zip Code:_____

Phone:_____

I understand the full import of this declaration, and I am emotionally and mentally competent to make this declaration.

Additional Instructions (optional):

_____

_____

_____

__(Signed)__

__Witness__

__Address__

__Phone__

__Witness__

__Address__

__Phone__

(2) The principal's failure to designate a surrogate shall not invalidate the living will.

Laws 1992, c. 92–199, § 4. Amended by Laws 1999, c. 99–6, § 35, eff. June 29, 1999; Laws 1999, c. 99–331, § 26, eff. Oct. 1, 1999; Laws 2000, c. 2000–295, § 12, eff. June 15, 2000; Laws 2015, c. 2015–153, § 15, eff. Oct. 1, 2015.

765.304. Procedure for living will

(1) If a person has made a living will expressing his or her desires concerning life-prolonging procedures, but has not designated a surrogate to execute his or her wishes concerning life-prolonging procedures or designated a surrogate under part II, the person's primary physician may proceed as directed by the principal in the living will. In the event of a dispute or disagreement concerning the primary physician's decision to withhold or withdraw life-prolonging procedures, the primary physician shall not withhold or withdraw life-prolonging procedures pending review under s. 765.105. If a review of a disputed decision is not sought within 7 days following the primary physician's decision to withhold or withdraw life-prolonging procedures, the primary physician may proceed in accordance with the principal's instructions.

(2) Before proceeding in accordance with the principal's living will, it must be determined that:

(a) The principal does not have a reasonable medical probability of recovering capacity so that the right could be exercised directly by the principal.

(b) The principal has a terminal condition, has an end-stage condition, or is in a persistent vegetative state.

(c) Any limitations or conditions expressed orally or in a written declaration have been carefully considered and satisfied.

Laws 1992, c. 92–199, § 4; Laws 1994, c. 94–183, § 10. Amended by Laws 1999, c. 99–331, § 27, eff. Oct. 1, 1999; Laws 2015, c. 2015–153, § 16, eff. Oct. 1, 2015.

765.305. Procedure in absence of a living will

(1) In the absence of a living will, the decision to withhold or withdraw life-prolonging procedures from a patient may be made by a health care surrogate designated by the patient pursuant to part II unless the designation limits the surrogate's authority to consent to the withholding or withdrawal of life-prolonging procedures.

(2) Before exercising the incompetent patient's right to forego treatment, the surrogate must be satisfied that:

(a) The patient does not have a reasonable medical probability of recovering capacity so that the right could be exercised by the patient.

(b) The patient has an end-stage condition, the patient is in a persistent vegetative state, or the patient's physical condition is terminal.

Laws 1992, c. 92–199, § 4. Amended by Laws 1999, c. 99–331, § 28, eff. Oct. 1, 1999; Laws 2000, c. 2000–295, § 13, eff. June 15, 2000.

765.306. Determination of patient condition

In determining whether the patient has a terminal condition, has an end-stage condition, or is in a persistent vegetative state or may recover capacity, or whether a medical condition or limitation referred to in an advance directive exists, the patient's primary physician and at least one other consulting physician must separately examine the patient. The findings of each such examination must be documented in the patient's medical record and signed by each examining physician before life-prolonging procedures may be withheld or withdrawn.

Laws 1992, c. 92–199, § 4; Laws 1994, c. 94–183, § 13. Amended by Laws 1999, c. 99–331, § 29, eff. Oct. 1, 1999; Laws 2000, c. 2000–295, § 14, eff. June 15, 2000; Laws 2015, c. 2015–153, § 17, eff. Oct. 1, 2015.

765.309. Mercy killing or euthanasia not authorized; suicide distinguished

(1) Nothing in this chapter shall be construed to condone, authorize, or approve mercy killing or euthanasia, or to permit any affirmative or deliberate act or omission to end life other than to permit the natural process of dying.

(2) The withholding or withdrawal of life-prolonging procedures from a patient in accordance with any provision of this chapter does not, for any purpose, constitute a suicide.

Laws 1992, c. 92–199, § 4.

PART IV. ABSENCE OF ADVANCE DIRECTIVE

765.401. The proxy

(1) If an incapacitated or developmentally disabled patient has not executed an advance directive, or designated a surrogate to execute an advance directive, or the designated or alternate surrogate is no longer available to make health care decisions, health care decisions may be made for the patient by any of the following individuals, in the following order of priority, if no individual in a prior class is reasonably available, willing, or competent to act:

(a) The judicially appointed guardian of the patient or the guardian advocate of the person having a developmental disability as defined in s. 393.063, who has been authorized to consent to medical treatment, if such guardian has previously been appointed; however, this paragraph shall not be construed to require such appointment before a treatment decision can be made under this subsection;

(b) The patient's spouse;

(c) An adult child of the patient, or if the patient has more than one adult child, a majority of the adult children who are reasonably available for consultation;

(d) A parent of the patient;

(e) The adult sibling of the patient or, if the patient has more than one sibling, a majority of the adult siblings who are reasonably available for consultation;

(f) An adult relative of the patient who has exhibited special care and concern for the patient and who has maintained regular contact with the patient and who is familiar with the patient's activities, health, and religious or moral beliefs; or

(g) A close friend of the patient.

(h) A clinical social worker licensed pursuant to chapter 491, or who is a graduate of a court-approved guardianship program. Such a proxy must be selected by the provider's bioethics committee and must not be employed by the provider. If the provider does not have a bioethics committee, then such a proxy may be chosen through an arrangement with the bioethics committee of another provider. The proxy will be notified that, upon request, the provider shall make available a second physician, not involved in the patient's care to assist the proxy in evaluating treatment. Decisions to withhold or withdraw life-prolonging procedures will be reviewed by the facility's bioethics committee. Documentation of efforts to locate proxies from prior classes must be recorded in the patient record.

(2) Any health care decision made under this part must be based on the proxy's informed consent and on the decision the proxy reasonably believes the patient would have made under the circumstances. If there is no indication of what the patient would have chosen, the proxy may consider the patient's best interest in deciding that proposed treatments are to be withheld or that treatments currently in effect are to be withdrawn.

(3) Before exercising the incapacitated patient's rights to select or decline health care, the proxy must comply with the provisions of ss. 765.205 and 765.305, except that a proxy's decision to withhold or withdraw life-prolonging procedures must be supported by clear and convincing evidence that the decision would have been the one the patient would have chosen had the patient been competent or, if there is no indication of what the patient would have chosen, that the decision is in the patient's best interest.

(4) Nothing in this section shall be construed to preempt the designation of persons who may consent to the medical care or treatment of minors established pursuant to s. 743.0645.

Laws 1992, c. 92–199, § 5; Laws 1994, c. 94–183, § 12. Amended by Laws 1999, c. 99–331, § 32, eff. Oct. 1, 1999; Laws 2000, c. 2000–295, § 15, eff. June 15, 2000; Laws 2001, c. 2001–250, § 7, eff. July 15, 2001; Laws 2001, c. 2001–277, § 136, eff. July 1, 2001; Laws 2002, c. 2002–195, § 13, eff. April 29, 2002; Laws 2003, c. 2003–57, § 5, eff. May 30, 2003.

765.404. Persistent vegetative state

For persons in a persistent vegetative state, as determined by the person's primary physician in accordance with currently accepted medical standards, who have no advance directive and for whom there is no evidence indicating what the person would have wanted under such conditions, and for whom, after a reasonably diligent inquiry, no family or friends are available or willing to serve as a proxy to make health care decisions for them, life-prolonging procedures may be withheld or withdrawn under the following conditions:

(1) The person has a judicially appointed guardian representing his or her best interest with authority to consent to medical treatment; and

(2) The guardian and the person's primary physician, in consultation with the medical ethics committee of the facility where the patient is located, conclude that the condition is permanent and that there is no reasonable medical probability for recovery and that withholding or withdrawing life-prolonging procedures is in the best interest of the patient. If there is no medical ethics committee at the facility, the facility must have an arrangement with the medical ethics committee of another facility or with a community-based ethics committee approved by the Florida Bio-ethics Network. The ethics committee shall review the case with the guardian, in consultation with the person's primary physician, to determine whether the condition is permanent and there is no reasonable medical probability for recovery. The individual committee members and the facility associated with an ethics committee shall not be held liable in any civil action related to the performance of any duties required in this subsection.

Added by Laws 1999, c. 99–331, § 33, eff. Oct. 1, 1999. Amended by Laws 2015, c. 2015–153, § 18, eff. Oct. 1, 2015.

PART V. ANATOMICAL GIFTS

UNIFORM ANATOMICAL GIFT ACT (2006)

Table of Jurisdictions Wherein Act Has Been Adopted

For text of Uniform Act, and variation notes and annotation materials for adopting jurisdictions, see Uniform Laws Annotated, Master Edition, Volume 8A.

Jurisdiction	Laws	Effective Date	Statutory Citation
Alabama[2]	2008, c. 453	11–1–2008	Code 1975, §§ 22–19–160 to 22–19–184.
Alaska	2008, c. 100	9–15–2008	AS 13.52.173 to 13.52.268.
Arizona	2007, c. 281	7–2–2007 *	A.R.S. §§ 36–841 to 36–864.

Jurisdiction	Laws	Effective Date	Statutory Citation
Arkansas	2007, c. 839	4–3–2007	A.C.A. §§ 20–17–1201 to 20–17–1227.
California	2007, c. 629	1–1–2008	West's Ann.Cal. Health & Safety Code, §§ 7150 to 7151.40.
Colorado	2007, c. 207	7–1–2007	West's C.R.S.A. §§ 12–34–101 to 12–34–125.
Connecticut	2010, P.A. 10-123	10–1–2010	C.G.S.A. §§ 19a–289 to 19a–289v.
District of Columbia	P.L. 17–145	4–15–2008	D.C. Official Code, 2001 Ed. §§ 7–1531.01 to 7–1531.28.
Florida	2009, c. 2009–218	7–1–2009	West's F.S.A. §§ 765.510 to 765.547.
Georgia	2008, Act 545	7–1–2008	O.C.G.A. §§ 44–5–140 to 44–5–159.4.
Hawaii	2008, c. 122	7–1–2008	HRS [§§ 327–1 to 327–26].
Idaho	2007, c. 30	7–1–2007	I.C. §§ 39–3401 to 39–3425.
Illinois[6]	2013, P.A. 98-172	1–1–2014	755 I.L.C.S. §§ 50/1–1 to 50/5-55.
Indiana	2007, c. 147	7–1–2007	West's A.I.C. 29–2-16.1–1 to 29–2–16.1-21.
Iowa	2007, S.F.509	4–5–2007 *	I.C.A. §§ 142C.1 to 142C.18.
Kansas	2007, c. 127	7–1–2007	K.S.A. 65–3220 to 65–3244.
Kentucky	2010, c. 161	7–15–2010	KRS 311.1911 to 311.1959.
Louisiana	2010, No. 937	7–1–2010	LSA–R.S. 17:2351 to 17:2359.
Maine	2008, c. 601	1–1–2009	22 M.R.S.A. §§ 2941 to 2965.
Maryland	2011, c. 541	10–1–2011	Code, Estates and Trusts, §§ 4–501 to 4–522.
Massachusetts	2012, c. 39	2–22–2012	M.G.L.A. 113A §§ 1 to 25.
Michigan	2008, No. 39	5–1–2008	M.C.L.A. §§ 333.10101 to 333.10123.
Minnesota	2007, c. 120	4–1–2008	M.S.A. §§ 525A.01 to 525A.25
Mississippi [3]	2008, c. 561	7–1–2008	Code 1972, §§ 41–39–101 to 41–39–149.
Missouri	2008, S.B. No. 1139	7–10–2008 *	V.A.M.S. §§ 194.210 to 194.294.
Montana	2007, c. 345	10–1–2007	MCA 72–17–101 to 72–17–312.
Nebraska	2010, L.B. 1036	1–1–2011	R.R.S. 1943, §§ 71–4824 to 71–4845.
Nevada	2007, c. 232	5–31–2007 *	N.R.S. 451.500 to 451.598.
New Hampshire	2010, c. 111	7–31–2010	RSA 291–A:1 to 291–A:25.
New Jersey	2008, c. 50	7–22–2008	N.J.S.A. 26:6–77 to 26:6–96.
New Mexico	2007, c. 323	7–1–2007	NMSA 1978 §§ 24–6B–1 to 24–6B–25.
North Carolina	2007, S.L. 2007–538	10–1–2007	G.S. §§ 130A–412.3 to 130A–412.33.
North Dakota	2007, c. 237	4–9–2007 *	NDCC 23–06.6–01 to 23–06.6–23.
Ohio	2008, H.B. No. 529	4–7–2009	R.C. §§ 2108.01 to 2108.35.
Oklahoma	2009, c. 139	11–1–2009	63 Okl.St.Ann. §§ 2200.1A to 2200.27A.
Oregon[5]	2007, c. 681	1–1–2008	ORS 97.951 to 97.985.
Rhode Island	2007, c. 476	7–6–2007	Gen.Laws 1956, §§ 23–18.6.1–1 to 23–18.6.1–25.
South Carolina	2009, No. 4	5–6–2009	Code 1976, §§ 44–43–300 to 44–43–420.
South Dakota	2007, c. 197	7–1–2007	SDCL 34–26–48 to 34–26–72.
Tennessee	2007, c. 428	7–1–2007	T.C.A. §§ 68–30–101 to 68–30–120.
Texas	2009, c. 186	9–1–2009	V.T.C.A. Health & Safety Code, §§ 692A.001 to 692A.023.
Utah	2007, c. 60	7–1–2007	U.C.A.1953, 26–28–101 to 26–28–125.
Vermont	2009, Adj. Sess., No. 119	7–1–2010	18 V.S.A. §§ 6001 to 6026.
Virgin Islands	2009, Act 7133	4	19 V.I.C. §§ 401 to 425.
Virginia	2007, cc. 92 and 907	1	Code 1950, §§ 32.1–291.1 to 32.1–291.25.
Washington	2008, c. 139	6–12–2008	West's RCWA 68.64.010 to 68.64.903.
West Virginia	2008, c. 191	6–5–2008	Code, §§ 16–19–1 to 16–19–23.
Wisconsin	2008, Act 106	4–1–2008	W.S.A. 157.06.

For Annotative Materials, see West's Florida Statutes Annotated

Jurisdiction	Laws	Effective Date	Statutory Citation
Wyoming	2009, c. 97	7–1–2009	Wyo.Stat.Ann. §§ 35–5–201 to 35–5–225.

* Date of approval.

[1] Virginia L.2007, c. 92, was approved February 23, 2007, and L.2007, c. 907, was approved April 4, 2007.

[2] Alabama has enacted the Revised Uniform Anatomical Gift Act (2006) and repealed the Uniform Anatomical Gift Act (1987) effective November 1, 2008, without repealing the Uniform Anatomical Gift Act (1968). Accordingly, Alabama is set forth in the tables for both the 1968 and 2006 acts.

[3] Mississippi section 41–39–149 provides for the repeal of sections 41–39–101 to 41–39–147 on July 1, 2014.

[4] Virgin Islands' amendment to this chapter became effective 60 days after its enactment on Nov. 25, 2009.

[5] Oregon has enacted the Revised Uniform Anatomical Gift Act (2006) and repealed, in part, the Uniform Anatomical Gift Act (1987), effective January 1, 2008. Accordingly, Oregon is set forth in the tables for both the 1987 and 2006 acts.

[6] Illinois has enacted the Revised Uniform Anatomical Gift Act (2006) and repealed, in part, the Uniform Anatomical Gift Act (1968), effective January 1, 2014. Accordingly, Illinois is set forth in the tables for both the 1968 and 2006 acts.

Cross References

Health care licensing, exemptions, see § 408.820.

765.510. Legislative declaration

Because of the rapid medical progress in the fields of tissue and organ preservation, transplantation of tissue, and tissue culture, and because it is in the public interest to aid the medical developments in these fields, the Legislature in enacting this part intends to encourage and aid the development of reconstructive medicine and surgery and the development of medical research by facilitating premortem and postmortem authorizations for donations of tissue and organs. It is the purpose of this part to regulate the gift of a body or parts of a body, the gift to be made after the death of a donor.

Laws 1974, c. 74–106, § 1; Laws 1975, c. 75–220, § 45; Laws 1984, c. 84–264, § 3. Renumbered from § 732.910, by Laws 2001, c. 2001–226, § 60, eff. Jan. 1, 2002.

Cross References

Sale of anatomical matter, see §§ 873.01, 873.05.

765.511. Definitions

As used in this part, the term:

(1) "Agency" means the Agency for Health Care Administration.

(2) "Anatomical gift" or "gift" means a donation of all or part of a human body to take effect after the donor's death and to be used for transplantation, therapy, research, or education.

(3) "Bank" or "storage facility" means a facility licensed, accredited, or approved under the laws of any state for storage of human bodies or body parts.

(4) "Death" means the absence of life as determined, in accordance with currently accepted medical standards, by the irreversible cessation of all respiration and circulatory function, or as determined, in accordance with s. 382.009, by the irreversible cessation of the functions of the entire brain, including the brain stem.

(5) "Decedent" means a deceased individual whose body or body parts may be, or are, the source of an anatomical gift.

(6) "Department" means the Department of Highway Safety and Motor Vehicles.

(7) "Disinterested witness" means a witness other than a person listed in s. 765.512(3) or other family member.

(8) "Document of gift" means any of the documents or mechanisms used in making an anatomical gift under s. 765.514.

(9) "Donor" means an individual who makes an anatomical gift of all or part of his or her body.

(10) "Donor registry" means a database that contains records of anatomical gifts and amendments to, or revocations of, such gifts.

(11) "Eye bank" means an entity that is accredited by the Eye Bank Association of America or otherwise regulated under federal or state law to engage in the retrieval, screening, testing, processing, storage, or distribution of human eye tissue.

(12) "Guardian" means a person appointed pursuant to chapter 744. The term does not include a guardian ad litem.

(13) "Hospital" means a hospital licensed, accredited, or approved under the laws of any state and includes a hospital operated by the United States Government or a state, or a subdivision thereof, although not required to be licensed under state laws.

(14) "Identification card" means an official identification card issued by a governmental entity, state agency, or subdivision thereof.

(15) "Organ procurement organization" means an entity that is designated as an organ procurement organization by the Secretary of the United States Department of Health and Human Services and that engages in the retrieval, screening, testing, processing, storage, or distribution of human organs.

(16) "Part of the body" or "body part" means an organ, eye, or tissue of a human being. The term does not include the whole body.

(17) "Physician" or "surgeon" means a physician or surgeon licensed to practice under chapter 458 or chapter 459 or similar laws of any state. "Surgeon" includes dental or oral surgeon.

(18) "Procurement" means any retrieval, recovery, processing, storage, or distribution of human organs or tissues for transplantation, therapy, research, or education.

(19) "Procurement organization" means an organ procurement organization, eye bank, or tissue bank.

(20) "Reasonably available" means able to be contacted by a procurement organization in a timely manner without undue effort, and willing and able to act in a manner consistent with existing medical protocols necessary for the making of an anatomical gift.

(21) "Record" means information that is inscribed on a tangible medium or that is stored in an electronic or other medium and is retrievable in perceivable form.

(22) "Sign" or "signed" means, with the present intent to authenticate or adopt a record, to execute or adopt a tangible symbol, or attach to or logically associate an electronic symbol, sound, or process with the record.

(23) "Tissue bank" means an entity that is accredited by the American Association of Tissue Banks or otherwise regulated under federal or state law to engage in the retrieval, screening, testing, processing, storage, or distribution of human tissue.

Laws 1974, c. 74–106, § 1; Laws 1975, c. 75–220, § 45; Laws 1997, c. 97–102, § 973; Laws 1998, c. 98–68, § 5. Renumbered from § 732.911, by Laws 2001, c. 2001–226, § 61, eff. Jan. 1, 2002. Amended by Laws 2009, c. 2009–218, § 1, eff. July 1, 2009.

765.512.   Persons who may make an anatomical gift

(1) Any person who may make a will may make an anatomical gift of his or her body.

(a) If the decedent makes an anatomical gift by one of the methods listed in s. 765.514(1), and in the absence of actual notice of contrary indications by the decedent, the document or entry in the donor registry is legally sufficient evidence of the decedent's informed consent to donate an anatomical gift.

(b) An anatomical gift made by a qualified donor and not revoked by the donor, as provided in s. 765.516, is irrevocable after the donor's death. A family member, guardian, representative ad litem, or health care surrogate may not modify, deny, or prevent a donor's wish or intent to make an anatomical gift after the donor's death.

(2) A health care surrogate designated by the decedent pursuant to part II of this chapter may give all or any part of the decedent's body for any purpose specified in s. 765.513 absent actual notice of contrary indications by the decedent.

(3) If the decedent has not made an anatomical gift or designated a health surrogate, a member of one of the classes of persons listed below, in the order of priority listed and in the absence of actual notice of contrary indications by the decedent or actual notice of opposition by a member of a prior class, may give all or any part of the decedent's body for any purpose specified in s. 765.513:

(a) The spouse of the decedent;

(b) An adult son or daughter of the decedent;

(c) Either parent of the decedent;

(d) An adult brother or sister of the decedent;

(e) An adult grandchild of the decedent;

(f) A grandparent of the decedent;

(g) A close personal friend, as defined in s. 765.101;

(h) A guardian of the person of the decedent at the time of his or her death; or

(i) A representative ad litem appointed by a court of competent jurisdiction upon a petition heard ex parte filed by any person, who shall ascertain that no person of higher priority exists who objects to the gift of all or any part of the decedent's body and that no evidence exists of the decedent's having made a communication expressing a desire that his or her body or body parts not be donated upon death.

Those of higher priority who are reasonably available must be contacted and made aware of the proposed gift and a reasonable search must be conducted which shows that there would have been no objection to the gift by the decedent.

(4) A donee may not accept an anatomical gift if the donee has actual notice of contrary indications by the donor or actual notice that an anatomical gift by a member of a class is opposed by a member of a prior class.

(5) The person authorized by subsection (3) may make the anatomical gift after the decedent's death or immediately before the decedent's death.

(6) An anatomical gift authorizes:

(a) Any examination necessary to assure medical acceptability of the gift for the purposes intended.

(b) The decedent's medical provider, family, or a third party to furnish medical records requested concerning the decedent's medical and social history.

(7) Once the anatomical gift has been made, the rights of the donee are paramount to the rights of others, except as provided by s. 765.517.

Laws 1974, c. 74–106, § 1; Laws 1975, c. 75–220, § 45; Laws 1984, c. 84–264, § 4; Laws 1985, c. 85–62, § 62; Laws 1995, c. 95–423, § 5; Laws 1997, c. 97–102, § 974; Laws 1998, c. 98–68, § 6; Laws 1999, c. 99–331, § 12. Renumbered from § 732.912, and amended by Laws 2001, c. 2001–226, § 62, eff. Jan. 1, 2002. Amended by Laws 2003, c. 2003–46, § 2, eff. July 1, 2003; Laws 2008, c. 2008–223, § 2, eff. July 1, 2008; Laws 2009, c. 2009–218, § 2, eff. July 1, 2009.

Cross References

Human remains, selling, buying, and conveying prohibited, see F.S.A. § 406.61.

765.513. Donees; purposes for which anatomical gifts may be made

(1) The following persons or entities may become donees of anatomical gifts of bodies or parts of them for the purposes stated:

(a) Any procurement organization or accredited medical or dental school, college, or university for education, research, therapy, or transplantation.

(b) Any individual specified by name for therapy or transplantation needed by him or her.

(c) The anatomical board or a nontransplant anatomical donation organization, as defined in s. 406.49, for donation of the whole body for medical or dental education or research.

(2) If multiple purposes are set forth in the document of gift but are not set forth in any priority order, the anatomical gift shall be used first for transplantation or therapy, if suitable. If the gift cannot be used for transplantation or therapy, the gift may be used for research or education.

(3) The Legislature declares that the public policy of this state prohibits restrictions on the possible recipients of an anatomical gift on the basis of race, color, religion, gender, national origin, age, physical disability, health status, marital status, or economic status, and such restrictions are void and unenforceable.

Laws 1974, c. 74–106, § 1; Laws 1975, c. 75–220, § 45; Laws 1994, c. 94–305, § 1; Laws 1997, c. 97–102, § 975; Laws 1998, c. 98–68, § 7. Renumbered from § 732.913 by Laws 2001, c. 2001–226, § 63, eff. Jan. 1, 2002. Amended by Laws 2009, c. 2009–218, § 3, eff. July 1, 2009; Laws 2013, c. 2013–138, § 20, eff. July 1, 2013.

765.514. Manner of making anatomical gifts

(1) A person may make an anatomical gift of all or part of his or her body under s. 765.512(1) by:

(a) Signing an organ and tissue donor card.

(b) Registering online with the donor registry.

(c) Signifying an intent to donate on his or her driver license or identification card issued by the department. Revocation, suspension, expiration, or cancellation of the driver license or identification card does not invalidate the gift.

(d) Expressing a wish to donate in a living will or other advance directive.

(e) Executing a will that includes a provision indicating that the testator wishes to make an anatomical gift. The gift becomes effective upon the death of the testator without waiting for probate. If the will is not probated or if it is declared invalid for testamentary purposes, the gift is nevertheless valid to the extent that it has been acted upon in good faith.

(f) Expressing a wish to donate in a document other than a will. The document must be signed by the donor in the presence of two witnesses who shall sign the document in the donor's presence. If the donor cannot sign, the document may be signed for him or her at the donor's direction and in his or her presence and the presence of two witnesses who must sign the document in the donor's presence. Delivery of the document of gift during the donor's lifetime is not necessary to make the gift valid. The following form of written document is sufficient for any person to make an anatomical gift for the purposes of this part:

UNIFORM DONOR CARD

The undersigned hereby makes this anatomical gift, if medically acceptable, to take effect on death. The words and marks below indicate my desires:

I give:

(a) _____ any needed organs, tissues, or eyes;

(b) _____ only the following organs, tissues, or eyes

                    [Specify the organs, tissues, or eyes]

for the purpose of transplantation, therapy, medical research, or education;

(c) _____ my body for anatomical study if needed. Limitations or special wishes, if any:

     (If applicable, list specific donee; this must be arranged in advance with the donee.)

Signed by the donor and the following witnesses in the presence of each other:

(Signature of donor)	(Date of birth of donor)
(Date signed)	(City and State)
(Witness)	(Witness)
(Address)	(Address)

(2) The anatomical gift may be made to a donee listed in s. 765.513, and the donee may be specified by name.

(3) Any anatomical gift by a health care surrogate designated by the decedent pursuant to part II of this chapter or a member of a class designated in s. 765.512(3) must be made by a document signed by that person or made by that person's witnessed telephonic discussion, telegraphic message, or other recorded message.

Laws 1974, c. 74–106, § 1; Laws 1975, c. 75–220, § 45; Laws 1983, c. 83–171, § 1; Laws 1994, c. 94–305, § 2; Laws 1995, c. 95–423, § 6; Laws 1997, c. 97–102, § 976; Laws 1998, c. 98–68, § 8; Laws 1999, c. 99–331, § 13. Renumbered from § 732.914 and amended by Laws 2001, c. 2001–226, § 64, eff. Jan. 1, 2002. Amended by Laws 2008, c. 2008–223, § 3, eff. July 1, 2008; Laws 2009, c. 2009–218, § 4, eff. July 1, 2009.

Cross References

Wills, competency of witnesses, see § 732.504.

765.515. Delivery of donor document

(1) If an anatomical gift is made pursuant to s. 765.521, the completed donor registration card shall be delivered to the department, and the department must communicate the donor's intent to the donor registry, but delivery is not necessary to the validity of the gift. If the donor withdraws the gift, the records of the department must be updated to reflect such withdrawal, and the department must communicate the withdrawal to the donor registry for the purpose of updating the registry.

(2) If an anatomical gift is made by the donor to a specified donee, the document of gift, other than a will, may be delivered to the donee to expedite the appropriate procedures immediately after death, but delivery is not necessary to the validity of the gift. The document of gift may be deposited in any hospital, bank, storage facility, or registry office that accepts such documents for safekeeping or to facilitate the donation of organs and tissue after death.

(3) At the request of any interested party upon or after the donor's death, the person in possession shall produce the document of gift for examination.

Laws 1974, c. 74–106, § 1; Laws 1975, c. 75–220, § 45; Laws 1983, c. 83–171, § 2; Laws 1987, c. 87–372, § 1; Laws 1995, c. 95–423, § 7; Laws 1996, c. 96–418, § 33; Laws 1998, c. 98–68, § 9; Fla.St.2000, Renumbered from § 732.915, and amended by Laws 2001, c. 2001–226, § 65, eff. Jan. 1, 2002. Amended by Laws 2008, c. 2008–9, § 17, eff. July 1, 2008; Laws 2008, c. 2008–223, § 4, eff. July 1, 2008; Laws 2009, c. 2009–218, § 5, eff. July 1, 2009.

765.5155. Donor registry; education program

(1) The Legislature finds that:

(a) There is a shortage of organ and tissue donors in this state willing to provide the organs and tissue that could save lives or enhance the quality of life for many persons.

(b) There is a need to encourage the various minority populations of this state to donate organs and tissue.

(c) A statewide donor registry having an online donor registration process coupled with an enhanced program of donor education will lead to an increase in the number of organ and tissue donors registered in this state, thus affording more persons who are awaiting organ or tissue transplants the opportunity for a full and productive life.

(2) The agency and the department shall jointly contract for the operation of a donor registry and education program. The contractor shall be procured by competitive solicitation pursuant to chapter 287, notwithstanding an exemption under s. 287.057(3)(e). When awarding the contract, priority shall be given to existing nonprofit groups that are based within the state, have expertise working with procurement organizations, have expertise in conducting statewide organ and tissue donor public education campaigns, and represent the needs of the organ and tissue donation community in the state.

(3) The contractor shall be responsible for:

(a) The development, implementation, and maintenance of an interactive web-based donor registry that, through electronic means, allows for online organ donor registration and the recording of organ and tissue donation records submitted through the driver license identification program or through other sources.

1. The registry must be maintained in a manner that allows, through electronic and telephonic methods, immediate access to organ and tissue donation records 24 hours a day, 7 days a week.

2. Access to the registry must be through coded and secure means to protect the integrity of the data in the registry.

(b) A continuing program to educate and inform medical professionals, law enforcement agencies and officers, other state and local government employees, high school students, minorities, and the public about the laws of this state relating to anatomical gifts and the need for anatomical gifts.

1. Existing community resources, when available, must be used to support the program and volunteers may assist the program to the maximum extent possible.

2. The contractor shall coordinate with the head of a state agency or other political subdivision of the state, or his or her designee, to establish convenient times, dates, and locations for educating that entity's employees.

(c) Preparing and submitting an annual written report to the agency by December 31 of each year. The report must include:

1. The number of donors on the registry and an analysis of the registration rates by location and method of donation;

2. The characteristics of donors as determined from registry information submitted directly by the donors or by the department;

3. The annual dollar amount of voluntary contributions received by the contractor;

4. A description of the educational campaigns and initiatives implemented during the year and an evaluation of their effectiveness in increasing enrollment on the registry; and

5. An analysis of Florida's registry compared with other states' donor registries.

(4) Costs for the donor registry and education program shall be paid by the agency from the funds deposited into the Health Care Trust Fund pursuant to ss. 320.08047 and 322.08, which are designated for maintaining the donor registry and education program. In addition, the contractor may receive and use voluntary contributions to help support the registry and provide education.

(5) The donor registry established by this section is designated as the "Joshua Abbott Organ and Tissue Registry."

Added by Laws 2008, c. 2008–223, § 5, eff. July 1, 2008. Amended by Laws 2009, c. 2009–218, § 6, eff. July 1, 2009; Laws 2010, c. 2010–151, § 40, eff. July 1, 2010; Laws 2013, c. 2013–154, § 20, eff. July 1, 2013.

765.51551. Donor registry; public records exemption

(1) Information held in the donor registry which identifies a donor is confidential and exempt from s. 119.07(1) and s. 24(a), Art. I of the State Constitution.

(2) Such information may be disclosed to the following:

(a) Procurement organizations that have been certified by the agency for the purpose of ascertaining or effectuating the existence of a gift under s. 765.522.

(b) Persons engaged in bona fide research if the person agrees to:

1. Submit a research plan to the agency which specifies the exact nature of the information requested and the intended use of the information;

2. Maintain the confidentiality of the records or information if personal identifying information is made available to the researcher;

3. Destroy any confidential records or information obtained after the research is concluded; and

4. Not directly or indirectly contact, for any purpose, any donor or donee.

Added by Laws 2008, c. 2008–222, § 1, eff. July 1, 2008. Amended by Laws 2009, c. 2009–218, § 7, eff. July 1, 2009; Laws 2013, c. 2013–65, § 1, eff. Oct. 1, 2013.

765.516. Donor amendment or revocation of anatomical gift

(1) A donor may amend the terms of or revoke an anatomical gift by:

(a) The execution and delivery to the donee of a signed statement witnessed by at least two adults, at least one of whom is a disinterested witness.

(b) An oral statement that is made in the presence of two persons, one of whom is not a family member, and communicated to the donor's family or attorney or to the donee. An oral statement is effective only if the procurement organization, transplant hospital, or physician or technician has actual notice of the oral amendment or revocation before an incision is made to the decedent's body or an invasive procedure to prepare the recipient has begun.

(c) A statement made during a terminal illness or injury addressed to the primary physician, who must communicate the revocation of the gift to the procurement organization.

(d) A signed document found on or about the donor's person.

(e) Removing his or her name from the donor registry.

(f) A later-executed document of gift which amends or revokes a previous anatomical gift or portion of an anatomical gift, either expressly or by inconsistency.

(g) By the destruction or cancellation of the document of gift or the destruction or cancellation of that portion of the document of gift used to make the gift with the intent to revoke the gift.

(2) Any anatomical gift made by a will may also be amended or revoked in the manner provided for the amendment or revocation of wills or as provided in paragraph (1)(a).

Laws 1974, c. 74–106, § 1; Laws 1975, c. 75–220, § 45; Laws 1983, c. 83–171, § 3; Laws 1995, c. 95–423, § 8; Laws 1997, c. 97–102, § 977; Laws 1998, c. 98–68, § 10. Renumbered from § 732.916, by Laws 2001, c. 2001–226, § 66, eff. Jan. 1, 2002. Amended by Laws 2003, c. 2003–46, § 3, eff. July 1, 2003; Laws 2008, c. 2008–223, § 6, eff. July 1, 2008; Laws 2009, c. 2009–218, § 8, eff. July 1, 2009; Laws 2015, c. 2015–153, § 19, eff. Oct. 1, 2015.

765.517. Rights and duties at death

(1) The donee, pursuant to s. 765.515(2), may accept or reject an anatomical gift. If the donee accepts a gift to be used for research or education purposes, the donee may authorize embalming and the use of the body in funeral services, subject to the terms of the gift. If the gift is of a part of the body, the donee shall cause the part to be removed without unnecessary mutilation upon the death of the donor and before or after embalming. After removal of the body part, custody of the remainder of the body vests in the surviving spouse, next of kin, or other persons under obligation to dispose of the body.

(2) The time of death shall be determined by a physician who attends the donor at the donor's death or, if there is no such physician, the physician who certifies the death. After death, those physicians or the donor's primary care physician may participate in, but may not obstruct, the procedures to preserve the donor's organs or tissues and may not be paid or reimbursed for such participation, nor be associated with or employed by, a procurement organization. These physicians may not participate in the procedures for removing or transplanting a part. Howev-

er, this subsection does not prevent a physician from serving in a voluntary capacity on the board of directors of a procurement organization or participating on any board, council, commission, or similar body related to the organ and tissue procurement system.

(3) The procurement organizations, or hospital medical professionals under the direction thereof, may perform any and all tests to evaluate the deceased as a potential donor and any invasive procedures on the deceased body in order to preserve the potential donor's organs. These procedures do not include the surgical removal of an organ or penetrating any body cavity, specifically for the purpose of donation, until:

(a) It has been verified that the deceased's consent to donate appears in the donor registry or a properly executed document of gift is located; or

(b) If a properly executed document of gift cannot be located or the deceased's consent is not listed in the donor registry, a person specified in s. 765.512(2) or (3) has been located, has been notified of the death, and has granted legal permission for the donation.

(4) All reasonable additional expenses incurred in the procedures to preserve the donor's organs or tissues shall be reimbursed by the procurement organization.

(5) A person who acts in good faith and without negligence in accord with the terms of this part or under the anatomical gift laws of another state or a foreign country, or attempts to do so, may not be subject to any civil action for damages, may not be subject to any criminal proceeding, and may not be subject to discipline, penalty, or liability in any administrative proceeding.

(6) The provisions of this part are subject to the laws of this state prescribing powers and duties with respect to autopsies.

(7) The person making an anatomical gift and the donor's estate are not liable for any injury or damages that result from the making or use of the gift.

(8) In determining whether an anatomical gift has been made, amended, or revoked under this part, a person may rely upon the representation of an individual listed in s. 765.512, relating to the individual's relationship to the donor or prospective donor, unless the person knows that the representation is untrue.

Laws 1974, c. 74–106, § 1; Laws 1975, c. 75–220, § 45; Laws 1983, c. 83–171, § 4; Laws 1995, c. 95–423, § 9; Laws 1997, c. 97–102, § 978; Laws 1999, c. 99–331, § 14. Renumbered from § 732.917 and amended by Laws 2001, c. 2001–226, § 67, eff. Jan. 1, 2002. Amended by Laws 2008, c. 2008–223, § 7, eff. July 1, 2008; Laws 2009, c. 2009–218, § 9, eff. July 1, 2009.

765.518. Eye banks

(1) Any state, county, district, or other public hospital may purchase and provide the necessary facilities and equipment to establish and maintain an eye bank for restoration of sight purposes.

(2) The Department of Education may have prepared, printed, and distributed:

(a) A form document of gift for a gift of the eyes.

(b) An eye bank register consisting of the names of persons who have executed documents for the gift of their eyes.

(c) Wallet cards reciting the document of gift.

Laws 1974, c. 74–106, § 1; Laws 1975, c. 75–220, § 45; Laws 1977, c. 77–147, § 462. Renumbered from § 732.918, by Laws 2001, c. 2001–226, § 68, eff. Jan. 1, 2002.

765.5185. Corneal removal by medical examiners

(1) In any case in which a patient is in need of corneal tissue for a transplant, a district medical examiner or an appropriately qualified designee with training in ophthalmologic techniques may, upon request of any eye bank authorized under s. 765.518, provide the cornea of a decedent whenever all of the following conditions are met:

(a) A decedent who may provide a suitable cornea for the transplant is under the jurisdiction of the medical examiner and an autopsy is required in accordance with s. 406.11.

(b) No objection by the next of kin of the decedent is known by the medical examiner.

(c) The removal of the cornea will not interfere with the subsequent course of an investigation or autopsy.

(2) Neither the district medical examiner nor the medical examiner's appropriately qualified designee nor any eye bank authorized under s. 765.518 may be held liable in any civil or criminal action for failure to obtain consent of the next of kin.

Laws 1977, c. 77–172, § 1; Laws 1978, c. 78–191, § 1; Laws 1997, c. 97–102, § 979; Fla.St.2000, § 732.9185. Renumbered from § 732.9185 by Laws 2001, c. 2001–226, § 69, eff. Jan. 1, 2002. Amended by Laws 2002, c. 2002–1, § 111, eff. May 21, 2002.

765.519. Enucleation of eyes by licensed funeral directors

With respect to a gift of an eye as provided for in this part, a licensed funeral director as defined in chapter 497 who has completed a course in eye enucleation and has received a certificate of competence from the Department of Ophthalmology of the University of Florida School of Medicine, the University of South Florida School of Medicine, or the University of Miami School of Medicine may enucleate eyes for gift after proper certification of death by a physician and in compliance with the intent of the gift as defined in this chapter. No properly certified funeral director acting in accordance with the terms of this part shall have any civil or criminal liability for eye enucleation.

Laws 1974, c. 74–106, § 1; Laws 1975, c. 75–220, § 45; Laws 1980, c. 80–157, § 1. Renumbered from § 732.919, by Laws 2001, c. 2001–226, § 70, eff. Jan. 1, 2002. Amended by Laws 2004, c. 2004–301, § 148, eff. Oct. 1, 2005.

765.521. Donations as part of driver license or identification card process

(1) The agency and the department shall develop and implement a program encouraging and allowing persons to make anatomical gifts as a part of the process of issuing identification cards and issuing and renewing driver licenses. The donor registration card distributed by the department shall include the information required by the uniform donor card under s. 765.514 and such additional information as determined necessary by the department. The department shall also develop and implement a program to identify donors which includes notations on identification cards, driver licenses, and driver records or such other methods as the department develops to clearly indicate the individual's intent to make an anatomical gift. A notation on an individual's driver license or identification card that the individual intends to make an anatomical gift satisfies all requirements for consent to organ or tissue donation. The agency shall provide the necessary supplies and forms from funds appropriated from general revenue or contributions from interested voluntary, nonprofit organizations. The department shall provide the necessary recordkeeping system from funds appropriated from general revenue. The department and the agency shall incur no liability in connection with the performance of any acts authorized herein.

(2) The department, after consultation with and concurrence by the agency, shall adopt rules to implement the provisions of this section according to the provisions of chapter 120.

(3) Funds expended by the agency to carry out the intent of this section may not be taken from funds appropriated for patient care.

Laws 1975, c. 75–71, § 1; Laws 1977, c. 77–16, § 1; Laws 1977, c. 77–147, § 463; Laws 1977, c. 77–174, § 1; Laws 1980, c. 80–134, § 1, 2; Laws 1983, c. 83–171, § 5; Laws 1995, c. 95–423, § 10. Renumbered from § 732.921 and amended by Laws 2001, c. 2001–226, § 71, eff. Jan. 1, 2002. Amended by Laws 2008, c. 2008–223, § 8, eff. July 1, 2008; Laws 2009, c. 2009–218, § 10, eff. July 1, 2009.

765.522. Duty of hospital administrators; liability of hospital administrators and procurement organizations

(1) If, based on accepted medical standards, a hospital patient is a suitable candidate for organ or tissue donation, the hospital administrator or the hospital administrator's designee shall, at or near the time of death, notify the appropriate procurement organization, which shall access the donor registry created by s. 765.5155 or any other donor registry to ascertain the existence of an entry in the registry which has not been revoked or a document of gift executed by the decedent. In the absence of an entry in the donor registry, a document of gift, or other properly executed document, the procurement organization shall request:

(a) The patient's health care surrogate, as authorized in s. 765.512(2); or

(b) If the patient does not have a surrogate, or the surrogate is not reasonably available, any of the persons specified in s. 765.512(3), in the order and manner listed,

to consent to the anatomical gift of the decedent's body for any purpose specified in this part. Except as provided in s. 765.512, in the absence of actual notice of opposition, consent need only be obtained from the person or persons in the highest priority class reasonably available.

(2) A document of gift is valid if executed in accordance with this part or the laws of the state or country where it was executed and where the person making the anatomical gift was domiciled, has a place of residence, or was a citizen at the time the document of gift was executed.

(3) The agency shall establish rules and guidelines concerning the education of individuals who may be designated to perform the request and the procedures to be used in making the request. The agency is authorized to adopt rules concerning the documentation of the request, where such request is made.

(4) If a document of gift is valid under this section, the laws of this state govern the interpretation of the document of gift.

(5) A document of gift or amendment of an anatomical gift is presumed to be valid unless it was not validly executed or was revoked.

(6) There shall be no civil or criminal liability against any procurement organization certified under s. 765.542 or against any hospital or hospital administrator or designee who complies with the provisions of this part and agency rules or if, in the exercise of reasonable care, a request for organ donation is inappropriate and the gift is not made according to this part and agency rules.

(7) The hospital administrator or a designee shall, at or near the time of death of a potential donor, directly notify the affiliated organ procurement organization of the potential organ donor. The organ procurement organization must offer any organ from such a donor first to patients on a Florida-based local or state organ sharing transplant list. For the purpose of this subsection, the term "transplant list" includes certain categories of national or regional organ

sharing for patients of exceptional need or exceptional match, as approved or mandated by the Organ Procurement and Transplantation Network, or its agent. This notification may not be made to a tissue bank or eye bank in lieu of the organ procurement organization unless the tissue bank or eye bank is also designated as an organ procurement organization.

Laws 1986, c. 86–212, § 1; Laws 1987, c. 87–372, § 2; Laws 1995, c. 95–423, § 13; Laws 1997, c. 97–102, § 980; Laws 1998, c. 98–68, § 12; Laws 1999, c. 99–331, § 15. Renumbered from § 732.922, and amended by Laws 2001, c. 2001–226, § 75, eff. Jan. 1, 2002. Amended by Laws 2003, c. 2003–1, § 104, eff. July 1, 2003; Laws 2008, c. 2008–223, § 9, eff. July 1, 2008; Laws 2009, c. 2009–218, § 11, eff. July 1, 2009.

Cross References

Organ and tissue donation, routine inquiry and certification for procurement activities, see § 395.2050.

765.53. Organ Transplant Advisory Council; membership; responsibilities

(1) A statewide technical Organ Transplant Advisory Council is created within the agency, consisting of twelve members who are physicians licensed under chapter 458 or chapter 459, to represent the interests of the public and the clients of the Department of Health or the agency. A person employed by the agency may not be appointed as a member of the council.

(2) The Secretary of Health Care Administration shall appoint all members of the council to serve a term of 2 years.

(3) The Secretary of Health Care Administration shall fill each vacancy on the council for the balance of the unexpired term. Priority consideration must be given to the appointment of an individual whose primary interest, experience, or expertise lies with clients of the Department of Health and the agency. If an appointment is not made within 120 days after a vacancy occurs on the council, the vacancy must be filled by the majority vote of the council.

(4) The members of the council shall elect a chairperson. The term of the chairperson shall be for 2 years, and an individual may not serve as chairperson for more than two consecutive terms.

(5) Members of the council shall receive no compensation, but shall be reimbursed for per diem and travel expenses by the agency in accordance with s. 112.061 while engaged in the performance of their duties.

(6) The responsibilities of the council shall be to recommend to the agency indications for adult and pediatric organ transplants. The council shall also formulate guidelines and standards for organ transplants and for the development of End Stage Organ Disease and Tissue/Organ Transplant programs. The recommendations, guidelines, and standards developed by the council are applicable only to those health programs funded through the agency.

(7) The council shall meet at least annually or upon the call of the chairperson or the Secretary of Health Care Administration.

Laws 1986, c. 86–208, § 1; Laws 1986, c. 86–220, § 88; Fla.St.1989, § 381.602; Laws 1991, c. 91–49, § 8; Laws 1991, c. 91–297, § 52; Laws 1994, c. 94–305, § 3; Laws 1997, c. 97–101, § 50. Amended by Laws 1999, c. 99–299, § 1, eff. Jan. 1, 2000; Laws 2000, c. 2000–305, § 6, eff. Oct. 1, 2000. Renumbered from § 381.0602, by Laws 2003, c. 2003–1, § 33, eff. July 1, 2003. Amended by Laws 2009, c. 2009–218, § 12, eff. July 1, 2009.

765.541. Certification of procurement organizations; agency responsibilities

The agency shall:

(1) Establish a program for the certification of organizations, corporations, or other entities engaged in the procurement of organs, tissues, and eyes for transplantation.

(2) Adopt rules that set forth appropriate standards and guidelines for the program in accordance with ss. 765.541–765.546 and part II of chapter 408. These standards and guidelines must be substantially based on the existing laws of the Federal Government and this state and the existing standards and guidelines of the United Network for Organ Sharing (UNOS), the American Association of Tissue Banks (AATB), the South-Eastern Organ Procurement Foundation (SEOPF), the North American Transplant Coordinators Organization (NATCO), and the Eye Bank Association of America (EBAA). In addition, the agency shall, before adopting these standards and guidelines, seek input from all procurement organizations based in this state.

(3) Collect, keep, and make available to the Governor and the Legislature information regarding the numbers and disposition of organs, tissues, and eyes procured by each certified procurement organization.

(4) Monitor procurement organizations for program compliance.

(5) Provide for the administration of the Organ and Tissue Procurement and Transplantation Advisory Board.

Laws 1991, c. 91–271, § 2; Laws 1994, c. 94–305, § 5. Renumbered from 381.6021 by Laws 2003, c. 2003–1, § 33, eff. July 1, 2003. Amended by Laws 2007, c. 2007–230, § 201, eff. July 1, 2007; Laws 2009, c. 2009–218, § 13, eff. July 1, 2009.

765.542. Requirements to engage in organ, tissue, or eye procurement

(1) The requirements of part II of chapter 408 apply to the provision of services that require licensure pursuant to ss. 765.541–765.546 and part II of chapter 408 and to entities licensed or certified by or applying for such licensure or certification from the agency pursuant to ss. 765.541–765.546. A person may not engage in the practice of organ procurement in this state without being designated as an organ procurement organization by the Secretary of the United States Department of Health and Human Services and being appropriately certified by the agency. A physician or organ procurement organization based outside this state is exempt from these certification requirements if:

(a) The organs are procured for an out-of-state patient who is listed on, or referred through, the United Network for Organ Sharing System; and

(b) The organs are procured through an agreement of an organ procurement organization certified by the state.

(2) A person may not engage in tissue procurement in this state unless it is appropriately certified as a tissue bank by the agency.

(3) A person may not engage in the practice of eye procurement in this state without being appropriately certified as an eye bank by the agency. Funeral directors or direct disposers who retrieve eye tissue for an eye bank certified under this subsection are exempt from the certification requirements under this subsection.

(4) A limited certificate may be issued to a tissue bank or eye bank, certifying only those components of procurement which the bank has chosen to perform. The agency may issue a

limited certificate if it determines that the tissue bank or eye bank is adequately staffed and equipped to operate in conformity with the rules adopted under this section.

Laws 1991, c. 91–271, § 3; Laws 1994, c. 94–305, § 6. Renumbered from 381.6022 by Laws 2003, c. 2003–1, § 33, eff. July 1, 2003. Amended by Laws 2007, c. 2007–230, § 202, eff. July 1, 2007; Laws 2009, c. 2009–218, § 14, eff. July 1, 2009.

765.543. Organ and Tissue Procurement and Transplantation Advisory Board; creation; duties

(1) There is hereby created the Organ and Tissue Procurement and Transplantation Advisory Board, which shall consist of 14 members who are appointed by and report directly to the Secretary of Health Care Administration. The membership must be regionally distributed and must include:

(a) Two representatives who have expertise in vascular organ transplant surgery;

(b) Two representatives who have expertise in vascular organ procurement, preservation, and distribution;

(c) Two representatives who have expertise in musculoskeletal tissue transplant surgery;

(d) Two representatives who have expertise in musculoskeletal tissue procurement, processing, and distribution;

(e) A representative who has expertise in eye and cornea transplant surgery;

(f) A representative who has expertise in eye and cornea procurement, processing, and distribution;

(g) A representative who has expertise in bone marrow procurement, processing, and transplantation;

(h) A representative from the Florida Pediatric Society;

(i) A representative from the Florida Society of Pathologists; and

(j) A representative from the Florida Medical Examiners Commission.

(2) The advisory board members may not be compensated for their services except that they may be reimbursed for their travel expenses as provided by law. Members of the board shall be appointed for 3–year terms of office.

(3) The board shall:

(a) Assist the agency in the development of necessary professional qualifications, including, but not limited to, the education, training, and performance of persons engaged in the various facets of organ and tissue procurement, processing, preservation, and distribution for transplantation;

(b) Assist the agency in monitoring the appropriate and legitimate expenses associated with organ and tissue procurement, processing, and distribution for transplantation and developing methodologies to assure the uniform statewide reporting of data to facilitate the accurate and timely evaluation of the organ and tissue procurement and transplantation system;

(c) Provide assistance to the Florida Medical Examiners Commission in the development of appropriate procedures and protocols to ensure the continued improvement in the approval and release of potential donors by the district medical examiners and associate medical examiners;

(d) Develop with and recommend to the agency the necessary procedures and protocols required to assure that all residents of this state have reasonable access to available organ and tissue transplantation therapy and that residents of this state can be reasonably assured that the statewide procurement transplantation system is able to fulfill their organ and tissue requirements within the limits of the available supply and according to the severity of their medical condition and need; and

(e) Develop with and recommend to the agency any changes to the laws of this state or administrative rules or procedures to ensure that the statewide organ and tissue procurement and transplantation system is able to function smoothly, effectively, and efficiently, in accordance with the Federal Anatomical Gift Act and in a manner that assures the residents of this state that no person or entity profits from the altruistic voluntary donation of organs or tissues.

Laws 1991, c. 91–271, § 4; Laws 1994, c. 94–305, § 7. Amended by Laws 2000, c. 2000–305, § 7, eff. Oct. 1, 2000. Renumbered from 381.6023 by Laws 2003, c. 2003–1, § 33, eff. July 1, 2003. Amended by Laws 2009, c. 2009–218, § 15, eff. July 1, 2009.

765.544. Fees; organ and tissue donor education and procurement

(1) In accordance with s. 408.805, an applicant or a certificateholder shall pay a fee for each application submitted under this part, part II of chapter 408, and applicable rules. The amount of the fee shall be as follows:

(a) An initial application fee of $1,000 from organ procurement organizations and tissue banks and $500 from eye banks.

(b) Annual fees to be used, in the following order of priority, for the certification program, the advisory board, maintenance of the donor registry, and the organ and tissue donor education program, which may not exceed $35,000 per organization:

1. Each organ procurement organization shall pay the greater of $1,000 or 0.25 percent of its total revenues produced from procurement activity in this state by the certificateholder during its most recently completed fiscal or operational year.

2. Each tissue procurement organization shall pay the greater of $1,000 or 0.25 percent of its total revenues from procurement and processing activity in this state by the certificateholder during its most recently completed fiscal or operational year.

3. Each eye bank shall pay the greater of $500 or 0.25 percent of its total revenues produced from procurement activity in this state by the certificateholder during its most recently completed fiscal or operational year.

(2) The agency shall specify by rule the administrative penalties for the purpose of ensuring adherence to the standards of quality and practice required by this chapter, part II of chapter 408, and applicable rules of the agency for continued certification.

(3)(a) Proceeds from fees, administrative penalties, and surcharges collected pursuant to this section must be deposited into the Health Care Trust Fund.

(b) Moneys deposited in the trust fund pursuant to this section must be used exclusively for the implementation, administration, and operation of the certification program and the advisory board, for maintaining the donor registry, and for organ and tissue donor education.

(4) As used in this section, the term "procurement activity in this state" includes the bringing into this state for processing, storage, distribution, or transplantation of organs or tissues that are initially procured in another state or country.

Laws 1991, c. 91–271, § 5; Laws 1994, c. 94–305, § 8; Laws 1996, c. 96–418, § 32. Amended by Laws 1998, c. 98–68, § 3, eff. May 21, 1998; Laws 1998, c. 98–68, § 4, eff. July 1, 1999; Laws 2002, c. 2002–1, § 54, eff. May 21, 2002. Renumbered from 381.6024 by Laws 2003, c. 2003–1, § 33, eff. July 1, 2003. Amended by Laws 2007, c. 2007–230, § 203, eff. July 1, 2007; Laws 2008, c. 2008–9, § 19, eff. July 1, 2008; Laws 2009, c. 2009–218, § 16, eff. July 1, 2009.

Cross References

Organ and tissue donation, delivery of donor registration card, see § 765.515.

765.545. Physician supervision of cadaveric organ and tissue procurement coordinators

Procurement organizations may employ coordinators who are registered nurses, physician's assistants, or other medically trained personnel who meet the relevant standards for procurement organizations adopted by the agency under s. 765.541, to assist in the medical management of organ donors or in the surgical procurement of cadaveric organs, tissues, or eyes for transplantation or research. A coordinator who assists in the medical management of organ donors or in the surgical procurement of cadaveric organs, tissues, or eyes for transplantation or research must do so under the direction and supervision of a physician medical director pursuant to rules and guidelines adopted by the agency. With the exception of organ procurement surgery, this supervision may be indirect supervision. For purposes of this section, the term "indirect supervision" means that the medical director is responsible for the medical actions of the coordinator, that the coordinator is operating under protocols expressly approved by the medical director, and that the medical director or his or her physician designee is always available, in person or by telephone, to provide medical direction, consultation, and advice in cases of organ, tissue, and eye donation and procurement. Although indirect supervision is authorized under this section, direct physician supervision is to be encouraged when appropriate.

Laws 1991, c. 91–271, § 6; Laws 1994, c. 94–305, § 9; Laws 1995, c. 95–148, § 1035. Renumbered from 381.6025 and amended by Laws 2003, c. 2003–1, § 34, eff. July 1, 2003. Amended by Laws 2009, c. 2009–218, § 17, eff. July 1, 2009.

765.546. Procurement of cadaveric organs for transplant by out-of-state physicians

Any physician currently licensed to practice medicine and surgery in the United States may surgically procure in this state cadaveric organs for transplant if:

(1) The organs are being procured for an out-of-state patient who is listed on, or referred through, the United Network for Organ Sharing System; and

(2) The organs are being procured through the auspices of an organ procurement organization certified in this state.

Laws 1991, c. 91–271, § 7. Renumbered from 381.6026 by Laws 2003, c. 2003–1, § 33, eff. July 1, 2003.

765.547. Cooperation between medical examiner and procurement organization

(1) A medical examiner and procurement organization shall cooperate with each other in order to maximize opportunities to recover anatomical gifts for the purpose of transplantation, therapy, research, or education.

(2) The Florida Medical Examiners Commission shall adopt rules establishing cooperative responsibilities between medical examiners and procurement organizations to facilitate and expedite completion of the medical examiner's responsibilities under chapter 406 in a manner that will maximize opportunities to recover anatomical gifts.

(3) This part does not supersede any part of chapter 406 relating to medical examiners and the disposition of dead bodies.

Added by Laws 2009, c. 2009–218, § 18, eff. July 1, 2009.

TITLE XLV

TORTS

Cross References

Combinations restricting trade or commerce, see § 542.15 et seq.
Commercial discrimination, see § 540.01 et seq.
Garnishment in tort actions, see § 77.02.
Husband and wife, joinder of claims, see § 46.031.
Interspousal tort immunity, abrogation, see § 741.235.
Limitation of actions, see § 95.11.
Sanitary nuisances, see § 386.01 et seq.
Wife's torts, husband's liability, see § 741.23.

CHAPTER 768

NEGLIGENCE

PART I.   GENERAL PROVISIONS

Cross References

Culpable negligence as criminal offense, see § 784.05.
Defense of civil actions against public officers, employees, or agents, see § 111.07.
Health professions and occupations, treatment programs for impaired practitioners, see § 456.076.
Manslaughter by culpable negligence, see § 782.07.

PART I.   GENERAL PROVISIONS

768.16.   Wrongful Death Act

Sections 768.16–768.26 may be cited as the "Florida Wrongful Death Act."
Laws 1972, c. 72–35, § 1. Amended by Laws 2003, c. 2003–1, § 105, eff. July 1, 2003.

768.17.   Legislative intent

It is the public policy of the state to shift the losses resulting when wrongful death occurs from the survivors of the decedent to the wrongdoer. Sections 768.16–768.26 are remedial and shall be liberally construed.
Laws 1972, c. 72–35, § 1. Amended by Laws 2003, c. 2003–1, § 106, eff. July 1, 2003.

768.18. Definitions

As used in ss. 768.16–768.26:

(1) "Survivors" means the decedent's spouse, children, parents, and, when partly or wholly dependent on the decedent for support or services, any blood relatives and adoptive brothers and sisters. It includes the child born out of wedlock of a mother, but not the child born out of wedlock of the father unless the father has recognized a responsibility for the child's support.

(2) "Minor children" means children under 25 years of age, notwithstanding the age of majority.

(3) "Support" includes contributions in kind as well as money.

(4) "Services" means tasks, usually of a household nature, regularly performed by the decedent that will be a necessary expense to the survivors of the decedent. These services may vary according to the identity of the decedent and survivor and shall be determined under the particular facts of each case.

(5) "Net accumulations" means the part of the decedent's expected net business or salary income, including pension benefits, that the decedent probably would have retained as savings and left as part of her or his estate if the decedent had lived her or his normal life expectancy. "Net business or salary income" is the part of the decedent's probable gross income after taxes, excluding income from investments continuing beyond death, that remains after deducting the decedent's personal expenses and support of survivors, excluding contributions in kind.

Laws 1972, c. 72–35, § 1; Laws 1977, c. 77–121, § 66; Laws 1977, c. 77–468, § 40; Laws 1981, c. 81–183, § 1; Laws 1989, c. 89–61, § 3; Laws 1990, c. 90–14, § 1. Amended by Laws 1997, c. 97–102, § 1167, eff. July 1, 1997; Laws 2003, c. 2003–1, § 107, eff. July 1, 2003.

Cross References

Minor, definition, see § 1.01.
Rights, privileges and obligations of persons 18 years of age or older, see § 743.07.

768.19. Right of action

When the death of a person is caused by the wrongful act, negligence, default, or breach of contract or warranty of any person, including those occurring on navigable waters, and the event would have entitled the person injured to maintain an action and recover damages if death had not ensued, the person or watercraft that would have been liable in damages if death had not ensued shall be liable for damages as specified in this act notwithstanding the death of the person injured, although death was caused under circumstances constituting a felony.

Laws 1972, c. 72–35, § 1.

Cross References

Felonies, defined, see § 775.08.
Offenses on navigable waters, see § 861.02 et seq.
Survival of actions, generally, see § 46.021.
Warranties, see § 672.314 et seq.

768.20. Parties

The action shall be brought by the decedent's personal representative, who shall recover for the benefit of the decedent's survivors and estate all damages, as specified in this act, caused by the injury resulting in death. When a personal injury to the decedent results in death, no action for the personal injury shall survive, and any such action pending at the time of death shall abate. The wrongdoer's personal representative shall be the defendant if the wrongdoer dies before or pending the action. A defense that would bar or reduce a survivor's recovery if she or he were the plaintiff may be asserted against the survivor, but shall not affect the recovery of any other survivor.

Laws 1972, c. 72–35, § 1. Amended by Laws 1997, c. 97–102, § 1168, eff. July 1, 1997.

Cross References

Guardianship law, see § 744.101 et seq.
Parties, generally, see Civil Procedure Rule 1.210.
Survival of actions, generally, see § 46.021.

768.21. Damages

All potential beneficiaries of a recovery for wrongful death, including the decedent's estate, shall be identified in the complaint, and their relationships to the decedent shall be alleged. Damages may be awarded as follows:

(1) Each survivor may recover the value of lost support and services from the date of the decedent's injury to her or his death, with interest, and future loss of support and services from the date of death and reduced to present value. In evaluating loss of support and services, the survivor's relationship to the decedent, the amount of the decedent's probable net income available for distribution to the particular survivor, and the replacement value of the decedent's services to the survivor may be considered. In computing the duration of future losses, the joint life expectancies of the survivor and the decedent and the period of minority, in the case of healthy minor children, may be considered.

(2) The surviving spouse may also recover for loss of the decedent's companionship and protection and for mental pain and suffering from the date of injury.

(3) Minor children of the decedent, and all children of the decedent if there is no surviving spouse, may also recover for lost parental companionship, instruction, and guidance and for mental pain and suffering from the date of injury. For the purposes of this subsection, if both spouses die within 30 days of one another as a result of the same wrongful act or series of acts arising out of the same incident, each spouse is considered to have been predeceased by the other.

(4) Each parent of a deceased minor child may also recover for mental pain and suffering from the date of injury. Each parent of an adult child may also recover for mental pain and suffering if there are no other survivors.

(5) Medical or funeral expenses due to the decedent's injury or death may be recovered by a survivor who has paid them.

(6) The decedent's personal representative may recover for the decedent's estate the following:

(a) Loss of earnings of the deceased from the date of injury to the date of death, less lost support of survivors excluding contributions in kind, with interest. Loss of the prospective net accumulations of an estate, which might reasonably have been expected but for the wrongful death, reduced to present money value, may also be recovered:

1. If the decedent's survivors include a surviving spouse or lineal descendants; or

2. If the decedent is not a minor child as defined in s. 768.18(2), there are no lost support and services recoverable under subsection (1), and there is a surviving parent.

(b) Medical or funeral expenses due to the decedent's injury or death that have become a charge against her or his estate or that were paid by or on behalf of decedent, excluding amounts recoverable under subsection (5).

(c) Evidence of remarriage of the decedent's spouse is admissible.

(7) All awards for the decedent's estate are subject to the claims of creditors who have complied with the requirements of probate law concerning claims.

(8) The damages specified in subsection (3) shall not be recoverable by adult children and the damages specified in subsection (4) shall not be recoverable by parents of an adult child with respect to claims for medical negligence as defined by s. 766.106(1).

Laws 1972, c. 72–35, § 1; Laws 1981, c. 81–183, § 2; Laws 1985, c. 85–260, § 1; Laws 1990, c. 90–14, § 2. Amended by Laws 1997, c. 97–102, § 1169, eff. July 1, 1997; Laws 2002, c. 2002–44, § 1, eff. April 16, 2002; Laws 2003, c. 2003–416, § 66, eff. Sept. 15, 2003.

Cross References

Limitation of actions other than for the recovery of real property, see F.S.A. § 95.11.
Wrongful death damages for civil actions to enforce rights of nursing home residents, see § 429.29.

768.22. Form of verdict

The amounts awarded to each survivor and to the estate shall be stated separately in the verdict.
Laws 1972, c. 72–35, § 1.

768.23. Protection of minors and incompetents

The court shall provide protection for any amount awarded for the benefit of a minor child or an incompetent pursuant to the Florida Guardianship Law.
Laws 1972, c. 72–35, § 1.

Cross References

Florida Guardianship Law, see § 744.101 et seq.
Survival of actions, see § 46.021.

768.24. Death of a survivor before judgment

A survivor's death before final judgment shall limit the survivor's recovery to lost support and services to the date of his or her death. The personal representative shall pay the amount recovered to the personal representative of the deceased survivor.
Laws 1972, c. 72–35, § 1. Amended by Laws 1997, c. 97–102, § 1170, eff. July 1, 1997.

Cross References

Parties, survival of actions, see Civil Procedure Rule 1.210.
Survival of actions, see § 46.021.

768.25. Court approval of settlements

While an action under this act is pending, no settlement as to amount or apportionment among the beneficiaries which is objected to by any survivor or which affects a survivor who is a minor or an incompetent shall be effective unless approved by the court.
Laws 1972, c. 72–35, § 1.

768.26. Litigation expenses

Attorneys' fees and other expenses of litigation shall be paid by the personal representative and deducted from the awards to the survivors and the estate in proportion to the amounts awarded to them, but expenses incurred for the benefit of a particular survivor or the estate shall be paid from their awards.

Laws 1972, c. 72–35, § 1.

FLORIDA RULES OF COURT
PROBATE RULES
PART I. GENERAL

PART II. PROBATE

PROBATE RULES

Effective Date

Rules of Probate and Guardianship promulgated by order of the Florida Supreme Court on July 26, 1967, to take effect on January 1, 1968, (201 So.2d 409), as amended, were superseded by the following rules adopted December 17, 1975, to take effect January 1, 1976 (324 So.2d 38).

Revision

The rules were revised March 31, 1977, effective July 1, 1977 (344 So.2d 828); September 29, 1988, effective January 1, 1989 (531 So.2d 1261); August 22, 1991, effective October 1, 1991 (584 So.2d 964); September 24, 1992, effective January 1, 1993 (607 So.2d 1306); September 28, 2000, effective January 1, 2001 (778 So.2d 272); October 11, 2001, effective October 11, 2001 (807 So.2d 622); May 2, 2002 (824 So.2d 849); revised June 19, 2003 (848 So.2d 1069); September 30, 2004, effective October 1, 2004 (887 So.2d 1090); September 29, 2005, effective January 1, 2006 (912 So.2d 1178); February 1, 2007 (948 So.2d 735); July 5, 2007, eff. January 1, 2008 (959 So.2d 1170); July 12, 2007 (964 So.2d 140); July 10, 2008 (986 So.2d 576); September 2, 2010 (50 So.3d 578); July 7, 2011 (67 So.3d 1035); September 28, 2011 (73 So.3d 205); September 28, 2011 (73 So.3d 205); October 1, 2011 (78 So.3d 1045); September 2, 2010, effective January 1, 2011 (50 So.3d 578); July 12, 2012, effective October 1, 2012 (95 So.3d 96); October 18, 2012, effective nunc pro tunc September 1, 2012 (102 So.3d 505); October 18, 2012, effective December 1, 2012, April 1, 2013, October 1, 2013 (102 So.3d 451); September 26, 2013, effective

January 1, 2014 (123 So.3d 31); November 27, 2013, effective November 27, 2013 (131 So. 3d 717); May 22, 2014, effective May 22, 2014 (139 So.3d 875).

PART I. GENERAL

Rule 5.010. Scope

These rules govern the procedure in all probate and guardianship proceedings and shall be known as the Florida Probate Rules and may be cited as Fla. Prob. R. Part I applies to all proceedings. Part II applies to probate alone, Part III applies to guardianship alone, and Part IV applies to expedited judicial intervention concerning medical treatment procedures. The Florida Rules of Civil Procedure apply only as provided herein.

Amended March 31, 1977, effective July 1, 1977 (344 So.2d 828); Sept. 29, 1988, effective Jan. 1. 1989 (531 So.2d 1261); Aug. 22, 1991, effective Oct. 1, 1991 (584 So.2d 964); Sept. 24, 1992, effective Jan. 1, 1993 (607 So.2d 1306).

Rules of Civil Procedure

The Rules of Civil Procedure applicable to probate and guardianship proceedings pursuant to Probate Rule 5.010, as provided for in Rule 5.080 are set out in an appendix following the text of these rules.

Committee Notes

Rule History

1975 Revision: These rules shall govern the procedures to be followed in all matters pending on or commenced after January 1, 1976, including procedures for the enforcement of substantive rights that have vested before that date. See section 731.011, Florida Statutes.

1977 Revision: The changes in these rules shall take effect on July 1, 1977.

1988 Revision: In the opinion reported at 460 So. 2d 906, the Florida Supreme Court directed the Probate and Guardianship Rules Committee to study the statutes and attempt to identify those portions of the Florida Probate Code, the Florida Guardianship Law, and other statutes that contained procedural provisions. When those procedural provisions were identified, the committee was charged to promulgate rules incorporating those procedures.

The committee has reviewed the statutes and has found a substantial measure of procedure that was contained only in the statutes for which there were no corresponding rules. The committee also determined that much of the procedure in the statutes already had a rule counterpart.

New rules added, or prior rules amended, in 1988 to add procedural matters previously found only in the statutes are rules 5.050, 5.122, 5.171, 5.180, 5.201, 5.235, 5.270, 5.275, 5.355, 5.360, 5.385, 5.386, 5.400, 5.440, 5.475, 5.490, and 5.510. With only one exception (see rule 5.050), the only portion of the statutes that has been reviewed in detail, and for which rules have been created, is the Florida Probate Code. Other portions of the statutes mentioned in the opinion cited above remain for the next cycle of this committee to review.

As the committee wrote rules to transfer the statutory procedure into these rules, an attempt was made to write the rule without changing the meaning of the statute. It was not possible or advisable to use the exact wording of the statute in some instances, and in those instances the committee rewrote the statutory language in the format used in the rules generally. Even under those circumstances, the committee attempted to transfer the entire procedural portion of the statute without changing its meaning. Where it was specifically intended in a few instances to add to existing statutory procedure, that fact is noted in the relevant committee note. The committee felt strongly that it would be detrimental to the orderly process of estate probate and related procedures if a rule specified a different procedure than was specified in the related statute, even though the statute must, under the Florida Constitution, yield to the rule when there is a conflict.

The committee, through the proper channels in The Florida Bar (initially, the Probate Law Committee of the Real Property, Probate and Trust Law Section), intends to ask the legislature to repeal those portions of the statutes that are procedural when there are similar rules already in place, or when similar new rules are added by this opinion. It is the opinion of the committee that continuing to maintain procedure in the statutes when there is a rule specifying that procedure is detrimental to the orderly process of the court and the public that it serves, especially when, over time, the statute and the rule may diverge.

Although the supreme court has adopted these recommended rules, it has not specifically determined that all of the provisions of the statutes that were procedural have now been adopted as a rule. This is a continuing project for the committee and although these new rules and changes represent a substantial transition of procedure into the rules, the committee does not suggest that the transition is complete. The court is not precluded from examining any particular statute or rule in the context of a particular actual dispute.

1991 Revision: Rule revised to reflect addition of new Part IV dealing with expedited judicial intervention concerning medical treatment procedures.

1992 Revision: In 1989, the Florida Legislature enacted a comprehensive revision to Florida's guardianship law. In response, the Florida Supreme Court appointed an ad hoc committee to recommend temporary rules of procedure for the new law. In an opinion at 551 So. 2d 452 (Fla. 1989), the court adopted the temporary rules recommended by the ad hoc committee, to replace Part III of the then-existing Florida Probate Rules, effective October 1, 1989. In its opinion, the court also directed the Florida Probate Rules Committee to review the new laws and, on a priority basis, to recommend permanent rules of procedure.

The committee reviewed the Florida Guardianship Law enacted in 1989, as well as revisions to the law enacted in 1990, and presented its rule recommendations to the court in 1991. The court, in an opinion at 584 So. 2d 964, adopted the recommendations with minor exceptions, to be effective October 1, 1991.

In 1990, the court also rendered its opinion in In re Guardianship of Browning, 568 So. 2d 4 (Fla. 1990), regarding a person's right to refuse life-prolonging medical procedures. In that decision, the court directed the committee to recommend a rule to provide for expedited judicial intervention. In response, the committee created a new Part IV of these rules and recommended rule 5.900, which was adopted by the court, with minor changes, in its opinion at 584 So. 2d 964, effective October 1, 1991.

The committee continued its efforts to review the Florida Probate Code and to promulgate or amend rules regarding any procedural portions of those statutes. As a result of those efforts, as well as the efforts described above, the committee recommended amendments to rules 5.010, 5.025, 5.040, 5.050, 5.200, 5.240, 5.310, 5.346, 5.400, 5.470, 5.550, 5.560, 5.590, 5.600, 5.610, 5.620, 5.630, 5.640, 5.650, 5.660, 5.670, 5.680, 5.695, 5.700, 5.710, and 5.800; creation of new rules 5.496, 5.540, 5.541, 5.555, 5.635, 5.636, 5.690, 5.696, 5.697, 5.705, and 5.900; and deletion of rule 5.495. In addition, the committee recommended editorial changes in virtually all the rules so that they would conform stylistically to one another and to all other rules promulgated by the supreme court.

2003 Revision: The committee has promulgated numerous changes in the rules and in the committee notes to many of the rules, in response to legislative amendments that deleted procedural aspects of a number of statutes in the Florida Probate Code, including deletion and re-titling of some statutes. See Ch. 2001–226, Laws of Fla.

Rule References

Fla. Prob. R. 5.025 Adversary proceedings.

Fla. Prob. R. 5.040(a)(3)(B) Notice.

Fla. Prob. R. 5.050 Transfer of proceedings.

Fla. Prob. R. 5.080 Discovery and subpoena.

Fla. Prob. R. 5.230(e) Commission to prove will.

Fla. R. App. P. 9.800 Uniform citation system.

Historical Notes

The Florida Supreme court in opinion of November 30, 1984, effective January 1, 1985, (458 So.2d 1079), provided:

"Those portions of chapters 731 through 735, Florida Statutes (Florida Probate Code), chapter 744, Florida Statutes (Florida Guardianship Law), chapter 737, Florida Statutes (pertaining to trust administration), and chapter 738, Florida Statutes (pertaining to principal and income) which are procedural are hereby adopted as temporary rules of procedure of this Court. The probate and guardianship rules committee is directed to study these temporary rules and to incorporate recommendations regarding them into the next quadrennial review of the probate and guardianship rules. These temporary rules of procedure will be effective immediately upon the filing of this opinion."

Cross References

Determination of substantive rights and procedures under probate code, see F.S.A. § 731.011.
Singular as including plural, see F.S.A. § 1.01.

Rule 5.015. General Definitions

(a) General. The definitions and rules of construction stated or referred to in sections 1.01 and 393.12, Florida Statutes, and chapters 731, 732, 733, 734, 735, 736, 738, 739, and 744, Florida Statutes, as amended from time to time, shall apply to these rules, unless otherwise defined in these rules.

(b) Specific Definitions. When used in these rules

(1) "Certified copy" means a copy of a document signed and verified as a true copy by the officer to whose custody the original is entrusted;

(2) "formal notice" means notice under rule 5.040(a);

(3) "informal notice" means notice under rule 5.040(b);

(4) "judge" means a judge of the circuit court, including any judge elected, appointed, substituted, or assigned to serve as judge of the court;

(5) "guardian advocate" means a person appointed for a person with a developmental disability pursuant to section 393.12, Florida Statutes;

(6) "guardian" means a person appointed pursuant to chapter 744, Florida Statutes, or a guardian advocate unless a rule indicates otherwise;

(7) "ward" means an individual for whom a guardian is appointed.

Amended March 31, 1977, effective July 1, 1977 (344 So.2d 828); Sept. 29, 1988, effective Jan. 1, 1989 (537 So.2d 500); Sept. 29, 1989, effective Oct. 1, 1989 (549 So.2d 665); Nov. 17, 1989 (551 So.2d 452); Sept. 24, 1992, effective Jan. 1, 1993 (607 So.2d 1306); Sept. 28, 2000, effective Jan. 1, 2001 (778 So.2d 272); July 12, 2007 (964 So.2d 140); July 10, 2008 (986 So.2d 576).

Committee Notes

Rule History

1977 Revision: No change in rule. Correction of typographical error in committee note.

This is intended to simplify drafting of these rules and should be liberally construed. See Fla. Prob. R. 5.190 and 5.540 and also §§ 731.201 and 744.102, Fla. Stat.

1988 Revision: Rule was expanded due to deletion of rule 5.190. Committee notes expanded. Citation form changes in rule and committee notes.

1992 Revision: Citation form changes in rule and committee notes.

2000 Revision: Subdivision (b)(2) amended to delete outdated reference to rule 5.550(c).

2007 Revision: Subdivision (a) amended to add reference to chapter 736, Florida Statutes, which was added to the statutes effective July 1, 2007 and which replaces deleted chapter 737, and to add reference to chapter 739, Florida Statutes, which was added effective July 1, 2005. Committee notes revised.

2008 Revision: Subdivision (a) amended to add reference to section 393.12, Florida Statutes, which governs guardian advocates for persons with developmental disabilities. As provided by section 744.102(11), the term "guardian advocate" as used in the Florida Guardianship Law and these rules does not include a guardian advocate appointed for a person determined to lack capacity to consent to treatment under section 394.4598, Florida Statutes. Subdivisions (b)(5) through (b)(7) added to reflect 2008 amendments to section 393.12, Florida Statutes. Committee notes revised.

Statutory References

§ 1.01, Fla. Stat. Definitions.

§ 393.063, Fla. Stat. Definitions.

§ 393.12, Fla. Stat. Capacity; appointment of guardian advocate.

§ 731.201, Fla. Stat. General definitions.

§ 736.0103, Fla. Stat. Definitions.

§ 738.102, Fla. Stat. Definitions.

§ 739.102, Fla. Stat. Definitions.

§ 744.102, Fla. Stat. Definitions.

Cross References

Definitions,
    Guardianship law, see F.S.A. § 744.102.
    Probate code, see F.S.A. § 731.201.
    Rules of probate, see Probate Rule 5.040.

Rule 5.020. Pleadings; Verification; Motions

(a) **Forms of Pleading.** Pleadings shall be signed by the attorney of record, and by the pleader when required by these rules. All technical forms of pleadings are abolished. No defect of form impairs substantial rights, and no defect in the statement of jurisdictional facts actually existing renders any proceeding void.

(b) **Petition.** A petition shall contain a short and plain statement of the relief sought, the grounds therefor, and the jurisdiction of the court where the jurisdiction has not already been shown.

(c) **Motions.** Any other application to the court for an order shall be by written motion, unless made orally during a hearing or trial. The motion shall state with particularity the grounds therefor and shall set forth the relief or order sought.

(d) **Rehearing.** A motion for rehearing of any order or judgment shall be served not later than 10 days after the date of filing the order or judgment with the clerk as shown on the face of the order or judgment.

(e) Verification. When verification of a document is required, the document filed shall include an oath, affirmation, or the following statement:

"Under penalties of perjury, I declare that I have read the foregoing, and the facts alleged are true, to the best of my knowledge and belief."

Amended March 31, 1977, effective July 1, 1977 (344 So.2d 828); Sept. 4, 1980, effective Jan. 1, 1981 (387 So.2d 949); Sept. 13, 1984, effective Jan. 1, 1985 (458 So.2d 1079); Sept. 29, 1988, effective Jan. 1, 1989 (537 So.2d 500); Sept. 24, 1992, effective Jan. 1, 1993 (986 So.2d 576).

Committee Notes

The time for determining when a motion for rehearing must be served has been clarified in view of Casto v. Casto, 404 So. 2d 1046 (Fla. 1981).

Rule History

1977 Revision: Editorial change (rule) and expansion of committee note. Subdivisions (a), (b), and (d) substantially the same as subdivisions (a), (b), and (f) of prior rule 5.030. Subdivision (c) taken from section 731.104, Florida Statutes. For adversary proceedings see new rule 5.025. Notice of administration is not a pleading within the meaning of this rule.

1980 Revision: Subdivisions (c) and (d) have been redesignated as (e) and (f). New subdivisions (c) and (d) are added to provide for the use of motions in probate proceedings other than adversary proceedings and to specifically authorize a procedure for rehearing.

1984 Revision: Minor editorial changes. Subdivision (f) of prior rule has been deleted as it is now covered under the adversary rules.

1988 Revision: Editorial change in caption of (a). Committee notes revised. Citation form change in committee notes.

1992 Revision: Editorial changes. Committee notes revised. Citation form changes in rule and committee notes.

2003 Revision: Committee notes revised.

2008 Revision: Committee notes revised.

2010 Revision: Committee notes revised.

Statutory References

§ 393.12, Fla. Stat. Capacity; appointment of guardian advocate.

§ 731.104, Fla. Stat. Verification of documents.

§ 731.201, Fla. Stat. General definitions.

§ 733.202, Fla. Stat. Petition.

§ 733.604(1), Fla. Stat. Inventories and accountings; public records exemptions.

§ 733.901, Fla. Stat. Final discharge.

§ 735.203, Fla. Stat. Petition for summary administration.

§ 744.104, Fla. Stat. Verification of documents.

§ 744.3085, Fla. Stat. Guardian advocates.

§ 744.3201, Fla. Stat. Petition to determine incapacity.

§ 744.331, Fla. Stat. Procedures to determine incapacity.

§ 744.334, Fla. Stat. Petition for appointment of guardian or professional guardian; contents.

Rule References

Fla. Prob. R. 5.025 Adversary proceedings.

Fla. Prob. R. 5.200 Petition for administration.

Fla. Prob. R. 5.205(b) Filing evidence of death.

Fla. Prob. R. 5.320 Oath of personal representative.

Fla. Prob. R. 5.330 Execution by personal representative.

Fla. Prob. R. 5.350 Continuance of unincorporated business or venture.

Fla. Prob. R. 5.370(a) Sales of real property where no power conferred.

Fla. Prob. R. 5.405(b) Proceedings to determine homestead real property.

Fla. Prob. R. 5.530 Summary administration.

Fla. Prob. R. 5.550 Petition to determine incapacity.

Fla. Prob. R. 5.560 Petition for appointment of guardian of an incapacitated person.

Fla. Prob. R. 5.600 Oath.

Fla. Prob. R. 5.649 Guardian advocate.

Cross References

Computation of time, see Civil Procedure Rule 1.090.
Perjury, see F.S.A. § 837.011 et seq.
Petitions,
    Definition, see F.S.A. § 731.201.
    Determination of beneficiaries, see F.S.A. § 733.105.
    Removal of personal representative, see F.S.A. § 733.505.
Verification of documents, see F.S.A. § 731.104.
Waiver of notice and consent to action or proceeding, see F.S.A. § 731.302.
Will construction, probate a prerequisite to petition, see F.S.A. § 733.213.

Rule 5.025. Adversary Proceedings

(a) **Specific Adversary Proceedings.** The following are adversary proceedings unless otherwise ordered by the court: proceedings to remove a personal representative, surcharge a personal representative, remove a guardian, surcharge a guardian, probate a lost or destroyed will or later-discovered will, determine beneficiaries, construe a will, reform a will, modify a will, cancel a devise, partition property for the purposes of distribution, determine pretermitted status, determine pretermitted share, determine amount of elective share and contribution, and for revocation of probate of a will.

(b) **Declared Adversary Proceedings.** Other proceedings may be declared adversary by service on interested persons of a separate declaration that the proceeding is adversary.

(1) If served by the petitioner, the declaration must be served with the petition to which it relates.

(2) If served by the respondent, the declaration and a written response to the petition must be served at the earlier of:

    (A) within 20 days after service of the petition, or

    (B) prior to the hearing date on the petition.

(3) When the declaration is served by a respondent, the petitioner must promptly serve formal notice on all other interested persons.

(c) **Adversary Status by Order.** The court may determine any proceeding to be an adversary proceeding at any time.

(d) **Notice and Procedure in Adversary Proceedings.**

(1) Petitioner must serve formal notice.

---

(2) After service of formal notice, the proceedings, as nearly as practicable, must be conducted similar to suits of a civil nature, including entry of defaults. The Florida Rules of Civil Procedure govern, except for rule 1.525.

(3) The court on its motion or on motion of any interested person may enter orders to avoid undue delay in the main administration.

(4) If a proceeding is already commenced when an order is entered determining the proceeding to be adversary, it must thereafter be conducted as an adversary proceeding. The order must require interested persons to serve written defenses, if any, within 20 days from the date of the order. It is not necessary to re-serve the petition except as ordered by the court.

(5) When the proceedings are adversary, the caption of subsequent pleadings, as an extension of the probate caption, must include the name of the first petitioner and the name of the first respondent.

Amended March 31, 1977, effective July 1, 1977 (344 So.2d 828); Sept. 13, 1984, effective Jan. 1, 1985 (458 So.2d 1079); Sept. 29, 1988, effective Jan. 1, 1989 (537 So.2d 500); Sept. 24, 1992, effective Jan. 1, 1993 (607 So.2d 1306); Oct. 11, 2001 (807 So.2d 622); Jan. 10, 2002 (816 So.2d 1095); Sept. 28, 2011 (73 So.3d 205).

Committee Notes

The court on its initiative or on motion of any party may order any proceeding to be adversary or nonadversary or enter any order that will avoid undue delay. The personal representative would be an interested person in all adversary proceedings. A prescribed form for the caption is provided that will facilitate the clerk's and the court's ability to segregate such adversary proceeding from other adversary proceedings and from the main probate file:

Court
Case #

In Re Estate of John B. Jones	)
	)
Julia Jones,	)
	)
Petitioner,	)
	)
v.	)
	)
Harold Jones, as Personal	)
Representative, et al.,	)
	)
Respondents.	)

Rule History

1975 Revision: New rule. 324 So. 2d 38.

1977 Revision: Editorial changes to (a)(1).

1984 Revision: Extensive changes, Committee notes revised and expanded.

1988 Revision: Changes in (a) add proceedings to remove a guardian and to surcharge a guardian to the list of specific adversary proceedings and delete proceedings to determine and award the elective share from the list. Change in (b)(4) clarifies on whom the petitioner must serve formal notice. Editorial change in (d)(2) and (d)(5). Committee notes revised. Citation form changes in committee notes.

1992 Revision: Deletion of (b)(3) as unnecessary. Former (b)(4) renumbered as new (b)(3). Committee notes revised. Citation form changes in committee notes.

2001 Revision: Change in (a) to add determination of amount of elective share and contribution as specific adversary proceedings. Committee notes revised.

2003 Revision: Committee notes revised.

2008 Revision: Committee notes revised.

2011 Revision: Subdivision (a) revised to add "reform a will, modify a will" and "determine pretermitted status." Subdivision (d)(2) modified to insure that an award of attorneys' fees in a probate or guardianship proceeding follows the law and procedures established for such proceedings, rather than the law and procedures for civil proceedings. *See Amendments to the Florida Family Law Rules of Procedure (Rule 12.525)*, 897 So. 2d 467 (Fla. 2005). Editorial changes to conform to the court's guidelines for rules submissions as set forth in Administrative Order AOSC06-14. Committee Notes revised.

Statutory References

§ 393.12, Fla. Stat. Capacity; appointment of guardian advocate.

§§ 732.201–732.2155, Fla. Stat. Elective share of surviving spouse.

§ 732.301, Fla. Stat. Pretermitted spouse.

§ 732.302, Fla. Stat. Pretermitted children.

§ 732.507, Fla. Stat. Effect of subsequent marriage, birth, adoption, or dissolution of marriage.

§§ 732.6005–732.611, Fla. Stat. Rules of construction.

§ 732.615, Fla. Stat. Reformation to correct mistakes.

§ 732.616, Fla. Stat. Modification to achieve testator's tax objectives.

§ 733.105, Fla. Stat. Determination of beneficiaries.

§ 733.107, Fla. Stat. Burden of proof in contests; presumption of undue influence.

§ 733.109, Fla. Stat. Revocation of probate.

§ 733.207, Fla. Stat. Establishment and probate of lost or destroyed will.

§ 733.208, Fla. Stat. Discovery of later will.

§ 733.504, Fla. Stat. Removal of personal representative; causes for removal.

§ 733.505, Fla. Stat. Jurisdiction in removal proceedings.

§ 733.506, Fla. Stat. Proceedings for removal.

§ 733.5061, Fla. Stat. Appointment of successor upon removal.

§ 733.603, Fla. Stat. Personal representative to proceed without court order.

§ 733.609, Fla. Stat. Improper exercise of power; breach of fiduciary duty.

§ 733.619(2), (4), Fla. Stat. Individual liability of personal representative.

§ 733.814, Fla. Stat. Partition for purpose of distribution.

§ 744.3085, Fla. Stat. Guardian advocates.

§ 744.474, Fla. Stat. Reasons for removal of guardian.

§ 744.477, Fla. Stat. Proceedings for removal of a guardian.

Rule References

Fla. Prob. R. 5.040 Notice.

Fla. Prob. R. 5.270 Revocation of probate.

Fla. Prob. R. 5.360 Elective share.

Fla. Prob. R. 5.365 Petition for dower.

Fla. Prob. R. 5.440 Proceedings for removal.

Fla. Prob. R. 5.649 Guardian advocate.

Fla. Prob. R. 5.660 Proceedings for removal of guardian.

Fla. Prob. R. 5.681 Restoration of rights of person with developmental disability.

Fla. R. Civ. P. 1.140 Defenses.

Fla. R. Civ. P. 1.160 Motions.

Fla. R. Civ. P. 1.200 Pretrial procedure.

Fla. R. Civ. P. 1.280 General provisions governing discovery.

Fla. R. Civ. P. 1.290 Depositions before action or pending appeal.

Fla. R. Civ. P. 1.310 Depositions upon oral examination.

Fla. R. Civ. P. 1.340 Interrogatories to parties.

Fla. R. Civ. P. 1.380 Failure to make discovery; sanctions.

Cross References

Default judgments, see Civil Procedure Rule 1.500.

Revocation of probate proceedings, see F.S.A. § 733.109.

Scope and application of civil procedure rules, see Civil Procedure Rule 1.010.

Rule 5.030. Attorneys

(a) **Required; Exception.** Every guardian and every personal representative, unless the personal representative remains the sole interested person, shall be represented by an attorney admitted to practice in Florida. A guardian or personal representative who is an attorney admitted to practice in Florida may represent himself or herself as guardian or personal representative. A guardian advocate is not required to be represented by an attorney unless otherwise required by law or the court.

(b) **Limited Appearance Without Court Order.** An attorney of record for an interested person in a proceeding governed by these rules shall be the attorney of record in all other proceedings in the administration of the same estate or guardianship, except service of process in an independent action on a claim, unless at the time of appearance the attorney files a notice specifically limiting the attorney's appearance only to the particular proceeding or matter in which the attorney appears. At the conclusion of that proceeding or matter, the attorney's role terminates upon the attorney filing notice of completion of limited appearance and serving a copy on the client and other interested persons.

(c) **Withdrawal or Limited Appearance With Court Order.** An attorney of record may withdraw or limit the attorney's appearance with approval of the court, after filing a motion setting forth the reasons and serving a copy on the client and other interested persons.

Amended March 31, 1977, effective July 1, 1977 (344 So.2d 828); June 14, 1979, effective July 1, 1979 (372 So.2d 449); Sept. 13, 1984, effective Jan. 1, 1985 (458 So.2d 1079); Sept. 29, 1988, effective Jan. 1, 1989 (537 So.2d 500); Sept. 24, 1992, effective Jan. 1, 1993 (607 So.2d 1306); Sept. 29, 2005, effective Jan. 1, 2006 (912 So.2d 1178); Feb. 1, 2007 (948 So.2d 735); July 10, 2008 (986 So.2d 576); Sept. 2, 2010, effective Jan. 1, 2011 (50 So.3d 578).

Committee Notes

The appearance of an attorney in an estate is a general appearance unless (i) specifically limited at the time of such appearance or (ii) the court orders otherwise. This rule does not affect the right of a party to employ additional attorneys who, if members of The Florida Bar, may appear at any time.

Rule History

1975 Revision: Subdivision (a) is same as prior rule 5.040 with added provision for withdrawal of attorney similar to Florida Rule of Appellate Procedure 2.3(d)(2). Subdivision (b) reflects ruling in case of State ex rel. Falkner v. Blanton, 297 So. 2d 825 (Fla. 1974).

1977 Revision: Editorial change requiring filing of petition for withdrawal and service of copy upon interested persons. Editorial change in citation forms in rule and committee note.

1984 Revision: Minor editorial changes and addition of subdivision (c). Committee notes expanded.

1988 Revision: Editorial changes and order of subdivisions rearranged. Committee notes expanded. Citation form changes in committee notes.

1992 Revision: Editorial changes. Committee notes revised. Citation form changes in committee notes.

2003 Revision: Committee notes revised.

2005 Revision: Committee notes revised.

2006 Revision: Committee notes revised.

2008 Revision: Subdivision (a) amended to reflect that a guardian advocate may not be required to be represented by an attorney in some instances. Committee notes revised.

2010 Revision: Subdivisions (b) and (c) amended to clarify the procedure for termination of an attorney's representation of an interested person either with or without court order.

2012 Revision: Committee notes revised.

Statutory References

§ 393.12, Fla. Stat. Capacity; appointment of guardian advocate.

§ 731.301, Fla. Stat. Notice.

§ 733.106, Fla. Stat. Costs and attorney's fees.

§ 733.212, Fla. Stat. Notice of administration; filing of objections.

§ 733.6175, Fla. Stat. Proceedings for review of employment of agents and compensation of personal representatives and employees of estate.

§ 744.108, Fla. Stat. Guardian's and attorney's fees and expenses.

§ 744.3085, Fla. Stat. Guardian advocates.

Rule References

Fla. Prob. R. 5.041 Service of pleadings and documents.

Fla. Prob. R. 5.110(b), (c) Resident agent.

Fla. R. Jud. Admin. 2.505 Attorneys.

Fla. R. Jud. Admin. 2.516 Service of pleadings and documents.

Fla. R. App. P. 9.440 Attorneys.

Rule 5.040. Notice

(a) Formal Notice.

(1) When formal notice is given, a copy of the pleading or motion shall be served on interested persons, together with a notice requiring the person served to serve written defenses on the person giving notice within 20 days after service of the notice, exclusive of the day of

---

service, and to file the original of the written defenses with the clerk of the court either before service or immediately thereafter, and notifying the person served that failure to serve written defenses as required may result in a judgment or order for the relief demanded in the pleading or motion, without further notice.

(2) After service of formal notice, informal notice of any hearing on the pleading or motion shall be served on interested persons, provided that if no written defense is served within 20 days after service of formal notice on an interested person, the pleading or motion may be considered ex parte as to that person, unless the court orders otherwise.

(3) Formal notice shall be served:

(A) by sending a copy by any commercial delivery service requiring a signed receipt or by any form of mail requiring a signed receipt as follows:

(i) to the attorney representing an interested person; or

(ii) to an interested person who has filed a request for notice at the address given in the request for notice; or

(iii) to an incapacitated person or a person with a developmental disability to the person's usual place of abode and to the person's legal guardian, if any, at the guardian's usual place of abode or regular place of business; or, if there is no legal guardian, to the incapacitated person or person with a developmental disability at the person's usual place of abode and on the person, if any, having care or custody of the incapacitated person or person with a developmental disability at the usual place of abode or regular place of business of such custodian; or

(iv) to a minor whose disabilities of nonage are not removed, by serving the persons designated to accept service of process on a minor under chapter 48, Florida Statutes; or

(v) on any other individual to the individual's usual place of abode or to the place where the individual regularly conducts business; or

(vi) on a corporation or other business entity to its registered office in Florida or its principal business office in Florida or, if neither is known after reasonable inquiry, to its last known address; or

(B) as provided in the Florida Rules of Civil Procedure for service of process; or

(C) as otherwise provided by Florida law for service of process.

(4) Service of formal notice pursuant to subdivision (3)(A) shall be complete on receipt of the notice. Proof of service shall be by verified statement of the person giving the notice; and there shall be attached to the verified statement the signed receipt or other evidence satisfactory to the court that delivery was made to the addressee or the addressee's agent.

(5) If service of process is made pursuant to Florida law, proof of service shall be made as provided therein.

(b) **Informal Notice.** When informal notice of a petition or other proceeding is required or permitted, it shall be served as provided in rule 5.041.

(c) **"Notice" Defined.** In these rules, the Florida Probate Code, and the Florida Guardianship Law "notice" shall mean informal notice unless formal notice is specified.

(d) **Formal Notice Optional.** Formal notice may be given in lieu of informal notice at the option of the person giving notice unless the court orders otherwise. When formal notice is given in lieu of informal notice, formal notice shall be given to all interested persons entitled to notice. When formal notice is given in lieu of informal notice, that notice does not modify any time period otherwise specified by statute or these rules.

Amended March 31, 1977, effective July 1, 1977 (344 So.2d 828); Sept. 4, 1980, effective Jan. 1, 1981 (387 So.2d 949); Sept. 13, 1984, effective Jan. 1, 1985 (458 So.2d 1079); Sept. 29, 1988, effective Jan. 1, 1989 (537 So.2d 500); Aug. 22, 1991, effective Oct. 1, 1991 (584 So.2d 964); Sept. 24, 1992, effective Jan. 1, 1993 (607 So.2d 1306); Oct. 3, 1996, effective Jan. 1, 1997 (683 So.2d 78); Sept. 28, 2000, effective Jan. 1, 2001 (778 So.2d 272); Sept. 29, 2005, effective Jan. 1, 2006 (912 So.2d 1178); Feb. 1, 2007 (948 So.2d 735); July 5, 2007, effective Jan. 1, 2008 (959 So.2d 1170); July 12, 2007 (964 So.2d 140); July 10, 2008 (986 So.2d 576); Sept. 2, 2010, effective Jan. 1, 2011 (50 So.3d 578); Oct. 18, 2012, effective, *nunc pro tunc*, Sept. 1, 2012 (102 So.3d 505).

Committee Notes

Formal notice is the method of service used in probate proceedings and the method of service of process for obtaining jurisdiction over the person receiving the notice. "The manner provided for service of formal notice" is as provided in rule 5.040(a)(3).

Informal notice is the method of service of notice given to interested persons entitled to notice when formal notice is not given or required.

Reference in this rule to the terms "mail" or "mailing" refers to use of the United States Postal Service.

Rule History

1975 Revision: Implements section 731.301, Florida Statutes.

1977 Revision: Reference to elisor.

1980 Revision: Editorial changes. Clarification of time for filing defenses after formal notice. Authorizes court to give relief to delinquent respondent from ex parte status; relief from service on numerous persons; allows optional use of formal notice.

1984 Revision: Editorial changes. Eliminates deadline for filing as opposed to serving defenses after formal notice; defines procedure subsequent to service of defenses after formal notice; new requirements for service of formal notice on incompetents and corporations; defines when service of formal notice is deemed complete; provisions relating to method of service of informal notice transferred to new rules 5.041 and 5.042; eliminates waiver of notice by will.

1988 Revision: Editorial changes. Committee notes revised. Citation form changes in committee notes.

1991 Revision: Subdivision (b) amended to define informal notice more clearly.

1992 Revision: Editorial changes. Committee notes revised. Citation form changes in committee notes.

1996 Revision: Subdivision (a) amended to permit service of formal notice by commercial delivery service to conform to 1993 amendment to section 731.301(1), Florida Statutes. Editorial changes.

2001 Revision: Editorial changes in subdivision (a)(3)(A) to clarify requirements for service of formal notice.

2003 Revision: Committee notes revised.

2005 Revision: Subdivision (a)(3)(A) amended to delete requirement of court approval of commercial delivery service.

2006 Revision: Committee notes revised.

2007 Revision: Committee notes revised.

2007 Revision: New subdivision (a)(3)(A)(iv) inserted in response to Cason ex rel. Saferight v. Hammock, 908 So.2d 512 (Fla. 5th DCA 2005), and subsequent subdivisions renumbered accordingly. Committee notes revised.

2008 Revision: Subdivision (a)(3)(A)(iii) revised to include "person with a developmental disability." Committee notes revised.

2010 Revision: Subdivision (d) amended to clarify that the optional use of formal notice when only informal notice is required does not modify any time period otherwise specified by statute or rule. Committee notes revised.

2012 Revision: Subdivision (b) revised to reflect amendment to rule 5.041.

Statutory References

§ 1.01(3), Fla. Stat. Definitions.

ch. 48, Fla. Stat. Process and service of process.

ch. 49, Fla. Stat. Constructive service of process.

§ 393.12, Fla. Stat. Capacity; appointment of guardian advocate.

§ 731.105, Fla. Stat. In rem proceeding.

§ 731.201(18), (22), Fla. Stat. General definitions.

§ 731.301, Fla. Stat. Notice.

§ 731.302, Fla. Stat. Waiver and consent by interested person.

§ 733.212, Fla. Stat. Notice of administration; filing of objections.

§ 733.2123, Fla. Stat. Adjudication before issuance of letters.

§ 733.502, Fla. Stat. Resignation of personal representative.

§ 733.613, Fla. Stat. Personal representative's right to sell real property.

§ 733.6175, Fla. Stat. Proceedings for review of employment of agents and compensation of personal representatives and employees of estate.

§ 733.901, Fla. Stat. Final discharge.

ch. 743, Fla. Stat. Disability of nonage of minors removed.

§ 744.106, Fla. Stat. Notice.

§ 744.301, Fla. Stat. Natural guardians.

§ 744.3085, Fla. Stat. Guardian advocates.

§ 744.3201, Fla. Stat. Petition to determine incapacity.

§ 744.331, Fla. Stat. Procedures to determine incapacity.

§ 744.3371, Fla. Stat. Notice of petition for appointment of guardian and hearing.

§ 744.441, Fla. Stat. Powers of guardian upon court approval.

§ 744.447, Fla. Stat. Petition for authorization to act.

§ 744.477, Fla. Stat. Proceedings for removal of a guardian.

Rule References

Fla. Prob. R. 5.025 Adversary proceedings.

Fla. Prob. R. 5.030 Attorneys.

Fla. Prob. R. 5.041 Service of pleadings and documents.

Fla. Prob. R. 5.042 Time.

Fla. Prob. R. 5.060 Request for notices and copies of pleadings.

Fla. Prob. R. 5.180 Waiver and consent.

Fla. Prob. R. 5.560 Petition for appointment of guardian of an incapacitated person.

Fla. Prob. R. 5.649 Guardian advocate.

Fla. Prob. R. 5.681 Restoration of rights of person with developmental disability.

Fla. R. Jud. Admin. 2.505 Attorneys.

Fla. R. Jud. Admin. 2.516 Service of pleadings and documents.

Fla. R. Civ. P. 1.070 Process.

Fla. R. Civ. P. Form 1.902 Summons.

Cross References

Claims against estate, notice, see F.S.A. § 733.701.
Constructive service, see F.S.A. § 49.011 et seq.
Deposition, notice to take, see Civil Procedure Rule 1.290.
Dismissal for insufficiency of process or service, see Civil Procedure Rule 1.140.
Formal notice defined, see F.S.A. § 731.201.
"Informal notice" or "notice" defined, see F.S.A. § 731.201.
Legal and official advertisements, see F.S.A. § 50.011 et seq.
Motion for issuance of process, see Civil Procedure Rule 1.160.
Notice, see F.S.A. § 731.301.
Numerous defendants, service of pleadings and papers, see Civil Procedure Rule 1.080.
Process generally, see Civil Procedure Rule 1.070.
Proof, notice of action, see F.S.A. §§ 49.10, 49.11.
Registered mail as including certified mail with return receipt requested, see F.S.A. § 1.01.
Service of pleadings and papers, see Civil Procedure Rule 1.080.
Service of process,
    Generally, see F.S.A. § 48.031.
    Constructive service, see F.S.A. § 49.011 et seq.
    Personal service outside state, see F.S.A. § 48.194.
    Publication, see F.S.A. §§ 49.011 et seq., 49.12.
Summons, see Civil Procedure Rule 1.070.
Time, computation and enlargement, see Civil Procedure Rule 1.090.
Waiver of notice and consent to action or proceeding, see F.S.A. § 731.302.

Rule 5.041. Service of Pleadings and Documents

Unless the court orders otherwise, every petition or motion for an order determining rights of an interested person, and every other pleading or document filed in the particular proceeding which is the subject matter of such petition or motion, except applications for witness subpoenas, shall be served on interested persons as set forth in Florida Rule of Judicial Administration 2.516 unless these rules, the Florida Probate Code, or the Florida Guardianship Law provides otherwise. No service need be made on interested persons against whom a default has been entered, or against whom the matter may otherwise proceed ex parte, unless a new or additional right or demand is asserted. For purposes of this rule an interested person shall be deemed a party under rule 2.516.

If the interested person is a minor whose disabilities of nonage are not removed, and who is not represented by an attorney, then service shall be on the persons designated to accept service of process on a minor under chapter 48, Florida Statutes.

Added Sept. 13, 1984, effective Jan. 1, 1985 (458 So.2d 1079). Amended Sept. 24, 1992, effective Jan. 1, 1993 (607 So.2d 1306); Oct. 3, 1996, effective Jan. 1, 1997 (683 So.2d 78); Sept. 28, 2000, effective Jan. 1, 2001 (778 So.2d 272); Sept. 29, 2005, effective Jan. 1, 2006 (912 So.2d 1178); Feb. 1, 2007 (948 So.2d 735); July 5, 2007, effective Jan. 1, 2008 (959 So.2d 1170); Oct. 18, 2012, effective, *nunc pro tunc*, Sept. 1, 2012 (102 So.3d 505).

Committee Notes

Derived from Florida Rule of Civil Procedure 1.080. Regulates the service of pleadings and papers in proceedings on petitions or motions for determination of rights. It is not applicable to every pleading and paper served or filed in the administration of a guardianship or decedent's estate.

Rule History

1984 Revision: New rule. Subdivision (c) is same as former rule 5.040(d).

1988 Revision: Committee notes revised. Citation form changes in committee notes.

1992 Revision: Editorial changes. Committee notes revised. Citation form changes in committee notes.

1996 Revision: Subdivision (b) amended to allow service to be made by facsimile. Committee notes revised.

2000 Revision: Subdivision (b) amended to clarify requirements for service of pleadings and papers. Subdivision (e) amended to clarify date of filing. Editorial changes in subdivision (f).

2003 Revision: Committee notes revised.

2005 Revision: Changes in subdivisions (b) and (f) to clarify service requirements, and editorial changes in (e).

2006 Revision: Committee notes revised.

2007 Revision: Provisions regarding service on a minor added in subdivision (b) in response to *Cason ex rel. Saferight v. Hammock*, 908 So.2d 512 (Fla. 5th DCA 2005). Committee notes revised.

2008 Revision: Committee notes revised.

2010 Revision: Committee notes revised.

2012 Revision: Portions of subdivision (b) and all of subdivisions (d), (e), (f), and (g) deleted in response to creation of Rule 2.516 of the Rules of Judicial Administration. Committee notes revised.

Statutory References

ch. 39, Fla. Stat. Proceedings relating to children.

ch. 48, Fla. Stat. Process and service of process.

ch. 61, Fla. Stat. Dissolution of marriage; support; time-sharing.

ch. 63, Fla. Stat. Adoption.

§ 393.12, Fla. Stat. Capacity; appointment of guardian advocate.

§ 731.201, Fla. Stat. General definitions.

§ 731.301, Fla. Stat. Notice.

§ 733.212, Fla. Stat. Notice of administration; filing of objections.

§ 733.2123, Fla. Stat. Adjudication before issuance of letters.

§ 733.705(2), (4), Fla. Stat. Payment of and objection to claims.

ch. 743, Fla. Stat. Disability of nonage of minors removed.

§ 744.3085, Fla. Stat. Guardian advocates.

§ 744.3201, Fla. Stat. Petition to determine incapacity.

§ 744.331, Fla. Stat. Procedures to determine incapacity.

§ 744.3371, Fla. Stat. Notice of petition for appointment of guardian and hearing.

§ 744.447, Fla. Stat. Petition for authorization to act.

ch. 751, Fla. Stat. Temporary custody of minor children by extended family.

Rule References

Fla. Prob. R. 5.020 Pleadings; verification; motions.

Fla. Prob. R. 5.025 Adversary proceedings.

Fla. Prob. R. 5.030 Attorneys.

Fla. Prob. R. 5.040 Notice.

Fla. Prob. R. 5.042 Time.

Fla. Prob. R. 5.150(c) Order requiring accounting.

Fla. Prob. R. 5.180 Waiver and consent.

Fla. Prob. R. 5.240(a) Notice of administration.

Fla. Prob. R. 5.340(d) Inventory.

Fla. Prob. R. 5.550 Petition to determine incapacity.

Fla. Prob. R. 5.560 Petition for appointment of guardian of an incapacitated person.

Fla. Prob. R. 5.649 Guardian advocate.

Fla. Prob. R. 5.681 Restoration of rights of person with developmental disability.

Fla. R. Civ. P. 1.080 Service of pleadings and papers.

Fla. R. Jud. Admin. 2.505 Attorneys.

Fla. R. Jud. Admin. 2.516 Service of pleadings and documents.

Rule 5.042. Time

(a) **Computation.** Computation of time shall be governed by Florida Rule of Judicial Administration 2.514.

(b) **Enlargement.** When an act is required or allowed to be done at or within a specified time by these rules, by order of court, or by notice given thereunder, for cause shown the court at any time in its discretion

(1) with or without notice may order the period enlarged if request therefor is made before the expiration of the period originally prescribed or as extended by a previous order, or

(2) on motion made and notice after the expiration of the specified period may permit the act to be done when failure to act was the result of excusable neglect. The court under this rule may not extend the time for serving a motion for rehearing or to enlarge any period of time governed by the Florida Rules of Appellate Procedure.

(c) **Service for Hearings.** A copy of any written petition or motion which may not be heard ex parte and a copy of the notice of the hearing thereon shall be served a reasonable time before the time specified for the hearing.

(d) **Additional Time after Service by Mail or E-mail.** Except when serving formal notice, or when serving a motion, pleading, or other document in the manner provided for service of formal notice, Florida Rule of Judicial Administration 2.514 shall apply to the computation of time following service.

Added Sept. 13, 1984, effective Jan. 1, 1985 (458 So.2d 1079). Amended Sept. 29, 1988, effective Jan. 1, 1989 (537 So.2d 500); Sept. 24, 1992, effective Jan. 1, 1993 (607 So.2d 1306); Sept. 29, 2005, effective Jan. 1, 2006 (912 So.2d 1178); July 12, 2012, effective Oct. 1, 2012 (95 So.3d 96).

Committee Notes

This rule is derived from Florida Rule of Civil Procedure 1.090.

Rule History

1984 Revision: New rule.

1988 Revision: Editorial changes in (a) and (b). Subdivision (a) enlarged to include closing of the clerk's office as a legal holiday. In *Clara P. Diamond, Inc. v. Tam–Bay Realty, Inc.*, 462 So. 2d 1168 (Fla. 2d DCA 1984), the Second District Court of Appeal suggested that Florida Rule of Civil Procedure 1.090(b) be clarified to leave no question that the court may not extend the time for rehearing, appeal, or petition for certiorari regardless of whether a request to enlarge the time therefor was made before the expiration of the time allowed. Because the format of rule 5.042(b) was substantially the same as the format of rule 1.090(b), subdivision (b) is amended to conform for the sake of clarity. Committee notes revised.

1992 Revision: Editorial changes. Committee notes revised. Citation form changes in committee notes.

2003 Revision: Committee notes revised.

2005 Revision: Subdivision (d) amended to clarify exception to mailing rule for service of formal notice and service in the manner provided for service of formal notice. Committee notes revised.

2008 Revision: Committee notes revised.

2012 Revision: Subdivision (a) revised to refer to Rule 2.514 and delete duplicative provisions. Subdivision (d) revised to incorporate service by e-mail and the filing and service of documents, rather than papers. Committee notes revised.

Statutory References

§ 393.12, Fla. Stat. Capacity; appointment of guardian advocate.

§ 683.01, Fla. Stat. Legal holidays.

§ 731.301, Fla. Stat. Notice.

§ 732.107, Fla. Stat. Escheat.

§ 732.2135, Fla. Stat. Time of election; extensions; withdrawal.

§ 732.402, Fla. Stat. Exempt property.

§ 732.901, Fla. Stat. Production of wills.

§ 733.104, Fla. Stat. Suspension of statutes of limitation in favor of the personal representative.

§ 733.212, Fla. Stat. Notice of administration; filing of objections.

§ 733.2121, Fla. Stat. Notice to creditors; filing of claims.

§ 733.701, Fla. Stat. Notifying creditors.

§ 733.702, Fla. Stat. Limitations on presentation of claims.

§ 733.705, Fla. Stat. Payment of and objection to claims.

§ 733.710, Fla. Stat. Limitations on claims against estates.

§ 733.816, Fla. Stat. Disposition of unclaimed property held by personal representatives.

§ 744.3085, Fla. Stat. Guardian advocates.

Rule References

Fla. Prob. R. 5.040(a)(1) Notice.

Fla. Prob. R. 5.150 Order requiring accounting.

Fla. Prob. R. 5.240 Notice of administration.

Fla. Prob. R. 5.241 Notice to creditors.

Fla. Prob. R. 5.340(a)–(b) Inventory.

Fla. Prob. R. 5.345 Accountings other than personal representatives' final accountings.

Fla. Prob. R. 5.395 Notice of federal estate tax return.

Fla. Prob. R. 5.400 Distribution and discharge.

Fla. Prob. R. 5.649 Guardian advocate.

Fla. Prob. R. 5.681 Restoration of rights of person with developmental disability.

Fla. Prob. R. 5.700 Objection to guardianship reports.

Fla. R. Civ. P. 1.090 Time.

Fla. R. Jud. Admin. 2.514 Computing and extending time.

Rule 5.043. Deposit of Wills and Codicils

Notwithstanding any rule to the contrary, and unless the court orders otherwise, any original executed will or codicil deposited with the court must be retained by the clerk in its original form and must not be destroyed or disposed of by the clerk for 20 years after submission regardless of whether the will or codicil has been permanently recorded as defined by Florida Rule of Judicial Administration 2.430.

Added Oct. 18, 2012, effective Dec. 1, 2012, April 1, 2013, Oct. 1, 2013 (102 So.3d 451).

Committee Notes

2012 Adoption. Florida Rule of Judicial Administration 2.525 requires that all documents be filed with the court electronically. Although the Florida Statutes direct the deposit of a will, rather than the filing of the will, the committee believes that original wills and codicils should be retained in their original form longer than other documents filed with the court due to the unique evidentiary aspects of the actual document. These unique aspects could be lost forever if the original document were converted to electronic form and the original destroyed.

Rule History

2012 Revision: New Rule.

Statutory References

§ 731.201(16), Fla. Stat. General definitions.

§ 732.901, Fla. Stat. Production of wills.

Rule References

Fla. R. Jud. Admin. 2.430 Retention of court records.

Fla. R. Jud. Admin. 2.525 Electronic filing.

Historical Notes

Publisher's Note

Florida Supreme Court Opinion No. SC11-399, revised Oct. 18, 2012, provides the following implementation schedule:

"First, the new electronic filing requirements the Court adopts will become effective in the civil, probate, small claims, and family law divisions of the trial courts, as well as for appeals to the circuit courts in these categories of cases, on April 1, 2013, at 12:01 a.m., except as may be otherwise provided by administrative order. Electronic filing will be mandatory in these divisions pursuant to rule 2.525 on that date. However, until the new rules take effect in these divisions, any clerk who is already accepting documents filed by electronic transmission under the current rules should continue to do so; attorneys in these

counties are encouraged to file documents electronically under the current rules.

"Next, the new electronic filing requirements the Court adopts will become effective in the criminal, traffic, and juvenile divisions of the trial courts, as well as for appeals to the circuit court in these categories of cases, on October 1, 2013, at 12:01 a.m., except as may be otherwise provided by administrative order. Electronic filing will be mandatory in these divisions under rule 2.525 on that date. The new e-filing requirements, as they apply in proceedings brought pursuant to the Florida Mental Health Act (Baker Act), Chapter 394, Part I, Florida Statutes, and the Involuntary Commitment of Sexually Violent Predators Act (Jimmy Ryce), Chapter 394, Part V, Florida Statutes, will also not be mandatory in these cases until October 1, 2013. As stated above, until the new rules take effect in these divisions and proceedings, any clerk who is already accepting electronically filed documents under the current rules should continue to do so; attorneys are again encouraged to utilize existing electronic filing procedures under the current rules.

"The new electronic filing procedures adopted in this case will become effective in this Court on December 1, 2012, at 12:01 a.m., except as may be otherwise provided by administrative order. E-filing will be mandatory in this Court under rule 2.525 on that date. Additionally, the e-filing rules will become effective and mandatory in the district courts of appeal on April 1, 2013, at 12:01 a.m. However, until the new rules and procedures take effect in the district courts, any clerk who is already accepting documents filed by electronic transmission may continue to do so; attorneys in these districts are encouraged to file documents electronically. Clerks will not be required to electronically transmit the record on appeal until July 1, 2013, at 12:01 a.m. Until July 1, we encourage clerks, whenever possible, to electronically transmit the record under the new rules and requirements."

Rule 5.050. Transfer of Proceedings

(a) Incorrect Venue. When any proceeding is filed laying venue in the wrong county, the court may transfer the proceeding in the same manner as provided in the Florida Rules of Civil Procedure. Any action taken by the court or the parties before the transfer is not affected because of the improper venue.

(b) Change of Residence of Ward. When the residence of a ward is changed to another county, the guardian of the person or the guardian advocate shall have the venue of the guardianship changed to the county of the acquired residence.

Amended Sept. 29, 1988, effective Jan. 1, 1989 (537 So.2d 500); Aug. 22, 1991, effective Oct. 1, 1991 (584 So.2d 964); July 10, 2008 (986 So.2d 576).

Committee Notes

Subdivision (b) of this rule represents a rule implementation of the procedure found in section 744.202(3), Florida Statutes.

Rule History

1975 Revision: Same as section 733.101(3), Florida Statutes.

1977 Revision: Title changed to indicate that the rule is one dealing with transfer.

1988 Revision: Prior rule renumbered as (a). New (b) is rule implementation of procedure in section 744.202(2), Florida Statutes. Editorial changes. Committee notes expanded. Citation form changes in rule and committee notes.

1991 Revision: Editorial changes.

1992 Revision: Committee notes revised. Citation form changes in committee notes.

2003 Revision: Committee notes revised.

2008 Revision: Change in (b) to add reference to guardian advocate. Committee notes revised.

Statutory References

ch. 47, Fla. Stat. Venue.

§ 393.12, Fla. Stat. Capacity; appointment of guardian advocate.

§ 733.101, Fla. Stat. Venue of probate proceedings.

§ 744.106, Fla. Stat. Notice.

§ 744.201, Fla. Stat. Domicile of ward.

§ 744.202, Fla. Stat. Venue.

§ 744.2025, Fla. Stat. Change of ward's residence.

§ 744.306, Fla. Stat. Foreign guardians.

§ 744.3085, Fla. Stat. Guardian advocates.

§ 744.3201, Fla. Stat. Petition to determine incapacity.

Rule References

Fla. Prob. R. 5.200(d) Petition for administration.

Fla. Prob. R. 5.240(b)(3), (d) Notice of administration.

Fla. Prob. R. 5.649 Guardian advocate.

Fla. R. Civ. P. 1.060 Transfers of actions.

Cross References

Change of venue, see F.S.A. § 47.091.

Transfers of actions, see Civil Procedure Rule 1.060.

Venue in civil actions, see F.S.A. § 47.011 et seq.

Venue of probate proceedings, see F.S.A. § 733.101.

Rule 5.060. Request for Notices and Copies of Pleadings

(a) Request. Any interested person who desires notice of proceedings in the estate of a decedent or ward may file a separate written request for notice of further proceedings, designating therein such person's residence and post office address. When such person's residence or post office address changes, a new designation of such change shall be filed in the proceedings. A person filing such request, or address change, must serve a copy on the attorney for the personal representative or guardian, and include a certificate of service.

(b) Notice and Copies. A party filing a request shall be served thereafter by the moving party with notice of further proceedings and with copies of subsequent pleadings and documents as long as the party is an interested person.

Amended Sept. 4, 1980, effective Jan. 1, 1981 (387 So.2d 949); Sept. 29, 1988, effective Jan. 1, 1989 (537 So.2d 500); Sept. 24, 1992, effective Jan. 1, 1993 (607 So.2d 1306); Sept. 26, 2013, effective Jan. 1, 2014 (123 So.3d 31).

Committee Notes

Rule History

1975 Revision: This rule substantially incorporates the provisions of prior rule 5.060 except that now a copy of the request shall be mailed by the clerk only to the attorney for the personal representative or guardian. Even though a request under this rule has not been made, informal notice as provided in rule 5.040(b)(3) may still be required.

1977 Revision: Editorial and citation form change in committee note.

1980 Revision: Caveat, the personal representative may want to give notice to parties even though not required, for example, where an independent action has been filed on an objected claim.

1988 Revision: Captions added to subdivisions. Committee notes expanded. Citation form changes in committee notes.

1992 Revision: Editorial changes. Committee notes revised. Citation form changes in committee notes.

2003 Revision: Committee notes revised.

2010 Revision: Committee notes revised.

2012 Revision: Committee notes revised.

2013 Revision: Subdivisions (a) and (b) revised to reflect service of documents, rather than papers. Subdivision (a) revised to shift responsibility for service of the request from the clerk to the interested person making the request for notice and copies. Editorial changes to conform to the court's guidelines for rule submissions as set forth in AOSC06–14.

Statutory References

§ 731.201, Fla. Stat. General definitions.

§ 733.604, Fla. Stat. Inventories and accountings; public records exemptions.

Rule References

Fla. Prob. R. 5.040 Notice.

Fla. Prob. R. 5.041 Service of pleadings and documents.

Fla. Prob. R. 5.340 Inventory.

Fla. Prob. R. 5.341 Estate information.

Fla. R. Jud. Admin. 2.516 Service of pleadings and documents.

Cross References

Legal and official advertisements, see F.S.A. § 50.011 et seq.

Method, time, and proof of notice, see F.S.A. § 731.301.

Registered mail defined to include certified mail with return receipt requested, see F.S.A. § 1.01.

Rule 5.065. Notice of Civil Action or Ancillary Administration

(a) Civil Action. A personal representative and a guardian shall file a notice when a civil action has been instituted by or against the personal representative or the guardian. The notice shall contain:

(1) the names of the parties;

(2) the style of the court and the case number;

(3) the county and state where the proceeding is pending;

(4) the date of commencement of the proceeding; and

(5) a brief statement of the nature of the proceeding.

(b) Ancillary Administration. The domiciliary personal representative shall file a notice when an ancillary administration has commenced, which notice shall contain:

(1) the name and residence address of the ancillary personal representative; and

(2) the information required in subdivisions (a)(2), (3), and (4) above.

(c) Copies Exhibited. A copy of the initial pleading may be attached to the notice. To the extent an attached initial pleading states the required information, the notice need not restate it.

Added Sept. 13, 1984, effective Jan. 1, 1985 (458 So.2d 1079). Amended Sept. 24, 1992, effective Jan. 1, 1993 (607 So.2d 1306); Sept. 28, 2000, effective Jan. 1, 2001 (778 So.2d 272).

Committee Notes

This rule reflects a procedural requirement not founded on a statute or rule.

Rule History

1984 Revision: New rule.

1988 Revision: Committee notes expanded.

1992 Revision: Editorial change. Citation form changes in committee notes.

2000 Revision: Subdivision (b) amended to eliminate requirement to set forth nature and value of ancillary assets.

Statutory References

§ 733.612(20), Fla.Stat. Transactions authorized for the personal representative; exceptions.

§ 744.441(11), Fla.Stat. Powers of guardian upon court approval.

Rule 5.080. Discovery and Subpoena

(a) Adoption of Civil Rules. The following Florida Rules of Civil Procedure shall apply in all probate and guardianship proceedings:

(1) Rule 1.280, general provisions governing discovery.

(2) Rule 1.290, depositions before action or pending appeal.

(3) Rule 1.300, persons before whom depositions may be taken.

(4) Rule 1.310, depositions upon oral examination.

(5) Rule 1.320, depositions upon written questions.

(6) Rule 1.330, use of depositions in court proceedings.

(7) Rule 1.340, interrogatories to parties.

(8) Rule 1.350, production of documents and things and entry upon land for inspection and other purposes.

(9) Rule 1.351, production of documents and things without deposition.

(10) Rule 1.360, examination of persons.

(11) Rule 1.370, requests for admission.

(12) Rule 1.380, failure to make discovery; sanctions.

(13) Rule 1.390, depositions of expert witnesses.

(14) Rule 1.410, subpoena.

(b) Limitations and Costs. In order to conserve the assets of the estate, the court has broad discretion to limit the scope and the place and manner of the discovery and to assess the costs, including attorneys' fees, of the discovery against the party making it or against 1 or more of the beneficiaries of the estate or against the ward in such proportions as the court determines, considering, among other factors, the benefit derived therefrom.

(c) Application. It is not necessary to have an adversary proceeding under rule 5.025 to utilize the rules adopted in subdivision (a) above. Any interested person may utilize the rules adopted in subdivision (a).

Amended March 31, 1977, effective July 1, 1977 (344 So.2d 828); Sept. 13, 1984, effective Jan. 1, 1985 (458 So.2d 1079); Sept. 29, 1988, effective Jan. 1, 1989 (537 So.2d 500); Sept. 24, 1992, effective Jan. 1, 1993 (607 So.2d 1306); Oct. 3, 1996, effective Jan. 1, 1997 (683 So.2d 78); May 2, 2002 (824 So.2d 849); Feb. 1, 2007 (948 So.2d 735); July 12, 2007 (964 So.2d 140).

Committee Notes

Subdivision (b) is not intended to result in the assessment of costs, including attorney's fees, in every instance in which discovery is sought. Subdivision (c) is not intended to overrule the holdings in *In re Estate of Shaw*, 340 So. 2d 491 (Fla. 3d DCA 1976), and *In re Estate of Posner*, 492 So. 2d 1093 (Fla. 3d DCA 1986).

Rule History

1975 Revision: This rule is the same as prior rule 5.080, broadened to include guardianships and intended to clearly permit the use of discovery practices in nonadversary probate and guardianship matters.

1977 Revision: Editorial change in citation form in committee note.

1984 Revision: Florida Rules of Civil Procedure 1.290, 1.300, 1.351, and 1.410 have been added.

1988 Revision: Subdivision (a)(15) deleted as duplicative of rule 5.070 Subpoena. Editorial change in (b). Citation form change in committee notes.

1992 Revision: Editorial changes. Committee notes revised. Citation form changes in committee notes.

1996 Revision: Reference to rule 1.400 eliminated because of deletion of that rule from the Florida Rules of Civil Procedure. Editorial change.

2002 Revision: Reference to rule 1.410 transferred to subdivision (a) from former rule 5.070. Subdivision (b) amended to give court discretion to assess attorneys' fees. Subdivision (c) added. Committee notes revised.

2006 Revision: Committee notes revised.

2007 Revision: Committee notes revised.

Statutory References

§ 731.201(23), Fla. Stat.   General definitions.

§ 733.106, Fla. Stat.   Costs and attorney's fees.

§ 744.105, Fla. Stat.   Costs.

§ 744.108, Fla. Stat.   Guardian's and attorney's fees and expenses.

Rule References

Fla. Prob.   R. 5.025 Adversary proceedings.

Fla. R. Jud. Admin. 2.535 Court reporting.

Rules of Civil Procedure

The Rules of Civil Procedure applicable to probate and guardianship proceedings pursuant to Probate Rule 5.010, as provided for in Rule 5.080, are set out in an appendix following the text of these rules.

Rule 5.095.   General and Special Magistrates

(a) **General Magistrates.** The court may appoint general magistrates as the court finds necessary. General magistrates shall be members of The Florida Bar and shall continue in office until removed by the court. The order making an appointment shall be recorded. Each general magistrate shall take the oath required of officers by the Florida Constitution. The oath shall be recorded before the magistrate begins to act.

(b) **Special Magistrates.** The court may appoint members of The Florida Bar as special magistrates for any particular service required by the court. Special magistrates shall be governed by all laws and rules relating to general magistrates, except special magistrates shall not be required to make oath unless specifically required by the court. For good cause shown, the court may appoint a person other than a member of The Florida Bar as a special magistrate.

(c) **Reference.** No referral shall be made to a magistrate without the consent of the parties. When a referral is made to a magistrate, either party may set the action for hearing before the magistrate.

(d) **General Powers and Duties.** Every magistrate shall act under the direction of the court. Process issued by a magistrate shall be directed as provided by law. All grounds for disqualification of a judge shall apply to magistrates.

(e) Bond. When not otherwise provided by law, the court may require magistrates who are appointed to dispose of real or personal property to give bond and surety conditioned for the proper payment of all money that may come into their hands and for the due performance of their duties. The bond shall be made payable to the State of Florida and shall be for the benefit of all persons aggrieved by any act of the magistrate.

(f) Hearings. Hearings before any magistrate may be held in the county where the action is pending or at any other place by order of the court for the convenience of the witnesses or the parties. The magistrate shall assign a time and place for proceedings as soon as reasonably possible after a referral is made and give notice to all parties. If any party fails to appear, the magistrate may proceed ex parte or may continue the hearing to a future day, with notice to the absent party. The magistrate shall proceed with reasonable diligence and the least practicable delay. Any party may apply to the court for an order directing the magistrate to accelerate the proceedings and to make a report promptly. Evidence shall be taken in writing or by electronic recording by the magistrate or by some other person under the magistrate's authority in the magistrate's presence and shall be filed with the magistrate's report. The magistrate may examine and take testimony from the parties and their witnesses under oath on all matters contained in the referral and may require production of all books, papers, writings, vouchers, and other documents applicable to those matters. The magistrate shall admit only evidence that would be admissible in court. The magistrate may take all actions concerning evidence that may be taken by the court. All parties accounting before a magistrate shall bring in their accounts in the form of accounts payable and receivable, and any other parties who are not satisfied with the account may examine the accounting party orally or by interrogatories or deposition as the magistrate directs. All depositions and documents that have been taken or used previously in the action may be used before the magistrate.

(g) Magistrate's Report. The magistrate's report shall contain a description of the matters considered and the magistrate's conclusion and any recommendations. No part of any statement of facts, account, charge, deposition, examination, or answer used before the magistrate shall be recited.

(h) Filing Report; Notice; Exceptions. The magistrate shall file the report and serve copies on the parties. The parties may serve exceptions to the report within 10 days from the time it is served on them. If no exceptions are filed within that period, the court shall take appropriate action on the report. All timely filed exceptions shall be heard on reasonable notice by either party.

(i) Application of Rule. This rule shall not apply to the appointment of magistrates for the specific purpose of reviewing guardianship inventories, accountings, and plans as otherwise governed by law and these rules.

Added July 5, 2007, effective Jan. 1, 2008 (959 So.2d 1170).

Committee Notes

Rule History

2007 Revision: This rule, patterned after Florida Rule of Civil Procedure 1.490, is created to implement the use of magistrates in probate and guardianship proceedings other than those specifically addressed in rule 5.697.

Rule References

Fla. Prob. R. 5.697 Magistrates' review of guardianship inventories, accountings, and plans.

Fla. R. Civ. P. 1.490 Magistrates.

Rule 5.100. Right of Appeal

Appeal of final orders and discretionary appellate review of non-final orders are governed by the Florida Rules of Appellate Procedure.

Amended Sept. 29, 1988, effective Jan. 1, 1989 (537 So.2d 500); Sept. 24, 1992, effective Jan. 1, 1993 (607 So.2d 1306); Oct. 3, 1996, effective Jan. 1, 1997 (683 So.2d 78); Sept. 28, 2000, effective Jan. 1, 2001 (778 So.2d 272).

Committee Notes

For purposes of appellate review, the service of a motion for rehearing postpones rendition of final orders only. A motion for rehearing of a non-final order does not toll the running of the time to seek review of that order.

Rule History

1975 Revision: Same as prior rule 5.100 with editorial changes.

1977 Revision: Citation form change in committee note.

1988 Revision: Committee notes expanded. Citation form changes in rule and committee notes.

1992 Revision: Editorial changes. Citation form changes in committee notes.

1996 Revision: Superseded by Florida Rule of Appellate Procedure 9.110(a)(2).

2000 Revision: Rewritten because former rule was superseded. Revisions to committee notes to amend text and to include cross-references to other rules.

2003 Revision: Committee notes revised.

Rule References

Fla. Prob. R. 5.020(d) Pleadings; verification; motions.

Fla. R. App. P. 9.020(h) Definitions.

Fla. R. App. P. 9.110(a)(2), (b) Appeal proceedings to review final orders of lower tribunals and orders granting new trial in jury and non-jury cases.

Fla. R. App. P. 9.130(b) Proceedings to review non-final orders and specified final orders.

Cross References

Supreme Court, jurisdiction, see Const. Art. 5, § 3.

Rule 5.110. Address Designation for Personal Representative or Guardian; Designation of Resident Agent and Acceptance

(a) **Address Designation of Personal Representative or Guardian.** Before letters are issued, the personal representative or guardian must file a designation of street address, and mailing address. If the personal representative or guardian is an individual, the designation must also include the individual's residence address. The personal representative or guardian must notify the court of any change in its residence address, street address, or mailing address within 20 days of the change.

(b) **Designation of Resident Agent.** Before letters are issued, a personal representative or guardian must file a designation of resident agent for service of process or notice, and the acceptance by the resident agent. A designation of resident agent is not required if a personal representative or guardian is (1) a corporate fiduciary having an office in Florida, or (2) a Florida Bar member who is a resident of and has an office in Florida. The designation must contain the name, street address, and mailing address of the resident agent. If the resident agent is an individual who is not an attorney, the designation must also include the individual's residence address.

(c) Residency Requirement. A resident agent, other than a member of The Florida Bar who is a resident of Florida, must be a resident of the county where the proceedings are pending.

(d) Acceptance by Resident Agent. The resident agent must sign a written acceptance of designation.

(e) Incorporation in Other Pleadings. The designation of the address of the personal representative or guardian, the designation of resident agent, or acceptance may be incorporated in the petition for administration, the petition for appointment of guardian, or the personal representative's or guardian's oath.

(f) Effect of Designation and Acceptance. The designation of and acceptance by the resident agent shall constitute consent to service of process or notice on the agent and shall be sufficient to bind the personal representative or guardian:

(1) in its representative capacity in any action; and

(2) in its personal capacity only in those actions in which the personal representative or guardian is sued personally for claims arising from the administration of the estate or guardianship.

(g) Successor Agent. If the resident agent dies, resigns, or is unable to act for any other reason, the personal representative or guardian must appoint a successor agent within 10 days after receiving notice that such event has occurred.

Amended Sept. 13, 1984, effective Jan. 1, 1985 (458 So.2d 1079); Sept. 29, 1988, effective Jan. 1, 1989 (537 So.2d 500); Sept. 24, 1992, effective Jan. 1, 1993 (607 So.2d 1306); September 28, 2000, effective Jan. 1, 2001 (778 So.2d 272); Sept. 2, 2010, effective Jan. 1, 2011 (50 So.3d 578); Sept. 26, 2013, effective Jan. 1, 2014 (123 So.3d 31).

Committee Notes

Rule History

1977 Revision: Change in committee note to conform to statutory renumbering.

Substantially the same as prior rule 5.210, except that under prior rule, designation was required to be filed within 10 days after letters issued.

1984 Revision: Captions added to subdivisions. New subdivision (b) added. Requires filing acceptance at the same time as filing designation. Committee notes revised.

1988 Revision: Change in (c) to clarify that the personal representative, if a member of The Florida Bar, may not also serve as resident agent for service of process or notice. Citation form change in committee notes.

1992 Revision: Editorial changes. Committee notes revised. Citation form changes in committee notes.

2000 Revision: Extensive editorial changes to rule. Rule reformatted for clarity and revised to permit an attorney serving as resident agent to designate a business address in lieu of a residence address.

2003 Revision: Committee notes revised.

2008 Revision: Committee notes revised.

2010 Revision: Subdivision (a) amended to require the personal representative or guardian to notify the court of any change of address to facilitate timely communication with the personal representative or guardian.

2013 Revision: Subdivision (b) amended to limit to individuals the requirement that the guardian or personal representative provide a designation of residence address, excluding corporate fiduciaries. Editorial changes to conform to the court's guidelines for rules submissions as set forth in AOSC06–14.

Rule References

Fla. Prob. R. 5.200 Petition for administration.

Fla. Prob. R. 5.320 Oath of personal representative.

Fla. Prob. R. 5.560 Petition for appointment of guardian of an incapacitated person.

Fla. Prob. R. 5.649 Guardian advocate.

Cross References

Guardians, oaths, see F.S.A. § 744.347; Fla.Prob.R. 5.600.
Personal representatives,
    Issuance of letters, bonds, see Fla.Prob.R. 5.235.
    Oaths, see Fla.Prob.R. 5.320.

Rule 5.120. Administrator Ad Litem and Guardian Ad Litem

(a) **Appointment.** When it is necessary that the estate of a decedent or a ward be represented in any probate or guardianship proceeding and there is no personal representative of the estate or guardian of the ward, or the personal representative or guardian is or may be interested adversely to the estate or ward, or is enforcing the personal representative's or guardian's own debt or claim against the estate or ward, or the necessity arises otherwise, the court may appoint an administrator ad litem or a guardian ad litem, as the case may be, without bond or notice for that particular proceeding. At any point in a proceeding, a court may appoint a guardian ad litem to represent the interests of an incapacitated person, an unborn or unascertained person, a minor or any other person otherwise under a legal disability, a person with a developmental disability, or a person whose identity or address is unknown, if the court determines that representation of the interest otherwise would be inadequate. If not precluded by conflict of interest, a guardian ad litem may be appointed to represent several persons or interests. The administrator ad litem or guardian ad litem shall file an oath to discharge all duties faithfully and upon the filing shall be qualified to act. No process need be served upon the administrator ad litem or guardian ad litem, but such person shall appear and defend as directed by the court.

(b) **Petition.** The petition for appointment of a guardian ad litem shall state to the best of petitioner's information and belief:

(1) the initials and residence address of each minor, person with a developmental disability, or incapacitated person and year of birth of each minor who has an interest in the proceedings;

(2) the name and address of any guardian appointed for each minor, person with a developmental disability, or incapacitated person;

(3) the name and residence address of any living natural guardians or living natural guardian having legal custody of each minor, person with a developmental disability, or incapacitated person;

(4) a description of the interest in the proceedings of each minor, person with a developmental disability, or incapacitated person; and

(5) the facts showing the necessity for the appointment of a guardian ad litem.

(c) **Notice.** Within 10 days after appointment, the petitioner shall serve conformed copies of the petition for appointment of a guardian ad litem and order to any guardian, or if there is no guardian, to the living natural guardians or the living natural guardian having legal custody of the minor, person with a developmental disability, or incapacitated person.

(d) Report. The guardian ad litem shall serve conformed copies of any written report or finding of the guardian ad litem's investigation and answer filed in the proceedings, petition for compensation and discharge, and the notice of hearing on the petition to any guardian, or in the event that there is no guardian, to the living natural guardians or the living natural guardian having legal custody of the minor, person with a developmental disability, or incapacitated person.

(e) Service of Petition and Order. Within 10 days after appointment, the petitioner for an administrator ad litem shall serve conformed copies of the petition for appointment and order to the attorney of record of each beneficiary and to each known beneficiary not represented by an attorney of record.

(f) Enforcement of Judgments. When an administrator ad litem or guardian ad litem recovers any judgment or other relief, it shall be enforced as other judgments. Execution shall issue in favor of the administrator ad litem or guardian ad litem for the use of the estate or ward and the money collected shall be paid to the personal representative or guardian, or as otherwise ordered by the court.

(g) Claim of Personal Representative. The fact that the personal representative is seeking reimbursement for claims against the decedent paid by the personal representative does not require appointment of an administrator ad litem.

Amended March 31, 1977, effective July 1, 1977 (344 So.2d 828); Sept. 29, 1988, effective Jan. 1, 1989 (537 So.2d 500); Sept. 24, 1992, effective Jan. 1, 1993 (607 So.2d 1306); Feb. 1, 2007 (948 So.2d 735); July 10, 2008 (986 So.2d 576); Oct. 18, 2012, effective, *nunc pro tunc*, Sept. 1, 2012 (102 So.3d 505); May 22, 2014, effective May 22, 2014 (139 So.3d 875).

Committee Notes

Rule History

1977 Revision: Editorial change in (a) limiting application of rule to probate and guardianship proceedings. In (b) the petition for appointment of a guardian need not be verified. Deletion of (g) as being substantive rather than procedural and changing former (h) to new (g). Change in committee note to conform to statutory renumbering.

This rule implements sections 731.303(5), 733.308, and 744.391, Florida Statutes, and includes some of the provisions of prior rule 5.230.

1988 Revision: Editorial changes; captions added to paragraphs. Citation form changes in committee notes.

1992 Revision: Addition of phrase in subdivision (a) to conform to 1992 amendment to section 731.303(5), Florida Statutes. Editorial changes. Committee notes revised. Citation form changes in committee notes.

2003 Revision: Committee notes revised.

2006 Revision: Committee notes revised.

2008 Revision: Subdivisions (a), (b), (c), and (d) amended to include persons with a developmental disability. Committee notes revised.

2012 Revision: The phrase "deliver or mail" in subdivisions (c), (d), and (e) has been replaced with the word "serve" to comply with other rules relating to service of pleadings and documents. Committee notes revised.

2014 Revision: Amends subdivision (b)(1) to conform to Fla. R. Jud. Admin. 2.425. Committee notes revised.

Statutory References

§ 393.12, Fla. Stat. Capacity; appointment of guardian advocate.

§ 731.303, Fla. Stat. Representation.

§ 733.308, Fla. Stat. Administrator ad litem.

§ 733.708, Fla. Stat. Compromise.

§ 744.3025, Fla. Stat. Claims of minors.

§ 744.3085, Fla. Stat. Guardian advocates.

§ 744.387, Fla. Stat. Settlement of claims.

§ 744.391, Fla. Stat. Actions by and against guardian or ward.

§ 744.446, Fla. Stat. Conflicts of interest; prohibited activities; court approval; breach of fiduciary duty.

Rule References

Fla. Prob. R. 5.041 Service of pleadings and documents.

Fla. R. Jud. Admin. 2.516 Service of pleadings and documents.

Fla. R. Jud. Admin. 2.425 Minimization of the Filing of Sensitive Information.

Cross References

Actions by and against guardian or ward, see F.S.A. § 744.391.
Administrator ad litem, appointment, see F.S.A. § 733.308.

Rule 5.122. Curators

(a) **Petition for Appointment.** The petition for appointment of a curator shall be verified and shall contain:

(1) the petitioner's name, address, and interest, if any, in the estate;

(2) the decedent's name, address, date and place of death, and state and county of domicile;

(3) the names and addresses of the persons apparently entitled to letters of administration and any known beneficiaries;

(4) the nature and approximate value of the assets;

(5) a statement showing venue;

(6) a statement as to why a curator should be appointed; and

(7) the name and address of any proposed curator.

The court may appoint a curator sua sponte.

(b) **Appointment.** Before letters of curatorship are issued, the curator shall file a designation of resident agent and acceptance, and an oath, as is required for personal representatives under these rules. The court shall issue letters of curatorship that shall entitle the curator to possess or control the decedent's property, which the court may enforce through contempt proceedings.

(c) **Notice.** Formal notice shall be given to the person apparently entitled to letters, if any. If it is likely that the decedent's property will be wasted, destroyed, or removed beyond the jurisdiction of the court and if the appointment of a curator would be delayed by giving notice, the court may appoint a curator without notice.

(d) **Powers.** By order, the court may authorize the curator to perform any duty or function of a personal representative, including publication and service of notice to creditors, or if a will has been admitted, service of notice of administration.

(e) Inventory and Accounting. The curator shall file an inventory within 30 days after issuance of letters of curatorship. When the personal representative is appointed, the curator shall account for and deliver all estate assets in the curator's possession to the personal representative within 30 days after issuance of letters of administration.

(f) Petition to Reconsider. If a curator has been appointed without notice, any interested party who did not receive notice may, at any time, petition to reconsider the appointment.

(g) Subject to Other Provisions. Curators shall be subject to the provisions of these rules and other applicable law concerning personal representatives.

Added Sept. 29, 1988, effective Jan. 1, 1989 (537 So.2d 500). Amended Sept. 24, 1992, effective Jan. 1, 1993 (607 So.2d 1306); June 19, 2003 (848 So.2d 1069).

Committee Notes

This rule implements the procedure found in section 733.501, Florida Statutes, as amended in 1997 and 2001. The rule has been modified, in part, to reflect the addition of new rule 5.241 regarding notice to creditors. Because the fundamental concern of curatorship is protection of estate property, the procedure facilitates speed and flexibility while recognizing due process concerns. It is not intended that this rule change the effect of the statute from which it has been derived, but the rule has been reformatted to conform to the structure of these rules. Furthermore, the Committee does not intend to create a new procedure, except that subdivision (d) specifies certain acts that the court may authorize the curator to perform. This specificity of example, while not included in the statute, is not intended to limit the authorized acts to those specified in the rule. The appointment of a curator without notice is tantamount to a temporary injunction. Thus, due process considerations suggest an expedited hearing to reconsider the appointment of a curator by any interested party who did not receive notice.

Rule History

1988 Revision: New rule.

1992 Revision: Editorial changes. Citation form changes in committee notes.

2003 Revision: Extensive changes to rule to clarify procedure for appointment of curator. Committee notes revised.

Statutory References

§ 733.402, Fla. Stat. Bond of fiduciary; when required; form.

§ 733.501, Fla. Stat. Curators.

Rule Reference

Fla. Prob. R. 5.020 Pleadings; verification; motions.

Rule 5.150. Order Requiring Accounting

(a) Accountings Required by Statute. When any personal representative or guardian fails to file an accounting or return required by statute or rule, the court on its own motion or on the petition of an interested person shall order the personal representative or guardian to file the accounting or return within 15 days from the service on the personal representative or guardian of the order, or show cause why he or she should not be compelled to do so.

(b) Accountings Not Required by Statute. On the petition of an interested person, or on its own motion, the court may require the personal representative or guardian to file an accounting or return not otherwise required by statute or rule. The order requiring an accounting or return shall order the personal representative or guardian to file the accounting or return within a specified time from service on the personal representative or guardian of the order, or show cause why he or she should not be compelled to do so.

(c) Service. A copy of the order shall be served on the personal representative or guardian and the personal representative's or guardian's attorney.

Amended Sept. 13, 1984, effective Jan. 1, 1985 (458 So.2d 1079); Sept. 24, 1992, effective Jan. 1, 1993 (607 So.2d 1306); Sept. 30, 2004, effective Oct. 1, 2004 (887 So.2d 1090).

Committee Notes

The court on its motion or on petition of an interested person may require a personal representative or guardian to file an accounting or return not otherwise required by statute.

Rule History

1977 Revision: Change in committee notes.

1984 Revision: Extensive editorial changes. Committee notes revised and expanded.

1992 Revision: Editorial changes. Committee notes revised. Citation form changes in committee notes.

2003 Revision: Committee notes revised.

2008 Revision: Committee notes revised.

Statutory References

§ 38.22, Fla. Stat. Power to punish contempts.

§ 38.23, Fla. Stat. Contempts defined.

§ 393.12(2)(h), Fla. Stat. Capacity; appointment of guardian advocate.

§ 733.5036, Fla. Stat. Accounting and discharge following resignation.

§ 733.508, Fla. Stat. Accounting and discharge of removed personal representatives upon removal.

§ 733.901, Fla. Stat. Final discharge.

ch. 738, Fla. Stat. Principal and income.

§ 744.3085, Fla. Stat. Guardian advocates.

§ 744.367, Fla. Stat. Duty to file annual guardianship report.

§ 744.3678, Fla. Stat. Annual accounting.

§ 744.3685, Fla. Stat. Order requiring guardianship report; contempt.

§ 744.369, Fla. Stat. Judicial review of guardianship reports.

§ 744.467, Fla. Stat. Resignation of guardian.

§ 744.511, Fla. Stat. Accounting upon removal.

§ 744.517, Fla. Stat. Proceedings for contempt.

§ 744.521, Fla. Stat. Termination of guardianship.

§ 744.524, Fla. Stat. Termination of guardianship on change of domicile of resident ward.

§ 744.527, Fla. Stat. Final reports and applications for discharge; hearing.

Rule References

Fla. Prob. R. 5.649 Guardian advocate.

Fla. Prob. R. 5.650 Resignation or disqualification of guardian; appointment of successor.

Fla. Prob. R. 5.660 Proceedings for removal of guardian.

Fla. Prob. R. 5.670 Termination of guardianship on change of domicile of resident ward.

Fla. Prob. R. 5.680 Termination of guardianship.

Fla. Prob. R. 5.681 Restoration of rights of person with developmental disability.

Fla. Prob. R. 5.695 Annual guardianship report.

Fla. Prob. R. 5.696 Annual accounting.

Fla. Prob. R. 5.697 Magistrates' review of guardianship accountings and plans.

Cross References

Accounting before final discharge, see F.S.A. § 733.901.
Contempts defined, see F.S.A. § 38.23.
Order requiring report of guardian, contempt, see F.S.A. § 744.3685.
Personal representative, accounting upon removal, see F.S.A. § 733.508.
Power to punish contempt, see F.S.A. § 38.22.
Removal of guardian, see Probate Rule 5.660.
Removal of personal representative, see Probate Rule 5.440.

Rule 5.160. Production of Assets

On the petition of an interested person, or on its own motion, the court may require any personal representative or guardian to produce satisfactory evidence that the assets of the estate are in the possession or under the control of the personal representative or guardian and may order production of the assets in the manner and for the purposes directed by the court.
Amended Sept. 13, 1984, effective Jan. 1, 1985 (458 So.2d 1079); Sept. 29, 1988, effective Jan. 1, 1989 (537 So.2d 500); Sept. 24, 1992, effective Jan. 1, 1993 (607 So.2d 1306).

Committee Notes

Rule History

1977 Revision: Change in committee notes.

1984 Revision: Minor editorial changes. Committee notes revised.

1988 Revision: Editorial changes.

1992 Revision: Editorial changes. Committee notes revised.

Statutory Reference

§ 744.373, Fla.Stat. Production of property.

Cross References

Production of assets, guardianship, see F.S.A. § 744.373.

Rule 5.170. Evidence

In proceedings under the Florida Probate Code and the Florida Guardianship Law the rules of evidence in civil actions are applicable unless specifically changed by the Florida Probate Code, the Florida Guardianship Law, or these rules.
Amended March 31, 1977, effective July 1, 1977 (344 So.2d 828); Sept. 13, 1984, effective Jan. 1, 1985 (458 So.2d 1079).

Committee Notes

Rule History

1977 Revision: New rule.

1984 Revision: To further clarify the intent of the rule to incorporate the provisions of the Florida Evidence Code (chapter 90, Florida Statutes) when not in conflict with the Florida Probate Code or Florida Guardianship Law, or rules applicable to these particular proceedings.

1992 Revision: Citation form changes in committee notes.

2003 Revision: Committee notes revised.

Statutory References

ch. 90, Fla. Stat. Florida Evidence Code.

§ 733.107, Fla. Stat. Burden of proof in contests; presumption of undue influence.

Cross References

Evidence as to death or status, see F.S.A. § 731.103.

Rule 5.171. Evidence of Death

In a proceeding under these rules, the following shall apply:

(a) Death Certificate. An authenticated copy of a death certificate issued by an official or agency of the place where the death purportedly occurred or by an official or agency of the United States is prima facie proof of the fact, place, date, and time of death and the identity of the decedent.

(b) Other Records. A copy of any record or report of a governmental agency, domestic or foreign, that a person is dead, alive, missing, detained, or, from the facts related, presumed dead is prima facie evidence of the status, dates, circumstances, and places disclosed by the record or report.

(c) Extended Absence. A person who is absent from the place of that person's last known domicile for a continuous period of 5 years and whose absence is not satisfactorily explained after diligent search and inquiry is presumed dead. The person's death is presumed to have occurred at the end of the period unless there is evidence establishing that death occurred earlier.

Added Sept. 29, 1988, effective Jan. 1, 1989 (537 So.2d 500). Amended Sept. 24, 1992, effective Jan. 1, 1993 (607 So.2d 1306).

Committee Notes

This rule represents a rule implementation of the procedure found in section 731.103, Florida Statutes. It is not intended to change the effect of the statute from which it was derived but has been reformatted to conform with the structure of these rules. It is not intended to create a new procedure or modify an existing procedure, except that additional language has been added which was not in the statute, to permit issuance of a death certificate by an official or agency of the United States. An example would be such a certificate issued by the Department of State or the Department of Defense.

Rule History

1988 Revision: New rule.

1992 Revision: Editorial changes. Committee notes revised. Citation form changes in committee notes.

Statutory References

§ 731.103, Fla.Stat. Evidence as to death or status.

§ 744.521, Fla.Stat. Termination of guardianship.

Rule References

Fla.Prob.R. 5.205   Filing evidence of death.

Fla.Prob.R. 5.680   Termination of guardianship.

Rule 5.180. Waiver and Consent

(a) Manner of Execution. A waiver or consent as authorized by law shall be in writing and signed by the person executing the waiver or consent.

(b) Contents. The waiver or consent shall state:

(1) the person's interest in the subject of the waiver or consent;

(2) if the person is signing in a fiduciary or representative capacity, the nature of the capacity;

(3) expressly what is being waived or consented to; and

(4) if the waiver pertains to compensation, language declaring that the waiving party has actual knowledge of the amount and manner of determining the compensation and, in addition, either:

(A) that the party has agreed to the amount and manner of determining that compensation and waives any objection to payment; or

(B) that the party has the right to petition the court to determine the compensation and waives that right.

(c) Filing. The waiver or consent shall be filed.

Amended March 31, 1977, effective July 1, 1977 (344 So.2d 828); Sept. 13, 1984, effective Jan. 1, 1985 (458 So.2d 1079); Sept. 29, 1988, effective Jan. 1, 1989 (537 So.2d 500); Sept. 24, 1992, effective Jan. 1, 1993 (607 So.2d 1306); Oct. 3, 1996, effective Jan. 1, 1997 (683 So.2d 78); Feb. 1, 2007 (948 So.2d 735).

Committee Notes

One person who serves in two fiduciary capacities may not waive or consent to the person's acts without the approval of those whom the person represents. This rule represents a rule implementation of the procedure found in section 731.302, Florida Statutes.

Rule History

1977 Revision: Extends right of waiver to natural guardian; clarifies right to waive service of notice of administration.

1984 Revision: Extends waiver to disclosure of compensation and distribution of assets. Committee notes revised.

1988 Revision: Procedure from section 731.302, Florida Statutes, inserted as new (1)(f), and a new requirement that the waiver be in writing has been added. Editorial changes. Committee notes expanded. Citation form changes in committee notes.

1992 Revision: Editorial changes. Committee notes revised. Citation form changes in committee notes.

1996 Revision: Addition of specific fee waiver disclosure requirements found in § 733.6171(9), Florida Statutes, and expanded to cover all fees. Committee notes revised.

2003 Revision: Committee notes revised.

2006 Revision: Rule extensively amended to remove references to interested persons' right to waive or consent, which is governed by section 731.302, Florida Statutes, and to address manner of execution and contents of waiver. Committee notes revised.

Statutory References

§ 731.302, Fla. Stat. Waiver and consent by interested person.

§ 731.303, Fla. Stat. Representation.

§ 733.6171, Fla. Stat. Compensation of attorney for the personal representative.

Cross References

Guardianship law, notice, see F.S.A. § 744.106.
Representation, see F.S.A. § 731.303.
Waiver of notice and consent to proceedings, see F.S.A. § 731.302.

PART II. PROBATE

Rule 5.200. Petition for Administration

The petition for administration shall be verified by the petitioner and shall contain:

(a) a statement of the interest of the petitioner, the petitioner's name and address, and the name and office address of the petitioner's attorney;

(b) the name and last known address of the decedent, last 4 digits of the decedent's social security number, date and place of death of the decedent, and state and county of the decedent's domicile;

(c) so far as is known, the names and addresses of the surviving spouse, if any, the beneficiaries and their relationship to the decedent and the year of birth of any beneficiaries who are minors;

(d) a statement showing venue;

(e) the priority, under the Florida Probate Code, of the person whose appointment as the personal representative is sought and a statement that the person is qualified to serve under the laws of Florida;

(f) a statement whether domiciliary or principal proceedings are pending in another state or country, if known, and the name and address of the foreign personal representative and the court issuing letters;

(g) a statement of the approximate value and nature of the assets;

(h) in an intestate estate, a statement that after the exercise of reasonable diligence the petitioner is unaware of any unrevoked wills or codicils, or if the petitioner is aware of any unrevoked wills or codicils, a statement why the wills or codicils are not being probated;

(i) in a testate estate, a statement identifying all unrevoked wills and codicils being presented for probate, and a statement that the petitioner is unaware of any other unrevoked wills or codicils or, if the petitioner is aware of any other unrevoked wills or codicils, a statement why the other wills or codicils are not being probated; and

(j) in a testate estate, a statement that the original of the decedent's last will is in the possession of the court or accompanies the petition, or that an authenticated copy of a will deposited with or probated in another jurisdiction or that an authenticated copy of a notarial will, the original of which is in the possession of a foreign notary, accompanies the petition.
Amended March 31, 1977, effective July 1, 1977 (344 So.2d 828); Sept. 29, 1988, effective Jan. 1, 1989 (537 So.2d 500); Sept. 24, 1992, effective Jan. 1, 1993 (607 So.2d 1306); May 2, 2002 (824 So.2d 849); July 5, 2007, effective Jan. 1, 2008 (959 So.2d 1170); July 12, 2007 (964 So.2d 140); Sept. 2, 2010, effective Jan. 1, 2011 (50 So.3d 578); Nov. 3, 2011, effective, *nunc pro tunc*, Oct. 1, 2011 (78 So.3d 1045); May 22, 2014, effective May 22, 2014 (139 So.3d 875).

Committee Notes

Rule History

1977 Revision: Addition to (b)(5) to require an affirmative statement that the person sought to be appointed as personal representative is qualified to serve. Committee note expanded to include additional statutory references.

Substantially the same as section 733.202, Florida Statutes, and implementing sections 733.301 through 733.305, Florida Statutes.

1988 Revision: Editorial changes. Committee notes revised.

1992 Revision: Addition of phrase in subdivision (b) to conform to 1992 amendment to section 733.202(2)(b), Florida Statutes. Reference to clerk ascertaining the amount of the filing fee deleted in subdivision (g) because of repeal of sliding scale of filing fees. The remaining language was deemed unnecessary. Editorial changes. Committee notes revised. Citation form changes in committee notes.

2002 Revision: Addition of phrases in subdivision (j) to add references to wills probated in Florida where the original is in the possession of a foreign official. Editorial changes. Committee notes revised.

2003 Revision: Committee notes revised.

2007 Revision: Committee notes revised.

2007 Revision: Editorial changes in (h) and (i).

2010 Revision: Editorial change in (e) to clarify reference to Florida Probate Code.

2011 Revision: Subdivision (b) amended to limit listing of decedent's social security number to last four digits.

2012 Revision: Committee notes revised.

2014 Revision: Subdivision (c) amended to conform to Fla. R. Jud. Admin. 2.425. Committee notes revised.

Statutory References

§ 731.201(23), Fla. Stat. General definitions.

§ 731.301, Fla. Stat. Notice.

§ 733.202, Fla. Stat. Petition.

§ 733.301, Fla. Stat. Preference in appointment of personal representative.

§ 733.302, Fla. Stat. Who may be appointed personal representative.

§ 733.303, Fla. Stat. Persons not qualified.

§ 733.304, Fla. Stat. Nonresidents.

§ 733.305, Fla. Stat. Trust companies and other corporations and associations.

Rule References

Fla. Prob. R. 5.020 Pleadings; verification; motions.

Fla. Prob. R. 5.040 Notice.

Fla. Prob. R. 5.041 Service of pleadings and documents.

Fla. Prob. R. 5.180 Waiver and consent.

Fla. Prob. R. 5.201 Notice of petition for administration.

Fla. R. Jud. Admin. 2.516 Service of pleadings and documents.

Fla. R. Jud. Admin. 2.425 Minimization of the Filing of Sensitive Information.

Cross References

Petition for administration, see F.S.A. § 733.202.
Removal of personal representative, see Probate Rule 5.440.
Revocation of letters, see F.S.A. § 733.504 et seq.

Rule 5.201. Notice of Petition for Administration

(a) **Petitioner Entitled to Preference of Appointment.** Except as may otherwise be required by these rules or the Florida Probate Code, no notice need be given of the petition for administration or the issuance of letters when it appears that the petitioner is entitled to preference of appointment as personal representative.

(b) **Petitioner Not Entitled to Preference.** Before letters shall be issued to any person who is not entitled to preference, formal notice must be served on all known persons qualified to act as personal representative and entitled to preference equal to or greater than the applicant, unless those entitled to preference waive it in writing.

(c) **Service of Petition by Formal Notice.** If the petitioner elects or is required to serve formal notice of the petition for administration prior to the issuance of letters, a copy of the will offered for probate must be attached to the notice.

Added Sept. 29, 1988, effective Jan. 1, 1989 (537 So.2d 500). Amended effective Dec. 9, 2010 (51 So.3d 1146).

Committee Notes

This rule represents a rule implementation of the procedure formerly found in section 733.203(2), Florida Statutes, which was repealed as procedural in 2001.

Rule History

1988 Revision: New rule.

1992 Revision: Committee notes revised. Citation form changes in committee notes.

2003 Revision: Committee notes revised.

2010 Revision: Subdivision (c) added to require service of a copy of the will offered for probate. This requirement was included in section 733.2123, Florida Statutes, but was removed in 2010 because it was deemed to be a procedural requirement. Committee notes revised. Editorial changes.

Statutory References

§ 731.301, Fla. Stat. Notice.

§ 733.212, Fla. Stat. Notice of administration; filing of objections.

§ 733.2123 Fla. Stat. Adjudication before issuance of letters.

Rule References

Fla. Prob. R. 5.040 Notice.

Fla. Prob. R. 5.060 Request for notices and copies of pleadings.

Fla. Prob. R. 5.200 Petition for administration.

Rule 5.205. Filing Evidence of Death

(a) **Requirements for Filing.** A copy of an official record of the death of a decedent shall be filed by the personal representative, if any, or the petitioner in each of the following proceedings and at the times specified:

(1) *Administration of decedent's estate*: not later than 3 months following the date of the first publication of the notice to creditors.

(2) *Ancillary proceedings*: not later than 3 months following the date of first publication of notice to creditors.

(3) *Summary administration*: at any time prior to entry of the order of summary administration.

(4) *Disposition without administration*: at the time of filing the application for disposition without administration.

(5) *Determination of beneficiaries*: at any time prior to entry of the final judgment determining beneficiaries.

(6) *Determination of protected homestead*: at any time prior to entry of the final judgment determining protected homestead status of real property.

(7) *Probate of will without administration*: at any time prior to entry of the order admitting will to probate.

(b) Waiver. On verified petition by the personal representative, if any, or the petitioner the court may enter an order dispensing with this rule, without notice or hearing.

(c) Authority to Require Filing. The court may, without notice or hearing, enter an order requiring the personal representative, if any, or the petitioner to file a copy of an official record of death at any time during the proceedings.

Added Sept. 4, 1980, effective Jan. 1, 1981 (387 So.2d 949). Amended Sept. 13, 1984, effective Jan. 1, 1985 (458 So.2d 1079); Sept. 29, 1988, effective Jan. 1, 1989 (537 So.2d 500); Sept. 24, 1992, effective Jan. 1, 1993 (607 So.2d 1306); May 2, 2002 (824 So.2d 849); June 19, 2003 (848 So.2d 1069).

Committee Notes

A short form certificate of death, which does not disclose the cause of death, should be filed.

Rule History

1980 Revision: This rule is intended to provide a uniform procedure for filing an official record of death in any judicial or statutory proceeding upon the death of a decedent. The court may, upon ex parte application, waive compliance with this rule or require filing at any stage in the proceedings.

1984 Revision: Captions and minor editorial changes. Committee notes revised.

1988 Revision: Editorial and substantive changes. Adds (a)(8) to require filing when will is admitted to probate without administration of the estate or an order disposing of property. Committee notes revised.

1992 Revision: Editorial changes. Committee notes revised. Citation form changes in committee notes.

2002 Revision: Replaces "homestead" with "protected homestead" in (a)(7) to conform to addition of term in section 731.201(29), Florida Statutes. Committee notes revised.

2003 Revision: Revises subdivision (a)(1) to change notice of administration to notice to creditors. Deletes subdivision (a)(3) referring to family administration, and renumbers subsequent subdivisions. Committee notes revised.

2010 Revision: Committee notes revised.

Statutory References

§ 28.222(3)(g), Fla. Stat. Clerk to be county recorder.

§ 382.008(6), Fla. Stat. Death and fetal death registration.

§ 731.103, Fla. Stat. Evidence as to death or status.

§ 733.2121, Fla. Stat. Notice to creditors; filing of claims.

Rule References

Fla. Prob. R. 5.042(a) Time.

Fla. Prob. R. 5.171 Evidence of death.

Fla. Prob. R. 5.241 Notice to creditors.

Rule 5.210. Probate of Wills Without Administration

(a) Petition and Contents. A petition to admit a decedent's will to probate without administration shall be verified by the petitioner and shall contain:

(1) a statement of the interest of the petitioner, the petitioner's name and address, and the name and office address of the petitioner's attorney;

(2) the name and last known address of the decedent, last 4 digits of the decedent's social security number, date and place of death of the decedent, and state and county of the decedent's domicile;

(3) so far as is known, the names and addresses of the surviving spouse, if any, the beneficiaries and their relationships to the decedent, and the name and year of birth of any who are minors;

(4) a statement showing venue;

(5) a statement whether domiciliary or principal proceedings are pending in another state or country, if known, and the name and address of the foreign personal representative and the court issuing letters;

(6) a statement that there are no assets subject to administration in Florida;

(7) a statement identifying all unrevoked wills and codicils being presented for probate and a statement that the petitioner is unaware of any other unrevoked wills or codicils or, if the petitioner is aware of any other unrevoked wills or codicils, a statement why the other wills or codicils are not being probated; and

(8) a statement that the original of the decedent's last will is in the possession of the court or accompanies the petition, or that an authenticated copy of a will deposited with or probated in another jurisdiction or that an authenticated copy of a notarial will, the original of which is in the possession of a foreign notary, accompanies the petition.

(b) Service. The petitioner shall serve a copy of the petition on those persons who would be entitled to service under rule 5.240.

(c) Objections. Objections to the validity of the will shall follow the form and procedure set forth in these rules pertaining to revocation of probate. Objections to the venue or jurisdiction of the court shall follow the form and procedure set forth in the Florida Rules of Civil Procedure.

(d) Order. An order admitting the will to probate shall include a finding that the will has been executed as required by law.

Amended Sept. 13, 1984, effective Jan. 1, 1985 (458 So.2d 1079); Sept. 29, 1988, effective Jan. 1, 1989 (537 So.2d 500); Sept. 24, 1992, effective Jan. 1, 1993 (607 So.2d 1306); Oct. 3, 1996, effective Jan. 1, 1997 (683 So.2d 78); May 2, 2002 (824 So.2d 849); July 5, 2007, effective Jan. 1, 2008 (959 So.2d 1170); Sept. 2, 2010, effective Jan. 1, 2011 (50 So.3d 578); Nov. 3, 2011, effective, *nunc pro tunc*, Oct. 1, 2011 (78 So.3d 1045); May 22, 2014, effective May 22, 2014 (139 So.3d 875).

Committee Notes

Examples illustrating when a will might be admitted to probate are when an instrument (such as a will or trust agreement) gives the decedent a power exercisable by will, such as the power to appoint a successor trustee or a testamentary power of appointment. In each instance, the will of the person holding the power has no legal significance until admitted to probate. There may be no assets, creditors' issues, or other need for a probate beyond admitting the will to establish the exercise or non-exercise of such powers.

Rule History

1975 Revision: Proof of will may be taken by any Florida circuit judge or clerk without issuance of commission.

1984 Revision: This rule has been completely revised to set forth the procedure for proving all wills except lost or destroyed wills and the title changed. The rule requires an oath attesting to the statutory requirements for execution of wills and the will must be proved before an order can be entered admitting it to probate. Former rules 5.280, 5.290, and 5.500 are included in this rule. Committee notes revised.

1988 Revision: Editorial and substantive changes. Change in (a)(3) to clarify which law determines validity of a notarial will; change in (a)(4) to clarify requirement that will of a Florida resident must comply with Florida law; adds new subdivision (b) to set forth required contents of petition for probate of will; moves former (b) to (c). Committee notes expanded; citation form change in committee notes.

1992 Revision: Editorial changes. Committee notes revised. Citation form changes in committee notes.

1996 Revision: Subdivision (a)(4) changed to allow authenticated copies of wills to be admitted to probate if the original is filed or deposited in another jurisdiction.

2002 Revision: Substantial revision to the rule setting forth the requirements of a petition to admit a will to probate when administration is not required. Self proof of wills is governed by the Florida Statutes. Former subdivision (a)(4) amended and transferred to new rule 5.215. Former subdivision (a)(5) amended and transferred to new rule 5.216.

2003 Revision: Committee notes revised.

2007 Revision: Existing text redesignated as subdivision (a) and editorial change made in (a)(7). New subdivisions (b) and (c) added to provide for service of the petition and the procedure for objections consistent with the procedures for probate of a will with administration. Committee notes revised.

2010 Revision: Subdivision (b) amended to reflect that service of the petition to admit a decedent's will to probate without administration shall be served on the persons who would be entitled to service of the notice of administration in a formal administration as set forth in rule 5.240. New subdivision (d) added to provide that any order admitting the decedent's will to probate without administration contain a finding that the will was executed as required by law. Committee notes revised.

2011 Revision: Subdivision (a)(2) amended to limit listing of decedent's social security number to last four digits.

2014 Revision: Subdivision (a)(3) amended to conform to Fla. R. Jud. Admin. 2.425. Committee notes revised.

Statutory References

§ 731.201, Fla. Stat. General definitions.

§ 731.301, Fla. Stat. Notice.

§ 732.502, Fla. Stat. Execution of wills.

§ 732.503, Fla. Stat. Self–proof of will.

§ 733.103, Fla. Stat. Effect of probate.

§ 733.201, Fla. Stat. Proof of wills.

---

§ 733.202, Fla. Stat. Petition.

§ 733.204, Fla. Stat. Probate of a will written in a foreign language.

§ 733.205, Fla. Stat. Probate of notarial will.

§ 733.206, Fla. Stat. Probate of will of resident after foreign probate.

§ 733.207, Fla. Stat. Establishment and probate of lost or destroyed will.

§ 734.104, Fla. Stat. Foreign wills; admission to record; effect on title.

Rule References

Fla. Prob. R. 5.015 General definitions.

Fla. Prob. R. 5.020 Pleadings, verification; motions.

Fla. Prob. R. 5.205(a)(7) Filing evidence of death.

Fla. Prob. R. 5.215 Authenticated copy of will.

Fla. Prob. R. 5.216 Will written in foreign language.

Fla. Prob. R. 5.230 Commission to prove will.

Fla. Prob. R. 5.240 Notice of administration.

Fla. Prob. R. 5.270 Revocation of probate.

Fla. R. Jud. Admin. 2.425 Minimization of the Filing of Sensitive Information.

Rule 5.215. Authenticated Copy of Will

An authenticated copy of a will may be admitted to probate if the original could be admitted to probate in Florida.

Added May 2, 2002 (824 So.2d 849).

Committee Notes

Rule History

2002 Revision: New rule, derived from former rule 5.210(a)(4).

2003 Revision: Committee notes revised.

Statutory References

§ 733.205, Fla. Stat. Probate of notarial will.

§ 733.206, Fla. Stat. Probate of will of resident after foreign probate.

§ 734.102, Fla. Stat. Ancillary administration.

§ 734.1025, Fla. Stat. Nonresident decedent's testate estate with property not exceeding $50,000 in this state; determination of claims.

§ 734.104, Fla. Stat. Foreign wills; admission to record; effect on title.

Rule References

Fla. Prob. R. 5.200 Petition for administration.

Fla. Prob. R. 5.210 Probate of wills without administration.

Fla. Prob. R. 5.470 Ancillary administration.

Fla. Prob. R. 5.475 Ancillary administration, short form.

Rule 5.216. Will Written in Foreign Language

A will written in a foreign language being offered for probate shall be accompanied by a true and complete English translation. In the order admitting the foreign language will to probate, the court shall establish the correct English translation. At any time during administration, any interested person may have the correctness of the translation redetermined after formal notice to all other interested persons.

Added May 2, 2002 (824 So.2d 849).

Committee Notes

Rule History

2002 Revision: New rule, derived from former rule 5.210(a)(5) and section 733.204(2), Florida Statutes.

Statutory Reference

§ 733.204, Fla. Stat. Probate of a will written in a foreign language.

Rule 5.230. Commission to Prove Will

(a) Petition. On petition the court may appoint a commissioner to take the oath of any person qualified to prove the will under Florida law. The petition must set forth the date of the will and the place where it was executed, if known; the names of the witnesses and address of the witness whose oath is to be taken; and the name, title, and address of the proposed commissioner.

(b) Commission. The commission must be directed to a person who is authorized to administer an oath by the laws of Florida, the United States of America, or the state or country where the witness may be found, and it shall empower the commissioner to take the oath of the witness to prove the will and shall direct the commissioner to certify the oath and file the executed commission, copy of the will, oath of the witness, and certificate of commissioner. An oath of the commissioner is not required.

(c) Mailing or Delivery. The petitioner or the petitioner's attorney must cause the commission, together with a copy of the will, the oath, and the certificate of commissioner, to be mailed or delivered to the commissioner.

(d) Filing. The executed commission, copy of the will, oath of the witness, and certificate of commissioner must be filed.

Amended Sept. 13, 1984, effective Jan. 1, 1985 (458 So.2d 1079); Sept. 29, 1988, effective Jan. 1, 1989 (537 So.2d 500); Sept. 24, 1992, effective Jan. 1, 1993 (607 So.2d 1306); Sept. 26, 2013, effective Jan. 1, 2014 (123 So.3d 31).

Committee Notes

Rule History

1975 Revision: Substantially the same as prior rule 5.130(a) and (b) and carries forward prior procedures as to a matter upon which Florida Probate Code is silent.

1984 Revision: This rule has been completely changed to set forth the procedure for the issuance and return of a commission. The rule has been broadened to allow anyone authorized by Florida Statutes or by the U.S. Code to be a commissioner as well as those authorized by the state or country where the witness resides.

The rule now provides that the petitioner or his attorney shall forward the commission to the commissioner. The rule also contemplates that a Florida notary may be appointed as commissioner to take the proof of a witness outside the State of Florida. Committee notes revised and expanded.

1988 Revision: Editorial and substantive changes. Change in (a) to provide that the commissioner may take the oath of not only the attesting witness to the will but also the oath of any other person qualified to prove the will; change in (c) to permit copies other than photographic copies to be furnished to the commissioner, and to permit delivery of documents in a manner other than by mailing; change in (d) to require the filing of documents with the court. Committee notes revised. Citation form changes in rule and committee notes.

1992 Revision: Editorial change. Committee notes revised. Citation form changes in committee notes.

2003 Revision: Committee notes revised.

2013 Revision: Subdivision (e) deleted because it duplicates subdivision (d) in Rule 5.240. Committee notes revised. Editorial changes to conform to the court's guidelines for rules submissions as set forth in AOSC06–14.

Statutory References

§ 92.50, Fla. Stat. Oaths, affidavits, and acknowledgments; who may take or administer; requirements.

§ 733.101, Fla. Stat. Venue of probate proceedings.

§ 733.201, Fla. Stat. Proof of wills.

§ 22 U.S.C. 4215 Notarial acts, oaths, affirmations, affidavits, and depositions; fees.

Rule References

Fla. Prob. R. 5.050 Transfer of proceedings.

Fla. R. Civ. P. 1.060 Transfers of actions.

Rule 5.235. Issuance of Letters, Bond

(a) **Appointment of Personal Representative.** After the petition for administration is filed and the will, if any, is admitted to probate:

(1) the court shall appoint the person entitled and qualified to be personal representative;

(2) the court shall determine the amount of any bond required. The clerk may approve the bond in the amount determined by the court; and

(3) any required oath or designation of, and acceptance by, a resident agent shall be filed.

(b) **Issuance of Letters.** Upon compliance with all of the foregoing, letters shall be issued to the personal representative.

(c) **Bond.** On petition by any interested person or on the court's own motion, the court may waive the requirement of filing a bond, require a personal representative or curator to give bond, increase or decrease the bond, or require additional surety.

Added Sept. 29, 1988, effective Jan. 1, 1989 (537 So.2d 500). Amended Sept. 24, 1992, effective Jan. 1, 1993 (607 So.2d 1306); Oct. 3, 1996, effective Jan. 1, 1997 (683 So.2d 78).

Committee Notes

This rule represents a rule implementation of the procedure formerly found in sections 733.401 and 733.403(2), Florida Statutes, both of which were repealed in 2001. It is not intended to change the effect of the statutes from which it was derived but has been reformatted to conform with the structure of these rules. It is not intended to create a new procedure or modify an existing procedure.

Rule History

1988 Revision: New rule.

1992 Revision: Editorial changes. Committee notes revised. Citation form changes in committee notes.

1996 Revision: Mandate in subdivision (a)(2) prohibiting charge of service fee by clerk deleted. Statutory references added.

2003 Revision: Committee notes revised.

2010 Revision: Committee notes revised.

Statutory References

§ 28.24(19), Fla. Stat. Service charges by clerk of the circuit court.

§ 28.2401, Fla. Stat. Service charges in probate matters.

§ 733.402, Fla. Stat. Bond of fiduciary; when required; form.

§ 733.403, Fla. Stat. Amount of bond.

§ 733.405, Fla. Stat. Release of surety.

§ 733.501, Fla. Stat. Curators.

Rule References

Fla. Prob. R. 5.110 Address designation for personal representative or guardian; designation of resident agent and acceptance.

Fla. Prob. R. 5.122 Curators.

Fla. Prob. R. 5.320 Oath of personal representative.

Rule 5.240. Notice of Administration

(a) **Service.** The personal representative shall promptly serve a copy of the notice of administration on the following persons who are known to the personal representative and who were not previously served under section 733.2123, Florida Statutes:

(1) the decedent's surviving spouse;

(2) all beneficiaries;

(3) a trustee of any trust described in section 733.707(3), Florida Statutes and each qualified beneficiary of the trust as defined in section 736.0103(16), if each trustee is also a personal representative of the estate; and

(4) persons who may be entitled to exempt property

in the manner provided for service of formal notice. The personal representative may similarly serve a copy of the notice on any devisee under another will or heirs or others who claim or may claim an interest in the estate.

(b) **Contents.** The notice shall state:

(1) the name of the decedent, the file number of the estate, the designation and address of the court in which the proceedings are pending, whether the estate is testate or intestate, and, if testate, the date of the will and any codicils;

(2) the name and address of the personal representative and of the personal representative's attorney, and that the fiduciary lawyer-client privilege in section 90.5021, Florida Statutes, applies with respect to the personal representative and any attorney employed by the personal representative;

(3) that any interested person on whom the notice is served who challenges the validity of the will, the qualifications of the personal representative, venue, or jurisdiction of the court must file

any objections with the court in the manner provided in the Florida Probate Rules within the time required by law or those objections are forever barred;

(4) that any person entitled to exempt property must file a petition for determination of exempt property within the time provided by law or the right to exempt property is deemed waived; and

(5) that an election to take an elective share must be filed within the time provided by law.

(c) Copy of Will. Unless the court directs otherwise, the personal representative of a testate estate must, upon written request, furnish a copy of the will and all codicils admitted to probate to any person on whom the notice of administration was served.

(d) Objections. Objections to the validity of the will shall follow the form and procedure set forth in these rules pertaining to revocation of probate. Objections to the qualifications of the personal representative shall follow the form and procedure set forth in these rules pertaining to removal of a personal representative. Objections to the venue or jurisdiction of the court shall follow the form and procedure set forth in the Florida Rules of Civil Procedure.

(e) Waiver of Service. For the purpose of determining deadlines established by reference to the date of service of a copy of the notice of administration in cases in which service has been waived, service on a person who has waived notice is deemed to occur on the date the waiver is filed.

Amended March 31, 1977, effective July 1, 1977 (344 So.2d 828); Sept. 13, 1984, effective Jan. 1, 1985 (458 So.2d 1079); Sept. 29, 1988, effective Jan. 1, 1989 (537 So.2d 500); Aug. 22, 1991, effective Oct. 1, 1991 (584 So.2d 964); Sept. 24, 1992, effective Jan. 1, 1993 (607 So.2d 1306); Oct. 3, 1996, effective Jan. 1, 1997 (683 So.2d 78); May 2, 2002 (824 So.2d 849); June 19, 2003, (848 So.2d 1069); Sept. 29, 2005, effective Jan.1, 2006 (912 So.2d 1178); July 12, 2007 (964 So.2d 140); Sept. 28, 2011 (73 So.3d 205); Nov. 27, 2013 (131 So.3d 717).

Committee Notes

Rule History

1977 Revision: Former subdivision (c) is deleted as being substantive rather than procedural.

1984 Revision: Editorial changes; new requirement to file proof of publication; new requirements as to form of objections to will and qualifications of personal representative. Committee notes revised.

1988 Revision: The obligation to mail notice of administration to all known or reasonably ascertainable creditors has been added to comply with the dictates of *Tulsa Professional Collection Services, Inc. v. Pope,* 485 U.S. 478, 108 S. Ct. 1340, 99 L. Ed. 2d 565 (1988).

This rule does not require sending notice of administration to creditors in estates where the time for filing claims has expired before the effective date of this rule. However, no opinion is offered whether such claims are barred by the provisions of section 733.702, Florida Statutes.

Committee notes revised. Citation form changes in committee notes.

1991 Revision: Subdivision (a) modified to make it consistent with recent changes to sections 733.212 and 733.702, Florida Statutes. Those statutes were amended to comply with the dictates of *Tulsa Professional Collection Services, Inc. v. Pope,* 485 U.S. 478, 108 S. Ct. 1340, 99 L. Ed. 2d 565 (1988). For the same reason, subdivision (e) was eliminated.

1992 Revision: Former subdivision (e) revised and reinstated to emphasize need for personal representative to determine all known or reasonably ascertainable creditors. Editorial changes; committee notes revised; citation form changes in committee notes.

1996 Revision: Subdivision (a) amended to require service of notice of administration on trustees of certain revocable trusts as defined by Florida statute. Editorial changes.

2002 Revision: Procedures for notifying creditors are now governed by new rule 5.241. Committee notes revised.

2003 Revision: Change in title of (a) to reflect elimination of publication of notice. Committee notes revised.

2005 Revision: Subdivision (a)(3) amended to make it consistent with 2003 change to section 733.212(1)(c), Florida Statutes, regarding when service on trust beneficiaries is required, and clarifying editorial change made in (a). New subdivision (b)(5) added regarding notice to file election to take elective share. Committee notes revised.

2007 Revision: Subdivision (a)(3) amended to replace reference to "beneficiary" with "qualified beneficiary" and to change reference from former section 737.303(4)(b) to new section 736.0103(14), which defines that term. Subdivision (b)(5) amended to delete the reference to the surviving spouse filing the election as another person can file the election on behalf of the surviving spouse. New subdivision (e) added to provide a deadline for objection by a person who waives service. Committee notes revised.

2011 Revision: Subdivision (b)(2) amended to conform to amendment to section 732.212, Florida Statutes, relating to attorney-client privilege for fiduciaries and their attorneys. Editorial changes to conform to the court's guidelines for rules submissions as set forth in Administrative Order AOSC06–14. Statutory reference to section 732.402, Florida Statutes, added. Committee Notes revised.

2013 Revision: Updated statutory reference in subdivision (a)(3). Committee notes revised.

Statutory References

§ 731.201(23), Fla. Stat. General definitions.

§ 731.301, Fla. Stat. Notice.

§ 731.302, Fla. Stat. Waiver and consent by interested person.

§ 732.2135, Fla. Stat. Time of election; extensions; withdrawal.

§ 732.402, Fla. Stat. Exempt property.

§ 732.5165, Fla. Stat. Effect of fraud, duress, mistake, and undue influence.

§ 733.101, Fla. Stat. Venue of probate proceedings.

§ 733.109, Fla. Stat. Revocation of probate.

§ 733.212, Fla. Stat. Notice of administration; filing of objections.

§ 733.2123, Fla. Stat. Adjudication before issuance of letters.

§ 733.302, Fla. Stat. Who may be appointed personal representative.

§ 733.303, Fla. Stat. Persons not qualified.

§ 733.305, Fla. Stat. Trust companies and other corporations and associations.

§ 733.504, Fla. Stat. Removal of personal representative; causes for removal.

§ 733.506, Fla. Stat. Proceedings for removal.

Rule References

Fla. Prob. R. 5.025 Adversary proceedings.

Fla. Prob. R. 5.040 Notice.

Fla. Prob. R. 5.050 Transfer of proceedings.

Fla. Prob. R. 5.180 Waiver and consent.

Fla. Prob. R. 5.270 Revocation of probate.

Fla. Prob. R. 5.440 Proceedings for removal.

Fla. R. Civ. P. 1.060 Transfers of actions.

Rule 5.2405. Service of Notice of Administration on Personal Representative

(a) Date Notice of Administration is Considered Served on Person who is Personal Representative. Unless service of the notice of administration is waived pursuant to Rule 5.240(e), when a person who is entitled to service of the notice of administration pursuant to Rule 5.240(a) is also a personal representative, the notice of administration shall be deemed served upon the person on the earliest of the following dates:

(1) the date on which the person acknowledges in writing receipt of the notice of administration;

(2) the date on which the notice of administration is first served on any other person entitled to service of the notice of administration (or the first among multiple persons entitled to service); or

(3) the date that is 30 days after the date letters of administration are issued.

(b) Date Other Notices are Considered Served on Person who is Personal Representative. When a person who is entitled to service of notice under these rules or the Florida Probate Code (other than the notice of administration) is also a personal representative, any notice shall be deemed as having been served on the personal representative on the earliest of the following dates:

(1) the date on which the person acknowledges in writing receipt of the notice;

(2) the date on which the notice is required to be served by the personal representative under these rules or the Florida Probate Code; or,

(3) the date on which the notice is first served by the personal representative on any other person entitled to service of the same notice.

Added Sept. 26, 2013, effective Jan. 1, 2014 (123 So.3d 31).

Committee Notes

This rule is intended to address situations in which the personal representative is also an interested person in an estate, but claims that he or she has not received the notice of administration, despite the personal representative being required to serve the notice. The receipt of the notice of administration can trigger time limits for the person receiving the notice with regard to certain rights, such as the right to claim an elective share.

Rule History

2013 Revision: New rule.

Statutory References

§ 731.201(23), Fla. Stat. General definitions.

§ 731.301, Fla. Stat. Notice.

§ 731.302, Fla. Stat. Waiver and consent by interested person.

§ 732.2135, Fla. Stat. Time of election; extensions; withdrawal.

§ 732.5165, Fla. Stat. Effect of fraud, duress, mistake, and undue influence.

§ 733.101, Fla. Stat. Venue of probate proceedings.

§ 733.109, Fla. Stat. Revocation of probate.

§ 733.212, Fla. Stat. Notice of administration; filing of objections.

§ 733.2123, Fla. Stat. Adjudication before issuance of letters.

§ 733.302, Fla. Stat. Who may be appointed personal representative.

§ 733.303, Fla. Stat. Persons not qualified.

§ 733.305, Fla. Stat. Trust companies and other corporations and associations.

§ 733.504, Fla. Stat. Removal of personal representative; causes for removal.

§ 733.506, Fla. Stat. Proceedings for removal.

Rule References

Fla. Prob. R. 5.025 Adversary proceedings.

Fla. Prob. R. 5.040 Notice.

Fla. Prob. R. 5.050 Transfer of proceedings.

Fla. Prob. R. 5.180 Waiver and consent.

Fla. Prob. R. 5.270 Revocation of probate.

Fla. Prob. R. 5.440 Proceedings for removal of personal representative.

Fla. R. Civ. P. 1.060 Transfers of actions.

Rule 5.241. Notice to Creditors

(a) **Publication and Service.** Unless creditors' claims are otherwise barred by law, the personal representative shall promptly publish a notice to creditors and serve a copy of the notice on all creditors of the decedent who are reasonably ascertainable and, if required by law, on the Agency for Health Care Administration. Service of the notice shall be either by informal notice, or in the manner provided for service of formal notice at the option of the personal representative. Service on one creditor by a chosen method shall not preclude service on another creditor by another method.

(b) **Contents.** The notice to creditors shall contain the name of the decedent, the file number of the estate, the designation and address of the court, the name and address of the personal representative and of the personal representative's attorney, and the date of first publication of the notice to creditors. The notice shall require all creditors to file all claims against the estate with the court, within the time provided by law.

(c) **Method of Publication and Proof.** Publication shall be made as required by law. The personal representative shall file proof of publication with the court within 45 days after the date of first publication of the notice to creditors.

(d) **Statement Regarding Creditors.** Within 4 months after the date of the first publication of notice to creditors, the personal representative shall file a verified statement that diligent search has been made to ascertain the name and address of each person having a claim against the estate. The statement shall indicate the name and address of each person at that time known to the personal representative who has or may have a claim against the estate and whether such person was served with the notice to creditors or otherwise received actual notice of the information contained in the notice to creditors; provided that the statement need not include persons who have filed a timely claim or who were included in the personal representative's proof of claim.

(e) **Service of Death Certificate.** If service of the notice on the Agency for Health Care Administration is required, it shall be accompanied by a death certificate.

Added May 2, 2002 (824 So.2d 849). Amended Sept. 29, 2005, effective Jan. 1, 2006 (912 So.2d 1178); July 5, 2007, effective Jan. 1, 2008 (959 So.2d 1170); July 12, 2007 (964 So.2d 140).

Committee Notes

It is the committee's opinion that the failure to timely file the proof of publication of the notice to creditors shall not affect time limitations for filing claims or objections.

On April 19, 1988, the United States Supreme Court decided *Tulsa Professional Collection Services, Inc. v. Pope*, 485 U.S. 478, 108 S. Ct. 1340, 99 L. Ed. 2d 565. This case substantially impacted the method for handling (and barring) creditors' claims. This case stands for the proposition that a creditor may not be barred by the usual publication if that creditor was actually known to or reasonably ascertainable by the personal representative, and the personal representative failed to give notice to the creditor by mail or other means as certain to ensure actual notice. Less than actual notice in these circumstances would deprive the creditor of due process rights under the 14th Amendment to the U.S. Constitution. Probably actual notice of the death (as in the case of a hospital where the decedent died as a patient) without notice of the institution of probate proceedings is not sufficient.

An elementary and fundamental requirement of due process in any proceeding which is to be accorded finality is notice reasonably calculated, under all the circumstances, to apprise interested persons of the pendency of the proceeding and afford them an opportunity to present their claims.

The steps to be taken by a personal representative in conducting a diligent search for creditors depends, in large measure, on how familiar the personal representative is with the decedent's affairs. Therefore, the committee believes it is inappropriate to list particular steps to be taken in each estate, since the circumstances will vary from case to case.

The statement required by this rule is not intended to be jurisdictional but rather to provide evidence of satisfaction (or lack thereof) of the due process requirements.

Rule History

2002 Revision: New rule to implement procedures consistent with new section 733.2121, Florida Statutes.

2003 Revision: Committee notes revised.

2005 Revision: Subdivision (a) amended to clarify approved methods of service on creditors. Committee notes revised.

2007 Revision: New subdivision (e) added to require service of a copy of the decedent's death certificate on the Agency for Health Care Administration, as is now required by section 733.2121(3)(d), Florida Statutes.

Statutory References

ch. 50, Fla. Stat. Legal and official advertisements.

§ 731.301, Fla. Stat. Notice.

§ 733.2121, Fla. Stat. Notice to creditors; filing of claims.

§ 733.702, Fla. Stat. Limitations on presentation of claims.

§ 733.703, Fla. Stat. Form and manner of presenting claim.

§ 733.704, Fla. Stat. Amendment of claims.

§ 733.705, Fla. Stat. Payment of and objection to claims.

§ 733.708, Fla. Stat. Compromise.

Rule Reference

Fla. Prob. R. 5.490 Form and manner of presenting claim.

Rule 5.260. Caveat; Proceedings

(a) Filing. Any creditor or interested person other than a creditor may file a caveat with the court. The caveat of an interested person, other than a creditor, may be filed before or after the death of the person for whom the estate will be, or is being, administered. The caveat of a creditor may be filed only after the person's death.

(b) Contents. The caveat shall contain the name of the person for whom the estate will be, or is being, administered, the last 4 digits of the person's social security number or year of birth, if known, a statement of the interest of the caveator in the estate, and the name and specific mailing address of the caveator.

(c) Resident Agent of Caveator; Service. If the caveator is not a resident of Florida, the caveator must file a designation of the name and specific mailing address and residence address of a resident in the county where the caveat is filed as the caveator's agent for service of notice. The written acceptance by the person appointed as resident agent must be filed with the designation or included in the caveat. The designation and acceptance shall constitute the consent of the caveator that service of notice upon the designated resident agent shall bind the caveator. If the caveator is represented by an attorney admitted to practice in Florida who signs the caveat, it shall not be necessary to designate a resident agent under this rule.

(d) Filing after Commencement. If at the time of the filing of any caveat the decedent's will has been admitted to probate or letters of administration have been issued, the clerk must promptly notify the caveator in writing of the date of issuance of letters and the names and addresses of the personal representative and the personal representative's attorney.

(e) Creditor. When letters of administration issue after the filing of a caveat by a creditor, the clerk must promptly notify the caveator, in writing, advising the caveator of the date of issuance of letters and the names and addresses of the personal representative and the personal representative's attorney, unless notice has previously been served on the caveator. A copy of any notice given by the clerk, together with a certificate of the mailing of the original notice, must be filed in the estate proceedings.

(f) Other Interested Persons; Before Commencement. After the filing of a caveat by an interested person other than a creditor, the court must not admit a will of the decedent to probate or appoint a personal representative without service of formal notice on the caveator or the caveator's designated agent. A caveator is not required to be served with formal notice of its own petition for administration.

Amended March 31, 1977, effective July 1, 1977 (344 So.2d 828); Sept. 13, 1984, effective Jan. 1, 1985 (458 So.2d 1079); Sept. 24, 1992, effective Jan. 1, 1993 (607 So.2d 1306); Sept. 2, 2010, effective Jan. 1, 2011 (50 So.3d 578); Subsecs. (a), (b), (d), (e), and (f) amended effective Dec. 9, 2010; Subsec. (c) amended effective Jan. 1, 2011 (51 So.3d 1146); Subsec. (b) amended effective July 7, 2011 (67 So.3d 1035); Nov. 27, 2013 (131 So.3d 717).

Committee Notes

Caveat proceedings permit a decedent's creditor or other interested person to be notified when letters of administration are issued. Thereafter, the caveator must take appropriate action to protect the caveator's interests.

This rule treats the creditor caveator differently from other caveators.

An attorney admitted to practice in Florida who represents the caveator may sign the caveat on behalf of the client.

Rule History

1977 Revision: Carried forward prior rule 5.150.

1984 Revision: Changes in (a), (b), and (d) are editorial. Change in (c) eliminates resident agent requirement for Florida residents and for nonresidents represented by a Florida attorney. Service on the attorney binds caveator. Former (e) is now subdivisions (e) and (f) and treats creditor caveator differently from other interested persons. Change in (f) requires formal notice. Committee notes revised.

1988 Revision: Committee notes revised. Citation form changes in committee notes.

1992 Revision: Addition of language in subdivision (b) to implement 1992 amendment to section 731.110(2), Florida Statutes. Editorial changes. Citation form changes in committee notes.

2003 Revision: Committee notes revised.

2010 Cycle Report Revision: Subdivision (c) amended to clarify that a state agency filing a caveat need not designate an agent for service of process, and to provide that a caveator who is not a resident of the county where the caveat is filed must designate either a resident of that county or an attorney licensed and residing in Florida as the caveator's agent. Editorial changes in (d) and (e). Committee notes revised.

2010 Out-of-Cycle Report Revision: Subdivisions (a) and (b) amended to conform with statutory changes. Subdivision (c) amended to read as it existed prior to SC10–171 (35 FLW S482) due to a subsequent legislative amendment (Chapter 2010–132, § 3, Laws of Fla.). Editorial changes in (d), (e), and (f). Committee notes revised.

2011 Revision: Subdivision (b) amended to replace language removed in 2010 out-of-cycle revision, to replace term "decedent" with "person for whom the estate will be, or is being, administered," and to limit listing of a social security number to the last four digits and a date of birth to the year of birth.

2013 Revision: Subdivision (f) is updated to provide that a caveator is not required to be served with formal notice of its own petition for administration. Committee notes revised.

Statutory Reference

§ 731.110, Fla. Stat. Caveat; proceedings.

Rule Reference

Fla. Prob. R. 5.040(a) Notice.

Cross References

Caveat, proceedings, see F.S.A. § 731.110.
Limitation of actions, see F.S.A. § 95.231.

Rule 5.270. Revocation of Probate

(a) Petition and Contents. A petition for revocation of probate shall state the interest of the petitioner in the estate and the facts constituting the grounds on which revocation is demanded.

(b) Continued Administration. Pending the determination of any issue for revocation of probate, the personal representative shall proceed with the administration of the estate as if no revocation proceeding had been commenced, except that no distribution may be made to beneficiaries in contravention of the rights of those who, but for the will, would be entitled to the property disposed of.

Amended Sept. 13, 1984, effective Jan. 1, 1985 (458 So.2d 1079); Sept. 29, 1988, effective Jan. 1, 1989 (537 So.2d 500); Sept. 29, 2005, effective Jan. 1, 2006 (912 So.2d 1178); July 12, 2007 (964 So.2d 140).

Committee Notes

This rule represents a rule implementation of the procedure found in section 733.109(2), Florida Statutes. It is not intended to change the effect of the statute from which it was derived but has

---

been reformatted to conform with the structure of these rules. It is not intended to create a new procedure or modify an existing procedure. The committee believes that subsections (1) and (3) of the statute are substantive, and have therefore not been included. Further, this rule revises subdivision (b) of the prior similar rule to track the language in the statute from which it was derived.

Rule History

1984 Revision: Extensive changes. Committee notes revised.

1988 Revision: Language of subdivision (b) of the rule rewritten to track the statute more closely. Committee notes expanded. Citation form change in committee notes.

1992 Revision: Committee notes revised. Citation form changes in committee notes.

2003 Revision: Committee notes revised.

2005 Revision: "Beneficiaries" substituted for "devisees" in subdivision (b) to conform language to section 733.109(2), Florida Statutes.

2007 Revision: Committee notes revised.

Statutory References

§ 731.201(23), Fla. Stat. General definitions.

§ 732.5165, Fla. Stat. Effect of fraud, duress, mistake, and undue influence.

§ 733.109, Fla. Stat. Revocation of probate.

§ 733.212, Fla. Stat. Notice of administration; filing of objections.

§ 733.2123, Fla. Stat. Adjudication before issuance of letters.

Rule References

Fla. Prob. R. 5.025 Adversary proceedings.

Fla. Prob. R. 5.040 Notice.

Fla. Prob. R. 5.240 Notice of administration.

Cross References

Revocation of letters, see F.S.A. § 733.504 et seq.
Revocation of probate proceedings, see F.S.A. § 733.109.

Rule 5.275. Burden of Proof in Will Contests

In all proceedings contesting the validity of a will, the burden shall be upon the proponent of the will to establish prima facie its formal execution and attestation. Thereafter, the contestant shall have the burden of establishing the grounds on which the probate of the will is opposed or revocation sought.

Added Sept. 29, 1988, effective Jan. 1, 1989 (537 So.2d 500).

Committee Notes

This rule represents a rule implementation of the procedure found in section 733.107, Florida Statutes. The presumption of undue influence implements public policy against abuse of fiduciary or confidential relationships and is therefore a presumption shifting the burden of proof under sections 90.301–90.304, Florida Statutes.

Rule History

1988 Revision: New rule.

1992 Revision: Citation form changes in committee notes.

2003 Revision: Committee notes revised.

Statutory References

§ 90.301, Fla. Stat. Presumption defined; inferences.

§ 90.302, Fla. Stat. Classification of rebuttable presumptions.

§ 90.303, Fla. Stat. Presumption affecting the burden of producing evidence defined.

§ 90.304, Fla. Stat. Presumption affecting the burden of proof defined.

§ 733.107, Fla. Stat. Burden of proof in contests; presumption of undue influence.

Rule 5.310. Disqualification of Personal Representative; Notification

Any personal representative who was not qualified to act at the time of appointment or who would not be qualified for appointment if application for appointment were then made shall immediately file and serve on all interested persons a notice describing:

(a) the reason the personal representative was not qualified at the time of appointment; or

(b) the reason the personal representative would not be qualified for appointment if application for appointment were then made and the date on which the disqualifying event occurred.

The personal representative's notice shall state that any interested person may petition to remove the personal representative.

Amended Sept. 24, 1992, effective Jan. 1, 1993 (607 So.2d 1306); May 2, 2002 (824 So.2d 849).

Committee Notes

Notification under this rule or section 733.3101, Florida Statutes, does not automatically affect the authority of the personal representative to act. The personal representative may resign or interested persons or the court must act to remove the personal representative.

Rule History

1975 Revision: This is same as old rule 5.220 and old section 732.47(3), Florida Statutes. The rule sets forth the imperative need for timely action and the inherent responsibility of a fiduciary to effect orderly succession. It further implies the inherent jurisdiction of the court to control by judicial overview the succession.

1977 Revision: Citation form change in committee note.

1988 Revision: Committee notes revised. Citation form changes in committee notes.

1992 Revision: Editorial changes to clarify rule. Committee notes revised. Citation form changes in committee notes.

2002 Revision: Rule amended to implement procedures found in section 733.3101, Florida Statutes. Committee notes revised.

Statutory References

§ 731.301, Fla. Stat. Notice.

§ 733.302, Fla. Stat. Who may be appointed personal representative.

§ 733.303, Fla. Stat. Persons not qualified.

§ 733.3101, Fla. Stat. Personal representative not qualified.

§ 733.502, Fla. Stat. Resignation of personal representative.

§ 733.504, Fla. Stat. Removal of personal representative; causes for removal.

§ 733.505, Fla. Stat. Jurisdiction in removal proceedings.

§ 733.506, Fla. Stat. Proceedings for removal.

Rule References

Fla. Prob. R. 5.040 Notice.

Fla. Prob. R. 5.430 Resignation of personal representative.

Fla. Prob. R. 5.440 Proceedings for removal.

Cross References

Persons not qualified to act as personal representative, see F.S.A. § 733.303.

Qualifications of personal representative, see F.S.A. § 733.302 et seq.

Removal of personal representative,

    Causes, see F.S.A. § 733.504.

    Jurisdiction, see F.S.A. § 733.505.

    Proceedings, see F.S.A. § 733.506.

Rule 5.320. Oath of Personal Representative

Before the granting of letters of administration, the personal representative shall file an oath to faithfully administer the estate of the decedent. If the petition is verified by the prospective personal representative individually, the oath may be incorporated in the petition or in the designation of resident agent.

Amended Sept. 24, 1992, effective Jan. 1, 1993 (607 So.2d 1306).

Committee Notes

It is contemplated the oath may be signed concurrently with the petition for administration and will be valid even if it predates the order appointing the personal representative.

Rule History

1977 Revision: No change in rule. Change in committee note to conform to statutory renumbering.

This rule establishes the uniform requirement for an oath of faithful performance of fiduciary duties within the permissiveness of section 733.401(1)(d), Florida Statutes. Should be taken together with new rule 5.110, Resident Agent.

1988 Revision: Committee notes expanded. Citation form changes in committee notes.

1992 Revision: Editorial change. Committee notes revised. Citation form changes in committee notes.

2003 Revision: Committee notes revised.

Rule References

Fla. Prob. R. 5.110 Address designation for personal representative or guardian; designation of resident agent and acceptance.

Fla. Prob. R. 5.235 Issuance of letters, bond.

Cross References

Oath of guardian, see F.S.A. § 744.347; Probate Rule 5.600.

Rule 5.330. Execution by Personal Representative

Notwithstanding any other provisions of these rules, the personal representative shall sign the:

(a) inventory;

(b) accountings;

(c) petition for sale or confirmation of sale or encumbrance of real or personal property;

(d) petition to continue business of decedent;

(e) petition to compromise or settle claim;

(f) petition to purchase on credit;

(g) petition for distribution and discharge; and

(h) resignation of personal representative.

Amended Sept. 29, 1988, effective Jan. 1, 1989 (537 So.2d 500); Sept. 24, 1992, effective Jan. 1, 1993 (607 So.2d 1306).

Committee Notes

Rule History

1975 Revision: Where the jurisdiction of the court is invoked voluntarily pursuant to section 733.603, Florida Statutes, or otherwise, the rule requires that the personal representative have actual knowledge of the more important steps and acts of administration.

1977 Revision: Citation form change in committee note.

1988 Revision: Editorial changes. Citation form changes in committee notes.

1992 Revision: Editorial changes. Committee notes revised. Citation form changes in committee notes.

2003 Revision: Committee notes revised.

2010 Revision: Committee notes revised.

Statutory References

§ 733.502, Fla. Stat. Resignation of personal representative.

§ 733.604, Fla. Stat. Inventories and accountings; public records exemptions.

§ 733.612(5), (22), (24), Fla. Stat. Transactions authorized for the personal representative; exceptions.

§ 733.613, Fla. Stat. Personal representative's right to sell real property.

§ 733.708, Fla. Stat. Compromise.

§ 733.901, Fla. Stat. Final discharge.

Rule References

Fla. Prob. R. 5.340 Inventory.

Fla. Prob. R. 5.345 Accountings other than personal representatives' final accountings.

Fla. Prob. R. 5.346 Fiduciary accounting.

Fla. Prob. R. 5.350 Continuance of unincorporated business or venture.

Fla. Prob. R. 5.370 Sales of real property where no power conferred.

Fla. Prob. R. 5.400 Distribution and discharge.

Fla. Prob. R. 5.430 Resignation of personal representative.

Cross References

Executions and levies upon property of estate, see F.S.A. § 733.706.

Inventory, see F.S.A. § 733.604.

Resignation of personal representative, see F.S.A. § 733.502.

Sale of real property, power of personal representative, see F.S.A. § 733.613.

Successor personal representative, powers and duties, see F.S.A. § 733.614.

Transactions authorized for personal representative, see F.S.A. § 733.612.

Rule 5.340. Inventory

(a) **Contents and Filing.** Unless an inventory has been previously filed, the personal representative shall file an inventory of the estate within 60 days after issuance of letters. The inventory shall contain notice of the beneficiaries' rights under subdivision (e), list the estate with reasonable detail, and include for each listed item (excluding real property appearing to be protected homestead property) its estimated fair market value at the date of the decedent's death. Real property appearing to be protected homestead property shall be listed and so designated.

(b) **Extension.** On petition the time for filing the inventory may be extended by the court for cause shown without notice, except that the personal representative shall serve copies of the petition and order on the persons described in subdivision (d).

(c) **Amendments.** A supplementary or amended inventory containing the information required by subdivision (a) as to each affected item shall be filed and served by the personal representative if:

(1) the personal representative learns of property not included in the original inventory; or

(2) the personal representative learns that the estimated value or description indicated in the original inventory for any item is erroneous or misleading; or

(3) the personal representative determines the estimated fair market value of an item whose value was described as unknown in the original inventory.

(d) **Service.** The personal representative shall serve a copy of the inventory and all supplemental and amended inventories on the surviving spouse, each heir at law in an intestate estate, each residuary beneficiary in a testate estate, and any other interested person who may request it in writing.

(e) **Information.** On request in writing, the personal representative shall provide the following:

(1) To the requesting residuary beneficiary or heir in an intestate estate, a written explanation of how the inventory value for an asset was determined or, if an appraisal was obtained, a copy of the appraisal.

(2) To any other requesting beneficiary, a written explanation of how the inventory value for each asset distributed or proposed to be distributed to that beneficiary was determined or, if an appraisal of that asset was obtained, a copy of the appraisal.

(f) **Notice to Nonresiduary Beneficiaries.** The personal representative shall provide to each nonresiduary beneficiary written notice of that beneficiary's right to receive a written explanation of how the inventory value for each asset distributed or proposed to be distributed to that beneficiary was determined or a copy of an appraisal, if any, of the asset.

(g) **Elective Share Proceedings.** Upon entry of an order determining the surviving spouse's entitlement to the elective share, the personal representative shall file an inventory of the property entering into the elective estate which shall identify the direct recipient, if any, of that property. The personal representative shall serve the inventory of the elective estate as provided in rule 5.360. On request in writing, the personal representative shall provide an interested person with a written explanation of how the inventory value for an asset was determined and shall permit an interested person to examine appraisals on which the inventory values are based.

(h) Verification. All inventories shall be verified by the personal representative.

Amended Sept. 4, 1980, effective Jan. 1, 1981 (387 So.2d 949); Sept. 13, 1984, effective Jan. 1, 1985 (458 So.2d 1079); Nov. 30, 1984, effective Jan. 1, 1985 (460 So.2d 906); Sept. 29, 1988, effective Jan. 1, 1989 (537 So.2d 500); Sept. 24, 1992, effective Jan. 1, 1993 (607 So.2d 1306); Oct. 11, 2001 (807 So.2d 622); Jan. 10, 2002 (816 So.2d 1095); May 2, 2002 (824 So.2d 849); Sept. 2, 2010, effective Jan. 1, 2011 (50 So.3d 578); Oct. 18, 2012, effective, *nunc pro tunc*, Sept. 1, 2012 (102 So.3d 505).

Committee Notes

Inventories of the elective estate under subdivision (f) shall be afforded the same confidentiality as probate inventories. § 733.604(1) and (2), Fla. Stat.

Inventories are still required to be filed. Once filed, however, they are subject to the confidentiality provisions found in sections 733.604(1) and (2), Florida Statutes.

Constitutional protected homestead real property is not necessarily a probatable asset. Disclosure on the inventory of real property appearing to be constitutional protected homestead property informs interested persons of the homestead issue.

Interested persons are entitled to reasonable information about estate proceedings on proper request, including a copy of the inventory, an opportunity to examine appraisals, and other information pertinent to their interests in the estate. The rights of beneficiaries to information contained in estate inventories is limited by section 733.604(3), Florida Statutes. Inventories of the elective estate under subdivision (f) affects a broader class of interested persons who may obtain information regarding the assets disclosed therein subject to control by the court and the confidentiality afforded such inventories under section 733.604(1) and (2).

Rule History

1980 Revision: Eliminated the time limit in requesting a copy of the inventory by an interested person or in furnishing it by the personal representative.

1984 (First) Revision: Extensive changes. Committee notes revised.

1984 (Second) Revision: Subdivision (a) modified to clarify or re-insert continued filing requirement for inventory.

1988 Revision: Editorial changes in (b) and (d). Committee notes revised. Citation form changes in committee notes.

1992 Revision: Editorial changes. Committee notes revised. Citation form changes in committee notes.

2001 Revision: Subdivision (a) amended to conform to statutory changes. Subdivision (d) amended to add requirement of filing of proof of service. Subdivision (e) amended to clarify personal representative's duty to furnish explanation of how inventory values were determined. Subdivision (f) added to require personal representative to file inventory of property entering into elective share. Subdivision (g) added to require verification of inventories. Committee notes revised.

2002 Revision: Subdivision (e) amended to conform to section 733.604(3), Florida Statutes. Subdivision (f) amended to establish procedures for interested persons to obtain information about assets and values listed in the inventory of the elective estate. Committee notes revised.

2003 Revision: Committee notes revised.

2010 Revision: Subdivisions (d) and (g) (former (f)) amended to delete the requirement to serve a copy of the inventory on the Department of Revenue. Subdivision (e) amended, and new (f) created, to limit the kind of information available to nonresiduary beneficiaries, and subsequent subdivisions relettered. Editorial changes in (a), (e), and (g). Committee notes revised.

2012 Revision: The last sentence of subdivision (d) is deleted to remove duplicative requirement of filing a proof of service for a document which includes a certificate of service as provided in

Fla. R. Jud. Admin. 2. 516. If service of the inventory is by service in the manner provided for service of formal notice, then proof of service should be filed as provided in rule 5.040(a)(5). Committee notes revised.

Constitutional Reference

Art. X, § 4, Fla. Const.

Statutory References

§ 732.401, Fla. Stat. Descent of homestead.

§ 732.4015, Fla. Stat. Devise of homestead.

§ 733.604, Fla. Stat. Inventories and accountings; public records exemptions.

Rule References

Fla. Prob. R. 5.041 Service of pleadings and documents.

Fla. Prob. R. 5.060 Request for notices and copies of pleadings.

Fla. Prob. R. 5.330 Execution by personal representative.

Fla. Prob. R. 5.360 Elective share.

Fla. Prob. R. 5.405 Proceedings to determine homestead real property.

Fla. R. Jud. Admin. 2.516 Service of pleadings and documents.

Cross References

Compensation of personal representative, see F.S.A. § 733.617.

Inventory, see F.S.A. § 733.604.

Inventory and appraisal, property of ward, see Probate Rule 5.620.

Rule 5.341. Estate Information

On reasonable request in writing, the personal representative shall provide an interested person with information about the estate and its administration.
Added May 2, 2002 (824 So.2d 849).

Committee Notes

This rule is not intended to overrule the holdings in *In re Estate of Shaw*, 340 So. 2d 491 (Fla. 3d DCA 1976), and *In re Estate of Posner*, 492 So. 2d 1093 (Fla. 3d DCA 1986).

Rule History

2002 Revision: New rule.

Rule 5.342. Inventory of Safe–Deposit Box

(a) Filing. The personal representative shall file an inventory of the contents of the decedent's safe-deposit box within 10 days of the initial opening of the box by the personal representative or the personal representative's attorney of record. The inventory shall include a copy of the financial institution's entry record for the box from a date that is six months prior to the decedent's date of death to the date of the initial opening by the personal representative or the personal representative's attorney of record.

(b) Verification. Each person who was present at the initial opening must verify the contents of the box by signing a copy of the inventory under penalties of perjury.

(c) Service. The personal representative shall serve a copy of the inventory on the surviving spouse, each heir at law in an intestate estate, each residuary beneficiary in a testate estate, and any other interested person who may request it in writing.

Added June 19, 2003 (848 So.2d 1069). Amended Oct. 18, 2012, effective, *nunc pro tunc*, Sept. 1, 2012 (102 So.3d 505).

Inventories and entry records, once filed, shall be afforded the same confidentiality as probate inventories.

If a safe-deposit box is opened pursuant to section 655.935 of the Florida Statutes, no written inventory of the box need be prepared or filed.

Rule History

2003 Revision: New rule.

2012 Revision: The last sentence of subdivision (c) is deleted to remove duplicative requirement of filing a proof of service for a document which includes a certificate of service as provided in Fla. R. Jud. Admin. 2. 516. If service of the inventory is by service in the manner provided for service of formal notice, then proof of service should be filed as provided in rule 5.040(a)(5). Committee notes revised.

Statutory References

§ 655.935, Fla. Stat. Search procedure on death of lessee.

§ 655.936, Fla. Stat. Delivery of safe-deposit box contents or property held in safekeeping to personal representative.

§ 733.6065, Fla. Stat. Opening safe-deposit box.

Rule References

Fla. Prob. R. 5.041 Service of pleadings and documents.

Fla. Prob. R. 5.340 Inventory.

Fla. R. Jud. Admin. 2.516 Service of pleadings and documents.

Rule 5.3425. Search of Safe Deposit Box

(a) **Petition for Order Authorizing Search.** The petition for an order authorizing the search of a safe deposit box leased or co-leased by a decedent must be verified and must contain:

(1) The petitioner's name, address, and interest, if any, in the estate;

(2) The decedent's name, address, date and place of death, and state and county of domicile;

(3) A description of the safe deposit box leased by the decedent and, if known, the name of any co-lessee;

(4) The name and address of the institution where the safe deposit box is located; and

(5) A statement that the petitioner believes that the decedent may have left in the safe deposit box one or more of the following:

(A) A will or codicil of the decedent, or a writing described in section 732.515 of the Code;

(B) A deed to a burial plot;

(C) A writing giving burial instructions; or

(D) Insurance policies on the life of the decedent.

(b) **Order.** If the Court determines that the petitioner is entitled to an order authorizing a search of the decedent's safe deposit box, it must enter an order

(1) authorizing the petitioner to open the safe deposit box in the presence of an officer of the lessor and, if requested by the petitioner, to remove and deliver

(A) to the court having probate jurisdiction in the county where the lessor is located any writing purporting to be a will or codicil of the decedent and any writing purporting to identify devises of tangible property;

(B) to the petitioner, any writing purporting to be a deed to a burial plot to give burial instructions; and

(C) to the beneficiary named therein, any document purporting to be an insurance policy on the life of the decedent.

(2) directing the officer of the lessor to make a complete copy of any document removed and delivered pursuant to the court order, together with a memorandum of delivery identifying the name of the officer, the person to whom the document was delivered, and the date of delivery, to be placed in the safe deposit box leased or co-leased by the decedent.

Added effective Dec. 9, 2010 (51 So.3d 1146).

Committee Notes

The search of the safe deposit box is not considered an initial opening and is not subject to the inventory requirements of rule 5.342.

Rule History

2010 Revision: New rule.

Statutory References

§ 655.935, Fla. Stat. Search procedure on death of lessee.

Rule 5.345. Accountings Other Than Personal Representatives' Final Accountings

(a) **Applicability and Accounting Periods.** This rule applies to the interim accounting of any fiduciary of a probate estate, the accounting of a personal representative who has resigned or been removed, and the accounting of a curator upon the appointment of a successor fiduciary. The fiduciary may elect to file an interim accounting at any time, or the court may require an interim or supplemental accounting. The ending date of the accounting period for any accounting to which this rule applies shall be as follows:

(1) For an interim accounting, any date selected by the fiduciary, including a fiscal or calendar year, or as may be determined by the court.

(2) For the accounting of a personal representative who has resigned or has been removed, the date the personal representative's letters are revoked.

(3) For a curator who has been replaced by a successor fiduciary, the date of appointment of the successor fiduciary.

(b) **Notice of Filing.** Notice of filing and a copy of any accounting to which this rule applies shall be served on all interested persons. The notice shall state that objections to the accounting must be filed within 30 days from the date of service of notice.

(c) **Objection.** Any interested person may file an objection to any accounting to which this rule applies within 30 days from the date of service of notice on that person. Any objection not filed within 30 days from the date of service shall be deemed abandoned. An objection shall be in writing and shall state with particularity the item or items to which the objection is directed and the grounds upon which the objection is based.

(d) **Service of Objections.** The objecting party shall serve a copy of the objection on the fiduciary filing the accounting and other interested persons.

(e) **Disposition of Objections and Approval of Accountings.** The court shall sustain or overrule any objection filed as provided in this rule. If no objection is filed, any accounting to which this rule applies shall be deemed approved 30 days from the date of service of the accounting on interested persons.

(f) Substantiating Papers. On reasonable written request, the fiduciary shall permit an interested person to examine papers substantiating items in any accounting to which this rule applies.

(g) Supplemental Accountings. The court, on its own motion or on that of any interested person, may require a fiduciary who has been replaced by a successor fiduciary to file a supplemental accounting, the beginning date of which shall be the ending date of the accounting as specified in subdivision (a) of this rule and the ending date of which is the date of delivery of all of the estate's property to the successor fiduciary, or such other date as the court may order.

(h) Verification. All accountings shall be verified by the fiduciary filing the accounting.

Amended March 31, 1977, effective July 1, 1977 (344 So.2d 828); Sept. 4, 1980, effective Jan. 1, 1981 (387 So.2d 949); Sept. 13, 1984, effective Jan. 1, 1985 (458 So.2d 1079); Sept. 24, 1992, effective Jan. 1, 1993 (607 So.2d 1306); May 2, 2002 (824 So.2d 849); Sept. 29, 2005, effective Jan. 1, 2006 (912 So.2d 1178).

Committee Notes

The personal representative is required to file a final accounting when administration is complete, unless filing is waived by interested persons. Additionally, a fiduciary of a probate estate may elect, but is not required, to file interim accountings at any time. An accounting is required for resigning or removed fiduciaries. The filing, notice, objection, and approval procedure is similar to that for final accounts.

Rule History

1977 Revision: Change in (a) to authorize selection of fiscal year.

1980 Revision: Change in (d) of prior rule to require the notice to state that the basis for an objection is necessary. Change in (e) of prior rule to require any person filing an objection to set forth the basis of such objection.

1984 Revision: Extensive changes. Committee notes revised.

1988 Revision: Citation form change in committee notes.

1992 Revision: Editorial change. Committee notes revised. Citation form changes in committee notes.

2002 Revision: Implements procedures for interim accountings and accountings by resigning or removed fiduciaries. Committee notes revised.

2003 Revision: Committee notes revised.

2005 Revision: Verification requirement added as new (h). Committee notes revised.

Statutory References

§ 733.3101, Fla. Stat. Personal representative not qualified.

§ 733.501, Fla. Stat. Curators.

§ 733.5035, Fla. Stat. Surrender of assets after resignation.

§ 733.5036, Fla. Stat. Accounting and discharge following resignation.

§ 733.508, Fla. Stat. Accounting and discharge of removed personal representatives upon removal.

§ 733.509, Fla. Stat. Surrender of assets upon removal.

ch. 738, Fla. Stat. Principal and income.

Rule References

Fla. Prob. R. 5.020 Pleadings; verification; motions.

Fla. Prob. R. 5.122 Curators.

Fla. Prob. R. 5.150 Order requiring accounting.

Fla. Prob. R. 5.330 Execution by personal representative.

Fla. Prob. R. 5.346 Fiduciary accounting.

Fla. Prob. R. 5.430 Resignation of personal representative.

Fla. Prob. R. 5.440 Proceedings for removal.

Cross References

Interim and final accountings, see F.S.A. § 733.901.

Rule 5.346. Fiduciary Accounting

(a) Contents. A fiduciary accounting shall include:

(1) all cash and property transactions since the date of the last accounting or, if none, from the commencement of administration, and

(2) a schedule of assets at the end of the accounting period.

(b) Accounting Standards. The following standards are required for the accounting of all transactions occurring on or after January 1, 1994:

(1) Accountings shall be stated in a manner that is understandable to persons who are not familiar with practices and terminology peculiar to the administration of estates and trusts.

(2) The accounting shall begin with a concise summary of its purpose and content.

(3) The accounting shall contain sufficient information to put interested persons on notice as to all significant transactions affecting administration during the accounting period.

(4) The accounting shall contain 2 values in the schedule of assets at the end of the accounting period, the asset acquisition value or carrying value, and estimated current value.

(5) Gains and losses incurred during the accounting period shall be shown separately in the same schedule.

(6) The accounting shall show significant transactions that do not affect the amount for which the fiduciary is accountable.

(c) Accounting Format. A model format for an accounting is attached to this rule as Appendix A.

(d) Verification. All accountings shall be verified by the fiduciary filing the accounting.

Added Sept. 29, 1988, effective Jan. 1, 1989 (537 So.2d 500). Amended Sept. 24, 1992, effective Jan. 1, 1993 (607 So.2d 1306); Oct. 3, 1996, effective Jan. 1, 1997 (683 So.2d 78); May 2, 2002 (824 So.2d 849); Sept. 29, 2005, effective Jan. 1, 2006 (912 So.2d 1178); July 12, 2007 (964 So.2d 140).

Committee Notes

This rule substantially adopts the Uniform Fiduciary Accounting Principles and Model Formats adopted by the Committee on National Fiduciary Accounting Standards of the American Bar Association: Section of Real Property, Probate and Trust Law, the American College of Probate Counsel, the American Bankers Association: Trust Division, and other organizations.

Accountings shall also comply with the Florida principal and income law, chapter 738, Florida Statutes.

Attached as Appendix B to this rule are an explanation and commentary for each of the foregoing standards, which shall be considered as a Committee Note to this rule.

Accountings that substantially conform to the model formats are acceptable. The model accounting format included in Appendix A is only a suggested form.

Rule History

1988 Revision: New rule.

1992 Revision: Editorial changes throughout. Rule changed to require compliance with the Uniform Fiduciary Accounting Principles and Model Formats for accounting of all transactions occurring on or after January 1, 1994. Committee notes revised. Citation form changes in committee notes.

1996 Revision: Committee notes revised.

1999 Revision: Committee notes revised to correct rule reference and to reflect formatting changes in accounting formats.

2002 Revision: Subdivisions (a) and (b) amended to clarify contents of accounting. Committee notes revised.

2003 Revision: Committee notes revised.

2005 Revision: Verification requirement added as new (d). Committee notes revised.

2007 Revision: Committee notes revised.

2010 Revision: Committee notes revised.

Statutory References

§ 733.501, Fla. Stat. Curators.

§ 733.5036, Fla. Stat. Accounting and discharge following resignation.

§ 733.508, Fla. Stat. Accounting and discharge of removed personal representatives upon removal.

§ 733.602(1), Fla. Stat. General duties.

§ 733.612(18), Fla. Stat. Transactions authorized for the personal representative; exceptions.

ch. 738, Fla. Stat. Principal and income.

Rule References

Fla. Prob. R. 5.020 Pleadings; verification; motions.

Fla. Prob. R. 5.040 Notice.

Fla. Prob. R. 5.122 Curators.

Fla. Prob. R. 5.180 Waiver and consent.

Fla. Prob. R. 5.330 Execution by personal representative.

Fla. Prob. R. 5.345 Accountings other than personal representatives' final accountings.

Fla. Prob. R. 5.400 Distribution and discharge.

Fla. Prob. R. 5.430 Resignation of personal representative.

Fla. Prob. R. 5.440 Proceedings for removal.

APPENDIX A

IN THE CIRCUIT COURT FOR _____ COUNTY, FLORIDA

IN RE: ESTATE OF   PROBATE DIVISION

                              File Number

         Deceased.   Division

_____ACCOUNTING OF PERSONAL REPRESENTATIVE(S)

From: _____, ___, Through: _____,_____

    The purpose of this accounting is to acquaint all interested persons with the transactions that have occurred during the period covered by the accounting and the assets that remain on hand. It consists of a SUMMARY sheet and Schedule A showing all Receipts, Schedule B showing all Disbursements, Schedule C showing all Distributions, Schedule D showing all Capital Transactions and Adjustments (the effect of which are also reflected in other schedules, if appropriate), and Schedule E showing assets on hand at the end of the accounting period.

    It is important that this accounting be carefully examined. Requests for additional information and any questions should be addressed to the personal representative(s) or the attorneys for the personal representative(s), the names and addresses of whom are set forth below.

    Under penalties of perjury, the undersigned personal representative(s) declare(s) that I (we) have read and examined this accounting and that the facts and figures set forth in the Summary and the attached Schedules are true, to the best of my (our) knowledge and belief, and that it is a complete report of all cash and property transactions and of all receipts and disbursements by me (us) as personal representative(s) of the estate of _____ deceased, from _____, ___ through _____, ___.

    Signed on _____, ___.

Attorney for Personal Representative:	Personal Representative:
_____	_____
Attorney	
	_____
	Name
Florida Bar No. _____	
	_____
_____	_____
(address)	(address)
Telephone: _____	[Print or Type Names Under All Signature Lines]

IN THE CIRCUIT COURT FOR _____ COUNTY, FLORIDA

IN RE: ESTATE OF   PROBATE DIVISION
                                         File Number

                   Deceased.   Division

_____ACCOUNTING OF PERSONAL REPRESENTATIVE

From: _____, ___, Through: _____,_____

SUMMARY

	Income	Principal	Totals

I. Starting Balance
   Assets per Inventory or on Hand at
   Close of Last Accounting Period   _____ _____ _____

II. Receipts
   Schedule A: _____ _____ _____

III. Disbursements
   Schedule B: _____ _____ _____

IV. Distributions
   Schedule C: _____ _____ _____

V. Capital Transactions and Adjustments
   Schedule D: Net Gain or (Loss) $_____

VI. Assets on Hand at Close of Accounting
   Period
   Schedule E: Cash and Other Assets   _____ _____ _____

NOTE: Refer to Fla. Prob. R. 5.330(b), 5.345, 5.346, and 5.400.

Also see Accountings, Chapter 12 of Practice Under Florida Probate Code (Fla. Bar CLE).

Entries on Summary are to be taken from totals on Schedules A, B, C, D and E.

The Summary and Schedules A, B, C, D and E are to constitute the full accounting. Every transaction occurring during the accounting period should be reflected on the Schedules.

All purchases and sales, all adjustments to the inventory or carrying value of any asset, and any other changes in the assets (such as stock splits) should be described on Schedule D.

The amount in the "Total" column for Item VI must agree with the total inventory or adjusted carrying value of all assets on hand at the close of the accounting period on Schedule E.

_____ACCOUNTING OF PERSONAL REPRESENTATIVE,

ESTATE OF _____

From:_____, ___, Through:_____,

SCHEDULE A   Receipts

Date	Brief Description of Items	Income	Principal

NOTE: Schedule A should reflect only those items received during administration that are not shown on the inventory. Classification of items as income or principal is to be in accordance with the provisions of the Florida Principal and Income Act, Chapter 738, Florida Statutes.

Entries involving the sale of assets or other adjustments to the carrying values of assets are to be shown on Schedule D, and not on Schedule A.

_____ACCOUNTING OF PERSONAL REPRESENTATIVE,

ESTATE OF _____

From:_____, ___, Through:_____,

SCHEDULE B		Disbursements	
Date	Brief Description of Items	Income	Principal

NOTE: Schedule B should reflect only those items paid out during the accounting period. Classification of disbursements as income or principal is to be in accordance with the provisions of the Florida Principal and Income Act, Chapter 738, Florida Statutes.

Entries involving the purchase of assets or adjustments to the carrying values of assets are to be shown on Schedule D, and not on Schedule B.

_____ACCOUNTING OF PERSONAL REPRESENTATIVE,

ESTATE OF _____

From:_____, ___, Through:_____,

SCHEDULE C   Distributions

Date	Brief Description of Items	Income	Principal

NOTE: Schedule C should reflect only those items or amounts distributed to beneficiaries during the accounting period. Assets distributed should be shown at their inventory or adjusted carrying values. Classification of distributions as income or principal is to be in accordance with the provisions of the Florida Principal and Income Act, Chapter 738, Florida Statutes.

Entries involving adjustments to the carrying values of assets are to be shown on Schedule D, and not on Schedule C.

_____ACCOUNTING OF PERSONAL REPRESENTATIVE,

ESTATE OF _____

From:_____, ___, Through:_____,

SCHEDULE D   Capital Transactions and Adjustments

(Does not include distributions. Distributions are shown on Schedule C.)

Date	Brief Description of Transactions	Net Gain	Net Loss

TOTAL NET GAINS AND
LOSSES

NET GAIN OR (LOSS)

NOTE: Schedule D should reflect all purchases and sales of assets and any adjustments to the carrying values of any assets.

Entries reflecting sales should show the inventory or adjusted carrying values, the costs and expenses of the sale, and the net proceeds received. The net gain or loss should be extended in the appropriate column on the right side of Schedule D.

Entries reflecting purchases should reflect the purchase price, any expenses of purchase or other adjustments to the purchase price, and the total amount paid. Presumably no gain or loss would be shown for purchases.

Entries reflecting adjustments in capital assets should explain the change (such as a stock split) and the net gain or loss should be shown in the appropriate column on the right side of Schedule D.

The NET gain or loss should be entered in the Principal column of the Summary.

_____ACCOUNTING OF PERSONAL REPRESENTATIVE,

ESTATE OF _____

From:_____, ___, Through:_____,

SCHEDULE E   Assets on Hand at Close of Accounting Period

(Indicate where held and legal description, certificate numbers or other identification.)

	Estimated Current Value	Carrying Value

ASSETS OTHER THAN CASH:

OTHER ASSETS TOTAL

CASH:

CASH TOTAL

TOTAL ASSETS (must agree with the Total for
Item VI on Summary)

NOTE: Schedule E should be a complete list of all assets on hand reflecting inventory values for each item, adjusted in accordance with any appropriate entries on Schedule D.

Current market values for any assets that are known to be different from the inventory or carrying values as of the close of the accounting period should be shown in the column marked "Current Value." The total inventory or adjusted carrying value (not Current Value) must agree with the Total for Item VI on Summary.

APPENDIX B

UNIFORM FIDUCIARY ACCOUNTING PRINCIPLES

I. ACCOUNTS SHOULD BE STATED IN A MANNER THAT IS UNDERSTANDABLE BY PERSONS WHO ARE NOT FAMILIAR WITH PRACTICES AND TERMINOLOGY PECULIAR TO THE ADMINISTRATION OF ESTATES AND TRUSTS.

Commentary: In order for an account to fulfill its basic function of communication, it is essential that it be stated in a manner that recognizes that the interested parties are not usually familiar with fiduciary accounts. It is neither practical nor desirable to require that accounts be tailored to meet individual disabilities of particular parties but any account should be capable of being understood by a person of average intelligence, literate in English, and familiar with basic financial terms who has read it with care and attention.

Problems arising from terminology or style are usually a reflection of the fact that people who become versed in a particular form of practice tend to forget that terms which are familiar and useful to them may convey nothing to someone else or may even be affirmatively misleading. For example, the terms "debit" and "credit" are generally incomprehensible to people with no knowledge of bookkeeping and many people who are familiar with them in other contexts would assume that in the context of fiduciary accounting, the receipt of an item is a "credit" to the fund rather than a "debit" to the fiduciary.

While the need for concise presentation makes a certain amount of abbreviation both acceptable and necessary, uncommon abbreviation of matters essential to an understanding of the account should be avoided or explained.

No position is taken for or against the use of direct print-outs from machine accounting systems. The quality of the accounts produced by these systems varies widely in the extent to which they can be understood by persons who are not familiar with them. To endorse or object to a direct print-out because it is produced by machine from previously stored data would miss the essential point by focusing attention upon the manner of preparation rather than the product.

II. A FIDUCIARY ACCOUNT SHALL BEGIN WITH A CONCISE SUMMARY OF ITS PURPOSE AND CONTENT.

Commentary: Very few people can be expected to pay much attention to a document unless they have some understanding of its general purpose and its significance to them. Even with such an understanding, impressions derived from the first page or two will often determine whether the rest is read. The use that is made of these pages is therefore of particular significance.

The cover page should disclose the nature and function of the account. While a complete explanation of the significance of the account and the effect of its presentation upon the rights of the parties is obviously impractical for inclusion at this point, there should be at least a brief statement identifying the fiduciary and the subject matter, noting the importance of examining the account and giving an address where more information can be obtained.

It is assumed that the parties would also have enough information from other sources to understand the nature of their relationship to the fund (e.g., residuary legatee, life tenant, remainderman), the function of the account, and the obligation of the fiduciary to supply further relevant information upon request. It is also assumed that notice will be given of any significant procedural considerations such as limitation on the time within which objections must be presented. This would normally be provided by prior or contemporaneous memoranda, correspondence, or discussions.

A summary of the account shall also be presented at the outset. This summary, organized as a table of contents, shall indicate the order of the details presented in the account and shall show separate totals for the aggregate of the assets on hand at the beginning of the accounting period; transactions during the period; and the assets remaining on hand at the end of the period. Each entry in the summary shall be supported by a schedule in the account that provides the details on which the summary is based.

III. A FIDUCIARY ACCOUNT SHALL CONTAIN SUFFICIENT INFORMATION TO PUT THE INTERESTED PARTIES ON NOTICE AS TO ALL SIGNIFICANT TRANSACTIONS AFFECTING ADMINISTRATION DURING THE ACCOUNTING PERIOD.

Commentary: The presentation of the information account shall allow an interested party to follow the progress of the fiduciary's administration of assets during the accounting period.

An account is not complete if it does not itemize, or make reference to, assets on hand at the beginning of the accounting period.

Illustration:

3.1 The first account for a decedent's estate or a trust may detail the items received by the fiduciary and for which the fiduciary is responsible. It may refer to the total amount of an inventory filed elsewhere or assets described in a schedule attached to a trust agreement.

Instead of retyping the complete list of assets in the opening balance, the preparer may prefer to attach as an exhibit a copy of the inventory, closing balance from the last account, etc., as appropriate, or may refer to them if previously provided to the interested parties who will receive it.

Transactions shall be described in sufficient detail to give interested parties notice of their purpose and effect. It should be recognized that too much detail may be counterproductive to making the account understandable. In accounts covering long periods or dealing with extensive assets, it is usually desirable to consolidate information. For instance, where income from a number of securities is being accounted for over a long period of time, a statement of the total dividends received on each security with appropriate indication of changes in the number of shares held will be more readily understandable and easier to check for completeness than a chronological listing of all dividends received.

Although detail should generally be avoided for routine transactions, it will often be necessary to proper understanding of an event that is somewhat out of the ordinary.

Illustrations:

3.2 Extraordinary appraisal costs should be shown separately and explained.

3.3 Interest and penalties in connection with late filing of tax returns should be shown separately and explained.

3.4 An extraordinary allocation between principal and income such as apportionment of proceeds of property acquired on foreclosure should be separately stated and explained.

3.5 Computation of a formula marital deduction gift involving non-probate assets should be explained.

IV. A FIDUCIARY ACCOUNT SHALL CONTAIN TWO VALUES, THE ASSET ACQUISITION VALUE OR CARRYING VALUE, AND CURRENT VALUE.

Commentary: In order for transactions to be reported on a consistent basis, an appropriate carrying value for assets must be chosen and employed consistently.

The carrying value of an asset should reflect its value at the time it is acquired by the fiduciary (or a predecessor fiduciary). When such a value is not precisely determinable, the figure used should reflect a thoughtful decision by the fiduciary. For assets owned by a decedent, inventory values or estate tax values – generally reflective of date of death – would be appropriate. Assets received in kind by a trustee from a settlor of an inter vivos trust should be carried at their value at the time of receipt. For assets purchased during the administration of the fund, cost would normally be used. Use of Federal income tax basis for carrying value is acceptable when basis is reasonably representative of real values at the time of acquisition. Use of tax basis as a carrying value under other circumstances could be affirmatively misleading to beneficiaries and therefore is not appropriate.

In the Model Account, carrying value is referred to as "fiduciary acquisition value." The Model Account establishes the initial carrying value of assets as their value at date of death for inventoried assets, date of receipt for subsequent receipts, and cost for investments.

Carrying value would not normally be adjusted for depreciation.

Except for adjustments that occur normally under the accounting system in use, carrying values should generally be continued unchanged through successive accounts and assets should not be arbitrarily "written up" or "written down." In some circumstances, however, with proper disclosure and explanation, carrying value may be adjusted.

Illustrations:

4.1 Carrying values based on date of death may be adjusted to reflect changes on audit of estate or inheritance tax returns.

4.2 Where appropriate under applicable local law, a successor fiduciary may adjust the carrying value of assets to reflect values at the start of that fiduciary's administration.

4.3 Assets received in kind in satisfaction of a pecuniary legacy should be carried at the value used for purposes of distribution.

Though essential for accounting purposes, carrying values are commonly misunderstood by laypersons as being a representation of actual values. To avoid this, the account should include both current values and carrying values.

The value of assets at the beginning and ending of each accounting period is necessary information for the evaluation of investment performance. Therefore, the account should show, or make reference to, current values at the start of the period for all assets whose carrying values were established in a prior accounting period.

Illustrations:

4.4 The opening balance of the first account of a testamentary trustee will usually contain assets received in kind from the executor. Unless the carrying value was written up at the time of distribution (e.g., 4.2 or 4.3 supra) these assets will be carried at a value established during the executor's administration. The current value at the beginning of the accounting period should also be shown.

4.5 An executor's first account will normally carry assets at inventory (date of death) values or costs. No separate listing of current values at the beginning of the accounting period is necessary.

Current values should also be shown for all assets on hand at the close of the accounting period. The date on which current values are determined shall be stated and shall be the last day of the accounting period, or a date as close thereto as reasonably possible.

Current values should be shown in a column parallel to the column of carrying values. Both columns should be totalled.

In determining current values for assets for which there is no readily ascertainable current value, the source of the value stated in the account shall be explained. The fiduciary shall make a good faith effort to determine realistic values but should not be expected to incur expenses for appraisals or similar costs when there is no reason to expect that the resulting information will be of practical consequence to the administration of the estate or the protection of the interests of the parties.

Illustrations:

4.6 When an asset is held under circumstances that make it clear that it will not be sold (e.g., a residence held for use of a beneficiary) the fiduciary's estimate of value would be acceptable in lieu of an appraisal.

4.7 Considerations such as a pending tax audit or offer of the property for sale may indicate the advisability of not publishing the fiduciary's best estimate of value. In such circumstances, a statement that value was fixed by some method such as "per company books," "formula under buy-sell agreement," or "300% of assessed value" would be acceptable, but the fiduciary would be expected to provide further information to interested parties upon request.

V. GAINS AND LOSSES INCURRED DURING THE ACCOUNTING PERIOD SHALL BE SHOWN SEPARATELY IN THE SAME SCHEDULE.

Commentary: Each transaction involving the sale or other disposition of securities during the accounting period shall be shown as a separate item in one combined schedule of the account indicating the transaction, date, explanation, and any gain or loss.

Although gains and losses from the sale of securities can be shown separately in accounts, the preferred method of presentation is to present this information in a single schedule. Such a presentation provides the most meaningful description of investment performance and will tend to clarify relationships between gains and losses that are deliberately realized at the same time.

VI. THE ACCOUNT SHALL SHOW SIGNIFICANT TRANSACTIONS THAT DO NOT AFFECT THE AMOUNT FOR WHICH THE FIDUCIARY IS ACCOUNTABLE.

Commentary: Transactions such as the purchase of an investment, receipt of a stock split, or change of a corporate name do not alter the total fund for which a fiduciary is accountable but must be shown in order to permit analysis and an understanding of the administration of the fund. These can be best shown in information schedules.

One schedule should list all investments made during the accounting period. It should include those subsequently sold as well as those still on hand. Frequently the same money will be used for a series of investments. Therefore, the schedule should not be totalled in order to avoid giving an exaggerated idea of the size of the fund.

A second schedule (entitled "Changes in Investment Holdings" in the Model Account) should show all transactions affecting a particular security holding, such as purchase of additional shares, partial sales, stock splits, change of corporate name, divestment distributions, etc. This schedule, similar to a ledger account for each holding, will reconcile opening and closing entries for particular holdings, explain changes in carrying value, and avoid extensive searches through the account for information scattered among other schedules.

Rule 5.350. Continuance of Unincorporated Business or Venture

(a) Separate Accounts and Reports. In the conduct of an unincorporated business or venture, the personal representative shall keep separate, full, and accurate accounts of all receipts and expenditures and make reports as the court may require.

(b) Petition. If the personal representative determines it to be in the best interest of the estate to continue an unincorporated business or venture beyond the time authorized by statute or will, the personal representative shall file a verified petition which shall include:

(1) a statement of the nature of that business or venture;

(2) a schedule of specific assets and liabilities;

(3) the reasons for continuation;

(4) the proposed form and times of accounting for that business or venture;

(5) the period for which the continuation is requested; and

(6) any other information pertinent to the petition.

(c) Order. If the continuation is authorized, the order shall state:

(1) the period for which that business or venture is to continue;

(2) the particular powers of the personal representative in the continuation of that business or venture; and

(3) the form and frequency of accounting by that business or venture.

(d) Petition by Interested Person. Any interested person, at any time, may petition the court for an order regarding the operation of, accounting for, or termination of an unincorporated business or venture, and the court shall enter an order thereon.

Amended Sept. 13, 1984, effective Jan. 1, 1985 (458 So.2d 1079); Sept. 29, 1988, effective Jan. 1, 1989 (537 So.2d 500).

Committee Notes

Rule History

1975 Revision: New rule, § 733.612, Fla.Stat.

1984 Revision: Extensive changes in rule and title. Clarifies procedural steps to be taken by a personal representative who determines it to be in the best interest of an estate to continue any unincorporated business beyond the time authorized by statute. Information required to be filed in a verified petition is specified, and normal information to be included in a court order is listed. Other pertinent information under (b)(6) may include provisions for insurance of business or venture, proposed professionals to be used in connection with such activities, how the business or venture shall be managed, the person or persons proposed for managerial positions, a list of all other employees, agents, or independent contractors employed by or affiliated with the business or venture, and proposed compensation for all such management personnel, agents, employees, and independent contractors. Committee notes revised and expanded.

1988 Revision: Editorial change in caption of (b). Committee notes revised. Citation form changes in committee notes.

1992 Revision: Committee notes revised. Citation form changes in committee notes.

2012 Revision: Committee notes revised.

Statutory References

§ 733.612(22), Fla.Stat. Transactions authorized for the personal representative; exceptions.

Rule References

Fla. Prob. R. 5.020 Pleadings; verification; motions.

Fla. Prob. R. 5.040 Notice.

Fla. Prob. R. 5.041 Service of pleadings and documents.

Fla. Prob. R. 5.330 Execution by personal representative.

Fla. R. Jud. Admin. 2.516 Service of pleadings and documents.

Cross References

Continuance of business of decedent, see F.S.A. § 733.612.

Continuance of business or venture of ward, see Probate Rule 5.640.

Rule 5.355. Proceedings for Review of Employment of Agents and Compensation of Personal Representatives and Estate Employees

After notice to all interested persons and upon petition of an interested person bearing all or a part of the impact of the payment of compensation to the personal representative or any person employed by the personal representative, the propriety of the employment and the reasonableness of the compensation or payment may be reviewed by the court. The petition shall state the grounds on which it is based. The burden of proving the propriety of the employment and the reasonableness of the compensation shall be upon the personal representative and the person employed by the personal representative. Any person who is determined to have received excessive compensation from an estate may be ordered to make appropriate refunds.

Added Sept. 29, 1988, effective Jan. 1, 1989 (537 So.2d 500). Amended Sept. 24, 1992, effective Jan. 1, 1993 (607 So.2d 1306); Oct. 3, 1996, effective Jan. 1, 1997 (683 So.2d 78); July 12, 2007 (964 So.2d 140).

Committee Notes

This rule represents a rule implementation of the procedure formerly found in section 733.6175, Florida Statutes. It is not intended to change the effect of the statute from which it was derived but has been reformatted to conform with the structure of these rules. It is not intended to create a new procedure or modify an existing procedure.

Rule History

1988 Revision: New rule.

1992 Revision: Editorial changes. Committee notes revised. Citation form changes in committee notes.

1996 Revision: Committee notes revised.

2003 Revision: Committee notes revised.

2007 Revision: Committee notes revised.

2012 Revision: Committee notes revised.

Statutory References

§ 731.201(23), Fla. Stat. General definitions.

§ 731.301, Fla. Stat. Notice.

§ 733.612(19), Fla. Stat. Transactions authorized for the personal representative; exceptions.

§ 733.617, Fla. Stat. Compensation of personal representative.

§ 733.6171, Fla. Stat.   Compensation of attorney for the personal representative.

§ 733.6175, Fla. Stat.   Proceedings for review of employment of agents and compensation of personal representatives and employees of estate.

Rule References

Fla. Prob. R. 5.040 Notice.

Fla. Prob. R. 5.041 Service of pleadings and documents.

Fla. R. Jud. Admin. 2.516 Service of pleadings and documents.

Rule 5.360.   Elective Share

(a) Election. An election to take the elective share may be filed by the surviving spouse, or on behalf of the surviving spouse by an attorney-in-fact or guardian of the property of the surviving spouse.

(1) *Election by Surviving Spouse.*   An electing surviving spouse must file the election within the time required by law and promptly serve a copy of the election on the personal representative in the manner provided for service of formal notice.

(2) *Election by Attorney-in-Fact or Guardian of the Property of Surviving Spouse.*

(A) Petition for Approval.   Before filing the election, the attorney-in-fact or guardian of the property of the surviving spouse must petition the court having jurisdiction of the probate proceeding for approval to make the election.   The petition for approval must allege the authority to act on behalf of the surviving spouse and facts supporting the election.

(B) Notice of Petition.   Upon receipt of the petition, the personal representative must promptly serve a copy of the petition by formal notice on all interested persons.

(C) Order Authorizing Election.   If the election is approved, the order must include a finding that the election is in the best interests of the surviving spouse during the spouse's probable lifetime.

(D) Filing the Election.   Upon entry of an order authorizing the filing of an election, the attorney-in-fact or guardian of the property must file the election within the later of the time provided by law or 30 days from service of the order and promptly serve a copy of the election on the personal representative in the manner provided for service of formal notice.

(b) Procedure for Election.

(1) *Extension.*   Within the period provided by law to make the election, the surviving spouse or an attorney-in-fact or guardian of the property of the surviving spouse may petition the court for an extension of time for making an election or for approval to make the election.   After notice and hearing the court for good cause shown may extend the time for election.   If the court grants the petition for an extension, the election must be filed within the time allowed by the extension.

(2) *Withdrawal of Election.*   The surviving spouse, an attorney-in-fact, a guardian of the property of the surviving spouse, or the personal representative of the surviving spouse's estate may withdraw the election within the time provided by law.

(3) *Service of Notice.*   Upon receipt of an election the personal representative must serve a notice of election within 20 days following service of the election, together with a copy of the election, on all interested persons in the manner provided for service of formal notice.   The notice of election must indicate the names and addresses of the attorneys for the surviving spouse and the personal representative and must state that:

(A) persons receiving a notice of election may be required to contribute toward the satisfaction of the elective share;

(B) objections to the election must be served within 20 days after service of the copy of the notice of election; and

(C) if no objection to the election is timely served, an order determining the surviving spouse's entitlement to the elective share may be granted without further notice.

(4) *Objection to Election.* Within 20 days after service of the notice of election, an interested person may serve an objection to the election which must state with particularity the grounds on which the objection is based. The objecting party must serve copies of the objection on the surviving spouse and the personal representative. If an objection is served, the personal representative must promptly serve a copy of the objection on all other interested persons who have not previously been served with a copy of the objection.

(c) Determination of Entitlement.

(1) *No Objection Served.* If no objection to the election is timely served, the court must enter an order determining the spouse's entitlement to the elective share.

(2) *Objection Served.* If an objection to the election is timely served, the court must determine the surviving spouse's entitlement to the elective share after notice and hearing.

(d) Procedure to Determine Amount of Elective Share and Contribution.

(1) *Petition by Personal Representative.* After entry of the order determining the surviving spouse's entitlement to the elective share, the personal representative must file and serve a petition to determine the amount of the elective share. The petition must

(A) give the name and address of each direct recipient known to the personal representative;

(B) describe the proposed distribution of assets to satisfy the elective share, and the time and manner of distribution; and

(C) identify those direct recipients, if any, from whom a specified contribution will be required and state the amount of contribution sought from each.

(2) *Service of Inventory.* The inventory of the elective estate required by rule 5.340, together with the petition, must be served within 60 days after entry of the order determining entitlement to the elective share on all interested persons in the manner provided for service of formal notice.

(3) *Petition by Spouse.* If the personal representative does not file the petition to determine the amount of the elective share within 90 days from rendition of the order of entitlement, the electing spouse or the attorney-in-fact or the guardian of the property or personal representative of the electing spouse may file the petition specifying as particularly as is known the value of the elective share.

(4) *Objection to Amount of Elective Share.* Within 20 days after service of the petition to determine the amount of the elective share, an interested person may serve an objection to the amount of or distribution of assets to satisfy the elective share. The objection must state with particularity the grounds on which the objection is based. The objecting party must serve copies of the objection on the surviving spouse and the personal representative. If an objection is served, the personal representative must promptly serve a copy of the objection on all interested persons who have not previously been served.

(5) *Determination of Amount of Elective Share and Contribution.*

(A) No Objection Served. If no objection is timely served to the petition to determine the amount of the elective share, the court must enter an order on the petition.

(B) Objection Served. If an objection is timely served to the petition to determine the amount of the elective share, the court must determine the amount of the elective share and contribution after notice and hearing.

(6) *Order Determining Amount of Elective Share and Contribution.* The order must:

(A) set forth the amount of the elective share;

(B) identify the assets to be distributed to the surviving spouse in satisfaction of the elective share; and

(C) if contribution is necessary, specify the amount of contribution for which each direct recipient is liable.

(e) Relief From Duty to Enforce Contribution. A petition to relieve the personal representative from the duty to enforce contribution must state the grounds on which it is based and notice must be served on interested persons.

Amended Sept. 13, 1984, effective Jan. 1, 1985 (458 So.2d 1079); Sept. 29, 1988, effective Jan. 1, 1989 (537 So.2d 500); Sept. 24, 1992, effective Jan. 1, 1993 (607 So.2d 1306); Oct. 11, 2001 (807 So.2d 622); Sept. 29, 2005, effective Jan. 1, 2006 (912 So.2d 1178); Dec. 9, 2010 (51 So.3d 1146).

Committee Notes

The extensive rewrite of this rule in 2001 is intended to conform it with and provide procedures to accommodate amendments to Florida's elective share statutes, §§ 732.201 *et seq.*, Fla. Stat. Proceedings to determine entitlement to elective share are not specific adversary proceedings under rule 5.025(a), but may be declared adversary at the option of the party. Proceedings to determine the amount of elective share and contribution are specific adversary proceedings under rule 5.025(a). Requirements for service are intended to be consistent with the requirements for formal notice. Rule 5.040. Service of process may be required to obtain personal jurisdiction over direct recipients who are not otherwise interested persons and who have not voluntarily submitted themselves to the jurisdiction of the court. Rule 5.040(a)(3)(C); ch. 48, Fla. Stat. Process and Service of Process; ch. 49, Fla. Stat., Constructive Service of Process. An inventory of the elective estate should be afforded the same confidentiality as other estate inventories. § 733.604(1) and (2), Fla. Stat. In fulfilling his or her obligations under this rule, a personal representative is not required to make impractical or extended searches for property entering into the elective estate and the identities of direct recipients. Preexisting rights to dower and curtesy formerly addressed in subdivision (e) of this rule are now governed by new rule 5.365.

Counsel's attention is directed to Fla. Ethics Opinion 76–16, dated April 4, 1977, for guidance regarding the duties of an attorney with respect to spousal rights.

Rule History

1984 Revision: Extensive changes. Clarifies information to be included in a petition for elective share filed by a personal representative and specifies information to be included in an order determining elective share. Committee notes revised and expanded.

1988 Revision: Extensive changes. A new procedure has been added providing for optional service of a notice of election together with a copy of the election and a procedure to expose objections to and determine right to entitlement, separate from the pre-existing procedure of determination of amount and setting aside. Subdivisions (c) and (d) represent rule implementation of procedure in statute. Committee notes revised and expanded. Citation form changes in committee notes.

1992 Revision: Editorial change. Committee notes revised. Citation form changes in committee notes.

2001 Revision: Entire rule rewritten. Committee notes revised.

2003 Revision: Committee notes revised.

2005 Revision: Subdivision (a) amended to require service in the manner of formal notice of the notice of election. Subdivision (b)(3) amended to provide time period for personal representative to service notice of election on interested persons, and title revised. Subdivision (d)(2) amended to provide time limit and service requirement for elective estate inventory and petition for determination of amount of elective share. Committee notes revised.

2010 Cycle Report Revision: Committee notes revised.

2010 Out-of-Cycle Report Revision: Subdivision (a)(2) amended to conform to an amendment to § 732.2125, Florida Statutes.

2012 Revision: Committee notes revised.

Statutory References

§ 732.201, Fla. Stat. Right to elective share.

§ 732.2025, Fla. Stat. Definitions.

§ 732.2035, Fla. Stat. Property entering into elective estate.

§ 732.2045, Fla. Stat. Exclusions and overlapping application.

§ 732.2055, Fla. Stat. Valuation of the elective estate.

§ 732.2065, Fla. Stat. Amount of the elective share.

§ 732.2075, Fla. Stat. Sources from which elective share payable; abatement.

§ 732.2085, Fla. Stat. Liability of direct recipients and beneficiaries.

§ 732.2095, Fla. Stat. Valuation of property used to satisfy elective share.

§ 732.2125, Fla. Stat. Right of election; by whom exercisable.

§ 732.2135, Fla. Stat. Time of election; extensions; withdrawal.

§ 732.2145, Fla. Stat. Order of contribution; personal representative's duty to collect contribution.

§ 733.604, Fla. Stat. Inventories and accountings; public records exemptions.

Rule References

Fla. Prob. R. 5.025 Adversary proceedings.

Fla. Prob. R. 5.040 Notice.

Fla. Prob. R. 5.041 Service of pleadings and documents.

Fla. Prob. R. 5.340 Inventory.

Fla. R. Jud. Admin. 2.516 Service of pleadings and documents.

Fla. R. App. P. 9.020(h) Definitions.

Cross References

Abolition of dower, see F.S.A. § 732.111.
Right to elective share, see F.S.A. § 732.201.

Rule 5.365. Petition for Dower

A widow may file an extraordinary petition for assignment of dower. The petition shall be filed in the court of each county where the widow's husband had conveyed land in which the widow had not relinquished her right of dower before October 1, 1973. Formal notice shall be served on persons adversely affected. The proceedings shall be as similar as possible to those formerly existing for the ordinary assignment of dower.
Added Oct. 11, 2001 (807 So.2d 622). Amended Jan. 10, 2002 (816 So.2d 1095).

Committee Notes

Rule History

2001 Revision: Derived from former rule 5.360(e).

Statutory Reference

§ 732.111, Fla.Stat. Dower and curtesy abolished.

Rule 5.370. Sales of Real Property Where No Power Conferred

(a) Petition. When authorization or confirmation of the sale of real property is required, the personal representative shall file a verified petition setting forth the reasons for the sale, a description of the real property sold or proposed to be sold, and the price and terms of the sale.

(b) Order. If the sale is authorized or confirmed, the order shall describe the real property. An order authorizing a sale may provide for the public or private sale of the real property described therein, in parcels or as a whole. An order authorizing a private sale shall specify the price and terms of the sale. An order authorizing a public sale shall specify the type of notice of sale to be given by the personal representative.

Amended Sept. 13, 1984, effective Jan. 1, 1985 (458 So.2d 1079); Oct. 3, 1996, effective Jan. 1, 1997 (683 So.2d 78).

Committee Notes

Petitions under the rule are governed by section 733.610, Florida Statutes, under which sales are voidable by interested persons if there was a conflict of interest without full disclosure and consent, unless the will or contract entered into by the decedent authorized the transaction or it was approved by the court after notice to all interested persons, and by section 733.609, Florida Statutes, involving bad faith actions by the personal representative. Note provision for attorneys' fees.

Rule History

1984 Revision: Extensive changes. Notice of hearing on any petition concerning sale of real property is required by statute unless waived. The requirement to record a certified copy of the order approving sale of real estate in each county where the real property or any part thereof is situated has been deleted. Committee notes revised and expanded.

1988 Revision: Committee notes expanded. Citation form changes in committee notes.

1992 Revision: Committee notes revised. Citation form changes in committee notes.

1996 Revision: Editorial changes.

2012 Revision: Committee notes revised.

Statutory References

§ 733.609, Fla.Stat. Improper exercise of power; breach of fiduciary duty.

§ 733.610, Fla.Stat. Sale, encumbrance or transaction involving conflict of interest.

§ 733.613(1), Fla.Stat. Personal representative's right to sell real property.

§ 733.810, Fla.Stat. Distribution in kind; valuation.

Rule References

Fla. Prob. R. 5.020 Pleadings; verification; motions.

Fla. Prob. R. 5.040 Notice.

Fla. Prob. R. 5.041 Service of pleadings and documents.

Fla. Prob. R. 5.180 Waiver and consent.

Fla. R. Jud. Admin. 2.516 Service of pleadings and documents.

Cross References

Powers of personal representative,
Generally, see F.S.A. § 733.608.
Improper exercise of power, see F.S.A. § 733.609.
Sales of real property, see F.S.A. § 733.613.
Transactions authorized, see F.S.A. § 733.612.

Rule 5.380. Compulsory Payment of Devises or Distributive Interests

(a) Petition. A beneficiary may file a petition setting forth the facts that entitle the beneficiary to compel payment of devises or distributive interests stating that the property will not be required for the payment of debts, family allowance, spouse's elective share, estate and inheritance taxes, claims, charges, and expenses of administration, or for providing funds for contribution or enforcing equalization in case of advancements.

(b) Order. If the court finds that the property will not be required for the purposes set forth in subdivision (a), it may enter an order describing the property to be surrendered or delivered and compelling the personal representative, prior to the final settlement of the personal representative's accounts, to do one or more of the following:

(1) Pay all or any part of a devise in money.

(2) Deliver specific personal property within the personal representative's custody and control.

(3) Pay all or any part of a distributive interest in the personal estate of a decedent.

(4) Surrender real property.

(c) Bond. Before the entry of an order of partial distribution, the court may require the person entitled to distribution to give a bond with sureties as prescribed by law.

Amended Sept. 13, 1984, effective Jan. 1, 1985 (458 So.2d 1079); Sept. 29, 1988, effective Jan. 1, 1989 (537 So.2d 500); Sept. 24, 1992, effective Jan. 1, 1993 (607 So.2d 1306).

Committee Notes

Rule History

1984 Revision: Extensive changes. Committee notes revised.

1988 Revision: Editorial change in caption of (a). Citation form change in committee notes.

1992 Revision: Editorial changes. Committee notes revised. Citation form changes in committee notes.

2003 Revision: Committee notes revised.

2012 Revision: Committee notes revised.

Statutory References

§ 731.301, Fla. Stat. Notice.

§ 733.802, Fla. Stat. Proceedings for compulsory payment of devises or distributive interest.

Rule References

Fla. Prob. R. 5.020 Pleadings; verification; motions.

Fla. Prob. R. 5.040 Notice.

Fla. Prob. R. 5.041 Service of pleadings and documents.

Fla. R. Jud. Admin. 2.516 Service of pleadings and documents.

Proceedings for compulsory payment of devises or distributive interest, see F.S.A. § 733.802.
Special provisions for distribution, see F.S.A. § 733.801 et seq.

Rule 5.385.　Determination of Beneficiaries and Shares

(a) Beneficiaries and Shares.　If a personal representative or other interested person is in doubt or is unable to determine with certainty beneficiaries entitled to an estate or the shares of any beneficiary of an estate, or a beneficiary entitled to any asset or interest in an estate, the personal representative or other interested person may petition the court to determine beneficiaries.

(b) Petition.　The petition shall include:

(1) the names, residences, and post office addresses of all persons who may have an interest, except creditors of the decedent, known to the petitioner or ascertainable by diligent search and inquiry;

(2) a statement of the nature of the interest of each person;

(3) designation of any person believed to be a minor or incapacitated, and whether any person so designated is under legal guardianship in this state;

(4) a statement as to whether petitioner believes that there are, or may be, persons whose names are not known to petitioner who have claims against, or interest in, the estate as beneficiaries.

(c) Order.　After formal notice and hearing, the court shall enter an order determining the beneficiaries or the shares and amounts they are entitled to receive, or both.

Added Sept. 29, 1988, effective Jan. 1, 1989 (537 So.2d 500).　Amended Sept. 24, 1992, effective Jan. 1, 1993 (607 So.2d 1306); May 2, 2002 (824 So.2d 849); June 19, 2003 (848 So.2d 1069); July 12, 2007 (964 So.2d 140).

Committee Notes

This rule represents a rule implementation of the procedure formerly found in section 733.105, Florida Statutes.　It is not intended to change the effect of the statute from which it was derived but has been reformatted to conform with the structure of these rules.　It is not intended to create a new procedure or modify an existing procedure.

Rule History

1988 Revision: New rule.

1992 Revision: Editorial changes.　Committee notes revised.　Citation form changes in committee notes.

2002 Revision: Subdivision (c) added to implement procedure formerly found in section 733.105(2), Florida Statutes.　Committee notes revised.

2003 Revision: Change in subdivision (c) to replace "heirs or devisees" with "beneficiaries" to incorporate term used in section 733.105, Florida Statutes.　Committee notes revised.

2007 Revision: Committee notes revised.

2012 Revision: Committee notes revised.

2014 Revision: Fla. R. Jud. Admin. 2.425(b)(6) provides an exception for the full name of any minor "in any document or order affecting minor's ownership of real property."　Committee notes revised.

Statutory References

ch. 49, Fla. Stat. Constructive service of process.

§ 731.201(2), (23), Fla. Stat. General definitions.

§ 731.301, Fla. Stat. Notice.

§ 733.105, Fla. Stat. Determination of beneficiaries.

Rule References

Fla. Prob. R. 5.025 Adversary proceedings.

Fla. Prob. R. 5.040 Notice.

Fla. Prob. Rule 5.041 Service of pleadings and documents.

Fla. Prob. R. 5.120 Administrator ad litem and guardian ad litem.

Fla. Prob. R. 5.205(a)(5) Filing evidence of death.

Fla. R. Jud. Admin. 2.516 Service of pleadings and documents.

Fla. R. Jud. Admin. 2.425 Minimization of the Filing of Sensitive Information.

Rule 5.386. Escheat

(a) Escheat Proceeding. If it appears to the personal representative that an estate may escheat or there is doubt about the existence of any person entitled to the estate, the personal representative shall institute a proceeding to determine beneficiaries within 1 year after letters have been issued to the personal representative, and notice shall be served on the Department of Legal Affairs. If the personal representative fails to institute the proceeding within the time fixed, it may be instituted by the Department of Legal Affairs.

(b) Court's Report. On or before January 15 of each year, each court shall furnish to the Department of Legal Affairs a list of all estates being administered in which no person appears to be entitled to the property and the personal representative has not instituted a proceeding for the determination of beneficiaries.

(c) Administration. Except as herein provided, escheated estates shall be administered as other estates.

Added Sept. 29, 1988, effective Jan. 1, 1989 (537 So.2d 500). Amended Sept. 24, 1992, effective Jan. 1, 1993 (607 So.2d 1306).

Committee Notes

This rule represents a rule implementation of the procedure formerly found in section 732.107, Florida Statutes. It is not intended to change the effect of the statute from which it was derived but has been reformatted to conform with the structure of these rules. It is not intended to create a new procedure or modify an existing procedure.

Rule History

1988 Revision: New rule.

1992 Revision: Editorial change. Committee notes revised. Citation form changes in committee notes.

2003 Revision: Committee notes revised.

2012 Revision: Committee notes revised.

Statutory References

§ 732.107, Fla. Stat. Escheat.

§ 733.105, Fla. Stat. Determination of beneficiaries.

§ 733.816, Fla. Stat. Disposition of unclaimed property held by personal representatives.

Rule References

Fla. Prob. R. 5.020 Pleadings; verification; motions.

Fla. Prob. R. 5.040 Notice.

Fla. Prob. R. 5.041 Service of pleadings and documents.

Fla. Prob. R. 5.042 Time.

Fla. Prob. R. 5.385 Determination of beneficiaries and shares.

Fla. R. Jud. Admin. 2.516 Service of pleadings and documents.

Rule 5.395. Notice of Federal Estate Tax Return

When a federal estate tax return is filed, required to be filed, or will be filed, the personal representative shall file a notice stating the due date of the return. The notice shall be filed within 12 months from the date letters are issued and copies of the notice shall be served on interested persons. Whenever the due date is subsequently extended, similar notice shall be filed and served.

Added Sept. 13, 1984, effective Jan. 1, 1985 (458 So.2d 1079). Amended Sept. 26, 2013, effective Jan. 1, 2014 (123 So.3d 31).

Committee Notes

The purpose of the rule is to require notification to the court and all interested persons that the time for closing the estate is extended when a federal estate tax return is required.

Rule History

1984 Revision: New rule.

1988 Revision: Citation form change in committee notes.

1992 Revision: Committee notes revised. Citation form changes in committee notes.

2003 Revision: Committee notes revised.

2013 Revision: Clarifies the available option to file a federal tax return even if one is not required by state or federal rule or law.

Rule Reference

Fla. Prob. R. 5.400 Distribution and discharge.

Rule 5.400. Distribution and Discharge

(a) Petition for Discharge; Final Accounting. A personal representative who has completed administration except for distribution shall file a final accounting and a petition for discharge including a plan of distribution.

(b) Contents.

The petition for discharge shall contain a statement:

(1) that the personal representative has fully administered the estate;

(2) that all claims which were presented have been paid, settled, or otherwise disposed of;

(3) that the personal representative has paid or made provision for taxes and expenses of administration;

(4) showing the amount of compensation paid or to be paid to the personal representative, attorneys, accountants, appraisers, or other agents employed by the personal representative and the manner of determining that compensation;

---

(5) showing a plan of distribution which shall include:

(A) a schedule of all prior distributions;

(B) the property remaining in the hands of the personal representative for distribution;

(C) a schedule describing the proposed distribution of the remaining assets; and

(D) the amount of funds retained by the personal representative to pay expenses that are incurred in the distribution of the remaining assets and termination of the estate administration;

(6) that any objections to the accounting, the compensation paid or proposed to be paid, or the proposed distribution of assets must be filed within 30 days from the date of service of the last of the petition for discharge or final accounting; and also that within 90 days after filing of the objection, a notice of hearing thereon must be served or the objection is abandoned; and

(7) that objections, if any, shall be in writing and shall state with particularity the item or items to which the objection is directed and the grounds on which the objection is based.

(c) Closing Estate; Extension. The final accounting and petition for discharge shall be filed and served on interested persons within 12 months after issuance of letters for an estate not filing a federal estate tax return, otherwise within 12 months from the date the return is due, unless the time is extended by the court for cause shown after notice to interested persons. The petition to extend time shall state the status of the estate and the reason for the extension.

(d) Distribution. The personal representative shall promptly distribute the estate property in accordance with the plan of distribution, unless objections are filed as provided in these rules.

(e) Discharge. On receipt of evidence that the estate has been fully administered and properly distributed, the court shall enter an order discharging the personal representative and releasing the surety on any bond.

Amended March 31, 1977, effective July 1, 1977 (344 So.2d 828); Sept. 4, 1980, effective Jan. 1, 1981 (387 So.2d 949); Sept. 13, 1984, effective Jan. 1, 1985 (458 So.2d 1079); Sept. 29, 1988, effective Jan. 1, 1989 (537 So.2d 500); Sept. 24, 1992, effective Jan. 1, 1993 (607 So.2d 1306); Oct. 3, 1996, effective Jan. 1, 1997 (683 So.2d 78); Sept. 29, 2005, effective Jan. 1, 2006 (912 So.2d 1178); Feb. 1, 2007 (948 So.2d 735); July 12, 2007 (964 So.2d 140); Sept. 26, 2013, effective Jan. 1, 2014 (123 So.3d 31).

Committee Notes

The rule establishes a procedure for giving notice and serving the final accounting, petition for discharge, and plan of distribution to all interested persons prior to distribution and discharge. No distinction is made in plans of distribution which distribute estate property in kind among multiple residual beneficiaries proportionate to their respective interests and those which include equalizing adjustments in cash or property and which do not make prorated distribution. If disclosure of the compensation or disclosure of the manner of determining the compensation in the petition for discharge is to be waived, the form of waiver must conform to rule 5.180(b).

Rule History

1980 Revision: Change in prior (a)(6) to require that an objection set forth the basis on which it is being made.

1984 Revision: This rule has been substantially revised. Portions of the prior rule are now incorporated in rules 5.400 and 5.401. The committee has included the procedure for filing and serving of objections to the final accounting, petition for discharge, plan of distribution, or compensation in rule 5.401.

1988 Revision: Subdivision (b)(1) is deleted to avoid duplication with rule 5.346. Subdivision (c) is amended to add the 12–month time specification of section 733.901(1), Florida Statutes. Committee notes revised. Citation form changes in committee notes.

1992 Revision: Subdivision (b)(5)(D) is added.   Editorial changes.   Committee notes revised. Citation form changes in committee notes.

1996 Revision: Addition in (a)(4) of specific attorney fee compensation disclosure requirements found in § 733.6171(9), Florida Statutes, and expanded to cover all compensation. Committee notes revised.

2003 Revision: Committee notes revised.

2005 Revision: Subdivision (f) deleted to avoid duplication with rule 5.180.

2006 Revision: Committee notes revised.

2007 Revision: Committee notes revised.

2012 Revision: Committee notes revised.

2013 Revision: Clarifies the available option to file a federal tax return even if one is not required by state or federal rule or law.

Statutory References

§ 731.201(12), (23), Fla. Stat.   General definitions.

§ 731.302, Fla. Stat.   Waiver and consent by interested person.

§ 733.809, Fla. Stat.   Right of retainer.

§ 733.810, Fla. Stat.   Distribution in kind; valuation.

§ 733.811, Fla. Stat.   Distribution; right or title of distributee.

§ 733.812, Fla. Stat.   Improper distribution or payment; liability of distributee or payee.

§ 733.901, Fla. Stat.   Final discharge.

Rule References

Fla. Prob. R. 5.020 Pleadings; verification; motions.

Fla. Prob. R. 5.040 Notice.

Fla. Prob. R. 5.041 Service of pleadings and documents.

Fla. Prob. R. 5.042 Time.

Fla. Prob. R. 5.180 Waiver and consent.

Fla. Prob. R. 5.330 Execution by personal representative.

Fla. Prob. R. 5.346 Fiduciary accounting.

Fla. Prob. R. 5.401 Objections to petition for discharge or final accounting.

Fla. R. Jud. Admin. 2.250(a)(1)(D) Time standards for trial and appellate courts and reporting requirements.

Fla. R. Jud. Admin. 2.516 Service of pleadings and documents.

Cross References

Final accounting and discharge, see F.S.A. § 733.901.

Rule 5.401.   Objections to Petition for Discharge or Final Accounting

(a) **Objections.**   An interested person may object to the petition for discharge or final accounting within 30 days after the service of the later of the petition or final accounting on that interested person.

(b) **Contents.**   Written objections to the petition for discharge or final accounting must state with particularity the items to which the objections are directed and must state the grounds on which the objections are based.

(c) Service. Copies of the objections shall be served by the objector on the personal representative and interested persons not later than 30 days after the last date on which the petition for discharge or final accounting was served on the objector.

(d) Hearing on Objections. Any interested person may set a hearing on the objections. Notice of the hearing shall be given to all interested persons. If a notice of hearing on the objections is not served within 90 days of filing of the objections, the objections shall be deemed abandoned and the personal representative may make distribution as set forth in the plan of distribution.

(e) Order on Objections. The court shall sustain or overrule any objections to the petition for discharge and final accounting and shall determine a plan of distribution.

(f) Discharge. On receipt of evidence that the estate has been distributed according to the plan determined by the court and the claims of creditors have been paid or otherwise disposed of, the court shall enter an order discharging the personal representative and releasing the surety on any bond.

Added Sept. 13, 1984, effective Jan. 1, 1985 (458 So.2d 1079). Amended Sept. 29, 1988, effective Jan. 1, 1989 (537 So.2d 500); Oct. 3, 1996, effective Jan. 1, 1997 (683 So.2d 78); July 12, 2007 (964 So.2d 140).

Committee Notes

Rule History

1984 Revision: New rule. Objections to the petition for discharge or final accounting were formerly under prior rule 5.400. Clarifies procedure for objections.

1988 Revision: Editorial changes in (a). Committee notes revised. Citation form changes in committee notes.

1992 Revision: Committee notes revised. Citation form changes in committee notes.

1996 Revision: Subdivision (d) amended to clarify that 90–day period pertains to service of hearing notice, not the actual hearing date.

2003 Revision: Committee notes revised.

2007 Revision: Committee notes revised.

2012 Revision: Committee notes revised.

Statutory References

§ 731.201(12), (23), Fla. Stat. General definitions.

§ 733.6175, Fla. Stat. Proceedings for review of employment of agents and compensation of personal representatives and employees of estate.

§ 733.901, Fla. Stat. Final discharge.

Rule References

Fla. Prob. R. 5.020 Pleadings; verification; motions.

Fla. Prob. R. 5.040 Notice.

Fla. Prob. R. 5.041 Service of pleadings and documents.

Fla. Prob. R. 5.042 Time.

Fla. Prob. R. 5.180 Waiver and consent.

Fla. Prob. R. 5.400 Distribution and discharge.

Fla. R. Jud. Admin. 2.516 Service of pleadings and documents.

Rule 5.402. Notice of Lien on Protected Homestead

(a) Filing. If the personal representative has recorded a notice of lien on protected home-stead, the personal representative shall file a copy of the recorded notice in the probate proceeding.

(b) Contents. The notice of lien shall contain:

(1) the name and address of the personal representative and the personal representative's attorney;

(2) the legal description of the real property;

(3) to the extent known, the name and address of each person appearing to have an interest in the property; and

(4) a statement that the personal representative has expended or is obligated to expend funds to preserve, maintain, insure, or protect the property and that the lien stands as security for recovery of those expenditures and obligations incurred, including fees and costs.

(c) Service. A copy of the recorded notice of lien shall be served on interested persons in the manner provided for service of formal notice.

Added Sept. 29, 2005, effective Jan. 1, 2006 (912 So.2d 1178).

Committee Notes

Rule History

2005 Revision: New rule.

2012 Revision: Committee notes revised.

Statutory References

§ 733.608, Fla. Stat. General power of the personal representative.

Rule References

Fla. Prob. R. 5.040 Notice.

Fla. Prob. R. 5.041 Service of pleadings and documents.

Fla. Prob. R. 5.403 Proceedings to determine amount of lien on protected homestead.

Fla. Prob. R. 5.404 Notice of taking possession of protected homestead.

Fla. Prob. R. 5.405 Proceedings to determine protected homestead real property.

Fla. R. Jud. Admin. 2.516 Service of pleadings and documents.

Rule 5.403. Proceedings to Determine Amount of Lien on Protected Homestead

(a) Petition. A personal representative or interested person may file a petition to determine the amount of any lien on protected homestead.

(b) Contents. The petition shall be verified by the petitioner and shall state:

(1) the name and address of the personal representative and the personal representative's attorney;

(2) the interest of the petitioner;

(3) the legal description of the real property;

(4) to the extent known, the name and address of each person appearing to have an interest in the property; and

(5) to the extent known, the amounts paid or obligated to be paid by the personal representative to preserve, maintain, insure, or protect the protected homestead, including fees and costs.

(c) Service. The petition shall be served on interested persons by formal notice.

Added Sept. 29, 2005, effective January 1, 2006 (912 So.2d 1178).

Committee Notes

Rule History

2005 Revision: New rule.

2012 Revision: Committee notes revised.

Statutory References

§ 733.608, Fla. Stat. General power of the personal representative.

Rule References

Fla. Prob. R. 5.040 Notice.

Fla. Prob. R. 5.041 Service of pleadings and documents.

Fla. Prob. R. 5.402 Notice of lien on protected homestead.

Fla. Prob. R. 5.404 Notice of taking possession of protected homestead.

Fla. Prob. R. 5.405 Proceedings to determine protected homestead real property.

Fla. R. Jud. Admin. 2.516 Service of pleadings and documents.

Rule 5.404. Notice of Taking Possession of Protected Homestead

(a) Filing of Notice. If a personal representative takes possession of what appears reasonably to be protected homestead pending a determination of its homestead status, the personal representative shall file a notice of that act.

(b) Contents of Notice. The notice shall contain:

(1) a legal description of the property;

(2) a statement of the limited purpose for preserving, insuring, and protecting it for the heirs or devisees pending a determination of the homestead status;

(3) the name and address of the personal representative and the personal representative's attorney;

(4) if the personal representative is in possession when the notice is filed, the date the personal representative took possession.

(c) Service of Notice. The notice shall be served in the manner provided for service of formal notice on interested persons and on any person in actual possession of the property.

Added May 2, 2002 (824 So.2d 849). Amended Sept. 29, 2005, effective Jan. 1, 2006 (912 So.2d 1178); Sept. 26, 2013, effective Jan. 1, 2014 (123 So.3d 31).

Committee Notes

Rule History

2002 Revision: New rule.

2005 Revision: Term "devisees" substituted for "beneficiaries" in subdivision (b)(2) to clarify the status of persons interested in protected homestead. Committee notes revised.

2013 Revision: Deletes subdivision (b)(4) because the required information is not appropriate for a Notice of Taking possession, nor does it comply with the Americans with Disabilities Act requirements.

Statutory References

§ 732.401, Fla. Stat. Descent of homestead.

§ 732.4015, Fla. Stat. Devise of homestead.

§ 733.608(2), Fla. Stat. General power of the personal representative.

Rule References

Fla. Prob. R. 5.402 Notice of lien on protected homestead.

Fla. Prob. R. 5.403 Proceedings to determine amount of lien on protected homestead.

Fla. Prob. R. 5.405 Proceedings to determine protected homestead real property.

Rule 5.405. Proceedings to Determine Protected Homestead Real Property

(a) Petition. An interested person may file a petition to determine protected homestead real property owned by the decedent.

(b) Contents. The petition shall be verified by the petitioner and shall state:

(1) the date of the decedent's death;

(2) the county of the decedent's domicile at the time of death;

(3) the name of the decedent's surviving spouse and the names of surviving descendants, and a statement as to whether the decedent had any minor children as of the date of death. If so, they should be identified with name and year of birth;

(4) a legal description of the property owned by the decedent on which the decedent resided; and

(5) any other facts in support of the petition.

(c) Order. The court's order on the petition shall describe the real property and determine whether any of the real property constituted the protected homestead of the decedent. If the court determines that any of the real property was the protected homestead of the decedent, the order shall identify by name the person or persons entitled to the protected homestead real property and define the interest of each.

Added Sept. 13, 1984, effective Jan. 1, 1985 (458 So.2d 1079). Amended Sept. 29, 1988, effective Jan. 1, 1989 (537 So.2d 500); Sept. 24, 1992, effective Jan. 1, 1993 (607 So.2d 1306); Oct. 3, 1996, effective Jan. 1, 1997 (683 So.2d 78); May 2, 2002 (824 So.2d 849); July 12, 2007 (964 So.2d 140); May 22, 2014, effective May 22, 2014 (139 So.3d 875).

Committee Notes

This rule establishes the procedure by which the personal representative or any interested person may petition the court for a determination that certain real property constituted the decedent's protected homestead property, in accordance with article X, section 4 of the Florida Constitution. The jurisdiction of the court to determine constitutional protected homestead property was established by *In re Noble's Estate*, 73 So. 2d 873 (Fla. 1954).

Rule History

1984 Revision: New rule.

1988 Revision: Editorial change in (a). Subdivision (b)(4) amended to conform to constitutional change. Committee notes revised. Citation form change in committee notes.

1992 Revision: Editorial change. Committee notes revised. Citation form changes in committee notes.

1996 Revision: Subdivision (c) amended to require description of real property that is the subject of the petition, description of any homestead property, and definition of specific interests of persons entitled to homestead real property.

2002 Revision: Replaces "homestead" with "protected homestead" throughout to conform to addition of term in section 731.201(29), Florida Statutes. Committee notes revised.

2003 Revision: Committee notes revised.

2007 Revision: Committee notes revised.

2010 Revision: Committee notes revised.

2012 Revision: Committee notes revised.

2014 Revision: Amends subdivisions (b)(3) and (c) to conform to Fla. R. Jud. Admin. 2.425. Committee notes revised.

Constitutional Reference

Art. X, § 4, Fla. Const.

Statutory References

§ 731.104, Fla. Stat. Verification of documents.

§ 731.201(33), Fla. Stat. General definitions.

§ 732.401, Fla. Stat. Descent of homestead.

§ 732.4015, Fla. Stat. Devise of homestead.

§ 733.607, Fla. Stat. Possession of estate.

§ 733.608, Fla. Stat. General power of the personal representative.

Rule References

Fla. Prob. R. 5.020 Pleadings; verification; motions.

Fla. Prob. R. 5.040 Notice.

Fla. Prob. R. 5.041 Service of pleadings and documents.

Fla. Prob. R. 5.205(a)(6) Filing evidence of death.

Fla. Prob. R. 5.340 Inventory.

Fla. Prob. R. 5.404 Notice of taking possession of protected homestead.

Fla. R. Jud. Admin. 2.516 Service of pleadings and documents.

Fla. R. Jud. Admin. 2.425 Minimization of the Filing of Sensitive Information.

Rule 5.406. Proceedings to Determine Exempt Property

(a) **Petition.** An interested person may file a petition to determine exempt property within the time allowed by law.

(b) **Contents.** The petition shall be verified by the petitioner and shall:

(1) describe the property and the basis on which it is claimed as exempt property; and

(2) state the name and address of the decedent's surviving spouse or, if none, the names and addresses of decedent's children entitled by law to the exempt property and the year of birth of those who are minors.

(c) Order. The court shall determine each item of exempt property and its value, if necessary to determine its exempt status, and order the surrender of that property to the persons entitled to it.

Added Sept. 13, 1984, effective Jan. 1, 1985 (458 So.2d 1079). Amended Sept. 29, 1988, effective Jan. 1, 1989 (537 So.2d 500); Oct. 3, 1996, effective Jan. 1, 1997 (683 So.2d 78); Sept. 2, 2010, effective Jan. 1, 2011 (50 So.3d 578); May 22, 2014, effective May 22, 2014 (139 So.3d 875).

Committee Notes

This rule establishes the procedure by which the personal representative or any interested person may petition the court for determination of exempt property in accordance with article X, section 4 of the Florida Constitution and section 732.402, Florida Statutes.

Section 732.402, Florida Statutes, specifies the time within which the petition to determine exempt property must be filed, within 4 months after the date of service of the notice of administration, unless extended as provided in the statute.

Rule History

1984 Revision: New rule.

1988 Revision: Subdivision (a) revised to reflect editorial changes and to require verification. Subdivision (b)(1) revised to require the basis for asserting exempt property status. Subdivision (b)(2) added the requirement of stating addresses of those entitled to exempt property. Subdivision (c) revised to reflect editorial changes and to require determination of the value of each item of exempt property. Committee notes revised.

1992 Revision: Committee notes revised. Citation form changes in committee notes.

1996 Revision: Editorial changes in rule to conform to similar language in rule 5.405. Committee notes revised.

2003 Revision: Committee notes revised.

2010 Revision: Subdivision (c) amended to limit the instances in which the value of the property claimed as exempt needs to be stated in the order.

2012 Revision: Committee notes revised.

2014 Revision: Subdivision (b)(2) amended to conform to Fla. R. Jud. Admin. 2.425 and provide the year of birth of a minor. Committee notes revised.

Statutory References

§ 731.104, Fla. Stat. Verification of documents.

§ 732.402, Fla. Stat. Exempt property.

Rule References

Fla. Prob. R. 5.020 Pleadings; verification; motions.

Fla. Prob. R. 5.040 Notice.

Fla. Prob. R. 5.041 Service of pleadings and documents.

Fla. Prob. R. 5.042 Time.

Fla. Prob. R. 5.420 Disposition of personal property without administration.

Fla. R. Jud. Admin. 2.516 Service of pleadings and documents.

Fla. R. Jud. Admin. 2.425 Minimization of the Filing of Sensitive Information.

Rule 5.407. Proceedings to Determine Family Allowance

(a) Petition. An interested person may file a petition to determine family allowance.

(b) Contents. The petition shall be verified by the petitioner and shall:

(1) state the names and addresses of the decedent's surviving spouse and the decedent's adult lineal heirs and the initials, address, and year of birth of the decedents' lineal heirs who are minors and who were being supported by the decedent or who were entitled to be supported by the decedent at the time of the decedent's death; and

(2) for each person for whom an allowance is sought, state the adult person's name, or minor child's initials, and relationship to the decedent, the basis on which the allowance is claimed, and the amount sought.

(c) Order. The order shall identify the persons entitled to the allowance, the amount to which each is entitled, the method of payment, and to whom payment should be made. Added June 19, 2003, effective Jan. 1, 2004 (848 So.2d 1069). Amended Oct. 18, 2012, effective, *nunc pro tunc*, Sept. 1, 2012 (102 So.3d 505); May 22, 2014, effective May 22, 2014 (139 So.3d 875).

Committee Notes

Rule History

2003 Revision: New rule.

2012 Revision: Editorial change in (b)(1) for gender neutrality. Committee notes revised.

2014 Revision: Subdivisions (b)(1) and (b)(2) are amended to conform to Fla. R. Jud. Admin. 2.425. Committee notes revised.

Statutory References

§ 731.104, Fla. Stat. Verification of documents.

§ 732.403, Fla. Stat. Family allowance.

Rule References

Fla. Prob. R. 5.020 Pleadings; verification; motions.

Fla. Prob. R. 5.040 Notice.

Fla. Prob. R. 5.041 Service of pleadings and documents.

Fla. R. Jud. Admin. 2.516 Service of pleadings and documents.

Fla. R. Jud. Admin. 2.425 Minimization of the Filing of Sensitive Information.

Rule 5.420. Disposition of Personal Property Without Administration

(a) Application. An interested person may request a disposition of the decedent's personal property without administration. An application signed by the applicant shall set forth:

(1) the description and value of the exempt property;

(2) the description and value of the other assets of the decedent;

(3) the amount of preferred funeral expenses and reasonable and necessary medical and hospital expenses for the last 60 days of the last illness together with accompanying statements or payment receipts; and

(4) each requested payment or distribution of personal property.

(b) Exempt Property. If the decedent's personal property includes exempt property, or property that can be determined to be exempt property, the application must also be signed by all persons entitled to the exempt property or by their representative.

(c) Preparation. On request, the clerk shall assist the applicant in the preparation of the required writing.

(d) Disposition. If the court is satisfied that disposition without administration is appropriate, the court may, without hearing, by letter or other writing authorize the payment, transfer, or disposition of the decedent's personal property to those persons entitled to it.

Amended March 31, 1977, effective July 1, 1977 (344 So.2d 828); Sept. 13, 1984, effective Jan. 1, 1985 (458 So.2d 1079); Sept. 29, 1988, effective Jan. 1, 1989 (531 So.2d 1261); Sept. 24, 1992, effective Jan. 1, 1993 (607 So.2d 1306).

Committee Notes

Section 732.402, Florida Statutes, requires persons entitled to exempt property, which excludes property specifically or demonstratively devised, to file timely a petition to determine exempt property. Accordingly, disposition of personal property under this rule should not be granted if decedent's personal property includes exempt property without all persons entitled thereto agreeing to such disposition.

Rule History

1977 Revision: Permits the clerk to perform limited ministerial acts in the completion of the application.

1984 Revision: Editorial changes. Delineates the required contents of the application. Committee notes revised.

1988 Revision: Subdivision (a)(3) changed to require applicant to attach accompanying statements or payment receipts regarding priority expenses. Subdivision (b) added to require persons entitled to exempt property to agree to the proposed disposition. Committee notes expanded.

1992 Revision: Editorial change. Committee notes revised. Citation form changes in committee notes.

2003 Revision: Committee notes revised.

Statutory References

§ 732.402, Fla. Stat. Exempt property.

§ 735.301, Fla. Stat. Disposition without administration.

Rule Reference

Fla. Prob. R. 5.205(a)(4) Filing evidence of death.

Cross References

Disposition without administration, see F.S.A. § 735.301.

Rule 5.430. Resignation of Personal Representative

(a) Resignation. A personal representative may resign with court approval.

(b) Petition for Resignation. The personal representative seeking to resign shall file a petition for resignation. The petition shall be verified and shall state:

(1) the personal representative desires to resign and be relieved of all powers, duties, and obligations as personal representative;

(2) the status of the estate administration and that the interests of the estate will not be jeopardized if the resignation is accepted;

(3) whether a proceeding for accounting, surcharge, or indemnification or other proceeding against the resigning personal representative is pending; and

(4) whether the appointment of a successor fiduciary is necessary. If the petition nominates a successor fiduciary, it shall state the nominee's priority under the Florida Probate Code, if any, and that the nominee is qualified to serve under the laws of Florida.

(c) Service. The petition shall be served by formal notice on all interested persons and the personal representative's surety, if any.

(d) Appointment of Successor. Before accepting the resignation, the court shall determine the necessity for appointment of a successor fiduciary. If there is no joint personal representative serving, the court shall appoint a successor fiduciary.

(e) Acceptance of Resignation. The court may accept the resignation and revoke the letters of the resigning personal representative if the interests of the estate are not jeopardized. Acceptance of the resignation shall not exonerate the resigning personal representative or the resigning personal representative's surety from liability.

(f) Delivery of Records and Property. The resigning personal representative shall immediately upon acceptance of the resignation by the court deliver to the remaining personal representative or the successor fiduciary all of the records of the estate and all property of the estate, unless otherwise directed by the court.

(g) Petition for Discharge; Accounting. The resigning personal representative shall file an accounting and a petition for discharge within 30 days after the date that the letters of the resigning personal representative are revoked by the court. The petition for discharge shall be verified and shall state:

(1) that the letters of the resigning personal representative have been revoked;

(2) that the resigning personal representative has surrendered all undistributed estate assets, records, documents, papers, and other property of or concerning the estate to the remaining personal representative or the successor fiduciary; and

(3) the amount of compensation paid or to be paid the resigning personal representative and the attorney and other persons employed by the resigning personal representative.

(h) Notice, Filing, and Objections to Accounting. Notice of, filing of, and objections to the accounting of the resigning personal representative shall be as provided in rule 5.345.

(i) Notice of Filing and Objections to Petition for Discharge.

(1) Notice of filing and a copy of the petition for discharge shall be served on all interested persons. The notice shall state that objections to the petition for discharge must be filed within 30 days after the later of service of the petition or service of the accounting on that interested person.

(2) Any interested person may file an objection to the petition for discharge within 30 days after the later of service of the petition or service of the accounting on that interested person. Any objection not filed within such time shall be deemed abandoned. An objection shall be in writing and shall state with particularity the item or items to which the objection is directed and the grounds on which the objection is based.

(3) The objecting party shall serve a copy of the objection on the resigning personal representative and other interested persons.

(4) Any interested person may set a hearing on the objections. Notice of the hearing shall be given to the resigning personal representative and other interested persons.

(j) Failure to File Accounting or Deliver Records or Property. The resigning personal representative shall be subject to contempt proceedings if the resigning personal representative fails to file an accounting or fails to deliver all property of the estate and all estate records under the control of the resigning personal representative to the remaining personal representative or the successor fiduciary within the time prescribed by this rule or by court order.

(k) Discharge. The court shall enter an order discharging the resigning personal representative and releasing the surety on any bond after the court is satisfied that the resigning personal representative has delivered all records and property of the estate to the remaining personal representative or the successor fiduciary; that all objections, if any, to the accounting of the resigning personal representative have been withdrawn, abandoned, or judicially resolved; and that the liability of the resigning personal representative has been determined and satisfied.

Amended Sept. 29, 1988, effective Jan. 1, 1989 (537 So.2d 500); Sept. 24, 1992, effective Jan. 1, 1993 (607 So.2d 1306); June 19, 2003 (848 So.2d 1069); July 12, 2007 (964 So.2d 140).

Committee Notes

In the event of resignation of a personal representative, if a joint personal representative is not serving, the successor fiduciary must file an oath and designation of a successor resident agent.

This rule was revised to implement the revisions to the probate code that govern resignation of personal representative. The committee intended to separate the procedure with respect to resignation from removal because these proceedings may differ in practice.

Rule History

1975 Revision: The rule provides for the orderly succession of personal representatives in the event a personal representative resigns or is removed.

1977 Revision: Editorial change in committee note.

1988 Revision: Editorial changes; captions added to subdivisions. Committee notes revised. Citation form changes in committee notes.

1992 Revision: Editorial changes. Committee notes revised. Citation form changes in committee notes.

2003 Revision: Rule completely revised to comply with statutory changes. Committee notes revised.

2007 Revision: Committee notes revised.

2012 Revision: Committee notes revised.

Statutory References

§ 731.104, Fla. Stat. Verification of documents.

§ 731.201(23), Fla. Stat. General definitions.

§ 733.101, Fla. Stat. Venue of probate proceedings.

§ 733.502, Fla. Stat. Resignation of personal representative.

§ 733.503, Fla. Stat. Appointment of successor upon resignation.

§ 733.5035, Fla. Stat. Surrender of assets after resignation.

§ 733.5036, Fla. Stat. Accounting and discharge following resignation.

Rule References

Fla. Prob. R. 5.020 Pleadings; verification; motions.

Fla. Prob. R. 5.040 Notice.

Fla. Prob. R. 5.041 Service of pleadings and documents.

Fla. Prob. R. 5.180 Waiver and consent.

Fla. Prob. R. 5.310 Disqualification of personal representative; notification.

Fla. Prob. R. 5.330 Execution by personal representative.

Fla. Prob. R. 5.345 Accountings other than personal representatives' final accountings.

Fla. Prob. R. 5.346 Fiduciary accounting.

Fla. Prob. R. 5.401 Objections to petition for discharge or final accounting.

Fla. R. Jud. Admin. 2.516 Service of pleadings and documents.

Cross References

Resignation of guardian, see Probate Rule 5.650.
Resignation of personal representative, see F.S.A. § 733.502.
Successor representative, appointment, see F.S.A. § 733.503.

Rule 5.440. Proceedings for Removal of Personal Representative

(a) Commencement of Proceeding. The court on its own motion may remove, or any interested person by petition may commence a proceeding to remove, a personal representative. A petition for removal shall state the facts constituting the grounds upon which removal is sought, and shall be filed in the court having jurisdiction over the administration of the estate.

(b) Accounting. A removed personal representative shall file an accounting within 30 days after removal.

(c) Delivery of Records and Property. A removed personal representative shall, immediately after removal or within such time prescribed by court order, deliver to the remaining personal representative or to the successor fiduciary all of the records of the estate and all of the property of the estate.

(d) Failure to File Accounting or Deliver Records and Property. If a removed personal representative fails to file an accounting or fails to deliver all property of the estate and all estate records under the control of the removed personal representative to the remaining personal representative or to the successor fiduciary within the time prescribed by this rule or by court order, the removed personal representative shall be subject to contempt proceedings.

Amended Sept. 4, 1980, effective Jan. 1, 1981 (387 So.2d 949); Sept. 13, 1984, effective Jan. 1, 1985 (458 So.2d 1079); Sept. 29, 1988, effective Jan. 1, 1989 (537 So.2d 500); Sept. 24, 1992, effective Jan. 1, 1993 (607 So.2d 1306); May 2, 2002 (824 So.2d 849); July 12, 2007 (964 So.2d 140); Dec. 9, 2010 (51 So.3d 1146).

Committee Notes

The revision of subdivision (a) of this rule by the addition of its final phrase represents a rule implementation of the procedure found in section 733.505, Florida Statutes. It is not intended to change the effect of the statute from which it was derived but has been reformatted to conform with the structure of these rules. It is not intended to create a new procedure or modify an existing procedure.

Rule History

1980 Revision: Subdivision (a) amended to require formal notice to interested persons and to delete requirement that court give directions as to mode of notice. Surety authorized to petition for removal.

1984 Revision: Editorial changes. Provisions in prior rule for contempt have been deleted since the court has the inherent power to punish for contempt. Committee notes revised.

1988 Revision: Last phrase of (a) added to implement the procedure found in section 733.505, Florida Statutes. Subdivision (b) amended to parallel interim accounting rules. Deletes ability to extend time to file and adds reference to court power to punish for contempt. Committee notes expanded. Editorial changes. Citation form changes in committee notes.

1992 Revision: Editorial changes. Committee notes revised. Citation form changes in committee notes.

2002 Revision: Entire rule amended. Contents of accountings by removed fiduciaries are now governed by rule 5.346. Editorial changes in (a), (c), and (d). Committee notes revised.

2003 Revision: Committee notes revised.

2007 Revision: Committee notes revised.

2010 Revision: Editorial change in title to clarify scope of rule.

2012 Revision: Committee notes revised.

Statutory References

§ 731.201(23), Fla. Stat. General definitions.

§ 733.504, Fla. Stat. Removal of personal representative; causes of removal.

§ 733.505, Fla. Stat. Jurisdiction in removal proceedings.

§ 733.506, Fla. Stat. Proceedings for removal.

§ 733.5061, Fla. Stat. Appointment of successor upon removal.

§ 733.508, Fla. Stat. Accounting and discharge of removed personal representatives upon removal.

§ 733.509, Fla. Stat. Surrender of assets upon removal.

Rule References

Fla. Prob. R. 5.020 Pleadings; verification; motions.

Fla. Prob. R. 5.025 Adversary proceedings.

Fla. Prob. R. 5.040 Notice.

Fla. Prob. R. 5.041 Service of pleadings and documents.

Fla. Prob. R. 5.042 Time.

Fla. Prob. R. 5.150 Order requiring accounting.

Fla. Prob. R. 5.310 Disqualification of personal representative; notification.

Fla. Prob. R. 5.345 Accountings other than personal representatives' final accountings.

Fla. Prob. R. 5.346 Fiduciary accounting.

Fla. R. Jud. Admin. 2.516 Service of pleadings and documents.

Cross References

Contempts defined, see F.S.A. § 38.23.
Power to punish contempts, see F.S.A. § 38.22.
Proceedings for removal of guardian, see Probate Rule 5.660.
Removal of personal representative,
    Accounting upon removal, see F.S.A. § 733.508.
    Causes for removal, see F.S.A. § 733.504.
    Jurisdiction, see F.S.A. § 733.505.
    Proceedings, see F.S.A. § 733.506.
    Surrender of assets, see F.S.A. § 733.509.

Rule 5.460. Subsequent Administration

(a) Petition. If, after an estate is closed, additional property of the decedent is discovered or if further administration of the estate is required for any other reason, any interested person may file a petition for further administration of the estate. The petition shall be filed in the same probate file as the original administration.

(b) Contents. The petition shall state:

(1) the name, address, and interest of the petitioner in the estate;

(2) the reason for further administration of the estate;

(3) the description, approximate value, and location of any asset not included among the assets of the prior administration; and

(4) a statement of the relief sought.

(c) Order. The court shall enter such orders as appropriate. Unless required, the court need not revoke the order of discharge, reissue letters, or require bond.

Amended Sept. 13, 1984, effective Jan. 1, 1985 (458 So.2d 1079).

Committee Notes

This rule establishes a procedure for further administration after estate is closed, which may be summary in nature.

Rule History

1984 Revision: Extensive changes. Committee notes revised.

1992 Revision: Citation form change in committee notes.

2003 Revision: Committee notes revised.

2012 Revision: Committee notes revised.

Statutory Reference

§ 733.903, Fla. Stat. Subsequent administration.

Rule References

Fla. Prob. R. 5.020 Pleadings; verification; motions.

Fla. Prob. R. 5.040 Notice.

Fla. Prob. R. 5.041 Service of pleadings and documents.

Fla. R. Jud. Admin. 2.516 Service of pleadings and documents.

Cross References

Subsequent administration, see F.S.A. § 733.903.

Rule 5.470. Ancillary Administration

(a) Petition. The petition for ancillary letters shall include an authenticated copy of so much of the domiciliary proceedings as will show:

(1) for a testate estate the will, petition for probate, order admitting the will to probate, and authority of the personal representative; or

(2) for an intestate estate the petition for administration and authority of the personal representative to act.

(b) Notice. Before ancillary letters shall be issued to any person, formal notice shall be given to:

(1) all known persons qualified to act as ancillary personal representative and whose entitlement to preference of appointment is equal to or greater than petitioner's and who have not waived notice or joined in the petition; and

(2) all domiciliary personal representatives who have not waived notice or joined in the petition.

(c) Probate of Will. On filing the authenticated copy of a will, the court shall determine whether the will complies with Florida law to entitle it to probate. If it does comply, the court shall admit the will to probate.

Amended Sept. 13, 1984, effective Jan. 1, 1985 (458 So.2d 1079); Sept. 24, 1992, effective Jan. 1, 1993 (607 So.2d 1306); Oct. 3, 1996, effective Jan. 1, 1997 (683 So.2d 78); Sept. 29, 2005, effective Jan. 1, 2006 (912 So.2d 1178).

Committee Notes

Rule History

1975 Revision: The rule sets out the procedural requirements for issuance of ancillary letters.

1984 Revision: Editorial changes with addition of notice requirement in (b). Committee notes revised.

1988 Revision: Committee notes revised.

1992 Revision: Changed rule to require that notice be given to persons qualified to act as ancillary personal representative whose entitlement to preference of appointment is equal to or greater than petitioner's and to all domiciliary personal representatives prior to entry of an order admitting the will to probate. Committee notes revised. Citation form changes in committee notes.

1996 Revision: The requirement that a filing of an authenticated copy of a will be a "probated" will is removed from subdivision (c). There may be circumstances in which a will is on deposit or file in a foreign jurisdiction but is not being offered for probate. That should not preclude an ancillary administration in Florida of that estate. This change is not intended to allow an authenticated copy of any document other than an original instrument to be filed under this rule and considered for probate.

2003 Revision: Committee notes revised.

2005 Revision: Committee notes revised.

2010 Revision: Committee notes revised.

2012 Revision: Committee notes revised.

Statutory References

§ 731.201(1), Fla. Stat. General definitions.

§ 733.212, Fla. Stat. Notice of administration; filing of objections.

§ 733.2121, Fla. Stat. Notice to creditors; filing of claims.

§ 734.102, Fla. Stat. Ancillary administration.

§ 734.1025, Fla. Stat. Nonresident decedent's testate estate with property not exceeding $50,000 in this state; determination of claims.

Rule References

Fla. Prob. R. 5.020 Pleadings; verification; motions.

Fla. Prob. R. 5.040 Notice.

Fla. Prob. R. 5.041 Service of pleadings and documents.

Fla. Prob. R. 5.042 Time.

Fla. Prob. R. 5.065(b) Notice of civil action or ancillary administration.

Fla. Prob. R. 5.205(a)(2) Filing evidence of death.

Fla. Prob. R. 5.215 Authenticated copy of will.

Fla. Prob. R. 5.240 Notice of administration.

Fla. Prob. R. 5.241 Notice to creditors.

Fla. Prob. R. 5.475 Ancillary administration, short form.

Fed. R. Civ. P. 44(a) Proving an official record.

Fla. R. Jud. Admin. 2.516 Service of pleadings and documents.

Cross References

Ancillary administration, see F.S.A. §§ 734.102, 734.1025.

Rule 5.475. Ancillary Administration, Short Form

(a) Filing Requirements. The foreign personal representative of a testate estate that meets the requirements of section 734.1025, Florida Statutes, may file with the clerk in the county where any property is located an authenticated copy of so much of the transcript of the foreign proceedings as will show:

(1) the probated will and all probated codicils of the decedent;

(2) the order admitting them to probate;

(3) the letters or their equivalent; and

(4) the part of the record showing the names of the beneficiaries of the estate or an affidavit of the foreign personal representative reciting that the names are not shown or not fully disclosed by the foreign record and specifying the names.

On presentation of the foregoing, the court shall admit the will and any codicils to probate if they comply with section 732.502(1) or section 732.502(2), Florida Statutes.

(b) Notice to Creditors. After complying with the foregoing requirements, the foreign personal representative may cause a notice to creditors to be published as required by these rules.

(c) Claims Procedure. The procedure for filing or barring claims and objecting to them and for suing on them shall be the same as for other estates, except as provided in this rule.

(d) Order. If no claims are filed against the estate within the time allowed, the court shall enter an order adjudging that notice to creditors has been duly published and proof thereof filed and that no claims have been filed against the estate or that all claims have been satisfied.

(e) Notification of Claims Filed. If any claim is filed against the estate within the time allowed, the clerk shall send to the foreign personal representative a copy of the claim and a notice setting a date for a hearing to appoint an ancillary personal representative. At the hearing, the court shall appoint an ancillary personal representative according to the preferences as provided by law.

(f) Objections to Claims. If an ancillary personal representative is appointed pursuant to this rule, the procedure for filing, objecting to, and suing on claims shall be the same as for other estates, except that the ancillary personal representative appointed shall have not less than 30 days from the date of appointment within which to object to any claim filed.

Added Sept. 29, 1988, effective Jan. 1, 1989 (537 So.2d 500). Amended Sept. 24, 1992, effective Jan. 1, 1993 (607 So.2d 1306); Sept. 29, 2005, effective Jan. 1, 2006 (912 So.2d 1178).

Committee Notes

This rule represents a rule implementation of the procedure found in section 734.1025, Florida Statutes. It is not intended to change the effect of the statute from which it was derived but has been reformatted to conform with the structure of these rules. It is not intended to create a new procedure or modify an existing procedure.

Rule History

1988 Revision: New rule.

1992 Revision: Editorial changes. Committee notes revised. Citation form changes in committee notes.

2003 Revision: Committee notes revised.

2005 Revision: Deletion of reference to intestate estates in subdivision (a) to conform to 2001 amendments to section 734.1025, Florida Statutes. Editorial changes throughout.

2012 Revision: Committee notes revised.

Statutory References

§ 733.2121, Fla. Stat. Notice to creditors; filing of claims.

§ 734.102, Fla. Stat. Ancillary administration.

§ 734.1025, Fla. Stat. Nonresident decedent's testate estate with property not exceeding $50,000 in this state; determination of claims.

Rule References

Fla. Prob. R. 5.020 Pleadings; verification; motions.

Fla. Prob. R. 5.040 Notice.

Fla. Prob. R. 5.041 Service of pleadings and documents.

Fla. Prob. R. 5.042 Time.

Fla. Prob. R. 5.065(b) Notice of civil action or ancillary administration.

Fla. Prob. R. 5.205(a)(2) Filing evidence of death.

Fla. Prob. R. 5.215 Authenticated copy of will.

Fla. Prob. R. 5.240 Notice of administration.

Fla. Prob. R. 5.241 Notice to creditors.

Fla. Prob. R. 5.470 Ancillary administration.

Fla. R. Jud. Admin. 2.516 Service of pleadings and documents.

Cross References

Recordation of probate records, see F.S.A. § 28.223.

Rule 5.490.   Form and Manner of Presenting Claim

(a) **Form.** A creditor's statement of claim shall be verified and filed with the clerk and shall state:

(1) the basis for the claim;

(2) the amount claimed;

(3) the name and address of the creditor;

(4) the security for the claim, if any; and

(5) whether the claim is currently due or involves an uncertainty and, if not due, then the due date and, if contingent or unliquidated, the nature of the uncertainty.

(b) **Copy.** At the time of filing the claim, the creditor shall also furnish the clerk with a copy thereof.

(c) **Mailing.** The clerk shall mail a copy of claims, noting the fact and date of mailing on the original, to the attorney for the personal representative unless all personal representatives file a notice directing that copies of claims be mailed to a designated personal representative or attorney of record.   Absent designation, a copy of claims shall be mailed to the attorney for the personal representative named first in the letters of administration.

(d) Validity of Claim.   Failure to deliver or receive a copy of the claim shall not affect the validity of the claim.

(e) Amending Claims.   If a claim as filed is sufficient to notify interested persons of its substance but is otherwise defective as to form, the court may permit the claim to be amended at any time.

(f) Service by Personal Representative.   If the personal representative files a claim individually, or in any other capacity creating a conflict of interest between the personal representative and any interested person, then at the time the claim is filed, the personal representative shall serve all interested persons with a copy of the claim and notice of the right to object to the claim.   The notice shall state that an interested person may object to a claim as provided by law and rule 5.496.   Service shall be either by informal notice or in the manner provided for service of formal notice.   Service on one interested person by a chosen method shall not preclude service on another interested person by another method.

Amended Sept. 13, 1984, effective Jan. 1, 1985 (458 So.2d 1079); Sept. 29, 1988, effective Jan. 1, 1989 (537 So.2d 500); July 5, 2007, effective Jan. 1, 2008 (959 So.2d 1170).

Committee Notes

Subdivision (e) of this rule represents a rule implementation of the procedure found in section 733.704, Florida Statutes.   It is not intended to change the effect of the statute from which it was derived but has been reformatted to conform with the structure of these rules.   It is not intended to create a new procedure or modify an existing procedure.

Rule History

1975 Revision: Sets forth the claims procedure to be followed and clarifies the matter of delivery of copies where there are multiple personal representatives or where the attorney of record desires to accept such delivery.

1984 Revision: Extensive editorial changes and requires furnishing of copy of claim to the attorney for the personal representative.   Committee notes revised.

1988 Revision: Clarifies the matter of delivery of copies and directs the clerk to mail the same to the attorney for the personal representative unless designations are filed by all personal representatives to the contrary.   Subdivision (e) added to implement the procedure found in section 733.704, Florida Statutes.   Editorial changes.   Committee notes expanded.   Citation form change in committee notes.

1992 Revision: Committee notes revised.   Citation form changes in committee notes.

1999 Revision: Reference to repealed rule deleted from committee notes.

2003 Revision: Committee notes revised.

2007 Revision: Editorial change in (a).   New (f) added, providing procedure for notice when personal representative files a claim individually or otherwise has a conflict of interest with any interested person regarding a claim.

Statutory References

§ 731.104, Fla. Stat. Verification of documents.

§ 733.2121, Fla. Stat. Notice to creditors; filing of claims.

§ 733.702, Fla. Stat. Limitations on presentation of claims.

§ 733.703, Fla. Stat. Form and manner of presenting claim.

§ 733.704, Fla. Stat. Amendment of claims.

§ 733.708, Fla. Stat. Compromise.

§ 733.710, Fla. Stat. Limitations on claims against estates.

§ 734.102, Fla. Stat. Ancillary administration.

Rule References

Fla. Prob. R. 5.020 Pleadings; verification; motions.

Fla. Prob. R. 5.241 Notice to creditors.

Fla. Prob. R. 5.470 Ancillary administration.

Fla. Prob. R. 5.475 Ancillary administration, short form.

Fla. Prob. R. 5.530 Summary administration.

Cross References

Form and manner of presenting claims, see F.S.A. § 733.703.

Rule 5.496. Form and Manner of Objecting to Claim

(a) Filing. An objection to a claim, other than a personal representative's proof of claim, shall be in writing and filed on or before the expiration of 4 months from the first publication of notice to creditors or within 30 days from the timely filing or amendment of the claim, whichever occurs later.

(b) Service. A personal representative or other interested person who files an objection to the claim shall serve a copy of the objection on the claimant. If the objection is filed by an interested person other than the personal representative, a copy of the objection shall also be served on the personal representative. Any objection shall include a certificate of service.

(c) Notice to Claimant. An objection shall contain a statement that the claimant is limited to a period of 30 days from the date of service of an objection within which to bring an action as provided by law.

Added Sept. 24, 1992, effective Jan. 1, 1993 (607 So.2d 1306). Amended June 19, 2003 (848 So.2d 1069); Sept. 29, 2005, effective Jan. 1, 2006 (912 So.2d 1178); July 5, 2007, effective Jan. 1, 2008 (959 So.2d 1170); Sept. 2, 2010, effective Jan. 1, 2011 (50 So.3d 578).

Committee Notes

This rule represents an implementation of the procedure found in section 733.705, Florida Statutes, and adds a requirement to furnish notice of the time limitation in which an independent action or declaratory action must be filed after objection to a claim.

Rule History

1992 Revision: New rule.

2003 Revision: Reference in (a) to notice of administration changed to notice to creditors. Committee notes revised.

2005 Revision: Removed provision for objections to personal representative's proof of claim, now addressed in rule 5.498, and subsequent subdivisions relettered. Reference to service on the claimant's attorney removed because service on the attorney is required by rule 5.041(b). Committee notes revised.

2007 Revision: Editorial change in (a). Second sentence of (b) added to specify that the objection must include a certificate of service.

2010 Revision: Subdivision (b) amended to delete the requirement to serve a copy of an objection to a claim within 10 days, and to clarify the requirement to include a certificate of service.

2012 Revision: Committee notes revised.

Statutory References

§ 731.201(4), Fla. Stat. General definitions.

§ 733.705, Fla. Stat. Payment of and objection to claims.

Rule References

Fla. Prob. R. 5.040 Notice.

Fla. Prob. R. 5.041 Service of pleadings and documents.

Fla. Prob. R. 5.498 Personal representative's proof of claim.

Fla. Prob. R. 5.499 Form and manner of objecting to personal representative's proof of claim.

Fla. R. Jud. Admin. 2.516 Service of pleadings and documents.

Cross References

Payment of and objections to claims, see F.S.A. § 733.705.

Rule 5.498. Personal Representative's Proof of Claim

(a) **Contents.** A personal representative's proof of claim shall state:

(1) the basis for each claim;

(2) the amount claimed;

(3) the name and address of the claimant;

(4) the security for the claim, if any;

(5) whether the claim is matured, unmatured, contingent, or unliquidated;

(6) whether the claim has been paid or is to be paid; and

(7) that any objection to a claim listed as to be paid shall be filed no later than 4 months from first publication of the notice to creditors or 30 days from the date of the filing of the proof of claim, whichever occurs later.

(b) **Service.** The proof of claim shall be served at the time of filing or promptly thereafter on all interested persons.

Added Sept. 29, 2005, effective Jan. 1, 2006 (912 So.2d 1178). Amended July 5, 2007, effective Jan. 1, 2008 (959 So.2d 1170).

Committee Notes

This rule represents an implementation of the procedure found in section 733.703(2), Florida Statutes, with respect to a proof of claim filed by the personal representative.

Rule History

2005 Revision: New rule.

2007 Revision: Subdivision (b) amended to eliminate the need to serve claimants listed as paid on the proof of claim, and clarifying editorial change.

2012 Revision: Committee notes revised.

Statutory References

§ 733.703(2), Fla. Stat. Form and manner of presenting claim.

§ 733.705, Fla. Stat. Payment of and objection to claims.

Rule References

Fla. Prob. R. 5.041 Service of pleadings and documents.

Fla. Prob. R. 5.499 Form and manner of objecting to personal representative's proof of claim.

Fla. R. Jud. Admin. 2.516 Service of pleadings and documents.

Rule 5.499. Form and Manner of Objecting to Personal Representative's Proof of Claim

(a) Filing. An objection to a personal representative's proof of claim shall be in writing and filed on or before the expiration of 4 months from the first publication of notice to creditors or within 30 days from the timely filing of the proof of claim, whichever occurs later.

(b) Contents. The objection shall identify the particular item or items to which objection is made. An objection to an item listed on the proof of claim as to be paid shall also contain a statement that the claimant is limited to a period of 30 days from the date of service of an objection within which to bring an independent action as provided by law.

(c) Items Listed as Paid. If an objection is filed to an item listed on the proof of claim as paid, it shall not be necessary for the claimant to file an independent action as to that item. Liability as between estate and the personal representative individually for claims listed on the proof of claim as paid, or for claims treated as if they were listed on the proof of claim as paid, shall be determined in the estate administration, in a proceeding for accounting or surcharge, or in another appropriate proceeding, whether or not an objection has been filed.

(d) Items Paid Before Objection. If an item listed as to be paid is paid by the personal representative prior to the filing of an objection as to that item, the item shall be treated as if it were listed on the proof of claim as paid.

(e) Service. The objector shall serve a copy of the objection on the personal representative and, in the case of any objection to an item listed as to be paid, shall also serve a copy on that claimant within 10 days after the filing of the objection. In the case of an objection to an item listed as to be paid, the objection shall include a certificate of service.

Added Sept. 29, 2005, effective Jan. 1, 2006 (912 So.2d 1178). Amended July 5, 2007, effective Jan. 1, 2008 (959 So.2d 1170).

Committee Notes

This rule represents an implementation of the procedure found in section 733.705, Florida Statutes, with respect to a proof of claim filed by the personal representative. The rule recognizes the different treatment between items listed on a proof of claim as having been paid versus items listed as to be paid. An objection to an item listed as to be paid is treated in the same manner as a creditor's claim and there is a requirement to furnish notice of the time limitation in which an independent action or declaratory action must be filed after objection to a claim.

Rule History

2005 Revision: New rule.

2007 Revision: Editorial change in (a). Extensive revisions to rest of rule to clarify the differences in procedure between items listed as paid and items listed as to be paid. Committee notes revised.

2012 Revision: Committee notes revised.

Statutory Reference

§ 733.705, Fla. Stat. Payment of and objection to claims.

Rule References

Fla. Prob. R. 5.040 Notice.

Fla. Prob. R. 5.041 Service of pleadings and documents.

Fla. Prob. R. 5.496 Form and manner of objecting to claim.

Fla. Prob. R. 5.498 Personal representative's proof of claim.

Fla. R. Jud. Admin. 2.516 Service of pleadings and documents.

Rule 5.510.　Establishment and Probate of Lost or Destroyed Will

(a) **Proceeding.**　The establishment and probate of a lost or destroyed will shall be in one proceeding.

(b) **Petition.**　The petition, in addition to reciting information required under these rules for petition for administration, shall include a statement of the facts constituting grounds on which relief is sought, and a statement of the contents of the will or, if available, a copy of the will.

(c) **Testimony.**　The testimony of each witness in the proceeding shall be reduced to writing and filed and may be used as evidence in any contest of the will if the witness has died or moved from the state.

(d) **Notice.**　No lost or destroyed will shall be admitted to probate unless formal notice has been given to those who, but for the will, would be entitled to the property thereby devised.

(e) **Order.**　The order admitting the will to probate shall state in full its terms and provisions.
Amended March 31, 1977, effective July 1, 1977 (344 So.2d 828); Sept. 13, 1984, effective Jan. 1, 1985 (458 So.2d 1079); Sept. 29, 1988, effective Jan. 1, 1989 (537 So.2d 500); May 2, 2002 (824 So.2d 849).

Committee Notes

This rule represents a rule implementation of the procedure formerly found in section 733.207, Florida Statutes. It is not intended to change the effect of the statute from which it was derived but has been reformatted to conform with the structure of these rules. It is not intended to create a new procedure or modify an existing procedure.

Rule History

1977 Revision: Editorial change in subdivision (c) of prior rule.

1984 Revision: Extensive changes. Committee notes revised.

1988 Revision: Rule rewritten to conform to statute. Committee notes expanded. Citation form change in committee notes.

1992 Revision: Committee notes revised. Citation form changes in committee notes.

2002 Revision: Subdivision (d) added to implement procedure formerly found in section 733.207(3), Florida Statutes. Committee notes revised.

2003 Revision: Committee notes revised.

2012 Revision: Committee notes revised.

Statutory Reference

§ 733.207, Fla. Stat. Establishment and probate of lost or destroyed will.

Rule References

Fla. Prob. R. 5.020 Pleadings; verification; motions.

Fla. Prob. R. 5.025 Adversary proceedings.

Fla. Prob. R. 5.040 Notice.

Fla. Prob. R. 5.041 Service of pleadings and documents.

Fla. Prob. R. 5.042 Time.

Fla. Prob. R. 5.200 Petition for administration.

Fla. R. Jud. Admin. 2.516 Service of pleadings and documents.

Cross References

Discovery of later will, see F.S.A. § 733.208.
Lost or destroyed wills, establishment, see F.S.A. § 733.207.
Revocation of will,
    Acts, see F.S.A. § 732.506.
    Revival by revocation, see F.S.A. § 732.508.
    Subsequent writings, see F.S.A. § 732.505.

Rule 5.530. Summary Administration

(a) Petition. The petition must be verified as required by law and must contain:

(1) a statement of the interest of each petitioner, each petitioner's name and address, and the name and office address of each petitioner's attorney;

(2) the name and last known address of the decedent, last 4 digits of the decedent's social security number, date and place of death of the decedent, and state and county of the decedent's domicile;

(3) so far as is known, the names and addresses of the surviving spouse, if any, and the beneficiaries and their relationship to the decedent and the year of birth of any who are minors;

(4) a statement showing venue;

(5) a statement whether domiciliary or principal proceedings are pending in another state or country, if known, and the name and address of the foreign personal representative and the court issuing letters;

(6) a statement that the decedent's will, if any, does not direct administration as required by chapter 733, Florida Statutes;

(7) a statement that the value of the entire estate subject to administration in this state, less the value of property exempt from the claims of creditors, does not exceed $75,000 or that the decedent has been dead for more than 2 years;

(8) a description of all assets in the estate and the estimated value of each, and a separate description of any protected homestead and exempt property;

(9) a statement either;

(A) that all creditors' claims are barred or

(B) that a diligent search and reasonable inquiry for any known or reasonably ascertainable creditors has been made and one of the following:

(i) A statement that the estate is not indebted.

(ii) The name and address of each creditor, the nature of the debt, the amount of the debt and whether the amount is estimated or exact, and when the debt is due. If provision for payment of the debt has been made other than for full payment in the proposed order of distribution, the following information must be shown:

(a) The name of the person who will pay the debt.

(b) The creditor's written consent for substitution or assumption of the debt by another person.

(c) The amount to be paid if the debt has been compromised.

(d) The terms for payment and any limitations on the liability of the person paying the debt.

(10) in an intestate estate, a statement that after the exercise of reasonable diligence each petitioner is unaware of any unrevoked wills or codicils;

(11) in a testate estate, a statement identifying all unrevoked wills and codicils being presented for probate, and a statement that each petitioner is unaware of any other unrevoked will or codicil; and

(12) a schedule of proposed distribution of all probate assets and the person to whom each asset is to be distributed.

(b) Service. The joinder in, or consent to, a petition for summary administration is not required of a beneficiary who will receive full distributive share under the proposed distribution. Any beneficiary and any known or reasonably ascertainable creditor not joining or consenting must receive formal notice of the petition.

(c) Testate Estate. In a testate estate, on the filing of the petition for summary administration, the decedent's will must be proved and admitted to probate.

(d) Order. If the court determines that the decedent's estate qualifies for summary administration, it must enter an order distributing the probate assets and specifically designating the person to whom each asset is to be distributed.

Amended March 31, 1977, effective July 1, 1977 (344 So.2d 828); Sept. 13, 1984, effective Jan. 1, 1985 (458 So.2d 1079); Sept. 29, 1988, effective Jan. 1, 1989 (537 So.2d 500); Sept. 24, 1992, effective Jan. 1, 1993 (607 So.2d 1306); May 2, 2002 (824 So.2d 849); Sept. 29, 2005, effective Jan. 1, 2006 (912 So.2d 1178); July 5, 2007, effective Jan. 1, 2008 (959 So.2d 1170); Nov. 3, 2011, effective, *nunc pro tunc*, Oct. 1, 2011 (78 So.3d 1045); Sept. 26, 2013, effective Jan. 1, 2014 (123 So.3d 31); May 22, 2014, effective May 22, 2014 (139 So.3d 875).

Committee Notes

Verification and service of a petition for summary administration are governed by rules 5.020, 5.040, and 5.041. Section 735.206(2), Florida Statutes, relating to diligent search for, and service of the petition for summary administration on, reasonably ascertainable creditors is substantive. Nothing in this rule is intended to change the effect of the statutory amendments.

Rule History

1977 Revision: Changes to conform to 1975 statutory revision. Established the requirements of a petition for summary administration and provided for the hearing thereon and the entry of the order of distribution of the assets.

1984 Revision: Extensive revisions and editorial changes. Committee notes revised.

1988 Revision: Editorial change in caption of (a). Committee notes revised.

1992 Revision: Editorial changes. Committee notes revised. Citation form changes in committee notes.

2002 Revision: Replaces "homestead" with "protected homestead" in (a)(2) to conform to addition of term in section 731.201(29), Florida Statutes. Committee notes revised.

2003 Revision: Committee notes revised.

2005 Revision: Subdivision (a)(3) amended to include requirements of section 735.206(2), Florida Statutes.

2007 Revision: Rule substantially rewritten to require petition to include essentially the same information required to be stated in a petition for administration and to require the petitioners to specify facts showing they are entitled to summary administration. New subdivision (b) added to provide for formal notice of the petition, and subsequent subdivisions relettered.

2011 Revision: Subdivision (a)(2) amended to limit listing of decedent's social security number to last four digits.

2012 Revision: Committee notes revised.

2013 Revision: Subdivision (a)(9) reorganized to avoid the misconception that a diligent search and reasonable inquiry for known or reasonably ascertainable creditors is required when creditor claims are barred. Committee notes revised. Editorial changes to conform to the court's guidelines for rules submissions as set forth in AOSC06–14.

2014 Revision: Subdivision (a)(3) amended to provide only the year of birth of a minor to conform to Fla. R. Jud. Admin. 2.425. Committee notes revised.

Statutory References

§ 731.104, Fla. Stat. Verification of documents.

§§ 735.201–735.2063, Fla. Stat. Summary administration.

Rule References

Fla. Prob. R. 5.020 Pleadings; verification; motions.

Fla. Prob. R. 5.040 Notice.

Fla. Prob. R. 5.041 Service of pleadings and documents.

Fla. Prob. R. 5.205(a)(3) Filing evidence of death.

Fla. R. Jud. Admin. 2.420 Public access to judicial branch records.

Fla. R. Jud. Admin. 2.425 Minimization of the filing of sensitive information.

Fla. R. Jud. Admin. 2.516 Service of pleadings and documents.

Cross References

Summary administration,
> Distribution, see F.S.A. § 735.206.
> Manner, see F.S.A. § 735.202.
> Maximum estate, increased statutory amount, see F.S.A. § 735.201.
> Nature, see F.S.A. § 735.201.
> Petition, see F.S.A. § 735.203.

PART III. GUARDIANSHIP

Rule 5.540. Hearings

(a) Application. All hearings under chapter 744 and under section 393.12, Florida Statutes, shall be open unless the alleged incapacitated person, adjudicated ward, or person alleged to have a developmental disability elects to have the hearing closed.

(b) Election. An election to close a hearing may be made before the hearing by filing a written notice. Subject to the court's approval, an election to close or reopen a hearing may be made at any time during the hearing by oral or written motion.

Added Aug. 22, 1991, effective Oct. 1, 1991 (584 So.2d 964). Amended July 10, 2008 (986 So.2d 576).

Committee Notes

This rule permits an alleged incapacitated person, adjudicated ward, or person alleged to have a developmental disability to elect to have all hearings open or closed at any time by oral or written election.

Rule History

1991 Revision: New rule.

1992 Revision: Committee notes revised.

2008 Revision: Subdivision (a) amended to include persons with a developmental disability. Committee notes revised.

Statutory References

§ 393.12, Fla. Stat. Capacity; appointment of guardian advocate.

§ 744.1095, Fla. Stat. Hearings.

§ 744.3085, Fla. Stat. Guardian advocates.

Rule References

Fla. Prob. R. 5.541 Recording of hearings.

Historical Notes

Former Provisions:

A former Rule 5.540, relating to definitions, was deleted Sept. 29, 1988, effective Jan. 1, 1989 (531 So.2d 1261).

Cross References

Definitions, see Probate Rule 5.015.
Guardianship law definitions, see F.S.A. § 744.102.
Minor, definition, see F.S.A. § 1.01.
Minors, removal of disabilities of nonage of minors over sixteen, see F.S.A. § 743.015.
Rights, privileges and obligations of persons 18 years of age or older, see F.S.A. § 743.07.

Rule 5.541. Recording of Hearings

Electronic or stenographic recordings shall be made of all hearings on the:

(a) adjudication of incapacity;

(b) appointment of a guardian;

(c) modification, termination, or revocation of the adjudication of incapacity;

(d) restoration of capacity; or

(e) restoration of rights.

Added Aug. 22, 1991, effective Oct. 1, 1991 (584 So.2d 964). Amended Sept. 24, 1992, effective Jan. 1, 1993 (607 So.2d 1306); July 10, 2008 (986 So.2d 576).

Committee Notes

This rule represents a rule implementation of the procedure found in sections 744.109 and 744.3031, Florida Statutes. It is not intended to change the effect of the statutes from which it is derived, or to create a new procedure or modify an existing procedure.

Rule History

1991 Revision: New rule.

1992 Revision: Editorial changes. Committee notes revised. Citation form change in committee notes.

2003 Revision: Committee notes revised.

2008 Revision: New subdivision (e) added for proceedings involving guardian advocates. Committee notes revised.

Statutory References

§ 393.12, Fla. Stat. Capacity; appointment of guardian advocate.

§ 744.109, Fla. Stat. Records.

§ 744.3031, Fla. Stat. Emergency temporary guardianship.

§ 744.3085, Fla. Stat. Guardian advocates.

§ 744.3371, Fla. Stat. Notice of petition for appointment of guardian and hearing.

Rule 5.550. Petition to Determine Incapacity

(a) **Contents.** The petition to determine incapacity shall be verified by the petitioner and shall state:

(1) the name, age, and present address of the petitioner and the petitioner's relationship to the alleged incapacitated person;

(2) the name, age, county of residence, and present address of the alleged incapacitated person, and specify the primary language spoken by the alleged incapacitated person, if known;

(3) that the petitioner believes the alleged incapacitated person to be incapacitated, the facts on which such belief is based, and the names and addresses of all persons known to the petitioner who have knowledge of such facts through personal observation;

(4) the name and address of the alleged incapacitated person's attending or family physician, if known;

(5) which rights the alleged incapacitated person is incapable of exercising to the best of the petitioner's knowledge; and, if the petitioner has insufficient experience to make that judgment, the petitioner shall so indicate;

(6) whether plenary or limited guardianship is sought for the alleged incapacitated person; and

(7) the names, relationships, and addresses of the next of kin of the alleged incapacitated person, specifying the year of birth of any who are minors, to the extent known to the petitioner.

(b) **Notice.**

(1) *Contents.* The notice of filing the petition to determine incapacity shall state:

(A) the time and place of the hearing to inquire into the capacity of the alleged incapacitated person;

(B) that an attorney has been appointed to represent such person; and

(C) that if the court determines that such person is incapable of exercising any of the rights enumerated in the petition a guardian may be appointed.

(2) *Service on Alleged Incapacitated Person.* The notice and a copy of the petition to determine incapacity shall be personally served by an elisor appointed by the court, who may be the court appointed counsel for the alleged incapacitated person. The elisor shall read the notice to the alleged incapacitated person, but need not read the petition. A return of service shall be filed by the elisor certifying that the notice and petition have been served on and the notice read to the alleged incapacitated person. No responsive pleading is required and no default may be entered for failure to file a responsive pleading. The allegations of the petition are deemed denied.

(3) *Service on Others.* A copy of the petition and the notice shall also be served on counsel for the alleged incapacitated person, and on all next of kin.

(c) Verified Statement. An interested person may file a verified statement that shall state:

(1) that he or she has a good faith belief that the alleged incapacitated person's trust, trust amendment, or durable power of attorney is invalid; and

(2) facts constituting a reasonable basis for that belief.

(d) Order. When an order determines that a person is incapable of exercising delegable rights, it shall specify whether there is an alternative to guardianship that will sufficiently address the problems of the incapacitated person.

Amended Sept. 4, 1980, effective Jan. 1, 1981 (387 So.2d 949); Sept. 13, 1984, effective Jan. 1, 1985 (458 So.2d 1079); Sept. 29, 1989, effective Oct. 1, 1989 (549 So.2d 665); Nov. 17, 1989 (551 So.2d 452); Aug. 22, 1991, effective Oct. 1, 1991 (584 So.2d 964); Feb. 1, 2007 (948 So.2d 735); May 22, 2014, effective May 22, 2014 (139 So.3d 875).

Committee Notes

Rule History

1980 Revision: Implements 1979 amendments to section 744.331, Florida Statutes.

1984 Revision: Change in title of rule. Editorial changes and adds a provision for service of petition. Committee notes revised.

1988 Revision: Committee notes revised. Citation form changes in committee notes.

1989 Revision by Ad Hoc Committee: The committee realized that formal notice as defined in rule 5.040(a)(1) requires the recipient of notice to file a responsive pleading within 20 days after the service of the notice. The committee believed that to impose such a requirement on the alleged incapacitated person would contravene the legislative intent of the 1989 revisions to chapter 744, Florida Statutes. The committee observed that the time required for appointment of mandatory appointed counsel might render a responsive pleading within 20 days impossible for the alleged incapacitated person. The committee concluded that, procedurally, notice upon the alleged incapacitated person should occur in the same manner as formal notice in rule 5.040, but the required response under that rule should not be imposed upon the alleged incapacitated person.

1991 Revision: Implements 1989 amendments to sections 744.3201 and 744. 331, Florida Statutes, and 1990 technical amendments.

1992 Revision: Citation form changes in committee notes.

2006 Revision: Subdivisions (c) and (d) added to incorporate 2006 amendment to section 744.441 and creation of section 744.462, Florida Statutes. Committee notes revised.

2014 Revision: Amends subdivision (a)(7) to conform with Fla. R. Jud. Admin. 2.425. Committee notes revised.

Statutory References

§ 744.3201, Fla. Stat. Petition to determine incapacity.

§ 744.331, Fla. Stat. Procedures to determine incapacity.

§ 744.3371, Fla. Stat. Notice of petition for appointment of guardian and hearing.

§ 744.441(11), Fla. Stat. Powers of guardian upon court approval.

§ 744.462, Fla. Stat. Determination regarding alternatives to guardianship.

Rule References

Fla. Prob. R. 5.020 Pleadings; verification; motions.

Fla. Prob. R. 5.040(a)(3) Notice.

Fla. Prob. R. 5.800(a) Application of revised chapter 744 to existing guardianships.

Fla. R. Jud. Admin. 2.425 Minimization of the Filing of Sensitive Information.

Cross References

Florida Mental Health Act, see F.S.A. § 394.451 et seq.
Procedures to determine incapacity, see F.S.A. § 744.331.

Rule 5.552. Voluntary Guardianship of Property

(a) **Petition for Appointment of Guardian.** The petition for voluntary guardianship shall be verified by the petitioner and shall state:

(1) the facts to establish venue;

(2) the petitioner's residence and post office address;

(3) that the petitioner although mentally competent is incapable of the care, custody, and management of the petitioner's estate by reason of age or physical infirmity, and is voluntarily petitioning to have a guardian of the petitioner's property appointed;

(4) whether the guardianship shall apply to all of the petitioner's property or less than all of the petitioner's property; and if less than all of the petitioner's property, the specific property to which the guardianship is to apply;

(5) the name and residence and post office address of any proposed guardian;

(6) that the proposed guardian is qualified to serve or that a willing and qualified proposed guardian has not been located; and

(7) the names and post office addresses of persons to whom the petitioner requests that notice of the hearing for the appointment of the guardian, and any petition for authority to act, be given.

(b) **Certificate of Licensed Physician.** The petition shall be accompanied by a certificate of a licensed physician as required by law.

(c) **Notice of Hearing.** Notice of hearing on the petition for appointment, and any petition for authority to act, shall be given to the ward and any person to whom the ward requests notice be given, which request can be made in the petition for appointment or a subsequent written request for notice signed by the ward.

(d) **Annual Report.** The annual report shall be accompanied by a certificate from a licensed physician as required by law.

(e) **Termination.** The ward may terminate a voluntary guardianship by filing a notice of termination. Copies of the notice shall be served on all interested persons. The guardian shall file a petition for discharge in accordance with these rules.

Added June 19, 2003, effective Jan. 1, 2004 (848 So.2d 1069); Feb. 1, 2007 (948 So.2d 735).

Committee Notes

Rule History

2003 Revision: New rule.

2006 Revision: New (d) added to incorporate 2006 amendment to section 744.341, Florida Statutes, requiring inclusion of physician's certificate in annual report, and subsequent subdivision relettered. Committee notes revised.

Statutory References

§ 744.341, Fla. Stat. Voluntary guardianship.

Rule References

Fla. Prob. R. 5.680 Termination of guardianship.

Fla. Prob. R. 5.695 Annual guardianship report.

Rule 5.555. Guardianships of Minors

(a) Application. This rule shall apply to any guardianship for a minor.

(b) Petition to Determine Incapacity. No petition to determine incapacity need be filed.

(c) Petition for Appointment of Guardian. The petition shall be verified by the petitioner and shall state:

(1) the facts to establish venue;

(2) the petitioner's residence and post office address;

(3) the name, age, and residence and post office address of the minor;

(4) the names and addresses of the parents of the minor and if none, the next of kin known to the petitioner;

(5) the name and residence and post office address of the proposed guardian, and that the proposed guardian is qualified to serve; or, that a willing and qualified guardian has not been located;

(6) the proposed guardian's relationship to and any previous association with the minor;

(7) the reasons why the proposed guardian should be appointed; and

(8) the nature and value of the property subject to the guardianship.

(d) Notice. Formal notice of the petition for appointment of guardian shall be served on any parent who is not a petitioner or, if there is no parent, on the persons with whom the minor resides and on such other persons as the court may direct.

(e) Initial and Annual Guardianship Reports.

(1) The initial guardianship report shall consist only of the verified inventory. The annual guardianship report shall consist only of the annual accounting.

(2) The guardian shall file an initial and annual guardianship plan as required by law.

(3) Unless otherwise ordered by the court or required by law, the guardian need not serve a copy of the initial guardianship report and the annual guardianship reports on the ward.

(f) Inspection of Inventory or Accounting. Unless otherwise ordered by the court for good cause shown, any inventory, amended or supplementary inventory, or accounting is subject to inspection only by the clerk, the ward or the ward's attorney, and the guardian or the guardian's attorney.

Added Aug. 22, 1991, effective Oct. 1, 1991 (584 So.2d 964). Amended Oct. 3, 1996, effective Jan. 1, 1997 (683 So.2d 78); Sept. 28, 2000, effective Jan. 1, 2001 (778 So.2d 272); June 19, 2003, effective Jan. 1, 2004 (848 So.2d 1069); Feb. 1, 2007 (948 So.2d 735).

Committee Notes

The provisions of chapter 744, Florida Statutes, and the guardianship rules enacted in 1989 leave some uncertainty with respect to the procedural requirements in guardianships for minors who are not incapacitated persons. This rule is intended to address only certain procedures with respect to the establishment and administration of guardianships over minors. The committee believes that certain provisions of the guardianship law and rules apply to both guardianships of minors as well as guardianships of incapacitated persons and no change has been suggested with respect to such rules. Because no adjudication of a minor is required by statute, it is contemplated that appointment of a guardian for a minor may be accomplished without a hearing. Initial and annual guardianship reports for minors have been simplified where all assets are on deposit with a designated financial institution under applicable Florida law.

Rule History

1991 Revision: New rule adopted to apply to guardianships over minors who are not incapacitated persons.

1992 Revision: Committee notes revised. Citation form changes in committee notes.

1996 Revision: Committee notes revised.

2000 Revision: Deletes requirement in subdivision (c) to report social security number of proposed guardian.

2003 Revision: Deletes requirement in subdivision (c) to report social security number of minor. Committee notes revised.

2006 Revision: Subdivision (e)(2) amended to conform to requirement in sections 744.362(1) and 744.3675, Florida Statutes, to file initial and annual guardianship plans. Subdivision (e)(3) amended to eliminate requirement of service on ward unless ordered by court or required by statute.

2014 Revision: Fla. R. Jud. Admin. 2.425(b)(4)—(5) provides exceptions for using the birth date of any minor "whenever the birth date is necessary for the court to establish or maintain subject matter jurisdiction," as well as using the full name in situations in which the "name of the minor in any order relating to parental responsibility, time-sharing, or child support." Committee notes revised.

Statutory References

§ 69.031, Fla. Stat. Designated financial institutions for assets in hands of guardians, curators, administrators, trustees, receivers, or other officers.

§ 744.3021, Fla. Stat. Guardians of minors.

§ 744.334, Fla. Stat. Petition for appointment of guardian or professional guardian; contents.

§ 744.3371(2), Fla. Stat. Notice of petition for appointment of guardian and hearing.

§ 744.342, Fla. Stat. Minors; guardianship.

§ 744.362, Fla. Stat. Initial guardianship report.

§ 744.363, Fla. Stat. Initial guardianship plan.

§ 744.365, Fla. Stat. Verified inventory.

§ 744.367, Fla. Stat. Duty to file annual guardianship report.

§ 744.3675, Fla. Stat. Annual guardianship plan.

§ 744.3678, Fla. Stat. Annual accounting.

§ 744.3679, Fla. Stat. Simplified accounting procedures in certain cases.

Rule References

Fla. Prob. R. 5.040 Notice.

Fla. Prob. R. 5.541 Recording of hearings.

Fla. Prob. R. 5.560 Petition for appointment of guardian of an incapacitated person.

Fla. Prob. R. 5.620 Inventory.

Fla. Prob. R. 5.636 Settlement of minors' claims.

Fla. Prob. R. 5.690 Initial guardianship report.

Fla. R. Jud. Admin. 2.425 Minimization of the Filing of Sensitive Information.

Rule 5.560. Petition for Appointment of Guardian of an Incapacitated Person

(a) Contents. The petition shall be verified by the petitioner and shall state:

(1) the facts to establish venue;

(2) the petitioner's residence and post office address;

(3) the name, age, and residence and post office address of the alleged incapacitated person;

(4) the nature of the incapacity, the extent of guardianship, either limited or plenary, requested for the alleged incapacitated person, and the nature and value of property subject to the guardianship;

(5) the names and addresses of the next of kin of the alleged incapacitated person known to the petitioner;

(6) the name and residence and post office address of the proposed guardian, and that the proposed guardian is qualified to serve, or that a willing and qualified guardian has not been located;

(7) the proposed guardian's relationship to and any previous association with the alleged incapacitated person;

(8) the reasons why the proposed guardian should be appointed;

(9) whether there are alternatives to guardianship known to the petitioner that may sufficiently address the problems of the alleged incapacitated person in whole or in part; and

(10) if the proposed guardian is a professional guardian, a statement that the proposed guardian has complied with the registration requirements of section 744.1083, Florida Statutes.

(b) Notice. Notice of filing the petition for appointment of guardian may be served as a part of the notice of filing the petition to determine incapacity, but shall be served a reasonable time before the hearing on the petition or other pleading seeking appointment of a guardian.

(c) Service on Public Guardian. If the petitioner requests appointment of the public guardian, a copy of the petition and the notice shall be served on the public guardian.

Amended Sept. 4, 1980, effective Jan. 1, 1981 (387 So.2d 949); Sept. 13, 1984, effective Jan. 1, 1985 (458 So.2d 1079); Dec. 23, 1987 (517 So.2d 675); Sept. 29, 1988, effective Jan. 1, 1989 (537 So.2d 500); Sept. 29, 1989, effective Oct. 1, 1989 (549 So.2d 665); Nov. 17, 1989 (551 So.2d 452); Aug. 22, 1991, effective Oct. 1, 1991 (584 So.2d 964); Oct. 3, 1996, effective Jan. 1, 1997 (683 So.2d 78); Sept. 28, 2000, effective Jan. 1, 2001 (778 So.2d 272); Feb. 1, 2007 (948 So.2d 140).

Committee Notes

Rule History

1975 Revision: Substantially the same as section 744.334, Florida Statutes, expanded to include provisions of section 744.302, Florida Statutes, and section 744.312, Florida Statutes, by reference.

1977 Revision: Change in committee notes to conform to statutory renumbering.

1980 Revision: Implements 1979 amendment to section 744.334, Florida Statutes.

1984 Revision: Combines rule 5.560 and part of prior rule 5.570. Editorial changes and committee notes revised.

1988 Revision: Editorial changes. Committee notes revised. Citation form changes in committee notes.

1989 Revision by Ad Hoc Committee: Subdivision (a)(4) of the former rule has been deleted altogether because the date and court of adjudication will probably not be known at the time of filing the petition for the appointment since petition for appointment will henceforth be filed contemporaneously with the petition to determine incapacity.

1991 Revision: Implements 1989 amendments to sections 744.334 and 744.331(1), Florida Statutes, and 1990 technical amendments. Subdivision (c)(1) deleted because rule 5.555(d) addresses service on parents.

1992 Revision: Citation form changes in committee notes.

1996 Revision: Deletes requirement in subdivision (a) to report social security number of alleged incapacitated person. Adds provision to subdivision (b) for notice before hearing when petition is not served simultaneously with petition to determine incapacity.

2000 Revision: Deletes requirement in subdivision (a) to report social security number of proposed guardian.

2003 Revision: Committee notes revised.

2006 Revision: New (a)(9) added to incorporate 2006 passage of section 744.462, Florida Statutes. Subdivision (a)(10) added to implement section 744.1083, Florida Statutes. Committee notes revised.

2014 Revision: Fla. R. Jud. Admin. 2.425(b)(4)—(5) provides exceptions for using the birth date of any minor "whenever the birth date is necessary for the court to establish or maintain subject matter jurisdiction," as well as using the full name in situations in which the "name of the minor in any order relating to parental responsibility, time-sharing, or child support." Committee notes revised.

Statutory References

§ 744.1083, Fla. Stat. Professional guardian registration.

§ 744.309, Fla. Stat. Who may be appointed guardian of a resident ward.

§ 744.312, Fla. Stat. Considerations in appointment of guardian.

§ 744.331, Fla. Stat. Procedures to determine incapacity.

§ 744.334, Fla. Stat. Petition for appointment of guardian or professional guardian; contents.

§ 744.3371(1), Fla. Stat. Notice of petition for appointment of guardian and hearing.

§ 744.341, Fla. Stat. Voluntary guardianship.

§ 744.344, Fla. Stat. Order of appointment.

§ 744.462, Fla. Stat. Determination regarding alternatives to guardianship.

§ 744.703, Fla. Stat. Office of public guardian; appointment, notification.

Rule References

Fla. Prob. R. 5.020 Pleadings; verification; motions.

Fla. Prob. R. 5.040 Notice.

Fla. Prob. R. 5.550 Petition to determine incapacity.

Fla. R. Jud. Admin. 2.425 Minimization of the Filing of Sensitive Information.

Cross References

Petition for appointment of guardian or professional guardian, see F.S.A. § 744.334.

Preference in appointment of guardian, see F.S.A. § 744.312.

Public Guardianship Act, see F.S.A. § 744.701 et seq.

Rule 5.590. Application For Appointment as Guardian; Disclosure Statement; Filing

(a) Individual Applicants.

(1) The application for appointment shall contain:

(A) the applicant's qualifications to serve as a guardian, including a statement indicating whether the applicant has ever been (i) arrested or (ii) convicted of a felony, even if the record of such arrest or conviction has been expunged, unless the expunction was ordered pursuant to section 943.0583, Florida Statutes; and

(B) the names of all wards who are adults and the initials of any ward who is a minor for whom the applicant is then acting as guardian, the court file number and circuit court in which each case is pending, and a statement as to whether the applicant is acting as a limited or plenary guardian of the person or property, or both, of each ward.

(2) The application for appointment shall be filed and served a reasonable time before the hearing on the appointment of a guardian.

(b) Nonprofit Corporate Guardians.

(1) No application for appointment shall be required of a nonprofit corporate guardian.

(2) A disclosure statement shall contain:

(A) the corporation's qualifications to serve as a guardian; and

(B) the names of all wards who are adults and the initials of any ward who is a minor for whom the corporation is then acting as guardian, the court file number and circuit court in which each case is pending, and a statement as to whether the corporation is acting as a limited or plenary guardian of the person or property, or both, of each ward.

(3) The disclosure statement of a nonprofit corporate guardian shall be filed quarterly with the clerk of the court for each circuit in which the corporation has been appointed, or is seeking appointment, as guardian.

(c) For Profit Corporations and Associations. No application for appointment or disclosure statement shall be required of any for profit corporation or association authorized to exercise fiduciary powers under Florida law.

(d) Public Guardians. No application for appointment or disclosure statement shall be required of a public guardian.

Added Sept. 29, 1989, effective Oct. 1, 1989 (551 So.2d 452). Amended Aug. 22, 1991, effective Oct. 1, 1991 (584 So.2d 964); Oct. 3, 1996, effective Jan. 1, 1997 (683 So.2d 78); Feb. 1, 2007 (948 So.2d 140); May 22, 2014, effective May 22, 2014 (139 So.3d 875); Nov. 6, 2014, effective Nov. 6, 2014 (150 So.3d 1100).

Committee Notes

Rule History

1988 Revision: Prior rule deleted; text of rule moved to rule 5.650.

1989 Revision: Rule reactivated with different title and text.

1991 Revision: Implements 1989 and 1990 amendments to section 744.3125, Florida Statutes.

1992 Revision: Citation form change in committee notes.

1996 Revision: Adds filing and service provisions consistent with rule 5.560. Corrects reference to corporations qualified to exercise fiduciary powers. Editorial changes. Adds statutory references.

2003 Revision: Committee notes revised.

2006 Revision: Committee notes revised.

2008 Revision: Committee notes revised.

2014 Revision: Amends subdivisions (a)(1)(B) and (b)(1)(B) to conform to Fla. R. Jud. Admin. 2.425. Creates a rule reference. Committee notes revised.

2014 Revision: Amends subdivision (a)(1)(A) to conform to sections 744.309(3), 943.0583, and 943.0585, Florida Statutes. Committee notes revised.

Statutory References

§ 393.063(17), Fla. Stat. Definitions.

§ 393.12, Fla. Stat. Capacity; appointment of guardian advocate.

§ 744.102(4), (9), (11), (14), (22) Fla. Stat. Definitions.

§ 744.3085, Fla. Stat. Guardian advocates.

§ 744.309, Fla. Stat. Who may be appointed guardian of a resident ward.

§ 744.3125, Fla. Stat. Application for appointment.

§ 744.331(1), Fla. Stat. Procedures to determine incapacity.

§ 744.3371, Fla. Stat. Notice of petition for appointment of guardian and hearing.

§ 943.0583, Fla. Stat. Human trafficking victim expunction.

§ 943.0585, Fla. Stat. Court-ordered expunction of criminal history records.

Rule References

Fla. R. Jud. Admin. 2.425 Minimization of the Filing of Sensitive Information.

Historical Notes

A former Rule 5.590, relating to disqualification of a guardian was deleted Sept. 29, 1988, effective Jan. 1, 1989 (531 So.2d 1261).

See, now, Probate Rule 5.650.

Cross References

Application for appointment as guardian, see F.S.A. § 744.3125.

Rule 5.600. Oath

Every guardian or emergency temporary guardian shall take an oath to perform faithfully the duties of guardian or emergency temporary guardian before exercising such authority. The oath may be incorporated in the petition for appointment of guardian, or petition for appointment of emergency temporary guardian, if verified by the prospective guardian.

Amended Sept. 13, 1984, effective Jan. 1, 1985 (458 So.2d 1079); Sept. 29, 1989, effective Oct. 1, 1989 (549 So.2d 665); Nov. 17, 1989 (551 So.2d 452); Aug. 22, 1991, effective Oct. 1, 1991 (584 So.2d 964); Sept. 24, 1992, effective Jan. 1, 1993 (607 So.2d 1306).

Committee Notes

Rule History

1977 Revision: Change in committee notes to conform to statutory renumbering. Rule permits oath of guardian to be incorporated in petition for appointment and in designation of resident agent.

1984 Revision: Editorial change and deletes genders.

1989 Revision: Prior rule adopted as temporary emergency rule.

1991 Revision: Permits oath to be incorporated in application for appointment of guardian, adds reference to temporary emergency guardian, and makes editorial change.

1992 Revision: Editorial changes.

2008 Revision: Committee notes revised.

Statutory References

§ 393.12, Fla. Stat. Capacity; appointment of guardian advocate.

§ 744.347, Fla. Stat. Oath of guardian.

Cross References

Oath of guardian, see F.S.A. § 744.347.
Oath of personal representative, see Probate Rule 5.320.

Rule 5.610.   Execution by Guardian

The guardian shall sign the:

(a) initial guardianship plan;

(b) inventory, amended inventory, or supplemental inventory;

(c) annual guardianship plan;

(d) annual accounting;

(e) guardian's petition for court approval required by law;

(f) petition for discharge;

(g) final report; and

(h) resignation of guardian.

Amended March 31, 1977, effective July 1, 1977 (344 So.2d 828); Sept. 29, 1988, effective Jan. 1, 1989 (537 So.2d 500); Sept. 29, 1989, effective Oct. 1, 1989 (549 So.2d 665); Nov. 17, 1989 (551 So.2d 452); Aug. 22, 1991, effective Oct. 1, 1991 (584 So.2d 964).

Committee Notes

Rule History

1975 Revision: Rule lists what guardian shall sign and includes any petition for court approval required by section 744.441, Florida Statutes. The rule requires that the guardian have actual knowledge of the more important steps and acts of administration.

1977 Revision: Change in statutory reference in rule and in committee note to conform to statutory renumbering.

1988 Revision: Editorial changes. Committee notes revised. Citation form changes in rule and committee notes.

1989 Revision: Prior rule deleted and replaced by temporary emergency rule.

1991 Revision: Changes to conform to 1989 and 1990 revisions to guardianship law. Adds additional documents to be signed by the guardian. Statutory references added.

2003 Revision: Committee notes revised.

2008 Revision: Committee notes revised.

Statutory References

§ 393.12, Fla. Stat. Capacity; appointment of guardian advocate.

§ 744.362, Fla. Stat. Initial guardianship report.

§ 744.363, Fla. Stat. Initial guardianship plan.

§ 744.365, Fla. Stat. Verified inventory.

§ 744.367, Fla. Stat. Duty to file annual guardianship report.

§ 744.3675, Fla. Stat. Annual guardianship plan.

§ 744.3678, Fla. Stat. Annual accounting.

§ 744.387, Fla. Stat. Settlement of claims.

§ 744.441, Fla. Stat. Powers of guardian upon court approval.

§ 744.446, Fla. Stat. Conflicts of interest; prohibited activities; court approval; breach of fiduciary duty.

§ 744.447, Fla. Stat. Petition for authorization to act.

§ 744.451, Fla. Stat. Order.

§ 744.467, Fla. Stat. Resignation of guardian.

§ 744.511, Fla. Stat. Accounting upon removal.

§ 744.521, Fla. Stat. Termination of guardianship.

§ 744.524, Fla. Stat. Termination of guardianship on change of domicile of resident ward.

§ 744.527(1), Fla. Stat. Final reports and application for discharge; hearing.

§ 744.534, Fla. Stat. Disposition of unclaimed funds held by guardian.

Cross References

Powers of guardian upon court approval, see F.S.A. § 744.441.

Rule 5.620. Inventory

(a) Inventory. Within 60 days after issuance of letters, the guardian of the property shall file a verified inventory as required by law. All property not in the guardian's possession as of the date the inventory is filed shall be so identified.

(b) Amended or Supplemental Inventory. If the guardian of the property learns of any property not included in the inventory, or learns that the description in the inventory is inaccurate, the guardian shall, within 30 days of this discovery, file a verified amended or supplemental inventory showing the change.

(c) Substantiating Papers. Unless ordered by the court, the guardian need not file the papers substantiating the inventory. Upon reasonable written request, the guardian of the property shall make the substantiating papers available for examination to those persons entitled to receive or inspect the inventory.

(d) Safe–Deposit Box Inventory. If the ward has a safe-deposit box, a copy of the safe-deposit box inventory shall be filed as part of the verified inventory.

(e) Guardian Advocates. This rule shall apply to a guardian advocate to the extent that the guardian advocate was granted authority over the property of the person with a developmental disability.

Amended Sept. 13, 1984, effective Jan. 1, 1985 (458 So.2d 1079); Sept. 29, 1988, effective Jan. 1, 1989 (537 So.2d 500); Sept. 29, 1989, effective Oct. 1, 1989 (549 So.2d 665); Nov. 17, 1989 (551 So.2d 452); Aug. 22, 1991, effective Oct. 1, 1991 (584 So.2d 964); Sept. 29, 2005, effective Jan. 1, 2006 (912 So.2d 1178); July 12, 2007 (964 So.2d 140); July 10, 2008 (986 So.2d 576).

Committee Notes

Rule History

1977 Revision: Change in committee notes to conform to statutory renumbering.

1984 Revision: Change to require inventory to be filed within 60 days after issuance of letters, rather than after appointment. Committee notes revised.

1988 Revision: Editorial changes. Committee notes revised. Citation form change in committee notes.

1989 Revision: Prior rule deleted and replaced by temporary emergency rule.

1991 Revision: Former rule 5.620(b) has been deleted as partly substantive and addressed in section 744.381, Florida Statutes, and the procedural part is unnecessary.

The committee recognizes the conflict between this rule and section 744. 362, Florida Statutes, which requires the filing of the initial guardianship report (which includes the inventory) within 60 days after appointment. The committee believes this provision, which attempts to regulate when a paper must be filed with the court, is procedural and that a guardian may not receive letters of guardianship empowering the guardian to act contemporaneously with the appointment. Therefore, the issuance of letters is a more practical time from which to measure the beginning of the time period for the accomplishment of this act.

1992 Revision: Citation form changes in committee notes.

2005 Revision: Editorial changes in (d).

2007 Revision: Committee notes revised.

2008 Revision: Adds reference to guardian advocate in new (e). Committee notes revised.

2012 Revision: Committee notes revised.

Statutory References

§ 393.12, Fla. Stat. Capacity; appointment of guardian advocate.

§ 744.362, Fla. Stat. Initial guardianship report.

§ 744.365, Fla. Stat. Verified inventory.

§ 744.3701, Fla. Stat. Inspection of report.

§ 744.381, Fla. Stat. Appraisals.

§ 744.384, Fla. Stat. Subsequently discovered or acquired property.

Rule References

Fla. Prob. R. 5.020 Pleadings; verification; motions.

Fla. Prob. R. 5.041 Service of pleadings and documents.

Fla. Prob. R. 5.060 Request for notices and copies of pleadings.

Fla. Prob. R. 5.610 Execution by guardian.

Fla. Prob. R. 5.649 Guardian advocate.

Fla. Prob. R. 5.690 Initial guardianship report.

Fla. Prob. R. 5.700 Objection to guardianship reports.

Fla. R. Jud. Admin. 2.516 Service of pleadings and documents.

Cross References

Annual guardianship plan, see F.S.A. § 744.3675.
Appraisals, property of the ward, see F.S.A. § 744.381.
Inventory, property of decedent, see Probate Rule 5.340.
Subsequently discovered property of ward, inventory, see F.S.A. § 744.384.
Verified inventory, see F.S.A. § 744.365.

Rule 5.625. Notice of Completion of Guardian Education Requirements

(a) **Filing.** Unless the guardian education requirement is waived by the court, each guardian, other than a professional guardian, shall file with the court within 4 months after the issuance of letters of guardianship or letters of guardian advocacy a notice of completion of guardian education requirements.

(b) Content. The notice shall state:

(1) that the guardian has completed the required number of hours of course instruction and training covering the legal duties and responsibilities of a guardian, the rights of a ward, the availability of local resources to aid a ward, and the preparation of habilitation plans and annual guardianship reports, including accountings;

(2) the date the course was completed;

(3) the name of the course completed; and

(4) the name of the entity or instructor that taught the course.

(c) Verification. The notice shall be verified by the guardian.

Added Sept. 29, 2005, effective Jan. 1, 2006 (912 So.2d 1178). Amended Feb. 1, 2007 (948 So.2d 735); July 10, 2008 (986 So.2d 576).

Committee Notes

Rule History

2005 Revision: New rule.

2006 Revision: Subdivision (a) amended to conform to 2006 amendment to section 744.3145(4), Florida Statutes.

2008 Revision: Adds reference in (a) to guardian advocacy. Committee notes revised.

Statutory References

§ 393.12, Fla. Stat. Capacity; appointment of guardian advocate.

§ 744.3145, Fla. Stat. Guardian education requirements.

Rule 5.630. Petition for Approval of Acts

(a) Contents. When authorization or confirmation of any act of the guardian is required, application shall be made by verified petition stating the facts showing:

(1) the expediency or necessity for the action;

(2) a description of any property involved;

(3) the price and terms of any sale, mortgage, or other contract;

(4) whether the ward has been adjudicated incapacitated to act with respect to the rights to be exercised;

(5) whether the action requested conforms to the guardianship plan; and

(6) the basis for the relief sought.

(b) Notice. No notice of a petition to authorize sale of perishable personal property or of property rapidly deteriorating shall be required. Notice of a petition to perform any other act requiring a court order shall be given to the ward, to the next of kin, if any, and to those persons who have filed requests for notices and copies of pleadings.

(c) Order.

(1) If the act is authorized or confirmed, the order shall describe the permitted act and authorize the guardian to perform it or confirm its performance.

(2) If a sale or mortgage is authorized or confirmed, the order shall describe the property. If a sale is to be private, the order shall specify the price and the terms of the sale. If a sale is to be public, the order shall state that the sale shall be made to the highest bidder and that the court reserves the right to reject all bids.

(3) If the guardian is authorized to bring an action to contest the validity of all or part of a revocable trust, the order shall contain a finding that the action appears to be in the ward's best interests during the ward's probable lifetime. If the guardian is not authorized to bring such an action, the order shall contain a finding concerning the continued need for a guardian and the extent of the need for delegation of the ward's rights.

Amended March 31, 1977, effective July 1, 1977 (344 So.2d 828); Sept. 4, 1980, effective Jan. 1, 1981 (387 So.2d 949); Sept. 29, 1988, effective Jan. 1, 1989 (537 So.2d 500); Sept. 29, 1989, effective Oct. 1, 1989 (549 So.2d 665); Nov. 17, 1989 (551 So.2d 452); Aug. 22, 1991, effective Oct. 1, 1991 (584 So.2d 964); Feb. 1, 2007 (948 So.2d 735); July 12, 2007 (964 So.2d 140).

Committee Notes

Rule History

1975 Revision: Substantially the same as sections 744.503, 744.447, and 744.451, Florida Statutes, with editorial changes.

1977 Revision: Change in statutory reference in rule and in committee note to conform to statutory renumbering.

1980 Revision: Implements 1979 amendment to section 744.447(2), Florida Statutes.

1988 Revision: Editorial changes; captions added to subdivisions. Committee notes revised. Citation form changes in rule and committee notes.

1989 Revision: Prior rule deleted and replaced by temporary emergency rule.

1991 Revision: Changes to conform to 1989 revised guardianship law.

1992 Revision: Committee notes revised. Citation form changes in committee notes.

2006 Revision: New (a)(6) added to incorporate 2006 amendment to section 744.441, Florida Statutes. New (c)(3) added to reflect passage of 2006 amendment to section 737.2065, Florida Statutes. Committee notes revised.

2007 Revision: Committee notes revised.

2008 Revision: Committee notes revised.

2012 Revision: Committee notes revised.

Statutory References

§ 393.12, Fla. Stat. Capacity; appointment of guardian advocate.

§ 736.0207, Fla. Stat. Trust contests.

§ 744.3215, Fla. Stat. Rights of persons determined incapacitated.

§ 744.441, Fla. Stat. Powers of guardian upon court approval.

§ 744.447, Fla. Stat. Petition for authorization to act.

§ 744.451, Fla. Stat. Order.

Rule References

Fla. Prob. R. 5.020 Pleadings; verification; motions.

Fla. Prob. R. 5.025 Adversary proceedings.

Fla. Prob. R. 5.040 Notice.

Fla. Prob. R. 5.041 Service of pleadings and documents.

Fla. Prob. R. 5.060 Request for notices and copies of pleadings.

Fla. Prob. R. 5.610 Execution by guardian.

Fla. Prob. R. 5.636 Settlement of minors' claims.

Fla. Prob. R. 5.649 Guardian advocate.

Fla. R. Jud. Admin. 2.516 Service of pleadings and documents.

Cross References

Order upon petition for authorization to act, see F.S.A. § 744.451.
Petition for authorization to act, see F.S.A. § 744.447.

Rule 5.635. Petition for Extraordinary Authority

(a) **Contents.** When authorization for extraordinary authority is sought as permitted by law, application shall be made by verified petition stating:

(1) the petitioner's interest in the proceeding;

(2) the specific authority requested; and

(3) the facts constituting the basis for the relief sought and that the authority being requested is in the best interest of the ward.

(b) **Notice.**

(1) The petition shall be served by formal notice. For good cause shown, the court may shorten the time for response to the formal notice and may set an expedited hearing.

(2) The petition shall be served on the guardian of the person, if the guardian is not the petitioner, the ward, the next of kin, if any, those interested persons who have filed requests for notices and copies of pleadings, and such other persons as the court may direct.

(c) **Hearing.** The hearing shall be at a time and place that will enable the ward to express the ward's views to the court.

Added Aug. 22, 1991, effective Oct. 1, 1991 (584 So.2d 964).

Committee Notes

Rule History

1991 Revision: New rule.

1992 Revision: Committee notes revised.

2008 Revision: Committee notes revised.

Statutory References

§ 393.12, Fla. Stat. Capacity; appointment of guardian advocate.

§ 744.3215(4), Fla. Stat. Rights of persons determined incapacitated.

§ 744.3725, Fla. Stat. Procedure for extraordinary authority.

Rule 5.636. Settlement of Minors' Claims

(a) **Time of Settlement.** Claims on behalf of minors may be settled either before or after an action is filed.

(b) **Petition.** The petition for approval of a settlement shall contain:

(1) the initials, residence address, and the year of birth of the minor;

(2) the name and address of any guardian appointed for the minor;

(3) the name and residence address of the natural guardians or other persons having legal custody of the minor;

(4) a statement disclosing the interests of any natural or court-appointed guardian whose interest may be in conflict with that of the minor;

(5) a description of the cause of action in which the minor's interest arises;

(6) a summary of the terms of the proposed settlement; and

(7) copies of all agreements, releases, or other documents to be executed on behalf of the minor.

(c) Notice. Notice of the petition shall be given to the court-appointed guardians for the minor, to the natural guardians or other persons with legal custody of the minor, to the minor if age 14 or older, and to the minor's next of kin if required by the court.

(d) Guardian Ad Litem. The court shall appoint a guardian ad litem on behalf of a minor, without bond or notice, with respect to any proposed settlement that exceeds $50,000 and affects the interests of the minor, if:

(1) there is no court-appointed guardian of the minor;

(2) the court-appointed guardian may have an interest adverse to the minor; or

(3) the court determines that representation of the minor's interest is otherwise inadequate.

(e) Valuation of Proposed Settlement. A proposed settlement is deemed to exceed $50,000 if the gross amount payable exceeds $50,000, without reduction to reflect present value or fees and costs.

(f) Report. A guardian ad litem appointed with respect to a proposed settlement affecting the interests of a minor shall, not later than 5 days prior to the hearing on a petition for order authorizing settlement, file and serve a report indicating the guardian ad litem's determination regarding whether the proposed settlement will be in the best interest of the minor. The report shall include:

(1) a statement of the facts of the minor's claim and the terms of the proposed settlement, including any benefits to any persons or parties with related claims;

(2) a list of the persons interviewed and documents reviewed by the guardian ad litem in evaluating the minor's claim and proposed settlement; and

(3) the guardian ad litem's analysis of whether the proposed settlement will be in the best interest of the minor.

A copy of the report shall be served on those persons on whom service is required in subdivision (c) of this rule.

Added Sept. 24, 1992, effective Jan. 1, 1993 (607 So.2d 1306). Amended Feb. 1, 2007 (948 So.2d 735); May 22, 2014, effective May 22, 2014 (139 So.3d 875).

Committee Notes

When a civil action is pending, the petition for approval of settlement should be filed in that civil action. In all other circumstances, the petition for approval of settlement should be filed in the same court and assigned to a judge who would preside over a petition for appointment of guardian of a minor.

The total settlement to be considered under subdivisions (d) and (e) is not limited to the amounts received only by the minor, but includes all settlement payments or proceeds received by all parties to the claim or action. For example, the proposed settlement may have a gross value of $60,000, with $30,000 payable to the minor and $30,000 payable to another party. In that instance the total proposed settlement exceeds $50,000. Further, the "gross amount payable" under subdivision (e) is the total sum payable, without reducing the settlement amount by fees and costs that might be paid from the proceeds of the settlement. For example, if the proposed settlement is $60,000 but $20,000 of that sum will be paid to the attorneys representing the minor's interest in the action, the "gross amount payable" still exceeds $50,000. Likewise, the "gross amount payable" cannot be reduced to reflect the present value of the proposed settlement on behalf of the minor.

Rule History

1992 Revision: New rule.

2003 Revision: Committee notes revised.

2006 Revision: Amended to reflect 2006 passage of new section 744.3025, Claims of Minors, increasing dollar figure from $25,000 to $50,000 as threshold amount requiring appointment of guardian ad litem if interests of minor are not otherwise adequately represented. Committee notes revised.

2014 Revision: Amends subdivision (b)(1) to conform to Fla. R. Jud. Admin. 2.425. Committee notes revised.

Statutory References

§ 744.3025, Fla. Stat. Claims of minors.

§ 744.387, Fla. Stat. Settlement of claims.

§ 744.391, Fla. Stat. Actions by and against guardian or ward.

§ 744.441, Fla. Stat. Powers of guardian upon court approval.

§ 744.446, Fla. Stat. Conflicts of interest; prohibited activities; court approval; breach of fiduciary duty.

§ 744.447, Fla. Stat. Petition for authorization to act.

§ 768.23, Fla. Stat. Protection of minors and incompetents.

§ 768.25, Fla. Stat. Court approval of settlements.

Rule References

Fla. Prob. R. 5.040 Notice.

Fla. Prob. R. 5.042 Time.

Fla. Prob. R. 5.120 Administrator ad litem and guardian ad litem.

Fla. Prob. R. 5.610 Execution by guardian.

Fla. Prob. R. 5.630 Petition for approval of acts.

Fla. R. Jud. Admin. 2.425 Minimization of the Filing of Sensitive Information.

Rule 5.640. Continuance of Unincorporated Business or Venture of Ward

(a) Continuance of Business. When the ward is adjudicated incapacitated while engaged in any unincorporated business or venture, or the court finds that a person with a developmental disability lacks capacity to manage an unincorporated business or venture, the court may authorize the guardian to continue the business or venture for a reasonable time under the supervision of the court.

(b) Petition. Before an order is made under subdivision (a), the guardian shall file a verified petition, alleging sufficient facts to make it appear that it is in the best interest of the ward's estate to continue the business or venture.

(c) Order. The order authorizing the continuance of the business or venture may empower the guardian to make contracts necessary to conduct the business or venture and to incur debts and pay out money in the proper conduct of the business or venture. The net profits only of the business or venture are to be added to the assets of the ward's estate.

(d) Accounts and Reports.   In the conduct of the business or venture, the guardian shall keep full and accurate accounts of all receipts and expenditures and make reports as the court requires.

(e) Discontinuance of Business.   Any person interested in the ward's estate may at any time petition the court for an order requiring the guardian to discontinue and to wind up the business or venture, and the court, after notice to the guardian, shall enter such order thereon as is in the best interest of the ward's estate.

Amended Sept. 29, 1988, effective Jan. 1, 1989 (537 So.2d 500); Sept. 29, 1989, effective Oct. 1, 1989 (549 So.2d 665); Nov. 17, 1989 (551 So.2d 452); Aug. 22, 1991, effective Oct. 1, 1991 (584 So.2d 964); July 10, 2008 (986 So.2d 576).

Committee Notes

Rule History

1975 Revision: Implements section 744.441(16), Florida Statutes. The rule is patterned after rule 5.350 pertaining to the continuation of a business of a decedent by a personal representative.

1977 Revision: No change in rule. Change in committee note to conform to statutory renumbering.

1988 Revision: Change in title of rule; captions added to subdivisions. Committee notes revised. Citation form changes in committee notes.

1989 Revision: Prior rule deleted and replaced by temporary emergency rule.

1991 Revision: Editorial changes in (a), (b), and (e).

1992 Revision: Citation form changes in committee notes.

2008 Revision: Subdivision (a) amended to include persons with a developmental disability. Committee notes revised.

Statutory References

§ 393.12, Fla. Stat. Capacity; appointment of guardian advocate.

§ 744.3085, Fla. Stat. Guardian advocates.

§ 744.441(13), Fla. Stat. Powers of guardian upon court approval.

§ 744.447, Fla. Stat. Petition for authorization to act.

Rule Reference

Fla. Prob. R. 5.350 Continuance of unincorporated business or venture.

Cross References

Continuance of unincorporated business of decedent, see Probate Rule 5.350.
Power of guardian to continue unincorporated business of ward, see F.S.A. § 744.441.

Rule 5.645.   Management of Property of Nonresident Ward by Foreign Guardian

(a) Petition.   A guardian of the property of a nonresident ward, duly appointed by a court of another state, territory, or country, who desires to manage any part or all of the property of the ward located in this state, may file a verified petition for authority to manage the property. The petition shall state:

(1) the circumstances of the guardian's appointment;

(2) a description of the property and its estimated value; and

(3) the indebtedness, if any, existing against the ward in this state.

(b) Designation of Resident Agent. The guardian shall designate a resident agent as required by these rules.

(c) Oath. The guardian shall file an oath as required by these rules.

(d) Filing of Authenticated Copies. The guardian shall file authenticated copies of:

(1) letters of guardianship or other authority to act as guardian; and

(2) bond or other security, if any.

(e) Order. The court shall determine if the foreign bond or other security is sufficient to guarantee the faithful management of the ward's property in this state. The court may require a new guardian's bond in this state in an amount it deems necessary. The order shall authorize the guardian to manage the property and shall specifically describe the property.

Added July 5, 2007, effective Jan. 1, 2008 (959 So.2d 1170).

Committee Notes

Rule History

2007 Revision: New rule.

Statutory References

§ 744.306, Fla. Stat. Foreign guardians.

§ 744.307, Fla. Stat. Foreign guardian may manage the property of nonresident ward.

Rule References

Fla. Prob. R. 5.110 Address designation for personal representative or guardian; designation of resident agent and acceptance.

Fla. Prob. R. 5.600 Oath.

Rule 5.646. Standby Guardians

(a) Petition for Appointment of Standby Guardian for Minor.

(1) *Contents*. A minor's guardian or the natural guardians of a minor may petition for the appointment of a standby guardian of the person or property of the minor. The petition shall be verified by the petitioner and shall state:

(A) the facts to establish venue;

(B) the petitioner's residence and post office address;

(C) the name, age, and residence and post office address of the minor;

(D) the names and addresses of the parents of the minor and, if none, the next of kin known to the petitioner;

(E) the name and residence and post office address of the proposed standby guardian, and that the proposed standby guardian is qualified to serve;

(F) the proposed standby guardian's relationship to and any previous association with the minor;

(G) the reasons why the proposed standby guardian should be appointed; and

(H) the nature and value of the property subject to the guardianship.

(2) *Notice and Waiver of Notice*. Notice of the hearing on the petition must be served on the parents, natural or adoptive, of the minor and on any guardian for the minor. Notice may be waived by those required to receive notice or by the court for good cause.

(b) Petition for Appointment of Standby Guardian for Incapacitated Person.

(1) *Contents.* A currently serving guardian may petition for the appointment of a standby guardian of the person or property of an incapacitated person. The petition shall be verified by the petitioner and shall state:

(A) the petitioner's residence and post office address;

(B) the name, age, and residence and post office address of the incapacitated person;

(C) the nature of the incapacity, the extent of guardianship, either limited or plenary, and the nature and value of property subject to the guardianship;

(D) the names and addresses of the next of kin of the incapacitated person known to the petitioner;

(E) the name and residence and post office address of the proposed standby guardian, and that the proposed standby guardian is qualified to serve;

(F) the proposed standby guardian's relationship to and any previous association with the incapacitated person; and

(G) the reasons why the proposed standby guardian should be appointed.

(2) *Notice.* Notice of the hearing on the petition must be served on the incapacitated person's next of kin.

(c) Petition for Confirmation.

(1) *Contents.* A standby guardian, not later than 20 days after the assumption of duties as guardian, shall petition for confirmation of appointment. The petition shall be verified by the petitioner and shall state:

(A) the petitioners's residence and post office address;

(B) the name, age, and residence and post office address of the adult incapacitated person or initials, year of birth, and residence address of minor;

(C) the nature of the incapacity, the extent of guardianship, either limited or plenary, and the nature and value of property subject to the guardianship;

(D) the names and addresses of the next of kin of the incapacitated person or minor known to the petitioner;

(E) the name and residence and post office address of the proposed guardian, and that the proposed guardian is qualified to serve;

(F) the proposed guardian's relationship to and any previous association with the incapacitated person or minor;

(G) the reasons why appointment of the proposed guardian should be confirmed; and

(H) if the proposed guardian is a professional guardian, a statement that the proposed guardian has complied with the educational requirements of section 744.1083, Florida Statutes.

(2) *Service.* The petition for confirmation and notice of hearing shall be served on the incapacitated person's next of kin a reasonable time before the hearing on the petition or other pleading seeking confirmation of the guardian.

Added Feb. 1, 2007 (948 So.2d 735). Amended May 22, 2014 (139 So.3d 875).

Committee Notes

The standby guardian must file an oath pursuant to rule 5.600 before commencing the exercise of authority as guardian. Prior to appointment, the standby guardian must file an application pursuant to rule 5.590.

Section 393.12(10), Florida Statutes, provides that a guardian advocate shall have all of the duties, responsibilities, and powers of a guardian under Chapter 744, Florida Statutes. However, section 744.304 authorizes the appointment of a standby guardian only for a minor or incapacitated person.

Rule History

2006 Revision: New rule.

2008 Revision: Committee notes revised.

2014 Revision: Subdivision (c)(1)(B) amended to conform to Fla. R. Jud. Admin. 2.425. Committee notes revised.

Statutory Reference

§ 744.304, Fla. Stat. Standby guardianship.

Rule References

Fla. Prob. R. 5.590 Application for appointment as guardian; disclosure statement; filing.

Fla. Prob. R. 5.600 Oath.

Fla. R. Jud. Admin. 2.425 Minimization of the Filing of Sensitive Information.

Rule 5.647. Surrogate Guardian

(a) **Petition for Designation of Surrogate Guardian.** A guardian may file a petition to designate a surrogate guardian to exercise the powers of the guardian if the guardian is unavailable to act. The surrogate must be a professional guardian. The petition shall state:

(1) the name and business address of the surrogate guardian;

(2) the requested duration of the appointment; and

(3) the powers to be exercised by the surrogate guardian.

(b) **Service.** The petition for appointment of a surrogate guardian shall be served on all interested persons and the ward, unless the ward is a minor.

(c) **Oath.** The surrogate guardian must file with the court an oath swearing or affirming that the surrogate guardian will faithfully perform the duties delegated.

(d) **Termination.** Prior to the expiration of the period granted by court order, the guardian may terminate the authority of the surrogate guardian by filing a written notice of the termination with the court and serving it on the surrogate guardian.

Added Feb. 1, 2007 (948 So.2d 735).

Committee Notes

Rule History

2006 Revision: New rule.

2008 Revision. Committee notes revised.

Statutory References

§ 393.12, Fla. Stat. Capacity; appointment of guardian advocate.

§ 744.442, Fla. Stat. Delegation of authority.

Rule 5.648. Emergency Temporary Guardian

(a) **Petition for Appointment of Emergency Temporary Guardian.** Prior to appointment of a guardian but after a petition for determination of incapacity has been filed, the alleged incapacitated person or any adult interested in the welfare of that person may petition for the appointment of an emergency temporary guardian of the person or property. The petition shall be verified and shall state:

(1) the petitioner's residence and post office address;

(2) the name, age, and residence and post office address of the alleged incapacitated person;

(3) that there appears to be imminent danger that the physical or mental health or safety of the alleged incapacitated person will be seriously impaired or that the alleged incapacitated person's property is in danger of being wasted, misappropriated, or lost unless immediate action is taken;

(4) the nature of the emergency and the reason immediate action must be taken;

(5) the extent of the emergency temporary guardianship, either limited or plenary, requested for the alleged incapacitated person, and, if known, the nature and value of the property to be subject to the emergency temporary guardianship;

(6) the names and addresses of the next of kin of the alleged incapacitated person known to the petitioner;

(7) the name and residence and post office address of the proposed emergency temporary guardian, and that the proposed emergency temporary guardian is qualified to serve, or that a willing and qualified emergency temporary guardian has not been located; and

(8) the proposed emergency temporary guardian's relationship to or any previous association with the alleged incapacitated person.

(b) Notice. Unless the court orders otherwise, notice of filing of the petition for appointment of an emergency temporary guardian and any hearing on the petition shall be served before the hearing on the petition on the alleged incapacitated person and on the alleged incapacitated person's attorney.

(c) Service on Public Guardian. If the petitioner requests appointment of the public guardian as emergency temporary guardian, a copy of the petition and notice shall be served on the public guardian.

(d) Order. The order appointing the emergency temporary guardian shall specify the powers and duties of the emergency temporary guardian.

(e) Extension of Authority. Prior to the expiration of the authority of the emergency temporary guardian, any interested person may file a verified petition for extension of authority of the emergency temporary guardian. The petition must show that the conditions that warranted the initial appointment of the emergency temporary guardian still exist. The petition shall be served on the ward's attorney and on the emergency temporary guardian.

(f) Final Report. An emergency temporary guardian shall file a final report no later than 30 days after the expiration of the emergency temporary guardianship. A copy of the final report shall be served on the successor guardian, if any, the ward, and the ward's attorney. With approval of the court, service on the ward may be accomplished by serving the attorney for the ward.

(1) If the emergency temporary guardian is a guardian of the property, the final report shall consist of a verified inventory of the ward's property as of the date letters of emergency temporary guardianship were issued, a final accounting that gives a full and correct account of the receipts and disbursements of all the ward's property over which the guardian had control, and a statement of the property on hand at the end of the emergency temporary guardianship.

(2) If the emergency temporary guardian is a guardian of the person, the final report shall summarize the activities of the guardian with regard to residential placement, medical condition, mental health and rehabilitative services, and the social condition of the ward to the extent of the authority granted to the emergency temporary guardian.

(3) If the emergency temporary guardian becomes the successor guardian of the property or person of the ward, the final report must satisfy the requirements of, and shall serve as, the initial report of the guardian of the property or person of the ward, as the case may be, as set forth in rule 5.690.

Added July 12, 2007 (964 So.2d 140).

Committee Notes

Rule History

2007 Revision: New rule.

Statutory References

§ 744.3031, Fla. Stat. Emergency temporary guardianship.

§ 744.344(4), Fla. Stat. Order of appointment.

Rule References

Fla. Prob. R. 5.600 Oath.

Fla. Prob. R. 5.690 Initial Guardianship Report.

Rule 5.649. Guardian Advocate

(a) Petition for Appointment of Guardian Advocate. A petition to appoint a guardian advocate for a person with a developmental disability may be executed by an adult person who is a resident of this state. The petition must be verified by the petitioner and must state:

(1) the name, age, and present address of the petitioner and the petitioner's relationship to the person with a developmental disability;

(2) the name, age, county of residence, and present address of the person with a developmental disability;

(3) that the petitioner believes that the person needs a guardian advocate and the factual information on which such belief is based;

(4) the exact areas in which the person lacks the ability to make informed decisions about the person's care and treatment services or to meet the essential requirements for the person's physical health or safety;

(5) the legal disabilities to which the person is subject;

(6) if authority is sought over any property of the person, a description of that property and the reason why management or control of that property should be placed with a guardian advocate;

(7) the name of the proposed guardian advocate, the relationship of the proposed guardian advocate to the person with a developmental disability, the relationship of the proposed guardian advocate with the providers of health care services, residential services, or other services to the person with developmental disabilities, and the reason why the proposed guardian advocate should be appointed. If a willing and qualified guardian advocate cannot be located, the petition must so state; and

(8) whether the petitioner has knowledge, information, or belief that the person with a developmental disability has executed an advance directive under chapter 765, Florida Statutes, or a durable power of attorney under chapter 709, Florida Statutes.

(b) Notice.

(1) Notice of the filing of the petition must be given to the person with a developmental disability, both verbally and in writing, in the language of the person and in English. Notice must also be given to the person with a developmental disability's next of kin, any designated health care surrogate, an attorney-in-fact designated in a durable power of attorney, and such other persons as the court may direct. A copy of the petition to appoint a guardian advocate must be served with the notice.

(2) The notice must state that a hearing will be held to inquire into the capacity of the person with a developmental disability to exercise the rights enumerated in the petition. The notice must also state the date of the hearing on the petition.

(3) The notice must state that the person with a developmental disability has the right to be represented by counsel of the person's own choice and the court must initially appoint counsel.

(c) Counsel. Within 3 days after a petition has been filed, the court must appoint an attorney to represent a person with a developmental disability who is the subject of a petition to appoint a guardian advocate. The person with a developmental disability may substitute his or her own attorney for the attorney appointed by the court.

(d) Order. If the court finds the person with a developmental disability requires the appointment of a guardian advocate, the order appointing the guardian advocate must contain findings of facts and conclusions of law, including:

(1) the nature and scope of the person's inability to make decisions;

(2) the exact areas in which the person lacks ability to make informed decisions about care and treatment services or to meet the essential requirements for the individual's physical health and safety;

(3) if any property of the person is to be placed under the management or control of the guardian advocate, a description of that property, any limitations as to the extent of such management or control, and the reason why management or control by the guardian advocate of that property is in the best interest of the person;

(4) if the person has executed an advance directive or durable power of attorney, a determination as to whether the documents sufficiently address the needs of the person and a finding that the advance directive or durable power of attorney does not provide an alternative to the appointment of a guardian advocate that sufficiently addresses the needs of the person with a developmental disability;

(5) if a durable power of attorney exists, the powers of the attorney-in-fact, if any, that are suspended and granted to the guardian advocate;

(6) if an advance directive exists and the court determines that the appointment of a guardian advocate is necessary, the authority, if any, the guardian advocate exercises over the health care surrogate;

(7) the specific legal disabilities to which the person with a developmental disability is subject;

(8) the name of the person selected as guardian advocate; and

(9) the powers, duties, and responsibilities of the guardian advocate, including bonding of the guardian advocate as provided by law.

(e) Issuance of Letters. Upon compliance with all of the foregoing, letters of guardian advocacy must be issued to the guardian advocate.

Added July 10, 2008 (986 So.2d 576). Amended Sept. 26, 2013, effective Jan. 1, 2014 (123 So.3d 31).

Committee Notes

Rule History

2008 Revision: New rule.

2013 Revision: New subdivisions (a)(6) and (d)(3) added to address situations in which the guardian advocate will have authority over the property of the person with a developmental disability. New subdivision (e) added to provide for the issuance of letters of guardian advocacy. Editorial changes to subdivisions (a)(7) and (b)(3). Editorial changes to conform to the court's guidelines for rules submissions as set forth in AOSC06–14.

Statutory References

§ 393.063(9), Fla. Stat. Definitions.

§ 393.12, Fla. Stat. Capacity; appointment of guardian advocate.

§ 709.08, Fla. Stat. Durable power of attorney.

§ 765.101, Fla. Stat. Definitions.

§ 765.104, Fla. Stat. Amendment or revocation.

§ 765.202, Fla. Stat. Designation of a health care surrogate.

§ 765.204, Fla. Stat. Capacity of principal; procedure.

§ 765.205(3), Fla. Stat. Responsibility of the surrogate.

§ 765.302, Fla. Stat. Procedure for making a living will; notice to physician.

§ 765.401, Fla. Stat. The proxy.

Rule References

Fla. Prob. R. 5.020 Pleadings; verification; motions.

Fla. Prob. R. 5.540 Hearings.

Fla. Prob. R. 5.681 Restoration of rights of person with developmental disability.

Rule 5.650. Resignation or Disqualification of Guardian; Appointment of Successor

(a) Resignation and Petition for Discharge. A guardian seeking to resign shall file a resignation and petition for discharge.

(b) Contents. The resignation and petition for discharge shall state:

(1) that the guardian wishes to resign and be relieved of all duties as guardian;

(2) the amount of compensation to be paid to the guardian and to the attorneys, accountants, or other agents employed by the guardian; and

(3) the names and addresses of the successor guardian and the successor guardian's attorney, or that a successor guardian has not yet been appointed or duly qualified.

(c) Final Report. A resigning guardian of the property shall file a final report showing receipts, disbursements, amounts reserved for unpaid and anticipated costs and fees, and other relevant financial information from the date of the previous annual accounting, and a list of assets to be turned over to the successor guardian.

(d) Notice. A notice shall be served stating that:

(1) any objection shall be in writing and shall state with particularity each item to which the objection is directed and the grounds on which the objection is based;

(2) any objection to the resignation, petition for discharge, or final report shall be filed within 30 days from the date of service of the petition for discharge; and

(3) within 90 days after filing of the objection, a notice of hearing thereon shall be served or the objection is abandoned.

(e) Service. A copy of the resignation, petition for discharge, final report, and notice of resignation and petition for discharge shall be served on the ward, any surety on the guardian's bond, any successor guardian, and such other persons as the court may direct.

(f) Objections. Objections shall be in the form and be filed within the time set forth in the notice of resignation and petition for discharge. A copy of the objections shall be served by the objector on the ward, all guardians, any surety on the guardian's bond, and any successor guardian.

(g) Disposition of Objections. Any interested person may set a hearing on the objections. Notice of the hearing shall be served on the guardian, the successor guardian, if any, and any other interested persons. If a notice of hearing on the objections is not served within 90 days of filing of the objections, the objections will be deemed abandoned.

(h) Discharge. The guardian's resignation shall not be accepted and the guardian shall not be discharged until all objections have been withdrawn, abandoned, or judicially resolved and a successor guardian has been appointed and duly qualified. After all objections have been withdrawn, abandoned, or judicially resolved, if the court is satisfied that the resigning guardian has faithfully discharged the duties of the guardianship and the interests of the ward are protected, and the resigning guardian of the property has delivered the assets of the ward, all guardianship records, and all money due to the ward from the guardian to the remaining or successor guardian, the court shall enter an order accepting resignation of guardian and granting discharge.

(i) Disqualification. Any guardian who is improperly appointed, or who becomes disqualified to act after appointment, shall immediately file a resignation and petition for discharge and proceed in accordance with this rule.

(j) Nonresident Guardians. Nonresident guardians appointed before October 1, 1989, shall not be automatically disqualified to serve and shall not be required to resign and initiate their own removal.

(k) Guardian Advocates. This rule shall apply to guardian advocates, except that a final report shall be required of a guardian advocate only if the guardian advocate's authority included the management of the property of the person with a developmental disability.

Amended Sept. 29, 1988, effective Jan. 1, 1989 (537 So.2d 500); Sept. 29, 1989, effective Oct. 1, 1989 (549 So.2d 665); Nov. 17, 1989 (551 So.2d 452); Aug. 22, 1991, effective Oct. 1, 1991 (584 So.2d 964); July 5, 2007, effective Jan. 1, 2008 (959 So.2d 1170); July 10, 2008 (986 So.2d 576).

Committee Notes

Rule History

1975 Revision: Substantially the same as sections 744.467 and 744.471, Florida Statutes, with editorial changes.

1977 Revision: No change in rule. Change in committee note to conform to statutory renumbering.

1988 Revision: Editorial changes in (a). Text of rule 5.590 inserted in (b). Editorial change in (c). Captions added to subdivisions. Committee notes revised. Citation form changes in committee notes.

1989 Revision: Prior rule deleted and replaced by temporary emergency rule.

1991 Revision: Substantial revision of entire rule to harmonize with procedure for termination of guardianship under rules 5.670 and 5.680. Subdivision (k) transferred from temporary emergency rule 5.800.

1992 Revision: Committee notes revised. Citation form changes in committee notes.

2007 Revision: Subdivision (i) deleted because right of waiver is substantive. Subsequent subdivisions relettered.

2008 Revision: Subdivision (k) added to include guardian advocates. Committee notes revised.

2012 Revision: Committee notes revised.

Statutory References

§ 393.12, Fla. Stat. Capacity; appointment of guardian advocate.

§ 744.102(11), Fla. Stat. Definitions.

§ 744.3085, Fla. Stat. Guardian advocates.

§ 744.467, Fla. Stat. Resignation of guardian.

§ 744.471, Fla. Stat. Appointment of successor.

Rule References

Fla. Prob. R. 5.040 Notice.

Fla. Prob. R. 5.041 Service of pleadings and documents.

Fla. Prob. R. 5.180 Waiver and consent.

Fla. Prob. R. 5.610 Execution by guardian.

Fla. Prob. R. 5.649 Guardian advocate.

Fla. Prob. R. 5.681 Restoration of rights of person with developmental disability.

Fla. R. Jud. Admin. 2.516 Service of pleadings and documents.

Cross References

Appointment of successor guardian, see F.S.A. § 744.471.
Reasons for removal of guardian, see F.S.A. § 744.474.
Resignation of guardian, see F.S.A. § 744.467.
Resignation of personal representative, see Probate Rule 5.430.

Rule 5.660. Proceedings for Removal of Guardian

(a) **Notice.** Proceedings for removal of a guardian may be instituted by a court, by any surety or other interested person, or by the ward, and formal notice of the petition for removal of a guardian must be served on all guardians, other interested persons, next of kin, and the ward. The pleading must state with particularity the reasons why the guardian should be removed.

(b) **Accounting.** A removed guardian must file with the court an accounting for the guardianship within 20 days after the guardian's removal. A copy of the accounting must be served on the successor guardian and the ward, unless the ward is a minor or has been determined to be totally incapacitated.

(c) **Transfer of Property and Records.** The removed guardian (or the guardian's heirs, personal representative, or surety) must turn over all the property of the ward in the removed guardian's control and all guardianship records to the duly qualified successor. The successor guardian must, or the ward may, demand of the removed guardian (or the guardian's heirs, personal representative, or surety) all of those items.

(d) Failure to Comply. If a removed guardian fails to file a true, complete, and final accounting for the guardianship or to turn over to the successor all property of the ward in the removed guardian's control and all guardianship records, the court must issue a show-cause order.

(e) Guardian Advocates. Subdivisions (b) through (d) of this rule apply to guardian advocates only to the extent that the guardian advocate was granted authority over the property of the person with a developmental disability.

Amended Sept. 4, 1980, effective Jan. 1, 1981 (387 So.2d 949); Sept. 13, 1984, effective Jan. 1, 1985 (458 So.2d 1079); Sept. 29, 1988, effective Jan. 1, 1989 (537 So.2d 500); Sept. 29, 1989, effective Oct. 1, 1989 (549 So.2d 665); Nov. 17, 1989 (551 So.2d 452); Aug. 22, 1991, effective Oct. 1, 1991 (584 So.2d 964); Feb. 1, 2007 (948 So.2d 735); July 10, 2008 (986 So.2d 576); Sept. 26, 2013, effective Jan. 1, 2014 (123 So.3d 31).

Committee Notes

Rule History

1977 Revision: No change in rule. Change in committee notes to conform to statutory renumbering.

1980 Revision: Subdivision (a) amended to specifically authorize any guardian or next of kin to file the petition and to require formal notice in conformity with rule 5.630(b).

1984 Revision: Subdivision (b) amended to conform to statute. Editorial changes and Committee notes revised.

1988 Revision: Subdivision (a) rewritten for clarity. Language in (b) deleted as surplusage. Editorial change in caption of (c). Committee notes revised. Citation form change in committee notes.

1989 Revision: Prior rule deleted and replaced by temporary emergency rule.

1991 Revision: Subdivision (a) amended to require that the petition allege specific reasons why the guardian should be removed and to require service of the petition on the ward. Otherwise, editorial changes in all subdivisions.

1992 Revision: Citation form changes in committee notes.

2006 Revision: Requirement in (b) to serve minors deleted to conform to 2006 amendment to section 744.511, Florida Statutes.

2008 Revision: Subdivision (e) added to include guardian advocates. Committee notes revised.

2012 Revision: Committee notes revised.

2013 Revision: Subdivision (b) revised to conform to section 744.511, Florida Statutes. Committee notes revised. Editorial changes to conform to the court's guidelines for rules submissions as set forth in AOSC06–14.

Statutory References

§ 393.12, Fla. Stat. Capacity; appointment of guardian advocate.

§ 744.3085, Fla. Stat. Guardian advocates.

§ 744.474, Fla. Stat. Reasons for removal of guardian.

§ 744.477, Fla. Stat. Proceedings for removal of a guardian.

§ 744.511, Fla. Stat. Accounting upon removal.

§ 744.514, Fla. Stat. Surrender of property upon removal.

§ 744.517, Fla. Stat. Proceedings for contempt.

Rule References

Fla. Prob. R. 5.025 Adversary proceedings.

Fla. Prob. R. 5.040 Notice.

Fla. Prob. R. 5.041 Service of pleadings and documents.

Fla. Prob. R. 5.649 Guardian advocate.

Fla. R. Jud. Admin. 2.420 Public access to judicial branch records.

Fla. R. Jud. Admin. 2.516 Service of pleadings and documents.

Cross References

Accounting upon removal of guardian, see F.S.A. § 744.511.

Proceedings for contempt upon failure to complete final accounting, see F.S.A. § 744.517.

Proceedings for removal of guardian, see F.S.A. § 744.477.

Proceedings for removal of personal representative, see Probate Rule 5.440.

Removal of guardian, reasons, see F.S.A. § 744.474.

Surrender of property upon removal of guardian, see F.S.A. § 744.514.

Rule 5.670. Termination of Guardianship on Change of Domicile of Resident Ward

(a) Petition for Discharge. The Florida guardian may file a petition for discharge when the domicile of a resident ward has changed to a foreign jurisdiction, the foreign court having jurisdiction over the ward at the ward's new domicile has appointed a foreign guardian, and the foreign guardian has qualified and posted a bond in the amount required by the foreign court.

(b) Contents of Petition. The petition for discharge shall state:

(1) that the grounds set forth in subdivision (a) have occurred;

(2) that the guardian has fully administered the Florida guardianship; and

(3) the amount of compensation to be paid to the guardian and to the attorneys, accountants, or other agents employed by the guardian.

(c) Final Report. The Florida guardian of the property shall file a final report showing receipts, disbursements, amounts reserved for unpaid and anticipated costs and fees, and other relevant financial information from the date of the previous annual accounting, and a list of the assets to be turned over to the foreign guardian.

(d) Notice. The Florida guardian of the property shall publish a notice as required by law, which shall state:

(1) the name of the ward;

(2) the file number of the guardianship;

(3) the designation and address of the court;

(4) the name and address of the guardian and the guardian's attorney;

(5) the name and address of the foreign guardian and the foreign guardian's attorney, if any;

(6) the date of first publication;

(7) that a petition for discharge has been filed upon the grounds of change of domicile of the ward;

(8) the date the guardian will apply for discharge;

(9) that the jurisdiction of the ward will be transferred to the foreign jurisdiction;

(10) that any objection shall be in writing and shall state with particularity each item to which the objection is directed and the grounds on which the objection is based;

(11) that any objection to the final report or the petition for discharge shall be filed within the later of 30 days from the date of service of the petition for discharge or the date of first publication of the notice; and

(12) that within 90 days after filing of the objection, a notice of hearing thereon shall be served or the objection is abandoned.

(e) Service. A copy of the petition for discharge and of the notice of petition for discharge shall be served on the foreign guardian and such other persons as the court may direct.

(f) Objections. Objections shall be in the form and be filed within the time set forth in the notice of petition for discharge. A copy of the objections shall be served by the objector on the Florida guardian and the foreign guardian.

(g) Disposition of Objections. Any interested person may set a hearing on the objections. Notice of the hearing shall be served on the Florida guardian, the foreign guardian, and any other interested persons. If a notice of hearing on the objections is not served within 90 days of filing of the objections, the objections will be deemed abandoned.

(h) Discharge. The Florida guardian may not be discharged until all objections have been withdrawn, abandoned, or judicially resolved. After all objections have been withdrawn, abandoned, or judicially resolved, if the court is satisfied that the Florida guardian has faithfully discharged the duties of the guardianship and the interests of the ward are protected, and the Florida guardian of the property has delivered the assets of the ward to the foreign guardian, the court shall enter an order of discharge.

Amended Sept. 13, 1984, effective Jan. 1, 1985 (458 So.2d 1079); Sept. 29, 1988, effective Jan. 1, 1989 (537 So.2d 500); Sept. 29, 1989, effective Oct. 1, 1989 (549 So. 2d 665); Nov. 17, 1989 (551 So.2d 452); Aug. 22, 1991, effective Oct. 1, 1991 (584 So.2d 964); July 5, 2007, effective Jan. 1, 2008 (959 So.2d 1170).

Committee Notes

Rule History

1977 Revision: Change in committee notes to conform to statutory renumbering.

1984 Revision: Adds 30–day requirement for filing objections. Editorial changes and Committee notes revised.

1988 Revision: Editorial change in (c). First and last sentences of (d) deleted and clarifying word added.

1989 Revision: Prior rule adopted as temporary emergency rule.

1991 Revision: Substantial revision of entire rule to harmonize with procedure for discharge of guardian under rule 5.680 and to conform to section 744.524, Florida Statutes.

1992 Revision: Committee notes revised. Citation form changes in committee notes.

2007 Revision: Subdivision (i) deleted because right of waiver is substantive. Committee notes revised.

2008 Revision: Committee notes revised.

2012 Revision: Committee notes revised.

Statutory References

§ 393.12, Fla. Stat. Capacity; appointment of guardian advocate.

§ 744.102(8), (9), Fla. Stat. Definitions.

§ 744.201, Fla. Stat. Domicile of ward.

§ 744.202, Fla. Stat. Venue.

§ 744.2025, Fla. Stat. Change of ward's residence.

§ 744.524, Fla. Stat. Termination of guardianship on change of domicile of resident ward.

§ 744.531, Fla. Stat. Order of discharge.

Rule References

Fla. Prob. R. 5.041 Service of pleadings and documents.

Fla. Prob. R. 5.180 Waiver and consent.

Fla. Prob. R. 5.610 Execution by guardian.

Fla. Prob. R. 5.680 Termination of guardianship.

Fla. R. Jud. Admin. 2.516 Service of pleadings and documents.

Cross References

Appointment of guardian of resident ward, qualifications, see F.S.A. § 744.309.

Termination of guardianship on change of domicile of resident ward, see F.S.A. § 744.524.

Rule 5.680. Termination of Guardianship

(a) Petition for Discharge. When the ward has become sui juris, has terminated a voluntary guardianship, has been restored to capacity, has had all rights restored, or has died, or when the guardian has been unable to locate the ward after diligent search, or, for a guardian of the property, when the property subject to the guardianship has been exhausted, the guardian shall file a petition for discharge. A guardian of the person is discharged without further proceeding upon filing a certified copy of the ward's death certificate.

(b) Contents of Petition. The petition for discharge shall state:

(1) the reason for termination of the guardianship;

(2) that the guardian has fully administered the guardianship; and

(3) the amount of unpaid and anticipated costs and fees to be paid to the guardian and to the attorneys, accountants, or other agents employed by the guardian.

(c) Final Report. The guardian of the property shall promptly file a final report. If the ward has died, the guardian must file the report no later than 45 days after he or she has been served with letters of administration, letters of curatorship, or an order of summary administration. The report shall show receipts, disbursements, amounts reserved for unpaid and anticipated disbursements, costs, and fees, including the amounts set forth in subdivision (b)(3), and other relevant financial information from the date of the previous annual accounting, and a list of the assets to be turned over to the person entitled to them.

(d) Notice. A notice shall be served stating:

(1) that any objection shall be in writing and shall state with particularity each item to which the objection is directed and the grounds on which the objection is based;

(2) that any objection to the final report or the petition for discharge shall be filed within 30 days from the date of service of the petition for discharge; and

(3) that within 90 days after filing of the objection, a notice of hearing thereon shall be served or the objection is abandoned.

(e) Service. The guardian applying for discharge shall serve a copy of the petition for discharge and final report on the ward, on the personal representative of a deceased ward, or if there are no assets justifying qualification of a personal representative for the estate of a deceased ward, on the known next of kin of the deceased ward, or such other persons as the court may direct; provided however, that a guardian of the property who is subsequently appointed personal representative shall serve a copy of the petition for discharge and final report on all beneficiaries of the ward's estate.

(f) Objections. All persons served shall have 30 days to file objections to the petition for discharge and final report. The objections shall state with particularity the items to which the objections are directed and shall state the grounds on which the objections are based. Copies of the objections shall be served by the objector on the guardian. Any interested person may set a hearing on the objections. Notice of the hearing shall be served on the guardian and any other interested persons. If a notice of hearing on the objections is not served within 90 days of filing of the objections, the objections will be deemed abandoned. The guardian may not be discharged until all objections have been withdrawn, abandoned, or judicially resolved, and the petition for discharge of the guardian is granted by the court.

(g) Discharge. The guardian may not be discharged until all objections are withdrawn, abandoned, or judicially resolved. After all objections are withdrawn, abandoned, or judicially resolved, and if it appears that the guardian has paid all amounts reserved to the persons entitled to them and has made full and complete distribution of the ward's assets to the persons entitled to them and has otherwise faithfully discharged the duties of the guardian, the court shall grant the petition for discharge and enter an order of discharge. If objections are filed and are not withdrawn, abandoned, or judicially resolved, the court shall conduct a hearing in the same manner as for a hearing on objections to annual guardianship plans. After hearing, if the court is satisfied that the guardian has faithfully discharged the duties of the guardianship and the interests of the ward are protected, and the guardian has rendered a complete and accurate final report and has delivered the assets of the ward to the person entitled to them, the court shall enter an order of discharge.

Amended Sept. 29, 1988, effective Jan. 1, 1989 (537 So.2d 500); Sept. 29, 1989, effective Oct. 1, 1989 (549 So.2d 665); Nov. 17, 1989 (551 So.2d 452); Aug. 22, 1991, effective Oct. 1, 1991 (584 So.2d 964); Sept. 24, 1992, effective Jan. 1, 1993 (607 So.2d 1306); Oct. 3, 1996, effective Jan. 1, 1997 (683 So.2d 78); June 19, 2003, effective Jan. 1, 2004 (848 So.2d 1069); Feb. 1, 2007 (948 So.2d 735); July 10, 2008 (986 So.2d 576).

Committee Notes

Rule History

1975 Revision: Implements sections 744.527 and 744.531, Florida Statutes, and also requires the guardian applying for discharge to do so by filing a petition for discharge and provides the procedure pertaining thereto.

1977 Revision: No change in rule. Change in committee note to conform to statutory renumbering.

1988 Revision: Captions added to subdivisions. Committee notes revised. Citation form changes in committee notes.

1989 Revision: Prior rule deleted and replaced by temporary emergency rule.

1991 Revision: Substantial revision of entire rule to harmonize with procedure for discharge of personal representatives under rules 5.400 and 5.401.

1992 Revision: Committee notes revised. Citation form changes in committee notes.

1996 Revision: Editorial changes to clarify that all anticipated costs and fees should be shown on final report and thereafter paid prior to transfer of assets and discharge of guardian.

2003 Revision: Subdivision (a) amended to reflect addition of rule 5.552 dealing with voluntary guardianship of property. Committee notes revised.

2006 Revision: Subdivision (c) amended to conform to 2006 amendments to section 744.527, Florida Statutes. Subdivision (h) deleted as unnecessary because substantive right of waiver is provided by section 731.302, Florida Statutes.

2008 Revision: Reference to restoration of rights added in subdivision (a). Committee notes revised.

2012 Revision: Committee notes revised.

Statutory References

§ 393.12, Fla. Stat. Capacity; appointment of guardian advocate.

§ 744.521, Fla. Stat. Termination of guardianship.

§ 744.527, Fla. Stat. Final reports and application for discharge; hearing.

§ 744.528, Fla. Stat. Discharge of guardian named as personal representative.

§ 744.531, Fla. Stat. Order of discharge.

§ 744.534, Fla. Stat. Disposition of unclaimed funds held by guardian.

Rule References

Fla. Prob. R. 5.040 Notice.

Fla. Prob. R. 5.041 Service of pleadings and documents.

Fla. Prob. R. 5.180 Waiver and consent.

Fla. Prob. R. 5.552 Voluntary guardianship of property.

Fla. Prob. R. 5.610 Execution by guardian.

Fla. Prob. R. 5.681 Restoration of rights of person with developmental disability.

Fla. R. Jud. Admin. 2.516 Service of pleadings and documents.

Cross References

Final reports and application for discharge, see F.S.A. § 744.527.
Order of discharge, see F.S.A. § 744.531.
Termination of guardianship, see F.S.A. § 744.521.

Rule 5.681. Restoration of Rights of Person With Developmental Disability

(a) **Suggestion of Restoration of Rights.** A suggestion of restoration of rights of a person with a developmental disability may be executed by any interested person, including the person with a developmental disability. The suggestion must contain:

(1) a statement that the person with a developmental disability is capable of exercising some or all of the rights that were granted to the guardian advocate;

(2) evidentiary support for the filing as provided by law; and

(3) the name and address of the attorney representing the person with a developmental disability, if any, known to the petitioner.

(b) **Counsel.** Within 3 days after the suggestion has been filed, the court must appoint an attorney to represent a person with a developmental disability who is not then represented by counsel as stated in the suggestion.

(c) **Notice.** Upon filing of the suggestion, if the name and address of the attorney representing the person with a developmental disability is listed in the suggestion, or upon the appointment of counsel, if no name and address of an attorney are listed in the suggestion, the clerk must immediately send notice of the filing of the suggestion, together with a copy of the suggestion, to the person with a developmental disability, the person's guardian advocate, the person's attorney, the attorney for the guardian advocate, if any, and any other interested person as directed by the court. The notice must contain a statement that all objections to the suggestion must be filed within 20 days after service of the notice. Formal notice must be served on the guardian advocate. Informal notice may be served on the other persons. Notice need not be served on the petitioner. The clerk must file proof of service.

(d) Objections. Any objection must be in writing and must state with particularity each item to which the objection is directed and the grounds on which the objection is based. The objector must serve notice of hearing on the objection and a copy of the objection on the person with the developmental disability, the person's attorney, the person's guardian advocate, the attorney for the guardian advocate, if any, the next of kin of the person with a developmental disability, and any other interested persons as directed by the court.

(e) Order.

The court must enter an order denying the suggestion or restoring all or some of the rights that were granted to the guardian advocate. If only some rights are restored to the person with a developmental disability, the order must state which rights are restored and amend the letters of guardian advocacy accordingly. The court need not hold a hearing prior to entering an order restoring rights if no objections are filed and the court is satisfied with the evidentiary support for restoration supplied by the petitioner.

(f) Additional Requirements. If personal rights are restored, the guardian advocate must file an amended plan within 60 days after the order restoring rights. If all property rights are restored, a guardian advocate previously granted management or control over property must file a final accounting within 60 days after the order restoring rights. A copy of any amended plan and accounting must be promptly served on the person with a developmental disability and the person's attorney.

Added July 10, 2008 (986 So.2d 576). Amended Sept. 26, 2013, effective Jan. 1, 2014 (123 So.3d 31).

Committee Notes

Rule History

2008 Revision: New rule.

2013 Revision: Substantial revisions to reflect the designation of the pleading as a Suggestion of Restoration of Rights; the requirement for a statement of evidentiary support, the identification and address of the attorney for the person with a developmental disability; procedures for service of objections; clarification of requirements following a restoration of rights; and editorial changes. Editorial changes to conform to the court's guidelines for rule submissions as set forth in AOSC06–14.

Statutory References

§ 393.063(9), Fla. Stat. Definitions.

§ 393.12, Fla. Stat. Capacity; appointment of guardian advocate.

§ 709.08, Fla. Stat. Durable power of attorney.

§ 765.101, Fla. Stat. Definitions.

§ 765.104, Fla. Stat. Amendment or revocation.

§ 765.202, Fla. Stat. Designation of a health care surrogate.

§ 765.204, Fla. Stat. Capacity of principal; procedure.

§ 765.205(3), Fla. Stat. Responsibility of the surrogate.

§ 765.302, Fla. Stat. Procedure for making a living will; notice to physician.

§ 765.401, Fla. Stat. The proxy.

Rule References

Fla. Prob. R. 5.020 Pleadings; verification; motions.

Fla. Prob. R. 5.540 Hearings.

Fla. Prob. R. 5.541 Recording of hearings.

Fla. Prob. R. 5.680 Termination of guardianship.

Rule 5.685. Determination Regarding Alternatives to Guardianship

(a) Reporting by Guardian. The guardian shall promptly file a report attaching a copy of a final order or judgment that determines the validity of a ward's durable power of attorney, trust, or trust amendment.

(b) Petition. At any time after the appointment of a guardian, the guardian, the ward, the ward's attorney, if any, or any other interested person may file a verified petition stating that there is an alternative to guardianship that will sufficiently address the problems of the ward.

(c) Contents of Petition. The petition to determine alternatives to guardianship shall state:

(1) the petitioner's interest in the proceeding; and

(2) the facts constituting the basis for the relief sought and that the proposed alternative to guardianship will sufficiently address the problems of the ward and is in the ward's best interest.

(d) Service. The petition shall be served on the guardian, the ward, the ward's attorney, if any, those interested persons who have filed requests for notices and copies of pleadings, and such other persons as the court may direct.

(e) Order. The order shall specify whether there is an alternative to guardianship that will sufficiently address the problems of the ward, the continued need for a guardian, and the extent of the need for delegation of the ward's rights.

Added Feb. 1, 2007 (948 So.2d 735).

Committee Notes

Rule History

2006 Revision: New rule.

Statutory References

§ 744.331, Fla. Stat. Procedures to determine incapacity.

§ 744.462, Fla. Stat. Determination regarding alternatives to guardianship.

Rule 5.690. Initial Guardianship Report

(a) Contents and Filing. An initial guardianship report shall be filed within 60 days after the issuance of letters of guardianship. The guardian of the property shall file the initial guardianship report consisting of the verified inventory. The guardian of the person shall file the initial guardianship report consisting of the guardianship plan.

(b) Service. Copies of the initial guardianship report shall be served on the ward, unless the ward is a minor under the age of 14 years or is totally incapacitated, and the attorney for the ward, if any. With approval of the court, service on the ward may be accomplished by serving the attorney for the ward.

Added Aug. 22, 1991, effective Oct. 1, 1991 (584 So.2d 964). Amended Sept. 24, 1992, effective Jan. 1, 1993 (607 So.2d 1306).

Committee Notes

The committee recognizes the conflict between this rule and section 744.362, Florida Statutes, which requires the filing of the initial guardianship report (which includes the inventory) within 60 days after appointment. The committee believes this provision, which attempts to regulate when a paper must be filed with the court, is procedural and that a guardian may not receive letters of guardianship empowering the guardian to act contemporaneously with the appointment. Therefore, the issuance of letters is a more practical time from which to measure the beginning of the time period for the accomplishment of this act.

In the event the guardian of the property and the guardian of the person are not the same entity or person, they shall make a good faith effort to jointly file the initial guardianship report.

Rule History

1991 Revision: New rule.

1992 Revision: Addition of phrase in subdivision (b) to conform to 1992 amendment to section 744.362(1), Florida Statutes. Citation form changes in committee notes.

2012 Revision: Committee notes revised.

Statutory References

§ 744.362, Fla.Stat. Initial guardianship report.

§ 744.363, Fla.Stat. Initial guardianship plan.

§ 744.365, Fla.Stat. Verified inventory.

§ 744.3701, Fla.Stat. Inspection of report.

§ 744.384, Fla.Stat. Subsequently discovered or acquired property.

Rule References

Fla. Prob. R. 5.020 Pleadings; verification; motions.

Fla. Prob. R. 5.041 Service of pleadings and documents.

Fla. Prob. R. 5.060 Request for notices and copies of pleadings.

Fla. Prob. R. 5.180 Waiver and consent.

Fla. Prob. R. 5.610 Execution by guardian.

Fla. Prob. R. 5.620 Inventory.

Fla. Prob. R. 5.700 Objection to guardianship reports.

Fla. R. Jud. Admin. 2.516 Service of pleadings and documents.

Cross References

Initial guardianship report, see § 744.362.

Rule 5.695. Annual Guardianship Reports

(a) Contents and Filing.

(1) *Guardian of the Person.* Unless the court requires reporting on a calendar year basis, the guardian of the person shall file an annual guardianship plan within 90 days after the last day of the anniversary month in which the letters of guardianship were issued. The plan shall be for

the year ending on the last day of such anniversary month. If the court requires reporting on a calendar year basis, the guardianship plan shall be filed on or before April 1 of each year.

(2) *Guardian of the Property.* Unless the court requires or authorizes reporting on a fiscal year basis, the guardian of the property shall file an annual accounting on or before April 1 of each year. The annual accounting shall cover the preceding annual accounting period. If the court requires or authorizes reporting on a fiscal year basis, the annual accounting shall be filed on or before the first day of the fourth month after the end of the fiscal year.

(b) Service. Copies of the annual plan and accounting shall be served on the ward, unless the ward is a minor or is totally incapacitated, and the attorney for the ward, if any. With the approval of the court, service on the ward may be accomplished by serving the attorney for the ward. The guardian shall serve copies on such other persons as the court may direct.

Former Rule 5.690. Amended Sept. 4, 1980, effective Jan. 1, 1981 (387 So.2d 949); Sept. 29, 1988, effective Jan. 1, 1989 (537 So.2d 500); Sept. 29, 1989, effective Oct. 1, 1989 (549 So.2d 665); Nov. 17, 1989 (551 So.2d 452). Renumbered as Rule 5.695 and amended Aug. 22, 1991, effective Oct. 1, 1991 (584 So.2d 964). Amended Sept. 24, 1992, effective Jan. 1, 1993 (607 So.2d 1306); Feb. 1, 2007 (948 So.2d 735).

Committee Notes

The annual guardianship report consists of the annual plan for the guardian of the person and the annual accounting for the guardian of the property.

For annual guardianship reports regarding minors, see rule 5.555.

With approval of the court, service on the ward may be accomplished by service on the attorney for the ward, if any. The committee was concerned that actual service on a ward of the accounting or guardianship plan may give uninterested persons access to financial or personal information to the detriment of the ward. The committee believes that under such circumstances, the guardian of the property could seek an order under section 744.371(5), Florida Statutes, even if the ward's circumstances were set out in detail in a pleading other than the annual guardianship report. Such court order may be sought in appropriate circumstances at the time of the initial hearing to determine incapacity.

Rule History

1975 Revision: Substantially the same as section 744.427(1), (2), and (4), Florida Statutes, and section 744.437, Florida Statutes, with editorial changes and providing for the waiving, by a ward who has become sui juris or by the personal representative of a deceased ward, of the filing of an annual accounting. The rule requires the guardian of the property of a ward to appear before the court at the time he files his annual accounting or at such time the court shall determine in order that the court may inquire as to any matter relating to the physical and financial well-being of the ward. This appears to be in conflict with section 744.437, Florida Statutes, which refers to "every guardian" but in the same sentence it refers to "at the time the guardian files his annual return" and only the guardian of the property is required to file an annual accounting.

1977 Revision: No change in rule. Change in committee note to conform to statutory renumbering.

1980 Revision: Subdivision (e) amended to avoid conflict with statutory changes in section 744.437, Florida Statutes (1979).

1988 Revision: Matter in (b) deleted; covered in sections 744.427(2) and 744.434, Florida Statutes. Subdivision (c) deleted; covered in section 744.427(4), Florida Statutes. Captions added to subdivisions. Committee notes revised. Citation form changes in committee notes.

1989 Revision: Prior rule deleted and replaced by temporary emergency rule.

1991 Revision: Substantial changes and rule renumbered.

1992 Revision: Addition of language in subdivisions (a)(1) and (a)(2) to implement 1992 amendments to sections 744.367(1) and (2), Florida Statutes. Committee notes revised. Citation form changes in committee notes.

2006 Revision: Requirement in (b) to serve minors age 14 and above deleted to conform to amendment to section 744.367(3), Florida Statutes. Committee notes revised.

2012 Revision: Committee notes revised.

Statutory References

§ 744.367, Fla. Stat. Duty to file annual guardianship report.

§ 744.3675, Fla. Stat. Annual guardianship plan.

§ 744.3678, Fla. Stat. Annual accounting.

§ 744.3685, Fla. Stat. Order requiring guardianship report; contempt.

§ 744.3701, Fla. Stat. Inspection of report.

§ 744.371, Fla. Stat. Relief to be granted.

§ 744.3735, Fla. Stat. Annual appearance of the guardian.

Rule References

Fla. Prob. R. 5.020 Pleadings; verification; motions.

Fla. Prob. R. 5.041 Service of pleadings and documents.

Fla. Prob. R. 5.060 Request for notices and copies of pleadings.

Fla. Prob. R. 5.180 Waiver and consent.

Fla. Prob. R. 5.552 Voluntary guardianship of property.

Fla. Prob. R. 5.555 Guardianships of minors.

Fla. Prob. R. 5.610 Execution by guardian.

Fla. Prob. R. 5.700 Objection to guardianship reports.

Fla. Prob. R. 5.800(b) Application of revised chapter 744 to existing guardianships.

Fla. R. Jud. Admin. 2.516 Service of pleadings and documents.

Cross References

Annual accounting, see F.S.A. § 744.3678.
Annual appearance of guardian, see F.S.A. § 744.3735.
Annual guardianship plan, see F.S.A. § 744.3675.
Removal of guardian, accounting, see Probate Rule 5.660.

Rule 5.696. Annual Accounting

(a) **Contents and Filing.** The guardian of the property must file an annual accounting as required by law. The annual accounting must include:

(1) a full and correct account of the receipts and disbursements of all of the ward's property over which the guardian has control and a statement of the ward's property on hand at the end of the accounting period; and

(2) a copy of the statements of all of the ward's cash accounts as of the end of the accounting period from each institution where the cash is deposited.

(b) **Substantiating Documents.** Unless otherwise ordered by the court, the guardian need not file the documents substantiating the annual accounting. Upon reasonable written request, the guardian of the property shall make the substantiating documents available for examination to persons entitled to receive or inspect the annual accounting.

(c) Interim Inspection of Records. Upon reasonable written request and notice, the guardian of the property shall make all material financial records pertaining to the guardianship available for inspections to those persons entitled to receive or inspect the annual accounting.

Added Aug. 22, 1991, effective Oct. 1, 1991 (584 So.2d 964). Amended Sept. 2, 2010, effective Jan. 1, 2011 (50 So.3d 578); Sept. 26, 2013, effective Jan. 1, 2014 (123 So.3d 31).

Committee Notes

Rule History

1991 Revision: New rule.

1992 Revision: Citation form changes in committee notes.

2010 Revision: Editorial change in (b) to delete redundant language.

2012 Revision: Committee notes revised.

2013 Revision: Subdivision (b) revised to substitute "documents" for "papers." Committee notes revised. Editorial changes to conform to the court's guidelines for rule submissions as set forth in AOSC06–14.

Statutory References

§ 744.367, Fla.Stat. Duty to file annual guardianship report.

§ 744.3678, Fla.Stat. Annual accounting.

§ 744.3701, Fla.Stat. Inspection of report.

§ 744.3735, Fla.Stat. Annual appearance of the guardian.

Rule References

Fla. Prob. R. 5.020 Pleadings; verification; motions.

Fla. Prob. R. 5.041 Service of pleadings and documents.

Fla. Prob. R. 5.060 Request for notices and copies of pleadings.

Fla. Prob. R. 5.610 Execution by guardian.

Fla. Prob. R. 5.695 Annual guardianship report.

Fla. Prob. R. 5.700 Objection to guardianship reports.

Fla. R. Jud. Admin. 2.516 Service of pleadings and documents.

Rule 5.697. Magistrates' Review of Guardianship Inventories, Accountings, and Plans

(a) General Magistrates. The court may appoint general magistrates to review guardianship inventories, accountings, and plans. General magistrates shall be members of The Florida Bar and shall continue in office until removed by the court. The order appointing a general magistrate shall be recorded. Each general magistrate shall take the oath required of officers of the court by the Florida Constitution. The oath shall be recorded before the magistrate begins to act.

(b) Special Magistrates. In connection with the court's review of guardianship inventories, accountings, and plans, the court may appoint members of The Florida Bar as special magistrates for any particular service required by the court. Special magistrates shall be governed by all laws and rules relating to general magistrates except special magistrates shall not be required to take an oath unless specifically required by the court. For good cause shown, the court may appoint a person other than a member of The Florida Bar as a special magistrate.

(c) General Powers and Duties. Every magistrate shall act under the direction of the court. Process issued by a magistrate shall be directed as provided by law. All grounds for disqualification of a judge shall apply to magistrates.

(d) Hearings. Hearings before any magistrate may be held in the county where the action is pending, or at any other place by order of the court for the convenience of the witnesses or the parties. A magistrate shall give notice of hearings to all parties. If any party fails to appear, the magistrate may proceed ex parte or may continue the hearing to a future day, with notice to the absent party. The magistrate shall proceed with reasonable diligence and the least practicable delay. Any party may apply to the court for an order directing the magistrate to accelerate the proceedings and to make a report promptly. Evidence shall be taken in writing or by electronic recording by the magistrate or by some other person under the magistrate's authority in the magistrate's presence and shall be filed with the magistrate's report. The magistrate may examine and take testimony from the parties and their witnesses under oath, on all matters authorized by the court for review by the magistrate and may require production of all books, papers, writings, vouchers, and other documents applicable to those matters. The magistrate shall admit only evidence that would be admissible in court. The magistrate may take all actions concerning evidence that may be taken by the court.

(e) Magistrate's Report. The magistrate's report shall contain a description of the matters considered and the magistrate's conclusions and any recommendations. No part of any statement of facts, account, charge, deposition, examination, or answer used before the magistrate shall be recited. The magistrate shall be required to file a report only if a hearing is held pursuant to subdivision (d) of this rule or if specifically directed to do so by the court.

(f) Filing Report; Service; Exceptions. The magistrate shall file a report with the court and serve copies on the parties. The parties may serve exceptions to the report within 10 days from the date the report is served on them. If no exceptions are timely filed, the court shall take appropriate action on the report. All timely filed exceptions shall be heard by the court on reasonable notice by any party.

Added Aug. 22, 1991, effective Oct. 1, 1991 (584 So.2d 964). Amended Sept. 24, 1992, effective Jan. 1, 1993 (607 So.2d 1306); Sept. 30, 2004, effective Oct. 1, 2004 (887 So.2d 1090); July 5, 2007, effective Jan. 1, 2008 (959 So.2d 1170).

Committee Notes

Rule History

1991 Revision: This is a new rule, patterned after Florida Rule of Civil Procedure 1.490.

1992 Revision: Editorial change. Citation form change in committee notes.

2004 Revision: Change in nomenclature from "master" to "magistrate" to track similar change in the Florida Statutes.

2007 Revision: Title of rule and subdivisions (a) and (b) amended to include inventories. "Shall" substituted for "may" in last sentence of subdivision (f). Committee notes revised.

Statutory Reference

§ 744.369(2), Fla. Stat. Judicial review of guardianship reports.

Rule References

Fla. Prob. R. 5.095 General and special magistrates.

Fla. R. Civ. P. 1.490 Magistrates.

Rule 5.700. Objection to Guardianship Reports

(a) Objections. The ward, or any other interested person, may file an objection to any part of a guardianship report within the time provided by law.

(b) Contents. Any objection shall be in writing and shall state with particularity each item to which the objection is directed and the grounds on which the objection is based.

(c) Service. The objector shall serve a copy of the objection on each guardian and on any other person as directed by the court.

Amended Sept. 29, 1988, effective Jan. 1, 1989 (537 So.2d 500); Sept. 29, 1989, effective Oct. 1, 1989 (549 So.2d 665); Nov. 17, 1989 (551 So.2d 452); Aug. 22, 1991, effective Oct. 1, 1991 (584 So.2d 964).

Committee Notes

Rule History

1975 Revision: Substantially the same as section 744.427(3), (5), and (6), Florida Statutes, with editorial changes.

1977 Revision: No change in rule. Change in committee note to conform to statutory renumbering.

1988 Revision: Captions added to subdivisions. Committee notes revised. Citation form change in committee notes.

1989 Revision: Prior rule deleted and replaced by temporary emergency rule.

1991 Revision: Revised to conform with new statutory requirements.

1992 Revision: Citation form changes in committee notes.

2008 Revision: Committee notes revised.

2012 Revision: Committee notes revised.

Statutory References

§ 393.12, Fla. Stat. Capacity; appointment of guardian advocate.

§ 744.362, Fla. Stat. Initial guardianship report.

§ 744.363, Fla. Stat. Initial guardianship plan.

§ 744.365, Fla. Stat. Verified inventory.

§ 744.367, Fla. Stat. Duty to file annual guardianship report.

§ 744.3675, Fla. Stat. Annual guardianship plan.

§ 744.3678, Fla. Stat. Annual accounting.

Rule References

Fla. Prob. R. 5.020 Pleadings; verification; motions.

Fla. Prob. R. 5.041 Service of pleadings and documents.

Fla. Prob. R. 5.060 Request for notices and copies of pleadings.

Fla. Prob. R. 5.180 Waiver and consent.

Fla. Prob. R. 5.610 Execution by guardian.

Fla. R. Jud. Admin. 2.516 Service of pleadings and documents.

Cross References

Annual accounting, see F.S.A. § 744.3678.

Rule 5.705. Petition for Interim Judicial Review

(a) Contents. A petition for interim judicial review shall be verified, state the petitioner's interest in the proceeding, state with particularity the manner in which the guardian's action or proposed action does not comply with or exceeds the guardian's authority under the guardian plan, and state why the action or proposed action of the guardian is not in the best interest of the ward.

(b) Service. The petition shall be served by formal notice.

(c) Hearing. The petitioner or any interested person may set the matter for hearing.

(d) Expedited Proceedings. For good cause shown, the court may shorten the time for response to the formal notice and may set an expedited hearing.

Added Aug. 22, 1991, effective Oct. 1, 1991 (584 So.2d 964). Amended September 28, 2000, effective Jan. 1, 2001 (778 So.2d 272).

Committee Notes

Rule History

1991 Revision: New rule.

2000 Revision: Subdivision (d) added to permit expedited proceedings.

2008 Revision: Committee notes revised.

Statutory References

§ 393.12, Fla. Stat. Capacity; appointment of guardian advocate.

§ 744.3715, Fla. Stat. Petition for interim judicial review.

Rule 5.710. Reports of Public Guardian

The public guardian, as the guardian of a ward, shall file:

(a) an initial report as required by law;

(b) annual guardianship reports, which shall include the dates of quarterly visits to the ward, as required by law;

(c) a report within 6 months of his or her appointment as guardian of a ward, which shall also be filed with the executive director of the Statewide Public Guardianship Office, stating:

(1) the public guardian's efforts to locate a family member or friend, other person, bank, or corporation to act as guardian of the ward; and

(2) the ward's potential to be restored to capacity;

(d) an annual report, filed with the Statewide Public Guardianship Office, by September 1 for the preceding fiscal year, on the operations of the office of public guardian; and

(e) a report of an independent audit by a qualified certified public accountant, to be filed with the Statewide Public Guardianship Office every 2 years.

Added effective Dec. 23, 1987 (517 So.2d 675). Amended Sept. 29, 1989, effective Oct. 1, 1989 (549 So.2d 665); Nov. 17, 1989 (551 So.2d 452); Aug. 22, 1991, effective Oct. 1, 1991 (584 So.2d 964); July 5, 2007, effective Jan. 1, 2007 (959 So.2d 1170); Sept. 2, 2010, effective Jan. 1, 2011 (50 So.3d 578).

Committee Notes

Rule History

1987 Revision: This is a new rule and was promulgated to establish procedures to accommodate the Public Guardian Act. See § 744.701, et seq., Fla. Stat. See also Fla. Prob. R. 5.560.

1989 Revision: Prior rule adopted as temporary emergency rule.

1991 Revision: Editorial changes.

1992 Revision: Citation form changes in committee notes.

2007 Revision: Rule extensively amended to specify reports a public guardian is required to file.

2010 Revision: Editorial change in (e).

Statutory Reference

§§ 744.701–744.709, Fla.Stat. Public Guardianship Act.

Rule Reference

Fla.Prob.R. 5.560 Petition for appointment of guardian of an incapacitated person.

Cross References

Public Guardianship Act, see F.S.A. § 744.701 et seq.

Rule 5.720. Court Monitor

(a) Appointment. Upon motion or inquiry by any interested person or upon its own motion, the court may appoint a court monitor in any proceeding over which it has jurisdiction.

(b) Order of Appointment. The order of appointment shall state the name, address, and phone number of the monitor and shall set forth the matters to be investigated. The order may authorize the monitor to investigate, seek information, examine documents, or interview the ward. The order of appointment shall be served upon the guardian, the ward, and such other persons as the court may determine.

(c) Report. The monitor shall file a verified written report with the court setting forth the monitor's findings. The report shall be served on the guardian, the ward, and such other persons as the court may determine.

(d) Protection of Ward. If it appears from the monitor's report that further action by the court to protect the interests of the ward is necessary, the court shall, after a hearing with notice, enter any order necessary to protect the ward or the ward's property, including amending the plan, requiring an accounting, ordering production of assets, or initiating proceedings to remove a guardian. Notice of the hearing shall be served on the guardian, the ward, and such other persons as the court may determine.

Added Feb. 1, 2007 (948 So.2d 735). Amended July 10, 2008 (986 So.2d 576).

Committee Notes

This rule applies to the non-emergency appointment of court monitors.

Rule History

2006 Revision: New rule.

2008 Revision: Editorial change in (d). Committee notes revised.

Statutory References

§ 393.12, Fla. Stat. Capacity; appointment of guardian advocate.

§ 744.107, Fla. Stat. Court monitors.

§ 744.3701, Fla. Stat. Inspection of report.

Rule 5.725. Emergency Court Monitor

(a) Appointment. Upon motion or inquiry by any interested person or upon its own motion, the court may appoint a court monitor on an emergency basis without notice in any proceeding over which it has jurisdiction.

(b) Order of Appointment. The order of appointment shall specifically find that there appears to be imminent danger that the physical or mental health or safety of the ward will be seriously impaired or that the ward's property is in danger of being wasted, misappropriated, or lost unless immediate action is taken. The scope of the matters to be investigated and the powers and duties of the monitor must be specifically enumerated in the order.

(c) Duration of Authority. The authority of a monitor expires 60 days after the date of appointment or upon a finding of no probable cause, whichever occurs first. The court may enter an order extending the authority of the monitor for an additional 30 days upon a showing that an emergency condition still exists.

(d) Report. Within 15 days after the entry of an order of appointment, the monitor shall file a verified written report setting forth the monitor's findings and recommendations. The report may be supported by documents or other evidence. The time for filing the report may be extended by the court for good cause.

(e) Review. Upon review of the report, the court shall enter an order determining whether there is probable cause to take further action to protect the person or property of the ward.

(1) If the court finds no probable cause, the court shall enter an order finding no probable cause and discharging the monitor.

(2) If the court finds probable cause, the court shall enter an order directed to the respondent stating the essential facts constituting the conduct charged and requiring the respondent to appear before the court to show cause why the court should not take further action. The order shall specify the time and place of the hearing with a reasonable time to allow for the preparation of a defense after service of the order. A copy of the order to show cause together with the order of appointment and report of the monitor shall be served upon the guardian, the ward, the ward's attorney, if any, and the respondent.

(f) Protecting Ward. If at any time prior to the hearing on the order to show cause the court enters a temporary injunction, a restraining order, an order freezing assets, an order suspending the guardian or appointing a guardian ad litem, or any other order to protect the physical or mental health, safety, or property of the ward, the order or injunction shall be served on the guardian, the ward, the ward's attorney, if any, and such other persons as the court may determine.

Added Feb. 1, 2007 (948 so.2d 735). Amended Sept. 2, 2010, effective Jan. 1, 2011 (50 So.3d 578).

Committee Notes

Rule History

2006 Revision: New rule.

2008 Revision: Committee notes revised.

2010 Revision: Editorial change in (c).

Statutory references

§ 393.12, Fla. Stat. Capacity; appointment of guardian advocate.

§ 744.1075, Fla. Stat. Emergency court monitor.

Rule 5.800. Application of Revised Chapter 744 to Existing Guardianships

(a) Prior Adjudication of Incompetency. When an adjudication of incompetency has taken place under chapter 744, Florida Statutes, before October 1, 1989, no readjudication of incapacity shall be required.

(b) Annual Guardianship Reports. Guardians appointed before October 1, 1989, shall file annual guardianship reports as required by law.

Added Sept. 29, 1989, effective Oct. 1, 1989 (549 So.2d 665); Nov. 17, 1989 (551 So.2d 452). Amended Aug. 22, 1991, effective Oct. 1, 1991 (584 So.2d 964).

Committee Notes

Rule History

1989 Revision by Ad Hoc Committee: The committee adopted a position that guardians appointed before the effective date of the 1989 revisions to chapter 744, Florida Statutes, should comply with all sections of the law that apply to future acts of the guardian. For example, all guardians will in the future file annual reports and will be responsible for the continuing well-being of their wards. The committee recognized a distinction between those actions that will necessarily occur on a continuing basis throughout the guardianship and those actions that happen at a particular moment in time but are not necessarily ongoing duties. There are two and only two specific examples to which the statutory reforms would not apply retrospectively if the above distinction is adopted. First, the initial adjudication of incapacity occurs only once in any guardianship. Although guardianships are reevaluated annually, the statute does not contemplate a complete readjudication procedure every year. Therefore, the committee concluded that the initial adjudicatory hearing need not be repeated for wards adjudicated incompetent before October 1, 1989. Second, as concerns nonresident guardians appointed before October 1, 1989, normally, a guardian is appointed only once at the beginning of the guardianship. While these nonresident guardians would be expected to obey all provisions of the law prospectively, they would not be required to initiate their own removal.

1991 Revision: Editorial changes in first sentence of (a), and rest of subdivision deleted as unnecessary. Subdivision (b) has been transferred to rule 5.650. Date reference no longer required in (c), and modified to make filing requirement of preexisting guardianships consistent with the current statutory provisions.

1992 Revision: Citation form changes in committee notes.

Statutory References

§ 744.367, Fla.Stat. Duty to file annual guardianship report.

§ 744.3675, Fla.Stat. Annual guardianship plan.

§ 744.3678, Fla.Stat. Annual accounting.

Rule References

Fla.Prob.R. 5.695 Annual guardianship report.

Fla.Prob.R. 5.696 Annual accounting.

PART IV. EXPEDITED JUDICIAL INTERVENTION CONCERNING MEDICAL TREATMENT PROCEDURES

Rule 5.900. Expedited Judicial Intervention Concerning Medical Treatment Procedures

(a) Petition. Any proceeding for expedited judicial intervention concerning medical treatment procedures may be brought by any interested adult person and shall be commenced by the filing of a verified petition which states:

(1) the name and address of the petitioner;

(2) the name and location of the person who is the subject of the petition (hereinafter referred to as the "patient");

(3) the relationship of the petitioner to the patient;

(4) the names, relationship to the patient, and addresses if known to the petitioner, of:

(A) the patient's spouse and adult children;

(B) the patient's parents (if the patient is a minor);

(C) if none of the above, the patient's next of kin;

(D) any guardian and any court-appointed health care decision-maker;

(E) any person designated by the patient in a living will or other document to exercise the patient's health care decision in the event of the patient's incapacity;

(F) the administrator of the hospital, nursing home, or other facility where the patient is located;

(G) the patient's principal treating physician and other physicians known to have provided any medical opinion or advice about any condition of the patient relevant to this petition; and

(H) all other persons the petitioner believes may have information concerning the expressed wishes of the patient; and

(5) facts sufficient to establish the need for the relief requested, including, but not limited to, facts to support the allegation that the patient lacks the capacity to make the requisite medical treatment decision.

(b) **Supporting Documentation.** Any affidavits and supporting documentation, including any living will or designation of health care decision-maker, shall be attached to the petition.

(c) **Notice.** Unless waived by the court, notice of the petition and the preliminary hearing shall be served on the following persons who have not joined in the petition or otherwise consented to the proceedings:

(1) the patient;

(2) the patient's spouse and the patient's parents, if the patient is a minor;

(3) the patient's adult children;

(4) any guardian and any court-appointed health care decision-maker;

(5) any person designated by the patient in a living will or other document to exercise the patient's health care decision in the event of the patient's incapacity;

(6) the administrator of the hospital, nursing home, or other facility where the patient is located;

(7) the patient's principal treating physician and other physicians believed to have provided any medical opinion or advice about any condition of the patient relevant to this petition;

(8) all other persons the petitioner believes may have information concerning the expressed wishes of the patient; and

(9) such other persons as the court may direct.

(d) **Hearing.** A preliminary hearing on the petition shall be held within 72 hours after the filing of the petition. At that time the court shall review the petition and supporting documentation. In its discretion the court shall either:

(1) rule on the relief requested immediately after the preliminary hearing; or

(2) conduct an evidentiary hearing not later than 4 days after the preliminary hearing and rule on the relief requested immediately after the evidentiary hearing.

Added Aug. 22, 1991, effective Oct. 1, 1991 (584 So.2d 964). Amended Sept. 24, 1992, effective Jan. 1, 1993 (607 So.2d 1306).

Committee Notes

This rule was submitted by the committee in response to the request contained in footnote 17 of *In re Guardianship of Browning*, 568 So.2d 4 (Fla. 1990). See also *Cruzan by Cruzan v. Director*, Missouri Department of Health, 497 U.S. 261, 110 S.Ct. 2841, 111 L. Ed.2d 224 (1990).

The promulgation of this rule is not intended to imply that judicial intervention is required to terminate life-prolonging procedures.

Practitioners should note that the criteria and standards of proof contained in Browning differ from the criteria and standards of proof presently existing in chapter 765, Florida Statutes.

Rule History

1991 Revision: New rule.

1992 Revision: This rule was created on an emergency basis and on further review, the committee decided it needed to clarify that the petition should include an allegation that the patient lacks capacity to make the requisite medical treatment decision, and that the patient should receive notice of the petition and hearing. Committee notes revised. Citation form changes in committee notes.

2008 Revision: Committee notes revised.

Constitutional Reference

Art. I, § 23, Fla. Const.

Statutory References

§ 393.12, Fla. Stat. Capacity; appointment of guardian advocate.

§ 709.08, Fla. Stat. Durable power of attorney.

§ 731.302, Fla. Stat. Waiver and consent by interested person.

§ 744.102, Fla. Stat. Definitions.

§ 744.104, Fla. Stat. Verification of documents.

§ 744.3115, Fla. Stat. Advance directives for health care.

ch. 765, Fla. Stat. Health care advance directives.

Rule References

Fla. Prob. R. 5.020 Pleadings; verification; motions.

Fla. Prob. R. 5.040 Notice.

APPENDIX

Rules of Civil Procedure

The Rules of Civil Procedure applicable to probate and guardianship proceedings pursuant to Probate Rule 5.010, as provided for in Rule 5.080 are set out in this appendix for the user's convenience.

Rule

Rule 1.280.   General Provisions Governing Discovery

(a) Discovery Methods.   Parties may obtain discovery by one or more of the following methods: depositions upon oral examination or written questions; written interrogatories; production of documents or things or permission to enter upon land or other property for inspection and other purposes; physical and mental examinations; and requests for admission. Unless the court orders otherwise and under subdivision (c) of this rule, the frequency of use of these methods is not limited, except as provided in rules 1.200, 1.340, and 1.370.

(b) Scope of Discovery.   Unless otherwise limited by order of the court in accordance with these rules, the scope of discovery is as follows:

(1) *In General.*   Parties may obtain discovery regarding any matter, not privileged, that is relevant to the subject matter of the pending action, whether it relates to the claim or defense of the party seeking discovery or the claim or defense of any other party, including the existence, description, nature, custody, condition, and location of any books, documents, or other tangible things and the identity and location of persons having knowledge of any discoverable matter. It is not ground for objection that the information sought will be inadmissible at the trial if the information sought appears reasonably calculated to lead to the discovery of admissible evidence.

(2) *Indemnity Agreements.* A party may obtain discovery of the existence and contents of any agreement under which any person may be liable to satisfy part or all of a judgment that may be entered in the action or to indemnify or to reimburse a party for payments made to satisfy the judgment. Information concerning the agreement is not admissible in evidence at trial by reason of disclosure.

---

(3) *Electronically Stored Information.* A party may obtain discovery of electronically stored information in accordance with these rules.

(4) *Trial Preparation: Materials.* Subject to the provisions of subdivision (b)(5) of this rule, a party may obtain discovery of documents and tangible things otherwise discoverable under subdivision (b)(1) of this rule and prepared in anticipation of litigation or for trial by or for another party or by or for that party's representative, including that party's attorney, consultant, surety, indemnitor, insurer, or agent, only upon a showing that the party seeking discovery has need of the materials in the preparation of the case and is unable without undue hardship to obtain the substantial equivalent of the materials by other means. In ordering discovery of the materials when the required showing has been made, the court shall protect against disclosure of the mental impressions, conclusions, opinions, or legal theories of an attorney or other representative of a party concerning the litigation. Without the required showing a party may obtain a copy of a statement concerning the action or its subject matter previously made by that party. Upon request without the required showing a person not a party may obtain a copy of a statement concerning the action or its subject matter previously made by that person. If the request is refused, the person may move for an order to obtain a copy. The provisions of rule 1.380(a)(4) apply to the award of expenses incurred as a result of making the motion. For purposes of this paragraph, a statement previously made is a written statement signed or otherwise adopted or approved by the person making it, or a stenographic, mechanical, electrical, or other recording or transcription of it that is a substantially verbatim recital of an oral statement by the person making it and contemporaneously recorded.

(5) *Trial Preparation: Experts.* Discovery of facts known and opinions held by experts, otherwise discoverable under the provisions of subdivision (b)(1) of this rule and acquired or developed in anticipation of litigation or for trial, may be obtained only as follows:

(A)(i) By interrogatories a party may require any other party to identify each person whom the other party expects to call as an expert witness at trial and to state the subject matter on which the expert is expected to testify, and to state the substance of the facts and opinions to which the expert is expected to testify and a summary of the grounds for each opinion.

(ii) Any person disclosed by interrogatories or otherwise as a person expected to be called as an expert witness at trial may be deposed in accordance with rule 1.390 without motion or order of court.

(iii) A party may obtain the following discovery regarding any person disclosed by interrogatories or otherwise as a person expected to be called as an expert witness at trial:

1. The scope of employment in the pending case and the compensation for such service.

2. The expert's general litigation experience, including the percentage of work performed for plaintiffs and defendants.

3. The identity of other cases, within a reasonable time period, in which the expert has testified by deposition or at trial.

4. An approximation of the portion of the expert's involvement as an expert witness, which may be based on the number of hours, percentage of hours, or percentage of earned income derived from serving as an expert witness; however, the expert shall not be required to disclose his or her earnings as an expert witness or income derived from other services.

An expert may be required to produce financial and business records only under the most unusual or compelling circumstances and may not be compelled to compile or produce nonexistent documents. Upon motion, the court may order further discovery by other means, subject to such restrictions as to scope and other provisions pursuant to subdivision (b)(5)(C) of this rule concerning fees and expenses as the court may deem appropriate.

(B) A party may discover facts known or opinions held by an expert who has been retained or specially employed by another party in anticipation of litigation or preparation for trial and who is not expected to be called as a witness at trial, only as provided in rule 1.360(b) or upon a showing of exceptional circumstances under which it is impracticable for the party seeking discovery to obtain facts or opinions on the same subject by other means.

(C) Unless manifest injustice would result, the court shall require that the party seeking discovery pay the expert a reasonable fee for time spent in responding to discovery under subdivisions (b)(5)(A) and (b)(5)(B) of this rule; and concerning discovery from an expert obtained under subdivision (b)(5)(A) of this rule the court may require, and concerning discovery obtained under subdivision (b)(5)(B) of this rule shall require, the party seeking discovery to pay the other party a fair part of the fees and expenses reasonably incurred by the latter party in obtaining facts and opinions from the expert.

(D) As used in these rules an expert shall be an expert witness as defined in rule 1.390(a).

(6) *Claims of Privilege or Protection of Trial Preparation Materials.* When a party withholds information otherwise discoverable under these rules by claiming that it is privileged or subject to protection as trial preparation material, the party shall make the claim expressly and shall describe the nature of the documents, communications, or things not produced or disclosed in a manner that, without revealing information itself privileged or protected, will enable other parties to assess the applicability of the privilege or protection.

(c) Protective Orders. Upon motion by a party or by the person from whom discovery is sought, and for good cause shown, the court in which the action is pending may make any order to protect a party or person from annoyance, embarrassment, oppression, or undue burden or expense that justice requires, including one or more of the following: (1) that the discovery not be had; (2) that the discovery may be had only on specified terms and conditions, including a designation of the time or place; (3) that the discovery may be had only by a method of discovery other than that selected by the party seeking discovery; (4) that certain matters not be inquired into, or that the scope of the discovery be limited to certain matters; (5) that discovery be conducted with no one present except persons designated by the court; (6) that a deposition after being sealed be opened only by order of the court; (7) that a trade secret or other confidential research, development, or commercial information not be disclosed or be disclosed only in a designated way; and (8) that the parties simultaneously file specified documents or information enclosed in sealed envelopes to be opened as directed by the court. If the motion for a protective order is denied in whole or in part, the court may, on such terms and conditions as are just, order that any party or person provide or permit discovery. The provisions of rule 1.380(a)(4) apply to the award of expenses incurred in relation to the motion.

(d) Limitations on Discovery of Electronically Stored Information.

(1) A person may object to discovery of electronically stored information from sources that the person identifies as not reasonably accessible because of burden or cost. On motion to compel discovery or for a protective order, the person from whom discovery is sought must show that the information sought or the format requested is not reasonably accessible because of undue burden or cost. If that showing is made, the court may nonetheless order the discovery from such sources or in such formats if the requesting party shows good cause. The court may

specify conditions of the discovery, including ordering that some or all of the expenses incurred by the person from whom discovery is sought be paid by the party seeking the discovery.

(2) In determining any motion involving discovery of electronically stored information, the court must limit the frequency or extent of discovery otherwise allowed by these rules if it determines that (i) the discovery sought is unreasonably cumulative or duplicative, or can be obtained from another source or in another manner that is more convenient, less burdensome, or less expensive; or (ii) the burden or expense of the discovery outweighs its likely benefit, considering the needs of the case, the amount in controversy, the parties' resources, the importance of the issues at stake in the action, and the importance of the discovery in resolving the issues.

(e) Sequence and Timing of Discovery. Except as provided in subdivision (b)(5) or unless the court upon motion for the convenience of parties and witnesses and in the interest of justice orders otherwise, methods of discovery may be used in any sequence, and the fact that a party is conducting discovery, whether by deposition or otherwise, shall not delay any other party's discovery.

(f) Supplementing of Responses. A party who has responded to a request for discovery with a response that was complete when made is under no duty to supplement the response to include information thereafter acquired.

(g) Court Filing of Documents and Discovery. Information obtained during discovery shall not be filed with the court until such time as it is filed for good cause. The requirement of good cause is satisfied only where the filing of the information is allowed or required by another applicable rule of procedure or by court order. All filings of discovery documents shall comply with Florida Rule of Judicial Administration 2.425. The court shall have the authority to impose sanctions for violation of this rule.

Amended July 26, 1972, effective Jan. 1, 1973 (265 So.2d 21); Sept. 13, 1984, effective Jan. 1, 1985 (458 So.2d 245); Oct. 6, 1988, effective Jan. 1, 1989 (536 So.2d 974); July 6, 1989 (545 So.2d 866); July 16, 1992, effective Jan. 1, 1993 (604 So.2d 1110); Oct. 31, 1996, effective Jan. 1, 1997 (682 So.2d 105); Oct. 5, 2000, effective Jan. 1, 2001 (773 So.2d 1098); Sept. 27, 2007, effective Jan. 1, 2008 (966 So.2d 943); Nov. 3, 2011, effective, *nunc pro tunc*, Oct. 1, 2011 (78 So.3d 1045); July 5, 2012, effective Sept. 1, 2012 (95 So.3d 76).

Committee Notes

1972 Amendment. The rule is derived from Federal Rule of Civil Procedure 26 as amended in 1970. Subdivisions (a), (b)(2), and (b)(3) are new. Subdivision (c) contains material from former rule 1.310(b). Subdivisions (d) and (e) are new, but the latter is similar to former rule 1. 340(d). Significant changes are made in discovery from experts. The general rearrangement of the discovery rule is more logical and is the result of 35 years of experience under the federal rules.

1988 Amendment. Subdivision (b)(2) has been added to enable discovery of the existence and contents of indemnity agreements and is the result of the enactment of sections 627.7262 and 627.7264, Florida Statutes, proscribing the joinder of insurers but providing for disclosure. This rule is derived from Federal Rule of Civil Procedure 26(b)(2). Subdivisions (b)(2) and (b)(3) have been redesignated as (b)(3) and (b)(4) respectively.

The purpose of the amendment to subdivision (b)(3)(A) (renumbered (b)(4)(A)) is to allow, without leave of court, the depositions of experts who have been disclosed as expected to be used at trial. The purpose of subdivision (b)(4)(D) is to define the term "expert" as used in these rules.

1996 Amendment. The amendments to subdivision (b)(4)(A) are derived from the Supreme Court's decision in *Elkins v. Syken*, 672 So. 2d 517 (Fla. 1996). They are intended to avoid annoyance, embarrassment, and undue expense while still permitting the adverse party to obtain relevant information regarding the potential bias or interest of the expert witness.

Subdivision (b)(5) is added and is derived from Federal Rule of Civil Procedure 26(b)(5) (1993).

2011 Amendment. Subdivision (f) is added to ensure that information obtained during discovery is not filed with the court unless there is good cause for the documents to be filed, and that information obtained during discovery that includes certain private information shall not be filed with the court unless the private information is redacted as required by Florida Rule of Judicial Administration 2.425.

2012 Amendment. Subdivisions (b)(3) and (d) are added to address discovery of electronically stored information.

The parties should consider conferring with one another at the earliest practical opportunity to discuss the reasonable scope of preservation and production of electronically stored information. These issues may also be addressed by means of a rule 1.200 or rule 1.201 case management conference.

Under the good cause test in subdivision (d)(1), the court should balance the costs and burden of the requested discovery, including the potential for disruption of operations or corruption of the electronic devices or systems from which discovery is sought, against the relevance of the information and the requesting party's need for that information. Under the proportionality and reasonableness factors set out in subdivision (d)(2), the court must limit the frequency or extent of discovery if it determines that the discovery sought is excessive in relation to the factors listed.

In evaluating the good cause or proportionality tests, the court may find its task complicated if the parties know little about what information the sources at issue contain, whether the information sought is relevant, or how valuable it may be to the litigation. If appropriate, the court may direct the parties to develop the record further by engaging in focused discovery, including sampling of the sources, to learn more about what electronically stored information may be contained in those sources, what costs and burdens are involved in retrieving, reviewing, and producing the information, and how valuable the information sought may be to the litigation in light of the availability of information from other sources or methods of discovery, and in light of the parties' resources and the issues at stake in the litigation.

Court Commentary

2000 Amendment. *Allstate Insurance Co. v. Boecher*, 733 So.2d 993, 999 (Fla. 1999), clarifies that subdivision (b)(4)(A)(iii) is not intended "to place a blanket bar on discovery from parties about information they have in their possession about an expert, including the party's financial relationship with the expert."

Cross References

Application to probate and guardianship proceedings, see Probate Rule 5.080.
Discovery in aid of execution, see Civil Procedure Rule 1.560.
Expert witnesses, see Civil Procedure Rule 1.390.
Order compelling discovery, see Civil Procedure Rule 1.380.
Persons before whom depositions may be taken, see Civil Procedure Rule 1.300.
Refusal to make discovery, see Civil Procedure Rule 1.380.

Rule 1.290. Depositions Before Action or Pending Appeal

(a) Before Action.

(1) *Petition.* A person who desires to perpetuate that person's own testimony or that of another person regarding any matter that may be cognizable in any court of this state may file a verified petition in the circuit court in the county of the residence of any expected adverse party.

The petition shall be entitled in the name of the petitioner and shall show: (1) that the petitioner expects to be a party to an action cognizable in a court of Florida, but is presently unable to bring it or cause it to be brought, (2) the subject matter of the expected action and the petitioner's interest therein, (3) the facts which the petitioner desires to establish by the proposed testimony and the petitioner's reasons for desiring to perpetuate it, (4) the names or a description of the persons the petitioner expects will be adverse parties and their addresses so far as known, and (5) the names and addresses of the persons to be examined and the substance of the testimony which the petitioner expects to elicit from each; and shall ask for an order authorizing the petitioner to take the deposition of the persons to be examined named in the petition for the purpose of perpetuating their testimony.

(2) *Notice and Service.* The petitioner shall thereafter serve a notice upon each person named in the petition as an expected adverse party, together with a copy of the petition, stating that the petitioner will apply to the court at a time and place named therein for an order described in the petition. At least 20 days before the date of hearing the notice shall be served either within or without the county in the manner provided by law for service of summons, but if such service cannot with due diligence be made upon any expected adverse party named in the petition, the court may make an order for service by publication or otherwise, and shall appoint an attorney for persons not served in the manner provided by law for service of summons who shall represent them, and if they are not otherwise represented, shall cross-examine the deponent.

(3) *Order and Examination.* If the court is satisfied that the perpetuation of the testimony may prevent a failure or delay of justice, it shall make an order designating or describing the persons whose depositions may be taken and specifying the subject matter of the examination and whether the deposition shall be taken upon oral examination or written interrogatories. The deposition may then be taken in accordance with these rules and the court may make orders in accordance with the requirements of these rules. For the purpose of applying these rules to depositions for perpetuating testimony, each reference therein to the court in which the action is pending shall be deemed to refer to the court in which the petition for such deposition was filed.

(4) *Use of Deposition.* A deposition taken under this rule may be used in any action involving the same subject matter subsequently brought in any court in accordance with rule 1.330.

(b) Pending Appeal. If an appeal has been taken from a judgment of any court or before the taking of an appeal if the time therefor has not expired, the court in which the judgment was rendered may allow the taking of the depositions of witnesses to perpetuate their testimony for use in the event of further proceedings in the court. In such case the party who desires to perpetuate the testimony may make a motion for leave to take the deposition upon the same notice and service as if the action was pending in the court. The motion shall show (1) the names and addresses of persons to be examined and the substance of the testimony which the movant expects to elicit from each, and (2) the reason for perpetuating their testimony. If the court finds that the perpetuation of the testimony is proper to avoid a failure or delay in justice, it may make an order allowing the deposition to be taken and may make orders of the character provided for by these rules, and thereupon the deposition may be taken and used in the same manner and under the same conditions as are prescribed in these rules for depositions taken in actions pending in the court.

(c) Perpetuation by Action. This rule does not limit the power of a court to entertain an action to perpetuate testimony.

Amended Oct. 9, 1980, effective Jan. 1, 1981 (391 So.2d 165); Sept. 13, 1984, effective Jan. 1, 1985 (458 So.2d 245); July 16, 1992, effective Jan. 1, 1993 (604 So.2d 1110).

Committee Notes

1980 Amendment. Subdivision (d) is repealed because depositions de bene esse are obsolete. Rules 1.280 and 1.310 with the remainder of this rule cover all needed deposition circumstances and do so better. Subdivision (d) was taken from former chapter 63, Florida Statutes, and is not a complete procedure without reference to the parts of the statute not carried forward in the rule.

Cross References

Arbitration proceedings, see F.S.A. § 682.08.
Consequences for refusal to make discovery, see Civil Procedure Rule 1.380.
Depositions upon oral examination, see Civil Procedure Rule 1.310.
Effect of errors and irregularities in depositions, see Civil Procedure Rule 1.330.
Expert witnesses, see Civil Procedure Rule 1.390.
Persons before whom depositions may be taken, see Civil Procedure Rule 1.300.
Summary procedure, civil actions, see F.S.A. § 51.011.
Uniform Foreign Depositions Law, see F.S.A. § 92.251.
Workers' compensation actions, see F.S.A. § 440.30.
Written questions, see Civil Procedure Rule 1.320.

Rule 1.300. Persons Before Whom Depositions May Be Taken

(a) **Persons Authorized.** Depositions may be taken before any notary public or judicial officer or before any officer authorized by the statutes of Florida to take acknowledgments or proof of executions of deeds or by any person appointed by the court in which the action is pending.

(b) **In Foreign Countries.** In a foreign country depositions may be taken (1) on notice before a person authorized to administer oaths in the place in which the examination is held, either by the law thereof or by the law of Florida or of the United States, (2) before a person commissioned by the court, and a person so commissioned shall have the power by virtue of the commission to administer any necessary oath and take testimony, or (3) pursuant to a letter rogatory. A commission or a letter rogatory shall be issued on application and notice and on terms that are just and appropriate. It is not requisite to the issuance of a commission or a letter rogatory that the taking of the deposition in any other manner is impracticable or inconvenient, and both a commission and a letter rogatory may be issued in proper cases. A notice or commission may designate the person before whom the deposition is to be taken either by name or descriptive title. A letter rogatory may be addressed "To the Appropriate Authority in _____ (name of country) _____." Evidence obtained in response to a letter rogatory need not be excluded merely for the reason that it is not a verbatim transcript or that the testimony was not taken under oath or any similar departure from the requirements for depositions taken within Florida under these rules.

(c) **Selection by Stipulation.** If the parties so stipulate in writing, depositions may be taken before any person at any time or place upon any notice and in any manner and when so taken may be used like other depositions.

(d) **Persons Disqualified.** Unless so stipulated by the parties, no deposition shall be taken before a person who is a relative, employee, attorney, or counsel of any of the parties, is a relative or employee of any of the parties' attorney or counsel, or is financially interested in the action.

Amended July 16, 1992, effective Jan. 1, 1993 (604 So.2d 1110).

Cross References

Certification and filing, see Civil Procedure Rule 1.310.
Depositions, objection to admissibility, see Civil Procedure Rule 1.330.
Depositions before foreign commissioners, see Civil Procedure Rule 1.410.
Record of deposition, see Civil Procedure Rules 1.310, 1.320.
Waiver as to disqualification, see Civil Procedure Rule 1.330.

Rule 1.310. Depositions Upon Oral Examination

(a) When Depositions May Be Taken. After commencement of the action any party may take the testimony of any person, including a party, by deposition upon oral examination. Leave of court, granted with or without notice, must be obtained only if the plaintiff seeks to take a deposition within 30 days after service of the process and initial pleading upon any defendant, except that leave is not required (1) if a defendant has served a notice of taking deposition or otherwise sought discovery, or (2) if special notice is given as provided in subdivision (b)(2) of this rule. The attendance of witnesses may be compelled by subpoena as provided in rule 1.410. The deposition of a person confined in prison may be taken only by leave of court on such terms as the court prescribes.

(b) Notice; Method of Taking; Production at Deposition.

(1) A party desiring to take the deposition of any person upon oral examination shall give reasonable notice in writing to every other party to the action. The notice shall state the time and place for taking the deposition and the name and address of each person to be examined, if known, and, if the name is not known, a general description sufficient to identify the person or the particular class or group to which the person belongs. If a subpoena duces tecum is to be served on the person to be examined, the designation of the materials to be produced under the subpoena shall be attached to or included in the notice.

(2) Leave of court is not required for the taking of a deposition by plaintiff if the notice states that the person to be examined is about to go out of the state and will be unavailable for examination unless a deposition is taken before expiration of the 30-day period under subdivision (a). If a party shows that when served with notice under this subdivision that party was unable through the exercise of diligence to obtain counsel to represent the party at the taking of the deposition, the deposition may not be used against that party.

(3) For cause shown the court may enlarge or shorten the time for taking the deposition.

(4) Any deposition may be recorded by videotape without leave of the court or stipulation of the parties, provided the deposition is taken in accordance with this subdivision.

(A) Notice. A party intending to videotape a deposition shall state in the notice that the deposition is to be videotaped and shall give the name and address of the operator. Any subpoena served on the person to be examined shall state the method or methods for recording the testimony.

(B) Stenographer. Videotaped depositions shall also be recorded stenographically, unless all parties agree otherwise.

(C) Procedure. At the beginning of the deposition, the officer before whom it is taken shall, on camera: (i) identify the style of the action, (ii) state the date, and (iii) swear the witness.

(D) Custody of Tape and Copies. The attorney for the party requesting the videotaping of the deposition shall take custody of and be responsible for the safeguarding of the videotape, shall permit the viewing of it by the opposing party, and, if requested, shall provide a copy of the videotape at the expense of the party requesting the copy.

(E) Cost of Videotaped Depositions. The party requesting the videotaping shall bear the initial cost of videotaping.

(5) The notice to a party deponent may be accompanied by a request made in compliance with rule 1.350 for the production of documents and tangible things at the taking of the deposition. The procedure of rule 1.350 shall apply to the request. Rule 1.351 provides the exclusive procedure for obtaining documents or things by subpoena from nonparties without deposing the custodian or other person in possession of the documents.

(6) In the notice a party may name as the deponent a public or private corporation, a partnership or association, or a governmental agency, and designate with reasonable particularity the matters on which examination is requested. The organization so named shall designate one or more officers, directors, or managing agents, or other persons who consent to do so, to testify on its behalf and may state the matters on which each person designated will testify. The persons so designated shall testify about matters known or reasonably available to the organization. This subdivision does not preclude taking a deposition by any other procedure authorized in these rules.

(7) On motion the court may order that the testimony at a deposition be taken by telephone. The order may prescribe the manner in which the deposition will be taken. A party may also arrange for a stenographic transcription at that party's own initial expense.

(8) Any minor subpoenaed for testimony shall have the right to be accompanied by a parent or guardian at all times during the taking of testimony notwithstanding the invocation of the rule of sequestration of section 90.616, Florida Statutes, except upon a showing that the presence of a parent or guardian is likely to have a material, negative impact on the credibility or accuracy of the minor's testimony, or that the interests of the parent or guardian are in actual or potential conflict with the interests of the minor.

(c) **Examination and Cross–Examination; Record of Examination; Oath; Objections.** Examination and cross-examination of witnesses may proceed as permitted at the trial. The officer before whom the deposition is to be taken shall put the witness on oath and shall personally, or by someone acting under the officer's direction and in the officer's presence, record the testimony of the witness, except that when a deposition is being taken by telephone, the witness shall be sworn by a person present with the witness who is qualified to administer an oath in that location. The testimony shall be taken stenographically or recorded by any other means ordered in accordance with subdivision (b)(4) of this rule. If requested by one of the parties, the testimony shall be transcribed at the initial cost of the requesting party and prompt notice of the request shall be given to all other parties. All objections made at time of the examination to the qualifications of the officer taking the deposition, the manner of taking it, the evidence presented, or the conduct of any party, and any other objection to the proceedings shall be noted by the officer upon the deposition. Any objection during a deposition shall be stated concisely and in a nonargumentative and nonsuggestive manner. A party may instruct a deponent not to answer only when necessary to preserve a privilege, to enforce a limitation on evidence directed by the court, or to present a motion under subdivision (d). Otherwise, evidence objected to shall be taken subject to the objections. Instead of participating in the oral examination, parties may serve written questions in a sealed envelope on the party taking the deposition and that party shall transmit them to the officer, who shall propound them to the witness and record the answers verbatim.

(d) **Motion to Terminate or Limit Examination.** At any time during the taking of the deposition, on motion of a party or of the deponent and upon a showing that the examination is being conducted in bad faith or in such manner as unreasonably to annoy, embarrass, or oppress the deponent or party, or that objection and instruction to a deponent not to answer are being made in violation of rule 1.310(c), the court in which the action is pending or the circuit court where the deposition is being taken may order the officer conducting the examination to ·cease forthwith from taking the deposition or may limit the scope and manner of the taking of the deposition under rule 1.280(c). If the order terminates the examination, it shall be resumed thereafter only upon the order of the court in which the action is pending. Upon demand of any party or the deponent, the taking of the deposition shall be suspended for the time necessary to make a motion for an order. The provisions of rule 1.380(a) apply to the award of expenses incurred in relation to the motion.

(e) Witness Review. If the testimony is transcribed, the transcript shall be furnished to the witness for examination and shall be read to or by the witness unless the examination and reading are waived by the witness and by the parties. Any changes in form or substance that the witness wants to make shall be listed in writing by the officer with a statement of the reasons given by the witness for making the changes. The changes shall be attached to the transcript. It shall then be signed by the witness unless the parties waived the signing or the witness is ill, cannot be found, or refuses to sign. If the transcript is not signed by the witness within a reasonable time after it is furnished to the witness, the officer shall sign the transcript and state on the transcript the waiver, illness, absence of the witness, or refusal to sign with any reasons given therefor. The deposition may then be used as fully as though signed unless the court holds that the reasons given for the refusal to sign require rejection of the deposition wholly or partly, on motion under rule 1.330(d)(4).

(f) Filing; Exhibits.

(1) If the deposition is transcribed, the officer shall certify on each copy of the deposition that the witness was duly sworn by the officer and that the deposition is a true record of the testimony given by the witness. Documents and things produced for inspection during the examination of the witness shall be marked for identification and annexed to and returned with the deposition upon the request of a party, and may be inspected and copied by any party, except that the person producing the materials may substitute copies to be marked for identification if that person affords to all parties fair opportunity to verify the copies by comparison with the originals. If the person producing the materials requests their return, the officer shall mark them, give each party an opportunity to inspect and copy them, and return them to the person producing them and the materials may then be used in the same manner as if annexed to and returned with the deposition.

(2) Upon payment of reasonable charges therefor the officer shall furnish a copy of the deposition to any party or to the deponent.

(3) A copy of a deposition may be filed only under the following circumstances:

(A) It may be filed in compliance with Florida Rule of Judicial Administration 2.425 and rule 1.280(f) by a party or the witness when the contents of the deposition must be considered by the court on any matter pending before the court. Prompt notice of the filing of the deposition shall be given to all parties unless notice is waived. A party filing the deposition shall furnish a copy of the deposition or the part being filed to other parties unless the party already has a copy.

(B) If the court determines that a deposition previously taken is necessary for the decision of a matter pending before the court, the court may order that a copy be filed by any party at the initial cost of the party, and the filing party shall comply with rules 2.425 and 1.280(f).

(g) Obtaining Copies. A party or witness who does not have a copy of the deposition may obtain it from the officer taking the deposition unless the court orders otherwise. If the deposition is obtained from a person other than the officer, the reasonable cost of reproducing the copies shall be paid to the person by the requesting party or witness.

(h) Failure to Attend or to Serve Subpoena; Expenses.

(1) If the party giving the notice of the taking of a deposition fails to attend and proceed therewith and another party attends in person or by attorney pursuant to the notice, the court may order the party giving the notice to pay to the other party the reasonable expenses incurred by the other party and the other party's attorney in attending, including reasonable attorneys' fees.

(2) If the party giving the notice of the taking of a deposition of a witness fails to serve a subpoena upon the witness and the witness because of the failure does not attend and if another party attends in person or by attorney because that other party expects the deposition of that witness to be taken, the court may order the party giving the notice to pay to the other party the reasonable expenses incurred by that other party and that other party's attorney in attending, including reasonable attorneys' fees.

Amended July 26, 1972, effective Jan. 1, 1973 (265 So.2d 21); Dec. 13, 1976, effective Jan. 1, 1977 (339 So.2d 626); June 14, 1979, effective July 1, 1979 (372 So.2d 449); Sept. 10, 1981, effective Jan. 1, 1982 (403 So.2d 926); Sept. 13, 1984, effective Jan. 1, 1985 (458 So.2d 245); Oct. 6, 1988, effective Jan. 1, 1989 (536 So.2d 974); July 16, 1992, effective Jan. 1, 1993 (604 So.2d 1110); Oct. 31, 1996, effective Jan. 1, 1997 (682 So.2d 105); Oct. 5, 2000, effective Jan. 1, 2001 (773 So.2d 1098); Sept. 27, 2007, effective Jan. 1, 2008 (966 So.2d 943); Sept. 8, 2010, effective Jan. 1, 2011 (52 So.3d 579); Nov. 3, 2011, effective, *nunc pro tunc*, Oct. 1, 2011 (78 So.3d 1045).

Committee Notes

1972 Amendment. Derived from Federal Rule of Civil Procedure 30 as amended in 1970. Subdivision (a) is derived from rule 1.280(a); subdivision (b) from rule 1.310(a) with additional matter added; the first sentence of subdivision (c) has been added and clarifying language added throughout the remainder of the rule.

1976 Amendment. Subdivision (b)(4) has been amended to allow the taking of a videotaped deposition as a matter of right. Provisions for the taxation of costs and the entry of a standard order are included as well. This new amendment allows the contemporaneous stenographic transcription of a videotaped deposition.

1988 Amendment. The amendments to subdivision (b)(4) are to provide for depositions by videotape as a matter of right.

The notice provision is to ensure that specific notice is given that the deposition will be videotaped and to disclose the identity of the operator. It was decided not to make special provision for a number of days' notice.

The requirement that a stenographer be present (who is also the person likely to be swearing the deponent) is to ensure the availability of a transcript (although not required). The transcript would be a tool to ensure the accuracy of the videotape and thus eliminate the need to establish other procedures aimed at the same objective (like time clocks in the picture and the like). This does not mean that a transcript must be made. As at ordinary depositions, this would be up to the litigants.

Technical videotaping procedures were not included. It is anticipated that technical problems may be addressed by the court on motions to quash or motions for protective orders.

Subdivision (c) has been amended to accommodate the taking of depositions by telephone. The amendment requires the deponent to be sworn by a person authorized to administer oaths in the deponent's location and who is present with the deponent.

1992 Amendment. Subdivision (b)(4)(D) is amended to clarify an ambiguity in whether the cost of the videotape copy is to be borne by the party requesting the videotaping or by the party requesting the copy. The amendment requires the party requesting the copy to bear the cost of the copy.

1996 Amendment. Subdivision (c) is amended to state the existing law, which authorizes attorneys to instruct deponents not to answer questions only in specific situations. This amendment is derived from Federal Rule of Civil Procedure 30(d) as amended in 1993.

2010 Amendment. Subdivision (b)(5) is amended to clarify that the procedure set forth in rule 1.351 must be followed when requesting or receiving documents or things without testimony, from nonparties pursuant to a subpoena. The amendment is intended to prevent the use of rules 1.310 and 1.410 to request documents from nonparties pursuant to a subpoena without giving the opposing party the opportunity to object to the subpoena before it is served on the nonparty as required by rule 1.351.

2011 Amendment. A reference to Florida Rule of Judicial Administration 2.425 and rule 1.280(f) is added to require persons filing discovery materials with the court to make sure that good cause exists prior to filing discovery materials and that certain specific personal information is redacted.

Court Commentary

1984 Amendment. Subdivision (b)(7) is added to authorize deposition by telephone, with provision for any party to have a stenographic transcription at that party's own initial expense.

Subdivision (d) is changed to permit any party to terminate the deposition, not just the objecting party.

Subdivision (e) is changed to eliminate the confusing requirement that a transcript be submitted to the witness. The term has been construed as requiring the court reporter to travel, if necessary, to the witness, and creates a problem when a witness is deposed in Florida and thereafter leaves the state before signing. The change is intended to permit the parties and the court reporter to handle such situations on an ad hoc basis as is most appropriate.

Subdivision (f) is the committee's action in response to the petition seeking amendment to rule 1.310(f) filed in the Supreme Court Case No. 62,699. Subdivision (f) is changed to clarify the need for furnishing copies when a deposition, or part of it, is properly filed, to authorize the court to require a deposition to be both transcribed and filed, and to specify that a party who does not obtain a copy of the deposition may get it from the court reporter unless ordered otherwise by the court. This eliminates the present requirement of furnishing a copy of the deposition, or material part of it, to a person who already has a copy in subdivision (f)(3)(A).

Subdivision (f)(3)(B) broadens the authority of the court to require the filing of a deposition that has been taken, but not transcribed.

Subdivision (g) requires a party to obtain a copy of the deposition from the court reporter unless the court orders otherwise. Generally, the court should not order a party who has a copy of the deposition to furnish it to someone who has neglected to obtain it when the deposition was transcribed. The person should obtain it from the court reporter unless there is a good reason why it cannot be obtained from the reporter.

Cross References

Rule 1.320. Depositions Upon Written Questions

(a) Serving Questions; Notice. After commencement of the action any party may take the testimony of any person, including a party, by deposition upon written questions. The attendance of witnesses may be compelled by the use of subpoena as provided in rule 1.410. The deposition of a person confined in prison may be taken only by leave of court on such terms as the court prescribes. A party desiring to take a deposition upon written questions shall serve them with a notice stating (1) the name and address of the person who is to answer them, if known, and, if the name is not known, a general description sufficient to identify the person or the particular class or group to which that person belongs, and (2) the name or descriptive title and address of the officer before whom the deposition is to be taken. A deposition upon written questions may be taken of a public or private corporation, a partnership or association, or a governmental agency in accordance with rule 1.310(b)(6). Within 30 days after the notice and written questions are served, a party may serve cross questions upon all other parties. Within 10 days after being served with cross questions, a party may serve redirect questions upon all other parties. Within 10 days after being served with redirect questions, a party may serve recross questions upon all other parties. The court may for cause shown enlarge or shorten the time.

(b) Officer to Take Responses and Prepare Record. A copy of the notice and copies of all questions served shall be delivered by the party taking the depositions to the officer designated in the notice, who shall proceed promptly to take the testimony of the witness in the manner provided by rules 1.310(c), (e), and (f) in response to the questions and to prepare the deposition, attaching the copy of the notice and the questions received by the officer. The questions shall not be filed separately from the deposition unless a party seeks to have the court consider the questions before the questions are submitted to the witness.

Amended July 26, 1972, effective Jan. 1, 1973 (265 So.2d 21); Sept. 10, 1981, effective Jan. 1, 1982 (403 So.2d 926); July 16, 1992, effective Jan. 1, 1993 (604 So.2d 1110).

Committee Notes

1972 Amendment. Derived from Federal Rule of Civil Procedure 31 as amended in 1970. The name of interrogatories has been changed to questions to avoid confusion with interrogatories to parties under rule 1.340. Language changes resulting from the rearrangement of the discovery rules have been inserted and subdivision (d) deleted.

Cross References

Application to probate and guardianship proceedings, see Probate Rule 5.080.
Errors and irregularities, see Civil Procedure Rule 1.330.
Failure to serve answers, effect, see Civil Procedure Rule 1.380.
Interrogatories to parties, see Civil Procedure Rule 1.340.
Recordation by officer presiding, see Civil Procedure Rule 1.310.
Refusal to make discovery, see Civil Procedure Rule 1.380.

Rule 1.330. Use of Depositions in Court Proceedings

(a) Use of Depositions. At the trial or upon the hearing of a motion or an interlocutory proceeding, any part or all of a deposition may be used against any party who was present or represented at the taking of the deposition or who had reasonable notice of it so far as admissible under the rules of evidence applied as though the witness were then present and testifying in accordance with any of the following provisions:

(1) Any deposition may be used by any party for the purpose of contradicting or impeaching the testimony of the deponent as a witness or for any purpose permitted by the Florida Evidence Code.

(2) The deposition of a party or of anyone who at the time of taking the deposition was an officer, director, or managing agent or a person designated under rule 1.310(b)(6) or 1.320(a) to testify on behalf of a public or private corporation, a partnership or association, or a governmental agency that is a party may be used by an adverse party for any purpose.

(3) The deposition of a witness, whether or not a party, may be used by any party for any purpose if the court finds: (A) that the witness is dead; (B) that the witness is at a greater distance than 100 miles from the place of trial or hearing, or is out of the state, unless it appears that the absence of the witness was procured by the party offering the deposition; (C) that the witness is unable to attend or testify because of age, illness, infirmity, or imprisonment; (D) that the party offering the deposition has been unable to procure the attendance of the witness by subpoena; (E) upon application and notice, that such exceptional circumstances exist as to make it desirable, in the interest of justice and with due regard to the importance of presenting the testimony of witnesses orally in open court, to allow the deposition to be used; or (F) the witness is an expert or skilled witness.

(4) If only part of a deposition is offered in evidence by a party, an adverse party may require the party to introduce any other part that in fairness ought to be considered with the part introduced, and any party may introduce any other parts.

(5) Substitution of parties pursuant to rule 1.260 does not affect the right to use depositions previously taken and, when an action in any court of the United States or of any state has been dismissed and another action involving the same subject matter is afterward brought between the same parties or their representatives or successors in interest, all depositions lawfully taken and duly filed in the former action may be used in the latter as if originally taken for it.

(6) If a civil action is afterward brought, all depositions lawfully taken in a medical liability mediation proceeding may be used in the civil action as if originally taken for it.

(b) Objections to Admissibility. Subject to the provisions of rule 1.300(b) and subdivision (d)(3) of this rule, objection may be made at the trial or hearing to receiving in evidence any deposition or part of it for any reason that would require the exclusion of the evidence if the witness were then present and testifying.

(c) Effect of Taking or Using Depositions. A party does not make a person the party's own witness for any purpose by taking the person's deposition. The introduction in evidence of the deposition or any part of it for any purpose other than that of contradicting or impeaching the deponent makes the deponent the witness of the party introducing the deposition, but this shall not apply to the use by an adverse party of a deposition under subdivision (a)(2) of this rule. At the trial or hearing any party may rebut any relevant evidence contained in a deposition whether introduced by that party or by any other party.

(d) Effect of Errors and Irregularities.

(1) *As to Notice.* All errors and irregularities in the notice for taking a deposition are waived unless written objection is promptly served upon the party giving the notice.

(2) *As to Disqualification of Officer.* Objection to taking a deposition because of disqualification of the officer before whom it is to be taken is waived unless made before the taking of the deposition begins or as soon thereafter as the disqualification becomes known or could be discovered with reasonable diligence.

(3) *As to Taking of Deposition.*

(A) Objections to the competency of a witness or to the competency, relevancy, or materiality of testimony are not waived by failure to make them before or during the taking of the deposition unless the ground of the objection is one that might have been obviated or removed if presented at that time.

(B) Errors and irregularities occurring at the oral examination in the manner of taking the deposition, in the form of the questions or answers, in the oath or affirmation, or in the conduct of parties and errors of any kind that might be obviated, removed, or cured if promptly presented are waived unless timely objection to them is made at the taking of the deposition.

(C) Objections to the form of written questions submitted under rule 1.320 are waived unless served in writing upon the party propounding them within the time allowed for serving the succeeding cross or other questions and within 10 days after service of the last questions authorized.

(4) *As to Completion and Return.* Errors and irregularities in the manner in which the testimony is transcribed or the deposition is prepared, signed, certified, or otherwise dealt with by the officer under rules 1.310 and 1.320 are waived unless a motion to suppress the deposition or some part of it is made with reasonable promptness after the defect is, or with due diligence might have been, discovered.

Amended July 26, 1972, effective Jan. 1, 1973 (265 So.2d 21); July 14, 1977, effective Sept. 1, 1977 (348 So.2d 325); Sept. 10, 1981, effective Jan. 1, 1982 (403 So.2d 926); July 16, 1992, effective Jan. 1, 1993 (604 So.2d 1110); Oct. 1, 1998 (718 So.2d 795).

Committee Notes

1972 Amendment. Derived from Federal Rule of Civil Procedure 32 as amended in 1970. Subdivisions (a), (b), and (c) are former rules 1.280(d), (f), and (g) respectively. Subdivision (d) is derived from the entire former rule 1.330.

1998 Amendment. Subdivision (a)(1) was amended to clarify that, in addition to the uses of depositions prescribed by these rules, depositions may be used for any purpose permitted by the Florida Evidence Code (chapter 90, Fla. Stat.). This amendment is consistent with the 1980 amendment to Rule 32 of the Federal Rules of Civil Procedure.

Cross References

Application to probate and guardianship proceedings, see Probate Rule 5.080.
Objections to taking deposition notation by officer, see Civil Procedure Rule 1.310.
Officer to sign deposition if witness fails to, see Civil Procedure Rule 1.310.
Proof of testimony or written admissions of a party, see F.S.A. § 90.957.

Rule 1.340. Interrogatories to Parties

(a) **Procedure for Use.** Without leave of court, any party may serve upon any other party written interrogatories to be answered (1) by the party to whom the interrogatories are directed, or (2) if that party is a public or private corporation or partnership or association or governmental agency, by any officer or agent, who shall furnish the information available to that party. Interrogatories may be served on the plaintiff after commencement of the action and on any other party with or after service of the process and initial pleading upon that party. The interrogatories shall not exceed 30, including all subparts, unless the court permits a larger number on motion and notice and for good cause. If the supreme court has approved a form of interrogatories for the type of action, the initial interrogatories on a subject included therein shall be from the form approved by the court. A party may serve fewer than all of the approved interrogatories within a form. Other interrogatories may be added to the approved forms without leave of court, so long as the total of approved and additional interrogatories does not exceed 30. Each interrogatory shall be answered separately and fully in writing under oath unless it is objected to, in which event the grounds for objection shall be stated and signed by the attorney making it. The party to whom the interrogatories are directed shall serve the answers and any objections within 30 days after the service of the interrogatories, except that a defendant may serve answers or objections within 45 days after service of the process and initial pleading upon that defendant. The court may allow a shorter or longer time. The party submitting the interrogatories may move for an order under rule 1.380(a) on any objection to or other failure to answer an interrogatory.

(b) **Scope; Use at Trial.** Interrogatories may relate to any matters that can be inquired into under rule 1.280(b), and the answers may be used to the extent permitted by the rules of evidence except as otherwise provided in this subdivision. An interrogatory otherwise proper is not objectionable merely because an answer to the interrogatory involves an opinion or contention that relates to fact or calls for a conclusion or asks for information not within the personal knowledge of the party. A party shall respond to such an interrogatory by giving the information the party has and the source on which the information is based. Such a qualified answer may not be used as direct evidence for or impeachment against the party giving the answer unless the court finds it otherwise admissible under the rules of evidence. If a party introduces an answer to an interrogatory, any other party may require that party to introduce any other interrogatory and answer that in fairness ought to be considered with it.

(c) **Option to Produce Records.** When the answer to an interrogatory may be derived or ascertained from the records (including electronically stored information) of the party to whom the interrogatory is directed or from an examination, audit, or inspection of the records or from a compilation, abstract, or summary based on the records and the burden of deriving or ascertaining the answer is substantially the same for the party serving the interrogatory as for the party to whom it is directed, an answer to the interrogatory specifying the records from which the answer may be derived or ascertained and offering to give the party serving the interrogatory a reasonable opportunity to examine, audit, or inspect the records and to make copies, compilations, abstracts, or summaries is a sufficient answer. An answer shall be in sufficient detail to permit the interrogating party to locate and to identify, as readily as can the party interrogated, the records from which the answer may be derived or ascertained, or shall identify a person or persons representing the interrogated party who will be available to assist the interrogating party in locating and identifying the records at the time they are produced. If the records to be produced consist of electronically stored information, the records shall be produced in a form or forms in which they are ordinarily maintained or in a reasonably usable form or forms.

(d) **Effect on Co-Party.** Answers made by a party shall not be binding on a co-party.

(e) **Service and Filing.** Interrogatories shall be arranged so that a blank space is provided after each separately numbered interrogatory. The space shall be reasonably sufficient to enable the answering party to insert the answer within the space. If sufficient space is not provided, the answering party may attach additional papers with answers and refer to them in the space provided in the interrogatories. The interrogatories shall be served on the party to whom the interrogatories are directed and copies shall be served on all other parties. A certificate of service of the interrogatories shall be filed, giving the date of service and the name of the party to whom they were directed. The answers to the interrogatories shall be served upon the party originally propounding the interrogatories and a copy shall be served on all other parties by the answering party. The original or any copy of the answers to interrogatories may be filed in compliance with Florida Rule of Judicial Administration 2.425 and rule 1.280(g) by any party when the court should consider the answers to interrogatories in determining any matter pending before the court. The court may order a copy of the answers to interrogatories filed at any time when the court determines that examination of the answers to interrogatories is necessary to determine any matter pending before the court.

Amended June 19, 1968, effective Oct. 1, 1968 (211 So.2d 206); July 26, 1972, effective Jan. 1, 1973 (265 So.2d 21); Dec. 13, 1976, effective Jan. 1, 1977 (339 So.2d 626); July 14, 1977, effective Sept. 1, 1977 (348 So.2d 325); Oct. 9, 1980, effective Jan. 1, 1981 (391 So.2d 165); Sept. 10, 1981, effective Jan. 1, 1982 (403 So.2d 926); Nov. 12, 1981, effective Jan. 1, 1982 (407 So.2d 197); Sept. 13, 1984, effective Jan. 1, 1985 (458 So.2d 245); Oct. 6, 1988, effective Jan. 1, 1989 (536 So.2d 974); July 16, 1992, effective Jan. 1, 1993 (604 So.2d 1110); Sept. 8, 2010, effective Jan. 1, 2011 (52 So.3d 579); Nov. 3, 2011, effective, *nunc pro tunc*, Oct. 1, 2011 (78 So.3d 1045); July 5, 2012, effective Sept. 1, 2012 (95 So.3d 76).

Committee Notes

1972 Amendment. Subdivisions (a), (b), and (c) are derived from Federal Rule of Civil Procedure 33 as amended in 1970. Changes from the existing rule expand the time for answering, permit interrogatories to be served with the initial pleading or at any time thereafter, and eliminate the requirement of a hearing on objections. If objections are made, the interrogating party has the responsibility of setting a hearing if that party wants an answer. If the interrogatories are not sufficiently important, the interrogating party may let the matter drop. Subdivision (b) covers the same matter as the present rule 1.340(b) except those parts that have been transferred to rule 1.280. It also eliminates the confusion between facts and opinions or contentions by requiring that all be given. Subdivision (c) gives the interrogated party an option to produce business records from which the interrogating party can derive the answers to questions. Subdivision (d) is former subdivision (c) without change. Former subdivision (d) is repealed because it is covered in rule 1.280(e). Subdivision (e) is derived from the New Jersey rules and is intended to place both the interrogatories and the answers to them in a convenient place in the court file so that they can be referred to with less confusion. The requirement for filing a copy before the answers are received is necessary in the event of a dispute concerning what was done or the appropriate times involved.

1988 Amendment. The word "initial" in the 1984 amendment to subdivision (a) resulted in some confusion, so it has been deleted. Also the total number of interrogatories which may be propounded without leave of court is enlarged to 30 from 25. Form interrogatories which have been approved by the supreme court must be used; and those so used, with their subparts, are included in the total number permitted. The amendments are not intended to change any other requirement of the rule.

2011 Amendment. A reference to Florida Rule of Judicial Administration 2.425 and rule 1.280(f) is added to require persons filing discovery materials with the court to make sure that good cause exists prior to filing discovery materials and that certain specific personal information is redacted.

2012 Amendment. Subdivision (c) is amended to provide for the production of electronically stored information in answer to interrogatories and to set out a procedure for determining the form in which to produce electronically stored information.

Court Commentary

1984 Amendment. Subdivision (a) is amended by adding the reference to approved forms of interrogatories. The intent is to eliminate the burden of unnecessary interrogatories.

Subdivision (c) is amended to add the requirement of detail in identifying records when they are produced as an alternative to answering the interrogatory or to designate the persons who will locate the records.

Subdivision (e) is changed to eliminate the requirement of serving an original and a copy of the interrogatories and of the answers in light of the 1981 amendment that no longer permits filing except in special circumstances.

Subdivision (f) is deleted since the Medical Liability Mediation Proceedings have been eliminated.

Cross References

Application to probate and guardianship proceedings, see Probate Rule 5.080.
Consequences for failure to serve answers, see Civil Procedure Rule 1.380.
Proof of written admissions of a party, see F.S.A. § 90.957.
Refusal to make discovery, see Civil Procedure Rule 1.380.

Rule 1.350. Production of Documents and Things and Entry Upon Land for Inspection and Other Purposes

(a) **Request; Scope.** Any party may request any other party (1) to produce and permit the party making the request, or someone acting in the requesting party's behalf, to inspect and copy any designated documents, including electronically stored information, writings, drawings, graphs, charts, photographs, phono-records, and other data compilations from which information can be obtained, translated, if necessary, by the party to whom the request is directed through detection devices into reasonably usable form, that constitute or contain matters within the scope of rule 1.280(b) and that are in the possession, custody, or control of the party to whom the request is directed; (2) to inspect and copy, test, or sample any tangible things that constitute or contain matters within the scope of rule 1.280(b) and that are in the possession, custody, or control of the party to whom the request is directed; or (3) to permit entry upon designated land or other property in the possession or control of the party upon whom the request is served for the purpose of inspection and measuring, surveying, photographing, testing, or sampling the property or any designated object or operation on it within the scope of rule 1.280(b).

(b) **Procedure.** Without leave of court the request may be served on the plaintiff after commencement of the action and on any other party with or after service of the process and initial pleading on that party. The request shall set forth the items to be inspected, either by individual item or category, and describe each item and category with reasonable particularity. The request shall specify a reasonable time, place, and manner of making the inspection or performing the related acts. The party to whom the request is directed shall serve a written response within 30 days after service of the request, except that a defendant may serve a response within 45 days after service of the process and initial pleading on that defendant. The court may allow a shorter or longer time. For each item or category the response shall state that inspection and related activities will be permitted as requested unless the request is objected to, in which event the reasons for the objection shall be stated. If an objection is made to part of an item or category, the part shall be specified. When producing documents, the producing party shall either produce them as they are kept in the usual course of business or shall identify them to correspond with the categories in the request. A request for electronically stored information may specify the form or forms in which electronically stored information is to be produced. If the responding party objects to a requested form, or if no form is specified in the request, the responding party must state the form or forms it intends to use. If a request for electronically stored information does not specify the form of production, the producing party must produce the information in a form or forms in which it is ordinarily maintained or in a reasonably usable form or forms. The party submitting the request may move for an order under rule 1.380 concerning any objection, failure to respond to the request, or any part of it, or failure to permit the inspection as requested.

(c) Persons Not Parties. This rule does not preclude an independent action against a person not a party for production of documents and things and permission to enter upon land.

(d) Filing of Documents. Unless required by the court, a party shall not file any of the documents or things produced with the response. Documents or things may be filed in compliance with Florida Rule of Judicial Administration 2.425 and rule 1.280(g) when they should be considered by the court in determining a matter pending before the court.

Amended July 26, 1972, effective Jan. 1, 1973 (265 So.2d 21); Oct. 9, 1980, effective Jan. 1, 1981 (391 So.2d 165); Sept. 10, 1981, effective Jan. 1, 1982 (403 So.2d 926); July 16, 1992, effective Jan. 1, 1993 (604 So.2d 1110); Nov. 3, 2011, effective, *nunc pro tunc*, Oct. 1, 2011 (78 So.3d 1045); July 5, 2012, effective Sept. 1, 2012 (95 So.3d 76).

Committee Notes

1972 Amendment. Derived from Federal Rule of Civil Procedure 34 as amended in 1970. The new rule eliminates the good cause requirement of the former rule, changes the time for making the request and responding to it, and changes the procedure for the response. If no objection to the discovery is made, inspection is had without a court order. While the good cause requirement has been eliminated, the change is not intended to overrule cases limiting discovery under this rule to the scope of ordinary discovery, nor is it intended to overrule cases limiting unreasonable requests such as those reviewed in *Van Devere v. Holmes*, 156 So.2d 899 (Fla.3d DCA 1963); *IBM v. Elder*, 187 So.2d 82 (Fla.3d DCA 1966); and *Miami v. Florida Public Service Commission*, 226 So.2d 217 (Fla.1969). It is intended that the court review each objection and weigh the need for discovery and the likely results of it against the right of privacy of the party or witness or custodian.

1980 Amendment. Subdivision (b) is amended to require production of documents as they are kept in the usual course of business or in accordance with the categories in the request.

2011 Amendment. A reference to Florida Rule of Judicial Administration 2.425 and rule 1.280(f) is added to require persons filing discovery materials with the court to make sure that good cause exists prior to filing discovery materials and that certain specific personal information is redacted.

2012 Amendment. Subdivision (a) is amended to address the production of electronically stored information. Subdivision (b) is amended to set out a procedure for determining the form to be used in producing electronically stored information.

Cross References

Application to probate and guardianship proceedings, see Probate Rule 5.080.
Consequences for failure to comply with order to produce, see Civil Procedure Rule 1.380.
Continuance to procure discovery opposing summary judgment, see Civil Procedure Rule 1.510.
Documents, production by witnesses, costs, see F.S.A. § 92.153.
Medical patient records, see F.S.A. §§ 395.3025 and 455.667.
Refusal to make discovery, see Civil Procedure Rule 1.380.
Subpoena duces tecum, see Civil Procedure Rule 1.410.
Tax returns and reports from department of revenue, see F.S.A. § 213.053.

Rule 1.351. Production of Documents and Things Without Deposition

(a) **Request; Scope.** A party may seek inspection and copying of any documents or things within the scope of rule 1.350(a) from a person who is not a party by issuance of a subpoena directing the production of the documents or things when the requesting party does not seek to depose the custodian or other person in possession of the documents or things. This rule provides the exclusive procedure for obtaining documents or things by subpoena from nonparties without deposing the custodian or other person in possession of the documents or things pursuant to rule 1.310.

(b) **Procedure.** A party desiring production under this rule shall serve notice as provided in rule 1.080 on every other party of the intent to serve a subpoena under this rule at least 10 days before the subpoena is issued if service is by delivery and 15 days before the subpoena is issued if the service is by mail or e-mail. The proposed subpoena shall be attached to the notice and shall state the time, place, and method for production of the documents or things, and the name and address of the person who is to produce the documents or things, if known, and if not known, a general description sufficient to identify the person or the particular class or group to which the person belongs; shall include a designation of the items to be produced; and shall state that the person who will be asked to produce the documents or things has the right to object to the production under this rule and that the person will not be required to surrender the documents or things. A copy of the notice and proposed subpoena shall not be furnished to the person upon whom the subpoena is to be served. If any party serves an objection to production under this rule within 10 days of service of the notice, the documents or things shall not be produced pending resolution of the objection in accordance with subdivision (d).

(c) **Subpoena.** If no objection is made by a party under subdivision (b), an attorney of record in the action may issue a subpoena or the party desiring production shall deliver to the clerk for issuance a subpoena together with a certificate of counsel or pro se party that no timely objection has been received from any party, and the clerk shall issue the subpoena and deliver it to the party desiring production. Service within the state of Florida of a nonparty subpoena shall be deemed sufficient if it complies with rule 1.410(d) or if (1) service is accomplished by mail or hand delivery by a commercial delivery service, and (2) written confirmation of delivery, with the date of service and the name and signature of the person accepting the subpoena, is obtained and filed by the party seeking production. The subpoena shall be identical to the copy attached to the notice and shall specify that no testimony may be taken and shall require only production of the documents or things specified in it. The subpoena may give the recipient an option to deliver or mail legible copies of the documents or things to the party serving the subpoena. The person upon whom the subpoena is served may condition the preparation of copies on the payment in advance of the reasonable costs of preparing the copies. The subpoena shall require production only in the county of the residence of the custodian or other person in possession of the documents or things or in the county where the documents or things are located or where the custodian or person in possession usually conducts business. If the person upon whom the subpoena is served objects at any time before the production of the documents or things, the documents or things shall not be produced under this rule, and relief may be obtained pursuant to rule 1.310.

(d) **Ruling on Objection.** If an objection is made by a party under subdivision (b), the party desiring production may file a motion with the court seeking a ruling on the objection or may proceed pursuant to rule 1.310.

(e) Copies Furnished. If the subpoena is complied with by delivery or mailing of copies as provided in subdivision (c), the party receiving the copies shall furnish a legible copy of each item furnished to any other party who requests it upon the payment of the reasonable cost of preparing the copies.

(f) Independent Action. This rule does not affect the right of any party to bring an independent action for production of documents and things or permission to enter upon land.

Added Oct. 9, 1980, effective Jan. 1, 1981 (391 So.2d 165). Amended July 16, 1992, effective Jan. 1, 1993 (604 So.2d 1110); Oct. 31, 1996, effective Jan. 1, 1997 (682 So.2d 105); Sept. 27, 2007, effective Jan. 1, 2008 (966 So.2d 943); Sept. 8, 2010, effective Jan. 1, 2011 (52 So.3d 579); Oct. 18, 2012, effective, *nunc pro tunc*, Sept. 1, 2012 (102 So.3d 505).

Committee Notes

1980 Adoption. This rule is designed to eliminate the need of taking a deposition of a records custodian when the person seeking discovery wants copies of the records only. It authorizes objections by any other party as well as the custodian of the records. If any person objects, recourse must be had to rule 1.310.

1996 Amendment. This rule was amended to avoid premature production of documents by nonparties, to clarify the clerk's role in the process, and to further clarify that any objection to the use of this rule does not contemplate a hearing before the court but directs the party to rule 1.310 to obtain the desired production. This amendment is not intended to preclude all communication between parties and nonparties. It is intended only to prohibit a party from prematurely sending to a nonparty a copy of the required notice or the proposed subpoena. This rule was also amended along with rule 1.410 to allow attorneys to issue subpoenas. See Committee Note for rule 1.410.

2007 Amendment. Subdivisions (b) and (d) were amended to permit a party seeking nonparty discovery to have other parties' objections resolved by the court.

2010 Amendment. Subdivision (a) is amended to clarify that the procedure set forth in rule 1.351, not rule 1.310, shall be followed when requesting or receiving documents or things, without testimony, from nonparties pursuant to a subpoena.

2012 Amendment. Subdivision (b) is amended to include e-mail service as provided in Fla. R. Jud. Admin. 2.516.

Cross References

Documents, production by witnesses, costs, see F.S.A. § 92.153.
Medical patient records, see F.S.A. §§ 395.3025 and 455.667.
Subpoena duces tecum, see Civil Procedure Rule 1.410.
Tax returns and reports, see F.S.A. § 213.053.

Rule 1.360. Examination of Persons

(a) Request; Scope.

(1) A party may request any other party to submit to, or to produce a person in that other party's custody or legal control for, examination by a qualified expert when the condition that is the subject of the requested examination is in controversy.

(A) When the physical condition of a party or other person under subdivision (a)(1) is in controversy, the request may be served on the plaintiff without leave of court after commencement of the action, and on any other person with or after service of the process and initial pleading on that party. The request shall specify a reasonable time, place, manner, conditions, and scope of the examination and the person or persons by whom the examination is to be made. The party to whom the request is directed shall serve a response within 30 days after service of the request, except that a defendant need not serve a response until 45 days after service of the process and initial pleading on that defendant. The court may allow a shorter or longer time. The response shall state that the examination will be permitted as requested unless the request is objected to, in which event the reasons for the objection shall be stated. If the examination is to be recorded or observed by others, the request or response shall also include the number of people attending, their role, and the method or methods of recording.

(B) In cases where the condition in controversy is not physical, a party may move for an examination by a qualified expert as in subdivision (a)(1). The order for examination shall be made only after notice to the person to be examined and to all parties, and shall specify the time, place, manner, conditions, and scope of the examination and the person or persons by whom it is to be made.

(C) Any minor required to submit to examination pursuant to this rule shall have the right to be accompanied by a parent or guardian at all times during the examination, except upon a showing that the presence of a parent or guardian is likely to have a material, negative impact on the minor's examination.

(2) An examination under this rule is authorized only when the party submitting the request has good cause for the examination. At any hearing the party submitting the request shall have the burden of showing good cause.

(3) Upon request of either the party requesting the examination or the party or person to be examined, the court may establish protective rules governing such examination.

(b) Report of Examiner.

(1) If requested by the party to whom a request for examination or against whom an order is made under subdivision (a)(1)(A) or (a)(1)(B) or by the person examined, the party requesting the examination to be made shall deliver to the other party a copy of a detailed written report of the examiner setting out the examiner's findings, including results of all tests made, diagnosis, and conclusions, with similar reports of all earlier examinations of the same condition. After delivery of the detailed written report, the party requesting the examination to be made shall be entitled upon request to receive from the party to whom the request for examination or against whom the order is made a similar report of any examination of the same condition previously or thereafter made, unless in the case of a report of examination of a person not a party the party shows the inability to obtain it. On motion, the court may order delivery of a report on such terms as are just; and if an examiner fails or refuses to make a report, the court may exclude the examiner's testimony if offered at the trial.

(2) By requesting and obtaining a report of the examination so ordered or requested or by taking the deposition of the examiner, the party examined waives any privilege that party may have in that action or any other involving the same controversy regarding the testimony of every other person who has examined or may thereafter examine that party concerning the same condition.

(3) This subdivision applies to examinations made by agreement of the parties unless the agreement provides otherwise. This subdivision does not preclude discovery of a report of an examiner or taking the deposition of the examiner in accordance with any other rule.

(c) Examiner as Witness. The examiner may be called as a witness by any party to the action, but shall not be identified as appointed by the court.

Amended July 26, 1972, effective Jan. 1, 1973 (265 So.2d 21); Oct. 6, 1988, effective Jan. 1, 1989 (536 So.2d 974); July 16, 1992, effective Jan. 1, 1993 (604 So.2d 1110); July 7, 1995, effective Jan. 1, 1996 (663 So.2d 1047); Nov. 22, 1995, effective Jan. 1, 1996 (663 So.2d 1049); Sept. 27, 2007, effective Jan. 1, 2008 (966 So.2d 943); Sept. 8, 2010, effective Jan. 1, 2011 (52 So.3d 579).

Committee Notes

1972 Amendment. Derived from Federal Rule of Civil Procedure 35 as amended in 1970. The good cause requirement under this rule has been retained so that the requirements of *Schlagenhauf v. Holder*, 379 U.S. 104, 85 S.Ct. 234, 13 L.Ed.2d 152 (1964), have not been affected. Subdivision (b) is changed to make it clear that reports can be obtained whether an order for the examination has been entered or not and that all earlier reports of the same condition can also be obtained.

1988 Amendment. This amendment to subdivision (a) is intended to broaden the scope of rule 1.360 to accommodate the examination of a person by experts other than physicians.

Cross References

Application to probate and guardianship proceedings, see Probate Rule 5.080.
Patient records, persons to whom copies are to be furnished, see F.S.A. § 455.667.
Refusal to permit discovery, see Civil Procedure Rule 1.380.

Rule 1.370. Requests for Admission

(a) Request for Admission. A party may serve upon any other party a written request for the admission of the truth of any matters within the scope of rule 1.280(b) set forth in the request that relate to statements or opinions of fact or of the application of law to fact, including the genuineness of any documents described in the request. Copies of documents shall be served with the request unless they have been or are otherwise furnished or made available for inspection and copying. Without leave of court the request may be served upon the plaintiff after commencement of the action and upon any other party with or after service of the process and initial pleading upon that party. The request for admission shall not exceed 30 requests, including all subparts, unless the court permits a larger number on motion and notice and for good cause, or the parties propounding and responding to the requests stipulate to a larger number. Each matter of which an admission is requested shall be separately set forth. The matter is admitted unless the party to whom the request is directed serves upon the party requesting the admission a written answer or objection addressed to the matter within 30 days after service of the request or such shorter or longer time as the court may allow but, unless the court shortens the time, a defendant shall not be required to serve answers or objections before the expiration of 45 days after service of the process and initial pleading upon the defendant. If objection is made, the reasons shall be stated. The answer shall specifically deny the matter or set forth in detail the reasons why the answering party cannot truthfully admit or deny the matter. A denial shall fairly meet the substance of the requested admission, and when good faith requires that a party qualify an answer or deny only a part of the matter of which an admission is requested, the party shall specify so much of it as is true and qualify or deny the remainder. An answering party may not give lack of information or knowledge as a reason for failure to admit or deny unless that party states that that party has made reasonable inquiry and that the information known or readily obtainable by that party is insufficient to enable that party to admit or deny. A party who considers that a matter of which an admission has been requested presents a genuine issue for trial may not object to the request on that ground alone;

the party may deny the matter or set forth reasons why the party cannot admit or deny it, subject to rule 1.380(c). The party who has requested the admissions may move to determine the sufficiency of the answers or objections. Unless the court determines that an objection is justified, it shall order that an answer be served. If the court determines that an answer does not comply with the requirements of this rule, it may order either that the matter is admitted or that an amended answer be served. Instead of these orders the court may determine that final disposition of the request be made at a pretrial conference or at a designated time before trial. The provisions of rule 1.380(a)(4) apply to the award of expenses incurred in relation to the motion.

(b) Effect of Admission. Any matter admitted under this rule is conclusively established unless the court on motion permits withdrawal or amendment of the admission. Subject to rule 1.200 governing amendment of a pretrial order, the court may permit withdrawal or amendment when the presentation of the merits of the action will be subserved by it and the party who obtained the admission fails to satisfy the court that withdrawal or amendment will prejudice that party in maintaining an action or defense on the merits. Any admission made by a party under this rule is for the purpose of the pending action only and is not an admission for any other purpose nor may it be used against that party in any other proceeding.

Amended June 19, 1968, effective Oct. 1, 1968 (211 So.2d 206); Oct. 1, 1970 (237 So.2d 151); July 26, 1972, effective Jan. 1, 1973 (265 So.2d 21); July 16, 1992, effective Jan. 1, 1993 (604 So.2d 1110); Oct. 23, 2003, effective Jan. 1, 2004 (858 So.2d 1013).

Committee Notes

1972 Amendment. Derived from Federal Rule of Civil Procedure 36 as amended in 1970. The rule is changed to eliminate distinctions between questions of opinion, fact, and mixed questions. The time sequences are changed in accordance with the other discovery rules, and case law is incorporated by providing for amendment and withdrawal of the answers and for judicial scrutiny to determine the sufficiency of the answers.

2003 Amendment. The total number of requests for admission that may be served without leave of court is limited to 30, including all subparts.

Cross References

Admissions on motion for summary judgment, see Civil Procedure Rule 1.510.
Application to probate and guardianship proceedings, see Probate Rule 5.080.
Expenses for refusal to admit, see Civil Procedure Rule 1.380.
Pre-trial procedure, see Civil Procedure Rule 1.200.
Refusal to make discovery, see Civil Procedure Rule 1.380.
Time, see Civil Procedure Rule 1.090.

Rule 1.380. Failure to Make Discovery; Sanctions

(a) Motion for Order Compelling Discovery. Upon reasonable notice to other parties and all persons affected, a party may apply for an order compelling discovery as follows:

(1) *Appropriate Court.* An application for an order to a party may be made to the court in which the action is pending or in accordance with rule 1.310(d). An application for an order to a deponent who is not a party shall be made to the circuit court where the deposition is being taken.

(2) *Motion.* If a deponent fails to answer a question propounded or submitted under rule 1.310 or 1.320, or a corporation or other entity fails to make a designation under rule 1.310(b)(6) or 1.320(a), or a party fails to answer an interrogatory submitted under rule 1.340,

or if a party in response to a request for inspection submitted under rule 1.350 fails to respond that inspection will be permitted as requested or fails to permit inspection as requested, or if a party in response to a request for examination of a person submitted under rule 1.360(a) objects to the examination, fails to respond that the examination will be permitted as requested, or fails to submit to or to produce a person in that party's custody or legal control for examination, the discovering party may move for an order compelling an answer, or a designation or an order compelling inspection, or an order compelling an examination in accordance with the request. The motion must include a certification that the movant, in good faith, has conferred or attempted to confer with the person or party failing to make the discovery in an effort to secure the information or material without court action. When taking a deposition on oral examination, the proponent of the question may complete or adjourn the examination before applying for an order. If the court denies the motion in whole or in part, it may make such protective order as it would have been empowered to make on a motion made pursuant to rule 1.280(c).

(3) *Evasive or Incomplete Answer.* For purposes of this subdivision an evasive or incomplete answer shall be treated as a failure to answer.

(4) *Award of Expenses of Motion.* If the motion is granted and after opportunity for hearing, the court shall require the party or deponent whose conduct necessitated the motion or the party or counsel advising the conduct to pay to the moving party the reasonable expenses incurred in obtaining the order that may include attorneys' fees, unless the court finds that the movant failed to certify in the motion that a good faith effort was made to obtain the discovery without court action, that the opposition to the motion was substantially justified, or that other circumstances make an award of expenses unjust. If the motion is denied and after opportunity for hearing, the court shall require the moving party to pay to the party or deponent who opposed the motion the reasonable expenses incurred in opposing the motion that may include attorneys' fees, unless the court finds that the making of the motion was substantially justified or that other circumstances make an award of expenses unjust. If the motion is granted in part and denied in part, the court may apportion the reasonable expenses incurred as a result of making the motion among the parties and persons.

(b) Failure to Comply with Order.

(1) If a deponent fails to be sworn or to answer a question after being directed to do so by the court, the failure may be considered a contempt of the court.

(2) If a party or an officer, director, or managing agent of a party or a person designated under rule 1.310(b)(6) or 1.320(a) to testify on behalf of a party fails to obey an order to provide or permit discovery, including an order made under subdivision (a) of this rule or rule 1.360, the court in which the action is pending may make any of the following orders:

(A) An order that the matters regarding which the questions were asked or any other designated facts shall be taken to be established for the purposes of the action in accordance with the claim of the party obtaining the order.

(B) An order refusing to allow the disobedient party to support or oppose designated claims or defenses, or prohibiting that party from introducing designated matters in evidence.

(C) An order striking out pleadings or parts of them or staying further proceedings until the order is obeyed, or dismissing the action or proceeding or any part of it, or rendering a judgment by default against the disobedient party.

(D) Instead of any of the foregoing orders or in addition to them, an order treating as a contempt of court the failure to obey any orders except an order to submit to an examination made pursuant to rule 1.360(a)(1)(B) or subdivision (a)(2) of this rule.

(E) When a party has failed to comply with an order under rule 1.360(a)(1)(B) requiring that party to produce another for examination, the orders listed in paragraphs (A), (B), and (C) of this subdivision, unless the party failing to comply shows the inability to produce the person for examination.

Instead of any of the foregoing orders or in addition to them, the court shall require the party failing to obey the order to pay the reasonable expenses caused by the failure, which may include attorneys' fees, unless the court finds that the failure was substantially justified or that other circumstances make an award of expenses unjust.

(c) **Expenses on Failure to Admit.** If a party fails to admit the genuineness of any document or the truth of any matter as requested under rule 1.370 and if the party requesting the admissions thereafter proves the genuineness of the document or the truth of the matter, the requesting party may file a motion for an order requiring the other party to pay the requesting party the reasonable expenses incurred in making that proof, which may include attorneys' fees. The court shall issue such an order at the time a party requesting the admissions proves the genuineness of the document or the truth of the matter, upon motion by the requesting party, unless it finds that (1) the request was held objectionable pursuant to rule 1.370(a), (2) the admission sought was of no substantial importance, or (3) there was other good reason for the failure to admit.

(d) **Failure of Party to Attend at Own Deposition or Serve Answers to Interrogatories or Respond to Request for Inspection.** If a party or an officer, director, or managing agent of a party or a person designated under rule 1.310(b)(6) or 1.320(a) to testify on behalf of a party fails (1) to appear before the officer who is to take the deposition after being served with a proper notice, (2) to serve answers or objections to interrogatories submitted under rule 1.340 after proper service of the interrogatories, or (3) to serve a written response to a request for inspection submitted under rule 1.350 after proper service of the request, the court in which the action is pending may take any action authorized under paragraphs (A), (B), and (C) of subdivision (b)(2) of this rule. Any motion specifying a failure under clause (2) or (3) of this subdivision shall include a certification that the movant, in good faith, has conferred or attempted to confer with the party failing to answer or respond in an effort to obtain such answer or response without court action. Instead of any order or in addition to it, the court shall require the party failing to act to pay the reasonable expenses caused by the failure, which may include attorneys' fees, unless the court finds that the failure was substantially justified or that other circumstances make an award of expenses unjust. The failure to act described in this subdivision may not be excused on the ground that the discovery sought is objectionable unless the party failing to act has applied for a protective order as provided by rule 1.280(c).

(e) **Electronically Stored Information; Sanctions for Failure to Preserve.** Absent exceptional circumstances, a court may not impose sanctions under these rules on a party for failing to provide electronically stored information lost as a result of the routine, good faith operation of an electronic information system.

Amended July 26, 1972, effective Jan. 1, 1973 (265 So.2d 21); Sept. 13, 1984, effective Jan. 1, 1985 (458 So.2d 245); Oct. 6, 1988, effective Jan. 1, 1989 (536 So.2d 974); July 16, 1992, effective Jan. 1, 1993 (604 So.2d 1110); Oct. 31, 1996, effective Jan. 1, 1997 (682 So.2d 105); Oct. 5, 2000, effective Jan. 1, 2001 (773 So.2d 1098); Oct. 23, 2003, effective Jan. 1, 2004 (858 So.2d 1013); Dec. 15, 2005, effective Jan. 1, 2006 (917 So.2d 176); July 5, 2012, effective Sept. 1, 2012 (95 So.3d 76); Nov. 14, 2013, effective Jan. 1, 2014 (131 So.3d 643).

1972 Amendment. Derived from Federal Rule of Civil Procedure 37 as amended in 1970. Subdivision (a)(3) is new and makes it clear that an evasive or incomplete answer is a failure to answer under the rule. Other clarifying changes have been made within the general scope of the rule to ensure that complete coverage of all discovery failures is afforded.

2003 Amendment. Subdivision (c) is amended to require a court to make a ruling on a request for reimbursement at the time of the hearing on the requesting party's motion for entitlement to such relief. The court may, in its discretion, defer ruling on the amount of the costs or fees in order to hold an evidentiary hearing whenever convenient to the court and counsel.

2005 Amendment. Following the example of Federal Rule of Civil Procedure 37 as amended in 1993, language is included in subdivision (a)(2) that requires litigants to seek to resolve discovery disputes by informal means before filing a motion with the court. This requirement is based on successful experience with the federal rule as well as similar local rules of state trial courts. Subdivision (a)(4) is revised to provide that a party should not be awarded its expenses for filing a motion that might have been avoided by conferring with opposing counsel. Subdivision (d) is revised to require that, where a party failed to file any response to a rule 1.340 interrogatory or a rule 1.350 request, the discovering party should attempt to obtain such responses before filing a motion for sanctions.

2012 Amendment. Subdivision (e) is added to make clear that a party should not be sanctioned for the loss of electronic evidence due to the good-faith operation of an electronic information system; the language mirrors that of Federal Rule of Civil Procedure 37(e). Nevertheless, the good-faith requirement contained in subdivision (e) should prevent a party from exploiting the routine operation of an information system to thwart discovery obligations by allowing that operation to destroy information that party is required to preserve or produce. In determining good faith, the court may consider any steps taken by the party to comply with court orders, party agreements, or requests to preserve such information.

2013 Amendment. This rule was amended to add "substantially" before "justified" in subdivisions (a)(4), (b)(2), and (d), to make the rule internally consistent and to make it more consistent with Federal Rule of Civil Procedure 37, from which it was derived.

Application to probate and guardianship proceedings, see Probate Rule 5.080.
Contempt,
    Definition, see F.S.A. § 38.23.
    Power to punish, see F.S.A. § 38.22.
Expenses, failure to attend or to serve subpoena, see Civil Procedure Rule 1.310.

Rule 1.390. Depositions of Expert Witnesses

  (a) Definition. The term "expert witness" as used herein applies exclusively to a person duly and regularly engaged in the practice of a profession who holds a professional degree from a university or college and has had special professional training and experience, or one possessed of special knowledge or skill about the subject upon which called to testify.

  (b) Procedure. The testimony of an expert or skilled witness may be taken at any time before the trial in accordance with the rules for taking depositions and may be used at trial, regardless of the place of residence of the witness or whether the witness is within the distance prescribed by rule 1.330(a)(3). No special form of notice need be given that the deposition will be used for trial.

  (c) Fee. An expert or skilled witness whose deposition is taken shall be allowed a witness fee in such reasonable amount as the court may determine. The court shall also determine a reasonable time within which payment must be made, if the deponent and party cannot agree. All parties and the deponent shall be served with notice of any hearing to determine the fee. Any reasonable fee paid to an expert or skilled witness may be taxed as costs.

(d) Applicability. Nothing in this rule shall prevent the taking of any deposition as otherwise provided by law.

Amended July 26, 1972, effective Jan. 1, 1973 (265 So.2d 21); Oct. 6, 1988, effective Jan. 1, 1989 (536 So.2d 974); July 16, 1992, effective Jan. 1, 1993 (604 So.2d 1110).

Committee Notes

1972 Amendment. This rule has caused more difficulty in recent years than any other discovery rule. It was enacted as a statute originally to make the presentation of expert testimony less expensive and less onerous to the expert and to admit the expert's deposition at trial regardless of the expert's residence. In spite of its intent, courts seem determined to misconstrue the plain language of the rule and cause complications that the committee and the legislature did not envisage. See *Owca v. Zemzicki,* 137 So.2d 876 (Fla.2d DCA 1962); *Cook v. Lichtblau,* 176 So.2d 523 (Fla.2d DCA 1965); and *Bondy v. West,* 219 So.2d 117 (Fla.2d DCA 1969). The committee hopes the amendment to subdivision (b) will show that the intent of the rule is to permit a deposition taken of an expert in conformity with any rule for the taking of a deposition to be admitted, if otherwise admissible under the rules of evidence, regardless of the residence of the expert. In short, the rule eliminates the necessity of any of the requirements of rule 1.330(a)(3) when the deposition offered is that of an expert.

1988 Amendment. Subdivision (c) has been amended to clarify the procedure to be used in paying an expert witness for his or her appearance at a deposition.

Cross References

Application to probate and guardianship proceedings, see Probate Rule 5.080.
Pre-trial procedure, see Civil Procedure Rule 1.200.

Rule 1.410. Subpoena

(a) Subpoena Generally. Subpoenas for testimony before the court, subpoenas for production of tangible evidence, and subpoenas for taking depositions may be issued by the clerk of court or by any attorney of record in an action.

(b) Subpoena for Testimony before the Court.

(1) Every subpoena for testimony before the court shall be issued by an attorney of record in an action or by the clerk under the seal of the court and shall state the name of the court and the title of the action and shall command each person to whom it is directed to attend and give testimony at a time and place specified in it.

(2) On oral request of an attorney or party and without praecipe, the clerk shall issue a subpoena for testimony before the court or a subpoena for the production of documentary evidence before the court signed and sealed but otherwise in blank, both as to the title of the action and the name of the person to whom it is directed, and the subpoena shall be filled in before service by the attorney or party.

(c) For Production of Documentary Evidence. A subpoena may also command the person to whom it is directed to produce the books, papers, documents (including electronically stored information), or tangible things designated therein, but the court, upon motion made promptly and in any event at or before the time specified in the subpoena for compliance therewith, may (1) quash or modify the subpoena if it is unreasonable and oppressive, or (2) condition denial of the motion upon the advancement by the person in whose behalf the subpoena is issued of the reasonable cost of producing the books, papers, documents, or tangible things. If a subpoena does not specify a form for producing electronically stored information, the person responding must produce it in a form or forms in which it is ordinarily maintained or in a reasonably usable form or forms. A person responding to a subpoena may object to discovery of electronically stored information from sources that the person identifies as not reasonably accessible because of undue costs or burden. On motion to compel discovery or to quash, the person from whom discovery is sought must show that the information sought or the form requested is not reasonably accessible because of undue costs or burden. If that showing is made, the court may nonetheless order discovery from such sources or in such forms if the requesting party shows good cause, considering the limitations set out in rule 1.280(d)(2). The court may specify conditions of the discovery, including ordering that some or all of the expenses of the discovery be paid by the party seeking the discovery. A party seeking a production of evidence at trial which would be subject to a subpoena may compel such production by serving a notice to produce such evidence on an adverse party as provided in rule 1.080. Such notice shall have the same effect and be subject to the same limitations as a subpoena served on the party.

(d) Service. A subpoena may be served by any person authorized by law to serve process or by any other person who is not a party and who is not less than 18 years of age. Service of a subpoena upon a person named therein shall be made as provided by law. Proof of such service shall be made by affidavit of the person making service except as applicable under rule 1.351(c) for the production of documents and things by a nonparty without deposition, if not served by an officer authorized by law to do so.

(e) Subpoena for Taking Depositions.

(1) Filing a notice to take a deposition as provided in rule 1.310(b) or 1.320(a) with a certificate of service on it showing service on all parties to the action constitutes an authorization for the issuance of subpoenas for the persons named or described in the notice by the clerk of the court in which the action is pending or by an attorney of record in the action. The subpoena shall state the method for recording the testimony. The subpoena may command the person to whom it is directed to produce designated books, papers, documents, or tangible things that constitute or contain evidence relating to any of the matters within the scope of the examination permitted by rule 1.280(b), but in that event the subpoena will be subject to the provisions of rule 1.280(c) and subdivision (c) of this rule. Within 10 days after its service, or on or before the time specified in the subpoena for compliance if the time is less than 10 days after service, the person to whom the subpoena is directed may serve written objection to inspection or copying of any of the designated materials. If objection is made, the party serving the subpoena shall not be entitled to inspect and copy the materials except pursuant to an order of the court from which the subpoena was issued. If objection has been made, the party serving the subpoena may move for an order at any time before or during the taking of the deposition upon notice to the deponent.

(2) A person may be required to attend an examination only in the county wherein the person resides or is employed or transacts business in person or at such other convenient place as may be fixed by an order of court.

(f) Contempt. Failure by any person without adequate excuse to obey a subpoena served upon that person may be deemed a contempt of the court from which the subpoena issued.

(g) Depositions before Commissioners Appointed in this State by Courts of Other States; Subpoena Powers; etc. When any person authorized by the laws of Florida to administer oaths is appointed by a court of record of any other state, jurisdiction, or government as commissioner to take the testimony of any named witness within this state, that witness may be compelled to attend and testify before that commissioner by witness subpoena issued by the clerk of any circuit court at the instance of that commissioner or by other process or proceedings in the same manner as if that commissioner had been appointed by a court of this state; provided that no document or paper writing shall be compulsorily annexed as an exhibit to such deposition or otherwise permanently removed from the possession of the witness producing it, but in lieu thereof a photostatic copy may be annexed to and transmitted with such executed commission to the court of issuance.

(h) Subpoena of Minor. Any minor subpoenaed for testimony shall have the right to be accompanied by a parent or guardian at all times during the taking of testimony notwithstanding the invocation of the rule of sequestration of section 90.616, Florida Statutes, except upon a showing that the presence of a parent or guardian is likely to have a material, negative impact on the credibility or accuracy of the minor's testimony, or that the interests of the parent or guardian are in actual or potential conflict with the interests of the minor.

Amended June 19, 1968, effective Oct. 1, 1968 (211 So.2d 206); July 26, 1972, effective Jan. 1, 1973 (265 So.2d 21); Dec. 13, 1976, effective Jan. 1, 1977 (339 So.2d 626); Oct. 9, 1980, effective Jan. 1, 1981 (391 So.2d 165); July 16, 1992, effective Jan. 1, 1993 (604 So.2d 1110); Oct. 31, 1996, effective Jan. 1, 1997 (682 So.2d 105); Sept. 27, 2007, effective Jan. 1, 2008 (966 So.2d 943); Sept. 8, 2010, effective Jan. 1, 2011 (52 So.3d 579); July 5, 2012, effective Sept. 1, 2012 (95 So.3d 76); Oct. 18, 2012, effective, *nunc pro tunc*, Sept. 1, 2012 (102 So.3d 505).

Committee Notes

1972 Amendment. Subdivisions (a) and (d) are amended to show the intent of the rule that subpoenas for deposition may not be issued in blank by the clerk, but only for trial. The reason for the distinction is valid. A subpoena for appearance before the court is not subject to abuse because the court can correct any attempt to abuse the use of blank subpoenas. Since a judge is not present at a deposition, additional protection for the parties and the deponent is required and subpoenas should not be issued in blank. Subdivision (d) is also modified to conform with the revised federal rule on subpoenas for depositions to permit an objection by the deponent to the production of material required by a subpoena to be produced.

1980 Amendment. Subdivision (c) is revised to conform with section 48.031, Florida Statutes (1979).

1996 Amendment. This rule is amended to allow an attorney (as referred to in Fla.R.Jud.Admin. 2.060(a)–(b)), as an officer of the court, and the clerk to issue subpoenas in the name of the court. This amendment is not intended to change any other requirement or precedent for the issuance or use of subpoenas. For example, a notice of taking the deposition must be filed and served before a subpoena for deposition may be issued.

2012 Amendment. Subdivision (c) is amended to reflect the relocation of the service rule from rule 1.080 to Fla. R. Jud. Admin. 2.516.

2012 Amendment. Subdivision (c) is amended to address the production of electronically stored information pursuant to a subpoena. The procedures for dealing with disputes concerning the accessibility of the information sought or the form for its production are intended to correspond to those set out in Rule 1.280(d).

Cross References

Discovery and production of documents and things, see Civil Procedure Rule 1.350.

COMBINED INDEX

Numerical References are to Florida Statutes Annotated
Unless Otherwise Preceded by Abbreviations Listed Below

Rule . . . . .Probate Rules
Civ.Proc. Rule . . . . .Civil Procedure Rules

ABANDONED OR UNCLAIMED PROPERTY—Cont'd

Life insurance policies, funds owing, **717.107**

Limitation of actions, **717.129**

List of abandoned property, notice and publication, **717.118**

Memoranda, credit memos, **717.1045**

Money orders, **717.104**

Negative or nothing owed report, **717.117**

Notice, **717.117, 717.118**
  Sales, **717.122**
  Violations, administrative rules and regulations, **717.132**

Omissions, claims, **717.124**

Owners,
  Conflicting claims, **717.1241**
  Filing of claim, **717.124**

Payment, **717.119**

Personal representatives,
  Claims, **717.12405**
  Powers and duties, **733.612**

Petitions, administrative hearings, **717.126**

Photography and pictures, identity and identification,
  Claims, **717.124**
  Purchase agreements, **717.1351**

Political subdivisions, property held by, **717.112, 717.113**

Power of attorney,
  Agreements, recovery, reported property, **717.135**
  Claims, payment, **717.124**
  Void, **717.1381**

Presumptions, **717.102 et seq.**
  Escheat, **717.1035**
  Trusts and trustees, **717.1125**

Private investigative, security and repossession services,
  Claims, filing, **717.124**
  Registration, **717.1400**

Production of books and records, **717.1301**

Public agencies, property held by, **717.112, 717.113**

Public utilities, deposits, **717.108**

Publication, notice, **717.118**

Purchase agreements, **717.1351**
  Void, **717.1381**

Reciprocal actions with other states, **717.133**

Records and recordation, **717.1311, 717.1315**

Recovery, persons wrongfully in possession, **717.1331, 717.1341**

Refunds, business associations, **717.109**

Registration, **717.1400**
  Revocation or suspension, **717.1322**

Reports, **717.117**
  Evidence, **717.1333**
  Failure to report, penalties, **717.134**
  Gift certificates, credit memos, **717.1045**
  Recovery, agreements, reported property, **717.135**

Representatives, claimants, registration, **717.1400**

Reprimands, **717.1322**

Returns, claims, **717.124**

Revocation or suspension, registration, **717.1322**

Rules and regulations, **717.138**

Sales, **717.122**
  Purchase agreements, **717.1351**

ABANDONED OR UNCLAIMED PROPERTY—Cont'd

Sales—Cont'd
  Time, **717.122**

Savings accounts, joint accounts, **717.12403**

Securities, joint tenants, **717.12406**

Shares and shareholders, **717.1101**
  Joint tenants, **717.12406**

Small estates, **717.1243**

Social security numbers, confidential or privileged information, **717.117**

State agencies, property held by, **717.1035, 717.112, 717.113**

State school fund, deposits, **717.123**

Statute of limitations, **717.129**

Stock, **717.1101**

Subpoenas, **717.1331**
  Hearings, **717.1301**

Telecommunications, lists, notice, **717.118**

Theme park tickets, exemptions, **717.1355**

Tickets, theme parks and entertainment complexes, exemptions, **717.1355**

Time,
  Checks, drafts and similar instruments, **717.105**
  Limitation of actions, **717.129**
  Presumption, **717.102 et seq.**
  Sales, **717.122**
  Travelers checks and money orders, **717.104**

Travelers checks and money orders, **717.104**

Value,
  Discount, purchase agreements, **717.1351**
  Less than expense of giving notice and sale, **717.127, 717.128**

Venue, administrative hearings, **717.126**

Void, power of attorney, purchase agreements, **717.1381**

Weapons, safe deposit boxes, **717.119**

Withdrawal, claims, **717.124**

Witnesses, **717.1301**

ABANDONMENT

Conveyances, forfeiture or reverter, **689.18**

Deeds and conveyances, forfeiture or reverter provisions, **689.18**

Forfeiture or reverter provisions, conveyances, **689.18**

Guardian and Ward, generally, this index

Power of attorney, **709.2120**

Property. Abandoned or Unclaimed Property, generally, this index

Reverter provisions, conveyances, **689.18**

ABATEMENT

Probate proceedings, surviving spouse, elective share, **732.2075**

Trusts and trustees, pollution, **736.0816**

ABATEMENT OF ACTIONS OR PROCEEDINGS

Guardian and ward, survival of actions, incapacity of ward, **744.394**

Wrongful death, **768.20**

ABBOTT, JOSHUA

Organ and tissue registry, **765.5155**

ADMISSIONS

Generally, **Civ.Proc. Rules 1.280, 1.370**
Agent, hearsay exceptions, **90.803**
Best Evidence Rule, writings or recordings, **90.957**
Coconspirator, hearsay exceptions, **90.803**
Hearsay exceptions, **90.803, 90.804**
Recordings, Best Evidence Rule, **90.957**
Request for admissions, rules of civil procedure, application, **Rule 5.080**
Servant, hearsay exceptions, **90.803**
Writings, Best Evidence Rule, **90.957**

ADOLESCENTS

Children and Minors, generally, this index

ADOPTION

Class gifts, probate proceedings, **732.608**
Evidence, hearsay exceptions, **90.804**
Guardian and ward, natural guardians, **744.301**
Hearsay exceptions, **90.804**
Intestate succession, **732.108**
  Termination of parental rights, **732.1081**
Natural guardians, **744.301**
Personal representatives, nonresidents, qualifications, **733.304**
Termination of parental rights, intestate succession, **732.1081**
Wills, subsequent adoption, **732.507**

ADULTS

Definitions, transfers to minors, **710.102**

ADVANCE DIRECTIVES FOR HEALTH CARE

Generally, **765.101 et seq.**
Living wills, designation of guardian, **744.3115**

ADVERSARY PROCEEDINGS

Generally, **Rule 5.025**

ADVERSE OR PECUNIARY INTEREST

Administrator ad litem, appointment, **733.308**
Appointment, administrator ad litem, **733.308**
Children and minors, trusts and trustees, **736.0303 et seq.**
Guardian and Ward, this index
Missing persons, trusts and trustees, **736.0304, 736.0305**
Power of attorney, **709.2114, 709.2116**
Powers of appointment, trusts and trustees, **736.0302**
Pregnancy, trusts and trustees, **736.0303 et seq.**
Probate proceedings, personal representative, **733.610**
Public guardians, **744.703**
Veterans, guardianship,
  Investments, **744.627**
  Judges, **744.618**

ADVERSE WITNESSES

Depositions, **Civ.Proc. Rule 1.330**

ADVISORY BOARDS AND COMMISSIONS

Anatomical gifts, **765.543**
Organ and tissue procurement and transplantation advisory board, **765.543**

ADVISORY COMMITTEES

Electronic recording advisory committee, **695.27**

ADVISORY COUNCILS

Anatomical gifts, **765.53**

ADVOCATES

Attorneys, generally, this index

AFFIDAVITS

Disposition without administration, application, **Rule 5.420**
Estate taxes, false or fraudulent affidavits, **198.38**
Foreign personal representatives, safe deposit boxes, access, **655.936**
Oath, form, probate proceedings, **731.104**
Physicians and surgeons, power of attorney, **709.2108**
Self proof, wills, **732.503**
Service, informal notice, **Rule 5.040**
Small estates, disposition without administration, **735.301**
Wills, self proof, **732.503, 733.107**

AFFILIATES

Power of attorney, **709.2116**

AFFINITY

Relatives, generally, this index

AFFIRMATIONS

Oaths and Affirmations, generally, this index

AFTER ACQUIRED PROPERTY

Guardian and ward, inventory, **744.384**
Wills, devises, **732.6005**

AFTER BORN HEIRS

Intestate succession, **732.106**

AGE

Civil rights. Discrimination, generally, this index
Discrimination, generally, this index
Power of attorney, **709.2105**
Wills, age of testator, **732.501**
Witnesses, depositions, **Civ.Proc. Rule 1.330**

AGED PERSONS

Abuse of Aged Persons, generally, this index
Civil rights. Discrimination, generally, this index
Convalescent homes. Nursing Homes, generally, this index
Crime victims, evidence, hearsay exception, **90.803**
Depositions, **Civ.Proc. Rule 1.330**
Depositions de bene esse, **Civ.Proc. Rule 1.290**
Discrimination, generally, this index
Long term care. Nursing Homes, generally, this index
Medical care and treatment. Nursing Homes, generally, this index
Nursing Homes, generally, this index
Residential care facilities. Nursing Homes, generally, this index
Rest homes. Nursing Homes, generally, this index
Witnesses,
  Depositions, **Civ.Proc. Rule 1.330**
  Hearsay exception, abuse of aged or handicapped persons, **90.803**

AGENT FOR SERVICE OF PROCESS
Generally, **Rule 5.110**

AGENTS AND AGENCIES
Confidential or privileged information, trade secrets, **90.506**
Convenience accounts, **655.80**
Definitions,
  Anatomical gifts, **765.511**
  Developmentally disabled persons, prevention and community services, **393.063**
  Power of attorney, **709.2102**
Guardian and ward, employment, **744.444**
Homestead, notice by agent to officer of property claimed as homestead, **222.02**
Personal representatives, adverse interest, sale of property, **733.610**
Power of Attorney, generally, this index
Resident agents, personal representatives or guardians, service of process, **Rule 5.110**
Safe deposit boxes, access, **655.933**
  Death or incapacity of lessee, **655.934**
Service of process, resident agents, personal representatives or guardians, **Rule 5.110**
State Agencies, generally, this index
Trade secrets, confidential information, **90.506**
Unclaimed property, **717.112**
  Disposition, **717.001 et seq.**

AGREEMENTS
Contracts, generally, this index

AGRICULTURAL PRODUCTS
Contracts, power of attorney, commodity futures contracts, **709.2208**
Power of attorney, commodity futures contracts, **709.2208**

AIDS
Real estate, sales, disclosures, **689.25**

AIR FORCE
Military Forces, generally, this index

ALCOHOLIC BEVERAGES
Curators, generally, this index

ALCOHOLICS AND CHEMICALLY DEPENDENT PERSONS
Confidential or privileged information, psychotherapist patient privilege, **90.503**
Guardian and ward, removal of guardian, **744.474**
Privileges and immunities, psychotherapist patient, **90.503**
Psychotherapist patient privilege, **90.503**

ALIAS WARRANTS
Inheritance and estate taxes, collection, **198.20**

ALIENS
Estate taxes, **198.04**
  Returns, filing, **198.13**
Inheritance and estate taxes, **198.04**
  Returns, filing, **198.13**
Intestate succession, **732.1101**

ALIENS—Cont'd
Probate proceedings,
  Nonresidents, location of assets, **731.106**
  Venue, **733.101**

ALIMONY
Bankruptcy exemption, **222.201**
Evidence, judicial notice, **90.204**

ALTERNATIVE DISPUTE RESOLUTION
Compromise and Settlement, generally, this index
Trusts and trustees, **736.0816**

AMBASSADORS AND CONSULS
Authentication, documents, **90.902**
Evidence, authentication, documents, **90.902**
Wills, notarial wills, authentication, **733.205**

AMERICANS WITH DISABILITIES ACT
Handicapped Persons, generally, this index

AMNESIA
Conservators and conservatorship, **747.01 et seq.**

ANATOMICAL GIFTS
Generally, **765.510 et seq.**
Acceptance, **765.517**
Access, registry, **765.5155**
  Hospitals, dying patients, **765.522**
Advisory boards and commissions, **765.543**
Advisory councils, **765.53**
Amendment, **765.516**
Attestation, **765.514**
Autopsy, application of law, **765.517**
Banks, eye banks, **765.518, 765.5185**
Cards. Donor cards, generally, post
Certificates and certification, procurement organizations, **765.541, 765.542**
Children and minors, **765.512**
Colleges and universities, eligibility, **765.513**
Confidential or privileged information, registry, **765.51551**
Conflict of laws, **765.522**
Consent, delivery of document, **765.515**
Coordinators, procurement organizations, **765.545**
Corneas, **765.5185**
Damages, **765.517**
  Enucleation of eyes, **765.519**
  Request for organ donation, **765.522**
Definitions, **765.511**
Delivery of consent, **765.515**
Dental schools, eligibility to receive, **765.513**
Deposit, document of consent, **765.515**
Discrimination, **765.513, 765.514**
District medical examiners, corneal removal, **765.5185**
Documents of gift, **765.515**
  Amendments, **765.516**
  Validity, **765.522**
Donees, eligibility, **765.513, 765.514**
Donor cards,
  Donor registration card, delivery, **765.515**
  Gifts to eye bank, **765.518**

ANATOMICAL GIFTS—Cont'd
Donor cards—Cont'd
  Issuance with drivers licenses on request, **765.521**
  Issuance with identification card, **765.521**
  Uniform donor card, **765.514**
  Wallets, eyes, **765.518**
Drivers licenses, donor cards, **765.514, 765.521**
Duties at death, donee, **765.517**
Education, **765.5155**
Eligibility, **765.513, 765.514**
  Transplant list, **765.522**
Execution, **765.514**
Expenses and expenditures, **765.517**
Eye banks, **765.518**
  Corneas, requests, **765.5185**
Eyes, enucleation, **765.519**
Fees, procurement organizations, **765.544**
Foreign states,
  Application of law, **765.517**
  Physicians and surgeons, procurement, **765.546**
Forms, **765.514**
Funds, procurement organizations, fees, **765.544**
Funeral directors and embalmers, enucleation of eyes, **765.519**
Guardian and ward, eligibility to give, **765.512**
Guidelines,
  Eligibility to receive, **765.513, 765.514**
  Requests for organ donation, dying patients, **765.522**
Handicapped persons, discrimination, **765.513, 765.514**
Identification cards, donor cards, **765.521**
Intent, donees, **765.514**
Internet, registry, **765.5155**
Joshua Abbott organ and tissue registry, **765.5155**
Manner of making gifts, **765.514**
Medical examiners, cooperation, procurement organizations, **765.547**
Medical management, organ and tissue procurement coordinators, **765.545**
Medical schools, eligibility to receive, **765.513**
Minors, **765.512**
Mutilation of body, **765.517**
Notice, procurement organizations, **765.522**
Ophthalmologic trainees, corneal removal, **765.5185**
Per diem, advisory councils, **765.53**
Persons eligible to give from body of deceased person, **765.512**
Physicians and surgeons,
  Foreign states, procurement, **765.546**
  Organ and tissue procurement coordinators, supervision, **765.545**
  Rights and duties at death, **765.517**
Presumptions, documents of gift, validity, **765.522**
Priorities and preferences, **765.513**
  Eligibility to give, **765.512**
Privileges and immunities, **765.517, 765.522**
Procurement organizations,
  Certificates and certification, **765.541, 765.542**
  Cooperation, medical examiners, **765.547**
  Coordinators, **765.545**

ANATOMICAL GIFTS—Cont'd
Procurement organizations—Cont'd
  Eligibility, **765.513**
  Fees, **765.544**
  Powers and duties, **765.522**
Public policy, **765.510**
Records and recordation, **765.514**
  Registry, confidential or privileged information, **765.51551**
Registry, **765.5155**
  Confidential or privileged information, **765.51551**
  Hospitals, access, dying patients, **765.522**
Rejection, **765.517**
Relatives, eligibility to give, **765.512**
Religious objections, **765.512**
Reports, registry, **765.5155**
Representatives ad litem, eligibility to give, **765.512**
Revocation, **765.516**
  Irrevocable after death, **765.512**
Rights and duties, death, **765.517**
Schools, medical schools, **765.513**
Signatures, manner of making gift, **765.514**
Specific donee, **765.513, 765.514**
Statements, amendments, **765.516**
Supervision, procurement organizations, coordinators, **765.545**
Surviving spouse, eligibility to give, **765.512**
Telegraphs and telephones, consent of gift over, **765.514**
Tort liability, enucleation of eyes, **765.519**
Travel expenses, advisory councils, **765.53**
Uniform donor card, **765.514, 765.521**
Universities, **765.513**
Verification, **765.517**
Wallet cards, gifts to eye bank, **765.518**
Wills, **765.514**

ANCESTORS
Anatomical gifts, eligibility, **765.512**
Intestate succession, shares, **732.103**

ANCIENT DOCUMENTS
Hearsay exceptions, **90.803**

ANCILLARY ADMINISTRATION
Estates, **734.102 et seq.**

ANIMALS
Burial, trusts and trustees, **736.0408**
Trusts and trustees, **736.0402, 736.0408**
  Beneficiaries, **736.0110**

ANNUITIES
Insurance, this index
Power of attorney, **709.2202**
Trusts and trustees, principal and income, receipts, allocations, **738.602**

ANNULMENT
Marriage, power of attorney, **709.2109**

ANSWER
Discovery, evasive answer, **Civ.Proc. Rule 1.380**

ANTENUPTIAL AGREEMENTS
Wills, **732.702**

ANTILAPSE STATUTE
Wills, **732.603**

APPEAL AND REVIEW
Generally, **Rule 5.100**
Abandoned or unclaimed property, administrative hearings, **717.126**
Advance directives for health care, **765.105**
Deposition pending appeal, **Civ.Proc. Rule 1.290**
Developmental disabilities prevention and community services, denial of application, **393.063**
Escheat, federal funds, **716.07**
Evidence, criminal conviction, impeachment, **90.610**
Guardian and Ward, this index
Probate proceedings, validity of wills, **733.103**
Trusts and trustees, principal and income, discretion, **738.105**

APPELLATE COURTS
Appeal and Review, generally, this index

APPOINTMENTS
Administrators ad litem, **Rule 5.120**
Agent for service of process, death of resident agent, successor agent, **Rule 5.110**
Curators, **Rule 5.122**
Guardian advocates, **Rule 5.649**
Guardians ad litem, **Rule 5.120**
Magistrates, **Rule 5.095**
  Guardian and ward, review of guardianship, **Rule 5.697**
Petition for guardian, **Rule 5.560**
Resident agents, personal representatives or guardians, **Rule 5.110**
Special magistrates, **Rule 5.095**
  Guardian and ward, review of guardianship, **Rule 5.697**
Successor, guardians, resignation, **Rule 5.650**

APPORTIONMENT
Principal and income, **738.301 et seq.**
Probate proceedings,
  Estate taxes, **733.817**
  Obligations of estate, priorities and preferences, **733.707**
Trusts and trustees, principal and income, **738.301 et seq.**
Veterans guardianship, benefits to dependents of ward, **744.625**

APPRAISAL AND APPRAISERS
Attachment, personal property exemptions, **222.061**
Estate taxes, **198.07 et seq.**
Execution, personal property exemptions, **222.061**
Garnishment, personal property exemptions, **222.061**
Guardian and ward, property of ward, **744.381; Rule 5.620**
Inheritance and estate taxes, **198.07 et seq.**
Probate proceedings, securities, distribution, **733.810**

APPROPRIATIONS
Developmental disabilities council, **393.002**
State Treasury, generally, this index

ARBITRATION AND AWARD
Probate proceedings, **731.401**
Trusts and trustees, **731.401, 736.0816**
Wills, **731.401**

ARCHITECTS AND ARCHITECTURE
Contracts, indemnity, **725.08**
Indemnity, **725.08**

ARMED FORCES
Military Forces, generally, this index

ARMY
Military Forces, generally, this index

ARREST
Order of court, disobeying, **Civ.Proc. Rule 1.380**

ASSAULT AND BATTERY
Abuse of Children, generally, this index
Children and minors. Abuse of Children, generally, this index
Sex Offenses, generally, this index

ASSESSMENTS
Probate proceedings, attorneys fees, costs, **733.106**
Trusts and trustees,
  Attorneys fees, **736.1005**
  Costs, **736.1006**

ASSETS
Interim accounting, statement, **Rule 5.345**
Production, order, **Rule 5.160**
Profits of business of decedent, adding to estate, **Rule 5.350**

ASSIGNMENT OF ERRORS
Appeal and Review, generally, this index

ASSIGNMENTS
Attorney client privilege, **90.502**
Bonds, premiums, expenses, **733.406**
Confidential or privileged information, accountant client privilege, **90.5055**
Disclaimer, property, **739.402**
Dower, widow, extraordinary petition, **Rule 5.365**
Intestate succession, assignment of claims, **732.107**
Land trust, real estate, ownership vesting in trustee, **689.071**
Lawyer client privilege, **90.502**
Privileges of lawyer client, **90.502**
Probate proceedings, claims against estates, **733.816**
Spendthrift trusts, **736.0105, 736.0501 et seq.**

ASSIGNMENTS FOR BENEFIT OF CREDITORS
Bonds (officers and fiduciaries), premiums, expenses, **733.406**

ASSISTED LIVING FACILITIES
Nursing Homes, generally, this index

ASSOCIATIONS AND SOCIETIES
Accountant client privilege, **90.5055**

BANK

BONDS

CHILD

CHILD CARE FACILITIES
Abuse of Children, generally, this index
Neglect. Abuse of Children, generally, this index

CHILD SUPPORT
Support, generally, this index

CHILDREN AND FAMILIES DEPARTMENT
Adoption, generally, this index

CHILDREN AND MINORS
Absentees, appointment of conservators, **747.02**
Abuse of Children, generally, this index
Accounts and accounting, transfers, **710.122**
Actions and proceedings, settlement of claims, guardian and ward, **744.387**
Adoption, generally, this index
Adverse or pecuniary interest, trusts and trustees, **736.0303 et seq.**
Afterborn heirs, intestate succession, **732.106**
Anatomical gifts, **765.512**
Assault and battery. Abuse of Children, generally, this index
Banks and banking,
    Deposits, **655.77**
    Joint accounts, survivorship, **655.78, 655.79**
Children Born Out of Wedlock, generally, this index
Claims, settlement, guardian and ward, **744.387**
Compensation and salaries,
    Custodians, transfers, **710.117**
    Deceased parents, exemptions, **222.15, 222.16**
Compromise and settlement, claims, guardian and ward, **744.387**
Crimes and offenses. Sex offenses, generally, post
Cruelty to children. Abuse of Children, generally, this index
Custody,
    Evidence, judicial notice, **90.204**
    Trusts and trustees, transfers, **736.0816**
Death,
    Custodian, transfers to minors, **710.121**
    Termination of custodianship, transfers to minors, **710.123**
    Wrongful death, **768.16 et seq.**
Debtors and creditors, transfers to minors, **710.108**
Definitions,
    Guardian and ward, **744.102**
    Molestation, **90.404**
    Probate proceedings, **731.201**
    Spendthrift trusts, **736.0503**
    Trusts and trustees, **736.0504**
    Wrongful Death Act, **768.18**
Deposits, financial institutions,
    Joint accounts, **655.79**
    Withdrawal, **655.77**
Disclaimer of interest, custodian, transfers to minors, **710.121**
Dissolution of marriage. Support, generally, this index
Distribution of estates, personal representatives, powers and duties, **733.602**
Domicile and residence, transfers to minors, **710.103**

CHILDREN AND MINORS—Cont'd
Evidence, hearsay exception, **90.803**
Exemptions, property, intestate succession, **732.402**
Exploitation,
    Disqualification as guardian, **744.309**
    Guardian and ward, court monitors, emergencies, **744.1075; Rule 5.725**
Family allowance, intestate succession, **732.403**
Fiduciaries, transfers to minors, **710.107**
Forms, transfers to minors, **710.111**
Garnishment, deceased parents, exemptions, **222.15, 222.16**
Gifts, Uniform Transfers to Minors Act, **710.101 et seq.**
Grandfather rights, transfers to minors, **710.125**
Guardian Ad Litem, generally, this index
Guardian and Ward, generally, this index
Hearsay exception, sexual abuse, witnesses, **90.803**
Homestead,
    Devise of, **732.4015**
    Remainders, **732.401**
Illegitimate children. Children Born Out of Wedlock, generally, this index
Income tax refunds, distribution, **735.302**
Interpreters, witnesses, **90.606**
Investments, custodial property, transfers to minors, **710.114**
Joint accounts, banks, survivorship, **655.79**
Judgments and decrees, settlement of claims, guardian and ward, **744.387**
Life insurance, exemption from creditors, **222.13**
Malicious treatment. Abuse of Children, generally, this index
Marriage. Support, generally, this index
Mentally ill persons, discharge, residential facilities, **393.115**
Molestation, definitions, **90.404**
Negligence,
    Abuse of Children, generally, this index
    Disqualification as guardian, **744.309**
Oaths and affirmations, witnesses, **90.605**
Paternity. Children Born Out of Wedlock, generally, this index
Personal representatives,
    Qualifications, **733.303**
    Transfers to minors, **710.107**
Power of appointment, transfers to minors, **710.105**
Probate Proceedings, this index
Rape. Sex offenses, generally, post
Receipts, transfers to minors, **710.109**
Refunds, income tax, **735.302**
Resignation, custodian, transfers to minors, **710.121**
Safe deposit boxes, **655.932**
    Death, **655.935**
Settlement of claims, guardian and ward, **744.387**
Sex offenses,
    Criminal prosecution, paternity determination, admissibility, **90.4025**
    Evidence,
        Hearsay exception, **90.803**

COMPENSATION FUND

Housing bonds as legal investments and security, **518.09**

COMPETENCY

Mentally Ill Persons, generally, this index

Mentally Retarded and Developmentally Disabled Persons, generally, this index

COMPILATION

Statutes, generally, this index

COMPREHENSIVE ASSESSMENTS

Definitions, developmental disabilities prevention and community services, **393.063**

COMPROMISE AND SETTLEMENT

Death, wrongful death actions, court approval, **768.25**

Estate taxes, receipts, **198.32**

Evidence, **90.408**

Guardian ad litem, damages, **744.3025**

Veterans guardianship, **744.646**

Wrongful death actions, court approval, **768.25**

CONDEMNATION

Probate proceedings, specifically devised property, **732.606**

CONFIDENTIAL OR PRIVILEGED INFORMATION

Generally, **90.501 et seq.**

Abandoned or unclaimed property,

Bank deposits and collections, inactive accounts, **717.117**

Investigations or examinations, **717.1301**

Accountant client privilege, **90.5055**

Adverse parties, **90.510**

Agents, trade secrets, **90.506**

Anatomical gifts, registry, **765.51551**

Application of law, **90.509**

Christian Science practitioners, **90.505**

Clinical social workers, psychotherapist patient privilege, **90.503**

Compulsion, erroneously, **90.508**

Consent, voluntary disclosure, **90.507**

Discovery, protective orders, **Civ.Proc. Rule 1.280**

Donor registry, **765.51551**

Error, compulsion, **90.508**

In camera inquiry, adverse parties, **90.510**

Lawyer client privilege, **90.502**

Marriage and family therapist, psychotherapist patient privilege, **90.503**

Mental health counselors, psychotherapist patient privilege, **90.503**

Ministers, privileged communications, **90.505**

Mistake, compelling erroneously, **90.508**

Motions, adverse parties, **90.510**

Nurse practitioners, psychotherapist patient privilege, **90.503**

Physicians and surgeons, deposition, **Civ.Proc. Rule 1.360**

Priest, privileged communications, **90.505**

Probate proceedings, accounts and accounting, inventory, **733.604**

CONFIDENTIAL OR PRIVILEGED INFORMATION
—Cont'd

Psychotherapist patient privilege, **90.503**

Rabbis, **90.505**

Refusal, **90.501**

Sexual assault counselor victim privilege, **90.5035**

Time, application of law, **90.509**

Trusts and trustees, securities, **736.0816**

Voluntary disclosure, **90.507**

Waiver, **90.507**

Wife husband privilege, **90.504**

CONFIRMATION OF SALES

Real property, **Rule 5.370**

Signatures, personal representatives, **Rule 5.330**

CONFLICT OF INTEREST

Adverse or Pecuniary Interest, generally, this index

CONFLICT OF LAWS

Anatomical gifts, **765.522**

Power of attorney, **709.2302**

Veterans guardianship, **744.602**

Wills, execution of instruments, **732.502**

CONGRESS

Judicial notice, laws or resolutions, **90.201, 90.202**

CONSANGUINITY

Relatives, generally, this index

CONSERVATORS AND CONSERVATORSHIP

See, also, Guardian and Ward, generally, this index

Absence and absentees, **747.01 et seq.**

Bonds (officers and fiduciaries), **747.034**

Discharge of conservator, **747.04**

Guardian ad litem, **747.031, 747.052**

Hearings,

Petitions to appoint, **747.031**

Termination of conservatorship, objections, **747.04**

Transfer of property, **747.052**

Incompetent, **747.011**

Jurisdiction, **747.02**

Lease of property, **747.052**

Mortgage of property, **747.052**

Notice,

Petition to appoint, hearings, **747.031**

Transfer of property, **747.052**

Oath, **747.033**

Objections, termination of conservatorship, **747.04**

Order of appointment, **747.032**

Orders of court, sale of property, **747.051**

Petitions, **747.03 et seq.**

Summary relief, **747.051**

Powers and duties, **747.035**

Resignation or removal, **747.036**

Sale or transfer of property, **747.052**

Summary procedure, **747.051, 747.052**

Termination of conservatorship, **747.04**

Appointments,

Absence and absentees, petition, **747.031**

CONTRACTS—Cont'd

Abandoned or unclaimed property—Cont'd
Recovery, reported property, **717.135**

Actions and proceedings, unenforceable obligations, voluntary payments, **725.04**

Anatomical gifts, **765.514**

Antenuptial agreements,
Pretermitted spouse, effect, **732.301**
Surviving spouse, waiver of rights, **732.702**

Continuance of business,
Decedents, personal representatives, power, **Rule 5.350**
Ward, **Rule 5.640**

Conveyances. Deeds and Conveyances, generally, this index

Cremation, application of law, **732.804**

Deeds and Conveyances, generally, this index

Definitions, real estate, military forces, termination, **689.27**

Exemptions, annuity contracts, attachment, garnishment, **222.14**

Forward contracts, power of attorney, **709.2208**

Guardian and Ward, this index

Liquidated obligations, written instrument for less than full amount due, satisfaction, **725.05**

Minerals, limitation of definitions, **689.20**

Personal representatives,
Individual liability, **733.619**
Powers and duties, **733.612**

Postnuptial agreements,
Pretermitted spouse, **732.301**
Surviving spouse, waiver of rights, **732.702**

Prenuptial agreements,
Pretermitted spouse, **732.301**
Surviving spouse, waiver of rights, **732.702**

Pretermitted spouse, prenuptial or postnuptial agreement, effect, **732.301, 732.702**

Simultaneous death, application of law, **732.601**

Statutes of frauds, **725.01 et seq.**

Trusts and Trustees, this index

Unenforceable contracts, **725.01 et seq.**

Voluntary payment as defense in action on, **725.04**

Wills,
Agreements not to make or revoke, **732.701**
Waiver of rights, consideration, **732.702**

Wrongful death, breach of contract, **768.16 et seq.**

CONTRIBUTIONS

Estate taxes, payments, **198.21**

Gifts, generally, this index

Housing bonds secured by pledge of contributions by United States, legal investments, **518.09**

Personal representatives, enforcement, **733.608**

Probate proceedings, distribution of estates, **733.802**

Trusts and trustees,
Breach of trust, **736.1002**
Debtors and creditors, claims, **736.0505**

Wills, abatement of devises, **733.805**

CONVALESCENT HOMES

Nursing Homes, generally, this index

CONVENIENCE ACCOUNTS

Financial institutions, **655.80**

CONVERSION

Attachment, fraudulent asset conversions, **222.30**

Definitions, attachment, fraudulent asset conversions, **222.30**

Executor de son tort, **733.309**

Garnishment, fraudulent asset conversion, **222.30**

Probate proceedings,
Executor de son tort, **733.309**
Improper distribution of assets, return, value of property, **733.812**

CONVEYANCES

Deeds and Conveyances, generally, this index

COOPERATIVE APARTMENTS

Repairs and maintenance, common expenses, **710.107**

COOPERATIVE ASSOCIATIONS

Abandoned or unclaimed property, banks and banking, **717.001 et seq.**

Credit Unions, generally, this index

Unclaimed or abandoned property, banks and banking, **717.001 et seq.**

COPARTNERS

Partnerships, generally, this index

COPIES

Administration, probate, notice, service, **Rule 5.240**

Ancillary administration, domiciliary proceedings, **Rule 5.470**

Claims against estate, probate, creditors, delivery, **Rule 5.490**

Notices,
Administration, probate, service, **Rule 5.240**
Requests, **Rule 5.060**

Order, sale, real property, **Rule 5.370**

Pleadings, requests, **Rule 5.060**

COPYRIGHTS

Trusts and trustees, principal and income, receipts, allocations, **738.603**

CORPORATIONS

Abandoned or unclaimed property, **717.1101**
Claims, **717.12404**
Dissolution, **717.111**

Acknowledgments, short form, **695.25**

Attorney client privilege, **90.502, 90.5055**

Confidential or privileged information, attorney client privilege, **90.5055**

Deeds and conveyances, **689.01 et seq.**

Depositions, **Civ.Proc. Rule 1.310 et seq.**

Directors, trusts and trustees, **736.0802**

Dissolution, abandoned or unclaimed property, **717.111**

Dividends, abandoned or unclaimed property, disposition, **717.001 et seq.**

Evidence, lawyer client privilege, **90.502**

Forms, acknowledgments, short form, **695.25**

Guardian and ward,
Bonds (officers and fiduciaries), **744.354**

CRIME

CRIME VICTIMS—Cont'd

Exclusion from hearings or trial, **90.616**

Presence, criminal prosecutions, exclusion from proceedings, **90.616**

Sex offenses,

Children or persons with mental retardation, hearsay exception, **90.803**

Counselor victim privilege, **90.5035**

Definitions, counselor victim privilege, **90.5035**

Witnesses, exclusion, **90.616**

CRIMES AND OFFENSES

Confessions, evidence, admissibility, **90.105**

Crime Victims, generally, this index

Death. Homicide, generally, this index

Evidence,

Accountant client privilege exception, **90.5055**

Lawyer client privilege exception, **90.502**

Photographs, property wrongfully taken, **90.91**

Similar facts, **90.404**

False pretenses. Fraud, generally, this index

Fraud, generally, this index

Guardian and Ward, this index

Homicide, generally, this index

Jury, generally, this index

Mentally Retarded and Developmentally Disabled Persons, this index

Murder. Homicide, generally, this index

Personal representatives,

Qualifications, **733.302, 733.303**

Removal from office, **733.504**

Property wrongfully taken, photographs, evidence, **90.91**

Rape. Sex Offenses, generally, this index

Sex Offenses, generally, this index

Unclaimed property, **717.134**

Victims. Crime Victims, generally, this index

Wrongfully taken property, photographs as evidence, **90.91**

CRIMINAL CODE

Crimes and Offenses, generally, this index

CRIMINAL HISTORY RECORD INFORMATION

Guardian and ward, **744.1085, 744.3135**

Registration, **744.1083**

Mentally retarded and developmentally disabled persons, care facilities, **393.067**

CRIMINAL PROCEDURE

Crimes and Offenses, generally, this index

CRIPPLED PERSONS

Handicapped Persons, generally, this index

CROSS CLAIMS

Probate proceedings, limitation of actions, **733.702**

CROSS INTERROGATORIES

Depositions upon written questions, **Civ.Proc. Rule 1.320**

CURATIVE AND VALIDATING ACTS

Partnership, limited partnership, deeds and conveyances, **689.045**

CURATIVE AND VALIDATING ACTS—Cont'd

Power of appointment, release, **709.05**

CURATORS

See, also,

Conservators and Conservatorship, generally, this index

Guardian and Ward, generally, this index

Generally, **733.501; Rule 5.122**

Accounts and accounting, **Rule 5.122**

Probate proceedings, **733.501**

Bonds (officers and fiduciaries), **733.501; Rule 5.122**

Extent of liability, **733.404**

Filing, **733.402**

Release of surety, **733.405**

Waiver, **733.403**

Definitions, probate proceedings, **731.201**

Estate taxes, names, **198.30**

Inheritance and estate taxes, names, **198.30**

Letters of curatorship, **Rule 5.122**

Powers and duties, **Rule 5.122**

Probate proceedings, **733.501**

CURRENCY

Money, generally, this index

CY PRES

Trusts and trustees, charities, **736.0413**

DAMAGES

Abandoned or unclaimed property, **717.134**

Buildings, construction, indemnity and indemnification, **725.06**

Construction, indemnity and indemnification, **725.06**

Contractors, construction contracts, indemnity and indemnification, **725.06**

Death, wrongful death actions, **768.16 et seq.**

Economic discrimination, **725.07**

Enucleation of eyes, funeral directors, **765.519**

Examination of property, **Civ.Proc. Rule 1.360**

Excavation, indemnity and indemnification, **725.06**

Guardian ad litem, compromise and settlement, **744.3025**

Guardian and ward, compromise and settlement, **744.3025**

Marital status, discrimination, **725.07**

Personal representatives, breach of duty, **733.609**

Power of attorney, third parties, **709.2120**

Probate proceedings,

Claims against estates, limitation of actions, **733.702**

Executor de son tort, **733.309**

Production of wills, **732.901**

Punitive damages, discrimination on basis of sex, marital status or race, economic discrimination, **725.07**

Race discrimination, **725.07**

Sex discrimination, **725.07**

Wills, production of wills, **732.901**

Wrongful Death, generally, this index

DEAD BODIES

Anatomical Gifts, generally, this index

Disposition, written instructions, **732.804**

DECEDENTS

DEPOSITS

DEPOSITS—Cont'd
Securities, generally, this index

DEPOSITS IN COURT
Abandoned or unclaimed property, disposition, **717.001 et seq.**

DERANGED PERSONS
Mentally Ill Persons, generally, this index

DERIVATIVES
Power of attorney, **709.2208**
Trusts and trustees, principal and income, receipts, allocations, **738.607**

DESCENT AND DISTRIBUTION
Generally, **732.101 et seq.**
Intestate Succession, generally, this index
Probate Proceedings, generally, this index

DESERTION
Guardian and Ward, generally, this index

DESTROYED WILLS
Generally, **Rule 5.510**

DEVELOPMENTAL DISABILITIES COUNCIL
Generally, **393.002**

DEVELOPMENTALLY DISABLED PERSONS
Mentally Retarded and Developmentally Disabled Persons, generally, this index

DEVISES AND DEVISEES
Wills, generally, this index

DISABLED PERSONS
Handicapped Persons, generally, this index

DISASTERS
Wills, specific devises, **732.606**

DISCHARGE
Guardian, application for discharge, **744.527**

DISCLAIMER
Beneficiaries, **739.101 et seq.**
Power of attorney, designated disclaimers, **709.2202**
Property, **739.101 et seq.**

DISCLAIMER OF PROPERTY INTERESTS ACT
Generally, **739.101 et seq.**

DISCLOSURE
Abandoned or unclaimed property,
 Purchase agreements, **717.1351**
 Recovery agreements, reported property, **717.135**
Charitable trusts, **736.1211**
Journalists, privilege against disclosure of sources or other information, **90.5015**
News reporters, privilege against disclosure of sources or other information, **90.5015**
Power of attorney, **709.2114**
Probate proceedings, accounts and accounting, inventory, **733.604**
Professional journalists, privilege against disclosure of sources or other information, **90.5015**

DISCLOSURE—Cont'd
Reporters, journalists, privilege against disclosure of sources or other information, **90.5015**
Split interest trusts, **736.1211**
Waiver, **Rule 5.180**

DISCOVERY
Generally, **Rule 5.080; Civ.Proc. Rule 1.280 et seq.**
Failure to comply, sanctions, **Civ.Proc. Rule 1.380**
Rules of civil procedure, application, **Rule 5.080**
Sanctions, **Civ.Proc. Rule 1.380**
Scope, **Civ.Proc. Rule 1.280**
Wills, later wills, **733.208**

DISCRIMINATION
Anatomical gifts, **765.513, 765.514**
Damages, sex, marital status or race, economic discrimination, **725.07**
Economic discrimination, sex, marital status or race, **725.07**
Marital status, economic discrimination, **725.07**
Organ donations, **765.513, 765.514**

DISEASES
Terminal diseases,
 Advance directives for health care, **765.101 et seq.**
 Living wills, **765.301 et seq.**

DISPOSABLE EARNINGS
Definitions, garnishment exemption, **222.11**

DISPOSITION OF UNCLAIMED PROPERTY ACT
Generally, **717.001 et seq.**

DISPOSITION WITHOUT ADMINISTRATION
Generally, **Rule 5.420**

DISQUALIFICATION
Guardians, **Rule 5.650**
Personal representatives, **Rule 5.310**

DISSENTING SHAREHOLDERS
Shares and shareholders. Corporations, this index

DISSOLUTION
Personal representatives,
 Powers and duties, **733.612**
 Voting rights, **733.612**

DISSOLUTION OF MARRIAGE
Marriage, this index

DISTRIBUTE
Definitions, probate proceedings, **731.201**

DISTRIBUTION OF ESTATES
Generally, **731.005 et seq., 733.801 et seq.**
Probate Proceedings, this index

DISTRICT COURTS OF APPEAL
Appeal and Review, generally, this index
Judgments and Decrees, generally, this index

DISTRICTS
Definitions, developmental disabilities prevention and community services, **393.063**

EVIDENCE

EXECUTIONS

GARNISHMENT—Cont'd
Surviving spouses, exemptions, **222.15, 222.16**
Transfers, fraudulent transfers, **222.29**

GENDER
Discrimination, generally, this index

GENERAL CORPORATION ACT
Corporations, generally, this index

GENERAL LAWS
Statutes, generally, this index

GENERAL MAGISTRATES
Generally, **Rule 5.095**
Guardian and ward, review of guardianship, **Rule 5.697**

GENERAL OBLIGATION BONDS
Bonds, generally, this index

GENERAL PARTNERSHIPS
Partnerships, generally, this index

GENERATION SKIPPING TRANSFER TAX
Inheritance and Estate Taxes, this index

GIFT CERTIFICATES
Abandoned or unclaimed property, **717.1045**

GIFTS
Ademption, **732.609**
Adverse or Pecuniary Interest, generally, this index
Anatomical Gifts, generally, this index
Certificates and certification, abandoned or unclaimed property, **717.1045**
Definitions, anatomical gifts, **765.511**
Developmental disabilities council, **393.002**
Family care councils, mentally retarded and developmentally disabled persons, **393.502**
Mentally retarded and developmentally disabled persons,
Family care councils, **393.502**
Trust funds, **393.23**
Power of attorney, **709.2114, 709.2202**
Public guardians, **744.7021**
Trusts and trustees, multigenerational classes, per stirpes, **736.1103**
Uniform Transfers to Minors Act, **710.101 et seq.**

GIFTS CAUSA MORTIS
Probate proceedings, inheritance and estate taxes, apportionment, **733.817**

GOOD FAITH
Guardian and ward, court monitors, **744.107**
Emergencies, **744.1075**
Power of attorney, **709.2109, 709.2111, 709.2114 et seq.**
Purchasers. Bona Fide Purchasers, generally, this index

GOOD FAITH PURCHASERS
Bona Fide Purchasers, generally, this index

GOODS, WARES AND MERCHANDISE
Sales, generally, this index

GOVERNMENTAL AGENCIES OR SUBDIVISIONS
Political Subdivisions, generally, this index

GOVERNOR
Appointments,
Family care councils, mentally retarded and developmentally disabled persons, **393.502**
Statewide public guardianship office, executive director, **744.7021**
Executive orders, developmental disabilities council, transfer to private nonprofit corporation, **393.002**
Statewide public guardianship office, executive director, appointments, **744.7021**
Support, generally, this index

GRAND JURY
Hearing impaired persons, interpreters, **90.6063**

GRANDFATHER RIGHTS
Children and minors, transfer to minors, **710.125**

GRANDPARENTS AND GRANDCHILDREN
Intestate succession, shares, **732.103**
Trusts and trustees, representation, **736.0303**
Wills,
Antilapse Statute, **732.603**
Per stirpes, distribution, **732.603**

GRANTS
Deeds and Conveyances, generally, this index
Developmental disabilities council, **393.002**
Family care councils, mentally retarded and developmentally disabled persons, **393.502**
Guardian and ward,
Joining forces for public guardianship grant program, **744.7101 et seq.**
Public guardians, **744.7021**
Mentally retarded and developmentally disabled persons, family care councils, **393.502**
Public guardians, **744.7021**
Joining forces for public guardianship grant program, **744.7101 et seq.**

GRATUITIES
Gifts, generally, this index

GROSS ESTATE
Inheritance and Estate Taxes, this index

GROUP ANNUITIES
Annuities. Insurance, this index

GUARANTY
Deeds and conveyances, **689.01 et seq.**
Wrongful death, breach of warranty, **768.16 et seq.**

GUARDIAN AD LITEM
Generally, **Rule 5.120**
Absentees property, conservators, appointment, **747.031**
Actions and proceedings,
Between guardian and ward, appointment of guardian ad litem, **744.391**
Compromise and settlement,
Claims, **744.301**
Damages, **744.3025**
Settlement of claims on behalf of minor, **Rule 5.636**
Wills, designated actions, fees, **733.1061**

GUARDIAN

GUARDIAN

GUARDIAN

GUARDIAN AND WARD—Cont'd

Notice—Cont'd
  Extraordinary authority of guardian, petition for, **Rule 5.635**
  Fees, **744.108**
  Incapacitated persons,
    Notice of all proceedings, **744.3215**
    Petitions to determine incapacity, **744.331; Rule 5.550**
  Inherent risk, waiver, **744.301**
  Medical treatment, expedited judicial intervention, petitions, **Rule 5.900**
  Petitions,
    Appointment, **Rule 5.560**
    Determination of incapacity, **Rule 5.550**
  Power of attorney, **709.2121**
    Revocation or suspension, before incapacity determination, **744.3203**
  Proceedings for removal, **744.477**
  Registration, denial, **744.1083**
  Relatives, failure to receive notice, removal of guardian, **744.474**
  Removal of guardian, proceedings, **744.477; Rule 5.660**
  Resident agents, **Rule 5.110**
  Resignation, **744.467; Rule 5.650**
  Sales, property, petitions, **744.447**
  Standby guardians, **744.304; Rule 5.646**
  Suggestion of capacity, **744.464**
  Surrogate guardians, **744.442; Rule 5.647**
  Termination of guardianship, **Rule 5.680**
    Change of residence, **744.524; Rule 5.670**
  Voluntary guardianship, **744.341; Rule 5.552**
  Waiver, **Rule 5.180**
    Probate proceedings, **731.302**
Oaths and affirmations, **744.347; Rule 5.600**
  Emergency temporary guardians, **744.3031**
  Preneed guardians, **744.3045, 744.3046**
  Resident agents, designation, **Rule 5.110**
  Standby guardians, **744.304**
  Surrogate guardians, **744.442; Rule 5.647**
  Verification of documents, **744.104**
Objections, **Rule 5.700**
  Discharge of guardian, **744.527**
    Change of domicile by ward, **Rule 5.670**
    Death of ward, guardian named as personal representative, **744.528**
  Final reports, termination of guardianship, **744.527**
  Initial guardianship report, **744.362**
  Judicial review of guardianships, **744.372**
  Reports, **Rule 5.700**
    Judicial review, **744.369**
  Resignation, **Rule 5.650**
  Suggestion of capacity, **744.464**
  Termination of guardianship, **Rule 5.680**
    Change of residence, **744.524**
Offenses. Crimes and offenses, generally, ante
Office of public guardian, **744.703**
Orders of court,
  Accounting, **Rule 5.150**

GUARDIAN AND WARD—Cont'd

Orders of court—Cont'd
  Alternatives to guardianship, **Rule 5.685**
  Amendments, annual guardianship report, **744.371**
  Appointment of guardian, **744.344**
  Assets of ward, restrictions, **744.344**
  Audits and auditors, production of books and papers, **744.368**
  Authorization of guardians actions, **Rule 5.630**
  Binding effect, **731.303**
  Continuance of business, wards, **Rule 5.640**
  Court monitors, **744.107; Rule 5.720**
    Emergencies, **744.1075; Rule 5.725**
  Dependents of ward, petition for support, **744.421**
  Discharge, **744.531**
  Disobedience, removal, **744.474**
  Incapacity of persons, **744.331**
  Mortgages of property, **744.451**
  Power of attorney, revocation or suspension, before incapacity determination, **744.3203**
  Prior authorization of guardians actions, **744.447**
  Production of property, **744.373**
  Reports,
    Approval or disapproval, **744.369**
    Failure to file, **744.3685**
  Restoration of capacity, **744.464**
  Sale of property, **744.451**
    Loans, **744.454**
  Settlement of claims, **744.387**
  Show cause orders, court monitors, emergencies, **744.1075**
  Support, payment to guardian, **744.374**
  Surrogate guardians, **744.442; Rule 5.647**
Parental rights of ward, termination, authority of guardian, **744.3215, 744.3725**
Parties, bound by orders of court, probate proceedings, **731.303**
Partition, powers and duties, **744.441**
Pensions and retirement, veterans benefits, support of dependents of ward, **744.421**
Periodic examination of ward, **744.3675**
Perishable property, sales, petition, **744.447**
Perjury, verification of documents, **744.104**
Persistent vegetative state, absence of advance directive, **765.404**
Personal injuries, settlement, **744.387**
Petitions,
  Adjudication, incompetency, **Rule 5.550**
  Adverse or pecuniary interest, authorization to act, **744.447; Rule 5.630**
  Alternatives to guardianship, **Rule 5.685**
  Approval of acts, **Rule 5.630**
  Authorization to act, **744.447; Rule 5.630**
  Capacity, determination of incapacity, **Rule 5.550**
  Change of residence, discharge of guardian, **Rule 5.670**
  Change of venue, **744.202**
  Children and minors, **Rule 5.555**
  Compromise and settlement, claims, **Rule 5.636**
  Confirmation acts of guardians, **Rule 5.630**

GUARDIAN

GUARDIAN AND WARD—Cont'd

Psychotherapist patient privilege, **90.503**

Public guardians, **744.701 et seq.**
  Appointment, **744.703, 744.704; Rule 5.560**
  Audits and auditors, **744.708**
  Bonds (officers and fiduciaries), **744.351, 744.709**
  Budget, **744.706**
  Commitment of ward, involuntary placement proceeding, **744.704**
  Community supported public guardianship programs, **744.7101 et seq.**
  Confidential or privileged information, **744.7081**
  Conflict of interest, **744.703**
  Contracts, **744.707**
  Costs, **744.705**
  Counties, community supported public guardianship programs, **744.7101 et seq.**
  Deposit, unclaimed funds held by guardian, **744.534**
  Expenses, **744.707**
  Financial assets of ward, eligibility, **744.704**
  Funds, **744.7021**
  Gifts, **744.7021**
  Grants, **744.7021**
    Joining forces for public guardianship grant program, **744.7101 et seq.**
  Indigent persons, joining forces for public guardianship grant program, **744.7101 et seq.**
  Joining forces for public guardianship grant program, **744.7101 et seq.**
  Legislative intent, **744.702**
  Lists, qualified persons, **744.703**
  Nonprofit corporations, restriction, **744.703**
  Notice, petition for appointment, **Rule 5.560**
  Office of public guardian, judicial circuits, **744.703**
  Plans and specifications, **744.7021**
  Powers and duties, **744.704**
  Procedures and rules, **744.707**
  Ratio of professional staff to wards, **744.708**
  Records and recordation, access, **744.7081**
  Reports, **744.708; Rule 5.710**
  Resignation, **744.704**
  Rules and regulations, **744.707**
  Standards, **744.708**
  Term of office, **744.703**
  Training, **744.7021**
Purchase, property by guardian, **744.454**
Purchasers, property, protection, **744.461**
Qualifications, guardians, **744.309, 744.3145**
Random field audits, **744.369**
Real estate,
  Joint tenants, sales, **744.457**
  Powers and duties, **744.441**
Receiver, appointment for corporate guardian, removal of guardian, **744.474**
Records and recordation, **744.109, 744.474**
  Actions and proceedings, **744.109**
  Annual accounting, **744.3678; Rule 5.690**
    Objections, **Rule 5.700**
  Foreign guardian, payment of indebtedness, **744.306**

GUARDIAN AND WARD—Cont'd

Records and recordation—Cont'd
  Hearings, **Rule 5.541**
  Inventory, initial inventory, **744.365**
  Public guardians, **744.708**
    Access, **744.7081**
  Resignation of guardian, **744.467**
Redemption, deposits or investments, **744.444**
Registration, professional guardians, **744.1083**
Reimbursement, costs incurred on behalf of ward, **744.108**
Relatives,
  Appointment of guardian, **744.309**
  Failure to receive notice, removal of guardian, **744.474**
Release,
  Claims, **744.387**
    Natural guardians, **744.301**
  Inherent risk, **744.301**
Relief to be granted, **744.371**
Religious organizations and societies, eligibility as guardian, **744.309**
Remainders, sale of property, valuation, **744.457**
Removal of guardian, **744.474; Rule 5.660**
  Accounting upon removal, **744.511**
    Failure to file, contempt, **744.517; Rule 5.660**
  Conflict of interest, **744.391, 744.446**
  Failure to file annual report, **744.367**
  Proceedings for removal, **744.477**
  Surrender of assets, **744.514**
    Contempt, failure to comply, **744.517**
Reports, **744.367**
  Abuse, **744.359**
  After acquired property, inventory, **744.384**
  Alternatives to guardianship, **Rule 5.685**
  Annual guardianship reports, **744.367; Rule 5.695**
    Amendments, **744.371**
    Appearance by guardian before court, **744.3735**
    Exemption, veterans guardianship, **744.653**
    Inspection, **744.3701**
    Objections, **Rule 5.700**
  Children and minors, guardianship of minors, **Rule 5.555**
  Compliance, failure to comply, **744.474**
    Failure to file, **744.3685**
    Removal, **744.474**
    Review, circuit court clerks, **744.368**
  Court monitors, **744.107 et seq.; Rules 5.720, 5.725**
  Disclosure, **744.3701**
  Emergency temporary guardianship, **744.3031; Rule 5.648**
  Examination committees, **744.331**
  Exploitation, **744.359**
  Failure to file, **744.3685**
  Final reports and application for discharge, **744.527**
  Financial statements and reports, generally, ante
  Initial guardianship reports, **744.362; Rule 5.690**
  Inspection, **744.3701**
  Inventory, **Rule 5.620**
  Judicial review, **744.369**
  Magistrates, review of guardianship accountings and plans, **Rule 5.697**

I-53

GUARDIAN

HEALTH FACILITIES—Cont'd

Fines and penalties, advance directives for health care, requirement or waiver, **765.110**

Hospitals, generally, this index

Licenses and permits,

Advance directives for health care, **765.110**

Mentally retarded and developmentally disabled persons, **393.067**

Life prolonging procedures, advance directives for health care, **765.101 et seq.**

Living wills, **765.301 et seq.**

Notice, advance directives for health care, **765.101 et seq.**

Nursing Homes, generally, this index

Pain and suffering, management, advanced directives for health care, **765.1103**

Palliative care, **765.101 et seq.**

Patients rights,

Advance directives for health care, **765.101 et seq.**

Health care surrogates, **765.201 et seq.**

Living wills, **765.301 et seq.**

Persistent vegetative state, right to decline life prolonging procedures, **765.302**

Privileges and immunities, withholding life prolonging procedures, **765.109**

Records and recordation,

Advance directives for health care, inclusion, **765.110**

Living wills, declining life prolonging procedures, **765.302**

Terminal illness,

Advance directives for health care, surrogates or proxies, **765.101 et seq.**

Living wills, **765.301 et seq.**

HEARING IMPAIRED PERSONS

Definitions, witnesses, **90.6063**

Grand jury, interpreters, **90.6063**

Interpreters,

Jury, **90.6063**

Witnesses, **90.6063**

Witnesses, interpreter service, **90.6063**

HEARSAY

Generally, **90.801 et seq.**

HEARTS

Anatomical Gifts, generally, this index

HEDGE FUNDS

Power of attorney, **709.2208**

HEIRS

Definitions, **731.201**

Financial institutions, pay on death accounts, **655.82**

Probate proceedings, **731.201**

Securities, transfer upon death of owner, **711.501**

Securities, Uniform Transfer on Death Security Registration Act, **711.50 et seq.**

HEIRS AT LAW

Definitions, **731.201**

HIGHER EDUCATION

Colleges and Universities, generally, this index

HIGHWAY SAFETY AND MOTOR VEHICLES DEPARTMENT

Driver licenses division, drivers licenses. Motor Vehicles, this index

HISPANICS

Discrimination, generally, this index

HOLDER

Definitions, abandoned or unclaimed property, **717.101**

HOLOCAUST VICTIMS

Intestate succession, evidence, heirs, **732.103**

HOLOGRAPHIC WILLS

Execution of instruments, **732.502**

Nonresidents, **732.502**

HOME AND COMMUNITY BASED SERVICES

Mentally retarded and developmentally disabled persons, **393.062 et seq.**

HOME HEALTH SERVICES

Mentally retarded and developmentally disabled persons, home and community based services, **393.062 et seq.**

HOMESTEAD

Generally, **222.01 et seq.**

Acreage included in homestead, **222.03**

Agent, notice to officer, portion of property claimed as homestead, **222.02**

Annulment of exemptions set apart, **222.10**

Attachment, exemptions, **222.01 et seq.**

Attorneys, notice by attorney to officer of property claimed as homestead, **222.02**

Circuit courts,

Injunction against sale, **222.09**

Jurisdiction to, enjoin sale, **222.09**

Jurisdiction to determine whether property is exempt, **222.10**

Jurisdiction to set apart, **222.08**

Debtors and creditors, exemptions, **222.01 et seq.**

Declaration of homestead, **222.01**

Deeds and conveyances,

Power of attorney, **689.111, 709.2201**

Probate proceedings, inter vivos transfer, **732.4017**

Survey at request of dissatisfied creditor, **222.04**

Definitions, community property, death of spouse, **732.227**

Designation and setting apart, inventory, estate of decedent, **Rule 5.340**

Determination, petitions, **Rule 5.405**

Domicile and residence, declarations, **222.17**

Dwelling house exempt from sale, **222.05**

Executions, exemptions, **222.01 et seq.**

Expenses of survey of homestead requested by creditor, **222.03**

Extent of homestead, **222.03**

Filing, exemption from execution, **222.01**

Forms, executions, exemption, **222.01**

Guardian and ward, powers, **744.441**

Homicide, survivorship rights, **732.802**

Injunctions,

Sale, **222.09**

INHERITANCE

INHERITANCE

INSOLVENCY

LETTERS AND OTHER CORRESPONDENCE
Best Evidence Rule, **90.951 et seq.**
Definitions, probate proceedings, **731.201**
Evidence, Best Evidence Rule, **90.951 et seq.**
Inspection, copying or photographing, **Civ.Proc. Rule 1.350**

LETTERS OF GUARDIANSHIP
Issuance, **744.345**

LETTERS ROGATORY
Deposition, foreign countries, **Civ.Proc. Rule 1.300**

LETTERS TESTAMENTARY OR OF ADMINISTRATION
Personal representatives. Probate Proceedings, this index

LEVY
Executions, generally, this index

LIBEL AND SLANDER
Negligence, generally, this index
Personal representatives, individual liability, **733.619**
Probate proceeding, executor de son tort, **733.309**
Small estates, summary administration distribution, **735.206**

LIBERTY BONDS
Escheat, **716.02**

LICENSES AND PERMITS
Care facilities, retardation prevention and community services, **393.067**
Comprehensive transitional education programs, mentally retarded and developmentally disabled persons, **393.067, 393.18**
Discrimination, generally, this index
Drivers licenses. Motor Vehicles, this index

LIENS AND INCUMBRANCES
Disclaimer, property, **739.402**
Group living homes, mentally deficient and mentally ill persons, **393.15**
Homestead, exemption, **222.01 et seq.**
Mentally retarded and developmentally disabled persons, foster care, group homes, developmental training, and supportive employment programs, **393.15**
Safe deposit boxes, nonpayment of rent, **655.94**
Signatures, personal representatives, **Rule 5.330**

LIFE ESTATES
Abolishment, Rule in Shelleys Case, **689.17**
Guardian and ward, valuation, **744.457**
Inheritance and estate taxes, apportionment, probate proceedings, **733.817**
Instrument purporting to create estate tail, **689.14**
Probate proceedings, inheritance and estate taxes, apportionment, **733.817**
Rule in Shelleys Case abolished, **689.17**
Shelleys case, abolishment, **689.17**
Surviving spouse, homestead, **732.401**

LIFE INSURANCE
Insurance, this index

LIFE PROLONGING PROCEDURES
Generally, **765.101 et seq.**
Living wills, **765.301 et seq.**

LIFE SUPPORT SERVICES
Advance directives for health care, **765.101 et seq.**
Guardian and ward, termination, authority of guardian, **744.3725**
Surrogates, health care surrogates, **765.201 et seq.**

LIMITATION OF ACTIONS
Abandoned or unclaimed property, **717.129**
Conservators and conservatorship, **747.04**
Escheat, **716.07**
Intestate succession, escheat, **732.107**
Probate Proceedings, this index
Trusts and Trustees, this index
Wills, objections, **733.212**

LIMITED APPEARANCE
Attorneys, **Rule 5.030**

LIMITED GUARDIANSHIP
Definitions, **744.102**

LIMITED LIABILITY COMPANIES
Investments, power of attorney, **709.2208**
Power of attorney, investments, **709.2208**
Real Estate Brokers and Sales Associates, generally, this index
Trusts and trustees, **736.0816**

LIMITED PARTNERSHIPS
Partnerships, this index

LIQUIDATION
Principal and income, receipts, allocations, **738.401**
Trusts and trustees, principal and income, receipts, allocations, **738.401**

LISTS
Abandoned or unclaimed property, **717.118**
Mentally retarded and developmentally disabled persons, intervention services, waiver, wait lists, **393.065**

LITERARY CORPORATIONS AND INSTITUTIONS
Conveyances, reverter or forfeiture provisions, **689.18**

LIVERS
Anatomical Gifts, generally, this index

LIVERY OF SEIZIN
Deeds, Statute of Uses, **689.09**

LOANS
Community resources development, mentally retarded and developmentally disabled persons, **393.15**
Discrimination, **725.07**
Family care program, mentally retarded and developmentally disabled persons, **393.068**
Foster care, group home, developmental training, and supportive employment programs, forgiveness, **393.15**
Home mortgages. Mortgages, generally, this index
Marital status, discrimination, **725.07**
Mortgages, generally, this index

LOANS

MEDICAL

MISDEMEANORS

Crimes and Offenses, generally, this index

MISREPRESENTATIONS

Fraud, generally, this index

MISSING PERSONS

Conservators and conservatorship, **747.01 et seq.**

Death, probate proceedings, **733.209**

Evidence as to death or status, **731.103**

Probate proceedings, **733.209**

   Presumption of death, **731.103**

Reported or listed as missing in action, absentee, **747.01**

MISTAKES

Depositions, **Civ.Proc. Rule 1.330**

MOBILE HOMES AND MOBILE HOME PARKS

Homesteads, exemptions, **222.01 et seq.**

Leases, homesteads, exemptions, **222.05**

MONEY

Estate taxes, tangible personal property, **198.01**

Investments, generally, this index

Mentally retarded and developmentally disabled persons, personal use and benefit, Bill of Rights, **393.13**

Principal and income, receipts, allocations, **738.401**

Probate proceedings, distribution in kind, **733.810**

Trusts and trustees, principal and income, receipts, allocations, **738.401, 738.501**

Wills, disposition, **732.515**

MONEY MARKET MUTUAL FUNDS

Guardian and ward, **744.444**

Power of attorney, **709.2208**

MONEY ORDERS

Abandoned or unclaimed property, **717.001 et seq.**

Power of attorney, **709.2208**

Unclaimed property, **717.001 et seq.**

MONUMENTS AND MEMORIALS

Evidence, hearsay exceptions, family engravings, **90.803**

Hearsay exceptions, evidence, **90.803**

MORTALITY AND ANNUITY TABLES

Guardian and ward, life estates remainder interest, valuation, **744.457**

MORTGAGES

   See, also, Loans, generally, this index

Assignments, husband and wife, estate by the entirety, **689.115**

Conservators and conservatorship, Absentees property, **747.02, 747.052**

Estate by the entirety, **689.115**

Estate taxes, intangible personal property, **198.01**

Guardian and Ward, this index

Inheritance and estate taxes,

   Intangible personal property, **198.01**

   Tangible personal property, **198.01**

Investments, fiduciaries, bonds, secured by mortgage insured by federal housing administrator, **518.07**

Land trusts, ownership vesting in trustee, **689.071**

MORTGAGES—Cont'd

Personal representatives, powers, **733.612**

Power of attorney, **709.2201**

Release, trust declaration, **689.07**

Satisfaction, trust declaration, **689.07**

Tangible personal property, transfer, trust declaration, **689.07**

Trusts and trustees, **736.0816**

   Addition of name creating lien, **689.07**

   Land trusts, **689.071**

MORTICIANS

Funeral Directors and Embalmers, generally, this index

MORTUARY SCIENCE

Funeral Directors and Embalmers, generally, this index

MOSQUES

Religious Organizations and Societies, generally, this index

MOTION PICTURES

Best Evidence Rule, **90.951 et seq.**

Evidence, Best Evidence Rule, **90.951 et seq.**

MOTIONS

   Generally, **Rule 5.020**

Delay, prevention, **Rule 5.025**

Discovery, order compelling discovery, **Civ.Proc. Rule 1.380**

Guardian and ward, revocation or suspension, power of attorney, before incapacity determination, **744.3203**

Judicial notice, **90.204**

Mental examinations, **Civ.Proc. Rule 1.360**

Physical examinations, **Civ.Proc. Rule 1.360**

Protective orders, discovery, **Civ.Proc. Rule 1.280**

Removal of personal representative, **Rule 5.440**

Withdrawal from case, attorney, **Rule 5.030**

MOTOR CARRIERS

Conveyances, reverter or forfeiture provisions, exemptions, **689.18**

Deeds and conveyances, reverter or forfeiture provisions, exemptions, **689.18**

MOTOR VEHICLES

Certificates and certification, tax anticipation certificates, investment, **518.15**

Chauffeurs. Drivers licenses, generally, post

Drivers licenses,

   Anatomical gifts, organ donor cards, **765.514, 765.521**

   Forms, anatomical gifts, **765.521**

   Organ donor cards, issuance with license on request, **765.514, 765.521**

   Uniform organ donor cards, issuance on request, **765.521**

Executions, attachment, exemption, **222.25**

Exemptions, attachment, **222.25**

Licenses and permits. Drivers licenses, generally, ante

Operators licenses. Drivers licenses, generally, ante

Probate proceedings, exempt property, **732.402**

Tax anticipation certificates, investments, **518.15, 518.16**

MULTIPLE PARTY ACCOUNTS

Definitions, pay on death accounts, **655.82**

MUNICIPAL CORPORATIONS
Municipalities, generally, this index

MUNICIPAL HOME RULE POWERS ACT
Municipalities, generally, this index

MUNICIPAL OFFICERS AND EMPLOYEES
Adverse or Pecuniary Interest, generally, this index

MUNICIPALITIES
Charters, judicial notice, **90.202**
Evidence, records, Best Evidence Rule, **90.955**
Investments,
   Commonwealth of Puerto Rico bonds or obligations, **518.152**
   Higher education bonds or certificates, **518.151**
   School bonds or motor vehicle tax anticipation certificates, **518.15**
Judicial notice, charters, **90.202**
Records and recordation, Best Evidence Rule, **90.955**

MURDER
Homicide, generally, this index

MUTUAL FUNDS
Definitions, trusts and trustees, **736.0816**
Power of attorney, **709.2208**

MUTUAL WILLS
Presumption of contract not to revoke, **732.701**

NAMES
Deeds and conveyances,
   Preparer of instruments, records, **695.26**
   Recorded instruments, variances, presumptions, **689.19**
Estate taxes, decedents, **198.30**
Inheritance and estate taxes, decedents, **198.30**
Records and recordation, preparer of instruments, **695.26**
Title to property, preparer of instruments, records, **695.26**

NATIONAL BANKS
Guardian and ward, qualification, **744.309**
Probate proceedings, personal representatives, **733.305**

NATIONAL MORTGAGE ASSOCIATIONS .
Investment by fiduciaries in securities, **518.07, 518.08**

NATIONAL ORIGIN
Discrimination, generally, this index

NATURAL GUARDIANS
Generally, **744.301**

NATURAL RESOURCES
Leases, trusts and trustees, **736.0816**
Principal and income, receipts, allocations, **738.604**
Trusts and trustees,
   Leases, **736.0816**
   Principal and income, receipts, allocations, **738.604**

NEGLIGENCE
Death, wrongful death, **768.16 et seq.**
Estate taxes, delinquent or deficient taxes, penalties, **198.18**
Evidence, subsequent remedial measures, **90.407**

NEGLIGENCE—Cont'd
Fiduciaries, investments, **518.11**
Inheritance or estate taxes, delinquent or deficient taxes, penalties, **198.18**
Net accumulations of estate, loss, damages, wrongful death, **768.21**
Personal representatives,
   Individual liability, **733.619**
   Removal from office, **733.504**
Remedial measures taken after injury, admissibility, **90.407**
Subsequent remedial measures, evidence, **90.407**
Wrongful death, **768.16 et seq.**

NEGOTIABLE INSTRUMENTS
Authenticity, **90.902**
Bank Deposits and Collections, generally, this index
Cashiers checks, power of attorney, **709.2208**
Checks,
   Abandoned or unclaimed property, **717.001 et seq.**
     Joint accounts, **717.12403**
   Certified checks,
     Abandoned or unclaimed property, disposition, **717.001 et seq.**
     Unclaimed property, disposition, **717.001 et seq.**
   Definitions, financial institutions, deposits and credits, **655.769**
   Joint accounts, abandoned or unclaimed property, **717.12403**
   Power of attorney, **709.2208**
Drafts,
   Checks, generally, ante
   Power of attorney, **709.2208**
Estate taxes,
   Intangible personal property, **198.01**
   Nonresidents, **198.03**
Evidence, authentication, **90.902**
Indorsements, power of attorney, **709.2208**
Inheritance and estate taxes,
   Intangible personal property, **198.01**
   Nonresidents, **198.03**
Mortgages, generally, this index
Power of attorney, **709.2208**
Probate proceedings, location of assets, **731.106**
Travelers checks,
   Abandoned or unclaimed property, **717.001 et seq.**
   Power of attorney, **709.2208**

NEWS REPORTERS
Evidence, privilege against disclosure of sources or other information, **90.5015**

NEWSPAPERS
See, also, Magazines, generally, this index
Authentication, **90.902**
   Evidence, **90.5015**
Evidence,
   Authentication, **90.5015, 90.902**
   Journalists, privilege against disclosure of sources or other information, **90.5015**
Journalists, evidence, privilege against disclosure of sources or other information, **90.5015**

PERSONAL

POPULAR

PROBATE

PROBATE

PROBATE

PROBATE

PROBATE

PROBATE

RACIAL

RACIAL DISCRIMINATION
Discrimination, generally, this index

RADIO
Television and Radio, generally, this index

RAPE
Sex Offenses, generally, this index

REAL ESTATE
Appraisal and Appraisers, generally, this index

Armed forces, purchase agreements, termination, **689.27**

Brokers. Real Estate Brokers and Sales Associates, generally, this index

Children and minors, transfers to minors, **710.101 et seq.**

Contracts for sale. Deeds and Conveyances, generally, this index

Conveyances. Deeds and Conveyances, generally, this index

Custodial property, retirement and pensions, **689.072**

Deeds and Conveyances, generally, this index

Disclaimer, **739.101 et seq.**

Dower, widow, assignment, extraordinary petition, **Rule 5.365**

Electronic records, **695.27, 695.28**

Estates by the entirety, mortgages, **689.115**

Fee simple,
Deeds and conveyances, words dispensed with, **689.10**
Trusts and trustees, title acquired, **689.07**

Frauds, Statute of, generally, this index

Hearings, sale of real property, **Rule 5.370**

Homestead, generally, this index

Individual retirement accounts, custodial property, **689.072**

Instruments affecting real estate, recording requirements, **695.26**

Interim accounting, identification, **Rule 5.345**

Investments, fiduciaries secured by real property, federal housing administrator insures, **518.06 et seq.**

Joint tenants, homicide, survivorship rights, **732.802**

Land trusts, ownership vesting in trustee, **689.071**

Leases, generally, this index

Liens and Incumbrances, generally, this index

Loans. Mortgages, generally, this index

Military forces, purchase agreements, termination, **689.27**

Mortgages, generally, this index

Personal representatives, sales, powers and duties, **733.613**

Purchase agreements, military forces, termination, **689.27**

Records and Recordation, generally, this index

Retirement and pensions, custodial property, **689.072**

Reverter or forfeiture provisions, limitation, exceptions, **689.18**

Sales. Deeds and Conveyances, generally, this index

Salespersons. Real Estate Brokers and Sales Associates, generally, this index

Secured transactions. Mortgages, generally, this index

Statute of Frauds. Frauds, Statute of, generally, this index

Tenancy by the Entireties, generally, this index

Title to Property, generally, this index

REAL ESTATE—Cont'd
Trusts and Trustees, this index

Tuberculosis hospitals, conveyance, educational purposes, **689.12**

Veterans guardianship,
Sale, petition, **744.631**
Schedules, **744.621**

REAL ESTATE BROKERS AND SALES ASSOCIATES
AIDS, disclosures, privileges and immunities, **689.25**

Death, disclosure, privileges and immunities, **689.25**

Disclosure,
AIDS, privileges and immunities, **689.25**
Death, privileges and immunities, **689.25**

Homicide, disclosure, privileges and immunities, **689.25**

Privileges and immunities, AIDS, death, disclosure, **689.25**

Suicide, disclosure, privileges and immunities, **689.25**

REAL ESTATE INVESTMENT TRUSTS
Power of attorney, **709.2208**

REAL ESTATE LICENSE LAW
Real Estate Brokers and Sales Associates, generally, this index

REAL ESTATE SALESPERSONS
Real Estate Brokers and Sales Associates, generally, this index

REAL PROPERTY
Real Estate, generally, this index

REAL PROPERTY ELECTRONIC RECORDING ACT
Generally, **695.27**

REBUTTAL
Depositions, **Civ.Proc. Rule 1.330**

RECEIPTS
Disclaimer, property, **739.301**

Principal and income, trusts and trustees, **738.103**

Safe deposit boxes, **655.931**

RECEIVERS AND RECEIVERSHIPS
Bonds (officers and fiduciaries), premiums, expense, **733.406**

Guardian and ward, appointment of receiver for corporate guardian, removal of guardian, **744.474**

Mentally retarded and developmentally disabled persons, care facilities, **393.0678**

Personal representatives, removal from office, **733.504**

RECIPROCAL AGREEMENTS
Support, generally, this index

RECIPROCAL EXEMPTION
Inheritance and estate taxes, **198.44**

RECIPROCITY
Abandoned or unclaimed property, **717.133**

RECORDS AND RECORDATION
Abandoned or unclaimed property, **717.1311, 717.1315**

RECORDS AND RECORDATION—Cont'd

Absence, entries, hearsay exceptions, **90.803**

Ancient documents, hearsay exceptions, **90.803**

Authentication, **90.901 et seq.**

Best Evidence Rule, **90.951 et seq.**

Confidential or Privileged Information, generally, this index

Deeds and Conveyances, this index

Definitions,
  Anatomical gifts, **765.511**
  Evidence, **90.951**
  Power of attorney, **709.2102**

Depositions upon oral examination, **Civ.Proc. Rule 1.310**

Developmental disabilities council, **393.002**

Disclaimer, property, **739.501**

Donor registry, confidential or privileged information, **765.51551**

Electronic records, real estate, **695.27, 695.28**

Escheat, federal funds, **716.06**

Evidence, this index

Guardian and Ward, this index

Identification, **90.901 et seq.**

Inheritance and Estate Taxes, this index

Instruments affecting real property, requirements of recording, **695.26**

Judicial notice, **90.202**
  Denial, **90.205**

Land trusts, ownership in trustee, undisclosed beneficiaries, **689.071**

Names, preparer of instruments, **695.26**

Power of appointment, release, **709.02**

Preparer of instruments, name and address, **695.26**

Principal and income,
  Distributions, **738.202**
  Receipts, allocations, **738.403**

Production of Books and Papers, generally, this index

Safe deposit boxes, leases, death, **655.935**

Self authentication, **90.902**

Standards, electronic recording, **695.27, 695.28**

Summaries, Best Evidence Rule, **90.956**

Trusts and Trustees, this index

Variance, names in recorded instruments, **689.19**

RED CROSS

Absentees, person reported missing, captured, serving with, **747.01**

REDEMPTION

Guardian and ward, deposits or investments, **744.444**

REEMPLOYMENT ASSISTANCE

Unemployment Compensation, generally, this index

REFORMATION

Trusts and trustees, mistakes, **736.0415**

Wills,
  Mistakes, **732.615, 733.1061**
  Rule Against Perpetuities, **689.225**

REFUNDS

Abandoned or unclaimed property, business associations, **717.109**

REFUNDS—Cont'd

Business associations, abandoned or unclaimed property, **717.109**

Income tax—federal, deceased taxpayer, **735.302**

REGIONAL NURSING HOME OMBUDSMAN COMMITTEE

Nursing Homes, generally, this index

REGISTERS

Definitions, securities, transfer upon death of owner, **711.501**

REGISTRATION

Abandoned or unclaimed property, **717.1400**
  Revocation or suspension, **717.1322**

Guardian and ward, professional guardians, **744.1083**

REGISTRY

Federal courts, escheat of unclaimed funds, **716.02**

RELATIVES

Absentees, appointment of conservators, **747.02**

Anatomical gifts, eligibility, **765.512**

Conservators and conservatorship, appointment, absentees, **747.02**

Definitions, developmental disabilities prevention and community services, **393.063**

Deposition, persons taking, **Civ.Proc. Rule 1.300**

Evidence, hearsay exceptions, family records, **90.803**

Guardian and ward, appointment, **744.309**

Hearsay exception, family records, **90.803**

Intestate succession, shares, **732.103**

Medical care and treatment, consent, absence of advance directive, **765.401**

Partnerships, trusts and trustees, damages, **736.1015**

Personal representatives, nonresidents, qualifications, **733.304**

Veterans guardianship, **744.634**
  Judges, appointment, **744.618**

RELEASE

Guardian and ward, claims, **744.387**
  Natural guardian, **744.301**

Mortgages, trust declarations, **689.07**

Power of appointment, **709.02 et seq.**

Veterans guardianship, benefits to dependents of ward, **744.625**

RELIGION

Anatomical gifts, religious objections, **765.512**

Associations and societies. Religious Organizations and Societies, generally, this index

Civil rights. Discrimination, generally, this index

Discrimination, generally, this index

Mentally retarded and developmentally disabled persons, freedom to practice, Bill of Rights, **393.13**

Organizations. Religious Organizations and Societies, generally, this index

Trusts and trustees, charities, **736.0405**

RELIGIOUS ASSOCIATIONS AND SOCIETIES

Religious Organizations and Societies, generally, this index

RELIGIOUS

RELIGIOUS DISCRIMINATION
Discrimination, generally, this index

RELIGIOUS ORGANIZATIONS AND SOCIETIES
Anatomical gifts, religious objections, **765.512**
Civil rights. Discrimination, generally, this index
Confidential or privileged information, **90.505**
Conveyances reverter or forfeiture provisions, exemptions, **689.18**
Deeds and conveyances, reverter or forfeiture revisions, exemptions, **689.18**
Discrimination, generally, this index
Evidence, hearsay exceptions, **90.803**
Exemptions, conveyances, reverter or forfeiture provisions, **689.18**
Guardians, appointment, **744.309**
Hearsay exceptions, records, **90.803**
Privileged communications, **90.505**
Records and recordation, evidence, hearsay exceptions, **90.803**

REMAINDERS AND REMAINDERMEN
Estate tail, instrument purporting to create, **689.14**
Guardian and ward, valuation, **744.457**
Homestead,
   Descent and distribution, **732.401**
   Surviving spouse, **732.401**
Probate proceedings, inheritance and estate taxes, apportionment, **733.817**
Rule in Shelleys Case, abolished, **689.17**
Shelleys case, abolishment, **689.17**

RENT
Principal and income, receipts, allocations, **738.502**
Rental agreements. Leases, generally, this index
Trusts and trustees, principal and income, receipts, allocations, **738.502**

RENTAL AGREEMENTS
Leases, generally, this index

REPORTERS
Professional journalists, evidence, privilege against disclosure of sources or other information, **90.5015**

REPORTS
Anatomical gifts, registry, **765.5155**
Court monitors, guardian and ward, **744.107 et seq.; Rules 5.720, 5.725**
Guardian and Ward, this index
Magistrates, **Rule 5.095**
Guardian and ward, review of accountings and plans, **Rule 5.697**
Power of attorney,
   Abuse, **709.2120**
   Guardian and ward, **744.462**
Public guardians, **744.708; Rule 5.710**

REPRESENTATIVES
Personal representatives. Probate Proceedings, this index

REPRESENTATIVES AD LITEM
Anatomical gifts, eligibility to make, **765.512**

REPUTATION
Character and Reputation, generally, this index

REQUESTS FOR ADMISSIONS
Generally, **Civ.Proc. Rule 1.370**
Rules of civil procedure, **Rule 5.080**

RES GESTAE
Hearsay exception, **90.803**

RESEARCH
Discovery, **Civ.Proc. Rule 1.280**

RESERVES
Trusts and trustees, termination, **736.0817**

RESIDENCE
Domicile and Residence, generally, this index

RESIDENT
Definitions, developmental disabilities prevention and community services, **393.063**

RESIDENT AGENTS
Agents and Agencies, generally, this index
Personal representative or guardian, **Rule 5.110**

RESIDENTIAL CARE FACILITIES
Nursing Homes, generally, this index

RESIDUARY ESTATE
Probate proceedings, inheritance and estate taxes, apportionment, **733.817**
Wills, failure of testamentary disposition, **732.604**

RESIGNATION
Guardians, **Rule 5.650**
   Petition, signature, **Rule 5.610**
Personal representatives, **Rule 5.430**
   Signatures, **Rule 5.330**

REST HOMES
Nursing Homes, generally, this index

RESTITUTION
Trusts and trustees, breach of trust, **736.1001**

RESTORATION
Power of attorney, **709.2117**

RESTORATION OF RIGHTS
Mentally retarded and developmentally disabled persons, **Rule 5.681**

RESTRAINING ORDER
Injunctions, generally, this index

RESTRAINTS
Definitions, developmentally disabled persons, prevention and community services, **393.063**

RESTRAINTS ON ALIENATION
Reverter or forfeiture provisions, limitation, **689.18**

RETAIL SALES
Sales, generally, this index

RETAINER
Distribution of estates, **733.809**

SAFE

SAFE DEPOSIT BOXES—Cont'd
Contents—Cont'd
Liens, nonpayment of rent, **655.94**
Death, lessee, **655.935**
Access,
Binding transactions, **655.934**
Joint lessees, **655.937**
Personal representatives, **655.933, 655.936**
Joint lessees, **655.937**
Personal representatives,
Access, **655.936**
Delivery of contents, **655.936**
Opening, **733.6065**
Definitions, **655.93**
Delinquent rent, remedies, **655.94**
Delivery, contents, death of lessee, **655.936**
Durable power of attorney, death or incapacity of lessee, binding transactions, **655.934**
Fines and penalties, abandoned or unclaimed property, delivery, **717.119**
Foreign personal representative, delivery of contents, **655.936**
Guardian and ward, initial inventory, **744.365**
Guardians inventory, **Rule 5.620**
Husband and wife, death, **655.935**
Inventory,
Death of lessee, **655.936, 733.604**
Personal representatives, **Rule 5.342**
Joint lessees, **655.937**
Liens and incumbrances, nonpayment of rent, **655.94**
Mentally deficient and mentally ill persons, access, binding transactions, **655.934**
Night depositories, **655.931**
Nonpayment of rent, **655.94**
Notice, nonpayment of rent, **655.94**
Orders of court,
Adverse claims, **655.938**
Death of lessee, access, **655.935**
Power of attorney, **655.934, 709.2208**
Procedure, access, limiting right of access for failure to comply, **655.939**
Receipts, **655.931**
Records and recordation, death, **655.935**
Rent, nonpayment of rent, **655.94**
Sales, nonpayment of rent, sale of contents, **655.94**
Security procedures, failure to comply, limiting access, **655.939**
Surviving spouse, **655.935**
Survivorship, joint lessees, **655.937**
Trusts and trustees, lessee as trustee, adverse claim by beneficiary, **655.938**
Two or more lessees, **655.937**
Unclaimed property, **717.116**
Disposition, **717.001 et seq.**
Wills, **655.935**

SAFE DEPOSIT COMPANIES
Safe Deposit Boxes, generally, this index

SAFETY
Guardian and ward, court monitors, emergencies, **744.1075; Rule 5.725**

SAFETY DEPOSIT BOXES
Safe Deposit Boxes, generally, this index

SAILORS
Military Forces, generally, this index

SALARIES
Compensation and Salaries, generally, this index

SALES
Absence and absentees, appointment of conservators, **747.02**
Bona Fide Purchasers, generally, this index
Checks. Negotiable Instruments, this index
Confirmation of sale, real property, **Rule 5.370**
Conservatorship of absentees property, **747.02**
Discrimination, generally, this index
Fraud, generally, this index
Frauds, statute of, **725.01**
Lands, **725.01**
Guardian and Ward, this index
Injunctions, exempt property, **222.09**
Real Estate Brokers and Sales Associates, generally, this index
Real property, confirmation of sale, **Rule 5.370**
Signatures, personal representatives, **Rule 5.330**
Wills, specific devises, **732.606**

SALESPERSONS
Real Estate Brokers and Sales Associates, generally, this index

SAVINGS AND LOAN ASSOCIATIONS
See, also, Savings Associations, generally, this index
Accounts and accounting, **655.769 et seq.**
Children and minors, **655.77**
Convenience accounts, **655.80**
Two or more names, deposit accounts, **655.78, 655.79**
Agents and agencies, convenience accounts, **655.80**
Certificates of deposit, two or more names, **655.78, 655.79**
Children and minors,
Deposits, **655.77**
Joint accounts, survivorship, **655.78, 655.79**
Convenience accounts, **655.80**
Death of customer, joint accounts, vesting, **655.79**
Definitions, deposits, **655.769**
Deposits, **655.769 et seq.**
Children and minors, **655.77**
Trust, **655.825**
Discharge, convenience accounts, **655.80**
Evidence, presumptions, joint accounts, vesting, **655.79**
Fiduciaries, legal investments, **518.01 et seq.**
Guardian and ward,
Children and minors, deposits, **655.77**
Convenience accounts, **655.80**
Qualification, **744.309**
Registration, professional guardians, **744.1083**
Investments,
Fiduciaries, **518.01 et seq.**
Higher education bonds or certificates, **518.151**
Joint accounts,
Convenience accounts, **655.80**

SCHOOL

SECURITY INTERESTS—Cont'd
Probate proceedings, improper distribution of property, protection of bona fide purchasers, **733.813**

SELL
Sales, generally, this index

SERVICE OF PROCESS
Generally, **Rule 5.041**
Agents and agencies, resident agents, personal representative or guardian, **Rule 5.110**
Books and papers, **Rule 5.041**
Copies, pleadings and motions, **Rule 5.020**
Informal notice, **Rule 5.040**
Motions, copies, **Rule 5.020**
Notice,
  Administration, **Rule 5.240**
  Formal, **Rule 5.040**
Petitions, formal notice, **Rule 5.040**
Pleadings, **Rule 5.041**
  Copies, **Rule 5.020**
Proof of service, **Rule 5.040**
Requests for notices and copies of pleadings, interested parties, **Rule 5.060**
Resident agents, personal representatives or guardians, **Rule 5.110**
Subpoenas, **Rule 5.080**
Time, computation, **Rule 5.042**
Withdrawal of attorney, motion or petition, **Rule 5.030**

SETOFF AND COUNTERCLAIM
Probate proceedings, **733.809**
  Limitation of actions, **733.702**

SETTLEMENT
Compromise and Settlement, generally, this index

SETTLOR
Generally, **736.0101 et seq.**

SEX
Discrimination, generally, this index

SEX OFFENSES
Children and Minors, this index
Confidential or privileged information, counselor victim privilege, **90.5035**
Counselors and counseling, privileges and immunities, **90.5035**
Definitions, evidence, prior offenses, **90.404**
Evidence,
  Second and subsequent offenses, **90.404**
  Sexual assault counselor victim privilege, **90.5035**
Second and subsequent offenses, evidence, **90.404**
Sexual assault counselor victim privilege, **90.5035**
  Evidence, **90.5035**
Volunteers, counselor victim privilege, **90.5035**

SEXUAL BATTERY
Sex Offenses, generally, this index

SEXUAL DISCRIMINATION
Discrimination, generally, this index

SEXUAL INTERCOURSE
Sex Offenses, generally, this index

SEXUAL OFFENDERS
Sex Offenses, generally, this index

SHARES AND SHAREHOLDERS
Abandoned or unclaimed property, joint tenants, **717.12406**
Corporations, this index
Options, power of attorney, **709.2208**
Power of attorney, **709.2201, 709.2208**
Securities, generally, this index

SHELLEYS CASE
Rule abolished, **689.17**

SHERIFFS
Attachment, generally, this index
Executions, generally, this index
Exempt property, injunction against sheriff against setting apart, **222.10**
Exemptions, injunction against setting apart exempt property by sheriff, **222.10**
Garnishment, generally, this index

SHIELD LAW
Professional journalists, privilege against disclosure of sources or other information, **90.5015**

SHORT TITLES
Popular Name Laws, generally, this index

SIGNATURES
Anatomical gifts, **765.514**
Disclaimer, property, **739.104**
Estate taxes, state employees, credentials, **198.07**
Guardians, **Rule 5.610**
Homestead, statement, **222.01**
Personal representatives, **Rule 5.330**
Pleadings, attorneys, **Rule 5.020**
Power of appointment, release, **709.02**
Property, disclaimer, **739.104**
Release, power of appointment, **709.02**
Trusts and trustees,
  Certificates and certification, **736.1017**
  Conveyances, **689.06**

SIGNS AND SIGNALS
Authentication, **90.902**
Evidence, authentication, **90.902**

SIMULTANEOUS DEATH LAW
Generally, **732.601**

SINKING FUND
Housing bonds, investments and security, **518.09**
Investments,
  Fiduciaries, commonwealth of Puerto Rico bonds or obligations, **518.152**
  Higher education bonds or certificates, **518.151**

SISTERS AND BROTHERS
Relatives, generally, this index

SLANDER

Libel and Slander, generally, this index

SOCIAL SECURITY

Bankruptcy exemptions, benefits, **222.201**

Numbers, deeds and conveyances, **689.02**

SOCIAL SERVICES

Adoption, generally, this index

Appeal and review, retardation prevention and community services, denial of application, **393.065**

Developmental disabilities prevention and community services, **393.062 et seq.**

Medical assistance,

Developmental disabilities prevention and community services, **393.062 et seq.**

Health care surrogates, application for assistance, **765.205**

Surrogates, health care decisions, application for assistance, **765.205**

SOLDIERS AND SAILORS

Military Forces, generally, this index

SOLE PROPRIETORS

Trusts and trustees, **736.0816**

SOLICITATION

Gifts, generally, this index

SOLICITORS

Attorneys, generally, this index

SOLVENCY

Insolvency, generally, this index

SPECIAL APPRAISERS

Estate taxes, **198.11**

SPECIAL DISTRICTS

Political Subdivisions, generally, this index

SPECIAL MAGISTRATES

Generally, **Rule 5.095**

Guardian and ward, review of guardianship, **Rule 5.697**

SPENDTHRIFT TRUSTS

Generally, **736.0501 et seq.**

SPLIT INTEREST TRUSTS

Generally, **736.1201 et seq.**

Amendments, powers and duties, **736.1206**

Application of law, **736.1202**

Choice of laws, **736.1209**

Construction of law, **736.1210**

Definitions, **736.1201**

Disclosure, **736.1211**

Distributions, **736.1211**

Donees, selections, powers and duties, release, **736.1208**

Elections, choice of laws, **736.1209**

Guardian and ward, wards will, federal estate tax charitable deduction, **744.441**

Notice, restrictive provisions, states attorney, **736.1205**

Orders of court, relief, restrictions, **736.1207**

Powers and duties,

Donees, selections, release, **736.1208**

SPLIT INTEREST TRUSTS—Cont'd

Powers and duties—Cont'd

Trustees, **736.1203, 736.1204**

Protections, **736.1211**

Release, powers and duties, donees, selections, **736.1208**

Relief, restrictions, orders of court, **736.1207**

Restrictive provisions, notice, states attorney, **736.1205**

Selections, donees, powers and duties, release, **736.1208**

SPOUSES

Husband and Wife, generally, this index

STANDARDS

Electronic transactions, records and recordation, **695.27, 695.28**

Records and recordation, electronic recording, **695.27, 695.28**

STANDBY GUARDIAN

Generally, **744.304; Rule 5.646**

STATE

Agencies. State Agencies, generally, this index

Buildings, generally, this index

Charters, judicial notice, **90.202**

Definitions,

Abandoned or unclaimed property, **717.101**

Deeds and conveyances, electronic recording, **695.27**

Inheritance and estate taxes, apportionment, **733.817**

Securities, transfer upon death of owner, **711.501**

Transfers, minors, **710.102**

Escheat, generally, this index

Estate taxes. Inheritance and Estate Taxes, generally, this index

Evidence, records, Best Evidence Rule, **90.955**

Foreign States, generally, this index

Funds. State Treasury, generally, this index

Inheritance and Estate Taxes, generally, this index

Investments,

Application of laws requiring security, **518.08**

Commonwealth of Puerto Rico bonds or obligations, **518.152**

Federal housing administrator insured bonds, **518.07**

Higher education bonds or certificates, **518.151**

Housing bonds as legal investment, **518.09**

Motor vehicle tax anticipation certificates, **518.15**

National mortgage associations securities, **518.07**

School bonds, **518.15**

Judicial notice, charters, **90.202**

Obligations, investment, fiduciaries, **518.01 et seq.**

Political Subdivisions, generally, this index

Probate proceedings, claims against estates, limitation of actions, **733.702**

Recreational complexes, naming, Best Evidence Rule, **90.955**

Spendthrift trusts, claims, exemptions, **736.0503**

Support, generally, this index

STATE AGENCIES

Abandoned or unclaimed property, property held by, **717.112, 717.113**

Death, probate proceedings, reports, **731.103**

STATE AGENCIES—Cont'd
Investments, commonwealth of Puerto Rico bonds or
obligations, **518.152**
Judicial notice, rules, **90.202**
Rules and regulations, judicial notice, **90.202**
Savings Associations, generally, this index

STATE BANKS
Banks and Banking, generally, this index

STATE BONDS
Fiduciaries, legal investments, **518.01 et seq.**
Investments, fiduciaries, **518.01 et seq.**

STATE COURTS SYSTEM
Courts, generally, this index

STATE DEPARTMENT
Corporations, generally, this index

STATE DEPARTMENTS
Definitions,
Developmental disabilities prevention and community
services, **393.063**
Estate taxes, **198.01**

STATE FUNDS
State Treasury, generally, this index

STATE HOSPITALS
Mental Institutions, generally, this index

STATE INSTITUTIONS
Colleges and Universities, generally, this index
Investments,
Application of laws requiring security, **518.08**
Bonds, issued or insured by federal housing administrator, **518.07**
Commonwealth of Puerto Rico bonds or obligations, **518.152**
National mortgage associations securities, **518.07**
Mental Institutions, generally, this index

STATE MENTAL INSTITUTIONS
Mental Institutions, generally, this index

STATE NURSING HOME OMBUDSMAN COMMITTEE
Nursing Homes, generally, this index

STATE TREASURY
Escheated funds, payments, **716.05**
Estate taxes, disposition, **198.34**
General revenue funds,
Estate taxes, disposition, **198.34**
Inheritance and estate taxes, disposition, **198.34**
Inheritance and estate taxes, disposition, **198.34**
Investments, commonwealth of Puerto Rico bonds or
obligations, **518.152**

STATISTICS
Vital Statistics, generally, this index

STATUTE OF FRAUDS
Frauds, Statute of, generally, this index

STATUTE OF LIMITATIONS
Limitation of Actions, generally, this index

STATUTE OF USES
Generally, **689.05 et seq.**

STATUTES
Construction of laws,
Advance directives for health care, **765.103, 765.107**
Evidence, **90.102**
Probate proceedings, construction against implied
repeal, **731.102**
Veterans guardianship, **744.602, 744.652**
Evidence, construction, **90.102**
Judicial notice, **90.201, 90.202**
Popular Name Laws, generally, this index

STATUTORY LIENS
Liens and Incumbrances, generally, this index

STATUTORY RAPE
Sex Offenses, generally, this index

STATUTORY RULE AGAINST PERPETUITIES
Generally, **689.225**

STAY
Appeals, **Rule 5.100**

STEPCHILDREN AND STEPPARENTS
Relatives, generally, this index

STERILIZATION
Advance directives for health care, consent by surrogate
or proxy, restrictions, **765.113**
Consent, incapacitated persons, surrogate or proxy, **765.113**
Guardian and ward, authority of guardian, **744.3215, 744.3725**
Incapacitated persons, consent by surrogate or proxy,
restrictions, **765.113**

STIPULATIONS
Depositions, persons to take, **Civ.Proc. Rule 1.300**
Elective share, spouse, payment, **Rule 5.360**

STOCK CORPORATIONS
Corporations, generally, this index

STOCK INSURERS
Insurance, generally, this index

STRUCTURES
Buildings, generally, this index

STUDENTS
Colleges and Universities, generally, this index

SUBDIVISIONS
Guardian and ward, powers and duties, **744.441**
Trusts and trustees, **736.0816**

SUBPOENA DUCES TECUM
Production of Books and Papers, generally, this index

SUBPOENAS
Generally, **Rule 5.080; Civ.Proc. Rule 1.410**

TENANCY

TRUSTS

TRUSTS

TRUSTS

UNIFORM

VETERANS

WILLS

WORDS

WORDS

WORDS

FOR REFERENCE
DO NOT REMOVE
FROM THIS ROOM

FOR REFERENCE
DO NOT REMOVE
FROM THIS ROOM